TANZANIA SAFARI

WITH KILIMANJARO, ZANZIBAR AND THE COAST

PHILIP BRIGGS
& CHRIS MCINTYRE

www.bradtguides.com

Bradt Guides Ltd, UK
The Globe Pequot Press Inc, USA

Bradt GUIDES
TRAVEL TAKEN SERIOUSLY

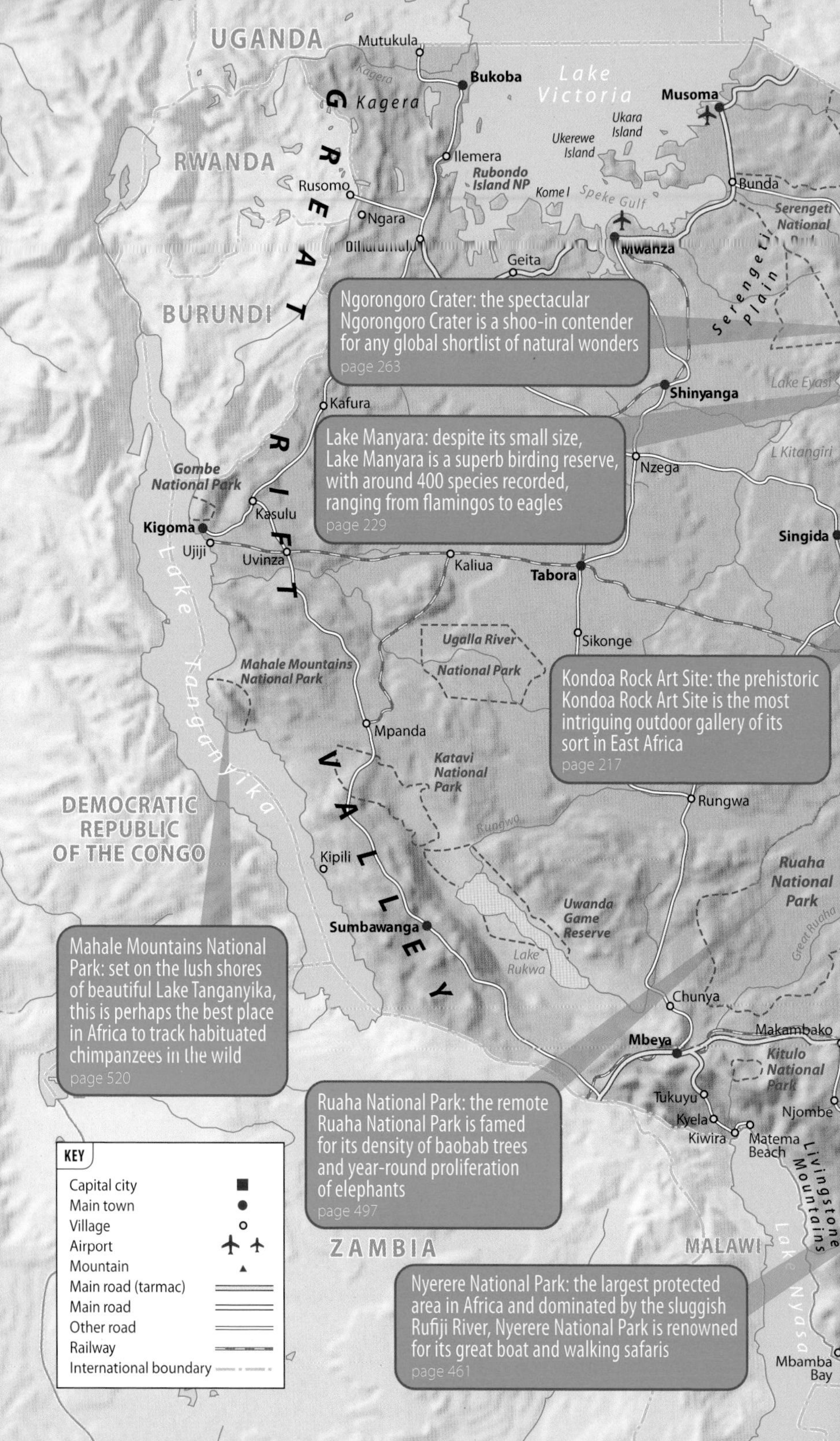

UGANDA
RWANDA
BURUNDI
DEMOCRATIC REPUBLIC OF THE CONGO
ZAMBIA
MALAWI
Lake Victoria
GREAT RIFT VALLEY
Lake Tanganyika
Mutukula
Bukoba
Kagera
Musoma
Ukara Island
Ukerewe Island
Ilemera
Rubondo Island NP
Rusomo
Ngara
Kome I
Speke Gulf
Bunda
Serengeti National Park
Mwanza
Geita
Serengeti Plain
Ngorongoro Crater: the spectacular Ngorongoro Crater is a shoo-in contender for any global shortlist of natural wonders
page 263
Shinyanga
Lake Eyasi
Kafura
Lake Manyara: despite its small size, Lake Manyara is a superb birding reserve, with around 400 species recorded, ranging from flamingos to eagles
page 229
Nzega
L Kitangiri
Gombe National Park
Kasulu
Kigoma
Ujiji
Uvinza
Kaliua
Tabora
Singida
Sikonge
Ugalla River National Park
Mahale Mountains National Park
Kondoa Rock Art Site: the prehistoric Kondoa Rock Art Site is the most intriguing outdoor gallery of its sort in East Africa
page 217
Mpanda
Katavi National Park
Rungwa
Kipili
Ruaha National Park
Great Ruaha
Uwanda Game Reserve
Sumbawanga
Lake Rukwa
Mahale Mountains National Park: set on the lush shores of beautiful Lake Tanganyika, this is perhaps the best place in Africa to track habituated chimpanzees in the wild
page 520
Chunya
Makambako
Mbeya
Kitulo National Park
Tukuyu
Njombe
Kyela
Kiwira
Matema Beach
Livingstone Mountains
Ruaha National Park: the remote Ruaha National Park is famed for its density of baobab trees and year-round proliferation of elephants
page 497
Lake Nyasa
Nyerere National Park: the largest protected area in Africa and dominated by the sluggish Rufiji River, Nyerere National Park is renowned for its great boat and walking safaris
page 461
Mbamba Bay
KEY
Capital city
Main town
Village
Airport
Mountain
Main road (tarmac)
Main road
Other road
Railway
International boundary

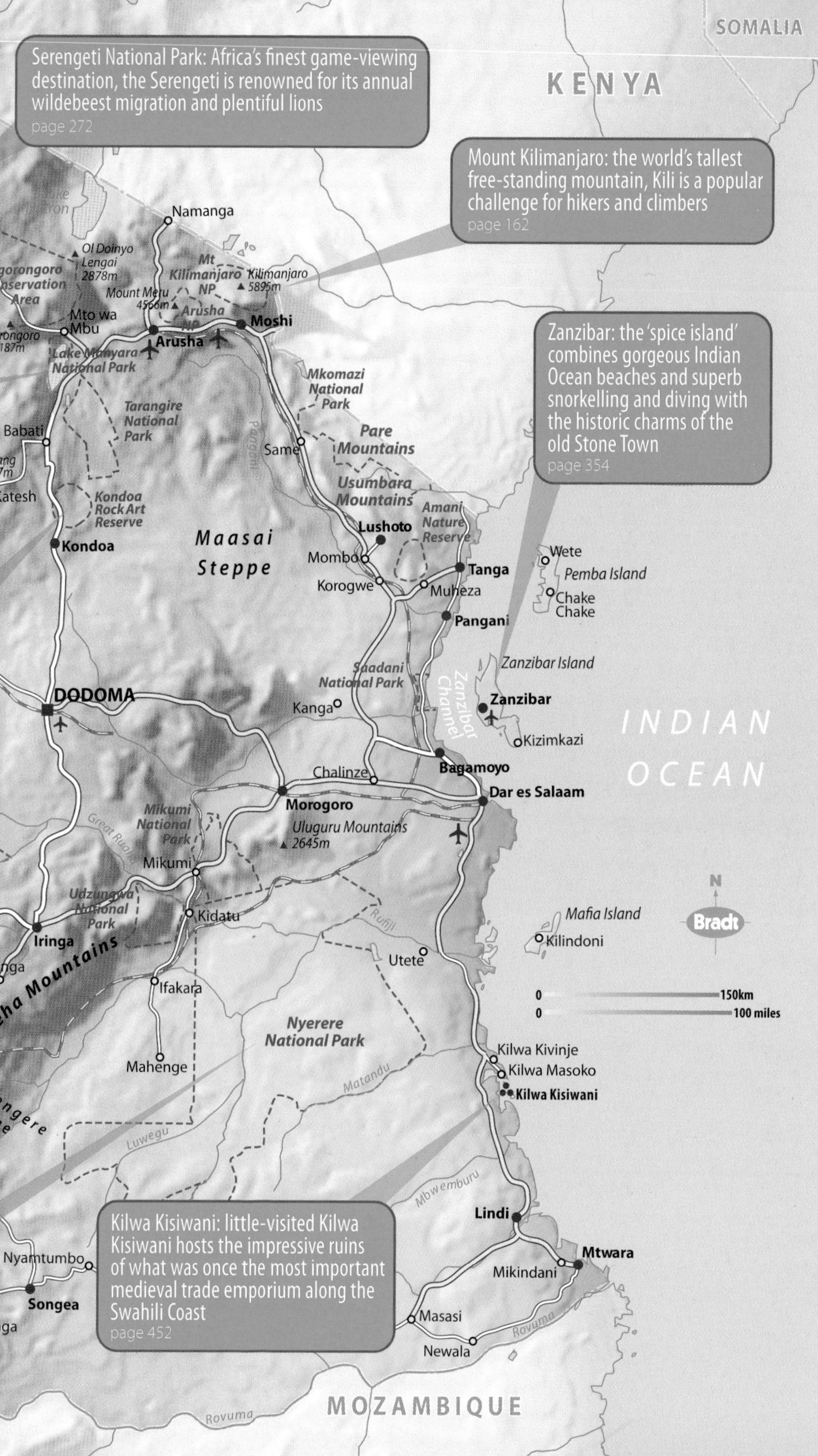

Serengeti National Park: Africa's finest game-viewing destination, the Serengeti is renowned for its annual wildebeest migration and plentiful lions
page 272
Mount Kilimanjaro: the world's tallest free-standing mountain, Kili is a popular challenge for hikers and climbers
page 162
Zanzibar: the 'spice island' combines gorgeous Indian Ocean beaches and superb snorkelling and diving with the historic charms of the old Stone Town
page 354
Kilwa Kisiwani: little-visited Kilwa Kisiwani hosts the impressive ruins of what was once the most important medieval trade emporium along the Swahili Coast
page 452
SOMALIA
KENYA
INDIAN OCEAN
MOZAMBIQUE
Namanga
Ol Doinyo Lengai 2878m
Mt Kilimanjaro NP
Kilimanjaro 5895m
Mount Meru 4566m
Arusha NP
Mto wa Mbu
Arusha
Moshi
Lake Manyara National Park
Tarangire National Park
Mkomazi National Park
Pare Mountains
Same
Babati
Katesh
Kondoa Rock Art Reserve
Kondoa
Usumbara Mountains
Amani Nature Reserve
Lushoto
Maasai Steppe
Mombo
Korogwe
Tanga
Muheza
Pangani
Wete
Pemba Island
Chake Chake
Zanzibar Island
Saadani National Park
Zanzibar Channel
Zanzibar
Kizimkazi
DODOMA
Kanga
Bagamoyo
Chalinze
Dar es Salaam
Morogoro
Mikumi National Park
Uluguru Mountains 2645m
Great Ruaha
Mikumi
Udzungwa National Park
Kidatu
Iringa
Rufiji
Mafia Island
Kilindoni
Utete
Ifakara
Bradt
N
0 150km
0 100 miles
Nyerere National Park
Mahenge
Matandu
Kilwa Kivinje
Kilwa Masoko
Kilwa Kisiwani
Luwegu
Mbwemburu
Lindi
Mtwara
Nyamtumbo
Mikindani
Songea
Masasi
Newala
Rovuma

TANZANIA
DON'T MISS...

TRADITIONAL CULTURE

The primal scenery of the Tanzanian interior is enhanced by the colourful presence of traditional pastoralists such as the Maasai and Barabaig. Pictured, Maasai women painting their faces with red ochre

PAGES 254 & 212

HIKING AND CLIMBING

Whether you summit the mighty Mount Kilimanjaro, scale the active volcano Ol Doinyo Lengai, or track chimpanzees in the forested Mahale Mountains, Tanzania is rife with hiking opportunities

PAGE 75

Climbers on Uhuru Peak, the summit of Mount Kilimanjaro

THE 'BIG FIVE'

National parks and reserves such as the Serengeti, Ruaha, Nyerere, Katavi and Ngorongoro offer an excellent opportunity for viewing the famous 'Big Five' PAGE 23

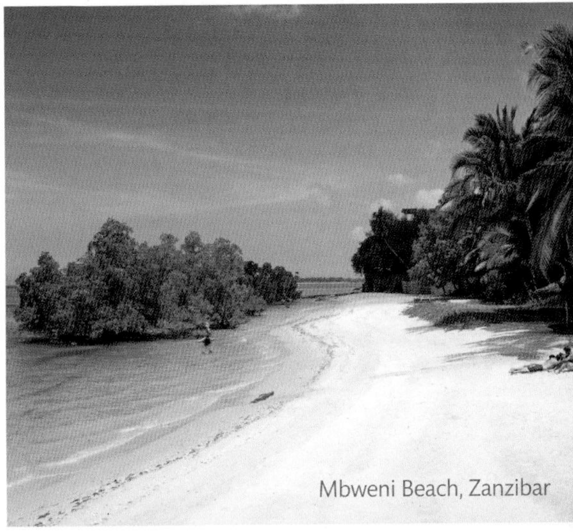

Mbweni Beach, Zanzibar

COASTAL DELIGHTS

Some of Africa's finest beaches line the coast of Zanzibar, an offshore island renowned for its snorkelling and diving opportunities, and traditional Swahili Stone Town PAGE 354

Lilac-breasted rollers

MAGNIFICENT BIRDLIFE

A checklist of more than 1,000 bird species includes brightly coloured lovebirds, rollers and bee-eaters, soaring eagles and buzzards, and 30-odd national endemics found nowhere else in the world PAGE 61

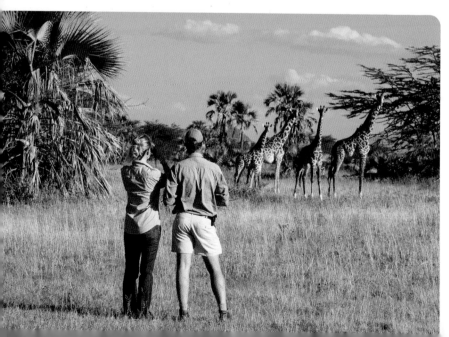

TANZANIA
IN COLOUR

above The Ngorongoro Crater is a mesmerising safari experience – made all the more spectacular by the striking backdrop of the 600m-high crater wall PAGE 257

below Lake Manyara National Park is a compact but ecologically varied area known for its tree-climbing lions, plentiful giraffes and prodigious birdlife PAGE 229

above Hot-air balloon rides in the Serengeti are an unforgettable experience. Gliding serenely above the trees as the sun rises allows you to see the expansive plains from a new and quite thrilling angle PAGE 284

right Tarangire National Park is best known for its density of baobab trees and year-round proliferation of elephants PAGE 201

below A boat trip on the Rufiji River is a must for any visitor to the Nyerere National Park PAGE 472

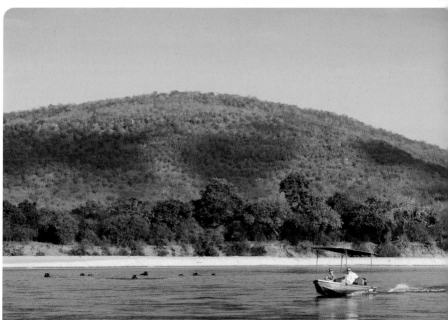

AUTHORS

Philip Briggs (e philip.briggs@bradtguides.com) has been exploring the highways and backwaters of Africa since he first backpacked there in 1986. In the 1990s, he authored pioneering Bradt guidebooks to several destinations then practically uncharted by the travel publishing industry, notably Tanzania, Uganda, Ethiopia, Malawi, Mozambique, Ghana and Rwanda. More recently, he wrote the Bradt Guides to Somaliland, Suriname, Sri Lanka and The Gambia. He spends at least four months travelling annually, usually accompanied by his wife, photographer Ariadne Van Zandbergen, and spends the rest of his time battering away at a keyboard in the coastal village of Wilderness in South Africa's Western Cape. Philip also acts as an advisor to specialist tour operator Expert Africa, helping to develop their programmes.

Chris McIntyre went to Africa in 1987, after reading Physics at Queen's College, Oxford. He taught with VSO in Zimbabwe for almost three years and travelled extensively, before writing his first guidebook in 1990. He has since written Bradt guides to Namibia, Botswana and Zambia, and co-authored (with his wife, Susie) the last four editions of Bradt's *Zanzibar* and (with Philip Briggs) the previous editions of *Tanzania* and *Northern Tanzania*. Since the late 1990s, Chris has also run specialist tour operator Expert Africa. Here he leads a team of dedicated Africa addicts – based in London, Cape Town, San Francisco and New Zealand – who provide impartial advice and guidance on great safaris to sub-Saharan Africa, including Tanzania. He can be contacted on e chris.mcintyre@expertafrica.com.

MAJOR CONTRIBUTORS

Ariadne Van Zandbergen, who took most of the photographs in this book and did much of the research for the sections on Kilimanjaro and Ol Doinyo Lengai, is a Belgian-born freelance photographer who first travelled through Africa in 1994–95 and now lives in South Africa. Her photographs have appeared in numerous travel and wildlife guides, coffee-table books, magazines and newspapers, and she runs her own website (**w** africaimagelibrary.com).

Susie McIntyre is co-author of Bradt's *Zanzibar*. Having worked in public relations for the travel industry since 1999, she created media campaigns for tourist boards worldwide before focusing on some of southern Africa's finest independent safari camps and boutique hotels. She continues to travel and to advise on Expert Africa's programme of trips to the Zanzibar archipelago and the Seychelles, with an increasing interest in adventurous family travel, thanks to the young McIntyres!

Emma Thomson (**w** ethomson.co.uk), former Commissioning Editor at Bradt Guides, is an award-winning freelance writer for the UK nationals and a Fellow of the Royal Geographical Society. She has spent time living with Rangi, Chagga and Maasai communities in Tanzania and has summited Kilimanjaro. She is also the author of Bradt's award-winning Flanders guide.

Christine Osborne, who wrote the original chapter on Mafia Island, has travelled widely as a writer and photographer. She is a member of the British Guild of Travel Writers.

AUTHOR'S STORY

Philip Briggs

We go back a bit, do Tanzania and I. Our first stilted encounter was back in 1986, when as a nervous novice traveller heading from Kenya to Zambia, I'd heard so much about the nightmarish black market, appalling public transport and obtuse officials that I decided to nip through Tanzania in less than a week, stopping only to catch my breath in the spectacularly rundown port of Dar es Salaam.

Two years later, I returned to Tanzania on a less intimidated footing, and followed a more adventurous route that incorporated side trips to somnolent Tanga and the fabulous ferry ride down Lake Tanganyika. But I guess the real romance began in 1992, when I spent four unforgettable months bussing the length and breadth of Tanzania to research what would become the first dedicated guidebook to this extraordinarily diverse – and at the time vastly underrated – country.

Updating duties have recalled me to Tanzania regularly since then, and every time I'm struck afresh at how much it has blossomed over the course of our acquaintance. The Tanzania I first encountered in 1986 was seemingly stuck in inextricable economic decline, with every aspect of its infrastructure, from roads and public transport to electricity and water supplies, tottering on the verge of collapse. Meanwhile, manufacture had ground to a standstill – simply tracking down a warm beer in Dar was an exercise that could take on epic proportions.

Back then, tourist facilities, such as they existed, were barely functional. And an insane fixed exchange rate ensured that travel was dominated by a risky black market. Had anybody then suggested that Tanzania might one day rank as the most diverse, the most friendly, and arguably the best safari destination anywhere in Africa, I'd have thought they were insane.

And how wrong I'd have been…for today, almost 40 years on, that's exactly what Tanzania is!

FEEDBACK REQUEST

At Bradt Guides we're aware that guidebooks start to go out of date on the day they're published – and that you, our readers, are out there in the field doing research of your own. You'll find out before us when a fine new family-run hotel opens or a favourite restaurant changes hands and goes downhill. So why not tell us about your experiences? Contact us on ☎ 01753 893444 or **e** info@bradtguides.com. We will forward emails to the author who may post updates on the Bradt website at **w** bradtguides.com/updates. Alternatively, you can add a review of the book to Amazon, or share your adventures with us on Facebook, Twitter or Instagram (@BradtGuides).

Contents

LIST OF MAPS

KEY TO SYMBOLS

Symbol	Meaning	Symbol	Meaning	Symbol	Meaning
	International boundary	$	Bank/ATM		Beach
	Tarred roads (town plans)		Post office		Viewpoint
	Tarred roads (regional maps)		Hospital/clinic		Archaeological site
	Other roads (regional maps)		Pharmacy		Spring/water hole
	Tracks/4x4 (regional maps)		Hotel/inn etc		Snorkel/scuba diving
	Footpath		Campsite		Woodland feature
	Railway/station		Resthouse/hut		Summit (height in metres)
	Airport/airstrip		Bar		Stadium/sports facility
	Pedestrian ferry & route		Restaurant, etc		Escarpment (rift valley)
	Bus station		Nightclub/casino		Crater
	Filling station/garage		Internet access		Glacier
	Tourist information		Telephone		Marsh
	Embassy		Church/cathedral		Coral
	Museum		Hindu temple		National park
	Theatre/cinema		Mosque		Forest park/reserve
	Important/historic building		Sikh temple		Urban market
	Castle/fortification		Garden		Urban park
	Statue/monument		Golf course		

HOW TO USE THIS GUIDE

AUTHORS' FAVOURITES Finding genuinely characterful accommodation or that unmissable off-the-beaten-track café can be difficult, so the authors have chosen a few of their favourite places throughout the country to point you in the right direction. These 'authors' favourites' are marked with a *.

LISTINGS Unless stated otherwise in the text, hotels and restaurants with entries in the *Where to stay* and *Where to eat and drink* sections in each chapter are listed alphabetically or, where applicable, by price bracket then alphabetically within each bracket. For accommodation and restaurant price codes, see pages 94 and 96 respectively.

MAPS

Keys and symbols Maps include alphabetical keys covering the locations of those places to stay, eat or drink that are featured in the book. Note that regional maps may not show all hotels and restaurants in the area: other establishments may be located in towns shown on the map.

Grids and grid references Several maps use gridlines to allow easy location of sites. Map grid references are listed in square brackets after the name of the place or sight of interest in the text, with page number followed by grid number, eg: [126 C3].

Introduction

Tanzania is Africa's ultimate safari destination. Statistics alone support this assertion eloquently. An unprecedented 38% of the country is protected in a network of conservation areas that incorporates the continent's most famous national park (Serengeti) and its largest (Nyerere). An estimated 10,000–15,000 lions still roam the country, three or four times as many as the nearest contender (South Africa with around 3,500), while the elephant population, estimated at 60,000 despite a devastating outbreak of commercial poaching over 2010–15, represents around 10% of the continental total. Less tangibly, it is thought that Tanzania supports something like 20% of Africa's large mammal biomass, much of it comprising the Serengeti's migratory herd of around 2 million wildebeest and zebra.

Moulded by the violent tectonic activity that created the Great Rift Valley, Tanzania is home to the continent's highest mountain, to the world's largest intact caldera, and to one of its most active volcanoes. It is bordered by Africa's largest three lakes: one of which is also the world's second most extensive freshwater body. These three inland seas vie with each other for the honour of harbouring the world's greatest diversity of freshwater fish. And if that were not enough, Tanzania also boasts Africa's second-longest bird checklist (after the Democratic Republic of Congo), with some 1,100 species recorded, including around 30 endemics.

So, the map of Tanzania is guaranteed to leave any statistician salivating. But, reading like a virtual litany of Africa's most evocative place names, it will also touch the heart of a poet. There's the magical offshore 'spice island' of Zanzibar. The snow-capped peak of Kilimanjaro rising dramatically above the surrounding scrubland. The endless plains of Serengeti National Park, the Edenesque vistas of Ngorongoro Crater, and the vast tracts of bush enclosed within the Nyerere National Park. Dusty Oldupai Gorge is the site of some of the most important hominid fossil finds ever, while lush Gombe National Park is where Jane Goodall embarked on her pioneering study of chimpanzees, our closest living relatives. There is the Maasai Steppe, where Africa's most charismatic pastoralists herd their cattle alongside fields of grazing wildlife. On the same map, you'll find an Indian Ocean coast lined by the modern port of Dar es Salaam and its legendary medieval forbear Kilwa, as well as the sky-blue expanses of lakes Victoria, Tanganyika and Natron, the last situated below the temperamental volcano Ol Doinyo Lengai.

Despite its great natural wealth, Tanzania was a relatively slow starter when it came to post-independence tourist development. In the early 1990s, tourist facilities were limited to a few government lodges whose dire standards reflected the sagging economic infrastructure and the anti-investor policies of the then-socialist government. Then, as now, Tanzania's profile as a safari destination is often overshadowed by that of neighbouring Kenya. But otherwise the situation has changed dramatically over the intervening two decades. Indeed, Tanzania today boasts some of the finest and most exclusive safari lodges and camps you'll find anywhere in Africa, as well as a world-class selection of city hotels and beach resorts, the latter concentrated on the islands of Zanzibar, Pemba and Mafia.

The evolution of the book you now hold in your hand reflects these changes. *The Bradt Guide to Tanzania* started life in 1993 as a pioneering warts-'n'-all manual to a country then practically uncharted by the guidebook industry and best suited to explorative, tolerant travellers. Over the course of its first six editions, the book trebled in length and gradually shifted in emphasis to reflect the ongoing expansion and upmarket drift that has characterised the county's tourist industry. Finally, with the seventh edition, we decided to acknowledge that Tanzania is now primarily a 'safari' and 'holiday' destination, as opposed to a 'travel' destination, by placing the emphasis squarely on genuine tourist attractions, both established and obscure, as well as on key urban travel hubs such as Arusha, Moshi and Dar es Salaam – a process that has been further refined and honed down for subsequent editions.

Structurally, the largest portion of this book (chapters 5–13) is devoted to Arusha and the northern safari circuit. Here, a well-defined tourist trail centres upon the world-famous Ngorongoro Crater and Serengeti, Lake Manyara and Tarangire national parks. But the region also boasts a wealth of more obscure highlights, among them ancient rock art of Kondoa, the hunter-gatherer cultures of Lake Eyasi, the biodiverse forests of Amani Nature Reserve and Rubondo Island National Park, and the primeval volcanic landscape of Lake Natron and Ol Doinyo Lengai. It is also a region that offers some fine hiking, most famously the sapping climb of Kilimanjaro, but also the scenic ascent up Mount Meru (the fifth highest in Africa) and limitless opportunities for rambling in the Usambara.

Safaris and wildlife viewing are also the primary concern of the portion of this book (chapters 18–21) dedicated to the southern and western safari circuits. Though not as well known as the Serengeti and other parks of the north, the south boasts three superb safari destinations, namely Nyerere, Ruaha and Mikumi national parks. These parks feel much untrammelled by comparison with the north, and Selous in particular is recommended to adventurous safari-goers who want to supplement conventional game drives with guided bush walks and boat trips on the Rufiji River. Wilder still is Katavi National Park, a superb plains reserve which, together with Mahale Mountains – the finest place in Africa to track chimpanzees – forms the cornerstone of the truly off-the-beaten-track western safari circuit.

Finally, as covered in chapters 14–17, there is the coast and offshore islands. This includes the country's largest city and former capital, the port of Dar es Salaam. But Tanzania's prime coastal attraction is the island of Zanzibar, with its atmospheric Swahili stone town, postcard-perfect beaches, and world-class diving and snorkelling opportunities. A similar bouquet of attractions is offered by the lesser-known islands of Pemba and Mafia, while those with a yen for exploration are pointed to the historic but little-visited old ports of Bagamoyo and Kilwa, or the bush-meets-the-beach anomaly that is Saadani National Park.

Part One

GENERAL INFORMATION

TANZANIA AT A GLANCE

Location East Africa, between 1° and 11°45'S, and 29°20' and 40°35'E
Size 945,166km^2
Climate Tropical along coast; temperate in the highlands
Status Republic
Ruling party Chama Cha Mapinduzi (CCM)
President Samia Suluhu Hassan
Population 63 million (2022 estimate)
Life expectancy 66
Capital Dodoma; 450,000 (2022 estimate)
Largest city Dar es Salaam; 6 million (2022 estimate)
Major exports Coffee, cotton, cashew nuts, sisal, tobacco, tea, diamonds, gold
Languages KiSwahili and English; over 100 regional languages
Religion 62% Christian, 35% Muslim, 3% traditional, other or none
Currency Tanzanian shilling (Tsh)
Exchange rate £1 = Tsh2,802, US$1 = Tsh2,328, €1 = Tsh2,488 (Feb 2023)
International telephone code +255
Time GMT + 3 hours
Electrical voltage 230v (60Hz). Round or square three-pin British-style plugs.
Weights and measures Metric
Flag Blue and green, with diagonal black-and-yellow stripe
Public holidays 1 January, 12 January, 7 April, 26 April, 1 May, 7 July, 8 August, 14 October, 9 December, 25–26 December. See also page 98.

1

Background Information

GEOGRAPHY

The bulk of East Africa is made up of a vast, flat plateau rising from a narrow coastal belt to an average height of about 1,500m. This plateau is broken dramatically by the 20-million-year-old Great Rift Valley, which cuts a trough up to 2,000m deep through the African continent from the Dead Sea to Mozambique. The eastern branch of the Rift Valley bisects Tanzania, while the western branch runs along the border with the Congo border. Lakes Natron, Manyara, Eyasi and Nyasa/Malawi are all in the eastern rift, Lake Tanganyika lies in the western branch, and Lake Victoria lies on an elevated plateau between them.

East Africa's highest mountains (with the exception of the Ruwenzori Mountains in Uganda) are volcanic in origin, created by the same forces that caused the emergence of the Rift Valley. Kilimanjaro is the most recent of these: it started to form about 1 million years ago, and was still growing as recently as 100,000 years ago. Mount Meru is older. Ngorongoro Crater is the collapsed caldera of a volcano that would once have been as high as Kilimanjaro is today. The only active volcano in Tanzania today is Ol Doinyo Lengai, which rises from the rift floor to the northeast of Ngorongoro.

SIZE AND LOCATION The United Republic of Tanzania came into being in 1964 when Tanganyika on the African mainland united with the offshore state of Zanzibar, the latter comprising the Indian Ocean islands of Unguja (Zanzibar) and Pemba. It lies on the East African coast between 1° and 11°45'S and 29°20' and 40°35'E, and is bordered by Kenya and Uganda to the north, Rwanda, Burundi and the Democratic Republic of Congo to the west, and Zambia, Malawi and Mozambique to the south. The country extends over 945,166km^2 (364,929 square miles), making it one of the largest countries in sub-Saharan Africa, covering a greater area than Kenya and Uganda combined. To place this in a European context, Tanzania is more than four times the size of Britain, while in an American context it's about 1.5 times the size of Texas.

CAPITAL Dodoma was earmarked as the future capital of Tanzania in 1973 and displaced Dar es Salaam as the official capital in 1996. All parliamentary sessions are held in Dodoma, and most government departments have relocated there, but Dar es Salaam remains the country's most important and largest city, and is the site of State House, the country's main international airport, most embassies and other diplomatic missions to Tanzania, and the majority of large businesses. The town of Arusha, set at the southern base of Mount Meru, is the country's unofficial safari capital and the main commercial centre in northern Tanzania.

CLIMATE

Tanzania on the whole has a pleasant tropical climate, but there are large regional climatic variations across the country, influenced by several factors, most significantly elevation. The hottest and most humid part of the country is the coast, where daytime temperatures typically hit around 30°C on most days, and are often higher. The high level of humidity exaggerates the heat on the coast, and there is little natural relief at night except from sea breezes – for which reason town centres often feel a lot hotter than nearby beaches.

Low-lying areas such as the Rift Valley floor, in particular the Lake Nyasa and Lake Tanganyika areas, are also hot, but far less humid, and thus more comfortable. At elevations of 1,000m or higher, daytime temperatures are warm to hot, and above 2,000m moderate to warm. Most parts of the interior cool down significantly at night, and montane areas such as the rim of the Ngorongoro Crater or Marangu on the foothills of Kilimanjaro can be downright chilly after dark. Alpine conditions and sub-zero night-time temperatures are characteristic of the higher slopes of Mount Meru and especially Kilimanjaro.

Tanzania is too near the Equator to experience the sort of dramatic contrast between summer and winter experienced in much of Europe or North America. The months between October and April are marginally hotter than May to September. In Dar es Salaam, for instance, the hottest month is February (average maximum 32°C; average minimum 23°C), and the coolest month is July (28°C; 18°C). Insignificant as this difference might look on paper, the coast is far more pleasant in the cooler months, while highland towns are far chillier.

Virtually all of Tanzania's rain falls between November and May. The rainy season is generally split into the short rains or *mvuli*, over November and December, and the long rains or *masika* from late February to early May. This pattern of two rainy seasons is strongest in coastal areas and in the extreme north around Arusha, where there is relatively little rainfall in January and February. Even then, there are years when the rain falls more continuously from November to May than is indicated by average rainfall figures. In many other parts of the country, figures suggest that rain falls fairly consistently between mid November and mid April.

For climate charts, see page 74.

HABITATS AND VEGETATION

The bulk of Tanzania is covered in open grassland, savannah (lightly wooded grassland) and woodland. The Serengeti Plains are an archetypal African savannah: grassland interspersed with trees of the acacia family – which are typically quite short, lightly foliated and thorny. Many have a flat-topped appearance. An atypical acacia, the yellow fever, is one of Africa's most striking trees. It is relatively large, has yellow bark and is often associated with water. *Combretum* is a genus of trees typical of many savannah habitats. The dry savannah of central Tanzania can be so barren during the dry season that it resembles semi-desert.

Woodland differs from forest in lacking an interlocking canopy. The most extensive woodland in Tanzania is in the miombo belt, which stretches from southern and western Tanzania to Zimbabwe. Miombo woodland typically grows on infertile soil, and is dominated by broad-leafed Brachystegia trees. You may come across the term 'mixed woodland': this refers to woodland with a mix of Brachystegia, acacia and other species. Many woodland habitats are characterised by an abundance of baobab trees.

True closed-canopy forest covers less than 1% of Tanzania's surface area, but is the most diverse habitat ecologically, with the forests of the Usambara, for instance, containing more than 2,000 plant species. Most of the forest in Tanzania is montane, associated with the Eastern Arc Mountains and other tall mountains. On the northern safari circuit, the habitat is represented by the montane forests of Kilimanjaro, Meru, Ngorongoro Crater rim and various lesser mountains, as well as the groundwater forests around Lake Duluti and in Lake Manyara. The lowland forests found in the extreme west of the country have strong affinities with the rainforests of Congo.

Other interesting but localised vegetation types are mangrove swamps (common along the coast, particularly around Kilwa) and the heath and moorland found on the higher slopes of Kilimanjaro and Meru.

HISTORY

Tanzania has a rich and fascinating history, but much of the detail is highly elusive. Specialist works often contradict each other to such an extent that it is difficult to tell where fact ends and speculation begins, while broader or more popular accounts are commonly riddled with obvious inaccuracies. This is partly because there are huge gaps in the known facts; partly because much of the available information is scattered in out-of-print or difficult-to-find books; and partly because once an inaccuracy gets into print it tends to spread like a virus through other written works. For whatever reason there is not, as far as I am aware, one concise, comprehensive and reliable book about Tanzanian history in print.

The following account attempts to provide a reasonably comprehensive and readable overview of the country's history. It is, to the best of my knowledge, as accurate as the known facts will allow, but at times I have had to decide for myself the most probable truth among a mass of contradictions, and I have speculated freely where speculation seems to be the order of the day. My goals are to stimulate the visitor's interest in Tanzanian history, and to give easy access to information that would have greatly enhanced my formative travels in Tanzania. Many of the subjects touched on in this general history are given more elaborate treatment elsewhere in the book, under regional history sections or in tinted boxes.

PREHISTORY OF THE INTERIOR The part of the Rift Valley passing through Ethiopia, Kenya and northern Tanzania is almost certainly where modern human beings and their hominine ancestors evolved. The two most common hominine genera on the fossil record are *Australopithecus* and *Homo*, the former extinct for at least a million years, and the latter now represented by only one species – *Homo sapiens* (modern man). The paucity of hominine fossils collected before the 1960s meant that for many years it was assumed that *A. africanus* (the most common Australopithecine in the fossil record) evolved directly into the genus *Homo* and was thus man's oldest identifiable ancestor.

This linear theory of human evolution became blurred when Richard and Mary Leakey, who were excavating Oldupai Gorge in northern Tanzania, discovered that at least two *Australopithecus* species had existed. Carbon dating and the skeletal structure of the two species indicated that the older *A. robustus* had less in common with modern man than its more lightly built ancestor *A. africanus*, implying that the *Australopithecus* line was not ancestral to the *Homo* line at all. This hypothesis was confirmed in 1972 with the discovery of a 2-million-year-old skull of a previously undescribed species *Homo habilis* at Lake Turkana in Kenya, providing conclusive evidence that *Australopithecus* and *Homo* species had lived alongside each other for at least 1 million years. As more fossils have come to light, including older examples of *Homo erectus* (the direct ancestor of modern humans), it has become clear that several different hominine species existed alongside each other in the Rift Valley until perhaps half a million years ago.

In 1974, Donald Johansen discovered an almost complete hominine skeleton in the Danakil region of northern Ethiopia. Named Lucy (the song 'Lucy in the Sky with Diamonds' was playing in camp shortly after the discovery), this turned out to be the fossil of a 3.5-million-year-old Australopithecine of an entirely new species dubbed *A. afarensis*. Lucy's anatomy demonstrated that bipedal hominines (or rather semi-bipedal, since the length of Lucy's arms suggest she would have been as comfortable swinging through the trees as she would have been on a morning jog) had evolved much earlier than previously assumed.

In the 1960s it was widely thought that humans and apes diverged around 20 million years ago. More recent molecular studies indicate that modern man and chimpanzees are far more closely related than previously assumed, and that the two evolutionary lines diverged from a common ancestor between 8 and 6 million years ago. The Afar region of Ethiopia has yielded the world's oldest undisputed hominine *Ardipithecus kadabba* (thought to be 5.5 million to 5.8 million years old). More controversial candidates for the title of the world's oldest known hominine fossil include the 6-million- to 7-million-year-old *Sahelanthropus tchadensis*, discovered in Chad in 2001, and the arboreal *Orrorin tugenensis*, which lived in Kenya about 6 million years ago and might represent a common ancestor of chimpanzees and hominines.

Thought to be the immediate ancestor of modern man, *Homo erectus* first appears on the fossil record about 2 million years ago. *Homo erectus* was the first hominine to surmount the barrier of the Sahara and spread into Europe and Asia, and is credited with the discovery of fire and the first use of stone tools and recognisable speech. Although modern man, *Homo sapiens*, has been around for around 300,000 years, only in the last 10,000 years have the African races recognised today more or less taken their modern form. Up until about 1000BC, East Africa was populated exclusively by hunter-gatherers with a physiology, culture and language similar to the modern-day Khoisan (or Bushmen) of southern Africa. Rock art accredited to these hunter-gatherers is found throughout East Africa, most notably in the Kondoa-Irangi region of central Tanzania.

The pastoralist and agricultural lifestyles that were pioneered in the Nile Delta in about 5000BC spread to parts of sub-Saharan Africa by 2000BC, most notably to the Cushitic-speaking people of the Ethiopian Highlands and the Bantu-speakers of West Africa. Cushitic-speakers first drifted into Tanzania in about 1000BC, closely followed by Bantu-speakers. Familiar with Iron Age technology, these migrants would have soon dominated the local hunter-gatherers. By AD1000, most of Tanzania was populated by Bantu-speakers, with Cushitic-speaking pockets in areas such as the Ngorongoro Highlands.

There is no detailed information about the Tanzanian interior prior to 1500, and even after that details are sketchy. Except for the Lake Victoria region, which supported large authoritarian kingdoms similar to those in Uganda, much of the Tanzanian interior is too dry to support large concentrations of people. In most of Tanzania, an informal system of ***ntemi*** chiefs emerged. The ntemi system, although structured, seems to have been flexible and benevolent. The chiefs were served by a council and performed a role that was as much advisory as it was authoritarian. By the 19th century there are estimated to have been more than 200 ntemi chiefs in western and central Tanzania, each with about 1,000 subjects.

The ntemi system was shattered when southern Tanzania was invaded by **Ngoni** exiles from what is now South Africa, refugees from the rampantly militaristic Zulu Kingdom moulded by Shaka in the early 19th century. The Ngoni entered southern Tanzania in about 1840, bringing with them the revolutionary Zulu military tactics based on horseshoe formations and a short stabbing spear. The new arrivals attacked the resident tribes, destroying communities and leaving survivors no option but to turn to banditry. Their tactics were observed and adopted by the more astute ntemi chiefs, who needed to protect themselves, but had to forge larger kingdoms to do so. The situation was exacerbated by the growing presence of Arab slave traders. Tribes controlling the areas that caravan routes went through were able to extract taxes from the slavers and to find work with them as porters or organising slave raids. This situation was exploited by several chiefs, most notably Mirambo of Unyamwezi and Mkwawa of the Uhehe, charismatic leaders who dominated the interior in the late 19th century.

THE COAST TO 1800 There have been links between the East African coast and the rest of the world for millennia, but only the barest sketch of events before AD1000 is possible. The ancient Egyptians believed their ancestors came from a southerly land called **Punt** and in about 2500BC an explorer called Sahare sailed off in search of this mysterious place. Sahare returned laden with ivory, ebony and myrrh, a booty that suggests he had landed somewhere on the East African coast, most likely in the north of present-day Somalia (but possibly further south). There is no suggestion that Egyptian boats traded regularly with Punt, but they did visit it again on several occasions. Interestingly, an engraving of the Queen of Punt, made after an expedition in 1493BC, shows her to have distinctly Khoisan features. The Phoenicians first explored the coast in about 600BC. According to the 1st-century *Periplus of the Ancient Sea* they traded with a town called Rhapta, which is thought to have lain upriver of a major estuary, possibly the Pangani or the Rufiji Delta.

Bantu-speakers arrived at the coast about 2,000 years ago. It seems likely they had trade links with the **Roman Empire**: Rhapta gets a name check in Ptolemy's 4th-century *Geography*, and a few 4th-century Roman coins have been found at the coast. The fact that the Romans knew of Kilimanjaro, and of the great lakes of the interior, raises some interesting questions. One hypothesis is that the coastal Bantu-speakers were running trade routes into the interior and that these collapsed at the same time as the Roman Empire, presumably as a result of the sudden dearth of trade partners. This notion is attractive and not implausible, but the evidence seems rather flimsy. The Romans could simply have gleaned the information from Bantu-speakers who had arrived at the coast recently enough to have some knowledge of the interior.

Historians have a clearer picture of events on the coast from about AD1000, by which time trade between the coast and the Persian Gulf was well established. The earliest-known Islamic buildings on the coast, which stand on Manda Island off Kenya, have been dated to the 9th century AD. Items sold to Arab ships at this time included ivory, ebony and spices, while a variety of oriental and Arabic goods were imported for the use of wealthy traders. The dominant item of export, however, was **gold**, mined in the Great Zimbabwe region, transported to the coast at Sofala (in modern-day Mozambique) via the Zambezi Valley, then shipped by local traders to Mogadishu, where it was sold to the Arab boats. The common assumption that Swahili language and culture was a direct result of Arab traders mixing with local Bantu-speakers is probably inaccurate. KiSwahili is a Bantu language, and although it did spread along the coast in the 11th century, most of the Arabic words that have entered the language did so at a later date. The driving force behind a common coastal language and culture was almost certainly not the direct trade with Arabs, but rather the internal trade between Sofala and Mogadishu.

More than 30 Swahili city-states sprung up along the East African coast between the 13th and 15th centuries, a large number of which were in modern-day Tanzania. This period is known as the **Shirazi era** after the sultans who ruled these city-states, most of whom claimed descent from the Shiraz region of Persia. Each city-state had its own sultan; they rarely interfered in each other's business. The Islamic faith was widespread during this period, and many Arabic influences crept into coastal architecture. Cities were centred on a great mosque, normally constructed in rock and coral. It has long been assumed that the many Arabs who settled on the coast before and during the Shirazi era controlled the trade locally, but this notion has been questioned in recent years. Contemporary descriptions of the city-states suggest that Africans formed the bulk of the population. It is possible that some African traders claimed Shirazi descent in order to boost their standing both locally and with Shirazi ships.

In the mid 13th century, probably due to improvements in Arab navigation and ship construction, the centre of the gold trade moved southward from Mogadishu to the small island of Kilwa. Kilwa represented the peak of the Shirazi period. It had a population of 10,000 and operated its own mint, the first in sub-equatorial Saharan Africa. The multi-domed mosque on Kilwa was the largest and most splendid anywhere on the coast, while another building, now known as Husuni Kubwa, was a gargantuan palace, complete with audience courts, several ornate balconies and even a swimming pool.

Although Mombasa had possibly superseded Kilwa in importance by the end of the 15th century, coastal trade was still booming. It came to an abrupt halt in 1505, however, when the **Portuguese** captured Mombasa, and several other coastal towns, Kilwa included, were razed. Under Portuguese control the gold trade collapsed and the coastal economy stagnated. It was dealt a further blow in the late 16th century when a mysterious tribe of cannibals called the Zimba swept up the coast to ransack several cities and eat their inhabitants before being defeated by a mixed Portuguese and local army near Malindi in modern-day Kenya.

In 1698, an Arabic naval force under the Sultan of Oman captured Fort Jesus, the Portuguese stronghold in Mombasa, paving the way for the eventual Omani takeover of the coast north of modern-day Mtwara. Rivalries between the new Omani and the old Shirazi dynasties soon surfaced, and in 1728 a group of Shirazi sultans went so far as to conspire with their old oppressors, the Portuguese, to overthrow Fort Jesus. The Omani recaptured the fort a year later. For the next 100 years an uneasy peace gripped the coast, which was nominally under Omani rule, but dominated in economic terms by the Shirazi Sultan of Mombasa.

SLAVERY AND EXPLORATION IN THE 19TH CENTURY The 19th century was a period of rapid change in Tanzania, with stronger links established between the coast and the interior as well as between East Africa and Europe. Over the first half of the 19th century, the most important figure locally was **Sultan Seyyid Said of Oman**, who ruled from 1804 to 1854. Prior to 1804, Britain had signed a treaty with Oman, and relations between the two powers intensified in the wake of the Napoleonic Wars, since the British did not want to see the coast fall into French hands. In 1827, Said's small but efficient navy captured Mombasa and overthrew its Shirazi sultan, to assert unambiguous control over the whole coast, with strong British support.

Having captured Mombasa, Sultan Said chose Zanzibar as his East African base, partly because of its proximity to Bagamoyo (the terminus of a caravan route to Lake Tanganyika since 1823) and partly because it was more secure against attacks from the sea or the interior than any mainland port. Said's commercial involvement with Zanzibar began in 1827 when he set up a number of clove plantations there, with scant regard for the land claims of local inhabitants. Said and his fellow Arabs had come to totally dominate all aspects of commerce on the island by 1840, the year in which the sultan permanently relocated his personal capital from Oman to Zanzibar.

The extent of the East African **slave trade** prior to 1827 is unclear. It certainly existed, but was never as important as the gold or ivory trade. In part, this was because the traditional centre of slave trading had always been West Africa, which was far closer than the Indian Ocean to the main markets of the Americas. In the early 19th century, however, the British curbed the slave trade out of West Africa, leaving the way open for Said and his cronies. By 1839, over 40,000 slaves were being sold from Zanzibar annually. These came from two sources: the central caravan route between Bagamoyo and the Lake Tanganyika region, and a southern route between Kilwa Kivinje and Lake Nyasa.

The effects of the slave trade on the interior were numerous. The **Nyamwezi** of the Tabora region and the **Yua** of Nyasa became very powerful by serving as porters along the caravan routes and organising slave raids and ivory hunts. Weaker tribes were devastated. Villages were ransacked; the able-bodied men and women were taken away while the young and old were left to die. Hundreds of thousands of slaves were sold in the mid 19th century. Nobody knows how many more died of disease or exhaustion between being captured and reaching the coast. Another long-term effect of the slave trade was that it formed the driving force behind the second great expansion of KiSwahili, which became the lingua franca along caravan routes.

Europeans knew little about the African interior in 1850. The first Europeans to see Kilimanjaro (Rebmann in 1848) and Mount Kenya (Krapf in 1849) were ridiculed for their reports of snow on the Equator. The Arab traders must have had an intimate knowledge of many parts of the interior that intrigued Europeans, but, oddly, at least in hindsight, nobody seems to have thought to ask them. In 1855, a German missionary, **James Erhardt**, produced a map of Africa, based on third-hand Arab accounts, which showed a large slug-shaped lake in the heart of the continent. Known as the Slug Map, it was wildly inaccurate, yet it did serve to fan interest in a mystery that had tickled geographers since Roman times: the source of the Nile.

The men most responsible for opening up the East African interior to Europeans were **David Livingstone**, **Richard Burton**, **John Speke** and, later, **Henry Stanley**. Livingstone, who came from a poor Scots background, left school at the age of ten, and educated himself to become a doctor and a missionary. He arrived in the Cape in 1841 to work in the Kuruman Mission, but, overcome by the enormity of the task of converting Africa to Christianity, he decided he would be of greater service opening up the continent so that other missionaries could follow. Livingstone was the first European to cross the Kalahari Desert, the first to cross Africa from west to east and the first to see Victoria Falls. In 1858, he stumbled across Africa's third-largest lake, Nyasa. Later in the same year, on a quest for the source of the Nile funded by the Royal Geographical Society, Burton and Speke were the first Europeans to see Lake Tanganyika, and Speke continued north to Lake Victoria. Speke returned to the northern shore of Lake Victoria in 1863 and concluded – correctly, although it would be many years before the theory gained wide acceptance – that Ripon Falls in modern-day Uganda formed the source of the Nile.

Livingstone had ample opportunity during his wanderings to witness the slave caravans at first hand. Sickened by what he saw – the human bondage, the destruction of entire villages, and the corpses abandoned by the traders – he became an outspoken critic of the trade. He believed the only way to curb it was to open up Africa to the three Cs: Christianity, commerce and civilisation. Though not an imperialist by nature, Livingstone had seen enough of the famine and misery caused by the slavers and the Ngoni in the Nyasa area to believe the only solution was for Britain to colonise eastern Africa.

In 1867, Livingstone set off from Mikindani to spend the last six years of his life wandering between the great lakes, making notes on the slave trade and trying to settle the Nile debate. He believed the source of the Nile to be Lake Bangweulu (in northern Zambia), from which the mighty Lualaba River flowed. In 1872, while recovering from illness at Ujiji, Livingstone was met by Henry Stanley and became the recipient of perhaps the most famous words ever spoken in Africa: 'Dr Livingstone, I presume.' Livingstone died near Lake Bangweulu in 1873. His heart was removed and buried by his porters, who then carried his cured body over 1,500km via Tabora to Bagamoyo, a voyage as remarkable as any undertaken by the European explorers.

Livingstone's quest to end the slave trade met with little success during his lifetime, but his death and highly emotional funeral at Westminster Abbey seem to have acted as a catalyst. Missions were built in his name all over the Nyasa region, while industrialists such as William Mackinnon and the Muir brothers invested in schemes to open Africa to commerce (which Livingstone had always believed was the key to putting the slavers out of business).

In the year Livingstone died, **John Kirk** was made the British Consul in Zanzibar. Kirk had travelled with Livingstone on his 1856–62 trip to Nyasa. Deeply affected by what he saw, he had since spent years on Zanzibar hoping to find a way to end the slave trade. In 1873, the British navy blockaded the island and Kirk offered Sultan Barghash full protection against foreign powers if he banned the slave trade. Barghash agreed. The slave market was closed and an Anglican church built over it. Within ten years of Livingstone's death, the volume of slaves was a fraction of what it had been in the 1860s. Caravans reverted to ivory as their principal trade, while many of the coastal traders started up rubber and sugar plantations, which turned out to be just as lucrative as their former trade. Nevertheless, a clandestine slave trade continued on the mainland for some years – 12,000 slaves were sold at Kilwa in 1875 – and even into the 20th century, only to be fully eradicated in 1918, when Britain took control of Tanganyika.

THE PARTITIONING OF EAST AFRICA The so-called **scramble for Africa** was entered into with mixed motives, erratic enthusiasm and an almost total lack of premeditation by the powers involved. Britain, the major beneficiary of the scramble, already enjoyed a degree of influence on Zanzibar, one that arguably approached informal colonisation, and it was quite happy to maintain this mutually agreeable relationship unaltered. Furthermore, the British government at the time, led by Lord Salisbury, was broadly opposed to the taking of African colonies. The scramble was initiated by two events. The first, the decision of King Leopold of Belgium to colonise the Congo Basin, had little direct bearing on events in Tanzania. The partitioning of East Africa was a direct result of an about-face by the German premier, Bismarck, who had previously shown no enthusiasm for acquiring colonies and probably developed an interest in Africa in the hope of acquiring pawns to use in negotiations with Britain and France.

In 1884, a young German metaphysician called **Carl Peters** arrived inauspiciously on Zanzibar and then made his way to the mainland to sign a series of treaties with local chiefs. The authenticity of these treaties is questionable, but when Bismarck announced claims to a large area between the Pangani and Rufiji rivers, it was enough to set the British government into a mild panic. Britain had plans to expand the Sultanate of Zanzibar, its informal colony, to include the fertile lands around Kilimanjaro. Worse, large parts of the area claimed by Germany were already part of the sultanate. Not only was Britain morally bound to protect these, it also did not want to surrender control of Zanzibar's annual import–export turnover of 2 million pounds.

Despite pressure put on the British government by John Kirk, angry that his promises to Barghash would not be honoured, there was little option but to negotiate with Germany. A partition was agreed in 1886, identical to the modern border between Kenya and Tanzania. (You may read that Kilimanjaro was part of the British territory before Queen Victoria gave it to her cousin, the Kaiser, as a birthday present. This amusing story, possibly dreamed up by a Victorian satirist to reflect the arbitrariness of the scramble, is complete fabrication.) In April 1888, the Sultan of Zanzibar unwillingly agreed to lease Germany the coastal strip south of the Umba River. Germany mandated this area to Carl Peters's **German East Africa Company (GEAC)**, which placed agencies at most of the coastal settlements north of Dar es Salaam. These agents demanded heavy taxes from traders and were encouraged to behave high-handedly in their dealings with locals.

The GEAC's honeymoon was short. Emil Zalewski, the Pangani agent, ordered the sultan's representative, the Wali, to report to him. When the Wali refused, Zalewski had him arrested and sent away on a German war boat. In September 1888, a sugar plantation owner called **Abushiri Ibn Salim** led an uprising against the GEAC. Except for Dar es Salaam and Bagamoyo, both protected by German war boats, the GEAC agents were either killed or driven away. A horde of 20,000 men gathered on the coast, including 6,000 Shambaa who refused to relinquish their right to claim tax from caravans passing the Usambara. In November, the mission at Dar es Salaam was attacked. Three priests were killed and the rest captured. The coast was in chaos until April 1889 when the Kaiser's troops invaded Abushiri's camp and forced him to surrender. The German government hanged Abushiri in Pangani; they withdrew the GEAC's mandate and banned Peters from ever setting foot in the area.

The 1886 agreement only created the single line of partition north of Kilimanjaro. By 1890, Germany had claimed an area north of Witu, including Lamu, and there was concern in Britain that they might try to claim the rich agricultural land around Lake Victoria, thereby surrounding Britain's territory. Undeterred by the debacle at Pangani (and with a nod and a wink from Bismarck), Carl Peters decided to force the issue. He slipped through Lamu and in May 1890, after a murderous jaunt across British territory, he signed a treaty with the King of Buganda entitling Germany to most of what is now southern Uganda. This time, however, Peters's plans were frustrated. Bismarck had resigned in March of the same year and his replacement, Von Kaprivi, wanted to maintain good relations with Salisbury's government. In any case, Henry Stanley had signed a similar treaty with the Baganda when he passed through the area in 1888 on his way from rescuing the Emin Pasha in Equatoria.

Germany had its eye on Heligoland, a small but strategic North Sea island that had been seized by Britain from Denmark in 1807. To some extent, German interest in Africa had always been related to the bargaining power it would give them in Europe. In 1890, Salisbury and Von Kaprivi knocked out the agreement that created the modern borders of mainland Tanzania (with the exception of modern-day Burundi

TRIBES

The word 'tribe' has fallen out of vogue in recent years, and I must confess that for several years I rigorously avoided the use of it in my writing. It has, I feel, rather colonial connotations, something to which I'm perhaps overly sensitive having lived most of my life in South Africa. Some African intellectuals have argued that it is derogatory, too, in so far as it is typically applied in a belittling sense to non-European cultures, where words such as 'nation' might be applied to their European equivalent.

All well and good to dispense with the word tribe, at least until you set about looking for a meaningful substitute. Nation, for instance, seems appropriate when applied in a historical sense to a large and cohesive centralised entity such as the Zulu or Hehe, but rather less so when you're talking about smaller and more loosely affiliated tribes. Furthermore, in any modern sense, Tanzania itself is a nation (and proud of it), just as are Britain and Germany, so that describing, for instance, the modern Chagga as a nation would feel as inaccurate and contrived as referring to, say, the Liverpudlian or Berliner nation.

It would be inaccurate, too, to refer to most African tribes in purely ethnic, cultural or linguistic terms. Any or all of these factors might come into play in shaping a tribal identity, without in any sense defining it. All modern tribes contain individuals with a diverse ethnic stock, simply through intermarriage. Most modern Ngoni, for instance, belong to that tribe through their ancestors having been assimilated into it, not because all or even any of their ancestors were necessarily members of the Ngoni band who migrated up from South Africa in the 19th century. And when the original Bantu-speaking people moved into present-day Tanzania thousands of years ago, local people with an entirely different ethnic background would have been assimilated into the newly established communities. Likewise, the linguistic and cultural differences between two neighbouring tribes are often very slight, and may be no more significant than dialectal or other regional differences within either tribe. The Maasai and Samburu, for instance, share a long common history, are of

and Rwanda, German territory until after World War I). In exchange for an island of less than 1km^2 in extent, Salisbury was guaranteed protectorateship over Zanzibar and handed the German block north of Witu, and Germany relinquished any claims it might have had to what are today Uganda and Malawi.

GERMAN EAST AFRICA The period of German rule was not a happy one. In 1891, Carl Peters was appointed governor. Peters had already proved himself an unsavoury and unsympathetic character: he boasted freely of enjoying killing Africans and, under the guise of the GEAC, his lack of diplomacy had already instigated one uprising. Furthermore, the 1890s were plagued by a series of natural disasters: a rinderpest epidemic at the start of the decade, followed by an outbreak of smallpox, and a destructive plague of locusts. A series of droughts brought famine and disease in their wake. Many previously settled areas reverted to bush, causing the spread of tsetse fly and sleeping sickness. The population of Tanganyika is thought to have decreased significantly between 1890 and 1914.

It took Peters a decade to gain full control of the colony. The main area of conflict was in the vast central plateau where, led by **Mkwawa**, the Hehe had become the dominant tribe. In 1891, the Hehe ambushed a German battalion led by Emil essentially the same ethnic stock, speak the same language and are culturally almost indistinguishable. Yet they perceive themselves to be distinct tribes, and are perceived as such by outsiders.

A few years ago, in mild desperation, I settled on the suitably nebulous term 'ethno-linguistic group' as a substitute for tribe. Clumsy, ugly and verging on the meaningless it might be, but it does sound impressively authoritative, without pinning itself exclusively on ethnicity, language or culture as a defining element, and it positively oozes political correctness. It's also, well, a little bit silly! Just as Tanzanians are unselfconscious about referring to themselves as black and to *wazungu* as white, so too do they talk about their tribe without batting an eyelid. For goodness sake, at every other local hotel in Tanzania, visitors are required to fill in the 'Tribe' column in the standard-issue guesthouse visitors' book. And if it's good enough for Tanzanians, who am I to get precious about it?

More than that, it strikes me that even in an African nation as united as Tanzania certainly is, the role of tribe in shaping the identity of an individual has no real equivalent in most Western societies. We may love – or indeed loathe – our home town, we might fight to the death for our loved ones, we might shed tears when our football team loses or our favourite pop group disbands, but we have no equivalent to the African notion of tribe. True enough, tribalism is often cited as the scourge of modern Africa, and when taken to fanatical extremes that's a fair assessment, yet to damn it entirely would be rather like damning English football, or its supporters, because of the actions of a fanatical extreme. Tribalism is an integral part of African society, and pussyfooting around it through an overdeveloped sense of political correctness strikes me as more belittling than being open about it.

So, in case you hadn't gathered, Tanzania's 120 ethno-lingual-cultural groupings are tribes for this edition of the guide, a decision that will hold at least for as long as I'm expected to fill in my tribe – whatever that might be – every time I check into a Tanzanian guesthouse.

Zalewski. They killed or wounded more than half of Zalewski's men, and made off with his armoury. Mkwawa fortified his capital near Iringa, but the Germans razed it in 1894. Mkwawa was forced to resort to guerrilla tactics, which he used with some success until 1898, when he shot himself rather than face capture by the Germans.

Germany was determined to make the colony self-sufficient. Sugar and rubber were well established on parts of the coast, coffee was planted in the Kilimanjaro region, a major base for settlers, and cotton grew well around Lake Victoria. The colony's leading crop export, sisal, was grown throughout the rest of the country. In 1902, Peters decided that the southeast should be given over to cotton plantations. This was an ill-considered move: the soils were not suitable for the crop and the scheme was bound to cause great hardship. It also led to the infamous and ultimately rather tragic **Maji-Maji rebellion**, which proved to be perhaps the most decisive event in the colony during German rule.

Carl Peters was fired from the colonial service in 1906. He believed his African mistress had slept with his manservant, so he flogged her close to death then hanged them both. After that, the German administration introduced a series of laws protecting Africans from mistreatment. To the disgust of the settler community, it also created an incentive-based scheme for African farmers. This made it worth their while to grow cash crops and allowed the colony's exports to triple in the period leading up to World War I.

When war broke out in Europe, East Africa also became involved. In the early stages of the war, German troops entered southern Kenya to cut off the Uganda Railway. Britain responded with an abortive attempt to capture Tanga. The balance of power was roughly even until **Jan Smuts** led the Allied forces into German territory in 1916. By January 1918, the Allies had captured most of German East Africa and the German commander, Von Lettow, retreated into Mozambique. The war disrupted food production, and a serious famine ensued. This was particularly devastating in the Dodoma region. The country was taken over by the League of Nations. The Ruanda-Urundi District, now the states of Rwanda and Burundi, was mandated to Belgium. The rest of the country was renamed Tanganyika and mandated to Britain.

TANGANYIKA The period of British rule between the wars was largely uneventful. Tanganyika was never heavily settled by Europeans so the indigenous populace had more opportunity for self-reliance than it did in many colonies. Nevertheless, settlers were favoured in the agricultural field, as were Asians in commerce. The Land Ordinance Act of 1923 secured some land rights for Africans, otherwise they were repeatedly forced into grand but misconceived agricultural schemes. The most notorious of these, the **Groundnut Scheme** of 1947, was an attempt to convert the southeast of the country into a large-scale mechanised groundnut producer. The scheme failed through a complete lack of understanding of local conditions; it caused a great deal of hardship locally and cost British taxpayers millions of pounds. On a political level, a system of indirect rule based around local government encouraged African leaders to focus on local rivalries rather than national issues between the wars. A low-key national movement called the **Tanganyika Africa Association (TAA)** was formed in 1929, but it was as much a cultural as a political organisation.

Although it was not directly involved in World War II, Tanganyika was profoundly affected by it. The country benefited economically. It saw no combat so food production continued as normal, while international food prices rocketed. Tanganyika's trade revenue increased sixfold between 1939 and 1949. World War II was a major force in the rise of **African nationalism**. Almost 100,000 Tanganyikans fought for the Allies. The exposure to other countries and cultures made it difficult for them to return home as second-class citizens. They had fought for non-racism and democracy in Europe, yet were victims of racist and non-democratic policies in their own country.

The dominant figure in the post-war politics of Tanganyika/Tanzania was **Julius Nyerere** (1922–99). Schooled at a mission near Lake Victoria, he went on to university in Uganda and gained a Master's degree in Edinburgh. After returning to Tanzania in 1952, Nyerere became involved in the TAA. This evolved into the more political and nationalist **Tanganyika African National Union (TANU)** in 1954. Nyerere became the president of TANU at the age of 32. By supporting rural Africans on grassroots issues and advocating self-government as the answer to their grievances, TANU gained a strong national following. By the mid 1950s, Britain and the UN were looking at a way of moving Tanganyika towards greater self-government, although over a far longer time-scale than TANU envisaged. The British governor, Sir Edward Twining, favoured a multi-racial system that would give equal representation to whites, blacks and Asians. TANU agreed to an election along these lines, albeit with major reservations. Twining created his own 'African party', the UTC.

In the 1958 election, there were three seats per constituency, one for each racial group. Electors could vote for all three seats, so in addition to putting forward candidates for the black seats, TANU indicated their preferred candidates in the white and Asian seats. Candidates backed by TANU won 67% of the vote; the UTC did not win a single seat. Twining's successor, Sir Richard Turnball, rewarded TANU by scrapping the multi-racial system in favour of open elections. In the democratic election of 1960, TANU won all but one seat. In May 1961, Tanganyika attained self-government and Nyerere was made prime minister. Tanganyika attained full **independence** on 9 December 1961. Not one life had been taken in the process. Britain granted Zanzibar full independence in December 1963. A month later the Arab government was toppled and in April 1964 the two countries combined to form Tanzania.

TANZANIA UNDER NYERERE At the very core of Tanzania's post-independence achievements and failures lies the figure of Julius Nyerere, who ruled Tanzania until his retirement in 1985. In his own country, where he remains highly respected, Nyerere is called *Mwalimu* – the teacher. In the West, he is a controversial figure, often portrayed as a dangerous socialist who irreparably damaged his country. This image of Nyerere doesn't bear scrutiny. He made mistakes and was intolerant of criticism – at one point Tanzania had more political prisoners than South Africa – but he is also one of the few genuine statesmen to have emerged from Africa, a force for positive change both in his own country and in a wider African context.

In 1962, TANU came into power with little policy other than their attained goal of independence. Tanganyika was the poorest and least economically developed country in East Africa, and one of the poorest in the world. Nyerere's first concerns were to better the lot of rural Africans and to prevent the creation of a money-grabbing elite. The country was made a one-party state, but had an election system that, by African standards, was relatively democratic. Tanzania pursued a policy of non-alignment, but the government's socialist policies and Nyerere's outspoken views alienated most Western leaders. Close bonds were formed with socialist powers, most significantly China, who built the Tanzam Railway (completed in 1975).

Relations with Britain soured in 1965. Nyerere condemned the British government's tacit acceptance of the Unilateral Declaration of Independence (UDI) in Rhodesia. In return, Britain cut off all aid to Tanzania. Nyerere also gave considerable vocal support to disenfranchised Africans in South Africa, Mozambique and Angola. The ANC and Frelimo both operated from Tanzania in the 1960s.

Nyerere's international concerns were not confined to white supremacism. In 1975, Tanzania pulled out of an Organisation of African Unity (OAU) conference in Idi Amin's Uganda saying: 'The refusal to protest against African crimes against Africans is bad enough…but…by meeting in Kampala…the OAU are giving respectability to one of the most murderous regimes in Africa.' Tanzania gave refuge to several Ugandans, including the former president Milton Obote and the current president Yoweri Museveni. Amin occupied part of northwest Tanzania in October 1978, and bombed Bukoba and Musoma. In 1979, Tanzania retaliated by invading Uganda and toppling Amin. Other African leaders condemned Tanzania for this action, despite Amin having been the initial aggressor. Ousting Amin drained Tanzania's financial resources, but it never received any financial compensation, either from the West, or from any other African country.

At the time of independence, most rural Tanzanians lived in scattered communities. This made it difficult for the government to provide such amenities as clinics and schools and to organise a productive agricultural scheme. In 1967, Nyerere embarked on a policy he called **villagisation**. Rural people were encouraged to form *Ujamaa* (familyhood) villages and collective farms. The scheme met with some small-scale success in the mid 1970s, so in 1975 Nyerere decided to forcibly re-settle people who had not yet formed villages. By the end of the year 65% of rural Tanzanians lived in Ujamaa villages. In many areas, however, water supplies were inadequate to support a village. The resultant mess, exacerbated by one of Tanzania's regular droughts, ended further villagisation. Ujamaa is often considered to have been an unmitigated disaster. It did not achieve what it was meant to, but it did help the government improve education and healthcare. Most reliable sources claim it did little long-term damage to agricultural productivity.

By the late 1970s Tanzania's economy was a mess. There were several contributory factors: drought, Ujamaa, rising fuel prices, the border closure with Kenya (to prevent Kenyan operators from dominating the Tanzanian safari industry), lack of foreign aid, bureaucracy and corruption in state-run institutions, and the cost of the Uganda episode. After his re-election in 1980 Nyerere announced he would retire at the end of that five-year term. In 1985, Nyerere was succeeded as President of Tanzania by **Ali Hassan Mwinyi**. However, he would stay on as chairman of **Chama Cha Mapinduzi (CCM)**, the party formed when TANU merged with the Zanzibari ASP in 1977, for another five years, only stepping down from that role in 1990. Nyerere remained active in international affairs, among other things serving as a UN mediator to end the civil war in Burundi in the late 1990s, almost until his death, aged 77, in 1999.

TANZANIA IN THE MULTI-PARTY ERA Tanzania moved away from socialism and authoritarianism under President Mwinyi. In 1986, an IMF-approved three-year Economic Recovery Plan was implemented, freeing up the exchange rate and encouraging private enterprise in order to help kickstart the economy. In 1990, attempts were made to rout corruption from the civil service, with surprisingly positive results. Two years later, with the support of ex-President Nyerere, the National Executive Committee of the CCM voted in favour of restoring the multi-party system that had been scrapped after the 1965 election.

The first multi-party election took place in October 1995. The CCM was returned to power with a majority of around 75% under the leadership of Benjamin Mkapa, who stood down in December 2005 following the country's third multi-party election. This, once again, was won by the CCM, which polled more than 80% of the 11.3 million votes under its new leader, Jakaya Kikwete. The CCM retained power under the 60-year-old Kikwete in the 2010 election, but with a vastly reduced majority, polling only 63% of the vote amongst the 42% of registered voters who turned out for the election. The main beneficiary of this significant electoral shift was the conservative **Chama cha Demokrasia na Maendeleo (CDM), popularly known as Chadema**, meaning Party for Democracy and Progress, whose leader Dr Willibrord Slaa took 27% of the vote. This trend continued in the 2015 presidential election, which was won by the new CCM candidate John Magufuli, but by a further reduced majority of 58.5% as opposed to the 40% of the vote garnered by the CDM under Edward Lowassa, who had served as prime minister during the first three years of Kikwete's first presidential term.

Widespread corruption is among the main reasons cited for the electoral swing away from the CCM, and this problem has been tackled head on by President Magufuli since he took power in July 2015. Nicknamed 'The Bulldozer', Magufuli signalled his intention to curb wasteful government spending early in his presidency, when he cancelled expensive Independence Day celebrations, reduced costs associated with the state dinner that marks the opening of parliament by 90%, placed a ban on first-class air travel by ministers, reduced the cabinet from 30 to 19 ministries, and cut his own monthly presidential salary from US$15,000 to US$4,000. Magufuli also came down strongly on corruption and allocated a far greater proportion of the budget to health care, education, road construction and other grassroots expenses.

On a less positive note, Magufuli proved to be intolerant of criticism and he placed significant curbs on free speech. He acquired a reputation for economic impulsiveness, one epitomised by the unexpected overnight implementation of 18% VAT on tourist-related services in July 2016. A devout Catholic, Magufuli was a vocal critic of birth control and family planning, attributing both practices to irreligious and immoral foreigners, and he urged Tanzanian women to 'set your ovaries free' in order to help grow the population. Magufuli was even more intolerant of homosexuality. When he had become president, this was already a crime punishable by 30 years in prison, but he cracked down harder by closing HIV clinics, by banning programmes and facilities designed to provide medical care to the gay community, and by appointing a committee of police, lawyers and doctors to identify and arrest homosexuals.

Magufuli's response to the Covid-19 pandemic was controversial, to put it mildly. On 19 April 2020, at which time only 500-odd cases of Covid-19 had been confirmed in Tanzania, he banned any further testing, as well as the use of face masks and vaccines, and refused to close churches and other places of worship, claiming that the disease was Satanic in origin and that the best treatment for it was prayer. The official policy of denialism means that no figures are available, but it is widely believed that many thousands of Tanzanians died as a direct result of these policies.

Despite all this, Magufuli remained a highly popular leader, and when general elections were held in 2020, he won a startling 84.4% of the presidential vote, up from 58.5% five years earlier. The CCM also increased their standing in the National Assembly to 350 of the 393 available seats (up from 260 in 2015), leaving the opposition in tatters.

On 17 February 2021, Seif Sharif Hamad, the Vice President of Zanzibar, died in hospital of complications associated with Covid-19. Ten days later, President Magufuli made his last public appearance, and when a Kenyan newspaper reported on 10 March that an unnamed African leader was being treated for Covid-19 at a Nairobi hospital, speculation about his health became rife. On 17 March 2021, it was announced that Magufuli had become the first President of Tanzania to die in office, officially due to a long-standing heart condition, but sceptics insisted that he had succumbed to the virus.

Magufuli's passing was marked by a 14-day period of national mourning during which at least 45 people died in a stampede at Dar es Salaam's Uhuru Stadium, where his body lay in state. He was succeeded by his Vice President Samia Suluhu Hassan, a Zanzibar-born CCM politician who was sworn in as Tanzania's first female president on 19 March 2021. Popularly known as Mama Samia, Suluhu took a more conventional approach to the pandemic, instituting a series of measures to curb the spread of the virus, and launching a vaccination campaign in July 2021 by being the first person to receive a jab in Tanzania, urging her compatriots to all follow her example. In her first 18 months in power, Suluhu has done much to restore press freedom and engage in dialogue with opposition leaders, while also ensuring that work continued on key development projects initiated under Magufuli. In May 2022, *Time* magazine named Suluhu on its list of the world's 100

Most Influential People, describing her leadership as 'a tonic [that] has made a big difference to Tanzania'.

As Africa experiences its sixth decade of post-colonialism, much of the continent suffers from the same tribal divisions it had at the time of independence. Tanzania is a striking exception to this generalisation, and hindsight demonstrates that Nyerere's greatest achievement was the tremendous sense of **national unity** he created by making KiSwahili the national language, by banning tribal leaders, by forcing government officials to work away from the area in which they grew up, and by his own example. True, Tanzania remains one of the world's least-developed countries, but most sources agree that the economic situation of the average Tanzanian has improved greatly since independence, with unusually high economic growth since the mid 1990s, as have adult literacy rates and health care. Furthermore, Tanzania has thus far navigated the tricky path from British colony to independent state to socialist dictatorship to free-market democracy with remarkably little internal conflict and bloodshed. This long history of adaptability, tolerance and stability should stand the country in good stead as the CCM faces fresh challenges to its political dominance.

GOVERNMENT AND POLITICS

The ruling party of Tanzania since independence has been **Chama Cha Mapinduzi (CCM)**. Up until 1995, Tanzania was a one-party state, under the presidency of Julius Nyerere and, after his retirement in 1985, Ali Hassan Mwinyi. Tanzania has held five multi-party elections since 1995, with the CCM winning them all – the first two under President Benjamin Mkapa, the next two under President Jakaya Kikwete, and the most recent under John Magufuli. The president and unicameral National Assembly of Tanzania are elected concurrently by popular vote, with 264 of the 393 seats in the National Assembly being elected directly, while 113 are allocated to women chosen by their parties (proportionate to each party's share of the electoral vote), another ten are nominated by the president, five are selected by the Zanzibar House of Representatives, and there is also one ex-officio Attorney General. The National Assembly is led by a prime minister, who is appointed by the president along with the cabinet. In 2015, 22 parties contested the general election, with the CCM taking 260 seats on the National Assembly, while the **Chama cha Demokrasia na Maendeleo (CDM)** claimed 70, the Civic United Front 42, and the two remainders each going to a different minor party. By contrast, in 2020, the election was contested by only five parties, and CCM won 350 seats, while 20 seats went to the CDM, five to the Alliance for Change and Transparency, and just two to the Civic United Front.

ADMINISTRATIVE REGIONS Tanzania is divided into 31 administrative regions, each with a local administrative capital. These are listed in the box shown opposite with population figures based on the most recent national census, undertaken in 2012.

ECONOMY

Immediately after independence, Tanzania became one of the most dedicated socialist states in Africa, and its economy suffered badly as a result of a sequence of well-intentioned but misconceived or poorly managed economic policies. By the mid 1980s, Tanzania ranked among the five poorest countries in the world.

ADMINISTRATIVE REGIONS

Region	Capital	Population (millions)	Area (km^2)	Number of districts
Arusha	Arusha	1.7	37,576	7
Dar es Salaam	Dar es Salaam	4.4	1,393	3
Dodoma	Dodoma	2.1	41,311	7
Geita	Geita	1.7	20,054	5
Iringa	Iringa	0.9	35,503	5
Kagera	Bukoba	2.5	25,265	8
Katavi	Mpanda	0.6	45,843	3
Kigoma	Kigoma	2.1	37,040	8
Kilimanjaro	Moshi	1.7	13,309	7
Lindi	Lindi	0.9	66,046	6
Manyara	Babati	1.4	44,522	6
Mara	Musoma	1.7	21,760	7
Mbeya	Mbeya	1.7	35,954	7
Morogoro	Morogoro	2.2	70,799	7
Mtwara	Mtwara	1.3	16,707	7
Mwanza	Mwanza	2.7	9,467	7
Njombe	Njombe	0.7	21,347	6
Pemba North	Wete	0.2	574	2
Pemba South	Chake Chake	0.2	335	2
Pwani	Kibaha	1.1	32,547	7
Rukwa	Sumbawanga	1.0	22,794	4
Ruvuma	Songea	1.4	63,670	6
Simiyu	Bariadi	1.6	25,212	5
Shinyanga	Shinyanga	1.5	18,900	5
Singida	Singida	1.4	49,341	6
Songwe	Vwaza	1	27,656	4
Tabora	Tabora	2.3	76,151	7
Tanga	Tanga	2.0	26,808	10
Zanzibar North	Mkokotoni	0.2	470	2
Zanzibar South	Mkoani	0.1	854	2
Zanzibar Urban	Zanzibar	0.6	230	2

The subsequent swing towards a free-market economy, making the country more attractive to investors, has resulted in dramatic improvement, and Tanzania today – while hardly wealthy – has managed to ascend out of the list of the world's 20 poorest countries. Indeed, with a GDP of US$70 billion in 2021, it now has the tenth-largest economy in Africa, and ranks 74th in the world. The mainstay of the economy is agriculture, and most rural Tanzanians are subsistence farmers who might also grow a few crops for sale. The country's major exports are traditionally coffee, cotton, cashew nuts, sisal, tobacco, tea and diamonds. Tanzania is also now the third-largest gold producer in Africa (after South Africa and Ghana), and a unique gem called tanzanite is of increasing importance to the export economy. Zanzibar and Pemba are important clove producers. The tourist industry that practically collapsed in the mid 1980s has since grown steadily, and now contributes around 13% of GDP and accounts for 11% of jobs countrywide. In the years immediately preceding the Covid-19 pandemic, the country has attracted around 1 million foreign visitors annually, and this has generated up to US$5 billion annually in foreign revenue, a 50-fold increase since 1990!

PEOPLE

The total population of Tanzania stood at 44.9 million in the most recent census undertaken in 2012, and is now estimated at around 63 million. The most densely populated rural areas tend to be the highlands, especially those around Lake Nyasa and Mount Kilimanjaro, and the coast. The country's largest city is Dar es Salaam, whose population, estimated at around 4.5 million, exceeds that of the country's next ten largest towns combined. Other large towns with populations exceeding 250,000 are Mwanza, Arusha, Dodoma, Mbeta, Morogoro and Tanga. There are roughly 120 tribes in Tanzania (page 12), each speaking their own language, and none of which exceeds 10% of the country's total population. The most numerically significant tribes are the Sukuma of Lake Victoria, Haya of northwest Tanzania, Chagga of Kilimanjaro, Nyamwezi of Tabora, Makonde of the Mozambican border area, Hehe of Iringa and Gogo of Dodoma.

LANGUAGE

More than 100 different languages are spoken across Tanzania, but the official languages are KiSwahili and English. Until recently, very little English was spoken outside of the larger towns, but this is changing rapidly and visitors can be confident

TRADITIONAL MUSICAL INSTRUMENTS

Tanzania's tribal diversity has meant that a vast array of very different – and, for that matter, very similar – traditional musical instruments are employed around the country under a bemusing number of local names. Broadly speaking, however, all but a handful of these variants can be placed in one of five distinct categories that conform to the classes of musical instrument used in Europe and the rest of the world.

The traditional music of many Tanzanian cultures is given its melodic drive by a *marimba* (also called a *mbira*), a type of instrument that is unique to Africa but could be regarded as a more percussive variant of the familiar keyboard instruments. The basic design of all marimbas consists of a number of metal or wooden keys whose sound is amplified by a hollow resonating box. Marimbas vary greatly in size from one region to the next. Popular with several pastoralist tribes of the Rift Valley and environs are small hand-held boxes with six to ten metal keys that are plucked by the musician. In other areas, organ-sized instruments with 50 or more keys are placed on the ground and beaten with sticks, like drums. The Gogo of the Dodoma region are famed for their marimba orchestras consisting of several instruments that beat out a complex interweave of melodies and rhythms.

The most purely melodic of Tanzanian instruments is the *zeze*, the local equivalent to the guitar or fiddle, used throughout the country under a variety of names. The basic zeze design consists of between one and five strings running along a wooden neck that terminates in an open resonating gourd. The musician rubs a bow fiddle-like across the strings, while manipulating their tone with the fingers of his other hand, generally without any other instrumental that almost anybody involved in the tourist industry will speak passable English. KiSwahili, indigenous to the coast, spread through the region along the 19th-century caravan routes, and is today spoken as a second language by most Tanzanians.

RELIGION

Christianity is the dominant religion, accounting for about 62% of Tanzania's total population. Among the more common denominations are Roman Catholic (around 50% of Christians), Lutheran (13%), Anglican (10%) and Pentecostal (10%).

Islam has had a long history on the coast and islands of Tanzania as evidenced by the presence of numerous ruined medieval mosques, some of which date back to the 12th century or earlier. It remains the main religion along the coast (for instance, more than 95% of Zanzibaris are Muslim), and it also has a stronghold in inland towns associated with the 19th-century Arab caravan routes, for example Ujiji and Tabora. It has been estimated that around 35% of Tanzanians are Muslim today, though no exact figures are available. Around 40% of the country's Muslims identify as Sunni, 20% as Shia and 15% as Ahmadi, while the remainder are non-denominational.

Traditional **animist** beliefs are followed by most other Tanzanians, in particular the Nilotic-speaking pastoralists of the Rift Valley. The Maasai traditionally worship a dualistic deity, Engai, who resides in the volcanic crater of Ol Doinyo Lengai, while Aseeta, the God of the Datoga, is said to live on Mount Hanang. Many practising Muslims or Christians in Tanzania concurrently adhere to traditional beliefs and will consult local healers and spiritualists in times of ill health or

accompaniment, but sometimes as part of an orchestra. Less widespread stringed instruments include the zither-like *enanga* of the Lake Tanganyika region and similar *bango* and *kinubi* of the coast, all of which are plucked like harps rather than stroked with a bow, to produce more defined melodic lines than the zeze.

The most important percussive instrument in African music is the drum, of which numerous local variations are found. Almost identical in structure and role to their European equivalent, most African drums are made by tightly stretching a membrane of animal hide across a section of hollowed tree trunk. A common and widespread type of drum, which is known in most areas as a *msondo* and is often reserved for important rituals, can be up to 1m tall and is held between the drummer's legs.

Percussive backing is also often provided by a variety of instruments known technically as idiophones. Traditionally, these might include the maraca-like *manyanga*, a shaker made by filling a gourd with dry seeds, as well as metal bells and bamboo scrapers. A modern variant on the above is the *chupa*: a glass soda bottle scraped with a piece of tin or a stick.

Finally, in certain areas, horned instruments are also used, often to supply a fanfare at ceremonial occasions. These generally consist of a modified animal horn with a blowing hole cut into its side, through which the musician manipulates the pitch using different mouth movements.

Readers with an interest in traditional music are pointed towards an excellent but difficult-to-locate booklet, *The Traditional Musical Instruments of Tanzania*, written by Lewis and Makala (Music Conservatoire of Tanzania, 1990), and the primary source of this boxed text.

SWAHILI NAMES

In KiSwahili, a member of a tribal group is given an 'M' prefix, the tribe itself gets a 'Wa' prefix, the language gets a 'Ki' prefix, and the traditional homeland gets a 'U' prefix. For example, an Mgogo person is a member of the Wagogo tribe who will speak Kigogo and live in Ugogo. The 'Wa' prefix is commonly but erratically used in English books; the 'M' and 'Ki' prefixes are rarely used, except in the case of KiSwahili, while the 'U' prefix is almost always used. There are no apparent standards; in many books the Swahili are referred to as just the Swahili while non-Swahili tribes get the 'Wa' prefix. I have decided to drop most of these prefixes: it seems as illogical to refer to non-Swahili people by their KiSwahili name when you are writing in English as it would be to refer to the French by their English name in a German book. I have, however, referred to the Swahili language as KiSwahili on occasion. I also refer to tribal areas – as Tanzanians do – with the 'U' prefix, and readers can assume that any place name starting with 'U' has this implication; in other words that Usukuma is the home of the Sukuma, and Unyamwezi is the home of the Nyamwezi.

misfortune. Tanzanians of Islamic and Christian persuasion generally live side by side without noticeable rancour, though both are often uncomfortable with the concept of atheism.

2

Tanzania Wildlife Guide

MAMMALS

More than 300 mammal species have been recorded in Tanzania, a list that includes about 80 so-called large mammals. For most first-time safari-goers, a major goal is to tick off the 'Big Five' – and even if doing so isn't a priority when you first arrive in Tanzania, conversations with lion-obsessed driver-guides and with other travellers are likely to make it one. Ironically, given its ubiquity in modern game-viewing circles, the term 'Big Five' originated with the hunting fraternity and it refers to those animals considered to be the most dangerous (and thus the best sport) back in the colonial era, namely lion, elephant, buffalo, leopard and black rhino. Of these, the first three are likely to be seen with ease on a safari of any significant duration. Leopards are more elusive, with the most reliable site in Tanzania being the Serengeti's Seronera Valley. The only parts of Tanzania where the black rhino remains reasonably visible are Mkomazi National Park, Ngorongoro Crater and parts of the northern Serengeti, but it is also present in a few other reserves.

In the listings that follow, an animal's scientific name is given in parentheses after its English name, followed by the Swahili (Sw) name. The Swahili for animal is *mnyama* (plural *wanyama*); to find out what animal you are seeing, ask '*Mnyama gani*?'

CARNIVORES This order of meat-eating mammals is represented in Tanzania by more than 30 species. These include cats such as the regal lion, along with dogs and jackals, hyenas and various smaller carnivores such as mongooses, otters and genets.

Cats Stealthy, secretive and inscrutable, the cats of the family Felidae are the most efficient killers among the carnivores, and the most strictly carnivorous. All cats conform to a similar anatomical plan to the familiar domestic tabby, the main physical difference between various species being coat pattern and size.

Lion (*Panthera leo*) Sw: *simba*. Shoulder height: 100–120cm; weight: 150–220kg. Africa's largest predator, the lion is the one animal that everybody hopes to see on safari. It is a sociable creature, living in prides of five to 20 animals (sometimes more) and defending a territory of between 20km^2 and 200km^2. Lions mostly hunt at night, and their favoured prey is large or medium bovids such as buffalo, wildebeest and impala. Most of the hunting is done by females, but dominant males normally feed first after a kill. Rivalry between males is intense, and battles to take over a pride are frequently fought to the death, for which reason two or more males often form a coalition. Young males are forced out of their home pride at three years of age, and male cubs are usually killed after a successful takeover. When not feeding or fighting, lions are remarkably indolent – they spend up to 23 hours of any given day at rest – so the anticipation of a lion sighting is often more exciting than the real thing. Lions naturally occur in any habitat but desert and rainforest, and once ranged across much of the Old World, but these days they are all but restricted to the larger conservation areas in sub-Saharan Africa (one remnant population exists in India). Essentially terrestrial, they seldom take to trees in most of their range, but this unusual behaviour is observed quite regularly in Lake Manyara and parts of the Serengeti National Park. Recent surveys indicate that Tanzania might host around 50% of the global population of roughly 20,000 free-ranging lions, and the Serengeti and the Ngorongoro Crater are arguably the best places in Africa to see these charismatic beasts.

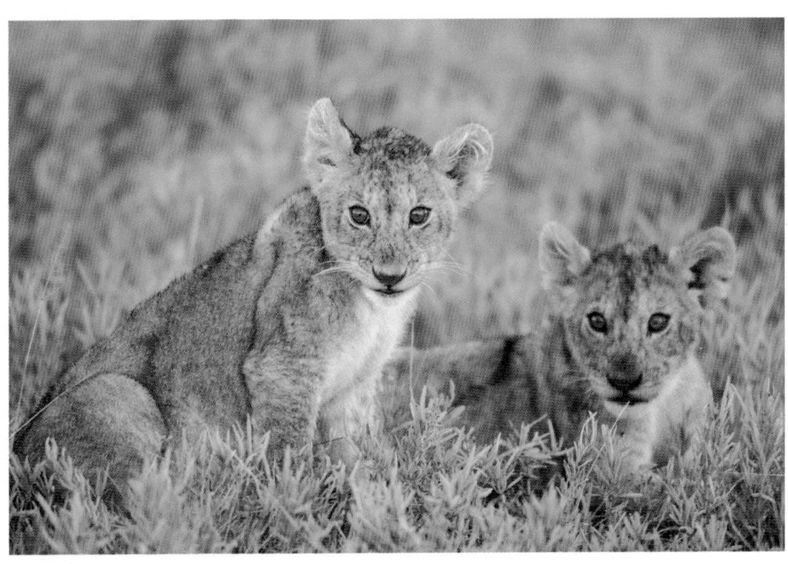

Leopard (*Panthera pardus*) Sw: *chui*. Shoulder height: 70cm; weight: 60–80kg. The powerful leopard is the most solitary and secretive of Africa's large cat species. It hunts using stealth and power, often getting to within 5m of its intended prey before pouncing, and it habitually stores its kill in a tree to keep it from hyenas and lions. The leopard can be distinguished from the superficially similar cheetah by its rosette-like spots, lack of black 'tear marks' and more compact, powerful build. Leopards occur in all habitats, favouring areas with plenty of cover such as riverine woodland and rocky slopes. There are many records of individuals living in close proximity to humans for years without being detected. The leopard is the most common of Africa's large felines, found throughout Tanzania, yet a good sighting must be considered a stroke of fortune. One relatively reliable spot for leopard sightings is the Seronera Valley in the Serengeti. Zanzibar's endemic leopard subspecies was presumed extinct for several decades prior to 2018, when nocturnal footage of a leopard – conceivably the escaped offspring of individuals transported to the island by traditional healers – was captured in Jozani Forest.

Cheetah (*Acinonyx jubatus*) Sw: *duma*. Shoulder height: 70–80cm; weight: 50–60kg. This remarkable spotted cat has a greyhound-like build, and is capable of running at 70km/h in bursts, making it the world's fastest land animal. It is often seen pacing the plains restlessly, either on its own or in a small family group comprising a mother and her offspring. A diurnal hunter, favouring the cooler hours of the day, the cheetah's habits have been adversely affected in areas where there are high tourist concentrations and off-road driving is permitted. Males are territorial, and generally solitary, though in the Serengeti they commonly defend their territory in pairs or trios. Despite superficial similarities, you can easily tell a cheetah from a leopard by its simple spots, disproportionately small head, streamlined build, diagnostic black 'tear marks', and preference for relatively open habitats. Widespread, but thinly distributed and increasingly rare outside of conservation areas, the cheetah is most likely to be seen in savannah and arid habitats such as the Serengeti Plains (where sightings are regular on the road to Seronera) but also occurs in Ruaha and Tarangire national parks.

Serval (*Leptailurus serval*) Sw: *mondo*. Shoulder height: 55cm; weight 12–15kg. Smaller than but with a similar build to a cheetah, the largely nocturnal serval has black-on-gold spots giving way to streaking near the head. It is widespread and quite common in moist grassland, reed beds and riverine habitats, but tends to be secretive. Ngorongoro Crater is probably the best place in Africa for serval sightings.

Caracal (*Felis caracal*) Sw: *simbamangu*. Shoulder height: 50cm; weight: 15–20kg. The caracal resembles the lynx with its short tail and tufted ears. It is a solitary hunter, feeding on birds, small antelope and livestock, and ranges throughout the country favouring relatively arid savannah habitats. It is nocturnal and seldom seen.

African wild cat (*Felis sylvestris*) Sw: *chapaku*. Shoulder height: 35cm; weight: 2.5-4.5kg. Ranging from the Mediterranean to the Cape of Good Hope, the African wild cat is similar in appearance to – and probably ancestral to – its domestic namesake. Like the caracal, it is common, but nocturnal, and infrequently seen. Though not threatened as such, the African wild cat regularly breeds with feral domestic cats and there are concerns its genetic pool is becoming increasingly diluted where the two regularly interact.

Leopard

Cheetah

Serval

Caracal

African wild cat

Dogs Five species of canid are present in Tanzania: the endangered African wild dog; the insectivorous bat-eared fox; and three species of jackal.

African wild dog (*Lycaon pictus*) Sw: *mbwa mwitu*. Shoulder height: 70cm; weight: 25kg. Also known as the African hunting dog or painted dog, the wild dog is distinguished from other African canids by its large size and cryptic black, brown and cream coat. Highly sociable, living in packs of up to 20 animals, the wild dog is a ferocious hunter that literally tears apart its prey on the run. Threatened with extinction as a result of its susceptibility to diseases spread by domestic dogs, it has become extinct or very rare in several areas where it was formerly abundant, for instance in the Serengeti and most other reserves in northern Tanzania. The global population of around 6,000 wild dogs – an increase of 50% since the turn of the millennium – is spread across much of eastern and southern Africa, but Nyerere National Park is the most important stronghold (estimated population 1,300) and Ruaha National Park also hosts a viable population. Wild dogs have been reported denning in Loliondo annually since 2008, and scattered sightings in Tarangire, Lake Manyara and the northern Serengeti indicate that this endangered creature is gradually recolonising the northern safari circuit. Wild dogs have also been reintroduced to Mkomazi National Park, where they are held in a caged breeding area and have yet to re-establish themselves in the wild.

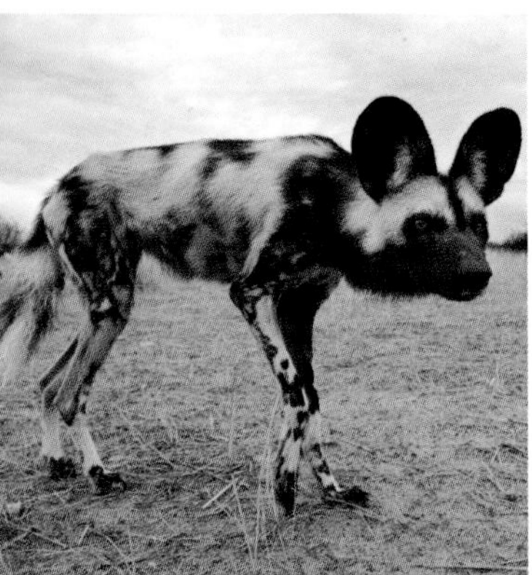

Bat-eared fox (*Otocyon megalotis*) Sw: *bweha masikio*. Shoulder height: 30–35cm; weight: 35kg. This small, silver-grey insectivore, unmistakable with its huge ears and black eye-mask, is most often seen in pairs or small family groups during the cooler hours of the day. Associated with dry open country, the bat-eared fox is quite common in the Serengeti and likely to be encountered at least once in the course of a few days' safari, particularly during the denning season (November and December).

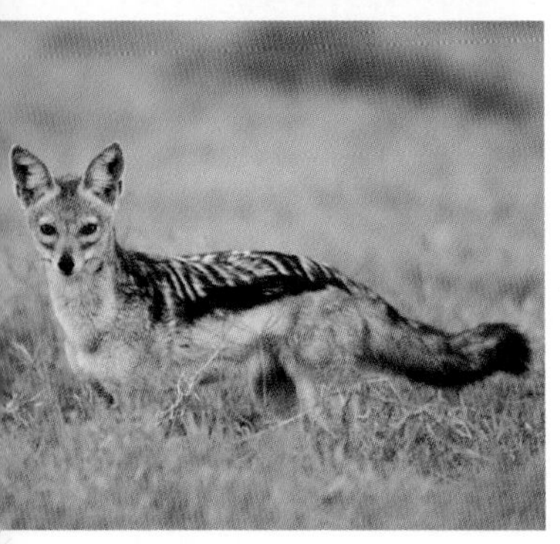

Black-backed jackal (*Lupulella mesomelas*) Sw: *mbweha*. Shoulder height: 35–45cm; weight: 8–12kg. The black-backed (or silver-backed) jackal is an opportunistic feeder capable of adapting to most habitats. Most often seen singly or in pairs at dusk or dawn, it is ochre in colour with a prominent black saddle flecked by a varying amount of white or gold. It is one of the most frequently observed small predators in Africa south of the Zambezi, and its eerie call is a characteristic sound of the bush at night. It is the commonest jackal in most Tanzanian reserves.

Side-striped jackal (*Lupulella adustus*) Sw: *mbweha*. Shoulder height: 35–50cm; weight: 8–12kg. More cryptic in colour than the otherwise very similar black-backed jackal, this species has an indistinct pale vertical stripe on each flank and a white-tipped tail. Nowhere very common, it is distributed throughout Tanzania, often favouring miombo woodland, but most likely to be seen in the southern reserves.

African golden jackal (*Canis lupaster*) Sw: *mbweha*. Shoulder height: 40–50cm; weight: 8–14kg. Formerly treated as a subspecies of the Eurasian common or golden jackal, this cryptically coloured canid is paler, less streaked and slightly larger than the black-backed or side-striped jackal, and has a black tail tip. A predominantly North African species whose range extends south to the Greater Serengeti, it is the most commonly seen canid on the Ngorongoro Crater floor, thanks to its relatively diurnal habits. Following a revelatory genetic study published in 2015, it is regarded to be a separate species from its Eurasian lookalike, one more closely related to wolves than to any other jackals.

Hyenas Hyenas are characterised by their bulky build, sloping back, brownish coat, powerful jaws and dog-like expression. Despite looking superficially canine, they are more closely related to mongooses and bears than to cats or dogs. Contrary to popular myth, hyenas are not exclusively scavengers: the spotted hyena in particular is an adept hunter capable of killing an animal as large as a wildebeest. Nor are they hermaphroditic, an ancient belief that stems from the false scrotum and penis covering the female hyena's vagina.

Spotted hyena (*Crocuta crocuta*) Sw: *fisi*. Shoulder height: 85cm; weight: 70kg. Sociable and fascinating to observe, the spotted hyena lives in loosely structured clans of about ten animals, led by females who are stronger and larger than males. It is the largest hyena, distinguished by its blotchily spotted coat, and it is probably the most common large predator in eastern and southern Africa. It is most frequently seen at dusk and dawn in the vicinity of game reserve lodges, campsites and refuse dumps, and is likely to be encountered on a daily basis in the Serengeti, Ngorongoro Crater and many other reserves.

Striped hyena (*Hyaena hyaena*) Sw: *fisi miraba*. Shoulder height: 65–75cm; weight: 45–50kg. A predominantly North African species, the striped hyena is pale brown with several dark vertical streaks and a striking off-black mane. It occurs alongside the spotted hyena in dry parts of Tanzania, but is far scarcer and more secretive.

Aardwolf (*Proteles cristatus*) Sw: *fisi ndogo*. Shoulder height: 40–50cm; weight: 10–15kg. This very secretive insectivore looks like a smaller striped hyena, being not much bigger than a jackal. It occurs in low numbers in drier parts of Tanzania.

Spotted hyena

Striped hyena

Aardwolf

© Joe McDonald/Shutterstock.com

African civet

© Superstock

Civets, mongooses and mustelids

African civet (*Civettictis civetta*) Sw: *fungo*. Shoulder height: 40cm; weight: 10–15kg. This stocky, long-haired, rather feline creature of the African night is primarily carnivorous, feeding on small animals and carrion as well as fruit. It has a similarly coloured coat to a leopard or cheetah, and this is densely blotched with large black spots becoming stripes towards the head. Civets are widespread and common in many habitats, but very rarely seen. The smaller and slenderer **tree civet** (*Nandinia binotata*) is a very seldom-seen arboreal forest animal whose dark-brown coat is marked with black spots.

Mongooses Sw: *nguchiro*. Several mongoose species occur in Tanzania, though some are too scarce and nocturnal to be seen by casual visitors. The largest, with a shoulder height of up to 40cm, is the **white-tailed mongoose** (*Ichneumia albicauda*) a widespread solitary nocturnal predator easily identified by its bushy white tail. More common is the diurnal and highly sociable **banded mongoose** (*Mungos mungo*; shoulder height: 20cm), which is dark brown except for a dozen black stripes across its back, and occurs in family groups in most wooded habitats and savannah. The **dwarf mongoose** (*Helogale parvula*) is a diminutive (shoulder height: 7cm) and highly sociable light-brown mongoose often seen in the vicinity of termite mounds, particularly in Tarangire National Park. The more solitary **marsh mongoose** (*Atilax

Dwarf mongoose

paludinosus) is large (shoulder height: 22cm), has a scruffy-looking brown coat, and is widespread in the eastern side of Africa where it is often seen in the vicinity of water. The **slender mongoose** (*Herpestes sanguinea*) is as widespread and also solitary, but it is very much smaller (shoulder height: 10cm) and has a uniform brown coat and black tail tip.

Genet (*Genetta* spp) Sw: *kanu*. Shoulder height: 20–40cm; weight: 1.5–3kg. Often but erroneously referred to as cats, the members of this taxonomically controversial genus are all very similar in appearance: low-slung, slender, with a grey to golden-brown coat marked with black spots, and an exceptionally long ringed tail. Most likely to be seen on nocturnal game drives or scavenging around game reserve lodges, the **large-spotted genet** (*G. tigrina*) is golden brown with very large spots and a black-tipped tail, whereas the **small-spotted genet** (*G. genetta*) is greyer with rather small spots and a pale tip to the tail.

Honey badger and other mustelids Sw: *nyegere*. Shoulder height: 30cm; weight: 12kg. Also known as the ratel, the **honey badger** (*Mellivora capensis*) is a black mustelid (member of the weasel family) with a puppyish face and grey-to-white back. It is an opportunistic feeder best known for its symbiotic relationship with a bird called the greater honeyguide, which leads it to a beehive, waits for it to tear the nest open, then feeds on the scraps. It is among the most widespread of African carnivores, but it is thinly distributed and rarely seen. Several other mustelids (mammals of the weasel family) occur in the region, including the **striped polecat** (*Ictonyx striatus*), a common but rarely seen nocturnal creature with black underparts and bushy white back, and the similar but much scarcer **striped weasel** (*Poecilogale albinucha*). The **Cape clawless otter** (*Aonyx capensis*) is a brown freshwater mustelid with a white collar, while the smaller **spotted-necked otter** (*Hydrictis maculicollis*) is darker with white spots on its throat.

Honey badger

PRIMATES The forests of Africa support somewhere between 60 and 100 primate species (taxonomic ambiguities make it impossible to be more exact), but diversity is far lower in the savannah habitats associated with most safari destinations. Despite this, western Tanzania is one of the best places in the world to track chimpanzee, while baboon and vervet monkey are common in most safari reserves, and the montane forests of the coast support several endemic monkey species.

Chimpanzee (*Pan troglodytes*) Sw: *sokwe-mtu*. Standing height: 100cm; weight: up to 55kg. This distinctive black-coated ape, along with the bonobo (*Pan paniscus*) of the southern Congo, is more closely related to humans than to any other living creature. The chimpanzee lives in large troops based around a core of related males dominated by an alpha male. Females aren't firmly bonded to their core group, so emigration between communities is normal. Primarily frugivores (fruit-eaters), chimpanzees eat meat on occasion, and though most kills are opportunistic, stalking of prey is not unusual. The first recorded instance of a chimp using a tool was at Gombe in Tanzania, where modified sticks were used to 'fish' in termite mounds. In West Africa, chimps have been observed cracking open nuts with a stone and anvil. In the USA, captive chimps have successfully been taught sign language and have created compound words such as 'rock-berry' to describe a nut. A widespread rainforest resident, the chimpanzee is thought to number 200,000 in the wild. In Tanzania, chimps are indigenous to the forested shore of Lake Tanganyika, where they can be tracked on foot in Mahale Mountains and Gombe national parks (the latter the site of the original research centre founded by primatologist Jane Goodall in the 1960s). In northern Tanzania, an introduced (but to all intents and purposes wild) population can be tracked on Rubondo Island in Lake Victoria.

Olive baboon

Baboon (*Papio* spp) Sw: *nyani*. Shoulder height: 50–75cm; weight: 25–45kg. This powerful terrestrial primate, distinguished from any other monkey by its much larger size, inverted U-shaped tail and distinctive dog-like head, is fascinating to watch from a behavioural perspective. It lives in large troops that boast a complex, rigid social structure characterised by matriarchal lineages and plenty of inter-troop movement by males seeking social dominance. Omnivorous and at home in almost any habitat, the baboon is the most widespread primate in Africa, frequently seen in most Tanzanian game reserves. There are several species of baboon in Africa, regarded by some authorities to be full races of the same species. Two species are present in Tanzania: the **olive** or **anubis baboon** (*P. anubis*), which is the darker and hairier green-brown baboon found in the west, and the **yellow baboon** (*P. cynocephalus*), a more lightly built and paler yellow-brown race whose range lies to the east of the Rift Valley.

Vervet monkey (*Chlorocebus (aethiops) pygerythrus*) Sw: *tumbili*. Length (excluding tail): 40–55cm; weight: 4–6kg. Tanzania's most widespread and conspicuous monkey is also rather atypical in that it inhabits savannah and woodland rather than true forest, and spends a high proportion of its time on the ground. In most of its range it could be confused only with the baboon, which is much larger and heavier. Where it occurs alongside the patas monkey, the vervet can be distinguished by its greyer coat, black face, white forehead band and the male's bright blue genitals. The vervet was until recently treated as a single species that ranged widely through sub-Saharan Africa, but it is now generally split into up to seven species, and the one found in Tanzania is also known as the tantalus monkey.

Red-tailed monkey

Patas monkey (*Erythrocebus patas*) Sw: unknown. Length (excluding tail): 75–85cm; weight: 7–12kg. This localised terrestrial monkey is larger and spindlier than the vervet, with an orange-tinged coat and black forehead stripe. Essentially a monkey of the dry northwestern savannah, the patas occurs in low numbers in the Mbalageti River region of the western Serengeti. It is very fast on the ground, attaining speeds of up to 55km/h.

Blue monkey (*Cercopithecus mitis*) Sw: *kima*. Length (excluding tail): 50–60cm; weight: 5–8kg. This most variable of African monkeys is also known as samango, silver or Sykes' monkey, or diademed or white-throated guenon. Several dozen races are recognised, divided by some authorities into more than one species. Taxonomic confusion notwithstanding, *C. mitis* is the most common forest guenon in eastern Africa, with one or another race occurring in just about any suitable habitat. Unlikely to be confused with another species in Tanzania, the blue monkey has a uniformly dark blue-grey coat broken by a white throat, which in some races extends all down the chest and in others around the collar. It lives in troops of up to ten animals and associates with other primates where their ranges overlap. It is common in Arusha and Lake Manyara national parks and in many forest reserves.

Red-tailed monkey (*Cercopithecus ascanius*) Sw: unknown. Length (excluding tail): 35–45cm; weight: 3–5kg. This small brown guenon has white whiskers, a red tail, and a distinctive white heart-shaped mark on its nose. In Tanzania, it is primarily restricted to western forests in the vicinity of lakes Tanganyika and Victoria.

Blue monkey

Patas monkey

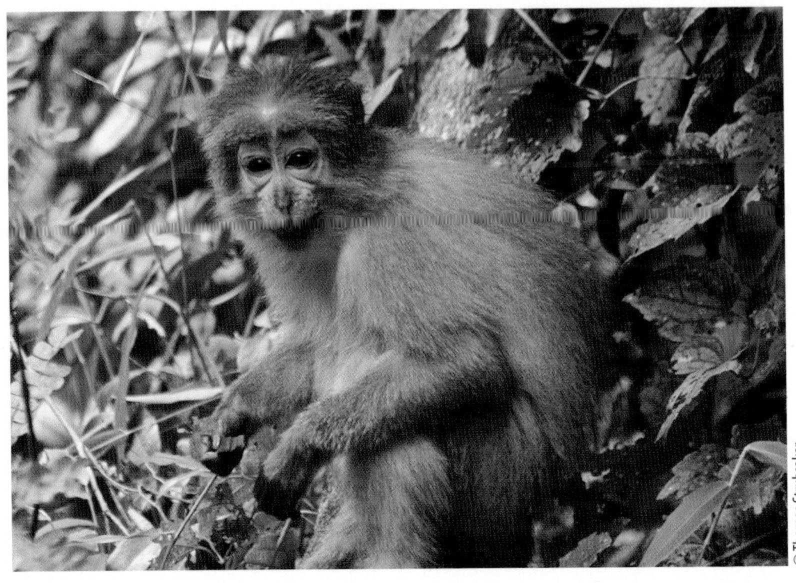
© Thomas Struhsaker

Sanje mangabey (*Cercocebus sanjei*) Sw: unknown. Length (excluding tail): 50–65cm; weight: 7–9kg. Essentially a west African monkey, this shaggy forest-dwelling relative of the baboons is represented by two extremely isolated populations in East Africa: one in Tanzania's Udzungwa Mountains and another along Kenya's Tana River. Both are classified as full species by most authorities.

Kipunji monkey (*Rungwecebus kipunji*) Sw: unknown. Length (excluding tail): 85–90cm; weight: 10–16kg. Discovered as recently as 2003, this large and critically endangered Tanzanian endemic is confined to the forests of the Udzungwa and Mount Rungwe.

© Tim Davenport

Black-and-white colobus

Angola colobus

Red colobus

Black-and-white colobus (*Colobus guereza*) Sw: *mbega mweupe*. Length (excluding tail): 60–70cm; weight: 10–16kg. This beautiful jet-black monkey has bold white facial markings and beard, a long white tail and in some races white sides and shoulders. Almost exclusively arboreal, it is capable of jumping up to 30m, a spectacular sight with fluffy white tail streaming behind. Several races have been described, and it seems likely that the Kilimanjaro colobus (*C. (g.) caudatus*), which is common on Mount Kilimanjaro and Meru, is a distinct species that's all but endemic to northeast Tanzania. Black-and-white colobus are also often seen along the Grumeti River in the Serengeti.

Angola colobus (*Colobus angolensis*) Sw: *mbega mweupe*. Length (excluding tail): 60–70cm; weight: 10–16kg. Although it is very similar in appearance to the black-and-white colobus, the Angola colobus differs in having a more streamlined and darker tail and no white on the beard. Both species are subdivided into a number of races, and the assignment of some is controversial, but three Tanzanian populations – those of the Eastern Arc Mountains (including the Usambara), southern highlands, and Lake Tanganyika forests – are now generally regarded to be Angola colobus.

Red colobus (*Procolobus badius*) Sw: *kima punju*. Length (excluding tail): 60cm; weight: 10kg. The status of this variable monkey is again controversial, with between one and ten species recognised by different authorities. Most populations have black on the upper back, red on the lower back, a pale tufted crown and a long-limbed appearance unlike that of any guenon or mangabey. This is the most conspicuous forest monkey in Mahale Mountains and Gombe national parks, where it is often preyed upon by chimps. Two isolated Tanzanian populations are now generally regarded to be endemic species. These are Kirk's red colobus (*P. kirkii*), which is confined to Zanzibar Island and readily observed in Jozani Forest, and the Uhehe red colobus (*P. gordonorum*), a fairly common and conspicuous resident of the Udzungwa Mountains in southern Tanzania.

Galagos (bushbabies) (*Galago* and *Otolemur* spp) Sw: *komba*. Length (excluding tail): up to 45cm; weight: up to 500g. This taxonomically controversial family (page 198), distantly related to the lemurs of Madagascar, is widespread in Tanzania, where around a dozen species in two genera are recognised. Most commonly seen, and easily identified due to their size, are the three species of **greater galago** (*Otolemur* spp). They occur all along the eastern side of Africa and produce a terrifying scream so loud you'd think it was emitted by a chimpanzee or gorilla. The **lesser bushbabies** of the genus *Galago* are more widespread and common but less readily seen, though they can sometimes be picked out by tracing the cry to a tree and shining a torch or spotlight in its general direction to look for its large eyes.

ANTELOPE AND OTHER BOVIDS The most characteristic mammals of the African savannah are antelope, with more than two dozen species present in Tanzania alone, ranging in size from the ox-like eland to the diminutive duikers. Taxonomists place antelope in the order Bovidae, along with cattle, buffalos and goats, as well as the deer, from which they most obviously differ in having permanent horns rather than seasonal antlers.

Large antelope

Roan antelope (*Hippotragus equinus*) Sw: *korongo*. Shoulder height: 120–150cm; weight: 250–300kg. This handsome horse-like antelope is uniform fawn-grey with a pale belly, short decurved horns and a light mane. It could be mistaken for the female sable antelope, but has a well-defined white belly, much larger horns and is more brown in facial markings. The roan is widespread but thinly distributed

in southern Tanzania, though rare in the north, with one small population known to occur (yet seldom seen) in the Serengeti.

Sable antelope (*Hippotragus niger*) Sw: *pala hala*. Shoulder height: 135cm; weight: 230kg. The male sable is jet black with a white-striped face, underbelly and rump, and long decurved horns. Females are chestnut brown with shorter horns. One of the main strongholds for Africa's sable population is the miombo woodland of southern Tanzania. It also occurs further north in Saadani National Park, but is virtually absent from northern Tanzania's safari circuit.

Fringe-eared oryx (*Oryx (beisa) callotis*) Sw: *choroa*. Shoulder height: 120cm; weight: 230kg. This regal, dry-country antelope is unmistakable with its ash-grey coat, bold black facial marks and flank strip, and unique long, straight horns. Within Tanzania, it is most common (though still scarce) in Mkomazi and Tarangire national parks, and the Lake Natron region.

Waterbuck (*Kobus ellipsiprymnus*) Sw: *kuro*. Shoulder height: 130cm; weight: 250–270kg. The waterbuck is easily recognised by its shaggy brown coat and the male's large lyre-shaped horns. The **Defassa waterbuck** (*K. e. defassa*) of the Rift Valley and areas further west has a full white rump, while the **common waterbuck** (*K. e. ellipsiprymnus*), found further east, has a white 'U' on its rump. The waterbuck is frequently seen in small family groups grazing near water in all but the most arid of game reserves in Tanzania.

Defassa waterbuck

Blue wildebeest (*Connochaetes taurinus*) Sw: *nyumbu*. Shoulder height: 130–150cm; weight: 180–250kg. This rather ungainly antelope, also called the brindled gnu, is easily recognised by its dark coat and bovine appearance. The superficially similar buffalo is far more heavily built. Immense herds of blue wildebeest occur on the Serengeti Plains, where the annual migration of more than a million heading into Kenya's Maasai Mara forms one of Africa's great natural spectacles. There are also significant wildebeest populations in the Ngorongoro Crater and Tarangire.

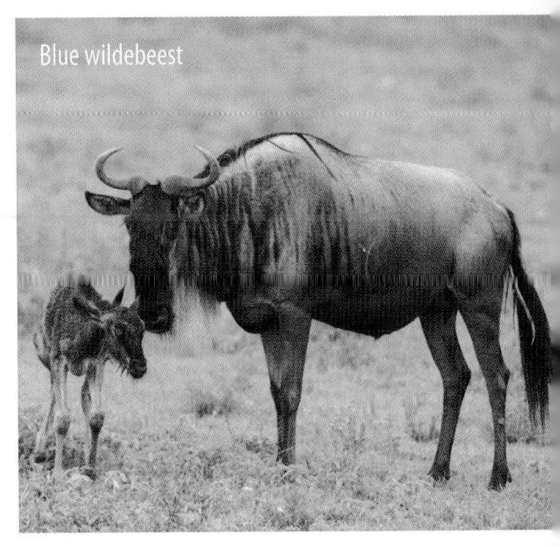
Blue wildebeest

Coke's hartebeest (*Alcelaphus buselaphus cokii*) Sw: *kongoni*. Shoulder height: 125cm; weight: 120–150kg. Hartebeests are ungainly antelopes, readily identified by the combination of high shoulders, a sloping back, red-brown or yellow-brown coat and smallish curved horns in both sexes. Numerous races are recognised, all of which are generally seen in small family groups in reasonably open country. The race found in Tanzania is Coke's hartebeest, which is common in open parts of the Serengeti and Ngorongoro.

Topi (*Damaliscus lunatus*) Sw: *topi*. Shoulder height: 125cm; weight: 120–150kg. Basically a darker version of the hartebeest but with striking yellow lower legs and straighter horns, this widespread but thinly and patchily distributed antelope, also known as the tsessebe, occurs alongside the much paler Coke's hartebeest in Serengeti National Park, where it is common.

Common eland (*Taurotragus oryx*) Sw: *pofu*. Shoulder height: 150–175cm; weight: 450–900kg. Africa's largest antelope, the common eland is light brown

Coke's hartebeest

Topi

Common eland

in colour, sometimes with a few faint white vertical stripes. It has a somewhat bovine appearance, accentuated by the relatively short horns, square frame and large dewlap. It is widely distributed in East and southern Africa, and small herds may be seen almost anywhere in grassland or light woodland. The eland is fairly common in Serengeti and Mkomazi national parks, but difficult to approach closely.

Greater kudu (*Tragelaphus strepsiceros*) Sw: *tandala*. Shoulder height: 140–155cm; weight: 180–250kg. In many parts of Africa, the greater kudu is the most readily observed member of the genus *tragelaphus*, a group of medium-to-large antelopes characterised by the male's large spiralling horns and a dark coat generally marked with several vertical white stripes. It is very large, with a grey-brown coat and up to ten stripes on each side, and the male has magnificent double-spiralled horns. A widespread animal occurring in most wooded habitats except for true forest, the greater kudu has been rare in most of Tanzania and Kenya since it was all but wiped out by a rinderpest epidemic in the late 19th century. However, it is quite common in Nyerere and Ruaha national parks, and might also be seen in Tarangire.

Lesser kudu (*Tragelaphus imberbis*) Sw: *tandala ndogo*. Shoulder height: 95–105cm, weight 60–100kg. This thinly distributed and skittish East African species is largely restricted to arid woodland. In Tanzania, it often occurs alongside the greater kudu, from which it can be distinguished by its smaller size, two white throat patches and greater number of stripes (at least 11). Nowhere common, it is most likely to be encountered in Tarangire, Ruaha and Mkomazi national parks.

Greater kudu

Lesser kudu

Sitatunga

Sitatunga (*Tragelaphus spekei*) Sw: *nzohe*. Shoulder height: 75–125cm, weight 50–120kg. This semi-aquatic antelope, notable for its specially adapted splayed hooves, is a widespread but infrequently observed inhabitant of African swamps from the Okavango in Botswana to the Sudd in South Sudan. Tanzania's Rubondo Island is one of the few places where it is readily observed. It is among the most sexually dimorphic of African antelopes. The tall and hefty male, with its large horns and shaggy fawn coat, is all but unmistakable in its habitat. The smaller female is variable in colour and might be mistaken for a bushbuck but is usually drabber.

Medium and small antelope

Bushbuck (*Tragelaphus scriptus*) Sw: *pongo*. Shoulder height: 70–80cm; weight: 30–45kg. This attractive antelope, a member of the same genus as the kudu and sitatunga, shows great regional variation in colouring. The male is dark brown, chestnut or, in parts of Ethiopia, black, while the much smaller female is generally pale red-brown. The male has relatively small, straight horns for a *Tragelaphus* antelope. Both sexes have similar throat patches to the lesser kudu, and are marked with white spots and sometimes stripes. One of the most widespread antelope species in Africa, the bushbuck occurs in forest and riverine woodland throughout Tanzania, where it is normally seen singly or in pairs. It tends to be secretive and skittish except where it is used to people, so it is not as easily seen as you might expect of a common antelope.

Thomson's gazelle (*Gazella thomsonii*) Sw: *swala tomi*. Shoulder height: 60cm; weight: 20–25kg. Gazelles are graceful, relatively small antelopes that generally occur in large herds in open country, and have fawn-brown upper parts and a white belly. Thomson's gazelle is characteristic of the East African plains, where it is the only gazelle to have a black horizontal flank stripe. It is common to abundant in the Serengeti and surrounds.

Grant's gazelle (*Gazella granti*) Sw: *swala granti*. Shoulder height: 75–95cm; weight: 35–75kg. Occurring alongside Thomson's gazelle in many parts of East Africa, the larger Grant's gazelle has a brown rather than black side stripe and comparatively large horns. It is common in the Serengeti but might be seen as far south as Ruaha National Park, which represents the most southerly part of its range.

Bushbuck

Thomson's gazelle

Grant's gazelle

Gerenuk (*Litocranius walleri*) Sw: *swala twiga*. Shoulder height: 90–105cm; weight: 35–50kg. This uncharacteristic gazelle is an arid-country species of Ethiopia, Kenya and northern Tanzania, similar in general colour to an impala but readily identified by its very long neck (the Swahili name translates as 'giraffe gazelle') and singular habit of feeding from trees standing on its hind legs. Nowhere common in Tanzania, the gerenuk is present in small numbers in Mkomazi, Tarangire, West Kilimanjaro and the Loliondo area.

Impala (*Aepyceros melampus*) Sw: *swala pala*. Shoulder height: 90cm; weight: 45kg. This slender, handsome antelope is superficially similar to some gazelles, but in fact belongs to a separate family. Chestnut in colour, the impala has diagnostic black and white stripes running down its rump and tail, and the male has large lyre-shaped horns. One of the most widespread antelope species in sub-equatorial Africa, the impala is normally seen in large herds in wooded savannah habitats, and it is one of the most common antelope in many Tanzanian reserves. Mixed impala herds typically comprise an alpha male and a vast harem of females and their offspring. Also common, unsurprisingly, are all-male bachelor herds.

Southern reedbuck

Reedbuck (*Redunca* spp) Sw: *tohe*. Shoulder height: 65–90cm; weight: 30–65kg. The three species of reedbuck are all rather nondescript fawn-grey antelopes generally seen in open grassland near water. The **mountain reedbuck** (*R. fulvorufula*) is the smallest and most distinct, with a clear white belly, tiny horns and an overall grey appearance. It has a broken distribution, occurring in mountainous parts of eastern South Africa, northern Tanzania, Kenya and southern Ethiopia. The **Bohor reedbuck** (*R. redunca*) is found in northern Tanzania, whereas the **southern reedbuck** (*R. arundinum*) occurs in southern Tanzania.

Klipspringer (*Oreotragus oreotragus*) Sw: *mbuze mawe*. Shoulder height: 60cm; weight: 13kg. The klipspringer is an agile antelope that's normally seen in pairs and is easily identified by its dark, bristly grey-yellow coat, slightly speckled appearance and unique habitat preference. Klipspringer means 'rock jumper' in Afrikaans, while the Swahili name means 'rock goat', both apt names for an antelope that occurs exclusively in mountainous areas and rocky outcrops. It is found throughout Tanzania, and is often seen around the Lobo Hills in the Serengeti and the Maji Moto area in Lake Manyara.

Steenbok (*Raphicerus campestris*) Sw: *tondoro*. Shoulder height: 50cm; weight: 11kg. This rather nondescript small antelope has red-brown upper parts and clear white underparts, and the male has short straight horns. It is probably the most commonly observed small antelope in Africa, though it has a broken range, and is absent from southern Tanzania despite being common in the north of the country and in southern Africa. Like most other antelopes of its size, the steenbok is normally encountered singly or in pairs and tends to 'freeze' when disturbed.

Oribi (*Ourebia ourebi*) Sw: *taya*. Shoulder height: 50–65cm; weight: 12–20kg. This widespread but uncommon grassland antelope looks much like a steenbok but stands about 10cm higher at the shoulder and has an altogether more upright bearing. It might be seen in almost any grassy habitat, usually in groups of two or three, but isn't very common anywhere in Tanzania.

Kirk's dik-dik (*Madoqua kirkii*) Sw: *digidigi*. Shoulder height: 35–45cm; weight: 6–8kg. Smaller than the steenbok and easily identified by its large white eye-circle, this adorably dainty antelope has a range focused primarily on Tanzania and Kenya. Usually seen in pairs in dry woodland, it is particularly common in Arusha and Ruaha National Parks.

Common duiker (*Sylvicapra grimmia*) Sw: *nysa*. Shoulder height: 50cm; weight: 20kg. This anomalous duiker holds itself more like a steenbok and is the only member of its family to occur outside of forests. Grey or grey-brown in colour, it is most easily separated from other small antelopes by the black tuft of hair that sticks up between its horns. It occurs throughout Tanzania, and tolerates most habitats except for true forest and very open country.

Forest duikers (*Cephalophus* spp) Sw: *nsya.* Duikers are small to diminutive antelope with slightly hunched backs and a preference for forest undergrowth, where they are less often seen than they are heard crashing through the undergrowth. The **red duiker** (*C. natalensis*) is the most likely of Africa's 12–20 'forest duikers' to be seen by tourists. It is deep chestnut in colour with a white tail and, in the case of the East African race *C. n. harveyi* (sometimes considered to be a separate species), a black face. The **blue duiker** (*C. monticola*) is easily told apart from the red duiker by its greyer colouring and much smaller size. The all-but-endemic **Abbott's duiker** (*C. spadix*) is a relatively large duiker, as tall as a klipspringer, and is restricted to a handful of montane forests in Tanzania, including those on Kilimanjaro and the Usambara, Udzungwa and Poroto mountains. The endangered **Ader's duiker** (*C. adersi*) is thought to be restricted to forested habitats on Zanzibar Island, where as few as 1,000 animals may survive, most of them in the Jozani Forest.

Red duiker

African buffalo (*Syncerus caffer*) Sw: *nyati.* Shoulder height: 140cm; weight: 700kg. Frequently and erroneously referred to as a water buffalo (an Asian species), the African buffalo is a distinctive ox-like animal that lives in large herds on the savannah and occurs in smaller herds in forested areas. Common and widespread in sub-Saharan Africa, herds of buffalo are likely to be encountered in most Tanzanian reserves and national parks. The best places to see large buffalo herds in Tanzania are the Ngorongoro Crater floor and Katavi National Park.

African elephant

OTHER LARGE UNGULATES

African elephant (*Loxodonta africana*) Sw: *tembo*. Shoulder height: 2.3–3.4m; weight: up to 6,000kg. The world's largest land animal, the African elephant is intelligent, social and often very entertaining to watch. Female elephants live in close-knit clans in which the eldest female plays matriarch over her sisters, daughters and granddaughters. Mother–daughter bonds are strong and may last for up to 50 years. Males generally leave the family group at around 12 years to roam singly or form bachelor herds. Under normal circumstances, elephants will range widely in search of food and water, but when concentrated populations are forced to live in conservation areas, the damage they cause to trees can have a serious environmental impact. Elephants are widespread in habitats ranging from desert to rainforest and, despite occasional outbreaks of heavy poaching, the Tanzanian population stands at more than 60,000 and they are likely to be seen on a daily basis in most larger national parks.

Black rhinoceros (*Diceros bicornis*) Sw: *kifaru*. Shoulder height: 160cm; weight: 1,000kg. This is the more widespread of Africa's two rhino species, an imposing, sometimes rather aggressive creature that has been poached to extinction in most of its former range and now has a global population of around 5,000. Contrary to its name, it has smooth grey skin, and is no darker in colour than the extra-limital white rhino (whose name is a derivative of the Dutch *weit* (wide), a reference to the square lips that enable it to crop grass so efficiently). Also known as the hook-lipped rhino, the black rhino occurs in many southern African reserves, but is now very localised in Tanzania, where it is most likely to be seen in the Ngorongoro Crater.

Hippopotamus (*Hippopotamus amphibius*) Sw: *kiboko*. Shoulder height: 150cm; weight: 2,000kg. Characteristic of Africa's sizeable rivers and lakes, this large, lumbering animal spends most of the day submerged, but emerges at night to graze. Strongly territorial, herds of ten or more animals are presided over by a dominant male who will readily defend his patriarchy to the death. Hippos are abundant in most protected rivers and water bodies, and they are still quite common outside of reserves, where they kill more people than any other African mammal.

Giraffe (*Giraffa camelopardalis*) Sw: *twiga*. Shoulder height: 250–350cm; weight: 1,000–1,400kg; see photo, page 54. The world's tallest and longest-necked land animal, a fully grown giraffe can measure up to 5.5m high. Quite unmistakable, the giraffe lives in loosely structured herds of up to 15, though herd members often disperse and are seen singly or in smaller groups. Formerly distributed throughout East and southern Africa, the giraffe is now more or less restricted to conservation areas, where it is generally common and easily seen.

Plains zebra (*Equus quagga*) Sw: *punda milia*. Shoulder height: 130cm; weight: 300–340kg; see photo, opposite. This attractive striped horse is common and widespread throughout most of East and southern Africa, where it is often seen in large herds alongside wildebeest. Tanzania's only wild equid, it is abundant in most conservation areas, especially the Serengeti where the population may be as high as half a million. The subspecies present in Tanzania are Crawshay's zebra (*E. q. crawshayi*) in the southeast and Grant's zebra (*E. q. boehmi*) in the rest of the country. Prior to a recent taxonomic revision, the plains zebra's Latin binomial was not *E. quagga* but *E. burchellii*, which is why guides in Tanzania still sometimes refer to it as Burchell's zebra, a name that now only applies to the extralimital subspecies *E. q. burchellii*.

Warthog (*Phacochoerus africanus*) Sw: *ngiri*. Shoulder height: 60–70cm; weight: up to 100kg. This widespread and often conspicuously abundant resident of the African savannah is grey in colour with a thin covering of hairs, wart-like bumps on its face, and rather large upward-curving tusks. Africa's only diurnal swine, the warthog is often seen in family groups, trotting off briskly with its tail raised stiffly (a diagnostic trait) and a determinedly nonchalant air. Two other swine species are present but seldom seen in Tanzania. The bulkier, hairier and browner **bushpig** (*Potamochoerus larvatus*) is as widespread as the warthog, but it's infrequently seen due to its nocturnal habits and preference for dense vegetation. Larger still, weighing up to 250kg, the **giant forest hog** (*Hylochoerus meinertzhageni*) is a primarily West African rainforest species known from a few highland forests in northern Tanzania, but the chance of a sighting is practically non-existent.

Plains zebra drinking, Mikumi National Park

Maasai giraffe, Mkomazi National Park

SMALL MAMMALS

Aardvark (*Orycteropus afer*) Sw: *muhanga*. Shoulder height: 60cm; weight: up to 70kg. This singularly bizarre nocturnal insectivore is unmistakable with its long snout and huge ears. It occurs practically throughout the region, but sightings are extremely rare, even on night drives.

Ground pangolin (*Smutsia temminckii*) Sw: *kakakuona*. Length: up to 35cm; weight 1.5–3kg. Also known as Temminck's pangolin, this widespread but very secretive nocturnal insectivore is known for its distinctive armour plating and tendency to roll up into an artichoke-like ball when disturbed. Individuals might be seen almost anywhere in Tanzania, but sightings are a once-in-a-lifetime event!

Cape porcupine (*Hystrix africaeaustralis*) Sw: *nungu*. Length: up to 80cm (excluding tail); weight up to 30kg. These common but infrequently seen nocturnal rodents are covered in long black-and-white quills that protect them from predators. They occasionally betray their presence by rattling as they walk.

Rock hyrax (*Procavia capensis*) Sw: *pimbi*. Shoulder height: 20–30cm; weight: 4kg. Rodent-like in appearance, hyraxes are more closely related to elephants. The rock hyrax and similar **bush hyrax** (*Heterohyrax brucei*) are often seen sunning in rocky habitats and become tame when used to people, for instance at Seronera and Lobo lodges in the Serengeti. The less common **tree hyrax** (*Dendrohyrax arboreus*) is a nocturnal forest creature, often announcing its presence with an unforgettable shrieking call.

Black and rufous elephant shrew

© Nigel Pavitt/AWL Images

Elephant shrew Sw: *sange*. These rodent-like nocturnal creatures look like miniature kangaroos with elongated noses. A number of species are recognised, but they are mostly secretive and nocturnal, so rarely seen. The smaller species are generally associated with savannah habitats, but the much larger sengis or 'giant' elephant shrews are resident in the Eastern Arc and other coastal forests.

© Nick Greaves/Shutterstock.com

Scrub hare (*Lepus saxatilis*) Sw: *sungura*. Weight: 2.7–4.5kg. This is the largest and most common African hare or rabbit. In some areas a short walk at dusk or drive after nightfall might reveal three or four scrub hares. They tend to freeze when disturbed.

Unstriped ground squirrel (*Xerus rutilus*) Sw: *squirrel ya ardhi*. Weight: 1.4kg. An endearing terrestrial animal of arid savannah, the unstriped ground squirrel is grey to grey-brown with a prominent white eye-ring and silvery black tail. It spends much time on its hind legs, and has the characteristic squirrel mannerism of holding food in its forepaws. In Tanzania, it is most likely to be seen in the Serengeti.

Bush squirrel (*Paraxerus cepapi*) Sw: *kidiri*. Weight: 1kg. This is the typical squirrel of the eastern and southern savannah, rusty-brown in colour with a silvery-black back and white eye-rings. A great many other arboreal or semi-arboreal squirrels occur in the region, but most are found in denser forest and difficult to tell apart in the field.

NILE CROCODILE (*Crocodylus niloticus*) Size/weight: up to 6m and 1,000kg (in extreme cases). The order *Crocodilia* dates back at least 150 million years, and fossil forms that lived contemporaneously with dinosaurs are remarkably unchanged from their modern counterparts, of which the Nile crocodile regularly grows to lengths of up to 6m. Widespread throughout Africa, the Nile crocodile was once common in most large rivers and lakes, but it has been exterminated in many areas in the past century – hunted professionally for its skin as well as by vengeful local villagers. Contrary to popular legend, Nile crocodiles generally feed mostly on fish, at least where densities are sufficient. They will also prey on drinking or swimming mammals where the opportunity presents itself, dragging their victim under water until it drowns. They also frequently eat carrion, such as a hippo that has died of natural causes in the water. A large crocodile is capable of killing a lion or wildebeest, or an adult human for that matter, and in certain areas such as the Mara or Grumeti rivers in the Serengeti, large mammals do form their main prey. Today, large crocodiles are mostly confined to protected areas within Tanzania.

Rock python

Puff adder

SNAKES A wide variety of snakes are found in Tanzania, though they are typically very shy and unlikely to be seen unless actively sought. One of the most likely to be seen on safari is Africa's largest, the **rock python** (*Python sebae*), which has gold-on-black mottled skin and sometimes grows to lengths exceeding 5m. Non-venomous, pythons kill their prey by strangulation, wrapping their muscular bodies around it until it cannot breathe, then swallowing it whole and dozing off for a couple of months while it is digested. Pythons feed mainly on small antelopes, large rodents and similar animals. They are harmless to adult humans, but could conceivably kill a small child.

One of the most commonly encountered venomous snakes is the **puff adder** (*Bitis arietans*), a large, thickset resident of savannah and rocky habitats. Although it feeds mainly on rodents, it will strike when threatened, and it is rightly considered the most dangerous of African snakes, not because it is especially venomous or aggressive but because its notoriously sluggish disposition means it is more often disturbed than other snakes. The related **Gabon viper** (*Bitis gabonica*) is possibly the largest African viper, growing up to 2m long, very heavily built, and with a beautiful cryptic, geometric gold, black and brown skin pattern that blends perfectly into the rainforest litter it inhabits. Although highly venomous, it is more placid and less likely to be encountered than the puff adder.

Several cobra species (*Naja* spp), including some of the **spitting cobras**, are present in Tanzania, most with characteristic hoods that they raise when they're about to strike, though they are all very seldom seen. Another widespread family is the mambas, of which the **black mamba** (*Dendroaspis polylepis*) – which will only attack when cornered, despite an unfounded reputation for unprovoked aggression – is the largest venomous snake in Africa, measuring up to 3.5m long. Theoretically, the most toxic of Africa's snakes is said to be the **boomslang** (*Dispholidus typus*). This variably coloured and largely arboreal snake is back-fanged and very non-aggressive, so while it has been known to inflict a fatal bite on snake handlers, it is not really a threat in the wild.

Most snakes are in fact non-venomous and not even potentially harmful to any other living creature much bigger than a rat. One of the non-venomous snakes in the region is the **green tree snake** (*Dendrelaphis punctulata*; sometimes mistaken for a boomslang, although the latter is never as green and more often brown), which feeds mostly on amphibians. The **mole snake** (*Pseudaspis cana*) is a common and widespread grey-brown savannah resident that grows up to 2m long, and feeds on moles and other rodents. The remarkable **egg-eating snake** (*Dasypeltis* spp) lives exclusively on bird eggs, dislocating its jaws to swallow the egg whole, before eventually regurgitating the crushed shell in a neat little package. Many snakes will take eggs opportunistically, for which reason large-scale agitation among birds in a tree is often a good indication that a snake (or small bird of prey) is around.

Speckled green snake

Flat-headed rock agama

Nile monitor

LIZARDS All African lizards are harmless to humans, with the arguable exception of the **giant monitor lizards**, which could in theory inflict a nasty bite if cornered. Two species of monitor occur in East Africa, the savannah (*Varanus exanthematicus*) and the water (*Varanus niloticus*), the former growing up to 2.2m long and occasionally seen in the vicinity of termite mounds, the latter slightly smaller but far more regularly observed by tourists, particularly around Lake Victoria. Their size alone might make it possible to fleetingly mistake a monitor for a small crocodile, but their more colourful yellow-dappled skin and smaller head precludes sustained confusion. Both species are predatory, feeding on anything from bird eggs to smaller reptiles and mammals, but will also eat carrion opportunistically.

Visitors to Tanzania will soon become familiar with the **common house gecko** (*Hemidactylus frenatus*), an endearing, bug-eyed, translucent white lizard, which reliably inhabits most houses as well as lodge rooms, scampering up walls and upside down on the ceiling in pursuit of pesky insects attracted to the lights. Also very common in some lodge grounds are various **agama** species, distinguished from other common lizards by their relatively large size of around 20–25cm, basking habits, and almost plastic-looking scaling – depending on the species, a combination of blue, purple, orange or red, with the flattened head generally a different colour from the torso. Another common family are the **skinks**: small, long-tailed lizards, most of which are quite dark and have a few thin black stripes running from head to tail. Tanzania is also home to around 20% of the world's chameleon species (page 188), a list that includes several very localised endemics, most associated with the Eastern Arc Mountains or other isolated forest habitats.

TORTOISES AND TERRAPINS These peculiar reptiles are unique in being protected by a prototypal suit of armour formed by their heavy exoskeleton. The most common of the terrestrial tortoises in the region is the **leopard tortoise** (*Stigmochelys pardalis*), named after its gold-and-black mottled shell, which can weigh up to 30kg, and has been known to live for more than 50 years in captivity. It is often seen motoring along in the slow lane of game reserve roads in northern Tanzania. Four species of terrapin – essentially the freshwater equivalent of turtles – are resident in East Africa, all somewhat flatter in shape than the tortoises, and generally with a plainer brown shell. They might be seen sunning on rocks close to water or peering out from roadside puddles. The largest is the **Nile soft-shelled terrapin** (*Trionyx triunguis*), which has a wide, flat shell and in rare instances might reach a length of almost 1m. In addition, five species of marine turtle have been recorded off Tanzania.

Leopard tortoise

1

2

BIRDS

Tanzania is one of the world's most bird-rich destinations. Indeed, the national checklist, which stood at below 1,000 species in 1980, now stands at more than 1,100 species, meaning that Tanzania now vies with Kenya as the African country with the second-most varied avifauna (after the Democratic Republic of Congo). Casual visitors will be stunned at the abundance and visibility of birds in the national parks: brilliantly coloured lilac-breasted rollers and superb starlings, numerous birds of prey, the giant ostrich – the list goes on. For more dedicated birdwatchers, Tanzania now stands second to South Africa among mainland African countries for its wealth of national endemics (species unique to the country). At present, up to 34 endemic species are recognised, including a couple of controversial splits, three species discovered and described in the 1990s, and four that still await formal description. Six of the national endemics are readily observed on the northern safari circuit, but a greater number are restricted to the Eastern Arc Mountains, together with about 20 eastern forest and woodland species whose core range lies within Tanzania. The forests of the Eastern Arc Mountains must therefore rank as the country's most important bird habitat, with the Amani Nature Reserve and Udzungwa Mountains National Park being among the most accessible sites for seeing some of the Eastern Arc specials. But virtually anywhere in Tanzania will offer rewarding birding: in many areas a reasonably competent novice to East African birds could hope to see up to 100 species in a day.

A full checklist of Tanzania's birds is downloadable at w tanzaniabirding.com. Another superb resource is Tanzanian Birds & Butterflies (w tanzaniabirds.net), which includes photographs of 1,052 species recorded in Tanzania, as well as detailed distribution maps based on data collected by the Tanzania Bird Atlas Project. A list of endemics and near endemics is included in *Appendix 3* (page 540). Elsewhere, species of local interest are noted under the relevant site throughout the main body of this guide.

1 Endemic to northern Tanzania, the robust **rufous-tailed weaver** (*Histurgops ruficauda*) is an unusual weaver placed in its own genus. Associated with acacia woodland in the Serengeti, Ngorongoro Crater and surrounds, it is typically seen bobbing around noisily in small babbler-like parties. **2** A favourite with first-time safari goers, the aptly named **superb starling** (*Lamprotornis superbus*) is one of around 20 starling species recorded in Tanzania. It has a distinctive semi-upright stance, terrestrial habits and a strong pointed bill, and is often seen at picnic sites and camps in the Serengeti. **3** **Fischer's lovebird** (*Agapornis fischeri*) is a sociable and noisy small parrot with a parakeet-like bill whose upper mandible almost completely hides the lower one. Near-endemic to northern Tanzania, it nests in tree cavities and is most common in the Serengeti.

BUSH AND FOREST BIRDS The wooded habitats of Tanzania support a particularly varied and colourful avifauna. Broadly, they break up into two main habitat types. The more localised of these is closed canopy forest, which accounts for just 1% of Tanzania's surface area, but due to its patchiness tends to be an important centre of biodiversity – indeed, more than 20 of the bird species endemic to Tanzania are forest specialists. A far more widespread habitat, and one that forms the core of most safari routes, is open-canopied woodland and savannah, which tends to be dominated by acacia trees in the north and by Brachystegia woodland in the south, and is typically home to a wide variety of colourful weavers, waxbills, cuckoos, hornbills, bee-eaters, barbets, woodpeckers and rollers.

European visitors to Tanzania during the months of October to March may be surprised to encounter many familiar species that overwinter in East Africa. Probably the most conspicuous of these is the barn swallow, but a great many other species of warbler, shrike and wheatear are also present during these months, as are numerous migrant waders and birds of prey. Ironically, many of Europe's most glamorous and sought-after birds – among them the stunning Eurasian roller and Eurasian bee-eater – are more likely to be seen overwintering in East Africa than in most parts of Europe.

1 The exquisite **little bee-eater** (*Merops pusillusi*) is probably the most widespread member of a family of colourful birds that hawk bees and other insects from a conspicuous perch. **2 Von der Decken's hornbill** (*Tockus deckeni*) is a member of a family of characterful medium-to-large forest and woodland species named for their curved, heavy bills – in this case red and yellow in the male and black in the female. **3 Hartlaub's turaco** (*Tauraco hartlaubi*) is a sensationally colourful forest dweller most likely to be seen in Arusha National Park or on the Ngorongoro Crater rim. **4** Another firm safari favourite, the lovely **lilac-breasted roller** (*Coracias caudate*) might be seen perching conspicuously in any wooded savannah habitat. **5** The strikingly coloured **red-and-yellow barbet** (*Tricholaema erythrocephalus*), often seen in Tarangire National Park, performs a trilling clockwork-like duet on termite mounds. **6** Of all the region's many kingfisher species, the gemlike **malachite kingfisher** (*Alcedo cristata*), often observed perched motionless on waterside reeds and shrubs, most strongly resembles its European namesake. **7** The **eastern golden weaver** (*Ploceus subaureusi*) lacks the black mask typical of many males in the genus (page 290). **8** The **eastern double-collared sunbird** (*Cinnyris mediocris*) is a typically brightly coloured member of a bird family whose long curved beaks are used to draw nectar from flowers.

3
4
5
6
7
8

BIRDS OF PREY The raptorial Falconiformes, with their strong hooked bills, sharp talons, powerful wings and keen eyesight, are perhaps the most charismatic of avian orders – the feathered equivalent of the lions and other mammalian carnivores that stride across African savannah. Large, intelligent, dashing and boldly marked, these birds of prey have exerted a fascination over humankind since prehistoric times, and even today their appeal extends beyond hardcore birdwatchers to casual safari-goers. So it's pleasing to report that the Accipitridae – incorporating eagles, kites, hawks and Old World vultures – is East Africa's most numerically diverse bird family, with 63 species recorded. In addition, there are 19 species of Falconidae, and a solitary representative of the monotypic family Sagittariidae. All of this makes Tanzania a mouth-watering destination for raptor enthusiasts, though occasionally frustrating when it comes to the identification of confusingly marked species.

1 Conspicuous along the shores of most rivers and lakes, the **African fish eagle** (*Hakliaeetus vocifer*) is a magnificent black-and-white raptor with a rich chestnut belly and yellow base to its large hooked bill. Its far-carrying banshee wail of a call, usually delivered as a duet with both birds throwing back their heads dramatically, is one of the most evocative sounds of the African bush. **2** Another unmistakable and widespread large eagle, the **bateleur** (*Terathopius ecaudatus*) is named for its unique tilting flight pattern, which is reminiscent of a tightrope walker wobbling along a suspended line, and is predominantly black, but offset by a striking bright red face mask, beak and legs. **3** Africa's largest raptor, the **lappet-faced vulture** (*Torgus tracheliotus*) is a massive bird, typically seen singly or in pairs on a carcass alongside some or all of the region's other five carrion-eating vulture species. Its habit of spreading open its heavy black wings like a cape reinforces its ghoulish presence. **4** One of the region's most conspicuous and handsome raptors, the medium–large **Auger buzzard** (*Buteo auger*) might have a black or white breast, but its short orange-red tail precludes confusion with any raptor other than the bateleur. **5** A nocturnal hunter, **Verreaux's eagle-owl** (*Bubo lacteus*), the largest of around 15 owl species resident in Tanzania, is often seen resting up in large trees by day, when black eyes distinguish it from other comparably sized species. **6** The largest and commonest of the region's all-brown raptors, the **tawny eagle** (*Aquila rapax*) has a 2m wingspan and a uniform plumage whose tone varies from dirty blond to buff to dark brown. **7** Associated with moist open savannah, the **dark (western) chanting goshawk** (*Melierax metabates*) has a distinctive upright perching stance and combination of grey back and finely barred underpart, pale rump and red legs. It is replaced by the similar but lighter pale (eastern) chanting goshawk (*M. poliopterus*) in drier habitats. **8** The **greater kestrel** (*Falco rupicolodes*), like other falcons and kestrel of the genus *Falco*, is a slim and cryptically marked small raptor often seen flying swiftly and directly in open country.

3
4
5
6
7
8

1
2
3
4
5
6

GROUND BIRDS The open grassland plains of the Serengeti are particularly rewarding for ground birds, a loosely defined term that embraces any species that spends most of its time foraging on the ground. These open-country specialists include the ostrich, the world's largest bird, whose immense bulk – up to 145kg – renders it incapable of flight. Many other large ground birds associated with the Serengeti and similar habitats are reluctant or clumsy flyers, a list headed by the Kori bustard, which weighs in at up to 19kg, making it the world's heaviest creature capable of taking flight. Smaller ground birds such as larks and pipits tend to be quite drab, as camouflage against predators in their open terrain.

1 Often seen scooting off towards the horizon on the open plains of the Serengeti, the **common ostrich** (*Struthio camelus*) might be the world's largest living bird, standing up to 2m tall, but in evolutionary terms it is a relatively petite relict of a once diverse order of hefty flightless birds known as ratites. Ostriches display strong sexual dimorphism, with the male being larger and very handsome with its striking black-and-white plumage, while the female is smaller, duller and scruffier. Ostrich eggs are the world's smallest in relation to the size of the adult bird, but still clock in at a whopping 1.5kg. **2** The **secretary bird** (*Sagittarius serpentarius*) is a bizarre and unmistakeable 1.5m-tall raptor with long skinny legs, a slender grey torso and long black wings and tail. It's often said that its name alludes to its flaccid black crest, which vaguely recalls the quills used by Victorian secretaries, but more likely that it's a corruption of the Arabic *saqr-et-tair* (hunting bird). Single birds and pairs stride purposefully though open grassland or savannah in search of their favoured prey of snakes, which are stamped to death in a flailing dance-like ritual. **3** The world's heaviest flying bird, the **kori bustard** (*Ardeotis kori*) is a widespread resident of grassland habitats and especially common in the Serengeti. **4** Typically seen marching through the savannah in small thuggish parties, the **southern ground hornbill** (*Bucorvus leadbeateri*) is a hefty and rather improbable turkey look-alike with a large casqued bill, conspicuous throat and eye wattles, and long fluttering eyelashes. A terrestrial hunter, it nests and roosts in trees. **5** The ubiquitous **helmeted guinea fowl** (*Numida meleagris*), named for its ivory crown, belongs to an endemic African family of large, gregarious fowls, all of which are spotted white-on-grey, and have bare blue heads. **6** With a range all but restricted to the Serengeti, the **grey-breasted spurfowl** (*Pternistis rufopictus*) is an endemic member of a widespread group of medium-to-small ground-dwelling fowls known as francolins and often seen calling conspicuously from a perch at dusk. **7** The most common and least water-dependent of Tanzania's storks is the **marabou** (*Leptoptilos crumeniferus*), a large and ungainly omnivore that can be distinguished by its scabrous bald head and inflatable flesh-coloured neck pouch, and is often attracted to carrion and rubbish dumps in both urban and natural environments. **8** The **yellow-throated longclaw** (*Macronyx croceus*) is the most common member of a group of colourful but inconspicuous long-tailed ground-dwellers affiliated to pipits and wagtails.

7

8

1
2
3
4
5
6

WATER BIRDS Tanzania's aquatic habitats embrace hundreds of kilometres of Indian Ocean frontage as well as vast freshwater marshes, tiny soda-crusted crater lakes, forest-fringed perennial rivers and a trio of expansive 'inland seas' in the form of lakes Victoria, Tanganyika and Nyasa-Malawi. These varied wetlands provide rich pickings for more than 100 species of non-passerine waterbirds, ranging from such widespread and familiar families as gulls, ducks and waders to engaging oddities such as pelicans, flamingos and spoonbills. Throughout Tanzania, waterbirds tend to be quite easy to observe and to identify, since most forage openly on the margins or in the shallows.

1 A unique bird with uncertain taxonomic affinities, the **hamerkop** (*Scopus umbretta*) is distinguished by the long flattened bill and angular crest that create the hammer-like appearance alluded to in its Afrikaans name (literally 'hammer head'). Its distinctive nest is a massive untidy construction built over several months using branches, sticks, mud, litter, natural debris and pretty much anything else it can lay its beak on. Abandoned hamerkop nests often acquire a veritable menagerie of squatters, including snakes, monitor lizards, owls and small mammals. **2** The tall and strikingly marked **grey crowned-crane** (*Balearica regulorum*) might be seen in moist wetlands throughout Tanzania. Listen out for its booing nasal call in the Ngorongoro Crater, where it is particularly common after the rains. **3** Herons and egrets are the most visible of East Africa's waterbird families, and the chestnut and purple-grey **goliath heron** (*Ardea goliath*) is the world's largest species, typically standing 1.5m tall. **4** The larger and more common of Tanzania's two pelican species, the larder-billed **great white pelican** (*Pelecanus onocrotalus*), weighing in at 15kg, is the region's bulkiest waterbird, often seen bobbing in flotillas of around ten individuals in the lakes of the Rift Valley and elsewhere. **5** Often seen in pink-tinged mixed flocks comprising many thousand birds, the **greater** and **lesser flamingo** (*Phoenicopterus ruber* and *P. minor*) are more or less resident on Lake Manyara and the saline lake at the centre of Ngorongoro Crater. They feed on algae and microscopic fauna sifted through filters contained within their unique down-turned bills. Their only known breeding site is remote Lake Natron in northern Tanzania. **6** Among the most common of 22 resident and migrant waterfowl species, the distinctive **white-faced whistling-duck** (*Dendocygna viduata*) is often seen in large flocks alongside the closely affiliated but plainer rufous whistling-duck (*D. bicolor*). **7** Closely related to the ibises, spoonbills are large all-white birds with distinctive long spatulate bills, which they sweep partially submerged from side to side in search of small fish and invertebrates. The **African spoonbill** (*Platalea alba*), a common resident, can be distinguished from its European counterpart, a very scarce migrant, by its reddish (as opposed to black) face and legs. **8** Also known as the lily-trotter, the **African jacana** (*Actophilornis africanus*) is totally unmistakeable with its rich chestnut torso and wings, and exceptionally widely spread toes that allow it to walk on lily pads and other light floating vegetation.

7

8

3

Practical Information

WHEN TO VISIT

Tourist arrivals to Tanzania are highest during the northern hemisphere winter, but the country can be visited throughout the year, since every season has different advantages, depending strongly on which parts of the country you plan to include in your travel itinerary. A regional overview follows, but for those with the option, it is worth emphasising that there is much to be said for trying to avoid peak tourist seasons, as the parks and other main attractions will be less crowded.

NORTHERN SAFARI CIRCUIT The focal point of most northern circuit safaris is Serengeti National Park, and wildlife movement here is highly seasonal. The most accessible parts of the Serengeti coming by road from Arusha are the southeastern and south-central plains around Ndutu and Seronera, where wildlife activity peaks over the rainy season, from early November to the end of May. The wildebeest migration disperses into the southern plains at this time of year, usually calving in February, and there is plenty of predator activity. It is also when the countryside is greenest, and it offers the best birdwatching, with resident species supplemented by Palaearctic and intra-African migrants.

The entire period between the Easter weekend and late September was once regarded as low season in northern Tanzania. However, a steady increase in tourist volumes, as well as the opening of several new camps in the far north and western corridor, has led to tourist seasons becoming more loosely defined. Indeed, many small camps and lodges in the western, central and northern Serengeti are actually busiest between June and October, since the migration is usually in the west/central Serengeti over June and July, and in the far north over August to October.

These days, April and May, the rainiest months, is the only period that could really be considered low season in northern Tanzania. Yet visiting at this time of year has its advantages. Lodges and camps tend to offer significantly cheaper low-season rates, which can greatly reduce the cost of a safari. And there is nothing wrong with the game viewing over April and May: plenty of wildlife can be seen in the south-central Serengeti, while Ngorongoro Crater and Lake Manyara, which are incorporated into most northern safaris, are not so strongly seasonal in terms of wildlife movements, but they are far less crowded with 4x4s and more enjoyable to visit outside of peak tourist seasons.

Aside from the Serengeti, the most seasonal of the northern circuit parks is Tarangire, where animal concentrations generally peak between July and the start of the rains in November or early December.

MOUNT KILIMANJARO AND MERU Trekking conditions are best in the dry seasons, which run from January to early March and from August to October.

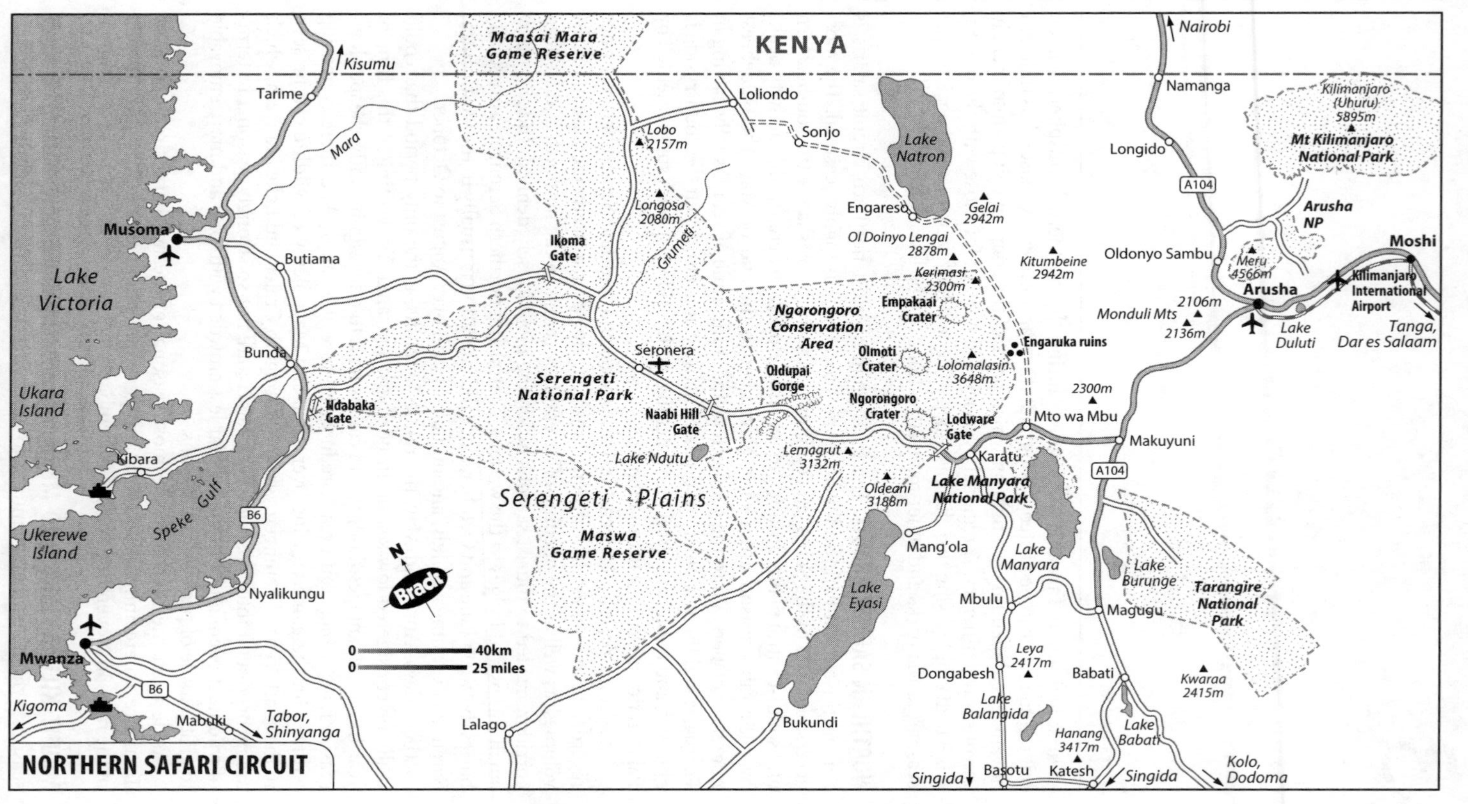
NORTHERN SAFARI CIRCUIT
KENYA
Maasai Mara Game Reserve
Kisumu
Nairobi
Tarime
Mara
Musoma
Lake Victoria
Butiama
Bunda
Ukara Island
Ukerewe Island
Kibara
Speke Gulf
B6
Nyalikungu
Mwanza
Kigoma
Mabuki
Tabor, Shinyanga
Lalago
Ndabaka Gate
Ikoma Gate
Grumeti
Lobo 2157m
Longosa 2080m
Loliondo
Sonjo
Seronera
Serengeti National Park
Naabi Hill Gate
Lake Ndutu
Serengeti Plains
Maswa Game Reserve
0 40km
0 25 miles
Bradt
N
Lake Natron
Engareso
Gelai 2942m
Ol Doinyo Lengai 2878m
Kerimasi 2300m
Kitumbeine 2942m
Ngorongoro Conservation Area
Empakaai Crater
Olmoti Crater
Oldupai Gorge
Ngorongoro Crater
Lolomalasin 3648m
Engaruka ruins
Lodware Gate
Lemagrut 3132m
Oldeani 3188m
Karatu
Lake Manyara National Park
Mang'ola
Lake Eyasi
Bukundi
Mto wa Mbu
2300m
Makuyuni
A104
Lake Manyara
Mbulu
Leya 2417m
Dongabesh
Lake Balangida
Hanang 3417m
Basotu
Katesh
Singida
Babati
Lake Babati
Magugu
Lake Burunge
Tarangire National Park
Kwaraa 2415m
Kolo, Dodoma
Namanga
Longido
Kilimanjaro (Uhuru) 5895m
Mt Kilimanjaro National Park
Arusha NP
Oldonyo Sambu
Meru 4566m
Arusha
Moshi
Kilimanjaro International Airport
Monduli Mts
2106m
2136m
Lake Duluti
Tanga, Dar es Salaam

There are several advantages to the period January to early March. The first is that it tends to be quieter in terms of tourists, an important consideration if you are following one of the more popular routes. The second is that it is probably the most beautiful time of year to climb, with the best chance of clear skies at higher altitudes. On the downside, it is also the coldest time of year on the mountain, though this does mean the snow cap tends be more extensive than in warmer months. The worst months for climbing in terms of weather are November and December.

ZANZIBAR AND THE COAST The coast can be visited throughout the year. However, the most pleasant time to be there is the long dry season, which runs from June to October. This is when temperatures are most comfortable (though still hot by European standards) and the humidity is lowest. There is also less chance of your holiday being disrupted by rain, and it is considerably safer than the wet season in terms of malaria and other mosquito-borne diseases. The wettest months of April and May are best avoided, while January to March, though drier, tend to be hot.

SOUTHERN AND WESTERN SAFARI CIRCUITS The parks of the south and west have a more clearly defined seasonal character than their northern counterparts. The best time to visit Nyerere, Ruaha, Mikumi and Katavi is during the long dry season, which runs from June to October or early November. This is when wildlife is spotted most easily as it congregates around perennial water sources, and also when road conditions are best and the risk of contracting malaria is lowest. Late November to early March sees showers, especially in the first two months. This makes wildlife more difficult to locate, but the scenery tends to be greener and avian activity peaks as migrant birds arrive from the northern hemisphere and resident birds go into breeding plumage. In January and early February, the scenery and birding is at its best, and whilst game densities seen will be lower, game viewing will still be good and you'll see very few other visitors. Late February to the end of May is best avoided, and roads are often washed out – indeed many camps and lodges in the south close for some or all of this period. Chimp tracking in Mahale and Gombe is also best during the dry season, though Gombe in particular could be visited at any time of year.

HIGHLIGHTS

Tanzania is truly a country of highlights, most of which are centred on the north, and it also contains a wealth of off-the-beaten-track opportunities. The list below, broken down by category, only skims the surface:

BEST PUBLIC WILDLIFE DESTINATIONS

Serengeti National Park The linchpin of the popular northern safari circuit, this world-renowned park harbours large numbers of predators, as well as being the site of a legendary migration comprising million-strong herds of wildebeest and zebra.

Ngorongoro Crater Centrepiece of the Ngorongoro Conservation Area, the world's largest intact caldera is superb Big Five territory. Lion, buffalo and large tuskers are all common, and it's the one of the best places in Tanzania to look for the endangered black rhinoceros.

CLIMATE CHARTS

ARUSHA

	Jan	Feb	Mar	Apr	May	Jun	Jul	Aug	Sep	Oct	Nov	Dec
Max (˚C)	29	29	28	25	22	21	20	22	25	27	28	28
Min (˚C)	10	12	12	14	11	10	10	9	9	10	10	10
Rain (mm)	50	85	180	350	205	20	10	15	15	20	105	100

DAR ES SALAAM

	Jan	Feb	Mar	Apr	May	Jun	Jul	Aug	Sep	Oct	Nov	Dec
Max (˚C)	32	32	33	30	29	28	27	28	29	30	31	31
Min (˚C)	25	25	26	26	25	24	23	23	23	25	25	26
Rain (mm)	50	65	140	310	290	45	25	25	35	60	180	135

IRINGA

	Jan	Feb	Mar	Apr	May	Jun	Jul	Aug	Sep	Oct	Nov	Dec
Max (˚C)	25	25	25	24	24	23	22	23	26	27	28	26
Min (˚C)	15	15	14	14	14	12	11	11	12	15	15	15
Rain (mm)	125	115	110	50	10	2	1	5	5	15	50	140

KIGOMA

	Jan	Feb	Mar	Apr	May	Jun	Jul	Aug	Sep	Oct	Nov	Dec
Max (˚C)	26	27	27	27	28	28	29	29	29	28	26	25
Min (˚C)	20	19	19	20	20	18	17	18	20	20	19	19
Rain (mm)	110	115	130	120	45	10	5	10	25	50	130	120

MOSHI

	Jan	Feb	Mar	Apr	May	Jun	Jul	Aug	Sept	Oct	Nov	Dec
Max (˚C)	36	35	34	30	29	29	28	30	31	32	34	34
Min (˚C)	15	15	15	16	14	13	12	12	13	14	14	15
Rain (mm)	50	60	120	300	180	50	20	20	20	40	60	50

NGORONGORO CRATER RIM

	Jan	Feb	Mar	Apr	May	Jun	Jul	Aug	Sep	Oct	Nov	Dec
Max (˚C)	23	23	22	21	20	19	19	20	21	22	22	22
Min (˚C)	10	10	10	11	10	8	8	8	8	9	10	10
Rain (mm)	110	90	135	220	100	20	10	15	15	55	115	135

SERONERA (SERENGETI NP)

	Jan	Feb	Mar	Apr	May	Jun	Jul	Aug	Sep	Oct	Nov	Dec
Max (˚C)	29	29	29	28	27	26	26	27	28	28	28	28
Min (˚C)	26	16	16	16	15	15	14	15	15	16	16	16
Rain (mm)	80	100	135	160	90	35	15	30	60	70	115	105

ZANZIBAR TOWN

	Jan	Feb	Mar	Apr	May	Jun	Jul	Aug	Sep	Oct	Nov	Dec
Max (˚C)	32	32	33	30	29	28	27	28	29	30	31	31
Min (˚C)	25	25	26	26	25	24	23	23	23	25	25	26
Rain (mm)	50	65	140	310	290	45	25	25	35	60	180	135

Tarangire National Park Less celebrated than the Serengeti – and, as a consequence, less heavily touristed – Tarangire preserves a classic chunk of dry savannah studded with plentiful baobabs and home to prodigious elephant herds, along with plenty of other wildlife.

Mahale Mountains and Gombe national parks These two mountainous parks on the forested shores of Lake Tanganyika vie with each other as Africa's top chimpanzee-tracking destination. Gombe is better suited to independent travellers, Mahale to those on pre-booked safaris.

Ruaha National Park Probably the most varied destination on the southern circuit in terms of large mammal and bird diversity, this southern counterpart to Tarangire is also the country's second-largest national park and combines great elephant and big-cat viewing with an untrammelled bush atmosphere.

Nyerere National Park Dominated by the Rufiji River, this vast reserve is the only place in Tanzania where almost all camps supplement game drives with guided walks and boat excursions. It also offers your best chance in East Africa of seeing the endangered African wild dog.

BEST EXCLUSIVE WILDLIFE CONCESSIONS

Klein's Camp Promising exclusive access to 100km^2 of hilly country bordering the northeast Serengeti, this long-established private reserve combines luxury and superb guiding with some of the best game viewing in Tanzania – it's particularly good for leopard and lion.

Grumeti Reserve North of the Serengeti National Park's Western Corridor lies an area of largely flat plains with the occasional hill. There are three very chic, high-quality lodges here: the grand, hilltop Sasakwa; the minimalist Faru Faru; and the old-Africa-style tented camp, Sabora Plains. Marketed by South Africa's top Singita team, these lodges in this very exclusive, private reserve command some of Tanzania's highest costs.

West Kilimanjaro Effectively the Tanzanian counterpart to Kenya's Amboseli National Park, but with little tourist traffic and no restrictions on walking, this game-controlled area is home to plenty of elephant alongside dry-country antelope such as gerenuk and oryx. It also lies right at the base of Kilimanjaro, offering fantastic views of the snow-capped icon along with several other distinctive northern Tanzanian mountains.

BEST HIKING AND WALKING

Mount Kilimanjaro National Park Encompassing the peaks and forested slopes of the continent's highest mountain, Kilimanjaro is climbed by thousands of tourists every year, not only to stand on the snow-capped pinnacle of Africa, but also to experience the other-worldly Afromontane moorland habitat of the upper reaches. For those with who are unwilling or unable to tackle a full hike (which requires at least five days, better six or more), a recommended taster is the Shira Plateau Day Hike.

West Usambara Mountains An affordable low-key alternative to Kilimanjaro, as well as being a good place to adapt to higher altitudes prior to a Kili climb, this beautiful mountain range southeast of Moshi offers unlimited opportunities for casual rambling.

Ol Doinyo Lengai Assuming it's not actually erupting when you visit, the affordable overnight ascent of Africa's most active volcano passes through some of the most dramatic rockscapes in the country.

Udzungwa Mountains National Park Protecting the largest of the Eastern Arc ranges, this pedestrian-oriented park offers the opportunity to hike to several lovely waterfalls, through lush forest inhabited by several rare monkey species and a variety of smaller endemics.

Arusha National Park The best-known hiking attraction here is the three- to four-day round ascent of Mount Meru, Africa's fifth-highest massif, but day hikes into Meru Crater or Ngurdoto Crater are both very worthwhile itinerary fillers out of Arusha town.

BEST FOR BIRDS

Lake Manyara National Park All of the northern safari circuit offers good birding, but for first-time visitors to Africa this is the jewel in the region's avian crown, offering a good opportunity to tick off 100 species – from flamingos and storks to eagles and barbets – in a day.

Amani Nature Reserve This reserve in the Eastern Usambara Mountains, inland of Tanga, protects some of the most important montane forest in Tanzania along with a wealth of rare and endemic birds. There's inexpensive accommodation and a good range of walking trails – and it's easily accessible by public transport, too.

Rubondo Island Situated in the southeastern waters of the vast Lake Victoria, this forested island supports several species with a limited distribution elsewhere in Tanzania, with African grey parrots and other forest dwellers vying for attention with fish eagles, herons and other water-associated species.

BEST FOR CULTURE AND HISTORY

Zanzibar Stone Town Like a living embodiment of *One Thousand and One Nights*, this traditional quarter of Zanzibar is as notable for its lovely Arab-influenced architecture as it is the pervasive laid-back vibe associated with traditional Swahili culture. It's emphatically worth spending a night or two here before heading out to one of the idyllic beaches that surround the island.

Kondoa Rock Art Sites Probably the least publicised of Tanzania's several UNESCO World Heritage Sites, the ancient paintings that adorn hundreds of rock shelters around Kondoa offer a good opportunity to stretch the legs whilst exploring this enigmatic facet of the country's rich prehistory.

Cultural programmes Numerous official cultural programmes operate around northern Tanzania, allowing visitors to interact with traditional pastoralists, farmers and hunter-gatherers. These range from hunting with the Hadza at Lake Eyasi to taking a camelback trip with the Maasai of Mkuru.

Kilwa Kisiwani This small offshore island south of Dar es Salaam, another UNESCO World Heritage Site, is the home of the substantial and well-preserved ruins of what was once the most important of several dozen Swahili city-states strung along the medieval coast of East Africa.

ITINERARY PLANNING

Tanzania has a well-defined tourist circuit. It would be no exaggeration to say that as many as 90% of visitors divide their time between the northern safari circuit and the island of Zanzibar. If this is what you plan on doing, then any good tour operator or safari company will be able to put together a package to meet your requirements. A ten- to 14-day trip is ideal for the Zanzibar/safari combination. Read the section *Organising a safari* below, before making contact with a tour operator. With Zanzibar, the main decision you need to make in advance is whether you want to be based at a hotel in the old Stone Town, or out on one of the beaches, or a combination of the two. For a short trip to Tanzania, it is advisable to fly between Arusha (the springboard for safaris in northern Tanzania) and Zanzibar. If you are really tight for time, you'll get more out of your safari by flying between lodges. A fly-in safari will also be less tiring than the more normal drive-in safari.

After the northern safari circuit and Zanzibar, Tanzania's main tourist attraction is Kilimanjaro, which is normally climbed over five to seven days. For a significant minority of travellers, climbing Kilimanjaro is the main reason for visiting Tanzania, but for the majority the multi-day hike is either too time-consuming to absorb into an itinerary, too costly, or of little interest. Kili climbs can be organised in advance through any number of tour and safari operators, but do ensure that the actual climb is being handled by a specialist company with a good ethical reputation (page 173). To combine a Kili climb with a few days on safari and a visit to Zanzibar you would need an absolute minimum of two weeks in the country, and even that would be very tight, allowing for no more than two nights on Zanzibar.

An increasingly popular alternative to a northern safari is the southern and/or western safari circuits. The national parks and reserves in these parts of the country cater mainly to the upper end of the price spectrum, and generally feel more untrammelled than the Serengeti and Ngorongoro, though game viewing isn't always in the same class. The most popular destinations in the south are Nyerere and Ruaha national parks, but for those who truly want to get away from the beaten track, the combination of Katavi and Mahale Mountains (the latter best known for its chimp tracking) is a great choice. For independent budget travellers, Mikumi, Udzungwa Mountains and Gombe national parks are relatively easy to visit affordably.

ORGANISING A SAFARI Several types of safari are on offer, with the major two variables being accommodation type (budget camping, larger lodges such as those operated by the Sopa and Serena chains, or more exclusive lodges and tented camps managed by the likes of Asilia, Sanctuary, Nomad and &Beyond) and transportation (ie: whether you drive between the reserves using one vehicle throughout, or fly between reserves and go on game drives provided by the lodge or camp). There is some room for overlap between these types of accommodation and transport, and there are also a few more offbeat options. For instance, you might want to travel with a company that specialises in walking safaris, spend part or all of your time in exclusive private concessions bordering the parks (which typically offer extras such as guided game walks and night drives), or visit more far-flung areas such as Lake Eyasi (home to the Hadza hunter-gatherers) or Lake Natron.

Finally, while most safaris concentrate on the quartet of superb reserves that comprise the northern circuit (Serengeti, Ngorongoro, Tarangire and Lake Manyara), the southern and western circuits (highlights of which are Nyerere, Ruaha, Katavi and Mahale Mountains national parks) form a viable alternative for visitors with a yen for less mainstream destinations. These southern and western reserves are seldom visited by budget campers, and they contain no large lodges, only small exclusive camps (typically 6–12 units each) catering mainly to fly-in clients, so they are only really worth considering if you can afford the higher parts of the price range.

Accommodation

Budget camping safaris These are generally designed to keep costs to a minimum, so they tend to make use of the cheapest camping options, often outside the national parks, and clients are normally expected to set up their own tents. Most backpackers and volunteers working in Tanzania go on budget camping safaris, although even with these there is a gap between the real shoestring operators (who'll skimp on everything) and those operators who offer a sensible compromise between affordability and adequate service. Given that high park fees, the introduction of VAT and an escalation in fuel costs have pushed the lowest realistic rate for a budget safari to US$200-plus per person per day, it really isn't worth going with a dodgy company to save a few dollars.

Group safaris staying at larger lodges These are usually fixed-itinerary trips that accommodate the largest volume of visitors, and generally cost around double the price of a budget camping safari. For the extra outlay you get a roof over your head at night, restaurant food and a far higher level of comfort. If you decide to go on a lodge safari, the probability is that the operator will decide which lodges you stay at. Should you have the choice, however, it's worth noting that the former government 'Wildlife Lodge' chain generally has the best natural settings but the poorest standards of accommodation and service, while Sopa and Serena lodges are more luxurious, better run and pricier.

Safaris to small lodges or tented camps If you think sleeping under canvas and eating under the stars might be comparable in price to a lodge safari, think again. Smart tented camps allow for a far more holistic and integrated safari experience than one will ever have sleeping in 'hotels in the bush' designed to insulate travellers from the wilderness, especially after dark. So this third and most costly type of safari accommodation in Tanzania comprises a multiplying selection of smaller and more exclusive lodges and seasonal, mobile or semi-permanent tented camps. These are generally as luxurious as any of the large lodges and at their best they can provide food, service and (where game drives are included) guiding to a much higher standard. They are, however, usually unfenced, have few permanent structures and are designed to maximise the bush experience, so nervous first-time safari-goers might find them a little daunting!

The cost of a safari like this depends on your exact requirements, but it will usually be a lot more than a comparable lodge safari. Indeed, the best mobile and tented camps (as operated by the likes of &Beyond, Asilia and Nomad), although absolutely superlative, are generally more than double the price of larger chain lodges, so not within most safari-goers' means. Fortunately, there are also a small handful of tented or other more low-key camps that offer a bush atmosphere at rates comparable to the chain lodges. These include Tarangire Safari Lodge, Kirurumu

Tented Camp and Ndutu Lodge, as well as the camps operated by Wayo Africa, Wild Frontiers and Tanganyika Wilderness Safaris, and are highly recommended to those seeking a bush experience at a relatively affordable price.

Getting around Regular scheduled flights connect all the main reserves in northern Tanzania, and an increasingly high proportion of safari-goers choose to fly around rather than bump along the long, dusty roads that separate the parks. Flying around will be particularly attractive to those who have bad backs or who tire easily, but it is more expensive and does dilute the sense of magic attached to driving through the vast spaces that characterise this region. Fly-in safaris allow you to see far more wildlife in a shorter space of time, because you don't lose hours on the road. Now that the road from Arusha is surfaced as far as Ngorongoro Conservation Area, a popular compromise is to cover the closer parks (Manyara, Tarangire and the NCA) by road, fly on to one or two locations in the Serengeti ecosystem, then fly directly back to Arusha, or possibly to drive one-way, into the Serengeti, and then fly out at the end.

The reserves of southern and western Tanzania are more dispersed than their northern counterparts, and it is probably fair to say that more than 95% of safaris in this region use the scheduled flights that connect the different reserves to each other and Dar es Salaam or Arusha. In isolation, it is also possible to visit the likes of Ruaha or Nyerere national parks by road, but a road safari through several parks will be quite an arduous experience; few travellers find this practical.

By private safari and car rental The most normal way of getting around northern Tanzania is on an **organised safari** by Land Cruiser, Land Rover or any other similarly hardy 4x4 with high clearance. It is standard procedure for safari companies to provide a driver/guide with a fair knowledge of local wildlife and road conditions, as well as some mechanical expertise. **Self-drive car hire**, although widely available in Zanzibar, isn't a popular option in mainland Tanzania. Should you wish to drive independently, however, Roadtrip Tanzania (w roadtriptanzania.com) provides RAV4 cars and Land Cruisers equipped with everything you need for a camping trip. The website is a great source of information and the 24/7 road support they promise gives peace of mind to explore Tanzania on your own.

Several **navigational apps** useful to self-drivers can be downloaded onto most smartphones and some GPS receivers. These include tracks4africa (w tracks4africa.co.za), Google maps, maps.me, guru maps and what3words. Be warned, however, that while these apps are exceptionally useful when accurate, they can also send you on major wild goose chases when information has been entered incorrectly.

Group size One factor that all visitors should consider is the size of the group doing the safari. It is almost invariably cheaper to go on safari as part of a group, but it can also ruin things if the people in that group are not compatible. A group safari will be highly frustrating to those who have a special interest such as birding or serious wildlife photography. And, frankly, it is probably unfair to impose this sort of interest on other passengers, who will have little interest in identifying every raptor you drive past, or in waiting for 2 hours at a lion kill to get the perfect shot. Another consideration is that non-stretch Land Rovers can feel rather cramped with four people in the back, especially when the luggage is in the vehicle, and jostling for head room out of the roof can be a nightmare when four cameras are vying for the best position.

A small proportion of companies – generally the large package tour operators – use minibuses as opposed to conventional 4x4s. These have several disadvantages, notably that the larger group size (typically around eight people) creates more of a package tour atmosphere, and that it is difficult for a large group to take proper advantage of the pop-up roofs that are usually found on safari vehicles. In any event, bouncing around rutted roads in a Land Rover is an integral part of the safari experience – it just wouldn't be the same in a minibus.

Finally, there is the question of aesthetics. Without wishing to wax too lyrical, the thrill of being on safari doesn't derive merely from the animals you see. There is an altogether more elusive (some might say spiritual) quality attached to simply being in a place as wild and vast and wonderful as the Serengeti, one that is most easily absorbed in silence, whether you travel on your own or with somebody with whom you feel totally relaxed. It isn't the same when you have to make small talk to new acquaintances, crack the rote jokes about who should be put out of the vehicle to make the lion move, decide democratically when to move on, listen to the driver's educational monotones, and observe social niceties that seem at odds with the surrounding wilderness.

Activities A typical day on safari is structured around a long (up to 6-hour) morning game drive and a shorter afternoon drive, returning to camp in between for a leisurely lunch and siesta. A full-day drive may be more appropriate if you want to travel further from camp, and it may be enforced on days when you need to travel between different lodges. Wherever possible, embark on your morning game drive shortly before sunrise and plan your afternoon game drive so that you return to camp at the last permitted hour, since this is when lions and other carnivores are most active and it usually offers the best photographic light. A safari diet of two daylight game drives is undoubtedly the best way to see and photograph a good variety of wildlife, but it can become repetitive, so where possible it is worth mixing it up with other activities such as night drives, guided walks and boat safaris.

Night drives These are now permitted in many national parks, provided you pay the dedicated night drive (US$50pp per activity), as well as in most private concessions bordering the official reserves. It is well worth doing at least one night drive to look for nocturnal species, which include leopard, genet, civet, white-tailed mongoose, greater and lesser galagoes, and the seldom-seen striped hyena, aardwolf and aardvark. Even if you don't see much wildlife, the African bush possesses an unforgettable haunted quality after dark, and the sparkling night sky can be utterly mesmerising.

Guided walks There is no more exciting way of seeing wildlife than on foot, and many national park and private reserves in Tanzania now allow camps to offer their guests morning game walks led by an experienced guide and armed park ranger. You'll generally see less wildlife than you would from a vehicle (not least because you cover far less distance), but being on foot can transform what would otherwise be a relatively mundane sighting (yet another wildebeest or impala) into something altogether inspirational, and it lends a definite edge to any encounter with lions, elephants, buffalos, rhinos or hippos. No less important, it provides a wealth of stimuli to senses that tend to be muted within the confines of a vehicle, and creates an opportunity to enjoy smaller creatures such as birds, bugs and butterflies, and to examine animal tracks and other spoor.

Boat trips Wildlife viewing from a boat is possible only in certain reserves. The best is undoubtedly Nyerere National Park, where boat trips on the Rufiji River and associated lakes invariably yield large numbers of hippos, crocodiles and water birds, and you might also see elephant or buffalo coming to drink or bathe. Canoe excursions in Arusha National Park and boat trips on Rubondo Island, though somewhat more low-key, are also highly recommended, especially to birders.

Balloon trips One of the most exciting ways to see the Serengeti is on an early-morning balloon trip, and these now run daily or seasonally from four launch sites within the park: Seronera, Ndutu, Kirawira and Kogatende. Balloon trips now also run in Tarangire National Park and plans to introduce them at Ruaha, though put on hold by the Covid-19 pandemic, should hopefully come to fruition during the lifespan of this edition.

Tipping In all categories of safari, the price you are quoted should include the vehicle and driver/guide, fuel, accommodation or camping equipment and fees, meals and park entrance fees. You are expected to tip the driver and cook. Around US$10 per day per party seems to be par, but you should check this with the company. Drivers and cooks are poorly paid; if they have done a good job, be generous.

MISCELLANEOUS TIPS AND WARNINGS **Malaria** is present in most parts of the region, with the notable exception of the Ngorongoro Crater rim, and the normal precautions should be taken. Aside from malaria, there are no serious health risks attached to visiting this area.

Tsetse flies are seasonally abundant in some well-wooded areas. Sleeping sickness is not a cause for serious concern, but the flies are sufficiently aggravating that it is worth applying insect repellent to your arms and legs before game drives (though this doesn't always deter tsetse flies) and avoiding the dark (in particular blue) clothing that tends to attract them.

You'll encounter some **rough roads** on safari, so if you have serious back problems or a low tolerance for bumping around in the back of a vehicle, you might want to consider flying between camps. If one member of a safari party has a particular need to avoid being bumped around, they will be best off in the front passenger seat or the central row of seats – the seats above the rear axle tend to soak up the most punishment.

The combination of **dust and glare** may create problems for those with sensitive eyes. Sunglasses afford some protection, and if you anticipate problems of this sort, then don't forget to pack eye drops. Many people who wear contact lenses suffer in these dusty conditions, so it is a good idea to wear glasses on long drives, assuming that you have a pair.

Dust and heat can damage sensitive **camera equipment**. Keep your equipment in a sealed bag and avoid exposing equipment to the sun when possible. Dust particles are most likely to gather on the sensor when changing lenses, so be careful when doing this. The sensor can be cleaned using special brushes and swabs made for this purpose, but this can also cause damage and should be done with the greatest care.

Finally, and at risk of stating the obvious, it is both illegal and foolhardy to get out of your safari vehicle in the presence of any wild animal, and especially buffalo, elephant, hippo and lion.

TOURIST INFORMATION

The **Tanzania Tourist Board** (TTB; **w** tanzaniatourism.go.tz) office in Arusha is a good source of information about the cultural tourism programmes, and its list of registered and blacklisted safari companies is a useful resource for budget travellers arranging a safari on the ground.

TOUR OPERATORS

Northern Tanzania is featured by a vast spectrum of tour operators. At the lower end of the price scale are companies that sell a handful of their own trips, and these are usually group trips with fixed itineraries and departure dates. If you're on a budget and are considering one of these trips, spend time comparing the companies who run them, as well as the actual itineraries, and see how past travellers have rated them.

At the higher-cost end of the market, many tour operators offer enticing trips to Tanzania, and some will be specialists with good knowledge of the country, backed by personal experience. Of those, a few will genuinely listen to what you want and do a good job of helping you choose the right places for your trip – offering a wide choice and unbiased advice. These companies are worth seeking out if you want the best trip possible.

Here we must, as authors, admit some personal interests in the tour-operating business. Chris runs Expert Africa (page 247), which is one of the leading tailor-made operators for Tanzania that organises trips for travellers to Africa from all over the world. Philip acts as an adviser to Expert Africa, complementing the company's team and helping to develop its programmes with the benefit of his high country knowledge. Booking your tailor-made trip with Expert Africa (or, indeed, many other tour operators) will usually cost you the same as, or less than, if you contacted Tanzania's upmarket camps directly – plus you have the benefit of independent advice, full financial protection and experts to make the arrangements for you.

For a fair comparison, the following international tour operators specialise in Tanzania. Safari companies based in Tanzania are found under their different regions in *Part Two*. Alternatively, **w** travellocal.com is a reputable UK-based agent whose website allows customers to communicate directly with selected local operators, as well as book their trips.

UK

Abercrombie & Kent **w** abercrombiekent.co.uk. Worldwide individual & group holidays; upmarket selection & prices to match.
Africa Travel **w** africatravel.com. Substantial operator to all of Africa, with specialist sports travel & flight-only sections.
Cazenove & Loyd Safaris **w** cazloyd.com. Top-end, tailor-made operator with worldwide options, including Tanzania.
Expert Africa **w** expertafrica.com. Specialists to southern & East Africa & Seychelles, with a comprehensive website & an ethical ethos. Run by one of this book's authors (Chris) & advised on Tanzania by the other (Philip), it has probably the most complete & detailed choice of the best Tanzanian lodges, camps & destinations available anywhere. Safaris are flexible & start from about US$3,000/£2,000pp for a week, including accommodation, meals & game activities, but excluding flights.
Explore Worldwide **w** explore.co.uk. Market leader in small-group, escorted trips worldwide.
Footloose **w** footlooseadventure.co.uk. Tailor-made tours, safaris & treks throughout Tanzania, including Zanzibar.
Gane & Marshall **w** ganeandmarshall.com. Long-established specialist to Africa with particularly strong ethics on Kilimanjaro climbs.

Hartley's Safaris w hartleys-safaris.co.uk. Reliable safaris to southern & East Africa, as well as diving & island holidays in the region.
Journeys by Design w journeysbydesign.com. Stylish approach to safaris across southern & East Africa.
Kusini Safaris w kusini-safaris.com. Safari experts with a passion for wildlife conservation, specialising in tailor-made, privately guided luxury safaris across Africa, including Tanzania.
Rainbow Tours w rainbowtours.co.uk. Africa & Latin America specialists, recently with an emphasis on responsible tourism.
Safari Consultants w safari-consultants.com. Long-established, knowledgeable tailor-made specialists to southern & East Africa, & the Indian Ocean islands.
Safari Drive w safaridrive.com. Self-drive Land Rover safaris & expedition with their own fleet, & tailor-made safaris; they know the ground very well.
Steppes Travel w steppestravel.com. Worldwide tailor-made specialists with a long Africa history.
Tanzania Odyssey w tanzaniaodyssey.com. The Tanzanian branch of African Odyssey, a company that offers tailor-made tours throughout Africa.
Tribes Travel w tribes.co.uk. Consciously ethical range covering the globe, including some unique Tanzania offerings.
Wildlife Worldwide w wildlifeworldwide.com. Tailor-made & small group trips worldwide.
World Odyssey w world-odyssey.com. Tailor-made trips across the globe.

USA

Abercrombie & Kent w abercrombiekent.com. A leader in luxury adventure travel.
Africa Adventure Consultants w adventuresinafrica.com. Small Africa specialist with good ethics.
Big Five Tours & Expeditions w bigfive.com. Luxury operator to Asia, Africa & South America.
Exodus w exodustravels.com. Provides safaris, treks, expeditions & active vacations worldwide.
Fair Trade Safaris w fairtradesafaris.com. Run by a Kenya-born philanthropist, this Austin-based luxury safari company donates 100% of profits to vetted conservation, community development & social impact projects.
Micato Safaris w micato.com. Smart, family-owned company, based in New York.
Naipenda Safaris w naipendasafaris.com. Small English- & French-speaking specialist operator to Tanzania, with bases in USA & Arusha.
Next Adventure w nextadventure.com. Small California-based operator with strong ties to Tanzania; also India & South America.
Thomson Safaris w thomsonsafaris.com. Long-established Tanzania specialist operating mostly set-departure small groups on fixed itineraries.

SOUTH AFRICA

Asilia Africa w asiliaafrica.com. This excellent operator manages some of the finest small camps & exclusive lodges in Tanzania & can now put together a full safari package including flights &/or road transfers between its properties.
Pulse Africa w pulseafrica.com. Specialist operator featuring Egypt, Gabon & southern & East Africa, including Zanzibar.
Wild Frontiers w wildfrontiers.com. Experienced Johannesburg-based tour operator notable for its range of air tickets & set-departure group trips, including specialist ornithological

safaris to East Africa. It also has its own Arusha office & runs several good-value tented camps in northern Tanzania.

AUSTRALASIA

Classic Safari Company w classicsafaricompany.com.au. Reliable old-school tour operator now organising tailor-made trips across Africa, India & Latin America.

Expert Africa w expertafrica.com. Antipodean office of African specialists whose Tanzania programme is run by author Chris McIntyre.

RED TAPE

Check well in advance that you have a valid **passport** and that it won't expire within six months of the date on which you intend to leave Tanzania. Should your passport be lost or stolen, it will generally be easier to get a replacement if you have a photocopy of the important pages.

If you want to drive or hire a vehicle while you're in the country, either bring your normal driving licence or organise an **international driving licence** through the AA. You may sometimes be asked at the border or international airport for an **international health certificate** showing you've had a yellow fever shot.

For security reasons, it's advisable to keep a record of all your important information. You can do this by detailing it on one sheet of paper, photocopying it, and distributing a few copies in your luggage, your money-belt, and among relatives or friends at home. Or alternatively, you can email yourself and a few close friends or family the relevant information. The sort of things you want to include are your travel insurance policy details and 24-hour emergency contact number, passport number, details of relatives or friends to be contacted in an emergency, bank and credit card details, camera and lens serial numbers, etc. See also page 86. For up-to-the-minute advice, check w gov.uk/foreign-travel-advice.

VISAS Visas are required by most visitors to Tanzania, including UK and US passport holders, and cost US$30–60, depending on your nationality. It is possible to obtain an e-visa online (visit w eservices.immigration.go.tz/visa) in advance of your visit, but easier perhaps just to buy a visa on arrival, a straightforward procedure that can be done at any international airport or border post. Other than a passport, no documents or photographs are required to buy a visa on arrival, but you must pay in hard currency. The visa is normally valid for three months after arrival, and it allows for multiple crossings into Uganda and Kenya during that period. Note, however, that the regional East African travel visa that can be issued by Kenya, Uganda and Rwanda, and that allows freedom of movement between these three countries, does not include Tanzania. For current information about visa requirements, visit w tanzaniatourism.go.tz or w eservices.immigration.go.tz.

EMBASSIES AND DIPLOMATIC MISSIONS Most embassies and high commissions are based in the former capital, Dar es Salaam, as opposed to Arusha (the main safari centre) or Dodoma (the capital). Generally they open mornings only (typically ⏲ 09.00–12.30) and close at weekends. A full list of embassies and other diplomatic missions in Tanzania is posted at w embassypages.com/tanzania.

GETTING THERE AND AWAY

BY AIR Three international airports are regularly used by visitors to Tanzania. Dar es Salaam's **Julius Nyerere International Airport** (IATA code: DAR; w jnia.

go.tz) is the traditional point of entry for international airlines, and it is generally convenient for business travellers but less so for tourists unless they are focused solely on the southern safari circuit. The more useful point of entry for tourists to northern Tanzania is **Kilimanjaro International Airport** (IATA code: JRO; w kilimanjaroairport.go.tz), which lies between Moshi and Arusha, and is now used by several international airlines. An increasing number of international flights also land at **Abeid Amani Karume International Airport** (IATA code: ZNZ; w zaa.go.tz) on the outskirts of Zanzibar Stone Town.

Budget travellers looking for flights to East Africa may well find it cheapest to use an airline that takes an indirect route. London is a good place to pick up a cheap ticket; many continental travellers buy their tickets there.

Airlines

Major international airlines that fly to at least 1 airport in Tanzania include the following:

EgyptAir w egyptair.com
Emirates w emirates.com
Ethiopian Airlines w flyethiopian.com
Kenya Airways w kenya-airways.com
KLM w klm.com
Oman Air w omanair.com
Qatar w qatarairways.com
Rwandair w rwandair.com
Swiss w swiss.com
Turkish Airlines w turkishairlines.com

Flight specialists

From the UK

Flight Centre w flightcentre.co.uk. An independent flight provider with over 450 outlets worldwide. It also has offices in Australia, New Zealand, South Africa & Canada.
Trailfinders w trailfinders.com. Has several offices in the UK. With origins in the discount flight market, Trailfinders now provides a one-stop travel service including visa & passport service, travel clinic & foreign exchange.
Travel Bag w travelbag.co.uk. Provides tailor-made flight schedules & holidays for destinations throughout the world.
WEXAS w wexas.com. More of a club than a travel agent. Membership is inexpensive, but for frequent fliers the benefits are many.

From the USA

Airtech w airtech.com. Standby seat broker that also deals in consolidator fares, courier flights & other travel-related services.
Council on International Educational Exchange w ciee.org. Focuses on work-exchange trips but also has a large travel department.
Worldtek Travel w worldtek.com. Operates a network of rapidly growing travel agencies.

From Canada

Flight Centre w flightcentre.ca. Has a network of branches around the country.
Travel CUTS w redtag.ca/travel-cuts. A student-based travel organisation with several offices throughout Canada.

From Australasia & South Africa

Flight Centre (Australia) w flightcentre.com.au; (New Zealand) w flightcentre.co.nz; (South Africa) w flightcentre.co.za. A good place to start for cheap air fares.

Web-based flight sites

Expedia w expedia.com. Worldwide with a number of local websites.
Lastminute.com w lastminute.com. Made its name selling last-minute trips.
Opodo w opodo.com. Pan-European family of flight sales sites.
Travelocity w travelocity.com. Another global travel company.

OVERLAND The viability of the established overland routes between Europe and East Africa depends on the current political situation. In recent years, it has often been possible to reach East Africa via Egypt, Sudan and Ethiopia. However, it's not easy to predict the local political situation in advance, so do some online research (a useful forum is f OverlandingAfrica) before setting off.

A route via the Sahara and West Africa used to be favoured by several overland truck companies but it has been impassable since the mid 1990s. The most popular overland route in Africa these days connects Kenya to South Africa via Tanzania and a combination of Mozambique, Malawi, Zambia, Zimbabwe, Botswana and Namibia. It is a good route for self-drivers, can be covered with ease using public transport, but is also serviced by a proliferation of overland truck companies – recommendations include **Acacia Expeditions** (w acacia-africa.com), **Dragoman** (w dragoman.com) and **Exodus** (w exodus.co.uk).

Border crossings Tanzania borders eight countries, but the only overland port of entry used with any regularity by fly-in safari-goers is the Namanga border between Nairobi and Arusha. A number of inexpensive shuttle companies such as Riverside (w riverside-shuttle.com) and Impala (w impalashuttles.co.tz) run daily minibus transfers between Arusha, Moshi and Nairobi. You can also travel between Nairobi and Arusha more cheaply (and more masochistically) in stages, catching a minibus between Nairobi and Namanga (these leave Nairobi from Ronald Ngala Road), crossing the border on foot, and then catching a shared taxi to Arusha. Expect this to take around 6 hours.

Provided that your papers are in order, Namanga is a very straightforward border crossing. There is a bank where you can change money during normal banking hours but at other times you'll have to change money with private individuals – don't change more than you need, as there are several con artists about.

SAFETY AND SECURITY

Crime exists in Tanzania as it does practically everywhere in the world, and tourists are inevitably at risk because they tend to be rather conspicuous and relatively wealthy. Despite this, Tanzania remains a lower crime risk than many countries, not least because the social taboo on theft is such that even a petty criminal is likely to be beaten badly should they be caught. With a bit of care, you would have to be unlucky to suffer from more serious crime while you are in Tanzania. Indeed, a far more serious concern is reckless and drunk driving, particularly on public transport along major roads. Generally buses are regarded to be safer than light vehicles such as minibuses, though this cannot be quantified statistically. Safari drivers are generally a lot more sedate and safe behind the wheel than bus and minibus drivers. Self-drivers should take a far more defensive attitude to driving than they would at home, and be alert to the road-hog mentality of many local drivers.

MUGGING There is nowhere in Tanzania where mugging is as commonplace as it is in, say, Nairobi or Johannesburg, but there are certainly several parts of the country where walking around alone at night would place you at some risk of being mugged. Mugging is generally an urban problem, with the main areas of risk being Dar es Salaam, Arusha and Zanzibar Town. Even in these places, the risk is often localised, so ask advice at your hotel, since the staff there will generally know of any recent incidents in the immediate vicinity. The best way to ensure that any potential mugging remains an unpleasant incident rather than a complete disaster is to carry as little as possible on your person. If you are mugged in Tanzania, the personal threat is minimal provided that you promptly hand over what is asked for.

CASUAL THEFT The bulk of crime in Tanzania consists of casual theft such as bag-snatching or pickpocketing. This sort of thing is not particularly aimed at tourists (and as a consequence it is not limited to tourist areas), but tourists will be considered fair game. In public places, you are less vulnerable if you carry little or nothing of value in your pockets or other easily accessible places. Most of the following points will be obvious to experienced travellers, but they are worth making:

- Casual thieves often operate in bus stations and markets, where you should keep a close watch on your belongings and avoid carrying valuables loose in a pocket or daypack.
- Keep valuables – passport, money, etc – in a money-belt that can be hidden under your clothes. Never use that money-belt to carry spending money you might need to access publicly.
- Many people carry a money-belt on their person at all times, but in certain circumstances it's probably safer to leave it in your hotel room, provided that you can secure it in a safe or lock it away in your luggage. True, hotel rooms are occasionally broken into by thieves, but this is far less common than being pickpocketed or mugged, at least in urban situations.
- Leave any jewellery of high personal or financial value at home.
- If you are robbed, think twice before you chase the thief, who is likely to be descended on by a mob and quite possibly beaten to death.

DOCUMENTATION The best insurance against complete disaster is to keep things well documented. Keep photos or scans of your passport and other important documents and paperwork on your phone, and email them to a trusted relative or friend as back up. You will have to report promptly to the police the theft of any item against which you wish to claim insurance.

SECURITY Tanzania is a very secure country, with a proud record of internal stability since independence. Those parts of Tanzania regularly visited by tourists have a good safety record, although occasional armed robberies might occur anywhere, and Zanzibar has experienced sporadic political instability.

WILD ANIMALS The dangers associated with Africa's wild animals have frequently been overstated since the days of the so-called Great White Hunters – who, after all, rather intensified the risk by shooting at animals that are most likely to turn nasty when wounded – and others trying to glamorise their chosen way of life. Contrary to the fanciful notions conjured up by images of rampaging elephants, man-eating lions and psychotic snakes, wild animals generally fear us more than we fear them, and their normal response to human proximity is to flee. That said, many travel guides have responded to the exaggerated ideas of the dangers associated with wild animals by being overly reassuring. The likelihood of a tourist being attacked by an animal is indeed very low, but it can happen and there have been a number of fatalities caused by such incidents in recent years, particularly in southern Africa.

The need for caution is greatest near water, particularly around dusk and dawn, when hippos are out grazing. Hippos are responsible for more human fatalities than any other large mammal, not because they are aggressive but because they tend to panic when something comes between them and the safety of the water. If you happen to be that something, then you're unlikely to live to tell the tale. Never consciously walk between a hippo and water, and never walk along riverbanks or through reed beds, especially in overcast weather or at dusk or dawn, unless you are certain that no hippos are present.

Watch out, too, for crocodiles. Only a very large crocodile is likely to attack a person, and then only in the water or right on the shore. Near towns and other settlements, you can be fairly sure that any such crocodile will have been consigned to its maker by its potential human prey, so the risk is greatest away from human habitation.

There are areas where hikers might still stumble across an elephant or a buffalo, the most dangerous of Africa's terrestrial herbivores. Elephants almost invariably mock charge and indulge in some hair-raising trumpeting before they attack in earnest. Provided that you back off at the first sign of unease, they are unlikely to take any further notice of you. If you see them before they see you, give them a wide berth, bearing in mind they are most likely to attack if surprised at close proximity. If an animal charges you, the safest course of action is to head for the nearest tree and climb it. Black rhinos are prone to charging without apparent provocation, but they're too rare in Tanzania to be a cause for concern. Elephants are the only animals to pose a potential danger to a vehicle, and much the same advice applies – if an elephant evidently doesn't want you to pass, then back off and wait until it has crossed the road or moved further away before you try again. In general, it's a good idea to leave your engine running when you are close to an elephant, and you should avoid letting yourself be boxed in between an elephant and another vehicle.

There are campsites in Tanzania where vervet monkeys and baboons have become pests. Feeding these animals is highly irresponsible, since it encourages them to scavenge and may eventually lead to them being shot. Vervet monkeys are too small to progress much beyond being a nuisance, but baboons are very dangerous and have often killed children and maimed adults with their teeth. Do not tease or underestimate them. If primates are hanging around a campsite and you wander off leaving fruit in your tent, don't expect the tent to be standing when you return. Chimpanzees are also potentially dangerous but are unlikely to be encountered except on a guided forest walk when there is little risk as long as you obey your guide's instructions at all times.

The dangers associated with large predators are often exaggerated. Most predators stay clear of humans and are only likely to kill accidentally or in self-defence. Lions are arguably the exception, but it is unusual for a lion to attack a human without cause. Should you encounter one on foot, the important thing is not to run since this is likely to trigger the instinct to give chase. Of the other cats, cheetahs represent no threat and leopards generally attack only when they are cornered. Hyenas are often associated with human settlements and are potentially very dangerous, but in practice aren't aggressive towards people and will most likely slink off into the shadows when disturbed. A slight but real danger when sleeping in the bush without a tent is that a passing hyena or lion might investigate a hairy object sticking out of a sleeping bag, and you might be decapitated through predatory curiosity. In areas where large predators are still reasonably common, sleeping in a sealed tent practically guarantees your safety – but don't sleep with your head sticking out and don't at any point put meat in the tent.

When all is said and done, the most dangerous animal in Africa, exponentially a greater threat than everything mentioned above, is the Anopheles mosquito, which carries the malaria parasite. Humans – particularly when behind a steering wheel – run them a close second!

CAR ACCIDENTS Dangerous driving is probably the biggest threat to life and limb in most parts of Africa. On a self-drive visit, drive defensively, being especially wary of stray livestock, gaping pot-holes, and imbecilic or bullying overtaking manoeuvres.

Many vehicles lack headlights and most local drivers are reluctant headlight-users, so avoid driving at night and pull over in heavy storms. On a chauffeured tour, don't be afraid to tell the driver to slow or calm down if you think he is too fast or reckless.

WOMEN TRAVELLERS

Women travellers in Tanzania have little to fear on a gender-specific level. Nevertheless, it would be prudent to pay some attention to how you dress in more conservative parts of the country, particularly along more remote parts of the Islamic coast, where people are unused to tourists, and skimpy clothing (shorts or skirts that reveal the knees, or shirts with bare shoulders) might cause offence. On safari, in larger towns, and in other areas where tourists are commonplace, you can dress as you like within reason. Women travellers should also be alert to the reality that, under certain circumstances, revealing clothes might be perceived to be provocative or to make an unintended declaration of availability.

Beach boys on Zanzibar can be persistent in declaring their affection to female travellers, but stick to your guns and they will eventually get the message and leave you alone.

LGBTQIA+ TRAVELLERS

Homosexuality is socially taboo in Tanzania and specific LGBTQIA+ rights are practically non-existent. Sexual acts between two men have been illegal since colonial times, and are currently punishable by up to 30 years in prison. Sexual activity between women is not addressed in mainland Tanzanian law, but it is illegal on Zanzibar, where the maximum penalty is five years' imprisonment. Oral sex or anal intercourse between any two people, irrespective of gender, is also illegal, though this law has seldom been enforced in the past. Same-sex marriage has never been recognised under Tanzanian law.

Official intolerance peaked under President John Magufuli, whose government launched a prominent campaign that led to the closure of health and community services catering to LGBTQIA+ people and to the arbitrary arrest, anal inspection and torture of numerous alleged homosexuals. This anti-gay agenda can to some extent be viewed as unabashed populism, insofar as it reflected a strong social taboo against homosexuality informed largely by the country's two main religions, Christianity and Islam. In 2007, 95% of Tanzanians declared that homosexuality should not be tolerated socially in a Pew Global Attitudes Project poll. An Afrobarometer poll taken ten years later indicated that only 10% would tolerate someone with a different sexuality as a neighbour. For more details, visit w equaldex.com/region/Tanzania.

INFORMATION ON TRAVELLING WITH A DISABILITY

The UK's **gov.uk** website (w gov.uk/government/publications/disabled-travellers/disability-and-travel-abroad) has a downloadable guide giving general advice and practical information for travellers with a disability (and their companions) preparing for overseas travel. The **Society for Accessible Travel and Hospitality** (w sath.org) also provides some general information. **Disabled Holidays** (w disabledholidays.com) is a specialist UK-based tour operator that offers trips to Tanzania.

These repressive laws and social attitudes have stifled LGBTQIA+ activism in Tanzania, and ensure there is no visible gay scene anywhere in the country. However, a great many LGBTQIA+ travellers and couples have visited Tanzania and been on a safari there without experiencing discrimination or any other problem, though a certain degree of circumspection would be advised.

WHAT TO TAKE

For road safaris, which often involve long, bumpy, dusty drives, carry your luggage in a tough, durable hard suitcase that seals well. For fly-around safaris, a better option is a waterproof duffel-bag that will easily squeeze into a light aircraft. If you plan on using much public transport or walking with your luggage, then the most practical option is a backpack. Whatever you use, make sure it is lockable (with a built-in lock or a padlock), not only for flights but also to deter opportunistic theft from upmarket hotels. A day pack or camera bag for game drives is also essential. If you will be flying between reserves on light aircraft, be aware that many carriers impose a 15kg (33lb) limit per passenger, which can be problematic for serious photographers (some book a second seat to get around it).

CAMPING EQUIPMENT On a budget safari or organised Kilimanjaro climb, camping equipment will be provided by the company you travel with. Taken together with the limited opportunities for camping outside of the safari circuit, this means that for most travellers a tent will be deadweight in Tanzania. An all-weather sleeping bag is required on Mount Meru or Kilimanjaro, and you may want to bring your own sleeping bag for any camping safari.

CLOTHES Clothing usually comprises the bulk of your luggage, so it is worth giving careful consideration to what you need. On a road safari using budget or mid-range lodges, you have no significant restrictions on luggage weight, dusty conditions enforce a daily change of clothes, and organising laundry can be a hassle, so it makes sense to pack a fresh T-shirt and underwear for every day you're on safari. By contrast, more upmarket camps catering to a fly-in clientele generally offer free laundry, in which case four or five outfit changes should suffice.

Many people kit themselves out with a suitcase full of dedicated khaki or green safari clothing, but this isn't really necessary. Ordinary cotton T-shirts, lightweight quick-dry travel trousers/shorts and cotton underwear and socks also work fine. For walking safaris, neutral brown, green and khaki is preferable to brighter colours, but avoid military-style camouflage gear. In areas with tsetse flies, be aware that these annoying creatures are reputedly attracted to blue and black clothing. Contrary to expectations, most safari destinations in Tanzania can be chilly at night, so bring a few layers of warm clothing and some sort of windbreaker. More serious alpine gear is necessary for climbing Kilimanjaro or Mount Meru.

As for footwear, bring one pair of sandals, flip-flops or other open shoes, as well as closed shoes for evenings, bush walks and hiking. Genuine hiking boots with good ankle support might be required for major mountain hikes (provided they have been broken in properly first), but in most other scenarios a solid pair of trainers or trail-running shoes is ideal.

Depending on where you travel in Tanzania, the sensibilities of the large Muslim population might factor into your dress choices. Women can wear shorts at most beach resorts, in game reserves and cities where locals are used to tourists, but in smaller coastal settlements it would be better to wear a skirt that covers your knees and a modest shirt that doesn't expose shoulders or cleavage. Shorts are acceptable for men, but trousers are considered more respectable in an urban setting, and walking around shirtless in a public place is unacceptable.

OTHER USEFUL ITEMS If you're staying at mid-range or upmarket lodges, basic **toiletries** such as soap, shampoo, conditioner and moisturiser are generally supplied, but it might be worth carrying a small back-up container of each, and you will definitely need to bring a toothbrush, toothpaste, razor, sunblock, mosquito repellent and any other more personal toiletries you require. On camping safaris, assume you will need to carry all your own toiletries. It's useful to keep handy a roll of **toilet paper**, which is widely available at shops and kiosks, but cannot always be relied upon to be present where it's most urgently needed.

In most situations, the torch and alarm clock on your smartphone should be all you require, but if you will be camping, then a proper **torch** and **penknife** are recommended. Carry a small **medical kit** (page 106). If you wear **contact lenses**, bring all the fluids you need, or if your eyes are sensitive to dusty, intense sun and dry air, consider reverting to glasses.

Binoculars are essential if you want to get a good look at birds, or to watch distant mammals in game reserves. For most purposes, lightweight 7x21 compact binoculars will be fine, although some might prefer traditional 7x35 binoculars for their larger field of vision. Serious birdwatchers will find a 10x30 or 10x50 magnification more useful, and should definitely carry a good field guide.

Don't forget to pack **charging cables** for your phone, tablet, e-reader, laptop, camera and/or any other electronic devices. Electric sockets are often different to those in Europe or the USA, so bring a universal adapter and whatever converters you might require. Many camps and lodges only have solar power, and charging facilities may be restricted to reception or other communal areas, so ensure everything is fully charged when you set off on safari, and carry a charged power bank as backup.

MONEY AND BANKING

The unit of currency is the Tanzanian shilling (pronounced *shillingi*), which is in theory divided into 100 cents. The Tanzanian shilling comes in Tsh10,000, 5,000, 1,000, 500 and 200 denomination bills. It is often very difficult to find change for larger denomination bills, so try always to have a fair spread of notes available. The bulky small denomination coins are worth considerably less than their weight in whatever leaden metal it is that's used to mint them! The rate of exchange has deteriorated against all hard currencies over the last two decades. Between 1999 and 2023, the exchange rate against the US dollar slid from Tsh670 to around Tsh2,330, a drop of around 10% annually. It is reasonable to expect a similar trend will persist during the lifespan of this edition. For rates of exchange, see page 2.

Most upmarket hotels and safari companies in Tanzania quote rates in US dollars. Some will also demand payment in this or another prominent hard currency, while others prefer payment in local currency. The situation with national parks and other conservation areas is variable, but if you expect to pay fees directly rather than through an operator, then you'll need a Visa or Mastercard (page 92). These exceptions noted, most things in Tanzania are best paid for in local currency, including restaurant bills, goods bought at a market or shop, mid-range and budget accommodation, public transport and most other casual purchases. Indeed, most service providers geared towards the local economy will have no facility for accepting any currency other than the Tanzanian shilling.

> **PAYING PARK FEES**
>
> Although it won't affect travellers on organised safaris, anybody doing a self-drive safari should be aware that none of Tanzania's national parks (including the Ngorongoro Conservation Area) will accept cash payments for entrance or other fees. The only form of payment accepted at entrance gates is Visa or Mastercard.

Note that most prices in this book are quoted in US dollars rather than Tanzanian shillings. This is because of the local currency's propensity for devaluation against hard currencies, which means that even where prices are quoted locally in shillings, a US dollar price is more likely to hold steady over the book's lifespan. However, in the few instances where a hotel quotes its rates in euros or sterling, we have followed suit.

CREDIT CARDS An international Visa or Mastercard (but not other brands of card) can be used to draw local currency at 24-hour ATMs associated with one or more of the NCB, NMB, CRDB, Exim, Barclays, Stanbic or Standard Chartered banks in most towns of any size and at all three international airports. Depending on the bank, a transaction limit of Tsh400,000 (around US$170) is imposed on ATM withdrawals, but it is usually possible to do several transactions in a row, to a maximum daily withdrawal limit of Tsh1,200,000–2,000,000 (around US$500–850). Visa and Mastercard can also be used to pay bills at most upmarket hotels, and at many restaurants and ships catering to a relatively affluent clientele, as well as for national park fees. Note that ATM facilities are not available in national parks, or in some smaller towns and beach resorts, and that cards are not generally accepted at budget hotels and restaurants or to pay for public transport. It's advisable to take along more than one card, in case one stops working or your bank decides to freeze it. It is also a good idea to carry some backup funds in hard currency **cash**, ideally US dollars although euros and pounds sterling are also widely accepted. Carry your hard currency and credit cards in a money-belt that can be hidden beneath your clothing. Your money-belt should be made of cotton or another natural fabric, and everything inside the belt should be wrapped in plastic to protect it against sweat.

FOREIGN EXCHANGE Foreign currencies can be changed into Tanzanian shillings at any bank during banking hours (generally 08.00–15.00 Mon–Fri, 08.00–noon Sat). If you need to change money outside banking hours, this can only be done formally at one of the three international airports (Dar es Salaam, Kilimanjaro and Zanzibar), though some hotels might help you out informally. The private bureaux de change (known locally as forex bureaux) that once proliferated all over Tanzania are now illegal. There is no longer a significant black market in Tanzania, and private individuals who offer a slightly better rate than the bank should be treated with suspicion.

GETTING AROUND

BY AIR Several private airlines run scheduled flights around Tanzania, most prominently Air Tanzania (w airtanzania.co.tz), Auric Air (w auricair.com), Coastal Aviation (w coastal.co.tz), Precision Air (w precisionairtz.com), Regional Air (w regionaltanzania.com), Safari Airlink (w flysal.com) and ZanAir (w zanair.com). Between them, these carriers offer reliable services to most parts of the country that regularly attract tourists, including Dar es Salaam, Zanzibar, Pemba,

Mafia, Kilimanjaro, Arusha, Serengeti, Ngorongoro, Lake Manyara, Mwanza, Rubondo Island, Kigoma and most of the southern parks. There are also regular flights between Kilimanjaro and the Kenyan cities of Mombasa and Nairobi. Several of the airlines now offer a straightforward online booking service.

BY PUBLIC TRANSPORT Good express coach services, typically travelling at faster than 60km/h, connect Arusha and Moshi to Dar es Salaam and Nairobi (Kenya). **Dar** and **Kilimanjaro Express** are particularly recommended, approaching (although far from attaining) Greyhound-type standards, and they operate several buses daily between Dar es Salaam and Arusha. Express coaches also connect Arusha to Moshi, Lushoto, Tanga, Mwanza and Dar es Salaam.

For long trips on major routes, ensure that you use an 'express bus', which should travel directly between towns, stopping only at a few prescribed places, rather than stopping wherever and whenever a potential passenger is sighted or an existing passenger wants to disembark. Be warned that as far as most touts are concerned, any bus that will give them commission is an express bus. The best way to counter this is to go to the bus station the day before you travel, and make enquiries and bookings in advance, when you're under less pressure and don't need to worry about keeping an eye on your luggage.

The alternative to buses on most routes is a *dalla dalla* – a generic name that seems to encompass practically any light public transport. On the whole, dalla dallas tend to be overcrowded by comparison with buses, and they are more likely to try to overcharge tourists, while the manic driving style results in regular fatal accidents.

When you check bus times, be conscious of the difference between Western time and Swahili time. Many Tanzanians will translate the Swahili time to English without making the 6-hour conversion – in other words, you might be told that a bus leaves at 11.00 when it actually leaves at 05.00. The best way to get around this area of potential misunderstanding is to confirm the time you are quoted in Swahili – for instance ask '*saa moja?*' if you are told a bus leaves at 13.00. See page 533 for more details.

BY PRIVATE SAFARI AND CAR RENTAL The most normal way of getting around northern Tanzania is on an **organised safari** by Land Cruiser, Land Rover or any other similarly hardy 4x4 with high clearance. It is standard procedure for safari companies to provide a driver/guide with a fair knowledge of local wildlife and road conditions, as well as some mechanical expertise. **Self-drive car hire** isn't a particularly attractive or popular option in northern Tanzania (although see page 79 for one option), but it is widely available in Zanzibar and Dar es Salaam.

ACCOMMODATION

The number of hotels in major urban tourist centres such as Zanzibar Town, Dar es Salaam, Arusha and Moshi is quite remarkable. So, too, is the variety in standard and price, which embraces hundreds of simple local guesthouses charging up to US$10 per night, as well as fantastic exclusive beach resorts and lodges charging in the ballpark of US$2,000 for a room – and everything in between. Unless otherwise stated, it can be assumed that all hotels and other accommodation options listed in this guide provide en-suite accommodation (or, as they say locally, 'self-contained') with hot showers, and offer free Wi-Fi to guests.

Accommodation listings in this guidebook are placed in one of five categories: exclusive, upmarket, moderate, budget, and camping. The purpose of this

ACCOMMODATION PRICE CODES

Accommodation price codes are based on the average cost of a standard double room.

$	under US$50	**$$$$$**	US$300–500
$$	US$50–100	**$$$$$$**	US$500–1,000
$$$	US$100–200	**$$$$$$$**	US$1,000+
$$$$	US$200–300		

categorisation is twofold: to break up long hotel listings that span a wide price range, and to help readers isolate the range of hotels that will best suit their budget and taste. The application of categories is not meant to be rigid. Aside from an inevitable element of subjectivity, hotels are categorised on their feel as much as their rates, and this is often influenced by the standard of other accommodation options in the same place – a budget option in some safari destinations might cost more than an upmarket lodge in an urban setting!

Before going into more detail about the different accommodation categories, it's worth noting a few potentially misleading quirks in local hotel-speak. In Swahili, the word *hoteli* refers to a restaurant while what we call a hotel is generally called a lodging, guesthouse or *gesti* – so if you ask a Tanzanian to show you a hotel, you might well be taken to an eatery. Another local quirk is that most Tanzanian hotels in all ranges refer to a room with an en-suite shower and toilet as being 'self-contained'. Finally, at most hotels in the moderate category or below, a single room will as often as not be one with a three-quarter or double bed, while a double room will be what we call a twin, with two single or double beds. 'B&B' refers to bed and breakfast, 'HB' to half board, 'FB' to full board.

For quick reference, a price-band symbol is appended to all hotel and other accommodation listings. This is usually based on the establishment's cheapest or standard high-season rate for a double unit. Where possible, we have also included exact room rates for hotel and other accommodation that regularly deal directly with the general public and fall in the **$–$$$** price range (ie: under US$200). Rack rates are not included for places in higher price brackets as they are almost invariably booked as part of a tour and often subject to complex seasonal and other discounts. Price bands are as follows:

EXCLUSIVE This category does not generally embrace conventional international-style hotels, but rather small and atmospheric tented camps, game lodges and beach resorts catering to the most exclusive end of the market. Lodges in this category typically (but not invariably) contain significantly fewer than 20 accommodation units built and decorated in a style that complements the surrounding environment. The management will generally place a high priority on personalised service and quality food and wine, with the main idea being that guests are exposed to a holistic 24-hour bush or beach experience, rather than just a hotel room and restaurant in a bush/beach location. In several instances, lodges that fall into the exclusive category might be less conventionally luxurious, in terms of air conditioning and the like, than their competitors in the upmarket category. It is the bush experience and not the range of facilities that lends lodges in this category a quality of exclusivity. Rack rates are typically upwards of US$1,000 all-inclusive for a double room, but many cost twice as much as that (with substantial discounts for operators).

This is the category to look at if you want authentic, atmospheric bush or beach accommodation and have few financial restrictions.

UPMARKET This category includes most hotels, lodges and resorts that cater almost entirely to the international tourist or business travel market. Hotels in this range would typically be accorded a two- to four-star ranking internationally, and they offer smart accommodation with en-suite facilities, mosquito netting, air conditioning or fans depending on the local climate, and satellite television in cities and some beach resorts. Hotels in this bracket might charge anything from under US$100 to upwards of US$600 for a double room, depending on quality and location, but they are generally at the higher end of that range in national parks and other safari destinations. As a rule, upmarket hotels in areas that see few foreign visitors are far cheaper than equivalent hotels in or around urban tourist centres such as Dar es Salaam and Arusha, which are in turn cheaper than beach hotels and lodges in national parks and game reserves. Room rates for city and beach hotels invariably include breakfast, while at game lodges they will also normally include lunch and dinner. Most package tours use accommodation in this range.

MODERATE In Tanzania, as in many African countries, there is often a wide gap in price and standard between the cheapest hotels geared primarily towards tourists and the best hotels geared primarily towards local travellers and budget travellers. For this reason, the moderate bracket is rather more nebulous than other accommodation categories, essentially consisting of hotels which, for one or another reason, couldn't really be classified as upmarket, but equally are too expensive or of too high quality to be considered budget lodgings. Many places listed in this range are superior local hotels that will suffice in lieu of any genuinely upmarket accommodation in a town that sees relatively few tourists. The category also embraces decent lodges or hotels in recognised tourist areas that charge considerably lower rates than their upmarket competitors, but are clearly a notch or two above the budget category. Hotels in this range normally offer comfortable accommodation in self-contained rooms with hot water, fan and possibly satellite television, and they will have decent restaurants and employ a high proportion of English-speaking staff. Prices for moderate city and beach hotels are generally in the US$50–150 range, more in some game reserves. This is the category to look at if you are travelling privately on a limited or low budget and expect a reasonably high but not luxurious standard of accommodation.

BUDGET Hotels in this category are aimed largely at the local market and definitely don't approach international standards, but are still reasonably clean and comfortable, and a definite cut above the basic guesthouses that proliferate in most towns. Hotels in this bracket will more often than not have a decent restaurant attached, English-speaking staff and comfortable rooms with en-suite facilities, running cold or possibly hot water, fans (but not air conditioning) and good mosquito netting. The hotels in this category typically charge up to US$80 for a self-contained double room, and may charge as little as US$15–20 in relatively out-of-the-way places. This is the category to look at if you are on a limited budget, but want to avoid total squalor!

CAMPING There are surprisingly few campsites in Tanzania, and those that do exist tend to be in national parks, where camping costs US$30 per person. Along the coast north of Dar es Salaam and in Moshi and Arusha, several private sites cater to backpackers and overland trucks. If you ask at moderate hotels in out-of-the-way places, you may sometimes be allowed to camp in their grounds for a small fee.

EATING AND DRINKING

FOOD Most visitors to Tanzania will eat at least 90% of their meals at game lodges or hotels that cater specifically to tourists and whose kitchens serve Western-style food, ranging in standard from adequate to excellent. Game lodges tend to offer a daily set menu with a limited selection, so it is advisable to have your tour operator specify in advance if you are a vegetarian or have other specific dietary requirements. First-time visitors to Africa might take note that most game lodges in and around the national parks have isolated locations, and driving within the parks is neither permitted nor advisable after dark, so that there is no realistic alternative to eating at your lodge. You will rarely be disappointed.

Most game lodges offer the option of a packaged breakfast and/or lunch box, so that their guests can eat on the trot rather than having to base their game-viewing hours around set meal times. The standard of the packed lunches is rather variable (and in some cases pretty awful), but if your first priority is to see wildlife, then taking a breakfast box in particular allows you to be out during the prime game-viewing hours immediately after sunrise. Packed meals must be ordered the night before you need them. It is best to ask your driver-guide to make this sort of arrangement, rather than doing it yourself.

When you are staying in towns such as Dar, Arusha and Moshi, there is a fair selection of eating-out options. Indian eateries are particularly numerous in most towns, thanks to the high resident Indian population, and good continental restaurants and pizzerias are also well represented. Seafood is excellent on the coast. Options tend to be more limited in smaller towns such as Lushoto and tanga, and very basic in villages off the main tourist trail. A selection of the better restaurants in each town is listed in the main part of the guide.

As for the local cuisine, it tends to consist of a bland stew eaten with one of four staples: rice, chapati, *ugali* or *batoke*. Ugali is a stiff maize porridge eaten throughout sub-Saharan Africa. Batoke or *matoke* is cooked plantain, served boiled or in a mushy heap. In the Lake Victoria region, batoke replaces ugali as the staple food. The most common stews are chicken, beef, goat and beans, and the meat is often rather tough. In coastal towns and around the great lakes, whole fried fish is a welcome change. The distinctive Swahili cuisine of the coast makes generous use of coconut milk and is far more spiced than other Tanzanian food.

Mandaazi, the local equivalent of doughnuts, are tasty when freshly cooked. They are served at hotelis and sold at markets. You can eat cheaply at stalls around markets and bus stations. Goat kebabs, fried chicken, grilled groundnuts and potato

RESTAURANT PRICE CODES

Restaurant price codes give a general indicator, based on the average cost of a main course, but there will often be plenty of variation outside that range:

Expensive	$$$	Most mains Tsh25,000/US$12+
Moderate	$$	Most mains in the Tsh15–25,000/US$7–11 bracket
Inexpensive	$	A good selection of mains under Tsh15,000/US$7

TRADITIONAL MBEGE BANANA BEER *Emma Thomson*

This party brew is prepared for many different Chagga ceremonies, but it is always drunk from a dried squash plant that has been hollowed out to form an enormous chalice, with the village landlord's clan name engraved upon it. Below is a rough recipe, as the measurements are only approximate.

INGREDIENTS
1kg mashed banana
1 litre water
1kg finger millet

METHOD Boil bananas in water until they turn red, and then cover for three days.

Meanwhile, wash the finger millet, cover and leave in a wet, warm and dark place for three to four days until the millet begins to sprout. Then grind the millet into flour.

From this, make porridge by mixing two parts flour to one part water. Next add ten parts of the boiled banana to one part porridge, mix and cover until the next day.

Let the celebrations begin. (The longer you leave it, the stronger the brew.)

chips are often freshly cooked and sold in these places. A very popular and filling (though not exactly healthy) street dish throughout Tanzania is *chipsi mayai*, which essentially consists of potato chips cooked in an omelette-like mix of eggs (mayai).

KiSwahili names for various foods are given on page 534.

DRINK The most widely drunk beverage is *chai*, a sweet tea where all ingredients are boiled together in a pot. Along the coast chai is often flavoured with spices such as ginger. In some places chai is served *ya rangi* or black; in others *maziwa* or milky. Sodas such as Coke, Pepsi, Sprite and Fanta are widely available, and normally cost less than US$0.50 in outlets geared towards locals, and up to five times that price in tourist-oriented lodges. In large towns you can often get fresh fruit juice. On the coast and in some parts of the interior, the most refreshing, healthy and inexpensive drink is coconut water, sold by street vendors who will decapitate the young coconut of your choice to create a natural cup, from which the juice can be sipped. Tap water in Tanzania is often dodgy, and most travellers try to stick to mineral water, which comes in 1.5-litre bottles that cost a few hundred shillings in supermarkets in Arusha but are very overpriced at game lodges – it is advisable to stock up with a dozen bottles or so before your safari leaves Arusha.

The two main alcoholic drinks are beer and *konyagi* (a cheap sugarcane spirit that tastes a bit strange on its own, but mixes well). Around ten different lager beers are now available, of which Safari, Kilimanjaro and Serengeti seem to be the most popular. Beers usually come in 500ml bottles and cost anything from under US$1 at a local bar to more than US$5 at a very upmarket hotel, although some lodges also serve smaller 330ml cans. A variety of imported spirits are available in larger towns. A varied selection of wines, usually South African in origin, is available at most mid-range and upmarket lodges and hotels, and generally quite reasonably priced by international standards. Wine bought at supermarkets is far cheaper than it is at lodges.

PUBLIC HOLIDAYS

Tourists visiting Tanzania should take note of public holidays, since all banks, forex bureaux and government offices will be closed. In addition to Good Friday, Easter Monday, Eid-al-Fitr, Islamic New Year and the Prophet's Birthday, which fall on different dates every year, the following public holidays are taken in Tanzania:

1 January	New Year's Day
12 January	Zanzibar Revolution Day
7 April	Karume Day (anniversary of the assassination of Vice President Abeid Amani Karume in 1972)
26 April	Union Day (anniversary of the union between Tanganyika and Zanzibar)
1 May	International Workers' Day
7 July	Saba Saba (Peasants') Day
8 August	Nane Nane (Farmers') Day
14 October	Nyerere Memorial Day
9 December	Independence Day
25 December	Christmas Day
26 December	Boxing Day

SHOPPING

Excellent chain supermarkets can be found in Dar es Salaam and Arusha, and there are reasonable private supermarkets in Zanzibar Stone Town and Moshi. These stock a wide range of imported foods, including packaged travel-friendly snacks (from dates and nuts to crisps and chocolate), fresh local produce, toiletries and some non-prescription medication, imported wine and spirits, and locally manufactured beers, soft drinks, juices and mineral water. A similar range of goods is available in most other large towns but generally the choice will be more limited and prices slightly inflated. Pharmacies are ubiquitous in most towns, and generally stock a fair range of medication and have competent English-speaking staff. Shopping hours are normally 08.30–18.00, sometimes with a lunch break between 13.00 and 14.00, but longer hours are kept by the small *dukas* (stalls) that are dotted around markets or line main roads throughout Tanzania.

CURIOS A variety of items specifically aimed at tourists is available: Makonde carvings, Tingatinga paintings (page 132), batiks, musical instruments, wooden spoons and various soapstone and malachite knick-knacks. Arusha is the best place to shop for curios, as prices are competitive and the quality is good. Prices in shops are fixed, but you may be able to negotiate a discount. At curio stalls, haggling is necessary. Unless you are good at this, and know the going rate for the thing you want to buy, then expect to pay more than you would in a shop. The colourful *vitenge* (the singular of this is *kitenge*) worn by most Tanzanian women can be picked up cheaply at any market in the country.

MEDIA AND COMMUNICATIONS

NEWSPAPERS The English-language *Daily News* (**w** dailynews.co.tz), *Citizen* (**w** thecitizen.co.tz) and *Guardian* (**w** guardian.co.tz) are all widely available in major towns (as well as having good websites) and carry a fair bit of syndicated international news along with detailed local news. Better still is the weekly *East African* (w theeastafrican.co.ke), which is published in Kenya but distributed throughout the countries to which it dedicates roughly equal coverage, ie: Kenya, Tanzania, Rwanda and Uganda.

CONNECTIVITY Network reception and internet access is increasingly widespread in Tanzania, even extending into many national parks, and mobile numbers have pushed landlines into virtual obsolescence. All but the most remote of hotels, lodges, camps and restaurants generally offer free Wi-Fi to their clients, but it is often slow or erratic, and doesn't allow you to go online when you are out and about. For this reason, it is worth investing in a Tanzanian SIM card, as well as local airtime and a data package allowing affordable internet usage from your smartphone. The investment is small (probably less than US$20 for the whole package), and it will work our far more cheaply than the hefty bill you're likely to rack up if you use your home phone number for calls and/or messages at roaming rates.

The most useful providers on the Tanzanian mainland are Vodacom (w vodacom.co.tz) and Airtel (w airtel.co.tz), whose SIM cards can be bought (along with airtime and data) at any of their service centres in Dar es Salaam, Zanzibar Town, Arusha, Moshi and elsewhere. If you are staying on Zanzibar only, then ZanTel (w zantel.co.tz) is recommended over Vodacom or Airtel. Legally, you have to register a new SIM for the number to be activated fully. This can be done on the spot in any Vodacom or Airtel service centre, provided you bring along your passport.

Assuming you have a single-SIM phone, a limitation of buying a local SIM card is that your home number will not work for the duration of your trip. One solution is to bring an old or spare mobile phone for your Tanzanian SIM card; another would be to buy a dual-SIM phone. Alternatively, if you don't need access to your home number while you are away, you can still communicate on WhatsApp with whatever number you ordinarily use, so ask friends or family to contact you that way.

Because WhatsApp is so cheap and convenient, it has caught on big time in Tanzania and is almost invariably the easiest and most reliable way to communicate with smaller hotels, guides, cultural tourism programmes, restaurants and other contacts that are unlikely to respond to emails. The overwhelming majority of mobile numbers provided in this edition are also linked to WhatsApp and it is easy enough to check any individual number by adding it to the contact list on your phone then switching to WhatsApp to search for it. Since mobile numbers require an international code to work on WhatsApp, they are listed in this format throughout the book.

Mobile money can be issued to pay for most things in Tanzania, so if you have a local SIM card and are travelling independently, it is well worth setting up this facility. The best service is Vodacom's m-pesa; for details visit w vodacom.co.tz/mpesa.

CULTURAL ETIQUETTE

Tanzania has perhaps the most egalitarian and tolerant mood of any African country that I've visited, and you'd have to do something pretty outrageous to commit a serious faux pas. But, like any country, Tanzania does have its rules of etiquette, and while allowances will always be made for tourists, there is some value in ensuring that they are not made too frequently.

GENERAL CONDUCT Perhaps the most important single point of etiquette in Tanzania is the social importance of formal greetings. Tanzanians tend to greet each other elaborately, and if you want to make a good impression on somebody who speaks English, whether they be a waiter or a shop assistant (and especially if they work in a government department), you would do well to follow suit. When you need to ask somebody directions, it is rude to blunder straight into interrogative mode without first exchanging greetings. Tanzanians will also readily greet passing strangers, particularly in rural areas. Adults will normally greet tourists with a cheerful '*Jambo*' or '*Mambo*' and children with a subdued '*Shikamu*' (a greeting

EATING THE NEWS

Emma Thomson

In the same way that it is rude not to greet a Tanzanian with the standard '*Hujambo*' or '*Mambo*', no Maasai will encounter another without going through the amusing paces of a ritual known as 'eating the news'. It is basically a quick catch-up on the health of the family, state of the livestock, etc. The aim is to race through these formalities as fast as possible so you can continue with the rest of the conversation. Bizarrely, even if you are on your deathbed, you must reply that all is well to maintain the front of warrior strength integral to Maasai psychology. Give it a go and they will be bowled over!

Man:	*Yeyio…*	Mother…
Woman:	*Eeu…*	Yes…
Man:	*Takwenya!*	I greet you!
Woman:	*Iko! Apaayia…*	Hello! Warrior…
Man:	*Ooe…*	Yes…
Woman:	*Supai!*	I greet you!
Man:	*Epa!*	Hello!
Woman:	*Ayia, koree indae?*	OK, how are you?
Man:	*Kiti …*	We are around…
Woman:	*Ee*	Uh-huh
Man:	*Kira sedan*	We are fine
Woman:	*Ee*	Uh-huh
Man:	*Kira biot*	We are healthy
Woman:	*Ee*	Uh-huh
Man:	*Supat inkera*	The children are well
Woman:	*Ee*	Uh-huh
Man:	*Biot inkishu*	The cattle are healthy
Woman:	*Ee*	Uh-huh
Man:	*Metii endoki torono*	There are no problems
Woman:	*Ayia*	OK
Woman:	*Kira siyook…*	As for us…
Man:	*Ee*	Uh-huh
Woman:	*Mekimweyaa*	We are not sick
Man:	*Ee*	Uh-huh
Woman:	*Biot inkera*	The children are healthy
Man:	*Ee*	Uh-huh
Woman:	*Supat indare*	The goats are well
Man:	*Ee*	Uh-huh
Woman:	*Ayia*	OK
Man:	*Ayia, enda serian*	OK, that's good news

reserved for elders). If you don't speak Swahili, replying '*Jambo*' with a smile and a nod of the head will be adequate.

Among Tanzanians, it is considered poor taste to display certain emotions publicly. It is frowned upon for members of the opposite sex to hold hands publicly, and kissing or embracing would be seriously offensive. By contrast, it is quite normal for friends of the same sex to walk around hand in hand. Male travellers who get into a long discussion with a male Tanzanian shouldn't be surprised if that person clasps them by the hand and retains a firm grip on their hand for several minutes. This is a warm gesture, one particularly appropriate when the person wants to make a point with which you might disagree.

MUSLIM CUSTOMS Visitors should be aware of the strong Muslim element in Tanzania, particularly along the coast and in Zanzibar. In Muslim society, it is insulting to use your left hand to pass or receive something or when shaking hands. If you eat with your fingers, it is also customary to use the right hand only. Even those of us who are naturally right-handed will occasionally need to remind ourselves of this (it may happen, for instance, that you are carrying something in your right hand and so hand money to a shopkeeper with your left). For left-handed travellers, it will require a constant effort. In traditional Muslim societies it is offensive for women to expose their knees or shoulders, a custom that ought to be taken on board by female travellers, especially on parts of the coast where tourists remain a relative novelty.

TIPPING AND GUIDES In Tanzania, it is customary to tip your guide at the end of a safari and/or a Kilimanjaro climb, as well as any cooks and porters who accompanied you. A figure of roughly US$10 per recipient per day is the benchmark, although it is advisable to check this with your safari company in advance, and acceptable to adjust the amount based on the quality of service. Bear in mind, however, that most guides, cooks and porters receive nominal salaries and are largely dependent on tips for their income, so a reasonable tip should be given in all but the most exceptional of circumstances.

Tipping around 10% is normal in smart restaurants and bars catering to a predominantly foreign clientele. It is not customary to tip in local bars and restaurants, though you may sometimes want to (in fact, given the difficulty of finding change, you may sometimes practically be forced into doing so).

TAKING PHOTOS It is unacceptable to photograph local people in Tanzania without permission, and many people will refuse to pose or will ask for a donation. In such circumstances, don't try to sneak photographs as you might get yourself into trouble. Even the most willing subject will often pose stiffly when a camera is pointed at them; relax them by making a joke, and take a few shots in quick succession to improve the odds of capturing a natural pose.

BARGAINING Tourists to Tanzania will sometimes need to bargain over prices, but generally this need exists only in reasonably predictable circumstances, for instance when chartering a private taxi, organising a freelance guide, or buying curios and to a lesser extent other market produce. Prices in hotels, restaurants and shops are generally fixed, and overcharging in such places is too unusual for it to be worth challenging a price unless it is blatantly ridiculous.

Bargaining is all but essential when buying curios at markets. What should be understood, however, is that the fact a curio seller is open to negotiation does not

PHOTOGRAPHING THE MAASAI

A surprisingly frequent cause of friction on safaris is the entrepreneurial Maasai attitude to being photographed by tourists. It's an issue that frequently leads visitors to conclude that the Maasai are 'too commercialised', a misguided allegation that reflects Western misconceptions and prejudices far more than it does any aspect of modern Maasai culture.

The root cause of this misunderstanding is a Western tendency to distinguish between 'authentic' traditional practices and more cosmopolitan influences, rather than recognising both as equally valid components in the ever-evolving hybrid that is modern African culture. To give one clearly identifiable example, you'll find that most Africans are devout Christians or Muslims, yet many also simultaneously adhere to an apparently conflicting traditional belief system. On the streets of Arusha, suited businessmen yapping into mobile phones and trendy safari guides brush past traditional Maasai street hawkers, a co-existence of modernity and traditionalism that seems contradictory to outsiders but is unremarkable to the country's inhabitants. What's more, the same slick businessmen or casually dressed safari guides might well visit traditional healers on occasion, or return home for tribal ceremonies dressed in traditional attire, to all outward purposes indistinguishable from less 'Westernised' relatives who always dress that way.

The point is that the Maasai, like us, are living in the 21st century, and a variety of external factors – among them, population growth, the gazetting of traditional grazing land as national parks, exposure to other Tanzanian cultures and exotic religions, the creation of a cash economy – have combined to ensure that their culture is not a static museum piece, but a dynamic, modern entity.

Another point of confusion is the only direct exposure to Maasai culture experienced by most visitors takes place in 'cultural villages' where tourists wander around as they please and photograph whomever they like after paying a fixed fee. There is nothing wrong with these villages, and much that is commendable about them, but they should be approached with realistic expectations – essentially, as cottage industries whose inhabitants derive a substantial portion of their living from tourist visits. And most such villages are long-standing Maasai settlements whose inhabitants live a largely traditional lifestyle. Indeed, it is we, the tourists, who are the distorting factor in their behaviour.

mean that you were initially being overcharged or ripped off. Curio sellers will generally quote a price knowing full well that you are going to bargain it down (they'd probably be startled if you didn't) and it is not necessary to respond aggressively or in an accusatory manner. It is impossible to say by how much you should bargain the initial price down. Some people say that you should offer half the asking price and be prepared to settle at around two-thirds, but my experience is that curio sellers are far more whimsical than such advice allows for. The sensible approach, if you want to get a feel for prices, is to ask at a few different stalls before you actually buy anything.

In fruit and vegetable markets and stalls, bargaining is the norm, even between locals, and the healthiest approach to this sort of haggling is to view it as an enjoyable part of the African experience. There will normally be an accepted price band for any particular commodity. To find out what it is, listen to what other people pay and try a few stalls. A ludicrously inflated price will always drop the moment you walk away. When buying fruit and vegetables, a good way to feel out the situation is to ask for a

Make no mistake, were you to wander off into a Maasai boma that doesn't routinely deal with tourists, the odds are that its inhabitants would simply refuse to be photographed no matter what payment you offered. What's more, you might well find a spear dangling from the end of your lens if you don't respect their wishes. So concluding that the Maasai are 'too commercialised' on the basis of an inherently contrived form of interaction is as daft as walking into a London shop and concluding that the English are 'too commercialised' because the assistant expects you to pay for the items you select.

There is a deeper irony to this cultural misunderstanding. Here we have well-off visitors from media-obsessed, materialistic Europe or North America fiddling with their iPhones, straightening their custom-bought safari outfits, and planning the diet they'll go on back home to compensate for the endless lodge buffets. They are confronted by a culture as resilient, non-materialistic and ascetic as that of the Maasai, and they accuse it with a straight face of being 'commercialised'. This genuinely concerns me: are we so culture bound, so riddled with romantic expectations about how the Maasai should behave, that any slight deviation from these preconceptions prevents us from seeing things for what they are?

So let's start again. The Maasai are proud and dramatically attired pastoralists who adhere almost entirely to the traditions of their forefathers. They fascinate us, but being the bunch of gadget-obsessed wazungu we are, our response is not to absorb their presence or to try to communicate with them, but to run around thrusting cameras in their faces. And this, I would imagine, irritates the hell out of those Maasai who happen to live along main tourist circuits, so they decide not to let tourists photograph them except for a fee or in the context of an organised tourist village. In theory, everybody should be happy. In practice, we somehow construe this reasonable attempt by relatively poor people to make a bit of honest money as rampant commercialism. OK, I recognise this is a bit simplistic, but we create the demand, the Maasai satisfy it, and if we pay to do so, that's just good capitalism, something the West has always been keen to encourage in Africa. If you don't like it, save space on your memory card and buy a postcard – in all honesty, you'll probably get a lot more from meeting these charismatic people if you leave your camera behind and enjoy the moment!

bulk discount or a few extra items thrown in. And bear in mind that when somebody is reluctant to bargain, it may be because they asked a fair price in the first place. And if you find yourself quibbling over a pittance with an old lady selling a few piles of fruit by the roadside, you might perhaps bear in mind that the notion of a fixed price is a very Western one. When somebody is desperate enough for money, or afraid that their perishable goods might not last another day, it may well be possible to push them down to a lower price than they would normally accept. In such circumstances, why not err on the side of generosity?

4

Health

With Dr Daniel Campion

Tanzania, like most parts of Africa, is home to several tropical diseases unfamiliar to people living in more temperate and sanitary climates. However, with adequate preparation, and a sensible attitude to malaria prevention, the chances of serious mishap are small. To put this in perspective, your greatest concern after malaria should not be the combined exotica of venomous snakes, stampeding wildlife, gun-happy soldiers or the Ebola virus, but something altogether more mundane: a road accident.

Private clinics, hospitals and pharmacies can be found in most large towns, and doctors generally speak good English. Consultation fees and laboratory tests are inexpensive when compared with most Western countries, so if you do fall sick, don't allow financial considerations to dissuade you from seeking medical help. Commonly required medicines such as broad-spectrum antibiotics, painkillers, asthma inhalers and various antimalarial treatments are widely available. If you are on any short-term medication prior to departure, or you have specific needs relating to a less common medical condition (for instance if you are allergic to bee stings or nuts), then bring necessary treatment with you.

PREPARATIONS

Sensible preparation will go a long way to ensuring your trip goes smoothly. Particularly for first-time visitors to Africa, this includes a visit to a travel clinic to discuss matters such as vaccinations and malaria prevention. A full list of current travel clinic websites worldwide is available on w istm.org. For other journey preparation information, consult w travelhealthpro.org.uk (UK) or w wwwnc.cdc.gov/travel (USA). All advice found online should be used in conjunction with expert advice received prior to or during travel.

The following summary points are worth emphasising:

- Don't travel without comprehensive medical **travel insurance** that will fly you home in an emergency.
- Make sure all your **immunisations** are up to date. Tanzania is not considered a risk for yellow fever but a yellow-fever certificate is required if you are coming from a yellow fever endemic zone or are transiting for more than 12 hours in an airport in a yellow fever endemic zone. When travelling in the tropics it's important to be up to date with tetanus, diphtheria and/or pertussis (usually now given as an all-in-one vaccine), typhoid and hepatitis A vaccines. Immunisation against hepatitis B, rabies and (rarely) tuberculosis or cholera may also be recommended.
- The biggest health threat is **malaria**. There is no vaccine against this mosquito-borne disease, but a variety of preventative drugs is available, including

mefloquine, atovaquone/proguanil (Malarone) and the antibiotic doxycycline. The start and stop times of the malaria tablets vary and can be as little as two days before and seven days after (Malarone) to two to three weeks before and four weeks after (mefloquine). The most suitable choice of drug varies depending on the individual and the country they are visiting, so visit your GP or a travel clinic for medical advice. If you will be spending a long time in Africa and visiting remote areas, consider taking an emergency treatment kit in addition to prophylaxis. It is worth noting that no homeopathic prophylactic for malaria exists, nor can any traveller acquire effective 'natural' immunity to malaria after infection. Those who don't make use of preventative drugs risk their life in a manner that is both foolish and unnecessary.

- Though advised for most travellers, a **pre-exposure rabies vaccination**, involving three doses taken over a minimum of 21 days, is particularly important if you intend to have contact with animals, or are likely to be more than 24 hours away from medical help.
- Anybody travelling away from major centres should carry a **personal first-aid kit**. Contents might include an antiseptic such as chlorhexidine, band-aids, suncream, insect repellent, aspirin or paracetamol, antifungal cream (e.g. Canesten), loperamide for diarrhoea (and possibly prescribed antibiotics for severe diarrhoea if you are at high medical risk), antibiotic eye drops, tweezers, condoms or femidoms, a digital thermometer and a needle-and-syringe kit with accompanying letter from a healthcare professional.
- Bring any **drugs or devices relating to known medical conditions** with you. That applies both to those who are on medication prior to departure, and those who are, for instance, allergic to bee stings, or are prone to attacks of asthma. You should also bring a copy of the prescription with you and ensure that medication is clearly labelled with your name.
- Prolonged immobility on long-haul flights can result in **deep-vein thrombosis (DVT)**, which can be dangerous if the clot travels to the lungs to cause pulmonary embolus. The risk increases with age, and is higher in obese or pregnant travellers, heavy smokers, those taller than 6ft/1.8m or shorter than 5ft/1.5m, and anybody with a history of clots, recent major operation or varicose veins surgery, cancer, a stroke or heart disease. If any of these criteria apply, consult a doctor before you travel.

ON THE ROAD

MALARIA This potentially fatal disease is widespread in tropical Africa. Within Tanzania, it is possible to catch malaria almost anywhere below the 2,000m contour, a category that incorporates all parts of the country except the upper slopes of high mountains such as Kilimanjaro and Meru. In mid-altitude locations, malaria is largely but not entirely seasonal, with the highest risk occurring during the rainy season. Moist and low-lying areas such as the coast are high risk throughout the year, but the risk is greatest during the rainy season. As such, all travellers to Tanzania should assume that they will be exposed to malaria and take suitable preventative drugs and other precautions throughout their trip.

Since no malaria prophylactic is 100% effective, it makes sense to take all reasonable precautions against being bitten by the nocturnal *Anopheles* mosquitoes that transmit the disease (page 109). Malaria usually manifests within two weeks of transmission, but it can take months, which means that short-stay visitors are most likely to experience symptoms after they return home. These typically include a rapid rise in temperature (over 38°C), and any combination of a headache, flu-like aches and pains, a general sense of disorientation, and possibly even nausea and diarrhoea. The earlier malaria is detected, the better it usually responds to treatment. So, if you display possible symptoms anything from seven days after being in a malaria area, *get to a doctor or clinic immediately*. A simple test is usually adequate to determine whether you have malaria. However, you need three negative tests to be sure that you don't have malaria so it may be necessary to stay around for further tests. While experts differ on the question of self-diagnosis and self-treatment, the reality is that if you think you have malaria and are not within easy reach of a doctor, it would be wisest to start treatment. If you use a self-treatment kit, you should still seek medical assistance as soon as possible, for definitive diagnosis and treatment.

TRAVELLERS' DIARRHOEA Many visitors to unfamiliar destinations suffer a dose of travellers' diarrhoea, usually as a result of imbibing contaminated food or water. Rule one in avoiding diarrhoea and other sanitation-related diseases is arguably to wash your hands regularly, particularly before snacks and meals, and after handling money. As for what food you can safely eat, a useful maxim is: 'peel it, boil it, cook it or forget it'. This means that fruit you have washed and peeled yourself should be safe, as should hot cooked foods. However, raw foods, cold cooked foods, salads, fruit salads prepared by others, ice cream and ice are all risky. It is rarer to get sick from drinking contaminated water but it happens. Bottled water is safe and widely available, although if you want to limit plastic waste, buying your own filter bottle such as Aquapure is an eco-friendly alternative.

If you suffer a bout of diarrhoea, it is dehydration that makes you feel awful, so drink lots of water and other clear fluids. These can be infused with sachets of oral rehydration salts, though any dilute mixture of sugar and salt in water will do you good, for instance a bottled soda with a pinch of salt. If diarrhoea persists beyond a couple of days, it is possible it is a symptom of a more serious sanitation-related illness (typhoid, cholera, hepatitis, dysentery, worms, etc), so get to a doctor. If the diarrhoea is greasy and bulky, and is accompanied by sulphurous (eggy) burps, one likely cause is giardia, which can persist but is treatable. Again, seek medical advice if you suspect this.

SCHISTOSOMIASIS Also known as bilharzia, schistosomiasis is an unpleasant parasitic disease transmitted by freshwater snails most often associated with reedy shores where there is lots of water weed. It cannot be caught in hotel swimming pools, but should be assumed to be present in any freshwater river, pond, lake or similar habitat, probably even those advertised as 'bilharzia free'. The riskiest shores will be within 200m of villages or other places where infected people use water and wash their clothes. Ideally, however, you should avoid swimming in any fresh water other than an artificial pool. Bilharzia is often asymptomatic in its early stages, but some people experience an intense immune reaction, including fever, cough, abdominal pain and an itching rash, around four to six weeks after infection. Later symptoms vary but often include a general feeling of tiredness and lethargy. Bilharzia can be tested for at specialist travel or tropical medicine clinics, ideally at least six weeks after likely exposure. Fortunately, it is easy to treat at present.

RABIES This deadly disease can be carried by any mammal and is usually transmitted to humans via a bite or scratch. Beware village dogs and habituated monkeys, but assume that *any* mammal that bites or scratches you (or even licks you over broken skin) might be rabid. First, scrub the wound with soap under a running tap, or while pouring water from a jug, then pour on a strong iodine or alcohol solution, which will guard against other infections and might reduce the risk of the rabies virus entering the body. Whether or not you underwent pre-exposure vaccination, it is vital to obtain post-exposure prophylaxis as soon as possible after the incident. Don't wait until you are back in your home country. Those who have not been immunised will need a full course of four or five vaccinations, as well as rabies immunoglobulin (RIG), but this product is expensive and may be hard to come by – another reason why pre-exposure vaccination should be encouraged. If you have had been vaccinated before exposure, then you should not usually need the RIG, just further doses of vaccine in most cases. It is important to tell the doctor if you have had pre-exposure vaccine – carry your vaccine record with you. Treatment may differ if your immune system is weakened, for example if you take immunosuppressant medication. Do take rabies seriously - death from rabies is probably one of the worst ways to go, and once you show symptoms it is too late to do anything. The mortality rate is close to 100%.

TETANUS Tetanus is caught through deep dirty wounds, including animal bites, so ensure that such wounds are thoroughly cleaned. Immunisation protects for ten years, provided you don't have an overwhelming number of tetanus bacteria on board. If you haven't had a tetanus shot in ten years, or you are unsure, get a booster immediately.

HIV/AIDS Rates of HIV infection are high in many parts of Africa, and other sexually transmitted infections are common. Condoms (or femidoms) greatly reduce the risk of transmission.

TICK BITES Ticks in Africa are not the rampant disease transmitters that they are in the Americas, but they may spread tickbite fever along with a few dangerous rarities. Ticks should ideally be removed complete, and as soon as possible, to reduce the chance of infection. You can use special tick tweezers, which can be bought in good travel shops; or, failing this, with your fingernails, grasping the tick as close to your body as possible, and pulling it away steadily and firmly at right angles to your skin without jerking or twisting. Applying irritants (eg: Olbas oil) or lit cigarettes is to be discouraged as a means of removal since they can cause the ticks to regurgitate and therefore increase the risk of disease. Once the tick is removed, if possible douse the wound with alcohol (any spirit will do), soap and water, or iodine. If you are travelling with small children, remember to check their heads, and particularly behind the ears, for ticks. Spreading redness around the bite and/or fever and/or aching joints after a tick bite imply that you have an infection that requires antibiotic treatment. In this case seek medical advice.

SKIN INFECTIONS Any mosquito bite or small nick is an opportunity for a skin infection in warm humid climates, so clean and cover the slightest wound in a good drying antiseptic such as dilute iodine, potassium permanganate or crystal (or gentian) violet. Prickly heat, most likely to be contracted at the humid coast, is a fine pimply rash that can be alleviated by cool showers, dabbing (not rubbing) dry and talc, and sleeping naked under a fan or in an air-conditioned room. Fungal infections also get a hold easily in hot moist climates, so wear 100% cotton socks and underwear and shower frequently.

EYE PROBLEMS Bacterial conjunctivitis (pink eye) is a common infection in Africa, particularly for contact-lens wearers. Symptoms are sore, gritty eyelids that often stick closed in the morning. They will need treatment with antibiotic drops or ointment. Lesser eye irritation should settle with bathing in salt water and keeping the eyes shaded. If an insect flies into your eye, extract it with great care, ensuring you do not crush or damage it, otherwise you may get a nastily inflamed eye from toxins secreted by the creature.

SUNSTROKE AND DEHYDRATION Overexposure to the sun can lead to short-term sunburn or sunstroke, and increases the long-term risk of skin cancer. Wear a T-shirt and waterproof sunscreen when swimming. When visiting outdoor historical sites or walking in the direct sun, cover up with long, loose clothes, wear a hat and use sunscreen. The glare and the dust can be hard on the eyes, so bring UV-protecting sunglasses. A less direct effect of the tropical heat is dehydration, so drink more fluids than you would at home.

SNAKE AND OTHER BITES All manner of venomous snakes occur in Tanzania, but they are unlikely to be encountered since they generally slither away when they sense the seismic vibrations made by a walking person. You should be most alert to snakes on rocky slopes and cliffs, particularly where you risk putting your hand on a ledge that you can't see. Rocky areas are the favoured habitat of the puff adder, which is not an especially venomous snake but is potentially lethal and unusual in that it won't always move off in response to human footsteps. Wearing good boots when walking in the bush will protect against the 50% of snake bites that occur below the ankle, and long trousers will help deflect bites higher up on the leg, reducing the quantity of venom injected. Lethal snake bites are a rarity – in South Africa, which boasts almost as many venomous snakes as Tanzania, more people are

AVOIDING MOSQUITO AND INSECT BITES

The *Anopheles* mosquitoes that spread malaria are active at dusk and after dark. Most bites can thus be avoided by covering up at night. This means donning a long-sleeved shirt, trousers and socks from around 30 minutes before dusk until you retire to bed, and applying a DEET-based insect repellent to any exposed flesh. It is best to sleep under a net, or in an air-conditioned room, though burning a mosquito coil and/or sleeping under a fan will also reduce (though not entirely eliminate) bites. Travel clinics usually sell a good range of nets and repellents, as well as Permethrin treatment kits. Permethrin (an insecticide) will render even the tattiest net a lot more protective, and helps prevent mosquitoes from biting through a net when you roll against it. These measures will also do much to reduce exposure to other nocturnal biters. Bear in mind, too, that most flying insects are attracted to light: leaving a lamp standing near a tent opening or a light on in a poorly screened hotel room will greatly increase the insect presence in your sleeping quarters.

It is also advisable to think about avoiding bites when walking in the countryside by day, especially in wetland habitats, which often teem with diurnal mosquitoes. Wear a long, loose shirt and trousers, preferably 100% cotton, as well as sturdy walking or hiking shoes with heavy socks (the ankle is particularly vulnerable to bites), and apply a DEET-based insect repellent to any exposed skin.

killed by lightning – but in the unlikely event you are bitten, it's worth knowing that a free snakebite clinic operates out of Meserani Snake Park (**w** meseranisnakepark.com) 25km from Arusha (page 139).

OTHER INSECT-BORNE DISEASES Although malaria is the insect-borne disease that attracts the most attention in Africa, and rightly so, there are others, most too uncommon to be a significant concern to short-stay travellers. These include dengue fever and other arboviruses (spread by day-biting mosquitoes), sleeping sickness (tsetse flies), and river blindness (blackflies). Bearing this in mind, however, it is clearly sensible, and makes for a more pleasant trip, to avoid insect bites as far as possible (page 109). Two nasty (though ultimately relatively harmless) flesh-eating insects associated with tropical Africa are *tumbu* or *putsi* flies, which lay eggs, often on drying laundry, that hatch and bury themselves under the skin when they come into contact with humans, and jiggers, which latch on to bare feet and set up home, usually at the side of a toenail, where they cause a painful boil-like swelling. Drying laundry indoors and wearing shoes are the best way to deter this pair of flesh-eaters.

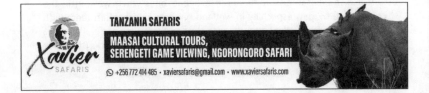

Part Two

THE GUIDE

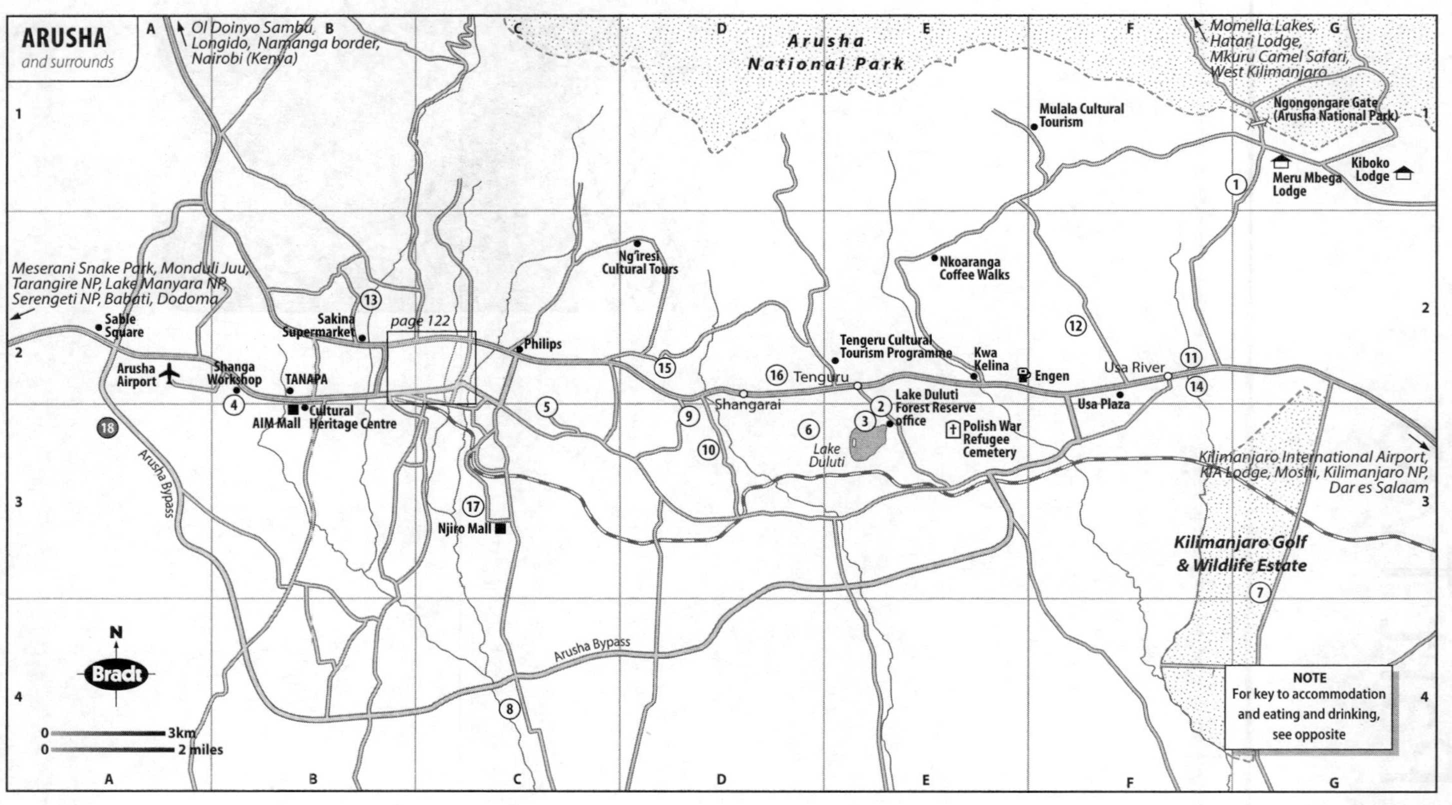
ARUSHA
and surrounds
Ol Doinyo Sambu, Longido, Namanga border, Nairobi (Kenya)
Arusha National Park
Momella Lakes, Hatari Lodge, Mkuru Camel Safari, West Kilimanjaro
Ngongongare Gate (Arusha National Park)
Mulala Cultural Tourism
Meru Mbega Lodge
Kiboko Lodge
Meserani Snake Park, Monduli Juu, Tarangire NP, Lake Manyara NP, Serengeti NP, Babati, Dodoma
Ng'iresi Cultural Tours
Nkoaranga Coffee Walks
Sable Square
Sakina Supermarket
page 122
Philips
Tengeru Cultural Tourism Programme
Kwa Kelina
Engen
Usa River
Arusha Airport
Shanga Workshop
TANAPA
AIM Mall
Cultural Heritage Centre
Tenguru
Shangarai
Lake Duluti Forest Reserve office
Polish War Refugee Cemetery
Usa Plaza
Lake Duluti
Kilimanjaro International Airport, KIA Lodge, Moshi, Kilimanjaro NP, Dar es Salaam
Arusha Bypass
Njiro Mall
Kilimanjaro Golf & Wildlife Estate
Bradt
0 3km
0 2 miles
NOTE
For key to accommodation and eating and drinking, see opposite

5

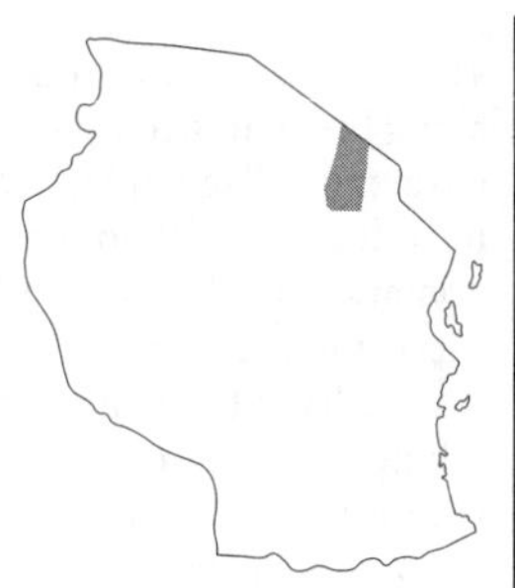

Arusha and Arusha National Park

Tanzania's third-largest city and unofficial safari capital, Arusha is the most popular springboard for visiting the Serengeti, Ngorongoro and other parks on the legendary northern safari circuit. It is an attractive green city with a northern skyline dominated – visibility permitting – by the imposing hulk of Mount Meru, a dormant volcano that rises to 4,566m, making it Africa's fifth-highest massif. Perched at an altitude of 1,350m in the mountain's fertile rain-shadow, Arusha also makes for an agreeably temperate – and, during the rainy season, often downright soggy – introduction to tropical Africa.

First impressions of Arusha are that practically everything revolves around the safari and tourist industries. Walking around the old town centre, it can feel like every second person wants to sell you something, be it a budget safari, a colourful batik, a Swahili phrase book or a wall map of Africa, and the roads are lined with trendy restaurants and cafés, and jammed with 4x4s adorned with safari company logos. And yet, despite this, Arusha's economic vitality is buoyed by several other factors, among them its fertile agricultural surrounds, the tanzanite mining boom, and its role as capital of the East African Community.

Architecturally, Arusha remains something of an African everytown, one where timeworn colonial-era structures rub shoulders with an ever-increasing number of more modern medium-rise edifices. In some respects, the wealth generated by the safari industry serves to accentuate both the vast economic gulf between the haves and have-nots, and the spectrum of cultural influences – traditionally dressed Maasai women selling colourful beadwork, besuited businessmen shouting into their mobile phones, trendy sunglass-shrouded 20-somethings – that play havoc with visitors seeking to pigeonhole the 'Real Africa'.

Paradoxically, while Arusha's status as Tanzania's safari capital is firmly entrenched, only a small proportion of fresh arrivals to Kilimanjaro International Airport, 45km further east, actually spends a night in town. Some arrive early enough to head out on

ARUSHA *and surrounds*

For listings, see from page 119

Where to stay

1	African View Lodge	G1
2	Arusha Serena	E3
3	Duluti Forest Club	E3
4	Elewana Arusha Coffee Lodge	B2
5	Karama Lodge & Spa	C3
6	Kigongoni Lodge	D3
7	Kili Villa	G3
8	Korona House	C4
9	Machweo & Onsea House	D3
10	Moivaro Coffee Plantation Lodge	D3
11	Mount Meru Game Lodge	F2
12	Ngare Sero Mountain Lodge	F2
13	Researchers Rest	B2
14	Rivertrees Country Inn	F2
15	Songota Falls Lodge	D2
16	Vijiji Center	D2
17	White House of Tanzania	C3
Off map		
	KIA Lodge	G3

Where to eat and drink

18	Blue Heron	A3
	Machweo Fine Dining	(see 9)

safari the same day, while others opt to stay at one of the many out-of-town lodges along the road from the airport. A particularly popular base is the amorphous but attractive village of Usa River, which flanks the Moshi road 20km east of Arusha near the turn-off to Arusha National Park, and hosts a cluster of countrified upmarket hotels that stand in lovely leafy grounds and offer sterling views to Mount Meru and the more distant snow-capped peak of Kilimanjaro.

Arusha is the closest town to Arusha National Park, an underrated safari and hiking destination that protects the upper slopes and peak of Mount Meru, along with a mosaic of lower-lying forests and wetlands and a wide variety of wildlife including elephant, buffalo, giraffe, various monkeys and a rich birdlife. Arusha National Park makes for an excellent and popular day trip out of Arusha, and it is also a worthwhile overnight destination in its own right, while the 4-day round hike to the summit of Mount Meru (page 146) is a fantastic adventure both in its own right and as a warm-up for Kilimanjaro.

HISTORY

Little is known about the Arusha area prior to the 17th century, when the Bantu-speaking Meru people – migrants from the west with strong linguistic and cultural affinities to the Chagga of Kilimanjaro – settled and farmed the fertile and well-watered northern foothills of Mount Meru. In 1830 or thereabouts, the southern slopes of the mountain verging on the Maasai Steppe were settled by the Arusha, a Maasai subgroup who lost their cattle and territory in one of the internecine battles characteristic of this turbulent period in Maasailand. The Arusha people speak the same Maa language as the plains Maasai and share a similar social structure based around initiated age-sets, but when they settled in the Mount Meru area they forsook their pastoralist roots, turning instead to agriculture as a primary source of subsistence.

The Arusha economy was boosted by the trade in agricultural produce – in particular tobacco – with the closely affiliated Maasai of the plains. The Arusha also became known as reliable providers of food and other provisions for the Arab slave caravans that headed inland from the Pangani and Tanga area towards modern-day Kenya and Lake Victoria. Invigorated by this regular trade, the Arusha had, by 1880, cleared the forested slopes of Mount Meru to an altitude of around 1,600m to make way for cultivation. As their territory expanded, however, the Arusha people increasingly came into contact with their northern neighbours, the Meru, resulting in several territorial skirmishes and frequent cattle raids between the two tribes.

In 1881, prompted by the need to defend their combined territories against the Maasai and other potential attackers, the incumbent warrior age-sets of the Arusha and Meru united to form a formidable military force. Since they were settled on the well-watered slopes of Mount Meru, and their subsistence was not primarily dependent on livestock, the Arusha and Meru people were less affected than the plains pastoralists by the devastating series of droughts and rinderpest epidemics of the 1880s and early 1890s. As a result, the combined army, known as the Talala – the Expansionists – was able to exert considerable influence over neighbouring Maasai and Chagga territories.

The Talala staunchly resisted German attempts to settle in their territory, killing the first missionaries to arrive there and repelling an initial punitive attack by the colonial army. In October 1896, however, the Arusha and Meru were soundly defeated by a military expedition out of Moshi led by Karl Johannes and consisting of 100 German troopers supported by some 5,000 Chagga warriors. In the aftermath of this defeat, the Germans drove home the point by razing hundreds of Arusha and Meru smallholdings, killing the men, confiscating the cattle and repatriating women of Chagga origin to the Kilimanjaro area.

In 1889, the Germans established a permanent settlement – modern-day Arusha town – on the border of Arusha and Maasai territories, and used forced Arusha and Maasai labour to construct the boma that can still be seen on the north end of Boma Road. Relations between the colonisers and their unwilling subjects remained tense, to say the least. During the construction of the fort, a minor dispute led to some 300 labourers being massacred while marching peacefully along present-day Boma Road, and several local chiefs from outlying areas were arbitrarily arrested and taken to Moshi to be hanged in the street.

Following the construction of the boma, Arusha quickly developed into a significant trading and administrative centre, with about two-dozen Indian and Arab shops clustered along what is today Boma Road. John Boyes, who visited Arusha in 1903, somewhat fancifully compared the boma to 'an Aladdin's Palace transported from some fairyland and dropped down in the heart of the tropics'. The town, he wrote, was 'a real oasis in the wilderness' and 'spotlessly clean', while 'the streets [were] laid out with fine sidewalks, separated by the road from a stream of clear water flowing down a cemented gully'.

At the outbreak of World War I, the small German garrison town was of some significance as a local agricultural and trade centre, but it remained something of a backwater in comparison to Moshi, which lay a week's ox-wagon trek distant at the railhead of the Tanga line. Much of the area around Arusha was, however, settled by German farmers, who had forcibly displaced the original Arusha and Meru smallholders. In 1916, British troops captured Arusha and expelled the German farmers, resulting in some resettlement by indigenous farmers, but the German farmland was eventually reallocated to British and Greek settlers. The British also set aside large tracts of land around Arusha for sisal plantations, which meant that by 1920, less than 20% of the land around Mount Meru was available to local farmers, most of it on dry foothills unsuited to cultivating the local staple of bananas.

Arusha grew steadily between the wars. The settler economy was boosted by the introduction of coffee, sisal and other export crops, and trade links were improved with the construction of road links to Moshi and Nairobi and the opening of the railway line to Moshi and the coast in 1929. Yet the land issues continued to simmer, eventually coming to a head after World War II, with the eviction of thousands of Meru farmers from north of Mount Meru to make way for a peanut production project overseen by 13 white farmers. The peanut project, aside from being a dismal and costly failure, resulted in the pivotal Meru Land Case, which not only caused great embarrassment to the UN Trusteeship Council, but also proved to be an important catalyst to the politicisation of the anti-colonial movement in Tanganyika.

Prior to independence, Arusha remained a relatively small town whose primary role was to service the surrounding agricultural lands. The official census of 1952 placed the urban population at fewer than 8,000 people, of which more than half were of Asian or European stock. All that changed in the post-independence era, when the town attracted, and continues to attract, large numbers of domestic migrants from surrounding rural areas and beyond. Indeed, by 1978 Arusha had become the ninth-largest town in Tanzania, supporting a population of 55,000. It was accorded city status in 2006, and recently overtook Dodoma as the country's third-largest settlement, with a population currently estimated at around 500,000.

Arusha's recent growth can be attributed to a number of factors, not least the town's location in the foothills of Mount Meru, whose drizzly sub-montane microclimate nurtures the rich volcanic soil to agricultural profligacy. There is also its proximity to the Mererani Hills, the only known source of the increasingly popular gemstone tanzanite. A more ephemeral economic boost was provided by the presence of UN and other NGO personnel linked to the United Nations Security Council's Rwandan War Crimes Tribunal, which operated out of the Arusha International Conference Centre from 1995 until its eventual completion in December 2015. Arusha has also served as the main administrative base of the East African Community [123 H3], a regionally significant international organisation comprising Tanzania, Kenya, Uganda, Burundi and Rwanda, since it was revived in 2000. The key to Arusha's modern economic growth, however, has undoubtedly been its role as the main urban pivot servicing a lucrative tourist industry focused on the likes of the Serengeti National Park, Ngorongoro Crater and lofty Mount Kilimanjaro.

GETTING THERE AND AWAY

BY AIR The main local point of entry is **Kilimanjaro International Airport** (w kilimanjaroairport.go.tz; often abbreviated to KIA, though the official airport code is JRO), which lies roughly 45km east of Arusha off the surfaced main road to Moshi. Several international carriers now fly to KIA, among them Ethiopian Airlines, Kenya Airways, KLM, Qatar, Rwandair and Turkish Airlines. Most new arrivals are collected by their hotel or safari company, but charter taxis are also available at the airport, at a negotiable fare of US$60. Travellers with problematic flight times might think about booking into KIA Lodge (page 125), which lies just 1km from the airport.

Most but not all domestic flights use the smaller **Arusha Airport** [112 A2] (airport code ARK), which lies about 5km out of town along the Serengeti road. Daily flights connect Arusha Airport to all major airstrips on the northern Tanzania safari circuit, including Manyara, Ngorongoro, Seronera, Grumeti and Lobo, as well as to Dar es Salaam and Zanzibar. There are also regular scheduled flights to the likes of Mwanza, Rubondo Island, Mafia Island and parks on the southern safari circuit.

Airlines

Most airlines that fly into KIA no longer maintain offices in Arusha, in which case we only list the website:

Air Excel Arusha Airport; m +255 784 455748; w airexcelonline.com
Air Tanzania [129 A5] Mafao Hse, Kanisa Rd; w airtanzania.co.tz
Auric Air Arusha Airport; m +255 746 986123; w auricair.com
Coastal Aviation Arusha Airport; m +255 699 999999; w coastal.co.tz
Ethiopian Airlines [126 C4] Boma Rd; w ethiopianairlines.com
Kenya Airways [126 C4] Boma Rd; w kenya-airways.com
KLM m +255 689 077307, +255 789 777213; w klm.com
Precision Air [126 B4] Ngorongoro Bldg, India Rd; w precisionairtz.com
Qatar m +255 787 770122/3; w qatarairways.com
Regional Air m +255 753 500300; w regionaltanzania.com
Rwandair m +255 782 039152; w rwandair.com
Turkish Airlines w turkishairlines.com
ZanAir Arusha Airport; w zanair.com

BY ROAD There are two main **bus stations**. Minibuses, dalla dallas and buses to local destinations such as Moshi, Namanga and Babati leave from the old bus station [122 C5] (Colonel Middleton Rd), which can be somewhat chaotic and

SAFETY

Arusha can be a daunting prospect on first contact, particularly if you arrive by bus. Competition between budget safari companies is fierce, and 'flycatchers' – the street touts who solicit custom for these companies – know that their best tactic is to hook travellers who don't have a pre-booked safari when they arrive. As a consequence, when you arrive in Arusha by bus you're likely to spend your first few minutes dodging the attention of a dozen yelling touts, all of whom will claim to be able to offer you the cheapest safari and room in town. In most cases, the touts probably will show you to a decent room, but allowing them to get involved like this does open the door to allowing your sense of obligation to be exploited later in your stay.

Fortunately, once you've run the bus station gauntlet, things do calm down somewhat, though the flock of flycatchers, newspaper vendors and curio sellers who hang around the old town centre can be a nuisance. Unlike in some other parts of Africa, however, it is unusual for such an exchange to descend into something truly unpleasant: most touts here seem capable of taking a good-humoured 'No' for an answer, especially one spoken in Swahili, and they will usually back down at any show of genuine irritation. Changing money on the street in Arusha (as elsewhere in Tanzania) is definitely a bad idea!

Such annoyances aside, Arusha is not a threatening city, though it is certainly not unheard of for tourists to be mugged after dark. The usual common-sense rules apply: avoid walking around singly or in pairs at night, especially on unlit roads and in parks, and avoid carrying valuables on your person or taking out significantly more money than you need for the evening. After dark, the dodgiest part of town for muggings is probably the quiet unlit roads of Kijenge, east of the Themi River. On the whole, Arusha is very safe by day, but do be wary of bag-snatchers and pickpockets in the Central market area.

intimidating, thanks to the high density of touts, who pose no serious threat but tend to be persistent. For longer hauls, Makao Mapya Station [122 A5], often referred to as Dar Express after its best-known operator, is far more orderly, quiet and hassle-free, though it is advisable to buy a ticket the day before you want to travel.

The best **coach services** for Dar es Salaam and other towns along the B1 are Dar Express [122 C3] (m +255 754 946155/487261/049395) and Kilimanjaro Express [122 D1] (m +255 767 334301/715 144301/765 064587). Both operate several coaches daily in either direction. Tickets cost US$17–19 depending on the type of coach, and the trip takes up to 14 hours. Cheaper bus services between Arusha and Dar es Salaam are plentiful but slower and less comfortable.

The best option between Arusha and Nairobi is a **minibus shuttle**. The reliable Riverside Shuttle (m +255 754 270089/757 091120; w riverside-shuttle.com) costs US$25 for non-residents and can be booked online. Also recommended is the Impala Shuttle (w impalashuttles.co.tz). Both leave from Simeon Road in front of Pablo Picasso Café [129 C4].

A steady stream of minibuses and buses connects Moshi and Arusha, taking up to 2 hours. Minibuses are faster than buses but more prone to accidents. There are also regular buses to other relatively local destinations such as Mto wa Mbu, Karatu, Mbulu, Babati and Kondoa; a reliable company servicing these routes is Mtei (m +255 755 717117).

BY RAIL Tanzania Railways Corporation recently resumed a thrice-weekly overnight train service between Arusha, Moshi and Dar es Salaam. Although the train is seldom used by international travellers, the schedule is posted at **w** trc.co.tz/pages/long-distance-train and bookings can be made at **w** booking.trc.co.tz/?lang=en.

ORIENTATION

Unlike Dar es Salaam or Zanzibar's labyrinthine Stone Town, Arusha is not a difficult town to familiarise yourself with. Its most significant geographical features are the Naura and Goliondoi rivers, which run parallel to each other through the town centre, cutting it into two distinct parts. To the east of the rivers lies the **'old' town** centre, a relatively smart area whose main north–south thoroughfares – Boma, India and Goliondoi roads – are lined with mid-range hotels, tourist-friendly restaurants, safari companies, curio shops and other tourist-related services. Major landmarks in this part of town include the Clock Tower [126 C5], the Old Boma [126 D2] (now a museum) and the Arusha International Conference Centre [126 D1] (AICC).

Connected to the old town centre by Sokoine Road in the south and Makongoro Road in the north, the more bustling **modern town** centre consists of a tight grid of roads west of the rivers centred on the market [122 D6] and the old central bus station south of the stadium [122 D4]. This area is well equipped with small budget hotels and affordable restaurants, but it boasts few facilities that approach international standards. Similar in feel, though more residential and less commercially orientated, is the suburb of Kaloleni immediately north of the stadium.

THE ARUSHA–MOSHI HIGHWAY

The most important – or at least the busiest – trunk road in northern Tanzania is the 80km tract of asphalt that connects Arusha to Moshi via Kilimanjaro International Airport. With the exception of nearby Lake Duluti and Arusha National Park, the highway boasts no tourist attractions of note. It's an attractive area, however – lush, fertile and bisected by numerous forest-fringed streams that rise on Mount Meru – and many tourists prefer to stay here instead of in Arusha or Moshi town, thanks to a proliferation of mid-range to upmarket accommodation, mostly set in large grounds offering views towards Mount Meru and Kilimanjaro.

For most of its length, the main road between Arusha and Moshi comprises a single lane running in either direction and is characterised by heavy congestion, impatient driving and regular police roadblocks and speed traps, so the going tends to be slow (not to mention costly for any self-driver who transgresses the limit of 50km/h imposed in all built-up areas). The one exception is the first 10km out of Arusha (running as far as Tengeru) which has been now upgraded to a dual carriageway, so tends not to be congested (though police are still plentiful). A longer but more appealing option than the main road, especially if you're heading to or from more westerly safari destinations such as Tarangire, Manyara or Serengeti, is a new, well-maintained and little-used southern bypass that connects Usa River to the western outskirts of Arusha. In Usa River, the bypass turns south more or less opposite the police station (⊕ -3.37136, 36.85840) and in the west it connects with the main road at a large traffic circle (⊕ -3.36380, 36.61406) between Arusha Airport and Sable Square Shopping Village.

Another important suburb is **Kijenge**, which lies to the southeast of the old town centre, and is reached by following Sokoine Road across a bridge over the Themi River to become the Old Moshi Road. Kijenge has a spacious, leafy character and it is dotted with half-a-dozen relatively upmarket hotels and numerous good restaurants, as well as an increasing number of safari company offices.

GETTING AROUND

BY TAXI AND TUK-TUK Taxis are plentiful and can be picked up at the market, both bus stations, the rank at the junction of Goliondoi and Joel Maeda roads [126 C5], and the open area at the north end of Boma and India roads [126 C3]. A taxi ride within the town centre should cost roughly US$4–6, though tourists are normally asked a slightly higher price. A taxi outside the town centre will cost more. Tuk-tuks are about half the price of taxis.

ON PUBLIC TRANSPORT A good network of minibus dalla dallas runs around the centre of town, though they are now banned from Sokoine Road, the main high street. Some of these continue west out of town past the Shoppers Centre, while others run east of the Clock Tower to the Impala Hotel [129 C5] (now closed) and beyond. There are also regular dalla dallas between the town centre and the main Nairobi–Moshi bypass. Fares are nominal, and it's easy enough to hop on or off any passing dalla dalla heading in your direction.

WHERE TO STAY

The choice of accommodation in and around Arusha is practically limitless, and the listings are necessarily highly selective. Accommodation is grouped by area: the city centre is recommended to those seeking an African urban experience while leafy Kijenge has a more suburban feel without being isolated from the city. The options listed under the *Suburban Arusha* and *Out of Town* headings are a mixed bag but tend to offer more individualistic experiences. Finally, if you are looking for a genuine bush experience, there is the option of staying at one of the lodges, resthouses or campsites set within or bordering Arusha National Park.

CITY CENTRE

Upmarket

Four Points by Sheraton Arusha [126 D5] Fire Rd; 027 297 7777; w marriott.com. The oldest & smartest hotel in the city centre (page 120), this Edwardian edifice stands opposite the Clock Tower in wooded grounds that run down towards the Themi River. The 86 spacious rooms & suites come with DSTV, nets, smoke detector, tea-/coffee-making facilities & optional AC. Amenities include 24hr room service, a business centre, a craft shop, a heated swimming pool, 3 bars, 2 restaurants & an airport shuttle service. **$$$$**

Budget

✷ Arusha Backpackers Hotel [122 B7] Sokoine Rd; m +255 715 377795; w booking.com. Safe, friendly & sociable hostel with small but clean rooms, 4-bed dorms, common showers & a relaxed rooftop bar & restaurant. *US$10/18 sgl/dbl or US$9pp dorm bed* B&B. **$**

Natron Palace Hotel [122 D5] Livingstone Rd; m +255 767 646569; w natronpalacehotel.com. This modern 9-storey block overlooking the central bus station is useful for early starts & late arrivals. The 30 comfortable rooms all have DSTV, AC, minibar & private balcony. *US$30/45 dbl/twin.* **$**

Pallson's Hotel [122 D6] Bandeni Rd; m +255 754 744882. Once a highly rated mid-range hotel, this medium-rise near the old bus station now offers clean budget rooms with fan, net & hot shower. Good value. *US$10/15 dbl/twin.* **$**

THE ARUSHA HOTEL

Symbolic of Arusha's growing significance in the 1920s was the opening of the New Arusha Hotel in lushly wooded grounds formerly occupied by the small town's only hostelry, the small boarding house operated by the Bloom family since the late 1890s. A 1929 government brochure eulogised the newly opened establishment as having 'hot and cold water in all bedrooms, modern sanitation, teak dancing floor, electric light and really excellent food, as well as golf, tennis, big game and bird shooting'. Less complimentary was the description included in Evelyn Waugh's amusingly acerbic travelogue *A Tourist in Africa* in 1960: it 'seeks to attract by the claim to be exactly midway between Cape Town and Cairo…I did not see any African or Indian customers. Dogs howled and scuffled under the window at night. Can I say anything pleasant about this hotel? Yes, it stands in a cool place in a well-kept garden and it stocks some potable South African wines in good conditions.' The New Arusha continued its slide, hosting the likes of John Wayne along the way, until finally it closed for overdue renovations only to reopen in 2004 as the Arusha Hotel. Now part of the Four Points by Sheraton chain (page 119), it remains the smartest establishment in the city centre and a recommended spot for pre-dinner drinks in historic surrounds.

KIJENGE

Upmarket

The African Tulip [129 C5] Serengeti Rd; **m** +255 783 714104; **w** theafricantulip.com. Owned & managed by Roy Safaris (page 135), this popular boutique hotel is set in a green suburban garden with a swimming pool, well-stocked gift shop & restaurant serving excellent Indian cuisine. The 22 rooms & 7 suites are large, attractively decorated with Zanzibar-style wooden furnishing & have good facilities including a safe, minibar, satellite TV & large bathroom with tub or shower. **$$$$**

Mount Meru Hotel [129 B1] 027 297 0256; **w** mountmeruhotel.co.tz. Set in large green grounds bordering a golf course, this veteran 7-storey landmark is geared more towards business travellers than tourists, but nevertheless offers some of the most comfortable accommodation & best facilities in Arusha. There are 3 restaurants, a large swimming pool with children's area, & large contemporary rooms with minibar, AC, DSTV & tea-/coffee-making facilities. 2 rooms are designed for travellers with disabilities. **$$$$**

Moderate

Milimani Lodge [129 D2] Off Simeon Rd; **m** +255 688 315222; **w** themilimanilodge.com. This quiet owner-managed lodge has 12 large & attractively decorated rooms split over 2 storeys surrounding a neat green courtyard. *US$100/120 sgl/dbl B&B.* **$$$**

Outpost Lodge [129 B6] Serengeti St; **m** +255 754 318523; **w** outpost-lodge.com. Originally the home of conservationist Bernhard Grzimek, this homely B&B set in a pretty suburban garden has been consistently popular since it opened in 1994. Rooms in the main house & garden bungalows all come with nets & DSTV, & there's a dedicated, wheelchair-friendly room for travellers with disabilities. Cheap & tasty lunches & dinners are available. *From US$55/73 sgl/dbl.* **$$**

Spices & Herbs [129 C4] Off Simeon Rd; **m** +255 754 313162; **w** arushaethiopianrestaurantandlodge.co.tz. Owned & managed by an Ethiopian family, this recently relocated lodge has 8 neat rooms with common showers & a lovely quiet garden setting. The attached restaurant serves excellent Ethiopian food. *US$45/55 sgl/dbl B&B.* **$$**

Budget

Green Garden Hostel [129 A6] Ingira Rd; **m** +255 784 474440; **w** booking.com. Set in a leafy secluded garden, this friendly hostel is a great place to meet other travellers. In addition to 6 dbl rooms, there's a 4-bed & 8-bed dorm, & a makuti-shaded outdoor restaurant/bar with comfortable sofas & inexpensive meals. *From US$25 dbl or US$12pp in a dorm B&B.* **$**

Pepe Hotel & Restaurant [129 A4] Kanisa Rd; **m** +255 769 747474/783 747474. Attached to a great little Italian garden restaurant, this sensibly priced place has 9 small but neat & comfortable rooms with hot shower, net & TV. *US$20/23 sgl/dbl B&B.* **$**

SUBURBAN ARUSHA

Exclusive

Elewana Arusha Coffee Lodge [112 B2] ⊕ -3.37425, 36.64398; m +255 784 250630; **w** elewanacollection.com. Situated on a large coffee estate on the western outskirts of town, Arusha Coffee Lodge justifiably billed itself as 'the first truly 5-star hotel in Arusha' when it first opened, & it still ranks among the most luxurious options around. The standalone split-level chalets & suites are distinguished by their elegant Victorian décor, hardwood floors, huge balconies, stunning fireplaces & in-room percolators to provide the true aroma of the coffee estate. An excellent restaurant stands in the original plantation houses & there's also a swimming pool & several Africa-themed boutiques & gourmet food outlets in the on-site Traders Walk (page 128). **$$$$$$**

Moderate

✷ **Karama Lodge & Spa** [112 C3] Old Moshi Rd; ⊕ -3.37984, 36.71450; **m** +255 754 475188; **w** karama-lodge.com. The Swahili word for 'blessing', Karama is fabulous eco-lodge with a genuine bush atmosphere, despite lying only 3km from central Arusha. Perched on a densely wooded hill, the grounds harbour Brachystegia-associated birds (including the rare brown-throated barbet prominent among them) & the nocturnal likes of bushbaby, genet & civet. The stilted wood-&-makuti units have Zanzibar-style beds with nets & a private balcony facing Kilimanjaro. There's also a good restaurant & highly rated spa. A recommended alternative to the bland upmarket city hotels that characterise central Arusha, though the sloping grounds are unsuited to travellers with limited mobility. *From US$117/140 sgl/dbl B&B.* **$$$**

✷ **Researchers Rest** [112 B2] ⊕ -3.3512, 36.67205; **m** + 255 753 858504/769 784621; **w** theresearchersrest.com. This refreshingly non-institutional guesthouse in Sakina is converted from a house built by two English ladies but now owned & managed by the long-serving Tanzanian staff. A great retreat for sociable single travellers & couples, it feels more like staying in somebody's home than in a hotel, thanks to the comfortable lounge (with its immense library & DVD/CD collection), delicious home-cooked meals & repeat clientele of researchers & other regular visitors to Tanzania. *From US$69/82 sgl/dbl B&B.* **$$–$$$**

Budget & camping

Korona House [112 C4] ⊕ -3.44907, 36.70747; **m** +255 687 666808; **w** koronahouse.com. This smart, friendly owner-managed B&B has a rather remote location near the Arusha Bypass, but it's very likeable & well-priced with thoughtfully decorated rooms, a swimming pool, a highly rated & brightly decorated restaurant & a homely feel. *From US$35 B&B.* **$–$$**

✷ **White House of Tanzania** [112 C3] ⊕ -3.40273, 36.70021; **m** +255 714 285823; **w** whitehouseoftanzania.com. Tucked away in the southeastern suburb of Njiro, this neat & friendly hostel offers the choice of private rooms or 4–8-bed dorms, all with en-suite bathrooms. Dorm beds all have their own power socket, mosquito net & reading light. There's a TV lounge & bar, & meals are eaten communally. *From US$35/40 twin/dbl or US$12pp dorm bed.* **$**

OUT OF TOWN

Exclusive

✷ **Machweo & Onsea House** [112 D3] Namasi Hill; ⊕ -3.38126, 36.74488; **m** +255 679 933207; **w** onseahouse.com. Owned & managed by the same Michelin-trained Belgian chef since they opened in 2006, these intimate boutique hotels are situated alongside each other on the slopes of Namasi Hill 10mins' drive from central Arusha. The older Onsea House consists of 5 rooms with funky but understated African décor, while Machweo offers the choice of 3 honeymoon suites or 6 semi-detached cottage suites decorated in classic contemporary style. All rooms have a minibar, walk-in netting, safe & flatscreen DSTV. Amenities include 2 swimming pools, a highly rated wellness centre & spa & a walking trail through the bird-rich forest behind the property. FB rates include meals at one of Tanzania's top restaurants, specialising in innovative European cuisine with an African twist (page 128). **$$$$$$**

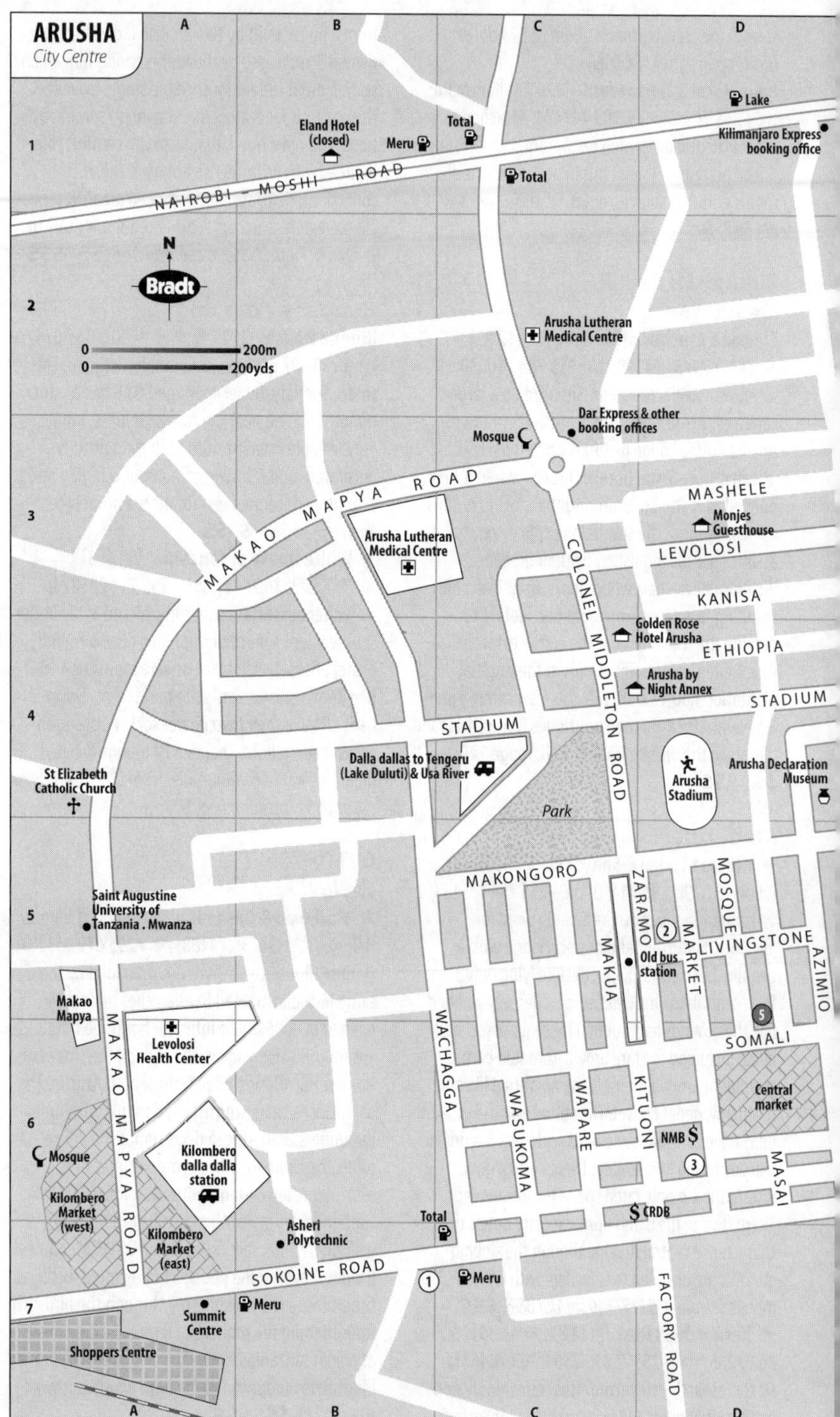

ARUSHA
City Centre
A
B
C
D
1
2
3
4
5
6
7
Lake
Kilimanjaro Express booking office
Eland Hotel (closed)
Total
Meru
Total
NAIROBI – MOSHI ROAD
N
Bradt
0
200m
0
200yds
Arusha Lutheran Medical Centre
Dar Express & other booking offices
Mosque
MAKAO MAPYA ROAD
Arusha Lutheran Medical Centre
MASHELE
Monjes Guesthouse
LEVOLOSI
KANISA
COLONEL MIDDLETON ROAD
Golden Rose Hotel Arusha
ETHIOPIA
Arusha by Night Annex
STADIUM
STADIUM
Dalla dallas to Tengeru (Lake Duluti) & Usa River
Arusha Stadium
Arusha Declaration Museum
St Elizabeth Catholic Church
Park
MAKONGORO
ZARAMO
MOSQUE
Saint Augustine University of Tanzania . Mwanza
2
LIVINGSTONE
MAKUA
Old bus station
MARKET
AZIMIO
Makao Mapya
WACHAGGA
5
SOMALI
MAKAO MAPYA ROAD
Levolosi Health Center
KITUONI
WAPARE
Central market
WASUKOMA
NMB
Mosque
Kilombero dalla dalla station
3
MASAI
Kilombero Market (west)
Total
CRDB
Kilombero Market (east)
Asheri Polytechnic
SOKOINE ROAD
1
Meru
FACTORY ROAD
Summit Centre
Meru
Shoppers Centre
A
B
C
D

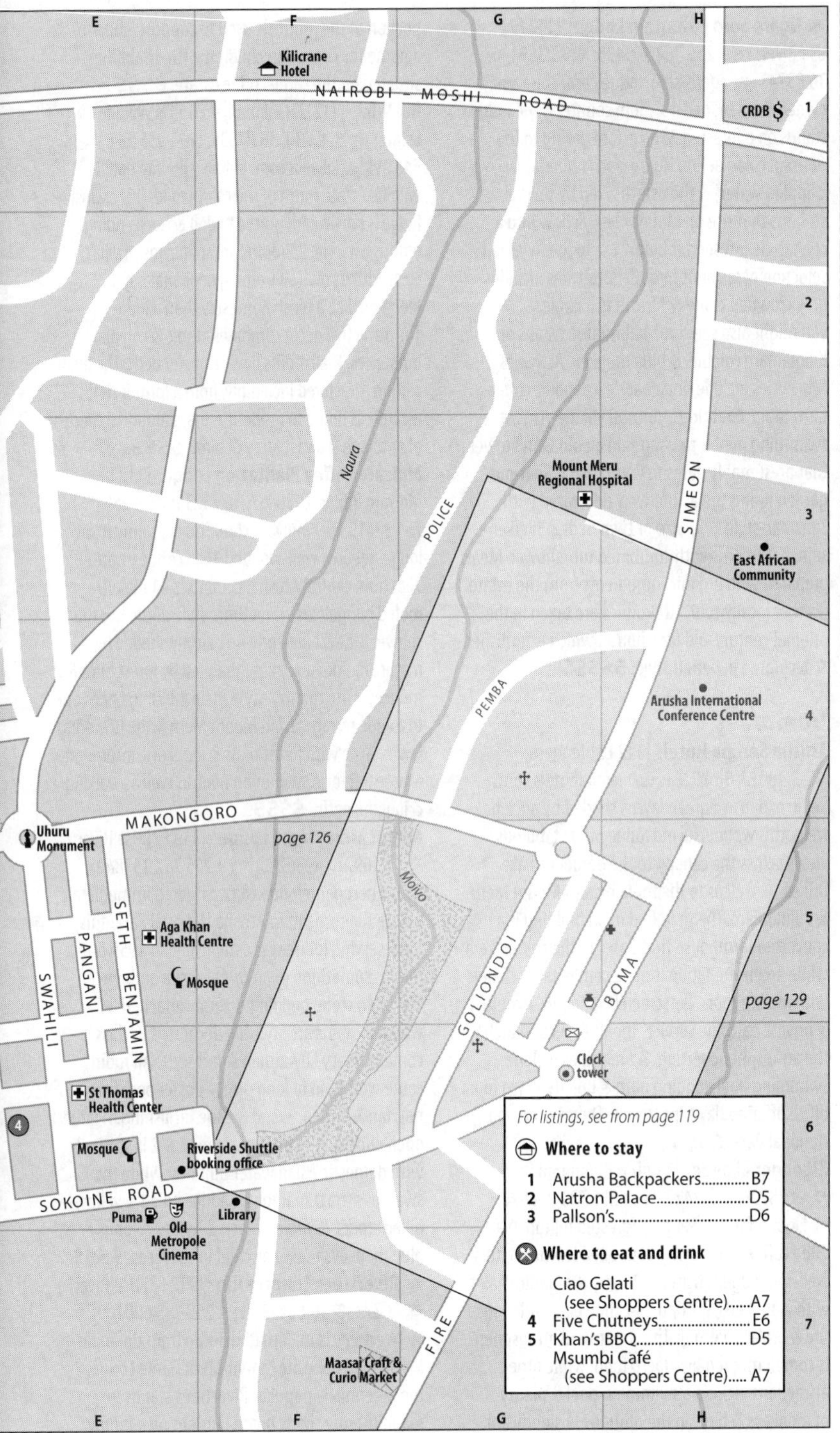
E
F
G
H
Kilicrane Hotel
NAIROBI – MOSHI ROAD
CRDB
1
2
Naura
POLICE
SIMEON
Mount Meru Regional Hospital
3
East African Community
PEMBA
Arusha International Conference Centre
4
MAKONGORO
Uhuru Monument
page 126
Moivo
SETH BENJAMIN
PANGANI
SWAHILI
Aga Khan Health Centre
Mosque
5
GOLIONDOI
BOMA
page 129
Clock tower
St Thomas Health Center
4
Mosque
Riverside Shuttle booking office
SOKOINE ROAD
Puma
Old Metropole Cinema
Library
6
FIRE
7
Maasai Craft & Curio Market
For listings, see from page 119
Where to stay
1 Arusha Backpackers.............B7
2 Natron Palace.........................D5
3 Pallson's.................................D6
Where to eat and drink
Ciao Gelati (see Shoppers Centre)......A7
4 Five Chutneys.........................E6
5 Khan's BBQ.............................D5
Msumbi Café (see Shoppers Centre)..... A7

✷ **Ngare Sero Mountain Lodge** [112 F2] Usa River; m +255 764 305435; ⊕ -3.359136, 36.83747; w ngare-sero-lodge.com. This family-owned & -managed 15-room country-style lodge stands on a forested 25ha estate dating to the German colonial era. Ngare sero is Maasai for 'dappled water', & the estate is fed by several streams that rise on Mount Meru & flow into a crystal-clear reservoir below the lodge. A varied selection of resident birds & butterflies includes grey crowned crane & African fish eagle, & you might also see semi-habituated troops of Kilimanjaro colobus & blue monkey. Activities & facilities include horseback excursions, coffee farm tours, boat rides, cultural village visits, a swimming pool & massages in an old watchtower that presumably dates to World War I. Spacious garden rooms are attractively decorated with Zanzibar-style king-size or twin beds & tiled en-suite bathrooms with combined tub/shower. Meals prepared with organic ingredients from the estate & other locally sourced produce are taken in the original century-old farmhouse, which is furnished & decorated in period style. **$$$$$**

Upmarket

Arusha Serena Hotel [112 E3] Tengeru; ⊕ -3.38022, 36.79261; w serenahotels.com. Set in expansive green lawns shaded by ancient trees, this wonderful old lodge offers fabulous views across the canopy to the gorgeous Lake Duluti, as well as to the more distant Mount Meru & Kilimanjaro. The thatched main building is a converted farmhouse that dates to the colonial era, while accommodation is in 42 comfortable chalets with makuti roofs, flatscreen DSTV, walk-in net & private balcony. Service, meals & décor match the atmospheric setting, & amenities include a swimming pool, jogging path & on-site Wayo Tours office offering day trips to Lake Duluti & Arusha National Park. **$$$$**

Kigongoni Lodge [112 D3] Kigongoni Rd; ⊕ -3.38238, 36.77423; m +255 732 978876; w kigongoni.net. Set on a forested hilltop in a 70ha coffee plantation 10km outside Arusha, this well-run lodge consists of 20 airy & organic chalets with 2 dbl beds, netting, hot shower & bath, log fire & private balcony. The countrified atmosphere is complemented by superb food, while other attractions include a swimming pool & plenty of monkeys & birds in the grounds. A significant portion of the profits is used to support Sibusiso, a home for Tanzanian children with disabilities, situated on the same coffee estate. **$$$$**

Kili Villa [112 G3] Kilimanjaro Golf & Wildlife Estate; ⊕ -3.42234, 36.87839; m +255 784 648144; w kilivilla.com. Set on a private golf & wildlife estate south of the Moshi road, this exclusive lodge is particularly suited to golf & horse-riding enthusiasts. The 15 rooms are split across 4 villas, each with its own swimming pool, making it feel more like a plush homestay than a lodge. The attractive décor combines ethnic & colonial influences, & all rooms have 4-poster beds. The bush setting – restored incredibly, from a former sisal estate – is home to resident zebra, around 10 species of antelope & a vast array of birds. **$$$$**

Moivaro Coffee Plantation Lodge [112 D3] Moivaro Rd; ⊕ -3.38857, 36.75235; m +255 754 324193; w moivaro.com. This elegantly rustic lodge, set on a well-wooded 16ha coffee estate 7km from central Arusha, comprises 41 makuti-roofed bungalows with ethnic-style décor, hot tub/shower & a secluded private balcony shaded by mature indigenous trees inhabited by forest birds & monkeys. The country-style main building opens out to a wide terrace facing Mount Meru & the flowering lawns, alive with forest birds & monkeys, incorporate a large freeform swimming pool, as well as walking & jogging paths. **$$$$**

Mount Meru Game Lodge [112 F2] Usa River; ⊕ -3.36977, 36.86286; m +255 752 131842; w mtmerugamelodge.co.tz. Situated immediately before the turn-off to Arusha National Park, this long-serving lodge was established in 1959 & it retains something of an *Out of Africa* ambience. The main stone building & semi-detached wooden cabins are stylishly decorated in classic contemporary Edwardian safari style. All rooms come with twin or king-size 4-poster bed, fitted net, fan & organic wood & cane furnishing. A large open enclosure in front of rooms 1 & 2 is stocked with domestic Asian water buffalos, while the swamps attract marabou, saddle-billed & yellow-billed storks, & vervet, black-&-white colobus & blue monkeys make mischief in the trees. **$$$$**

✷ **Rivertrees Country Inn** [112 F2] Usa River; ⊕ -3.37338, 36.86433; m +255 743 600160; w rivertrees.com. Situated 300m from the main Moshi road opposite Mount Meru Game Lodge, the perennially popukar Rivertrees stands in magnificently shady green gardens on a family estate bounded by the forest-fringed Usa River & offering great views of Mount Meru & Kilimanjaro. Centred on a rambling old farmhouse, the inn has 24 spacious en-suite rooms with large wooden 4-poster beds. Facilities include a swimming pool & a highly rated restaurant serving hearty country food, while activities include massage services, village tours, mountain biking & bird walks. **$$$$**

Moderate

African View Lodge [112 G1] Usa River; ⊕ -3.32432, 36.87341; m +255 784 419232; w african-view.com. Owned & managed by a hands-on German & English couple with years of hospitality experience in the area, this comfortable & well-priced lodge stands about 2km from Arusha National Park's Ngongongare Gate. The 20 brightly decorated & individually themed semi-detached bungalows stand in a large, well-wooded property with a swimming pool, beer garden, spa, TV room, gift shop & restaurant. The owners are active mountain guides with plenty of experience setting up Kilimanjaro & Meru climbs. *From US$100/140 sgl/dbl B&B.* **$$$**

KIA Lodge [112 G3] Kilimanjaro International Airport; ⊕ -3.42148, 37.07710; m + 255 754 780125; w kialodge.co.tz. This comfortable 40-room lodge is a useful option for visitors with unusual or inconvenient flight times out of Kilimanjaro International Airport, but the noise from overhead flights makes it less than ideal for an extended stay. Otherwise, it's an attractive enough set-up, with a good makuti-roofed restaurant, hilltop swimming pool, plentiful birdlife & views towards Kilimanjaro (the mountain, that is). The staff is used to monitoring flight arrivals & departures. **$$$**

✷ **Vijiji Center** [112 D2] Nguruma; ⊕ -3.37201, 36.76773; m +754 322664; w vijijicenter.com. Set in green 2-acre gardens, this attractive & friendly lodge arguably ranks as the best-value mid-range option close to Arusha & all profits help fund a nearby primary school. The 12 makuti-roofed cottages come with king-size or twin beds, fitted nets, hot shower & private veranda, while facilities include a swimming pool, an open-sided restaurant serving mostly organic & free-range fare, & an on-site operator offering cultural day trips & longer safaris. *US$96/120 sgl/dbl B&B.* **$$$**

Budget & camping

Duluti Forest Club [112 E3] Tengeru; ⊕ -3.38497, 36.78271; m +255 743 751260; f dulutiforestclub. This open-sided restaurant on the forested shore of Lake Duluti has a campsite with hot showers & boats for hire. *US$10pp.* **$**

Songota Falls Lodge [112 D2] ⊕ -3.36716, 36.74195; m +255 754 095576; w songotafallslodge.co.tz. Situated along a rough 1.5km dirt road that runs north from the Moshi road, Songota Falls Lodge consists of a few unfussy but clean en-suite bungalows overlooking the large green valley below the Songota Waterfall – to which guided walks are offered when underfoot conditions are reasonably dry. This refreshingly unpretentious set-up is owned & managed by a friendly Tanzanian woman with years of experience in the hotel trade. *From US$52 dbl B&B.* **$$**

ARUSHA NATIONAL PARK *Map, page 144*

Exclusive

✷ **Hatari Lodge** ⊕ -3.22491, 36.85732; w hatari.travel. This sumptuous & characterful owner-managed lodge stands in a patch of moist fever-tree woodland that lies within the national park following a recent boundary extension & is frequently visited by giraffes & other wildlife. The lodge is named after the 1961 movie *Hatari!* (danger) & is situated on a property formerly owned by Hardy Kruger, one of the film's co-stars. Accommodation is in 8 rooms & chalets with king-size beds, tall makuti ceilings & individualistic décor that blends a classic African bush feel with imaginative retro touches. The lounge & restaurant are littered with *Hatari!* memorabilia & overlook a swamp inhabited by buffalo, waterbuck, grey crowned crane & other water birds. There are also stirring views across to nearby Mount Meru & Kilimanjaro. The excellent meals embody the German owners' commitment to the Slow Food movement, with an emphasis on using organic ingredients sourced from traditional Tanzanian home gardens. Activities on offer include game drives, canoeing on the Momella Lakes, birdwatching excursions & day hikes into the Meru Crater & on Kilimanjaro's Shira Plateau. **$$$$$$**

Moderate

Kiboko Lodge ⊕ -3.32106, 36.91340; w kibokolodge.nl. Situated on the southern border

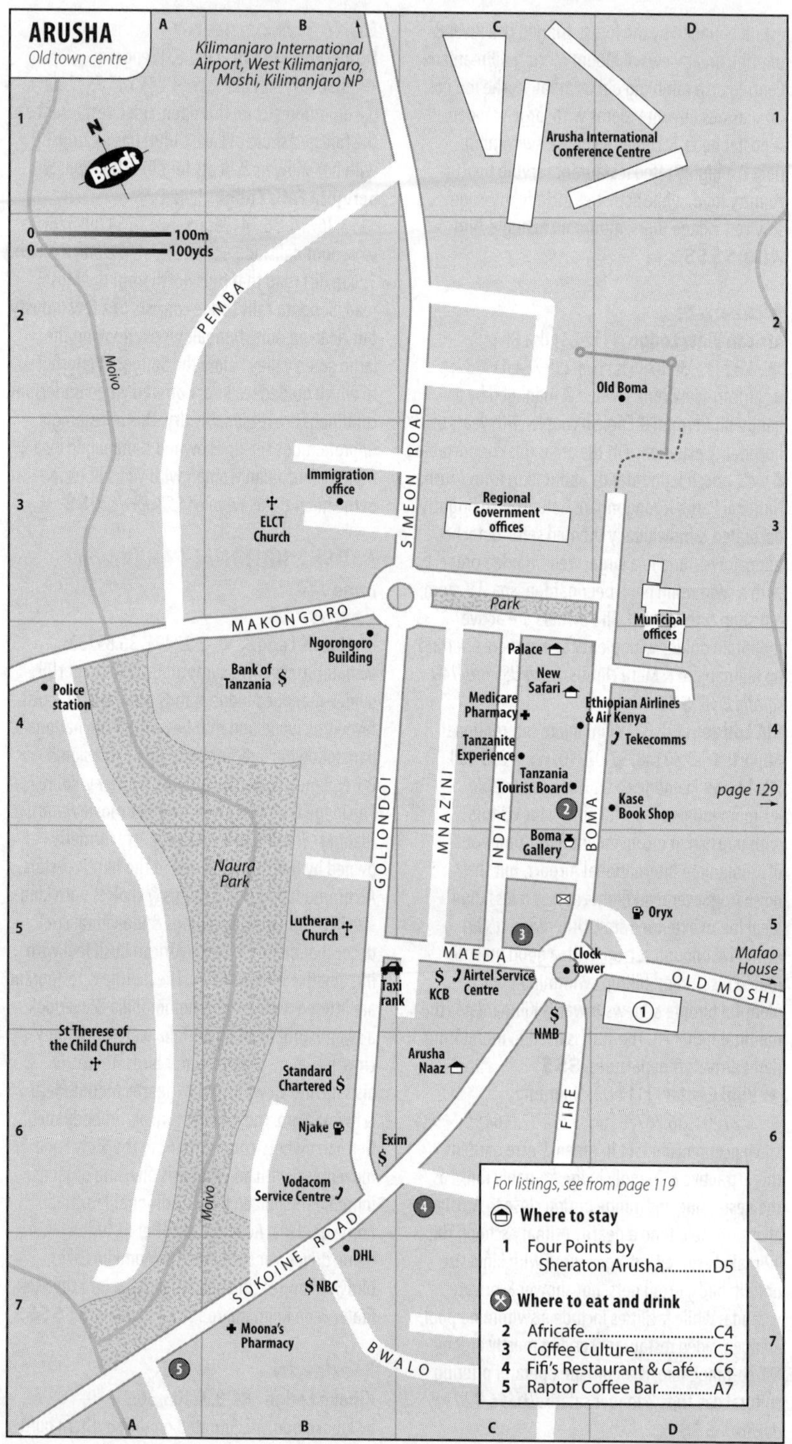
ARUSHA
Old town centre
Kilimanjaro International Airport, West Kilimanjaro, Moshi, Kilimanjaro NP
Arusha International Conference Centre
PEMBA
Moivo
SIMEON ROAD
Old Boma
Immigration office
ELCT Church
Regional Government offices
MAKONGORO
Park
Municipal offices
Ngorongoro Building
Bank of Tanzania
Palace
New Safari
Police station
Medicare Pharmacy
Ethiopian Airlines & Air Kenya
Tekecomms
Tanzanite Experience
Tanzania Tourist Board
page 129
MNAZINI
INDIA
BOMA
Kase Book Shop
Boma Gallery
GOLIONDOI
Naura Park
Oryx
Lutheran Church
MAEDA
Clock tower
Mafao House
Taxi rank
KCB
Airtel Service Centre
OLD MOSHI
NMB
St Therese of the Child Church
Arusha Naaz
Standard Chartered
FIRE
Njake
Exim
Vodacom Service Centre
SOKOINE ROAD
DHL
NBC
Moona's Pharmacy
BWALO
For listings, see from page 119
Where to stay
1 Four Points by Sheraton Arusha.............D5
Where to eat and drink
2 Africafe.....................................C4
3 Coffee Culture...........................C5
4 Fifi's Restaurant & Café.....C6
5 Raptor Coffee Bar..............A7

of Arusha National Park, this attractively rustic lodge comprises 21 chalets linked by a wooden boardwalk over a swamp inhabited by the solitary hippo (*'kiboko'*) for which it is named. It also offers great views of Mount Meru & excellent birding, with several species of weaver & bishop breeding there seasonally. Profits help fund a Dutch NGO dedicated to educating former street children, & most of the staff are graduates of the school. *US$172 dbl B&B*. **$$$**

Meru Mbega Lodge ⊕ -3.31310, 36.88585; w mt-meru.com. This unpretentious family-friendly set-up has 12 comfortable rooms in a dbl-storey building that offer views over a small pond towards Mount Meru, & 8 larger cottages with private balconies facing the national park boundary – which means that quite a bit of game comes past seasonally. An attractive makuti structure serves as the bar & restaurant. It's a good place to arrange Meru climbs. *From US$76/93 B&B*. **$$**

Budget & camping

National park campsites w tanzaniaparks.go.tz. A number of scenically located national park campsites are scattered around the park, all with drop toilets & firewood. *US$30pp*. **$$**

National Park Resthouse ⊕ -3.24860, 36.84999; w tanzaniaparks.go.tz. This quaint resthouse, set in a grassy clearing 1km east of the main road through Arusha National Park, was originally built in the 1920s as the home of Martha Margaret Trappe. It retains plenty of period character & amenities include a kitchen & hot showers. Elephants & leopards are quite often seen in the vicinity. *US$30pp*. **$$**

 WHERE TO EAT AND DRINK

Arusha's cosmopolitan culinary scene caters to most tastes and budgets. Cafés and restaurants in the **city centre** are geared mostly towards local business people, office workers and volunteers, so they tend to be relatively affordable and busiest at lunch, but most also stay open late enough for an early dinner. Restaurants in the leafy suburb of **Kijenge** are generally more diverse and upmarket. A handful of **out-of-town** restaurants offer something more unique to foodies.

CITY CENTRE

Africafe [126 C4] Boma Rd; m +255 656 799229; ⌚ 07.30–21.00 daily. Ever-popular brunch & lunch spot serving fresh coffee & juices, freshly baked goodies & a long list of burgers, salads, sandwiches & other meals. No alcohol. **$$$**

Ciao Gelati [122 A7] Shoppers Centre; m +255 627 905070; f. Renowned for its freshly made ice cream, this Italian restaurant also serves pizzas, paninis, burgers & excellent pasta dishes & salads. Coffee, smoothies, beer & wine are also available. **$$**

Coffee Culture [126 C5] Joel Maeda Rd; m +255 765 016230; f coffeecultureclocktower; ⌚ 08.00–21.00 Mon–Sat, 08.00–18.00 Sun. This sedate coffee shop opposite the Clock Tower has attractive modern décor, gentle music in the background & an extensive menu of pizzas, burgers, curries, stews & wraps. Light snacks include pies, croquettes, pastries & cakes. **$–$$**

✱ **Fifi's Restaurant & Café** [126 C6] Themi Rd; m +255 788 462232; w fifi-s-restaurant-cafe.business.site; ⌚ 08.00–21.30 daily. This friendly, characterful & cheerfully decorated local restaurant is always busy at lunch. The menu has something for everyone: salads, pizzas from a wood-fired oven, international dishes (from chilli con carne to mushroom-&-pea curry), as well as Tanzanian specialities. Vegetarians are well catered for & it serves cocktails, shooters, wine & beer. **$$**

✱ **Five Chutneys** [123 E6] Azimio St; m +255 783 505505; w fivechutneys.com; ⌚ 08.00–20.00 Mon–Sat, 09.00–17.00 Sun. Delicious authentic Gujarati cuisine is the speciality at this unpretentious, popular & affordable Indian vegetarian restaurant near the market. No alcohol. **$**

✱ **Khan's BBQ** [122 D5] Mosque St; m +255 754 652747; ⌚ 18.00–23.00. This singular eatery near the market is a motor spares shop by day & street BBQ in the evening. Specialities include flame-grilled ½ chicken & beef & mutton kebabs accompanied by a huge selection of salads, naan bread & the like. No alcohol. **$**

Msumbi Café [122 A7] Shoppers Centre; m +255 784 318242; w msumbicoffees.com;

⌚ 08.00–19.00 daily. Excellent freshly brewed coffee, a varied selection of teas, & b/fasts & light lunches are all on offer at this clean & modern-looking patisserie. $

Raptor Coffee Bar [126 A7] Sokoine Rd; m +255 683 864044; f TheRaptorcafetz; ⌚ 07.30–23.00 daily. This friendly little café has an appealing fan-cooled wood-dominated interior & serves great coffee, smoothies & juices, as well as a tempting selection of inexpensive burgers, wraps & pasta & vegetarian dishes. $

KIJENGE

✷ **George's Tavern** [129 B4] Haile Selassie Rd; m +255 782 943690; w georges.co.tz; ⌚ 11.00–23.00 Tue-Sun. Owned & managed by a Greek family, this likeable garden taverna has a globetrotting menu incorporating traditional Greek & Italian dishes, sushi, burgers & Tanzanian specialities such as Swahili chicken curry to Arusha-style beef & banana stew. $$$

✷ **Hot Tandoori Village** [129 B6] Serengeti Rd; m +255 620 559075; ⌚ 11.00–23.00 Tue–Sun. Offering the choice of dining in the leafy garden or a converted suburban house, this pan-Asian restaurant & bar specialises in delicious meat-based & vegetarian Indian cuisine but it also serves a range of Chinese, Manchurian & Malay dishes. Tasty & good value. $–$$

Pablo Picasso Café [129 C4] Simeon Rd; m +255 748 000786; f pablopicassocafe; ⌚ 10.00–23.00 daily. Despite its location in a parking lot, this stylish café could be transplanted from Italy or France & it serves a sumptuous & imaginative selection of cakes, pastries, filled crepes, salads & more substantial mains. It serves good coffee & has a great wine list. $$

Peace Chinese [129 B2] Kanisa Rd; m +255 763 597989; ⌚ 11.30-22.30 daily. Situated alongside the Gymkhana Club, the former Chinese Dragon is probably Arusha's oldest Chinese restaurant &, despite the new name & management, it remains a popular, informal & well-priced venue with plenty of choice for vegetarians & meat eaters alike. $–$$

Pepe Hotel & Restaurant [129 A4] Kanisa Rd; m +255 769 747474/783 747474; ⌚ 09.00–22.00 daily. The speciality at this informal open-air Italian-owned restaurant is pizzas straight from a wood-fired oven, but it also serves a varied choice of pasta dishes, seafood & grills. $–$$

✷ **Spices & Herbs** [129 C4] Off Simeon Rd; m +255 754 313162; w arushaethiopianrestaurantandlodge.co.tz; ⌚ 09.00–22.00 daily. This long-serving & reliable family-run Ethiopian restaurant recently changed venue but it remains a great place to try distinctive Ethiopian staples such as spicy *kai wat* stew served with *injera* (flat round sour bread). The terrace seating is very pleasant & vegans are well catered for. $–$$

Uzunguni City Park [129 A5] Off Simeon Rd; m +255 766 306006; w uzungunicitypark.business.site; ⌚ 07.00–23.00 daily (later at w/ends). This perennially popular terrace restaurant, set in sprawling gardens at the end of a short cul de sac, is essentially an upmarket variation of a typical Tanzanian *nyama choma* (grilled meat) & beer joint. In addition to flame-barbecued chicken & *mishkaki* (beef kebabs), local specialities include foil-wrapped whole tilapia & various stews. The atmosphere is informal & welcome, & it's a great place to people watch or catch live football on the big screen. $–$$

OUT OF THE CITY

✷ **Blue Heron Restaurant** [112 A3] ⊕ -3.38235, 36.61243; m +255 783 885833, w blueheron.co.tz; ⌚ 10.00–22.00 Thu–Sun. Recently relocated to larger gardens near Arusha Airport, this popular & stylish contemporary restaurant is renowned for its pizzas, pasta of the day, Fri-night pork & lamb spit BBQ & sumptuous buffet b/fast on Sun. There's also local craft beer & a good wine & cocktail menu. $$$

✷ **Machweo Fine Dining** [112 D3] ⊕ -3.38126, 36.74488; w onseahouse.com; ⌚ lunch & dinner daily. Situated in the boutique hotel of the same name, Machweo is widely regarded to offer Tanzania's top fine-dining experience. The brainchild of Michelin-trained Belgian chef Axel Janssens, it serves a different 4-course set menu every night, accompanied by specially selected wines. Bookings are mandatory for those not staying at the hotel. $$$

Traders Walk [112 B2] w elewanacollection.com; ⌚ 10.00–14.30 daily. In the grounds of the Elewana Arusha Coffee Lodge (page 121), this 'African experience centre' houses a coffee shop (Kahawa) & an African restaurant (Jikoni), the Shanga Workshop (page 130), plus a jewellers & a gift shop. $$

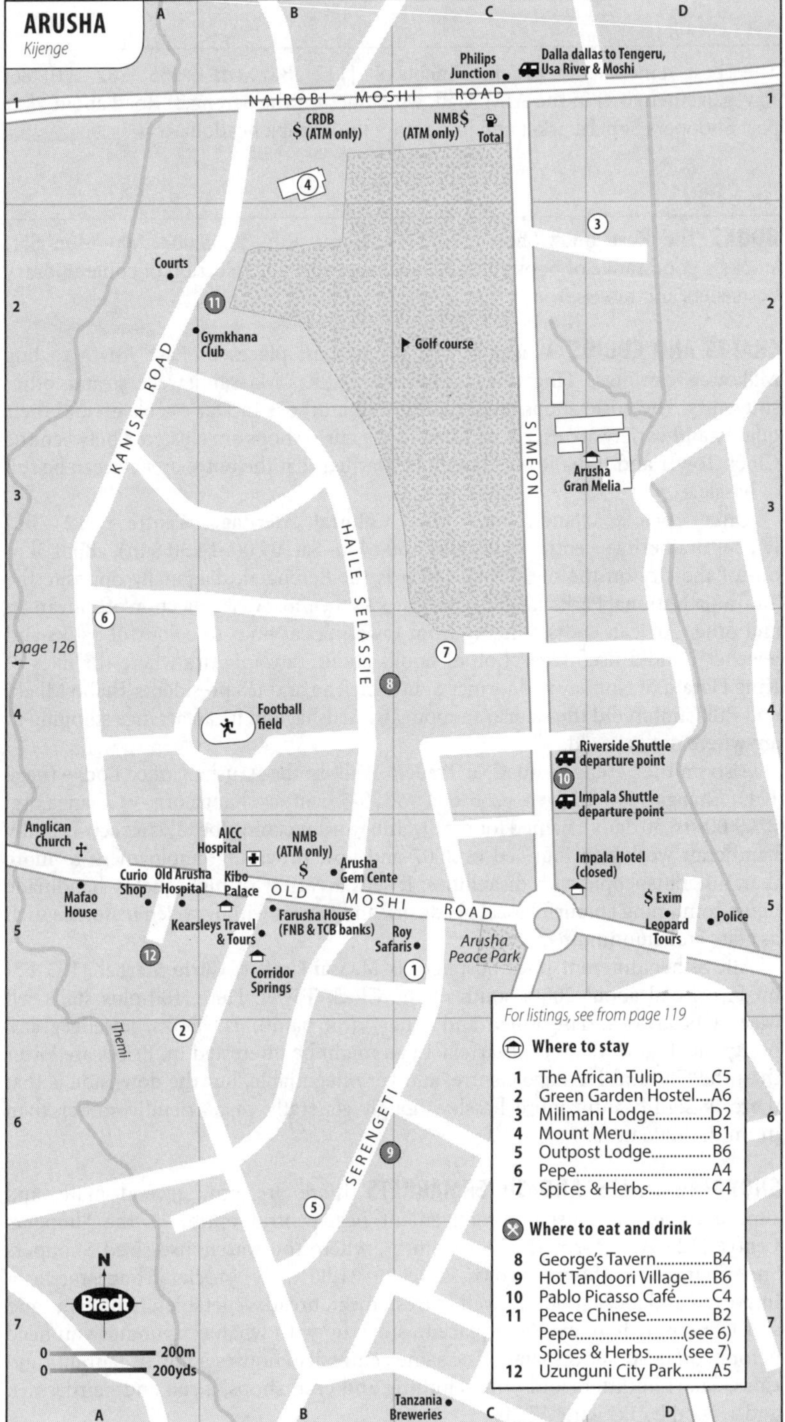

ARUSHA
Kijenge
Philips Junction
Dalla dallas to Tengeru, Usa River & Moshi
NAIROBI – MOSHI ROAD
CRDB (ATM only)
NMB (ATM only)
Total
Courts
Gymkhana Club
Golf course
KANISA ROAD
SIMEON
Arusha Gran Melia
HAILE SELASSIE
page 126
Football field
Riverside Shuttle departure point
Impala Shuttle departure point
Anglican Church
AICC Hospital
NMB (ATM only)
Arusha Gem Cente
Impala Hotel (closed)
Curio Shop
Old Arusha Hospital
Kibo Palace
OLD MOSHI ROAD
Mafao House
Kearsleys Travel & Tours
Farusha House (FNB & TCB banks)
Roy Safaris
Exim
Leopard Tours
Police
Arusha Peace Park
Corridor Springs
Themi
SERENGETI
Bradt
200m
200yds
Tanzania Breweries
For listings, see from page 119
Where to stay
1 The African Tulip.............C5
2 Green Garden Hostel....A6
3 Milimani Lodge...............D2
4 Mount Meru....................B1
5 Outpost Lodge................B6
6 Pepe...............................A4
7 Spices & Herbs................C4
Where to eat and drink
8 George's Tavern...............B4
9 Hot Tandoori Village.......B6
10 Pablo Picasso Café.......C4
11 Peace Chinese................B2
Pepe..............................(see 6)
Spices & Herbs.........(see 7)
12 Uzunguni City Park........A5

ENTERTAINMENT

The best cinema is **Regalz Cinemaxx** [112 B3] (m +255 782 110786; f regalzcinemaxx) in the AIM Mall, which lies on the Serengeti Road about 2km past Shoppers Supermarket and just before the Tanapa headquarters.

SHOPPING

BOOKS The **Kase Book Shop** [126 D4] (Boma Rd; ⌚ 09.00–17.00 Mon–Sat) stocks a good range of books about Tanzania and a fair selection of contemporary bestsellers and novels.

CRAFTS AND CURIOS Arusha is one of the best places in East Africa to buy Makonde carvings, Tingatinga paintings, batiks, Maasai jewellery and other souvenirs. The curio shops are far cheaper than those in Dar es Salaam and their quality and variety are excellent. Most of the curio shops are clustered between the Clock Tower and India Road, though be warned that the outdoor stalls can be full of hassle.

Three places stand out. The **Cultural Heritage Centre** [112 B3] (f culturalheritagecentre; ⌚ 09.00–17.30 Mon–Sat, 09.00–14.30 Sun), about 3km out of the city on the main road towards the Serengeti, diagonally opposite the Tanzania National Parks' headquarters, stocks the most vast collection of Tanzanian and other African crafts, ranging from towering carvings to colourful batiks and jewellery, and a useful selection of books about Tanzania. It's where the likes of King Harald of Norway and former South African and US presidents Thabo Mbeki and Bill Clinton did their curio shopping in Arusha, and it can arrange shipping to anywhere in the world.

Also on the Serengeti Road, at Traders Walk in the Arusha Coffee Lodge (page 121), **Shanga** [112 B2] (m +255 684 793204; e info@shanga.org; w shanga.org; ⌚ 09.00–16.30 daily), named for the Swahili word meaning 'bead', is an eco-friendly handicraft workshop founded in 2007 and now providing employment to more than 40 craftspeople with disabilities. It sells a variety of high-quality handmade items combining colourful local beadwork and fabrics with recycled materials such as glass and aluminium.

Altogether different in atmosphere is **Maasai Craft & Curio Market** [123 F7] on Fire Road about 200m south of the Clock Tower. Here, 100-plus stalls sell Maasai beadwork, Tingatinga and other local paintings, batiks, jewellery and pretty much any other ethno-artefact you might be interested in. Prices are lower than the Cultural Heritage Centre, and very negotiable, but the downside is that there is significantly more hassle, though generally of a friendly rather than intimidating nature.

SHOPPING MALLS AND SUPERMARKETS There are now several malls and supermarkets in Arusha. A convenient near-central option is the **Shoppers Centre** [122 A7] (formerly TFA Centre), where the warehouse-sized Shoppers Supermarket (w shoppers.co.tz; ⌚ 08.00–21.00 daily) stocks a huge range of imported and local goods, as well as fresh meat, bread, vegetables, fruit, wine and spirits, making it an excellent place to stock up with whatever goodies you need before you head out on safari. The same centre also houses a few restaurants and cafes, safari outfitters and other clothing and craft shops, a spa and hairdresser, and several banks with ATMs.

MAKONDE CARVINGS

The Makonde of the Tanzania–Mozambique border area are the finest traditional sculptors in East Africa. According to oral tradition the males of this matrilineal society have been practising this craft to woo their women for at least 300 years. Legend has it that the first person on earth, not yet male or female, living alone in the foothills of the Makonde Plateau, carved a piece of wood into the shape of a human figure. The carver left his creation outside his home overnight, and awoke to find it had been transformed into a living woman. Twice the woman conceived, but both times the child died after three days. Each time, the pair moved higher on to the plateau, believing this would bring them luck. The third child lived, and became the first true Makonde. The mother is regarded to be the spiritual ancestor of all the Makonde, and the legend is sometimes said to be a parable for the difficulty of creation.

In their purest form, the intricate, stylised carvings of the Makonde relate to this ancestral cult of womanhood, and are carried only by men, as a good-luck charm. Traditional carvings almost always depict a female figure, sometimes surrounded by children, and the style was practically unknown outside of Tanzania until a carving workshop was established at Mwenge in suburban Dar es Salaam during the 1950s. Subsequently, like any dynamic art form, Makonde sculpture has been responsive to external influences and subject to changes in fashion, with new styles of carvings becoming increasingly abstract and incorporating wider moral and social themes.

The most rustic of the new styles is the Binadamu sculpture, which depicts traditional scenes such as old men smoking pipes or women fetching water in a relatively naturalistic manner. Altogether more eerie and evocative is the Shetani style, in which grotesquely stylised human forms, sometimes with animal-like features, represent the impish and sometimes evil spirits for which the style is named. Many Makonde and other East Africans leave offerings for Shetani sculptures, believing them to be possessed by ancestral spirits. Most elaborate of all are the naturalistic Ujamaa sculptures, which depict many interlocking figures and relate to the collective social policy of Ujamaa fostered by the late President Nyerere. Also known as People Poles or Trees of Life, these statues sometimes incorporate several generations of the carver's family, rising in circular tiers to be up to 2m high. A newer style called Mawingu – the Swahili word for clouds – combines human figures with abstract shapes to represent intellectual or philosophical themes. Today, the finest examples of the genre fetch prices in excess of US$5,000 from international collectors.

The Makonde traditionally shape their creations exclusively from *Dalbergia melanoxylon*, a hardwood tree known locally as *mpingo* and in English as African blackwood or (misleadingly) African ebony. The carver – always male – will first saw a block of wood to the required size, then create a rough outline by hacking away excess wood with an instrument called an adze. The carving is all done freehand, with hammers, chisels and rasps used to carve the fine detail, before the final sculpture is sanded and brushed for smoothness. A large Ujamaa sculpture can take several months to complete, with some of the carving – appropriately – being undertaken communally. Traditionally, the craft was more or less hereditary, with sons being apprenticed to their fathers from a young age, and different families tending to work specific subjects related to their own traditions.

Another 8km out of town on the Serengeti road, just past Arusha Airport, stands the more sedate and upmarket **Sable Square Shopping Village** [112 A2] (**m** +255 678 133841; **w** sablesquare.com). Here you will find the superb Food Lover's Market, a branch of a South African chain that easily ranks as Arusha's best supermarket, stocking a similar range of goods to Shoppers, but generally superior when it comes to quality and choice. Sable Square also houses several ATMs, a coffee shop, a fitness centre, a pharmacy, a spa and several safari companies and craft shops.

The more out-of-town **Njiro Mall** [112 C3] also boasts several eateries, as well as the excellent Village Supermarket, but the selection of shops is limited. **AIM Mall**

TINGATINGA PAINTINGS

The brightly coloured paintings of fabulous creatures you might notice at craft stalls in Arusha and elsewhere in the region are Tingatinga paintings, a school of painting that is unique to Tanzania and named after its founder Edward Tingatinga. The style arose in Dar es Salaam in the early 1960s, when Tingatinga fused the vibrant and popular work of Congolese immigrants with art traditions indigenous to his Makua homeland in the Mozambique border area (a region well known to aficionados of African art as the home of Makonde carving). When Tingatinga died in 1972, the accidental victim of a police shoot-out, his commercial success had already spawned a host of imitators, and shortly after that a Tingatinga art co-operative was formed with government backing.

In the early days, Tingatinga and his followers produced fairly simple paintings featuring a large, bold and often rather surreal two-dimensional image of one or another African creature on a monotone background. But as the paintings took off commercially, a greater variety of colours came into play, and a trend developed towards the more complex canvases you see today. Modern Tingatinga paintings typically depict a menagerie of stylised and imaginary birds, fish and mammals against a backdrop of natural features such as Kilimanjaro or an abstract panel of dots and whorls. An offshoot style, reputedly initiated by Tingatinga himself, can be seen in the larger, even more detailed canvases that depict a sequence of village or city scenes so busy you could look at them for an hour and still see something fresh.

Tingatinga painters have no pretensions to producing high art. On the contrary, the style has been commercially driven since its inception: even the largest canvases are produced over a matter of days and most painters work limited variations around favourite subjects. It would be missing the point altogether to talk of Tingatinga as traditional African art. With its bold, bright images – tending towards the anthropomorphic, often subtly humorous, always accessible and evocative – Tingatinga might more appropriately be tagged Africa's answer to Pop Art.

Labels aside, souvenir hunters will find Tingatinga paintings to be a lively, original and surprisingly affordable alternative to the identikit wooden animal carvings that are sold throughout East Africa (and, one suspects, left to gather dust in cupboards all over Europe). Take home a Tingatinga panel, and you'll have a quirky but enduring memento of your African trip, something to hang on your wall and derive pleasure from for years to come.

[112 B3], on the Serengeti Road between Shoppers and Sable Square, is of interest mainly for its modern cinema (page 130).

OTHER PRACTICALITIES

BANKS, ATMS AND FOREIGN EXCHANGE Most major banks in Arusha double as bureaux de change, where you can change US dollars, euros, pounds sterling and other major currencies into Tanzanian shillings. You may be offered a better rate on the streets, but don't be tempted, as you are sure to be ripped off.

There are numerous 24-hour ATMs where local currency can be drawn against a Visa or Mastercard. These include the ATMs at the **Standard Chartered Bank** on Goliondoi Road [126 B6], the **Stanbic Bank** on Bwalo Road [126 B7], various ATMs operated by the NBC, NMB and Exim Bank, and the ATMs in **Sable Square Mall** and **Shoppers Centre** [122 A7]. Most ATMs impose a transaction limit of Tsh400,000 (around US$170) but you can usually do several transactions if required.

A NOTE ON ATMS

Travellers heading off on safari should be aware that Arusha will offer the first and last chance to reliably draw money against a credit card. ATM facilities are available in Mto wa Mbu and Karatu, but these cannot be relied upon 100%.

COMMUNICATIONS The main **post office** [126 C5] and **telecommunications centre** [126 D4] are both on Boma Road. Almost all the hotels and restaurants listed from page 119 offer free Wi-Fi to clients. If you want to buy a local SIM card, as well as airtime and a data bundle, the best place to do so is the **Vodacom service centre** [126 B6] at the junction of Sokoine and Goliondoi roads, or the **Airtel service centre** [126 C5] on Joel Maeda Road. In both cases, it is very inexpensive, but do remember to bring your passport as proof of identity.

MEDICAL The **Arusha Lutheran Medical Centre** [122 B3] (ALMC; off Colonel Middleton Rd; m +255 736 502376/737 212629; w almc.or.tz) is generally regarded to be the best in Arusha. For other recommendations, consult your hotel reception or safari company.

TOURIST INFORMATION

The **Tanzania Tourist Board** (TTB) office [126 C4] (⏲ 08.00–16.00 Mon–Fri, 08.30–13.00 Sat) on Boma Road is refreshingly helpful and well informed. It stocks a useful colour road map of Tanzania, as well as a great street plan of Arusha, both given free of charge to tourists, and maintains a regularly updated list of registered and blacklisted safari and trekking companies.

The TTB has been actively involved in the development of cultural tourism programmes in Ng'iresi, Mulala, Mkuru, Longido, Mto wa Mbu, Usambara, North Pare and South Pare, as well as several projects further afield. The Arusha office stocks informative pamphlets about these programmes, and can help out with information on prices and access. Details are also available at the **Cultural Tourism Programme** office in the Old Boma [126 D2] (m +255 713 230134/786 703010; w tanzaniaculturaltourism.com).

The head office of **Tanzania National Parks** [112 B2] (TANAPA; 📞027 250 3471; w tanzaniaparks.go.tz) is located in the Mwalimu J K Nyerere Conservation Centre about 3km out of town along the Serengeti road, roughly opposite the Cultural Heritage Centre.

The **Ngorongoro Conservation Area Authority** [126 B4] (NCAA; w ncaa.go.tz) has a helpful information office on the ground floor of the new Ngorongoro Building. In addition to some worthwhile displays on the conservation area, it sells a good range of books and booklets about the northern circuit. Fees for the NCA can also be paid in advance here.

SAFARI OPERATORS

The list given here is not definitive, but it provides a good cross-section of the sort of services that are on offer and sticks to companies that have maintained high standards over the years. The listed companies generally specialise in northern circuit safaris, but most can also set up Kilimanjaro and Meru climbs, fly-in safaris on the southern safari circuit, and excursions to Zanzibar.

&Beyond w andbeyond.com. Operating some of the most sumptuous lodges in northern Tanzania, &Beyond arranges fly-in, drive-in (or mixed) safaris throughout northern Tanzania, as well as mobile safaris using seasonal camps in the 'Under Canvas' brand.

Africa Dream Safaris w africadreamsafaris.com. An award-winning outfit specialising in upmarket customised safaris for serious wildlife enthusiasts & photographers, using intimate tented camps & knowledgeable driver/guides who place strong emphasis on early-morning & full-day game drives, avoiding circuits that suffer from overcrowding.

Asilia Africa w asiliaafrica.com. This excellent operator manages some of Tanzania's most exclusive camps & lodges, & puts together safari packages including flights &/or road transfers between its properties.

Bush2Beach Safaris w bush2beach.com. With almost 20 years' experience designing custom-made safaris, B2B offers good value for money for safaris, mountain climbs & beach holidays.

Fahari Safari w faharisafari.com. With a focus on immersive & transformative experiences & sustainable luxury, this operator arranges bespoke itineraries including safari, wildebeest migration, Kilimanjaro trekking, Zanzibar & Ngorongoro Crater.

Fair Travel Tanzania w fairtravel.com. This admirable company is strongly committed to ecologically sound travel that pays fair wages to drivers & other staff, channels profits into community projects & offers competitive rates to its clients.

Hoopoe Safaris w hoopoe.com. This long-serving owner-managed company specialises in personalised luxury camping & lodge safaris. It is also a good contact for trekking & walking safaris in Natron & the Ngorongoro Highlands.

Kearsleys Travel & Tours w kearsleys.com. Established in 1948, this is the oldest safari company in Tanzania, with dynamic management & staff, & well-maintained vehicles.

Leopard Tours w leopard-tours.com. Founded in 1985, this large & very reliable operation specialises in mid-range safaris concentrating on the bigger lodges in game-viewing areas.

Nature Discovery w naturediscovery.com. This eco-friendly operator is widely praised for its top-end Kilimanjaro climbs. It also arranges standard northern circuit safaris & trekking expeditions in the Ngorongoro Highlands & elsewhere.

Roy Safaris [129 C5] w roysafaris.com. One of the few Arusha-based operators to still maintain a walk-in office (next to the African Tulip Hotel), this dynamic & efficient owner-managed company has been offering reliable & reasonably priced budget & mid-range safaris since the early 1990s.

Safari Infinity w safari-infinity.com. Reliable tailor-made upmarket safaris throughout the northern safari circuit.

Safari Makers w safarimakers.com. Good for budget & mid-range camping & lodge safaris, as well as visits to cultural programmes outside Arusha.

Summits Africa w summits-africa.com. A small adventure-orientated company that specialises in Kilimanjaro & Meru climbs, often using the less well-known routes. It's also a great contact for Lake Natron & Ol Doinyo Lengai.

Tropical Trails w tropicaltrails.com. This eco-friendly budget-oriented company arranges lodge-based & camping safaris, walking excursions on the fringes of the main national parks & Kili climbs.

Wayo Africa w wayoafrica.com. This environmentally minded operator specialises in walking safaris & bush camps in wilderness areas within the Serengeti & other national parks. The standard of guiding can be exceptional, & it's highly recommended to active travellers seeking a genuine wilderness experience at reasonable rates.

Wild Frontiers w wildfrontiers.com. Based in South Africa but with its own ground operation in Arusha, this well-established & flexible company offers a varied range of motorised, walking & combination safaris using its own tented camps. Recommended to those seeking a relatively unpackaged safari at a reasonable price.

Wild Things Safaris w wildthingsafaris.com. Operating all over the country & highly experienced in both northern & southern circuits, Wild Things offers high-quality, well-priced tailor-made safaris to anywhere you want to go. They are also a great source of information for adventures to less-visited & more remote destinations.

WHAT TO SEE AND DO

Arusha is better known as a springboard for safaris than as a destination in its own right, but the town and its immediate environs offer some worthwhile sightseeing. These range from a trio of urban museums to the gorgeous Lake Duluti and a number of engaging community-based cultural programmes scattered in the surrounding countryside. Further afield, a day trip to Arusha National Park, covered under its own heading on page 141, is highly recommended.

AROUND TOWN None of the three museums detailed below could be described as a 'must see', but all are worth a passing look if you're in the area.

National Natural History Museum

[126 D2] (Boma Rd; f NNHMArusha; ⌚ 09.00–18.00 daily; entrance US$6 payable by card only) Housed in the old German Boma, this might more accurately be renamed the Archaeological or Palaeontological Museum. The limited displays – you can walk around the museum in a minute – include a selection of animal and hominid fossils unearthed at Oldupai and Laetoli in the Ngorongoro Conservation Area, as well as life-size models of *Australopithecus* hunter-gatherers at play.

Arusha Declaration Museum

[122 D4] (Uhuru Monument Circle; f ArushaDeclaration; ⌚ 09.00–17.30; entrance US$6 payable by card only) Dedicated primarily to 20th-century developments in Tanzania, this has some interesting displays on the colonial and post-independence Nyerere era. It also contains a few decent ethnographic displays, but seems overpriced for what it is.

The Tanzanite Experience [126 C4] (3rd Fl, Blue Plaza, India Rd; m +255 767 600991; w tanzaniteexperience.com; ⌚ 08.30–17.30 Mon–Fri, 09.00–15.00 Sat; free entrance) Operated by the world's largest tanzanite mining company, this

ALL THAT GLISTERS...

In 1962, local legend tells, a Maasai cattle herder called Ali Juyawatu was walking through the Mererani Hills after a bush fire, and noticed some unusual blue crystals lying on the ground. Ali picked up the beautiful stones and took them to the nearby town of Arusha, from where they somehow made their way to the New York gemstone dealer Tiffany & Co, which had never seen anything like them before. In 1967, Tiffany launched the newly discovered gem on the market, naming it tanzanite in honour of its country of origin.

Tanzanite is by any standards a remarkable stone. A copper-brown variety of zoisite, it is rather dull in its natural condition, but responds to gentle heating, transforming into a richly saturated dark-blue gem, with purple and violet undertones that have been compared among other things to the eyes of Elizabeth Taylor! Tanzanite comes only from Tanzania's Mererani Hills – rumours of a second deposit in Usangi, 75km from Arusha, have yet to be confirmed – and it is a thousand times rarer than diamonds. Despite its upstart status in the jewellery world, tanzanite has rocketed in popularity since its discovery. By 1997, 30 years after its launch, it had become the second most popular gemstone in the North American market, second to sapphires and ahead of rubies and emeralds, generating an annual trade worth US$300 million in the USA alone.

Remarkable, too, is the degree of controversy that the tanzanite trade has attracted in recent years. In the late 1990s, the Tanzanian government, comparing international tanzanite trade figures against their documented exports, realised that as much as 90% of the tanzanite sold in the USA was being smuggled out of Tanzania, resulting in a huge loss of potential government revenue in taxes and royalties. The ease with which the stones were being smuggled was clearly linked to the unregulated nature of the workings at Mererani, which consisted of more than 300 small claims operating in what has been described by more than one observer as a Wild West atmosphere. For the small claim holders, rather than distributing the stones they collected through legitimate sources, it was more profitable – and considerably more straightforward – to sell them for cash to illicit cross-border traders.

The lack of regulations at Mererani, or at least the lack of a body to enforce what regulations do exist, is also largely to blame for a series of tragedies that has dogged the workings in recent years. The greatest single catastrophe occurred during the El Niño rains of 1998, when one of the shafts at Block D flooded and at least 100 miners drowned. But it has been estimated that a similar number of miners died underground subsequent to this mass tragedy, as a result of suffocation, inept dynamite blasting, or periodic outbreaks of violent fighting over disputed claims. Aside from such incidents, it has long been rumoured that miners who are down on their luck will kidnap and sacrifice children from neighbouring villages, in the hope it will bring them good fortune and prosperity.

modern museum provides a fascinating overview of the discovery and extraction of this exquisite blue gem, which occurs in Tanzania only. Imaginative multi-media displays and enthusiastic staff are complemented by many examples of rough and cut tanzanite (and other striking local rocks). There is also the chance to purchase certified gemstones direct from source, along with tanzanite and diamond jewellery.

In 1999, the Tanzanian government put out to tender a lease on Block C, the largest of the four mining blocks, accounting for about 75% of the known tanzanite deposit. The rights were acquired by a South African company – with a 25% Tanzanian stake – called African Gem Resources (AFGEM), which reputedly pumped US$20 million into establishing the mine with the intention of going online in early 2000. This goal proved to be highly optimistic, as local miners and stakeholders, understandably hostile to the corporate intrusion on their turf, not to mention the threat it posed to the illicit tanzanite trade, attempted to disrupt the new project and persuade AFGEM to withdraw.

The long-simmering tensions erupted in April 2001, when a bomb was set off in the new mining plant, killing nobody, but causing large-scale material damage nonetheless. Later in the same month, AFGEM security guards opened fire on a group of 300 irate miners who had invaded the plant, killing one trespasser and causing serious injury to nine. When the Minister for Energy and Minerals visited the scene a few days later, the trespassers claimed to have been protesting against AFGEM's alleged complicity in the alleged death of 20 miners who were buried alive. AFGEM refuted the claims as pure fabrication, part of a smear campaign designed to discredit them and protect the illicit tanzanite trade. The result of the official investigation into the incident has yet to be released.

The tanzanite plot took a new and wholly unexpected twist in late December 2001, when press reports linked four of the men convicted on charges relating to the 1998 US embassy bombings in Nairobi and Dar es Salaam with the illicit tanzanite trade. Amid wild speculation that the underground tanzanite trade was funding Osama bin Laden and his al-Qaeda organisation, three major US jewellery dealers announced a total boycott on the purchase or sale of the gem. Among them, ironically, was the retailer that had first placed it in the spotlight back in 1967. Tiffany & Co publicly conceded a lack of hard evidence supporting the bin Laden link, but announced that it 'troubled' them regardless. By the end of January 2002, the price of tanzanite dropped to a third of its 2001 level.

The Tanzanian government elected to suspend operations at Mererani until the claims were investigated. At a Tucson trade fair in February 2002, the American Gem Trade Association and the Tanzanian Minister of Energy and Minerals signed a protocol that placed significant new controls on local access to the tanzanite mines. After the protocol was signed, the US State Department praised Tanzania for having 'done everything in its power to assist us in the war against terrorism' and declared it had 'seen no evidence that…any terrorist group is currently using tanzanite sales to finance its efforts or launder money'. Sales of the gem have since boomed, and many specialist stores line the streets of Arusha, while a new museum called the Tanzanite Experience (page 136) has raised the gem's profile. Prices remain volatile, reaching as high as US$750 per carat, depending on the size and quality of the individual gemstone.

TENGERU AND LAKE DULUTI Straddling the Moshi Highway some 10km east of Arusha, Tengeru is an impressively hectic market town reached along a dual carriageway that can usually be covered in 20 minutes in a private vehicle and is serviced by a non-stop stream of dalla dallas (easily picked up at Philips junction). The main attraction here is Lake Duluti, but Tengeru is also the site of a poignant Polish refugee cemetery dating to World War II. It is also home to the Tengeru Cultural Tourism Programme [112 E2] (m +255 754 960176; f tengeru-cultural-tourism), a well-run community-based organisation that offers canoeing trips on and guided hikes around Lake Duluti, Tengeru market tours (Wed & Sat only) and full-day banana and coffee tours leading through valleys, rivers and waterfalls to a local market with an optional overnight stay (US$50pp).

Lake Duluti Nestled in a volcanic crater 12km east of Arusha, pretty Lake Duluti is fed by subterranean springs that rise on the southern footslopes of Mount Meru. Around 60ha in extent and claimed to be hundreds of metres deep, the lake is lined with papyrus beds while the crater walls support a gallery of riparian forest comprising more than 50 tree species. Wildlife associated with this forest includes blue and vervet monkey, monitor lizard and birds such as Hartlaub's turaco, crowned hornbill, silvery-cheeked hornbill, Narina trogon, brown-breasted barbets, African broadbill, little greenbul, black-throated wattle-eye, African paradise flycatcher, white-starred robin and black-breasted apalis. On clear days, good views of Mount Meru and Kilimanjaro can be had from the lakeshore.

The relatively developed northern shore is open to the public and you can enjoy it from the lakeside Duluti Forest Club (page 125), which comprises a restaurant/bar and campsite. For those with an interest in monkeys and birds, a more rewarding option is the 3km circular walking trail through the small but beautiful **Lake Duluti Forest Reserve** [112 E3] (office: ⊕ -3.38298, 36.79286; entrance US$10pp), which protects the southern, eastern and western shores. Services of an optional guide are included in the entrance fee, but a tip will be expected.

Lake Duluti lies on the southern outskirts of Tengeru, from where it is about 1.5km to Duluti Forest Club or the entrance to Lake Duluti Forest Reserve

Canoe trips on Duluti cost around US$35–40 and are operated by **Wayo Africa** (page 135) and the **Tengeru Cultural Tourism Programme** (page 138).

Polish War Refugee Cemetery [112 E3] During World War II, Tengeru was selected as the site of a refugee camp whose 5,000 Polish inhabitants had been deported to Siberian work camps following the German and Russian invasion of Poland in 1939, but then released in 1942 in the wake of Russia's decision to side with the Allies. Around 18,000 Polish refugees were shipped to Mombasa to start a new life in Britain's East African colonies, where Tengeru became the largest of half-a-dozen refugee camps established in what was then Tanganyika. By 1944, the camp at Tengeru was a well-organised agricultural settlement comprising about ten schools, a few hospitals, several Orthodox and Catholic churches, and one synagogue catering to the small Jewish community. The refugees were permitted to go back to Europe after the war ended, but many had little reason to return, and decided to stay on in Tengeru. A well-signposted and well-tended Polish War Cemetery housed within a magnolia-shaded compound in the former refugee camp (now a Livestock Training Institute) contains 143 Christian and five Jewish graves, most of which date to the 1940s, when many freshly arrived refugees succumbed to malaria or influenza. Others are more recent. Indeed, the last surviving member of the refugee community, Edward Wojtowicz, who stayed on in Tengeru for the rest of his days, was buried there in March 2015 following his death at the age of 85.

The cemetery lies about 3km south of Tengeru close to the Old Moshi Road (⊕ -3.38415, 36.80827); a boda-boda from Tengeru market will cost around US$1. Visits can also be arranged through the **Tengeru Cultural Tourism Programme** (page 138).

NKOARANGA COFFEE WALKS [112 E2] A company called **Wild Tracks** (m +255 784 420342/416317; w wild-tracks.com) runs informative coffee walks on a local organic and fair-trade farm in the village of Nkoaranga, which lies on the fertile Mount Meru footslopes 25km east of Arusha. Tours incorporate a visit to the oldest Lutheran church on Mount Meru, a visit to a primary or secondary school and to small subsistence farms (shambas) where local people grow various vegetables and fruits. The farms visited are all part of the organic Aranga co-operative and you'll be shown the entire process from planting saplings to picking the beans and roasting and grinding them. Groups of 1/2/3/4/5+ pay a fee of US$120/70/60/48/43 per person, inclusive of a traditional buffet lunch, a bag of fresh Tanzanian coffee and pickup from your hotel.

MESERANI SNAKE PARK [112 A2] (m + 255 0754 440800; w meseranisnakepark.com; ⌚ 07.30–18.00 daily; entrance US$15pp) Situated 25km out of Arusha along the main Serengeti Road, this long-serving establishment combines a snake park (home to more than 40 species including the deadly venomous black mamba and red spitting cobra) with a Maasai Cultural Museum. It also operates a free snakebite clinic. Other facilities include a popular campsite (US$8pp) and a characterful bar and restaurant serving inexpensive burgers, toasted sandwiches and the like.

CULTURAL TOURISM PROGRAMMES A number of cultural tourism programmes have been implemented around Arusha and any one of them makes for an excellent half- or full-day excursion offering an opportunity to experience something of rural Africa away from the slick lodges and main safari circuit. Several of these programmes also offer the opportunity to spend a night in a village, although it should be stressed that accommodation of this sort is not up to accepted tourist-class standards. Of the various programmes, the one at Longido can be easily visited on public transport, but the rest are only realistically visited in a private vehicle. Alternatively, ask your operator to tag a visit to a cultural programme onto your main safari. Half-day to full-day modules and activities offered by the various programmes typically cost around US$30–60 per person, in many cases dependent to some extent on group size. For more details, visit the Cultural Tourism Office in the Old Boma (page 133) or check out the detailed website w tanzaniaculturaltourism.com.

Mkuru Camel Safari [112 F2] (m +255 784 472475/724498; w tanzaniaculturaltourism.com) This well-organised set-up specialises in camelback treks ranging from a day outing into the wildlife-rich plains towards Longido to a week-long trek to Ol Doinyo Lengai and Lake Natron. Activities run out of the down-to-earth and reasonably priced Mkuru Camel Camp, which lies 55km from Arusha, on the northern border of Arusha National Park, at the northern base of Mount Meru, near the village of Ngare Nanyuki. The camp stands close to the pyramidal Ol Doinyo Landare (literally 'Mountain of Goats') and offers great views towards Kilimanjaro and Meru.

Longido [112 A1] (**m** +255 788 295390; **e** touryman1@yahoo.com; **w** tanzaniaculturaltourism.com; **f** longidoculturaltourism) Very accessible to independent travellers, Longido is a great option for those who want to spend time among the Maasai. There are three different modules: a half-day bird walk through the Maasai Plains, a full-day ascent of the 2,637m peak of Mount Longido, and a two-day variant that involves camping out overnight in the green Kimokouwa Valley. On all modules, you can expect to see a variety of birds, as well as larger game (gazelle, lesser kudu and giraffe) and you'll have an opportunity to interact with local Maasai and learn about their culture. It is worth trying to be in Longido on Wednesday, when a hectic cattle market is held on the village outskirts.

Longido straddles the main road to the Namanga border roughly 100km from Arusha, and there's plenty of public transport there. The tourist project maintains an inexpensive guesthouse 100m from the main road, or you can arrange to pitch a tent at a Maasai boma. Cheap Tanzanian fare and cold beers are available from a few small restaurants and bars on the main road.

Ng'iresi [112 D2] (**m** + 255 754 320966; **w** arusha-ngiresi.com) Situated 7km from Arusha town, the traditional Wa-Arusha village of Ng'iresi lies on the Mount Meru foothills and is surrounded by fast-flowing streams, small waterfalls and relict forest patches. Nearby Lekimana Hill offers good views over the Maasai Steppe (all the way to Kilimanjaro on a clear day), while Kivesi Hill is an extinct volcano whose forested slopes support a variety of birds and small mammals. Three different walking modules offer insights into the local culture and agricultural practices, and are inclusive of meals prepared by the Juhudi Women's Group and guided activities. There is no public transport to Ng'iresi, so you must either set up a visit through a safari company or make arrangements with a private vehicle.

Mulala [112 F1] (**m** +255 763 969742/767 378951; **w** agapetourism.com) Mulala, set at an altitude of 1,450m on the footslopes of Mount Meru about 30km from Arusha, has a well-organised cultural tourism programme run by the local Agape Women's Group. Several short walks can be undertaken in this fertile agricultural area, which produces coffee, bananas and other fruit and vegetables. Landmarks include the forest-fringed Marisha River, which is home to a variety of birds and monkeys, and to Mazungu Lake, where it is said that a mzungu (white person) was

TANZANIA'S GREAT TREK

Among Germany's more improbable – and less successful – attempts to populate the Arusha area with Europeans was the sponsored settlement of 100 Boer families, mostly of German descent, in the aftermath of South Africa's divisive Anglo–Boer War. In 1904, the Germans arranged for the Boers to be taken by boat to Tanga, from where they travelled to Arusha by ox-wagon. When the oxen all succumbed to tsetse-borne disease, the Germans provided the Boers with teams of local Africans as a substitute. The families were granted large ranches, mainly around Ol Doinyo Sambu on the northern slopes of Mount Meru, but most of them fell out with their benefactors and eventually packed up their ox-wagons to head across the border into Kenya, where several settled in the Eldoret area. A neatly whitewashed stone monument to this latter-day Great Trek still stands in a field near Ol Doinyo Sambu, visible from the road between Arusha and Longido.

once lured to his death by a demon. Another local place of interest is Mama Anna's dairy, which supplies cheese to several upmarket hotels in Arusha.

Monduli Juu [112 A2] (m + 255 786 799688; f mondulijuucultural) Situated 50km west of Arusha, the Monduli Hills rise to an altitude of 2,660m from the Rift Valley floor and offer superb views to Kilimanjaro, Meru and Ol Doinyo Lengai. Monduli Juu is the collective name for a cluster of four Maasai villages, one of which stands alongside a sacred crater that betrays the volcanic origins of the hills. The cultural programme here offers programmes ranging from a few hours to several days in duration. The hike to Monduli Peak passes through montane forest that supports plenty of monkeys, birds and butterflies, as well as relict populations of elephant and buffalo (an armed ranger is mandatory). Other attractions include visits to a traditional healer, Naramatu bead factory and a Maasai boma visit. In addition to guiding tours, the cultural tourism programme here can arrange transport from Arusha, meals and camping sites.

ARUSHA NATIONAL PARK

Northern Tanzania's most accessible wildlife destination, Arusha National Park (m +255 689 262363; e arusha@tanzaniaparks.go.tz) lies a mere 45 minutes' drive from the eponymous town, and it's even closer to the many lodges in the vicinity of Tengeru and Usa River, making it an easy target for a half- or full-day trip at the start of a safari. Despite this, it remains somewhat neglected by the safari industry. The main reason for this is that the park offers relatively limited possibilities to see the so-called Big Five: buffalos are common here, and you stand a fair chance of seeing elephants, but leopards are scarce, and lion and rhino absent altogether.

This one perceived failing aside, however, Arusha National Park is a quite extraordinary conservation area. Established in 1960 and recently extended to cover a total of 542km², the park is dominated by Mount Meru, which rises on the western boundary to an altitude of 4,562m, making it Africa's fifth-highest massif. Meru is a popular goal for walkers, whether they opt for a half-day stroll into the partially collapsed volcanic caldera or undertake a multi-day hike to the jagged summit. For non-hikers, a cluster of attractive lakes can be explored by road or on organised canoe trips, with stirring views of Kilimanjaro looming large on the eastern skyline, while the spectacular forest-swathed Ngurdoto Crater is an intact caldera reminiscent of a smaller version of Ngorongoro.

FLORA AND FAUNA Despite its relatively small size, Arusha National Park incorporates a diversity of habitats reflecting its wide altitudinal variations. Lower-lying areas support a cover of moist savannah, but the slopes of Mount Meru and Ngurdoto are swathed in evergreen montane rainforest, giving way to alpine moorland at higher altitudes. The forest around Ngurdoto is one of the best places in Tanzania to see forest primates such as Kilimanjaro colobus and blue monkey. Elsewhere, other common mammals include hippo, giraffe, zebra, buffalo, warthog, bushbuck, common waterbuck and olive baboon. Look out, too, for Kirk's dik-dik, an attractively marked small antelope which is usually seen in pairs and seems to be less skittish here than elsewhere in Tanzania. Around 200 elephants are more or less resident in the park, but they tend to stick to the forest zone of Mount Meru. Elephant sightings used to be infrequent, but these days they are quite often encountered in the far south, especially when the Ridon Track is open to vehicles.

WEST KILIMANJARO

Also sometimes referred to as South Amboseli, this vaguely defined area is essentially the wedge of dry savannah country that divides the northwestern base of Kilimanjaro from the legendary Amboseli National Park in neighbouring Kenya. Some 2–3 hours' drive northeast of Arusha, it consists of several blocks of Maasai community land that recently amalgamated to form the 1,800km^2 Enduimet Wildlife Management Area (EWMA), where local pastoralists live alongside the wildlife that ranges through this cross-border ecosystem. A major attraction here is the superb close-up view of Kilimanjaro, but the vast horizon is studded with several other notable peaks, including Mount Meru, Mount Longido and Namanga Mountain (on the Kenyan side of the eponymous border crossing to Nairobi). The area also retains a genuine wilderness feel, since only two small permanent tented camps are situated within it.

Despite being surrounded by dramatic peaks, much of West Kilimanjaro is composed of very flat land where the fine volcanic soil once formed the bed of Lake Amboseli (then twice as big as present-day Lake Manyara) before it started to dry up some 10,000–15,000 years ago. As the lake dried it left calcareous deposits that were later mined by the Germans in order to make the famous meerschaum tobacco pipes. The abandoned pits left behind by the open-cast mines are now an important part of the ecosystem, since they trap rainwater, thereby providing drinking water for the Maasai cattle as well as the wildlife at the driest times of the year.

Ecologically, the EWMA supports a near-pristine cover of lightly wooded acacia savannah where Maasai herdsmen co-exist with a remarkable variety of wildlife, including wildebeest, zebra, eland, impala, Grant's gazelle, hartebeest and yellow baboon, as well as one of the few Tanzanian populations of the remarkable stretch-necked gerenuk. Predator densities are low, but cheetah and lion are still present and quite often observed. The area also forms part of a migration corridor

The only large predators are leopard and spotted hyena. More than 400 bird species have been recorded, including a wide variety of aquatic and forest specialists.

FEES AND FURTHER INFORMATION A detailed booklet, *Arusha National Park*, containing information on every aspect of the park's ecology and wildlife, is widely available in Arusha. All fees, including the park entrance fee of US$50 (dropping to US$45 from 15 March to 15 May) plus 18% VAT per person per 24 hours, as well as camping or guide fees as applicable, must be paid with a Visa or Mastercard, or one of the Tanapa cards that can be issued at any Exim Bank. No other cards are accepted, nor is cash.

GETTING THERE AND AWAY Ngongongare Gate lies on the park's southern boundary about 30km (1hr) from Arusha on a good surfaced road. To get there, follow the Moshi Highway east to Usa River, then take the turn-off signposted for Arusha National Park and continue north for 8km to the gate. From here, it's another 15km on a fair dirt road (normally navigable in an ordinary saloon car, but a 4x4 may be necessary after rain) to Hatari Lodge. Technically, it is possible to reach Ngongongare Gate on public transport, but it would be practically impossible to explore beyond this without private transport.

Most people visit Arusha National Park on an organised half- or full-day safari, which can be arranged through any operator in Arusha town. Day hikes into Meru used by the local elephant population – noted for its even temperament and the immense tusks of the bulls – to cross between the Kenyan part of the Amboseli ecosystem and the forested slopes of Kilimanjaro. Many impressive bulls are resident throughout the year, but numbers peak in June and July, after the rains, when the smaller family groups merge to form 100-strong herds. This also is when mating takes place, and irascible bulls follow the family herds accompanied by a fanfare of trumpeting.

WHERE TO STAY

Kambi ya Tembo ⊕ -2.82455, 37.18771; w twctanzania.com. Literally translating as 'Camp of Elephants', this aptly named lodge lies in the Sinya Concession bordering Amboseli National Park. Comfortable standing tents have walk-in nets, hot showers & private balconies facing Kilimanjaro or the Amboseli Plains. Activities include game drives, hikes on the Kilimanjaro foothills & Maasai village visits. **$$$$$$**

Shu'mata Camp ⊕ -2.84337, 36.92417; w hatari.travel. With the same dynamic owners as Hatari Lodge (page 125), this exclusive tented camp sprawls across the eponymous hill, whose Maasai name translates as something close to 'heaven'. It offers panoramic views over plains capped by Kilimanjaro to the southeast & Longido & Namanga to the northwest, marred only by the fierce winds that often blow in from the direction of Kilimanjaro. The 5 large & stylish standing tents all have a writing desk, colourful drapes & matting & a curvaceous adobe-style hot shower. The camp has a flexible attitude to activities, which include game drives (night & day), guided walks & cultural visits. Game densities don't compare with the national parks but there is plenty of wildlife around & the immersive sense of isolation more than compensates. **$$$$$$$**

Crater can usually be arranged on arrival at Ngongongare Gate, but overnight climbs, which require a minimum of three days, must be arranged in advance through a registered safari operator.

WHERE TO STAY AND EAT *Map, page 144*

Arusha National Park is no more than an hour's drive from any of the accommodation options listed earlier in this chapter, so the vast majority of visitors overnight in Arusha or Usa River and explore the park on half- or full-day safari from there. However, if you are seeking a bush experience, there's a lot to be said for staying at one of the handful of lodges based within the park or on along its borders, as listed on page 125.

WHAT TO SEE AND DO If your time is limited, you can get a pretty good feel for the park's two most accessible geographic features – Ngurdoto Crater and the Momella Lakes – on one extended morning or afternoon game drive. Those with a full day, or who are staying in the park overnight, should also think about the wonderful and surprisingly undemanding day hike into Meru Crater. The full ascent of Mount Meru takes at least three days and is covered separately on page 146.

Ngurdoto Crater Coming from Arusha, a good first goal is this fully intact 3km-wide, 400m-deep volcanic caldera, which has often been described as a mini

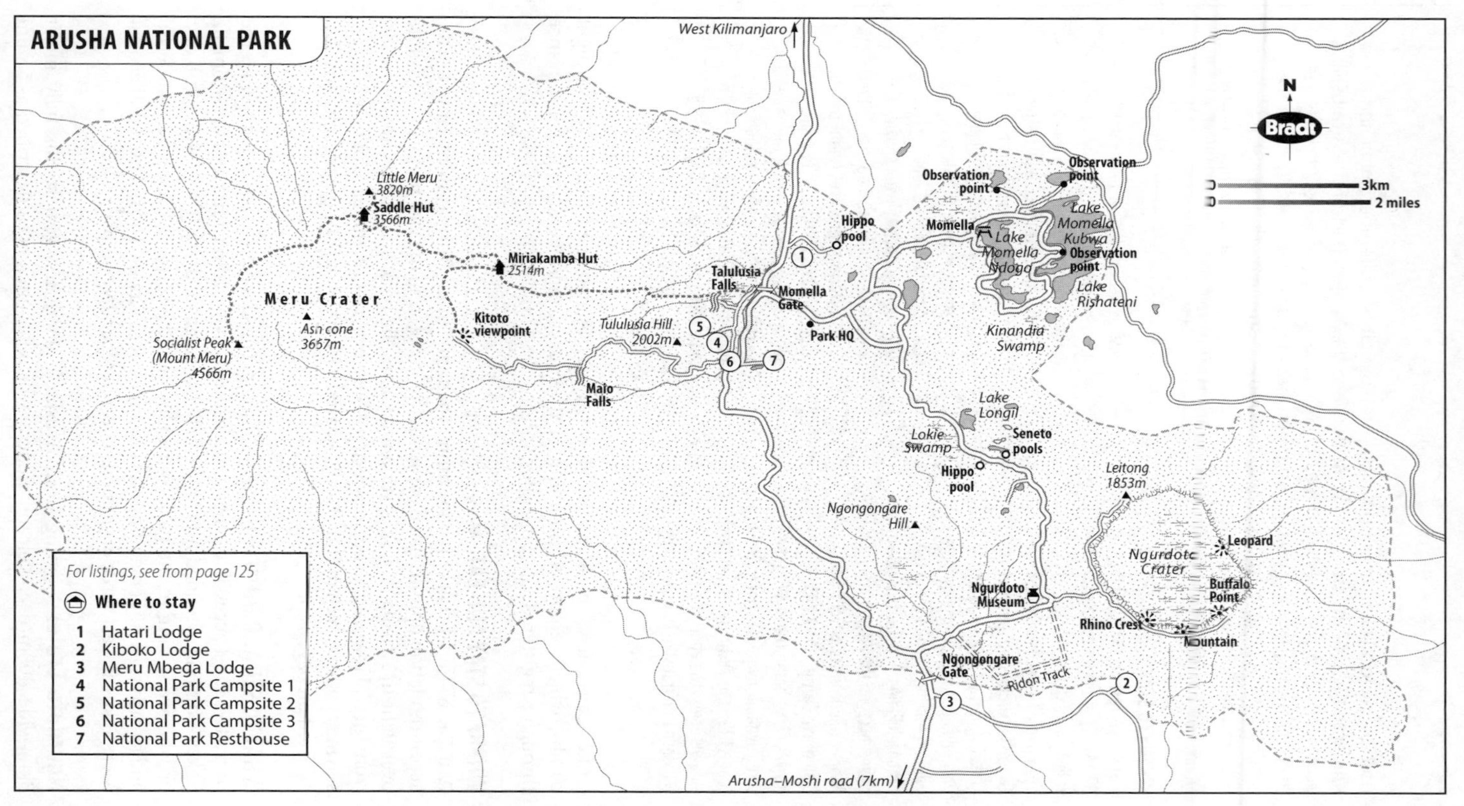

ARUSHA NATIONAL PARK
West Kilimanjaro
N
Bradt
3km
2 miles
Little Meru 3820m
Saddle Hut 3566m
Miriakamba Hut 2514m
Meru Crater
Ash cone 3657m
Socialist Peak (Mount Meru) 4566m
Kitoto viewpoint
Tululusia Hill 2002m
Maio Falls
Talulusia Falls
Momella Gate
Park HQ
Hippo pool
Observation point
Observation point
Observation point
Momella
Lake Momella Ndogo
Lake Momella Kubwa
Lake Rishateni
Kinandia Swamp
Lake Longil
Lokie Swamp
Seneto pools
Hippo pool
Ngongongare Hill
Leitong 1853m
Ngurdoto Crater
Leopard
Buffalo Point
Rhino Crest
Mountain
Ngurdoto Museum
Ngongongare Gate
Ridon Track
Arusha–Moshi road (7km)
For listings, see from page 125
Where to stay
1 Hatari Lodge
2 Kiboko Lodge
3 Meru Mbega Lodge
4 National Park Campsite 1
5 National Park Campsite 2
6 National Park Campsite 3
7 National Park Resthouse

Ngorongoro. No roads descend into the crater, but the views from the forest-fringed rim over the lush crater floor are fantastic. A large herd of buffalo is usually resident on the crater floor, and with binoculars it is normally possible to pick out other mammals, such as warthog, baboon and various antelope. Look out, too, for augur buzzard, Verreaux's eagle and other cliff-associated raptors soaring above the crater. The forest around the crater rim harbours many troops of Kilimanjaro colobus and blue monkey, as well as a good variety of birds including several types of hornbill and the gorgeous Hartlaub's turaco and cinnamon-chested bee-eater. If the view from the top isn't sufficient, the park offers guided hikes to the crater floor in the dry season; these cost US$30 per person, take around 3 hours return, and should be booked at Ngongongare Gate at last one day in advance.

Momella Lakes Underground streams feed this group of shallow alkaline lakes, which lie to the north of Ngurdoto; each lake has a different mineral content and is slightly different in colour. In the late evening and early morning, it is often possible to stand at one of the viewpoints over the lakes and see Kilimanjaro on the eastern horizon and Mount Meru to the west. This is the best part of the park for large mammals such as buffalo and hippo, while a wide variety of aquatic birds can be seen, including various herons, waterfowl (this is the best site in Tanzania for the otherwise uncommon maccoa duck), waders, flamingos, pelicans and little grebe. A very tranquil way to enjoy the birdlife and scenery is the canoe safaris offered by Wayo Africa (US$35pp; page 135).

Meru Crater drive and hike Best undertaken with a reasonably early start and a packed lunch, this half- to full-day outing will be a highlight of any visit to Arusha National Park, though an armed ranger (US$20pp) must be collected at one of the entrance gates if you want to hike into the crater or drive further up the mountain than Kitoto. The first leg, about an hour's drive to Kitoto, climbs through a beautiful stretch of primary forest with lots of tall trees, ferns and epiphytes, a good place to look for elephant, Kilimanjaro colobus, blue monkey, eastern tree hyrax, Harvey's red duiker (a small antelope associated with montane forests of the East African interior) and the raucous and very beautiful Hartlaub's turaco. At one point the road passes through the famous **Fig Tree Arch**, a natural formation at the base of an immense strangler fig large enough for a Land Cruiser to pass under (provided no heads are sticking out of the roof, take note). It is also worth diverting to the pretty Maio Waterfall, which lies about 50m from the ascent road and forms a nice spot for a picnic lunch.

From Kitoto Car Park (⊕ -3.24260, 36.79157), which lies at 2,490m, a popular option is a walking loop to Miriakamba Hut (the first overnight stop used by hikers to the summit), which covers about 3km in each direction and should take around 2 hours in total. The hike is not too demanding in terms of climbing, because the maximum elevation you reach on the collapsed eastern crater wall is 2,600m. Assuming conditions aren't too misty, the scenery is truly spectacular and embraces close-up views of the 3,667m-high ash cone at the centre of the crater, as well as the towering 1,500m cliff that forms the crater's western wall and incorporates Mount Meru's highest peak. The first half of the walk passes through Afromontane forest, but once you breach the crater wall, you'll be in more open vegetation. Wildlife is scarce at this altitude, but you may well see pairs of klipspringer on the rock slopes, as well as cliff-nesting raptors such as Verreaux's eagle, augur buzzard, and the scarce and eagerly sought lammergeier (bearded vulture).

HIKING MOUNT MERU

Arusha National Park's tallest landmark and most publicised attraction is Mount Meru, an active stratovolcano whose upper slopes and peak lie within its boundaries. The Arusha and Meru people deify Mount Meru as a rain god, but it is unlikely that any local person actually reached the peak prior to Fritz Jaeger's pioneering ascent in 1904. Mount Meru, like nearby Kilimanjaro, is a product of the volcanic activity that formed the Great Rift Valley 15 million–20 million years ago, and it attained a height similar to that of its loftier neighbour until 250,000 years ago, when a massive eruption tore out its eastern wall. The most recent major eruption on Meru took place around 7,800 years ago, when the current ash cone was formed. A less cataclysmic lava flow was documented as recently as 1879, and while there is no particular reason to suppose anything dramatic will happen in the foreseeable future, a recurrence is possible at any time, with potentially devastating results for people living in the vicinity.

Often overlooked by tourists because it is 'only' the fifth-highest mountain in Africa, Meru is no substitute for Kilimanjaro for achievement-orientated travellers. On the other hand, those who climb both mountains invariably enjoy Meru more. Also going in its favour, Meru is less crowded than Kilimanjaro, considerably less expensive and – although steeper and almost as cold – less likely to engender the health problems associated with Kilimanjaro's higher altitude. Meru is just as interesting as Kilimanjaro from a biological point of view and, because comparatively few people climb it, you are more likely to see forest animals and plains game on the lower slopes.

Meru can technically be climbed in two days, but three or four days is normal, allowing time to explore Meru Crater and to look at wildlife and plants. All climbs must be arranged through a registered safari company (page 134). The going rate for a budget three- to four-day hike is around US$750–1,100 per person, a large chunk of which is swallowed up by national park fees. Meru is very cold at night, and you will need to bring clothing adequate for alpine conditions. In the rainy season, mountain boots are necessary. At other times, good walking shoes will probably be adequate. The best time to climb is from December to February, but June to August is also good. Accommodation is in simple but comfortable bunkhouses at Miriakamba Hut and Saddle Hut. These might be fully booked during peak seasons, in which case the only alternative is camping.

DAY 1: MOMELLA GATE (1,500M) TO MIRIAKAMBA HUT (2,514M) This relatively gentle 14km ascent usually takes around 4 hours and passes through well-developed woodland where there is a good chance of seeing large animals such as giraffe. At an altitude of about 2,000m you enter the forest zone. This gives way to more open vegetation as you breach the collapsed eastern crater wall about an hour before arriving at Miriakamba Hut. If you leave Momella early, there will be ample time in the afternoon to explore Meru Crater, the centrepiece of which is an ash cone that rises more that 1,000m above the crater floor. Even taller is the 1,500m cliff that forms the western crater wall. The ash cone is an hour from Miriakamba Hut, and can be climbed.

DAY 2: MIRIAKAMBA HUT (2,514M) TO SADDLE HUT (3,566M) Shorter than the previous day's hike at 6km, but considerably steeper and at higher altitude, this hike should take around 3 hours. It initially passes through forest, where there is a good chance of seeing Kilimanjaro colobus. At about 3,000m, you enter a moorland zone similar to that on Kilimanjaro. It is not unusual to see Kilimanjaro peeking above the clouds from Saddle Hut. If you feel energetic, you can climb Little Meru (3,820m) in the afternoon. It takes about an hour each way from Saddle Hut.

DAY 3: SADDLE HUT (3,566M) TO THE SUMMIT (4,562M) AND BACK You will need to rise very early to ascend the 4,562m peak, probably at around 02.00. This ascent follows a very narrow ridge above the inner crater and takes 4–5 hours. It is then a 2–3-hour walk back down to Saddle Hut.

DAY 4: SADDLE HUT (3,566M) TO MOMELLA GATE (1,500M) The last day retraces the route taken on the first two days, but in reverse, and usually takes about 4 hours.

6

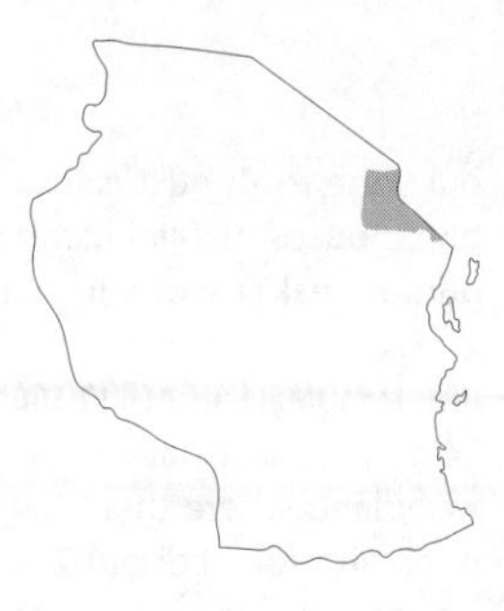

Moshi and the Kilimanjaro Foothills

Situated at the heart of a major coffee-growing region 80km east of Arusha, the smaller town of Moshi – population around 200,000 – is an intrinsically unremarkable commercial centre salvaged from anonymity by its spectacular location below Mount Kilimanjaro.

When the white-helmeted dome of Africa's tallest mountain emerges from its customary blanket of cloud, most usually at dusk or dawn, Moshi boasts a backdrop as imposing and dramatic as any in Africa. And yet, the teasing proximity of that iconic snow-capped silhouette notwithstanding, Moshi is not the cool, breezy highland settlement you might expect it to be. Indeed, situated at an altitude of 810m, it is generally far hotter than Arusha, and not as drizzly, with a hint of stickiness in the air that recalls the coast.

Stirring views of Kilimanjaro aside, there is little to do or see in Moshi that you couldn't do or see in any similarly sized African market town. But it's a pleasant enough place to explore on foot, with an interesting central market area, and far less tourist-oriented than Arusha, despite the inevitable attention paid to any visiting *mazungu* by a coterie of (mostly very affable) flycatchers offering relatively cheap 'n' dodgy safaris and Kilimanjaro climbs.

In addition to being an established springboard for multi-day Kilimanjaro hikes (a subject covered more fully from page 165), Moshi is a useful base for several worthwhile day trips in the vicinity of the mountain. These include cultural tours and waterfall tours in the forest-fringed village of Marangu, a visit to the spectacular Lake Chala (nested in an old volcanic caldera) and a high-altitude day hike on the Shira Plateau on Kilimanjaro's western slopes, and are covered later in this chapter from page 156.

HISTORY

Moshi and the slopes of nearby Kilimanjaro are home to the Chagga, a Bantu-speaking agricultural people whose ancestors probably settled there in the 15th century. Traditionally, the Chagga have no tradition of central leadership, and prior to the mid 19th century the area was carved up into around three dozen small patrilineal Umangi (chieftaincies) that co-existed reasonably peacefully.

This changed under the rule of Mangi (King) Rindi Mandara, who came to power in the late 1850s and whose capital, Moshi (now known as Old Moshi), stands on the footslopes of Kilimanjaro 10km northeast of its modern namesake. Like so many other 19th-century leaders in the Tanzanian interior, Mandara consolidated

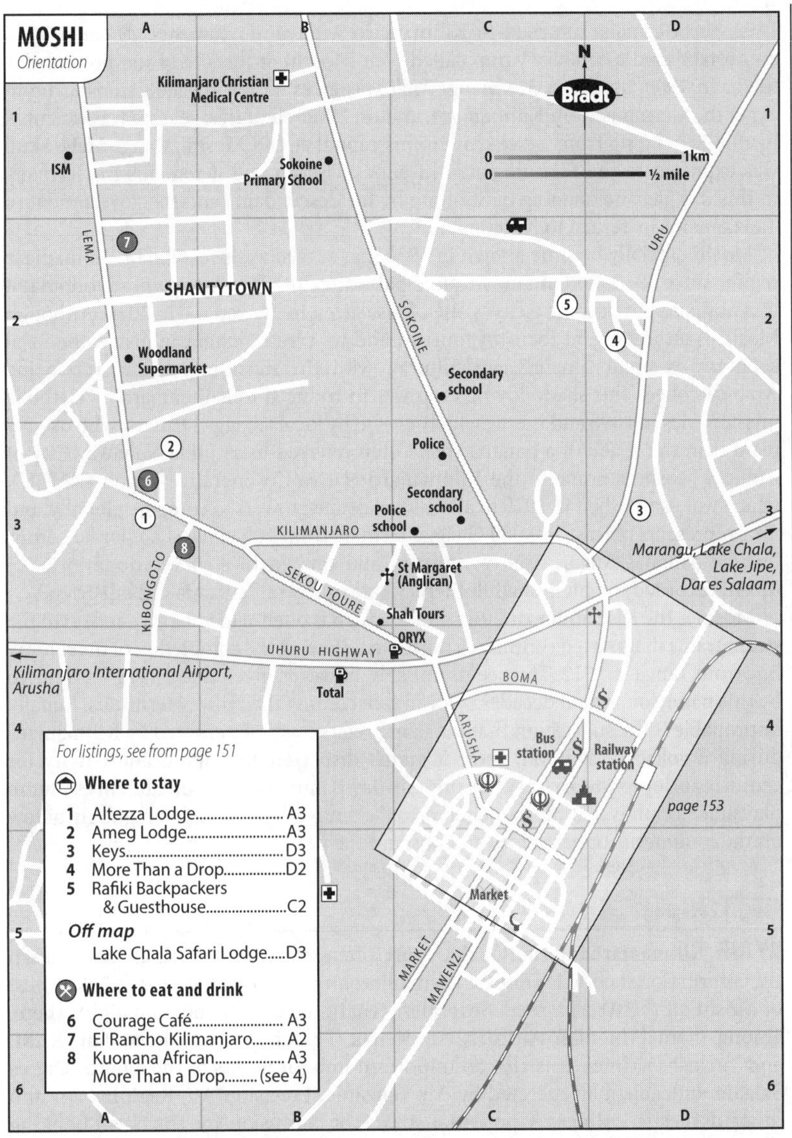

his power through his links with the Arab slavers, leading ruthless raids on rival villages to sell the captives to passing traders for firearms and other imported valuables, and levying high taxes from caravans that passed through Chagga territory to avoid Maasailand. A skilled diplomat, Mandara made a favourable impression on John Kirk, the British Consul in Zanzibar in the 1870s and 1880s, and signed a treaty with Carl Peters in 1885, one that led to the Germans offering him support in crushing his main local political rival, Mangi Sina of Kibosha.

Mandara died of natural causes in 1891 and was succeeded by his son Meli, a staunch opponent of colonialism who led a successful attack on the Germans in 1892, killing their governor and expelling them from Kilimanjaro region. In August

1893, the Germans returned to Kilimanjaro with reinforcements, defeated Meli, and established a military camp called Neu-Moschi at the site of the present-day town. In 1900, aged just 33, Mangi Meli was arrested for allegedly conspiring to expel the Germans from Kilimanjaro, and on 2 March of that year he was executed by public hanging from a tree close to his capital at Old Moshi. Mangi Meli's skull was exported to the Ethnological Museum of Berlin and it remains in Germany to this day, despite ongoing petitioning by his descendants and the government of Tanzania for its return to Kilimanjaro.

Moshi officially became a town in 1956, has served as the capital of Kilimanjaro region since 1963, and attained municipal status in 1988. Along with Dodoma, it was upgraded to become a city – one of just seven in Tanzania – in 2016. Although Moshi is an important focus of tourism and to a lesser extent industry, the local economy is predominantly agricultural, with the most important crop being Arabica coffee. This shade-loving crop was introduced to Kilimanjaro by Catholic missionaries in 1898 and is now widely grown by local Chagga farmers, who usually plant it in the shade of a banana tree. Often referred to as Jiji la Kahawa (City of Coffee), Moshi is home to the Kilimanjaro Native Co-operative Union (KNCU), which was established in 1929 to allow local coffee growers to compete globally, and now represents at least 150,000 Chagga farmers from 100 villages. Other key crops include bananas, sugar, sisal, pyrethrum and timber. In a survey done in 2005, Moshi recorded the highest adult literacy rate of any of Tanzania's 129 districts.

Moshi is the Kiswahili word for smoke, which is often said to be an allusion to the steam trains that started running to the town following the completion of the railway line from Tanga in 1912. This seems unlikely, however, given that Moshi was known by this name for several decades prior to it becoming the railway terminus. Equally improbable is the suggestion that the name refers to smoke emitted by Kilimanjaro during a volcanic eruption, since it hadn't displayed any significant activity for centuries prior to the arrival of its present-day Bantu-speaking inhabitants. A more plausible notion is that the name refers to the smoke-like mists that regularly billow on the mountain's upper slopes and obscure the peak.

GETTING THERE AND AWAY

BY AIR **Kilimanjaro International Airport**, often referred to locally as KIA, though the international code is JRO (**w** kilimanjaroairport.go.tz), lies about 35km west of Moshi off the Arusha road. Several international carriers operate flights there, among them Ethiopian Airlines, Air Kenya, Flydubai, Qatar, Rwandair, KLM, and Turkish Airlines. It is also an important hub for flights to the likes of Dar es Salaam and Zanzibar operated by Air Tanzania, Precision Air, Regional Air and other domestic airlines. A potential source of confusion for travellers booking their own flights is that flights to the Serengeti and other national parks on the northern safari circuit don't leave from KIA, but from **Arusha Airport** on the outskirts of Arusha.

Most tourists flying into KIA are met by their hotel or safari company. However, there are plenty of **taxis** waiting to meet all flights, and these usually charge around US$30 for a transfer to Moshi.

BY ROAD The town centre runs southwards from the main surfaced road to Dar es Salaam 80km east of Arusha. The driving time from Arusha in a **private vehicle** is at least 90 minutes, but it may take longer in heavy traffic, or if you are stopped for speeding (watch out for those 50km/h signs at the start of most villages) or under any other pretext at one of the many police blocks en route. It is possible to drive from Nairobi (Kenya) to Moshi via Namanga and Arusha in about 6 hours. The driving time between Moshi and Dar es Salaam is at least 8 hours.

Express coaches between Dar es Salaam and Moshi take 8–10 hours, usually with a 20-minute lunch break in Korogwe or Mombo. The best operators are Dar Express (m +255 754 946155/487261/049395) and Kilimanjaro Express (m +255 767 334301/715 144301/765 064587), which operate luxury and VIP services for around US$15–18 per person. Alternatively, numerous cheaper and inferior bus services leave from the chaotic main bus station [153 C4], mostly in the morning.

There are also plenty of direct buses between Moshi and Tanga, which can drop you off at Same, Mombo, Muheza and other junction towns en route. In addition, a steady flow of **buses** and **dalla dallas** connects Arusha to Moshi, charging around US$3 and taking up to 2 hours, as well as to Marangu. There is no need to book ahead for these routes as vehicles will leave when they fill up, but be warned that there is a high incidence of accidents, particularly with minibuses.

Most **shuttle bus** services between Nairobi and Arusha continue on to Moshi, or start there, a total journey time of 6–7 hours, and charge around US$25 per person. The pick is the **Riverside Shuttle** (m +255 754 270089/757 091120; w riverside-shuttle.com) which leaves Moshi at 06.30 and Nairobi at 08.00 daily.

WHERE TO STAY

Moshi's compact town centre is liberally scattered with dozens of budget hotels, the pick of which are listed on page 152. Smarter hotels are mostly concentrated in Shantytown, a misleadingly named residential suburb whose leafy avenues lie a short walk north of the town centre and the main Arusha Highway. For those who prefer not to stay in town, we also list a few select properties in Marangu, Machame and elsewhere on the footslopes of Kilimanjaro.

UPMARKET

Ameg Lodge [149 A3] Off Lema Rd; m +255 754 058268; w ameglodge.com. Probably the top place to stay in Moshi, this stylish modern lodge in Shantytown comprises 20 large, airy semi-detached rooms set in a 2ha plot with views of Kilimanjaro. Rooms have DSTV, fan & private balcony. Amenities include a swimming pool, gym & good restaurant serving Indian & continental cuisine. *From US$85/130 sgl/dbl B&B.* **$$$**

MODERATE

✷ **Altezza Lodge** [149 A3] Sekou Touré Way; m +255 694 407676; w altezza-lodge.com. The closest thing in Moshi to a boutique hotel, Altezza stands in attractive tropical grounds with a tempting swimming pool, & the 9 stylish rooms all come with AC. There's a good restaurant & lounge decorated with colourful local artworks. It's very competitively priced for a hotel of this quality & often full, so book early. *From US$65/75 sgl/dbl B&B.* **$$**

Bristol Cottages [153 B3] Rindi Ln; m +255 693 975139; w bristolcottages.com. Located close to the bus station, this neat lodge has 17 spacious rooms & cottages with AC, satellite TV, nets & attractive modern décor. Despite the central location, the manicured gardens are secure & peaceful & offer safe parking. An open-sided restaurant serves Asian & continental dishes. *From US$65/95 sgl/dbl B&B.* **$$**

Keys Hotel [149 D3] Uru Rd; m +255 755 486377; w keyshotelstz.com. This long-serving family-run hotel stands in attractive suburban grounds with a swimming pool 1km from the Clock Tower. Popular & well-priced, it offers the choice of rooms in the dbl-storey main building or makuti-roofed garden cottages, all with satellite TV & nets. From *US$86/98 sgl/dbl B&B.* **$$**

Kilimanjaro Crane Hotel [153 C2] Kaunda St; m +255 272 751114; w kilimanjarocranehotel.co.tz. This well-run central high-rise has 30 spacious rooms equipped with AC, DSTV, fridge, private balcony, netting, fan & tub. There's also a green garden, a swimming pool, great rooftop views of Kilimanjaro, a cosmopolitan restaurant, & a well-stocked book & souvenir shop. Good value. *From US$60/80 sgl/dbl B&B*. **$$**

✷ **More Than a Drop** [149 D2] Off Uru Rd; m +255 768 460567; w bnb.morethanadrop.org. There's a real home-away-from-home feel to this unpretentious but very comfortable B&B set in a converted family house in sprawling green grounds (complete with organic vegetable garden) along a quiet side road in Shantytown. All 5 guest rooms are brightly decorated in African style & the attached vegetarian restaurant (page 155) is one of the best in Moshi. Proceeds fund an on-site hospitality school that provides vocational training to disadvantaged young Tanzanian women. *US$43/63 en-suite sgl/dbl or US$39/58 using shared amenities*. **$$**

Moshi Leopard Hotel [153 B7] Market St; w booking.com. Adequate central multi-storey hotel whose 47 clean, tiled rooms have AC, fan, TV & netting. *US$70/80/100 sgl/dbl/suite B&B*. **$$**

BUDGET

Buffalo Hotel [153 C6] New Rd; m +255 765 068295; w booking.com. This clean medium-rise is currently the pick of a cluster of adequate budget hotels dotted around New & Nyerere rds a short walk south of the main bus station. Tiled rooms have fans & nets. The attached restaurant serves tasty Indian & Chinese meals. *From US$10/14 sgl/dbl B&B*. **$**

Climbers Corner [153 B6] Cnr Guinea & Nyerere; m +255 758 555554; w climberscornermoshi.com. Signposted as Kilimanjaro Climbers, this new central hostel has a variety of clean & colourfully decorated private rooms & dorms with fans & nets. The fabulous rooftop bar & restaurant has a sociable vibe & serves a great selection of inexpensive meat & vegetarian dishes. The location is quite noisy, so ask for a room away from the road. *US$8pp dorm. US$25/40 en-suite sgl/dbl or US$20/35 using shared amenities*. **$**

✷ **Rafiki Backpackers & Guesthouse** [149 C2] Off Uru Rd; m +255 714 422500; w rafikibackpackers.com. Set in a quiet corner of Shantytown, this funky & sociable backpackers offers a variety of clean & comfortable dorms & private rooms with nets & fans. There's also a rooftop terrace with views to Kilimanjaro, an affordable bar & restaurant, a swimming pool & an inhouse operator offering competitively priced safaris & mountain climbs. *From US$8pp dorm, US$20/30 sgl/dbl shared bathroom*. **$**

FURTHER AFIELD *Map, page 162, unless otherwise stated*

✷ **Aisha Machame Hotel** Machame road, 20km from Moshi & 35km from Kilimanjaro International Airport; m +255 786 221788; w aishi-machame.com. Formerly part of South Africa's Protea chain, this peaceful retreat comprises 30 well-equipped motel-style rooms, a solar-heated swimming pool & large, thatched restaurant/bar area facing a patch of indigenous forest alive with monkeys & birds. It arranges reliable Kilimanjaro hikes & a variety of day excursions. Good value. *From US$80/90 sgl/dbl B&B*. **$$**

Babylon Lodge Central Marangu, 40km from Moshi; m +255 762 016016; w babylonlodge.com. Situated 500m from Marangu's post office, this compact owner-managed hotel has small but immaculate rooms with a combination tub/shower & ethnic décor. Good value. *From US$60/80 sgl/dbl B&B*. **$$**

Honey Badger Lodge 6km from Moshi on the road to Dar es Salaam; m +255 767 551190; w honeybadgerlodge.com. This friendly family-run lodge stands in a large green compound & combines a rustic, eco-friendly ethos with comfortable accommodation & excellent facilities including a swimming pool, ample parking & a characterful lounge, restaurant & bar. Management can arrange traditional drumming performances & lessons, & day hikes & longer climbs on Kilimanjaro. Proceeds fund the Second Chance Education Centre, which provides secondary schooling to disadvantaged children. *From US$90/110 sgl/dbl B&B*. **$$$**

Kaliwa Lodge Machame road, 25km from Moshi & 40km from Kilimanjaro International Airport; m +255 762 620707; w kaliwalodge.com. This highly praised German owner-managed boutique hotel juxtaposes a stylish modernist Bauhaus architecture against a rural setting on leafy footslopes that offer great views of Kilimanjaro's snow-capped peak. The dining area serves excellent set menus & is decorated with interesting collages & a vast library of English & German books. Listen out for bushbabies calling at night. *US$99/198 sgl/dbl B&B*. **$$$**

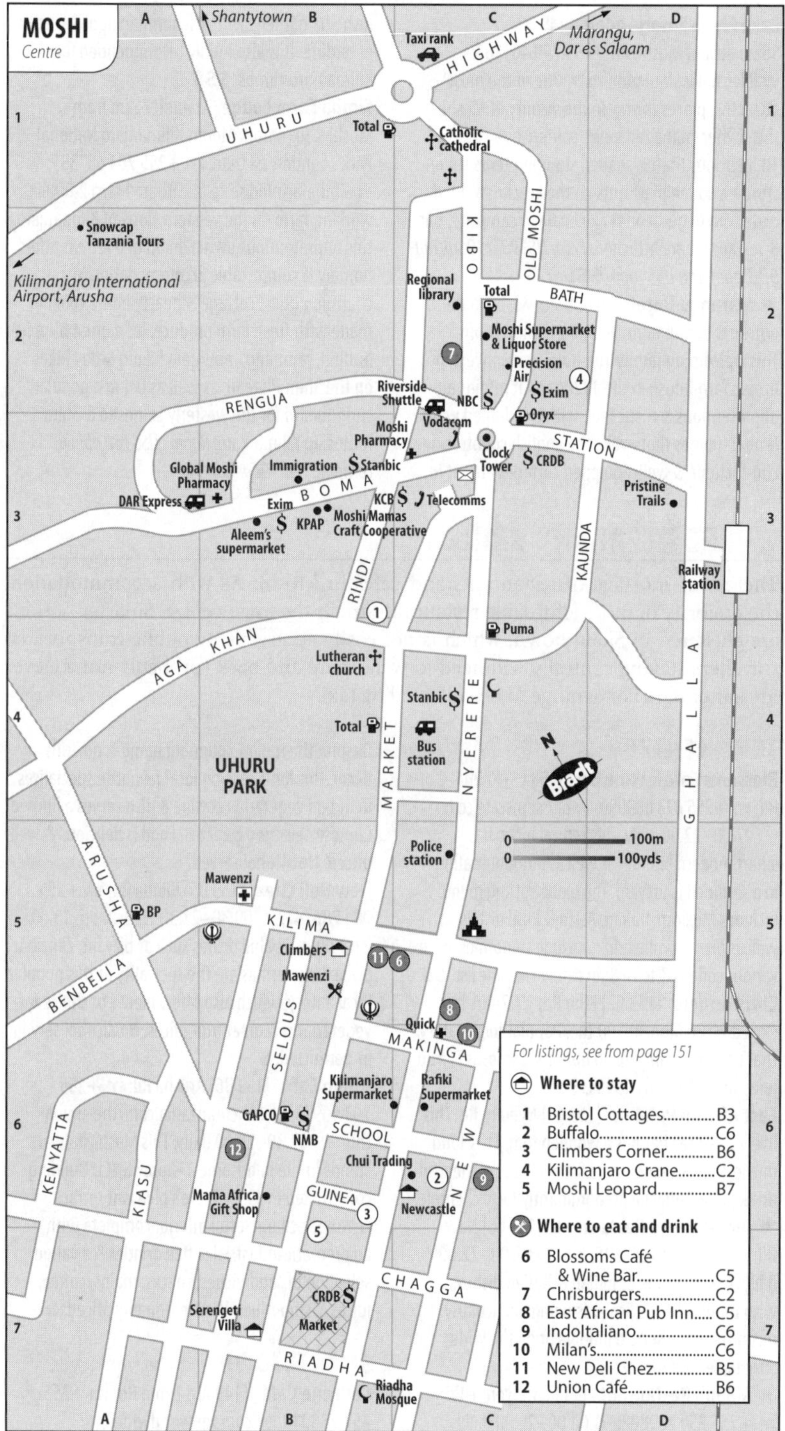
MOSHI
Centre
Shantytown
Marangu,
Dar es Salaam
Kilimanjaro International
Airport, Arusha
Taxi rank
HIGHWAY
UHURU
Total
Catholic
cathedral
Snowcap
Tanzania Tours
KIBO
OLD MOSHI
Regional
library
Total
BATH
Moshi Supermarket
& Liquor Store
Precision
Air
Exim
RENGUA
Riverside
Shuttle
NBC
Oryx
Vodacom
Moshi
Pharmacy
Clock
Tower
STATION
CRDB
Global Moshi
Pharmacy
Immigration
Stanbic
DAR Express
BOMA
Exim
KCB
Telecomms
KPAP
Moshi Mamas
Craft Cooperative
Aleem's
supermarket
Pristine
Trails
KAUNDA
Railway
station
RINDI
AGA KHAN
Puma
Lutheran
church
Stanbic
Total
Bus
station
MARKET
NYERERE
GHALLA
UHURU
PARK
Bradt
0 100m
0 100yds
Police
station
ARUSHA
Mawenzi
BP
KILIMA
BENBELLA
Climbers
Mawenzi
SELOUS
Quick
MAKINGA
Kilimanjaro
Supermarket
Rafiki
Supermarket
GAPCO
NMB
SCHOOL
Chui Trading
MWEN
KENYATTA
KIASU
Mama Africa
Gift Shop
GUINEA
Newcastle
CHAGGA
CRDB
Serengeti
Villa
Market
RIADHA
Riadha
Mosque
For listings, see from page 151
Where to stay
1 Bristol Cottages B3
2 Buffalo C6
3 Climbers Corner B6
4 Kilimanjaro Crane C2
5 Moshi Leopard B7
Where to eat and drink
6 Blossoms Café & Wine Bar C5
7 Chrisburgers C2
8 East African Pub Inn C5
9 IndoItaliano C6
10 Milan's C6
11 New Deli Chez B5
12 Union Café B6

Lake Chala Safari Lodge [149 D3] 50km east of Moshi; m +255 759 463107; w lakechalasafarilodge.co.tz. One of the most attractive places to stay in the vicinity of Moshi, this owner-managed lodge comprises a string of 10 luxurious thatch-shaded standing tents set on sturdy wooden platforms on the acacia-studded crater rim of gorgeous Lake Chala. A campsite, bar & restaurant are attached. *From US$90/130 sgl/dbl B&B; camping US$16pp*. **$$$**

✷ **Marangu Hotel** 35km from Moshi on the outskirts of Marangu; w maranguhotel.com. This welcoming family-run hotel was converted from a farmhouse in the 1920s and it retains an unpretentious & rustic feel, with ivy-draped walls & neat hedges that evoke the English countryside. Comfortable & well-equipped cottages are set in lush 5ha gardens with a swimming pool & plenty of birdlife. It is also highly recommended for Kilimanjaro climbs. **$$$**

Simba Farm Lodge Matadi, 75km from Moshi & 9km from Mount Kilimanjaro National Park's Londorossi Gate; m +255 784 687335; w simbafarmlodge.co.tz. Situated on a 2,000ha working farm on the western slope of Kilimanjaro, this unpretentious owner-managed retreat offers homely & comfortable accommodation in a charming guest cottage & hearty home cooking made with fresh farm produce. It's a great base for birding, rambling, mountain biking & day hikes on the Shira Plateau, as well as being a popular springboard for the westerly Lemosho & Shira routes up Kilimanjaro. *Rooms US$160 dbl FB; camping US$10pp*. **$$$**

WHERE TO EAT AND DRINK

There's no shortage of restaurants and cafes in Moshi. As with accommodation, the majority of more affordable restaurants are in the town centre. Smarter options are clustered in Shantytown, which is not easily accessible by public transport, so travellers staying centrally will need to walk there and back (probably not a clever idea after dark) or arrange to be collected by taxi.

TOWN CENTRE

Blossoms Café & Wine Bar [153 C5] Kilima Rd; m +255 623 689090; w blossomscafe.co.tz; ⏲ 07.00–22.00 daily. This central bistro has a smart modern interior, as well as outdoor seating in a secluded courtyard. The globetrotting menu includes Mexican, Italian, Asian & local dishes, as well as pizzas, while drinks include smoothies, juices, various coffees & teas, & an extensive wine list. **$$**

Chrisburgers [153 C2] Kibo Rd; ⏲ 24hrs but closed 22.00 Mon–07.00 Tue. Popular local eatery that's been serving cheap burgers, samosas & fruit juice since the early 1990s. **$**

East African Pub Inn [153 C5] Nyerere Rd. This lively, 2-storey bar has a wooden roof, TV & loud music. It keeps long hours & the cheap 'n' cheerful drink prices reflect a predominantly local clientele.

✷ **IndoItaliano Restaurant** [153 C6] New Rd; m +255 784 843535; f; ⏲ 07.00–22.00 daily. A wide range of Indian & Italian dishes, with tandoori grills & pizzas being particularly recommended, served indoors or on the wide streetside veranda. **$$**

✷ **Milan's Restaurant** [153 C6] Nyerere Rd; m +255 754 269802; ⏲ 08.00–20.00 daily. Despite the Italian-sounding name & no-frills décor, this long-serving local favourite specialises in Indian vegetarian cuisine & also serves a limited Chinese selection & pizzas. Food is delicious & well priced. No alcohol served. **$**

New Deli Chez [153 B5] Kilima Rd; m +255 784 786241; ⏲ 09.30–21.30 Wed–Mon, 13.00–21.30 Tue. Swahili dishes such as biryani, Zanzibar pizza & shwarmas are the speciality at this popular local eatery, which also offers plenty of choice for vegetarians, & great fruit juices. No alcohol served or permitted. **$**

Union Café [153 B6] Arusha Rd; m +255 763 969731; w kncutanzania.com/the-union-café; ⏲ 07.30–20.00 daily. This Moshi stalwart stands in the handsome 1-storey KNCU Building constructed in 1939. There's pleasant terrace seating, a characterful interior complete with an aromatic industrial coffee grinder & a varied selection of sandwiches, snacks, mains, coffee, juices & smoothies. Very reasonably priced. **$**

SHANTYTOWN

Courage Café [149 A3] Lema Rd; m +255 757 758018; w courageworldwide.org;

08.00–20.00 Mon–Sat. Set on a large lawn shaded by tropical trees, this lovely café funds a Moshi- & California-based anti-trafficking NGO called Courage Worldwide. The coffee is great & it serves an excellent selection of tacos, salads, steaks, Swahili dishes & wood-fired pizzas. $$

El Rancho Kilimanjaro [149 A2] Off Lema Rd; m +255 782 149502; f erkrestaurant; noon–23.00 daily. This top-notch Indian restaurant/bar stands in a converted old house in a large garden & serves a broad selection of vegetarian & meat-based mains. $

* **Kuonana African Restaurant** [149 A3] Kibongoto Rd; m + 255 762 152929; w kuonana.com; 08.30–22.00 daily. This upmarket take on a traditional *nyama choma* (grilled meat) joint is justifiably popular with well-heeled Tanzanians, but also a great place for visitors to enjoy the local cuisine in a relaxed outdoors atmosphere. In addition to flame-grilled chicken, pork, beef & fish, it serves a variety of tasty Swahili curries, *makange* stews & salads. There's a fair wine list too. Vegetarian options are limited. $

* **More Than a Drop** [149 D2] Off Uru Rd; m +255 768 460567; w bnb.morethanadrop.org; 18.00–22.00 daily, lunch by appt only. Set in the leafy garden of a hospitality school for Tanzanian women, this NGO-run restaurant specialises in vegetarian fare – including curries, vegetable lasagne & vegan burgers – made almost entirely using organic ingredients grown on the property. $

SHOPPING

CRAFTS AND SOUVENIRS Moshi's main concentration of craft shops lies close to the central market along Nyerere and Chagga roads. Prices tend to be a bit lower than in Arusha, as does the pushiness factor. Elsewhere in the town centre, two highly recommended outlets specialising in ethically sourced local crafts are **Mama Africa Gift Shop** [153 B6] (Selous St; w mamaafricagiftshop.com) and **Moshi Mamas Craft Cooperative** [153 B3] (Boma Rd; w giveahearttoafrica.org).

SUPERMARKETS Following the closure of the Moshi branch of the international Nakumatt chain, the best options for grocery shopping are **Aleem's supermarket** [153 B3] (Boma Rd), **Kilimanjaro Supermarket**, [153 C6] (Nyerere Rd), **Rafiki Supermarket** [153 C6] (Nyerere Rd) and **Moshi Supermarket & Liquor Store** [153 C2] (Kibo Rd).

OTHER PRACTICALITIES

BANKS, ATMS AND FOREIGN EXCHANGE The National Bank of Commerce (NBC) located opposite the Clock Tower [153 C3] changes cash at the usual rate of commission, but there are usually long queues. There are now many **24-hour ATMs** where up to Tsh400,000 cash can be withdrawn with Mastercard or Visa. These include the CRDB [153 C3], NBC [153 C2], KCB [153 C3] and Stanbic [153 B3].

MEDICAL The best place to head to in the case of a medical emergency is Shantytown's **Kilimanjaro Christian Medical Centre** [149 B1] (KCMC; m +255 658 450642; w kcmc.ac.tz), which lies 5km north of the town centre.

IMMIGRATION The immigration office [153 B3] (Kibo Hse, Boma Rd; 08.00–15.00 Mon–Fri) processes visa extensions on the spot during office hours.

SWIMMING You can swim in the pools at **Keys Hotel** (page 151), **Kilimanjaro Crane Hotel** (page 151) and out-of-town **Honey Badger Lodge** (page 152) for a small fee.

TOURIST INFORMATION AND TOUR OPERATORS

There's no tourist information office in Moshi; the closest is in Arusha (page 133). The companies listed below all specialise foremost in Kilimanjaro climbs, but most also arrange safaris and Zanzibar stays.

Honey Badger Page 152. Based out of the eponymous lodge, this operator is recommended both for its prices & for its socially conscious treatment of porters & guides.
Keys Hotel Page 151. Based at one of the town's best-known hotels, this experienced operator offers reasonably priced packages inclusive of 1 night's HB accommodation before & after the hike.
Marangu Hotel Page 154. This family-run hotel near Marangu has been organising reliable & well-priced Kilimanjaro climbs since 1932.
Mawenzi Adventures m +255 754 755086; w mawenziadventures.com. Run by an energetic Belgian-Tanzanian couple, this is a good contact for day trips to the likes of Materuni, Kikuletwa & lakes Jipe & Chala, as well as day hikes on Kilimanjaro.
Pristine Trails [153 D3] NHC Bldg, Ghala Rd; w pristinetrails.com. Highly rated company operating group & private Kilimanjaro climbs.
Shah Tours [149 B3] Sekou Touré Way; w shah-tours.com.
Snowcap Tanzania Tours [153 A2] CCM Bldg, Uhuru Rd; w snowcap.co.tz.
Viva Africa Tours [149 C2] Off Uru Rd; w vivaafricatours.com. The on-site operator at Rafiki Backpackers (page 152) specialises in affordable group tours & safaris.

WHAT TO SEE AND DO

The most popular tourist destination in the vicinity of Moshi is of course Mount Kilimanjaro, the upper slopes and ascent of which are detailed in *Chapter 7*. Other lesser attractions in the region include the villages of Marangu and Machame; Chagga ecotourism projects in the Kilimanjaro foothills; and a spectacular crater lake called Chala on the Kenyan border. The closest safari destinations are Arusha National Park (page 141) and Mkomazi National Park (page 176).

OLD MOSHI The former capital of Mangi (King) Mandara and his successor Meli stands at an altitude of 1,750m on the Kilimanjaro footslopes about 10km northeast of what is now central Moshi. Guided cultural tours of the forest-fringed village, which is steeped in oral history and offers great views over its modern namesake, can be arranged through Old Moshi Cultural Tourism (w oldmoshiculturaltour.com) and provide a great introduction to traditional Chagga agricultural practices.

As of March 2019, a video and photographic exhibition called **Mangi Meli Remains**, formerly exhibited in Berlin and Dar es Salaam, is now permanently housed in a building that once served as Old Moshi's courthouse (⊕ -3.315230, 37.404618). The installation is a collaboration between Tanzanian historian Sarita Mamseri and German artist Konradin Kunze, and it includes some fascinating 19th-century documents and photographs relating to the eponymous king (who was hanged by the Germans at Old Moshi in 1900; page 150) and his Chagga subjects. The tree where Mangi Meli was hanged still stands and is signposted close to the old courthouse.

MATERUNI FALLS Cascading 80m down a single cliff face on the southern slopes of Kilimanjaro, Materuni is probably the most impressive and beautiful of the many waterfalls associated with Africa's tallest mountain, and it has a lovely natural swimming pool at its base. The waterfall stands at an altitude of 1,700m near the village of Materuni, some 15km north of Moshi, and can be visited as part of a half-

or full-day package put together by Materuni Village Cultural Tourism (m +255 759 410470/752 191326; w materuni.com). The 3.5km hike from the village to the waterfall is quite steep but very scenic, and usually takes about 1 hour in either direction. For a full-day trip, the hike can be combined with a village tour or coffee tour, and you can extend it further with an overnight homestay at Mama Agnes's home. Tours include a hot Chagga-style lunch, and rates depend on group size, but start at US$35 per person for groups of six or more inclusive of transport from Moshi, or for solo travellers who self-drive or make their way to Materuni on one of the dalla dallas that run there quite regularly from Moshi (except on Sunday).

CULTURAL TOURS AROUND MOSHI

Several cultural tourism projects operate in the Kilimanjaro foothills in association with local communities. In addition to offering insights into Chagga culture and the opportunity to limber up the limbs before a full-on ascent of Kilimanjaro, these cultural tours allow non-climbers to get a good look at the scenic Kilimanjaro foothills, with a chance of catching a glimpse of the snow-capped peak itself.

MACHAME CULTURAL TOURISM (w machameculturaltourism.com) This programme is based at the village of Kyalia, close to the Machame Gate of Kilimanjaro National Park. A good day tour for those with a strong interest in scenery is the 5-hour Sieny-Ngira Trail, which passes through the lush montane forest to a group of large sacred caves, a natural rock bridge over the Marire and Namwi rivers, and a nearby waterfall. For those with a greater interest in culture, the 5-hour Nronga Tour, which visits a milk purification and processing co-operative run by women, is best done on Monday, market day in Kyalia village. Of similar duration, the Nkuu Tour focuses instead on agriculture, in particular coffee production. Longer excursions include the two-day Ng'uni Hike and three-day Lyamungo Tour. In a private vehicle, Kyalia can be reached by following the Arusha road out of Moshi for 12km, then following the turn-off signposted for Machame Gate and driving for another 14km. The road to Kyalia is surfaced in its entirety, and regular dalla dallas run to Kyalia from the junction on the Moshi–Arusha road.

MAMBA AND MARANGU CULTURAL TOURISM (f mambamarangu) This programme offers a variety of half-day trips taking in various natural and cultural sites on the surrounding slopes. Popular goals include the Kinukamori or Kilasia Falls, as well as the first coffee tree planted in Tanzania more than a century ago, and a traditional conical Chagga homestead. Few prospective climbers will be unmoved by the grave of the legendary Yohanu Lauwo, who guided Hans Meyer to the summit of Kilimanjaro back in 1889, continued working as a guide into his seventies, and reputedly lived to the remarkable age of 124! Other walks lead to nearby Mamba and Makundi, known for their traditional Chagga blacksmiths and woodcarvers, and for the Laka Caves, where women and children were hidden during the frequent 19th-century clashes with the Maasai of the surrounding plains. Guided tours can be arranged through most hotels and operators in Marangu or Moshi.

If you're driving yourself, head north out of Moshi on Ura Road, and continue for around 11km past Keys Hotel to the cultural tourism office close to Materuni Catholic Church (⊕ -3.26567, 37.39239).

KIKULETWA HOT SPRINGS (⊕ -3.44369, 37.19363; ⊙ 08.00–18.30 daily) Situated 40km southwest of Moshi by road, Kikuletwa (also known as Chemka) is a paradisial oasis-like pool of crystal-clear water, fed by bubbling hot springs and surrounded by a small jungle-like stand of palms, in the otherwise arid surrounds of a village called Rundugai. The pool offers safe and pleasant swimming and you can also enjoy a natural pedicure courtesy of a type of small toe-nibbling fish that inhabit its waters. Blue monkeys might also be seen in the fringing palm forest. Any tour operator in Moshi can arrange a half-day trip to Kikuletwa (often combined with a half-day in Materuni Falls) or talk directly to the well-organised Rundugai Cultural Tourism Enterprise (m +255 654 523090; w rundugaiculturaltourism.com). If you are driving from Moshi, head west along the Arusha Highway for 23km as far as Boma Ngombe, then turn left onto a dirt road that passes through Rundugai after 11km and arrives at the springs after another 4km. Occasional public transport runs to Rundugai, from Moshi, and Rundugai Cultural Tourism can arrange camping and homestays in the village.

MARANGU The village of Marangu, whose name derives from a Chagga word meaning 'spring water', is situated at an altitude of 1,800m on the forested slopes of Kilimanjaro 40km from Moshi and 5km south of the most frequently used entrance gate to Mount Kilimanjaro National Park. Cooler and moister than lower-lying Moshi, Marangu is surrounded by lush Afromontane vegetation and bisected by a babbling mountain stream, making it a pleasant goal for those wanting to explore the footslopes of the great mountain.

Marangu's most central tourist attraction, Kinukamori Waterfall (⊕ -3.276454, 37.519643; entrance US$10) lies on the Unna River 20 minutes' walk from town. Clearly signposted, the waterfall stands in a small park maintained by the district council as an ecotourism project in collaboration with two nearby villages. It's a pretty spot, and the wooded riverbanks above the falls harbour a variety of forest birds and regularly attract troops of Kilimanjaro colobus. A legend associated with Kinukamori – which means 'Little Moon' – relates to an unmarried girl called Makinuka, who discovered she was pregnant, a crime then punishable by death in Chagga society, and decided to take her own life by jumping over the waterfall. When Makinuka arrived at the waterfall and looked over the edge, she changed her mind and turned to go home to plead for mercy. As she did so, however, she came face to face with a leopard and ran back screaming in fear, forgetting about the gorge behind her, to plunge to an accidental death. A statue of Makinuka and her feline nemesis stands above the waterfall. The waterfall can be visited independently, or by arrangement with your hotel as part of a longer sightseeing tour.

More remote than Kinukamori, the spectacular Kilasia Falls (⊕ -3.289206, 37.493391; entrance US$10) is the centrepiece of a new ecotourism community project that includes a guided nature walk. Approximately 30m high, the waterfall tumbles into the base of a sheer-sided gorge before running through a set of violent rapids into a lovely pool that's said to be safe for swimming. The waterfall is at its most powerful during the rains, but it flows solidly throughout the year – the name Kilasia derives from a Chagga word meaning 'without end', reputedly a reference to its reliable flow. The path to the base of the falls, though no more than 500m long, is very steep and potentially dangerous when wet. The rocky gorge below the waterfall is lined with ferns and evergreen trees, and a troop of blue monkeys often passes through in the early morning and late afternoon.

If you are driving the 40km from Moshi to Marangu in a **private vehicle**, follow the surfaced A23 towards the Taveta border east for 26km, then turn left at the junction village of Himo. Regular **buses** and **dalla dallas** between Moshi and Marangu leave when full and generally take about 1 hour.

LAKE CHALA Straddling the Kenyan border on the eastern footslopes of Kilimanjaro, this roughly circular crater lake, a full 3km wide yet invisible until you virtually topple over the rim, is one of northern Tanzania's true off-the-beaten-track scenic gems. The brilliant turquoise water, hemmed in by sheer cliffs draped in tropical greenery, is an arresting sight at any time, and utterly fantastic when Kilimanjaro emerges from the clouds to the immediate west. Not for the faint-hearted, a very steep footpath leads from the rim to the edge of the lake, its translucent waters plunging near-vertically to an undetermined depth from the rocky shore.

Abundant birdlife aside, wildlife at Chala is in short supply, though in common with many other African crater lakes, the water is said locally to harbour a quota of

SHIRA PLATEAU DAY HIKE

Ideal for those who want a close-up look at Kilimanjaro but don't want to dedicate the time, money or effort required for a full-blown multi-day ascent to the summit, a great alternative is the Shira Plateau Day Hike on the western slopes. Roughly 8.5km in length, the circular trail starts at a parking area (⊕ -2.98641, 37.23056) set at an altitude of 3,400m some 12km inside Londorossi Gate and climbs as far as Shira Camp One, which stands at around 3,510m. The trail leads through an open plateau of Afroalpine moorland characterised by tussocked grassland, heather shrubs and occasional giant lobelia. Eland and other large mammals are very occasionally recorded in the area, and birders can look out for Alpine chat, the heavyweight white-necked raven and the beautiful nectar-feeding scarlet-tufted malachite sunbird. But the real star, weather permitting, is the spectacular frame-filling views of the Kibo massif and snow-capped Uhuru Peak, which lies about 8km to the east as the crow flies.

The guided day hike is well marked and relatively flat and easy, despite crossing a few small but steep river ravines, and can be covered comfortable in 2 hours or so. You may feel some slight effects of altitude, so drink plenty of water and try to walk at a relaxed pace. Even in warm weather, you should also carry some extra clothes in case the mist or rain suddenly closes in. The ideal time to visit is in the early to mid morning, setting off from the car park before 09.00, when you are most likely to have clear views of the peak.

A specialist operator that regularly runs Shira day hikes is Hatari Travel (w hatari.travel), which also runs Hatari Lodge in Arusha National Park and Shu'mata Camp in West Kilimanjaro. The hike is offered as a day trip from either of these lodges or as an activity when travelling between them. It would also be possible to arrange it as a standalone activity with any operator based in Arusha, Moshi or environs. Allow 3 hours to get to the car park coming from Arusha or 2½ hours from Moshi. Note that, because the trail lies within Mount Kilimanjaro National Park, hikers must pay the park entrance fee of US$70 per person per day, plus VAT.

mysterious and malignant Nessie-like beasties. A less fantastic threat, should you be thinking of dipping a toe in the water, is the crocodiles that were introduced into Chala in the 1930s and killed a British volunteer off the Kenyan shore in 2002. According to the management of Lake Chala Safari Lodge, local fishermen have since eradicated all the lake's crocodiles.

For the time being, the only practical way to reach Chala is on an **organised day or overnight trip** out of Moshi, or in a **private 4x4 vehicle**. If you're driving, follow the A23 towards the Taveta border for 33km, then turn left onto the rough road signposted for Lake Chala Safari Lodge, and you'll arrive at the crater rim after another 16km. Accommodation, meals and camping are available at the Lake Chala Safari Lodge. The lodge also offers day visitors guided walks for around US$6 per person and kayak rental at around US$4 per person per hour. Lake Chala now falls within a Wildlife Management Area and an entrance fee (US$25/20 plus 18% VAT for adults/children, credit card only) must be paid at the entrance barrier.

LAKE JIPE Shallow, narrow and enclosed by dense beds of tall papyrus, Lake Jipe runs for 10km along a natural sump on the Kenyan border south of Kilimanjaro, which is the main source of its water. It's an atmospheric body of water, overlooked by the Pare Mountains to the south, Chala's crater rising from the flat plain to the north, all capped – when the clouds clear – by Kilimanjaro's glacial peak. Because Jipe's northern shore lies within Kenya's Tsavo West National Park, the area hosts a fair bit of wildlife, most conspicuously hippos, crocodiles and various antelope, but also occasionally elephant and possibly even lion and cheetah. The fringing papyrus beds harbour several localised birds including lesser jacana, African water rail, pygmy goose and black egret. The lovely impala lily, a succulent shrub known for its bright pink-and-white flowers, is common in the dry acacia plains approaching the lake.

Lake Jipe lies about 55km (1½ hrs) from Moshi by road. The junction town is Kifaru, which straddles the B1 to Dar es Salaam 38km southeast of Moshi. From Kifaru, drive east along a reasonable dirt road towards Kiwakuku, then after 15km turn left on to a track that arrives at Makuyuni and the lakeshore after another 2km. Once at Makuyuni, it's straightforward enough to arrange to be poled on to the lake in a local dugout canoe, whether you want to fish, watch birds, look for hippo or just enjoy the lovely scenery and hope for glimpses of big game on the Kenyan shore. Expect to pay around US$5–10 for a short excursion or US$15 for a full day. The best time to head out is in the early morning or late afternoon, when it's not too hot, game is more active and Kilimanjaro is most likely to be visible. There is no accommodation or formal campsite in the vicinity of the lake.

The only operator we're aware of that offers day tours to Lake Jipe from Moshi is Mawenzi Adventures (page 156).

7

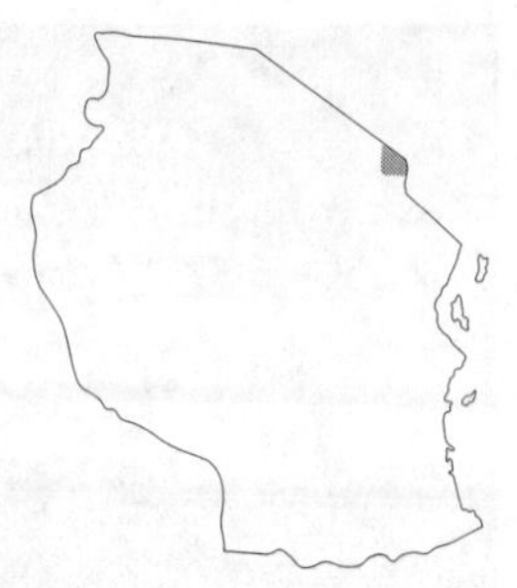

Kilimanjaro National Park

Dominating the skyline north of Moshi, the 1,688km² Kilimanjaro National Park (**m** +255 739 767679; **e** kinapa@tanzaniaparks.go.tz) protects the upper slopes of Africa's highest mountain, whose snow-capped Uhuru Peak summits at 5,895m (19,340ft). Kilimanjaro also ranks as the tallest free-standing mountain anywhere in the world, and its distinctive volcanic silhouette – rising a full 5km above the surrounding plains – is a truly breathtaking apparition, at least on those precious occasions when it emerges fully from its customary veil of clouds. For hikers, Kilimanjaro has the added allure of being the highest mountain in

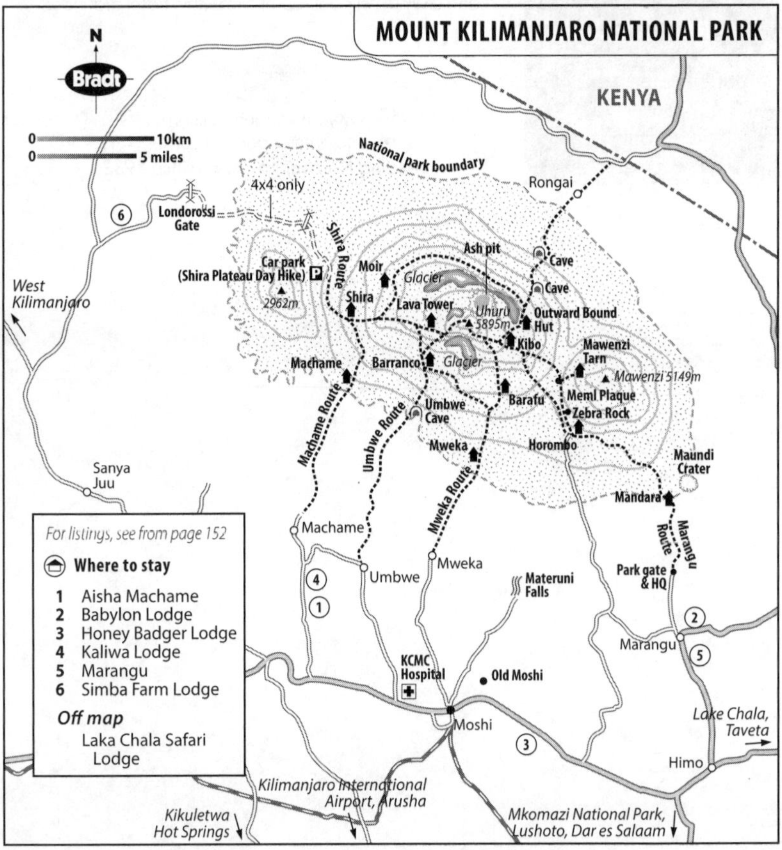

MOUNT KILIMANJARO NATIONAL PARK

For listings, see from page 152

Where to stay

1 Aisha Machame
2 Babylon Lodge
3 Honey Badger Lodge
4 Kaliwa Lodge
5 Marangu
6 Simba Farm Lodge

Off map

Laka Chala Safari Lodge

WHAT'S IN A NAME?

Nobody is sure about the meaning of the name Kilimanjaro, or even whether it is Swahili, Maasai or Chagga in origin. That the term 'kilima' is Swahili for little mountain (a joke?) is not in doubt. But 'njaro' could derive from the Chagga word for caravan (the mountain was an important landmark on the northern caravan route), or from the Maasai word 'ngare' meaning water (it is the source of most of the region's rivers), or the name of a Swahili demon of cold. Another unrelated version of the name's origin is that it's a bastardisation of the phrase 'kilemakyaro' (impossible journey), the initial Chagga response to European queries about trekking to the peak!

the world that can be ascended by inexperienced climbers without specialist mountaineering equipment.

Kilimanjaro straddles the border with Kenya, but the upper slopes and peaks all fall within Tanzania and can only be climbed from within the country. There are several routes up the mountain, all of which take at least five days, though a day or two longer is recommended for acclimatisation. Most people use the Marangu Route, which is relatively easy and affordable, and has the best facilities (including overnight huts instead of campsites), but tends to be crowded. Next most popular is the Machame Route, which used to be very quiet but can become quite busy these days. A number of other routes are available but generally only used by specialist trekking companies. Kilimanjaro can be climbed at any time of year, but the hike is more difficult in the rainy months, especially between March and May.

For those who'd like to get close to Kilimanjaro but opt not to do a full-blown multi-day hike to the summit, a highly recommended alternative is the Shira Plateau Day Hike described on page 159.

GEOLOGY

In geological terms, Kilimanjaro is a relatively young mountain. Like most other large mountains near the Rift Valley, it was formed by volcanic activity, first erupting about 1 million years ago. The 3,962m-high Shira Peak collapsed around half a million years ago, but the 5,895m-high Uhuru Peak on Mount Kibo (the higher of Kilimanjaro's two main peaks) and 5,149m-high Mawenzi Peak continued to grow until more recently. Shira Plateau formed 360,000 years ago, when the caldera was filled by lava from Kibo after a particularly violent eruption. Kibo is now dormant, and nobody knows when it last displayed any serious volcanic activity. The Kilimanjaro National Park, gazetted in 1977, protects the entire Tanzanian part of the mountain above the 2,700m contour, an area of 756km^2.

HISTORY

Blessed by fertile volcanic soil and reliable rainfall, the lower slopes of Kilimanjaro have probably been a magnet for human settlement for hundreds of millennia. Ancient stone tools of indeterminate age have been found on the lower slopes, as have the remains of pottery artefacts thought to be at least 2,000 years old. Archaeological evidence suggests that, between 1,000 and 1,500 years ago, Kilimanjaro was the centre of an Iron Age culture spreading out to the coastal belt between Pangani and Mombasa. Before that, it's anybody's guess really, but

A ROYAL VISIT

An unsubstantiated legend holds that Emperor Menelik I of Ethiopia, the illegitimate son of King Solomon and the Queen of Sheba, visited Kilimanjaro about 3,000 years ago while returning from a successful military campaign in East Africa. The emperor camped on the saddle for a night, and then ascended Kibo, where he suddenly fell ill and died, possibly from exposure and/or altitude-related causes. Menelik's slaves buried the imperial corpse in the snowy crater, where the story says it remains to this day, together with a royal cache of jewels, religious scrolls and other treasures. An extension of this legend prophesies that a descendant of Menelik I will one day ascend Kibo, find the frozen body and claim the seal ring of Solomon worn by it, thereby endowing himself with the wisdom of Solomon and heroic spirit of Menelik. Pure apocrypha, as far as I can ascertain, is the story that the ancient Ethiopian emperor's 19th-century successor and namesake Menelik II once climbed Kilimanjaro in an unsuccessful bid to fulfil this centuries-old prophecy.

references in Ptolemy's *Geography* and the *Periplus of the Erythraean Sea* suggest that the mountain was known to the early coastal traders, and might even have served as the terminus of a trade route starting at modern-day Pangani and following the eponymous river inland. Kilimanjaro is also alluded to in an account written by a 12th-century Chinese trader, and by 16th-century Spanish geographer Fernandes de Encisco.

These ancient allusions fired the curiosity of 19th-century geographers, who outdid each other in publishing wild speculations about the African interior. In 1848, locals told Johan Rebmann, a German missionary working in the Taita Hills, about a very large silver-capped mountain known to the Maasai as Ol Doinyo Naibor – White Mountain – and reputedly protected by evil spirits that froze anybody who tried to ascend it. When Rebmann visited the mountain, he immediately recognised the spirit-infested silver cap to be snow, but this observation, first published in 1849, was derided by European experts, who thought it ludicrous to claim there was snow so near the Equator. Only in 1861, when an experienced geologist, Von der Decken, saw and surveyed Kilimanjaro, was its existence and that of its snow-capped peaks accepted internationally. Oral tradition suggests that no local person had successfully climbed Kilimanjaro – or at least returned to tell the tale – before Hans Meyer and Ludwig Purtscheller reached the summit in 1889.

VEGETATION AND BIOLOGY

There are five vegetation zones on Kilimanjaro: the cultivated lower slopes; the forest; heath and moorland; alpine; and the barren arctic summit zone. Vegetation is sparse higher up due to lower temperatures and rainfall.

The **lower slopes** of the mountain were probably once forested, but are now mainly cultivated. The volcanic soils make them highly fertile and they support a dense human population. The most biologically interesting aspect of the lower slopes is the abundance of wild flowers, seen between Marangu and the park entrance gate.

The **montane forest zone** of the southern slopes lies between the altitudes of 1,800m and 3,000m. Receiving up to 2,000mm of rainfall annually, this zone displays a high biological diversity, and still supports a fair amount of wildlife. The most frequently seen mammals are the Kilimanjaro colobus and blue monkeys, while typical forest antelope include three duiker species and the beautifully marked bushbuck. Leopard, bushpig and porcupine are fairly common but seldom encountered by hikers, while eland, buffalo and elephant are present in small numbers. The forest is home to many varieties of butterfly, including four endemic species. The forests of Kilimanjaro are less rich in birds (particularly endemics) than the more ancient forests of the Eastern Arc Mountains, but some 40 species peculiar to Afromontane forest have been recorded. Most forest birds are quite difficult to observe, but trekkers should at least hear the raucous silvery-cheeked hornbill and beautiful Hartlaub's turaco.

The semi-alpine **heath and moorland zone**, which lies between 3,000m and 4,000m, is characterised by heath-like vegetation and abundant wild flowers. As you climb into the moorland, two distinctive plants become common. These are *Lobelia deckenii*, which grows to 3m high, and the groundsel *Senecio kilimanjarin*, which grows up to 5m high and can be distinguished by a spike of yellow flowers. The moorland zone supports a low density of mammals, but pairs of klipspringer are quite common on rocky outcrops and several other species are recorded from time to time. Alpine chat and scarlet-tufted malachite sunbird are two birds whose range is restricted to the moorland of large East African mountains. Other localised birds include lammergeier, augur buzzard and alpine swift, and you're also bound to see white-necked raven – the world's second-largest passerine – scavenging around camps. Because the moorland is so open, the views are stunning.

The **alpine zone** between 4,000m and 5,000m is classified as a semi-desert because it receives an annual rainfall of less than 250mm. The ground often freezes at night, but ground temperatures may soar to above 30°C by day. Few plants survive in these conditions: only 55 species are present, many of them lichens and grasses. Six species of moss are endemic to the higher reaches of Kilimanjaro. Large mammals have been recorded at this altitude, most commonly eland, but none is resident.

Approaching the summit, the **arctic zone** starts at an altitude of around 5,000m. This area receives virtually no rainfall, and supports little permanent life other than the odd lichen. Two remarkable records concern a frozen leopard discovered here in 1926, and a family of hunting dogs seen in 1962. The most notable natural features at the summit are the inner and outer craters of Kibo, surrounding a 120m-deep ash pit, and the Great Northern Glacier, which has retreated markedly since Hans Meyer and Ludwig Purtscheller first saw it in 1889. Indeed, since that historic ascent, it is thought that Kilimanjaro's distinctive snow cap has retreated by up to 90%, probably as a result of global warming, and some experts predict that it will vanish completely by 2040.

CLIMBING KILIMANJARO

As Africa's highest peak and most identifiable landmark, Kilimanjaro offers an irresistible challenge to many tourists. Dozens of visitors to Tanzania set off for Uhuru Peak every day, ranging from teenagers to pensioners, and those who make it generally regard the achievement to be the highlight of their time in the country. A major part of Kilimanjaro's attraction is that any reasonably fit person stands a fair chance of reaching the top. The ascent requires no special climbing skills or experience; on the contrary, it basically amounts to a long uphill slog over four (or more) days, followed by a more rapid descent.

FAMILY INTRIGUES

The names of Kilimanjaro's two main peaks, Kibo and Mawenzi, derive from local Chagga words respectively meaning 'cold' and 'jagged'. According to Chagga legend, the peaks are sisters and both were once as smoothly shaped as the perfect dome of Kibo is today. But the younger sister Mawenzi was habitually too lazy to collect her own firewood and kept borrowing from Kibo until one day the elder sister instructed her to go out and gather her own. When Mawenzi refused, the enraged Kibo reached into her woodpile, grabbed the largest log there, and started beating her over the head, resulting in the jagged shape of the younger sister today.

The relative ease of climbing Kilimanjaro should not lull travellers into thinking of the ascent as some sort of prolonged Sunday stroll. It is a seriously tough hike, with potentially fatal penalties for those who are inadequately prepared or who belittle the health risks attached to being at an altitude of above 4,000m. It should also be recognised that there is no such thing as a cheap Kilimanjaro climb (page 169). A five-day Marangu climb generally costs at least US$1,250 per person, depending to some extent on group size, while six-day climbs start at around US$1,500. People using high-quality operators and/or more obscure routes should expect to pay considerably more.

MARANGU ROUTE Starting at the Marangu Gate some 5km from the village of the same name, the so-called 'tourist route' is the most popular way to the top of Kilimanjaro, largely because it is less arduous than most of the alternatives, as well as having better facilities and being cheaper to climb. Marangu is also probably the safest route, due to the volume of other climbers and good rescue facilities relative to more obscure routes, and it offers a better chance of seeing some wildlife. It is the only route where you can sleep in proper huts throughout, with bathing water and bottled drinks normally available, too. The main drawback of the Marangu Route is that it is heavily trampled by comparison with other routes, for which reason many people complain that it can feel overcrowded.

Day 1: Marangu to Mandara Hut (12km; 4hrs) On an organised climb you will be dropped at the park entrance gate a few kilometres past Marangu. There is a high chance of rain in the afternoon, so it is wise to set off on this 4-hour hike as early in the day as you can. Foot traffic is heavy along this stretch, which means that although you pass through thick forest, the shy animals that inhabit the forest are not likely to be seen. If your guide will go that way, use the parallel trail, which meets the main trail halfway between the gate and the hut. Mandara Hut (2,700m) is an attractive collection of buildings with room for 200 people.

Day 2: Mandara Hut to Horombo Hut (15km; 6hrs) You continue through forest for a short time before reaching the heath and moorland zone, from where there are good views of the peaks and Moshi. The walk takes up to 6 hours. Horombo Hut (3,720m) sleeps up to 120 people. It is in a valley and surrounded by giant lobelia and groundsel. If you do a six-day hike, you will spend a day at Horombo to acclimatise.

Day 3: Horombo Hut to Kibo Hut (15km; 6–7hrs) The vegetation thins out as you enter the desert-like alpine zone, and when you cross the saddle Kibo Peak comes into view. This 6–7-hour walk should be done slowly: many people start to feel the effects of altitude. Kibo Hut (4,703m) is a stone construction that sleeps up to 120 people. Water must be carried from a stream above Horombo. You may find it difficult to sleep at this altitude, and as you will have to rise at around 01.00 the next morning, many people feel it is better not to bother trying.

Days 4 and 5: Kibo Hut to the summit to Marangu (5km; 6hrs) The best time to climb is during the night, as it is marginally easier to climb the scree slope to Gillman's Point on the crater rim when it is frozen. This ascent typically takes about 6 hours, so you need to get going between midnight and 01.00 to stand a chance of reaching the summit in time to catch the sunrise. From Gillman's Point it is a further 2-hour round trip along the crater's edge to Uhuru Peak, the highest point in Africa. From the summit, it's a roughly 7-hour descent with a break at Kibo Hut to Horombo Hut, where you will spend your last night on the mountain. The final day's descent from Horombo to Marangu generally takes 7–8 hours, so you should arrive in Marangu in the mid afternoon.

OTHER ROUTES Although the majority of trekkers stick to the Marangu Route, which is both the easiest and quickest ascent route up Kilimanjaro, with the best overnight facilities, an increasing proportion opt for one of five relatively off-the-beaten-track alternatives. While the merits and demerits of avoiding the Marangu Route are hotly debated, there is no doubt about two things: first, that you'll see relatively few other tourists on the other routes; and, second, that you'll pay considerably more for this privilege. Aesthetic and financial considerations aside, an unambiguous logistical disadvantage of the less-used routes is that, with the exception of Rongai, they are tougher going (though only the Umbwe is markedly so). Also, huts are non-existent, which enforces camping.

Machame Route In recent years, the Machame Route has grown greatly in popularity. It is widely regarded to be the most scenic viable ascent route, with great views across to Mount Meru, and as a whole it is relatively gradual, requiring at least six days for the full ascent and descent. Short sections are steeper and slightly more difficult than any part of the Marangu Route, but this is compensated for by the longer period for acclimatisation.

The route is named after the village of Machame, from where it is a 2-hour walk to the park gate (1,950m). Most companies will provide transport as far as the gate (at least when the road is passable), and then it's a 6–8-hour trek through thick forest to Machame Hut, which lies on the edge of the moorland zone at 2,890m. The Machame Hut is now a ruin, so camping is necessary, but water is available. The second day of this trail consists of a 9km, 4–6-hour hike through the moorland zone of Shira Plateau to Shira Hut (3,840m), which is near a stream. Once again, this hut has fallen into disuse, so the options are camping or sleeping in a nearby cave.

From Shira, a number of options exist: you could spend your third night at Lava Tower Hut (4,630m), 4 hours from Shira, but the ascent to the summit from here is tricky and only advisable if you are experienced and have good equipment. A less arduous option is to spend your third night at Barranco Campsite (3,950m), a tough 12km, 6-hour hike from Shira, then to go on to Barafu Hut (4,600m) on the fourth day, a walk of approximately 7 hours. From Barafu, it is normal to begin the steep 7–8-hour clamber to Stella Point (5,735m) at midnight, so that you arrive at sunrise, with the option of continuing on to Uhuru Peak, a 2-hour round trip, before hiking back down to Mweka Hut via Barafu in the afternoon. This day can involve up to 16 hours of walking altogether. After spending your fifth night at Mweka Hut (3,100m), you will descend the mountain on the sixth day via the Mweka Route, a 4–6-hour walk.

The huts along this route are practically unusable, but any reliable operator will provide you with camping equipment and employ enough porters to carry the camp and set it up.

Mweka Route This is the steepest and fastest route to the summit. There are two huts along it – Mweka (3,100m) and Barafu (4,600m), each sleeping up to 16 people – though neither is habitable at the time of writing. There is water at Mweka but not at Barafu. This route starts at the Mweka Wildlife College, 12km from Moshi. From there it takes about 8 hours to get to Mweka Hut, then a further 8 hours to Barafu, from where it replicates the Machame Route. The Mweka Route is not recommended for ascending the mountain, since it is too short for proper acclimatisation, but is often used as a descent route by people climbing the Machame or Shira routes.

Shira Route Although this route could technically be covered in five days by driving to the high-altitude trailhead, this would allow you very little time to acclimatise, and greatly decrease the odds of reaching the summit. A minimum of six days is recommended, but better seven so that you can spend a full day at Shira Hut to acclimatise. The route starts at Londorossi Gate on the western side of the mountain, from where a 19km track leads to the trailhead at around 3,500m. It is possible to motor to the trailhead in a 4x4, but for reasons already mentioned it would be advisable to walk, with an overnight stop to camp outside Simba Cave, which lies in an area of moorland where elephants and buffalo are regularly encountered. From the trailhead, it's a straightforward 4km to the campsite at the disused Shira Hut. If you opt to spend two nights at Shira in order to acclimatise, there are some worthwhile day walks in the vicinity. From Shira Hut, the route is identical to the Machame Route, and it is normal to return along the Mweka Route.

Rongai Route The only route ascending Kilimanjaro from the northeast, the Rongai Route starts close to the Kenyan border and was closed for several years due to border sensitivity. In terms of gradients, it is probably less physically demanding than the Marangu Route, and the scenery, with views over the Tsavo Plains, is regarded to be as beautiful. The Rongai Route can be covered over five days, with equally good if not better conditions for acclimatisation than the Marangu Route,

PORTER TREATMENT GUIDELINES

The Kilimanjaro Porters Assistance Project (KPAP) is an initiative of the International Mountain Explorers Connection (w mountainexplorers.org), a non-profit organisation based in the USA, aimed at ensuring the fair treatment of porters on Kilimanjaro. We would recommend that all prospective climbers visit their website (w kiliporters.org) for further information, including guidelines for porter treatment and tipping, and a list of local and international operators that it regards to be committed to responsible treatment of porters. You are also welcome to drop in to their Moshi office [153 B3], on Boma Road opposite Immigration, for more information. After your climb, you are also encouraged to report any instances of abuse or neglect through the contact form on their website, or by visiting the office.

COSTING A CLIMB

The reason why climbing Kilimanjaro is so expensive boils down to the prescribed park fees charged by Tanapa. For the 2022–23 season, the daily entrance fee is US$70 per person, then there's a hut fee of US$60 or camping fee of US$50 per person per night, as well as a one-off rescue fee of US$20 per person per climb, plus 18% VAT. This creates a fixed cost of US$670–700 per person for a five-day hike up Marangu, plus an additional US$140 per person per extra day, before any actual services are provided. On top of this, there are set fees of US$20 per guide and US$15 per cook per party per day, and US$10 per porter per day, which would for example add another US$187.50 per person (plus VAT) for two people taking a five-day hike with two porters each, or US$112.50 per person (plus VAT) for four people taking a six-day hike with one porter each. Or to put it another way, an operator charging US$1,200 per person for two people to climb via the Marangu Route will be forking out at least US$800 in fees and other fixed costs, even before budgeting for transportation, food, equipment, etc, as well as the general running costs attached to operating any business.

It is worth noting that hikers should set aside around 10% of the cost of their climb to tipping guides, cooks and porters at the end of the trip. Usual tipping guidelines per day per party are around US$10–20 per guide, US$8–15 per cook and US$5–10 per porter.

though as with Marangu the odds of reaching the summit improve if you opt for an additional day.

The route starts at the village of Nale Moru (2,000m) near the Kenyan border, from where a footpath leads through cultivated fields and plantation forest before entering the montane forest zone, where Kilimanjaro colobus monkeys are frequently encountered. The first campsite is reached after 3–5 hours, and lies at about 2,700m on the frontier of the forest and moorland zones. On the five-day hike, the second day involves a gentle 5–6-hour ascent, through an area of moorland where elephants are sometimes seen, to Third Cave Campsite (3,500m). On the third day, it's a 4–5-hour walk to School Campsite (4,750m) at the base of Kibo, with the option of camping here or else continuing to the nearby Kibo Hut, which is more crowded but more commodious. The ascent from here is identical to the Marangu Route. A six-day variation on the above route involves spending the second night at Kikelewa Caves (*3,600m, 6–7hr walk*), a night at Mawenzi Tarn near the synonymous peak (*4,330m, 4hr walk*), then crossing the saddle between Mawenzi and Kibo to rejoin the five-day route at School Campsite.

Umbwe Route This short, steep route, possibly the most scenic of the lot, is not recommended as an ascent route as it is very steep in parts and involves one short stretch of genuine rock climbing. It is occasionally used as a descent route, and can be tied in with almost any of the ascent routes, though many operators understandably prefer not to take the risk, or charge a premium for using it. Umbwe Route descends from Barranco Hut, and comes out at the village of Umbwe. It is possible to sleep in two caves on the lower slopes along this route.

ARRANGING A CLIMB The only way to go about climbing Kilimanjaro is through a reliable specialised operator. Readers who pre-book a climb through a known

CHAGGA HOME GARDENS

Emma Thomson

For decades the Chagga have been making use of the fertile soil that lies at the foot of Kilimanjaro. Originally, the land was divided into family allotments or shamba (usually 0.68ha) and passed from father to son. Later on land was seized by the state, and reallocated depending on the size of the family. These lush plots are used to grow coffee, plantain, bananas and medicinal herbs, allowing the Chagga to be self-sufficient. This cropping system remained stable for at least a century, and only recently has it come under pressure from rapid population growth, diminishing land resources, changes in dietary habits and economic pressures for improved housing and schooling. These pressing needs have forced the younger generations to travel into the towns in search of paid work. However, this migration of youngsters to urban areas not only leads to labour shortages on the farms but also disrupts the traditional transmission from one generation to the next of the knowledge and experience required for the successful management of the farms.

tour operator in their own country can be reasonably confident that they will be going with a reputable ground operator in Tanzania. Readers who want to make their arrangements online or after they arrive in Tanzania will find an almost infinite number of trekking companies operating out of Moshi, Arusha and to

MOUNTAIN HEALTH

with Dr Daniel Campion

Although Kilimanjaro is a popular travel destination – and the ascent does not require mountaineering skills or equipment – don't underestimate how challenging it can be. You should not attempt the climb unless you are reasonably fit, or if you have heart or lung problems (although asthma sufferers should be all right). Bear in mind, however, that very fit people are more prone to altitude sickness because they ascend too fast.

Above 3,000m you may not feel hungry, but you should try to eat. Carbohydrates and fruit are recommended, whereas rich or fatty foods are harder to digest. You should drink plenty of liquids, at least three litres of water daily, and will need enough water bottles to carry this. Dehydration is one of the most common reasons for failing to complete the climb. If you dress in layers, you can take off clothes before you sweat too much, thereby reducing water loss.

Few people climb Kilimanjaro without feeling some of the symptoms of altitude sickness: headaches, nausea, fatigue, breathlessness, sleeplessness and swelling of the hands and feet. You can reduce these by allowing yourself time to acclimatise by taking an extra day over the ascent, eating and drinking properly, and trying not to push yourself. If you walk slowly and steadily, you will tire less quickly than if you try to rush each day's walk. Acetazolamide (Diamox) helps speed acclimatisation and many people find it useful. We would usually prescribe 125mg – half a tablet – twice a day for around five days, starting two or three days before reaching 3,500m. However, the side effects from this drug can be inconvenient and may resemble altitude sickness. Therefore it is advisable to try the medication for a couple of days about two weeks before the trip to see if it suits you.

Should symptoms become severe, and especially if they are clearly getting worse, then descend immediately. Even going down 500m is enough to start a lesser extent Marangu, and they should be able to negotiate a far better price by cutting out the middleman, but should also be circumspect about dealing with any company that lacks a verifiable pedigree. A list of respected operators is included in the box on page 173, and while such a list can never be close to comprehensive, it is reasonable to assume that anybody who can offer you a significantly cheaper package than the more budget-friendly companies on this list is not to be trusted.

Kilimanjaro climbs do not come cheaply (page 169). Five-day Marangu climbs with a reliable operator start at an all-inclusive price of around US$1,200–1,600 per person for two people. You may be able to negotiate the price down slightly, especially for a larger group, but when you are paying this sort of money, it strikes me as sensible to shop around for quality of service rather than a fractional saving. A reputable operator will provide good food, experienced guides and porters, and reliable equipment – all of which go a long way to ensuring not only that you reach the top, but also that you come back down alive. You can assume that the cost of any package with a reputable operator will include a registered guide, two porters per person, park fees, food, and transport to and from the gate. It is, however, advisable to check exactly what you are paying for, and (especially for larger parties) to ensure that one porter is also registered as a guide, so that if somebody has to turn back, the rest of the group can still continue their climb.

The standard duration of a climb on the Marangu Route is five days. Many people with repeated experience of Kilimanjaro recommend adding a sixth day to

recovery. Sleeping high with significant symptoms is dangerous; if in doubt descend to sleep low.

Pulmonary and cerebral oedema are more severe forms of altitude sickness that can be rapidly fatal if you do not descend. Symptoms of pulmonary oedema include shortness of breath when at rest, coughing up frothy spit or even blood, and undue breathlessness compared with accompanying friends. Symptoms of high-altitude cerebral oedema (ie: swelling of the brain) are headaches, poor co-ordination, staggering as if you were drunk, disorientation, poor judgement and even hallucinations. The danger is that the sufferer usually doesn't realise how sick he/she is and may argue against descending. The only treatment for altitude sickness is descent.

Altitude-related illness is also a potential problem on Mount Meru, and similar precautions should be taken. Other mountains in Tanzania are not high enough for it to be a cause for concern.

Hypothermia is a lowering of body temperature usually caused by a combination of cold and wet. Mild cases usually manifest themselves as uncontrollable shivering. Put on dry, warm clothes and get into a sleeping bag; this will normally raise your body temperature sufficiently. Severe hypothermia is potentially fatal: symptoms include disorientation, lethargy, mental confusion (including an inappropriate feeling of well-being and warmth!) and coma. In severe cases the rescue team should be summoned.

A US$20 rescue fee is paid by all climbers upon entering the national park. The rescue team ordinarily covers the Marangu Route only; if you use another route their services must be organised in advance.

CHAGGA FAMILIES

Emma Thomson

Clan identity is highly important to the Chagga – to the extent that when individuals address each other, they will mention their clan name before revealing their first name or family name.

This sense of solidarity and membership is reinforced within the family unit, where every son is appointed a specific role. The first-born must protect and care for his grandmother, by visiting her at least once a month. The second son is raised to inherit the role of the father and must apply himself to his father's bidding. The third son must protect and cherish his mother.

Every year, between Christmas and the New Year, all family members must return to their home villages for at least three days, so they can be accounted for and to introduce new family members. If unable to attend, an absentee must provide a valid excuse, or from then on be considered an outsider.

acclimatise at Horombo Hut. The majority opinion among operators and mountain experts is that this will improve the odds of reaching the summit by as much as 20%. However, other operators say that that the extra day makes little difference except that it adds a similar figure to the cost of the climb. No meaningful statistics are available to support one view or the other, but we would certainly recommend those can who afford it to take an extra day or two over the ascent.

In this context, it is worth noting that the exhaustion felt by almost all hikers as they approach the peak is not merely a function of altitude. On the Marangu Route, for instance, most people hike for 6–8 hours on day three, and then after a minimal dose of sleep (if any at all), rise at around midnight to start the final 5–6-hour ascent to the peak. In other words, when they reach the peak, they will usually have been walking for up to 14 of the last 20-odd hours, without any significant sleep – something that would tire out most people even if they weren't facing an altitudinal increase of around 2,000m! On that basis alone, an extra night along the way would have some value in pure recuperative terms. And certainly, my firm impression is that travellers who spend six days on the mountain enjoy the climb far more than those who take five days, whether or not they reach the peak.

RECORD KILIMANJARO CLIMBS

First recorded ascent: Hans Meyer and Ludwig Purtscheller, 1889
Fastest ascent: Karl Egloff (Switzerland–Ecuador) in 4 hours, 56 minutes, (Mweka Route), 2014
Fastest ascent by a woman: Kristina Shoo Madsen (Denmark) in 6 hours 52 minutes, 54 seconds (Umbwe Route) 2018
Fastest ascent and descent: Karl Egloff (Switzerland–Ecuador) in 6 hours 42 minutes, 24 seconds (Mweka Route), 2014
Youngest person to summit: Coaltan Tanner (USA), aged 6 years, 1 month and 4 days, 2018
Oldest person to summit: Anne Lorimor (USA), 89 years and 267 days, 2015
Oldest man to summit: Dr Fred Distelhorst (USA), 88 years and 201 days, 2014

Of the less popular routes up Kilimanjaro, the one most frequently used by tourists, the Machame Route, requires a minimum of six days. Most operators will charge at least US$1,600 per person for this route, which requires far more outlay insofar as camping equipment must be provided, along with a coterie of porters to carry and set up the makeshift camp. The same problem exists on all routes except Marangu, so that any off-the-beaten-track climb will be considerably more costly than the standard one. Should you decide to use a route other than Marangu, it is critical that you work through an operator with experience of that route.

The dubious alternative to using a reputable company is to take your chances with a small operator or private individual who approaches you on the street. These will be marginally cheaper than using an established operator, but the risks are greater, accountability is lower, and you can be almost certain that porters and

KILIMANJARO: RECOMMENDED LOCAL OPERATORS

Almost any international agent selling safaris to Tanzania can also arrange a Kilimanjaro climb through a reliable local operator. However, travellers who want to book their climb direct through a local operator, whether they do it online or after arriving in Tanzania, will soon realise that there are a daunting number of options, ranging from costly quality operators with vast experience of the mountain through to small local operators offering cut-throat prices and similar services – and pretty much every gradation in between. It is impossible for a guidebook of this sort to attempt to assess every last operator in such a busy and competitive market, but the following, well-established, companies can all be recommended as reputable and reliable, and are listed as Partners for Responsible Travel on w kiliporters.org and w mountainexplorers.org.

MOSHI It is difficult to walk far in some parts of Moshi without having a local guide or self-styled tour operator trying to persuade you to arrange a climb. These guys may offer marginally cheaper rates than established operators, but they are notoriously unreliable. Our advice is to ignore anybody who approaches you on the street in favour of a proper travel agency, of which Pristine Trails, Snowcap Tanzania Tours and Shah Tours stand out (page 156).

MARANGU The family-run Marangu Hotel has been taking people up Kilimanjaro for decades, and they have an impeccable reputation. The standard packages aren't the cheapest available, but they are pretty good value, and the standard of service and equipment is very high.

ARUSHA Most safari operators in Arusha arrange Kilimanjaro climbs, and any company listed in the Arusha chapter (page 134) should be reliable. Particularly recommended are **Summits Africa**, **Hoopoe Safaris** and **Nature Discovery**, all of which have a long track record of organising ascents along the lesser-known routes, and are well worth contacting if you're prepared to pay a premium for top guides and equipment. These are also the companies we would recommend for longer climbs that include an overnight stay in Kibo Crater, from where you can explore the peaks area and ash cone at relative leisure.

guides will be underpaid to help cut costs. A crucial point when comparing this situation with the similar one that surrounds arranging a safari out of Arusha is that you're not merely talking about losing a day through breakdown or a similar inconvenience. With Kilimanjaro, you could literally die on the mountain. Stories abound of climbers being supplied with inadequate equipment and food, and even being abandoned by their guide mid climb. The very least you can do, if you make arrangements of this sort, is to verify that your guide is registered; he should have a small wallet-like document to prove it, though even this can be faked.

OTHER PREPARATIONS Two climatic factors must be considered when preparing to climb Kilimanjaro. The obvious one is the cold. Bring plenty of warm clothes, a windproof jacket, a pair of gloves, a balaclava, a warm sleeping bag and an insulation mat. During the rainy season, a waterproof jacket and trousers will come in useful. A less obvious factor is the sun, which is fierce at high altitudes. Bring sunglasses, sunscreen and a hat.

Other essentials are water bottles, and solid shoes or preferably boots that have already been worn in. Most of these items can be hired in Moshi or at the park gate, or from the company you arrange to climb with. We've heard varying reports about the condition of locally hired items, but standards seem to be far higher than they were only a few years back.

A good medical kit is essential, especially if you are climbing with a cheap company. You'll go through plenty of plasters if you acquire a few blisters (assume that you will), and can also expect to want headache tablets.

You might want to buy biscuits, chocolate, sweets, glucose powder and other energy-rich snacks to take with you up the mountain. No companies supply this sort of thing, and although they are sometimes available at the huts, you'll pay through the nose for them.

ABBOTT'S DUIKER

An antelope occasionally encountered by hikers on Kilimanjaro is Abbott's duiker (*Cephalophus spadix*), a montane forest species known as *minde* in Swahili. Formerly quite widespread in suitable East African habitats, it is today endemic only to eastern Tanzania due to environmental loss and poaching elsewhere in its natural range. After Ader's duiker, a lowland species of the East African coastal belt, Abbott's is the most threatened of African duikers, categorised as Endangered in the IUCN Red List for 2016, but based on present trends it is likely to decline to a status of Critically Endangered in the foreseeable future. Abbott's duiker is today confined to five forested montane 'islands' in eastern Tanzania, namely Kilimanjaro, Usambara, Udzungwa, Uluguru and Rungwe. It is a notoriously secretive creature (the first photograph of one was taken in 2003) and the total population is unknown, but the most recent estimates place the total at fewer than 1,500. Either way, Udzungwa probably harbours the most substantial and secure single population, followed by Kilimanjaro. Should you be lucky enough to stumble across this rare antelope, it has a glossy, unmarked off-black torso, a paler head and a distinctive red forehead tuft. Its size alone should, however, be diagnostic: the shoulder height of up to 75cm is the third largest of any duiker species, and far exceeds that of other more diminutive duikers that occur in Tanzania.

MAPS AND FURTHER READING Trekkers are not permitted on the mountain without a registered guide, and all sensible trekkers will make arrangements through a reliable operator, which means that there is no real need for detailed route descriptions once you're on the mountain. Nevertheless, many trekkers will benefit from the detailed practical advice and overview of route possibilities provided in Henry Stedman's superb 408-page *Kilimanjaro: The Trekking Guide to Africa's Highest Mountain* (Trailblazer, 5th edition 2018).

8

Mkomazi National Park and the Usambara Mountains

The Tanzanian interior southeast of Moshi and northwest of Tanga is home to two of the country's most underrated off-the-beaten-track natural attractions. Mkomazi National Park, a Tanzanian extension of Kenya's immense Tsavo National Park, is an emergent safari destination that hosts small numbers of all the Big Five, and ranks as the best place in the country to see the Endangered black rhino. Further south, the hiker-friendly Usambara is a single geological range split into discrete eastern and western components by a deeply incised river valley. The Western Usambara, centred on the attractive town of Lushoto, offers some great scenic walks and opportunities for cultural interaction, while the Eastern Usambara's Amani Nature Forest Reserve supports a diverse selection of forest wildlife including several endemic and localised species of bird. Visited separately or in combination with each other, Mkomazi and the Usambara make a great add-on or alternative to the northern safari circuit for those wanting to get away from the crowds.

MKOMAZI NATIONAL PARK

One of Tanzania's most underrated national parks, Mkomazi (**m** +255 624 333888; **e** mkomazi@tanzaniaparks.go.tz) is an emergent safari destination whose main attractions are its untrammelled atmosphere and the exciting opportunity to see the Endangered black rhino in a special drive-in sanctuary that opened in 2021. It extends across 3,234km^2 of dry scrubland to the southeast of Kilimanjaro and immediate north of the Pare Mountains, and is effectively a southern extension of Kenya's vast Tsavo National Park. As such, it forms part of one of East Africa's most important semi-arid savannah ecosystems and harbours a great many dry-country species rare or absent elsewhere in Tanzania.

Although Mkomazi has been a game reserve since 1951, it was subject to considerable pressure by an ever-growing human population around its peripheries prior to 2008, when it was upgraded to national park status. For several years after this, wildlife remained thinly distributed and skittish, and even today Mkomazi doesn't host animal densities comparable to the more established likes of the Serengeti and Tarangire. However, populations of most key species are tangibly on the increase, with giraffe, buffalo, zebra, eland and Coke's hartebeest being particularly conspicuous.

For many years, an obstacle to exploring Mkomazi was a lack of tourist development, but the park now boasts a decent choice of accommodation, and the

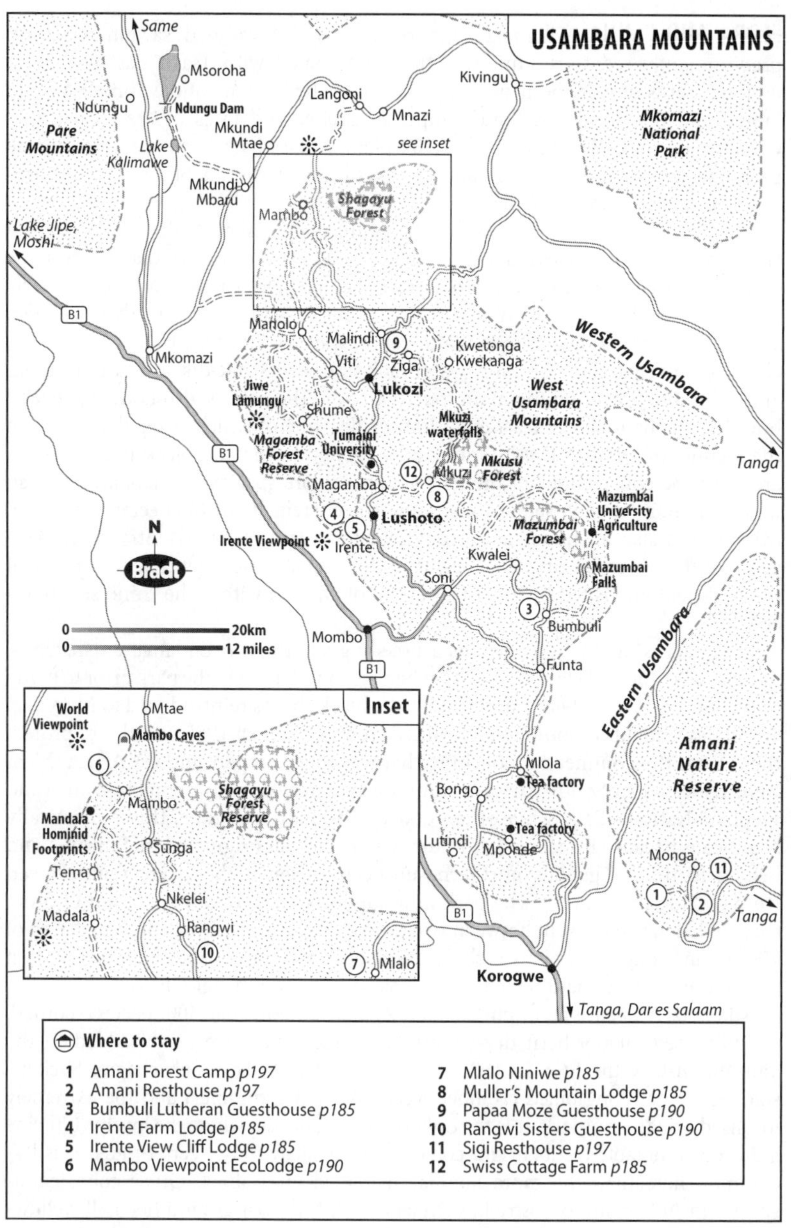

main reason why it is included on so few safari itineraries is probably logistical – coming from Arusha or Moshi, it lies in the opposite direction to the other major parks on the northern circuit. If you decide to buck the trend, Mkomazi's main drawcard is probably the near-certainty of seeing black rhinos, but other attractions include the presence of all the Big Five, the wilderness feel, the impressive birdlife and the enclosing mountainous scenery, often capped by Kilimanjaro to the northwest at dawn and dusk.

FLORA AND FAUNA Mkomazi supports a cover of wooded savannah set on predominantly red soils similar to those associated with Tsavo East and West national parks in neighbouring Kenya. It is classified as part of the Somali-Maasai biome and the dominant flora comprises grasses and trees of the Acacia and Commiphora families. More than 1,300 plant species have been identified in the park but none is endemic to it, and the overall impression is of a rather uniform cover of dense scrubby woodland.

In 1992, when Mkomazi was still a struggling game reserve, a detailed ecological study by the Royal Geographical Society (RGS) determined that most large mammal species present in Tsavo were either resident in the park or regularly migrated there from Kenya. Wildlife populations have increased greatly since then, and large numbers of giraffe, buffalo, zebra, warthog, impala, Coke's hartebeest, eland, Grant's gazelle, common waterbuck and Kirk's dik-dik are now resident and commonly seem on the main tourist circuit. The park is also home to several hundred elephant and at least eight lion prides, one of which is regularly seen in the vicinity of Dindira Dam. Lions aside, spotted hyena and black-backed jackal are most the conspicuous of the park's 20 carnivore species, but leopard are also quite common (though seldom seen) and the current status of cheetah is unclear. Mkomazi is also an important stronghold for a trio of dry-country antelope – gerenuk, fringe-eared oryx and lesser kudu – that are concentrated in parts of the park seldom visited by tourists, but are often seen within the rhino sanctuary at Mbula.

Mkomazi is now best known as a breeding site for two Endangered species – African wild dog and black rhino – that had become extinct in the park prior to being reintroduced in the 1990s. Interestingly, the black rhinos reintroduced to Mkomazi are all descendants of individuals airlifted from the area in 1985 in order to protect them from the commercial poaching that was then rampant in East Africa. Most were relocated to South Africa to found a new black rhino population in Addo Elephant National Park, while others ended up in European zoos. This is genetically significant because it means that Mkomazi's rhinos all originated in Tanzania and belong to the indigenous northern subspecies, even if they were reintroduced from outside the country. The park now supports a breeding population of more than 30 black rhinos, split between two fenced enclosures with a combined area of 70km^2, and long-term plans include the relocation of a few individuals to tourist sanctuaries in other national parks such as Nyerere and Burigi-Chato.

Mkomazi is listed as an Important Bird Area, with more than 400 species recorded, including several northern dry-country endemics that were newly added to the Tanzania list by the RGS in 1992 – for instance three-streaked tchagra, Shelley's starling, Somali long-billed crombec, yellow-vented eremomela and the extremely localised Friedmann's lark. It is the only place in Tanzania where the lovely vulturine guineafowl, notable for its bright cobalt chest, is likely to be seen, though it is less common here than the more familiar helmeted guineafowl. Other conspicuous species include common ostrich, secretary bird, southern ground hornbill, yellow-throated spurfowl, bare-faced go-away bird, African grey hornbill, lilac-breasted roller, Taita fiscal, rosy-patched bush-shrike and white-headed buffalo-weaver. The birdlife is particularly impressive in the rainy season, when weavers, whydahs and widows enter their breeding plumage, and resident species are joined by migrants such as the prolific European roller.

FEES AND FURTHER INFORMATION The entrance fee for non-residents/residents is US$30/15 per person per 24 hours. Overnight fees are US$30 per person to camp,

US$35 per person to stay in a national park banda, or US$25 per person if you are staying at a private camp or lodge. Guided safaris in open 4x4s into Mkomazi Black Rhino Tourist Sanctuary at Mbula cost US$30 per person while a similar activity in Kisima Rhino Breeding Sanctuary costs US$200 per person. In both cases, the activity fee includes an optional stop at the African wild dog enclosure at Kisima. All fees attract a charge of 18% VAT.

GETTING THERE AND AWAY Mkomazi is among the most accessible of Tanzania's national parks. The gateway town Same straddles the main Dar es Salaam Highway 105km southeast of Moshi, a drive that shouldn't take longer than 2 hours. From Same, a clearly signposted 5km dirt road runs to the park's Zange Entrance Gate, where you need to pay the entrance fee. Although several more easterly entrance gates exist, they may not have facilities to accept entrance fees, which makes it difficult to explore the eastern two-thirds of the national park at the time of writing.

Agencies that offer day safaris to Mkomazi from the Western Usambara are Lushoto's Shambaa Eco Tours (page 186) and Mambo Viewpoint EcoLodge (page 190).

WHERE TO STAY AND EAT

Upmarket

Mkomazi View Camp ⊕ -4.01524, 37.81214; m +255 684 346748; w african-view.com. This intimate, well-priced & down-to-earth camp comprises 6 solar-powered twin or dbl tents scattered along the slopes of a hilly amphitheatre overlooking a riverine valley that often attracts large herds of elephant, giraffe & zebra. Despite the secluded location at the end of a cul-de-sac, it is well positioned for game drives to Dindira Dam & Mbula Rhino Sanctuary. **$$$$$**

Mkomazi Wilderness Retreat ⊕ -3.93407, 37.80037; m +255 684 346748; w mkomaziwilderness.com. Boasting a superb hillside location overlooking Dindira Dam, this camp was under construction when we visited in 2022 but is expected to comprise 7 solar-powered luxury tents with sliding glass front doors & hot showers. The dam is a magnet for wildlife, there are distant views of Kilimanjaro on a clear day & meals are prepared using organic produce from the owners' farm near Morogoro. **$$$$$$**

Budget & camping

Amani Lutheran Centre m +255 784 894140. Situated 200m uphill from Same's bus station, this long-serving hostel consists of around a dozen rooms enclosing a small green courtyard. It's a friendly set-up with canteen & safe parking. *US$12/15 dbl/twin B&B*. **$**

Elephant Motel ⊕ -4.07086, 37.75103; m +255 754 839545; w elephantmotel.com. Situated 1.5km south of Same on the B1 to Dar es Salaam, this agreeable hotel has clean rooms with netting, TV & hot showers & a restaurant serving Indian, Tanzanian & Western meals in the restaurant or shady green garden. It's less than 15mins drive from here to Mkomazi's Zange Gate. *From US$40/45 sgl/dbl*. **$**

Mkomazi Cottages ⊕ -4.05581, 37.78865; m +255 624 333888; w tanzaniaparks.go.tz. Situated immediately outside Zange Gate, this national park-run complex comprises 6 semi-detached bandas, all with dbl bed, fitted net, AC, TV, hot shower & balcony. A restaurant serves simple & inexpensive meals & cold beers, & the surrounding bush is rattling with birdlife. *US$35pp + 18% VAT*. **$$**

Zange Campsite ⊕ -4.04900, 37.79901; m +255 624 333888; w tanzaniaparks.go.tz. This public campsite has a lovely bush location about 400m from the main road just inside Zange Gate. There's an ablution block & a dining boma. *US$35pp + 18% VAT*. **$$**

WHAT TO SEE AND DO

Game drives The main focal point for game-viewing is Dindira Dam and the various roads that connect it to Zange Gate. This takes you through a mixture of open grassland and thicker woodland where you should see plenty of giraffe, zebra, hartebeest, eland, dik-dik, gazelle and waterbuck, and might also encounter lion, buffalo and elephant. It is worth lingering at Dindira Dam, especially in the dry season, when it attracts a steady stream of thirsty wildlife from further afield. This drive can be extended by a couple of hours by looping northeast from Dindira Dam to Norbanda Dam via Vitewari Viewing Point, passing through well-wooded slopes where you might see impala and lesser kudu

The thicker bush further southeast, though somewhat less accessible, is the main population centre for dry-country antelope such as fringe-eared oryx, lesser kudu and gerenuk.

Mkomazi Black Rhino Tourist Sanctuary A highlight of any visit to Mkomazi is a guided safari into this 16km² fenced rhino sanctuary, which opened at Mbula, about an hour's drive south of Zange Gate or Dindira Dam, in 2021. Five adult black rhinos have been relocated here from the main breeding sanctuary at Kisima, and it is hoped they will eventually produce more offspring. Guided tours cost US$30 per person and are conducted in open-sided 4x4s for an authentic safari experience. Locating the rhinos can be surprisingly difficult, even in this relatively confined area, but it is rare not to find at least one of them, and you will be introduced to various aspects of rhino ecology and behaviour as you search for them. Other dangerous animals such as buffalo, elephant and lion were cleared from the sanctuary before it was fenced, but plenty of other wildlife is trapped inside, and it's a good place to look for more unusual species such as gerenuk and lesser kudu.

Kisima Rhino Breeding Sanctuary Mkomazi's main 54km² rhino breeding sanctuary can be found at Kisima, about an hour's drive southeast of Mbula. It is home to around 30 adult black rhinos, which are split between four different enclosures to keep rival males from different lineages from engaging in potentially deadly fights. Unlike its newer counterpart at Mbula, the sanctuary here is not primarily designed for tourists, but it is permitted to visit on a similar guided tour for US$200 per person. This is highly recommended to photographers, or anybody who wants to see rhino interaction, especially if you visit in the mid afternoon (around 15.00) when several thirsty individuals usually cluster around a small watering point overlooked by an excellent hide.

Kisima Wild Dog Sanctuary The fee for visiting either rhino sanctuary includes an optional side trip to a caged enclosure housing a pack of around 20 African wild dogs at Kisima. Sadly, unlike visiting the rhino sanctuaries, which are large enough that their inhabitants can range and forage freely within them, the wild dog sanctuary has a decidedly zoo-like feel, and we can't honestly recommend it.

LUSHOTO AND THE SOUTHWEST USAMBARA

Set at an elevation of 1,400m (4,550ft), Lushoto is the principal town of northern Tanzania's most densely populated and heavily cultivated mountain range: the Western Usambara. The modern town was founded in the 1890s under the name Wilhelmstal (after Kaiser Wilhelm II) and peaked in significance during German colonial times, when its temperate climate provided weekend relief for settlers farming the dry, dusty plains below. Architecturally, the main road through Lushoto, lined as it is with early-20th-century buildings, retains the slightly anachronistic aura of an Alpine village. Culturally, however, the town is unambiguously African,

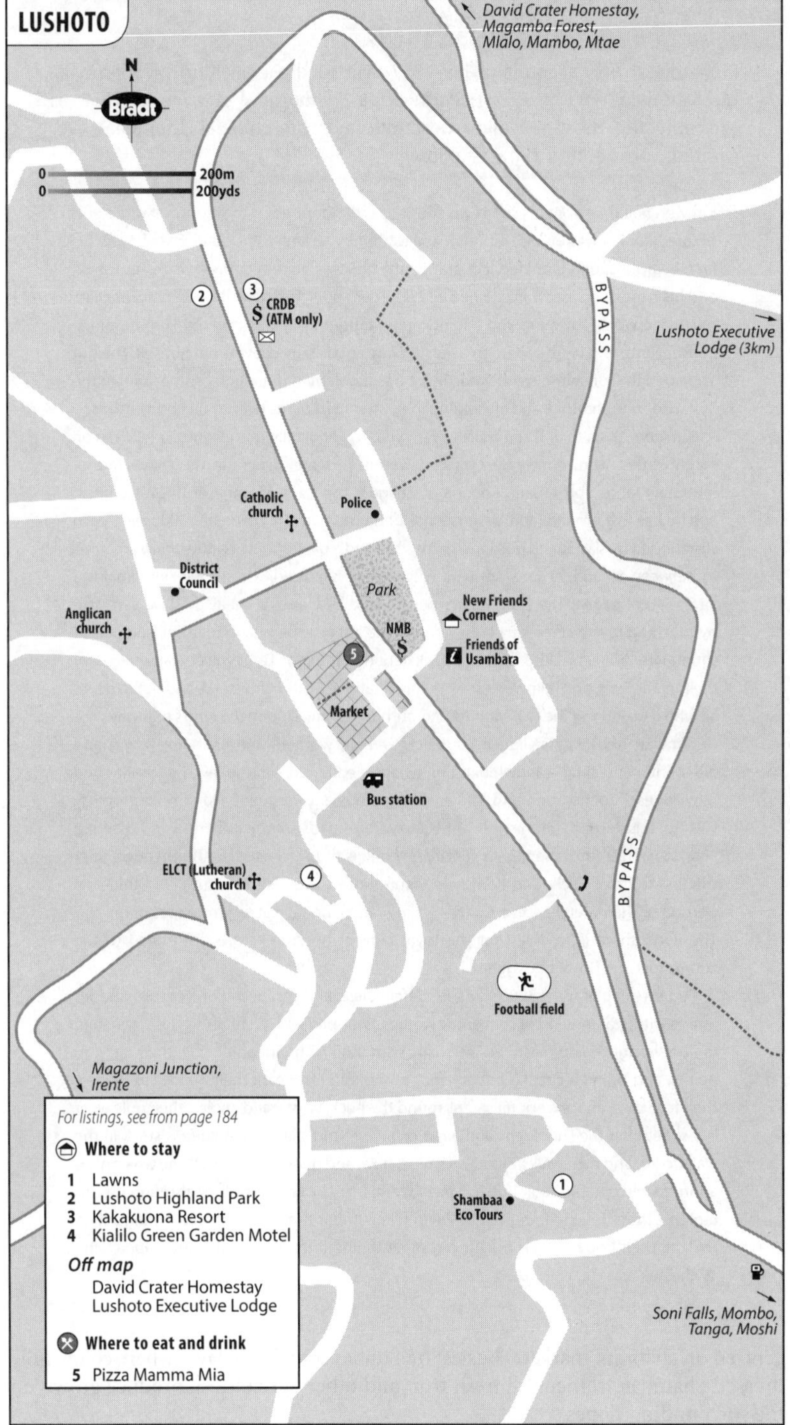
LUSHOTO
N
Bradt
0 200m
0 200yds
David Crater Homestay, Magamba Forest, Mlalo, Mambo, Mtae
BYPASS
Lushoto Executive Lodge (3km)
CRDB (ATM only)
Catholic church
Police
District Council
Park
Anglican church
New Friends Corner
NMB
Friends of Usambara
Market
Bus station
ELCT (Lutheran) church
BYPASS
Football field
Magazoni Junction, Irente
Shambaa Eco Tours
Soni Falls, Mombo, Tanga, Moshi
For listings, see from page 184
Where to stay
1 Lawns
2 Lushoto Highland Park
3 Kakakuona Resort
4 Kialilo Green Garden Motel
Off map
David Crater Homestay
Lushoto Executive Lodge
Where to eat and drink
5 Pizza Mamma Mia

PORTRAIT OF A LION KING

Richard Burton's account of his 1857 visit to the Lion King of Shambaai, published in Volume 83 of *Blackwood's Edinburgh Magazine* in 1858, is probably the most revealing description of pre-colonial Shambaai ever printed. Some edited extracts follow:

> Kimweri half rose from his cot as we entered, and motioned us to sit upon dwarf stools before him. He was an old, old man, emaciated by sickness. His head was shaved, his face beardless, and wrinkled like grandam's; his eyes were red, his jaws disfurnished, and his hands and feet were stained with leprous spots. The royal dress was a Surat cap, much the worse for wear, and a loinwrap as tattered. He was covered with a double cotton cloth, and he rested upon a Persian rug, apparently coeval with himself. The hut appeared that of a simple cultivator, but it was redolent of dignitaries, some fanning the Sultan, others chatting, and all holding long-stemmed pipes with small ebony bowls.
>
> Kimweri, I was told, is the fourth of a dynasty...originally from Nguru, a hilly region south of the river...Kimweri, in youth a warrior of fame, ranked in the triumvirate of mountain kings above Bana Rongua of Chagga, and Bana Kizunga of the Wakuafy. In age he has lost ground [and] asserts kinghood but in one point: he has 300 wives, each surrounded by slaves, and portioned with a hut and a plantation. His little family amounts to between 80 and 90 sons, some of whom have Islamised, whilst their sire remains a 'pragmatical pagan'. The Lion [King]'s person is sacred; even a runaway slave saves life by touching royalty. Presently [Kimweri] will die, be wrapped up in matting, and placed sitting-wise under his deserted hut, a stick denoting the spot. Dogs will be slaughtered for the funeral-feast, and [Kimweri's son] Muigni Khatib will rule in his stead, and put to death all who dare, during the two months of mourning, to travel upon the king's highway.
>
> Kimweri rules...by selling his subjects – men, women, and children, young and old, gentle and simple, individually, or, when need lays down the law, by families and by villages...Confiscation and sale are indigenous and frequent. None hold property without this despot's permission...In a land where beads are small change, and sheeting and 'domestics' form the higher specie, revenue is thus collected. Cattle-breeders offer the first fruits of flocks and herds; elephant-hunters every second tusk; and traders a portion of their merchandise. Cultivators are rated annually at ten measures of grain... The lion's share is reserved for the royal family; the crumbs are distributed to the councillors and [royal bodyguards].
>
> Fuga, a heap of some 3000 souls, [is] defenceless, and composed of...circular abodes [made with] frameworks of concentric wattles, wrapped with plantain-leaves...fastened to little uprights, and plastered internally with mud...The [people]...file their teeth to points, and brand a circular beauty-spot in the mid-forehead; their heads are shaven, their feet bare, and, except talismans round the neck, wrists, and ankles, their only wear is a sheet over the shoulders, and a rag or hide round the loins. A knife is stuck in the waist-cord, and men walk abroad with pipe, bow, and quiverless arrows. The women are adorned with charm-bags; and collars of white beads – now in fashion throughout this region – from three to four pounds weight, encumber the shoulders of a 'distinguished person'. Their body-dress is the African sheet bound tightly under the arms, and falling to the ankles...

centred on a vibrant market – busiest on Sunday and Thursday – where colourfully dressed Shambaa women sell fresh fruit and other agricultural produce grown on the surrounding slopes.

The vegetation around Lushoto is similarly dichotomous. Broad-leafed papaya and banana trees subvert neat rows of exotic pines and eucalyptus, which in turn are interspersed by patches of lush indigenous forest alive with the raucous squawking of silvery-cheeked hornbills and the banter of monkeys. These scenic highlands form superb walking country, riddled with small footpaths and winding roads, and studded with spectacular viewpoints over the low-lying plains below.

Situated less than an hour's drive from the main road between Moshi and Dar es Salaam, Lushoto has developed into the focal point of a travel scene that feels delightfully down to earth in comparison with the hype, hustle and extravagant prices associated with the likes of Arusha and Zanzibar. Indeed, a plethora of guides, community tourism projects and affordable guesthouses aimed at independent travellers makes it an ideal diversion for anybody interested in experiencing everyday Tanzanian culture.

HISTORY The name Usambara derives from that of the Shambaa, a Bantu-speaking agriculturalist people whose modern population totals around 600,000. Their origin is difficult to ascertain. Some clans claim they have always lived in the mountains, others that they moved there during times of drought, or in response to the 18th-century Maasai invasion of the plains. Quite possibly, these divergent accounts simply reflect divergent clan histories, since the ancestral Shambaa had a reputation for welcoming refugees, and the loosely structured political system that characterised the region until about 300 years ago would have encouraged the peaceful assimilation of newcomers.

Prior to the 18th century, Shambaa social structure was similar to the ntemi chieftaincies of western Tanzania. Each clan lived in a clearly defined territory with its own petty leadership. A regional council of elders had the authority to settle disputes between different clans, and to approve marriages that would help cement inter-clan unity. According to tradition, the move towards centralised power – probably a response to the threat posed by the Maasai – was led by an outsider called Mbegha, the first Simba Mwene (Lion King) of the Shambaa.

That Mbegha is a genuine historical figure is not in doubt, and the oral traditions of neighbouring tribes support the local story that he moved to the mountains from the plains below and became king after resolving a major crisis there. Quite how Mbegha achieved his leonine coup is open to question. One – rather implausible – local tradition has it that, as a hunter of renown, Mbegha was called upon by a delegation of elders to rid the mountains of the bushpigs that were destroying all their crops, and was so effective in his campaign that he was appointed ruler of all the Shambaa.

Mbegha went on to forge regional unity by taking a wife from each major clan and placing their firstborn son in charge of it. The Shambaa invested Mbegha and the Kilindi dynasty of Lion Kings that succeeded him with supernatural powers, believing among other things that they were able to control the elements. The dynasty consolidated power under the rule of Mbegha's grandson Kinyashi, who adopted a militaristic policy with the aim of forging the most important state between the coast and the great lake region. This ambition was realised by Kinyashi's son and successor, Kimweri, the greatest Simba Mwene of them all. Towards the end of his reign, Kimweri was held in sufficient esteem outside his kingdom that the explorer Richard Burton undertook the trek inland from Pangani to visit the Shambaa capital of Fuga (now more often called Vuga), close to modern-day Bumbuli (page 187).

Kimweri's death, a few years after Burton's visit, was the catalyst for the first major rift in Shambaa. Vuga was too deep in the mountains to have attracted regular contact with the Kilimanjaro-bound caravans. Not so the Shambaa town of Mazinde, on what is now the main Moshi–Dar es Salaam road, whose chief Semboja exerted considerable influence over passing traders and was able to stockpile sufficient arms to overthrow Kimweri's successor at Vuga. This event split the Shambaa into several different splinter groups, and although Semboja retained nominal leadership of Shambaa, he controlled a far smaller area than Kimweri had before him.

Shambaa unity was further divided under German rule. Although the people of the Usambara played a leading role in the Abushiri Uprising of 1888–89, their resistance crumbled after Semboja's son and successor Mputa was hanged by the Germans in 1898. The Kilindi dynasty has, however, retained a strong symbolic role in modern Shambaa culture. Mputa's grandson Kimweri Mputa Magogo, who took the throne in 1947 and died in September 2000, was one of the most respected traditional leaders in Tanzania prior to the title being abolished in 1962 following independence.

GETTING THERE AND AWAY Coming from almost anywhere else in Tanzania, the gateway to Lushoto is **Mombo**, a nondescript junction town that straddles the B1 on the plains below. Mombo (not to be confused with the similarly named Mambo on the northwest Usambara) is connected to Lushoto by a surfaced 33km road that offers splendid views in all directions, passing en route through Soni with its famous waterfall; the trip takes 40–60 minutes by car, depending on how cowed the driver is by the precipitously steep drop-offs. Depending on your starting point, allow 6 hours to reach Lushoto from Arusha or Dar es Salaam, 4 hours from Moshi, or 3 hours from Tanga or Same.

If you're bussing, a recommended operator is Kibomboi Royal Class (f Kibomboi Royal Class KRC; m +255 783 808081; fares in the US$7–10 range), which runs daily buses in either direction connecting Lushoto to Arusha, Moshi and Dar es Salaam, and continuing on to Mtae or Mlalo. Another good option to or from Dar es Salaam is Kiluwa Luxury Bus (kiluwa_luxury_coach). Alternatively, take an express service such as Dar Express or Kilimanjaro Express and ask to be dropped off at Mombo, from where regular dalla dallas (US$2) run through to Lushoto. Coming from Tanga, there are no buses but plenty of dalla dallas (US$3).

WHERE TO STAY *Map, page 181*

David Crater Homestay w booking.com. Situated in a leafy garden 1.5km north of the town centre off the road to Magamba, this friendly owner-managed B&B offers the choice of brightly decorated private rooms or a 4-bed mixed dorm. Meals are eaten communally & it's a great place to meet other travellers. *From US$32 dbl B&B or US$20pp dorm bed.* **$**

Kakakuona Resort f kakakuonalodge; m +255 754 006969. This well-priced lodge behind the post office has comfortable modern rooms with TV & hot shower. An excellent balcony restaurant (one of the few in Lushoto to serve alcohol) overlooks a tree-fringed stream & serves a varied selection of inexpensive grills & stews. *US$13/16 sgl/dbl.* **$**

Kialilo Green Garden Motel m +255 762 143468; w kialilomotel.wordpress.com. The pick of several cheap local lodgings scattered on the slopes west of the town centre, this has simple but clean rooms with hot shower, ¾ bed & net, as well as a neat little garden with a nice view. *US$10/13 sgl/dbl.* **$**

✷ **Lawns Hotel** m +255 652 315914; w lawnshotel.com. Lushoto's most characterful lodge is centred on a c1900 German homestead that's been owned & managed by the same Greek family since the 1970s, though a dynamic new generation took the reins in 2016. It stands in large sloping gardens 500m south of the town centre & has a cheerful bar decorated with quirky paraphernalia, a spa offering Finnish sauna &

massage, an on-site tour operator in the form of Shambaa Eco Tours, & a good restaurant housed in an old colonial-era cinema. Rooms retain a period feel & come with piping-hot showers, while the campsite is popular with overland trucks. Rooms are variable in size & standard. *From US$40–90 dbl B&B, camping US$5pp.* **$–$$**

Lushoto Executive Lodge m +255 677 985265; w lushotoexecutivelodge.co.tz. Set in large forested gardens 3km out of town, this lovely lodge, centred on an old German homestead built in 1902, doesn't quite live up to its potential, but the spacious rooms are reasonably priced & come with hot shower & DSTV. *From US$49/62 dbl B&B.* **$$**

Lushoto Highland Park Hotel m +255 789 428911; w lushotohighlandhotels.co.tz. This multi-storey hotel is probably the smartest option in the town centre but equally characterless & relatively pricey at the inflated non-resident rate. Small but clean rooms have TV & hot shower. The restaurant is OK but service is slow. *US$35/40 sgl/dbl B&B.* **$**

Further afield *Map, page 177*

Irente

✷ **Irente Farm Lodge** ⊕ -4.79399, 38.26675; m +255 788 503002; w irentefarmlodge.com. Signposted en route to Irente Viewpoint 5km west of Lushoto, this popular retreat is set within the 6ha Irente Biodiversity Reserve, which has been replanted with indigenous trees & forms part of a 200ha working farm that started life as a German experimental coffee estate in 1896. The farm was bought by the ELCT Lutheran Church in 1963 & now doubles as an orphanage & school for the blind, funded partially by proceeds from the lodge & associated home produce shop. Accommodation includes en-suite bandas, twin rooms using shared bathrooms, & a 6-bed self-catering lodge. Tasty home-cooked meals are available, along with superb picnic lunches (see below). The farm is clearly signposted 1.5km before Irente Viewpoint. From *US$15pp B&B (shared showers) & US$50 en-suite dbl HB.* **$–$$**

Irente View Cliff Lodge ⊕ -4.80198, 38.25847; m +255 784 866877; w irenteview.com. This modern lodge at Irente, 6km west of Lushoto, boasts an impressive thatched roof, an erratically decent restaurant & a stunning clifftop location. The rooms are comfortable & come with DSTV, hot shower & balcony, but are let down by poor-quality fittings. *From US$65 dbl B&B.* **$**

Bumbuli

Bumbuli Lutheran Guesthouse ⊕ -4.86363, 38.47048; m +255 784 205805. Set in the Lutheran mission hospital grounds 10mins' walk uphill from Bumbuli town centre, this characterful restored building reputedly dates back to the 1930s. The neat rooms use a common shower, & there's a lounge & a self-catering kitchen. Cheap meals are available. *US$10pp.* **$**

Migambo (near Magamba Nature Forest Reserve)

✷ **Muller's Mountain Lodge** ⊕ -4.76052, 38.33441; m +255 757 500999; w mullersmountainlodge.co.tz. This family-run 1930s farm cottage, set in flowering gardens bordering Magamba 14km from Lushoto, is one of the most attractive places to stay anywhere in the Usambara & an excellent base for birdwatchers. The 16 rooms are cosy & comfortable, home-cooked meals can be enjoyed in the restaurant or garden, & several day trails lead out from the property. *US$45/60 sgl/dbl B&B.* **$$**

Swiss Cottage Farm ⊕ -4.75482, 38.33041; m +255 715 700813; w swiss-farm-cottage.co.tz. Situated 13km from Lushoto, this peaceful retreat stands on a working farm close to Magamba. Accommodation is very comfortable & excellent meals are prepared with organic farm produce. *From US$95 dbl B&B.* **$$**

Mlalo

Mlalo Niniwe Hotel ⊕ -4.58003, 38.35081; m +255 753 214898; w mlaloniniwehotel.com. This simple family-run hotel 700m from Mlalo's bus station has comfortable tooms with hot showers & an adequate restaurant. *US$25/35 sgl/dbl B&B.* **$**

WHERE TO EAT

Irente Farm Lodge [map, page 177] See also above; m +255 788 503002; w irentefarmlodge.com; ⏲ 10.00–14.00 Mon–Sat. A popular stop on the hike between Lushoto & Irente, Irente Farm Lodge can provide delicious picnic lunch hampers with homemade rye bread & cheese, organic vegetables, fruit juice & other fresh farm produce. The picnics cost around US$6pp, but you should call in advance to book. Alternatively, an attached farm shop sells an array of cheese & other local produce for consumption off the premises.

Pizza Mamma Mia [map, page 181] m +255 717 787888; f mammamialushoto; ⌚ 11.30–21.00 Tue–Sat, 14.30–21.00 Sun–Mon. Lushoto's funkiest restaurant has retro 1950s décor, diner-style seating & a varied menu that includes exceptional pizzas, as well as curries, grills, pasta dishes & salads. Drinks include freshly brewed coffee, smoothies, juices, beer & wine. It can also prepare lunch boxes for hikers. *Mains US$6–8.* **$$**

OTHER PRACTICALITIES The **CRDB** and **NMB** both have ATMs where you can draw normally local currency on foreign cards. The CRDB also has a **foreign exchange** bureau.

TOURIST INFORMATION AND TOUR OPERATORS In addition to the organisations recommended below, several other semi-official and private small agencies are dotted around Lushoto. We would advise circumspection about taking on any guide who doesn't operate out of a proper office.

Friends of Usambara m +255 787 094725; w usambaratravels.com; ⌚ 08.00–18.00 daily. This prominently signposted TTB-endorsed cultural tourism enterprise has been arranging reliable guided trips throughout the Usambara region since the 1990s. The staff are willing to offer advice without being pushy about paid services, so it is also a great source of tourist information. The fee structure for guided day trips is rather complex, & linked strongly to group size, but most day outings work out at around US$15–25pp, while the daily rate for overnight excursions is about double that. The office also arranges bicycle, tent, sleeping bag & roll-mat hire. All profits go towards community projects.

Magamba Eco-Cultural Tourism ⊕ -4.74707, 38.28865; m +255 783 688844; w magambaculturaltourism.com. Situated 10km from Lushoto & 1km from the office for Magamba Nature Forest Reserve, this agency specialises in forest hikes & visits to remote Mlalo.

Shambaa Eco Tours m +255 744 114115; w shambaaecotours.co.tz. Founded in 2020, the only fully registered tour company in Lushoto is based in the grounds of Lawns Hotel. Guided outings range from a 1½hr historical tour of the town centre, cooking & dance classes, & a half-day ramble to Irente Viewpoint to multi-day hikes deeper into the mountains. It also runs day & overnight safaris to Mkomazi National Park. Rates are comparable to Friends of Usambara & it offers substantial discounts to guests staying at Lawns Hotel.

WHAT TO SEE AND DO Lushoto is a useful base for a number of guided or unguided day and excursions. Most popular of these is the relatively undemanding and scenic day hike to Irente Viewpoint west of Lushoto, while other common goals for day trips include the pretty Soni Falls and wildlife-rich Magamba Forest. More off-the-beaten track possibilities are the small and little-visited villages of Bumbuli and Mlalo. Lushoto is also a good starting point for visits to Mambo, Mtae and the Northwest Usambara Escarpment, which is covered separately on page 190.

Irente Viewpoint and Farm Perched on the Usambara's western escarpment edge 6.5km from Lushoto by road, Irente Viewpoint (⊕ -4.80364, 38.25748) offers an absolutely fantastic view across the Maasai Steppe as it rolls towards a vast horizon 1,000m below. The viewpoint is situated alongside the well-signposted Irente View Cliff Lodge and it's perfectly possible to walk there unguided from Lushoto, allowing 1½ hours in either direction. Starting at the Catholic Church, head west for 250m to the ELCT (Lutheran) church, then turn left and follow the main road as it winds uphill for another 1.2km to Magazoni Junction, where you need to take a sharp right. It's another 5km from here to the viewpoint, passing Irente Farm to your right after about 3.5km, and there's no serious likelihood of getting lost. However, most travellers opt to arrange a guided tour with Friends of Usambara or Shambaa Eco Tours, as this allows you to use a more interesting route following backroads and footpaths.

We would recommend two add-ons to the Irente hike. The first is a diversion to Yoghoi Viewpoint, which lies 1km from Irente, following a clear footpath south along the escarpment. From Yoghoi, you can cut east onto a small road that returns directly to Lushoto via Magazoni Junction, a distance of about 6km in total. Alternatively, a popular option is to combine the hike to Irente with a picnic at Irente Farm Lodge (page 185), which also has a great shop (🕘 08.00–16.00 daily) selling an array of yummy fresh farm produce. The birding at Irente can be rewarding, with more than 80 species recorded in the area.

Soni Falls Straddling the surfaced road between Mombo and Lushoto, the small town of Soni is of interest primarily for the attractive waterfall with which it shares a name. Although it is visible from the main road to Lushoto, the waterfall can only be seen properly from its rocky base, which is accessed by a steep 500m path leading downhill from the grounds of what used to be the Soni Falls Hotel but is now the Soni Education Centre (⊕ -4.84736, 38.36361). The drive between Lushoto and Soni takes no more than 30 minutes, and there are plenty of dalla dallas. It is possible to visit independently but guided day trips with Friends of Usambara also take in a peak called Kwa Mongo, which is known for its colourful butterflies, as well as the 300-year-old grave of King Mbegha and the so-called Magila Growing Rock (whose base is exposed further every year as a result of soil erosion).

Bumbuli Situated 23km from Soni near the eastern rim of the Western Usambara, Bumbuli is reputedly where King Mbegha entered the mountains some 300 years ago. A small waterfall can be found on the outskirts of the town, close to the Soni road, and the Saturday market is very colourful. Locally, Bumbuli is best known for its hospital, which lies in the leafy grounds of a Lutheran Mission established in 1927, and also contains a characterful old guesthouse (page 185). The town lies in the shadow of Mazumbai Peak, whose upper slopes are protected in a 3.2km² forest reserve inhabited by Angola colobus and blue monkey, as well as a variety of localised birds, including the endemic banded green sunbird. Several direct buses run daily between Bumbuli and Korogwe, Mombo or Lushoto (all passing through Soni), so it is possible to visit independently, but if you want to explore Mazumbai Forest Reserve, it's best to organise an overnight guided hike with Friends of Usambara and Shambaa Eco Tours.

Magamba Nature Forest Reserve (⊕ -4.74323, 38.28444 (reserve office); w nature-reserves.go.tz; entrance fee US$10pp; guide fee US$15 per group; camping US$10/15 for 1/2 people) Only 10km north of Lushoto, the most accessible indigenous forest in the Western Usambara covers the slopes of its highest peak, the 2,230m Mount Magamba. Protected in a 93km² nature forest reserve, it is of great interest to birders as the best place to look for Usambara weaver and Usambara akalat (both of which are endemic to the Western Usambara), while other localised and endemic forest residents include Usambara eagle-owl, Usambara nightjar, Usambara thrush, spot-throat, red-capped forest warbler, black-fronted bush-shrike, Fülleborn's boubou and Usambara double-collared sunbird. A variety of mammals also live in this forest, most conspicuously Angola colobus and blue monkey, and it's an important stronghold for the endemic Western Usambara two-horned chameleon.

Several day trails run through Magamba Nature Forest Reserve, ranging in distance from the 6.5km Juma Kahema Trail to the 23km Shume Skyline Trail. The most productive option for birding is generally regarded to be the first 7km of the Shume Skyline Trail (also known as the Old Sawmill Trail), which starts at the reserve office then runs northwest through the heart of the forest for 7km to a lovely but unfacilitated camping and picnic site next to an abandoned sawmill. For non-birders, a popular goal for relaxed day walks is a small but pretty waterfall on the forest-fringed Mkuzu River about 2km from Migambo village.

Guided hikes into the forest, inclusive of transport from Lushoto, can be arranged through any of the agencies listed on page 186. It is also possible to

CHAMELEONS

Common and widespread in Tanzania, but not easily seen unless they are actively searched for, chameleons are arguably the most intriguing of African reptiles. True chameleons of the family Chamaeleonidae are confined to the Old World, with the most important centre of speciation being the island of Madagascar, to which about half of the world's 120 recognised species are endemic. Aside from two species of chameleon apiece in Asia and Europe, the remainder are distributed across mainland Africa.

Chameleons are best known for their capacity to change colour, a trait that is often exaggerated in popular literature, and which is generally influenced by mood more than the colour of the background. Some chameleons are more adept at changing colour than others, with the most variable being the **common chameleon** (*Chamaeleo chamaeleon*) of the Mediterranean region, with more than 100 colour and pattern variations recorded. Many African chameleons are typically green in colour but will gradually take on a browner hue when they descend from the foliage to more exposed terrain, for instance while crossing a road. Several change colour and pattern far more dramatically when they are confronted by a rival of the same species. Different chameleon species also vary greatly in size, the largest being **Oustalet's chameleon** (*Furcifer oustaleti*) and **Parson's chameleon** (*Calumma parsonii*), both of which are endemic to Madagascar and can reach a length of almost 70cm.

A remarkable physiological feature common to all true chameleons is their protuberant round eyes, which offer a potential 180° vision on both sides and are able to swivel around independently of each other. Only when one of them isolates a suitably juicy-looking insect will the two eyes focus in the same direction as the chameleon stalks slowly forward until it is close enough to use the other unique weapon in its armoury. This is its sticky-tipped tongue, which is typically about the same length as its body and remains coiled up within its mouth most of the time, to be unleashed in a sudden, blink-and-you'll-miss-it lunge to zap a selected item of prey. In addition to their unique eyes and tongues, many chameleons are adorned with an array of facial casques, flaps, horns and crests that enhance their already somewhat fearsome prehistoric appearance.

In Tanzania, you're most likely to come across a chameleon by chance when it is crossing a road, in which case it should be easy to take a closer look at it, since visit independently in a private vehicle and make arrangements at the reserve office. Using public transport, you could catch a dalla dalla from Lushoto to any town further north (for instance Lukozi, Mtae or Mlalo) and ask to be dropped just past the Sebastian Kolowa Memorial University, from where it is 1.5km to the reserve office.

Mlalo This bizarre town sprawls over a large valley some 50km from Lushoto along a road that forks from the Mtae road at Malindi, 30km from Lushoto. Mlalo has an insular, almost otherworldly feel, epitomised by the unusual style of many of the buildings: two-storey mud houses whose intricately carved wooden balconies show German or Swahili influences. The small Lutheran Church here reputedly dates to the 1890s and the surrounding area also offers some interesting off-the-beaten-track hiking. At least three buses run daily between Lushoto and Mlalo, and the trip takes around 2 hours.

most chameleons move painfully slowly and deliberately. Chameleons are also often seen on night game drives, when their ghostly nocturnal colouring shows up clearly under a spotlight – as well as making it pretty clear why these strange creatures are regarded with both fear and awe in many local African cultures. More actively, you could ask your guide if they know where to find a chameleon – a few individuals will be resident in most lodge grounds.

The **flap-necked chameleon** (*Chamaeleo dilepis*) is probably the most regularly observed species in savannah and woodland habitats in East Africa. Often observed crossing roads, the flap-necked chameleon is generally around 15cm long and bright green in colour with few distinctive markings, but individuals might be up to 30cm in length and will turn tan or brown under the right conditions. Another closely related and widespread savannah and woodland species is the similarly sized **graceful chameleon** (*Chamaeleo gracilis*), which is generally yellow-green in colour and often has a white horizontal stripe along its flanks.

Characteristic of East African montane forests, **three-horned chameleons** form a closely allied species cluster of some taxonomic uncertainty. Typically darker than the savannah chameleons and around 20cm in length, the males of all taxa within this cluster are distinguished by a trio of long nasal horns that project forward from their face. The most widespread three-horned chameleon in Tanzania is **Johnston's chameleon** (*Trioceros johnstoni*), while the most localised is the **Ngosi three-horned chameleon** (*Trioceros fuelleborni*), confined to the forested slopes of Ngosi Volcano in the Poroto Mountains. Perhaps the most alluring of East Africa's chameleons is the **giant one-horned chameleon** (*Trioceros melleri*), a bulky dark-green creature with yellow stripes and a small solitary horn, mainly associated with the Eastern Arc forests, where it feeds on small reptiles (including snakes) as well as insects.

Usambara ranks among most the most important hotspots of chameleon diversity in East Africa. Eastern Arc or Usambara endemics that occur here include the Usambara three-horned chameleon (*Trioceros deremensis*), West Usambara two-horned chameleon (*Kinyongia multituberculata*), East Usambara two-horned chameleon (*Kinyongia matschiei*), Usambara soft-horned chameleon (*Kinyongia tenuis*) and several different pygmy chameleons.

MAMBO, MTAE AND THE NORTHWEST USAMBARA ESCARPMENT

Though it traditionally sees less tourism than Lushoto, the most scenic part of the Western Usambara is undoubtedly the far north, where the high escarpment offers scintillating views across expansive plains towards Lake Kalimawe, the Pare Mountains, Mkomazi National Park and even Kilimanjaro, which is 250km distant but still a striking sight on a clear morning. Tourist activity is focused on Mambo Viewpoint EcoLodge, which lies on the escarpment at the eponymous village, and offers an exciting range of guided and unguided hikes, as well as vehicle-based activities organised through its in-house tour operator. Highlights include the nearby village of Mtae, which is surely one of the most scenically located settlements in Africa, as well as a variety of day walks along the escarpment and on the nearby forested slopes of Mount Shagayu.

GETTING THERE AND AWAY Mtae and Mambo lie 65km north of Lushoto by road, a 2-hour drive. If you are **driving** yourself, follow the main road north out of Lushoto for 7km to Magamba, then turn left. After 16km, you'll reach Lukozi, where the main road to Mtae and Mambo branches left, but the road to Papaa Moze or Rangwi Sisters entails going straight through town along a rougher road that reconnects with the main road after about 23km at Nkelei. From Nkelei, it's another 10km to Mtae, or a similar distance to Mambo, turning left at a signposted junction about 3km before Mtae. Using **public transport**, a few local buses connect Lushoto to Mtae and Mambo, usually leaving between noon and 14.00, and charging around US$3 per person.

Coming from Arusha or Moshi in a **4x4** or on a **motorbike**, a scenic shortcut entails following the B1 for about an hour south of Same to the village of Mkomazi (not to be confused with the eponymous national park), where a dirt road to the left is signposted for Mambo Viewpoint. Allow 2 hours for the 50km drive between Mkomazi and Mambo, which ascends a very scenic pass that requires a 4x4 at all times and should not be attempted after heavy rain.

For **independent travellers**, it is also possible to do the trip between Lushoto and Mambo in stages, stopping en route at small settlements such as Lukozi (which hosts a big Monday market), Malindi and Rangwi and overnighting at one of the lodges listed below under the heading *En route from Lushoto*. Alternatively, both Friends of Usambara or Shambaa Eco Tours in Lushoto (page 186) can arrange tailormade multi-day guided tours terminating in Mambo.

WHERE TO STAY AND EAT *Map, page 177*

En route from Lushoto

Papaa Moze Guesthouse ⊕ -4.63228, 38.30038; m +255 784 599019. This friendly owner-managed guesthouse is set in a small but leafy garden in the village of Malindi, 4km north of Lukozi. It has a campsite, restaurant, bar & shop, along with clean & cosy rooms with hot shower. *US$12pp inc b/fast & dinner.* **$**

Rangwi Sisters Guesthouse ⊕ -4.57138, 38.25095; m +255 629 412217. Situated 20km north of Lukozi, just before the junction village of Nkelei, this long-serving guesthouse, set in a Catholic Mission, offers the most comfortable accommodation en route from Lushoto to Mtae & also serves good home cooking. *US$13pp inc b/fast & dinner.* **$**

Mambo & Mtae

Mambo Viewpoint EcoLodge ⊕ -4.50401, 38.21720; m +255 769 522420; w mamboviewpoint.org. Dutch-founded but now under Tanzanian management, this socially conscious lodge has a spectacular escarpment setting, perched at an altitude of 1,900m on the outskirts of Mambo village. It offers cottages, luxury tents, dorm beds & camping, as well as delicious home-cooked meals that are eaten communally. The striking West Usambara 2-horned chameleon lives in the grounds & the rare Taita falcon nests on the cliffs below. It arranges a variety of overnight hiking & biking trips to/from other villages, ranging from 1 to 6 nights in duration. *Luxury tent US$40/60 sgl/dbl B&B, rooms from US$65/80 sgl/dbl B&B, camping US$5pp; dorm US$15pp.* **$–$$**

WHAT TO SEE AND DO

Mtae This small but sprawling village has perhaps the most spectacular location in the Western Usambara. Boasting several fine examples of traditional Shambaa mud houses, it runs for about 2km along what is in effect a dry peninsula, jutting out to the north of the range, and with a drop of several hundred metres on either side offering breathtaking views. The name Mtae translates as 'Place of Counting', a reference to its strategic importance to the Shambaa people during the 19th-century Maasai wars, when it was the site of several battles won by the Shambaa, who were able to see and count any raiding Maasai war party from afar.

The striking Lutheran church that stands in the middle of the town was built in the late 19th century on a site where, formerly, the most powerful ancestral spirits were believed to reside. The story is that the local chief showed this site to the missionaries, expecting them to flee in fear. Instead, the missionaries were unmoved, and the chief – concluding that they must be in touch with more powerful spirits – granted them permission to build a church there.

Mambo Several day hikes run from Mambo Viewpoint (page 190) to sites on the nearby escarpment. The hike to the **Mambo Caves**, on the cliffs below the ecolodge, entails a 400m ascent and descent over 4km and takes around 3 hours, with a good chance of spotting cliff-nesting raptors, including the rare Taita falcon.

Another very scenic hike of similar length leads to the so-called **Mandala Hominid Footprints**, which some local sources reckon were imprinted in volcanic ash by early hominid inhabitants of the area perhaps a million years ago – an unlikely claim, given that the bedrock here is very ancient and non-volcanic in origin, and the impressions look a lot more like a function of weathering than they do footprints. Mambo Viewpoint can also arrange a cultural day tour encompassing a visit to a local healer, lunch with a local family, and meetings with local farmers.

Shagayu Forest Reserve The second-largest indigenous forest in the Western Usambara, Shagayu extends over some 60km² along the slopes of the eponymous mountain, which rises to an altitude of 2,228m a few kilometres east of Mtae and Mambo. The forest here is thought to be in more pristine condition than the larger Magamba Forest, and it harbours a rich and varied forest birdlife, including the colourful Hartlaub's turaco, eagerly sought bar-tailed trogon, and Eastern Arc endemics such as Usambara akalat, Usambara double-collared sunbird, white-chested alethe and Usambara weaver. Visits to the forest can be arranged inexpensively through Mambo Viewpoint (page 190). These include dedicated birding walks with knowledgeable guides, while non-birders can follow the scenic route to the **Kidhege Waterfall**, set deep in the forest, or undertake an overnight camping trip to the peak.

AMANI NATURE FOREST RESERVE AND THE EASTERN USAMBARA

The Eastern Usambara is one of the smallest of the Eastern Arc ranges, as well as one of the lowest, barely exceeding 1,500m in elevation. It also ranks among the Eastern

AN AFRICAN GALÁPAGOS?

Dr Jon Lovett coined the phrase 'Eastern Arc' in the mid 1980s to describe a string of 13 physically isolated East African mountain ranges that share a very similar geomorphology and ecology. All but one of these crystalline ranges lies within Tanzania, forming a rough crescent that runs from Pare and Usambara in the north to Udzungwa and Mahenge in the south. Following a fault line that runs east of the more geologically recent Rift Valley, these are the oldest mountains in East Africa, having formed at least 100 million years ago, making them 30 times older than Kilimanjaro.

For the past 30 million years, the Eastern Arc has supported a cover of montane forest, one that flourished even during the drier and colder climatic conditions that have periodically affected the globe, thanks to a continuous westerly wind that blew in moisture from the Indian Ocean. It was during one such dry phase, ten million years ago, that these became isolated from the lowland rainforest of western and central Africa. More recently, each of the individual forested ranges became a discrete geographical entity, transforming the Eastern Arc into an archipelago of forested islands jutting out from an ocean of low-lying savannah. And as with true islands, these isolated ancient forests became veritable evolutionary hotspots.

The Eastern Arc Mountains host an assemblage of endemic races, species and genera with few peers anywhere in the world. In the two Usambara ranges alone, more than 2,850 plant species have been identified, a list that includes 680 types of tree, a greater tally than that of North America and Europe combined. At least 16 plant genera and 75 vertebrate species are endemic to the Eastern Arc forests. Their invertebrate wealth can be gauged by the fact that 265 invertebrate species are thus far known from just one of the 13 different ranges – an average of 20 endemics per range. Little wonder that the Eastern Arc is classified among the world's 20 top biodiversity hotspots, and is frequently referred to as the Galápagos of Africa.

Eastern Arc endemics fall into two broad categories: old endemics are modern relics of an ancient evolutionary lineage, while new endemics represent very recently evolved lineages. A clear example of a 'living fossil' falling into the former category are the giant elephant shrews of the genus *Rhynchocyon*, whose five extant species are almost identical in structure to more widespread 20-million-year-old ancestral fossils. In many cases, these older, more stable endemics are affiliated to extant West African species from which they have become isolated: Abbott's duiker (page 174) and the endemic monkey species of Udzungwa are cases in point.

The origins of new endemics are more variable. Some, such as the African violets, probably evolved from an ancestral stock blown across the ocean from Madagascar in a freak cyclone. Others, including many birds and flying insects, are local variants on similar species found in neighbouring savannah habitats or in other forests in East Africa. The origin of several other Eastern Arc endemics is open to conjecture: four of the endemic birds show sufficient affiliations to Asian species to suggest they may have arrived there at a time when moister coastal vegetation formed a passage around the Arabian Peninsula.

The forests of the Eastern Arc vary greatly in extent, biodiversity and the degree to which they have been studied and accorded official protection. A 1998 assessment by Newmark indicates that the Udzungwa range retains almost 2,000km^2 of natural forest, of which 20% has a closed canopy, while the forest cover on Kenya's Taita Hills is reduced to a mere 6km^2. The most significant forests in terms of biodiversity are probably Udzungwa, East Usambara and Uluguru. However, ranges such as Nguru and Rubeho remain little studied compared with the Usambara and Udzungwa, so they may host more endemics than is widely recognised.

The Eastern Arc forests are of great interest to birdwatchers as the core of the so-called Tanzania–Malawi Mountains Endemic Bird Area (EBA). This EBA includes roughly 30 forest pockets scattered across Malawi, Mozambique and Kenya, but these outlying forests cover a combined 500km² as compared with 7,200km² of qualifying forest in Tanzania. Of the 37 range-restricted bird species endemic to this EBA, all but five occur in Tanzania, and roughly half are confined to the country. In terms of avian diversity, Udzungwa leads the pack with 23 regional endemics present, including several species found nowhere else or shared only with the inaccessible Rubeho Mountains. For first-time visitors, however, Amani Nature Forest Reserve has the edge over Udzungwa in terms of ease of access to prime birding areas.

Distribution patterns of several range-restricted bird species within the EBA illuminate the mountains' pseudo-island ecology, with several species widespread on one particular range being absent from other apparently suitable ones. The Usambara akalat, for instance, is confined to the Western Usambara, while Loveridge's sunbird and the Uluguru bush-shrike are unique to the Uluguru. The most remarkable distribution pattern belongs to the long-billed forest warbler (aka tailorbird), a Critically Endangered forest-fringe species confined to two ranges set an incredible 2,000km apart – the Eastern Usambara in northern Tanzania and Mount Namuli in central Mozambique. Stranger still is the case of the forest partridges of the genus *Xenoperdix*. Discovered as recently as 1991, this evolutionary relic comprises two recognised species, one endemic to Udzungwa and the other to Rubeho, with stronger genetic affiliations to Asian hill partridges than to any other African birds.

The Eastern Arc has suffered extensive forest loss and fragmentation in the past century, primarily due to unprecedented land use pressure – the population of the Western Usambara, for instance, increased twentyfold in the 20th century. Of the 12 Eastern Arc ranges within Tanzania, only one – the inaccessible Rubeho massif – has retained more than half of its original forest cover, while five have lost between 75% and 90% of their forest in the last two centuries. Fortunately, none of Tanzania's Eastern Arc forests has yet approached the crisis point reached in Kenya's Taita Hills, where a mere 2% of the original forest remains.

Given that many Eastern Arc species are highly localised and that animal movement between forest patches is inhibited by fragmentation, it seems likely that 30% of Eastern Arc endemics have become extinct in the last century, or might well do so in the immediate future. True, the salvation of a few rare earthworm taxa might be dismissed as bunny-hugging esoterica, but the preservation of the Eastern Arc forests as water catchment areas is an issue of clear humanitarian concern. Most of the extant Eastern Arc forests are now protected as forest reserves. The proclamation of a large part of the Udzungwa Mountains as a national park in 1992 is a further step in the right direction. Even more encouraging is the recent creation of Amani Nature Forest Reserve as part of a broader effort to introduce sustainable conservation and ecotourism with the involvement of local communities in the Eastern Usambara.

Anybody wishing to come to grips with the fascinating phenomenon of 'island' ecology in the Eastern Arc Mountains (and elsewhere on the African mainland) is pointed to Jonathon Kingdon's superb book *Island Africa*.

Arc's most ecologically important components, since it supports extensive tracts of evergreen forest sustained by the annual rainfall of up to 2,000mm. In places, the indigenous vegetation has been replaced by tea plantations, and there has also been more recent encroachment by subsistence farmers, but at least 500km² of reasonably undisturbed forest remains. In common with the other montane forests of eastern Tanzania, the Eastern Usambara is cited as a biodiversity hotspot, characterised by a high level of endemism (page 192), as well as being a vital catchment area that provides fresh water to some 200,000 people.

The main tourist focus in the Eastern Usambara is the quirky village of Amani, which was settled in 1902 by German scientists, who established the 3km² Amani Botanical Garden (reputedly the second-largest such entity in the world) as an agricultural research station and arboretum specialising in long-term botanical trials for exotic plant species. Lying at an elevation of roughly 900m, Amani remains a biological and medical research station of note, and the old village – dominated by buildings that date to the German and British colonial eras – has the genteel but rather ramshackle appearance of a European country village transplanted to the African jungle. The development of ecotourism has been a high priority since 1997, when the Amani Nature Forest Reserve (Amani NFR), protecting 84km² of relatively undisturbed forest, was amalgamated from various pre-existing forest reserves, as well as the Amani Botanical Garden and a further 10km² of forest managed by local tea estates. Today, Amani ranks among the most underrated reserves anywhere in northern Tanzania, offering the combination of excellent walking, beautiful forest scenery and a wealth of animal life.

FLORA AND FAUNA The Eastern Usambara supports some 220km² of lowland forest and 280km² of submontane forest, both of which are protected within Amani NFR. The most common of several near-endemic tree species found around the old botanical garden is *Allanblackia stuhlmannii*, which can be distinguished by its foot-long fruits, whose kernels produce a hard white fat used as soap or for cooking. As might be expected, many exotic trees planted by the Germans also flourish around the botanical gardens, but mostly these have not penetrated through to the forest interior. Smaller plants found in the forest around Amani include various endemic wild coffee species, and the well-known African violets of the genus *Saintpaulia* (page 195).

In the early colonial era, elephants, buffalo and leopards still roamed the forests of the Eastern Usambara. Large mammals are relatively poorly represented today, the most conspicuous exception being Angola colobus and blue monkey, both of which are common and draw attention to themselves with their regular vocalisations, as does the smaller but very pretty Tanganyika mountain squirrel. At night, various bushbabies and the eastern tree hyrax are more often heard than seen, while 16 species of bat flit through the forest. Other range-restricted mammals associated with Amani NFR include the impressive black-and-rufous elephant shrew and rather less striking lesser pouched rat. More than 100 forest-associated bird species have been recorded in the reserve, several of them endemic or near-endemic (page 196).

Amani NFR is particularly impressive when it comes to less glamorous wildlife. A long list of reptiles includes at least 25 snake and seven chameleon species. Particularly impressive are the Usambara three-horned chameleon (*Trioceros deremensis*), a near-endemic that can grow to 35cm in length, and the Eastern Usambara two-horned chameleon (*Kinyongia matschiei*), an endemic subspecies that occasionally attains a length of 40cm. These and several other smaller species might be encountered on a guided 'chameleon walk' out of Amani Forest Camp (page 197).

Amani NFR's checklist of 34 amphibian species includes eight endemics, most notably the spectacular Usambara blue-bellied frog (*Hoplophryne rogersi*), which is sometimes seen in leaf litter in Amani Forest Camp. Amani supports a rare wealth of invertebrates, and although these are relatively poorly documented, those families that have been studied show a high level of endemism – of the 40 millipede species recorded at Amani, for instance, around three-quarters are known only from the Eastern Usambara. Among the more conspicuous insects, *Hypolimnas antevorta* is a large black, blue and white butterfly endemic to the Eastern Usambara, while the Amani flatwing (*Amanipodagrion gilliesi*), placed in a monotypic genus and endemic to fast-flowing streams that run downhill from Amani to Sigi, is a

THE GENUS *SAINTPAULIA*

Of the 3,500 species of vascular plants recorded in the Usambara Mountains, more than 25% are thought to be endemic or near-endemic. Without doubt the most familiar of these unique taxa is a small flowering plant first collected in the Eastern Usambara in 1892 by the District Commissioner of Tanga, Baron Walter von Saint Paul Illaire. Subsequently described as *Saintpaulia ionantha* in honour of its discoverer, the African violet (as it is more commonly known) was made commercially available in 1927, when ten different blue-flowered strains were put on the market. It is today one of the world's most popular perennial pot plants, with thousands of cultivated strains generating a global trade worth tens of millions of US dollars, and yet few enthusiasts realise that the wild flower is threatened within its natural range.

Although they vary greatly in shape and colour, most cultivated strains of African violet are hybrids of the original seeds collected by Baron Saint Paul, which belonged to two highly malleable races, *S. i. ionantha* and *S. i. grotei*. The specific taxonomy of the genus *Saintpaulia* is controversial: at one time more than 20 species were recognised but a 2006 study has reduced that number to six. The genus is unique to the Eastern Arc Mountains, and its main strongholds are the Eastern Usambara and Nguru Mountains.

Not affiliated to the true violets, *Saintpaulia* is a relatively recently evolved genus whose ancestral stock was most likely blown across from Madagascar in a cyclone (a flowering plant in the genus *Streptocarpus* has been cited as the probable ancestor). The wild *Saintpaulia* has probably never enjoyed a wide distribution or a high level of habitat tolerance. In the wild, as in the home, most species require continuous shade and humidity in order to flourish and because it depends on surface rather than underground moisture, *Saintpaulia* has an unusually shallow root system. It typically grows in moist cracks in porous rocks close to streams running through closed-canopy forest – though some specimens do lead an epiphytic existence on cycad trunks or the shady branches of palms.

The main threat to the wild *Saintpaulia* is the logging of tall trees, which creates breaks in the closed canopy. Researchers in the Eastern Usambara have come across dead or dying plants at several established *Saintpaulia* sites where the canopy has been broken due to logging. One of the many positive effects of the gazetting of Amani NFR in 1997 is that it should help secure the future of the genus – or at least those species that are resident within the reserve. Local guides will be able to show you the wild flowers on several of the established walking and driving trails.

critically endangered damselfly whose unusually long slender abdomen ends in a conspicuous white tip.

FEES AND FURTHER INFORMATION Access to Amani NFR is via the Sigi Visitors Centre (m +255 084 587805/716 535038; ⌚ 07.00–18.00 daily), which is also known as Zigi or Kisiwani, and lies some 7km before Amani village on the main road coming from Muheza. The rehabilitated German stationmaster's house doubles as an entrance gate, ticket office and information centre, while an adjoining resthouse offers visitors a lower-elevation site from which to explore the forest. Guided hikes can be arranged at the conservation office next to the Amani Resthouse, but this is closed on Sunday.

BIRDING IN AMANI

Eastern Usambara takes second place to the Udzungwa as the most important avian site in the Eastern Arc Mountains, but it is still one of the most significant birding sites anywhere in East Africa. Amani in particular has several logistical advantages over the best birdwatching sites in the Udzungwa, namely relative ease of access, proximity to the established tourist circuit of northern Tanzania, and a superior tourist infrastructure and quality of guides. The Eastern Usambara's avifauna has received far more scientific attention than that of the other Eastern Arc ranges, dating from 1926 to 1948 when Amani was the home of the doyen of Tanzania ornithology, Reginald Moreau, credited with discovering and describing several new species including the long-billed forest warbler (also known as Mrs Moreau's tailorbird). This extensive study is reflected in a checklist of 340 bird species, including 12 that are globally threatened and 19 that are either endemic to the Eastern Arc Mountains or to the East African coastal biome.

The temptation on first arriving at Amani might be to rush off along one of the trails into the forest interior. In fact some of the most productive general birdwatching is to be had in the gardens and forest fringe around Amani village, slow exploration of which is likely to yield up to 50 forest-associated species including half-a-dozen genuine rarities. One of the more conspicuous and vocal residents around the resthouses is the green-headed oriole, a colourful bird that is restricted to a handful of montane forests between Tanzania and Mozambique. The flowering gardens are a good site for three of the four range-restricted sunbirds associated with the Eastern Usambara (ie: Amani, banded green and Uluguru violet-backed sunbird). The rare long-billed tailorbird has been discovered breeding at two sites in Amani village.

Having explored the resthouse area, the guided Turaco and Mbamole Hill trails are recommended for sighting further montane forest specials. Noteworthy birds resident in the forest around Amani include the Usambara eagle owl, southern banded snake eagle, silvery-cheeked hornbill, half-collared kingfisher, African green ibis, Fischer's turaco, African broadbill, East Coast akalat, white-chested alethe, Kenrick's and Waller's starlings, and several forest flycatchers. It is also worth noting that several of the more interesting Usambara specials are lowland forest species, more likely to be seen in and around Sigi than at Amani. Among the birds to look out for on the trails around Sigi are eastern green tinkerbird, African cuckoo-hawk, square-tailed drongo, bar-tailed trogon and chestnut-fronted helmet-shrike.

Entrance costs US$10 per person per day and is valid for the full duration of your stay. Other fees include a daily vehicle entrance fee equivalent to around US$3/6 for a tare of less/more than 2,000kg (or US$15/25 if the vehicle is foreign-registered), and an additional charge of US$15 per party per day for the services of a guide.

GETTING THERE AND AWAY The springboard for Amani NFR is **Muheza**, a small town situated 40km west of Tanga on the main road to Moshi. From Muheza, the unsurfaced road to Amani should take about 90 minutes in a private vehicle, passing through Sigi after an hour.

Muheza is easily reached on public transport, whether you're coming from Tanga, Arusha, Lushoto or Dar es Salaam. Three buses daily run from Muheza to Sigi, leaving between noon and the mid afternoon, and one continues to Amani, arriving there in the late afternoon, then continuing for 8km to the Konkoro Tea Estate, passing the turn-off 3.5km from Amani Forest Camp en route. The return bus from Konkoro Tea Estate to Muheza passes through Amani at about 06.30 and Sigi 30 minutes later.

More straightforwardly, a trickle of dalla dallas runs back and forth between Muheza and Amani throughout the day, charging around US$2 per person. A boda-boda will cost US$5–15 one-way, and a taxi around US$30–40.

WHERE TO STAY AND EAT *Map, page 177*

Amani Forest Camp ⊕ -5.11232, 38.61037; m +255 758 844228; w amaniforestcamp.com. Situated outside the nature reserve about 7km from Amani village, this environmentally responsible camp (formerly Emau Hill) offers the choice of en-suite stone or tented cottages or camping in your own tent. Monkeys are regular visitors & all the key endemic bird species have been recorded in the immediate vicinity, along with various African violets. The camp operates a good network of trails outside the reserve: these can be walked unguided for free, or a guide can be supplied for US$10pp. The camp can also arrange expert bird guides to accompany serious twitchers, while early-evening walks often yield up to 4 species of chameleon. *From US$112/176 en-suite sgl/dbl B&B.* **$$$–$$$$**

Amani Resthouse (18 rooms) m +255 784 587805/716 535038. This comfortable no-frills resthouse, situated next to the conservation office in Amani, has adequate rooms, a canteen & a bar. *US$10–15pp.* **$**

Sigi Resthouse (8 rooms) m +255 784 587805/716 535038. Sigi's resthouse is similar in standard to the one at Amani, but feels more modern. Clean twin rooms have fitted nets, writing desk & hot shower. There's a canteen & bar. *US$10pp.* **$**

WHAT TO SEE AND DO Nine walking trails have been demarcated in the reserve, ranging from 3km to 12km, and leaflets with trail descriptions are available at the entrance gate. The directions in these are reportedly not 100% accurate, so it might be worth hiking with a trained guide, who will also help you to spot birds and monkeys. It is worth consulting with the guides about the trail most suited to your specific interest.

The 10km **Konkoro Trail**, which can be covered on foot or in a vehicle, is good for African violets, and it cuts through several different forest types, as well as passing a viewpoint and terminating in an overnight campsite in the heart of the forest. The shorter **Turaco** and **Mbamole Hill** trails are recommended first options for birdwatchers. There is also much to be seen along the roads and paths that lie within the research centre and botanical garden. Wandering around the forest-fringed village, you are likely to encounter a variety of birds, as well as Angola colobus and blue monkey – and you might even catch a glimpse of the bizarre and outsized Zanj elephant shrew.

GALAGO DIVERSITY IN TANZANIA

The Prosimian galago family is the modern representative of the most ancient of Africa's extant primate lineages, more closely related to the lemurs of Madagascar than to any other mainland monkeys or apes. With their wide round eyes and agile bodies, they are also – as their alternative name of bushbaby suggests – uniquely endearing creatures, bound to warm the heart of even the least anthropomorphic of observers. And no natural history lover could fail to feel some excitement at the revolution in the taxonomy of the galago family that has taken place over recent years, largely due to research undertaken in the forests of Tanzania by the Nocturnal Primate Research Group (NPRG; w nprg.org) of Oxford Brookes University.

In 1975, only six species of galago were recognised. Today, it is thought that there may be up to 40, a quarter of which are confirmed or likely to occur in Tanzania, including three national endemics. This explosion of knowledge is largely due to galagos' nocturnal habits, which makes identification tricky, particularly in forested habitats. Previously biologists based their definition of galago species largely on superficial visual similarities. It has been recently recognised, however, that the distinctive vocal repertoires of different populations, as well as differences in the penile structure, provide a more accurate indicator of whether two populations would or could interbreed given the opportunity – in other words, whether they should be regarded as discrete species.

By comparing the calls, penile structures and DNA of dwarf galago populations around Tanzania, the NPRG has discovered several previously undescribed species since the early 1990s. These are Grant's galago (*Galago granti*; coastal woodland south of the Rufiji River); Matundu galago (*G. udzungwensis*; Udzungwa Mountains); Zanzibar galago (*G. zanzibaricus*; Zanzibar); Uluguru galago (*G. orinus*; Uluguru and Usambara Mountains); and Rondo galago (*G. rondoensis*). The last of these was initially thought to be confined to the Rondo Plateau inland of Lindi but has since been discovered in the Pugu Hills, outside Dar es Salaam, Tanzania's largest city. Nevertheless, the IUCN lists it as Critically Endangered and as one of the 'World's 25 Most Endangered Primates'. It is not so much possible as certain that further galago species await discovery: in East Africa alone populations that require further study are found in southeast Tanzania, in the isolated forests of Mount Marsabit in northern Kenya, and in the mountains along the northern shores of Lake Nyasa-Malawi.

Simon Bearder of the Nocturnal Primate Research Group argues convincingly that the implications of these fresh discoveries in galago taxonomy might extend to other 'difficult' groups of closely related animals. He points out that our most important sense is vision, which makes it easiest for us to separate species that rely primarily on vision to recognise or attract partners. It becomes more difficult for us to separate animals that attract their mates primarily by sound and scent, more so if they use senses we do not possess such as ultrasound or electric impulses. 'Such "cryptic" species', Bearder writes, 'are no less valid than any other, but we are easily misled into thinking of them as being much more similar than would be the case if we had their kind of sensitivity. The easiest way for us to distinguish between free-living species is to concentrate on those aspects of the communication system that the animals themselves use to attract partners.'

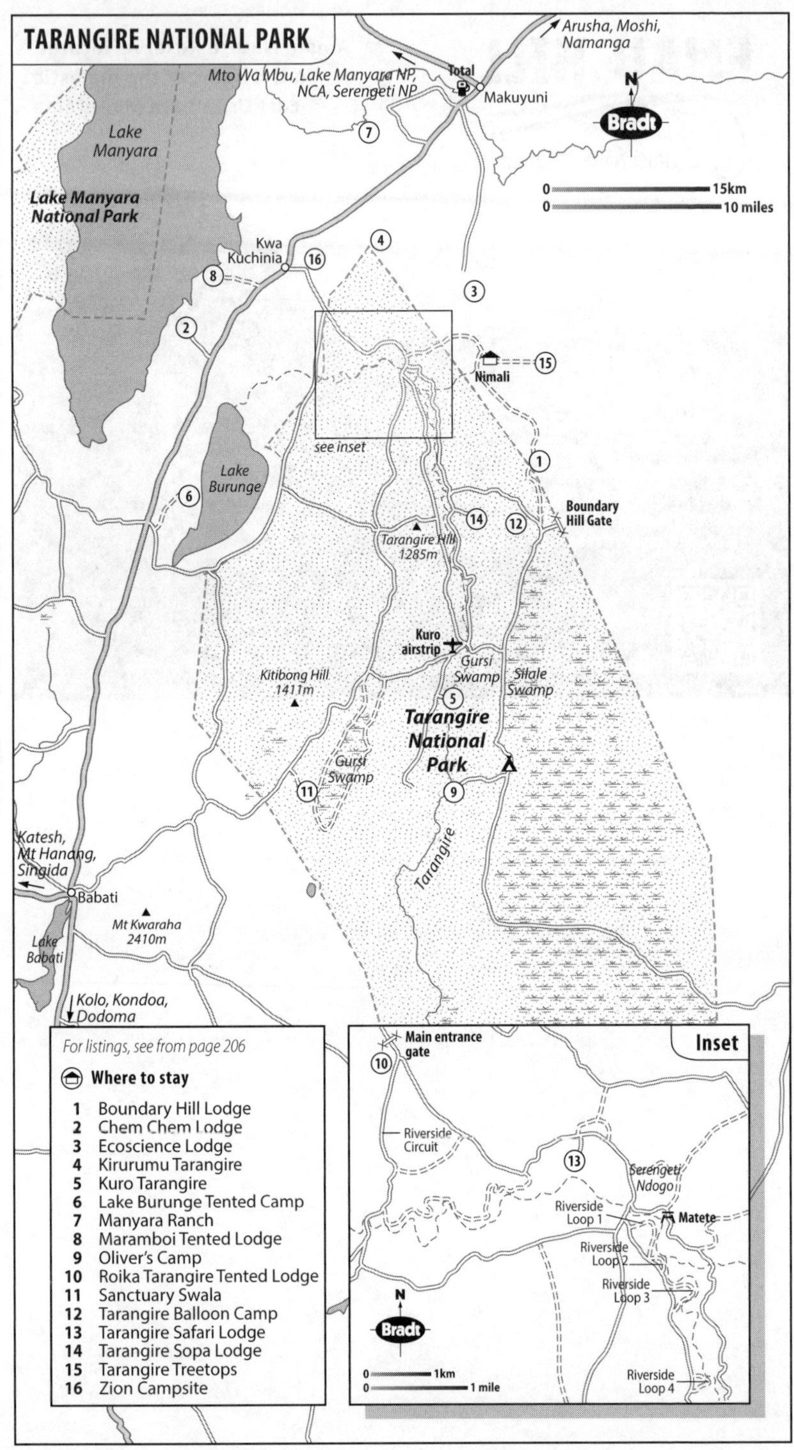
TARANGIRE NATIONAL PARK
Arusha, Moshi, Namanga
Mto Wa Mbu, Lake Manyara NP, NCA, Serengeti NP
Total
Makuyuni
Lake Manyara
Lake Manyara National Park
0 15km
0 10 miles
Kwa Kuchinia
Nimali
see inset
Lake Burunge
Boundary Hill Gate
Tarangire Hill 1285m
Kuro airstrip
Gursi Swamp
Silale Swamp
Kitibong Hill 1411m
Tarangire National Park
Gursi Swamp
Tarangire
Katesh, Mt Hanang, Singida
Babati
Mt Kwaraha 2410m
Lake Babati
Kolo, Kondoa, Dodoma
For listings, see from page 206
Where to stay
1 Boundary Hill Lodge
2 Chem Chem Lodge
3 Ecoscience Lodge
4 Kirurumu Tarangire
5 Kuro Tarangire
6 Lake Burunge Tented Camp
7 Manyara Ranch
8 Maramboi Tented Lodge
9 Oliver's Camp
10 Roika Tarangire Tented Lodge
11 Sanctuary Swala
12 Tarangire Balloon Camp
13 Tarangire Safari Lodge
14 Tarangire Sopa Lodge
15 Tarangire Treetops
16 Zion Campsite
Inset
Main entrance gate
Riverside Circuit
Serengeti Ndogo
Riverside Loop 1
Matete
Riverside Loop 2
Riverside Loop 3
Riverside Loop 4
0 1km
0 1 mile

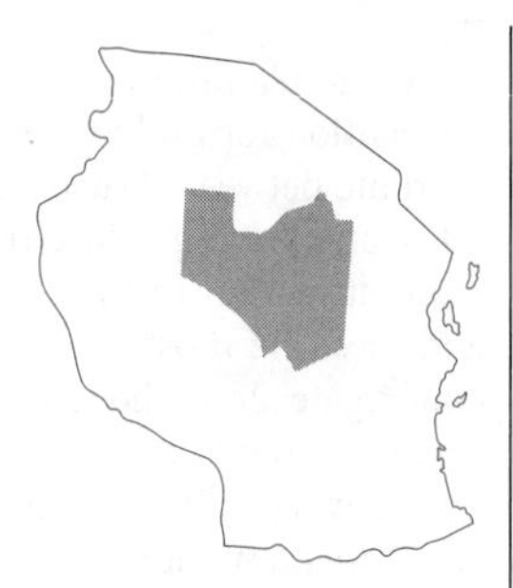

Tarangire and the Central Rift Valley

The semi-arid Central Rift Valley south of Arusha has two main points of touristic interest. The better known and busier of these is Tarangire National Park, a world-class wildlife-viewing destination best renowned for its daunting concentrations of baobab trees and elephants, supplemented by influxes of migrant grazers during the dry season (July to November), when it is appended to most northern safari itineraries and also forms a worthwhile goal for a short self-standing safari out of Arusha. Although most tourists confine their exploration of the area to Tarangire and surrounds, another important (albeit relatively obscure) attraction is the Kondoa Rock Art, an alfresco collection of 150-plus prehistoric artworks inscribed as a UNESCO World Heritage Site in 2006. Other geographic landmarks include pretty Lake Babati and the volcanic Mount Hanang. The area is also notable for its traditional pastoralist inhabitants, most famously the Maasai, whose traditional grazing grounds enclose Tarangire National Park, but also the Barabaig and other sub-groups of the Datoga who live further southwest.

TARANGIRE NATIONAL PARK

Named after the perennial river that forms its lifeblood, Tarangire National Park (**m** +255 689 062248; **e** tnp@tanzaniaparks.go.tz) extends for 2,850km² across the scrubby semi-arid plains and baobab-studded slopes of the Maasai Steppe southwest of Arusha. Less publicised than Serengeti or Ngorongoro, Tarangire is nevertheless a highly rewarding wildlife destination and a recommended inclusion on any safari itinerary through northern Tanzania. The park is best known for its year-round abundance of elephants, but it is also home to plenty of other wildlife, including lion, leopard, cheetah, buffalo and giraffe, along with an exceptional variety of birds.

Tarangire National Park lies at the core of a 20,000km² migratory ecosystem that runs east across the Maasai Steppe from the base of the Rift Valley escarpment between Manyara and Engaruka. Known as the Tarangire–Manyara ecosystem, it hosts East Africa's second-largest ungulate migration, comprised – like its better-known counterpart in the Serengeti–Mara – mainly of wildebeest and zebra. Since 2006, much of the region bordering the national park has been protected in Wildlife Management Areas (WMAs) created in consultation with Maasai and other resident communities. These include the northerly Randileni WMA, northwesterly Levolosi WMA, westerly Burunge WMA and 5,372km² Makame WMA to the south. But while wildlife ranges widely across the ecosystem during the rains, it tends to congregate along the Tarangire River from July to November, when other sources of drinking water are scarce and game viewing in the national park can be truly spectacular.

When planning your Tarangire itinerary, be conscious that it is now the convention for budget-conscious operators to visit the park on a quick day safari en route between Arusha and an overnight stop elsewhere, typically arriving after 10.00 and leaving before 16.00. In one sense, this makes a lot of sense, as the park's main attraction in the context of the northern circuit is large herds of elephant, and these are most likely to be seen in the midday and afternoon heat, when they congregate along the river to drink. But it also means that Tarangire's main game-viewing circuits tend to be very congested with tourist traffic at lunchtime, but are unexpectedly quiet before 09.00 and after 15.00. For this reason, we highly recommend spending a night in Tarangire, or staying close enough that you can still do a game drive in the late afternoon and/or early morning, in order to experience this wonderful park at its undiluted best.

FLORA AND FAUNA The Tarangire–Manyara ecosystem tends to be drier and more densely vegetated than the Serengeti, supporting a tangle of semi-arid acacia and mixed woodland. Its dominant geographic feature, bisecting the national park, is the Tarangire River, which is flanked by dense patches of elephant grass and a sporadic ribbon of riparian woodland dotted with the occasional palm tree. A striking feature of the park's flora is the abundance of massive bulbous baobab trees that line the slopes away from the river.

Mammals Tarangire National Park is an important stronghold for elephants, with a count of almost 2,500 individuals in a census undertaken in 2009. There has been no significant poaching in the area since then, so the population now probably stands at 3,000–4,000, meaning that along with the Serengeti, it is one if the few places in Tanzania where elephant numbers are on the increase. The elephants of Tarangire have been less keen to cross outside the park boundaries in recent seasons, presumably as a result of an increased risk of poaching, but within the park they tend to be very relaxed around safari vehicles, especially along the busier riverside game drive routes. Indeed, it is no exaggeration to say that you might see 500 elephants over the course of a day in this part of the park.

It is difficult to put reliable figures on other wildlife populations associated with Tarangire, as the most recent census was completed in the 1980s, but there is no reason to suppose that the numbers recorded then – including 25,000 wildebeest, 30,000 zebra, 6,000 buffalo, 2,700 giraffe, 5,500 eland, 30,000 impala and 2,000 warthog – are significantly changed. More localised antelope associated with Tarangire include fringe-eared oryx, gerenuk and lesser kudu, but none of them is seen with great regularity.

The most conspicuous carnivores are lions, with a population of around 150 individuals split across at least 15 prides. Spotted hyena and leopard are also common, though less visible than in some other parks, while the cheetah population, now estimated at 30, tends to prefer open grassland such as the Small Serengeti Plain near the main entrance gate. Of the park's smaller carnivores, the highly sociable dwarf mongoose is characteristic and often seen on the termite hills where it lives in colonial burrows.

As with Serengeti–Ngorongoro, the Tarangire-Manyara ecosystem is characterised by significant seasonal migratory movement. During the dry season, between July and November, elephant numbers can be little short of phenomenal, and large herds of zebra, wildebeest, antelope and other grazers are attracted to life-giving waters of the Tarangire River. This isn't to say that Tarangire is without merit at other times of the year. True, a lot of wildlife disperses outside the park during the wetter months – wildebeest and zebra northwest to the Rift Valley floor between Manyara and Natron, other species southward across the Maasai Steppe – but the landscape is greener and more scenic during the rains, and the birdlife can be astounding. Also, contrary to expectations, lions seem to be easier to locate in the wet season, possibly because the tall grass makes them more inclined to walk and hunt along roads, and to rest up on them at night.

Birds Tarangire is a great park for birdwatching, with around 500 species recorded to date. Characteristic acacia birds include yellow-necked spurfowl, orange-bellied parrot, Von der Decken's hornbill, barefaced go-away bird, red-fronted barbet, little bee-eater, silverbird, superb starling and white-headed buffalo-weaver. A good starting point for acacia dwellers is the grounds of Tarangire Safari Lodge, where many common woodland species – hornbills, woodpeckers, swallows, starlings, weavers and the like – are very habituated and approachable. As you drive around the park, look out for termite mounds stained white with bird droppings – these are often perches where pairs of the spectacular red-and-yellow barbet perform their quaintly comical clockwork duet.

Tarangire hosts a wide range of resident raptors including bateleur, African fish eagle, palmnut vulture, eastern chanting goshawk and pygmy falcon, while the river supports saddle-billed stork, yellow-billed stork and several other water birds. Another good spot for wetland species is Silale Swamp, whose margins often host the likes of long-tailed lapwing, African jacana, squacco heron, kob-billed duck and spur-winged goose.

Tarangire's location at the western limit of the Somali-Maasai biome means it harbours several dry-country bird species at the extremity of their range, among them vulturine guineafowl, Donaldson-Smith's nightjar, pink-breasted lark, northern pied babbler and mouse-coloured penduline tit. It is also the easiest place to observe a pair of bird species endemic to the dry heartland of central Tanzania: the lovely yellow-collared lovebird (often seen in fast-flapping neon-green flocks flashing between trees) and the very common but somewhat drabber ashy starling.

FEES AND FURTHER INFORMATION The park entrance fee is US$50 per person per 24 hours (dropping to US$45 between 15 March and 15 May), while those staying overnight in the park must pay a separate fee of US$30 per person (ordinary campsite), US$40 per person (hotel) or US$60 per person (special campsite). All fees attract 18% VAT and must be paid by Visa or Mastercard (cash is not accepted; page 92).

People staying at lodges set within any of the bordering WMAs require a separate permit, which is usually incorporated in the room price.

A detailed booklet, *Tarangire National Park*, is widely available in Arusha and some of the park's lodges.

GETTING THERE AND AWAY Most people tag a visit to Tarangire on to a longer safari, but if time or money is limited, a one- or two-day standalone safari would be a viable option, since the park is less than 2 hours' drive south of Arusha. In principle, any public transport running along the Babati road could drop you at the junctions mentioned from page 204, but there is no realistic way of exploring the park itself without private transport.

There are three main access points, the most useful of which depends on which lodge or camp you are booked into.

ANIMAL TAXONOMY

In this book, I've made widespread use of taxonomic terms such as genus, species and race. Some readers may not be familiar with these terms, so a brief explanation follows.

Taxonomy is the branch of biology concerned with classifying living organisms. It uses a hierarchical system to represent the relationships between different animals. At the top of the hierarchy are kingdoms, phyla, sub-phyla and classes. All vertebrates belong to the animal kingdom, phylum Chordata, sub-phylum Vertebrata. There are five vertebrate classes: Mammalia (mammals), Aves (birds), Reptilia (reptiles), Amphibia (amphibians) and Pisces (fish). Within any class, several orders might be divided in turn into families and, depending on the complexity of the order and family, various sub-orders and sub-families. All baboons, for instance, belong to the Primate order, sub-order Catarrhini (monkeys and apes), family Cercopithecoidea (Old World monkeys) and sub-family Cercopithecidae (cheek-pouch monkeys, ie: guenons, baboons and mangabeys).

Taxonomists accord every living organism a Latin binomial (two-part name) indicating its genus (plural genera) and species. Thus the savannah baboon (*Papio cyenephalus*) and hamadrayas baboon (*Papio hamadrayas*) are different species of the genus *Papio*. Some species are further divided into races or sub-species. For instance, taxonomists recognise four races of savannah baboon: yellow baboon, olive baboon, chacma baboon and Guinea baboon. A race is indicated by a trinomial (three-part name), for instance *Papio cyenephalus cyenephalus* for the yellow baboon and *Papio cyenephalus anubis* for the olive baboon. The identical specific and racial designation of *cyenephalus* for the yellow baboon make it the nominate race – a label that has no significance other than that it would most probably have been the first race of that species to be described by taxonomists.

Taxonomic constructs are designed to approximate the real genetic and evolutionary relationships between various living creatures, and on the whole they succeed. But equally the science exists to help humans understand a reality that is likely to be more complex and less absolute than any conceptual structure used to contain it. This is particularly the case with speciation – the evolution of two or more distinct species from a common ancestor – a gradual process that might occur over many thousands of generations and lack for any absolute landmarks.

Simplistically, the process of speciation begins when a single population splits into two mutually exclusive breeding units. This can happen as a result of geographic isolation (for instance mountain and lowland gorillas), habitat differences (forest and savannah elephants) or varied migratory patterns (the six races of yellow wagtail intermingle as non-breeding migrants to Africa during the northern winter, but they all have discrete Palaearctic breeding grounds). Whatever the reason, the two breeding communities will share an identical gene

The main entrance gate lies about 7km east of the main Arusha–Dodoma road. Coming from Arusha, the road is surfaced as far as the clearly signposted turn-off at Kwa Kuchinja, a small village situated about 100km south of Arusha and 25km past Makuyuni (the junction for Manyara and the Serengeti). This is the best approach for most lodges and camps set within the park, as well as those set along the northwestern boundary close to the main gate.

Coming from Arusha, the three lodges set in the Randileni WMA (Tarangire Treetops, Nimali and EcoScience) are all best reached by following the Arusha–

pool when first they split, but as generations pass they will accumulate a number of small genetic differences and eventually marked racial characteristics. Given long enough, the two populations might even deviate to the point where they wouldn't or couldn't interbreed, even if the barrier that originally divided them was removed.

The taxonomic distinction between a full species and a sub-species or race of that species rests not on how similar the two taxa are in appearance or habit, but on the final point above. Should it be known that two distinct taxa freely interbreed and produce fertile hybrids where their ranges overlap, or it is believed that they would in the event that their ranges did overlap, then they are classified as races of the same species. If not, they are regarded as full species. The six races of yellow wagtail referred to above are all very different in appearance, far more so, for instance, than the several dozen warbler species of the genus *Cisticola*, but clearly they are able to interbreed, and they must thus be regarded as belonging to the same species. And while this may seem a strange distinction on the face of things, it does make sense when you recall that humans rely mostly on visual recognition, whereas many other creatures are more dependent on other senses. Those pesky cisticolas all look much the same to human observers, but each species has a highly distinctive call and in some cases a display flight that would preclude crossbreeding whether or not it is genetically possible.

The gradual nature of speciation creates grey areas that no arbitrary distinction can cover – at any given moment in time there might exist separate breeding populations of a certain species that have not yet evolved distinct racial characters, or distinct races that are on their way to becoming full species. Furthermore, where no conclusive evidence exists, some taxonomists tend to be habitual 'lumpers' and others eager 'splitters' – respectively inclined to designate any controversial taxon racial or full specific status. For this reason, various field guides often differ in their designation of controversial taxa.

Among African mammals, this is particularly the case with primates, where in some cases up to 20 described taxa are sometimes lumped together as one species and sometimes split into several specific clusters of similar races. The savannah baboon is a case in point. The four races are known to interbreed where their ranges overlap but they are also all very distinctive in appearance, and several field guides now classify them as different species. The olive baboon, for instance, is designated *Papio anubis* as opposed to *Papio cyenephalus anubis*. Such ambiguities can be a source of genuine frustration, particularly for birdwatchers obsessed with ticking 'new' species, but they also serve as a valid reminder that the natural world is, and will always be, a more complex, mysterious and dynamic entity than any taxonomic construct designed to label it.

Dodoma road for about 5km past Makuyuni junction, then turning left on to a signposted dirt road that reaches the Mswakini Juu checkpoint after 20 minutes and the lodges after another 30–45 minutes. Access to the national park from these lodges is via the westerly Boundary Hill Gate.

The relatively new and little-used Sandayuwa Gate lies about 8km east of the Arusha–Dodoma road along a side road signposted about 35km south of the turn-off for the main gate. The camps around Lake Burunge lie just outside this gate, which also provides an alternative access point for more southerly camps within the park.

 **WHERE TO STAY AND EAT** *Map, page 200*

Tarangire is now serviced by the best part of 20 lodges and camps. All else being equal, we would give preference to those properties situated within the national park, as they generally have the best locations for wildlife viewing.

Inside Tarangire National Park

Exclusive

Kuro Tarangire ⊕ -4.05832, 36.07177; **m** +250 787 595908; **w** nomad-tanzania.com; ⏲ closed late Mar–late May. This exclusive low-footprint camp comprises just 6 spacious luxury tents with veranda, solar lighting, bucket showers & flush eco-toilets, spread across an acacia grove on the west bank of the Tarangire River. It is sufficiently far south from the main game-viewing circuit to retain some distance from the crowds, but close enough to ensure top-notch game viewing, particularly in the dry season. An open-sided thatched lounge & dining room furnished with hides & colourful local fabrics serves superb food. **$$$$$$$**

✷ **Oliver's Camp** ⊕ -4.13390, 36.07687; **w** asiliaafrica.com; ⏲ closed Apr–mid May. Overlooking the expansive Silale Swamp, which has hosted a permanent lake since the rains of 2019, this classic luxury bush camp lies far enough south of the main tourist circuit that activities can usually be undertaken without seeing other vehicles. The 15 thatch-shaded tents are very spacious inside, set far apart for maximum privacy & each has a wide wooden balcony with a clearing & bird bath in front. Game drives are the main activity but the guides are very experienced when it comes to guided bush walks & night drives. Food is excellent. 2 new features are a 200m-long canopy walk that provides incredible views to the river & large (& very welcome) freeform infinity swimming pool. **$$$$$$$**

✷ **Sanctuary Swala** ⊕ -4.12958, 35.95341; **w** sanctuaryretreats.com; ⏲ closed Apr–May. Situated in the south of the park, this isolated camp comprises 12 luxurious standing tents scattered widely in a shady acacia grove overlooking Gurusi Swamp (which has been transformed into a lake since the heavy rains of 2019). The remote location means you won't often see other vehicles in the vicinity, but wildlife is plentiful. The swala (impala) after which the camp are named are much in evidence, accompanied by a noisy entourage of vervet monkeys, guineafowl & various plovers, buffalo-weavers & starlings. Regular visitors include elephant, a near-resident lion pride & more occasionally leopard. The food is excellent & optional activities include guided bush walks, night drives & canoeing on the lake. **$$$$$$$**

Upmarket

Tarangire Balloon Camp ⊕ -3.90424, 36.13608; **w** madahotels.com. This isolated bush camp has a lovely – albeit rather tsetse-ridden – location on a slope close to Boundary Hill Gate. The 16 spacious standing tents have 4-poster beds, walk-in nets & private balcony, there's a fabulous swimming pool set in the rocks, & it's the base of Adventures Aloft (the only company that offers balloon safaris in Tarangire; page 210). **$$$$$$**

✷ **Tarangire Safari Lodge** ⊕ -3.77002, 36.02130; **m** +255 658 820030; **w** tarangiresafarilodge.com. Founded in 1985, this unpretentious owner-managed lodge is the oldest in the park, & one of the most characterful, boasting a sublime location on a tall bluff overlooking the Tarangire River. The grounds are also highly attractive to birders, & inhouse game viewing can be stupendous with large herds of elephants, hippo, giraffe, etc, coming down to drink at the river below. The 35 standing tents & 5 bungalows are comfortable rather than luxurious & come with solar-heated shower, flush toilet & private balcony. Buffet meals are to an unusually high standard & amenities include a swimming pool, a spa with a sensational river view & a well-stocked gift shop. The lodge is ideally located for game drives, being only minutes from the grassland of the Small Serengeti & the various riverside circuits & loops. Arguably the best-value lodge on the northern circuit; highly recommended. **$$$$$**

Tarangire Sopa Lodge ⊕ -3.90777, 36.09506; **m** +255 784 250630; **w** sopalodges.com. Tarangire's largest, most conventionally luxurious & least 'bush' lodge comprises 75 well-equipped suites (2 of which are wheelchair accessible), a swimming pool & attractive restaurant serving good buffet meals. The indifferent location, alongside a small & normally dry watercourse, is compensated for by direct access to some of the park's best game-viewing roads. **$$$$$$**

Camping

Campsites within Tarangire National Park are strong on bush atmosphere but short on facilities. Public campsites cost US$30pp & special campsites US$60pp.

West of the national park

The places listed below are mostly set within Burunge or Levolosi WMAs, which extend westward from Tarangire National Park towards Lake Manyara. Managed in consultation with local Maasai communities, these WMAs form part of the historically important wildlife corridor between Tarangire and Lake Manyara, whose respective northern and southeastern tips lie only 20km apart but are separated by ranchland and the surfaced Arusha–Dodoma Highway. Of particular note are Manyara Ranch and Chem Chem, a pair of exclusive private camps set in private concessions that have played an important role in reopening the wildlife corridor to migratory elephants and other wildlife, but also offer visitors an opportunity to combine guided walks and drives within the concession with day trips to Tarangire.

Exclusive

✷ **Chem Chem Lodge** ⊕ -3.75234, 35.84192; **w** chemchemsafari.com; ⌚ closed Apr–mid May. This sophisticated owner-managed lodge lies on an unfenced 40km² concession in a WMA in the wildlife corridor connecting Tarangire to Lake Manyara. Linked by stilted wooden walkways, the 8 ultra-spacious & earthily stylish cottages have canvas walls & roof, king-size bed, walk-in net, indoor & outdoor shower & 2 private balconies. The lodge overlooks a grassy plain on the southeast shore of Lake Manyara & the tall escarpment above it. Guided walking safaris offer an opportunity to get close to plenty of plains wildlife & to experience the superb birdlife associated with the tangled acacia scrub & the open floodplain (good for wading birds such as flamingos, coursers, pratincoles, storks & avocets). It is also a useful springboard for day safaris to Tarangire National Park & the little-visited south of Lake Manyara National Park. 2 other smaller lodges recently opened on the same property: Little Chem Chem & Forest Chem Chem. **$$$$$$$**

Manyara Ranch ⊕ -3.58466, 36.00184; **m** +255 683 918888; **w** manyararanch.com; ⌚ closed Apr–May. Established as a cattle ranch during the colonial era, this 120km² conservancy was acquired by the African Wildlife Foundation in 2000 & it now doubles as conservancy in the wildlife corridor connecting Manyara to Tarangire. Set in a shady acacia grove alive with birds, the wonderfully rustic & intimate camp comprises 6 classic safari tents with hardwood floor, king-size bed, hot shower & private balcony overlooking a floodplain that frequently attracts wildlife. Guided game walks regularly offer close encounters with elephant, giraffe, wildebeest, zebra & more localised antelope such as fringe-eared oryx, eland & lesser kudu. Night drives come with a chance of lion, spotted hyena & bat-eared fox. Birdlife is varied, thanks to a wide variety of habitats ranging from open grassland to lush riparian forest. It is also a good base for day trips to Tarangire & Lake Manyara national parks, both of which lie a 30–45min drive way. **$$$$$$$**

Upmarket

Kirurumu Tarangire ⊕ -3.67809, 36.01384; **m** +255 774 533198; **w** kirurumu.net. Set on the national park boundary less than 30mins' drive from the main park gate, unpretentious Kirurumu comprises 10 spacious tented cottages raised on solid stone bases & suspended under thatch. It stands in a patch of dense bush frequented by elephant & other large mammals & also offers Maasai-guided nature walks & village visits. Good value. **$$$$**

Lake Burunge Tented Camp ⊕ -3.88733, 35.85690; **m** + 255 785 069944; **w** twctanzania.com. Overlooking seasonal Lake Burunge, this lodge lies in the eponymous WMA around 10mins' drive outside the park boundary, some distance south of the main Tarangire tourist circuit. The 30 spacious & attractively rustic tents are built on stilted platforms & shaded by makuti roofs. It is well positioned for game drives, guided nature walks & canoe trips (when the lake holds water). **$$$$$**

✷ **Maramboi Tented Lodge** ⊕ -3.70076, 35.86394; **m** + 255 785 069944; **w** twctanzania.com. Set within a private concession overlooking the eastern floodplain of Lake Manyara, Maramboi comprises 44 spacious tents set on wooden platforms & equipped with walk-in nets, electricity, ceiling fans, hot showers & private balconies looking towards the lake & Rift Escarpment. Unless your budget stretches to Chem Chem or Manyara Ranch, we'd rate this attractive & well-managed accommodation as the best option outside Tarangire, not least because morning game drives into the park can be supplemented with Maasai-guided afternoon nature walks on the property, which supports plenty of giraffe, zebra, antelope & birds. **$$$$$**

Moderate

Roika Tarangire Tented Lodge ⊕ -3.74020, 35.96912; **m** +255 754 001444; **w** tarangireroikatentedlodge.com. Situated in a stand of tangled acacia scrub close to the main park entrance gate, this relatively affordable lodge comprises 21 comfortable standing tents with makuti roofs, stilted wooden platforms & simple safari-style décor undermined somewhat by the tackily sculpted animal-shaped baths. The main building is thatched with open sides & overlooks a large swimming pool. Good value. **$$$$**

Camping

Zion Campsite **m** +255 765 870079. This very basic camp stands about 2km along the road between Kwa Kuchinja & the main entrance gate. There's a bar but no restaurant. *US$10pp.* **$**

Lodges east of the national park The concession lodges and camps below all lie outside the eastern park boundary within the thick bush of the Randileni WMA, which attracts fair volumes of wildlife during the dry season. Access to Tarangire is via the Boundary Hill Gate, which lies about an hour's drive through tsetse-infested bush from all the lodges except nearby Boundary Hill Lodge, which makes them relatively inconvenient for game drives within the national park. On the plus side, because they lie outside the national park, game walks and night drives are permitted and can be very rewarding.

Exclusive

Ecoscience Lodge ⊕ -3.72095, 36.09525; **m** +255 752 324140; **w** ecoscience.co.tz. Owned by a Belgian volcanologist & his wife, this unique property is divided into 2 camps: 1 a conventional lodge aimed at tourists, the other a science centre offering medium-term stays to scientists & researchers. The fabulous domed central building, tastefully decorated with local & imported antique furniture, resembles a futuristic version of a local African hut. The circular lodge rooms have a similar aesthetic of minimalist luxury & come with king-size bed, large dressing room, hot shower & private balcony, while standing tents in the science camp are equally comfortable but more conventionally laid out & decorated. The food is excellent & wildlife is seasonally plentiful, but the USP is the opportunity to interact with visiting scientists or explore a science centre dedicated to the volcanology of East Africa. **$$$$$**

Tarangire Treetops ⊕ -3.77510, 36.15397; **w** elewana.com; ⌚ closed Apr–May. Situated in a WMA northeast of the national park, this architecturally innovative lodge consists of 20 luxurious but uncluttered 65m² stilted treehouses that offer great birding opportunities soundtracked by a lively night chorus led by bushbabies. Because the lodge lies on private land, diurnal game drives can be supplemented by guided game walks, birding walks along a nearby watercourse, night drives & mountain-biking. The quality of game viewing in the immediate vicinity varies seasonally. Ideal for honeymooners, this is also a wonderful place to recover from jetlag at the start of a safari, or to stretch your legs at the end. **$$$$$$$**

Moderate

Boundary Hill Lodge ⊕ -3.86485, 36.14913; **m** +255 687 723488; **w** tanzanianhorizons.com. Set on a rocky hilltop just outside Boundary Hill Gate, this well-priced lodge was the first in Tanzania to have a community shareholding, with the Maasai village of Lokisale owning 50%. The 8 spacious solar-powered suites are individually designed & lavishly decorated, & have private sitting areas & wide balconies offering spectacular views over the Silale & Gosuwa swamps, where elephant & buffalo are resident. In addition to daytime game drives into the national park, the lodge offers night drives & Maasai-guided game walks. The concession lies on a migration route & is particularly busy with wildlife Nov–Mar. **$$$$**

WHAT TO SEE AND DO The main activity in Tarangire is daylight game drives, but most camps set within the park or in neighbouring WMAs now also offer night drives (which, if done within the park, attract an additional park fee – US$40 + 18% VAT) to look for leopards, genets, bushbabies and other nocturnal oddities. Many camps also now offer guided bush walks.

Game drives Most people spend only one day (or a part thereof) in Tarangire and thus concentrate on the game-viewing roads in the far north close to the main entrance gate. These roads undoubtedly offer the best general game viewing in the park, and they can be truly magical in the early morning or late afternoon, but tend to become quite hectic with day trippers between 10.00 and 16.00, which is when the park's prolific elephant tend to congregate along the river to drink and occasionally play in the water.

An excellent route for those with limited time is the main road that runs south from Tarangire Safari Lodge towards Tarangire Sopa Lodge west of the Tarangire River. This road offers access to several small riverside loops that go right down to the riverbank. You are almost certain to see elephant, buffalo, giraffe, wildebeest, zebra, impala, gazelle, warthog and yellow baboon along this road, and it is also often a good place to look for lions and leopards. If you don't want to return the way you came, a parallel on the east side of the river also offers good game viewing, and access to Matete Picnic Site (⊕ -3.78371, 36.04729), which has a spectacular location on a low cliff overlooking a popular elephant crossing and drinking point.

Another great road is the Riverside Circuit that runs for roughly 20km south of the main road between the main entrance gate and Tarangire Safari Lodge. This road stays close to the Tarangire River for most of its length and is supplemented by several short loops that go closer to the river. Lions are often seen here in the early morning, while elephants come down to drink throughout the day. A worthwhile spot to stop for a few minutes is a permanent waterhole (⊕ -3.77114, 35.96932) on the east side of the road about 3km south of the entrance gate. Allow at least 3 hours for this loop.

Altogether different in feel is the area of open grassland nicknamed Serengeti Ndogo (Small Serengeti). Situated immediately north of the main road between the main entrance gate and Matete Picnic Site, this is another good place to look for lions in the early morning, and it is probably the most reliable part of the park for cheetah and fringe-eared oryx (though neither is common).

Those who stay at camps south of the main tourist circuit, or who have sufficient time to do a full-day drive, will it find it to be refreshingly quiet compared with the far north in terms of tourist traffic. Overall, however, wildlife viewing is more erratic as you head further south, and some areas are seasonally riddled with tsetse flies. The Lake Burunge area offers the best chance of seeing bushbuck and lesser kudu, while Kitibong Hill is home to large herds of buffalo, and Silale Swamp is excellent for water birds and may also sometimes support a few hippos. The Lamakau Road running east from Oliver's Camp is a good place to look for localised antelope such as fringe-eared oryx, gerenuk, greater kudu and lesser kudu, but it is also very rough and a notorious tsetse hotspot, so not for the faint of heart!

Balloon trips Hot-air balloon trips over Tarangire are now offered by Adventures Aloft (m +255 272 543300; w aaballoonsafari.com), which is based out of Tarangire Balloon Camp (page 206) and sets off at around 06.30 daily, though pre-dawn transfers can be arranged from most other lodges in the vicinity. The trip lasts for up to 1 hour and includes a champagne bush breakfast.

BABATI

Set below the prominent Mount Kwaraha, the bustling and fast-growing market town of Babati straddles the Arusha–Dodoma road some 70km south of Kwa Kuchinja (the junction for the main gate to Tarangire National Park) and 95km north of Kondoa. For those using public transport, the junction town is a useful springboard for climbing Mount Hanang, which overlooks the Singida Road near the small town of Katesh 75km to the west, or continuing southward to the Kondoa Rock Art Sites around Kolo. Further justification for stopping over here is the eponymous Lake Babati, which lies on the town's southern outskirts and hosts large numbers of birds and hippos, and – if you are in the area at the right time – the impressive all-day livestock and general market held about 5km along the Kondoa Road on the 17th and 26th of every month.

GETTING THERE AND AWAY Babati lies 170km south of Arusha on a good surfaced road. It shouldn't take longer than 2½ hours to cover the full distance in a **private vehicle**. **Buses** in either direction leave throughout the day, taking 3–4 hours, and tickets cost around US$5. The best service is Mtei Express Coaches; hourly buses from Arusha to Babati leave from their own station on Makao Mapya Road hourly between 06.00 and 16.00. There are also several buses daily to Katesh in the west, as well as to Kondoa via Kolo in the south.

WHERE TO STAY AND EAT

Ango Tree Guesthouse ⊕ -4.18483, 35.75440; m +255 624 859443; w angotreehotel.co.tz. On the east side of the Arusha Rd 2km north of Babati, this pleasant guesthouse lies in pretty green gardens & offers a wide variety of twin or dbl rooms with fitted net, AC, flatscreen DSTV, tea-/coffee-making facilities & hot shower. A good restaurant is attached. *From US$70 dbl/twin.* **$$**

Asmorein Hotel ⊕ -4.22286, 35.72037; m +255 628 008008; e asmoreinhotel@gmail.com. Tucked away but well signposted in a backroad 3km southwest of the town centre, this unexpectedly plush new hotel has 20 comfortable modern rooms with all mod cons, a decent restaurant/bar & even a swimming pool. The staff can help arrange cultural tours in & around Babati. *US$60/80 sgl/dbl B&B.* **$$**

Winners Hotel m +255 684 18282. Situated a block east of the main road close to the bus station, this smart little hotel has 12 clean tiled rooms with nets, DSTV & hot shower. The attached restaurant serves inexpensive meat, fish & chicken dishes, as well as pizzas & salads. *US$15/24 sgl/dbl.* **$$**

TOURIST INFORMATION AND OPERATORS

Kahembe Trekking m +255 748 397477; w kahembeculturalsafaris.com. Founded as a private ecotourism concern in the 1990s & formalised into an official cultural tourism project, Kahembe's arranges a wide variety of informative day & overnight trips which – though not luxurious by any standard – offer an unforgettable glimpse into African traditions. These include 3- & 2-day Mount Hanang climbs, a 3-day Barabaig walking safari & 7- & 8-day walking itineraries that visit several local bomas, as well as incorporating walks on the game-rich verges of Lake Manyara & Tarangire national parks.

WHAT TO SEE AND DO

Lake Babati Measuring almost 10km from north to south, but nowhere more than 2km wide, serpentine Lake Babati lies immediately south of the eponymous town, and is easily reached by walking along the Kondoa road for about 10 minutes. The papyrus-fringed stretch of shore alongside the road supports a good selection of water birds – egrets, waders and storks – while flotillas of pelican sail pompously across the open water. The lake is also known for its large numbers of hippo, which sometimes venture close to town by night, but are unlikely to be seen by day unless you take a boat out on to the water. Boat trips can be arranged with Kahembe Trekking (page 210) or by chatting to local fishermen.

Mount Kwaraha Rising to a peak of 2,415m about 5km east of Babati, this prominent mountain has a rather volcanic appearance, but is in fact a granite inselberg. Its upper slopes are protected in the Ufoime Forest Reserve and give rise to around two-dozen springs that flow westward into Lake Babati. The mist forest above the 1,800m contour is still home to small numbers of elephant and buffalo, as well as a profusion of birds and monkeys. Inexpensive guided day or (better) overnight hikes, inclusive of the US$10 per person forestry permit, can be arranged through Kahembe Trekking.

MOUNT HANANG

Tanzania's fourth-highest mountain after Kilimanjaro, Meru and Lolmalasin (in the Crater Highlands), volcanic Mount Hanang is a product of the same geological upheavals that sculpted the Great Rift, and it is the only one of these mountains to actually rise from the valley floor. The dormant caldera towers to an elevation of 3,418m above the low-lying plains, and is visible from hundreds of kilometres away on a clear day. Not surprisingly, this imposing free-standing mountain is revered by the Barabaig who inhabit its lower slopes, and it features prominently in their myths. Hanang supports its own distinct microclimate and forms an important local watershed, with most of the rain falling on the northern and eastern slopes.

Seldom visited by tourists, Hanang forms a very affordable alternative or supplementary montane hike to Kilimanjaro or Meru. It lies outside the national park system, but the slopes above the 1,860m contour support a mosaic of Afromontane forest and grassland which is now protected in the 58km² Mount Hanang Nature Forest Reserve (**m** +255 784 922255/756 076552; **w** nature-reserves.go.tz). These forests still support elusive populations of bushbuck, duiker, bushpig and various monkeys, as well as a wide range of forest birds. The upper slopes also offer excellent views over a stretch of the Rift Valley studded with smaller volcanic cones and shallow lakes.

The attractions of the Hanang area are not restricted to the mountain. On the contrary, the primal scenery of the surrounding plains is enhanced by the colourful presence of traditional pastoralists such as the Barabaig, people who have consciously retained their traditional way of life. Several substantial lakes also lie in the vicinity of Katesh, the normal base for climbs. These include the shallow and highly saline Lake Balangida, which is set at the base of the Rift Valley scarp immediately north of Mount Hanang, and more remote Lake Basotu. The area is home to the Hanang mole-rat (*Fukomys hanangensis*), a presumed endemic first described in 2017.

GETTING THERE AND AWAY Most aspirant hikers place themselves in the experienced hands of Kahembe Trekking (page 210), who will take care of

THE BARABAIG

The Barabaig are the most populous of a dozen closely related tribes, collectively known as the Datoga or Tatoga. At around 100,000, the Datoga are one of Tanzania's smaller ethno-linguistic groupings, but their territory, centred on Mount Hanang, extends into large semi-arid tracts within Arusha, Dodoma and Singida.

Superficially similar to, and frequently confused with, their Maasai neighbours by outsiders, the Barabaig are dedicated cattle-herders, speaking a Nilotic tongue, who have steadfastly resisted external pressure to forsake their semi-nomadic pastoralist ways. Unlike the Maasai, however, the Barabaig are representatives of the earliest-known Nilotic migration into East Africa from southwest Ethiopia. Their forebears probably settled in western Kenya during the middle of the first millennium AD, splitting into two groups. One – the Kalenjin – stayed put. The other, the proto-Datoga, migrated south of Lake Natron 500 to 1,000 years ago to the highlands of Ngorongoro and Mbulu, and Rift Valley plains south towards Dodoma.

Datoga territory was greatest before 1600, thereafter being eroded by migrations of various Bantu-speaking peoples into northern and central Tanzania. The most significant incursion came in the early 19th century, with the arrival of the Maasai. Oral traditions indicate that several fierce territorial battles were fought between the two pastoralist groups, resulting in the Maasai taking over the Crater Highlands and Serengeti Plains, and the Datoga retreating to their modern homeland near Mount Hanang. The Lerai Forest in Ngorongoro Crater is said to mark the grave of a Datoga leader who fell in battle in about 1840, and the site is still visited by Datoga elders from the Lake Eyasi area. The Maasai call the Barabaig the 'Mangati' (feared enemies), and the Barabaig territory around Mount Hanang is sometimes referred to as the Mangati Plains.

The Barabaig used to move around the plains according to the feeding and watering requirements of their herds. They tend a variety of livestock, including goats, donkeys and chickens, but their culture and economy revolve around cattle, which are perceived to be a measure of wealth and prestige, and every part and product of the animal, including the dung, is ingested, or worn or used in rituals. In recent years, agriculture has played an increasingly significant support role in the subsistence of the Barabaig, which together with increased population pressures has more or less put paid to the nomadic lifestyle.

Barabaig territory receives an average annual rainfall of less than 500mm, which means that water is often in short supply. Although the area is dotted with numerous lakes, most are brackish and unsuitable to drink from. Barabaig women often walk kilometres every day to collect gourds of drinking water, much of which comes from boreholes dug with foreign aid. The cattle cannot drink from the lakes directly when water levels are low and salinity is high, but the Barabaig get around this by digging wells on the lakes' edges and allowing the water to filter through the soil. Even so, the herders won't let their cattle drink from these wells on successive days for fear that it will make them ill.

Barabaig social structure is not dissimilar to that of the Maasai, although it lacks the rigid division into hierarchical age-sets pivotal to Maasai and other East African pastoralist societies. The Barabaig do not recognise one centralised leader, but are divided into several hereditary clans, each answering to a chosen elder who sits on a tribal council. The central unit of society is the family homestead or *gheida*, dwelt in by one man, his wives and their unwed offspring. This consists of a tall outer protective wall, built of thorny acacia branches and shaped like a figure of eight, with one outer gate entered through a narrow passage. Within this wall stand several small rectangular houses – low, thick-roofed constructions of wooden poles plastered with mud – and the all-important cattle stockade. Different huts are reserved for young men, young women, wives and elders. A number of gheida may be grouped together to create an informal community, and decisions are made communally rather than by a chief.

Patrilineal polygamy is actively encouraged. Elders accumulate four or more wives, up to three of which might share one hut, but marriage within any given clan is regarded to be incestuous. The concept of divorce is not recognised, but a woman may separate from her husband and return to her parents' home under some circumstances. The Barabaig openly regard extramarital sex to be normal, even desirable, although a great many taboos and conventions dictate just who may have intercourse with whom, and where they can perform the act. Traditionally, should a married woman bear a child whose biological father is other than her husband, the child remains the property of the husband – even when husband and wife are separated.

The appearance of the Barabaig is striking. The women wear heavy ochre-dyed goatskin or cowhide dresses, tasselled below the waist, and decorated with colourful yellow and orange beads. They adorn themselves with brass bracelets and neck-coils, tattoo circular patterns around their eyes, and some practise facial scarification. Men are less ornate, with a dyed cotton cloth draped over the shoulders and another around the waist. Traditionally, young men would prove themselves by killing a person (other than a Datoga) or an elephant, lion or buffalo, which might be used as the base of a ceremonial headdress along with the pelts of other animals they had killed.

The Barabaig are monotheists who believe in a universal creator whom they call Aseeta. The sun – to which they give the same name – is the all-seeing eye of Aseeta, who lives far away and has little involvement in their lives. Barabaig legend has it that they are descended from Aseeta's brother Salohog, whose eldest son Gumbandaing was the first true Datoga. Traditionally, most Barabaig elders can trace their lineage back over tens of generations to this founding father, and ancestral worship plays a greater role in their spiritual life than direct worship of God. Oddly, given the arid nature of their homeland, the Barabaig have a reputation as powerful rainmakers. It is said that only 1% of the Barabaig have abandoned their traditional beliefs in favour of exotic religions – a scenario which, judging by the number of internet sites devoted to the state of the Barabaig's souls, has spun quite a few evangelical types into a giddy froth.

The above statistic is indicative of the Barabaig's stubborn adherence to a traditional way of life. In the colonial era, the Barabaig refused to be co-opted into the migrant labour system, on the not unreasonable basis that they could sell one good bullock for more than the typical labourer would earn in a year. Other Tanzanians tend to view the Barabaig as embarrassingly primitive and ignorant – when the Nyerere government outlawed the wearing of traditional togas in favour of Westernised clothing, the Barabaig resolutely ignored them. Even today, few have much formal education or speak a word of English – it would, for that matter, be pretty unusual to meet a Barabaig who could hold a sustained conversation in Swahili.

all aspects of the climb including transport from Babati. The springboard for independent climbs is Katesh, which lies at the mountain's southern base 75km southwest of Babati along the surfaced road to Singida. In a **private vehicle**, the drive from Arusha to Katesh takes about 4 hours, and from Babati it's slightly longer than 1 hour. For those dependent on **public transport**, buses run between Babati and Singida via Katesh throughout the day, and there are also a few direct buses from Arusha, the pick being Mtei Express Coaches.

WHERE TO STAY AND EAT If you need to overnight in Katesh, the basic **Summit Hotel** (⊕ -4.51840, 35.39085; m +255 787 242424; US$10 dbl; **$**) near the municipal offices is the established favourite with travellers, with basic but decent en-suite rooms, and a good place to ask about guides and other local travel advice. Other more basic options include the Colt Guesthouse (⊕ -4.52154, 35.38118; 027 253 0030; US$4 dbl; **$**) opposite the market.

FEES All fees for Mount Hanang Nature Forest Reserve are payable at the Katesh Forestry Office, which is in the municipal office near the Summit Hotel. Entrance costs US$10 per person per day and a mandatory guide is US$15 per group per day. There is also a village fee equivalent to around US$1.50 per person. If you camp overnight on the mountain, you'll also need to pay a camping fee from US$10/15 per night for one/two people. Porters are optional and charge around US$5–10 per day.

WHAT TO SEE AND DO

Climbing Mount Hanang Several ascent routes exist, but only two are suited to first-time climbers. Marginally the easiest, especially for those making their own arrangements, is the 8.5km Jorodom (or Katesh) Route, which starts at the eponymous village on the southern slopes about 3km from Katesh, and takes anything from 5 to 8 hours to summit. The Gitting Route starts on the wetter eastern slopes 10km out of town, and is more densely forested, but also more slippery underfoot during the rains. Other tougher routes include the Himit River Trail, which passes mostly through forest and is of particular interest to birders, and the short but very steep Barjomot Trail.

Hanang can be climbed as a full-day round trip out of Katesh, but this reduces the hike to something of an endurance test, with little opportunity to enjoy the scenery. What's more, while a very fit hiker could complete the full ascent and descent in 12 hours, others may struggle. An overnight climb is therefore recommended. There are several good places to pitch a tent, or you can sleep in the caves on the Gitting Route (checking in advance that your guide knows their location). Either way, the upper slopes of Hanang get very chilly at night, so you'll need a good sleeping bag or thick blanket, and enough warm clothes.

No permanent water source exists on the mountain, so bring all the drinking water you'll require. This is an *absolute* daily minimum of four litres per climber, more during the hot, dry season. Bottled mineral water is available in Katesh, but not in Gitting or Jorodom.

Hanang climbs can be arranged through a specialist local operator. Katesh-based Thomas Safaris (aka Mount Hanang Safaris; m +255 784 503300/758 345240; w sites.google.com/site/hanangsafaris/home) comes highly recommended and charges US$80/120 per person for a day/overnight hike inclusive of meals, forest reserve fees, accommodation in Katesh and an experienced English-speaking guide. Another option is Kahembe Trekking (page 210), which arranges similar all-inclusive portered climbs out of Babati. Alternatively, you could arrange your own climb at the Forestry Office in Katesh, but this won't save you much money, there's a risk of being given an inexperienced guide, and you'll need to arrange your own food and water.

Climbers intending to use the **Jorodom Route** will need to walk the 3km from Katesh to Jorodom village. From Jorodom, the hike to a good campsite on the lower ridge takes about 6 hours. The upper ridge looks deceptively close at this point, but is in fact at least 4 hours distant. It is thus advisable to camp at the top of the lower ridge, then tackle the final ascent and full descent the next day.

To get to the trailhead for the **Gitting Route**, follow the Babati road out of Katesh for 5km to Nangwa, then turn left on to a side road and continue for another 4km to the village of Gitting. The Forestry Department has an office here where you can arrange a guide and porters at the same rate charged in Katesh or Jorodom. There's no accommodation in Gitting, but you can camp in the Forestry Department compound.

Mount Hanang road loop A loop of rough road near Katesh circles around the north side of Mount Hanang, making for an interesting half-day drive for motorised travellers who don't particularly want to climb the mountain. The scenery along this road is lovely, passing through cultivated montane meadows and lower-lying acacia scrub, with the mountain looming to the south and Lake Balangida and the Rift Valley Escarpment about 5km to the north. A diversion to the lake and its hinterland offers good birding and the opportunity to seek out some little-known rock paintings, as well as exposure to rustic Barabaig and Iraqw villages.

Leave Katesh along the Babati road, and after 5km you'll reach Nangwa, a small settlement noted locally for its Catholic church with impressive stained-glass windows. A left turn at Nangwa leads you on to the loop road and, after about 4km, the semi-urban sprawl of Gitting, also the trailhead for the Hanang ascent route of that name. From Gitting, you'll probably need to ask somebody to point you in the right direction for Barjomet, which lies another 5–6km along the loop. The cultivated highlands between Gitting and Barjomet buffer the forest zone of Hanang, and once you reach Barjomet, a small crater, clearly visible from the road, hosts a seasonal lake where local villagers bring cattle and sheep to drink. Moving on from Barjomet, the road deteriorates and becomes little more than a rough track as it descends into a hot valley, densely covered in acacia woodland. After about 5km and 10km respectively, it passes through the small traditional villages of Gendabi and Dawar, with fine views of Lake Balangida to the north. About 2km past Dawar, the loop road emerges on the main road between Katesh (to the left) and Basotu (to the right).

A worthwhile **side trip** from this loop, best undertaken in the company of a local guide and about 5km long in either direction, leads from Gitting to Gidawira and the shore of Lake Balangida. This shallow body of water, far too saline to drink, is set in the sweltering depression that divides Hanang from the Rift Valley scarp, and it frequently harbours substantial concentrations of flamingos. In recent years, Balangida has often been reduced to a puddle, or has dried up entirely, during the dry season. When this happens, the extensive white flats are exposed, and the local Barabaig can be seen extracting coarse salt by the bucket load. Also of interest are some faded rock paintings, depicting both animals and people, which can be reached by scrambling up a rock face close to Gidawira. This is a hot walk, with no potable water to be found along the way, so do bring some bottled water with you.

Lake Basotu The little-known but very accessible Lake Basotu lies about 40km northwest of Katesh, and is reached via a scenic road that ascends the Rift Valley scarp north of Mount Hanang and Lake Balangida before passing through grassy highlands populated by Barabaig and Bulu pastoralists. Lake Basotu is a lovely, atmospheric spot, fringed by stands of papyrus and tall yellow fever trees, with Hanang towering on the eastern horizon. Large numbers of hippo are resident in the shallows, and troops of vervet monkey commandeer the wooded shore. The birdlife is fabulous, too, particularly on the far eastern shore, where a ghostly forest of waterlogged trunks supports a seasonal breeding colony of reed cormorant, pink-backed pelican and black-headed, grey and squacco heron.

The aforementioned heronry can be explored on foot at the point where the road from Katesh first skirts the eastern shore of the lake. This is also a favourite watering spot for traditionally attired Barabaig, Bulu and Maasai, who march their cattle here from many kilometres away. Directly opposite this stretch of shore, only 50m from the road but invisible until you stand on the wooded rim, is a small green crater lake with waters too saline to support any fish. The cattle herders who congregate here don't see many tourists and, based on our experience, are likely to be more than willing to show you the lake – ask for it by the Barabaig name of Gida Monyot (Salt Lake). Assuming you have a fair grasp of Swahili, you might also want to enquire about the folklore surrounding the lake. It is said that the local Barabaig used to throw their dead into it, because it is so deep, and also that when a woman had sexual intercourse outside of marriage she would undress and wade into the lake up to her shoulders to cleanse herself of wrongdoing.

After reaching the eastern part of Lake Basotu, the road from Katesh continues roughly parallel to the shore for about 3km before reaching the town of Basotu, which sprawls across a pretty peninsula on the southern shore of the lake. Today a sleepy and unexpectedly traditionalist small fishing town, though somewhat more bustling on Monday, the main market day, Basotu was the scene of the decisive battle in the German campaign to coerce the resistant Barabaig into their colony before World War I. The German garrisons at Singida and Mbulu marched into Barabaig territory, converging on Basotu, where after a short battle they hanged 12 leading elders and the most revered of the Barabaig medicine men, leaving the bodies dangling from the scaffold to discourage future resistance.

BARABAIG WINE

Brian Doench

The Barabaig are enthusiastic beekeepers, and their unique wine Gesuda is made from honey, together with a rare local root that is gathered on the upper slopes of Mount Hanang and said to lend the drink a medicinal property. Gesuda is fermented in huge gourds, the size of a half keg, and it takes a week to reach perfection, during which period entry to the room in which it is being made is restricted to the brewers.

Reserved for special occasions, the drinking of Gesuda is governed by a complex and rigid set of rules and procedures. The wine is traditionally drunk from hollowed cow horns, and since the drinking rules revolve around age and rank, the most important people are served using the biggest horns. The man who supplies the honey for any given batch of Gesuda will monitor the drinking, and you need his invitation – or to be a member of his family – to join a drinking party. A close friend or brother of the host will be designated wine pourer, in charge of keeping the guests' horns filled, and of refusing to refill the horn of any man who is obnoxious or drinking irresponsibly. Any outsider who is offered the drink should regard it to be a great honour.

Whether in a private vehicle or on public transport, it is perfectly feasible to visit Basotu as a self-standing day trip out of Katesh. The drive takes about 60–90 minutes, following the Singida road for a few kilometres out of Katesh and then turning right at the first major intersection. A bus service runs between Katesh and Haidom (about 50km past Basotu) daily except for Sundays. This leaves from Katesh in the early morning, passes through Basotu 2 or 3 hours later, then passes through again in the early to mid afternoon on the return trip, allowing you a good 4 or 5 hours to explore the area. Should you choose to overnight in Basotu, there's at least one guesthouse, and a couple of no-frills restaurants serve fresh fish from the lake.

SINGIDA

Some 90km west of Katesh, Singida is a fast-growing town and eponymous regional capital set at an elevation of 1,500m on the Rift Valley floor. The main point of local interest, on the town's northeast outskirts, the shallow and hypersaline Lake Singida is a rather surreal apparition of eerie green waters offset by a shimmering white salt-encrusted shore and weird rock formations. Together with the more southerly Lake Kindai, it is listed as an Important Bird Area and attracts large flocks of waders – including thousands of lesser flamingo – when water levels are suitable. The only other attraction here is the small Singida Regional Ethnographical Museum, which is (temporarily?) closed at the time of writing. A recent mushrooming of adequate hotels, evidently aimed mainly at the conference market, makes this well-equipped town a useful overnight stop for those driving between Arusha and the new northwestern cluster of national parks described on page 304.

GETTING THERE AND AWAY Coming from the east, Singida lies 325km from Arusha via Babati and Katesh along a good surfaced road that takes 5–6 hours in a private vehicle. Mtei Express Coach operates several buses along this route daily.

WHERE TO STAY AND EAT

Regency Hotel & Resort Singida ⊕ -4.79493, 34.74093; m +255 789 310887/767 820145; w booking.com. This well-run lakeshore hotel has small but modern rooms with AC, TV & hot shower, a swimming pool & a good restaurant with indoor & outdoor seating. Great value. *From US$38/40 sgl/dbl.* **$**

Stanley Motel Majengo St; m +255 754 476785; w stanleygroupofhotels.com. Set at the base of a large rock outcrop, this central stalwart has a good restaurant & comfortable rooms with net, fan, hot shower & TV. There's a similar quality annex closer to the lake. *From US$15/20 sgl/dbl.* **$**

KONDOA ROCK ART SITES

Inscribed as a UNESCO World Heritage Site in 2006, the prehistoric rock art that adorns the Maasai Escarpment south of Tarangire is the most intriguing outdoor gallery of its sort in East Africa, and among the most ancient and stylistically varied anywhere on the continent. The best-known panels are centred around the blink-and-you'll-miss-it village of Kolo, which straddles the Arusha–Dodoma road between Kondoa and Babati, but the World Heritage Site extends across an area of 2,335km^2, and more remote sites are still being discovered, most recently a cluster of more than 50 undocumented panels in the Swaga Swaga Game Reserve southwest of Kondoa.

The rock art around Kolo and Kondoa is the most prolific in equatorial Africa. This is partly due to the lay of the land. Like the equally rich uKhahlamba-Drakensberg region in South Africa, Kondoa is endowed with numerous granite outcrops tailor-made for painting. The major rock art panels here are generally sited within small caves or beneath overhangs aligned to an east–west axis, a propensity that might reflect the preferences of the artists, or might have provided the most favourable conditions for preservation against the elements. The age of the paintings is tentatively placed at between 200 and 4,000 years, but their intent is a matter of speculation (page 222).

The pigments for the paintings were made with leaf extracts (yellow and green), powdered ochre and manganese (red and black) and possibly bird excrement (white), bound together by animal fat. Subjects and styles vary greatly. The most widely depicted animals are giraffe (26%) and eland (14%), which may have held mystical significance to the artists, or might simply have been their favoured prey. A large number of panels also contain human figures, generally highly stylised and often apparently engaged in ritual dances or ceremonies. At some sites, particularly those of the relatively recent and unformed 'late white' style, readily identifiable subjects are vastly outnumbered by abstract or geometric figures, the significance of which can only be guessed at. A common feature of the more elaborate panels is the jumbled superimposition of images, which is now widely thought to be a deliberate ploy to associate two or more significant images with each other.

The proposal to enshrine the Kondoa Rock Art as a UNESCO World Heritage Site stated that 'in terms of conservation, most of the sites are stable and relatively well preserved although there are a variety of problems including salt encrustation, erosion, water damage, and fading caused by sunlight'. Exposure to the elements notwithstanding, the rock art has been left undisturbed by locals in the past because it is regarded as sacred or taboo. In 1931, a government employee, A T Culwick, documented an example of one such taboo, so deeply ingrained that its source had evidently been forgotten. When Culwick needed to climb Ilongero Hill near Singida on official business, the chief of the village at the base warned him off, saying that the hill was inhabited by a demon. Culwick eventually persuaded the reluctant chief and entourage to accompany him on the ascent, where he discovered a large shelter covered with ancient rock art. The fear displayed by the villagers before climbing, combined with their startled reaction to the rock panel, left Culwick in no doubt that they had never suspected the existence of the paintings.

The erosion of traditional beliefs in recent years places the art at greater threat of local interference. Already, a few sites are partially defaced by graffiti or scratching, while other paintings are deteriorating as a result of unofficial guides splashing water on them to bring out the colours, or through repeated exposure to flash photography, which damages sensitive organic pigments. More bizarrely, a local legend that the Germans buried a hoard of gold near one of the rock art sites during World War I has resulted in fortune-seekers manually excavating and dynamiting close to several rock sites. Under such circumstances, UNESCO's inscription of the rock art as a World Heritage Site is welcome indeed, although more formal protection is overdue.

GETTING THERE AND AWAY Although very few people do so, it is perfectly feasible to tag a visit to Kondoa Rock Art onto a standard northern circuit safari, whether you do so as a day trip from Tarangire National Park or overnight somewhere more close by. The rock art site's office is in the small junction village of Kilo, which straddles the surfaced Dodoma Road 240km south of Arusha, 80km south of Babati and 25km north of Kondoa. Allow up to 4 hours driving all the way from Arusha,

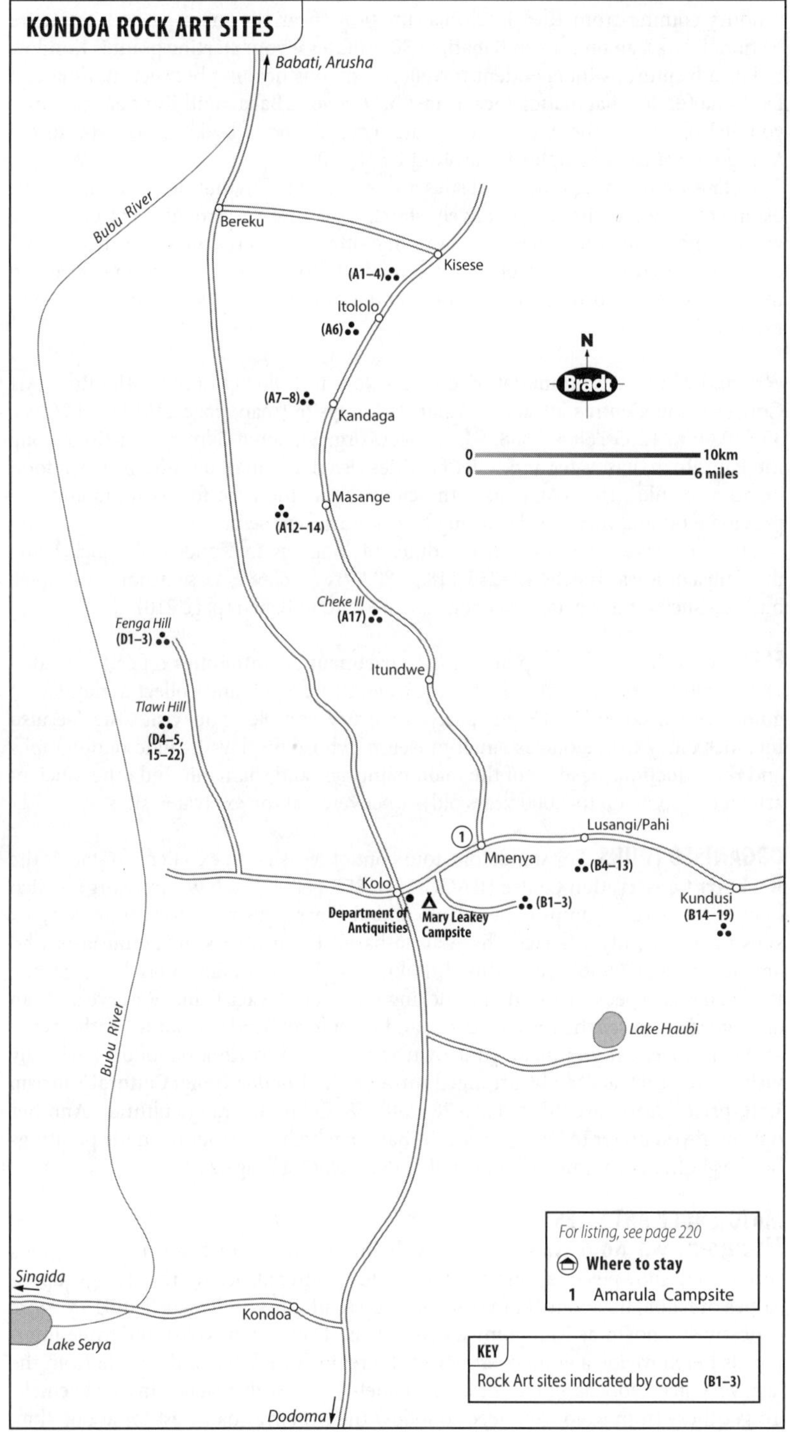
KONDOA ROCK ART SITES
Babati, Arusha
Bubu River
Bereku
Kisese
(A1–4)
Itololo
(A6)
(A7–8)
Kandaga
N
Bradt
0 10km
0 6 miles
Masange
(A12–14)
Cheke III
(A17)
Fenga Hill
(D1–3)
Itundwe
Tlawi Hill
(D4–5, 15–22)
1
Lusangi/Pahi
Mnenya
(B4–13)
Kolo
(B1–3)
Kundusi
(B14–19)
Department of Antiquities
Mary Leakey Campsite
Lake Haubi
Bubu River
For listing, see page 220
Where to stay
1 Amarula Campsite
Singida
Kondoa
Lake Serya
KEY
Rock Art sites indicated by code (B1–3)
Dodoma

2 hours coming from Kwa Kuchinja junction (near the main gate to Tarangire National Park), an hour from Babati, or 30 minutes if your starting point is Kondoa.

For adventurous independent travellers, any bus heading between Arusha and Dodoma (or, for that matter, local transport between Babati and Kondoa) can drop you at Kolo. Once there, the guides can arrange a boda-boda to take you to the Mungomi wa Kolo complex for around US$8–10.

Details on reaching individual sites are provided below, but be aware that while distances between sites are relatively short, roads are very rough (4x4 only) and visiting most sites will entail some walking, often on steep slopes. For this reason, even motorised travellers will find it unrealistic to visit more than one cluster in the space of one morning or afternoon, and a full three days would be required to explore the lot.

WHERE TO STAY Accommodation options close to Kolo are limited. The Rock Art Conservation Centre's attractive **Amarula Campsite** [map, page 219] (⊕ -4.70130, 35.86984; m +255 768 475868; f; w racctz.org; **$**), about 5km east of Kolo along the Pahi Road, has water and toilet facilities (even a sauna), but doesn't stock food or other drinks. The RACC uses the campsite as the base for its tours and can provide tents and full-board catering by prior arrangement.

Further afield, there are a few indifferent lodgings in Kondoa, the pick being the **Samsudi Royal Hotel** (m +255 718 728087/784 768689; w samsudi-royal-hotel.business.site; **$**) but a better selection can be found in Babati (page 210).

FEES All visitors must stop at Kolo's **Department of Antiquities** office (🕘 07.00–18.00 daily) to pay an entrance fee equivalent to US$12, and collect a mandatory guide, which costs US$15 per party for every complex you visit. The fee also includes entry to the office's small museum, whose displays include photographs and reproductions of some of the main paintings, and shamanic and other ancient artefacts – some up to 7,000 years old – uncovered at the excavated sites.

ORGANISED TOURS For standalone tours out of Arusha, an excellent contact is the **Rock Art Conservation Centre** (RACC; m + 255 768 475868; w racctz.org), which operates Amarula Campsite near Kolo and also arranges visits to various rock art sites in the vicinity. Managed by Arusha-based Finnish rock art enthusiasts who are dedicated to publicising this little-known aspect of Tanzania's heritage, the RACC has also been involved in exploring the Swaga Swaga Game Reserve and can arrange visits to see the rock art there, and meet local Sandawe hunter-gatherers.

Alternatively, if you make your own way to head to Kondoa, budget-friendly visits to the rock art can be arranged through the **Kondoa Irangi Cultural Tourism Enterprise** (Usandawe Rd; m +255 784 948858; f kondoairangicultural). Another option, if you prefer to base yourself in Babati, which is further from the paintings but has better accommodation, is **Kahembe Trekking** (page 210).

MAJOR ROCK ART SITES

Mungomi wa Kolo Most visitors with limited time are taken to the region's recognised showpiece, a cluster of ten sites scattered across the craggy upper slopes of Ichoi Hill about 10km from Kolo by road. Prosaically labelled B1–3, more evocatively known as Mungomi wa Kolo (The Dancers of Kolo), the three finest panels here provide a good overview of the region's rock art, and – aside from the last, very steep, foot ascent to the actual panels – it is easily reached in a 4x4 vehicle. To get there from Kolo, you need to follow the Mnenya road west for about 4km, crossing the normally dry Kolo River on the way, before turning right on to a rough 4x4 track that reaches the base of the hill after about 6km.

Probably the most intriguing of the panels is **B2**, which lies in a tall overhang right at the top of the hill. This panel includes more than 150 figures, including several fine, but very faded, paintings of animals (giraffe, leopard, zebra and rhino), as well as some abstract designs and numerous humanoid forms. Richard Leakey regarded this site as representing a particularly wide variety of superimposed styles and periods, and it must surely have been worked over hundreds if not thousands of years. One striking scene, which Mary Leakey dubbed 'The Abduction', depicts five rather ant-like humanoid forms with stick bodies, spindly limbs and distended heads. The two figures on the right have elongated heads, while the two on the left have round heads, as does the central figure, which also appears to have breasts and whose arms are being held by the flanking figures. Leakey interpreted the painting as a depiction of an attempted abduction, with the central female figure being tugged at by two masked people on the right, while friends or family try to hold on to her from the left. Of course, a scene such as this is open to numerous interpretations, and it could as easily depict a ritual dance as an abduction. And why stop there? I once stumbled across a web page that made an oddly compelling case for this haunting scene, and other paintings in Kondoa, providing evidence of extraterrestrial visits to the region in the distant past. If this sort of speculation tickles you, the long-snouted figures to the right, according to this interpretation, are alien abductors, while a separate scene to the right shows another alien standing in a hot-air balloon!

Panel **B1**, also in an overhang, is even larger and more elaborate, though most of the paintings have been partially obliterated by termite activity. Prominent among several animal portraits are those of elephants and various antelope. The most striking scene consists of three reposed humanoid figures with what appear to be wild, frizzy hairstyles (some form of headdress?) and hands clutching a vertical bar. A small cave in front of the panel is used for ceremonial purposes by local rainmakers, and sacrifices are still sometimes left outside the shelter. Finally, near the base of the mountain, the most accessible of the three main panels, **B3**, depicts the animated humanoids that gave rise to the local name, along with a few faded animal figures, including a cheetah and buffalo.

Pahi, Lusangi and Kinyasi Panels B4–13 all lie close to the base of the escarpment near the twin villages of Lusangi and Pahi, about 12km from Kolo. To reach them from Kolo, follow the same road you would to get to Mungomi wa Kolo, but instead of turning right after crossing the river, keep straight on the main road, passing through Mnenya until you reach Lusangi. This site is normally accessible in any vehicle, though a 4x4 may be useful after rain. Lusangi can be reached by dalla dalla from Kolo, and there is a guesthouse about 1km away in Pahi. A 1km piste leads from the main road to the base of the escarpment, from where a flat 100m footpath leads to three shelters about 20m apart.

The art at Lusangi is not as impressive as that at Mungomi wa Kolo, but it is probably a more suitable goal for those unwilling or unable to climb steep footpaths. Several figures do stand out, however, the most notable being a 70cm-high outlined giraffe superimposed on a very old painting of a rhino. Below this, a red and yellow figure of an eland-like antelope with a disproportionately small head is regarded by archaeologists as one of the very oldest paintings known in Kondoa region. Only a couple of clear humanoid figures are found at these sites, and several of the panels are dominated by bold, childlike patterns in the 'late white' style and are

BUT WHAT DOES IT MEAN?

There is a strangely eerie sensation attached to emerging from a remote and nondescript tract of bush to be confronted by an isolated panel of primitive paintings executed by an artist or artists unknown, hundreds or maybe thousands of years before the time of Christ. Faded as many of the panels are, and lacking the perspective to which modern eyes are accustomed, you can still hardly fail to be impressed by the fine detail of many of the animal portraits, or to wonder at the surrealistic distortion of form that characterises the human figures. And, almost invariably, first exposure to these charismatic works of ancient art prompts three questions: how old are they, who were the artists and what was their intent?

When, who and why? The simple answers are that nobody really knows. The broadest time frame, induced from the absence of any representations of extinct species in the rock galleries of Kondoa, places the paintings at less than 20,000 years old. The absence of a plausible tradition of attribution among the existing inhabitants of the area – a Gogo claim that the paintings were the work of the Portuguese can safely be discounted – makes it unlikely that even the most modern paintings are less than 200 years old. Furthermore, experts have noted a clear progression from the simplest early styles to more complex, expressive works of art, and a subsequent regression to the clumsy graffiti-like finger painting of the 'late white' phase, indicating that the paintings were created over a substantial period of time.

Early attempts at dating the Kondoa Rock Art concentrated on categorising it chronologically based on the sequence of superimposition of different styles on busy panels. The results were inconclusive, even contradictory, probably because the superimposition of images was an integral part of the art, so that a foreground image might be roughly contemporaneous with an image underneath it. It is also difficult to know the extent to which regional style, or even individual style, might be of greater significance than chronological variation. The most useful clue to the age of the paintings is the stratified organic debris deposited alongside red ochre 'pencils' at several sites. Carbon dating of a handful of sites where such deposits have been found suggests that the earliest-surviving paintings might be up to 7,000 years old, but that the artists were most active about 3,000 years ago. The crude 'late white' paintings, on the other hand, are widely agreed to be hundreds rather than thousands of years old, and there is evidence to suggest that some underwent ritual restoration by local people who held them sacred into historical times.

The identity of the artists is another imponderable. In the first half of the 20th century, the rock art of southern Africa was solely attributed to 'Bushmen' hunter-gatherers, a people whose click-based Khoisan tongue is unrelated to Bantu and who are of vastly different ethnic stock from any Bantu-speakers. True, the Bushmen are the only people who practised the craft in historical times, but much of the rock art of southern Africa (like that of eastern Africa) dates back thousands of years. Coincidentally, two of East Africa's few remaining click-tongued hunter-gatherers, the Sandawe and the Hadzabe, both live in close proximity to the main concentration of Tanzanian rock art, but neither has a tradition relating to the paintings.

Given that the archaeological record indicates east-southern Africa was populated entirely by hunter-gatherers when the paintings were probably executed, furthermore that a succession of human migrations has subsequently passed through the region, postulating an ancestral link between the artists of Kondoa and modern hunter-gatherers would be tenuous in the extreme.

If anything, the probable chronology of the rock art points in the opposite direction. Assuming that creative activity peaked some 3,000 years ago, it preceded the single most important known migration into East Africa: the mass invasion of the Bantu-speakers who today comprise the vast majority of Tanzania's population. Most probable, then, that a Bantu- or perhaps Nilotic-speaking group, or another group forced to migrate locally as a ripple effect of the Bantu invasion, moved into the Kondoa region and conquered or assimilated the culture responsible for the rock art, resulting in the gradual stylistic regression noted by archaeologists. All that can be said about the artists with reasonable certainty is that they were hunter-gatherers whose culture, were it not for the painted testament left behind on the granite faces of Kondoa, would have vanished without trace.

The most haunting of the questions surrounding the rock art of Kondoa is the intent of its creators. In determining the answer to this, one obstacle is that nobody knows just how representative the surviving legacy might be. Most extant rock art in Kondoa is located in caves or overhangs, but the small number of faded paintings that survive on more open sites must be a random subset of similarly exposed panels that have been wiped clean by the elements. We have no record, either, of whether the artists dabbled on canvases less durable than rock, but unless one assumes that posterity was a conscious goal, it seems wholly presumptuous to think otherwise. The long and short of it, then, is that the extant galleries might indeed represent a sufficiently complete record to form a reliable basis for any hypothesis, but they might just as easily represent a fraction of a percentage of the art executed at the time. Furthermore, there is no way of telling whether rocks were painted only in specific circumstances – it is conceivable that the rock art would maker greater sense viewed in conjunction with other types of painting that have not survived.

Two broad schools of thought surround the interpretation of Africa's ancient rock art. The first has it that the paintings were essentially recreational, documentary and/or expressive in intent – art for art's sake, if you like – while the second regards them to be mystical works of ritual significance. It is quite possible that the truth of the matter lies between these poles of opinion. A striking feature of the rock art of Kondoa is the almost uniform discrepancy in the styles used to depict human and non-human subjects. Animals are sometimes painted in stencil form, sometimes filled with bold white or red paint, but – allowing for varying degrees of artistic competence – the presentation is always naturalistic. The people, by contrast, are almost invariably heavily stylised in form, with elongated stick-like bodies and disproportionately round heads topped by a forest of unkempt hair. Some such paintings are so downright bizarre that they might be more reasonably described as humanoid than human (a phenomenon that has not gone unnoticed by UFO theorists searching for prehistoric evidence of extraterrestrial visits; page 221).

The discrepancy between the naturalistic style favoured for animals and highly stylised presentation of humans has attracted numerous theoretical explanations. Most crumble under detailed examination of the evidence, but all incline towards supporting the mystical or ritualistic school of interpretation. Ultimately, however, for every tentative answer we can provide, these enigmatic ancient works pose a dozen more questions. It is an integral part of their charisma that we can speculate to our heart's content, but will never know the whole truth.

often superimposed over older and more finely executed portraits. From Pahi it is possible to drive another 12km to Kinyasi, where sites B14–19 are situated in a valley below the 1,000m-high Kome Mountain. The most interesting of these sites is a 1m² panel of small, finely executed antelope, which also includes one of the few known examples of a painting depicting a homestead.

Mnenya to Kisese Sites A1–18 all lie along the stretch of the Maasai Escarpment that runs immediately east of the reasonable dirt road connecting Mnenya to Kisese. This road itself runs roughly parallel to, and about 10km east of, the Great North Road, and is connected to it by a roughly 8km road between Kolo and Mnenya in the south and about a 15km road between Bereku and Kisese in the north. Ideally, travellers driving southwards from Babati or Arusha along the Great North Road would explore sites A1–18 by turning on to the Kisese road at Bereku, then following the Mnenya road south and returning to the Great North Road at Kolo. Unfortunately, however, it is mandatory to pass through Kolo first to pay fees and collect a guide, which will enforce quite a bit of backtracking for southbound travellers (but makes no real difference to travellers driving north from Kondoa). There isn't much public transport on the Mnenya–Kisese road, but a few dalla dallas run along it daily, and there is basic accommodation in Masange.

Running northwards from Mnenya, the direction in which regulations practically force you to travel, the first major site is **A17** or Cheke III, which lies about 5km along the Kisese road. This extensive, intricate panel contains at least 330 figures, is rich in superimposition, and is studded with various animals as well as surreal humanoids with circular heads and pincer legs and a couple of unusually robust human figures seemingly draped in robes. The shelter is dominated by the so-called Dance of the Elephant, a red painting of a solitary elephant surrounded by perhaps a dozen people – who might as easily be worshipping or hunting the elephant as dancing around it. Getting to Cheke III involves following a 2km track west of the main road, followed by a short but steep ascent to the actual panel.

About 5km further along the road, you arrive at Masange village, from where a roughly 1km-long side road leads to the base of the escarpment, and another 5–10 minutes' climb brings you to sites **A12–14**. The most compelling panel in this cluster is A13, another elaborately decorated overhang with numerous superimposed paintings, but A14 is of interest for its solitary painting of ten faded human figures in a row. Most of the sites between Masange and Kisese lie some distance from the main road, but site **A9** or Kandaga III, 6km past Masange, consisting of a series of geometric representations in the 'late white' style first described in 1931 by Julian Huxley, is particularly recommended to serious enthusiasts. The excellent and well-preserved site dubbed Kisese II or **A4** lies another 8km past Kandaga on a tall rock no more than 10 minutes' walk from the road.

Bubu River sites Unlike the other rock art sites within the proposed reserve, this cluster lies to the west of the Great North Road, overlooking the Bubu River about 12km from Kolo. Short of walking there and back from Kolo, this is the one cluster that cannot easily be reached without private transport, ideally a 4x4. It is, nevertheless, perhaps the best cluster of them all, with several panels in close proximity and in a particularly good state of preservation.

Of the three panels D1–3 situated on Fenga Hill, the most worthwhile is **D3**, sometimes referred to as the Trapped Elephants. Covered in a jumble of superimposed red features, including several slim humanoid figures with distended heads and headdresses, this panel is named for the central painting of two elephants surrounded by a stencilled oblong line. Some experts believe that this depicts an elephant trap, a theory supported by three fronds below the elephants that might well represent branches used to camouflage a pit. Others believe that it might have a more mystical purpose, placing the elephants in a kind of magic circle. A trickle of circles dripping from the left base of the picture could be blood, or the elephants' spoor.

About 3km south of Fenga Hill, the immediate vicinity around Twali Hill hosts at least ten panels, numbered D4–5 and D15–22. A dedicated enthusiast could easily devote half a day to this cluster of very different sites. Panel **D19** is notable for an almost life-size and unusually naturalistic attempt to paint a human figure in a crouched or seated position, and it also contains some finely executed paintings of animals, including a buffalo head and a giraffe leaning forward. Directly opposite this panel, site **D20** depicts several seated human figures, while 500m further away site **D22** is also known as the Red Lion for the striking painting of a lion, with a stencilled black outline and red fill, that dominates the shelter.

BACKGROUND TO THE ROCK ART OF KONDOA DISTRICT

Outside attention was first drawn to the rock art of Kondoa District in the 1920s, although it would be several decades before the full extent of its riches was grasped. In 1923, District Commissioner Bagshawe visited and described the two main shelters at Mungomi wa Kolo, and six years later several of the sites on and around Twali Hill were visited by Dr T Nash. In the early 1930s, the eminent archaeologists Louis and Mary Leakey explored a handful of new sites, notably Cheke III, on which was based Louis Leakey's formative attempt at stylistic categorisation and relative chronology, published in his 1936 book *Stone Age Africa*.

By the late 1940s, enthusiasts and archaeologists had located 75 sites in the Kondoa region, and their discoveries led to the publication in 1950 of a unique special edition of *Tanganyika Notes and Records* dedicated solely to the rock art. The first intensive survey of the region was undertaken in 1951 by Mary Leakey, who boosted the tally of known panels for A sector alone from 17 panels to 186, of which one-third were sufficiently well preserved to be studied. Leakey traced and redrew 1,600 figures and scenes, an undertaking that formed the basis of her 1983 book *Africa's Vanishing Art: The Rock Paintings of Tanzania*. Leakey said of her time in the Kondoa region, 'No amounts of stone and bone could yield the kinds of information that the paintings gave so freely…here were scenes of life, of men and women hunting, dancing, singing and playing music'. Bizarrely, the only major excavations to have taken place since then were undertaken by Ray Inskeep in 1956.

The two works mentioned above are out of print, but Mary Leakey's book is freely available through online vendors such as AbeBooks and Amazon. Also worth the small asking price, however, is the National Museums of Tanzania's Occasional Paper No 5 *The Rock Art of Kondoa and Singida*, written by Fidelis Masao and available at the National Museum in Dar es Salaam. A newer book with detailed coverage of the Kondoa Rock Art placed within a broader African context, is *African Rock Art: Paintings and Engravings on Stone* by David Coulson and Alec Campbell, published by Harry N Abrams in 2000.

LEGEND OF THE CAT

Emma Thomson

To maintain the balance of power between the sexes, the Rangi people of Kondoa have devised an ingenious plan. From sunrise to sunset the men are in charge, but come sunset the rule of power shifts to the women, allowing them to reign supreme until daybreak.

This female empowerment was established following the legend of the cat, told to me by a village member one starry night near Kelema:

The cat was looking for a hero. While walking through the jungle one day he befriended a cheetah. 'This cheetah is surely the strongest and fastest animal in the forest – he will be my hero,' exclaimed the cat.

The next day, while walking with the cat through the undergrowth, the cheetah encountered a lion. They fought until the cheetah fell to the ground dead. 'The lion then must be the strongest and fiercest animal in the forest – he will be my new hero,' decided the cat.

The following day the two felines encountered an elephant foraging in the trees. Startled, the elephant charged, killing the lion. Bemused, the cat approached the elephant: 'You truly are the king of the jungle – will you be my hero?'

One day the elephant and cat were surprised by a man hunting. In fear the man killed the elephant and after cutting the meat from the body he turned for home. The cat decided to follow this beast that could defeat an animal without even touching it.

On arriving home the man approached his wife who took the elephant meat from him and set to work in the kitchen. The cat gasped: 'This woman surely must be the queen of all beasts – an animal that can take from another without fighting! She will forever be my hero.' From that day on, the cat is always to be found in the kitchen admiring its heroine.

Five minutes' walk along the same ridge towards the Bubu River brings you to a pair of shelters called **D17** or The Hunter, for a rare action painting of a hunter killing a large antelope – presumably an eland – with his bow and arrow. Several other interesting human figures are found on these twin shelters. Another 10–20 minutes' walk downhill towards the river stand two large rock faces, **D4 and D5**, respectively known as The Rhino and The Prancing Giraffe. The former is named for the 60cm-long portrait of a rhino with a rather narrow head, and it also depicts what appears to be a herd of antelope fleeing from human pursuers. The nominated painting at site D5 is a strikingly lifelike depiction of a giraffe with its front legs raised as if cantering or rearing, but no less interesting is a tall pair of very detailed, shaggy-headed human figures sometimes referred to as The Dancers.

Swaga Swaga Game Reserve This 870km² game reserve, situated about 15km southwest of Kondoa, was revealed to the outside world as a new centre of rock art in 2018, when Dr Maciej Grzelczyk documented more than 50 painting sites there. Many of these panels are in poor shape, but a handful rank among the finest examples of the genre to be seen anywhere in East Africa, and the area is still inhabited by Sandawe hunter-gatherers whose ancient dances are connected to the paintings. Of particular interest is Amak'hee 4, an elaborate diorama whose multi-layered images include a trio of unusual anthropomorphic figures with buffalo heads. Swaga Swaga is not currently developed for tourism, but visits can be arranged through the RACC (page 220), and since it is also home to significant numbers of lion and elephant, there is talk of upgrading it to become a national park.

DODOMA

Situated at an elevation of 1,135m on the windswept, drought-prone plains of the central plateau, Dodoma is the principal town of the Gogo people. It was an important stopover on the 19th-century caravan route between the coast and Lake Tanganyika, and it became a regional administration centre after Germany built a railway station there in 1910. As the country's most central town, it was chosen as the designate capital of Tanzania in 1974, a role that was formalised in 1996 when parliament relocated there (though most government offices stayed in Dar es Salaam and many are still there today).

The name Dodoma is derived from the Gogo word *idodomya*, which means 'place of sinking'. The most widely accepted explanation for this name is that it was coined by a group of villagers who came down to a stream to collect water, to find an elephant stuck irretrievably in the muddy bank. Another version of events is that a local clan stole some cattle from a neighbouring settlement, slaughtered and ate the stolen beasts, then placed their dismembered tails in a patch of swamp. When a search party arrived, the thieves claimed that the lost animals had sunk in the mud. Whether or not anybody actually believed this unlikely story goes unrecorded!

Since becoming the capital, Dodoma has experienced a high influx of people from surrounding rural areas, but it remains unremittingly small-town in atmosphere and of no specific interest to tourists (unless perhaps there are those who collect capital cities as others collect passport stamps). Dodoma is also the focal point of Tanzania's low-key viniculture industry, founded by an Italian priest in 1957, though the product is as readily available in Arusha and other tourist centres.

GETTING THERE AND AWAY Dodoma lies 430km/7 hours south of Arusha on a surfaced road through Babati and 440km/8 hours inland of Dar es Salaam on a surfaced road through Morogoro. Buses are plentiful along both routes. Trains from Dar es Salaam to Tabora and Kigoma stop at Dodoma, often for several hours.

WHERE TO STAY AND EAT

Christian Council of Tanzania (CCT) Hostel Railway St; w cct-tz.org. This long-serving hostel is only 300m from the railway station. *From US$10 dbl.* **$**

New Dodoma Hotel Railway St; 026 232 1641; w newdodomahotel.com-tanzania.com. Built more than a century ago as a German colonial rest house, this smart hotel now comprises 96 comfortable rooms with AC & DSTV, as well a gym, swimming pool, health club, internet café, hair salon & 2 restaurants. *From US$50/70 standard sgl/dbl.* **$$**

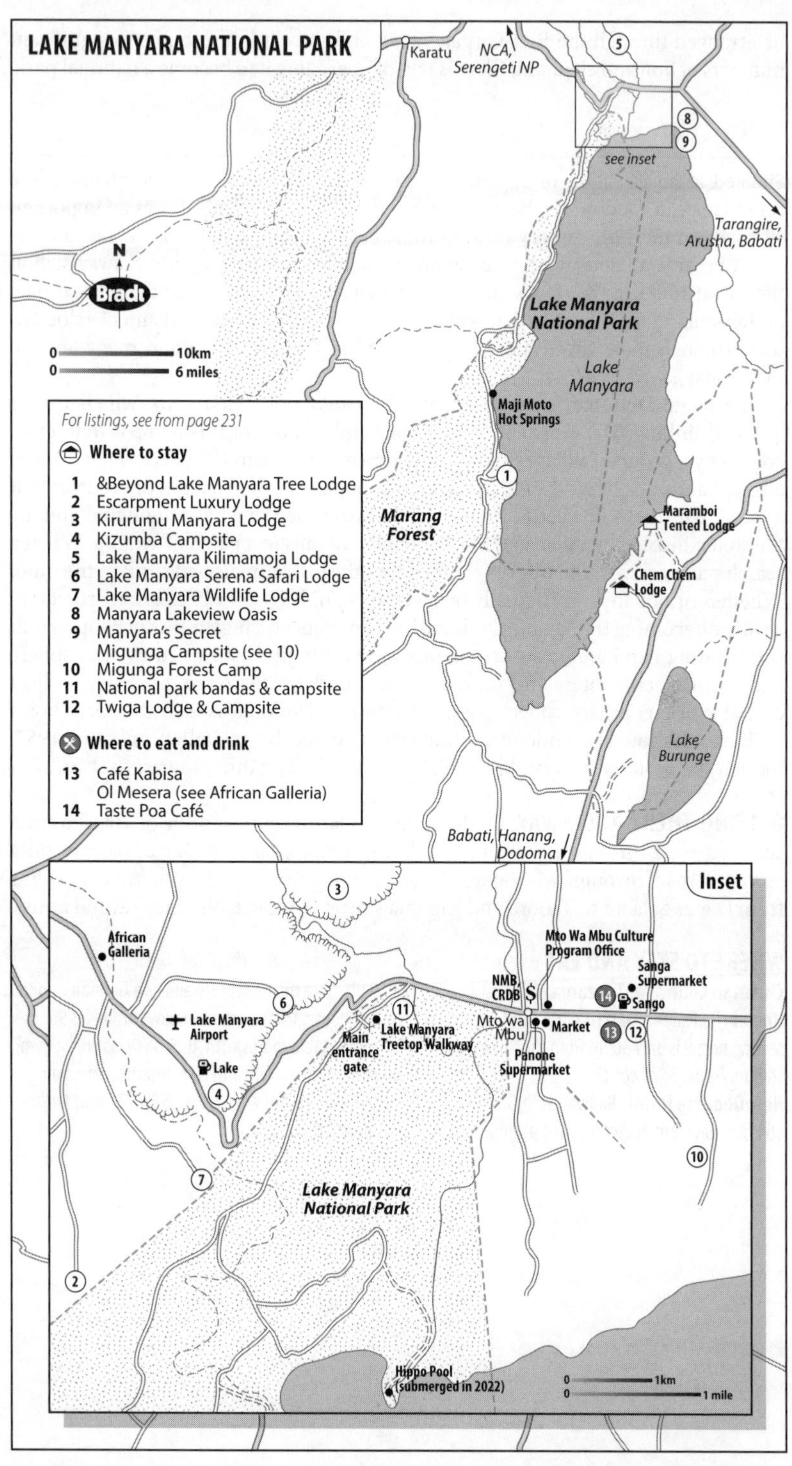
LAKE MANYARA NATIONAL PARK
Karatu
NCA, Serengeti NP
see inset
Tarangire, Arusha, Babati
Lake Manyara National Park
Lake Manyara
Maji Moto Hot Springs
Marang Forest
Maramboi Tented Lodge
Chem Chem Lodge
Lake Burunge
Babati, Hanang, Dodoma
0 10km
0 6 miles
For listings, see from page 231
Where to stay
1 &Beyond Lake Manyara Tree Lodge
2 Escarpment Luxury Lodge
3 Kirurumu Manyara Lodge
4 Kizumba Campsite
5 Lake Manyara Kilimamoja Lodge
6 Lake Manyara Serena Safari Lodge
7 Lake Manyara Wildlife Lodge
8 Manyara Lakeview Oasis
9 Manyara's Secret
Migunga Campsite (see 10)
10 Migunga Forest Camp
11 National park bandas & campsite
12 Twiga Lodge & Campsite
Where to eat and drink
13 Café Kabisa
Ol Mesera (see African Galleria)
14 Taste Poa Café
Inset
African Galleria
Lake Manyara Airport
Lake
Main entrance gate
Lake Manyara Treetop Walkway
Mto Wa Mbu Culture Program Office
NMB, CRDB
Sanga Supermarket
Sango
Mto wa Mbu
Market
Panone Supermarket
Lake Manyara National Park
Hippo Pool (submerged in 2022)
0 1km
0 1 mile

10

Lake Manyara and the Northern Rift Valley

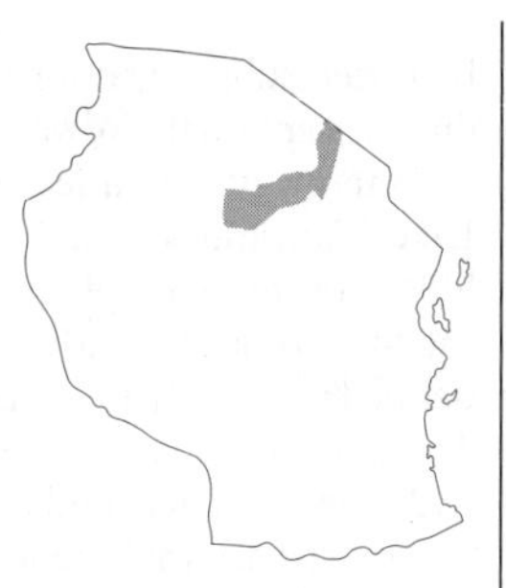

The dramatic stretch of the Rift Valley separating Arusha from the Ngorongoro Highlands supports a chain of shallow mineral-rich lakes of which the largest three – Eyasi, Natron and Manyara – all attain a length of 50km or greater when full. The most accessible and popular of these scenic landmarks is Lake Manyara, which lies only 2 hours' drive from Arusha town (along the same asphalt road that continues to Ngorongoro and the Serengeti), and whose northwestern shores are protected in an ecologically varied national park famed for its dense elephant population, tree-climbing lions and prodigious birdlife. The other two lakes are considerably more remote but still form worthwhile off-the-beaten-track deviations from a standard northern safari itinerary. Lake Eyasi, south of Manyara, is of interest primarily for the Hadza hunter-gatherers and Datoga pastoralists who inhabit its dry hinterland. To the north of Manyara, inhospitable Lake Natron – which nudges up to the border with Kenya along a little-used back route to the northern Serengeti – stands in the shadow of Ol Doinyo Lengai, a majestic (and climbable) active volcano whose Maasai name translates as 'God's Mountain'.

LAKE MANYARA NATIONAL PARK

Gazetted in 1960 and centrepiece of an eponymous UNESCO Biosphere Reserve since 1981, Lake Manyara National Park (**m** +255 767 536137; **e** manyara@tanzaniaparks.go.tz) is a popular and scenic first port of call on many safaris. The park is named after its dominant geographic feature, a shallow alkaline Rift Valley lake that extends across 470km² when full. The lake's name, a corruption of *emanyara*, the spiky protective fence of cactus-like euphorbias that traditionally encloses a Maasai family compound, alludes to the imposing cliffs of the Rift escarpment that rises to its west. In addition to protecting the northwest portion of Lake Manyara, the national park contains a rich diversity of terrestrial habitats, one that seems all the more remarkable when you consider that water comprised up to two-thirds of the park's 330km² surface area prior to the recent incorporation of the largely inaccessible 250km² Marang Forest Reserve.

Home to four of the Big Five (the exception being rhino), Lake Manyara National Park is probably best known for its tree-climbing lions, sightings of which are most likely on a morning game drive, but far from certain. Other highlights include the large troops of habituated baboon that inhabit the groundwater forest, an enjoyable canopy walkway near the entrance gate, the unusually dark giraffes that graze on the lake floodplain, an excellent hippo pool (which, when this edition was researched, had been submerged for three years following the heavy rains of 2019) and some quite exceptional birdwatching.

In terms of amenities, only one (very exclusive) permanent lodge stands within Lake Manyara National Park. Most people stay instead at one of the upmarket lodges on the escarpment above the lake, or at a cheaper lodging or campsite in the town of Mto wa Mbu near the entrance gate. Although Manyara and its well-defined game-viewing circuit kick off a high proportion of safaris through northern Tanzania, it gets mixed feedback: some find it rather low-key and boring compared with the Serengeti and Ngorongoro, while others relish the opportunity to see several species that are less common or shyer elsewhere in the region. Certainly, those with time or budgetary restrictions could consider passing by Manyara in order to spend more time in the likes of the Serengeti or Tarangire.

FLORA AND FAUNA The accessible terrestrial portion of Lake Manyara National Park is dominated by open grassland on the lake floodplain and denser acacia woodland towards the rocky escarpment that runs along its western boundary. An important feature of the park is the dense groundwater forest, dominated by shady *ficus* trees, that extends for about 5km south of the entrance gate. There is also some impressive forest in the far south, and a 250km² tract of escarpment forest, formerly protected in the Marang Forest Reserve, was annexed to the park in 2012.

This habitat diversity is reflected in Manyara's varied mammalian fauna. Among the more commonly seen large mammals are buffalo, giraffe, hippo, olive baboon, blue monkey and various antelope, all of which are likely to be sighted in the course of any game drive. Large predators include a dense but skittish leopard population, while the lions of Manyara are renowned for their conspicuous tree-climbing ways (page 234), though these days this behaviour is probably more likely to be seen in the Serengeti.

The elephants of Manyara were immortalised by Iain Douglas-Hamilton, author of *Amongst the Elephants*, in the 1970s, and while the population suffered a slight decline in the 1980s due to poaching, this was not as severe as in many larger parks in southern Tanzania. By the 1990s, the Manyara population had recovered fully, and its elephants were generally well endowed on the tusk front, and very relaxed around vehicles, making for great viewing. Sadly, on all our visits over the ten years prior to 2022, we were struck by how skittish and bad-tempered Manyara's elephants have become, and how few large tuskers we observed.

Manyara, despite its small size, is a great birding reserve, with around 400 species recorded. As Duncan Butchart, writing in the &Beyond *Ecological Journal*, once noted, 'If a first-time birdwatcher to Africa had the time to visit only a single reserve in Tanzania, then Manyara must surely be it.' It's perfectly feasible for a casual birder to see 100 species here in a day, ranging from a variety of colourful bee-eaters, barbets, kingfishers and rollers to the gigantic ground hornbill and white-backed pelican. Substantial flocks of flamingo are also present when the water level is suitable. In rainy years, the trees around the entrance gate often support large and pungent breeding colonies of the handsome yellow-billed stork and pink-backed pelican between February and June.

A remarkable 51 diurnal raptor species are known from the park, of which 28 are resident or regular. Two unusual species worth looking out for are crowned eagle, which is commonly observed in the forests close to the entrance gate, and African hawk-eagle, which often rests up on rocks and stumps immediately south of the hot springs. Also common is the African fish eagle and superficially similar palmnut vulture, the latter often associated with doum palms. In addition, six species of owl are regularly recorded.

The recent annexation of Marang Forest Reserve has not only expanded Lake Manyara National Park's area by almost 80%, but it has also helped secure an ancient elephant migration corridor connecting the lake to the highlands to its west. Marang, though relatively unexplored, hosts a selection of highland forest birds similar to those associated with the Crater Highlands, so in time it will greatly increase the already impressive bird checklist for this small national park.

FEES AND FURTHER INFORMATION Several locally published booklets, providing detailed coverage of the park's flora and fauna, can be bought from street vendors and shops in Arusha and elsewhere on the northern safari circuit. The park entrance fee of US$50 per person per 24 hours (discounted to US$45 from 15 March to 15 May) plus 18% VAT can be paid by Mastercard or Visa. No other cards are accepted, and neither is cash.

Lake Manyara National Park operates a one-entry rule, which means that visitors staying outside the park who want to do separate morning and afternoon game drives within the same 24-hour period will need to pay two sets of entrance fees. If you have the choice, we would recommend a morning game drive, as the park tends to be quieter then, and wildlife is more conspicuous. Better still, take a packed lunch and spend a full day in the park, which allows you to explore southern areas visited by few safaris.

GETTING THERE AND AWAY The main entrance gate lies at the park's northern tip bordering the small town of Mto wa Mbu. The 2-hour drive from Arusha, surfaced in its entirety, entails following the Babati road south for 80km to Makuyuni, then turning right at a prominently signposted junction, from where it's about 35km to Mto wa Mbu.

A second, very little-used entrance gate lies in the far south of the park, close to &Beyond Lake Manyara Tree Lodge. To get there from outside the park, follow the surfaced Babati road south past Makuyuni for 54km, then turn right on to an unsurfaced road that leads to the gate after another 35km.

WHERE TO STAY *Map, page 228*

The only permanent accommodation set within the park boundaries is &Beyond Lake Manyara Tree Lodge, which functions almost as a private concession in the far south, a long way from the busy northern circuit near Mto wa Mbu. Also situated within the park are a number of special campsites favoured as sites for temporary camps by operators that want to offer clients a true bush experience. Otherwise, national park bandas and campsites aside, all the accommodation servicing Manyara lies outside the park, either on the Rift Valley Escarpment overlooking the lake, or in and around Mto wa Mbu. Listed under Tarangire as they are closer to that park (page 201), the exclusive Chem Chem and Manyara Ranch both lie in the wildlife corridor connecting Tarangire and Lake Manyara national parks and make a feasible base for day trips to Manyara.

Within the park

Exclusive

✷ &Beyond Lake Manyara Tree Lodge
-3.668227, 35.745985; w andbeyond.com; closed Apr. Offering the ultimate Manyara experience, this exclusive property stands deep in a mahogany forest 20mins' drive south of Maji Moto hot springs. The 10 treehouse-like hardwood suites have banana leaf roofs, large bathrooms

with indoor tub & outdoor shower, & private decks offering intimate views into the forest, which supports a wealth of birds & bushbabies that call throughout the night. Guiding standards are exceptional & the lodge is sufficiently remote (45km south of main entrance gate) that you feel you have this beautiful park pretty much to yourself, especially during prime game-viewing hours. Night drives, village visits & exclusive lakeshore sundowners are also offered, while facilities include a swimming pool & personal butler. **$$$$$$$**

Budget & camping

✷ **National park bandas & campsite** ⊕ -3.372268, 35.839330; m +255 767 536137; w tanzaniaparks.go.tz. Situated in a lovely forest glade immediately outside the main entrance gate, the brick bandas at this attractive & well-priced facility have hot showers but no net (the latter a serious omission in the swampy vicinity), so bring a good insect repellent. Facilities include a kitchen, a dining area & an elevated treehouse looking into the forest canopy. *US$30pp plus 18% VAT banda or camping.* **$$**

Mto wa Mbu and the Rift Valley floor The small town of Mto wa Mbu is the funnel through which almost all tourist traffic to Lake Manyara National Park must pass. Pronounced 'mtowambu' like it's one word, the name literally means 'River of Mosquitoes', and if you do spend the night here, then you'll be in no doubt as to why. Several decent budget lodges are scattered around the one-street town, while the likes of Manyara Lakeview Oasis, Manyara's Secret and Migunga Forest Camp provide more rustic upmarket accommodation on the nearby Rift Valley floor.

Upmarket

Manyara Lakeview Oasis ⊕ -3.403428, 35.890195; m +255 782 908815; w manyaralakeview.com. Set in lovely wooded grounds on the northeast lake floodplain 10mins' drive from the park entrance gate, the former Manyara Wildlife Safari Camp offers excellent views across the lake to the escarpment from its thatched dining area & swimming pool. Standing tents are set on stilted wooden platforms below a cool thatch roof & come with rustic wooden furniture, while 2-storey cottages have a more solid feel but lack the view. Nothing special but well located, comfortable & good value. **$$$$$**

✷ **Manyara's Secret** ⊕ -3.413772, 35.889294; m +255 710 730257; w manyarassecret.com. Opened in 2021, this stunning boutique lodge stands on the western shore of Lake Manyara, about 15mins' drive from the main entrance gate. Accommodation is in 4 stylish & spacious thatched solar-powered villas, each with between 1 & 4 bedrooms, a private infinity pool & a terrace with a wonderful view across the lake towards the escarpment. Service & food are of the highest quality too. **$$$$$**

Moderate

Migunga Forest Camp ⊕ -3.386607, 35.873271; m +255 754 324193; w moivaro.com. Set in an atmospheric fever-tree forest 2km from Mto wa Mbu, the 21 comfortable standing tents at this underrated camp are an excellent compromise between price & comfort, with the added bonus that reedbuck, bushbuck & buffalo sometimes pass through, vervet monkey & banded mongoose are resident, bushbabies are often heard at night, & 70-odd acacia-associated bird species have been recorded. **$$$$**

Budget & camping

Migunga Campsite m +255 754 324193; w moivaro.com. Situated alongside the eponymous tented camp & under the same management (see above), this campsite boasts a stunning setting amid the yellow-fever trees, & facilities include hot showers. Highly recommended. *US$8pp.* **$**

Twiga Lodge & Campsite ⊕ -3.374322, 35.865160; m +255 784 901497; e twigalodgecampsite@gmail.com. This long-serving & ever-reliable lodge in the heart of Mto wa Mbu has neatly cropped gardens, a good restaurant serving lunch & dinner for US$10pp each, a large clean swimming pool, a spacious campsite & serviceable rooms with hot water & net. *US$60 dbl B&B; camping US$10pp.* **$$**

Escarpment lodges The lodges below all stand on the cultivated escarpment overlooking Lake Manyara and most offer fabulous views over the national park or its surrounds.

Exclusive

✷ **Escarpment Luxury Lodge** ⊕ -3.40128, 35.80482; m +255 767 804856; w escarpmentluxurylodge.co.tz. The escarpment's most stylish & exclusive lodge has funky but organic interiors with a contemporary African feel & a swimming pool with a luxuriant setting & stunning views over the national park. The 16 state-of-the-art suites are super-spacious & come with wooden floor, fan, AC, internet access, king-size bed with walk-in netting, large bathroom with indoor tub & outdoor shower, & private deck with a view. In addition to game drives, activities include cycling, bird walks & village visits. **$$$$$$**

Lake Manyara Kilimamoja Lodge ⊕ -3.34574, 35.83440; m +255 688 058365; w wellworthcollection.co.tz. This swanky escarpment lodge boasts massive gardens (guests are transported around in a golf cart) & an impressive array of facilities including a spa, gym, cinema & large swimming pool. The 49 thatched chalets are also very impressive, coming as they do with king-size bed, walk-in net, stone fireplace, old-style bathtub, outdoor & indoor shower & much else besides. The ostentatious décor aims for an Edwardian safari look – plenty of mock zebra-stripe & leopard-spot fabrics – but arguably overshoots the mark. Still, if you're after unabashed luxury, this place has it in spades, at relatively realistic rates. **$$$$$$**

Upmarket

Kirurumu Manyara Lodge ⊕ -3.36037, 35.83315; m +255 774 533198; w kirurumu.net. Rustic & unpretentious, this long-serving tented lodge has far more of a bush feel than other more built-up lodges on the Rift Escarpment, complemented by a grand view across the Rift Valley plains north of Lake Manyara. There's plenty of small wildlife around: bush squirrels, foot-long yellow-speckled plated lizards & abundant birds by day, while hedgehogs & bushbabies come past by night. The secluded & comfortable standing tents all have hot showers & a private veranda – higher numbered rooms generally have the best views! **$$$$**

✷ **Lake Manyara Serena Safari Lodge** ⊕ -3.37215, 35.82731; w serenahotels.com. You can't go wrong with this smart & perennially popular lodge, which stands in large escarpment grounds overlooking the lake & run through by a small wooded stream that attracts a wide range of birds including chattering flocks of breeding weavers. Like other Serena lodges, it is very appealing & well set-up, offering accommodation in 67 attractively furnished ethnic-looking *rondawels* (round African-style huts) with private balconies. There's a large swimming pool & the food – buffets when it's busy, à la carte when quiet – is very good. **$$$$$**

Lake Manyara Wildlife Lodge ⊕ -3.38905, 35.81772; ☎ 027 254 4595; w hotelsandlodges-tanzania.com. The oldest & most spectacularly located property on the escarpment, this former government lodge feels a bit old-fashioned & the 100 rooms are on the small side, but all come with tub/shower, private balcony, safe & tea-/coffee-making facilities. The attractively wooded grounds are centred on a large swimming pool with peerless view over Manyara's groundwater forest & lake. With binoculars, you should be able to pick out elephant, giraffe & buffalo on the Rift Valley floor; closer to home, there is good birding within the lodge grounds. Food is variable. **$$$$$**

Budget & camping

✷ **Kizumba Campsite** ⊕ -3.38219, 35.82008; m +255 767 264373. This friendly & well-organised new campsite stands in green grounds alongside the main surfaced road towards Karatu just above the escarpment. Small standing tents include simple bedding & have a light inside & there are clean ablution blocks. A restaurant/bar serves chilled drinks & inexpensive meals, there's Tanzanian music & dancing after dinner most nights & even Wi-Fi (which you might not expect at a place this simple). *US$15pp (significantly cheaper if you pay in Tsh)*. **$**

WHERE TO EAT AND DRINK *Map, page 228*

Most people will eat at their lodge, since full-board packages are the norm, but there are a few decent standalone restaurants in and around Mto wa Mbu.

Cafe Kabisa m +255 759 171132; w cafekabisa.com; ⌚ 06.00–18.00 daily. Also situated close to Twiga Lodge, this café serves the best coffee in Mto wa Mbu, blended from Arabica beans grown on the slopes of Kilimanjaro. The fresh muffins are great too. $

Ol Mesera Restaurant m +255 717 10737; w olmesera.co.tz; ⌚ 07.30–17.30 daily. Situated in the African Galleria complex on Karatu Rd about 2km past the top of the escarpment, this stylish modern restaurant specialises in Swahili & other Tanzanian dishes with a modern/fusion twist. $$

Taste Poa Café m +255 752 261683; f taste-poa-café; ⌚ 06.00–23.00 daily. Despite its inauspicious setting alongside Sango filling station, this open-sided restaurant, almost opposite Twiga Lodge, has garden seating, a pleasant ambience, a well-stocked bar, a proper coffee machine & a varied menu of pizzas, burgers, grills & Swahili dishes in the US$4–6 range. $

OTHER PRACTICALITIES Mto wa Mbu, less than 1km from the main park entrance, is a well-equipped town with a busy craft and fresh produce market and several

THE TREE-CLIMBING LIONS OF MANYARA

Lake Manyara National Park is famous for its tree-climbing lions, which habitually rest up in the branches for most of the day, to the excitement of those lucky tourists who chance upon them. But while the tree-climbing phenomenon is well documented, the explanation behind it remains largely a matter of conjecture.

In the 1960s, Stephen Makacha undertook research into lion behaviour at Manyara to compare with similar studies being conducted by George Schaller in the Serengeti. In Schaller's book, *The Serengeti Lion: A Study of Predator–Prey Relations*, he noted that:

> The lions in the Lake Manyara National Park climbed trees far more often than those in the Serengeti. They were resting in trees on two-thirds of the occasions on which we encountered them during the day. The reason why Manyara lions rest in trees so often is unknown. Fosbrooke noted that lions in the Ngorongoro Crater ascended trees during an epidemic of biting flies, but this is an unusual situation…and the vegetation in the various parks is in many respects so similar that no correlation between it and tree climbing is evident. The Manyara lions sometimes escaped from buffalo and elephant by climbing trees, but there would seem to be no reason for lions to remain in them all day because of the remote chance that they might have to climb one. I think that the behaviour represents a habit, one that may have been initiated by for example, a prolonged fly epidemic, and has since been transmitted culturally.

Schaller's suggestion that the lions were climbing trees to avoid flies made the most sense to me, but I had also heard that the lions climbed to enjoy the cool breezes that came off the lake, and to keep a lookout for prey and threats. So I decided to make notes whenever I saw the lions in order to explore these theories. For every sighting, I noted whether flies were present on the ground or in the trees; the temperature and breeze conditions; whether buffalo or elephant were in the vicinity; how high up the tree the lions were and the view it afforded; and the species of tree.

In the 1960s, Iain Douglas-Hamilton noted that on 80% of the occasions when tree-climbing lions were observed, they were in one of just 17 individual trees. These favoured trees were so well known to park guides at the time that they were given particular names and – to protect them from debarking and destruction by elephants – wrapped in coils of wire mesh. My observations indicated a similar pattern. Lions were found to be resting in trees on about half of the times they supermarkets. For a pre-safari stock-up, try the Sango Supermarket, next to the eponymous filling station, which sells a good range of imported goods, as well as wine & beer. For quality local handicrafts and art, a highly recommended stop, signposted on the right side on the Karatu Road some 2km after it climbs the escarpment, is African Galleria (**m** +255 786 026461; **w** africangalleriatz.com), which stocks a superb range of individually crafted items and also offers tanzanite and woodcarving tours. Banks include branches of the NMB and CRDB, both with an ATM outside.

EXPLORING LAKE MANYARA

Game drives For logistical reasons, most safari operators visit the national park in the afternoon, but there's much to be said for doing a morning game drive instead (or in addition), starting as soon as possible after the entrance gate opens at 06.30. Manyara is wonderfully and unexpectedly peaceful at this time, and you'll

were sighted, and although six different tree species were used, three – *Acacia tortilis*, *Kigelia africana* and *Balanites aegyptiaca* – accounted for 90% of sightings. Specific trees were usually favoured, and the lions often moved a considerable distance to reach them.

In most cases the lions were seen to be resting during the heat of the day, and they would usually come down at dusk. Only 5% of sightings coincided with hot weather and breezy conditions, and at most sightings there was no significant breeze, so it seems unlikely that the lions climb to escape the heat. Although buffalo have been documented killing lions at Manyara, there was never any sign of the lions taking to trees to avoid harassment. Most of the time the lions were found to be resting approximately 5–6m above the ground, which afforded them a better view of their surroundings, but since the trees were normally in densely vegetated areas, it would have been difficult for them to observe any potential prey or threat.

My conclusions were similar to those of Makacha and Schaller. Although lions that I found resting on the ground were apparently not greatly concerned by biting flies, lions observed in trees were surrounded by flies in only 10% of cases, when flies were present on the ground below them about 60% of the time. Because the lions generally rested above 5m and flies were seldom encountered at this height, it seems likely that the behaviour was originally initiated during a fly epidemic, and it has since been passed on culturally. I observed the cubs of the Maji pride begin their attempts to climb up to the adults when they were about seven or eight months old. It seemed definitely to be a case of 'lion see, lion do', as there was no apparent reason as to why they should have climbed. Once they had mastered climbing, they too spent a lot of time playing and climbing up and down the trees. More thorough research would be required to fully understand the reasons for this unusual and fascinating behaviour.

Edited from Notes on Tree-climbing Lions of Manyara *by Kevin Pretorius, a former manager of Lake Manyara Tree Lodge, as originally published in the* &Beyond Ecological Journal, *volume 2:79–81 (2000). Interestingly, since it was written, tree climbing has become less frequent among the lions of Manyara, and more frequent in the Serengeti, particularly during the rains, evidently confirming the behaviour is essentially cultural and habitual.*

probably see fewer other vehicles over 2 or 3 hours than you would in 5 minutes in the late afternoon. By being the first car through the gate, you also stand a chance of disturbing one of the park's plentiful but skittish leopards before it vanishes into the thickets for the day.

Unless you are staying overnight in the park, all game drives start at the entrance gate, which lies on the northern boundary near Mto wa Mbu. From here, the main road winds for several kilometres through a cool, lush, mature groundwater forest dominated by large Ficus trees and a tangle of green epiphytes. With appropriate jungle noises supplied by outsized silvery-cheeked hornbills, this is one part of the northern safari circuit that might conjure up images of Tarzan swinging into view. It's a good place to see olive baboons (Manyara supports a density of 2,500 baboons in $100km^2$), which plonk themselves down alongside the road, often in the company of the smaller and more beautiful blue monkey, which is also common in the forest. The shy bushbuck might also be encountered here, but otherwise the main point of faunal interest is the diversity of birds and butterflies.

The road emerges from the forest on to the northern floodplain, where a series of small pools on the Mto wa Mbu River supports a wide variety of birds, notably giant kingfisher and African and painted snipe. This is a lovely spot, too, with the Rift Valley Escarpment rising to the west, and the sparsely vegetated floodplain of Lake Manyara stretching to the south. Giraffes are common in this area, many of them so dark in colour that they appear to be almost melanistic. This is also where you'll (hopefully) find the hippo pool referred to on page 229.

For large mammals, the best road runs inland of the lake to the Maji Moto (literally 'Hot Water') springs in the south. The tangled acacia woodland here – quite dry for most of the year, but spectacularly lush after the rains – offers views across the floodplain, where you should see large herds of zebra and wildebeest, and the occasional warthog, impala, Kirk's dik-dik and giraffe. The acacia woodland is the place to look out for the famous tree-climbing lions of Manyara (page 234), although on an afternoon game drive the safari driver grapevine is bound to ensure that you know about any arboreal lions long before you encounter them. As you head further south, several large seasonal waterfalls tumble over the escarpment, most visibly during the rainy season. The marshy area around the hot springs

MANYARA'S HIPPO POOL

The Mto wa Mbu river as it runs through northern Manyara hosts a famous hippo pool that has been an erratic presence in recent years. It was submerged by the main lake for several years in the late 1990s and early 2000s as a result of flooding, then again by rising lake waters following the heavy rains of 2019, and it had yet to re-emerge when this edition was researched in 2022. Assuming the lake has receded sufficiently by the time you visit, the pool will still hopefully be overlooked by a stilted viewing platform from where you might see around a dozen soaking, yawning hippos. For birders, the final stretch of road to the pool used to be flanked by a marshy area that offered good photography opportunities for aquatic species. In addition to larger birds such as yellow-billed stork and pink-backed pelican, the reed beds formed a nesting site for a variety of passerines (including yellow bishop, thick-billed weaver and Jackson's golden-backed weaver), while the shallows supported waders such as glossy ibis, common snipe, black crake, collared pratincole and various lapwings and sandpipers.

reliably harbours waterbuck and plenty of buffalo, while several pairs of klipspringer are resident on the rocky escarpment base towards the southern end of the park.

If you arrive in Mto wa Mbu without a vehicle, Wayo Africa (w wayoafrica.com) charges from US$150 per person for a full-day game drive, inclusive of vehicle, driver-guide, fuel and the driver and vehicle entrance fee, but exclusive of personal park entrance fees.

Cultural tours Mto wa Mbu, said locally to be the only place where representatives of all Tanzania's 120-odd tribes are resident, is the starting point for a clutch of walking and cycling tours (w tanzaniaculturaltourism.com) that run out of the Red Banana Café on the main road through town. One of the most interesting of these walks is the papyrus lake tour, which takes you to the Miwaleni Waterfall, as well as to a papyrus lake where Rangi people collect basket- and mat-weaving material, and to the homesteads of Sandawe hunter-gatherers. Other tours take you to Balaa Hill, which boasts excellent views over the village and lake, and to Chagga farms and Maasai bomas.

Less formally, at least half-a-dozen Maasai *manyattas* (settlements) signposted along the road between Makuyuni and Mto wa Mbu welcome tourist visits. The going rate is US$20–30 per vehicle irrespective of the group size.

Other activities Mto wa Mbu is the focal point of a range of adventure activities run exclusively by Wayo Africa (w wayoafrica.com). These include **mountain biking** down the Rift escarpment, an **afternoon walk** through groundwater forest in the Kirurumu Gorge, and a **village walk** with a local guide through surrounding agricultural areas. Most of these activities cost US$35–40 per person including equipment.

Unique to Wayo Africa, **night drives** within Lake Manyara cost from US$55 per person, depending on group size, excluding the park entrance fee and the night drive fee (an additional US$100pp plus 18% VAT).

Wayo Africa operates Tanzania's first **treetop walkway** just inside the main gate. This 370m canopy walkway crosses a series of nine suspended bridges to reach an 18m-high viewing deck offering a monkey's-eye view into the canopy. The walk takes about an hour and costs US$30 per person, though an additional fee of US$15 plus 18% VAT is levied by Tanapa.

LAKE EYASI AND THE YAEDA VALLEY

Situated below a magnificent 800m-high stretch of the Rift escarpment, Eyasi is a shallow alkaline lake that can extend for 80km from north to south in years of plentiful rain, but also sometimes dries out completely to form a forbidding expanse of caked soda. Most of the time, the lake falls somewhere between the two extremes: an eerily bleak and windswept body of water surrounded by a muddy white soda crust and tangled dry acacia scrub. In the middle of the day, it can have a rather desolate appearance, but it is very beautiful in the softer light of early morning and late afternoon, especially when the sun sets dramatically behind the escarpment that hems it in.

Verging the southern border of the Ngorongoro Conservation Area, the remote Eyasi hinterland – also known as Yaeda Valley, after the eponymous river – was sparsely populated in prehistoric times, since it was unsuited to cultivation, and tsetse flies made it unattractive to livestock farmers. Back then, the only semi-permanent inhabitants were the Hadza, hunter-gatherers who still live in the area today, and practise a largely traditional lifestyle (page 238), despite several more recent human influxes, most significantly the Datoga, a pastoralist people with

THE LAST HUNTER-GATHERERS

The Hadza (or Hadzabe) of the Lake Eyasi hinterland, which lies to the east of Karatu, represent a unique – and increasingly fragile – link between modern East Africa and the most ancient of the region's human lifestyles and languages. Numbering at most 1,200 individuals, the Hadza are Tanzania's only remaining hunter-gatherers, and their unique language isn't closely related to any other extant African tongue.

The Hadza live in nomadic family bands, typically numbering about 20 adults and a coterie of children. Their rudimentary encampments of light grass shelters are erected in the space of a couple of hours, and might be used as a base for anything from ten days to one month before the inhabitants move on. These movements, though often rather whimsical, might be influenced by changes in the weather or local game distribution, and a band will also often relocate close to a fresh kill that is sufficiently large to sustain them for several days. The Hadza are fairly indiscriminate about what meat they eat – anything from mice to giraffe are fair game, and we once saw a family roasting a feral cat, fur and all, on their campfire – but baboons are regarded to be the ultimate delicacy and reptiles are generally avoided. Hunting with poisoned arrows and honey gathering are generally male activities, while women and children collect roots, seeds, tubers, fruit and other vegetarian fodder, which actually accounts for about 80% of the food intake.

The Hadza have a reputation for living for the present and they care little for conserving food resources, probably because their lifestyle inherently places very little stress on the environment. This philosophy is epitomised in a popular game of chance, which Hadza men will often play – and gamble valuable possessions on – to while away a quiet afternoon. A large master disc is made from baobab bark, and each participant makes a smaller personal disc, with all discs possessing distinct rough and smooth faces. The discs are stacked and thrown in the air, an action that is repeated until only one of the small discs lands with the same face up as the large disc, deciding the winner.

Many Hadza people still dress in the traditional attire of animal skins – women favour impala hide, men the furry coat of a small predator or baboon – which are often decorated with shells and beads. Hadza social groupings are neither permanent nor strongly hierarchical: individuals and couples are free to move between bands, and there is no concept of territorial possession. In order to be eligible for marriage, a Hadza man must kill five baboons to prove his worth. Once married, a couple might stay together for several decades or a lifetime, but there is no taboo against separation and either partner can terminate the union at any time by physically abandoning the other partner.

The Hadza might reasonably be regarded as a sociological and anthropological equivalent of a living fossil, since they are one of the very few remaining adherents

many cultural affinities to the Maasai (page 254). In addition, the Yaeda Valley is now the most important onion-growing area in East Africa, thanks to a colonial era irrigation scheme, and the main supplier of this crop to both Nairobi and Arusha. Eyasi is also an important source of fish for Arusha, and when the water is high enough, it often hosts temporary fishing encampments populated by people from all over northern Tanzania.

Lake Eyasi supports large seasonal concentrations of water birds, including hundreds of thousands of flamingos at some times of year. Otherwise, little wildlife is resident, and most of what is around – lesser kudu, Kirk's dik-dik and to the hunter-gatherer lifestyle that sustained the entire human population of the planet for 98% of its history. In both the colonial and post-independence eras, the Hadza have resolutely refused to allow the government to coerce them into following a more settled agricultural or pastoral way of life. The last concerted attempt to modernise Hadza society took place in the 1960s, under the Nyerere government, when a settlement of brick houses with piped water, schools and a clinic was constructed for them alongside an agricultural scheme. Within ten years, the model settlement had been all but abandoned as the Hadza returned to their preferred lifestyle of hunting and gathering. The government, admirably, has since tacitly accepted the right of the Hadza to lead the life of their choice; a large tract of communal land fringing Lake Eyasi has been set aside for their use and they remain the only people in Tanzania automatically exempt from taxes!

The Hadza tongue, sometimes referred to as Hadzane, is thought to be an isolated relic of a click-based linguistic family that was widely spoken in eastern and southern Africa until perhaps 3,000 years ago. It is sometimes contentiously classified as part of the Khoisan family (a group of tongues associated with Southern Africa's San or Bushmen hunter-gatherers) on account of its similar use of click-based sounds. As Bantu-speaking agriculturists and pastoralists swept into the region from the northwest, however, most hunter-gatherer communities were assimilated into Bantu-speaking societies or forced to retreat into arid and montane territories ill-suited to herding and cultivation. This slow but steady process of marginalisation has continued into historical times: it has been estimated that of Africa's 100 documented Khoisan and other click-based languages, only 30 are still in use today, and that the total number of people speaking them is fewer than 200,000.

That most click-based languages, if not already extinct, are headed that way, takes on an added poignancy if, as a minority of linguists suggested throughout the 20th century, those clicks are a preserved element of the very earliest human language. In order to investigate this possibility, the anthropological geneticists Alec Knight and Joanna Mountain analysed the chromosome content of samples taken from the geographically diverse San and Hadza, and concluded that they 'are as genetically distant from one another as two populations could be'. Discounting the somewhat improbable scenario that the clicking noises of the Hadza and San languages arose independently, this wide genetic gulf would imply a very ancient common linguistic root indeed. Several linguists dispute Knight and Mountain's conclusion, but if it is correct, then Hadzane, along with Africa's dying Khoisan languages, might represent one last fading echo of the first human voices to have carried across the African savannah.

olive baboon – tends to be rather shy. Overall, Lake Eyasi is less of interest for its wildlife than the opportunities for cultural interaction. Guided visits to Datoga homesteads and Hadza encampments are easily arranged through the tourist office in Mang'ola (also known as Ghorofani), an overgrown village that qualifies as the most important settlement in the area, and it is also possible to go hunting with the Hadza or visit an onion farm.

GETTING THERE AND AWAY Mang'ola lies about 50km from Karatu (on the surfaced road connecting Lake Manyara National Park to the Ngorongoro Conservation

Area) along a fair dirt road that shouldn't take much longer than an hour to drive. Once at Mang'ola, it's easy enough to arrange a guided visit to a Hadza encampment. Most visitors stay in the area overnight, but it could be visited as a full- or half-day trip out of Karatu. The recent growth in the onion farming industry means that Mang'ola is now reasonably accessible by **public transport**: a few 4x4s run back and forth to Karatu daily (US$2.50; 1½hrs) and there are also two daily buses from Arusha (US$5; 5hrs), leaving at around 05.00.

WHERE TO STAY AND EAT

Kisima Ngeda Camp ⊕ -3.47447, 35.34930; m +255 764 558839; w entara.co.tz. This remote camp, comprising 8 tented chalets, has a scenic location in a palm-shaded grove near the east shore of Lake Eyasi & makes an excellent base for visiting a Hadza encampment. The structures around the en-suite tents are made entirely from organic local materials & the excellent food includes fresh lake tilapia. **$$$$$$**

Lake Eyasi Ng'ula Sunset Safari Camp ⊕ -3.50117, 35.39957; m +255 759 160232; w lakeeasysafaricamp.business.site. Opened in 2020, this well-wooded campsite stands in the village of Gorfan, 8km from Mang'ola on the road back towards Karatu. Facilities include a small ablution block with hot showers. *US$10pp*. **$**

Lake Eyasi Safari Lodge ⊕ -3.48752, 35.36109; m +255 758 563354; w lakeeyasi.com. Set on an acacia-studded slope offering a fabulous view over the lake, this place has the only swimming pool in the Eyasi area & offers accommodation in 16 solar-powered stone cottages with fitted nets, private balcony & hot shower. **$$$$$**

TOURIST INFORMATION The **Lake Eyasi Cultural Tourism Programme** (LECTP; w tanzaniaculturaltourism.com) operates a tourist office at the road barrier where you enter Mang'ola coming from Karatu. You need to stop here to pay the mandatory entrance fee of US$20 per vehicle, and it is also where all activities and guides must be arranged.

WHAT TO SEE AND DO All cultural activities in the area must be arranged through the tourist office operated by the Lake Eyasi Cultural Tourism Programme. This offers a number of guided activities, including Hadza hunts and visits, Datoga village excursions, and visits to a Datoga blacksmith (who makes copper and tin jewellery from recycled car parts, broken padlocks and other junk). All activities cost US$20 for a party of up to ten, plus a guide fee of US$30 per party covering all activities undertaken.

The definite must-do here is a visit to a Hadza encampment. The people struck us as being very warm and unaffected, and going on an actual hunt is a primal and exciting experience – though do be warned that a temporary conversion to vegetarianism might be in order should you come back with a baboon or another large mammal and be offered the greatest delicacy, which is the raw liver. It might be expected that regular exposure to tourists could erode the traditional lifestyle of certain Hadza bands, but we have seen no sign of this over repeated visits, perhaps because the Hadza have chosen their nomadic lifestyle despite the attempts by successive governments to settle them.

NORTH OF MANYARA

The vast majority of Serengeti safaris head directly west from Manyara along the asphalt road that climbs the Rift Valley Escarpment into the Ngorongoro Highlands, and then return to Arusha exactly the same way. An offbeat alternative to this well-trodden route, one that will transform your safari itinerary into a genuine loop, is the spine-jarring 250km road that connects Mto wa Mbu to the northern Serengeti via the parched stretch of the Rift Valley abutting the border with Kenya. This is not, it should be stressed, a route that should instil any great enthusiasm in anybody who nurses a dodgy back or chronic agoraphobia, or who has limited tolerance for simple travel conditions. But equally this half-forgotten corner of northern Tanzania also possesses some genuinely alluring off-the-beaten-track landmarks in the form of the ruined city of Engaruka, the brooding Lake Natron, and above all perhaps the fiery volcanic majesty of Ol Doinyo Lengai.

Technically, it is possible to travel between Mto wa Mbu and the northern Serengeti via Natron in one (very long) day, but this would rather defeat the point of the exercise. More realistic is to split the drive over two days, stopping for a night at the lakeshore village of Engaresero, or two nights if you intend to climb Ol Doinyo Lengai or undertake any other exploration of the region. It is common practice to tag this area on to the end of a safari, but there is a strong case for slotting it in between the Tarangire/Manyara and Ngorongoro/Serengeti legs of your itinerary, if for no other reason than it will break up the vehicle-bound regime of game drives with a decent leg-stretch – whether you opt for a gentle stroll around the Engaruka ruins or the southern shore of Natron, the slightly more demanding hike to the Engaresero Waterfall in the escarpment west of Natron, or the decidedly challenging nocturnal ascent of Ol Doinyo Lengai.

ENGARUKA RUINS (Entrance US$5.50pp inc guide fee) Situated below the Rift Valley Escarpment 65km north of Manyara, Engaruka is the Maasai name for the extensive ruins of a mysterious terraced city and irrigation system constructed at least 500 years ago by a late Iron Age culture in the eastern foothills of Mount Empakaai. Nobody knows for sure who built the city: some say it was the Mbulu, who inhabited the area immediately before the Maasai arrived there; others that it was built by Datoga settlers from the north. Locally, the city is said to have been home to forebears of the Sukuma, whose greeting 'Mwanga lukwa' was later bastardised to Engaruka by the Maasai – more likely, however, is that the name of this well-watered spot has roots in the Maasai word 'ngare' (water).

The discovery of the ruins by outsiders is generally credited to Dr Fischer, who followed the base of the Rift Valley through Maasailand in 1883, and wrote how: 'peculiar masses of stone became suddenly apparent, rising from the plain to heights up to ten feet. Partly they looked like mouldering tree trunks, partly like the tumbled down walls of ancient castles.' An older reference to Engaruka can be found on the so-called Slug Map drawn up by the missionaries Krapf and Erhardt in 1855. The first person to excavate the site was Hans Reck in the early 20th century, followed by the legendary Louis Leakey, who reckoned it consisted of seven large villages containing roughly 1,000 homes apiece and thought the total population must have exceeded 30,000.

The ruined villages overlook a complex stone-block irrigation system that extends over some 25km² and is fed by the perennial Engaruka River. This highly specialised and integrated agricultural community was abandoned in the 18th century, probably due to a combination of changes in the local hydrology and the immigration of more militaristic pastoralist tribes from the north. Yet Engaruka is unique only in scale, since a number of smaller deserted sites in the vicinity form part of the same cultural and agricultural complex, and radiocarbon dating suggests it might be older than has been assumed in the past – possibly as old as the 4th century AD, which would make it a likely precursor to the great centralised empires that thrived in pre-colonial Uganda and Rwanda.

The floor plan of the main village is still quite clear, and a few of the circular stone houses remain more or less intact to around waist level, their floors strewn with shards of broken earthenware. Substantial sections of the irrigation canal are still in place, as are some old burial mounds that might or might not be related to the war with the Maasai that caused the village to be abandoned.

Getting there and away The ruins lie about 5km west of the village of Engaruka Chini, which lies 50km (about 1hr's drive) north of Mto wa Mbu on the dirt road towards Engaresero. Turn left at Engaruka Chini and continue through a semi-urban sprawl to Engaruka Juu, from where it's a 10-minute walk to the nearest ruin. At least one bus connects Arusha to Engaruka via Mto wa Mbu daily, but it is very slow and crowded, so better to bus to Mto wa Mbu and then pick up local transport to Engaruka. This is most prolific on Monday and Wednesday, respectively the main market days in Engaruka Juu and Engaruka Chini.

Where to stay and eat

Magofu Hill Campsite ⊕ -3.00106, 35.96559; f magofutrails; m +255 752 036059. Under construction at the time of writing, this rustic new campsite should be fully operational by the time you read this. Run by the family of the main guide at Engaruka Ruins, it stands on a hillside outside Engaruka Juu & facilities will include an ablution block & a bar/restaurant. *US$10pp*. **$**

LAKE NATRON There are but a handful of places where the Rift Valley evokes its geologically violent origins with graphic immediacy. Ethiopia's Danakil Desert is one such spot; the volcanic Virunga Range in the Albertine Rift is another. And so, too, is the most northerly landmark in the Tanzanian Rift Valley, the low-lying Lake Natron, a shallow sliver of exceptionally alkaline water that extends southward from the Kenyan border near Mount Shompole for 58km. The Natron skyline is dominated by the textbook volcanic silhouette of Ol Doinyo Lengai, which rises more than 2km above the surrounding Rift Valley floor to an altitude of 2,962m, its harsh black contours softened by an icing of white ash that glistens brightly below the sun, as if in parody of Kilimanjaro's snows. Then there is the lake itself, a thrillingly primordial phenomenon whose caustic waters are enclosed by a crust of sodden grey volcanic ash and desiccated salt, punctuated by isolated patches of steamy, reed-lined swamp where the hot springs that sustain the lake bubble to the surface.

Thought to be about 1.5 million years old, Natron is a product of the same tectonic activity that formed the Ngorongoro Highlands and Mount Gelai, the latter being a 2,941m-high extinct volcano that rises from the eastern lakeshore. Nowhere more than 50cm deep, it has changed shape significantly since that time, largely as a result of volcanic activity associated with the creation of Ol Doinyo Lengai to its immediate south. It lies at an altitude of 610m in an unusually arid stretch of the rift floor, receiving an average of 400mm of rainfall annually, and it would have probably dried out centuries ago were it not also fed by the freshwater Ewaso Ngiro River, which has its catchment in the central Kenyan Highlands, and the hot springs that rise below its floor. The alkaline level has also increased drastically over the millennia, partially because of the high salinity of ash and lava deposits from Lengai, partially because the lake's only known outlet is evaporation. Today, depending on recent rainfall, the viscous water has an average pH of 9–11, making it almost as caustic as ammonia when the level is very low, and it can reach a temperature of up to 60°C in extreme circumstances.

Fauna The area around Lake Natron supports a thin population of large mammals typical of the Rift Valley. Zebra and giraffe are quite common in the vicinity of Engaresero, and other wildlife includes wildebeest, zebra, fringe-eared oryx, Grant's and Thomson's gazelle, and even the odd lion and cheetah. Natron's hyper-salinity makes it incapable of sustaining any but the most specialised life forms. The only resident vertebrates are a few species of small fish, notably the endemic white-lipped tilapia (*Oreochromis alcalica*) that congregate near hot-spring inlets where the water temperature is around 36–40°C. The microbiology of the lake is dominated by halophytic (salt-loving) organisms such as spirulina, a form of blue-green algae whose red pigments make the salt-encrusted flats in the centre of the lake look bright red when seen from the air. Natron is also the only known breeding ground for East Africa's 2.5 million lesser flamingos, which usually congregate there between August and October, feeding on the abundant algae (whose pigments are responsible for the birds' trademark pink hue). The breeding ground's inhospitality to potential predators makes it an ideal flamingo nursery, but it also makes it difficult for human visitors to access – situated in the centre of the lake, it was discovered as recently as the 1950s and it can only be seen from the air today. In addition to the flamingos, Natron attracts up to 100,000 migrant water birds during the European winter.

Getting there and away The centre of tourist activity on Natron is the small lakeshore village of Engaresero (also spelled Ngare Sero), bisected by the wooded Mikuyu River from whence derives its Maasai name ('black water', 'clear water', 'dappled water' or 'forest of water', depending on who does the translating). Engaresero lies about 90km (3hrs) north of Mto wa Mbu along an unsurfaced road through Engaruka Chini. Coming to/from the northern Serengeti, Engaresero is about 160km from Klein's Gate, a drive that takes 5–6 hours without stops, and involves a spectacular ascent/descent of the Rift Escarpment to the west of the lake.

The only **public transport** to Engaresero are the Coastline and Loliondo buses that run daily between Arusha and Loliondo town. These leave Arusha from opposite the Namanga bus station at 06.00 daily, and take around 4–5 hours to get to Engaresero. In the opposite direction you'll need to get your lodge or camp to reserve you a seat from Loliondo.

A trio of council roadblocks on the road between Engaruka and Natron each levies a toll fee of US$10–15 per person to non-Tanzanian passengers, whether they travel by bus or on a private vehicle. As you enter Natron, you will also need to pay the Wildlife Management Area entrance fee of US$25 plus 18% VAT per person per night.

A more ambitious approach to Lake Natron would be **on foot**, via one of several overnight trekking routes that lead there from Empakaai Crater and elsewhere in the Ngorongoro Conservation Area. For more details, see page 267, or contact Lake Natron Camp (see below), which specialises in setting up this kind of trip.

Where to stay

Upmarket

✱ Lake Natron Camp ⊕ -2.55507, 35.92189; **m** +255 787 850000; **w** lake-natron-camp.com. Set around a spring-fed oasis in a 315ha Maasai concession on the soda flats that hem in the southern lakeshore, this old-style eco-friendly bush camp doesn't offer the sort of under-canvas luxury you associate with Tanzania's top tented camps, but it will appeal greatly to those seeking an isolated wilderness experience in arguably the most spectacular stretch of the Tanzanian Rift Valley. The 11 net-shaded safari tents contain an outdoor sitting area, queen-size beds (with walk-in nets), compost toilets & hot showers. There is no swimming pool, but it is great fun to swim in the clear & rather soapy spring-fed stream that runs in front of the sleeping tents, though be warned that the white-lipped tilapia here enjoy nibbling gently on dead skin, a sensation that can be disconcerting at first, but rather addictive, like a natural pedicure, once you get used to it. The camp offers superb views of Mounts Lengai & Gelai, wonderful star-studded night skies, a good chance of sighting zebras & other ungulates, & access to some of the oldest hominid footprints yet discovered (see below), as well as to a section of the lakeshore rich in flamingos & other birds. It also arranges a range of activities further afield, including Natron climbs. **$$$$$$**

Moderate

Lake Natron Tented Camp ⊕ -2.59624, 35.91806; **m** +255 754 324193; **w** moivaro.com. Established in 1989, this low-key camp, set in wooded grounds on the outskirts of Engaresero, has a spectacular position 4km from the southern lakeshore & offers great views across the floodplain to Mount Gelai. Though somewhat no-frills compared with most tented camps & lodges in Tanzania, it has a welcoming swimming pool & pleasant restaurant & bar area. It can arrange inexpensive guided climbs of Ol Doinyo Lengai. **$$$$$**

Lengai Safari Lodge ⊕ -2.63607, 35.87613; **m** +255 758 314396; **w** lengaisafarilodge.com. Perched on a slope near the start of the waterfall trail, this out-of-town lodge offers great views towards Lengai, a swimming pool & a 2-storey restaurant decorated with Tingatinga-style paintings. **$$$$**

Budget & camping

✷ **Maasai Giraffe Eco-Lodge** ⊕ -2.62312, 35.89149; **m** +255 785 227010; **w** maasaigiraffe.com. This friendly budget lodge stands in large wooded grounds near the junction of the main road from Mto wa Mbu & feeder road to Lake Natron Camp. Simple but comfortable thatched cottages have nets, en-suite shower & private balcony. A range of guided activities is offered & it's only 45mins on foot to the southern lakeshore & hominid footprints. *US$150 dbl FB; camping US$10pp in your own tent or US$20pp in theirs.* **$$$**

Where to eat and drink If you are not eating at your camp, a few simple bars and restaurants serving local staples, along with nyama choma and chips, line the short main road through Engaresero. Cold beers and other bottled drinks are served at several places; rather unexpectedly, a few shops even stock imported wine.

What to see and do The activities described below can be arranged through the various camps and campsites in the area, or directly through the **Engaresero Cultural Tourism Program** (ECTP; f engareserotourism; **m** +255 688 568245). A community fee of US$20 per person is charged to visit each of the sites except Ol Doinyo Lengai, where the climbing fee is US$100 per person for one or two people or US$70 per person for larger parties (see opposite).

Southern lakeshore To reach the southern lakeshore from Engaresero, you need to drive for around 5km to an unofficial parking spot about 1km from the water's edge, then walk for about 10 minutes across salt-encrusted flats to a series of pockmarked black volcanic protrusions that serve as vantage points over the water. It's a lovely spot with Lengai looming in the background, and it hosts a profusion of water birds, most visibly large flocks of the pink-tinged lesser flamingo but also various pelicans, egrets, herons and waders. Wildebeest and zebra are also often seen in the area. If your driver doesn't know the way to the lakeshore – it's a rather obscure track – then ask for a local guide at one of the campsites. Whatever else you do, don't let the driver take the vehicle beyond the tracks left behind by his predecessors, or you run a serious risk of getting stuck in the treacherously narrow saline crust that surrounds the lake.

Engaresero human footprints One of the most important sites of its type in the world, this set of 58 human footprints is embedded in a layer of tuff-like compressed ash close to the southern shore of Natron. Although much older hominid fossil footprints have been discovered elsewhere in East Africa, these might well be the earliest-known ones associated with *Homo sapiens*. The prints were discovered by a Maasai herder in 1998 but only investigated properly by scientists about ten years later. It is thought that they were made by a party of 18 adults and children as they traipsed through a field of muddy ash when Lengai erupted around 120,000 years ago. The footprints are remarkably clear (although they can be obscured below a layer of fine dust) and their presence here only goes to underscore the prehistoric feel of this vast volcanic stretch of the Rift Valley. The site lies on the concession operated by Lake Natron Camp, about 10 minutes' walk from the camp itself, but is open to day visitors provided they are accompanied by a guide from the ECTP. Try to visit in the early morning or the very late afternoon, as shoes must be taken off before you enter the fenced-off site, and walking barefoot on the sun-baked black rocks is all but impossible during the heat of the day.

Engaresero Waterfall The Engaresero River forms a series of pretty waterfalls as it descends from the Nguruman Escarpment west of Lake Natron, a kilometre or two south of the village of Engaresero. The lowest two falls can be reached by driving out to Waterfall Campsite, then following the river upstream on foot for 45–60 minutes through the gorge it has carved into the escarpment wall. If you are not already sufficiently doused by the time you reach the second waterfall, there's a chilly natural swimming pool below it. There is no clear footpath through the gorge: you will need to wade across the river several times (potentially dangerous after heavy rain) and can also expect to do a fair bit of clambering along ledges and rocks. This walk can only be recommended to reasonably fit and agile travellers, and a guide is now mandatory.

Ol Doinyo Lengai Estimated to be around 350,000–400,000 years old, 2,962m-high Ol Doinyo Lengai – the Maasai 'Mountain of God' – is one of the youngest volcanoes in East Africa and possibly the most active. Its crater is known to have experienced almost continuous low-key activity since 1883, when Dr Fischer, the first European to pass through this part of Maasailand, observed smoke rising from the summit and was told secondhand that the mountain regularly emitted rumbling noises. At least a dozen minor or major eruptions have occurred since then. An interesting feature of Lengai is that it is the only active volcano known to emit carbonate lava, a form of molten rock that contains almost no silicon, is about 50% cooler than other forms of lava at around 500°C, and is also exceptionally fluid, with a viscosity comparable to water.

During an eruption in 2004, plumes in the crater could be seen from as far away as Engaresero and many local Maasai herdsmen moved their livestock out of the area. The mountain once again experienced a high level of volcanic activity between July 2007 and June 2008. On 18 July 2007, tremors emanating from the mountain measured 6.0 on the Richter scale and were felt as far away as Nairobi city. Ol Doinyo Lengai erupted spectacularly on 4 September 2007, emanating an ashen steamy plume almost 20km downwind and sending fresh lava flows along the north and west flanks. Activity continued intermittently into mid 2008, with further eruptions occurring in March, April and August. Lengai has been relatively quiet since then, but the crater formed by the 2007–08 eruptions is gradually filling with lava; it released several small flows over September 2018 to August 2019, and another eruption might occur at any time.

Climbing Ol Doinyo Lengai The ascent of Lengai is a popular hike with adventurous travellers, and it forms an excellent budget alternative to climbing Kilimanjaro, at least when the volcano is sufficiently placid. The ascent passes through some magnificently arid scenery and offers spectacular views back towards the Rift Valley,

THE 1966 ERUPTION

The most impressive eruption of Ol Doinyo Lengai in recorded history occurred in the latter part of 1966, when ash fall was reported as far away as Seronera, more than 100km to the west, as well as at Loliondo and Shombole, both some 70km further north. It is believed that the otherwise inexplicable death of large numbers of game around Empakaai Crater in that year was a result of an ash fall that coated the grass up to 2cm deep, though it is unclear whether the animals starved to death or they succumbed to a toxin within the ash. The effect on Maasai livestock was also devastating according to Tepilit Ole Saitoti, who recalled the incident as follows in his excellent book *The Worlds of a Maasai Warrior*:

> In the year 1966, God, who my people believe dwells in this holy mountain, unleashed Her fury unsparingly. The mountain thunder shook the earth, and the volcanic flame, which came from deep down in the earth's crust, was like a continuous flash of lightning. During days when the eruption was most powerful, clouds of smoke and steam appeared. Many cattle died and still more would die. Poisonous volcanic ash spewed all over the land as far as a hundred miles away, completely covering the pastures and the leaves of trees. Cattle swallowed ash each time they tried to graze and were weakened. They could not wake up without human assistance. We had to carry long wooden staffs to put under the fallen animals to lift them up. There must have been more than enough reason for God to have unleashed Her anger on us, and all we could do was pray for mercy. My pastoral people stubbornly braved the gusting warm winds as they approached the flaming mountain to pray. Women and men dressed in their best walked in stately lines towards God, singing. The mountain was unappeased and cattle died in the thousands. Just before the people started dying too, my father decided to move; as he put it: 'We must move while we still have children, or else we will all lose them'.

before leading to the bleakly visceral lunar landscape of the crater, studded with ash cones, lava pools, steam vents and other evidence of volcanic activity. Suitable only for reasonably fit and agile travellers, the normal northern ascent route to the top of Lengai is very steep, climbing in altitude from around 800m to around 2,900m, while the descent on loose scree can be very tough on knees and ankles. The climb normally takes 5–6 hours along slopes practically bereft of shade, for which reason many locals recommend leaving late at night (around 23.00–midnight) to avoid the intense heat and to reach the crater rim in time for sunrise. If you ascend by day a 05.00 start is advised, and precautions should be taken against dehydration and sunstroke. Either way, the descent takes about 2 hours.

Most adventure safari operators in Arusha offer guided Lengai climbs (page 245), but it is also possible to arrange a one-day climb locally, either at the ECTP or at one of the camps dotted around Engaresero village. The mountain lies outside any conservation area so no park fees are charged, but a fixed fee of US$100 per person for one or two people or US$70 per person for larger parties is levied by the ECTP. This includes the services of an experienced guide, who will need to be tipped.

All hikers should be aware that the cones on the crater floor can easily collapse under pressure and they often cover deadly lava lakes. Under no circumstances should you climb on a cone, or walk inside a partially collapsed cone. It is inadvisable (and may be forbidden) to climb the mountain during periods of high activity.

11

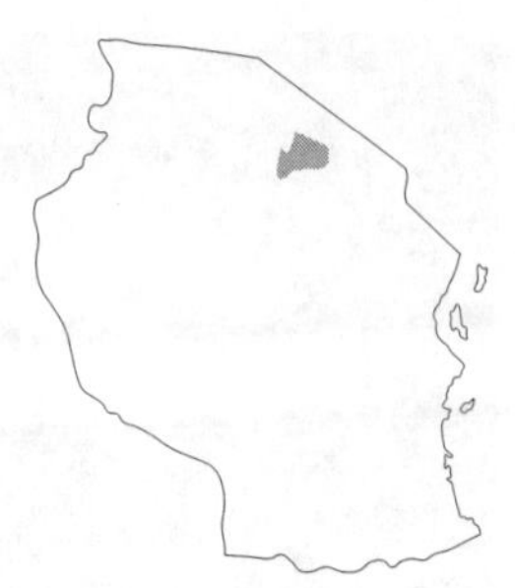

Ngorongoro and the Crater Highlands

Immediately west of Lake Manyara, the main road towards the Serengeti switchbacks up a spectacular stretch of the Rift Valley Escarpment to reach the fertile slopes of the volcanically formed Crater Highlands, which rise to a maximum altitude of 3,648m and are pockmarked with dormant and extinct calderas, most famously the wondrous Ngorongoro Crater. Much of the Crater Highlands is protected within the Ngorongoro Conservation Area (NCA), a vast biosphere reserve where Maasai cattle-herders still live alongside a bewildering diversity of wildlife, from the lions and elephants that strut fearlessly across the floor of Ngorongoro Crater to the secretive forest birds that flit through its jungle-swathed rim. Coming from Arusha or Lake Manyara, the urban gateway to the NCA, only 12km before Loduare Entrance Gate, is Karatu, a small but rapidly expanding agricultural town whose immediate environs support an ever-growing number of hotels, lodges and campsites designed to supplement the relatively limited options situated within the NCA itself.

KARATU AND SURROUNDS

Set at an altitude of 1,500m along the main road to Ngorongoro, Karatu outstrips Mto wa Mbu as the largest settlement between Arusha and the Serengeti, supporting a population estimated at around 20,000. This fast-growing town is the administrative capital of Karatu District, whose dominant ethnolinguistic group is the agriculturalist Iraqw, whose ancestors are credited with constructing the terraced Engaruka Ruins in the Rift Valley north of Lake Manyara (page 241).

OLOIBONI *Emma Thomson*

The *oloiboni* acts as a spiritual psychiatrist within Maasai communities, using stones to divine past, present and future events. Members of the homestead are able to consult him about family or mental and physical health problems, the answers to which come to the oloiboni in dreams. A reading involves the patient sitting cross-legged before him, spitting on the stones to infuse them with his/her spirit, and waiting for the results.

The skills are only passed on through the patrilineal line, and even then sons are not permitted to practise their powers of mediation until their twentieth birthday.

Intriguingly, two oloibonis are forbidden to meet each other, so if a neighbouring spiritual leader appears to be stealing business or enjoying good trade, villagers will claim that their oloiboni will send lions to attack the offending culprit.

MODERN-DAY MAASAI

Emma Thomson

The future of the Maasai seems an uncertain one. The Tanzanian government regards them as primitive and criticises them for 'holding the country back'. They are banned from wearing their distinctive *rubega/shuka* (robes) on public transport and in order to attend primary or secondary school the children are forced to remove their elaborate bead jewellery, and dress in Western-style clothes, while boys must shave off their long hair. All this follows a scheme launched by the government in the 1960s named the 'official national ideology of development', whose unspoken aims were to integrate the Maasai forcibly into mainstream society and settle them so the government could implement taxation.

Originally transhumant pastoralists, alternating the movement of their cattle between established wet- and dry-season pastures, the Maasai have now lost these latter areas to commercial farmers and wildlife conservation. Increasingly unpredictable rains leave grass and cattle dehydrated, and freak outbreaks of rinderpest and east coast fever (brought by explorers in the early 19th century) combine to often wipe out herds all together.

Squeezed into this bottleneck of depleted herds and land, the Maasai have had to overcome one of their greatest taboos – the ban on 'breaking the ground' and destroying grass, believed to have been sent by the Creator as sacred food for the cattle – in order to grow crops. Skills were acquired from nearby neighbours, the Chagga and Meru, and recent studies show that less than half of the Maasai in East Africa live purely on the traditional diet of milk, blood and meat, while the majority trade meat for beans and maize.

Unfortunately, when farming fails as a result of nutrient-poor soil, members of the family come back into the towns in search of paid work to supplement the unavoidable financial needs of providing for their families in the modern world. Men often find employment as nightwatchmen, while the women may have to resort to petty trading, beer brewing and, increasingly, prostitution.

However, the Maasai are both resourceful and resilient and the developing tourist industry brings new opportunities. Gemma EnoLengila, co-founder of the NGO Serian UK, stresses that 'the real challenge lies in creating sustainable projects that are developed in partnership with (traditional) communities, in a way that empowers rather than oppresses them'.

The Iraqw's ancestors probably migrated from southern Ethiopia to present-day Tanzania some 2,000 years ago and their Cushitic language, now something of an isolate, is more closely related to Oromo, Somali, Afar and other tongues from the Horn of Africa than to any other major Tanzanian or Kenyan language.

As Karatu's local nickname 'Safari Junction' suggests, the town is a minor route focus, situated close to the junction for Lake Eyasi (page 237) and another road leading via Mbulu to Mount Hanang (page 211). For most safari-goers, however, Karatu is of note mainly for providing the last straightforward opportunity to stock up on the likes of drinking water, snacks, local currency and fuel before heading into the wilds of Ngorongoro and the Serengeti. Fortunately, a fair selection of tourist facilities are dotted around town: there are several lodgings and restaurants, as well as a few filling stations, supermarkets, ATMs, and banks offering foreign exchange facilities (including a branch of the CRDB where those not carrying a Visa or Mastercard can pay entrance and other fees for the NCA; page 257).

MEANINGS OF THE MAASAI BEADS

Maasai jewellery beads are composed of nine main colours. It's a common misconception that the colours are blended to create complex messages. In fact, while the colours carry meaning, the combinations are randomly selected, mainly for beauty. It's often possible to tell the age of some necklaces according to the fashionable arrangement of colours that vary from year to year. Tendons extracted from the meat consumed originally served as string to hold these intricate designs together but these have now been replaced with shredded plastic bags.

The meanings for each colour vary from area to area but in general they mean the following:

black	God/rain	orange	rainbow
blue	water	red	warrior/blood/bravery
dark blue	God in the sky	white	milk/peace
gold	ground water	yellow	sun
green	life/spring		

The fertile slopes running from Karatu north and west towards the forested NCA border also host at least a dozen tourist lodges that are routinely used as bases for game drives into Ngorongoro Crater.

GETTING THERE AND AWAY Karatu lies about 30km from Mto wa Mbu along a good surfaced road that can be covered in 30 minutes. Coming directly from Arusha, the 140km drive takes 2½ hours. There is plenty of **public transport**: minibus-taxis depart from Arusha throughout the day and cost around US$3, while the best of several slightly cheaper bus services is probably Dar Express, which leaves Arusha from the new bus terminus a few hundred metres west of the central bus station.

If you arrive in Karatu without transport, Ngorongoro Camp & Lodge; (**w** ngorongorolodgetz.com; page 252) is a good contact for affordable day tours to Ngorongoro Crater and other local points of interest.

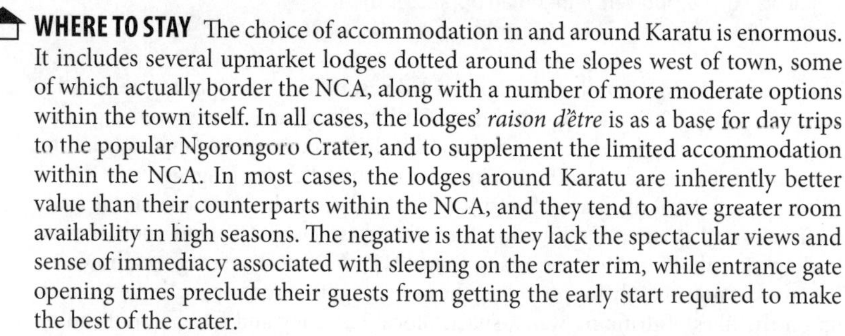

WHERE TO STAY The choice of accommodation in and around Karatu is enormous. It includes several upmarket lodges dotted around the slopes west of town, some of which actually border the NCA, along with a number of more moderate options within the town itself. In all cases, the lodges' *raison d'être* is as a base for day trips to the popular Ngorongoro Crater, and to supplement the limited accommodation within the NCA. In most cases, the lodges around Karatu are inherently better value than their counterparts within the NCA, and they tend to have greater room availability in high seasons. The negative is that they lack the spectacular views and sense of immediacy associated with sleeping on the crater rim, while entrance gate opening times preclude their guests from getting the early start required to make the best of the crater.

In & around town

Upmarket

* **Acacia Farm Lodge** [251 D3] **m** +255 759 331772; **w** karatuacacialodge.com. This exceptional all-suite lodge lies 2km from Karatu on a wooded hill offering views towards Ngorongoro. High standards of hospitality are complemented by stylish contemporary African décor, while

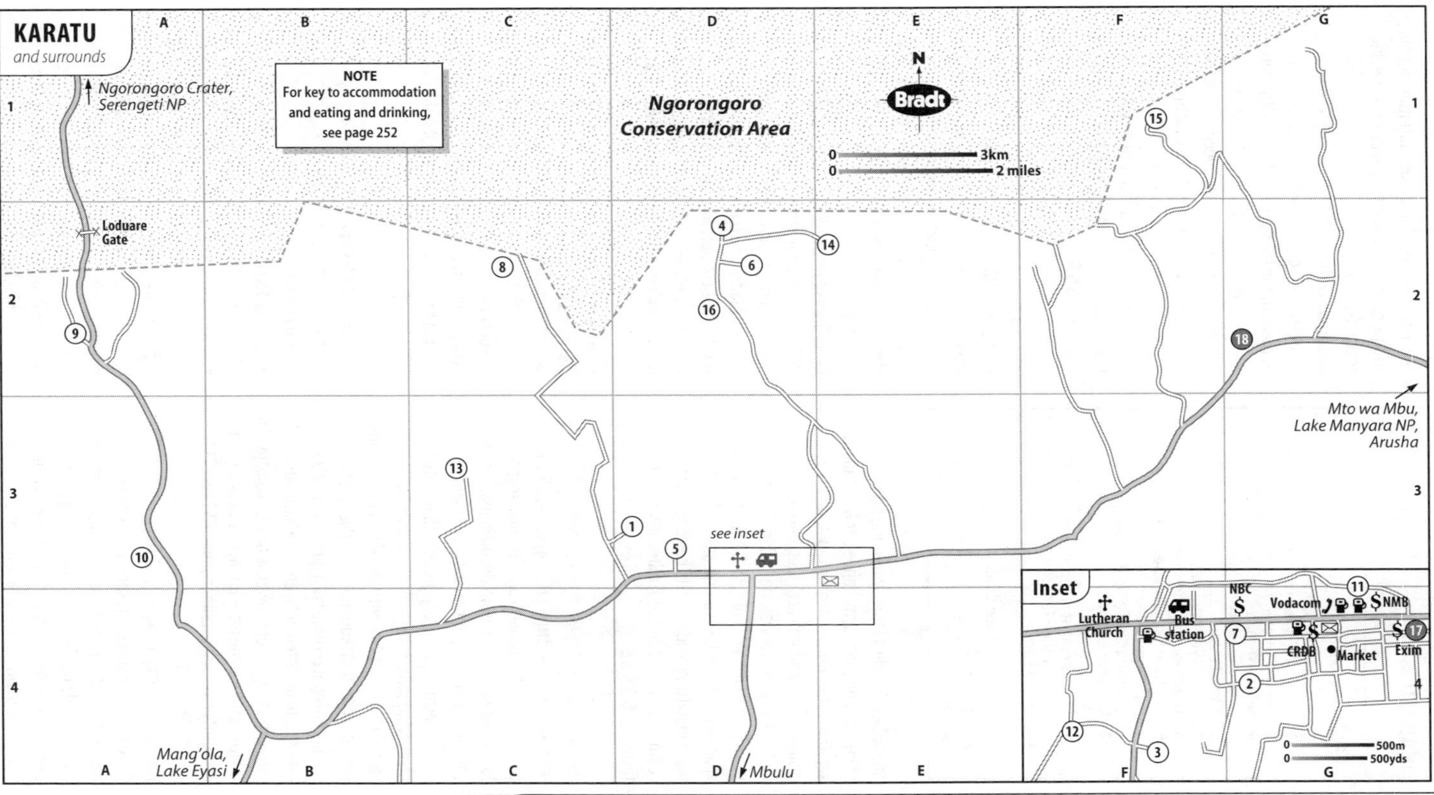
KARATU
and surrounds
Ngorongoro Crater, Serengeti NP
NOTE
For key to accommodation and eating and drinking, see page 252
Ngorongoro Conservation Area
N
Bradt
3km
2 miles
Loduare Gate
see inset
Mto wa Mbu, Lake Manyara NP, Arusha
Mang'ola, Lake Eyasi
Mbulu
Inset
Lutheran Church
Bus station
NBC
Vodacom
NMB
CRDB
Market
Exim
500m
500yds

KARATU *and surrounds*
For listings, see from page 250

Where to stay

1 Acacia Farm Lodge........D3
2 Crater Rim View Inn........G4
3 Eileen's Trees Inn........F4
4 Gibb's Farm........D2
5 Karatu Country Lodge........D3
6 Kitela Lodge........D2
7 Lilac Elevate Inn........G4
8 The Manor at Ngorongoro........C2
9 Neptune Ngorongoro........A2
10 Ngorongoro Farm House........A3
11 Ngorongoro Camp & Lodge........G4
12 Octagon Lodge........F4
13 Plantation Lodge........C3
14 The Retreat at Ngorongoro........E2
15 Rhotia Valley Tented Lodge........F1
16 Tloma Lodge........D2

Where to eat and drink

17 Lilac Café........G4
18 Rhotia Valley's Coffee Corner........G2

amenities include a large swimming pool, children's pool, spa, gym, coffee bar & restaurant serving home-grown organic vegetables. It can also arrange children's activities, bird walks, coffee-farm visits & waterfall hikes. Decorated in understated shades of grey & blue, the extra-spacious cottages have a king-size bed with walk-in netting, wide private balcony & sitting room with flatscreen DSTV, minibar & tea/coffee facilities. **$$$$$**

Moderate

✷ **Eileen's Trees Inn** [251 F4] m +255 755 656502; w eileenstrees.com. This owner-managed lodge, set back 500m from the main road, is easily the most appealing option in Karatu town. It sprawls across quiet leafy grounds that feature an inviting swimming pool & a plantation-style stilted restaurant/bar with wooden floor, upstairs dining room, & makuti roof. The 20 large rooms are uncluttered & come with queen-size or 2 ¾ 4-poster beds, fitted nets, en-suite bathroom with terracotta tiles & hot shower, & private balcony. All rooms are the same price but newer ones are larger & slightly smarter. Excellent value. *US$100/150 sgl/dbl FB.* **$$$**

Karatu Country Lodge [251 D3] m +255 757 235858; w countrylodgekaratu.com. Situated 1km out of town, this well-managed lodge is set around a large shady garden with a swimming pool & plenty of lounger beds. The spacious & earthily decorated rooms come with 4-poster bed, fitted net, banana-leaf ceiling, wood furniture, fireplace, fridge, balcony, en-suite hot shower & dressing room. **$$$$**

Octagon Lodge [251 F4] m +255 784 650324; w octagonlodge.com. Set in compact green gardens in the backstreets of Karatu, this long-serving & reasonably priced lodge comprises 15 airy wooden cottages with queen-size or twin beds, walk-in nets, colourful but earthy décor & private balcony. The characterful 'Irish Bar' actually has more of an African feel with its thatched roof. From *US$105/150 sgl/dbl B&B, with low-season discounts.* **$$$**

Budget

Crater Rim View Inn [251 G4] w booking.com. There's nothing flash about this neat little lodge, but it stands in pleasant green gardens & the clean rooms come with 4-poster bed, net, DSTV & hot shower. There's a decent restaurant. *From US$40pp B&B.* **$$**

Lilac Elevate Inn [251 G4] m +255 744 931632; w lilactanzania.com/elevate-inn. This 5-storey hotel near the bus station lacks for any semblance of a bush feel, but the 24 rooms & suites are comfortable, well-equipped & reasonably priced. There's also a decent 1st-floor restaurant. *From US$49/64 sgl/dbl B&B.* **$$**

Camping

Ngorongoro Camp & Lodge [251 G4] w ngorongorolodgetz.com. Avoid the overpriced rooms at this well-established complex, but it has the best campsite in Karatu & amenities include a heated swimming pool, supermarket & restaurant serving tasty Indian & continental dishes. *Camping US$10pp.* **$**

Towards Ngorongoro Conservation Area

Exclusive

✷ **Gibb's Farm** [251 D2] m +255 272 970438; w gibbsfarm.com. Situated 6km from Karatu along a rough road, this long-serving & sumptuous boutique hotel stands on an active coffee estate bordering a swathe of indigenous forest protected within the NCA. The main building here is a converted 1920s farmhouse that retains a strong period feel with its red polished floor, tall bay windows & leather & wood furnishing. The 17 exquisite & very spacious guest cottages all combine a contemporary look with farmhouse rusticity & have a private terrace with lovely views. Hearty home-style 4-course meals are prepared with fresh farm produce. Activities include bird walks, cultural & farm excursions, a 2hr hike to a waterfall & cave made by elephants on the forested slopes of the crater, & a spa offering traditional massages by a Maasai elder. There is no TV or swimming pool. **$$$$$$**

The Manor at Ngorongoro [251 C2] w elewanacollection.com. Boasting a magnificent hilltop setting on a coffee estate bordering the forests of the NCA, this handsome lodge – all whitewashed exteriors, tall gables, slate-tiled roofs & neatly tended gardens – is reminiscent of the Cape Dutch architecture associated with South Africa's wine estates. The semi-detached cottages each contain 2 large split-level open-plan suites with king-size or twin beds, comfortable sitting area, fireplace, large windows & an old-fashioned tub & shower. Excellent service & top-quality food makes this one of the most covetable places to stay in the Ngorongoro area. **$$$$$$$**

Upmarket

Kitela Lodge [251 D2] m +255 785 069944; w twctanzania.com. The most exclusive of 3 Tanganyika Wilderness Camps properties near Karatu, Kitela lies on a coffee estate & offers good views to the neighbouring forests of the Crater Highlands. The massive cottages, decorated in understated colonial style, incorporate a king-size bed, walk-in net, writing desk, private balcony & spacious bathroom with tub, shower & 2 sinks. **$$$$$$**

Neptune Ngorongoro [251 A2] w neptunehotels.com. This plush lodge literally borders the NCA & lies only 2km by road from Loduare Gate. The 20 spacious, airy & uncluttered cottages all have a makuti-thatch roof, wooden floor, lounge with fireplace, large bedroom with king-size or twin ¾ beds, spacious private balcony & hot tub or shower. There's a spa & large swimming pool with a great view. **$$$$**

Ngorongoro Farm House [251 A3] +255 785 069944; w twctanzania.com. Situated on a coffee farm halfway between Karatu & the NCA, this luxurious lodge comprises 3 separate camps of semi-detached thatched cottages with views to the forested slopes of Ngorongoro. There's a pleasant swimming pool area & the restaurant serves good country-style cooking. Guided nature walks, mountain biking & other leg-stretching activities are on offer. **$$$$$**

✱ **Plantation Lodge** [251 C3] m +255 753 743378; w plantation-lodge.com. In refreshingly individual contrast to the many chain lodges on the northern circuit, this beautiful & perennially popular property has been owned & managed by the same welcoming & hands-on German couple since it first opened in the late 1990s. It stands in large flowering gardens & has a classic whitewash-&-thatch exterior complemented by the stylish décor of the 24 spacious rooms & suites. All food is grown on site or sourced from local suppliers. It's only 15mins' drive from the NCA & there's an on-site swimming pool & spa. **$$$$$$**

The Retreat at Ngorongoro [251 E2] m +255 688 300600; w theretreatatngorongoro.com. Set in lovely green 12ha grounds bordering the NCA, this modern boutique lodge comprises 27 spacious & stylish family & dbl cottages. All bedrooms have a king- & queen-size bed, walk-in nets, private terrace, fireplace & large bathrooms. Amenities include a large swimming pool, 200m jogging path, well-equipped gym, spa & table tennis rooms. It can also arrange day hikes to a nearby elephant cave in the NCA. **$$$$$**

✱ **Rhotia Valley Tented Lodge** [251 F1] m +255 784 446579; w rhotiavalley.com. This low-key hilltop lodge abuts the NCA, but lies 30–45mins from the entrance gate along a 5km feeder road signposted from the main road between Karatu & Mto wa Mbu. The 16 standing tents are small but cosy, with balconies facing Ngorongoro's forested slopes. The restaurant is a wonderful open-sided thatched construction whose stylish but down-to-earth décor has a European-countryside-meets-classic-safari feel. Home-cooked meals are made largely from organic ingredients grown in the sprawling vegetable & herb garden. Several nature trails run through the property, which also has a swimming pool & receives occasional visits from elephants & other wildlife from the NCA. Proceeds support an eponymous Dutch-run orphanage & school that accommodates around 50 parentless or homeless children; visits are encouraged & usually take place at 17.30. **$$$$$**

THE MAASAI

The northern safari circuit is the homeland of the Nilotic-speaking Maasai, whose reputation as fearsome warriors ensured that the 19th-century slave caravans studiously avoided their territory, which was one of the last parts of East Africa ventured into by Europeans. The Maasai today remain the most familiar of African people to outsiders, a reputation that rests as much on their continued adherence to a traditional lifestyle as on past exploits. Instantly identifiable, Maasai men drape themselves in toga-like red blankets, carry long wooden poles, and often dye their hair with red ochre and style it in a manner that has been compared to a Roman helmet. And while the women dress similarly to many other Tanzanian women, their extensive use of beaded jewellery is highly distinctive, too.

The Maasai are often regarded to be the archetypal East African pastoralists, but are in fact relatively recent arrivals to the area. Their language Maa (Maasai literally means 'Maa-speakers') is affiliated to those languages spoken by the Nuer of southwest Ethiopia and the Bari of southern Sudan, and oral traditions suggest that the proto-Maasai started to migrate southward from the lower Nile area in the 15th century. They arrived in their present territory in the 17th or 18th century, forcefully displacing earlier inhabitants such as the Datoga and Chagga, who respectively migrated south to the Hanang area and east to the Kilimanjaro foothills. The Maasai territory reached its greatest extent in the mid 19th century, when it covered most of the Rift Valley from Marsabit (Kenya) south to Dodoma. Over the 1880s/90s, the Maasai were hit by a series of disasters linked to the arrival of Europeans – rinderpest and smallpox epidemics exacerbated by a severe drought and a bloody secession dispute – and much of their former territory was recolonised by tribes whom they had displaced a century earlier. During the colonial era, a further 50% of their land was lost to game reserves and settler farms. These territorial incursions notwithstanding, the Maasai today have one of the most extensive territories of any Tanzanian tribe, ranging across the vast Maasai Steppe to the Ngorongoro Highlands and Serengeti Plains.

The Maasai are monotheists whose belief in a single deity with a dualistic nature – the benevolent Engai Narok (Black God) and vengeful Engai Nanyokie (Red God) – has some overtones of the Judaic faith. They believe that Engai, who resides in the volcano Ol Doinyo Lengai, made them the rightful owners of all the cattle in the world, a view that has occasionally made life difficult for neighbouring herders. Traditionally, this arrogance does not merely extend to cattle: agriculturist and fish-eating peoples are scorned, while Europeans' uptight style of clothing earned them the Maasai name Iloredaa Enjekat – Fart Smotherers! Today, the Maasai co-exist peacefully with their non-Maasai compatriots, but while their tolerance for their neighbours' idiosyncrasies has increased in recent decades, they show little interest in changing their own lifestyle.

The Maasai measure a man's wealth in terms of cattle and children rather than money – a herd of about 50 cattle is respectable, the more children the

Moderate

✷ **Tloma Lodge** [251 D2] **m** +255 785 069944; **w** twctanzania.com. Situated 1km from Gibb's Farm & sharing a similar view over the forested Ngorongoro footslopes, this attractive & competitively priced lodge stands in spacious grounds that lead down to a wooden deck enclosing a large swimming pool. The 34 better, and a man who has plenty of one but not the other is regarded as poor. Traditionally, the Maasai will not hunt or eat vegetable matter or fish, but feed almost exclusively off their cattle. The main diet is a blend of cow's milk and blood, the latter drained – it is said painlessly – from a strategic nick in the animal's jugular vein. Because the cows are more valuable to them alive than dead, they are generally slaughtered only on special occasions. Meat and milk are never eaten on the same day, because it is insulting to the cattle to feed off the living and the dead at the same time. Despite the apparent hardship of their chosen lifestyle, many Maasai are wealthy by any standards. On one safari, our driver pointed out a not unusually large herd of cattle that would fetch the market equivalent of three new Land Rovers.

The central unit of Maasai society is the age-set. Every 15 years or so, a new and individually named generation of warriors or Ilmoran will be initiated, consisting of all the young men who have reached puberty and are not part of a previous age-set – most boys aged between 12 and 25. Every boy must undergo the Emorata (circumcision ceremony) before he is accepted as a warrior. If he cries out during the 5-minute operation, which is performed without any anaesthetic, the post-circumcision ceremony will be cancelled, the parents spat on for raising a coward, and the initiate taunted by his peers for several years before he is forgiven. When a new generation of warriors is initiated, the existing Ilmoran graduate to become junior elders, who are responsible for all political and legislative decisions until they in turn graduate to become senior elders. All political decisions are made democratically, and the role of the chief elder or Laibon is essentially that of a spiritual and moral leader.

Maasai girls are permitted to marry as soon as they have been initiated, but warriors must wait until their age-set has graduated to elder status, which will be 15 years later, when a fresh warrior age-set has been initiated. This arrangement ties in with the polygamous nature of Maasai society: in days past, most elders would typically have acquired between three and ten wives by the time they reached old age. Marriages are generally arranged, sometimes even before the female party is born, as a man may 'book' the next daughter produced by a friend to be his son's wife. Marriage is evidently viewed as a straightforward, child-producing business arrangement: it is normal for married men and women to have sleeping partners other than their spouse, provided that those partners are of an appropriate age-set. Should a woman become pregnant by another lover, the prestige attached to having many children outweighs any minor concerns about infidelity, and the husband will still bring up the child as his own. By contrast, although sex before marriage is condoned, an unmarried girl who falls pregnant brings disgrace on her family, and in former times would have been fed to the hyenas.

For further details about Maasai society and beliefs, get hold of the coffee-table book *Maasai*, by the photographer Carol Beckwith and Maasai historian Tepilit Ole Saitoti (Harry N Abrams, New York, reprinted 1993).

cottages are earth-coloured with colonial-style green corrugated-iron roofs & have screed floors, wood ceilings, fireplaces, 4-poster king-size or twin beds & a large bathroom. Also on offer are birdwatching tours, massages, village walks, coffee plantation demonstrations & Ngorongoro Crater day safaris. **$$$$$**

BUTTERFLIES

Tanzania's wealth of invertebrate life, though largely overlooked by visitors, is perhaps most easily appreciated in the form of butterflies and moths of the order Lepidoptera. Almost 1,000 butterfly species have been recorded in the country, compared with roughly 650 in the whole of North America, and a mere 56 in the British Isles. Several forests in Tanzania harbour 300 or more butterfly species, and one might easily see a greater selection in the course of a day than one could in a lifetime of exploring the English countryside. Indeed, I've often sat at one roadside pool in an East African forest and watched ten to 20 clearly different species converge there over the space of 20 minutes.

The Lepidoptera are placed in the class Insecta, which includes ants, beetles and locusts among others. All insects are distinguished from other invertebrates, such as arachnids (spiders) and crustaceans, by their combination of six legs, a pair of frontal antennae, and a body divided into a distinct head, thorax and abdomen. Insects are the only winged invertebrates, though some primitive orders have never evolved wings, and other more recently evolved orders have discarded them. Most flying insects have two pairs of wings, one of which, as in the case of flies, might have been modified beyond immediate recognition. The butterflies and moths of the order Lepidoptera have two sets of wings and are distinguished from all other insect orders by the tiny ridged wing scales that create their characteristic bright colours.

The most spectacular of all butterflies are the **swallowtails** of the family Papilionidae, of which roughly 100 species have been identified in Africa. Named for the streamers that trail from the base of their wings, swallowtails are typically large and colourful, and relatively easy to observe when they feed on mammal dung deposited on forest trails and roads. Sadly, this last generalisation doesn't apply to the African giant swallowtail (*Papilio antimachus*), a powerful flier that tends to stick at canopy level and seldom alights on the ground. With a wingspan known to exceed 20cm, this black, orange and green gem is the largest butterfly on the continent, and possibly the world.

The Pieridae is a family of medium-sized butterflies, generally smaller than the swallowtails and with wider wings, of which almost 100 species are present in Tanzania, several as seasonal intra-African migrants. Most species are predominantly white in colour, with some yellow, orange, black or even red and blue markings on the wings. One widespread member of this family is the

WHERE TO EAT AND DRINK The selection of bespoke eateries in Karatu itself is rather limited, but several small establishments serve the usual local staples, and there are more cosmopolitan restaurants at Eileen's Trees Inn, Crater View Inn and Ngorongoro Camp & Lodge.

Lilac Café [251 G4] m +255 746 822243; w lilactanzania.com/lilac-cafe; ⏲ 08.00–21.00 Mon–Wed, 08.00–22.00 Fri–Sat. Vibrantly decorated with Makonde sculptures, local paintings & wine barrels, this lively new café with indoor & garden seating serves a variety of pizzas, salads, sandwiches & curries in the US$5–6 range. Also available is freshly brewed coffee, juices, wine & beer, plus cocktails from 16.00 on Tue & Sat. Clean toilets, free Wi-Fi & speedy service are added attractions if you're looking for a quick lunch stop en route to the NCA. $

Rhotia Valley's Coffee Corner [251 G2] m +255 784 446579; w rhotiavalley.com/our-food; ⏲ 08.00–18.00 daily. Under the same management as Rhotia Valley Tented Lodge, this oddly named **angled grass yellow** (*Eurema desjardinsii*), which has yellow wings marked by a broad black band, and is likely to be seen in any savannah or forest fringe habitat. The orange and lemon *Eronia leda* also has yellow wings, but with an orange upper tip, and it occurs in open grassland and savannah countrywide.

The most diverse of African butterfly families is the Lycaenidae, which accounts for almost one-third of the continental tally of around 1,500 recorded species. Known also as **gossamer wings**, this varied family consists mostly of small- to medium-sized butterflies, with a wingspan of 1–5cm, dull underwings, and brilliant violet blue, copper or rufous-orange upper wings. The larvae of many Lycaenidae species have a symbiotic relationship with ants – they secrete a fluid that is milked by the ants and are thus permitted to shelter in their nests. A striking member of this family is *Hypolycaena hatita*, a small bluish butterfly with long tail streamers, often seen on forest paths throughout Tanzania.

Another well-represented family in Tanzania is the Nymphalidae, a diversely coloured group of small to large butterflies, generally associated with forest edges or interiors. The Nymphalidae are also known as brush-footed butterflies, because their forelegs have evolved into non-functional brush-like structures. One of the more distinctive species is the **African blue tiger** (*Tirumala petiverana*), a large black butterfly with about two-dozen blue-white wing spots, often observed on forest paths, near puddles or feeding from animal droppings. Another large member of this family is the **African queen** (*Danaus chrysippus*), which has a slow, deliberate flight pattern, orange or brown wings, and is as common in forest edge habitats as it is in cultivated fields or suburbia.

The family Charaxidae, regarded by some authorities to be a subfamily of the Nymphalidae, is represented by roughly 200 African species. Typically large, robust, strong fliers with one or two short tails on each wing, the butterflies in this family vary greatly in coloration, and several species appear to be scarce and localised since they inhabit forest canopies and are seldom seen. Rather less spectacular are the 200–300 **grass-skipper** species of the family Hersperiidae, most of which are small and rather drably coloured, though some are more attractively marked in black, white and/or yellow. The grass-skippers are thought to form the evolutionary link between butterflies and the generally more nocturnal moths, represented in Tanzania by several families of which the most impressive are the boldly patterned **giant silk moths** of the family Saturniidae.

roadside eatery 5km east of Karatu is the ideal place to break for lunch en route from Mto wa Mbu or Arusha. It serves burgers, chicken skewers, pasta, salads & soups in the US$5–7 range, as well as smoothies, coffee & juices. Further assets include a friendly welcome, clean toilets, Wi-Fi & lovely view from the balcony. $$

NGORONGORO CONSERVATION AREA

Listed as a UNESCO World Heritage Site and International Biosphere Reserve, the Ngorongoro Conservation Area (NCA) extends over 8,292km^2 to the southeast of the Serengeti National Park, with which it shares a border of roughly 80km. Its dominant feature is the geological marvel known as the Ngorongoro Crater – the world's largest intact volcanic caldera, and a shoo-in contender for any global shortlist of natural wonders thanks to its gobsmacking scenic beauty and the wildlife that teems across its verdant 260km^2 floor. The rest of the NCA can be divided into two distinct parts: the eastern Crater Highlands comprise a sprawling volcanic massif studded with craggy peaks and gaping craters, while the lower-lying western plains are essentially a continuation of the Serengeti ecosystem, supporting a cover of short grass that attracts immense concentrations of grazers during the rainy season.

Coming from the direction of Arusha, the road ascent of Ngorongoro Crater is a sensational scene setter, switchbacking through densely forested slopes to Heroes Point, where most visitors will catch their first breathtaking view from the rim to the crater floor 600m below. Even at this distance, it is often possible to pick out hundred- or even thousand-strong ant-like formations foraging across the crater floor – herds of wildebeest, zebra and buffalo – and with binoculars you might also pick out some of the elephants that haunt the fringes of Lerai Forest. The drive along the crater rim to your lodge will be equally riveting: patches of forest interspersed with sweeping views back across to a patchwork of farmland around Karatu, and the possibility of encountering buffalo, zebra, bushbuck, elephant and even the occasional leopard.

The Ngorongoro Crater is the main focal point of tourist activity in the NCA but those who have the time can explore any number of less-publicised natural features further afield. Oldupai Gorge, for instance, is the site of some of Africa's most important hominid fossil finds, and can easily be visited en route from the crater rim to the Serengeti. Other highlights include the Empakaai Crater and (to a lesser extent) Olmoti Crater in the northern NCA, while the crater rim is highly rewarding for montane forest birds.

GEOLOGY With an altitudinal span of 1,230m to 3,648m, the NCA ranks among the most geologically spectacular protected areas in Africa. The southwest NCA comprises flat short-grass plains similar to those in the neighbouring Serengeti, while the low rocky granite outcrops of the Gol Range, which formed some 500 million years ago, rise in the northwest. But the NCA's dominant feature is the more easterly Crater Highlands, a volcanic range of free-standing mountains, undulating plateaus and gaping calderas whose formation is linked to the same tectonic process responsible for the creation of the Rift Valley. Most of the Crater Highlands stands above the 2,000m contour, and the tallest peak – 3,648m Lolmalasin – is actually the third-highest mountain in Tanzania after Kilimanjaro and Meru.

Ngorongoro Crater itself is the relic of an immense shield volcano that attained a similar height to that of Kilimanjaro before it imploded violently some 2 million to 3 million years ago. It is the world's sixth-largest volcanic caldera, and the most expansive anywhere on the planet to have an unbroken wall. Eight smaller craters in the NCA, most notably Olmoti and Empakaai, are the product of similar eruptions. The Crater Highlands are no longer volcanically active, but free-standing Ol Doinyo Lengai to the immediate northeast ranks among the world's most active volcanoes, having erupted on several occasions since the late 19th century.

HISTORY Based on fossil evidence unearthed at Oldupai Gorge in the western NCA, we know that various hominid species have occupied the area for at least 3 million years. It was the domain of hunter-gatherers until a few thousand years ago, when pastoralists moved in. The fate of these early pastoralists is unknown, because a succession of immigrants replaced them: the ancestors of the Cushitic-speaking Iraqw and Mbulu some 2,000 years ago and those of the Nilotic-speaking Datoga about 300 years ago. A century later the militaristic Maasai drove both of

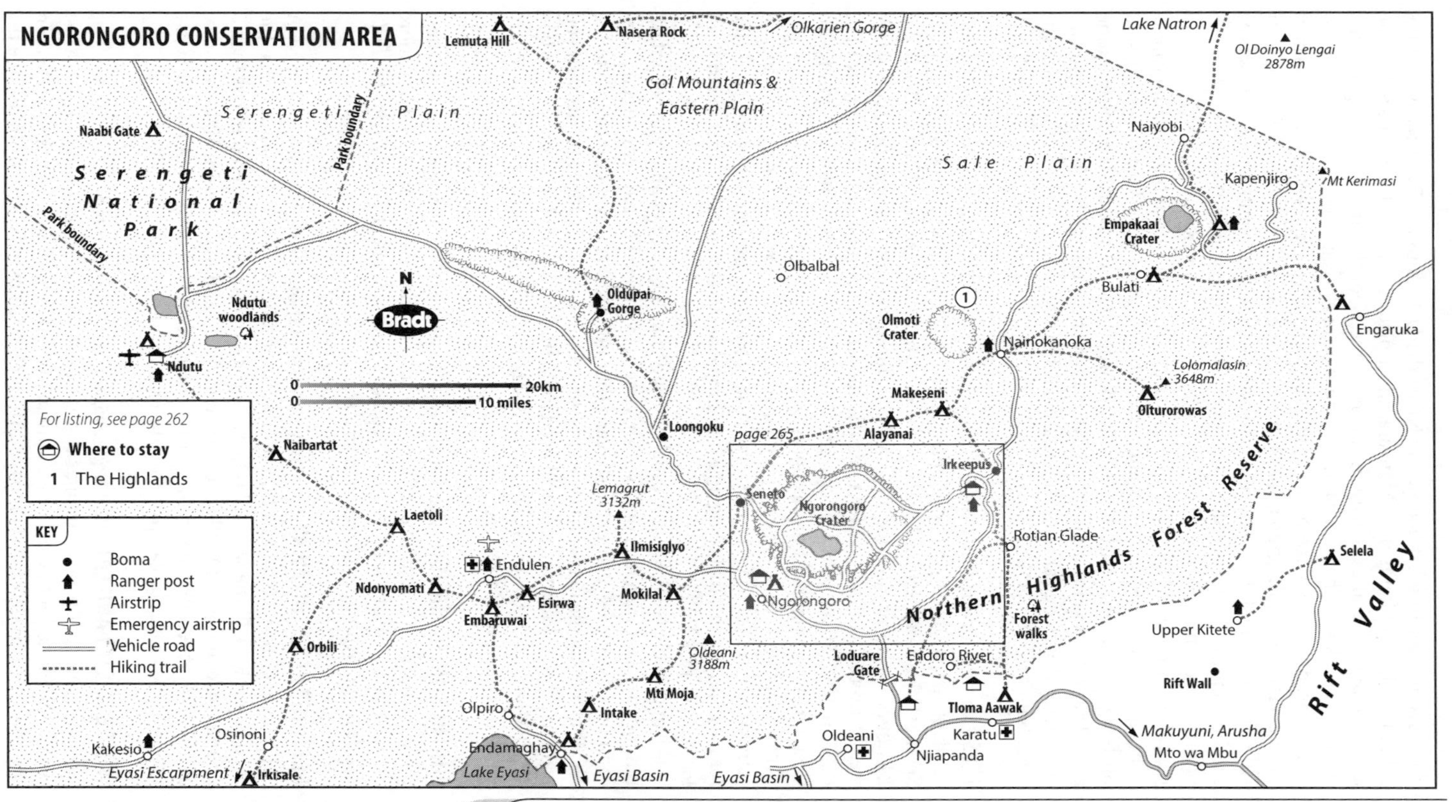
NGORONGORO CONSERVATION AREA
Lemuta Hill
Nasera Rock
Olkarien Gorge
Lake Natron
Ol Doinyo Lengai 2878m
Gol Mountains & Eastern Plain
Serengeti Plain
Park boundary
Naabi Gate
Serengeti National Park
Naiyobi
Sale Plain
Kapenjiro
Mt Kerimasi
Empakaai Crater
Olbalbal
Bulati
Oldupai Gorge
Ndutu woodlands
Bradt
N
Olmoti Crater
Engaruka
Nainokanoka
Ndutu
0 20km
0 10 miles
Lolomalasin 3648m
Makeseni
Olturorowas
Loongoku
page 265
Alayanai
For listing, see page 262
Where to stay
1 The Highlands
Naibartat
Irkeepus
Reserve
Lemagrut 3132m
Seneto
Ngorongoro Crater
Laetoli
Forest
Rotian Glade
Selela
Ilmisiglyo
Highlands
KEY
Boma
Ranger post
Airstrip
Emergency airstrip
Vehicle road
Hiking trail
Endulen
Ndonyomati
Esirwa
Mokilal
Ngorongoro
Northern
Forest walks
Upper Kitete
Rift Valley
Embaruwai
Orbili
Oldeani 3188m
Loduare Gate
Endoro River
Mti Moja
Rift Wall
Tloma Aawak
Intake
Olpiro
Karatu
Makuyuni, Arusha
Osinoni
Oldeani
Kakesio
Endamaghay
Njiapanda
Mto wa Mbu
Lake Eyasi
Eyasi Escarpment
Irkisale
Eyasi Basin
Eyasi Basin

these groups out of what is now the NCA: the Datoga to the Eyasi Basin and the Mbulu to the highlands near Manyara. Most place names in the area are Maasai, and although several explanations for the name Ngorongoro are floating around, the most credible is that it is named after a type of Maasai bowl.

Europeans settled in the NCA around the turn of the 20th century. Two German brothers farmed on the crater floor until the outbreak of World War I. One of their old farmhouses is still used by researchers, and a few sisal plants dating to this time can be seen in the northeast of the crater. Tourism began in the 1930s when the original Ngorongoro Crater Lodge was built on the crater rim. The NCA formed part of the original Serengeti National Park as gazetted in 1951, but Maasai protests at being denied access to such a huge tract of their grazing land led to it being split off from the national park in 1959 and downgraded to a multi-use conservation area. The NCA was inscribed as a UNESCO World Heritage Site in 1979, and two years later it was declared an International Biosphere Reserve, together with the neighbouring Serengeti.

FEES An entrance fee of US$30/60 per person per 24 hours for residents/non-residents is payable by all who enter the NCA, even those in transit to or from Serengeti National Park. A vehicle fee of Tsh20,000 (around US$8)/US$40 per 24 hours is also payable for all Tanzanian/foreign-registered vehicles with a tare weight up to 2,000kg (heavier tares pay more). In addition, a Crater Service Fee (CSF) of US$250 per vehicle is charged for each and every descent into Ngorongoro Crater. For overnight visitors, a concession or camping fee is also levied: US$50 per person per night for a lodge or permanent camp or US$30/60 for a public/special campsite. Entrance to Oldupai Gorge costs US$30 per person, while the guide fee for a walking safari, including a visit to Empakaai Crater, is US$20 per person. All fees attract 18% VAT.

All applicable NCA fees are usually included in the price of an organised safari, but independent travellers on a self-drive safari will need to pay fees directly. This can now be done by Visa or Mastercard (but not cash) at any entrance gate to the NCA, assuming the network is working, or at the NCA head office in Arusha. If you want to pay US dollars cash, you'll need to do this during banking hours (🕘 08.00–15.00 Mon–Fri, 09.00–noon Sat) at the NMB or CRDB in Arusha or Karatu, where you'll be issued with a receipt.

FURTHER INFORMATION The official NCA website (**w** ncaa.go.tz) is the best place to check time-sensitive information such as changes in park fees. For a more detailed overview of the NCA, buy Veronica Roodt's excellent *Tourist Travel & Field Guide to the Ngorongoro Conservation Area*.

GETTING THERE AND AWAY The only access point on the eastern side of the NCA is Loduare Gate, which lies 12km northwest of Karatu. Coming from Arusha, the road is surfaced all the way to Loduare, and it can usually be covered in less than 3 hours. Once in the NCA, all roads are unsurfaced and may require high clearance and/or 4x4, especially after rain. Allow 30–60 minutes to drive from Loduare Gate to any of the lodges or campsites on the crater rim.

WHERE TO STAY AND EAT *Map, page 265, unless otherwise stated*
No accommodation or camping facilities exist within Ngorongoro Crater. Most people either stay at one of the handful of upmarket lodges and camps perched on the crater rim, as described on page 261, or else visit as a day trip from outside the

NCA, basing themselves at a lodge or camp in the vicinity of Karatu (page 250) or Lake Manyara (page 231).

Both these approaches have their pros and cons. Accommodation is generally a lot cheaper in Karatu or Mto wa Mbu than it is within the NCA, and you'll also avoid the seriously chilly nights and misty mornings typical of the crater rim. But assuming your budget runs to it, and you carry plenty of warm clothing, we would recommend staying on the crater rim as the more immersive experience, thanks to the stirring views, the wilder atmosphere and the relative ease of doing an early morning game drive on the crater floor.

Two main clusters of accommodation stand on the crater rim. Most of the larger and more established lodges are situated on the southwest edge, while the remainder are in the east close to or inside Lemala Gate. A big advantage of the eastern cluster is that the combined ascent and descent road here offers by far the quickest access to the crater floor, which makes it relatively easy to avoid the crowds by starting morning drives earlier and ending evening drives later. Conversely, if you opt to visit Ngorongoro Crater as a day trip from Karatu, or elsewhere outside the NCA, you'll have no choice but to arrive in the crater as part of the post-breakfast crush.

Two rather anomalous lodges within the NCA are Asilia's The Highlands and the independent Ndutu Lodge. The Highlands lies on the rim of Olmoti Crater about 45 minutes from Lemala Gate, and is therefore treated as one of the 'eastern rim' lodges on page 262. Ndutu, set immediately inside the western border of the NCA, is not a realistic base from which to explore Ngorongoro Crater, so it is covered in the chapter on the Serengeti, to which it is closer in both geographic and ecological terms.

Southwestern Rim

✷ &Beyond Ngorongoro Crater Lodge ⊕ -3.23987, 35.49696; w andbeyond.com. Founded in 1934 but rebuilt from scratch after it was acquired by &Beyond in 1995, this innovative creation largely lives up to its billing as 'the finest safari lodge in Africa'. The standalone suites resemble Maasai huts distorted in Dadaist style, while the eclectic interiors combine elements of Baroque, classical, African & colonial décor. For all its architectural flourishes, however, the lodge never loses sight of its spectacular location – the crater is almost constantly in sight, even from the baths & toilets. The guides are immensely knowledgeable about the crater & wildlife in general, & the food is world class – from the sumptuous packed b/fasts taken on early-morning drives to the mouthwatering homemade chocolate in the room. Though it's not bush enough for some tastes, this unique lodge is difficult to fault taken on its own playfully ostentatious terms. **$$$$$$$**

Ngorongoro Rhino Lodge ⊕ -3.25690, 35.52511; ☎ 022 212 8485; w rhino.co.tz. Formerly the home of the first conservator of NCA & later managed as a guesthouse by the NCA, this modest low-rise lodge is far & away the most affordable on the crater rim. It lacks a direct crater view, but the surrounding mist-swathed forest has a charm of its own & is very convenient for game drives. The 24 rooms are comfortable & have hot showers, while buffet meals are taken in a cosy dining room heated by log fire. **$$$$**

Ngorongoro Serena Safari Lodge ⊕ -3.20903, 35.47882; w serenahotels.com. Meeting the usual high Serena standards, this is the pick of the more conventional lodges on the crater rim in terms of facilities, & it receives consistent praise from tourists & from within the safari industry. It is also the closest lodge to the western descent road, a decided advantage for those who want to reach the crater floor as early as possible. The setting is a secluded wooded valley rustling with birdlife & offering a good view over the crater. The facilities, food & service are all of a high standard, & rooms are centrally heated. **$$$$$$**

Ngorongoro Wildlife Lodge ⊕ -3.24384, 35.51277; w hotelsandlodges-tanzania.com. This former government hotel has the most scenic location of all the crater rim lodges, directly above Lerai Forest. Comfortably functional rooms have piping-hot baths & windows facing the crater, while the grounds support a fair range of forest birds. The monolithic architecture is rather dated & décor, service & food are not up the standard of its competitors, but this is reflected in the relatively low rates. **$$$$**

Eastern Rim

The Highlands [map, page 259] ⊕ -2.99706, 35.63809; w asiliaafrica.com. This blissfully isolated luxury tented camp stands on the forested wall of Olmoti Crater 45mins' drive from the Lemala ascent/descent road. Accommodation is in unique domed tented structures set on wooden platforms designed to combine a contemporary bush feel with the degree of natural incubation suited to this relatively chilly climate. **$$$$$$$**

Lemala Ngorongoro Tented Camp ⊕ -3.12929, 35.67037; m +255 682 933933; w lemalacamp.com. This semi-permanent luxury tented camp stands in an atmospheric acacia forest immediately inside Lemala Gate. The 9 spacious tents are decorated in classic safari style & have solar-powered lighting & hot water. An excellent choice for outdoorsy types who don't mind braving the chilly crater rim under canvas at night. **$$$$$$**

Lion's Paw Camp ⊕ -3.12547, 35.66138; m +255 789 193333; w karibucamps.com. Also situated inside Lemala Gate, this camp offers accommodation in 15 luxurious hybrid tents that combine canvas walls with tiled roofs. Each unit is perched on a stilted platform with a private

THE RHINOS OF NGORONGORO

Ngorongoro Crater has always been noted for its density of black rhinos. Back in 1892, Dr Oscar Baumann, the first European to visit the area, remarked on the large numbers of rhino, particularly around Lerai Forest – and he shot seven of the unfortunate beasts to prove his point. More recently, in 1964, the biologist John Goddard estimated the resident population at greater than 100. Sadly, by 1992, poaching had reduced the crater's rhino population to no more than ten individuals, although this number had increased to 18 by 1998, including a mother and calf relocated from South Africa's Addo National Park to boost the local genetic pool. Sadly, five of these rhinos died soon after, one taken by a lion and the remainder thought to be victims of a tick-borne disease linked to the low rainfall of 2000/01. Since then, numbers have gradually recovered: the crater's resident population stood at around 20 individuals in 2008 and it has most likely doubled since then, though exact numbers are undisclosed. Rhinos in the crater all have a tracking device implanted in their horns, to discourage poachers and to enable the rangers to monitor their movements.

Despite the overall decline in the crater's black rhino numbers since the 1960s, it remains the second-best place in Tanzania (after Mkomazi National Park) to look for these endangered animals. For many visitors to Ngorongoro, therefore, rhino sightings are a very high priority. For most of the year, the rhinos tend to sleep in Lerai Forest at night and forage around Lake Magadi in daylight hours, and they are often seen moving between the two in the early morning. In the wet season, rhinos are also often encountered in the vicinity of the Ngoitokitok Springs and the base of the road to Lemala Gate.

Ngorongoro's rhinos display a couple of local quirks. The black rhino (unlike its 'white' cousin) is normally a diurnal browser, which makes it rather odd to see them spending most of the day in open grassland, but the story is that they mostly feed by night while they are in the forest. Baumann noted that the crater's rhinos were unusually pale in colour, a phenomenon that is still observed today and is due to their predilection for bathing and rolling in the saline lake and fringing salt flats.

terrace, & includes 4-poster queen/twin beds with fitted net & small desk. There's a welcome campfire at night & good food. **$$$$$$$**

✷ **Ngorongoro Sopa Lodge** ⊕ -3.15382, 35.67663; w sopalodges.com. The largest & most built-up lodge on the eastern rim accommodates guests in large semi-detached suites with a wide bay window facing the crater & Ol Mokarot Mountain. There is a swimming pool in front of the bar & the food & service are excellent. In addition to the useful location near Lemala Gate, the forested grounds are great for Afromontane forest birds, with sunbirds (tacazze, golden-winged & eastern double-collared) well represented & a variety of weavers, seedeaters & robins present. **$$$$$$**

✷ **Sanctuary Ngorongoro Crater Camp** ⊕ -3.12438, 35.66503; w sanctuaryretreats.com. Nestled within a fairy-tale forest of ancient flat-topped acacias swathed in 'old man's beard' lichen, this intimate bush camp is located about 3km inside Lemala Gate, meaning it is perfectly based for early-morning game drives into the crater. The chilly location is offset by a roaring campfire on the deck outside the dining area & a combination of gas heater & electric blankets in the cosy tents. The 10 luxurious tents also have hot showers, charging points & secluded terraces from where you can enjoy the forest birdlife. **$$$$$$$**

Camping

Simba Campsite A ⊕ -3.22810, 35.49009; w ncaa.go.tz. The only public campsite on the rim offers wonderful views over the crater, & amenities include a good ablution block & a stall selling hot coffee & other drinks. *US$30pp.* **$$**

WHAT TO SEE AND DO

Ngorongoro Crater floor The 260km^2 floor of Ngorongoro Crater ranks among Africa's most rewarding safari destinations, both in terms of scenery and wildlife viewing, and a game drive there is simply not to be missed. There are few places where you can see so reliably such large concentrations of wildlife all year round, and your game viewing (and photography) will only be enhanced by the striking backdrop of the 600m-high crater wall. The crater is also excellent Big Five territory: lions, elephants and buffalos are all but guaranteed, black rhinos are regularly seen, and leopards are chanced upon from time to time.

Several notable geographic features punctuate the crater. **Lerai Forest** consists almost entirely of tall fever trees, a swamp-loving species of acacia noted for the jaundiced shade of its bark (it was once thought that this tree, which tends to occur in habitats favoured by breeding mosquitoes, was the cause of yellow fever and malaria). To the north of this forest, **Lake Magadi** is a shallow soda lake that varies greatly in extent depending on the season. Standing close to the lakeshore is a cluster of **burial cairns** that show some similarities with the tombs at the Engaruka Ruins further east, and are presumably a relic of the Datoga occupation of the crater prior to the arrival of the Maasai. To the south and east of this, the **Gorigor Swamp** also varies in extent seasonally, but it seldom, if ever, dries up completely. There is a permanent hippo pool at the **Ngoitokitok Springs** at the eastern end of the swamp. The northern half of the crater is generally drier, though it is bisected by the **Munge River**, which is lined by thickets and forms a seasonally substantial area of swamp to the immediate north of Lake Magadi.

The open grassland that covers most of the crater floor supports large concentrations of wildebeest and zebra (the population of these species is estimated at 10,000 and 5,000 respectively), and smaller numbers of buffalo, tsessebe, Thomson's gazelle and Grant's gazelle. The vicinity of Lerai Forest is the best area in which to see waterbuck, bushbuck and eland. The forest and adjoining Gorigor Swamp are the main haunt of the crater's elephant population, which typically stands at around 70. All the elephants resident in the crater are old males (although females and families sometimes pass through), and you stand a good chance of seeing big tuskers of the

NOT A ZOO

You won't spend long in northern Tanzania before you hear somebody complain that Ngorongoro Crater is 'like a zoo'. It's a common allegation, but one as facile as it is nonsensical. The defining quality of a typical zoo is surely its total artificiality: the captive inmates have been placed there by people largely for entertainment, a high proportion are exotic to the zoo's location, they are invariably confined within enclosures of some sort (with different species, particularly predator and prey, normally kept apart), and most are fed artificially like pets.

Ngorongoro Crater could scarcely be more different from a typical zoo. The wildlife you see in the crater is neither caged nor fed by people. Indeed, with the exception of a few reintroduced black rhinos, it is all 100% indigenous and free to come and go as it pleases, forming part of the same cohesive ecosystem that includes the Serengeti and Maasai Mara.

The only respect in which the crater is faintly zoo-like is that the wildlife mostly seems very relaxed. But that doesn't mean it is tame, merely habituated to vehicles (in the same way that the mountain gorillas of Rwanda and Uganda are habituated to people on foot). This creates superb opportunities to observe wildlife interaction and behaviour at close quarters – trust me, an infinitely more satisfying experience than travelling through a reserve where the wildlife is so skittish that most sightings amount to little more than a rump disappearing into the bush.

The notion of Ngorongoro as a glorified zoo also stems from the high volume of tourist traffic. This undoubtedly dilutes the crater's wilderness character and has some potential for environmental damage, but it probably has little impact on the well-being of the animals. Indeed, wildlife in Ngorongoro Crater is clearly less affected by the presence of vehicles than its counterparts in more remote and little-visited reserves where many animals display clear signs of distress at the approach of a vehicle.

So, no, Ngorongoro Crater is not a zoo. It's nothing like one. But the high tourist volume within its confines can jar against our sense of aesthetics – especially when game spotting entails looking for a group of vehicles clustered together in the distance rather than looking for an actual animal! Personally, I feel that the scenery and abundance of animals more than makes up for the mild congestion, but if crowds put you off then there are other places to visit in Tanzania. Instead of adding to the tourist traffic and then moaning about it, why not give the crater a miss? Or better still, make the effort to be in the crater first thing in the morning when, for a brief hour or so before the post-breakfast crowds descend, it really does live up to every expectation of untrammelled beauty.

sort that have been poached away elsewhere in East Africa. Two curious absentees from the crater floor are impala and giraffe, both of which are common in the surrounding plains. Some researchers attribute the absence of giraffes to a lack of suitable browsing fodder, others to their presumed inability to descend the steep crater walls. Quite why there are no impalas in the crater is a mystery.

The crater floor supports Africa's densest concentration of large carnivores. The lion population typically stands at between 50 and 100 individuals, but it has fluctuated greatly since records were maintained, partly as a result of migration in and out of the crater, but also because of vulnerability to epidemics. It hit an all-time low in 1962, when numbers plummeted from around 90 individuals to fewer than 20 as a result of a disease spread by biting flies. The most recent census counted 12 prides of between 6 and 22 individuals each, suggesting a total population of greater than 100, and anecdotal accounts suggest it has increased since then. Lions might be encountered just about anywhere in the crater, and are generally very relaxed around vehicles.

Several leopards are resident in the crater, but they tend to be shy and are seldom encountered – your best chance of a sighting is in the patch of riparian forest associated with the Munge River. Cheetahs are a more erratic presence, which is quite surprising given that much of the crater floor comprises textbook cheetah habitat of open grassland, but can probably be attributed to the high density of hyenas and other competing predators. After a long period of total absence, two different female cheetahs colonised the crater floor in 2000, to establish a small resident population which was regularly encountered over the next decade or so. However, in 2022 it had once again been some years since a cheetah was sighted. The crater floor is perhaps the most reliable place anywhere in Africa to see the serval, a long-limbed blotchy cat that tends to favour open

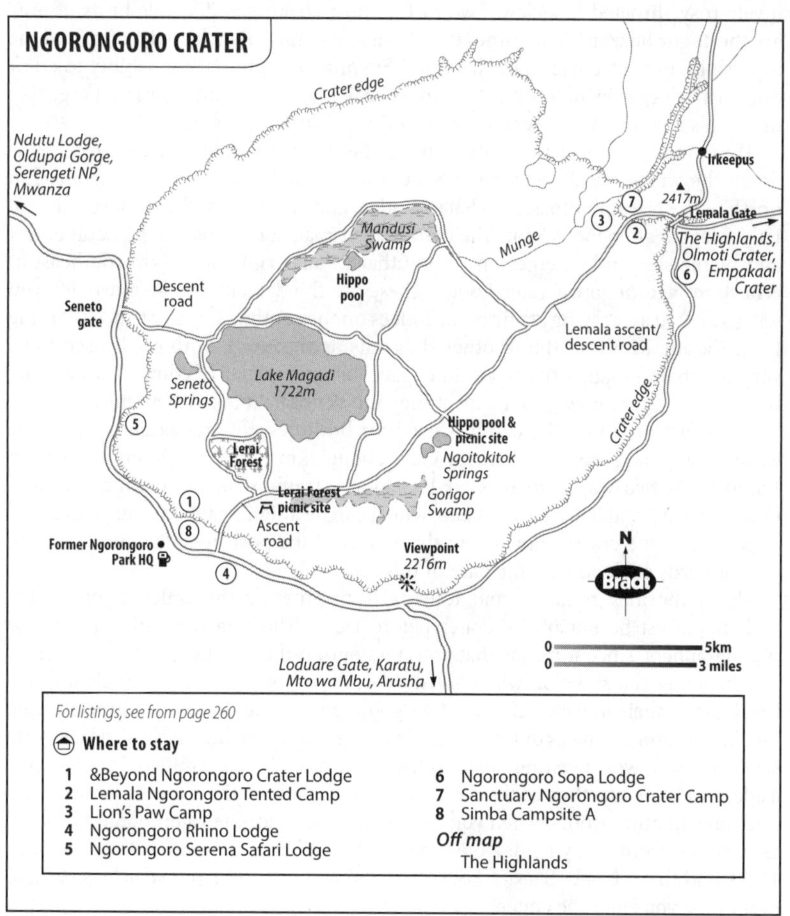

country close to swamps and streams, and might be mistaken for a miniature cheetah at a glance.

The most populous large carnivore in Ngorongoro is the spotted hyena, the population of which is estimated at around 400. You won't spend long in the crater without seeing a hyena: they often rest up on the eastern shore of Lake Magadi during the day, sometimes trying – and mostly failing – to sneak up on the flamingos in the hope of a quick snack. Other common carnivores are golden jackal and black-backed jackal, with the former being more frequently encountered due to its relatively diurnal habits.

The crater floor offers some great birding. Lake Magadi normally harbours large flocks of flamingo, giving its edges a pinkish tinge when seen from a distance. The pools at the Mandusi Swamp can be excellent for water birds, with all manner of waders, storks, ducks and herons present. The grassland is a good place to see a number of striking ground birds. One very common resident is the kori bustard, which is the world's heaviest flying bird, and spectacular if you catch it during a mating dance. The ostrich is also common, along with the gorgeously garish crowned crane, and (in the rainy season) huge flocks of migrant storks. Less prominent, but common, and of great interest to more dedicated birders, is the lovely rosy-throated longclaw. Two of the most striking and visible birds of prey are the augur buzzard, sometimes seen here in its unusual melanistic form, and the foppish long-crested eagle. The localised Egyptian vulture – whose ability to crack open ostrich eggs by holding a stone in its beak makes it the only bird that arguably uses tools – is sometimes seen in the vicinity of Mungu Stream.

Three roads connect the crater rim to the floor. The main descent road runs down the western wall, starting at Seneto in the Malanja Depression about 8km north of the Ngorongoro Serena Safari Lodge, and connects to the western shore of Lake Magadi after about 5km. The main ascent road starts close to the Lerai Forest and picnic site, and emerges on the southern crater rim about 1km southeast of &Beyond Ngorongoro Crater Lodge. These are the descent and ascent roads you will use if you are staying at any of the lodges on the southwest crater rim, or coming from Karatu, Mto wa Mbu or other sites outside the NCA. Both roads used to be very rough and many drivers would engage 4x4 as a matter of course before using them, but they are now paved with stones and very safe if taken at a sensible speed.

The third road into the crater – used for both descent and ascent – is on the eastern wall, and starts at Lemala Gate about 2km north of Ngorongoro Sopa Lodge. This two-way road sees far less tourist traffic than the main ascent and descent roads, and it is also less steep, which can be a significant advantage in terms of getting to the crater floor before the arrival of the post-breakfast hordes. Look out for herds of eland near the base of this road.

The authorities rigidly forbid tourists from entering the crater before 07.00, and they must be out of the crater before 18.00. This is a frustrating ruling for photographers, since it means that you miss out on the best light of the day, and it has encouraged a situation where most safari drivers suggest that their clients take breakfast in their lodge or camp before going on a game drive, and carry a picnic lunch. This programme is difficult to avoid on a group safari, but for those on a private safari it is well worth getting down to the crater as early as permitted. Photography aside, this is the one time of the day when you might have the crater to yourself, the one time, in other words, when you can really experience the Ngorongoro Crater of television documentary land. Note that it is forbidden to descend to the floor after 16.00, and that a Crater Service Fee of US$250 plus 18% VAT per vehicle is payable every time you enter the crater.

HIKING IN NGORONGORO CONSERVATION AREA

Because the NCA lies outside the national park system, it is permissible to walk and hike along a number of trails covering most main points of interest (but not the crater floor) in the company of an authorised guide. Indeed, you could theoretically spend a fortnight exploring the NCA along a trail network that connects Lake Eyasi in the south to Lake Natron in the north, as well as running west across the plains towards Laetoli and Lake Ndutu and northwest to Oldupai Gorge. Other possible targets for hikers include the Olmoti and Empakaai craters, Mount Lolmalasin (the third-highest in Tanzania), and the remote Gol Mountains. At least five different one-day hiking trails from the crater rim can be arranged at the headquarters at short notice, though it's best to make contact in advance to make sure an armed ranger is available (this can be done through the NCA Information Centre on Boma Road in Arusha; see page 134 for contact details).

Trekking expert Akë Lindstrom notes: 'More ambitiously, multi-day treks from one to six days all the way from Lake Eyasi to Lake Natron via the Crater Highlands are possible. For those with limited time, a superlative option would be to start at Empakaai Crater in the east and trek down to the base of Ol Doinyo Lengai over two days, then transfer by vehicle to the Lake Natron area. Lightweight camps supported by donkeys are the norm as it is very remote and the views are quite simply stunning. A number of tour operators offer this route and there are options of both public and private campsites on this sector.' For more details, contact Akë via Lake Natron Camp (page 243).

If you do take lunch in the crater, there are two main picnic sites. The most popular overlooks a hippo pool at Ngoitokitok Springs, and tends to be enlivened by a flock of black kites that have become adept at swooping down on tourists and snatching the food from their hands. The other picnic site is in Lerai Forest close to the start of the main ascent road. Both sites now have clean ablution blocks and there is also a stall selling freshly brewed coffee and other drinks at Ngoitokitok Springs.

Empakaai and Olmoti craters The NCA protects two major craters other than Ngorongoro, both relicts of the volcanic activity that have shaped the Crater Highlands over the past few million years. These are the Empakaai and Olmoti craters, and while both are dwarfed in size and reputation by the peerless Ngorongoro, they are also well worth a visit, offering a welcome opportunity to break the typical safari regime of twice-daily game drives with a stiff steep walk in lovely mountain scenery. Furthermore, the view from the rim of Empakaai has to rank among the most spectacular in East Africa.

The more alluring of the two craters is **Empakaai**, which is around 540m deep and has a diameter of almost 8km. The crater floor, enclosed by sheer forested cliffs, supports a sparkling soda lake that covers about half of its area and has a depth of around 60m. The emerald lake's shallows are frequently tinged pink with thousands of flamingos, and a variety of other aquatic birds are common, too. As for mammals, elephant and leopard are still present in the area, but bushbuck, buffalo and blue monkey are more likely to be seen, especially on the crater rim.

The drive from Ngorongoro to Empakaai takes around 90 minutes, leaving from the crater rim close to the Sopa Lodge. A 4x4 is required, and if you want to hike to the crater floor you need to stop en route at Nainokanoka village to pick up a mandatory armed ranger for US$20. Past Nainokanoka, the road descends to the grassy bowl of the Embulbul Depression, which dips to a low point of 2,325m at the bases of the 3,260m Mount Losirua and 3,648m Lolmalasin (the highest point in the Crater Highlands, and third-highest peak in Tanzania). The road then climbs Empakaai's outer slopes, passing through alpine moorland and lush Afromontane forest, before reaching the rim and its fantastic views over the crater to Ol Doinyo Lengai and, on very clear days, Kilimanjaro and Lake Natron.

A road circles part of the forested rim, which reaches an elevation of 3,200m in the east. An excellent footpath to the crater floor was constructed in 2008 – a steep but wonderful walk that takes around 45 minutes each way, longer if you're looking out for the (plentiful) forest birds – which definitely requires decent walking shoes. There is a campsite with rustic ablution facilities on the crater rim a few metres from the start of the footpath, but no other accommodation in the area.

If that walk hasn't sapped your energy, the smaller and less dramatic **Olmoti Crater**, a sunken caldera situated close to Nainokanoka, is worth a stop on the way back to Ngorongoro. A motorable track leads from Nainokanoka to a ranger post further west, from where the crater rim can only be reached on foot, following a footpath through montane forest that takes about 30 minutes up and 20 minutes back down. From the ranger post it is a half-hour walk to the rim. This is a shallow crater, covered in grass and bisected by a river valley, and it offers good grazing for Maasai cattle and also sometimes supports a few antelope. From the viewpoint at the rim, you're bound to see pairs of augur buzzard cartwheeling high in the sky, and might also catch a glimpse of the mighty cliff-loving Verreaux's eagle. On a clear day, the viewpoint also offers glimpses of the distant southern wall of Ngorongoro Crater, and you can follow a short footpath to the seasonal Munge Waterfall, where the eponymous river leaves the crater.

Oldupai Gorge It's difficult to believe today perhaps, but for much of the past 2 million years the seasonally parched plains around Oldupai – the Maasai name for the sisal plant, often but incorrectly transcribed as Olduvai – were submerged beneath a lake that formed an important watering hole for local animals and our hominid ancestors. This was a fluctuating body of water, at times expansive, at other times drying up altogether, creating a high level of stratification accentuated by sporadic deposits of fine ash from the volcanoes that surrounded it. Then, tens of thousands of years ago, volcanic activity associated with the rifting process caused the land to tilt, and a new lake formed to the east. The river that flowed out of this new lake gradually incised a gorge through the former lakebed, exposing layers of stratification up to 100m deep. Oldupai Gorge thus cuts through a chronological sequence of rock beds preserving a practically continuous fossil record of life on the plains over the past 2 million years.

The significance of Oldupai Gorge was first recognised by the German entomologist Professor Katwinkle, who stumbled across it in 1911 while searching for insect specimens. Two years later, Katwinkle led a palaeontological expedition to the gorge, and unearthed a number of animal fossils before the excavations were abandoned at the outbreak of World War I. In 1931, the palaeontologist Louis Leakey visited the long-abandoned diggings and realised that the site provided ideal conditions for following the hominid fossil record back to its beginnings. Leakey found ample evidence demonstrating that ancient hominids had occupied the site, but lacking financial backing, his investigations went slowly and frustratingly refused to yield any truly ancient fossilised hominid remains.

The pay-off for the long years of searching came in 1959 when Louis's wife, Mary Leakey, an accomplished palaeontologist in her own right, discovered a heavy fossilised cranium whose jawbone displayed unambiguous human affinities but was also clearly unlike any other fossil documented at the time. Nicknamed 'nutcracker man' in reference to its bulk, the cranium proved to belong to a robust Australopithecine that lived and died on the ancient lakeshore around 1.75 million years earlier (hominid taxonomy being a somewhat fluid science, the Leakeys named their discovery *Zinjanthropus boisei*, but it was later reclassified as *Australopithecus boisei*, and is now usually designated *Paranthropus boisei*). And while 'nutcracker man' would later be superseded by more ancient fossils unearthed elsewhere in East Africa, it was nevertheless a critical landmark in the history of palaeontology: the first conclusive evidence that hominid evolution stretched back over more than a million years and had been enacted on the plains of East Africa.

This important breakthrough shot the Leakeys' work to international prominence, and with proper funding at their disposal, a series of exciting new discoveries followed, including the first fossilised remains of *Homo habilis*, a direct ancestor of modern man that would have dwelt on the lakeshore contemporaneously with its Australopithecine cousin. After Louis's death in 1972, Mary Leakey continued working in the area until she retired in 1984. In 1976, at the nearby site of Laetoli, she discovered the 3.6-million-year-old footprints made by a party of early hominids that had walked through a bed of freshly deposited volcanic ash – still the most ancient hominid footprints ever found.

Reopened in 2018 following extensive reconstruction and expansion, the excellent Oldupai Gorge Museum (⊕ -2.99471, 35.35169; **w** ncaa.go.tz/pages/the-archaeological-sites; entrance US$30pp) makes for a thoroughly rewarding diversion when driving between the Crater Highlands and Serengeti National Park. The museum comprises a circular sequence of five huts housing various displays relating to major palaeontological finds at Oldupai and elsewhere in East Africa. These include a replica of the Laetoli footprints, dioramas of early hominids, reproductions of several important hominid fossils (including 'nutcracker man', the Taung skull from South Africa and Ethiopia's even older 'Lucy') and fossils of extinct wildlife including gigantic species of buffalo, hippo and gelada, a giraffe with elaborate antlers and a bizarre antelope with long decurved horns. There's also a viewpoint over the gorge, and the entrance fee includes optional guided visits to the Mary Leakey Living Museum and *Zinjanthropus boisei* discovery site, both of which lie within the gorge, as well as a peculiar isolated dune known as the Shifting Sands some 10km to the northwest.

To get to Oldupai Gorge and the museum from Ngorongoro, follow the main road towards the Serengeti's Naabi Hill Gate for 22km past the top of the Seneto descent road until you see the prominent roadside Oldupai Gorge Monument to your right. Turn right here, and you'll reach the museum after 5km. There is a small coffee shop in the museum, and a picnic site outside where evolutionary diversity is represented by the variety of colourful – and very alive – dry-country birds including red-and-yellow barbet, slaty-coloured boubou, rufous chatterer, speckle-fronted weaver and purple grenadier.

12

Serengeti National Park

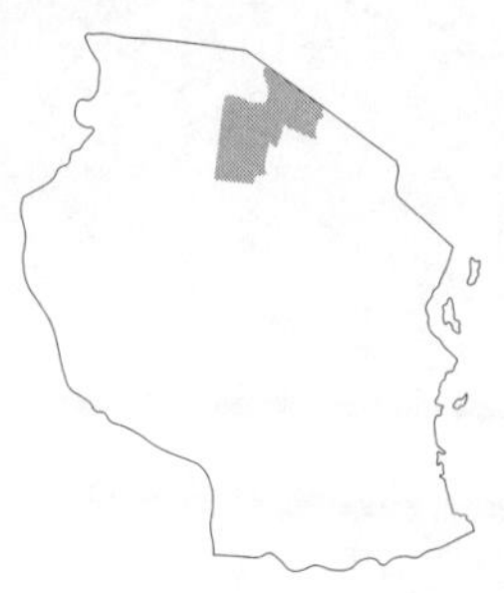

Tanzania's oldest and most famous national park, the 14,763km^2 Serengeti (m +255 689 062243; e serengeti@tanzaniaparks.go.tz) is the centrepiece of a twice-larger cross-border savannah ecosystem that hosts an unimpeded 1,000km annual migration comprising at least 4 million wildebeest and other ungulates. A UNESCO World Heritage Site since 1981, Serengeti National Park also probably stands as Africa's finest all-round safari destination, thanks not only to its singularly spectacular wildebeest migration but also to the unusually dense populations of lions and other large carnivora that inhabit its plains. Sceptics might fear that such a heavily hyped destination is unlikely to match expectations, but our experience over more than a dozen Serengeti safaris over the last 30 years is that this iconic park seldom disappoints: the variety and volume of its wildlife truly is second to none, as is the liberating sense of space attached to exploring its immense plains.

HISTORY

Much of the area now protected within Serengeti National Park was formerly inhabited by the Maasai (page 254), who grazed their cattle on the eastern plains, but had a more sporadic presence in the west due to the seasonal profusion of tsetse flies, which carry the parasite responsible for *nagama* (a disease that can be fatal to cows). The Maasai are actually relatively recent arrivals to the region, having migrated there from the north in the 17th century, when they forcefully displaced their Datoga predecessors. The name Serengeti derives from the Maa word 'siringit', meaning 'Endless Plain', and it most properly refers to the short-grass plains of the southeast rather than the whole park. The notorious inhospitality of the Maasai meant that the Serengeti remained little known to outsiders until after World War I, when the first European hunters moved in to bag its plentiful wildlife.

Serengeti National Park was gazetted in 1951 and in its original incarnation it also incorporated what is now the Ngorongoro Conservation Area (NCA). However, when the area's Maasai residents realised they were threatened with forceful eviction from the entirety of the newly gazetted park, they staged widespread protests that led to a compromise wherein the NCA was excised from the park and the Maasai were allowed to live and graze their cattle there. The Serengeti became world famous partly as a result of the pioneering work of German zoologist Professor Bernhard Grzimek (pronounced 'Jimek'), who served as president of the Frankfurt Zoological Society (FZS) for 40 years prior to his death in 1987. Grzimek was the author and director of the book and Academy Award-winning film *Serengeti Shall Not Die*, both of which were released to public acclaim in 1959. Tragically, Bernhard's son Michael died in an aeroplane crash over the Serengeti aged just 24, and is buried at Heroes Point on the Ngorongoro Crater rim. The FZS still plays an important role in conservation and research within the national park.

FLORA

Much of the Serengeti comprises flat plains whose fertile soil is essentially volcanic soil deposited by Ngorongoro and other calderas in the Crater Highlands to the east. The main vegetation type is open grassland, with the two most common species being *Sporobolus ioclados* and *Digitaria macroblephora*, both of which have shallow roots and form the main diet for the ecosystem's abundant grazers. Another common species in some areas is *Themeda triandra*, a taller grass that turns dark red when dry, and is consumed by wildebeest when more nutritious shorter grasses are unavailable. Parts of the Serengeti – particularly in the north and west – support a denser cover of deciduous woodland dominated by the gum-bearing African myrrh (*Commiphora africana*) and acacia trees such as the iconic umbrella thorn (*Vachellia tortilis*) and shrubbier whistling thorn (*Vachellia drepanolobium*).

There is little permanent water in the Serengeti, though perennial rivers such as the Mara and Grumeti support narrow strips of evergreen woodland, usually comprising various palms and fruiting ficus trees, the yellow-barked fever-tree (*Vachellia xanthophloea*), and the sausage tree (*Kigelia africana*), which is named for its heavy (up to 5kg) elongated fruits much favoured by elephants. Many parts of the Serengeti are studded with *koppies* (a Dutch or Afrikaans word literally meaning 'little heads'), isolated granitic outcrops that rise above the surrounding blanket of flat volcanic soil. Two magnificent trees commonly associated with koppies are fruiting rock figs such as *Ficus abutilifolia*, whose strong roots have been known to split boulders, and the cactus-like candelabra tree (*Euphorbia candelabrum*), a succulent whose deadly white latex was once harvested as a poison by hunter-gatherers.

The most conspicuous and worrying of several invasive species found in the Serengeti is the Mexican gold poppy (*Argemone mexicana*), a yellow-flowered perennial introduced to the Crater Highlands a few years back as a stowaway in a shipment of wheat seeds. This aggressive weed has spread profusely in recent years,

SERENGETI NATIONAL PARK

For listings, see from page 283

Where to stay

1 &Beyond Grumeti Serengeti Tented Camp ... D3
2 &Beyond Klein's Camp ... F2
3 Dunia Camp ... E5
4 Faru Faru Lodge ... D3
5 Four Seasons Safari Lodge ... E3
6 Ikoma Bush Camp ... E3
7 Kirawira Luxury Serena Camp ... C3
8 Lake Masek Camp ... F6
9 Lamai Serengeti ... E2
10 Lemala Kuria Hills Lodge ... E2
11 Little Okavango ... C3
Lobo Campsite ... (see 12)
12 Lobo Wildlife Lodge ... H2
Mapito Tented Camp ... (see 6)
13 Mbalageti Serengeti ... D4
14 Mbuzi Mawe Tented Camp ... F3
Mkombe's House ... (see 8)
15 Namiri Plains ... F4
16 Ndutu Safari Lodge ... E6
17 Sabora Camp ... C3
18 Sanctuary Kusini ... E6
19 Sasakwa Lodge ... D3
20 Sayari Camp ... E2
21 Serengeti Central Wilderness Camp ... E4
22 Serengeti Migration Camp ... F3
23 Serengeti Sametu Camp ... C5
24 Serengeti Serena Lodge ... E4
25 Serengeti Sopa Lodge ... E4
26 Seronera Wildlife Lodge ... A5
27 Speke Bay Lodge ... B4
Tanapa Resthouse & campsites ... (see 26)

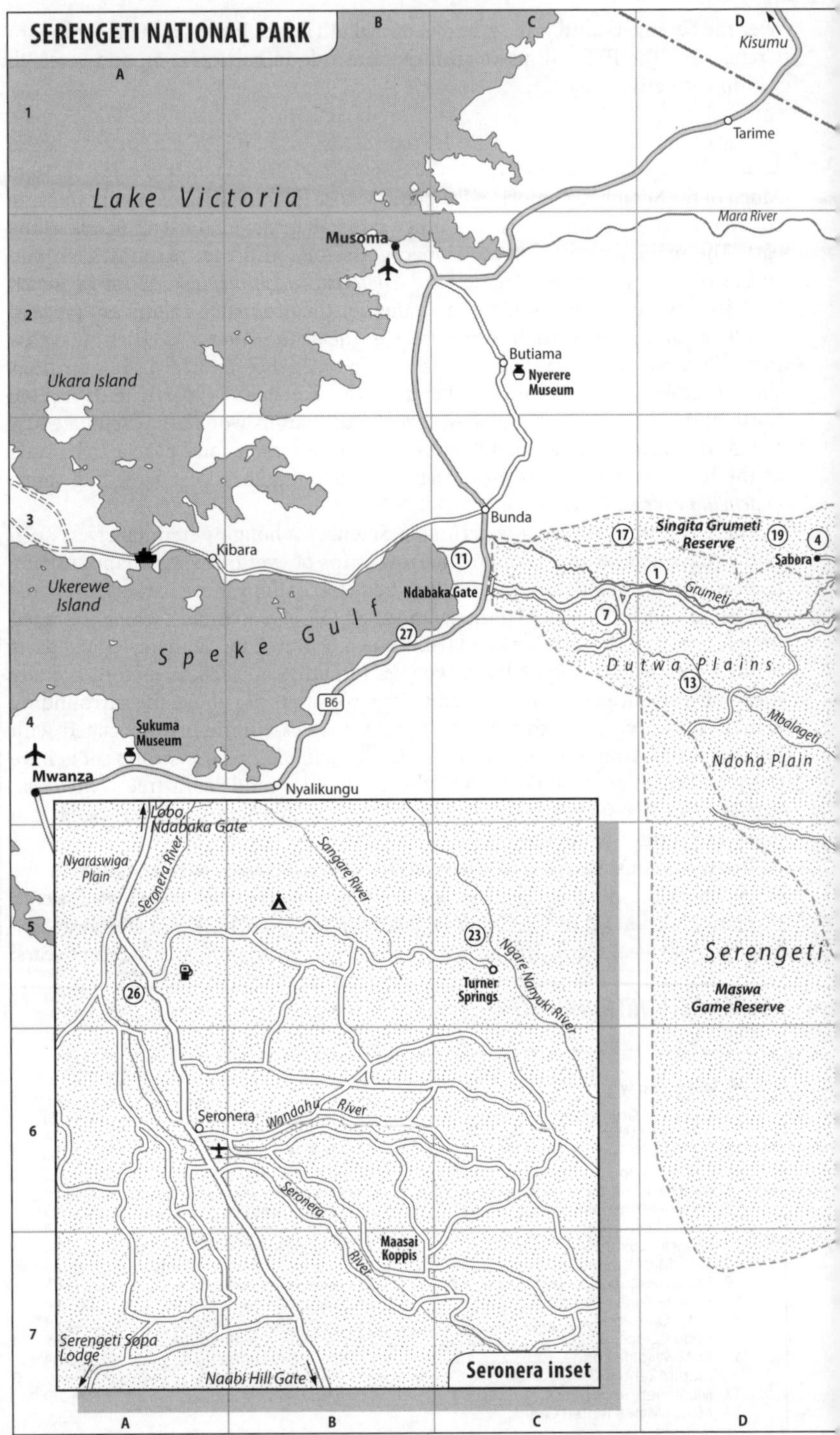
SERENGETI NATIONAL PARK
Kisumu
Tarime
Lake Victoria
Mara River
Musoma
Butiama
Nyerere Museum
Ukara Island
Bunda
Kibara
Singita Grumeti Reserve
Sabora
Ukerewe Island
Ndabaka Gate
Grumeti
Speke Gulf
Dutwa Plains
B6
Mbalageti
Sukuma Museum
Ndoha Plain
Mwanza
Nyalikungu
Lobo, Ndabaka Gate
Nyaraswiga Plain
Seronera River
Sangare River
Turner Springs
Ngare Nanyuki River
Serengeti
Maswa Game Reserve
Seronera
Wandahu River
Seronera River
Maasai Koppis
Serengeti Sopa Lodge
Naabi Hill Gate
Seronera inset

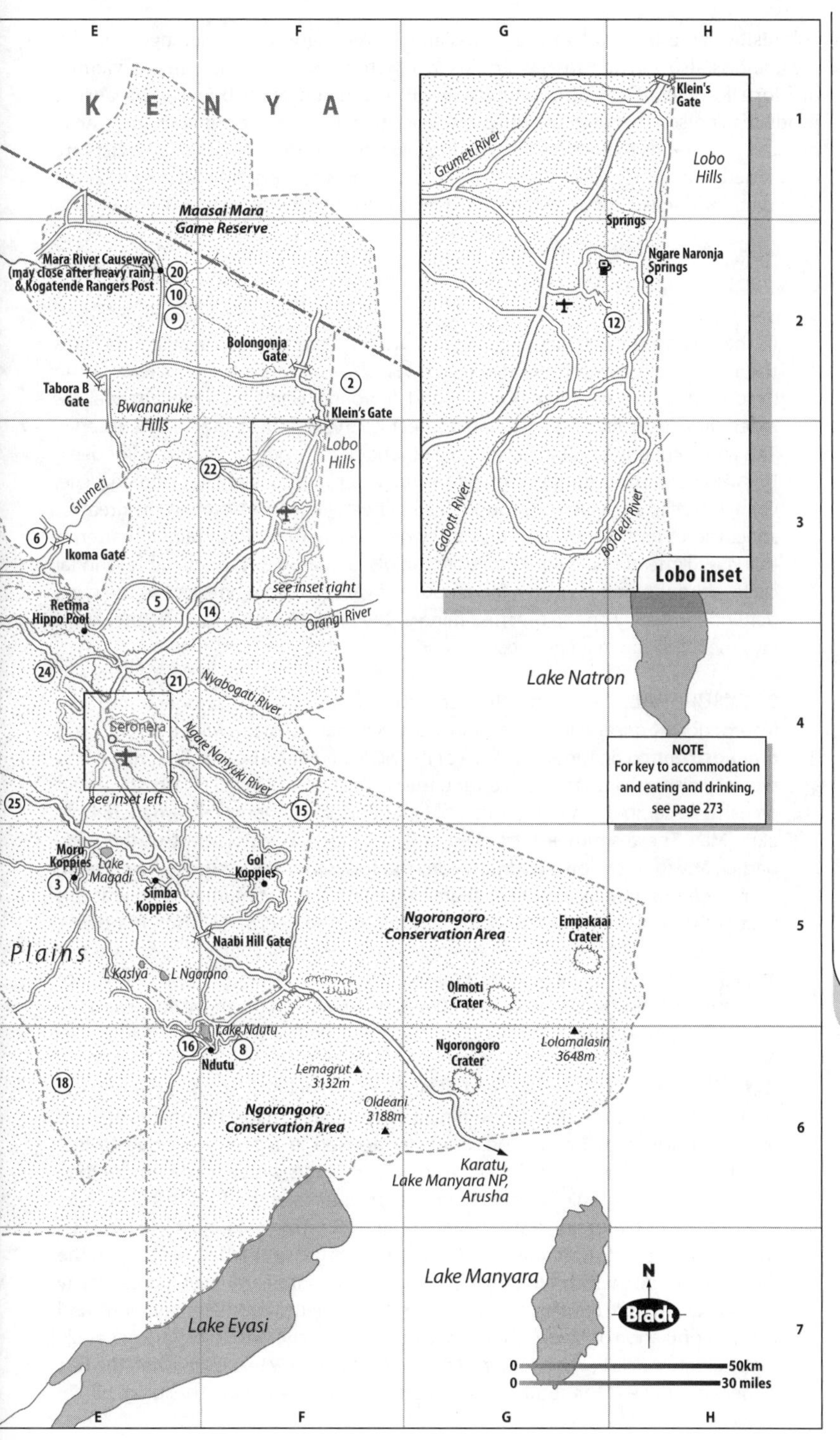
KENYA
Maasai Mara Game Reserve
Mara River Causeway (may close after heavy rain) & Kogatende Rangers Post
Bolongonja Gate
Tabora B Gate
Bwananuke Hills
Klein's Gate
Lobo Hills
Grumeti
Ikoma Gate
see inset right
Retima Hippo Pool
Orangi River
Nyabogati River
Seronera
Ngare Nanyuki River
see inset left
Moru Koppies
Lake Magadi
Simba Koppies
Gol Koppies
Naabi Hill Gate
Plains
L Kasiya
L Ngorono
Lake Ndutu
Ndutu
Lemagrut 3132m
Oldeani 3188m
Ngorongoro Conservation Area
Karatu, Lake Manyara NP, Arusha
Lake Eyasi
Lake Manyara
Lake Natron
Empakaai Crater
Olmoti Crater
Ngorongoro Crater
Lolomalasin 3648m
Klein's Gate
Grumeti River
Lobo Hills
Springs
Ngare Naronja Springs
Gabott River
Boldedi River
Lobo inset
NOTE
For key to accommodation and eating and drinking, see page 273
N
Bradt
0 50km
0 30 miles

colonising large tracts of former grassland in the Ngorongoro-Serengeti border area, and is also starting to appear closer to Seronera, for instance in the vicinity of Moru Koppies. The exotic poppy's spread is difficult to curb, partly because it produces a poison that impedes the growth of naturally occurring grasses, and partly because it responds to burning by growing back even more profusely. Ecologists are concerned that it might eventually replace large tracts of the grassland on which the Serengeti's immense ungulate biomass depends to survive.

THE GREAT MIGRATION

Serengeti National Park is the largest and most ecologically important component in the unfenced 31,000km^2 Serengeti–Mara ecosystem, which also incorporates the more easterly Ngorongoro Conservation Area, the southerly Maswa Game Reserve and the westerly Grumeti and Ikorongo Game Reserves, as well as extending north across the Kenyan border into the Maasai Mara National Reserve. The annual migration of at least 2 million ungulates – predominantly wildebeest but also large concentrations of zebra and lesser numbers of Thomson's gazelle, Grant's gazelle and eland – through the Serengeti–Mara ecosystem is the greatest spectacle of its type anywhere in the world. Dictated by local rainfall patterns, this 1,000km annual migration does follow a reasonably predictable annual cycle, although there is also a fair amount of variation from one year to the next, dependent mainly on the precise timing of the rainy seasons. The cycle breaks up into the following main periods:

DECEMBER–APRIL The plains that stretch southeast from Seronera into the Ngorongoro Conservation Area form the Serengeti's main wildebeest calving grounds, centred on the Ndutu area of the NCA–Serengeti border. The wildebeest typically disperse into this area during the short rains, which fall in late November or early December, and stay put until the end of the long rains, generally in early May. These southeastern plains are the most accessible part of the park, particularly for those on a budget safari, and this is a fantastic time to be on safari in the Serengeti thanks to the lush green scenery. The optimum time to visit this area is the peak calving season (usually centred on February) when hundreds, even thousands, of calves are dropped daily, and predator concentrations are also at their peak. In March and April, you won't see the migration itself, but it's not uncommon to encounter herds of 10,000-plus animals on the move, following the rain to greener pastures.

MAY–JULY Usually towards the end of April, the wildebeest and their entourage start to congregate on the southern plains in preparation for the long northward migration. The actual migration, regularly delayed in recent years due to late rain, might start any time from late April to early June, with a herd of more than a million migrating animals marching in a braying column of up to 40km long, one of the most impressive spectacles in the world. The major obstacle faced by the wildebeest on this migration is the crossing of the Grumeti River through the Western Corridor, which typically occurs from June into early July. A great many animals die in the crossing, many of them taken by the Grumeti's ravenous and prolific population of outsized crocodiles, and the first herds to cross are generally at the greatest risk. For this reason, it can take up to two weeks from when the first wildebeest arrive at the southern bank of the river for the actual crossing to begin,

FAUNA

Although the most recent full census for Serengeti National Park was undertaken way back in the 1980s, it can safely be said that it supports the highest large mammal biomass remaining anywhere in Africa. Ungulate populations associated with the greater Serengeti include around 2 million wildebeest, 300,000 plains zebra, 750,000 Thomson's gazelle, 30,000 Grant's gazelle, 70,000

by which time thousands upon thousands of wildebeest are congregated in the Western Corridor.

AUGUST–NOVEMBER Following the great northward sweep across the Grumeti, the ungulates usually cross the Mara River in August, before dispersing across the plains of the northwest. Conventional wisdom has it that August–October is a bad time to visit the Serengeti, because the wildebeest have crossed the Kenyan border into the Maasai Mara National Reserve. In reality, however, about half of the wildebeest stay in the northwest Serengeti over these months, and game viewing can be excellent, assuming that you can afford to base yourself at one of the exclusive tented camps in the Mara River area. Here, relatively small herds of wildebeest – typically between 500 and a few thousand – frequently travel back and forth between the northern and southern banks of the Mara River in response to changes in the local rainfall pattern, a truly spectacular event. In October, sometimes earlier, the animals generally cross the Mara River one last time and start to plod back southward to the short-grass plains of the southeast, and there is a good chance of catching the southward migration in the Lobo area between late October and mid-November. The wildebeest usually reach the short-grass plains around Ndutu in late November, when the cycle starts all over again.

WHEN SHOULD YOU VISIT? Whether it is worth planning your safari dates around the migration is a matter of choice. With the best will in the world, it would be practically impossible to ensure that a few days in the Serengeti will coincide with the exact date of a major river crossing, which is the most spectacular event in the migration calendar. On the other hand, if you choose the right part of the Serengeti – the southeast from December–May, the Western Corridor from May–July, the Mara River area from July–October, and the Lobo area from October–November – large herds of grazers should be easy enough to locate and there's a fair chance of witnessing a more spectacular migrational movement or river crossing.

On the other hand, bearing in mind that most predators and ungulate species other than zebra and wildebeest are strongly territorial and do not stray far from their core territory over the course of any given year, there is a lot to be said for avoiding the migration. Most lodges and camps now charge substantially lower rates during April and May, with a knock-on effect on the rates offered by safari companies that suddenly become hungry for business. Furthermore, the safari circuit as a whole is far less crowded outside of peak seasons, and in our experience the Serengeti, irrespective of season, will still offer game viewing to equal that of any game reserve in Africa.

SERENGETI BIRDS

The Serengeti National Park, although popularly associated with grassland and open savannah, is in fact a reasonably ecologically varied entity. The western part of the national park consists of broken savannah, interspersed with impenetrable stands of whistling thorns and other acacias, and run through by the perennial Grumeti River and an attendant ribbon of riparian forest. The north, abutting Kenya's Maasai Mara National Reserve, is unexpectedly hilly, particularly around Lobo, and it supports a variety of more or less wooded savannah habitats. So, while the actual Serengeti Plains in the southeast of the park do support the relatively limited avifauna you tend to associate with open grassland, the national park ranks with the best of them in terms of avian variety. A working Serengeti checklist compiled by Schmidt in the 1980s tallied 505 species, and at least 30 new species have been added since 1990.

The Serengeti–Mara ecosystem is one of Africa's Endemic Bird Areas (EBA), hosting five bird species found nowhere else, some of which are confined to the Tanzanian portion of the ecosystem. These 'Serengeti specials' are easy to locate and identify within their restricted range. The **grey-throated spurfowl**, a common roadside bird around the park headquarters at Seronera, is easily distinguished from the similar red-throated spurfowl by the white stripe below its red mask. In areas of woodland, parties of exquisite **Fischer's lovebird** draw attention to themselves by their incessant screeching and squawking as they flap energetically between trees. If the endemic spurfowl and lovebird are essentially local variations on a more widespread generic type, not so the **rufous-tailed weaver**, a fascinating bird placed in its own genus, but with nesting habits that indicate an affiliation to the sparrow-weavers. The rufous-tailed weaver is significantly larger and more sturdily built than most African ploceids, and its scaly feathering, pale eyes and habit of bouncing around boisterously in small flocks could lead to it being mistaken for a type of babbler – albeit one with an unusually large bill!

impala, 30,000 topi, 15,000 Coke's hartebeest, 7,000 eland, 3,000 waterbuck and 4,000 Maasai giraffe. Other less conspicuous antelope species include Kirk's dik-dik, klipspringer, and small numbers of roan, oryx, oribi and waterbuck. There are also significant numbers of warthog, hippo, olive baboon and vervet monkey. The Western Corridor is home to two localised primate species: an isolated and seldom-seen population of the largely terrestrial patas monkey, as well as the troops of black-and-white colobus that haunt the riparian woodland along the Grumeti River.

As recently as the turn of the millennium, elephants were quite scarce in the Serengeti, but an aerial survey undertaken in 2014 counted more than 8,000 individuals in the Serengeti–Mara ecosystem, as compared with the 1986 tally of around 2,000. Some sources attribute this massive increase to greater persecution outside protected areas, but whatever the cause, elephants are visibly more common than they were even ten years ago, with the greatest concentrations to be found in the north. The same survey indicated that the buffalo population probably stands at 50,000–70,000. The park's black rhino population today stands at fewer than 50 individuals, as compared with 700 in the mid 1970s, and is restricted to the vicinity of Moru Koppies in the far southeast, and the Mara River area in the far north.

Of the two other Serengeti–Mara EBA endemics, the most visible and widespread is the **Usambiro barbet**, a close relative of the slightly smaller D'Arnaud's barbet, which also occurs in the region but lacks the full white-on-black spotted chest band. Altogether more elusive is the **grey-crested helmetshrike**, which strongly resembles the more widespread white-crested helmetshrike but is larger, has a more upright grey crest, and lacks an eye wattle. Although this striking bird indulges in typically conspicuous helmet-shrike behaviour, with small parties streaming noisily from one tree to the next, it is absent from the southern Serengeti, and thinly distributed in the north, where it is often associated with stands of whistling thorns. Another localised species associated with whistling thorns, the Karamoja apalis is most likely to be seen in the Western Corridor.

Endemic chasing will be a priority of any serious birding visit to the Serengeti, but the mixed woodland and grassland offers consistently good birdwatching, including many species that will delight non-birders. The world's largest bird, the ostrich, is common; indeed it is thought that the Serengeti supports the largest remaining wild population of these flightless giants. It is also an important stronghold for other primarily terrestrial heavyweights such as Kori bustard, secretary bird and southern ground hornbill. Perhaps the most distinctive of the park's smaller birds is the lilac-breasted roller, often seen perched on trees alongside the road. Highlights are inevitably subjective, but include a breeding colony of Jackson's golden-backed weaver at &Beyond Grumeti Serengeti Tented Camp, the magnificent black eagle soaring above the cliffs at Lobo, and up to six different vulture species squabbling over a kill. And there is always the chance of an exciting 'first'. Recent additions to the Tanzanian bird list from the Serengeti include European turtledove (1997), short-eared owl (1998), long-tailed nightjar, black-backed cisticola and swallow-tailed kite (2000). In 2001, close to the Grumeti River, we were fortunate enough to see (and photograph) the first golden pipit ever recorded in the national park.

The success of most first-time safaris lies in the number and quality of the big cat encounters. There is something infinitely compelling about these animals, a fascination that seems to affect even the most jaded of safari drivers, many of whom are leopard obsessives, content to drive up and down the Seronera Valley all day in the search for a tell-tale tail dangling from a tree. And when it comes to big cats, the Serengeti rarely disappoints. The Tanzanian side of the greater Serengeti ecosystem supports an estimated 2,500–3,000 lions, probably the largest single population left anywhere in Africa, and hundreds of resident lions stalk the plains around Seronera, as well as Simba, Moru and Gol koppies close to the main Ngorongoro road. Here, it's normal to see two or three prides in the course of one game drive. Sociable, languid and deceptively pussycat-like, lions are most often seen lying low in the grass or basking on rocks, though several Serengeti prides are increasingly given to languishing in the trees on hot days.

Leopard numbers are unknown, due to their secrecy, but a recent estimate would suggest the national park supports between 750 and 1,000 individuals. Leopards are present throughout the park, but most likely to be seen in the Seronera Valley, where they are highly habituated and might spend hours languishing conspicuously on an acacia bough, seemingly unperturbed by the presence of dozens of safari vehicles and their noisy passengers. Cheetahs, too, are frequently sighted: the park's estimated population of 250–500 is densest in the open grasslands around Seronera and further east towards Ndutu. In direct contrast to their more languid cousins, these streamlined, solitary creatures are most normally seen pacing the plains with the air of an agitated greyhound.

The real rarity among the Serengeti's larger predators is the African wild dog, which was very common there until the 1970s. By 1991, however, the park's wild dog population had dwindled to near-extinction as a result of canid-borne diseases, persecution by farmers living on the park's periphery, and possibly competition from lions and hyenas. Fortunately, wild dogs are very mobile and wide-ranging animals, and sightings have been reported with increased frequency over recent years, particularly in the far north and the adjacent Loliondo Game Controlled Area. Indeed, following a series of reintroductions from elsewhere, the wild dog population of the Tanzanian part of the Serengeti–Mara ecosystem is thought to stand at around 120 adults split between 10 packs, most of whose territory is focussed on Loliondo.

Of the other predators that can be seen in the Serengeti, spotted hyenas are very common, perhaps more numerous than lions. Golden jackals and bat-eared foxes appear to be the most abundant canid species on the plains around Seronera, while black-backed jackals are reasonably common in the thicker vegetation towards

AVOIDING THE CROWDS

Many visitors whose experience of the Serengeti is limited to the Seronera area complain that the park is uncomfortably crowded, and that any worthwhile sighting attracts a gaggle of safari vehicles within a few minutes. To some extent, this reputation is justified: Seronera is the most accessible part of the park, coming from the direction of Arusha, and it boasts the highest concentration of camping and lodge facilities, so that game-viewing roads within a 5–10km radius tend to carry an uncharacteristically high level of vehicular traffic.

This situation is exacerbated by the tendency of the budget safari companies that favour Seronera to impose heavy budgetary restrictions on drivers, discouraging them from burning excess fuel to explore further afield. Furthermore, some of the safari industry's obsession with the Big Five and large predators has created a mindset where drivers tend to rely heavily on radio messages from other drivers to locate the animals they think their clients most want to see. As a result, all vehicles within radio earshot tend to congregate on any such sighting within minutes. Sadly, this all goes to create the common misperception that one of Africa's wildest and most wonderful parks is far more crowded with tourists than is actually the case.

What can you do about this? Well, for one, assuming that you can afford it, it's a good idea to split the Serengeti leg of your safari between two lodges or camps, one set in the heart of the migration – and tourist – action, the other somewhere unseasonal, for instance the far north between November and June, or the western corridor between August and October. It's best to arrange your safari through a company that specialises in more offbeat areas of the park, and whose budget incorporates unlimited mileage. If you work with a cheaper company, try to avoid being based at Seronera. True, this area does usually offer the best wildlife viewing in the park, but many other parts of the Serengeti are almost as good, whilst carrying a significantly lower tourist volume. Failing that, should your itinerary include Seronera, speak to the safari company about what, if any, fuel restrictions they impose on drivers and try to reach an understanding in advance.

Lobo. Driving at dusk or dawn, you stand the best chance of seeing nocturnal predators such as civet, serval, genet and African wildcat.

FEES AND FURTHER INFORMATION

Several guides to the park are available locally. They include the official 72-page booklet *Serengeti National Park*, with good maps and introductory information, and the newer and glossier *Serengeti* published by African Publishing House. Far more detailed is Veronica Roodt's *Tourist Travel & Field Guide to the Serengeti*, which is strong on maps, photographs, GPS points and other information, making it especially useful to self-drivers (see also maps on w tracks4africa.co.za).

The park entrance fee of US$70 per person per 24 hours (discounted to US$60 from 15 March to 15 May) plus 18% VAT can be paid only by Mastercard or Visa. No other cards are accepted, nor is cash. For overnight visitors, a concession or camping fee is also levied: US$60 per person per night for a lodge, special camp or permanent camp in peak season (July to September), dropping to US$50 from October to June) or US$30 per person for a public campsite. For more details, see page 92.

It's also worth bearing in mind that roads around Seronera tend to be busiest during peak game-viewing hours of 07.30–10.00 and 14.00–16.30. So instead of breakfasting in camp, take a packed breakfast and head out as early as possible – game drives are permitted from 06.00 onwards, and even if you ignore the crowding issue, the first hour of daylight is the best time to see predators on the move. Also, bearing in mind that drivers tend to place emphasis on seeking out big cats because they think it's what their clients want, travellers with different priorities should talk them through with the driver – more radically, ask him to switch off his radio, stop worrying about what everybody else might be seeing, and just enjoy what animals you happen to chance upon.

WALKING SAFARIS Wayo Africa (w wayoafrica.com) now offers multi-day walking safaris in designated wilderness sectors of the Serengeti that are all but inaccessible to other tourists. These safaris usually take place out of a simple but well-equipped mobile camp – dome tents with mattresses and bedding, safari-style hot bucket shower, mess tent with food cooked by a trained chef – which serve as a base for long morning hikes and shorter afternoon walks with an experienced armed guide. Alternatively, they can also set up more elaborate four- to ten-night semi-portered itineraries using a moveable camp that relocates daily, though guests need to carry their own tent, blow-up mattress, sleeping bag, clothes and personal toiletries. Generally, the routes follow watercourses so there is no need to carry water. On either type of trek, close-up encounters with the Big Five are commonplace, birding is great, and the night sky dazzling – but the biggest attraction is the opportunity to experience Africa's greatest national park at its most raw and untrammelled, far away from the crowding that often characterises the busier road circuits. Rates start around US$450 per person per day inclusive of transport, guiding, park fees and gear.

NDUTU AND THE SOUTHEASTERN PLAINS

The short-grass plains stretching from the western extreme of the Ngorongoro Conservation Area through the southeast of the national park might be termed the 'classic' Serengeti: a vast open expanse teeming with all manner of wild creatures ranging from the endearing bat-eared fox to the imperious lion, from flocks of habitually panicked ostrich to strutting pairs of secretary birds, and from the gigantic eland antelope to the diminutive mongooses. Except during the rainy season, it is a dry and thinly vegetated area, supporting only two notable lakes: seasonal Ndutu on the Ngorongoro–Serengeti border and the smaller but perennial Masek set entirely within the NCA less than 2km further east. Both lakes are alkaline, but not so salty as to prevent Maasai watering their cattle in them, and form part of the same basin as the paleontologically renowned Oldupai Gorge a short distance further north (page 268).

The southern plains are interspersed with several clusters of rocky hills known as koppies, each of which forms a microhabitat inhabited by non-plains wildlife such as klipspringer, rock hyrax, leopard, rock agama, rock thrushes, mocking chat and various cliff-nesting raptors. As the name suggests, **Simba Koppies**, which straddles the main road between the NCA and Seronera, is particularly good for lion, while the grassland around the more easterly **Gol Koppies** is excellent for cheetah and lion. Although trees flourish on the sides of these koppies, a striking feature of the surrounding plains is its paucity of trees. The most likely explanation for this quirk is that the soil, which consists of volcanic deposits from an ancient eruption of Ngorongoro, is too hard for most roots to penetrate, except where it has been eroded by flowing water.

The southeastern Serengeti is well populated with wildlife all year through, but it's especially rewarding between December and April, when the rains act as a magnet to the migrant herds of wildebeest and zebra. At this time of year, the prime game-viewing area is usually around Lake Ndutu, which lies at the epicentre of the wildebeest dispersal, and offers truly dramatic game viewing during and after the calving season. The acacia woodland around the lakes also supports a quite different selection of birds from other parts of the Serengeti, with the brilliantly coloured Fischer's lovebird being particularly conspicuous in the vicinity of the dead trees where it roosts.

MAASAI ROCK ART

An unusual relic of the Serengeti's former Maasai inhabitants is to be found at Moru Koppies in the form of some well-preserved rock paintings of animals, shields and other traditional military regalia near the base of a small koppie. This is one of the few such sites associated with the Maasai, and the paintings, which are mostly red, black and white, may well have been inspired by the more ancient and more accomplished rock art of the Kondoa area (page 217) – although it's anybody's guess whether they possess some sort of ritual significance, or are purely decorative. On another koppie not far from the rock paintings is an ancient rock gong thought to have been used by the Datoga predecessors of the Maasai – a short but steep scramble up a large boulder leads to the rock gong and a close-by rock whose face is decorated with carved cupolas. Both sites should be inspected carefully from below before you climb the rocks, as lions frequently rest up there.

 **WHERE TO STAY AND EAT** It may cause some confusion that the listings below include all lodges and several seasonal camps based in the Ndutu area, even though some of these technically lie within Ngorongoro Conservation Area. This is because the Ndutu area is an ecological extension of the southern Serengeti Plains, and it essentially provides a 'Serengeti experience' of open plains and large wildebeest herds (especially between December and April). Indeed, despite lying within the NCA, Ndutu isn't well positioned for visiting Ngorongoro Crater. It should be noted, however, that if you stay at a lodge on the NCA side of the border, then crossing over to the Serengeti will attract a separate national park entrance fee. That said, dedicated photographers might be quite happy to skip paying national park fees and stick within the NCA, since – unlike in most parts of the Serengeti – off-road driving is permitted.

Exclusive

Bush Rover Suites Mobile; m +255 713 323318; w tentwithaview.com. This unique & very likeable mobile camp consists of 6 2-storey standing tents whose ground floor comprises a toilet & shower built into the Land Rover used to transport the unit between sites, while the upper floor contains a comfortable tented bedroom with a balcony. This ultimate rooftop tent experience has the added bonus that you can safely watch wildlife from the balcony or stargaze after dark. It usually sets up in the Kusini area from Nov to mid-Mar for the calving season. **$$$$$$**

Lemala Ndutu/Mara Tented Camp Mobile; m +255 682 933933; w lemalacamps.com. This luxury mobile tented camp is situated close to Ndutu airstrip from Dec to Mar, when it is well positioned to catch the migration during calving season. The 12 spacious tents are decorated in classic safari style, with twin or king-size beds, solar-powered lighting & hot water. **$$$$$$$**

✷ **Olakira Camp** Mobile; w asiliaafrica.com. This classic mobile camp is based near Ndutu from Dec to Mar to coincide with the wildebeest calving season. The 9 standing tents have king-size or twin beds, private veranda & en-suite flush toilet & hot shower. **$$$$$$$**

Sanctuary Kichakani Serengeti Camp Mobile; w sanctuaryretreats.com. Taking the exclusive mobile camp concept to its luxurious extreme, Kichakani – a Swahili word meaning 'in the bush' – comprises 10 well-equipped tents whose handsome handcrafted furnishings evoke the Edwardian-style safari experience. It's actually hard to believe the dining area & lounge – a massive wooden deck shaded by a billowing canvas roof & plenty of comfortable seating – belong to a mobile camp rather than a permanent one. Kichakani is based in the southern Serengeti, not far from Kusini, from Dec to Mar, in order to catch the calving season. **$$$$$$$**

✷ **Sanctuary Kusini** [275 E6] ⊕ -3.02267, 34.71629; w sanctuaryretreats.com; ⌚ closed Apr–May. Spaciously laid-out Kusini has a fantastic location among a series of tall black boulders. It is the most remote & exclusive place to stay in the southern Serengeti & especially rewarding over Feb & Mar when immense herds of wildebeest & zebra converge on the area. Elephant, giraffe & buffalo are quite common all year round, while the open plains 30mins' drive away are renowned for cheetah sightings, and a large lion pride resident in the surrounding koppies provides an exciting nocturnal soundtrack. The 12 spacious & luxurious tents each lead out to a wide private balcony with a couch where you can rest up between game drives. Sundowners are usually taken on a rock offering views to Ngorongoro. Kusini lies about 2hrs' drive south of Ndutu or Moru Koppies, but most guests fly in to the eponymous airstrip. **$$$$$$$**

Serengeti Safari Camp Mobile; m +255 787 595908; w nomad-tanzania.com. Established in the early 1990s, Serengeti's oldest mobile camp offers an authentic old-school bush experience in 6 comfortable standing tents with eco-flush toilets & bucket showers. It relocates seasonally in accordance with the predicted movements of the wildebeest migration & is generally located close to Ndutu from Dec to Apr. **$$$$$$$**

Upmarket

Lake Masek Camp [275 F6] ⊕ -3.02909, 35.04722; m +255 785 069944; w twctanzania.com. Blessed with a perfect location overlooking perennial Lake Masek, this friendly camp

SERENGETI BALLOON SAFARIS

Serengeti Balloon Safaris is – no prizes for guessing – the name of a highly reputable company that has been running balloon safaris in the Serengeti since 1989. The safaris leave daily at 06.00 from four different launch sites: Seronera (year-round), Ndutu (Dec–Mar), Kogatende (Jul–Oct) and the Western Corridor (Jun–Oct). Although not cheap, a balloon safari is definitely worth the expense if you can afford it. Gliding serenely above the trees as the sun rises allows you to see the expansive plains from a new and quite thrilling angle. It also offers the chance to see secretive species such as bushbuck and reedbuck, and, because you leave so early in the morning, you are likely to spot a few nocturnal predators. That said, any images you have of sweeping above innumerable wildebeest and zebra may prove a little removed from reality unless you are in the right place at the right time. Launching from Ndutu over December to March, the odds are pretty good, as the large herds tend to congregate there throughout that period. In Seronera or the Western Corridor, you'll only see large herds of ungulates during the exact week or two when animals concentrate in the immediate vicinity – though if you do get lucky, as we did in the Western Corridor in July 2022, the experience is pretty mind-boggling.

The package costs US$599 per person inclusive of a national park ballooning fee of US$50. It includes the transfer from your lodge or camp to the balloon site, a balloon trip of roughly an hour's duration, and a champagne breakfast. The breakfast is set up at a different site every day, depending on which way the balloons are blown, and it's presented with some flourish by the immaculately uniformed waiters who conjure up images of the safaris of old.

Be prepared for a very early start (the transfer from Seronera leaves at 05.30 and from the other lodges at around 04.30), and take some warm clothing, as well as a bag in which you can secure cameras, binoculars, etc, during take-off and landing. Reservations can be made through any safari company or lodge, or directly with Serengeti Balloon Safaris, either online (w balloonsafaris.com) or else at their office at the Seronera visitors' centre. If you want to be certain of a place, it is advisable to book in advance, particularly during high season.

comprises 30 spacious thatch-shaded standing tents set on wooden decks. Photographers will appreciate the early b/fast (from 06.00) & there's a tempting swimming pool. **$$$$$$**

✷ **Ndutu Safari Lodge** [275 E6] ⊕ -3.02001, 34.99705; ☎ 027 254 5856; w ndutu.com. Set within the NCA, this long-serving family-owned retreat, set in thick acacia woodland overlooking seasonal Lake Ndutu, has a low-key bush atmosphere lacking from most other comparably priced lodges in the Serengeti. The 34 small & unfussy stone chalets have netting, hot water & private veranda, while the open-sided bar/restaurant is frequented by a legion of genets by night & Fischer's lovebird nests in the parking area. A great base over Dec–Apr, when the surrounding plains are teeming with wildebeest, Ndutu offers good general game viewing away from the crowds at other times of year. Great value. **$$$$$**

Ndutu Wilderness Camp Mobile; m +255 754 842466; w tanzaniawildernesscamps.com. This sensibly priced mobile camp stands close to Lake Ndutu over Dec-Mar. The standing tents have solar lighting, eco-friendly toilets & comfortable but unpretentious furnishings. It's one of the few camps to offer day & overnight guided walks in the NCA. **$$$$$$**

SERONERA AND THE SOUTH-CENTRAL PLAINS

Serengeti's main focal point of tourist (and other human) activity is the park headquarters at Seronera. This is the site of the park's oldest tourist lodge, as well as a cluster of public and special campsites, the staff village, various research projects, and a visitor information centre that incorporates a small site museum, a picnic area, a coffee shop, and an elevated wooden walkway leading through an informative open-air display.

Ecologically, the plains running immediately southeast from Seronera form a continuum with the Ndutu and NCA border area described on page 276 comprising open grassland interspersed with several clusters of koppies. Wildlife viewing here is superb throughout the year, but peaks from March to May, when the post-calving wildebeest herds can usually be found in the vicinity. As the name suggests, **Simba Koppies**, which straddles the main road between the NCA and Seronera, is particularly good for lion, while the scenic **Moru Koppies**, closer to Seronera, is also reliable for lion and cheetah sightings. Moru Koppies is also home to an estimated 25 black rhinos, descended from a small herd that was reintroduced in the 1990s, but these are unlikely to be seen unless you obtain a special rhino-viewing permit (US$100pp).

The two main waterways in the region are the small but perennial Mbalageti and Seronera rivers, both of which support a thin strip of riparian woodland. The sausage trees and umbrella thorns of the Seronera River Valley rank among the best places in Africa to search for leopards – there are simply too few tall trees for these normally elusive creatures to be as well-hidden as they tend to be in dense woodland. More surprisingly, several lion prides resident along the Seronera River have taken to the trees with increasing regularity in recent years, particularly during the rains, when arboreal lion sightings are possibly more frequent than terrestrial ones.

Fed by the Mbalageti River immediately northeast of Moru Koppies, the small, saline **Lake Magadi** (a common name for lakes, as 'magadi' just means soda or salt) often supports large numbers of aquatic birds, including thousands of flamingos when the water level is suitable. A small hippo pool lies on the Seronera River about 5km south of Seronera along the road back towards the NCA. Far more impressive, however, is the **Retima Hippo Pool**, where up to 100 of these aquatic animals can be seen basking near the confluence of the Seronera and Grumeti rivers about 15km north of the park headquarters.

WHERE TO STAY AND EAT The most established and central accommodation here is the stalwart Seronera Wildlife Lodge, but several other lodges, including Serengeti Serena and Sopa, are also well positioned for exploring the southern plains. The area is home to an ever-growing number of seasonal and semi-permanent tented camps.

Exclusive

✷ **Dunia Camp** [275 E5] ⊕ -2.65612, 34.74334; w asiliaafrica.com. The first & currently only camp in Tanzania to be managed & staffed entirely by women, stylish Dunia offers great year-round game viewing thanks to its proximity to Moru Koppies, with ungulate numbers peaking over Dec–Mar. The 8 spacious tents come with king-size or twin beds, unobtrusive décor brightened up by Maasai fabrics & a spacious veranda with comfortable seating. Hospitality, food & guiding are to the highest standard. **$$$$$$$**

Four Seasons Safari Lodge [275 E3] ⊕ -2.23443, 34.91937; w fourseasons.com. Set amid rocky hills 35km north of Seronera, this opulent lodge is as luxurious as it gets in northern Tanzania (the 77 rooms all come with flatscreen

DSTV, fan, AC, walk-in net, laminate floor & stone-tiled bathroom with tub & shower) but feels more like a misplaced city hotel than a bush camp. Still, taken on its own terms it's a magnificent set-up & ideal for 1st-time safari-goers terrified at the prospect of sharing a tent with lizards or having nothing but canvas separating them from passing lions & elephants. Amenities include an infinity pool overlooking a waterhole that attracts a steady stream of thirsty wildlife, a choice of 3 restaurants, facilities for travellers with disabilities, gym, massage & spa, & a superb exploration centre with cultural, geological & wildlife displays. **$$$$$$$**

✷ **Namiri Plains** [275 F4] ⊕ -2.54742, 35.09903; **w** asiliaafrica.com. Spaced out along the Ngare Nanyuki River 40km east of Seronera, this super-exclusive lodge has an isolated location in an untrammelled corner of the park renowned for offering superb lion & cheetah sightings that guests will often have to themselves. Accommodation is in 10 large & organic-looking cottages constructed with locally sourced stones, decorated with basketwork made by local women & shaded by massive canvas shells. Guiding & cuisine are to the highest standard, while amenities include a swimming pool & spa. **$$$$$$$**

Nomad Serengeti Safari Camp Mobile; page 283. This mobile camp is usually located in the vicinity of Moru Koppies or Seronera over May, early Jun & Nov. **$$$$$$$**

Serengeti Sametu Camp [274 C5] ⊕ -2.47443, 34.99237; **w** karibucamps.com. This exclusive camp comprises 8 comfortable en-suite tents strung out along a wooded ridge overlooking the Ngare Nanyuki River 20km east of Seronera. The proximity to Seronera allows you to conduct some game drives in this wildlife-rich area, but you can also explore the more off-the-beaten-track circuits towards Barafu & Sametu koppies, both of which often host lions & leopards. **$$$$$$$**

Upmarket

Mbuzi Mawe Tented Camp [275 F3] ⊕ -2.22508, 34.96991; **w** serenahotels.com. This pleasant & well-run Serena camp is set among a cluster of ancient granite koppies inhabited by klipspringer antelope (for which the camp is named) & rock hyraxes that lounge on the footpaths like well-fed domestic cats. The 16 spacious en-suite standing tents each contain 2 dbl beds & have a private stone patio. It is a popular base for exploring the Seronera circuit, about an hour's drive to the south, but there is also often excellent wildlife viewing – lion, elephant & large herds of ungulates – on the nearby & relatively quiet Togara Plains, off the road towards Lobo. This is supplemented by the wildebeest migration as it heads southwards in Nov or Dec. **$$$$$$**

✷ **Serengeti Central Wilderness Camp** [274 E4] ⊕ -2.38651, 35.02211; **m** +255 754 842466; **w** tanzaniawildernesscamps.com. This down-to-earth camp comprises 12 en-suite tents with solar lighting, eco-friendly toilets & comfortable furnishings. The central location on the Nyabogati River about 20km east of Seronera offers good year-round game viewing. It can be used as a base for multi-day wilderness trails. **$$$$$$**

Serengeti Serena Lodge [275 E4] ⊕ -2.38192, 34.70308; **w** serenahotels.com. Situated on a hilltop 20km west of Seronera, this attractive 66-room lodge comprises a village-like cluster of Maasai-style dbl-storey *rondawels*, built with slate, wood & thatch to create a pleasing organic feel. The spacious rooms each have 1 sgl & 1 king-size bed, net, fan & hot shower. There is a swimming pool & the buffet meals are exceptional. Game viewing in the surrounding scrub is poor except for when the migration passes through, & it's a good half-hour drive before you reach the main game-viewing circuit east of Seronera Wildlife Lodge. **$$$$$**

Serengeti Sopa Lodge [275 E4] ⊕ -2.59668, 34.67880; **w** sopalodges.com. This ostentatious lodge lies on the slopes of the Nyarboro Hills some 30mins' drive south of Seronera, close to Moru Koppies. The 77 suites each have 2 dbl beds, a small sitting room, a large bathroom, a private balcony & a large window offering a grandstand view over the plains at sunset. Facilities include a swimming pool & game viewing in the vicinity is good, with a high chance of encountering tree-climbing lions on the road north to Seronera & relatively little traffic. **$$$$$$**

Seronera Wildlife Lodge [274 A5] ⊕ -2.43617, 34.82058; **w** hotelsandlodges-tanzania.com. The Serengeti's oldest, most central & largest lodge (with a total of 100 rooms) boasts an unbeatable year-round location for game drives. Built around a granite koppie in the early 1970s, it utilises the natural features to create an unmistakably African character. Unfortunately, the tired-looking décor & indifferent service & food don't quite match the location. **$$$$$**

Moderate

Ikoma Bush Camp [275 E3] ⊕ -2.17608, 34.71118; **m** +255 754 324193; **w** moivaro.com. This unpretentious camp stands in a glade of acacias roughly 3km from the national park outside Ikoma Gate. The land is leased from the nearby village of Robanda & proceeds help fund the local school, water pump, clinic & other community projects. The old-style dbl & twin tents have hot showers & small verandas. Because it lies in a concession outside the park, guided game walks are on offer, while night drives come with a chance of encountering the likes of leopard, genet & more occasionally aardvark. It offers good year-round game viewing but is best in Jun when the migration passes through. Very reasonably priced. **$$$$$**

Mapito Tented Camp [275 E3] ⊕ -2.17864, 34.68065; **m** +255 747 157777; **w** mapito-camp-serengeti.com. Similar in feel to Ikoma Bush Camp & also situated outside Ikoma Gate, this likeable & very affordable camp comprises 12 simple standing tents furnished with a strong African touch & hot showers. The solar-lit mess tent serves hearty home-style meals. There's plenty of avian & mammal activity in the immediate vicinity & activities include guided walks & night drives. **$$$$$**

Budget

Tanapa Resthouse & campsites [274 A5] **m** +255 689 062243; **e** serengeti@tanzaniaparks.go.tz. Some simple bandas & a cluster of 7 **campsites** can be found at the Seronera park headquarters 5km from Seronera Wildlife Lodge. *Both US$30pp*. **$$**

THE WESTERN CORRIDOR

The relatively narrow arm of the Serengeti that stretches westward from Seronera almost as far as the shore of Lake Victoria is generally flatter than the more northerly parts of the park, but moister and more densely vegetated than the southern plains. Aside from a few small isolated mountain ranges, the dominant geographic feature of the Western Corridor is a pair of rivers, the Grumeti and Mbalageti, whose near-parallel west-flowing courses, which run less than 20km apart, support tall ribbons of riparian forest before eventually exiting the national park to empty into Lake Victoria. The characteristic vegetation of the Western Corridor is park-like woodland, interspersed with areas of open grassland and dense stands of the ghostly grey 'whistling thorn' acacias.

Game viewing is pretty good here throughout the year. The broken savannah to the south of the Grumeti River supports substantial resident populations of giraffe, elephant, wildebeest, zebra and other typical plains animals, while the little-visited vistas of open grassland north of the river are especially good for cheetah. The area is also home to the famous 50-strong Grumeti lion pride, which is reputedly the largest anywhere in Africa. The riverine forest along the two rivers harbours a few troops of the exquisite black-and-white colobus monkey, and the Grumeti is also home to plenty of hippos, crocodiles and water-associated birds. The side road to Mbalageti Serengeti is a good place to look for the localised Coke's hartebeest, and the acacia woodland around the junction with the main road is the one place in Tanzania where the localised patas monkey is regularly seen.

Few camping safaris make it this far west, and permanent accommodation is limited to a handful of smallish lodges and camps, so tourist traffic tends to be low. The exception is from late May to July when the migration usually passes through the Western Corridor (although it may stick further east in years of heavy rain) and several mobile camps set up in the vicinity. The crossing of the Grumeti River, usually in late June or early July, is one of the most dramatic sequences in the annual wildebeest migration, and a positive bonanza for a dense population of gargantuan crocodiles.

WHERE TO STAY

Exclusive

✱ **&Beyond Grumeti Serengeti Tented Camp** [274 D3] ⊕ -2.15767, 34.21948; w andbeyond.com; ⌚ closed Apr. The last word in down-to-earth bush luxury, this plush tented camp overlooks an oxbow lake fed by the Grumeti River. Home to a resident hippo pod, it also attracts a steady stream of thirsty wildlife, while the prolific birdlife includes the black-headed gonolek & the localised Karamoja apalis. At night, the place comes alive with a steady chorus of insects & frogs, while hippo & buffalo graze noisily around the tents. Facilities include an outdoor boma for evening meals & a circular swimming pool. The massive standing tents incorporate a king-size bed, walk-in nets, a minibar, a spectacular waterside balcony & outdoor hot showers. The atmosphere is very informal, exceptional food is complemented by excellent house wines, & the service is world class. Expertly guided game drives offer a good chance of encounters with the Grumeti lion pride & venture into little-visited areas inhabited by large herds of elands, topi & buffalo, as well as offering regular sightings of cheetah & spotted hyena. **$$$$$$$**

Bush Rover Suites Mobile; page 283. This unique mobile camp is located in the Western Corridor from May to mid-Jul. **$$$$$$**

Kirawira Luxury Serena Camp [274 C3] ⊕ -2.20807, 34.13591; w serenahotels.com. This plush tented camp, set on an acacia-covered hill offering sweeping views over the Western Corridor, has a distinct *Out of Africa* feel. Each of the 25 standing tents is set on a stilted platform & decorated in classic Edwardian safari style. Facilities include a large swimming pool complete with a small waterfall from a higher plunge pool – it's a lovely place to relax. **$$$$$$**

Nomad Serengeti Safari Camp Mobile; page 283. This top mobile camp is usually located in the Western Corridor over late Jun & Jul. **$$$$$$$**

Singita Grumeti w singita.com. The legendary South African operator Singita has exclusive traversing rights to the 1,400km^2 Grumeti Game Reserve, a northern extension of the Western Corridor, where it operates a trio of 5-star lodges aimed at affluent travellers seeking an exclusive safari experience. The flagship **Sasakwa Lodge** [274 D3] on the eponymous hill offers dramatic elevated views across the verdant plains of the Western Corridor, while the chic, minimalist **Faru Faru Lodge** [274 D3] lies in a wooded area noted for its high mammal & bird diversity, & the more earthy **Sabora Camp** [274 C3] is a tented camp set in the open plains. The wildlife in this formerly undeveloped corner of the greater Serengeti is similar to other parts of the vast ecosystem, but notable population increases have been recorded since 2003. The enterprise employs 600 people, mostly from surrounding communities, & it offers cultural visits to nearby villages. Although wildlife viewing is good all year through, it peaks during Jul–Sep, when the migration is in the area. **$$$$$$$**

Upmarket

Little Okavango [274 C3] ⊕ -2.17282, 33.84532; m +255 713 323318; w tentwithaview.com. This unique new lodge stands outside the national park on a swampy stretch of the Lake Victoria shoreline about 10mins' drive from Ndabaka Gate. Named after Botswana's Okavango swamp, it comprises 7 comfortable stilted bandas connected by a network of wooded walkways above the swamp. Boat trips to a lookout tower & the open waters of the lake are a treat for birders, who can expect to see a wide range of weavers, kingfishers & other swamp-dwellers (a shoebill was recorded close by in August 2022). It's also a great base for game drives in the Western Corridor. **$$$$$**

✱ **Mbalageti Serengeti** [274 D4] ⊕ -2.34021, 34.30903; m +255 622 320042; w mbalageti.co.tz. Perched on the northwestern slopes of Mwamnevi Hill, this relatively large lodge lies 16km south of the main road through the Western Corridor, via the game-rich Dutwa plain & Mbalageti River. There are 14 standard rooms, 24 more luxurious tented chalets & 2 huge executive family suites, all secluded in evergreen woodland running along the ridge & offering a superb view over the river to the Dutwa Plains. The dining area & bar are centred on a swimming pool, which also offers breathtaking views The food is excellent, with different theme buffets every night. Good value. **$$$$$**

Moderate

Speke Bay Lodge [274 B4] ⊕ -2.26700, 33.79673; w spekebay.com. Set on the eastern shore of Lake Victoria, this lovely beachfront lodge has been under the same Dutch owner-managers since it was founded in the mid 1990s. It forms an excellent overnight stop for those coming to the Serengeti from western Kenya or the Lake Victoria region, as well as offering an opportunity for those on lengthy safaris to take a day or 2's break from bouncing through the dusty bush to enjoy the moister environment alongside Africa's largest lake. Only 15mins' drive outside the Ndabaka Entrance Gate, the lodge lies in 40ha of lakeshore woodland close to the Mbalageti River mouth. It offers good birdwatching (250 species recorded, including red-chested sunbird, swamp flycatcher, black-headed gonolek, slender-billed weaver & other lake specials unlikely to be seen in the Serengeti proper), as well as cultural visits by dugout to a nearby fishing village. The cottages have a thatched roof, stone floor, king-size bed, lake-facing balcony & high-quality hardwood & wrought-iron furnishing & finishes. There are also cheaper & more basic standing tents using common showers. *US$270/430 sgl/dbl en-suite bungalow; US$110/200pp sgl/dbl safari tent. All rates FB.* **$$$–$$$$$**

LOBO, LOLIONDO AND THE NORTH-CENTRAL SERENGETI

Wildly beautiful, and relatively untrammelled in comparison to the southern Serengeti, the undulating plains of the North-Central Serengeti are characterised by green hills capped by some spectacular granite outcrops, particularly in the vicinity of Lobo. Here, you will also encounter dense acacia woodland interspersed with tracts of more open grassland, as well as lush ribbons of riparian woodland along the eastern Grumeti River and its tributaries. Partially due to the relatively dense foliage, the North-Central Serengeti doesn't generally match up to the far south in terms of game viewing, but it feels far more remote and carries a relatively low tourist volume.

Wildlife viewing around Lobo generally comes into its own during September and October, when the wildebeest pass through on the southward migration from Kenya to the Serengeti Plains. The area also sometimes hosts large numbers of wildebeest in July, especially in wetter years, when the northward migration tends to use a more easterly route than normal. But even at other times of year, there is plenty to see. The North-Central Serengeti supports most of the park's elephant population, while the Lobo Hills are known for hosting several large lion prides. Cheetah, leopard, spotted hyena and bat-eared fox are also quite common, as is the exquisite serval, a small spotted cat most often seen darting through open grassland shortly after sunrise.

Extending over 4,000km^2 along the northeastern border of the Serengeti and northern border of the NCA, the **Loliondo Game Controlled Area (LGCA)**, reached via Klein's Gate 20km north of Lobo, is an integral part of the wildebeest migration route through the greater Serengeti. Inhabited by the pastoralist Maasai, it effectively functions as a buffer zone to the national park, where cattle herds are frequently seen grazing alongside wild animals. Several lodges lie within the LGCA, on concessions that range in extent from a few dozen to a few thousand hectares. The largest and best of these concessions – indeed, one of the finest game-viewing destinations anywhere in Tanzania – is Klein's Camp, which effectively functions as an exclusive private reserve, and offers superb game viewing as well as optional extras such as night drives and game walks. The LGCA also offers your best chance of seeing African wild dogs in the greater Serengeti ecosystem.

WHERE TO STAY AND EAT

Exclusive

✷ &Beyond Klein's Camp [274 F2] ⊕ -1.83508, 35.24596; **w** andbeyond.com. Set within the LGCA on a hilly 100km^2 private concession bordered by the Serengeti National Park & Grumeti River, Klein's offers a maximum of 20 guests some of the finest & most exclusive wildlife viewing in northern Tanzania. Wildlife is similar to the neighbouring Serengeti, with at least 1 pride of around 20 lions resident & a good chance of encountering 1 of several habituated leopards, but off-road driving is permitted. The hillside camp comprises 10 luxurious bandas with hot shower, king-size bed, walk-in net & a private balcony offering panoramic views. Facilities include a swimming pool & a well-stocked gift shop. Food, service & guiding are to the highest standard. **$$$$$$$**

Serengeti Migration Camp [275 F3] ⊕ -1.92745, 35.01888; **w** elewanacollection.com. Set in the Ndasiata Hills about 20km northeast of Lobo, this exclusive lodge provides accommodation in 20 spacious luxury wood-&-canvas chalets with classic Edwardian-style safari décor & with large balconies overlooking the Grumeti River. The lushly wooded grounds are rustling with birds & lizards, a hippo pool can be seen on the river & the surrounding area supports plenty of lion, leopard, elephant & buffalo. Facilities include a swimming pool, jacuzzi, cocktail bar, library, lounge & a

WEAVERS

Placed by some authorities in the same family as the closely related sparrows, the weavers of the family Ploceidae are a quintessential part of Africa's natural landscape, common and highly visible in virtually every habitat from rainforest to desert. The name of the family derives from the intricate and elaborate nests – typically but not always a roughly oval ball of dried grass, reeds and twigs – that are built by the dextrous males of most species.

It can be fascinating to watch a male weaver at work. First, a nest site is chosen, usually at the end of a thin hanging branch or frond, which is immediately stripped of leaves, probably to prevent snakes from reaching the nest undetected. The weaver then flies back and forth to the site, carrying the building material blade by blade in his heavy beak, first using a few thick strands to hang a skeletal nest from the end of a branch, then gradually completing the structure by interweaving numerous thinner blades of grass into the main frame. Once completed, the nest is subjected to the attention of his chosen partner, who will tear it apart if the result is less than satisfactory, and so the process starts all over again.

All but 12 of the 113 described weaver species are resident on the African mainland or associated islands, with at least 45 represented within Tanzania, all but six of which have a range extending into the north of the country. A full 20 of these Tanzanian species are placed in the genus *Ploceus* (true weavers), which is surely the most characteristic of all African bird genera. Most of the *Ploceus* weavers are slightly larger than a sparrow, and display a strong sexual dimorphism. Females are with few exceptions drab buff- or olive-brown birds, with some streaking on the back, and perhaps a hint of yellow on the belly.

Most male *Ploceus* weavers conform to the basic colour pattern of the 'masked weaver' – predominantly yellow, with streaky back and wings, and a distinct black facial mask, often bordered with orange. Seven Tanzanian weaver species fit this masked weaver prototype more or less absolutely, and a similar number approximate it rather less exactly, for instance by having a chestnut-brown mask, or a full black head, or a black back, or being more chestnut than yellow on the belly. Identification of the masked weavers can be tricky without experience – useful clues are the exact shape of the mask, the presence and extent of the fringing orange, and the colour of the eye and the back.

The golden weavers, of which only four species are present in Tanzania, are also brilliant yellow and/or light orange with some light streaking on the back, but they lack a mask or any other strong distinguishing features. Forest-associated *Ploceus* weavers, by contrast, tend to have quite different and very striking colour patterns, and although sexually dimorphic, the female is often as boldly marked as the male. The most aberrant among these is Vieillot's black weaver, the males viewing platform for sundowners & private meals. Guided game walks can be undertaken along several trails leading out from camp. **$$$$$$$**

Upmarket

✷ **Lobo Wildlife Lodge** [275 H2] ⊕ -2.00304, 35.16753; w hotelsandlodges-tanzania.com. Built in the late 1960s when most tourism to Serengeti came directly from Kenya, this architecturally impressive 75-room former government hotel is built around a koppie crawling with hyraxes & colourful agama lizards, & it offers a fantastic view over the surrounding plains. The location is compromised by mediocre service, food & maintenance, but if you can live with that, the excellent game viewing, innovative architecture, fabulous setting, relative isolation & reasonable rates make it a definite pick. **$$$$$**

of which are totally black except for their eyes, while the extralimital black-billed weaver reverses the prototype by being all black with a yellow face-mask. Among the more conspicuous *Ploceus* species in northern Tanzania are the Baglafecht, spectacled, vitelline masked, lesser masked and black-headed weavers – for the most part gregarious breeders forming single- or mixed-species colonies of hundreds, sometimes thousands, of pairs, often in reed beds and waterside vegetation. Most weavers don't have a distinctive song, but they compensate with a rowdy jumble of harsh swizzles, rattles and nasal notes that can reach deafening proportions near large colonies. One more cohesive song you will often hear seasonally around weaver colonies is a cyclic 'dee-dee-dee-Diederik', often accelerating to a hysterical crescendo when several birds call at once. This is the call of the Diederik cuckoo, a handsome green-and-white cuckoo that lays its eggs in weaver nests.

Oddly, while most East African *Ploceus* weavers are common, even abundant, in suitable habitats, seven highly localised species are listed as range-restricted, and three are regarded to be of global conservation concern. These include the Taveta palm weaver, which is restricted to the plains immediately below Kilimanjaro and is most common in the West Kilimanjaro–Amboseli area and around Lake Jipe, and the Usambara and Kilombero weavers, both endemic to a limited number of sites in eastern Tanzania.

Most of the colonial weavers, perhaps relying on safety in numbers, build relatively plain nests with a roughly oval shape and an unadorned entrance hole. The nests of certain more solitary weavers, by contrast, are far more elaborate. Several weavers, for instance, protect their nests from egg-eating invaders by attaching tubular entrance tunnels to the base – in the case of the spectacled weaver, sometimes twice as long as the nest itself. The grosbeak weaver (a peculiar larger-than-average, brown-and-white weaver of reed beds, distinguished by its outsized bill and placed in the monospecific genus *Amblyospiza*), constructs a large and distinctive domed nest, which is supported by a pair of reeds, and woven as precisely as the finest basketwork, with a neat raised entrance hole at the front.

By contrast, the scruffiest nests are built by the various species of sparrow- and buffalo-weaver, relatively drab but highly gregarious dry-country birds that occur throughout northern Tanzania. The most striking bird in the group is the white-headed buffalo-weaver, which despite its name is most easily identified by its unique bright-red rump. The endemic rufous-tailed weaver, a close relative of the buffalo-weavers, is a common resident of Tarangire, Serengeti and Ngorongoro Conservation Area.

Camping

Lobo Campsite [275 H2] ⊕ -1.99997, 35.16943; **m** +255 689 062243; **e** serengeti@tanzaniaparks.go.tz. Situated a few hundred metres from Lobo Wildlife Lodge, this relatively little-used campsite has a similarly scenic location, an ablution block & rubbish pit. If you decide to stay, you can pop into the lodge for a drink or meal. **$$**

THE MARA RIVER AND THE FAR NORTHWEST

Almost matching the southern Serengeti plains for general game viewing, the northwestern Lamai Wedge is a 100km^2 triangle of sloping grassland that divides the Mara River from the Kenyan border. Accessed from the south via a concrete causeway near Kogatende Rangers Post, this extension of the legendary Maasai Mara National Reserve supports prodigious herds of elephant, eland, topi, gazelle, zebra, wildebeest, buffalo, etc, throughout the year, as well as significant numbers of lion and cheetah, and a small but regularly seen population of black rhino.

Game viewing either side of the Mara River can be little short of mind-boggling when the migration moves into the vicinity between July and September. During this time, large herds of wildebeest frequently gather on one or other side of the river, sometimes milling around for hours, even days, before one brave or foolish individual initiates a sudden river crossing, often for no apparent reason – indeed, it's not unusual for the same group of wildebeest to cross back in the opposite direction within hours of the initial crossing, suggesting that these slow-witted beasts are firm adherents to the maxim that the grass is always greener on the other side.

Prior to the late 1970s, when most safaris entered the Serengeti from Kenya, the far north was quite busy with tourist traffic. The closure of the border between the Serengeti and Maasai Mara to non-residents led to a long lull in casual tourism to the region, partly due to its remoteness from any lodge, and partly due to a period of regular banditry and poaching. The northwest effectively reopened to tourism in 2005, following the opening of Sayari Camp in 2005, and the region is now serviced by quite a number of small camps and lodges, most of which lie to the south of the Mara River near Kogatende and the causeway.

Though it's not as remote as it was 20 years ago, the northwest remains perhaps the most untrammelled and exciting part of the Serengeti, except during the migration season, when the main wildebeest crossing points can be a magnet for large numbers of safari vehicles. Things can get uncomfortably circus-like when an actual crossing takes place, especially if the build-up is slow enough for word of an imminent crossing to spread on the driver grapevine. If you want to see a crossing, it might be difficult to avoid the overcrowding, but given that most of the vehicles are coming from further afield – Lobo and possibly even as far south as Seronera – and are only present from mid morning to mid afternoon, it will help to stay at a camp close to the river and to be out and about in the early morning and late afternoon.

WHERE TO STAY

Exclusive

Bush Rover Suites Mobile; **w** tentwithaview.com; page 283. This exceptional mobile camp moves to the Mara River area over mid-Jul to Oct. **$$$$$$$**

✱ **Lamai Serengeti** [275 E2] ⊕ -1.64537, 34.92183; **m** +255 787 595908; **w** nomad-tanzania.com. This luxurious lodge, situated in the Nyamarumbwa ('Many animal') Hills 12km south of Kogatende, comprises a dozen luxurious & well-lit chalets, with minimalist pastel décor, king-size beds, walk-in netting, massive en-suite bathrooms & large balconies offering grandstand views in all directions. The camp supports plenty of gaudy agama lizards, hyraxes, & many birds (including several localised barbet species) & offers access to a game-viewing circuit through an impressive group of koppies where leopards & lions are often seen sprawled out on the granite boulders. It is also well placed to explore the road network around the Mara River, which is home to a resident group of black rhino & site of frequent wildebeest crossings in migration season. The large swimming pool is a welcome luxury on hot days. **$$$$$$$**

Lemala Kuria Hills Lodge [275 E2] ⊕ -1.64869, 34.88933; **m** +255 682 933933; **w** lemalacamp.com; ⏲ closed Apr & May. This permanent tented camp has a great location in the Kuria Hills about 30mins' drive south of the Mara River. The glass-fronted tented suites are very spacious & all have twin or king-size beds & 24hr electricity, plunge pool & hot water. **$$$$$$$**

Lemala Ndutu/Mara Tented Camp Mobile; page 283. This luxury mobile tented camp relocates from Ndutu to the Mara River area over Jul–Oct, when it is close to 2 major crossing points. **$$$$$$$**

Mkombe's House [275 E2] ⊕ -1.64537, 34.92183; **m** +255 787 595908; **w** nomad-tanzania.com. An extension of Lamai Serengeti, this unique family-oriented lodge comprises a large 4-bedroom house offering expansive views across the distant Mara River into Kenya. Resembling a stylish beach house transplanted to the bush, it has a cool & airy feel, & is decorated in light pastel shades offset by bright splashes of African colour. Some rooms have an optional star-bed where you can sleep outside on the veranda below a glittering night sky. Amenities include a swimming pool, TV/DVD room, library & plentiful seating in the lounge & veranda. **$$$$$$$**

Nomad Serengeti Safari Camp Mobile; **w** nomad-tanzania.com; page 283. This mobile camp is usually located in the Mara River region over late Jul–Nov. **$$$$$$$**

Olakira Camp Mobile; **w** asiliaafrica.com; page 283. Over Jun–Oct, this wonderful mobile camp moves close to the Mara & Bolongonja confluence, near a frequently used wildebeest crossing point. **$$$$$$$**

✱ Sanctuary Kichakani Serengeti Camp Mobile; **w** sanctuaryretreats.com; page 283. From Jun to mid-Nov, this luxurious 10-tent mobile camp is situated in the Lamai Wedge, & offers great access to the remote north bank of the Mara River. **$$$$$$$**

✱ Sayari Camp [275 E2] ⊕ -1.58495, 34.92666; **w** asiliaafrica.com ⏲ closed Apr–May. Set amid a group of rocky hills 2km south of the Mara River, this stylish camp offers excellent access to the Lamai Wedge & is ideally placed to catch wildebeest crossings over Aug–Oct. Spaced so far apart that guests are transported to the dining area by car after dark, the 15 luxury tents are stylishly decorated with hardwood floors, walk-in nets, king-size beds, private balconies & hot showers. The genuine wilderness atmosphere & high-quality guiding typical of Asilia make this a real gem. **$$$$$$$**

Upmarket

Serengeti North Wilderness Camp Mobile; **m** +255 754 842466; **w** tanzaniawildernesscamps.com. This down-to-earth & reasonably priced mobile camp moves from Ndutu to a location north of the Mara River from Jul to Oct. The en-suite tents have solar lighting, eco-friendly toilets & comfortable but unpretentious furnishings. **$$$$$$**

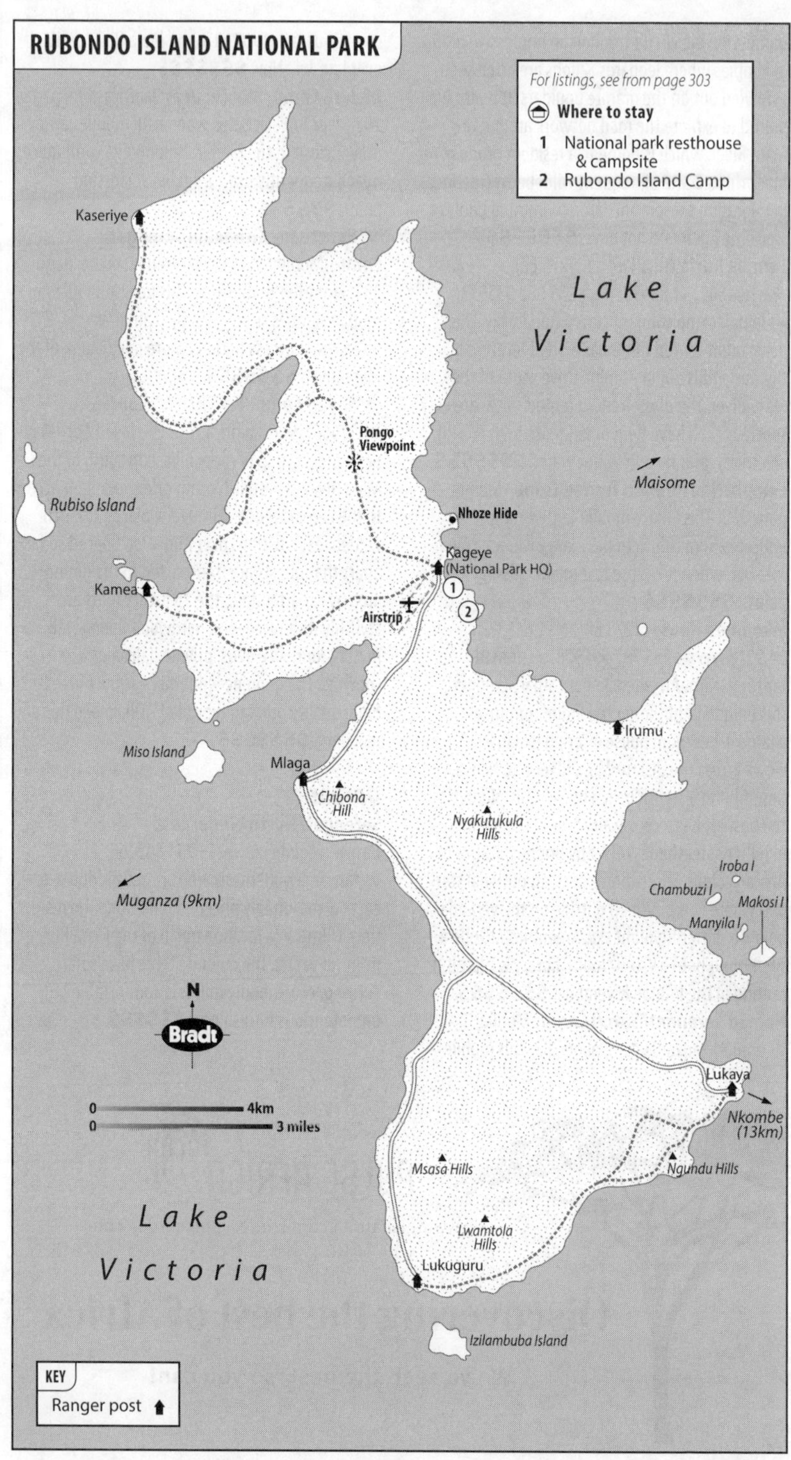
RUBONDO ISLAND NATIONAL PARK
For listings, see from page 303
Where to stay
1 National park resthouse & campsite
2 Rubondo Island Camp
Lake Victoria
Kaseriye
Pongo Viewpoint
Maisome
Rubiso Island
Nhoze Hide
Kageye (National Park HQ)
Kamea
Airstrip
Irumu
Miso Island
Mlaga
Chibona Hill
Nyakutukula Hills
Iroba I
Chambuzi I
Makosi I
Manyila I
Muganza (9km)
N
Bradt
Lukaya
Nkombe (13km)
0 4km
0 3 miles
Msasa Hills
Ngundu Hills
Lake Victoria
Lwamtola Hills
Lukuguru
Izilambuba Island
KEY
Ranger post

13

Rubondo Island and the Northwest Safari Circuit

The far northwest of Tanzania is dominated by Lake Victoria, a vast inland sea that extends over almost 60,000km^2, making it the largest freshwater body on the African continent. Although it practically borders the western Serengeti, Lake Victoria has never featured prominently on Tanzania's tourist circuit, and very few visitors to the country catch so much as a glimpse of its oceanic expanses. The one significant wildlife attraction associated with the lake is pedestrian-friendly Rubondo Island National Park, which protects an archipelago of forested islands whose varied fauna includes elephant, giraffe, a conspicuous population of the otherwise secretive sitatunga antelope, and almost 300 forest- and water-associated bird species. Rubondo's main attraction, however, is the opportunity to track chimpanzees, which are not yet quite so as habituated as their counterparts in Mahale Mountains or Gombe, but are far more easily tagged on as a fly-in (or even drive-down) extension to a northern Tanzania safari package.

For adventurous travellers, the far northwest of Tanzania is also the site of four new national parks gazetted in 2019. Three of these parks, namely Burigi-Chato, Rumanyika-Karagwe and Ibanda-Kyerwa, lie in remote Kagera District, a 35,686km^2 wedge of moist and hilly land bordered by Rwanda and Burundi to the west, Uganda to the north, and Lake Victoria to the east. The fourth and largest of these national parks is Kigosi, which lies immediately south of the main road that runs west towards Kagera from Singida and elsewhere in eastern Tanzania. None of these parks is yet fully developed for tourism, but this will hopefully change during the lifespan of this edition, and for the time being they make for interesting off-the-beaten-track goals, particularly for overlanders driving between Tanzania and Uganda or Rwanda. The northwest is also home to the Minziro Nature Forest Reserve, which easily ranks as the most important site in Tanzania for forest wildlife endemic to the Guinea–Congo biome.

RUBONDO ISLAND NATIONAL PARK

Situated in the far southwest corner of Lake Victoria, 200km from the Serengeti as the crow flies, this 457km^2 national park was gazetted in 1977 to protect the undulating forests of the 240km^2 Rubondo Island, along with another 11 islets (none much larger than 2km^2) and the surrounding waters. One of Tanzania's most low-profile and underrated safari destinations, Rubondo is a lovely retreat, offering the combination of a near-perfect climate, atmospheric jungle-fringed beaches, some unusual wildlife viewing (including chimp tracking), and the opportunity to explore it all on foot or by boat. Sadly, very few tourists actually make it to here, partly because its attractions are more low key and esoteric than those of Tanzania's

THE ECOLOGY OF LAKE VICTORIA

Set in an elevated basin between the eastern and western arms of the Rift Valley, Lake Victoria is the world's second-largest freshwater body after Lake Superior in North America. Half of its 59,950km^2 surface area falls within Tanzania, while the remainder is split between Uganda and Kenya. With a maximum depth of 80m, it is a relatively shallow lake, enclosing four of the world's 20 largest freshwater islands (Rubondo included), and much of its 7,000km shoreline is marshy. The largest and longest of several inflowing rivers is the Kagera, which rises in the highlands of Rwanda and Burundi before crossing into Tanzania. The Kagera thus also qualifies as the most remote source of the Nile, the world's longest river, which exits Lake Victoria in Uganda.

Victoria naturally supports a greater variety of fish than any other lake in the world aside from Tanganyika and Malawi-Nyasa. This includes an estimated 500 endemic haplochromine cichlid species, of which only 200 have been described. All these cichlids evolved from a mere five ancestral species since the lake dried out 10,000–15,000 years ago, representing the most recent comparable explosion of vertebrate adaptive radiation anywhere in the world.

Lake Victoria has been afflicted by a series of manmade ecological disasters since the early colonial era, when large tracts of indigenous vegetation were cleared and natural swamps drained to make way for sugar, tea and coffee plantations. One result of this was an increase in the amount of topsoil washed into the lake, so that the water became progressively muddier and murkier during the 20th century. More serious was the wash-off of toxic pesticides and other agricultural chemicals, which in addition to polluting the water contain nutrients that promote algae growth, which leads to a decrease in oxygenation levels. The foundation of several large lakeshore cities and plantations attracted migrant labourers from around the region, many of whom settled at the lake, leading to a high population increase and overfishing.

By the early 1950s, the above factors had conspired to create a noticeable drop in fishing yields, in particular the two indigenous tilapia species *Oreochromis esculentus* and *O. variabilis* (known locally as *ngege*), which are both listed as Near-threatened by the IUCN. The colonial authorities introduced the similar Nile tilapia *O. niloticus*, which restored the diminishing yield without noticeably affecting the ecological balance of the lake. More disastrous, however, was the controversial introduction of the Nile perch *Lates niloticus*, a voracious predator that feeds almost exclusively on smaller fish, and frequently reaches a length of 2m and a weight exceeding 100kg. Nile perch were probably first released into the lake's Ugandan waters in the early 1950s, followed by a more deliberate programme of introductions initiated in the early 1960s.

It would be another 20 years before the full impact of this introduction policy became clear. In a UN survey undertaken in 1971, indigenous haplochromine cichlids constituted 80% of Lake Victoria's fish biomass, while introduced perch and tilapia had effectively displaced the indigenous tilapia species without otherwise altering the ecological balance. By contrast, a similar survey undertaken ten years later revealed that the perch's share of the lake fish biomass had grown to 80%. Around 40% of Victoria's endemic cichlid species disappeared during this period, an event described by Les Kauffman of Boston University as 'the greatest vertebrate mass extinction in recorded history'.

Despite this, the introduction of the invasive Nile perch could be considered a success on its own terms. It ensured that Lake Victoria remained Africa's largest inland fishery, with the majority of the perch catch being exported from East Africa to the EU and other international markets, generating an annual revenue that peaked at US$400 million in 2008. Tanned perch hide is used locally as a leather substitute for shoes, belts and purses, and the dried swim bladders, used to filter beer and make fish stock, are also exported commercially. That said, since the perch is too large to roast on a fire and too fatty to dry in the sun, it does not really meet local needs as well as tilapia. Furthermore, the thriving export market made it difficult for local fishing communities to compete against larger and better-equipped commercial companies, and it diverted an important source of protein away from lakeside households.

Ironically, perch numbers have declined considerably since 2008, probably through a combination of overfishing and a decrease in prey availability, and the latest reports suggest that endemic cichlids now comprise around 65% of the lake's fish biomass. Opinion is divided as to whether this should be seen as a corrective development that will partially restore the lake's natural ecological equilibrium, or an economic disaster for an industry that employed more than 1 million lakeshore residents at its peak.

The introduction of perch is not the only factor to have altered Lake Victoria's ecology. Since the 1960s, vast amounts of agricultural chemicals, untreated sewage and industrial waste have been dumped into the lake daily, leading to a massive increase in the volume of nutrients that promote the growth of plankton and algae and a corresponding decrease in oxygen levels. The lower level of the lake now consists of dead water – lacking any oxygenation or fish activity below about 30m – and the water quality closer to the surface has deteriorated markedly since the 1960s.

A clear indicator of this deterioration was the rapid spread of water hyacinth after it first entered Lake Victoria via the Kagera River in the late 1980s. An exotic South American species that thrives in polluted conditions, hyacinth tends to deplete water oxygenation levels further by forming an impenetrable mat over the surface. It colonised vast tracts of the lake's surface over the course of the 1990s and clogged up several harbours, since when it has been kept under control by measures such as manual harvesting and the deployment of hyacinth-eating insects. And for those who adhere to the 'if life gives you lemons' philosophy, it will be reassuring to learn that, as of 2018, the exotic hyacinth has been harvested for biogas production at the Kenyan port of Dunga.

As is so often the case with ecological issues, what might at first be dismissed by some as an esoteric concern for environmentalists in fact has wider implications for the 40-plus million people resident in the Lake Victoria basin. The infestation of hyacinth and rapid decrease in indigenous snail-eating fish has led to a growth in the number of bilharzia-carrying snails. The deterioration in water quality, exacerbated by sewage pumping, has increased the risk of sanitary-related diseases such as cholera. The change in the fish biomass has encouraged commercial fishing for export outside of the region, in the process depressing the local semi-subsistence fishing economy. And if not properly managed in the future, there is a risk that Africa's largest lake will eventually be reduced to a vast expanse of dead water, with no fish in it at all – with ecological, economic and humanitarian ramifications that scarcely bear thinking about.

THE FLOATING ZOO

Rubondo Island is unique among Tanzania's national parks not only in its aquatic location, but also in that it was conceived less as a game reserve than as a sort of 'floating zoo'. Proclaimed a forest reserve in German times, the island was upgraded to a game reserve in 1966, at the behest of Professor Bernhard Grzimek of the Frankfurt Zoological Society. Grzimek, best known for his tireless efforts to protect the Serengeti, believed that the forested island would make an ideal sanctuary for the breeding and protection of introduced populations of endangered Congolese rainforest species such as golden cat, okapi, bongo and lowland gorilla.

This plan never quite attained fruition, even though several chimpanzees were introduced to the island along with small numbers of elephant, giraffe, roan antelope, suni, Kilimanjaro colobus monkey and black rhinoceros – most of which would not normally be regarded as forest-specific species. This arbitrary introduction programme was abandoned in 1973, only to be resurrected briefly in July 2000, when a flock of 37 grey parrots – captured in Cameroon for sale in Asia and confiscated in transit at Nairobi – were released onto the island.

Not all of the mammal reintroductions were a success. The 16 black rhinoceros relocated from the Serengeti in 1965 were poached in the 1970s, while five roan antelope introduced in 1967 died of natural causes before reproducing. By contrast, six sub-adult elephants released over 1972–73 have bred up to 80 individuals, with the larger herds concentrated in the south and lone bulls ranging all over the island. Some concern has been expressed that an elephant overpopulation could lead to the destruction of the natural forest, but the population would need to pass 200 for this to be a real threat, at which point contraception would be an option.

Relocated to Rubondo from Mount Meru, an introduced population of Kilimanjaro colobus has also proliferated, though these striking monkeys remain less common than the naturally occurring vervet. The giraffe herd, estimated at around 100 individuals, is most likely to be encountered in the restricted area of acacia woodland around Lukaya, some distance south of the lodge and park headquarters. The small and secretive suni is the most elusive of the introduced species.

Between 1966 and 1969, eight male and nine female chimpanzees were released on to the island, all of them born wild in the Guinean rainforest belt but captured when young to be taken to European zoos and circuses. Some had been held in good zoos where they had the company of other chimpanzees, while others were caged inadequately or in solitary confinement. Several individuals were regarded as troublesome and had regularly attacked or bitten their keepers, and two of the males were shot after they attacked people living on the island. The others settled down quickly. Two newborn chimps were observed in 1968, and the population now stands at around 70, all of them at least second generation, and split between two separate communities.

high-profile savannah reserves, but also because its relative inaccessibility makes it a challenging goal for any but the most intrepid or wealthy of visitors. This is a real shame, because this forested park can be recommended without reservation to anybody with a strong interest in birds, walking or game fishing – or simply a yen to escape to a blissfully uncrowded peaceful tropical paradise.

Measuring about 28km from north to south but nowhere more than 10km wide, the forested island for which the national park is named comprises a partially submerged quartet of volcanic hills linked by three flattish isthmuses. The park headquarters, airstrip and all accommodation facilities lie within 2km of one another at Kageye, which stands on the east shore of the central isthmus that forms the narrowest part of the island about 10km from its northernmost tip. About 8km southwest, Mlaga jetty, on the western shore facing the mainland port of Kasenda, is the landing point for most boats. The highest point is Msasa Hill. which reaches an elevation of 1,486m in the far south of the island, meaning it rises 350m above the lakeshore.

Recent years have seen quite a number of exciting developments at Rubondo. These include the acquisition of Rubondo's only private camp by the highly regarded Asilia group, the reintroduction of daily scheduled flights from Arusha, Serengeti and elsewhere on the northern circuit, and a huge improvement in road accessibility. More importantly, chimpanzee tracking is also now offered at Rubondo, with a success rate of almost 100% in 2022. What's more, the introduction of scheduled Coastal Aviation flights between Rubondo and Kigali, the capital of Rwanda, means that the island can now easily be incorporated into an itinerary that combines a Serengeti safari with mountain gorilla tracking in Rwanda or Uganda.

Rubondo has a pleasant year-round climate, with temperatures seldom falling outside the 20–25°C range by day or by night. The average annual rainfall is around 1,200mm, with the driest months being January, February and June to September. The dry months are the perfect time to visit Rubondo, but the park and lodge are open all year, and there is no serious obstacle to visiting during the rains.

The entrance fee is US$30 per 24 hours. Activity fees are US$25 daily for fishing, US$10 for canoeing, US$20 for boat safaris, US$10/20 per person for walks of less/more than 4 hours, or US$135 per person for the chimp habituation experience. An additional 18% VAT is levied on all fees.

FLORA AND FAUNA Closed-canopy lowland forest covers about 80% of Rubondo Island's surface. This is interspersed with patches of open grassland and acacia woodland, the latter all but restricted to the Lukaya area. The eastern lakeshore is characterised by rocky areas and sandy beaches (such as those in front of the lodge and camp), while the western shore supports extensive papyrus swamps, often lined with wild date palms. Between December and March, an estimated 40 terrestrial and epiphytic orchid species come into bloom, as do gloriosa and fireball lilies. The red coral tree, which flowers almost all year round, is also a spectacular sight.

Mammals Rubondo's wildlife doesn't offer the easy thrills of many savannah reserves, but many large mammals are present, most alluring perhaps the introduced populations of chimpanzee and elephant (page 298). However, the presence of these glamour boys shouldn't shift the focus away from the island's interesting assemblage of naturally occurring residents, including the aquatic sitatunga antelope (page 302), hippopotamus, crocodile and water monitor. Vervet monkeys are numerous and easily seen all over Rubondo, but no other primate species occurs here naturally. This is difficult to explain, given the variety of primates that are present in similar island habitats on the Ugandan part of the lake, and given that the lake dried up fully in the biologically recent past, which would have allowed a free flow of species between the island and mainland forests. The only terrestrial predators that occur on the island are the marsh mongoose and large-spotted genet, and the latter sometimes

LAKE VICTORIA AND THE RIDDLE OF THE NILE

The first European to see Lake Victoria was John Hanning Speke, who marched from Tabora to the site of present-day Mwanza in 1858 following his joint 'discovery' of Lake Tanganyika with Richard Burton the previous year. Speke named the lake for Queen Victoria, but prior to that Arab slave traders called it Ukerewe (still the name of its largest island). It is unclear what name was in local use, since the only one used by Speke is Nyanza, which simply means lake.

A major goal of the Burton–Speke expedition had been to solve the great geographical enigma of the age, the source of the White Nile. Speke, based on his brief glimpse of the southeast corner of Lake Victoria, somewhat whimsically proclaimed his 'discovery' to be the answer to that riddle. Burton, with a comparable lack of compelling evidence, was convinced that the great river flowed out of Lake Tanganyika. The dispute between the former travelling companions erupted bitterly on their return to Britain, where Burton – the more persuasive writer and respected traveller – gained the backing of the scientific establishment.

Over 1862–63, Speke and Captain James Grant returned to Lake Victoria, hoping to prove Speke's theory correct. They looped inland around the western shore of the lake, arriving at the court of King Mutesa of Buganda, then continued east to the site of present-day Jinja, where a substantial river flowed out of the lake after tumbling over the cataract that Speke named Ripon Falls. From here, the two explorers headed north, sporadically crossing paths with the river throughout what is today Uganda, before following the Nile to Khartoum and Cairo.

Speke's declaration that 'The Nile is settled' met with mixed support back home. Burton and other sceptics pointed out that Speke had bypassed the entire western shore of his purported great lake, had visited only a couple of points on the northern shore, and had not attempted to explore the east. Nor, for that matter, had he followed the course of the Nile in its entirety. Speke, claimed his detractors, had seen several different lakes and different stretches of river, connected only in Speke's deluded mind. The sceptics had a point, but Speke had nevertheless gathered sufficient geographical evidence to render his claim highly plausible, and his notion of one great lake, far from being mere whimsy, was backed by anecdotal information gathered from local sources along the way.

Matters were scheduled to reach a head on 16 September 1864, when an eagerly awaited debate between Burton and Speke – in the words of the former, 'what silly tongues called the "Nile Duel"' – was due to take place at the Royal Geographic Society (RGS). And reach a head they did, but in circumstances more tragic than anybody could have anticipated. On the afternoon of the debate, Speke went out shooting with a cousin, only to stumble while crossing a wall, in the process discharging a barrel of his shotgun into his heart. The subsequent inquest recorded a verdict of accidental death, but it has often been suggested – purely on the basis of the curious timing – that Speke deliberately took his own life rather than face up to Burton in public. Burton, who had seen Speke less than 3 hours earlier, was by all accounts deeply troubled by Speke's death, and years later he was quoted as stating 'the uncharitable [say] that I shot him' – an accusation that seems to have been aired only in Burton's imagination.

Speke was dead, but the 'Nile debate' would keep kicking for several years. In 1864, Sir Stanley and Lady Baker were the first Europeans to reach Lake Albert and nearby Murchison Falls in present-day Uganda. The Bakers, much to the delight of the anti-Speke lobby, were convinced that this newly named lake was a source of the Nile, although they openly admitted it might not be the only one. Following the Bakers' announcement, Burton put forward a revised theory, namely that the most remote source of the Nile was the Rusizi River, which he believed flowed out of the northern head of Lake Tanganyika and emptied into Lake Albert.

In 1865, the RGS followed up on Burton's theory by sending Dr David Livingstone to Lake Tanganyika. Livingstone, however, was of the opinion that the Nile's source lay further south than Burton supposed, and so he struck out towards the lake along a previously unexplored route. Leaving from Mikindani in the far south of present-day Tanzania, Livingstone followed the Rovuma River inland, continuing westward to the southern tip of Lake Tanganyika. From there, he ranged southward into present-day Zambia, where he came across a new candidate for the source of the Nile, the swampy Lake Bangweulu and its major outlet, the Lualaba River. It was only after his famous meeting with Henry Stanley at Ujiji, in November 1871, that Livingstone (in the company of Stanley) visited the north of Lake Tanganyika and Burton's cherished Rusizi River, which, it transpired, flowed into the lake. Burton, nevertheless, still regarded Lake Tanganyika to be the most likely source of the Nile, while Livingstone was convinced that the answer lay with the Lualaba River. In August 1872, Livingstone headed back to the Lake Bangweulu region, where he fell ill and died six months later, the great question still unanswered.

In August 1874, ten years after Speke's death, Stanley embarked on a three-year expedition every bit as remarkable and arduous as those undertaken by his predecessors, yet one whose significance is often overlooked. Partly, this is because Stanley cuts such an unsympathetic figure, the grim caricature of the murderous pre-colonial White Man blasting and blustering his way through territories where Burton, Speke and Livingstone had relied largely on diplomacy. It is also the case, however, that Stanley set out with no intention of seeking out headline-making fresh discoveries. Instead, he was determined to test out the various theories that had been advocated by Speke, Burton and Livingstone about the Nile's source. First, Stanley sailed around the circumference of Lake Victoria, establishing that it was indeed as vast as Speke had claimed. Stanley's next step was to circumnavigate Lake Tanganyika, which, contrary to Burton's long-held theories, clearly boasted no outlet sufficiently large to be the source of the Nile. Finally, and most remarkably, Stanley took a boat along Livingstone's Lualaba River to its confluence with an even larger river, which he followed for months with no idea as to where he might end up.

When, exactly 999 days after he left Zanzibar, Stanley emerged at the Congo mouth, the shortlist of plausible theories relating to the source of the Nile had been reduced to one. Clearly, the Nile did flow out of Lake Victoria at Ripon Falls, before entering and exiting Lake Albert at its northern tip to start its long course through the sands of the Sahara. Stanley's achievement in putting to rest decades of speculation about how the main rivers and lakes of East Africa linked together is estimable indeed. He was nevertheless generous enough to concede that: 'Speke now has the full glory of having discovered the largest inland sea on the continent of Africa, also its principal affluent as well as its outlet. I must also give him credit for having understood the geography of the countries we travelled through far better than any of us who so persistently opposed his hypothesis.'

STALKING THE SITATUNGA

Two closely related antelope species occur naturally on Rubondo Island: the swamp-dwelling sitatunga and forest-dwelling bushbuck. Of these, the more interesting is the sitatunga – a widespread but localised species with uniquely splayed hooves that allow it to manoeuvre through swampy habitats – since Rubondo is one of only two East African parks where it is easily observed (the other being Saiwa Swamp in Kenya). The males of both these antelopes are very handsome, with large spiralled horns, but the sitatunga is larger, shaggier in appearance, and grey where the bushbuck is chestnut brown. The females of both species are smaller and less striking, but easily distinguished from one another, since the bushbuck is striped on its sides, whereas the sitatunga is unmarked.

Rubondo's sitatunga population probably exceeds ten individuals per square kilometre, and is not so habitat-specific as elsewhere, apparently – and unexpectedly – outnumbering bushbuck even in the forest. Researchers have noted that the sitatunga of Rubondo's forests are more diurnal than is normally the case, and have less-splayed feet and darker coats than those resident in the swamps – whether this is genetically influenced, or a function of wear and sun bleaching, is difficult to say. A possible explanation for this anomalous situation is that sitatunga colonised the island and expanded into forested habitats before there were any bushbuck around.

comes to feed around the lodge at dinnertime. Also present in good numbers is the spotted-necked otter, a diurnal predator that feeds mainly on fish and frogs. A few pairs of otter are resident in the rocky bay around the lodge and camp, and can sometimes be seen from the breakfast area.

Birds With its combination of aquatic and forested habitats, Rubondo Island is an alluring destination for birdwatchers, especially as it can so easily be explored on foot. The bird checklist currently stands at 286 species, but it seems likely that a substantial number of resident forest species and regular visitors have thus far gone unrecorded.

The main avian attraction for casual visitors will be the concentrations of large water birds that occur along the island's swampy shores. Rubondo hosts Lake Victoria's densest population of African fish eagles – 638 individuals were recorded in a 1995 census – as well as large numbers of open-billed and yellow-billed storks. An excellent spot for varied water birds (as well as aquatic mammals and reptiles) is Mlaga Bay on the western side of the island, where some of the more prominent species are Goliath, purple and squacco heron, long-toed lapwing, blue-headed coucal, swamp flycatcher and various weavers. Of interest less for their variety than for their high number of birds are the so-called Bird Islands, a pair of tiny rocky islets that lie about 1km off the east shore of Rubondo, and support breeding colonies of various cormorants, egrets and ibises.

Dedicated birders are likely to be most interested in forest and other terrestrial species. These include Vieillot's black weaver and black-and-white casqued hornbill, both of which are Guinea–Congo biome species with a limited range elsewhere in Tanzania. The lodge grounds and adjacent road and forest loop are as good a place as any to seek out other forest birds. Among the more interesting species commonly seen in this area are palmnut vulture, blue-breasted kingfisher, African pygmy kingfisher, tambourine dove, green malkoha, grey-winged akalat, snowy-headed robin-chat, African paradise flycatcher, brown-throated wattle-eye and green twinspot. The area around the lodge is also the main stomping – and screeching – ground for the recently introduced flock of African grey parrots.

GETTING THERE AND AWAY

By air Most visitors fly with **Coastal Aviation** (w coastal.co.tz) which operates daily flights (with a minimum inducement of six seats) connecting Rubondo to from Arusha, Manyara and most airstrips in the Serengeti, as well as thrice-weekly flights to/from Kigali in Rwanda.

By road Rubondo Island is now readily accessible by road, with the springboard for independent visits being the mainland national park office at Kasenda (⊕ -2.35263, 31.75672; 028 289314; e sitatunga@tanzaniaparks.go.tz), from where a twice-daily boat service runs to Mlaga costing US$100 per perosn (inclusive of a road transfer to Kageye). Kasenda lies just 3km from the junction village of Muganza along an excellent new surfaced road connecting Bwanga to Bukoba via Chato, and it can be reached in any vehicle, or for that matter by bus from Bwanga or Bukoba. With an early start, self-drivers should be able to cover the 385km between the Serengeti's Ndabaka Gate and Kasenda in one day. At the time of writing, you need to allow 8–10 hours for this trip, the major variable being how long you wait for the Kigongo–Busisi ferry across Mwanza Gulf, but once a new toll bridge is complete (hopefully by the time you read this), you should be looking at around 7 hours. If you are coming from the southeast, allow 9–10 hours to cover the 550km from Singida. From the north, Kasenda lies about 170km (up to 3hrs) from Bukoba.

WHERE TO STAY AND EAT *Map, page 294, unless otherwise stated*

Chato Beach Resort [map, page 305] ⊕ -2.61620, 31.74970; m +255 737 562788; w chatobeachresort.co.tz. Boasting an attractive lakeshore setting in the small town of Chato 35km south of the park office at Kasenda, this well-run beach resort is an attractive overnight option for self-drivers before/after crossing to/from Rubondo. It has comfortable rooms with queen-size beds & AC, a decent restaurant & a swimming pool & spa. *From US$39 dbl.* **$–$$**

National park resthouse & campsite This clean resthouse & lovely campsite stand on a forest-fringed beach 1km north of Rubondo Island Camp & a similar distance from park headquarters. No meals are available, & it's advisable to bring most of what you will need with you, but a shop in the park headquarters does sell a few basic foodstuffs (essentially what the national park staff would eat), as well as warm beers & sodas. A cook can be arranged on request. *US$35pp resthouse or US$30pp camping.* **$$**

✷ **Rubondo Island Camp** w asiliaafrica.com; ⌚ closed Apr–May. This attractive & immensely tranquil lodge comprises 8 luxury thatched cottages laid out along a fabulous sandy beach fringed by rocky outcrops & hemmed in by tall gallery forest. The communal areas are spread across a rocky outcrop that overlooks a stretch of lakeshore where kingfishers hawk for food, African paradise flycatchers flutter in the trees & the occasional otter swims past. There's also a lovely swimming pool, built in a natural rock outcrop, outstanding food, super-friendly staff & a varied selection of boat & foot excursions including chimp tracking & catch-&-release fishing for Nile perch. **$$$$$$$**

WHAT TO SEE AND DO The most popular activity on Rubondo is chimpanzee tracking, which is usually done on the north of the island, where a community of around 40 individuals is now at an advanced stage of being habituated to tourists. The habituated chimps here are not yet quite as relaxed as their counterparts in Mahale Mountains or Gombe, and the hike can be relatively demanding owing to the tangled undergrowth and lack of footpaths, but visitors who are patient and reasonably fit can be almost 100% confident of finding them. Typically, the outing takes 4–6 hours (including boat transfers from Kageye), and the chimps are most easily located during the dry months of June to August, when the vegetation is less thick and the chimps often feed on fruiting bungo (*Saba* spp) and barkcloth (*Antiaris toxicaria*) trees. Unlike in Mahale and Gombe, once the chimps have been located, you can theoretically spend as long as you like with them, as tracking here is still regarded to be part of the habituation process.

Guided forest walks can be undertaken anywhere in the park. A popular option, taking up to 6 hours depending on how often you stop, is the **Pongo Viewpoint Trail**, where you can expect to see plenty of birds, as well as sitatunga and – very occasionally – elephant. **Game drives** to the south of the island offer your best chance of seeing giraffe, colobus monkey and bushpig, and you should also see plenty of sitatunga and bushbuck, along with a good variety of forest and water birds. **Boat trips** to the swampy Mlaga Bay or Bird Island offer excellent aquatic birding and you should see plenty of hefty crocodiles, some pods of hippo, and possibly otters swimming in the lake or elephants coming down to drink. The main goal of catch-and-release **game fishing expeditions** is the heavyweight Nile perch – the all-time record at Rubondo is a 108kg Nile perch, but the heaviest catch in recent years is 48kg.

NORTHWEST SAFARI CIRCUIT

The far northwest of Tanzania became the setting for the country's newest safari circuit – or, more accurately, nascent safari circuit – in June 2019, when then-President John Magufuli, who hailed from the region, upgraded six former game reserves to become a quartet of national parks with a combined area almost as large as Serengeti. Three of these new parks – Burigi-Chato, Rumanyika-Karagwe and Ibanda-Kyerwa – lie to the west of Lake Victoria in Magufuli's homeland district of Kagera, whose rolling green hills, marshy valleys and matoke plantations bear strong scenic, cultural and historical affinities with neighbouring Rwanda and Uganda. Other wildlife destinations in the northwest are Minziro Nature Forest Reserve, which lies on the Uganda border close to the port of Bukoba and protects more than 50 species of forest bird unknown from elsewhere in Tanzania, and the remote and relatively inaccessible Kigosi National Park to the south of Kagera. Planned tourist development of the new safari circuit has been stalled by the Covid-19 pandemic and by the death of Magufuli in 2021, so as things stand visitors are few and far between, but all the parks can be visited with varying degrees of effort, and it is to be hoped that further development will take place during the lifespan of this edition.

BURIGI-CHATO NATIONAL PARK Tanzania's fifth largest national park, Burigi-Chato was amalgamated from a contiguous trio of former game reserves – Biharamulo, Burigi and Kimisi – in 2019. It extends across 4,707km² from the Lake Victoria shore opposite Rubondo Island to the Kagera River as it flows north along on the border with southern Rwanda. Being more inherently accessible than swampy Kigosi and ten times larger than Ibanda-Kyerwa and Rumanyika-Karagwe combined, Burigi-Chato has the greatest immediate potential as a safari destination of all the national parks in the northwest. It helps that the park is already home to quite a bit of wildlife, including four of the Big Five, that it is close enough to Rubondo for the two to be visited in tandem, and that an extensive road system and tourist accommodation are in the process of being completed at the time of writing.

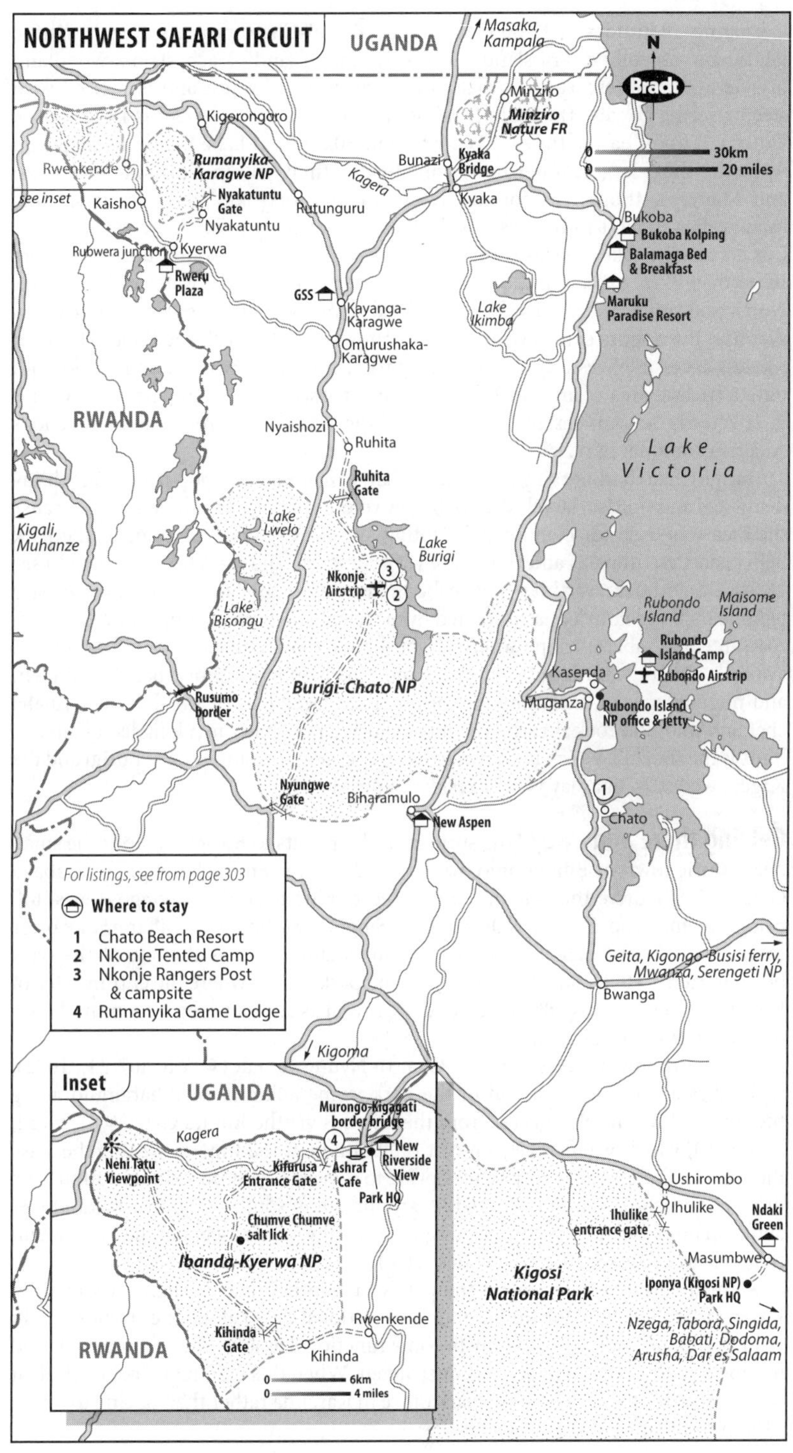
NORTHWEST SAFARI CIRCUIT
UGANDA
Masaka, Kampala
Minziro
Minziro Nature FR
Kigorongoro
Rumanyika-Karagwe NP
Rwenkende
see inset
Kaisho
Nyakatuntu Gate
Nyakatuntu
Rutunguru
Kagera
Bunazi
Kyaka Bridge
Kyaka
0 30km
0 20 miles
Bukoba
Bukoba Kolping
Balamaga Bed & Breakfast
Maruku Paradise Resort
Rubwera junction
Kyerwa
Rweru Plaza
GSS
Kayanga-Karagwe
Omurushaka-Karagwe
Lake Ikimba
RWANDA
Nyaishozi
Ruhita
Ruhita Gate
Lake Victoria
Kigali, Muhanze
Lake Lwelo
Lake Burigi
Nkonje Airstrip
Lake Bisongu
Rubondo Island
Maisome Island
Rubondo Island Camp
Rubondo Airstrip
Kasenda
Muganza
Rubondo Island NP office & jetty
Burigi-Chato NP
Rusumo border
Nyungwe Gate
Biharamulo
New Aspen
Chato
For listings, see from page 303
Where to stay
1 Chato Beach Resort
2 Nkonje Tented Camp
3 Nkonje Rangers Post & campsite
4 Rumanyika Game Lodge
Geita, Kigongo-Busisi ferry, Mwanza, Serengeti NP
Bwanga
Kigoma
Inset
UGANDA
Murongo-Kigagati border bridge
Kagera
Nehi Tatu Viewpoint
Kifurusa Entrance Gate
Ashraf Cafe
New Riverside View
Park HQ
Chumve Chumve salt lick
Ibanda-Kyerwa NP
Kihinda Gate
Rwenkende
Kihinda
RWANDA
0 6km
0 4 miles
Ushirombo
Ihulike
Ihulike entrance gate
Ndaki Green
Masumbwe
Iponya (Kigosi NP) Park HQ
Kigosi National Park
Nzega, Tabora, Singida, Babati, Dodoma, Arusha, Dar es Salaam

Spanning altitudes of 1,100m to 1,700m, Burigi-Chato protects a near-pristine landscape of rolling grassland, acacia savannah and Brachystegia woodland bisected by a tall escarpment that runs from north to south and is incised with steep riverine gorges. The main focal point of tourist development is Lake Burigi, which lies to the east of the escarpment, some 30km from Lake Victoria, and is said to be the third-largest water body contained entirely within Tanzania after Eyasi and Manyara (though its commonly cited extent of 70km^2 contradicts satellite images that show it to be closer to 200km^2). Essentially a flooded riverine basin, this serpentine lake measures roughly 50km from north to south, but is nowhere more than 8km wide, and the lack of any outflow has left the water mildly saline. North and south of the open lake, the flooded valley contains some large papyrus swamps. Even more extensive are the wetlands associated with the Kagera River in the less accessible western sector of the park, Here, lakes Bisongu and Lwelo both have a surface area of around 20km^2, while a massive network of papyrus swamps is effectively a southeastern extension of the ecosystem protected in Rwanda's Akagera National Park.

Burigi-Chato harbours a good variety of large mammals but populations are thinly distracted and skittish, largely due to the low volume of tourist traffic, but also because the area was used for commercial hunting and heavily poached prior to the park being gazetted. Impalas and zebras are very common, and it is also quite easy to see Defassa waterbuck, warthog, olive baboon and vervet monkey. Other more elusive wildlife includes lion, leopard, spotted hyena, elephant, buffalo, hippo, giraffe, eland, roan antelope, sable antelope, topi, oribi, bushbuck and sitatunga. Little information is available about the birdlife, but the park most likely supports more than 400 resident and migrant species, including the localised red-faced barbet, Ross's turaco, Ruaha chat and miombo rock thrush. The most alluring possibility in a long list of aquatic birds is the shoebill, which is known to be an occasional visitor to Lake Burigi and the Kagera wetlands, but may well be resident in the latter.

Getting there and away The springboard for visits to Burigi-Chato is the small but historic town of Biharamulo, which lies 370km from the Serengeti's Ndabaka Gate (a 7–8hr drive that should be reduced to 6hrs once the Kigongo–Busisi toll bridge opens) and 530km (10hrs) from Singida. Stopping in Biharamulo prior to visiting Burigi-Chato is more or less mandatory, as it is the site of the park headquarters (☎ 028 298 3024; e bc@tanzaniaparks.go.tz) where the entrance fee of US$30 per person plus 18% VAT per day (as well as any camping, accommodation or guide fees) must be paid.

The main point of access to Burigi-Chato is Nyungwe Gate (⊕ -2.64407, 31.01082), which lies at the southern end of the park, some 80km from Biharamulo along the surfaced B6 and B3. Access from the north is via the Ruhita Gate (⊕ -1.95754, 31.15079), which is effectively an exit-only option at the time of writing, because there is nowhere nearby to pay fees prior to a visit. If you do exit via Ruhita, the drive to Nyaishozi (on the main B182, around 25km south of Omurushaka), takes about an hour and involves a very rough but equally scenic ascent of the escarpment (high clearance essential and 4x4 desirable).

A third entrance gate lies on the park's eastern boundary roughly 10km from Kasenda (the jetty site for Rubondo Island National Park) along the surfaced main road to Bukoba, but this will only become functional as and when an internal road linking it to the rest of the park is constructed. When this does happen, hopefully it will be possible to pay fees at the park office in Kasenda rather than having to divert 115km to Biharamulo.

Where to stay and eat *Map, page 305*

Two potentially very attractive accommodation facilities are currently under construction on the lakeshore. These are a cluster of en-suite bandas at **Nkonje Rangers Post** (⊕ -2.08867, 31.28966) and the five-unit **Nkonje Tented Camp** (⊕ -2.16626, 31.29264) about 10km further south. Until such time as these open, it is possible for self-sufficient visitors to camp at Nkonje Rangers Post, where amenities include clean ablution facilities and a shaded picnic area. Camping costs US$30 per person plus 18% VAT, and when the bandas and tented camp do open, rates are likely to be in line with the US$30–50 per person plus 18% VAT charged in other national parks.

Outside the park, the pick of Biharamulo's somewhat motley selection of lodges is the **New Aspen** (⊕ -2.64298, 31.32054; m +255 692 730673/753 349114; from US$13 dbl B&B; **$**), which has clean rooms with hot showers and a decent garden bar and restaurant. As and when the gate near Kasenda becomes operational, the attractive **Chato Beach Resort** (page 303), in the lakeshore town of the same name, might be a useful springboard for exploring the park.

What to see and do The main activity at the time of writing is game drives. Nyungwe and Ruhita gates are connected by a well-maintained unsurfaced road that runs through the heart of the park for roughly 120km. A few 4x4-only game-viewing roads run either side of this main road, the most worthwhile being the Lakeview Circuit, which leads to Lake Burigi, Nkonje Rangers Post, and the main airstrip, and also offers good wildlife viewing and birding. It is also possible to arrange guided walks with the rangers, and plans exist to start operating boats and canoes on the lake.

KARAGWE The northwest safari circuit's most important urban route pivot is Karagwe, an eponymous district administrative capital that comprises two small towns, southerly Omurushaka and northerly Kayanga, situated 7km apart along the B182 between Biharamulo and Kyaka/Bukoba. Both towns have plenty of banks, filling stations, guesthouses and restaurants. Should you need to overnight, your best option is Kayanga's friendly and well-run GSS Hotel (⊕ -1.52544, 31.14801; m +255 673 858274; w gsshotel.wordpress.com; US$25 dbl; **$**), which has a quiet location 500m west of the main road, small but pleasant rooms with net, TV, water dispenser and hot shower, a good restaurant, a garden bar and safe parking.

BUKOBA The administrative capital of and largest town in Kagera, Bukoba stands on the lush and hilly western shore of Lake Victoria some 50km south of the border with Uganda. It was founded in 1890 as a German administrative outpost and captured and looted 25 years later in an amphibious raid that represented the first World War I victory for the Allied Forces in what is now Tanzania. Today, this pleasant lakeshore town supports a population estimated at 150,000 in an agricultural region known for its thriving coffee industry and proliferation of batoke (or matoke), a large green cooking banana that is the main staple crop of Kagera. At the lake end of Jamhuri Road stands a cluster of German-era buildings, including the old boma, magistrate's court and post office; but the town's most impressive edifice is the Catholic Cathedral built by Bishop Hirth between 1893 and 1904. The marshy area between the town and the lake supports large numbers of pied kingfisher and other waterbirds. Further afield, the Bwanjai Rock Art Site, about 25km northwest of Bukoba and linked to it by erratic dalla dallas, is dominated by strange geometric shapes but also includes some heavily stylised human figures.

Getting there and away Bukoba has one of the most remote locations of any town in Tanzania but it is connected to the rest of the country by several good roads – the best maintained being the 250km (4hrs) surfaced road from Bwanga via Chato and Muganza (for Rubondo Island) – and plenty of buses. There are also weekly ferries from Mwanza on the southeast lakeshore.

Tour operators The long-serving **Kiroyera Tours** (m +255 759 424933; w kiroyeratours.com) and newer **Bukoba Cultural Tours** (m +255 713 568276; f BukobaTours) can arrange guided tours to Bwanjai, Minziro and all three national parks in Kagera.

Where to stay *Map, page 309*

✱ **Balamaga B&B** Maruku Rd; m +255 787 757289; w balamagabb.com. Perched on Balamaga Hill 3km out of town, this homely & welcoming German-Tanzanian B&B is a converted suburban house whose leafy garden is alive with birdsong & offers great views towards the lake. Rooms are spacious & airy, there's a cosy lounge with satellite TV & the freshly prepared b/fasts are excellent. *From US$35/50 sgl/dbl B&B.* **$–$$**

Bukoba Coop Hotel Shore Rd; m +255 687 471188. This lakeshore cheapie looks offputtingly rundown from the outside but the rooms are clean, good value & come with net, TV, fridge & hotel shower. A restaurant & waterfront bar are attached. *US$8 dbl B&B.* **$**

Bukoba Kolping Hotel Maruku Rd; m +255 756 967965; w bukobakolpinghotel.com. A few doors down from Balamaga B&B, this church-run hotel has clean, comfortable rooms & a decent restaurant with indoor & outdoor seating. *From US$15 dbl B&B.* **$**

Maruku Paradise Beach m +255 759 424933; w marukuparadisebeach.com. Affiliated to Kiroyera Tours, this peaceful lakeside retreat, set in the village of Maruku about 20km south of Bukoba, has simple rooms, a campsite that's popular with overlanders & a relaxing terrace bar & restaurant. *From US$8pp.* **$$**

Victorious Perch Hotel Jamhuri Rd; m +255 756 189475. Despite the odd name, this efficient hotel is the best central option. The 20 rooms all come with AC, sat TV & fridge, & there's a good restaurant on the ground floor. *From US$22 dbl B&B.* **$**

Where to eat and drink *Map, page 309*

Fruit Filly Juice Bar Jamhuri Rd. Great fresh fruit juice, plain or blended, for around US$1.

Rock Bar Shore Rd. This popular garden bar stands close to the lake.

TRS Café & Health Club Jamhuri Rd; m +255 745 947001. This bright café with indoor & outdoor seating has a long & varied menu of healthy & not-so-healthy meals, including curries, sizzler plates, pasta dishes, burgers, soups & salads, as well as smoothies, freshly brewed coffee, wine & beer. Portions are generous & you can work them off in the attached gym, followed by a sauna or steam bath. $

MINZIRO NATURE FOREST RESERVE *Dr Terry Oatley, with additional information and updates by Philip Briggs*

Bounded by the Kagera River to the east and Uganda's Malabigambo Forest to the north, the 248km² Minziro Nature Forest Reserve (w nature-reserves.go.tz; entrance US$10pp) is unique within Tanzania for the predominantly West African affinities of its fauna and remarkable birdlife. Situated about 20km inland of Lake Victoria, the reserve stands at an elevation of around 1,150m and is subject to seasonal flooding from the Kagera between October and May. Groundwater forest predominates, with a tree composition divided equally between western lowland and eastern montane species, but other habitats include patches of open grassland, a scattering of small rocky hills, and the extensive papyrus beds that line the riverbank.

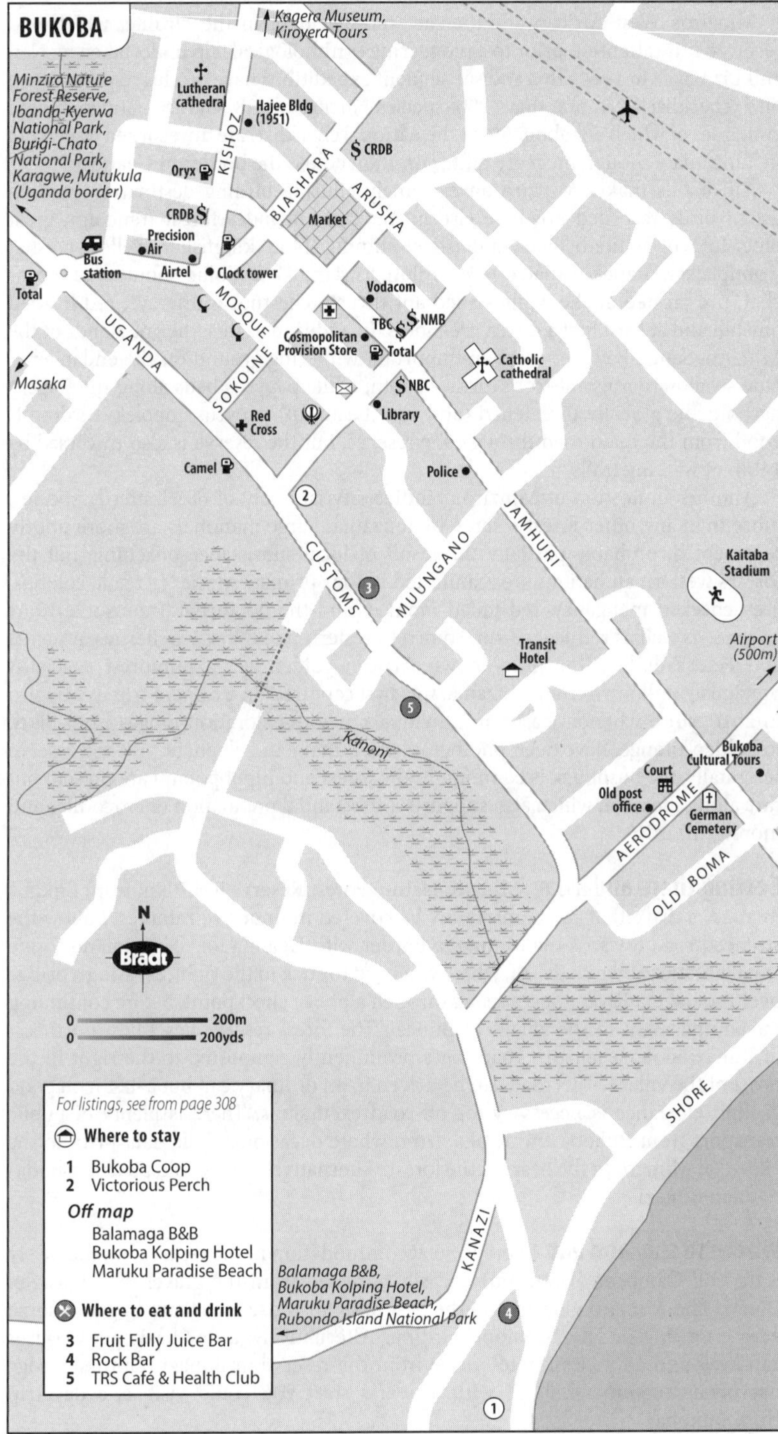
BUKOBA
Kagera Museum, Kiroyera Tours
Minziro Nature Forest Reserve, Ibanda-Kyerwa National Park, Burigi-Chato National Park, Karagwe, Mutukula (Uganda border)
Lutheran cathedral
Hajee Bldg (1951)
KISHOZ
Oryx
CRDB
BIASHARA
ARUSHA
Market
CRDB
Precision Air
Bus station
Airtel
Clock tower
Total
Vodacom
MOSQUE
UGANDA
TBC
NMB
Cosmopolitan Provision Store
Total
Catholic cathedral
Masaka
SOKOINE
NBC
Library
Red Cross
Camel
Police
CUSTOMS
MUUNGANO
JAMHURI
Kaitaba Stadium
Airport (500m)
Transit Hotel
Kanoni
Bukoba Cultural Tours
Court
Old post office
AERODROME
German Cemetery
OLD BOMA
N
Bradt
0 200m
0 200yds
SHORE
KANAZI
Balamaga B&B, Bukoba Kolping Hotel, Maruku Paradise Beach, Rubondo Island National Park
For listings, see from page 308
Where to stay
1 Bukoba Coop
2 Victorious Perch
Off map
Balamaga B&B
Bukoba Kolping Hotel
Maruku Paradise Beach
Where to eat and drink
3 Fruit Fully Juice Bar
4 Rock Bar
5 TRS Café & Health Club

Minziro's West African affinities are most evident in the birdlife, which had received little attention prior to a pioneering ornithological trip undertaken by Neil and Liz Baker in 1984. This and subsequent expeditions have produced a formative bird checklist of more than 250 species, including 58 Guinea–Congo biome endemics of which 56 (about 5% of the national checklist) are unrecorded elsewhere in Tanzania – though most are quite common across the border in Uganda

All of this makes Minziro an extremely alluring birding destination. A long list of birds recorded nowhere else in Tanzania includes forest francolin, great blue turaco, white-bellied kingfisher, shining blue kingfisher, yellow-crested woodpecker, orange-throated forest robin, lowland akalat, blue-shouldered robin-chat, fire-crested alethe, white-tailed ant thrush, chestnut wattle-eye, red-headed bluebill and at least half a dozen greenbuls. In addition to this, the grasslands of the Minziro–Sango Bay area form an important wintering ground for the endangered blue swallow, a migrant from further south, while papyrus beds along the Kagera harbour the globally threatened (and very beautiful) papyrus gonolek. Birding is good from the main road through the reserve, but the reserve is also traversed by 14km of walking trails.

Another indication of Minziro's biodiversity is a tally of 600 butterfly species, more than any other forest reserve in Tanzania. Large mammals are more poorly represented, probably partially the result of local subsistence poaching, but the forest's western affiliations are manifested in four primate species (Angola colobus, grey-cheeked mangabey, red-tailed monkey and the nocturnal Thomson's dwarf galago), as well as red-legged sun squirrel, western tree hyrax (vociferous at night) and Peter's duiker. The little-known African golden cat, a rainforest specialist previously unknown from Tanzania, was first captured on a camera trip in Minziro in 2016, since when at least ten individuals, whose coloration ranges from black to golden-orange, have been photographed. Buffalo and elephant visit the reserve seasonally, the bushbuck is common in the forest and hippopotami are present but rare along the river, which also supports a substantial population of crocodiles and monitor lizards.

Getting there and away Minziro Nature Forest Reserve lies 70km from Bukoba by road, a drive that can comfortably be covered in under 90 minutes. Follow the surfaced road towards the Mutukula border with Uganda for 55km inland to the small junction town of Kyaka, where you need to stick to the right, crossing a bridge over the Kagera River, then passing through a police checkpoint, before continuing for another 5km to the village of Bunazi. The forest reserve lies 14km northeast of Bunazi along a fair dirt road that's prominently signposted to the right in the heart of the village. This road can be driven in an ordinary car, but a 4x4 with good ground clearance is necessary for off-road excursions. There is plenty of public transport from Bukoba and Kyaka, from where occasional dalla dallas run to the village of Minziro in the heart of the forest. Alternatively, you could pick up a boda-boda in Bunazi.

Where to stay and eat There is no accommodation in the reserve but the lovely Kere Hill Campsite (US$10pp) is easily accessed from the gravel road between Bunazi and Minziro villages and the best base for those who want to get in some early-morning or late-afternoon birding. Alternatively, a few basic guesthouses can be found only 20 minutes' drive from the reserve in Bunazi (Optima Lodge has been recommended) or with an early start you could visit as a day trip from Bukoba.

above The Momella Lakes in Arusha National park support a wide variety of aquatic birds including flamingo PAGE 145

left A cyclist overlooking Lake Manyara, Tanzania's finest spot for birdwatching PAGE 230

below Approximately 30m high, the spectacular Kilasia waterfall flows solidly throughout the year PAGE 158

The annual migration of more than a million blue wildebeest forms one of Africa's great natural spectacles PAGE 276 — above

A kayaker along the mangroves and palm-lined beach in Pangani PAGE 344 — right

The montane forests of Usambara are alive with the raucous squawking of hornbills and the banter of monkeys PAGES 187 & 191 — below

above The Maasai traditionally worship a dualistic deity, Engai, who resides in the volcanic crater of Ol Doinyo Lengai PAGE 254

left A homestead in the traditional Wa-Arusha village of Ng'iresi, on the slopes of Mount Meru PAGE 140

below A wedding celebration of the Barabaig, a tribe of traditional pastoralists who live on the slopes of Mount Hanang PAGE 212

above Brightly coloured Tingatinga paintings are prevalent among craft stalls across Tanzania, particularly in Dar es Salaam PAGE 132

right Colourfully dressed Shambaa women sell fresh fruit and vegetables at the vibrant Lushoto market PAGE 182

below Seaweed farming is a vital source of income for coastal villagers on Zanzibar, and is one of the island's biggest exports PAGE 403

above The mysterious Kaole Ruins serve as a powerful physical reminder of Africa's forgotten past PAGE 340

left The fascinating and myriad painted shelters around Kondoa allow you to explore this enigmatic facet of Tanzania's prehistory PAGE 217

below The Great Mosque, which would have been the focal point of spiritual life in medieval Kilwa, is the largest coastal mosque of its period PAGE 454

The Bavarian style of the Lutheran Church makes it one of Dar es Salaam's most striking and attractive landmarks PAGE 329 above left

The Uhuru Monument in Arusha celebrates Tanzania's independence above right

Built in 1872, the church within the grounds of the Holy Ghost Mission is reputedly the oldest on the East African mainland PAGE 339 below

above Sunset dhow cruises are a popular activity on Zanzibar

below left Stone Town's Anglican Cathedral stands on the site of a 19th-century slave market. Pictured, a sculpture of slaves chained in a pit PAGE 377

below right Nungwi is the centre of Zanzibar's dhow-building industry; generations of skilled craftsmen have worked on the beach outside the village PAGE 395

IBANDA-KYERWA NATIONAL PARK Bounded by the Kagera River as it flows along the Rwanda border to the west then the Uganda border to the north, 294km² Ibanda-Kyerwa (e ibandakyerwa@tanzaniaparks.go.tz) was upgraded from a game reserve to a national park in 2019. It protects a scenic tract of rolling hills covered in undulating grassland, patches of acacia woodland and narrow ribbons of riverine forest. When it was originally set aside as a game reserve in the 1970s, Ibanda hosted all the Big Five and it formed part of a thriving wildlife-rich cross-border ecosystem whose much larger Rwandan component was protected in Akagera National Park. Sadly, since Akagera's borders were redrawn in the late 1990s, Ibanda has been completely isolated from other conservation areas and it has also been subject to extensive poaching. As a result, black rhino, elephant and giraffe have long been absent, the last lion was observed in 2007, and the once prolific buffalo population is now greatly reduced.

Today, the most common and conspicuous large mammals in Ibanda-Kyerwa are impala, topi and olive baboon. The park also supports around 30 roan antelope, an estimated 500 eland, and three herds of buffalo totalling around 100 individuals. In addition, a few pods of hippos are present in the Kagera, blue monkeys inhabit the riverine forests, leopards retain a typically furtive presence, and tentative plans exist to translocate zebra, wildebeest and other wildlife from the Serengeti. Conspicuous and notable on a bird checklist of more than 200 species are augur buzzard, black coucal, the stunning Ross's turaco and more elusive papyrus gonolek.

Getting there and away The semi-urban gateway to Ibanda-Kyerwa is Murongo, a remote and monumentally scruffy little border town connected to Uganda by a bridge across the Kagera River. Two scenic unsurfaced roads, both around 115km in length and taking up to 3 hours, connect Murongo to Karagwe. Marginally the better is the road from Omurushaka via Kyerwa, which runs to the west of Rumanyika-Karagwe National Park and offers some memorable views over Lake Rushwa and other wetlands flanking the Kagera River as it flows north along the Rwanda border. The alternative route runs from Kayanga along a scenic escarpment to the east of Rumanyika-Karagwe and offers spectacular views over the Kagera River as it arcs back southeast towards Kyaka and Lake Victoria. Once in Murongo, you can pay your entrance fee (US$30pp) and pick up an optional guide at the prominently signposted park headquarters, from where it is only 3km to Kifurusa Entrance Gate.

Where to stay and eat

New Riverside View Hotel ⊕ -1.0684, 30.65261. The only hotel in Murongo itself stands in small but quite attractive hillside grounds but rooms are basic & rundown. **$**

Rumanyika Game Lodge [map, page 305] ⊕ -1.07304, 30.62591; m +255 757 240102; f visitkagera. Situated about halfway along the 3km road between Murongo & Kifurusa Gate, this rustic owner-managed camp occupies large bushy, bird-filled grounds that run down to the marshy bank of the Kagera River. Spacious bungalows come with nets & hot showers. Inexpensive meals & cold beers can be ordered in a stilted wooden building that offers great views over the river. It's a little rundown, true, but far better than you could reasonably expect in such a remote & untouristed location. *From US$35 dbl B&B.* **$**

Ashraf Café This local place next to the park headquarters will dish up a plate of beef stew & rice for around US$2.

What to see and do Self-drivers can explore Ibanda-Kyerwa along a small but quite well-maintained network of game-viewing roads. The 21km main road connects Kifurusa Entrance Gate to the hillside Nehi Tatu Viewpoint (⊕ -1.07469,

30.46932), which as its name (literally 'Three Countries') indicates, overlooks the three-way border between Tanzania, Uganda and Rwanda. About 7km along the main road (⊕ -1.08743, 30.56674), a 26km loop branches south through Milima Tohe (Hill of Reedbuck) and the Chumve Chumve salt lick (a good spot for roan antelope) then arcs back north to reconnect with the main road at a junction (⊕ -1.07715, 30.48071) 2km before Nehi Tatu Viewpoint. From the southernmost point of the loop road (⊕ -1.16305, 30.54115), another 6km road runs southeast to Kihinda Gate then on to the small town of Rwenkende on the Omurushaka–Murongo road.

It is possible to arrange guided walks in the national park, and future plans include canoe trips on the Kagera River.

RUMANYIKA-KARAGWE NATIONAL PARK The former Rumanyika-Orugundu Game Reserve protects a lush and magnificently scenic 247km² tract of forested mountains that rise to above 1,700m either side of a marshy valley flowed through by the Kishanda River (a tributary of the Kagera) and an associated series of lakes. Gazetted as a national park in 2019, it is named after Omukama (King) Rumanyika I Orugundu and the Karagwe Kingdom over which he reigned from 1855 to 1882. Greatly reduced in area from the original 800km² reserve created in 1965, Rumanyika-Karagwe used to be an important stronghold for elephants, which are now locally extinct as a result of land encroachment and illegal hunting. The park still harbours significant numbers of leopard, buffalo, Defassa waterbuck, bushbuck, olive baboon, vervet monkey and blue monkey, as well as a varied selection of forest and aquatic birds. The rainforests of Rumanyika-Karagwe include many plants eaten by Africa's great apes, and there has been some talk of introducing a habituated population of eastern lowland gorilla, partly to help boost tourism to this little visited region, but also to help protect these Critically Endangered creatures, which are naturally confined to a politically volatile area of the DR Congo where the population has declined by more than 50% since the 1990s.

There are two entrances to Rumanyika-Karagwe: Nyakatuntu Gate in the south and Rugasha Gate in the north. Both gates provide access to around 20km of 4x4-only tracks that don't connect with each other due to the rugged terrain. The more interesting option is Nyakatuntu, which offers access to a series of beautiful forest-fringed lakes. Nyakatuntu Gate is reached via an unsignposted 20km track that runs northeast from the Omurushaka-Murongo Road at Rubwera (⊕ -1.37683, 30.76006; marked on some maps as Rwenkorongo), which lies on the northern outskirts of the small town of Kyerwa some 300m north of the Tanesco District Office. Rugasha Gate is accessed along a rough feeder road that runs southwest from the Kayanga–Murongo Road village of Kigorogoro (⊕ -1.11875, 30.83246). Rather inconveniently, you need to visit the park headquarters at Murongo (e ibandakyerwa@tanzaniaparks.go.tz) to pay the daily entrance fee (US$30pp) before you head to either gate.

There is no accommodation or campsite in the park. The closest option is Rweru Plaza Hotel (⊕ -1.399320, 30.75411; m +255 713 415089/783 500816; US$30 dbl B&B; **$**), which lies in central Kyerwa 3km from Rubwera junction and 45 minutes' drive from Nyakatuntu Gate. Alternatively, the park could be visited as a day trip from Murongo (but not, as things stand, from Karagwe town, as you'd need to divert to Murongo to pay fees).

KIGOSI NATIONAL PARK Gazetted in 2019 as Tanzania's fourth-largest national park, the former Kigosi Game Reserve protects an 8,265km² mosaic of Brachystegia woodland and wetlands bordered to the west by the Moyowosi (sometimes spelt Muyovozi) River and 11,430km² Moyowosi Game Reserve. The contiguous national park and game reserve both form part of East Africa's largest wetland complex Malagarasi-Muyovozi, a vast mosaic of open lakes, papyrus swamps and seasonal floodplains designated as a 32,500km² Ramsar site in April 2000. The wetlands incorporate the 425km Malagarasi River, Tanzania's second-longest, which flows along the western boundary of Moyowosi Game Reserve before emptying into Lake Tanganyika some 40km south of Kigoma.

Malagarasi-Muyovozi ranks as one of the most ecologically important wetlands anywhere in Africa, particularly when it comes to IUCN red-listed aquatic birds. An estimated 1,000–2,500 shoebills represents up to 20% of the global population of these charismatic swamp-specialists, and the wetland also supports up to 5% of the world's wattled crane, and large numbers of Goliath heron, great white egret, saddle-billed stork, African pygmy goose, African fish eagle, palmnut vulture, osprey and African marsh harrier. Other notable aquatic wildlife includes one of East Africa's largest protected populations of sitatunga and Cape clawless otter, and the easternmost population of the localised slender-snouted crocodile. The wetlands and associated protected areas also support the likes of lion, leopard, spotted hyena, elephant, buffalo, giraffe, warthog, zebra hippo and around a dozen antelope species.

Alluring as it sounds on paper, Malagarasi-Muyovozi is almost totally undeveloped for tourism and the swampy terrain makes much of it inaccessible by road. The creation of Kigosi National Park, which protects the most easterly and driest part of the ecosystem, can be seen as a first step towards opening up the wetlands to adventurous visitors, but the road network and other amenities are very limited at the time of writing. According to staff at the park headquarters in Iponya, the likes of giraffe, zebra, greater kudu, sable antelope, bushbuck, topi and Defassa waterbuck are all quite common in the park, and hippos are plentiful along the Nkuba River, but the probable presence of lion, leopard, elephant and buffalo has yet to be 100% confirmed. It is also unclear whether shoebills and other key aquatic birds are resident east of the Moyowosi River or confined the larger papyrus swamps further west.

If you want to explore Kigosi, your first port of call should be the Iponya park headquarters (⊕ -3.69675, 32.11898; **m** +255 739 589599; **e** kigosi@tanzaniaparks.co.tz), which lies about 8km from the surfaced B3 along a bumpy dirt road that runs southwest from the small town of Masumbwe. Here you can pay your park fees (US$30pp entrance & US$30pp to camp, plus 18% VAT) and ask the helpful staff for up-to-date advice and information. The main park entrance gate at Ihurike lies about 40km from Masumbwe, continuing northwest along the B3 for 27km to Ushirombo, then following a signposted turn-off to the left for 13km. From Ihurike, it is about 25km to Mirambo Rock, a prominent outcrop associated with the eponymous mid-19th century Nyamwezi king, then another 90km to the Nkuba River, which is a good place to look for hippos, other large mammals and aquatic birds. Tentative plans exist to build accommodation at a yet-to-be-determined site, to introduce canoe safaris, to improve the existing tracks, and to construct a new road through the south of the park to Tabora; but for the time being Kigosi is dedicated 4x4 country and the only overnight option is to camp wild at Mirambo Rock or close to the Nkuba River. There are also a few lodges in Masumbwe, the pick being the Ndaki Green Hotel (⊕ -3.64777, 32.16580), which stands opposite the NMB bank and has decent en-suite rooms and a restaurant.

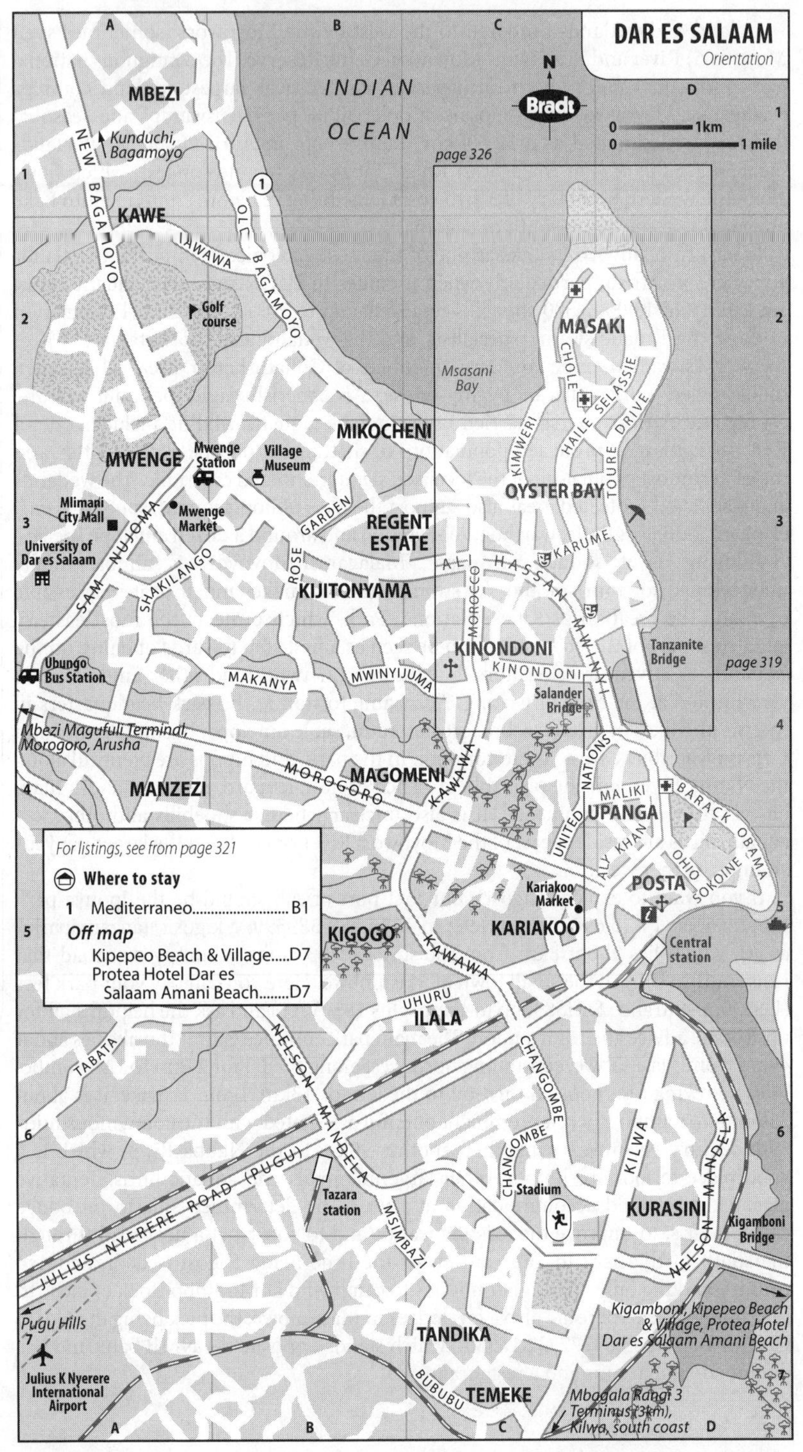
DAR ES SALAAM
Orientation
INDIAN OCEAN
Bradt
0 1km
0 1 mile
page 326
page 319
MBEZI
Kunduchi, Bagamoyo
NEW BAGAMOYO
KAWE
OLD BAGAMOYO
Golf course
MASAKI
Msasani Bay
MIKOCHENI
MWENGE
Mwenge Station
Village Museum
Mlimani City Mall
Mwenge Market
University of Dar es Salaam
OYSTER BAY
REGENT ESTATE
KIJITONYAMA
KINONDONI
Tanzanite Bridge
Ubungo Bus Station
Salander Bridge
Mbezi Magufuli Terminal, Morogoro, Arusha
MAGOMENI
MANZEZI
UPANGA
POSTA
Kariakoo Market
KARIAKOO
KIGOGO
Central station
ILALA
Stadium
Tazara station
KURASINI
Kigamboni Bridge
TANDIKA
TEMEKE
Pugu Hills
Julius K Nyerere International Airport
Kigamboni, Kipepeo Beach & Village, Protea Hotel Dar es Salaam Amani Beach
Mbagala Rangi 3 Terminus (3km), Kilwa, south coast
For listings, see from page 321
Where to stay
1 Mediterraneo.......................... B1
Off map
Kipepeo Beach & Village.....D7
Protea Hotel Dar es Salaam Amani Beach........D7

14

Dar es Salaam and the North Coast

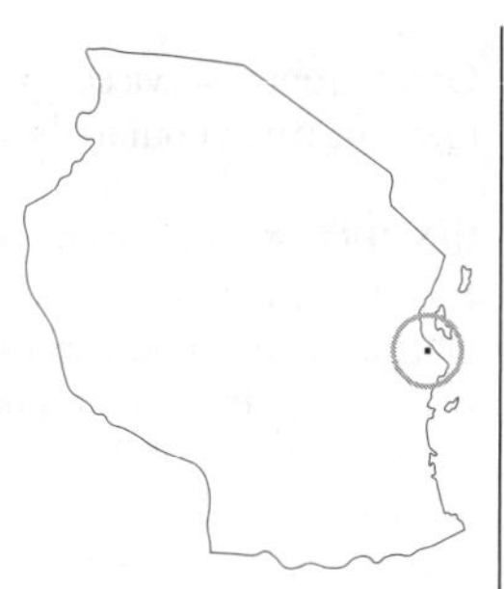

Capital of Tanzania from 1887 to 1973, the port of Dar es Salaam, set on the Indian Ocean mainland about 30km southwest of Zanzibar, remains the country's most populous, prosperous and vibrant city. It is also the site of the country's largest international airport, and while this has been replaced by Kilimanjaro/Arusha as the main port of entry and springboard for the northern safari circuit, Dar es Salaam remains the obvious starting point for safaris to southern Tanzania, and the main funnel for flights and ferries to Zanzibar and the islands. In terms of amenities, Dar es Salaam is geared primarily towards business travellers, and has a relatively low tourist profile, thanks to the ease with which fly-in visitors can pass through its international airport without setting foot in the city itself. Despite this, the old city centre doesn't lack for character or historic interest, and it is flanked by some attractive beaches, though neither deserves to be mentioned in the same breath as its counterparts on Zanzibar. Rather more compelling, only an hour's drive north of Dar es Salaam, is the small port town of Bagamoyo, a former slaving entrepôt steeped in history and equipped with beachfront accommodation catering to most budgets. Further north still, Saadani National Park is the only East African wildlife reserve lapped by the waves of the Indian Ocean, and its lodges make a fine wilderness alternative to a more conventional beach resort at the end of a dusty safari.

DAR ES SALAAM

The *ipso facto* commercial and social capital of Tanzania, Dar es Salaam is a lively, bustling Indian Ocean port whose maritime significance within East Africa is rivalled only by Mombasa. Affectionately nicknamed 'Bongo' and often abbreviated to plain 'Dar', it is the focal point of East Africa's largest urban agglomeration, with a population estimated at almost 7 million in 2022. Despite this, Dar es Salaam features on relatively few tourist itineraries to Tanzania. The main reason for this is logistical: quite simply, for those heading to the popular northern safari circuit, Dar es Salaam's Julius Nyerere International Airport is a far less convenient port of entry than Kilimanjaro International Airport, which stands between the northern safari hubs of Arusha and Moshi. As for those tourists who do land at Dar, the vast majority will be in transit to Zanzibar (a 20min air hop to the northeast), or to Kilimanjaro/Arusha (90mins north) or to one of the national parks on the southern safari circuit. Still, while it would be disingenuous to punt Dar es Salaam as an essential addition to a Tanzanian safari, it is a likeable and interesting city, one with a distinct sense of place. Architecturally, the city centre's burgeoning forest of modern high-rises hides an understorey of older buildings that display a rich mix of German, British, Asian and Arabian influences, while the superficial hustle and bustle overlies a laidback, friendly atmosphere typical of old Swahili ports. And whether or not the city itself appeals, Dar es Salaam's Indian

Ocean front is serviced by some excellent hotels and restaurants and flanked by some lovely beaches, both to the north and to the south.

HISTORY A modern city by coastal standards, Dar es Salaam was founded by Sultan Majid of Zanzibar in the 1860s, close to what was then the insignificant fishing village of Mzizima (on the site of present-day Ocean Road Hospital). The city's name dates to Majid's tenancy and is usually cited as an abbreviation of Bandari Salaam (Haven of Peace), reflecting the sultan's great love of the site. More likely, however, is that it is a corruption of Dari Salaam (House of Peace), the name Majid gave his palace in reference to nearby Mzizima, which means 'healthy' or 'tranquil place' in the local dialect.

Before Majid Prior to 1862, Mzizima was a typical coastal fishing village, ruled by small-time self-styled Sultans of the Shomvi and Pazi clans with a peripheral interest in the coastal trade. The only evidence of medieval maritime trade out of Dar es Salaam harbour is a quantity of 13th-century Chinese pottery unearthed at Kivukoni, near the present-day ferry terminal. The absence of structural ruins or more modern artefacts indicates that this site was abandoned before the 14th century, when stone buildings became the vogue on the coast. Otherwise, the area's most important pre-1860s ports, respectively about 30km north and 15km south of the modern city, were Kunduchi and Mbwamaji, both of which house the remains of Shirazi mosques and Omani pillar tombs.

Modern writers sometimes treat it as an oversight on the part of the Shirazi and Portuguese that Dar es Salaam, with its fine harbour, stood alone among modern Tanzanian ports in being unused during the great eras of coastal trade. In reality, however, the harbour's main assets to modern ships – its depth and shelter – would not have been significant advantages to the relatively small seafaring vessels used in earlier eras. Furthermore, the approach to the harbour is unusually hazardous to small ships, as noted by the 19th-century explorer Joseph Thomson, who described it as 'a narrow, zigzag dangerous channel [where] a false turn of the wheel or a mistaken order would bring [a ship] to grief'.

Dar under Majid and Barghash Local tradition has it that Sultan Majid was encouraged to visit Mzizima by Said bin Abdullah, the illegitimate son of a prominent Zanzibari merchant and a high-ranking local Pazi woman. Said originally sailed from Mzizima to Zanzibar to seek the sultan's counsel with regard to the unpunished murder of a local merchant's son. Majid, impressed by his guest's description, decided to join him on the return voyage to Mzizima, and was so enamoured that he immediately arranged to lease land there. Three years later, Majid returned with a small garrison and several artisans, and set about building a palace, hotel, fort and other stone buildings along present-day Sokoine Drive. Majid's new capital officially opened in September 1867, when the English, French, American and German consuls attended a large banquet held in the new palace.

Majid's relocation to Mzizima was not quite as whimsical as folklore suggests. It is likely that the sultan believed moving his capital away from Zanzibar would reduce his vulnerability to domestic political intrigues and to the influence of various European consuls sited there. Majid evidently also intended to replace Bagamoyo as the main mainland centre of trade opposite Zanzibar. A letter written in November 1866 by Dr Seward of the British Consulate on Zanzibar notes that Majid 'hopes to form the nucleus of a trading port, whence caravan routes shall radiate into the interior, and which bye and bye roads along the coast may connect with Kilwa and Lamu'. One factor in this decision might have been that Dar es Salaam's harbour was more suitable to large European ships than Bagamoyo. Seward noted that 'the capacity of this new port for shipping is of the best' and that although 'the narrowness of the leading channel is a drawback which only a steam tug can countervail…this want has been anticipated and a powerful tug has been ordered from Hamburg'.

We shall never know whether Majid would have realised his grand plans for Dar es Salaam. In 1870, the sultan slipped in his new palace, broke several bones and punctured a lung, and was hastily taken for medical treatment to Zanzibar, where he died a few days later. His successor Barghash decided to retain Zanzibar as his capital and to stick with the existing trade network through the mainland ports of Bagamoyo and Kilwa Kivinje. Barghash did retain an agent at Dar es Salaam, and his abode – a two-storey building that still stands on Sokoine Drive – was well maintained, but the palace and other buildings were abandoned. By 1873, Majid's capital had become something approaching a ghost town.

The modern rise of Dar es Salaam In 1877, the anti-slaver Sir William Mackinnon proposed Dar es Salaam as the starting point for the construction of 'Mackinnon's Road', intended to encourage legitimate trade between the coast and Lake Nyasa, but eventually abandoned after 112km had been completed. In the same year, a GEAC station was established there under an administrator called Leue, who penned a brief but vivid description of his posting: 'a town of ruins [that] had sunk as quickly as it had risen under Majid…Streets were overgrown with grass and bush [and] teeming with snakes, scorpions, centipedes and other pests…In the halls of the Sultan's palace lived bats…part of the palace was used as a gaol and…where once the harem ladies' tender feet had trodden, now clanked the prisoners' chains.'

Ironically, it would be the German colonists who revived and realised Majid's grand plans for Dar es Salaam. Ten years after Leue first set foot there, the 'town of ruins' replaced Tanga as capital of German East Africa. Between 1893 and 1899 several departments of the colonial government were established there, along with a Roman Catholic cathedral in 1898. The arrival of the central railway consolidated Dar es Salaam's position; by 1914, when the line was completed, Dar was the country's most significant harbour and trading centre. After World War I, when German East Africa became Tanganyika, Dar es Salaam remained the capital, and its importance has never been challenged – although the national capital is now Dodoma, Dar remains the country's economic hub, with a population that increased from about 1,000 people in 1867 to 20,000 in 1900, 270,000 in 1967, and passed the 1 million mark in the early 1990s. An annual population increase of 5.6% since 2002 makes it Africa's third fastest-growing city, with a population estimated at almost 7 million.

Along with the rest of Tanzania, Dar es Salaam slumped to an economic nadir during the socialist 1970s. By the early 1980s, its streets were acneous with potholes, shops had long given up the pretence of having anything to sell, water ran for about an hour on a good day, and 'tourist traffic' was limited to the occasional overland traveller crossing between eastern and southern Africa. Since then, the city has staged a remarkable recovery. True, many of its buildings could use a scrub and a whitewash, and poverty remains as rife as in any large African city. But the overall impression on visiting Dar today is that of a modern, vibrant city: smoothly surfaced streets, pavements spilling over with pedlars and colourful informal markets, well-stocked shops, a rapidly increasing number of smart high-rise buildings, and water and electricity supplies as reliable as you could hope for.

ORIENTATION

City centre The city centre straddles a **claw-shaped peninsula** bounded by the Indian Ocean to the northeast, Kurusini Creek and harbour to the south, and Bibi Titi Mohamed Street to the northwest. The main southwest–northeast thoroughfare **Samora Avenue** and its southeast–northwest counterpart **Azikiwe** (or Maktaba) **Street** intersect at a roundabout guarded by the well-known **Askari Monument**. West of the monument, waterfront **Sokoine Drive** is flanked by several important landmarks including the **Zanzibar Ferry Terminal**. East of the Askari Monument, Kivukoni Front angles southeast to provide access to the **Kivukoni–Kigamboni Ferry Terminal** and **Kivukoni Fish Market**.

Azikiwe (Maktaba) Street divides central Dar es Salaam into two very different halves. The leafy and relatively sedate **old colonial administrative quarter** to the east comprises a neat grid of roads dotted with old colonial buildings such as Ocean Road Hospital, State House and the National Museum. By contrast, the westerly **old Indian and Arab quarter** is a chaotic labyrinth of narrow roads lined by a miscellany of colourful Hindu temples, domed mosques, modern skyscrapers, and early-20th-century Indian and Arabic buildings.

Suburban Dar es Salaam West of the city centre, densely inhabited **Kariakoo**, the city's oldest indigenous quarter (its name is a Swahili corruption of the 'Carrier Corps' that was based here after Britain captured the city from Germany in World War I) has housed the city's main market since 1923. Bounding Kariakoo to the north, **Morogoro Road** connects Dar es Salaam not only to Morogoro but also to other inland towns, from Iringa and Dodoma to Moshi and Arusha, and it is flanked by **Ubungo Station**, the city's most important long-haul bus terminal, some 8km from the city centre. On the southern boundary of Kariakoo, **Julius Nyerere** (or Pugu) **Road** runs southwest for 10km to **Julius Nyerere International Airport**.

The main thoroughfare running north out of the city centre is **Ali Hassan Mwinyi Drive**, which after 2km leads across **Selander Bridge** to become the **New Bagamoyo Road**. This road is frequently very congested, a situation that was somewhat alleviated in February 2022 by the opening of the nippy new 673m-long Tanzanite Bridge, which runs offshore parallel to Selander Bridge. East of the New Bagamoyo Road, the upmarket seafront suburbs of **Oyster Bay** start immediately north of Selander and Tanzanite bridges, while the more northerly **Msasani Peninsula** (often referred to just as 'The Peninsula') hosts several of the city's most prestigious hotels and a cluster of upmarket bars and restaurants that cater to expats, tourists and wealthy locals. Several other important landmarks lie alongside or close to the New Bagamoyo Road, among them the **US Embassy** and vast **Mlimani City Mall**.

GETTING THERE AND AWAY

Dar es Salaam has good local and international transport links. Details of transport to other parts of the country are given throughout this guide, under the relevant town or area, but a brief overview follows.

By air The **Julius Nyerere International Airport** [314 A7] (w taa.go.tz), 10km from the city centre, is served by flights from many African and European cities, as well as domestic flights to most large Tanzanian towns. The airport is a 30–60-minute taxi ride from the city centre, depending on traffic, with a negotiable fare of US$15–20. A list of international and domestic airlines serving the airport can be found on page 356.

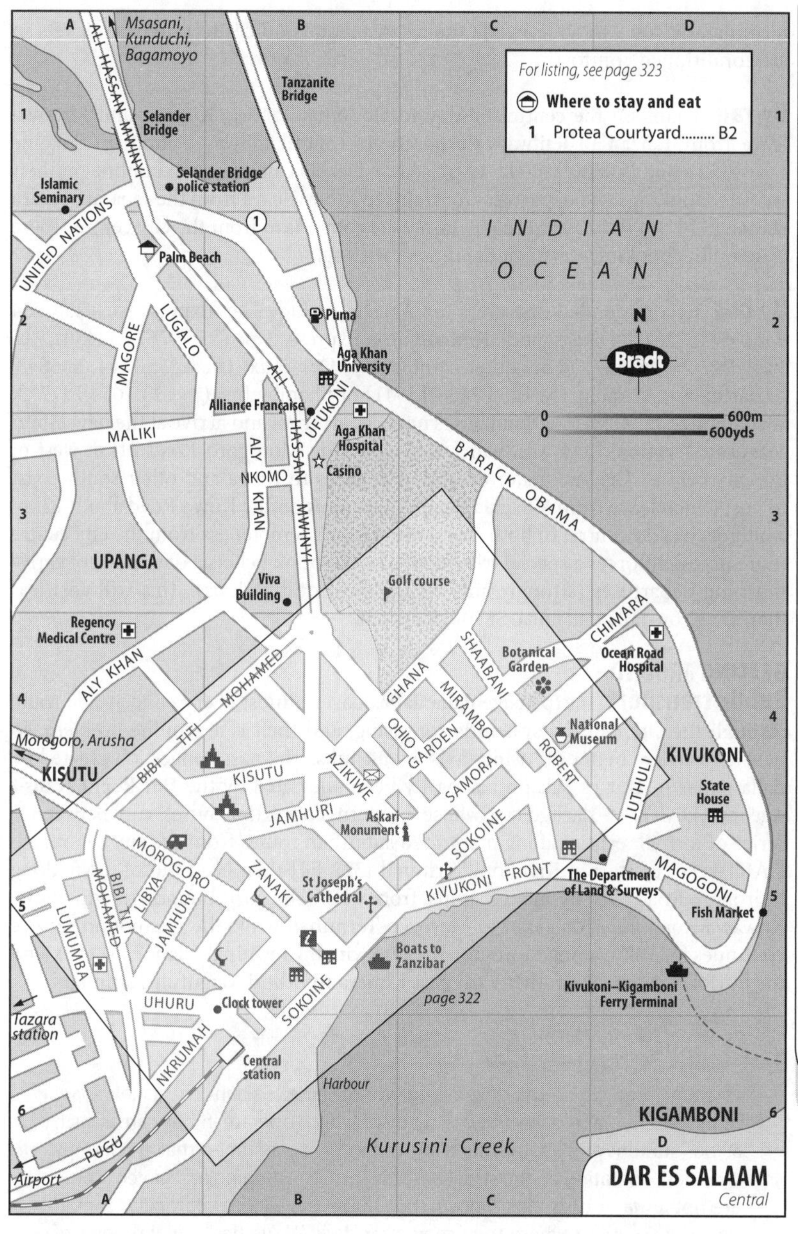

By boat Several boats run between Dar es Salaam and Zanzibar daily. All the boat operators have kiosks clustered centrally on Sokoine Drive, so it's easy to shop around for prices, which start at around US$25 one-way. Most reliable are Azam Marine (022 2123324; w azammarine.com) and Zan Fast Ferries [322 D4] (m +255 674 151427; w zanfastferries.co.tz), which between them cross up to six times daily in either direction, taking 45–90 minutes. Booking online spares you the hassle of dealing with the hustlers who hang out outside the ferry terminal, or you can slide inside their conspicuous offices to purchase tickets in air-conditioned comfort.

By rail Trains on the central railway to Dodoma, Tabora, Kigoma and Mwanza leave from **Tanzanian Railways Corporation**'s central railway station on Sokoine Drive [322 B3] (0800 110042; w trc.co.tz). Tickets can be booked online on their website. Bookings and departures for trains to Mbeya leave from the separate **Tazara station** [314 B6] (022 2861163; w tazarasite.com), 4km from the city centre. There is no online booking service at the time of writing.

By bus Recommended operators for Arusha include Dar Express (m +255 754 946155/487261/049395) and Kilimanjaro Express (m +255 767 334301/715 144301/765 064587). For other routes try Dar Lux (m +255 744 666643; f darluxco), Al Saedy (m +255 713 013541) or Shabiby Bus (m +255 654 777773; w shabiby.co.tz. Most long-haul buses now depart from and arrive at the new **Mbezi Magufuli Terminal** [314 A4], which lies alongside Morogoro Road 21km west of the city centre. The one major exception is buses to Kilwa and other south-coast towns, which leave from **Mbagala Rangi 3 Terminus** on the Kilwa Road about 12km south of the city centre. In both cases, the station's remoteness from the city centre more or less enforces a special trip out of town to book tickets a day ahead of early-morning departures (strongly advised for most destinations). This will cost less than US$1 by dalla dalla or US$10–15 by taxi.

GETTING AROUND

Public transport Inexpensive **dalla dallas** cover almost every conceivable route through the city, but the system is confusing, and theft is a genuine problem, so new arrivals are better off using taxis or tuk-tuks. The past congestion created by dalla dallas in Dar es Salaam has partly been alleviated by the **Dar Rapid Transit Agency** (DART; w dart.go.tz), whose modern concertina buses run between a series of formal termini along prescribed suburban routes from the city centre. All DART services start at Kivukoni Terminal [322 E4] then head out of town along Morogoro Road to Magomeni Mapipa, from where the northbound line runs along Kuwawa Road for about 3km to Morocco Terminal, while the westbound service continues for 10km along Morogoro Road to Kimara Terminal. Plans exist to extend the DART service for another 7km past Kimara to Mbezi Magufuli Terminal.

A WORD OF WARNING

Like any large city in the developing world, Dar es Salaam has its fair share of pickpockets and petty thieves, many of whom operate in busy areas such as bus stations and ferry terminals. It can safely be assumed that any money changers operating on the street are scam artists. Mugging and violent crime are not a major cause for concern, but single travellers in particular should be sensible about where they stray after dark. We've had a few reports of seemingly friendly scammers befriending travellers then offering them a lift in a car or taxi, where they are driven to a quiet place and robbed or abused. As with most large cities, it is reasonable to assume that any overly friendly stranger might have another agenda, but be particularly wary on Maktaba Street (around the post office) and Sokoine Drive (around the ferry terminals) and in the vicinity of Kariakoo Market and Coco Beach.

Taxis and tuk-tuks There are taxis all over the place. The standard price for a taxi within the city centre is around US$3, though you'll probably be asked for more at first. For rides further afield, the fare will vary from US$5 to US$10 to Oyster Bay or the Msasani Peninsula, and will be more like US$15–20 to the airport. If you are jumping in a taxi at the port, make sure it's a reputable taxi with the correct plates. The airport is more reliable in terms of taxi regulation. Tuk-tuks are cheaper but slower.

WHERE TO STAY There is no shortage of accommodation in and around Dar es Salaam, and the following highly selective list covers the city centre and seaside suburbs running north from Oyster Bay to Msasani Peninsula. For genuine beach resorts, head to the more rustic coastline immediately south of the city, or to more distant Bagamoyo, all of which are covered later in the chapter.

Exclusive

✷ **Oyster Bay Hotel** [326 C5] Touré Dr; **w** theoysterbayhotel.com. All billowing white drapes, stylish sculptures & African minimalism, the super-exclusive Oyster Bay is easily Dar es Salaam's top boutique hotel. The 8 spacious suites are beautifully decorated & come with king-size bed, walk-in netting, flatscreen DSTV, wooden writing desk & balcony with a sea view. Food is tailored around guests' preferences, but is reliably superb. There is a small swimming pool in the garden. **$$$$$$**

Upmarket

Hyatt Regency Kilimanjaro [322 F4] Kivukoni Front; **w** hyatt.com. Built on the seafront in the 1950s, the 'Kili' has undergone several subsequent transformations but remains the most upmarket option in the city centre. The ostentatious angular architecture, glazed over by arctic AC, stands in surreal contrast to the superb view over the tropical harbour. Still, if 5-star facilities are what you are after, 5-star is what you get – the 180 rooms are immense & come with all mod cons & 24hr room service, while facilities include a 20m swimming pool, gym, spa, casino, several restaurants & bars & an in-house shopping mall. **$$$$**

Sea Cliff Hotel [326 D1] Touré Dr; **m** +255 764 700600; **w** hotelseacliff.com. Perched on a cliff at the northern tip of Msasani Peninsula, this comfortable & stylish hotel comprises 114 large rooms with wooden floors, hardwood furnishings, king-size bed, flatscreen DSTV & marble fittings in the bathroom. Facilities include a franchise of the popular Alcove Restaurant, a coffee shop, a swimming pool with ocean view & a gym. A nearby mall has ATMs, several good restaurants & cafés, & a massage centre. **$$$$**

✷ **Serena Hotel Dar es Salaam** [322 E1] Ohio St; **w** serenahotels.com. Set in lush tropical grounds bordering the city centre, the Serena is popular with business travellers but also regarded as offering the best value in its range by many tour operators. Service is excellent & the 230 spacious rooms have all the facilities you'd expect, including DSTV & AC. Facilities include 2 restaurants, a beauty salon, a gymnasium, a jogging track, a sauna & an outdoor swimming pool. **$$$$**

Moderate

✷ **Coral Beach Hotel** [326 C2] Yacht Club Rd; **m** +255 744 287554; **w** coralbeach-tz.com. This well-run resort-like hotel stands in compact green gardens with a swimming pool & ocean frontage. The 62 large (& mostly sea-facing) rooms have queen-size beds with walk-in nets, DSTV, AC & writing desk. An excellent restaurant, specialising in seafood & curries, offers the choice of eating indoors or alfresco as the sun sets over Msasani Bay. Good value. *From US$130/140 sgl/dbl B&B.* **$$$**

✷ **Mediterraneo Hotel & Restaurant** [314 B1] Tuari Rd; **m** +255 754 812567; **w** mediterraneotanzania.com. Situated on Msasani Bay's west shore 12km north of the city centre, this refreshingly non-corporate hotel has 42 spacious rooms with contemporary Afro-Mediterranean décor (terracotta tiles, wrought-iron furniture, colourful local artworks) as well as AC, fitted nets, DSTV & private balconies. It stands in large rambling beachfront gardens with a swimming pool, views across the bay to

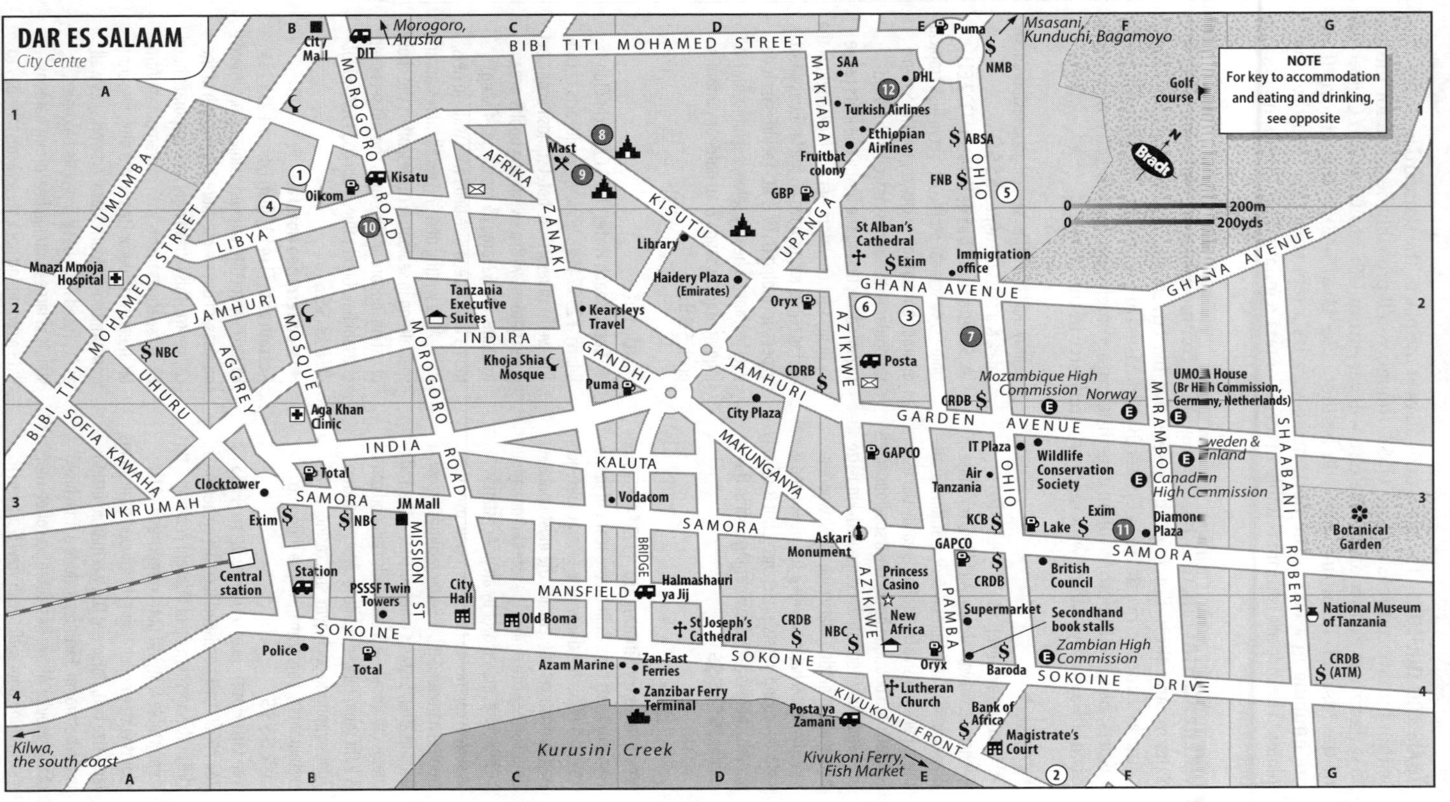
DAR ES SALAAM
City Centre
Morogoro, Arusha
Msasani, Kunduchi, Bagamoyo
NOTE
For key to accommodation and eating and drinking, see opposite
Golf course
Bradt
0 200m
0 200yds
BIBI TITI MOHAMED STREET
LUMUMBA
LIBYA
JAMHURI
MOSQUE
AGGREY
UHURU
BIBI SOFIA KAWAHA
NKRUMAH
MOROGORO ROAD
AFRIKA
ZANAKI
KISUTU
UPANGA
MAKTABA
OHIO
GHANA AVENUE
INDIRA
GANDHI
INDIA
KALUTA
MAKUNGANYA
AZIKIWE
GARDEN AVENUE
MIRAMBO
SHAABANI ROBERT
SAMORA
MISSION ST
BRIDGE
MANSFIELD
PAMBA
SOKOINE
SOKOINE DRIVE
KIVUKONI FRONT
City Mall
DIT
Oilkom
Kisatu
Mnazi Mmoja Hospital
NBC
Tanzania Executive Suites
Khoja Shia Mosque
Aga Khan Clinic
Total
Clocktower
Exim
JM Mall
Central station
Station
PSSSF Twin Towers
City Hall
Old Boma
Police
Mast
Library
Haidery Plaza (Emirates)
Kearsleys Travel
Puma
Vodacom
Halmashauri ya Jij
St Joseph's Cathedral
Azam Marine
Zan Fast Ferries
Zanzibar Ferry Terminal
Kurusini Creek
Kilwa, the south coast
Posta ya Zamani
Kivukoni Ferry, Fish Market
SAA
DHL
Turkish Airlines
Ethiopian Airlines
Fruitbat colony
GBP
ABSA
FNB
NMB
St Alban's Cathedral
Immigration office
Oryx
CDRB
Posta
City Plaza
CRDB
Mozambique High Commission
Norway
GAPCO
IT Plaza
Air Tanzania
KCB
Wildlife Conservation Society
Lake
Askari Monument
Princess Casino
New Africa
Supermarket
Secondhand book stalls
British Council
Zambian High Commission
Baroda
Lutheran Church
Bank of Africa
Magistrate's Court
Botanical Garden
National Museum of Tanzania
CRDB (ATM)

the Msasani Peninsula & a popular restaurant specialising in Italian fare & fresh grills. *From US$85/95 sgl/dbl B&B.* **$$–$$$$**

Onomo Hotel [322 E2] Ghana Rd; w onomohotels.com. In refreshing contrast to the rather staid mid-range hotels that otherwise dot the city centre, this modern high-rise stands out for its contemporary African feel & décor. The brightly decorated rooms come with sat TV, minibar & AC, while amenities include a good & well-priced restaurant, a rooftop bar with a fabulous view over the city, a swimming pool & a gym. The location is central but quiet. *From US$116/133 sgl/dbl B&B.* **$$$**

Protea Courtyard Hotel [319 B2] Barack Obama Dr; w marriott.com. Bordering the city centre but close to the beach, this comfortable chain hotel started life in 1948 as the Seaview, & hosted the likes of presidents Kenyatta (Kenya) & Kaunda (Zambia) in its pomp, as well as the South African ANC leader Oliver Tambo. Today, it has comfortable rooms with queen-size bed, walk-in net, DTSV & AC, along with an excellent restaurant, a 24hr coffee shop & a small courtyard swimming pool. *US$98/112 sgl/dbl B&B.* **$$$**

Budget

Econo Lodge [322 B1] Off Libya Rd; m +255 684 947010; e econolodgetanzania@gmail.com. This well-established hotel has a convenient central location. The comfortable rooms with hot shower & fan or AC are good value. *US$16/20 sgl/dbl with fan, US$30/33 sgl/dbl with AC B&B.* **$**

Safari Inn [322 B1] Off Libya Rd; m +255 683 128933; e safari-inn@outlook.com. One of the city centre's longest-serving & most popular budget hotels, tucked away along a quietish cul de sac, this has 40 clean tiled rooms with hot shower, net & AC or fan. The hands-on management is a reliable source of bus & taxi recommendations. *US$18/20 dbl with fan/AC B&B.* **$**

✷ The Slow Leopard [326 C3] Chole Rd; m +255 757 029244; w theslowleopard.com. Dar's most appealing budget option, this funky hostel on Msasani Peninsula offers the choice of private rooms or 5- & 10-bed dorms, all with AC, fan, net & access to a common shower & balcony. The vibe is relaxed & sociable, the attached sports bar & restaurant are great for hanging out & it can arrange affordable safaris, as well as excursions to Kilwa (where it also has a hostel, page 452). *From US$15pp dorm bed & US$40 dbl B&B.* **$**

YWCA [322 E2] Off Maktaba St; m +255 677 061606. The YWCA has long been a central favourite with couples & single women travelling on the cheap. Single men are not accommodated. Clean rooms come with nets & fans. A canteen serves inexpensive if unexciting meals. *US$22 dbl B&B.* **$**

DAR ES SALAAM *City Centre*
For listings, see from page 321

Where to stay

1	Econo Lodge	B1
2	Hyatt Regency Kilimanjaro	F4
3	Onomo	E2
4	Safari Inn	B1
5	Serena Hotel Dar es Salaam	E1
6	YWCA	E2

Where to eat and drink

7	Akemi Revolving	E2
	The Alcove (see Haidery Plaza)	D2
8	Chili & Lime	C1
9	Chowpatty	C1
10	Mamboz Corner BBQ	B2
	Old Boma Seaview (see Old Boma)	C4
11	Samaki Samaki	F3
12	Subway	E1

Beaches south of Dar A great alternative to staying in Dar es Salaam itself, the coast to the immediate south feels several worlds apart rather than a mere kilometre or two from the city. The south coast is separated from the city centre by Dar es Salaam's main harbour, and linked to it by the Kivukoni–Kigamboni motor ferry at the harbour entrance and Nyerere Bridge, which opened in 2016 some 4km to the south. South of this, a surfaced road travels through rustic fields overlooking a series of idyllic beaches pockmarked with mushroom-shaped coral outcrops. The Kivukoni–Kigamboni ferry, which leaves from Kivukoni Front every 15 minutes, and takes about 5 minutes, is the best way to get here on public transport (you'll have no problem finding a dalla dalla on to Kipepeo Beach). Nyerere Bridge is the quicker option for self-drivers.

✷ **Kipepeo Beach & Village** m +255 754 276178; w kipepeobeach.com. Situated on a lovely beach at Mjimwema, along a short side road signposted from the main road 7km south of the ferry terminal, this ever-popular budget resort offers the choice of 2-storey bandas with net & fan, simpler beach bandas with no fan but a reliable sea breeze, or pitching a tent in the campsite. The seaside restaurant is popular with day trippers from the city, while Dekeza Dhow (w kipepeobeach.com/dekeza-dhow), offers a variety of marine activities including snorkelling, fishing, kayaking & sailing. *US$21/32 sgl/dbl without fan, US$60/75 sgl/dbl with fan; camping US$10pp.* **$–$$**

Protea Hotel Dar es Salaam Amani Beach m +255 782 410033; w marriott.com. Situated above a lovely sandy beach 30km south of the ferry, this isolated beach hotel comprises 10 large Swahili-style chalets with king-size 4-poster bed, walk-in nets, AC, fan, private sea-facing balcony & en-suite bathroom with tub & shower. The lushly vegetated gardens are teeming with birds & monkeys, fishing & other watersports are available, & there's a swimming pool & a tennis court. Good value. **$$$$**

WHERE TO EAT AND DRINK Dar es Salaam has a good range of restaurants, and food is generally of a high standard and well-priced by international standards (though costly for Tanzania). The city centre is dominated by good-value places catering primarily to local Swahili and Indian palates and budgets, while Msasani Peninsula and environs hosts the main concentration of more cosmopolitan restaurants catering to deeper wallets.

City centre

✷ **Akemi Revolving Restaurant** [322 E2] Ohio St; m + 255 753 360360; ⌚ 11.00–22.30 daily. Set on the 21st floor of Golden Jubilee Towers, Dar's only revolving restaurant offers constantly changing views over the city & a classy fine-dining experience with a varied globetrotting menu. **$$$**

The Alcove [322 D2] Haidery Plaza, Kisutu St; m +255 769 213744; e alcovetz.com; ⌚ noon–15.30 & 19.00–22.30 daily. This city-centre stalwart has been serving world-class Indian & Chinese food since it was founded in 1987. Food is tasty & good value, but the venue lacks in character. **$$**

Chili & Lime [322 C1] Kisutu Rd; m +255 738 860850; w chiliandlime.co.tz; ⌚ 09.00–22.00 Wed–Mon, 09.00–17.00 Tue. Situated almost opposite Chowpatty, this fabulous little Hindu-owned restaurant specialises in vegan South Indian fare & delicious sweets & desserts. No alcohol served. **$**

✷ **Chowpatty** [322 C1] Kisutu Rd; m +255 712 469546; f ChowpattyTZ; ⌚ 11.30–22.30 daily. Tucked in between the Hindu temples of Kisutu Rd, this well-priced vegetarian restaurant specialises in Indian & Chinese dishes. It's very popular with local Hindi families & the thaal is exceptional value at around US$5. If you visit on a Sat, it may be closed for cleaning, in which case the neighbouring Mast Restaurant has the same owners & serves a similar menu. **$**

Mamboz Corner BBQ [322 B2] Cnr Morogoro & Libya sts; m +255 784 243735; w mambozbbq-dsm-streetfood.business.site; ⌚ 18.30–midnight daily. The smartest & most popular of several informal street-side BBQ joints dotted around the city centre, this serves great grilled chicken tikka, tangy garlic naan bread & plenty else besides. The yummy fruit juices compensate for the no-alcohol policy. **$**

✷ **Old Boma Seaview Restaurant** [322 C4] Sokoine Dr; m +255 622 979804/735 577 833; ⌚ 07.00–22.00 Mon–Sat. A must-visit simply for its historic & scenic setting, this breezy restaurant on the roof of Dar's oldest building (now somewhat dwarfed by modern skyscrapers) offers a commanding view over the harbour. The menu is dominated by unexceptional but very affordable Swahili seafood, meat & vegetarian dishes, not all of which might be available on any given day. Even if you don't eat here, it's a fabulous spot for a mid-morning coffee or beer & wine at sundowners. **$**

Subway [322 E1] Upanga Rd; ☎ 022 212 6258; ⌚ 09.00–21.00 daily. This American franchise serves fresh baguettes with a wide selection of tasty hot & cold fillings. Good for an inexpensive lunch. **$**

Suburban

✷ **305 Karafuu** [326 A6] Karafuu St; m + 255 754 277188; w 305karafuu.co.tz; ⌚ 18.00–22.30 Tue–Sun. Despite its inauspicious setting in the owner's former garage in downmarket Kinondoni, this funky restaurant is Dar's closest thing to a culinary must-do, thanks to the sunny décor, innovative Swahili fusion cuisine, great dessert menu & interesting wine list. $$

✷ **Addis in Dar** [326 A5] Ursino St; m +255 713 266299; w addisindar.com; ⌚ 18.00–22.30 Mon–Sat. Founded in 1998, this family-run favourite near the US embassy specialises in spicy meat & vegan Ethiopian dishes. $$$

Anatolia [326 C3] The Slipway; m +255 748 406099; ⌚ 08.00–22.00 daily. This excellent Turkish restaurant with indoor & outdoor seating serves a varied selection of tasty meat-oriented light & full meals. $$–$$$

Barbecue Village [326 B4] Off Kimweri Av; m + 255 784 320736; f bbqvillage; ⌚ 18.00–23.30 Tue–Sun. This relaxed & affordable restaurant, with rooftop & garden dining areas, serves seafood, Indian & Chinese dishes. $$

Cape Town Fish Market [326 B3] Msasani Bay; m +255 758 555366; w ctfm.co.tz; ⌚ 11.00–23.00 daily, bar until 02.00 at w/ends. Boasting a fabulous seaside setting on the southern Msasani Peninsula & some of the best seafood in Tanzania, this upmarket restaurant also serves sushi, steaks & an extensive selection of South African wines. $$$

Épi d'Or [326 C2] Sea Cliff Village; m +255 786 669889; w epidor.co.tz; ⌚ 07.30–22.30 Tue–Sun. This French & Lebanese bakery on the Msasani Peninsula is great for b/fast – excellent coffee, & a good range of fresh croissants & pastries. There are also sandwiches, pizzas & other mains at lunch & dinner. $$

✷ **Samaki Samaki** [322 F3] Haile Selassie Rd; m +255 686 257503; w samakisamaki.com; ⌚ 09.00–late daily. Set in a massive thatched construction with coral rock walls & tables made from old wooden dhows, this vibey restaurant feels like a cross between a beach café & sports bar. Samaki is the Kiswahili word for fish, & fresh seafood is very much the speciality here, but there is also plenty of choice for meat-eaters (less so vegetarians), a well-priced selection of cocktails, wine & beer, & a big screen for major football matches. $$–$$$

The Waterfront [326 C3] The Slipway; m +255 769 467272; w hotelslipway.com; ⌚ 11.00–midnight daily. This popular & relaxed open-air grill stands on a deck next to the Indian Ocean. Specialities include salads, seafood, steaks & pizzas from the wood-fired oven. $$$

BARS, ENTERTAINMENT AND NIGHTLIFE

Bars and pubs There is something of a dearth of decent bars in the centre of Dar, presumably due to the strong Muslim presence, and many hotels and restaurants don't serve alcohol. A recommended exception, the characterful Old Boma Seaview Restaurant (page 324) serves chilled beers and affordable wine on a rooftop overlooking the harbour, making it a perfect sundowner spot, with the option of staying on for dinner. Less down to earth and far pricier, the rooftop **Level 8 Bar** at the Hyatt Regency Kilimanjaro [322 F4], also has a killer view and a superb selection of cocktails, wine and beer.

Further out of town, several good places for a drink inhabit the Msasani Peninsula and Oyster Bay area. If it's an old-fashioned English-style pub you're after, try the **George and Dragon** [326 D3] (m +255 717 8000021; f gndpubtz; ⌚ 13.00–late Tue–Sun), which has a well-stocked bar, a menu of typical pub grub, and more contemporary music than appearances might lead you to expect. Equally lively is **The Slow Leopard** [326 C3] (page 323; ⌚ 09.00–23.00 daily), which has a well-stocked bar with craft beer on tap, a pub menu dominated by gourmet burgers, occasional live music and big screens for major sporting events. The informal **Coco Beach Bar** [326 D4] (⌚ until late daily) at Oyster Bay is a good place to while away a day sipping cold beers and eating *mishkaki* kebabs on the Indian Ocean, and also features regular karaoke evenings. Nearby, on Haile Selassie Road, **Jackie's Pub** [326 C4] is a pleasant informal local bar with outdoor seating and inexpensive beers.

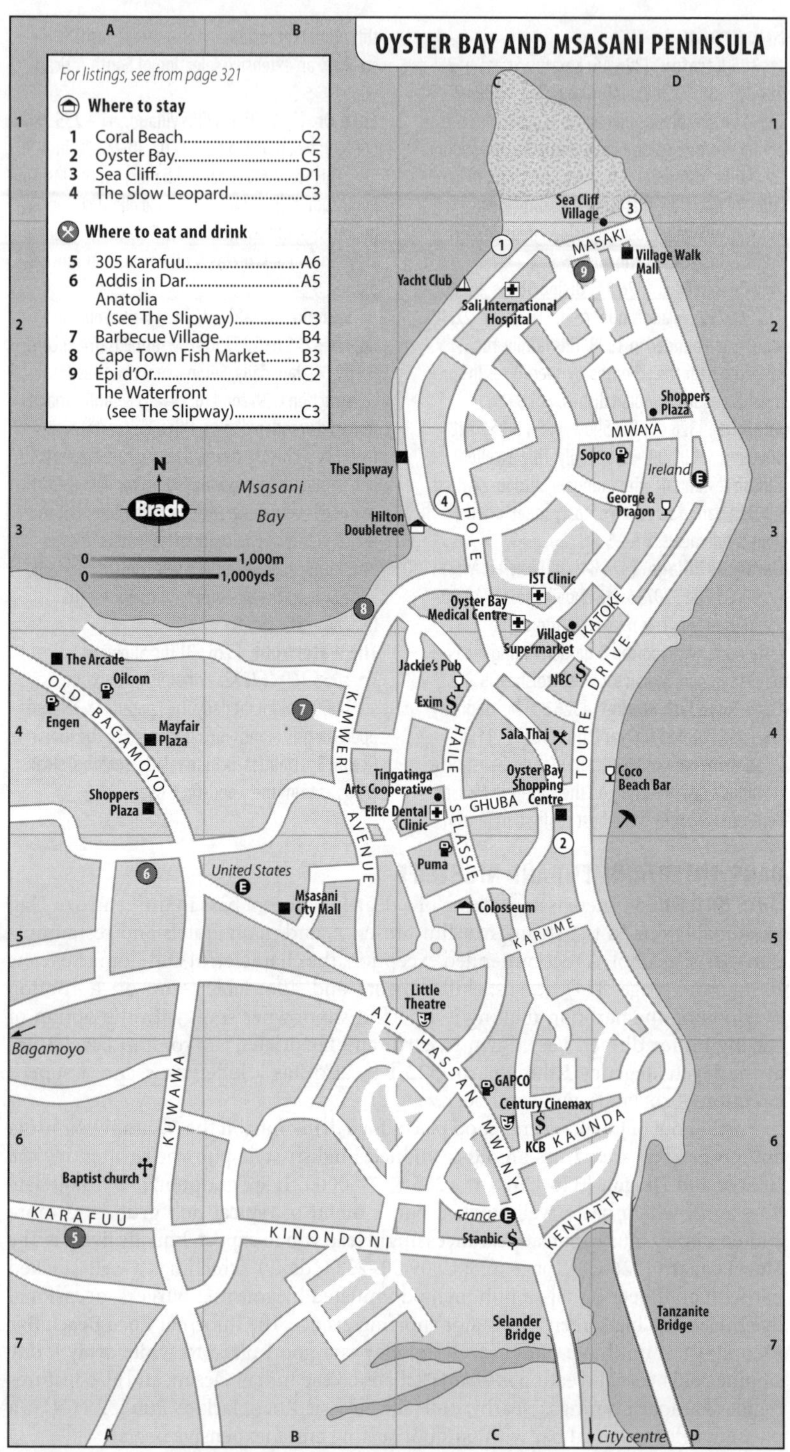
OYSTER BAY AND MSASANI PENINSULA
For listings, see from page 321
Where to stay
1 Coral Beach....C2
2 Oyster Bay....C5
3 Sea Cliff....D1
4 The Slow Leopard....C3
Where to eat and drink
5 305 Karafuu....A6
6 Addis in Dar....A5
Anatolia (see The Slipway)....C3
7 Barbecue Village....B4
8 Cape Town Fish Market....B3
9 Épi d'Or....C2
The Waterfront (see The Slipway)....C3
Msasani Bay
1,000m
1,000yds
Sea Cliff Village
MASAKI
Village Walk Mall
Yacht Club
Sali International Hospital
Shoppers Plaza
MWAYA
Sopco
Ireland
The Slipway
George & Dragon
Hilton Doubletree
CHOLE
IST Clinic
Oyster Bay Medical Centre
Village Supermarket
KATOKE
The Arcade
Oilcom
OLD BAGAMOYO
Engen
Mayfair Plaza
Jackie's Pub
Exim
NBC
TOURE DRIVE
KIMWERI AVENUE
HAILE SELASSIE
Sala Thai
Coco Beach Bar
Shoppers Plaza
Tingatinga Arts Cooperative
Elite Dental Clinic
GHUBA
Oyster Bay Shopping Centre
United States
Puma
Msasani City Mall
Colosseum
KARUME
Little Theatre
Bagamoyo
ALI HASSAN MWINYI
KUWAWA
GAPCO
Century Cinemax
KCB
KAUNDA
Baptist church
KARAFUU
KINONDONI
France
Stanbic
KENYATTA
Selander Bridge
Tanzanite Bridge
City centre

Cinema and theatre There are two branches of the multi-screen Century Cinemax (w centurycinemaxtanzania.com), one on Ali Hassan Mwinyi Road [326 C6] and one in the Mlimani City Mall [314 A3]. Both show current Western movies for around US$5. Oyster Bay's Little Theatre [326 C5] (off Haile Selassie Rd; f thelittletheatredaressalaam; m +255 716 221652) is a 180-seat auditorium that was founded in 1947 and still holds regular performances.

SHOPPING

Shopping malls and supermarkets Numerous shopping malls are dotted around suburban Dar es Salaam, the most useful to tourists staying in Msasani or the Oyster Bay area being **The Slipway** [326 C3] (w hotelslipway.com/slipway), which occupies a prime seafront position on the north end of the peninsula. In addition to four waterfront restaurants, this mall contains an excellent bookshop, a good chain supermarket and several ATMs. It is also the site of The Souk, a cluster of handicraft stalls selling high-quality local and Asian produce, and the mainland departure point for ferries to Bongoyo Island.

The largest mall in Dar es Salaam, Ubungo's 19,000m² **Mlimani City Mall** [314 A3] (Sam Nujoma Rd; w mlimanicity.co.tz) is air-conditioned throughout and hosts the Century Cinemax movie theatre, several South African chain stores, an excellent supermarket, several ATMs and a few restaurants.

On Msasani Peninsula, the air-conditioned **Shoppers Supermarket** [326 D2] (Shoppers Plaza, Haile Selassie Rd; w shoppers.co.tz; ⌚ 08.30–22.00 daily) stocks an excellent range of imported goods, South African and other wines, and fresh fruit and meat. Inside the supermarket you'll also find a bakery, while the plaza houses several ATMs, a pharmacy, a beauty salon, a phone repair shop and a terrace café.

Crafts and souvenirs Though many craft stalls can be found in the city centre, especially in the vicinity of the Askari Monument, and most upmarket hotels also have craft shops, produce tends to be expensive when compared with Arusha. Nevertheless, a few places are worth checking out. Several clothes shops and fruit stalls line Zanaki Street, but the most colourful place to buy this sort of thing is **Kariakoo Market** [314 C5] (page 330). Showcasing the best of modern Tanzanian design, **The Green Room** [326 C3] (w thegreenroomtz.com) at The Slipway sells fresh and inspiring interior design and art, many by local artists, which make great gifts.

An art form specifically associated with Dar es Salaam is Tingatinga painting (page 132), and there is no better place to shop for these than the sprawling cluster of stalls and shops centred on the **Tingatinga Arts Cooperative** [326 C4] (Haile Selassie Rd; w tingatinga.org; ⌚ 08.30–17.30 daily). Situated alongside the original Morogoro Store, where the genre's pioneer Edward Tingatinga displayed his art, the co-operative has thousands of works on display, and is well worth a visit even if you have no intention of buying.

Books The best bookshop, **A Novel Idea** [326 C3] (The Slipway; w anovelidea.co.tz; ⌚ 10.00–18.00 daily) stocks a great selection of novels, field and travel guides, and local interest books. In the city centre, an eclectic selection of inexpensive secondhand books can be bought at negotiable prices at a few **secondhand bookstalls** along Samora Avenue and Pamba Road [322 E4].

OTHER PRACTICALITIES

Communications The central **post office** is on Azikiwe Street [322 C1]. Several kiosks outside sell postcards, envelopes and writing paper.

To buy a **local SIM card** for your mobile phone, it is best to head to a bona fide Airtel or Vodacom service centre, and get the staff there to test your connection, rather than just buying from a street vendor or small shop. The most central Airtel centre is in the JM Mall [322 B3] (Samora Av; w airtel.co.tz) and there is also a Vodacom centre on the same road [322 D3] (Samora Av; w vodacom.co.tz). Both providers also have shops in the Mlimani City Mall.

Medical The **Aga Khan Hospital** [319 B2] (Ocean Rd; ☎ 022 211 5151/3; w agakhanhospitals.org) and suburban **International School of Tanzania (IST) Clinic** [326 C3] (m +255 754 783393/746 499411; w istclinic.com) are recommended for emergencies. For malaria and other blood tests, try **Regency Medical Centre** [319 A4] (m +255 784 417500; w regencymedicalcentre.com). For dental emergencies, try the **Elite Dental Clinic** [326 C4] (m +255 788 938740/764 616993; w elitedental.co.tz).

Money Visa and Mastercards can be used to draw up to Tsh400,000 of local currency per transaction (and usually up to Tsh2,000,000 daily) at countless ATMs in central and suburban Dar es Salaam.

Swahili courses **Kiswahili na Utamaduni (KIU) Swahili & Culture Trainers** (m +255 713 440045; w swahilicourses.com) offers a variety of beginners and advanced courses, as well as cultural familiarisation courses, translation and other linguistic services.

TOURIST INFORMATION There is no longer a tourist office in Dar es Salaam. A useful monthly booklet called Dar Life (m +255 784 434929; f) covers current events and listings in the city, and can be picked up at most hotels or downloaded at w issuu.com/darlife.

TOUR OPERATORS Most tour operators in Dar es Salaam specialise in visits to the southern reserves. The following companies are recommended:

Authentic Tanzania m +255 786 019965; w authentictanzania.com. Private 'bush' camping safaris, often with an emphasis on walking, in the south & west of Tanzania, as well as in more remote parts of the north.

Foxes African Safaris w tanzaniasafaris.info. These southern safari specialists run several camps on the southern circuit, as well as Safari AirLink, which operates charter & scheduled flights to the major southern & western reserves.

Hippo Tours & Safaris m +255 754 267706; w hippotours.com. This long-standing operator specialises in Selous & other southern safaris.

Kearsleys Travel [322 C2] Zanaki St; m +255 762 224499; w kearsleys.com. Still based in the heart of the city centre, Dar es Salaam's oldest safari operator, founded in 1948, has years of experience in arranging safaris throughout Tanzania, & the dynamic management makes it an excellent first point of contact for safaris in the south.

WHAT TO SEE AND DO Dar es Salaam offers little in the way of conventional sightseeing. The harbour area and back streets between Maktaba Road and the station house several old German buildings, as does the area around the national museum and botanical gardens. If you have a couple of days to kill in Dar es Salaam, you might want to spend them at the beaches north or south of the city centre, or around Bagamoyo, both of which are covered later in this chapter. The beaches immediately north or south of Dar also form realistic goals for a day trip from the city centre.

Historical buildings and monuments Several relics of Dar es Salaam's early days are dotted around the city centre. The oldest is the **Old Boma** [322 C4] on the corner of Morogoro Road and Sokoine Drive, a plain, rather austere whitewashed monolith, built using coral rubble in the traditional coastal style, and distinguished by its inscribed Zanzibari door. It was built in 1867 as a hotel to house visitors to the court of Sultan Majid, whose palace stood alongside it. Between 1870 and 1887, the building was the residence of the Sultan of Zanzibar's local agent, and it subsequently served as the GEAC's first administrative headquarters in Dar es Salaam, and the police charge office. It was recently restored as the rooftop Old Boma Seaview Restaurant (page 324), which also offers guided city tours.

Several late 19th-century German buildings have survived into modern times. The **Ocean Road Hospital** [319 D4], which lies east of the city centre at the end of Samora Avenue, was built in 1897, and is notable for its twin domed towers. Nearby **State House** [319 D4] also dates to a similar time, though it was heavily damaged in World War I, and the modern building, restored in 1922, bears little resemblance to photographs of the original.

The area between Ocean Road and Azikiwe Street, though increasingly populated by modern high-rises, is also notable for its pre-1914 German buildings, recognisable by their red-tiled roofs. The **Botanical Garden** [322 G3], established in 1906, is now pretty rundown, but if you walk back to town along Kivukoni Front, you will be rewarded by good views of the city and harbour. Kivukoni Front also leads you to the city's most impressive building, the **Lutheran Church** [322 E4] on the corner of Sokoine Drive and Azikiwe Road. This was built in 1898 in the Bavarian style, and following the restoration of its exterior, it's a striking and attractive landmark, best viewed from the park on Sokoine Drive.

A block away, at the junction of Azikiwe Road and Samora Avenue, the **Askari Monument** [322 E3] comprises a bronze statue of a soldier carrying a rifle and bayonet that point towards the harbour. Unveiled in 1927, it commemorates the 'askaris' (African soldiers) who fought in the British Carrier Corps in World War I.

Back on Sokoine Drive, a few blocks west of the Lutheran Church, the Gothic-influenced **St Joseph's Cathedral** [322 D4] was built between 1897 and 1902. Other buildings dating from the German era include the **City Hall** [322 C4] (on Sokoine Drive opposite the Old Boma), several ex-civil servants' residences around the botanical garden, and the buildings housing the Department of Lands and Surveys and Magistrate's Court on Kivukoni Front [322 E4].

For a very different architectural experience, the area around India Road is dotted with Indian- and Arabic-influenced buildings dating to the mid 20th century, as well as ornate mosques reflecting its predominantly Islamic population. Nearby Kisutu Road is lined with pretty Hindu temples and low-key Indian eateries. The road is particularly colourful during festivals such as Diwali, when the city's substantial Hindu community turns out in force.

National Museum of Tanzania [322 G4] (w nmt.go.tz; ⌚ 09.30–18.00 daily; entrance US$5) Located near the Botanical Gardens on Shaabani Robert Street, the National Museum originally opened in 1940 as the King George VI Museum and underwent major renovations in 2012. The section on early hominid development contains some of the world's most important fossils, while the upstairs history displays include a good selection of exhibits dating back to the era of European exploration and German occupation. If you plan to visit Kilwa Kisiwani, don't miss the display of coins, pottery and other artefacts found during excavations there.

Kivukoni Fish Market [319 D5] Situated on Barack Obama Drive between State House and the Kigamboni Ferry Terminal, this traditional market is well worth visiting, especially in the early morning, when dhows laden with the night's catch stream into the adjacent harbour, offering great photographic opportunities at sunrise. It is also a hive of no-nonsense commerce, with larger fish often attracting some heated auctioneering, and plenty of bargaining over more routine catches. Almost all the seafood you'll eat in Dar is sourced from here – indeed, self-caterers might well want to head down early to score some fresh fish – but be warned that the action peaks shortly after dawn, and it is pretty much all over by 08.00.

Kariakoo Market [314 C5] A huge variety of clothes, foodstuffs, spices and traditional medicines can be bought at this lively and colourful covered market, which extends on to the surrounding streets in the form of a chaotic miscellany of stalls. It is situated in the suburb of Kariakoo, one of the oldest populated parts of Dar es Salaam – indeed, a contemporary census indicated that about 60% of the city's African population lived in this quarter in 1913. Kariakoo is a bastardisation of 'Carrier Corps', the name of the division of indigenous Africans formed to support the British military campaign in East Africa during World War I, and which was stationed in the area after the city was captured from Germany in 1916.

Village Museum and Mwenge Market The **Village Museum** [314 B3] (w nmt.go.tz; ⌚ 09.30–18.00 daily; entrance US$5) consists of 16 life-size replicas of huts built in architectural styles from all over Tanzania. The best time to visit is between 14.00 and 16.00 on weekends and public holidays, when a traditional dance performance is held; an additional US$2 is charged to see the dance. Nearby **Mwenge Market** [314 A3], often referred to as the Makonde Market, is a cluster of around 50 craft stalls that also houses a traditional Makonde carving community. It is one of the best places to buy these unique sculptures (page 131), but in other respects it is pretty much just another craft market, and not really worth the lengthy trip out of town.

Both are along the Bagamoyo road, 10km and 13km from the city centre respectively. To get there on public transport, pick up a dalla dalla from the post office to Makumbusha bus stand.

Bongoyo Island Bongoyo lies within the Dar es Salaam Marine Reserve, which was gazetted in 1975 to protect a group of small offshore islands to the north of the city centre. It has a pretty beach where – unusually for Tanzania – swimming is possible at any time of day, owing to the absence of an offshore reef. A motorised dhow service runs between the island and The Slipway [326 C3] (m +255 713 328126/311424); boats leave for Bongoyo at 09.30, 10.30, 11.30, 13.30 and 15.30, and the last one back returns at 17.00 The return trip costs US$13 per person exclusive of the US$16 marine park entrance fee.

Kunduchi Ruins Situated in the seaside village of Kunduchi about 25km north of central Dar es Salaam, this intriguing Swahili ruin is all that remains of the oldest known settlement in the vicinity of the modern city. Little is known about the ruin's history, but at least one old building, a mosque, dates to the 16th century. The main point of interest, set amongst a grove of baobab trees, is an 18th-century graveyard containing East Africa's most extensive assemblage of pillar tombs, several of which are decorated with porcelain plates and inscribed in a manner that is unique among

Swahili graveyards of this period. Pottery collected at the site suggests the town was wealthy and had trade links with China and Britain. To get there, follow the Bagamoyo Road out of town for around 25km, then turn right along the side road

DHOWS OF THE SWAHILI COAST

The word 'dhow', commonly applied by Europeans to any traditional seafaring vessel used off the coast of East Africa, is generally assumed to be Arabic in origin. There is, however, no historical evidence to back up this notion, nor does it appear to be an established Swahili name for any specific type of boat. Caroline Sassoon, writing in *Tanganyika Notes & Records* in 1970, suggests that the word is a corruption of *não*, used by the first Portuguese navigators in the Indian Ocean to refer to any small local seafaring vessel, or of the Swahili *kidau*, a specific type of small boat described below.

The largest traditional sailing vessel in wide use off the coast of East Africa is the *jahazi*, which measures up to 20m long and whose large billowing sails are a characteristic sight off Zanzibar and other traditional ports. With a capacity of about 100 passengers, the jahazi is mainly used for transporting cargo and passengers over relatively long distances or in open water, for instance between Dar es Salaam and Zanzibar. Minor modifications in the Portuguese and Omani eras notwithstanding, the design of the modern jahazi is pretty much identical to that of similar seafaring vessels used in medieval times and before. The name jahazi is generally applied to boats with cutaway bows and square sterns built on Zanzibar and nearby parts of the mainland. Similar boats built in Lamu and nearby ports in Kenya are called *jalbut* (possibly derived from the English 'jolly boat' or Indian 'gallevat') and have a vertical bow and wineglass-shaped stern. Smaller but essentially similar in design, the *mashua* measures up to 10m long, has a capacity of about 25 passengers, and is mostly used for fishing close to the shore or as local transport.

The most rudimentary and smallest type of boat used on the Swahili coast is the *mtumbwi*, which is basically a dugout canoe made by hollowing out the trunk of a large tree – the mango tree is favoured today – and used for fishing in mangrove creeks and other still-water environments. The mtumbwi is certainly the oldest type of boat used in East Africa, and its simple design probably replicates that of the very first boats crafted by humans. A more elaborate and distinctive variation on the mtumbwi is the *ngalawa*, a 5–6m-long dugout supported by a narrow outrigger on each side, making it sufficiently stable to be propelled by a sail. The ngalawa is generally used for fishing close to shore as well as for transporting passengers across protected channels such as the one between Mafia and Chole islands in the Mafia Archipelago.

The largest traditional boats of the Indian Ocean, the ocean-going dhows that were once used to transport cargo between East Africa, Asia and Arabia, have become increasingly scarce in recent decades owing to the advent of foreign ships and other, faster modes of intercontinental transport. Several distinct types of ocean-going dhow are recognised, ranging from the 60-ton *sambuk* from Persia to 250-ton boats originating from India. Oddly, one of the larger of these vessels, the Indian *dengiya*, is thought to be the root of the English word 'dinghy'. Although a few large dhows still ply the old maritime trade routes of the Indian Ocean, they are now powered almost exclusively with motors rather than by sails.

signposted for Kunduchi Beach Hotel. Dalla dallas run to Kunduchi from the city centre and a taxi will cost US$20–25 one-way.

Pugu Hills Nature Forest Reserve (⊕ -6.90104, 39.09276 (reserve office); **w** nature-reserves.go.tz; entrance US$10pp) The main water catchment for Dar es Salaam, the forested Pugu Hills lie 25km southwest of the city centre and receive a significantly higher rainfall owing to their greater elevation. In 1954, a roughly 20km² tract of evergreen forest here was set aside as a forest reserve, much of which has since been destroyed or severely degraded from a combination of commercial logging, planting of exotic eucalyptus trees, and local subsistence exploitation for charcoal, firewood and timber. Today, less than 5km² of pristine forest remains, supporting a surprisingly varied fauna. Although Pugu attracts few foreign tourists, the reserve is crossed with trails and roads, making it one of the most accessible coastal forests in Tanzania.

Large mammals include vervet and blue monkey, bushpig, suni antelope, checkered elephant-shrew and Rondo galago, while lion, spotted hyena and elephant pass through from time to time. A bird checklist of more than 100 species includes localised forest dwellers such as spotted ground thrush and east-coast akalat, as well as crowned eagle and southern banded snake-eagle. A wealth of butterflies can be seen, as with luck can chameleons. Of particular interest is a large artificial cave in a disused limestone quarry that harbours around 100,000 bats – the whole flock streams out of the cave entrance at dusk, a quite spectacular phenomenon. Other points of interest include a small bamboo forest and the swampy Minaki Wetlands.

To get to Pugu Hills, follow the Pugu Road out past Julius Nyerere International Airport for around 15km to the reserve boundary. Here, a 2.5km dirt road to the right leads to the village of Minaki, which is enclosed by the forest, and is the site of the reserve office, where entrance fees must be paid. Guided hikes and camping trips in the forest, as well as other cultural programmes, can be arranged with Pugu Hills Eco Cultural Tourism (⊕ -6.89836, 39.10839; **m** +255 653 901193; **w** puguhills.co.tz), which is run by local Zaramo women and has an office just before you reach the reserve boundary coming from Dar es Salaam.

BAGAMOYO

Historic Bagamoyo, 70km north of Dar es Salaam, was the mainland terminus for the slave caravan route linking Lake Tanganyika to Zanzibar for much of the 19th century. The old port slipped backwards in economic terms throughout the 20th century, all the while retaining an absorbing museum-like quality that has never quite generated the tourist interest one might expect, despite its location on a superb white beach and proximity to Dar es Salaam. Post-millennial Bagamoyo has, however, enjoyed a modest economic revival, one sparked initially by the rehabilitation of the once-appalling main road from Dar es Salaam and a flurry of beachfront hotel construction aimed mainly at the lucrative conference market. A more recent development is the rejuvenation of the old stone quarter, known locally as Dunda or Mji Mkongwe. Several of Bagamoyo's more venerable buildings have been restored as houses or hotels by investors, while the rehabilitated Old Fort and Caravanserai now operate as museums, and the German Boma is likely to follow suit during the lifespan of this edition. More unexpectedly, Bagamoyo's old quarter has also acquired a mini cluster of rather Bohemian tourist facilities in the form of the Firefly Boutique Lodge and nearby Poa Poa and Nashe's Restaurant. As a result,

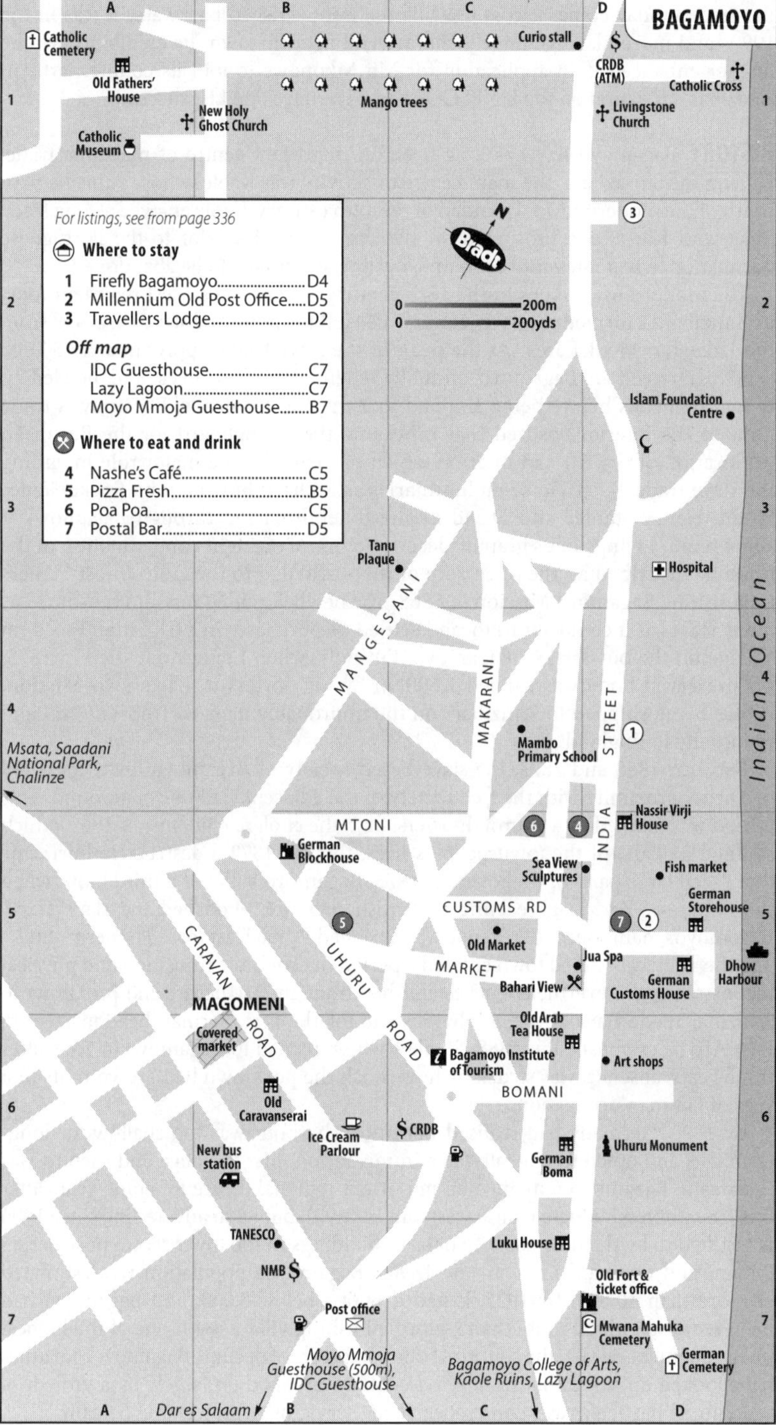
BAGAMOYO
For listings, see from page 336
Where to stay
1 Firefly Bagamoyo........D4
2 Millennium Old Post Office.....D5
3 Travellers Lodge........D2
Off map
IDC Guesthouse........C7
Lazy Lagoon........C7
Moyo Mmoja Guesthouse........B7
Where to eat and drink
4 Nashe's Café........C5
5 Pizza Fresh........B5
6 Poa Poa........C5
7 Postal Bar........D5
Catholic Cemetery
Old Fathers' House
New Holy Ghost Church
Catholic Museum
Mango trees
Curio stall
CRDB (ATM)
Catholic Cross
Livingstone Church
Islam Foundation Centre
Hospital
Tanu Plaque
MANGESANI
MAKARANI
INDIA STREET
Indian Ocean
Mambo Primary School
Msata, Saadani National Park, Chalinze
MTONI
German Blockhouse
Nassir Virji House
Sea View Sculptures
Fish market
German Storehouse
CUSTOMS RD
Old Market
Jua Spa
Dhow Harbour
MARKET
Bahari View
German Customs House
CARAVAN ROAD
UHURU ROAD
MAGOMENI
Covered market
Old Arab Tea House
Bagamoyo Institute of Tourism
Art shops
BOMANI
Old Caravanserai
Ice Cream Parlour
CRDB
New bus station
German Boma
Uhuru Monument
TANESCO
Luku House
NMB
Old Fort & ticket office
Post office
Mwana Mahuka Cemetery
Moyo Mmoja Guesthouse (500m), IDC Guesthouse
Bagamoyo College of Arts, Kaole Ruins, Lazy Lagoon
German Cemetery
Dar es Salaam
0 200m
0 200yds

Bagamoyo today comes across less like the impoverished backwater it was in the 1990s and more like a genuinely characterful historic town. Its credibility will be further enhanced if an application for Mji Mkongwe to join its counterparts on Zanzibar and Lamu on the UNESCO World Heritage Site List succeeds.

HISTORY Bagamoyo Bay has long been an important centre of maritime trade. During the Shirazi era, the main centre of activity was Kaole, whose ruins lie 5km south of the modern town. Founded in the 12th century, Kaole enjoyed strong trade links with Kilwa, and prospered for the three centuries prior to the Portuguese occupation, when it fell into economic decline, eventually to be abandoned.

The modern town dates to the 18th century, and as the closest mainland port to Zanzibar, it formed the 19th-century coastal terminus for slave caravans from the Lake Tanganyika area. At the peak of the slave trade, approximately 50,000 captives arrived in Bagamoyo annually, chained neck-to-neck and horded in dingy dungeons before being shipped to Zanzibar. Ironically, Bagamoyo's trade links to the interior ensured that it became the springboard for the European exploration of the African interior, which in turn played a major role in ending the slave trade. Such Victorian luminaries as Richard Burton, John Speke, James Grant, Henry Stanley and David Livingstone all passed through Bagamoyo at some point. Livingstone's graphic descriptions and outright condemnation of the trade he described as 'the open sore of the world' led to the Holy Ghost Fathers establishing Bagamoyo Mission in 1868. The newly founded mission ransomed as many slaves as it could afford to, and settled its purchases in a Christian Freedom Village on the outskirts of Bagamoyo. Fittingly, when Livingstone died in 1873, his preserved body was carried 1,600km by his porters to Bagamoyo Mission, before being shipped to Zanzibar (on the improbably named HMS *Vulture*) and eventually to England.

Between 1868 and 1873, the slave-based society of Bagamoyo town coexisted in uneasy proximity with the free society of the adjacent Catholic compound. This period was marked by a pair of disasters: first, the cholera epidemic of 1869, which claimed 25–30% of the townspeople's lives; then in 1872 a destructive hurricane that razed large parts of the town. In 1873, Bagamoyo suffered a third blow, when the Sultan of Zanzibar, reacting to British pressure, abolished the slave trade. Bagamoyo's main source of revenue was curtailed – or at least forced underground – and the already battered town entered a period of economic transition and physical reconstruction. Nevertheless, its established trade infrastructure and proximity to Zanzibar made Bagamoyo the obvious site for the first German headquarters in East Africa, established in 1888. Stanley, who returned to Bagamoyo in 1889 after three years' absence, was struck by how much the port town had grown in its first year of German occupation.

By 1890, Germany had realised Bagamoyo harbour was too shallow for long-term use, and opted to relocate the administration, first to Tanga and then to Dar es Salaam. Bagamoyo remained an important regional centre for some years after this (the impressive State House was built in 1897), but its steady decline since 1900 is testified to by the near absence of large buildings in the town centre post-dating Omani and German times. In the 1890s, Bagamoyo's population was estimated at more than 10,000. By 1925, it had dropped below 5,000, and Bagamoyo had been reduced to little more than a glorified fishing village, with one of the highest unemployment rates in the country. Following years of decline, Bagamoyo's fortunes have looked up somewhat in the 21st century, propped up largely by a growth of tourism, in particular as a conference venue servicing nearby Dar es Salaam.

THE BURDEN OF BAGAMOYO

In a pattern repeated all along the East African coast, the modern town of Bagamoyo is essentially a 19th-century entity, constructed by Omani slave traders close to the ruins of a medieval Shirazi town (in this case Kaole) that fell into disuse during the Portuguese era. The name Bagamoyo, too, dates to the 19th century, and is clearly linked to the town's role in the iniquitous slave trade, though the precise meaning is debatable. A Victorian explorer claimed that Bagamoyo referred to the port's role as the gateway to the African interior. Today, it is more widely accepted to be a corruption of the phrase *bwaga moyo*, at least a dozen translations of which have been published, falling into two broad categories.

The first set of interpretations, variations on 'lose heart' or 'lay down my heart', would have the phrase as the refrain of a slave lament: although the captives were to be shipped from the African mainland, their hearts would be left behind, in Bagamoyo. The second is that the phrase translates as 'lay down the burden of your heart' or similar, and was coined by caravan porters for whom Bagamoyo afforded an opportunity to lay down their burden at the end of the arduous trek from the Lake Tanganyika hinterland. The traditional Swahili porter's song, displayed in the Catholic Museum and loosely translated below, would certainly back up the second theory:

Be happy, my soul, release all cares, for we soon reach the place you yearn for
The town of palms, Bagamoyo!
When you were far away, how my heart ached when I thought of you, you pearl
You place of happiness, Bagamoyo!
The women wear their hair parted; you can drink palm wine all year through
In the gardens of love of Bagamoyo!
The dhows arrive with streaming sails to take aboard the treasures of Europe
In the harbour of Bagamoyo!
Oh, such delight to hear the drums and the lovely girls swaying in dance
All night through in Bagamoyo!
Be quiet, my heart, all cares are gone. Let the drumbeats rejoice:
We are reaching Bagamoyo!

GETTING THERE AND AWAY The 70km road between Dar es Salaam and Bagamoyo is surfaced in its entirety and the drive should take no longer than an hour, depending greatly on traffic on the city outskirts. Regular minibuses from Dar es Salaam to Bagamoyo leave from Mwenge Station [314 A3] on the New Bagamoyo Road north of the city centre (2hrs; US$2).

Until recently, no other passable road of note exited Bagamoyo, but that has changed with the construction of a new surfaced 65km road linking Bagamoyo to Msata, a small junction town on the main north–south road connecting Dar es Salaam, Chalinze and points further south to Moshi and Arusha in the north. For self-drivers heading between Dar es Salaam and the northern safari circuit, this route through Bagamoyo and Msata carries far less traffic and is significantly quicker than the conventional route through Chalinze. Using public transport, regular dalla dallas link Chalinze to Bagamoyo via Msata.

For details of roads and transport along the coastal route north of Bagamoyo, see page 342.

WHERE TO STAY Although a great many mid-range hotels service Bagamoyo, most are rather uninspiring and rundown set-ups catering almost entirely to the conference market. The places listed below stand out for their individuality or (at the bottom end of the range) affordability.

Exclusive

Lazy Lagoon [333 C7] w tanzaniasafaris.info. This beautiful oceanic retreat stands on Ras Lwale Island, at the isolated tip of a long spit hemming in the Mbegani Lagoon south of Bagamoyo. The 10 makuti beach chalets, separated by the thick coastal scrub, are the epitome of barefoot luxury. Chill out at the beach or next to the swimming pool, pamper yourself at a spa offering massage, pedicure, manicure & henna decoration, & enjoy seafood beach dinners below a sparkling night sky, with the lights of Bagamoyo twinkling in the distance. More active guests can enjoy snorkelling & kayaking close to the lodge, or walk around the island to look for wildlife such as bushpig, genet, suni antelope, red duiker & plentiful birds. Day trips to Mwambakuni Reef (for snorkelling), Bagamoyo, Kaole & elsewhere can also be arranged. Boat transfers from the FETA compound, 7km south of Bagamoyo, take 20mins and should be booked in advance. **$$$$**

Upmarket

Millennium Old Post Office Hotel [333 D5] India St; m +255 767 200900; w millennium.co.tz. An extension of the old post office overlooking the old customs house, this high-rise blot on Dunda's historic urban landscape has spacious en-suite rooms offering superb views over the old dhow harbour & market, though it goes slightly against the grain to support a development of such reckless insensitivity. *US$100/120 sgl/dbl B&B.* **$$$**

Moderate

✷ **Firefly Bagamoyo** [333 D4] India St; m +255 762 519612; w fireflybagamoyo.com. This wonderful small hotel in the heart of the old stone town is focused on Abdun's Palace, an 1850s mansion that had been uninhabited for 30 years prior to being restored by the energetic owner-manager. Boasting a Bohemian shabby-chic aesthetic befitting of an upmarket backpacker lodge, Firefly espouses an eco-conscious philosophy & is involved in promoting recycling & better waste management in Bagamoyo. Rooms are restored in period style, with mangrove-pole ceilings, rough whitewashed limestone walls & traditional wooden doors, but would be better described as characterful than as smart. The garden incorporates a small circular swimming pool, several shaded sitting areas & a restaurant serving healthy & inexpensive meals, always with a few vegetarian options. There's also a campsite, yoga sessions & a spa. From *US$50 dbl B&B, US$16pp dorm; US$10pp camping.* **$–$$**

Travellers Lodge [333 D2] m +255 754 855485; w travellers-lodge.com. Established in the 1990s, this appealing German-owned lodge is set in large green grounds that sprawl down to an attractive beach within easy walking distance of the town centre & Holy Ghost Mission. The 25 spacious cottages are simply decorated with large beds, netting, AC & private balcony. Free laundry. A good restaurant & bar are attached. *US$60/80 sgl/dbl B&B.* **$$**

Budget

IDC Guesthouse [333 C7] Jakaya Dr; w booking.com. This very friendly & helpful guesthouse has a 4-bed dorm & private rooms, all with fan & AC. There's a swimming pool, a shared TV lounge & kitchen, & plenty of restaurants nearby. *From US$38 dbl, US$15pp dorm.* **$**

Moyo Mmoja Guesthouse [333 C7] m +255 754 978628; w moyommoja.org. Set in a leafy compound opposite a football field about 500m from the beach & a similar distance south of the town centre, this small NGO-run guesthouse, proceeds from which support a project for orphans, has obliging staff, a self-catering kitchen, shared bathrooms & the choice of sleeping in a room in the main house or garden hut, all brightly decorated with nets & fans. *From US$13/18 sgl/dbl, camping US$4pp.* **$**

WHERE TO EAT AND DRINK Most hotels listed above have restaurants, most notably Firefly Bagamoyo, which also hosts live traditional Swahili music on

Friday night (entrance US$2.50pp). The standout standalone eateries are listed here.

Nashe's Café [333 C5] Off India St; m +255 676 506705; f Nashes-Cafe; ⌚ 08.00–22.00 daily. Named after its energetic owner-manager, Nashe's stands in a restored 19th-century town house opposite Poa Poa & has a similar feel with its indoor courtyard, rooftop seating, & furniture made from old dhow planks. Seafood is the speciality, but it also serves b/fasts, coffee, wine & beer. $

Pizza Fresh [333 B5] m +255 766 440962; ⌚ 10.00–21.00 Tue–Sun. This pleasant open-sided thatch-roofed eatery close to the Old Caravanserai has an Italian-dominated menu, with pizza, pasta & salads, but it also serves dirt-cheap Tanzanian staples, coffee & beer. $

Poa Poa [333 C5] Off India St; m +255 768 300277; f PoaPoaRestaurant; ⌚ 09.00–22.00 daily. This funky little gem, set in a restored old house, has a stylishly decorated interior, a large courtyard & a breezy umbrella-shaded rooftop. Renowned for its superb pizzas, it also serves a selection of grills, chapati wraps & sandwiches, as well as coffee, fruit juices, beers & spirits. There's live music on Tue. $

Postal Bar [333 D5] 023 244 0303. Converted from what was once the first post office on the Tanzanian mainland, this is the most characterful place for a chilled beer in Dunda, despite its affiliation to the Millennium Old Post Office Hotel.

TOURIST INFORMATION All visitors are technically required to drop into the official tourist office in the restored Old Fort [333 D7] (⌚ 08.30–18.00 daily) to pay a 'Stone Town' entrance fee equivalent to US$9 that covers all historic sites listed in this section apart from the Old Caravanserai, the Holy Ghost Mission and the out-of-town Kaole Ruins, all of which charge separate entrance fees. The office can also arrange reliable guides to show you around the historic sites in town, and to attractions further afield such as the Kaole Ruins, at an asking rate of around US$50 per party per day. All the beach resorts offer good advice and can also organise the same tours and activities. For more information, check the useful website maintained by the German–Tanzanian Bagamoyo Friendship Society (w bagamoyo.com).

ACTIVITIES AND EXCURSIONS

Swimming The entire waterfront of Bagamoyo amounts to one long swimming beach, though wandering around public parts of the beach in swimming trunks or a bikini probably wouldn't be appreciated.

A SNAPSHOT OF BAGAMOYO c1890

Caravan trade in Bagamoyo was of little importance. The old caravanserai below the station has been evacuated; it will no longer be used, for hygienic reasons. A new location has been chosen to lodge the caravans, further above the station, within the palms. While slave trade in general can be regarded as suppressed, in singular cases, men deep-rooted in the slave trade try to catch free men and ship them from smaller coastal places in the vicinity of Bagamoyo. A certain Ibrahim, who has been arrested for slave trade last year, but who had succeeded in escaping from the prison, was again brought in by natives a few weeks ago, as, with a few aides, he had ambushed free men, killed some, captured the others and sold them as slaves. As his crimes were proven by numerous witness reports, he was hanged on September 23rd.

Extracted from a report by the Deputy Commissioner of German East Africa, September 1890

Town walking tour Dunda, the old town of Bagamoyo, warrants a few hours' exploration. Local guides can be arranged at any of the beach hotels, or you can wander around independently. A blanket entrance fee, equivalent to US$9, must be paid at the Old Fort before you visit any or all of the historic sites in the old town, as well as outlying sites such as the German Boma, German Cemetery or hanging tree, but the requirement is seldom enforced on visitors who just wander around unguided. The fee excludes entrance to the Old Caravanserai, Holy Mission Church and Kaole Ruins.

The main thoroughfare through Dunda is India Street, which has changed little in shape since the late 19th century, and houses most of the town's old buildings and administrative offices. It also retains a singularly Swahili atmosphere, and a tangible sense of community exists among its estimated 1,000 residents. At the junction of India Street and Customs Road, the **old post office** [333 D5], now the Postal Bar (page 337), was the first such institution to be established on the Tanzanian mainland and was used for this purpose until as recently as 1995. Opposite the old post office is one of the oldest and most ornate of several carved **Zanzibari doors** that decorate the façades of India Street.

From the intersection with India Street, Customs Road leads down to the main port, still dominated by the **German Customs House** [333 D5] built in 1895, opposite which stands the remains of a **German Storehouse** [333 D5] built in 1888. The old beachfront slave market is today a **fish market** [333 D5], and the white sands in front of it are lined with picturesque fishing dhows and scuttled across by legions of ghostly white crabs at dusk. Two interesting buildings just north of this are **Nassir Virji House** [333 D5], which stands next to Firefly and is named after the wealthy Indian merchant and outfitter who built it in the late 19th century, and the German-founded **Mambo Primary School** [333 C4], which dates to 1896.

Continuing south for a few hundred metres, India Street runs past a trio of noteworthy buildings. First up is the **Old Arab Tea House** [333 C6], which possibly predates the German occupation, and has authentic carved Zanzibari doors. Close by, the once-dilapidated **German Boma** [333 C6], an impressive two-storey building with a fortified roof built in 1897 as the regional headquarters, has ostensibly been undergoing restoration work for years, and may possibly reopen as a museum during the lifespan of this edition.

Opposite the Boma, in front of an abandoned bandstand, stands the **Uhuru Monument** [333 D6] celebrating Tanzania's independence in 1961, together with a plaque commemorating Burton and Speke's departure from Bagamoyo on their expedition to lakes Tanganyika and Victoria. The third building of note, **Luku House** [333 C7], is a pre-colonial two-storey construction appropriated to serve as Germany's first East Africa headquarters from 1888 to 1891 (see opposite).

A short distance south of this, the **Old Fort** [333 D7] incorporates the oldest extant house in Bagamoyo. Originally a slave prison, what is now the ground floor was built by the Arab trader Abdullah Suleimen Marhabi in 1860, when a subterranean passage linked it to a landing point where slaves were herded to dhows. In 1870, Sultan Barghash of Zanzibar acquired and fortified the building, which he used as a slave chamber and customs house. In 1886, it was taken over by the Germans, who used it as a military base and constructed the upper floor. The building served as a jail from 1919 to 1974, then as a police station until 1990, prior to being restored by the Department of Antiquities over 1992–94. Its most striking feature is the ornate Zanzibari entrance door, fitted by Sultan Barghash in 1874.

Near the fort, in the grounds of the long defunct (but for some reason still signposted) Badeco Beach Hotel, a plaque identifies the **hanging tree** where the Germans executed any African considered insufficiently sympathetic to their

THE EMIN PASHA'S FALL

In 1889, the renowned explorer Henry Stanley marched into Bagamoyo at the end of a three-year trek across Africa that had seen his original party of 700 reduced to fewer than 200. With him was the Emin Pasha, the German-born Governor of Equatoria Province (then nominally part of Egypt, now part of South Sudan), who against all odds had managed to defend his isolated territory against the Mahdist onslaught for three years following the fall of Khartoum in 1885. The German garrison at Bagamoyo, then at the height of the Abushiri Rebellion, must have embraced any excuse for a bit of festivity. Stanley and the Emin Pasha were welcomed with open arms – and a stockpile of open bottles – culminating in a wild party at the headquarters in present-day Luku House. The festivities ended in tragedy, as the Emin Pasha – presumably drunk at the time, and certainly short-sighted at the best of times – celebrated his safe return from the trials of Equatoria and a trans-Africa march with a fall from the balcony of Luku House to the street below. Scheduled to sail to Zanzibar with Stanley the next day, the Governor of Equatoria instead spent the next six weeks in the Holy Ghost Mission hospital recuperating from head injuries. The offending balcony, still present in 1992, appears to have been removed during the subsequent restoration of Luku House.

rule. Immediately south of this, the Muslim **Mwana Mahuka Cemetery** [333 D7] houses the oldest tomb in Bagamoyo, dating to 1793, while the **German Cemetery** [333 D7] is the last resting place for 20 German soldiers who died in the late 19th century. Further south, perhaps 100m along the Kaole Road, the **Bagamoyo College of Arts** or **Chuo Cha Sanaa** [333 C7] (☎ 023 244 0149; **w** tasuba.ac.tz) is a striking example of modern architecture constructed entirely from traditional materials. At weekends, students often stage local plays or put on a show of traditional music, dancing and mime.

Northwest of the Old Fort along Caravan Road, the relatively modern settlement of **Magomeni** is home to more than 95% of Bagamoyo's population. The bustling market and bus station are situated alongside each other here, as are numerous local guesthouses, but the only historical building is the **German Blockhouse** [333 B5] (also known as Dunda Tower), a well-preserved circular coral rag structure built by Von Wissman to protect Bagamoyo against the Abushiri rebellion of 1889.

Situated around the corner from the modern bus station, the **Old Caravanserai** [333 B6] (🕘 08.00–18.00 daily; entrance US$8), is where caravan parties assembled and stocked up before trekking into the interior. In its prime, it comprised an open central courtyard surrounded by low-rise market stalls and shops – not dissimilar, in fact, from many modern bus terminals in Tanzania. Now partially restored, it houses the town's official museum (something of a work in progress, and less illuminating than its counterpart at the Holy Ghost Mission), as well as an internet café.

Holy Ghost Mission and Livingstone Church Situated on the outskirts of town, and reached via a mango-lined avenue planted by missionaries in 1871, the Holy Ghost Mission houses several buildings dating to the late 19th century. The double-storey Sisters' House, built in 1876, now houses the superb **Catholic Museum** [333 A1] (🕘 10.00–17.00 daily; entrance US$4), which provides a good overview of the history of Bagamoyo and Kaole, and sells an extensive selection of books and booklets about Bagamoyo past and present.

Also within the mission grounds, the original **Holy Ghost Church**, built in 1872, is reputedly the oldest church on the East African mainland. Opposite, the wide-balconied three-storey **Old Fathers' House** [333 A1] is a fine, though somewhat deteriorated, example of a style of pre-colonial mission architecture more normally associated with West Africa. In front of it stands the **New Holy Ghost Church** [333 A1], constructed shortly before World War I and more imposing than its predecessor. A few hundred metres past the main mission buildings is the **cemetery** [333 A1] where the early missionaries are buried, and a **grotto** built in 1876 by the emancipated slaves living in the mission grounds. Several of the exotic trees in the wooded grounds were the first of their type to be planted in Tanzania.

At the junction of Ocean Road and the mango-lined avenue to the mission stands the unimposing tin-roofed **Livingstone Church** [333 D1], which is where Livingstone's sun-dried body, after an initial night in the Holy Ghost Mission, was stored before it was shipped to Zanzibar in 1874. On the seafront, about 200m behind this church, a green marble monument and cross, erected in the 1870s and replanted in 1993, marks the spot where Father Horner landed in 1868 to establish the Holy Ghost Mission.

Kaole Ruins [333 C7] (🕘 08.00–16.00 daily; entrance US$8) On the outskirts of Kaole village, 5km south of Bagamoyo, stand the brooding ruins of the urban precursor to modern Bagamoyo, a relatively minor but wealthy trading settlement that peaked in prosperity at about the same time as Kilwa Kisiwani and Mtangata (Tongoni). The main ruins consist of one large mosque with a well-preserved outer staircase and ornate engraved *mihrab*, surrounded by a cemetery of 22 graves including four tall pillar tombs that stand up to 7m high. Close to the mosque stand a footbath and well, the latter still containing water. Some 300m away, a second mosque and a building of unknown purpose stand in total isolation.

Surprisingly little is known about medieval Kaole. No reference survives in the chronicles of the Shirazi or early Portuguese era, and it is highly unlikely it was called Kaole – or Bagamoyo, for that matter – in its commercial heyday. Even the dating of the ruins is controversial. The main mosque displays features consistent with 7th-century construction, which would make it the oldest surviving mosque on the East African mainland, but the 12th or 13th century seems more probable. Based on its humpback topography and the absence of secular buildings, it has been suggested that Kaole was not a town but a religious retreat set on a holy offshore highland.

Kaole was abandoned in the 16th century, presumably due to the intervention of the Portuguese or the appetite of the Zimba. It enjoyed a revival as a military and administrative centre for the Sultan of Zanzibar in the late 18th century, though the actual ruins bear little trace of this resettlement. By the early 19th century, the main centre of trade had relocated to Bagamoyo, whose larger harbour could hold a greater number of ships, while Kaole's had become increasingly clogged by mangrove swamps.

While the major buildings at Kaole don't stand comparison to the splendid architecture of Kilwa – or even the Gedi Ruins in Kenya – the decorated tombs are perhaps the best preserved on the Swahili coast. A better reason to visit, perhaps, is the aura of mystery that surrounds the ruins: crumbling relics of an undocumented centre of international trade, one that must have flourished for three centuries or longer – a powerful physical reminder of Africa's forgotten past.

With a private vehicle, Kaole can be reached by following the coastal road south out of Bagamoyo, past the Art College, for 5km. In Kaole village, a signposted

600m turn-off leads to the ruins. Unfortunately, no dalla dallas head out this way, so the options are walking (about an hour each way), cycling (ask your hotel to arrange a bike), or hanging around the junction to wait for a lift with one of the very occasional pick-up trucks that run along this road. If you're walking or cycling, leave all valuables and extra cash behind.

SAADANI NATIONAL PARK

Situated on the mainland directly opposite Zanzibar and about 100km north of Dar es Salaam, Saadani (**m** +255 698 062276; **e** saadani@tanzaniaparks.go.tz) is the closest national park to both these places, and the only wildlife sanctuary in East Africa graced with an Indian Ocean beachfront. The 1,100km^2 park retains a low profile by comparison with the likes of the Serengeti and Ruaha, and certainly it doesn't bear comparison to Tanzania's finest when it comes to conventional wildlife viewing. That said, a concerted clampdown on poaching in recent years has led to a steady increase in Saadani's large mammal populations, which now includes an estimated 150–200 elephants, 50 lions, significant numbers of giraffe, buffalo and hippo, and a wide range of antelope. Other attractions include the prolific birdlife, boat trips up the atmospheric Wami River, guided bush walks and the relative scarcity of other tourists. All in all, while Saadani might not find its way on to too many bucket lists, it's a thoroughly worthwhile and enjoyable retreat, combining the hedonistic pleasures of a sandy beach idyll with some erratic but often rewarding game viewing by boat, on foot and from a vehicle.

HISTORY The village of Mkwaja, in the north of the park, was a minor Swahili trading post from the 9th century AD, when it was first settled by Omani traders, right through until the Portuguese occupation of the early 17th century. The village of Saadani, 40km south of Mkwaja, emerged as a slave- and ivory-trade outpost in the 19th century, when it briefly rivalled Bagamoyo in stature and was considered as a possible site for the London Missionary Society's first East African mission. However, the port's growth was inhibited by a defensive wall built to protect against the warring Wadoe and Wazigua clans, whose ongoing fighting also dissuaded caravans from passing through the Saadani hinterland. Saadani maintained a proud tradition of independence under the late 19th-century leadership of Bwana Heri bin Juma, who defeated an occupational force sent across by the Sultan of Zanzibar in 1882 and also played an important role in the anti-imperial Abushiri Uprising in 1888. Saadani was bombarded and captured by the Germans in 1889, whose brief rule is survived by a crumbling old customs house and a clutch of late 19th-century graves. Saadani went into decline in the early 20th century, despite the development of the surrounding land agriculture, in particular sisal and cashew production. In 1952, the vast Mkwaja cattle ranch was founded, partly as a source of meat for workers at the sisal and other plantations in the area. The original 200km^2 Saadani Game Reserve was established alongside Mkwaja cattle ranch in 1969, and upgraded to become a national park in 2006, when the ranch was incorporated to extend the total area to 1,100km^2. Today, the village of Saadani, one of several semi-urban enclaves along the park's coastline, supports a population of fewer than 1,000, most of whom are dependent on fishing or salt production in the evaporation pans immediately to the south.

FLORA AND FAUNA The 60km of Indian Ocean frontage associated with Saadani is lined with a succession of palm-lined beaches, mangrove stands and riverine estuaries. A mere 20km of this coastline is actually protected within the national park; the remainder is divided into community-owned land associated with various ancient fishing villages. Inland, the Saadani supports a low-lying park-like cover of open grassland interspersed with stands of acacia trees and knotted coastal thicket. Several perennial and seasonal rivers flow east through the park before draining into the Indian Ocean, the largest being the Wami close to the southern boundary, and these are mostly fringed by lush riparian woodland. The park also incorporates the eastern portion of the 200km^2 Zaraninge Forest, one of the most biodiverse habitats of its type in Tanzania.

Typical and frequently observed savannah wildlife includes elephant, giraffe, buffalo, warthog, yellow baboon, vervet monkey, impala, common waterbuck, Bohor reedbuck and Lichtenstein's hartebeest. Quite common, but less easily seen, are greater kudu and eland. Something of a Saadani special, the red duiker is a diminutive and normally very shy antelope found in coastal scrub and forest. Saadani also harbours a small population of Roosevelt's sable, a localised race otherwise found in Nyerere National Park and Kenya's Shimba Hills. In the 1970s, several species not indigenous to the coastal region were introduced to Saadani, among them white-bearded wildebeest, eland, zebra and oryx, though the last of these didn't survive. Lion, leopard, spotted hyena and black-backed jackal are all around, along with the usual small nocturnal predators. Game densities are highest in January–February and June–August, when the plains hold more water.

Forest mammals include Angola colobus, blue monkey, Matundu dwarf galago and black-and-rufous elephant shrew. The beaches of Saadani are the only Tanzanian turtle-nesting site north of Dar es Salaam, with green turtle being the most regular visitor. The official bird checklist for Saadani totals around 260 species but this evidently excludes many localised forest dwellers associated with Zaraninge.

FEES AND FURTHER INFORMATION Park entrance costs US$30 per person plus 18% VAT per 24 hours. Access is often problematic over April and May, when the black cotton soil roads tend to become waterlogged. Several publications about the park, including a full bird checklist, can be downloaded from **w** wildlife-baldus.com/saadani.html.

GETTING THERE AND AWAY

By air There are no scheduled flights to Saadani airstrip, but air charters can be arranged through any of the lodges.

By road The erection of a bridge over the Wami River in 2012 opened up the direct coastal road between Bagamoyo and Saadani for the first time since the original Wami Ferry sank in the 1980s. As a result, it is now possible to drive directly from Dar es Salaam to Saadani, a 3-hour trip that entails following the surfaced Msata road west of Bagamoyo for about 15km to Makurunge, then branching north on to an unsurfaced road that leads to Saadani village and the park headquarters after about 60km.

Using **public transport**, one rather beat-up bus runs between Saadani and Dar es Salaam daily, leaving Saadani at 04.00 and Dar es Salaam at noon and taking at least 4 hours in either direction. There are also occasional dalla dallas from Chalinze and Bagamoyo, but not along the road north to Mkwaja. Once there, options for exploring the park are limited, and you would be required to pay the full entrance fee for the duration of your stay.

WHERE TO STAY AND EAT

Bab's Camp ⊕ -5.92094, 38.79985; m +255 713 323318; w tentwithaview.com. Situated about 12km south of Simply Saadani & under the same management, this 2-bedroom satellite camp stands on community land that's enclosed by the national park & regularly visited by lion, elephant, giraffe & other wildlife. An isolated watchtower-like construction, it incorporates a private 3rd-floor restaurant & 4th-floor viewing platform that offer fabulous views across the plain to the palm-lined Indian Ocean. It is not luxurious in a conventional sense, but the rooms are very comfortable & the experience feels very exclusive. The steep stairs are not suited to people with limited mobility. **$$$$$$**

✱ **Miseni Retreat** ⊕ -6.17120, 38.62961; m +255 621 555678; w kijanicollection.com. The flagship for an NGO that supports various local community projects, eco-friendly Miseni Retreat stands outside the national park on a sacred hill in Gongo Forest, a short distance southwest of Saadani's pristine Zaraninge forest. The rustic wooden bandas are simple but comfortable & come with nets & solar-heated water. There's also standing tents, a dorm & a restaurant looking into the forest. Management can arrange road transfers from Dar es Salaam & 4x4 excursions into the national park. *From US$45/50 sgl/dbl or US$40pp dorm bed B&B.* **$–$$**

Saadani Bandas ⊕ -6.02897, 38.77832; w tanzaniaparks.go.tz. These newly built semi-detached bandas are arranged in a semi-circle around a lawn that runs down to a lovely beach 2km north of Saadani village. All rooms have dbl or twin bed, AC, fan, fitted nets & a modern bathroom, while a restaurant/dar serves inexpensive meals. Super value, *US$40pp for a room or US$30pp to camp.* **$$**

Saadani Safari Lodge ⊕ -6.03414, 38.77849; m +255 776 355352; w saadanisafarilodges.com. This intimate tented camp, which runs attractively along a palm-fringed beach about 1km north of Saadani village, comprises 15 framed canvas tents with a stilted wooden base, makuti roof, en-suite facilities, solar electricity & twin or dbl bed, as well as a 2nd netted bed on the balcony should you want to sleep outside. There is no AC but the constant sea breeze keeps the rooms cool. The open dining area serves fresh seafood, while a treehouse overlooks a waterhole regularly visited by wildlife. There are 2 swimming pools & activities include game drives, guided walks with a ranger & Wami River boat trips . **$$$$$**

✱ **Simply Saadani** ⊕ -5.82375, 38.83307; m +255 713 323318; w tentwithaview.com. This stunning beachfront camp stands in community land near Mkwaja some 30km north of Saadani village. Standing tents on stilted wooden platforms are spaced out in the coastal scrub immediately behind the beach. Activities include game drives (the surrounding area is good for elephant sightings), walking trails in the coastal scrub & canoeing in Mafuwe Creek (home to mangrove kingfisher). The camp runs several conservation projects from its dedicated wildlife research centre. **$$$$$$**

WHAT TO SEE AND DO Game drives are the main activity. The most productive wildlife-viewing circuit comprises the roads running inland and south of Saadani Safari Lodge. Here, you are all but certain to encounter large numbers of yellow baboon, vervet monkey, Bohor reedbuck, common waterbuck, Lichtenstein's hartebeest and giraffe. With luck, you should also see buffalo and elephant, but neither is guaranteed. A couple of lion prides are resident in the area, but sightings tend to be sporadic – they might be seen several days in a row in one area, then vanish elsewhere for a few weeks. Birders should divert to the salt evaporation pools around Saadani village – a great site for wading birds in general and flamingos in particular. Guided walks offer a good chance of seeing various antelope and representatives of Saadani's rich variety of woodland birds.

A must-do activity, boat trips on the Wami River cost US$50 per person plus 18% VAT, which must be paid for at the parks office in Saadani village before driving 12km south to the riverside jetty (⊕ -6.12924, 38.81344). Hippos and crocodiles are plentiful in the river and most conspicuous at low tide, while Angola colobus monkeys are often observed foraging in the trees. Marine and riverine birds likely to be seen include African fish eagle, saddle-billed stork, whimbrel, African skimmer and the localised mangrove kingfisher. The spectacular Pel's fishing owl is resident but seldom seen in daylight. The road between Saadani village and the jetty passes through a traditional salt extraction plant whose extensive saline ponds often host large flocks of avocet and greater and lesser flamingo.

PANGANI AND USHONGO

One of the most important 19th-century trade ports along the Swahili Coast, Pangani retains an overtly traditional Swahili character complemented by its attractive setting on the north bank of the forest-fringed Pangani River mouth. Despite its antiquity, the old town is strikingly undeveloped for tourism, but not so the flanking coastline, which supports a scattering of low-key resorts catering more to Arusha-based expats seeking a seaside break than to bona fide tourists. The finest of these resorts can be found 12km south of Pangani at Ushongo, whose fabulous and practically deserted beach ranks as one of the best-kept secrets on the Tanzanian coast.

GETTING THERE AND AWAY

By air **Coastal Aviation** (w coastal.co.tz) can fly to Pangani or Ushongo as a scheduled stop on its daily flight network connecting Dar es Salaam, Zanzibar, Arusha and Tanga.

By boat Emayani Beach Lodge offers a daily morning transfer between Zanzibar (leaves from Kendwa Rocks) and Ushongo or Pangani. For details of timings and prices, see w emayanilodge.com/boat-transfers.

By road Coming from the south, an erratic 80km dirt road connects Saadani village in the eponymous national park to the south bank of the Pangani River opposite the eponymous town. The drive should take under 2 hours in dry conditions but might

PANGANI IN 1857

The following edited extracts from Richard Burton's *Zanzibar and Two Months in East Africa*, originally published in 1858 in Blackwood's *Edinburgh Magazine* (vol 83), provide a vivid impression of Pangani in the mid 19th century:

> Pangani boasts of 19 or 20 stone houses. The remainder is a mass of cadjan huts, each with its wide mat-encircled yard, wherein all the business of life is transacted…Pangani, with the three other villages, may contain a total of 4,000 – Arabs, Muslim Swahili, and heathens. Of these, female slaves form a large proportion. I am told it exports 35,000lb of ivory, 1,750lb of rhinoceros's horn, and 16lb of hippopotamus's teeth annually. Twenty Banyans manage the lucrative ivory trade…These merchants complain loudly of their porters, who receive 10 dollars for the journey, half paid down, the remainder upon return; and the proprietor congratulates himself if, after payment, only 15% run away. The Hindus' profits, however, must be enormous. I saw one man to whom 26,000 dollars were owed by the people. Like all settlements upon this coast, Pangani belongs, by right of succession, to the [Sultan] of Zanzibar, who confirms and invests the governors and diwans. At Pangani, these officials are *par congé d'elire* selected by Kimweri [the king of Usambara], whose ancestors received tribute and allegiance from para to the seaboard.

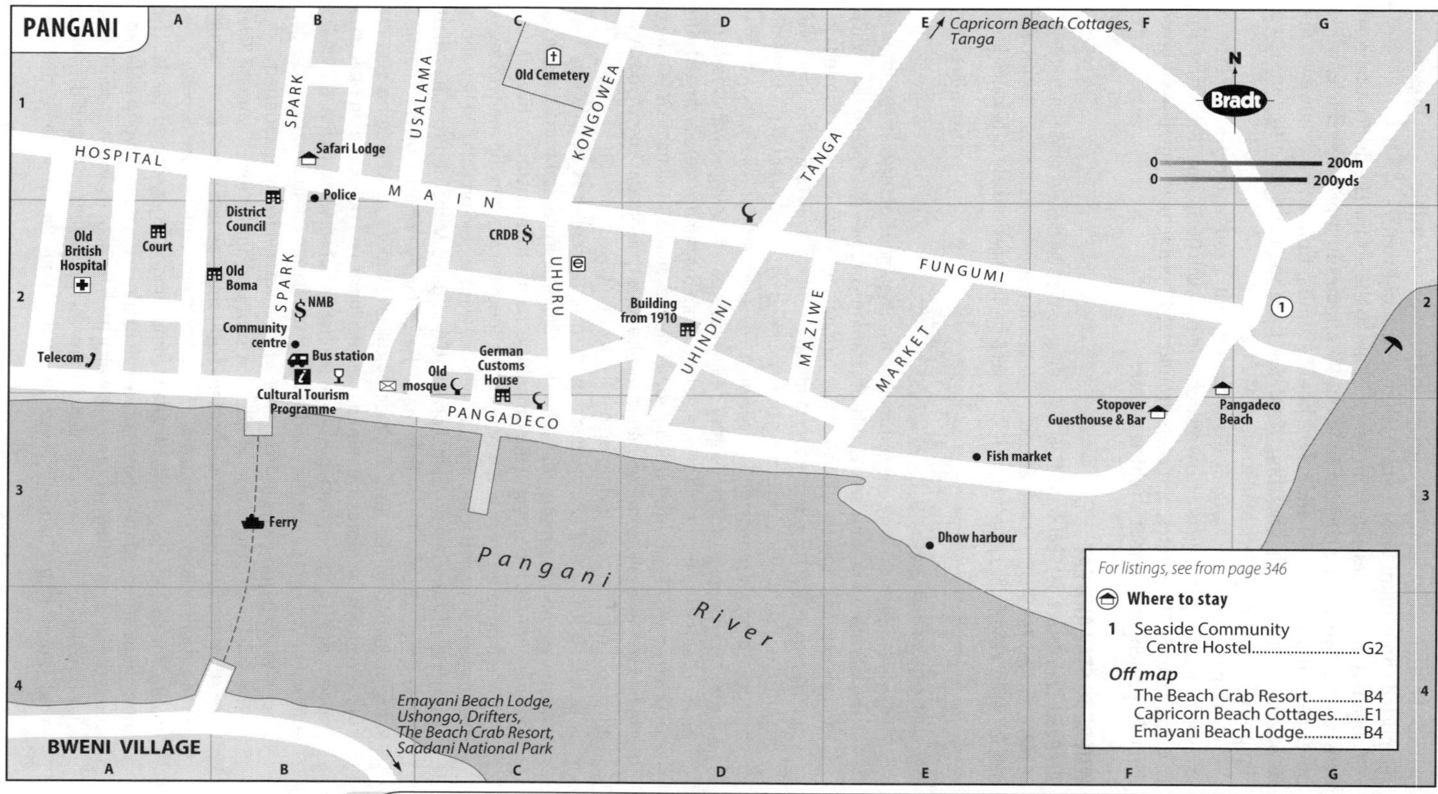
PANGANI
Capricorn Beach Cottages, Tanga
N
Bradt
0 200m
0 200yds
Old Cemetery
HOSPITAL
SPARK
USALAMA
KONGOWEA
TANGA
Safari Lodge
Police
MAIN
District Council
Old British Hospital
Court
CRDB
Old Boma
UHURU
NMB
Community centre
Building from 1910
UHINDINI
MAZIWE
MARKET
FUNGUMI
Telecom
Bus station
Old mosque
German Customs House
Cultural Tourism Programme
PANGADECO
Stopover Guesthouse & Bar
Pangadeco Beach
Fish market
Ferry
Dhow harbour
Pangani River
For listings, see from page 346
Where to stay
1 Seaside Community Centre Hostel.......G2
Off map
The Beach Crab Resort.......B4
Capricorn Beach Cottages.......E1
Emayani Beach Lodge.......B4
Emayani Beach Lodge, Ushongo, Drifters, The Beach Crab Resort, Saadani National Park
BWENI VILLAGE

be trickier after heavy rain. The turn-off to Ushongo, accessible in any weather, is signposted about 10km before you reach the Pangani River.

Pangani is more accessible from Tanga, 53km to the north. The dirt coastal road between the two can be covered in about 90 minutes in a private vehicle, while buses cost around US$1.50 and take 2 hours. Coming from Arusha, however, the most direct route entails branching southeast from the main road to Tanga at a signposted junction in the small town of Muheza.

No bridge crosses the Pangani River mouth, but a motor ferry is in place to carry vehicles and passengers across on demand between 06.30 and 18.30 daily. The crossing takes 5–10 minutes, and costs around US$2 per vehicle. Small local boats can take passengers without a vehicle across.

WHERE TO STAY AND EAT

The Beach Crab Resort [345 B4] ⊕ -5.54236, 38.96878; **m** +255 767 543700; **w** thebeachcrab.com. This laidback & idyllic budget resort in Ushongo offers the choice of simple safari-style tents with shared showers or en-suite bandas with net & fan. The large thatched-roof beachside bar

PANGANI AND THE RIDDLE OF RHAPTA

Pangani has been cited by one historian as 'the Bagamoyo of the first 18 centuries of the Christian era'. In a sense, this description is rather misleading. For while Pangani was an important 19th-century terminus for slave caravans to the Lake Victoria region, the town that now stands on the north bank of the Pangani River mouth is not particularly old, having been founded by Omani Arabs in the late 18th century and totally rebuilt in 1810 following a destructive flood. Likely, too, that the very name Pangani is of 19th-century derivation – 'panga' being a Swahili word for 'arrange', and Pangani the place where slaves from the interior were arranged into groups by their Arab captors (though other sources suggest the name is far older, alluding to the locally common *panga* shellfish or a type of boat known locally as *mtepe* but referred to by an English naval offer in 1608 as *pangaia*).

But even if Pangani is a relatively modern settlement, it is equally true that the eponymous river mouth has played a major role in coastal trade for several centuries. Prior to the arrival of the Omani, the main settlement on the river mouth was Bweni, situated then, as it is now, on the south bank facing the modern town. Prior to that, a larger trading post, Muhembo, was situated on Pangani Bay about 2km north of the present town. Local tradition dates Muhembo to the earliest Shirazi times, circa AD900, when the El Harth family, who reputedly founded Pangani, landed in the area. Archaeological excavations at Muhembo suggest that, aside from its impressive ruined mosque, it was less built up than Mtangata (modern-day Tongoni), and probably politically subservient to it. Muhembo suffered heavily in 1588 at the hands of the cannibalistic Zimba, and was razed in a punitive Portuguese raid in 1635, after which it was evidently abandoned.

The most intriguing historical question surrounding the lower Pangani River is whether it was the site of the ancient trade settlement referred to in the 1st-century *Periplus of the Erythraean Sea* and Ptolemy's 2nd-century *Geography* as Rhapta. The case for Pangani as Rhapta is compelling, if largely circumstantial. The anonymous author of the *Periplus* places Rhapta 'two days' sail' beyond a 'flat and wooded' island he calls Menouthesias, which itself lay 'slightly south of southwest after a voyage of two days and nights' from 'the Pyralaae Islands and the island called Diorux [the Channel]'. These vague directions lack any name that has

& restaurant offers a set daily menu. Activities include windsurfing, diving, snorkelling, mountain biking & beach volleyball. *US$45/80 sgl/dbl, US$20pp safari tents.* **$–$$**

Capricorn Beach Cottages [345 E1] ⊕ -5.37276, 39.03217; m +255 768 811511; w capricornbeachcottages.com. This relaxed Italian owner-managed beach resort stands alongside the Tanga road about 13km north of Pangani. The comfortable self-catering beach chalets have a kitchenette, fridge, coffee press & hot shower & the restaurant is famed for its wood-fired pizzas & seafood. *From US$75/114 sgl/dbl.* **$$$**

✷ Emayani Beach Lodge [345 B4] ⊕ -5.52122, 38.97818; m +255 782 457668; w emayanilodge.com. This wonderful boutique resort consists of a dozen breeze-cooled chalets made entirely from organic material & spaced out along a long, deserted stretch of sandy beach at Ushongo. It's a great place to chill out with a beach towel & novel, the beach is good for swimming at high tide, & you can retreat to the swimming pool when the tide recedes to expose shallow reefs & mudflats that offer decent snorkelling. Sea kayaks can be used to explore a mangrove-lined creek 1km north of the lodge, & windsurfers & a catamaran are also available. Good value. **$$$$**

Seaside Community Centre Hostel [345 G2] m +255 766 580423; e seasidehostelpangani@yahoo.com. By far the most attractive of the limited accommodation options in Pangani town,

survived into the modern era, and are open to interpretation, but they do seem to point to Menouthesias as either Pemba or Mafia Island, respectively making the most likely location of Rhapta to be Pangani or the Rufiji Delta.

Ptolemy's *Geography*, based on the firsthand and secondhand observations of three different sailors, talks of Rhapta as 'the metropolis of Barbaria, set back a little from the sea' on the river Rhapton, but – contradicting the *Periplus* – it places Menouthias Island (presumably the same as Menouthesias) considerably further south. More intriguingly, based on information gathered by a Greek merchant called Diogenes, Ptolemy talks of two snow-capped peaks and two large lakes lying 25 days' trek up the river Rhapton. The Pangani River has its source near Moshi, at the base of snow-capped Kilimanjaro.

No trace of an appropriately ancient settlement has ever been found near Pangani, which would not be entirely surprising had Rhapta been situated upriver and lacked the permanent stone structures of later medieval ports. Several other possible locations for Rhapta have been suggested, including Ras Kimbiji near Dar es Salaam and more plausibly the Rufiji Delta, the latter so vast and labyrinthine that the remains of a 2,000-year-old settlement would be difficult to locate and might well be submerged. To further complicate the picture, many historians regard it as unlikely that Rhapta was the local name for a port, since it appears to derive from *ploiaria rhapta*, the Greek name for the same type of boat later referred to by an English navigator as *pangaia*. Furthermore, given that these two ancient documents were written centuries apart, and appear to contradict each other on several details, there's every chance that the Rhapta of the *Periplus* is a totally different port from the Rhapta described by Ptolemy's sources.

Whatever the truth, it does seem certain that the Pangani River has long formed an important route for exploration of the interior, largely because it provides a reliable source of fresh water as far inland as Moshi. It almost certainly served as an important inland trade corridor for Mtangata and Muhembo in the Shirazi era, and could as easily have done so 2,000 years ago. Ptolemy's information about the Rhapton River and the African interior, flawed and confusing as it may have been, seems too close to the truth to be dismissed as mere coincidence.

this purpose-built church-run hostel stands in lovingly tended gardens that lead down to a safe swimming beach. Clean & comfortable tiled twin rooms have fans, nets & private balcony, & there's a huge thatched dining room. Great value. *US$5/6 sgl/dbl B&B, or US$6/8 with AC.* **$**

TOURIST INFORMATION AND TOURS The **Pangani Cultural Tourism Programme** [345 B2] (**m** +255 717 463871) has an office close to the ferry jetty and offers bicycle rental for US$3/day as well as walking tours around the old town, snorkelling trips to the islands and river cruises. The beach lodges to the north and south of town can arrange the same activities.

ACTIVITIES AND EXCURSIONS IN AND AROUND PANGANI

Pangani town Several buildings dating to the 19th and early 20th century still stand close to the town's old waterfront. The Old Boma, complete with original carved Zanzibar-style doors, is a rectangular two-storey building constructed in 1810 as the residence of an Omani trader who reputedly had several slaves buried alive underneath to ensure it had strong foundations. Further east along

A FORGOTTEN REVOLUTIONARY

Pangani was the birthplace and home of Abushiri ibn Salim al-Harthi, the African–Arabic trader who masterminded the first and most successful indigenous uprising against German rule. On 20 September 1888, Abushiri's hastily assembled troops evicted the German East Africa Company from Pangani and several other minor German stations along the coast. On 22 September, Abushiri personally led a force of 8,000 men in an assault on Bagamoyo, at that time the German capital, and days of intense fighting resulted in the destruction of much of the town before a German Marine detachment of 260 men deflected Abushiri's army. Nevertheless, by the end of the month, only Bagamoyo and Dar es Salaam remained fully under German control, while Kilwa Kivinje was under permanent siege.

In the face of this onslaught, the trading company appealed to its government for support. A ragbag army of 21 German officers, 40 NCOs and 1,000 African mercenaries assembled by the German commander Hermann von Wissmann recaptured a number of the ports following naval bombardments that drove the occupying forces away, but the spirit of revolt remained high. The naval force was able to further secure the coast by setting up a blockade preventing arms and equipment from reaching the rebels. In May 1889, the Germans attacked Abushiri's fort at Jahazi (also called Nzole), between Pangani and Bagamoyo. Using artillery fire, Wissmann drove the defenders back from the 2m-high fortifications, and then led a charge in which more than 100 Arabs were killed and Jahazi was captured. Abushiri escaped, to launch a new series of mostly unsuccessful assaults assisted by Yao and Shambaa recruits.

Von Wissmann, realising he would not be able to wrest control of the hinterland while the revolution's leader remained at large, put a price of 10,000 rupees on Abushiri's head. This rich bounty persuaded a local chief who had been harbouring Abushiri to hand him over to the German commander. On 15 December 1889, Abushiri was taken to his hometown of Pangani, paraded through the streets clad in a skimpy loincloth, and hanged later the same day. The town bears no trace of the revolutionary's existence today.

COCONUT PALMS

Industry and associated opportunities for formal employment are thin on the ground in Pangani, but the surrounding district is self-sufficient in food, thanks to its fertile soil and the rich bounty of the ocean. Cashew and sisal – the latter introduced by a German botanist in 1892 – form the region's main export crops, but Pangani is also known for its extensive coconut palm plantations. The coconut plantations around Pangani are significant employers (monthly salaries are equivalent to US$40), and also provide an estimated 50% of Tanzania's coconut yield.

Even on a casual stroll around Pangani, the ubiquity of coconuts is striking. Vendors selling young nuts provide travellers with a refreshing and nutritious alternative to bottled soft drinks. Near the harbour, you'll see large piles of drying husks, the debris of nuts shipped to other parts of the country. Women wander home from the market carrying their goods in palm fronds converted with a few deft strokes into disposable shopping baskets.

No part of the coconut palm goes unused. The flesh of the mature nut, harvested twice annually, is not only a popular snack, but also an important ingredient in Swahili cuisine, and a source of cooking oil. The fibrous husks surrounding the nut are twined to make rope and matting, or dried for fire fuel. Palm fronds form the basis of the makuti roofs characteristic of the Swahili coast, and are also used as brooms. The sap and flowers are brewed to make a popular local wine, and the timber is used for furniture. A multi-faceted resource indeed!

the waterfront stands a castellated double-storey Slave Depot dating to the 1850s, and a fort-like German Customs House built in 1910 and still used for its original purpose today. A few metres inland, India Street, the main shopping drag, is lined with old double-storey Indian residences adorned with ornate iron balconies, while the dense bush 500m west of town is scattered with 17th-century Portuguese and 19th-century German graves. Inexpensive guided tours of the old town are offered by the Pangani Cultural Tourism Programme.

Pangani river trip Boat trips up the forested Pangani River are of interest primarily for the scenery and birds such as the mangrove kingfisher, though some large mammals still occur in the area, most visibly vervet monkeys. In the wet season, you can boat upriver to the base of the Pangani Falls, now swallowed by a hydro-electric plant, though pools at the base harbour crocodiles and hippos. Boat trips can be arranged through any of the beach resorts at Ushongo, and the tourist office in Pangani charges around US$80 (for one to four people) to arrange the boat, plus the guide and development fees.

Maziwe and Fungu islands These two small offshore islands south of Pangani form the centrepieces of a recently proclaimed marine park. Maziwe was once regarded as the most important nesting site on the Tanzanian coast for sea turtles, but it has been abandoned since the 1980s due to erosion of the beach, which causes it to be submerged at high tide. Today, the main attraction is the snorkelling on the offshore reefs, where the usual host of colourful reef fish can be observed. It is important to time a visit so you arrive at low tide, when the snorkelling is best. Boat trips to the islands can be arranged through the resorts at Ushongo, which generally charge US$35–40 per person for a minimum of three people to charter a large local dhow. The tourist office in Pangani arranges trips for US$120 (one to five people) inclusive of gear. A nominal park entrance fee is levied.

TANGA

An intriguing port town whose compact and somnambulant centre is lined with timeworn pastel-shaded German and Asian buildings, Tanga practically dropped off the East African travel map following the termination of passenger train services from Moshi and Dar es Salaam in the late 1990s. Not much is known about the port's early history, but it emerged as a substantial centre of ivory trade in the mid 19th century, one that was less important than Pangani but sufficiently profitable to be governed by an agent of the Sultan of Zanzibar. Tanga was selected as the administrative centre of German East Africa in 1890, but relinquished this status to Dar es Salaam a year later. Nevertheless, its deep and well-protected natural harbour ensured that it was earmarked for colonial development. The first school in German East Africa was built at Tanga in 1893, and several other impressive buildings on the modern waterfront date back to the German era. The completion of a railway line to Moshi in 1911 and introduction of several profitable sisal plantations sealed Tanga's role as the country's second busiest seaport in the colonial era, but it has since fallen into decline and is now largely bypassed by travellers and commerce alike. Despite this, the characterful town centre is studded with architectural gems, notably the original Tanga School, the old German Boma (now the Urithi Tanga Museum) and the German-built two-storey Usambara Courthouse. There are two World War I cemeteries: the German Sakarani Cemetery on Swahili Street and Commonwealth War Cemetery on Bombo Road. Attractions further afield include the Amboni Caves and medieval Tongoni Ruins.

GETTING THERE AND AWAY

By air **Coastal Aviation** (w coastal.co.tz) operates daily flights connecting Tanga to Arusha, Dar es Salaam, Zanzibar and Pemba. The airport is about 3km west of the town centre.

By road A good surfaced 70km road connects Tanga to Segera, the junction town on the main road between Arusha and Dar es Salaam. Regular **buses** run between

THE BATTLE FOR TANGA

In late 1914, German Tanga was the setting of a tragically farcical British naval raid. Suffering from seasickness after a long voyage from India, 8,000 Asian recruits were instructed to leap ashore at Tanga, only to become bogged down in the mangroves, then stumble into a swarm of ferocious bees, and finally trigger off German trip-wires. The raid was eventually aborted, but not before 800 British troops lay dead, and a further 500 were wounded. In the confusion, 455 rifles, 16 machine guns and 600,000 rounds of ammunition were left on the shore – a major boon for the Germans. This battle forms a pivotal scene in William Boyd's excellent novel, *An Ice-Cream War*. The Germans were eventually forced out of Tanga in 1916, when the British, better prepared this time, launched a land offensive from Moshi on the weakened German outpost.

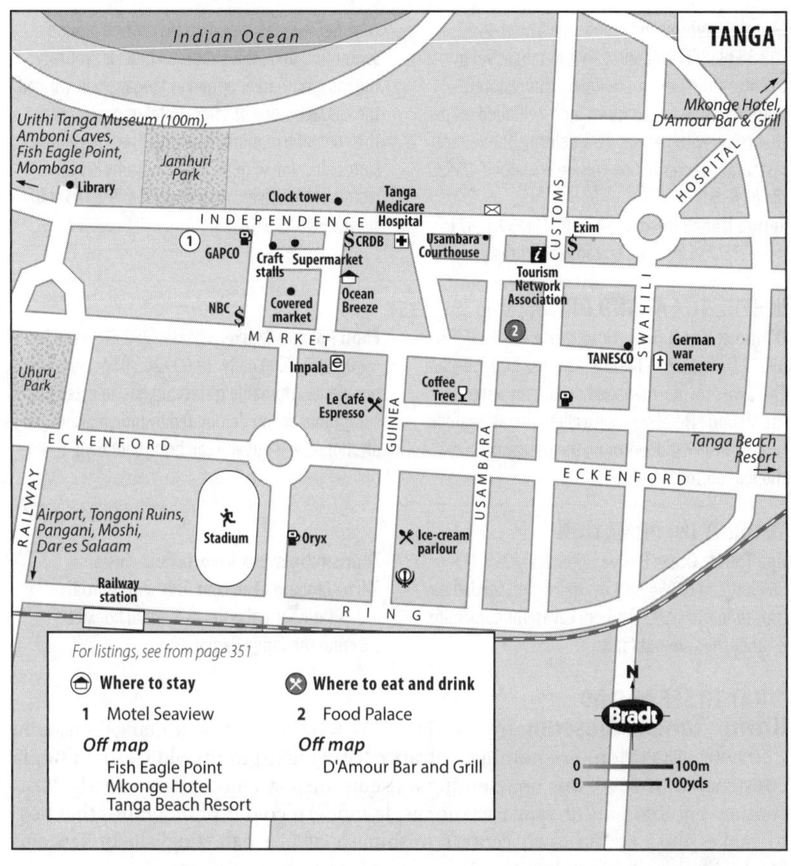

Tanga, Arusha and Dar es Salaam. Coming from either, it might be preferable to use a superior company such as Kilimanjaro or Dar Express as far as Segera, and then pick up local transport from there. Local buses and minibuses also connect Tanga to Lushoto, Pangani and Muheza. All buses and dalla dallas leave from and arrive at the main bus station, 500m from the town centre on the main road to Segera.

WHERE TO STAY *Map, page 351*

As a barometer of its 21st-century descent into backwater status, Tanga is the only town in Tanzania where fewer central hotel rooms are available today than was the case when the first edition of this guide was researched 30 years ago.

Fish Eagle Point -4.84091, 39.21244; m +255 687 680890; w fisheaglepoint.com. This lovely lodge on the remote baobab-lined beach of Manza Bay stands 48km north of Tanga off the main road to Mombasa (Kenya). It has an idyllic unspoilt setting, far from any other beach resort. Snorkelling, fishing & coastal birding are all on offer. *From US$80pp B&B.* **$$$**

Mkonge Hotel Hospital Rd; m +255 753 248611; w booking.com. Built in the 1950s, this former government hotel stands in attractive gardens overlooking the harbour. The 45 characterful rooms have wooden floors, twin or king-size beds, AC, satellite TV & hot water. Facilities include a restaurant & swimming pool. Good value. *From US$36/45 sgl/dbl B&B.* **$**

Motel Seaview Independence Av; m +255 713 383868; f Motel-sea-view-tanga. Set in a century-old German building, this restored seafront lodge has spacious high-ceilinged rooms that come with net, sat TV & balcony. The terrace restaurant serves Indian cuisine & seafood. *US$20 dbl B&B.* **$$**

Tanga Beach Resort ⊕ -5.07711, 39.12571; m +255 785 171717; w tangabeachresort.com. Set in small lush gardens centred around a swimming pool, this suburban hotel is probably the most upmarket option in Tanga, albeit with all the character of a business hotel transplanted to the edge of a mangrove swamp. The 118 rooms & suites all come with AC, DSTV, balcony & fridge. A restaurant & spa are attached. *From US$105/130 sgl/dbl B&B.* **$$$**

WHERE TO EAT AND DRINK *Map, page 351*

D'Amour Bar & Grill Hospital Rd; m +255 786 395391; ⌚ 11.30–14.00 & 18.30–23.00 Tue–Sun. This Swiss owner-managed restaurant opposite the Mkonge Hotel serves excellent pizzas, seafood & meat dishes indoors or on the breezy makuti-shaded rooftop. *Mains US$6–8.* **$**

Food Palace Market St; m + 255 715 418824; ⌚ 07.30–16.00 daily, 19.00–20.30 Fri–Sun. This popular & affordable restaurant has an extensive & sumptuous menu dominated by Indian dishes. No alcohol served but you can bring your own. **$**

TOURIST INFORMATION

Ilya Tours Ocean Breeze Hotel; m +255 713 560569/784 660569; w ilyatours.com. Guided day trips to Toten Island, Amboni Caves, Tongoni Ruins & other sites around Tanga.

Tourism Network Association Customs Rd; w tangatourism.com. This semi-official organisation usually stocks a useful booklet covering the Tanga Region.

WHAT TO SEE AND DO

Urithi Tanga Museum (m +255 784 440068; f urithitanga.museum; ⌚ 09.00–17.00 Mon–Fri; nominal entrance fee) Housed in the old German Boma constructed in 1890, this unassuming museum displays monochrome early 20th-century photographs of Tanga set alongside modern colour photographs that help to make sense of the town centre's mishmash of German, English, Indian and Swahili architectural styles.

Toten Island This tiny uninhabited island in Tanga harbour is dotted with overgrown relics of earlier Islamic settlements, including two medieval mosques, one of which was renovated during the late 18th century and has a well-preserved ornamental mihrab. It can be reached by boat as a 3–4-hour round-trip excursion from Tanga. Ilya Tours (see above) can arrange guided tours.

Amboni Caves (⌚ 08.00–17.00 daily; entrance US$8pp inc the services of an English-speaking guide & use of a good torch) The limestone Amboni Caves are reputedly the most extensive in East Africa, said locally to be more than 200km long, though a comprehensive survey undertaken by a German–Turkish expedition in 1994 explored ten caves and found them all to be less than 1km deep. The tourist route through Amboni leads through a succession of narrow passages and larger caverns to some striking natural limestone sculptures including the so-called *Madonna* and *Statue of Liberty*. Close to the entrance, the Mkulimuzi River runs through a coastal forest patch that supports black-and-white colobus monkey as well as the African violet in its wild state. The caves lie 7km north of Tanga off the Mombasa road. Using public transport, dalla dallas between Tanga and Amboni village (2km further along the Mombasa road), will drop passengers at the junction, from where it's a 30-minute walk to the caves.

Tongoni Ruins (🕘 08.00–17.00 daily; entrance US$8) Tongoni means 'Place of Ruins', and the village of that name, situated alongside the Pangani road 20km south of Tanga, stands adjacent to the remains of an abandoned Swahili town known contemporaneously as Mtangata. Little is known about the early history of this settlement, but it must have been founded before the late 14th century (one unverifiable local tradition relates that it was founded at the same time as Kilwa, and by the same family). During its 15th-century commercial peak, Mtangata was the most prosperous trade centre for 100km in any direction. It also became one of the first places in East Africa to be visited by Europeans when three Portuguese ships under the command of Vasco da Gama ran aground there in 1498. Traditionally hostile to Mombasa, Mtangata maintained a good relationship with the Portuguese until they were evicted from the coast in 1698, but was abandoned shortly thereafter. Today, the ruins comprise a well-preserved 150m² mosque, several disused wells and walls, and a cemetery of 40 pillar tombs, a type of construction unique to the Swahili Coast. To reach the ruins from Tanga, follow the Pangani road south for 18km to Tongoni village, then turn left at the signposted junction and follow this motorable track for 1km. Any bus heading to Pangani can drop you at the junction.

15

Zanzibar

Chris and Susie McIntyre

Zanzibar is one of those magical travel names, richly evocative even to the many Westerners who would have no idea where to start looking for it on a global map. Steeped in history, and blessed with a sultry tropical climate – warm to hot all year round and often very humid; it receives more rainfall and is windier than the mainland – and a multitude of idyllic beaches, Zanzibar is also that rare travel destination that genuinely does live up to every expectation. Whether it's a quick cultural fix you're after, scintillating diving, or just a palm-lined beach where you can laze away the day, some time on Zanzibar is the perfect way to round off a dusty safari on the Tanzanian mainland.

A separate state within Tanzania, Zanzibar consists of two large islands, Unguja or Zanzibar Island and Pemba, plus several smaller islets. Zanzibar Island is about 85km long and between 20km and 30km wide; Pemba is about 75km long and between 15km and 20km wide. Both are flat and low-lying, surrounded by coasts of rocky inlets or sandy beaches, with lagoons and mangrove swamps, and coral reefs beyond the shoreline. Farming and fishing are the main occupations, and most people live in small villages. Cloves are a major export, along with coconut products and other spices. The capital, and by far the largest settlement, is Zanzibar Town (usually known as Stone Town) on the west coast.

For many, the highlight of a stay is the old Stone Town, with its traditional Swahili atmosphere and wealth of fascinating buildings. For others, it is the sea and the coral reefs, which offer diving, snorkelling and game fishing to compare with anywhere in East Africa. And then there are the clove and coconut plantations that cover the interior of the 'Spice Island', the dolphins of Kizimkazi, the colobus monkeys of Jozani, and the giant sea turtles of Nungwi. And above all, some will say, those seemingly endless tropical beaches.

For a detailed and dedicated guide to these incredible islands, see our comprehensive *Zanzibar, Pemba & Mafia: the Bradt Guide* (tenth edition, 2022).

HISTORY

Zanzibar has been trading with ships from Persia, Arabia and India for approximately 2,000 years. From about the 10th century AD, groups of immigrants from Shiraz (Persia) settled on Zanzibar and mingled with the local Swahili. The Portuguese established a trading station on the site of Zanzibar Town in the early 16th century. At the end of the 17th century, the Sultan of Oman's navy ousted the Portuguese from the island.

In 1840, Sultan Said of Oman relocated his capital in Muscat to Zanzibar. Many Omani Arabs settled on Zanzibar as rulers and landowners, forming an elite group, while Indian settlers formed a merchant class. The island became an Arab state, an important centre of regional politics, and the focus of a booming slave trade.

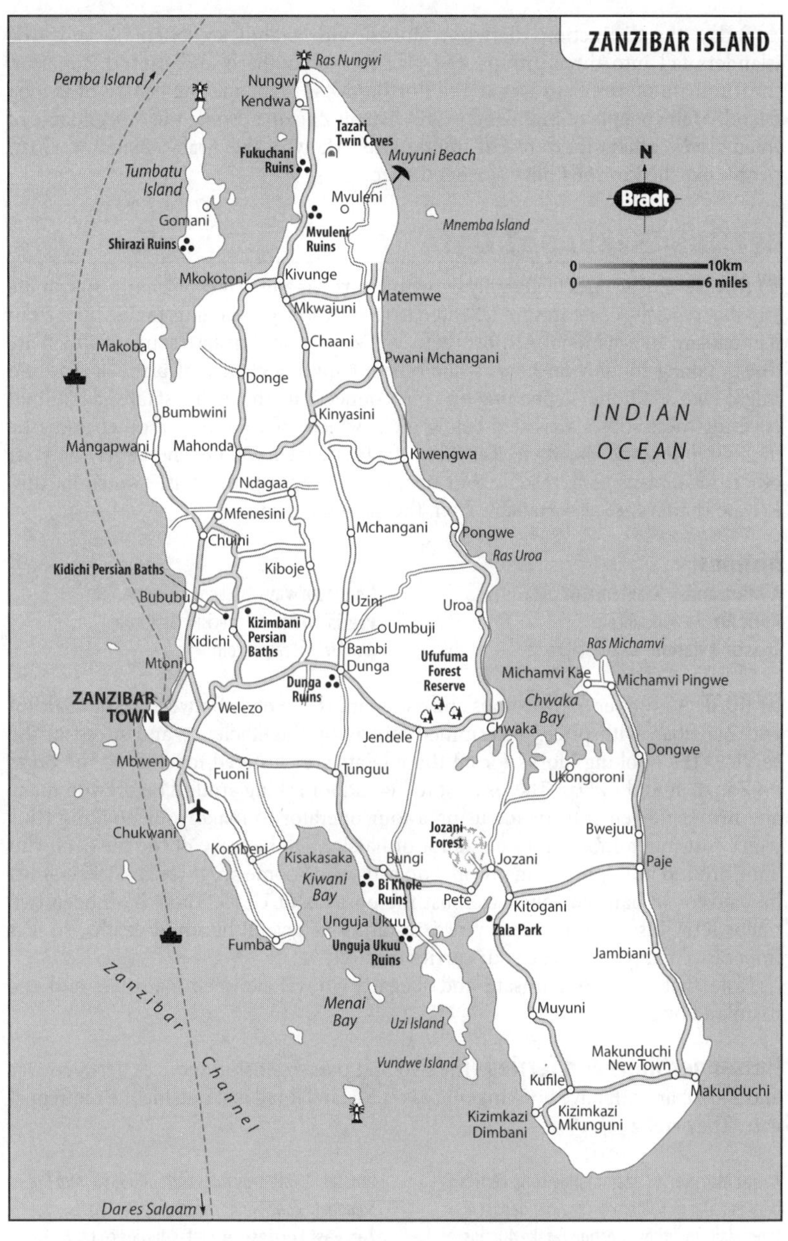

Britain had interests in Zanzibar throughout the 19th century; explorers such as Livingstone, Speke and Burton began their expeditions into the African interior from there. In 1890, Zanzibar became a British protectorate.

Zanzibar gained independence from Britain in December 1963. In 1964, the sultan was overthrown in a revolution and nearly all Arabs and Indians were expelled. Later the same year, Zanzibar and Tanganyika combined to form the United Republic of Tanzania.

Today, the distinctions between Shirazi and Swahili are often blurred. The islanders fall into three groups: the Hadimu of southern and central Zanzibar, the Tumbatu of Tumbatu Island and northern Zanzibar, and the Pemba of Pemba Island. Many people of mainland origin live on Zanzibar, some the descendants of freed slaves, others more recent immigrants. Many of the Arab, Asian and Goan people expelled in 1964 have since returned.

GETTING THERE AND AWAY

BY AIR Several airlines fly directly between Zanzibar and Dar es Salaam, a 30-minute trip that typically costs around US$80. There are also regular flights to Zanzibar from Kilimanjaro International Airport (between Moshi and Arusha), some of which are direct, taking roughly an hour, while others require a change of plane at Dar and might take 3–4 hours depending on your connection. The main established airlines covering these routes are listed below, all of which offer a range of other domestic flights, while some also fly to Kenya, so the best choice will depend largely on your other travel plans. Any reliable tour operator will be able to advise you about this. Private charters are also available from the main safari spots.

Airlines

Air Tanzania w airtanzania.co.tz
Auric Air w auricair.com
Coastal Aviation w coastal.co.tz
Kenya Airways w kenya-airways.com
Precision Air w precisionairtz.com
ZanAir w zanair.com

BY BOAT A number of hydrofoils and catamarans run daily between Dar es Salaam and Zanzibar, with prices determined largely by the efficiency and speed of the service. The booking kiosks for all these boats are clustered together at the ports on Zanzibar and in Dar. There's a lot to be said for asking around before you make any firm arrangements, or for using a tour operator to make your booking (this won't cost much more and saves a lot of hassle). Do be wary of the hustlers who hang around both ports – many are con artists and some are thieves. Tickets must be paid for in hard currency, as must the port tax of US$5. There have been two major ferry disasters in recent years, resulting in several hundred deaths, so it is imperative that you choose your carrier carefully.

Note that it is both unsafe and illegal to travel between Zanzibar and the mainland by dhow.

Passenger ships and ferries The two best passenger ship services between Dar and Zanzibar both have booking offices on Malawi Road just outside the main port gate. They are:

Azam Marine w azammarine.com. Ferries between Dar es Salaam & Zanzibar depart 4 times daily in either direction & take 40mins. Ferries between Zanzibar & Pemba run 4 times weekly, & there's also a weekly service between Tanga & Pemba. Check the website for the current timetable. *One-way fares start at US$35 from Dar es Salaam to Zanzibar or Zanzibar to Pemba.*

Zan Fast Ferries w zanfastferries.co.tz. 2 crossings in either direction daily, leaving from Zanzibar at 07.00 & 14.00 & from Dar es Salaam at 10.30 & 17.00. *Fares start at US$25pp.*

ORGANISED TOURS Most international tour operators (page 82) offering safaris to Tanzania can append a flight to Zanzibar (or a full travel package to the island) to your safari arrangements. Likewise, most safari companies based in Arusha are able to set up excursions to Zanzibar. If you are booking a safari in advance, there is a lot to be said for making all your travel arrangements through the same company.

VISAS AND TAXES Visitors who fly to Zanzibar from mainland Tanzania do not need to complete an immigration card or show their passport and visa, but they may be asked to produce a yellow fever certificate. If you arrive by ferry from the mainland, however, all documentation must be shown and an immigration card completed.

Many travellers flying into Zanzibar from outside Tanzania obtain an e-visa online at w eservices.immigration.go.tz/visa. It is also possible to buy a **visa on arrival** at the airport. The **airport tax** for international and domestic flights in to or out of Zanzibar is now almost invariably incorporated into the price of a ticket.

If you lose your passport while on Zanzibar, you will need to have an Emergency Travel Document issued at the Ministry of Home Affairs (☎024 223 9148). This will allow you to travel back to the mainland (where nationals of most countries will find diplomatic representation in Dar es Salaam) or directly to your home country.

GETTING AROUND

BUSES, PUBLIC MINIBUSES AND DALLA DALLAS Local minibuses and dalla dallas cover many routes around Zanzibar Island, and are the quickest way to get around. Buses are also available, but often there is only one daily to any given destination and journeys can be very slow. In all cases, fares are cheap, typically about US$0.50 for destinations close to Zanzibar Town and a few dollars to cross the island.

Buses and dalla dallas from outlying villages heading for Zanzibar Town tend to leave very early in the morning but, apart from that, most vehicles simply leave when they're full. Be aware that the last buses to some coastal villages will leave Zanzibar Town by mid afternoon. The dalla dalla destinations are written on the front of the vehicle, but it's also worth telling the driver where you're going.

There are four **main terminals** in Zanzibar Town. Darajani Station on Creek Road (opposite the market) is where you will find transport to Nungwi, Matemwe, Kiwengwa and elsewhere in the north, while Mnazi Moja, opposite the eponymous hospital, services the airport, Bububu and other relatively local destinations. The more out-of-town Mwana Kwerekwe is the terminus for transport to Paje, Jambiani, Jozani Forest, Kizimkazi and elsewhere in the southeast, while Mwembe Ladu services Uroa, Pongwe and Chwaka. Mwana Kwerekwe and Mwembe Ladu are a few kilometres from Stone Town and best accessed by a short hop on a dalla dalla from Darajani.

CAR HIRE To hire a car, SUV or scooter, contact one of the island's tour operators (page 360). A car or SUV for a day will cost US$50–100, excluding fuel. **Insurance cover** is in theory comprehensive, but check this thoroughly. Note that driving standards on Zanzibar are not good, and the roads can be pot-holed, so think very carefully before hiring a car. You should be aware that, unlike on the mainland, you need an **international driving licence** and a **local permit** to drive a vehicle on Zanzibar. Your tour operator can help organise a local permit (best to give 24 hours' notice), and you should insist that they do to avoid roadside police fines. Petrol and diesel are readily available island-wide nowadays.

TAXIS Taxis are fairly widely available. A short hop within Zanzibar Town costs just over US$3, while the trip to Mtoni costs up to US$10 one-way; to Jozani or the east coast US$20–25 one-way or US$30–35 return. To Nungwi or Bwejuu is around

US$40–50 one-way. The going rate for transfers between the airport and Zanzibar Town is US$10–15.

BICYCLE HIRE Some tour operators in Zanzibar Town can arrange bicycle hire. The current rate for a heavy Chinese bike is from US$10 per day, while mountain bikes go for around US$15. Keen cyclists might like to contact Blue Bikes (page 360) or Mreh Tours (page 360) – the only companies as far as we know to offer specific cycle tours out of Stone Town.

ZANZIBAR TOWN

Zanzibar's old quarter, usually called Stone Town, is a fascinating maze of narrow streets and alleyways that lead the visitor past numerous old houses and mosques, ornate palaces, and shops and bazaars. Many buildings in Stone Town date from the 19th-century slave boom. Houses reflect their builder's wealth: Arab houses have plain outer walls and large front doors leading to an inner courtyard; Indian houses have a more open façade and large balconies decorated with railings and balustrades. Most are still occupied.

A striking feature of many houses is the brass-studded doors with their elaborately carved frames. The size of a door and the intricacy of its design was an indication of the owner's wealth and status. The use of studs probably originated in Persia or India, where they helped prevent doors being knocked down by war elephants. In Zanzibar, studs were purely decorative.

The area outside Stone Town used to be called Ng'ambo ('The Other Side'), and is still often referred to as such, though its official name is actually Michenzani (New City). Attempts have been made to modernise it and at the centre of Michenzani are some ugly apartment blocks, built by East German engineers as part of an international aid scheme.

TOUR OPERATORS A number of tour companies operate out of Zanzibar Town, offering tours as well as transfers and general tourist information. The better companies can set up bespoke excursions, as well as make hotel reservations and onward travel arrangements. For straightforward day trips and transfers, there is no real need to make bookings before you arrive in Zanzibar as they can easily be set up at the last minute. If, however, you want to have all your travel arrangements organised in advance through one company, or you have severe time restrictions, then it would be sensible to make advance contact with one of the companies with good international connections, such as those shortlisted on page 82.

While prices vary greatly depending on standard of service, season and group size, typical costs per person for the most popular outings are: City Tour (US$20); Prison Island Tour (US$30); Dolphin Tour (US$40); Spice Tour (US$28); Jozani Forest Tour (US$35). All these rates are per person (based on four people sharing) but for the tour only, and do not include extras like entrance fees (ie: for the Palace Museum this is US$2, for Prison Island US$4, for Jozani Forest US$4). Prices are negotiable, particularly out of season, but do be wary of unregistered companies and individuals offering substandard trips at very low rates.

It's also possible to arrange many of the standard tours more cheaply through taxi drivers or independent guides (nicknamed *papaasi* after a type of insect). With spice tours, this may often turn out to be a false economy, in that the guide will lack any botanical knowledge and may cut the excursion short, rendering the whole exercise somewhat pointless.

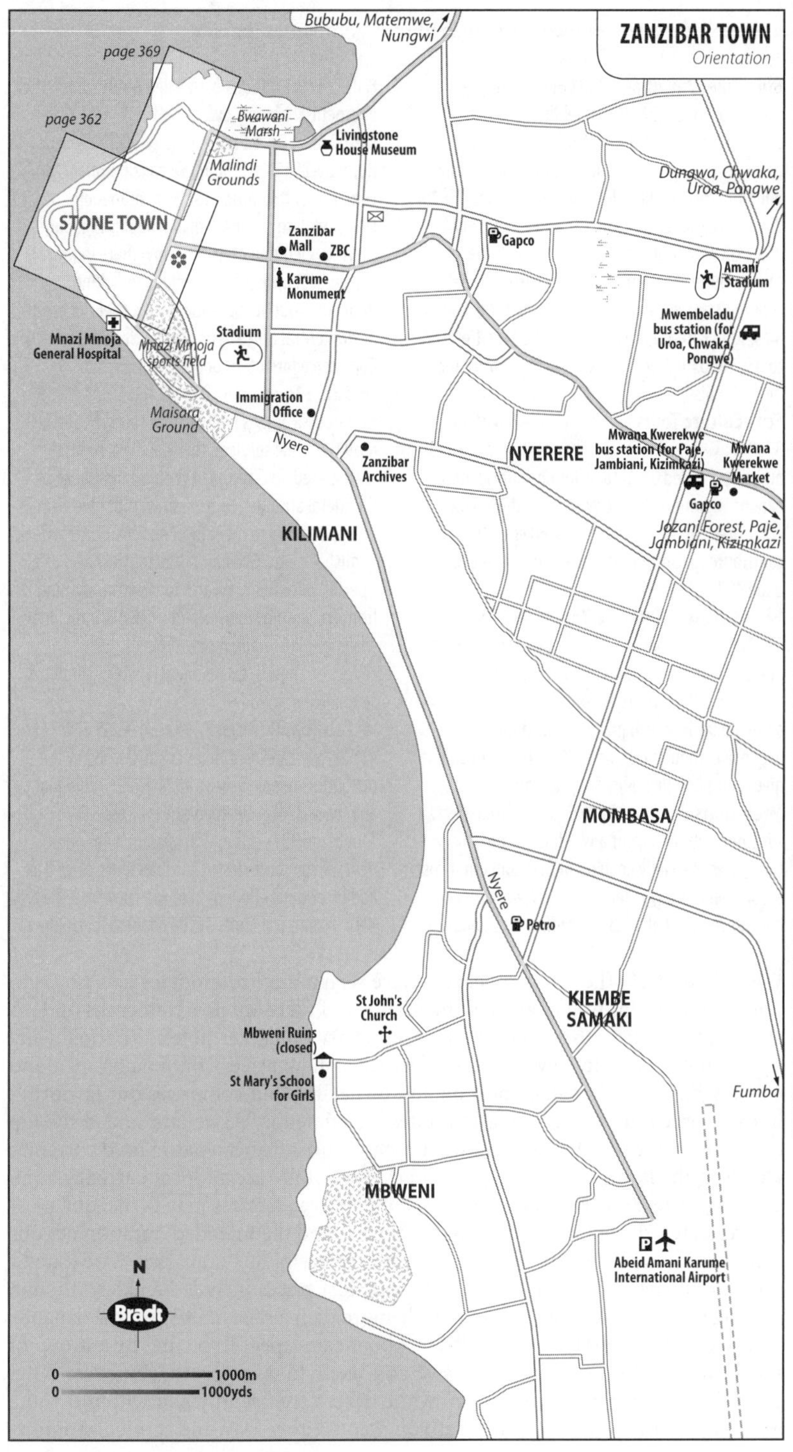
ZANZIBAR TOWN
Orientation
Bububu, Matemwe, Nungwi
page 369
page 362
Bwawani Marsh
Livingstone House Museum
Malindi Grounds
Dungwa, Chwaka, Uroa, Pongwe
STONE TOWN
Zanzibar Mall
ZBC
Gapco
Amani Stadium
Karume Monument
Mwembeladu bus station (for Uroa, Chwaka, Pongwe)
Stadium
Mnazi Mmoja General Hospital
Mnazi Mmoja sports field
Immigration Office
Maisara Ground
Nyere
Zanzibar Archives
NYERERE
Mwana Kwerekwe bus station (for Paje, Jambiani, Kizimkazi)
Mwana Kwerekwe Market
Gapco
Jozani Forest, Paje, Jambiani, Kizimkazi
KILIMANI
MOMBASA
Nyere
Petro
KIEMBE SAMAKI
St John's Church
Mbweni Ruins (closed)
St Mary's School for Girls
Fumba
MBWENI
N
Bradt
Abeid Amani Karume International Airport
0 1000m
0 1000yds

Zanzibar ZANZIBAR TOWN

15

Recommended and well-established tour companies include:

Blue Bikes Zanzibar [369 C6] Kiponda St; m +255 776 828385; w bluebikeszanzibar.com. An offshoot of the KAWA Guides Training Centre & situated on the ground floor of the same building, this excellent little set-up charges US$10/day for bicycle rental & also arranges a variety of inexpensive guided day & overnight cycle tours around the island, taking in various urban locations, as well as spice farms & the little-known Masingini Forest. Rates start at US$25 for 1 person to US$15pp for 3 or more. Check the website for more details.

Eco+Culture Tours [363 E1] m +255 755 873066; w ecoculture-zanzibar.com. A respected, ethically minded operator offering slightly more expensive but excellent day trips for those who want to avoid the more established circuits & contribute to community development. See also page 407.

Island Express Safaris & Tours m +255 774 111222; w islandexpress.co.tz. A smart, efficient operation offering a more personal service than most. Tours & transfers are only ever arranged on a private basis, which makes them slightly more expensive, though not prohibitively so, & of course gives complete flexibility for your trip.

Mreh Tours 024 223 3476; e mrehtours@zanzinet.com. This company offers all the usual tours, & is especially keen on bicycle tours that cost around US$50/day including bike, food, drink & backup vehicle. Call in at their office on Baghani St & discuss the options with Saleh Mreh Salum, the energetic & friendly owner.

One Ocean Dive Shop [362 B3] Off Kenyatta Rd; m +255 774 310003; w zanzibaroneocean.com. Under the same Australian management since 1999, this 5* PADI dive school is the longest serving operation of its type anywhere in Tanzania & your best option for diving & snorkelling excursions out of Stone Town. Visit their website or the central office opposite the National Bank of Commerce for details of activities & rates.

✱ **Sama Tours** [362 D2] m +255 777 430385; samatours.com. As well as spice tours, boat trips & all the usual services, the friendly & helpful team based on Gizenga St (behind the House of Wonders) arranges cultural tours that give visitors an opportunity to meet local people. Guides speak English, French, German & Italian. They also offer 'special' spice tours, & cater to groups (anything from cruise ships to overland trucks) & individuals seeking tailor-made tours, airport & port collection, hotels, excursions, transfers, car hire & so on. Recommended.

✱ **Zanzibar Different** [362 D3] +255 777 430117; w zanzibardifferent.com. Owned by the delightful Stefanie Schoetz of Mrembo Traditional Spa (page 374) & creator of the Princess Salme Tour (page 381), this ethical operation has put a new spin on some classic Zanzibari tours, as well as adding original offerings in music, cookery & the arts. Very flexible & all tours can be adapted for children.

WHERE TO STAY The last two decades have seen a mushrooming of new hotels in Zanzibar Town, as well as around the island, and there are now numerous options at every level, from basic guesthouses to smart upmarket hotels. The following selection of places to stay is not exhaustive, as new places continually open and existing ones change name, location and ownership, but comprises our favourites in each price range. As a rule, room rates are quoted in US dollars, and at the top end of the range the management will probably insist that you pay in hard currency. Hotels at the lower end of the price bracket generally accept local currency at an exchange rate similar to those given at forex bureaux. Rates may be negotiable at budget hotels depending on how busy they are and the intended duration of your stay. It is advisable to make an advance reservation for any upmarket, moderate or popular budget hotel during peak seasons. Most prices include breakfast, though at budget hotels this may amount to little more than a slice of bread and a banana.

Travellers who arrive on Zanzibar by boat can expect to be met by a group of hotel touts. Some are quite aggressive and likely to take you to whichever hotel gives them the largest commission, while others are friendly and will find you a suitable hotel if you tell them what you want. Either way, the service shouldn't cost you anything, since the tout will get a commission from the hotel, and it may save a lot of walking in the confusing alleys of Stone Town. Given the difficulty of getting past the touts and the general aura of chaos around the ferry port, there is probably a lot to be said for taking the path of least resistance when you first arrive. Should you not like the place to which you are first directed, you can always look around yourself once your bags are securely locked away, and change hotel the next day.

However you arrive, many of the hotels in Stone Town cannot be reached by taxi. You are liable to get lost if you strike out on foot without a guide, though we found that people were always very helpful when it came to pointing us in the right direction (bearing in mind that the right direction may change every few paces). Most taxi drivers will be prepared to walk you to the hotel of your choice, but they will expect a decent tip.

Shangani Waterfront and Southwest Stone Town Many of Stone Town's premier hotels, among them the opulent Park Hyatt, stylish Jafferji House and landmark Zanzibar Serena Hotel, run along the waterfront west of Forodhani Gardens or in the adjoining alleys. The poshest and most touristy part of Stone Town, this area incorporates the historic district of Shangani, whose long triangular waterfront lies to the west of Kenyatta Road, and is the most plentifully endowed part of the city when it comes to restaurants and cafés, craft and souvenir shops, and other tourist amenities. Although the overall feel of the area is relatively upmarket, it also incorporates a popular cluster of budget hostels along the alley running immediately east of and parallel to Kenyatta Road.

The southwest and northwest borders of the area included in this section are more or less naturally defined, with boundaries lapped by the Indian Ocean. The eastern border is rather more arbitrary but essentially comprises an imaginary line that runs south from House of Wonders to High Court through St Joseph's Catholic Cathedral. In terms of the map on page 362, that means everything within columns A to C on the left page.

Upmarket

✷ **Park Hyatt Zanzibar** [362 A4] Shangani St; w hyatt.com. This imposing hotel is hard to beat when it comes to grandeur & elegance. It also boasts a prestigious oceanfront location on quiet & leafy Shangani St only mins on foot from the city hustle. The hotel spans 2 buildings: the UNESCO-listed Mambo Msiige mansion & the brand-new Zamani Residence, & offers a contemporary take on Swahili architecture,

STONE TOWN *South*

For listings, see from page 360

Where to stay

1 Dhow Palace........C5
2 Emerson on Hurumzi........E2
3 Emerson Spice........F1
4 Jafferji House........C3
5 Jambo Guesthouse........F4
6 Kisiwa House........C5
7 Lost & Found Hostel........B4
8 Maru Maru........D2
9 Park Hyatt Zanzibar........A4
10 Shoki Shoki Hostel........D3
11 Stone Town B&B........C4
12 The Swahili House........F1
13 Upendo House........D1
14 Zanzibar Coffee House........F2
15 Zanzibar Serena........A5

Where to eat and drink

16 6°South........B6
17 Abyssinian Maritim........D6
18 Baboo Beach Café........C6
19 Beach House........B5
20 Cape Town Fish Market........B2
Emerson Spice Tea House........(see 3)
21 Krishna Food House........C3
22 La Taverna........G4
23 Lazziz Bakery........D6
24 Mzee Husa........C4
25 New Monsoon........C3
26 Puzzle Coffee Shop........C5
Stone Town Café........(see 11)
27 The Secret Garden........F1
28 Travellers Café Zanzibar........A5
Zanzibar Coffee House Café........(see 14)

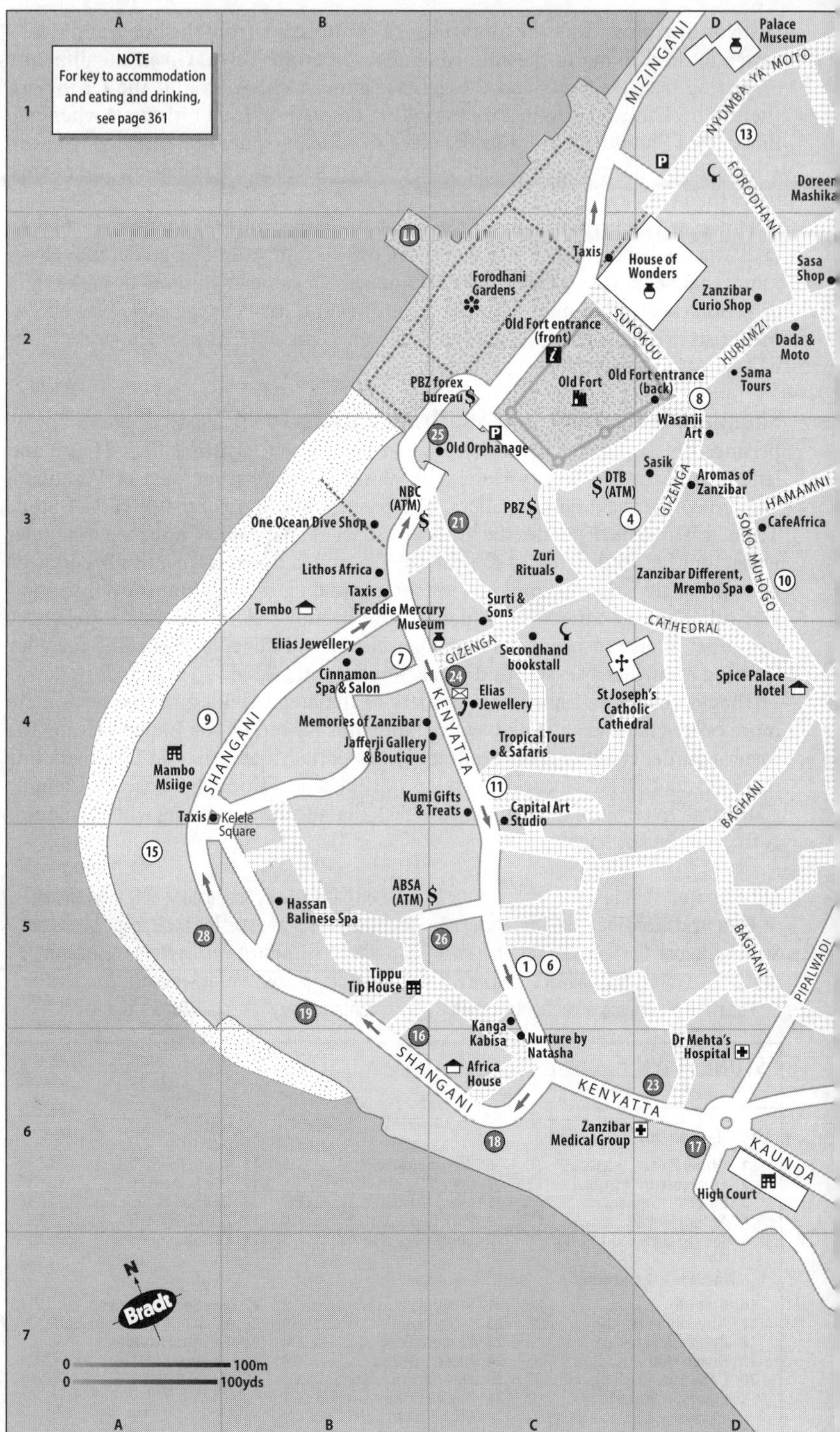
NOTE
For key to accommodation and eating and drinking, see page 361
MIZINGANI
Palace Museum
NYUMBA YA MOTO
FORODHANI
Doreen Mashika
Taxis
House of Wonders
Sasa Shop
Forodhani Gardens
Zanzibar Curio Shop
SUKOKUU
HURUMZI
Dada & Moto
Old Fort entrance (front)
Sama Tours
Old Fort
Old Fort entrance (back)
PBZ forex bureau
Wasanii Art
Old Orphanage
Sasik
Aromas of Zanzibar
DTB (ATM)
HAMAMNI
NBC (ATM)
PBZ
GIZENGA
SOKO MUHOGO
CafeAfrica
One Ocean Dive Shop
Zuri Rituals
Lithos Africa
Zanzibar Different, Mrembo Spa
Taxis
Tembo
Freddie Mercury Museum
Surti & Sons
CATHEDRAL
Elias Jewellery
Secondhand bookstall
GIZENGA
Cinnamon Spa & Salon
Elias Jewellery
St Joseph's Catholic Cathedral
Spice Palace Hotel
KENYATTA
Memories of Zanzibar
SHANGANI
Jafferji Gallery & Boutique
Tropical Tours & Safaris
Mambo Msiige
Kumi Gifts & Treats
Capital Art Studio
BAGHANI
Taxis
Kelele Square
ABSA (ATM)
Hassan Balinese Spa
BAGHANI
PIPALWADI
Tippu Tip House
Kanga Kabisa
Nurture by Natasha
Dr Mehta's Hospital
SHANGANI
Africa House
KENYATTA
Zanzibar Medical Group
KAUNDA
High Court
Bradt
0 100m
0 100yds

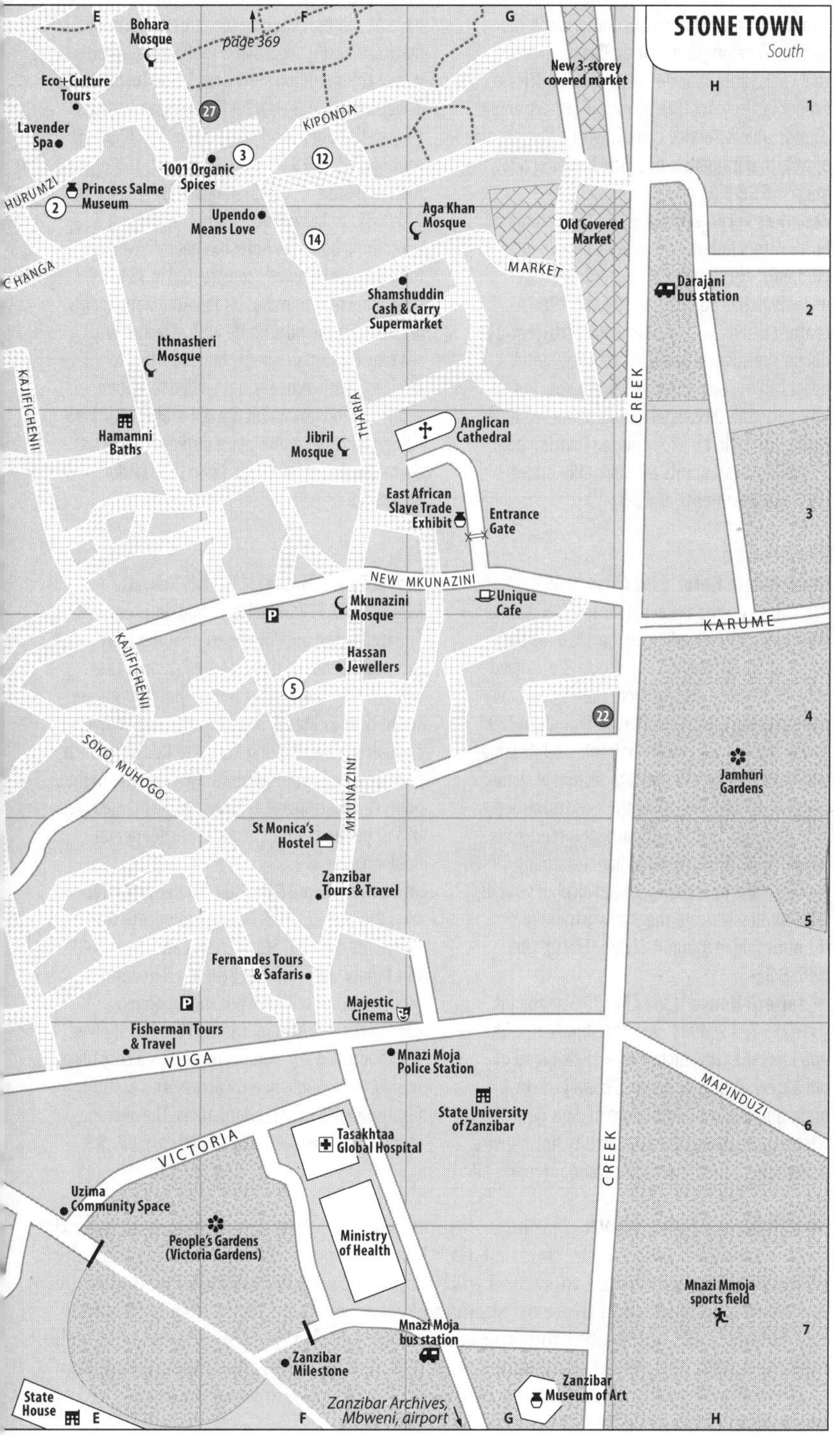

STONE TOWN
South

page 369

Bohara Mosque
Eco+Culture Tours
Lavender Spa
1001 Organic Spices
Princess Salme Museum
Upendo Means Love
Aga Khan Mosque
Old Covered Market
New 3-storey covered market
Darajani bus station
Shamshuddin Cash & Carry Supermarket
Ithnasheri Mosque
Hamamni Baths
Jibril Mosque
Anglican Cathedral
East African Slave Trade Exhibit
Entrance Gate
Mkunazini Mosque
Unique Cafe
Hassan Jewellers
Jamhuri Gardens
St Monica's Hostel
Zanzibar Tours & Travel
Fernandes Tours & Safaris
Majestic Cinema
Fisherman Tours & Travel
Mnazi Moja Police Station
State University of Zanzibar
Tasakhtaa Global Hospital
Uzima Community Space
People's Gardens (Victoria Gardens)
Ministry of Health
Mnazi Mmoja sports field
Mnazi Moja bus station
Zanzibar Milestone
Zanzibar Museum of Art
State House
Zanzibar Archives, Mbweni, airport

KIPONDA
HURUMZI
CHANGA
MARKET
KAJIFICHENII
THARIA
CREEK
NEW MKUNAZINI
KARUME
SOKO MUHOGO
MKUNAZINI
VUGA
MAPINDUZI
VICTORIA

with modernist whitewashed interiors & high ceilings set alongside soaring Omani arches, cool courtyards, marbled corridors & intricate timber latticework. The 67 rooms are extremely comfortable & service is slick, with a distinct air of wealth permeating both the building & its guests. **$$$$$**

Zanzibar Serena Hotel [362 A5] Shangani St; w serenahotels.com. A well-known local landmark, this impressive oceanfront hotel on leafy Kelele Sq incorporates the 19th-century Extelcoms building & an 18th-century doctor's residence. The staff are excellent & it boasts all the facilities that you'd expect of an international-class establishment, including AC & satellite TV in all 51 rooms, an inviting pool, 2 excellent restaurants & reasonably priced massage treatments. **$$$$**

Moderate

Dhow Palace Hotel [362 C5] m +255 777 878088; w dhowpalace-hotel.com. This excellent 30-room hotel started life in the 1550s as the house of Sheikh Mushin bin Mujbia & was lived in by his descendants for more than 3 centuries prior to being sold to the Barwani family in 1899. Newer rooms have private balconies, while larger original rooms access a private section of shared balcony; all have Persian baths & are furnished with Zanzibari beds & antiques, plus mod-cons including AC. The stylised Indian restaurant overlooks the pool courtyard (no alcohol served). All is spotlessly clean, the staff are friendly & the atmosphere tranquil. *US$85/120 sgl/dbl B&B*. **$$$**

✷ **Jafferji House** [362 C3] 170 Gizenga Rd; m +255 773 284084; w jafferjihouse.net. This hotel has the wow factor: an artistic blend of old & new. Zanzibari doors, old wall clocks & gramophones are reminiscent of days gone by, while warm colours & a top-quality finish give a modern feel. The 8 suites & 2 standard rooms all have AC, baths, exquisite furniture & traditional fabrics. B/fast is served at a rooftop restaurant with a commanding view over Stone Town. Warm & welcoming, it feels a bit like a home, albeit a very stylish one. Good value. *From US$126/135 sgl/dbl B&B*. **$$$**

Kisiwa House [362 C5] Baghani St; ☎ 024 223 0685; w kisiwahouse.com. This elegant & welcoming boutique hotel has been converted from a house originally constructed in 1840 by the Omani merchant Nassor ibn Abdullah. Rooms are decorated in pure white with splashes of sea blue & most are simply huge (perfect for families). With a cheery, light-filled reception, sunny rooftop restaurant & a dbl-storey courtyard lounge for chilling, this place displays calm, class & imagination throughout. *From US$152 dbl B&B*. **$$$**

Budget

Lost & Found Hostel [362 B4] Kenyatta Rd; m +255 777 086940; w booking.com. Situated in the bustling heart of Stone Town, this popular hostel has 2 16-bed dorms, 1 for women only & the other mixed. Both dorms are stylishly decorated & have AC, en-suite showers & a balcony overlooking Kenyatta Rd, while each pod-style bed comes with its own curtain, night light, charging socket & locker. Walk-in rates are US$15 per bed but it's often a lot cheaper on Booking.com. **$**

✷ **Stone Town B&B** [362 C4] Kenyatta Rd; m +255 627 880808; w stonetowncafe.com. Above the bustling Stone Town Café (page 368), this family-owned & run B&B has 5 delightful modern rooms with dbl polished wooden Zanzibari beds, AC, fan, fridge, TV & hot shower. Cool floors & warm colours make this a cosy place to stay, while high-quality accessories & sturdy furniture raise the standard above the average Stone Town cheapie. *From US$70 dbl B&B*. **$$**

Southeast Stone Town The labyrinthine heart of Stone Town, running inland from Forodhani Gardens to chaotic Creek Road, supports far fewer hotels than the southwest. But it is home to several mid-range to exclusive hotels that tend to be less overtly touristy than those on Shangani Waterfront, and to feel more physically and thematically integrated into the alleys from which they rise. The area is well endowed with restaurants and shops, and it is also home to the historic Anglican Cathedral and bustling market. All hotels listed here are shown in columns D to H of the map on page 362.

Upmarket

Emerson on Hurumzi [363 E2] Hurumzi St; m +255 779 854225; w emersonzanzibar.com. Reincarnated many times, this Stone Town institution sprawls across 3 venerable buildings dating from 1840 & decorated with antique Zanzibari furniture & carpets. Each of the 15 rooms is unique, but none, very deliberately, has phone, TV or fridge. Some have AC, others natural cooling – shutters, shades, deep balconies & a sea breeze. B/fast is taken at the rooftop restaurant, and since this is the 2nd-highest building in Zanzibar Town, you'll enjoy fine views. **$$$$$**

✷ **Emerson Spice** [363 F1] Tharia St; m +255 774 483483; w emersonzanzibar.com. This vibrant hotel has striking theatrical rooms, each with a colourful twist on traditional Swahili design. Ceilings are immense, vibrant colours adorn the walls, & potted plants, stained-glass windows & intricately carved wooden doors add to the atmosphere. Rooms are kitted out with open-plan bathrooms, fans & AC, fridges & mosquito nets, & some even have dramatic hand-painted murals. There's now also a cool, palm-filled walled garden & 2 enchanting restaurants: Secret Garden (page 368) & rooftop Emerson Spice Tea House (page 367), the latter also where b/fast is served. One of the best choices for an atmospheric stay in Stone Town. **$$$$**

✷ **Upendo House** [362 D1] Hurumzi Rd; m +255 748 417737; w upendozanzibar.com. Situated close to the seafront & around the corner from the Old Arab Fort, this stylish new boutique hotel comprises 8 comfortable & well-equipped rooms with bright modern décor, AC & in some cases a private balcony. There's also a funky rooftop restaurant & swimming pool with ocean views & a good spa on the 1st floor. **$$$$**

Moderate

Maru Maru [363 D2] Gizenga St; m +255 774 007003; w marumaruzanzibar.com. On the site of an old Hindu temple, Maru Maru is a large, spotless, well-finished & bright hotel. Modern rooms all have en suites (some with traditional hammam baths), AC, fridge & flatscreen TV. There's a choice of 2 dining areas – The Bakery, in the fountain courtyard, for snacks & afternoon teas, & the rooftop Terrace Restaurant, popular for sundowner cocktails followed by spicy Indian suppers. One of the few hotels in Stone Town with a lift. Parking provided. *US$100/150 sgl/dbl B&B*. **$$$**

The Swahili House [363 F1] Kiponda St; m +255 778 919525; w theswahilihousezanzibar.com. Converted from a towering 19th-century Indian merchant's house, this elegant & well-managed 4-storey hotel encloses a roofed courtyard & boasts an authentic Zanzibari feel. Rooms are decked out in locally produced furniture & antiques, with polished stone floors, narrow wooden balconies & a touch of modernity thrown in in the form of AC & fans. Rooms nearest the top offer excellent views over the alleyways of Stone Town, as does the rooftop restaurant, with its long bar, cushion-covered benches & jacuzzi. *US$90/130 sgl/dbl B&B*. **$$$**

✷ **Zanzibar Coffee House** [363 F2] Tharia St; m +255 773 061532; w zanzibarcoffeehouse.com. Housed in an 1885 Arabic home, this unpretentious haven stands above the excellent café of the same name (page 368). The 8 rooms have traditional Zanzibari 4-poster beds & AC, & are mostly en suite, but a few share facilities. Gracious staff provide a friendly service, & the tower-top terrace offers one of Stone Town's best b/fast views. Good value. *From US$90/130 sgl/dbl B&B*. **$$$**

Budget

Jambo Guesthouse [363 F4] Mkunazini St; m +255 653 943548; w jamboguesthouse.co.tz. Set in a peaceful quarter of Stone Town, this straightforward but good-value hotel has been justifiably popular with backpackers for many years. The 9 rooms have coconut-wood beds, fitted nets, AC & fans. Shared bathrooms are small but the water is always hot. Book 2 nights in advance & the rate includes a free pick-up from the port or airport. *US$30/45 sgl/dbl B&B*. **$**

✷ **Shoki Shoki Hostel** [362 D3] Soko Muhogo St; m +255 658 179187; w shokishokihouse.com/shoki-shoki-hostel. Opened in Jun 2022, this excellent & beautifully decorated hostel occupies a tall old house close to the landmark Mrembo Spa. There are 3 private rooms & 2 8-bed mixed dorms, all with solid wood beds, AC & fan. All rooms use common toilets & hot showers, which are very clean, & there is a kitchen for self-caterers. *From US$30 dbl or US$10pp dorm bed*. **$**

Northern Stone Town and Zanzibar Port The most northern part of Stone Town has a far more lived-in and down-to-earth feel than the busy south. Away from a few main roads, tourists are relatively few here, and the atmosphere often recalls Zanzibar as it was before the post-millennium tourist boom took hold. Unlike the south, the waterfront here is not lined with hotels and restaurants but is altogether more functional, comprising as it does a pair of traditional dhow harbours bookending the island's main port in the north and the ferry jetty for Dar es Salaam and Pemba to its south. Immediately inland, the districts of Malindi, Kiponda and Kokoni support a scattering of hotels, most of them catering to the budget end of the market, though there are also a few small boutique hotels, notably Kholle House, The Seyyida and Zanzibar Palace. Eating out and shopping opportunities in this part of Stone Town are relatively limited. All hotels listed here are shown on the map on page 369.

Upmarket

✷ **Kholle House** [369 B5] Off Malindi St; m +255 772 161033; w khollehouse.com. This traditionally inspired boutique bolthole has been converted from an 1860 mansion that once belonged to Princess Kholle, sister of Sultan Barghash & Princess Salme. Princess Kholle displayed her most treasured possessions of artwork & ceramics here, & the house makes the most of its fascinating past by including many original historic features. Great thought has gone into the high-quality furnishings, with antique chests, French ceramics, glass lanterns & Zanzibari beds complementing a warm ochre colour scheme. Rooms are split into 3 categories, varying in size, but all with Zanzibari beds, mosquito nets, fans & AC. B/fast is à la carte overlooking the small garden, where loungers & cushions surround the swimming pool – a precious rarity in Stone Town & a welcome relief after a hot day's sightseeing. Kholle House can be something of a mission to find but is most easily located by following the alley that runs south from Malindi St from behind a prominent sweet almond tree immediately west of the Old Dispensary. *From US$158/178 sgl/dbl B&B*. **$$$**

Moderate

Mizingani Seafront Hotel [369 A6] Mizingani Rd; ☎ 024 223 5396; w mizinganiseafront.co.tz. Constructed in 1865 as a palace for royal honeymooners & repurposed as the Customs House in 1928, this immaculately restored waterfront hotel offers a good balance between comfort, character & value. Furnished with antique & traditional pieces, the 31 rooms have tall mangrove-pole & plaster ceilings, 4-poster Zanzibari bed, walk-in net, AC, fan, TV & fridge. The 1st-floor restaurant makes the most of the waterfront location & there's also a lovely courtyard swimming pool. *US$95/130 sgl/dbl B&B*. **$$$**

Budget

✷ **Kiponda B&B** [369 A7] Nyumba ya Moto Rd; m +255 777 431665; w kiponda.com. Formerly a sultan's harem, this quiet 12-room hotel has been renovated in period style & its entrance comprises an original carved wooden door & well-preserved traditional *daka* (a deep arched porch that predates the arrival of the Omani & Indians on Zanzibar). Simply decorated in traditional style, the clean rooms all have 4-poster Zanzibar beds, fitted nets & ceiling fan. Some also have AC &, while most are en suite, 2 have private bathrooms with separate entrance. Good b/fasts are served in the airy rooftop restaurant, which mutates into a casual lounge from 11.00 to 18.00. The friendly hands-on Zanzibari management team has good connections with Sama Tours (page 360), so can help with travel arrangements & excursions. *From US$35/60 sgl/dbl. B&B*. **$$**

✷ **Pyramid Hotel** [369 C6] Kokoni St; w pyramidhotel.co.tz. Situated in a quiet & little-touristed area of Stone Town, just behind Malindi's Ijumaa Mosque a short walk from the seafront, this characterful old hotel has been a budget travellers' favourite for many years, & deservedly so. It gets its name from the very steep & narrow staircases (almost ladders) that lead to the upper floors. Traditionally furnished rooms come with 4-poster beds, fitted nets, AC, fan & hot water, but vary in atmosphere, so choose carefully. The long-serving manager

Ibrahim & his staff are very friendly & the rooftop restaurant does great b/fasts. An excellent budget choice. *US$40/50 sgl/dbl B&B.* **$**

WHERE TO EAT AND DRINK

WHERE TO EAT AND DRINK The dining experience in Stone Town has recently taken a dramatic turn for the better, with the opening of some stylish evening eateries and a burgeoning selection of cool cafés.

We have only listed a selection here; there are plenty more to choose from, and the level of competition for custom means that standards are generally reflected by prices.

The cheapest place to eat in Stone Town is at the night market in **Forodhani Gardens** [362 C2], along the seafront, where dozens of vendors serve freshly grilled meat, chicken, fish, calamari and prawns with salad and chips or naan bread. This is far and away the best street food we've come across anywhere in southern and East Africa, and offers excellent value. The stalls cater primarily to locals and travellers, and many return night after night. Even if you aren't hungry or an adventurous eater, it's worth visiting for the spectacle.

Top end

Abyssinian Maritim [362 D6] Kenyatta Rd; m +255 772 293836; f AbyssinianMaritim; ⌚ noon–15.00 & 18.00–22.30 daily exc Thu. Popular with Zanzibari expats & visitors alike, this exceptional Ethiopian restaurant specialises in spicy meat or vegan 'wat' stews eaten with a pancake-like staple called injera. It's a welcome culinary departure from Swahili curries & seafood. (vegan) **$$** / (meat & fish) **$$$**

Beach House [362 B5] Shangani St; ☎ 024 550 1234; w beachhousezanzibar.com. Set in a renovated 2-storey 19th-century building perfectly positioned to watch the sun set over the Indian Ocean, this slick new restaurant is entered via a palm-shaded courtyard & offers the choice of sitting in the chic AC interior or on a breezy wooden deck framed by sweet almond trees. A cosmopolitan menu includes dishes from various cultures associated with the Indian Ocean over the centuries, including Omani, Portuguese, Swahili, Indian &, err, British (read: fish 'n' chips). It also serves pizzas & light snacks, & has a great dessert menu. The bar has extensive cocktail & gin menus, as well as a good wine list. **$$$**

Cape Town Fish Market [362 B2] Forodhani Gardens; m +255 628 796977; w ctfmzanzibar.co.tz; ⌚ 11.00–23.00 daily. This recently opened branch of its popular namesake in Dar es Salaam has an unbeatable location on a stilted jetty on the Forodhani ocean front. Known for its excellent fresh sushi & other seafood, it also serves steaks & other grills, along with an extensive menu of South African wines. **$$$**

✷ **Emerson Spice Tea House** [363 F1] Tharia St; m +255 779 854225; w emersonspice.com; ⌚ cocktails 18.00 & dinner 19.00. This intimate dining experience offers a lovely bird's-eye vista from the rooftop of Emerson Spice (page 365). Expect a buzzing atmosphere & 5-course degustation menu of delicious Swahili fusion cuisine. It's open every night, but for a single sitting only, so book to avoid disappointment. A real treat! *US$40pp.* **$$$**

Medium to expensive

✷ **6°South** [362 B6] Shangani St; m +255 620 644611; w 6degreessouth.co.tz; ⌚ 10.00–01.00 daily. 'Quirky. Imaginative. Breezy. This culinary hotspot is all degrees of cool': a claim many of the cocktail-sipping diners would concur. This expansive restaurant overlooks the waterfront from 3 levels. The striking street-level restaurant, complete with soaring arched glass roof, serves a selection of Zanzibari favourites & grills, while upstairs is the popular 2-storey cocktail bar, a perfect sundowner & late-night hangout. **$$**

New Monsoon Restaurant [362 C3] Forodhani Gardens; m +255 777 410410; w newmonsoonrestaurant.com; ⌚ 07.00–22.30 daily. This Stone Town stalwart shed some personality following a recent change in ownership (there's no longer a shisha bar, live *taarab* or *ngoma* music), but the shady terrace remains a great spot for people-watching, the Swahili & Indian cuisine is decent value, & the bar is well stocked. **$$**

✷ **La Taverna** [363 G4] Creek Rd; m +255 776 650301; w latavernazanzibar.com; ⌚ 10.00–23.00 Mon–Sat. A little off the main tourist trail, this is a gem of a restaurant whose Italian owners hail from a family with 3 generations of culinary experience. The homemade pasta/pizza is consistently tasty & the inexpensive & free-flowing wine adds to the relaxed vibe. $$

Mzee Husa [362 C4] Kenyatta Rd; m +255 774 227078; w mzeehusa.com; ⌚ noon–22.00 Mon-Sat. This new restaurant has a large but sparse modernist interior leading out to a breezy balcony above Shangani Post Office. The Swedish chef specialises in Nordic-Swahili fusion cuisine, with a strong emphasis on tapas, seafood & vegetarian fare. $$$

✷ **The Secret Garden** [363 F1] Tharia St; m +255 779 854225; w emersonzanzibar.com; ⌚ noon–16.00 & 17.00–22.00 daily. Secret Garden is simply magical. Part of Emerson Spice (page 365), this tumbledown, former Swahili marketplace has been transformed into an utterly enchanting open-air restaurant. The flickering light of candles illuminate the crumbling windows & arches & help create the impression of a grand opera set. And here, an impeccable experience awaits: efficient waiters serve chilled glasses of wine at neat triangular tables & aromatic waves of spiced Swahili dishes drift from an open BBQ. Highly recommended. (lunch) $$ / (dinner) $$$

Cheap to medium

Baboo Beach Café [362 C6] Shangani St; m +255 787 499297. Tucked under 2 sweet almond trees, this unpretentious small café is a friendly hangout with a seafront terrace offering great sunset views. Engaging service under the guidance of owner Baboo & tasty Swahili food courtesy of his wife, Mariam, make for happy customers. Iced coffees, freshly squeezed juices, salads, seafood & curries are all on offer. $$

✷ **Krishna Food House** [362 C3] Off Forodhani Rd; m +255 788 809153; ⌚ 09.00–22.00 daily exc Wed. This vegetarian restaurant serves delicious Gujarati-style Indian fare & the filling thali (comprising 2 curries, dhal, rice, roti, poppadom & lassi) is great value at around US$6. You can also get savoury snacks such as samosas & spring rolls, cakes & sweets, fresh juices & beer. $

Lazziz Bakery [362 D6] Kenyatta Rd; m +255 776 721244; ⌚ 09.00–21.00. Zanzibari's top bakery offers a great selection of fresh bread, mini pizzas, pies, cakes, croissants & other sweet & savoury goodies.

Puzzle Coffee Shop [362 C5] Suicide Alley, off Kenyatta Rd; m +255 714 699117; w puzzlecoffeeshop.com; ⌚ 08.30–18.00 Mon–Sat. This welcoming Brazilian-owned & -managed cafe serves some of the best coffee in Stone Town, plus brownies, cookies & other snacks. All coffee is roasted on site & it also hosts coffee workshops for up to 6 people with 24hrs' notice. $

Stone Town Café [362 C4] Kenyatta Rd; m +255 627 880808; w stonetowncafe.com; ⌚ 08.00–22.00 daily. The scents of spiced tea & falafel waft from this buzzing Aussie–Zanzibari-run café. Marked out by lush potted plants, passers-by queue for unfussy, tasty dishes served by friendly staff. All-day b/fasts, cheesy pizzas, fresh fruit shakes, smoothies & tasty teatime treats are recommended. $–$$

Travellers Café Zanzibar [362 A5] Shangani St; m +255 682 4016241; ⌚ 08.00–22.00 daily. Perfectly located for sundowners, this fabulous new café has a breezy, palm-shaded beachfront setting alongside the Serena. There's a good cocktail menu, as well as beer & wine. Pasta, pizzas & seafood dominate a very varied menu. $$

Zanzibar Coffee House Café [363 F2] Tharia St; m +255 773 061532; w zanzibarcoffeehouse.com; ⌚ 08.00–18.00 daily. This friendly café is an excellent place for a strong cup of freshly ground coffee & a light snack – the glass cabinet boasts a deliciously tempting array of fresh cakes, pies, pastries, croissants & sandwiches. The café is filled with heavy wooden kitchen-style tables that are perfect for gossiping groups, as well as intimate tables for 2. $

ENTERTAINMENT AND NIGHTLIFE Although a largely Muslim island, most tourist restaurants serve African beers and many of the larger hotels have separate bars. Their atmosphere and quality vary considerably.

For cocktails the current top picks are the **Terrace Bar** at the Park Hyatt (page 361) and the upstairs bar at 6°South (page 367). **Mercury's** [369 A5] (m +255 777 413081), **Lulu Rooftop Restaurant** at the Seyyida [369 A7] (w theseyyida-zanzibar.com) and **Baboo Beach Café** (see above) all have a sea view and a decidedly more low-key vibe.

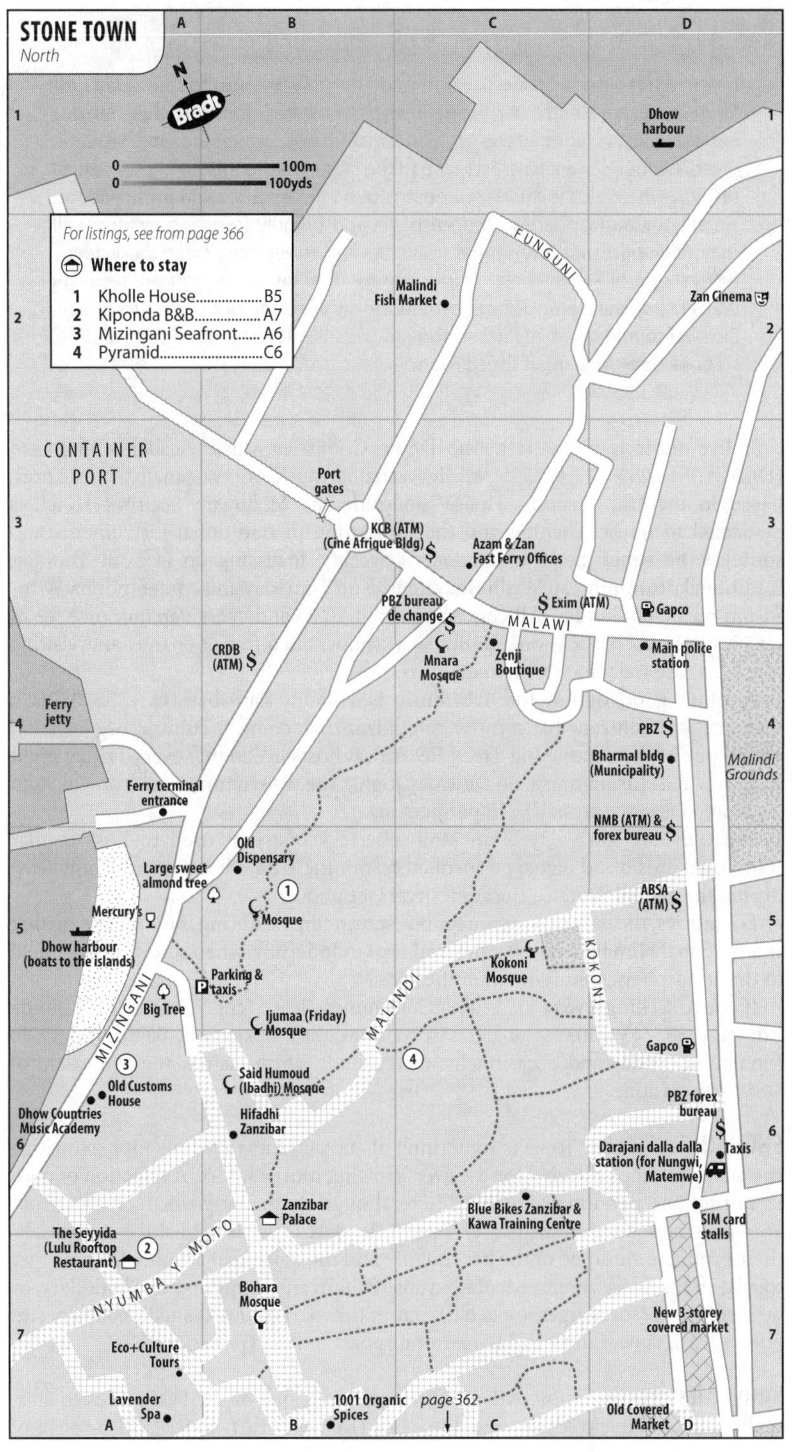
STONE TOWN
North
Bradt
0 100m
0 100yds
For listings, see from page 366
Where to stay
1 Kholle House.................B5
2 Kiponda B&B.................A7
3 Mizingani Seafront......A6
4 Pyramid..........................C6
A
B
C
D
1
2
3
4
5
6
7
Dhow harbour
FUNGUNI
Malindi Fish Market
Zan Cinema
CONTAINER PORT
Port gates
KCB (ATM) (Ciné Afrique Bldg)
Azam & Zan Fast Ferry Offices
PBZ bureau de change
Exim (ATM)
Gapco
MALAWI
CRDB (ATM)
Mnara Mosque
Zenji Boutique
Main police station
Ferry jetty
PBZ
Bharmal bldg (Municipality)
Malindi Grounds
Ferry terminal entrance
NMB (ATM) & forex bureau
Old Dispensary
Large sweet almond tree
Mosque
ABSA (ATM)
Mercury's
Dhow harbour (boats to the islands)
Kokoni Mosque
KOKONI
Parking & taxis
MIZINGANI
Big Tree
Ijumaa (Friday) Mosque
MALINDI
Gapco
Said Humoud (Ibadhi) Mosque
Old Customs House
PBZ forex bureau
Dhow Countries Music Academy
Hifadhi Zanzibar
Darajani dalla dalla station (for Nungwi, Matemwe)
Taxis
Zanzibar Palace
Blue Bikes Zanzibar & Kawa Training Centre
SIM card stalls
The Seyyida (Lulu Rooftop Restaurant)
NYUMBA Y MOTO
Bohara Mosque
New 3-storey covered market
Eco+Culture Tours
Lavender Spa
1001 Organic Spices
page 362
Old Covered Market

SAUTI ZA BUSARA – ZANZIBAR'S ANNUAL MUSIC FESTIVAL

If you're heading to Stone Town in mid-February, be sure to buy tickets for Sauti Za Busara. Centred on Stone Town's atmospheric Old Fort, this four-day extravaganza celebrates the best of African music, traditional and modern. Over 200 musicians and artists take to the stage during this highly successful festival, which also includes screenings of documentaries and music videos. An electric atmosphere of African beats and friendly festival-goers from all over the world, plus a variety of souvenirs and street food, make this eclectic festival one of Africa's best. Tickets can be purchased through the festival's website, (w busaramusic.org), or bought on the door, but expect to queue. Do bear in mind that city accommodation sells out fast around festival time, so book early for a guaranteed room.

If **live music** is of interest, The Dhow Countries Music Academy [369 A6] (DCMA; m +255 777 416529; e info@zanzibarmusic.org; w zanzibarmusic.org), based in the Old Customs House alongside the Mizingani Seafront Hotel, is dedicated to music teaching and the promotion of traditional instruments and sounds. The venue hosts four concerts weekly, focussing on jazz on Tuesday, traditional drumming on Wednesday, *taarab* on Thursday and contemporary Afro-fusion music on Sunday. All concerts start at 20.00 and charge an entrance fee of US$5. It also hosts occasional public workshops, often free of charge, and visiting musicians are welcomed with open arms.

Another good option for live music is Hifadhi Zanzibar (m +255 077123; e contact@hifadhizanzibar.com; w hifadhizanzibar.com), a cultural organisation set a block back from the Big Tree [369 A5]. It hosts live *taarab* every Friday night and Zanzibari fusion music on Saturday night. The programme runs from 20.30 to 23.30 and entrance costs US$12 per person.

The Old Fort [362 C3] is an atmospheric venue that used to host regular traditional music and dance performances, but these days it is generally only used during the annual Sauti Za Busara festival (see above).

For **movies**, the only real option for big-screen films is during the annual **Zanzibar International Film Festival** (w ziffestival.org) in June/July, when screenings are held in the atmospheric Old Fort amphitheatre.

If you're seeking a **yoga** fix, Uzima Community Space (cnr Victoria St & Kaunda Rd; m +255 743 940596; w uzimaspace.com) has sessions at 08.00 and 17.30 Monday to Friday and occasionally at weekends. Drop-ins pay the equivalent of US$9 per session.

SHOPPING Zanzibar Town is something of an Aladdin's cave for shoppers, with a vast array of shops catering for the ever-growing tourist influx. A selection of both favourites and perennials are listed here, though particularly worth checking out are those mentioned in the box on page 371; aside from their positive credentials, their products are some of the best quality and most original around. In the larger tourist shops, prices are fixed and payable in Tanzanian shillings or US dollars, or by credit card (surcharges are usual), but in the market and at smaller, locally run outlets, cash is necessary and bargaining is part of the experience.

Souvenirs For souvenirs without the bargaining, one of the best places to start is the Jafferji Gallery & Boutique [362 C4] (Kenyatta Rd), which sells a range of

MADE IN ZANZIBAR – FAIR-TRADE AND HIGH QUALITY

There has been a welcome trend recently towards training members of the local community, especially women, to produce high-quality, well-designed clothing and accessories for sale to tourists. The women benefit from a new skill and a fair price for their efforts. Several of the brands belong to the 'Made in Zanzibar' producers' network (w madeinzanzibar.com), a collective aiming to cross-promote quality products from Zanzibar to support the local 'economy' and provide an identifiable brand for visitors.

Currently, the best projects, products and shopping outlets are:

CafeAfrica [362 D3] w vassalam.org. Individually crafted cloth dolls, handbags & clothes.
Dada [362 D2] Wholesome tropical preserves & cosmetics.
Fahari [362 C5] w fahari-zanzibar.com. Stylish leatherwork.
Kanga Kabisa [362 C5] w kangakabisa.com; 🕘 09.00–19.00 daily. Nordic fashion in kanga print.
Malkia Several hotel shops; f malkiazanzibar. Funky fashion.
Moto [362 D2] w motozanzibar.wordpress.com. Basketry.
Sasa Shop [362 D2] f safisanagroup. High-quality handmade clothes, handbags & day packs using bright African fabrics.
Sasik [362 D3] w sasikzanzibar.blogspot.co.uk. Appliqué.
Surti & Sons [362 C4] w surtiandsons.wordpress.com; 🕘 09.00–14.00 & 14.30–19.00 daily. Bespoke leather sandals.
Upendo Means Love [363 F2] f UpendoMeansLoveZanzibar; 🕘 09.00–17.00 Mon–Sat. Gorgeous island kidswear.
Zenji Boutique [369 C4] w zenjihotel.com. Pan-African craft selection.
Zuri Rituals [362 C3] w zurirituals.com. Organic skincare & cosmetic products.

carvings, clothes, maps, antiques and a good selection of books. Another good all-rounder is Memories of Zanzibar [362 B4] (Kenyatta Rd; w memories-zanzibar.com), where you can pick up anything from beaded flip-flops and silver bracelets to carvings and CDs.

Gizenga Street and **Hurumzi Street** are the hub of tiny local souvenir shops and pavement traders, where you'll find carvings, Tingatinga paintings, assorted jewellery, packets of spices, coconut-shell mobiles, twisted wire bikes and much more at every turn.

Antiques Around Zanzibar Town there are also several shops selling antiques from Arabia and India, dating from Omani and British colonial times. One of the best is the enthusiastically staffed Zanzibar Curio Shop [362 D2] (Hurumzi St), which has a great range of timber souvenirs from doors to carvings. There are several more options on the street between St Joseph's Cathedral and Soko Muhogo crossroads.

Art and local crafts Probably Stone Town's best art gallery, **Wasanii Art** [362 D3] (Gizenga St; m +255 788 054760; e anitasita@gmail.com) displays and sells a good selection of high-quality contemporary art from Zanzibar and elsewhere in East Africa, all selected and organised by style and artist by the knowledgeable owner and curator, Anita.

Postcards, newspapers and books The best bookshop is the Jafferji Gallery & Boutique [362 C4] on Kenyatta Road, which has a good selection of fiction, field guides and coffee-table books on Zanzibar and other parts of Africa.

For light holiday reading material, Aromas of Zanzibar [362 D3] stocks a huge selection of English and other language secondhand novels at a uniform price equivalent to around US$3.50 per item.

Jewellery If a more precious purchase is what you're after, **Hassan Jewellers** [363 F4] (Mkunazini St; m +255 773 453575), close to the market, is reliable and reputable. The family team here stocks a good range of tanzanite and is able to supply authentication certificates. Be aware that tanzanite is a soft stone that scratches easily; better to have it set as earrings or in a necklace than as a ring. For something more contemporary and unique, **Elias Jewellery** (m +255 629 990467; w eliasjewellers.com) is certainly worth a look. Founded in 1963, it currently has two branches, one on Kenyatta Road [362 C4] above the post office and another opposite Tembo Hotel [362 B4]. A family business, you'll find tanzanite set in gold and silver, as well as some unusual pieces incorporating materials such as ebony wood and recycled rubber. For serious sparkle, with a dazzling price tag, **Lithos Africa** [362 B3] (w lithosafrica.com), set in a 19th-century building that served as the British Consulate in the days of Livingstone, Stanley and Kirk, may fit the bill.

Food shopping If you are self-catering or just going on a picnic for the day, Zanzibar Town has a large market selling a vast array of exotic fruit and vegetables, plus fresh fish and meat, though the latter is not for the faint-hearted. Among the best supermarkets is the **Shamshuddin Cash & Carry Supermarket** [363 F2], off Creek Road, near the market.

If you fancy returning home with some organic Zanzibari spices, whether as a gift for a culinarily-minded friend or for your own kitchen, head to **1001 Organic Spices** [363 F1] (Tharia St; w 1001organic.com/en; ⌚ 09.00–18.00 daily), which stands in the heart of Stone Town next to the landmark Emerson Spice Hotel.

OTHER PRACTICALITIES

Banks and money changing Major credit cards (ie: Visa and Mastercard) are now accepted by most hotels, large restaurants, tourist-oriented shops and tour operators in Stone Town, though usually at a surcharge of around 5%. They are generally not accepted by smaller restaurants and shops, or by institutions that don't usually deal with tourists. Local currency cash can be drawn at several ATMs dotted around Stone Town, notably the National Bank of Commerce (NBC) [362 B3] on Kenyatta Road, ABSA [369 D5] (formerly Barclays) on Creek Road, the Kenya Commercial Bank (KCB) [369 C3] in the Cine Afrique building on Malawi Road, the CRDB [369 B4] outside the ferry terminal on Mizingani Road, and the Diamond Trust Bank (DTB) [362 C3] behind the Old Fort. Note that the Umoja ATMs operated by the People's Bank of Zanzibar (PBZ) do not normally accept foreign cards. There are also a few ATMs at the airport but few elsewhere on the island, so it's safest to draw as much as you need while you are in Stone Town or at the airport. The maximum withdrawal at most ATMs is around Tsh400,000–600,000, but multiple withdrawals are permitted.

Following the closure of private bureaux de change in Tanzania in 2018, hard-currency cash can be changed into local currency only at banks or official bureaux de change operated by them. These include the PBZ 'forex bureaux' opposite Forodhani Gardens, near the Gapco filing station on Creek Road, and below Stone

View Inn on Malawi Road, which operate during normal banking hours (⌚ 08.30–15.30 Mon–Fri & 08.30–12.30 Sat). Most service providers will accept payments in hard currency if you are unable to change it into local currency.

Mobile phones, email and internet Wi-Fi is free and easy to access at practically all cafés, hotels and restaurants in Zanzibar Town these days. Speeds and reliability vary considerably, but while that might limit download speeds, it is not a problem for ordinary browsing and seldom presents an obstacle to making free international calls on WhatsApp, FaceTime, Skype and other such apps.

If you don't want to be dependent on hotel and restaurant Wi-Fi, a Tanzanian SIM card costs around US$2 and gives you a local number, while airtime cards are available in units of Tsh1,000–5,000. For the best coverage on the islands at present, we recommend you purchase a Zantel or Holotel SIM card. The easiest place to do this is at the airport, upon arrival; failing that, head to one of the numerous small vendors around Darajani bus station [363 H2] and the market area of Creek Road. International text messages and calls out of Tanzania are seriously cheap, especially if you use data-based apps for your calls. By contrast, you can expect to rack up a hefty bill very quickly by using your home SIM, since in most instances these are charged at international rates out of your home country, even when you are phoning home.

Medical facilities Zanzibar's private medical clinics, where staff speak English and drugs are more readily available, are usually a better option for visitors than the public Mnazi Mmoja General Hospital. There are pharmacies at the medical centres as well as in Stone Town.

Dr Mehta's Hospital [362 D6] Pipalwadi St; emergency m + 255 777 419999; f. For 24hr medical treatment.

Tasakhtaa – Global Hospital Zanzibar [363 F6] emergency ☎ 0800 0000001; w tasakhtaahospital.co.tz. Relatively new hospital open 24hrs for emergencies.

Police The main police station [369 D4] (☎ 112 or 024 223 0772) is in the Malindi area, on the north side of Stone Town. Robberies can be reported here (travel insurance companies usually require you to provide a copy of the basic report on the incident from the local police if you are making a claim), but you should not expect any real action to be taken as the police are not particularly well motivated and corruption is rife.

Spas and salons A number of spas and beauty salons have sprung up in Stone Town over recent years. The most engaging, original and quintessentially Zanzibari of these is Mrembo Traditional Spa (page 374) but a few equally professional options, many staffed by Thai therapists, are listed here.

Cinnamon Spa & Salon [362 B4] Shangani St; w cinnamonspa.net; ⌚ 08.00–22.00 daily. Under the same management as Jafferji House & situated right opposite the Park Hyatt, this large, professional spa offers a wide variety of relatively pricey treatments, from massage & facials to pedicures & epicures, using locally sourced natural products where possible.

Hassan Balinese Spa [362 B5] Shangani St; m +255 779 181440; w balinesespazanzibar.com; ⌚ 08.00–20.00 daily. This professional spa opposite the Zanzibar Serena offers a wide range of massages & other treatments.

Lavender Spa [363 E1] Hurumzi St; ⌚ 09.30–18.00. Situated opposite Emerson on Hurumzi,

MREMBO TRADITIONAL SPA

[362 D3] (Call or visit to book appointments; ☎ 024 223 0004; m + 255 777 430117; w mrembospa.com; ⌚ 09.30–18.00 daily) In an old antique store halfway along Soko Muhogo Street, close to St Joseph's Cathedral, Mrembo is a small, wonderfully unassuming place offering the finest traditional treatments from Zanzibar and Pemba. Their flagship treatment, singo, is a natural exfoliating scrub traditionally used when preparing Zanzibari girls for marriage. Prepared by hand with a pestle and mortar (kinu), the fresh jasmine, ylang ylang, rose petals, mpompia (geranium), mrehani (sweet basil) and liwa (sandalwood) combine to create the most wonderfully aromatic blend. Perfuming the skin for days after treatment and leaving it soft as silk, it's equally popular with honeymoon brides today. For men, the clove-based scrub vidonge is said by Pemba islanders to increase libido and stamina, and is even offered in souvenir packages. Hot sand massages, authentic henna painting and beauty treatments are available too, with all the herbal products coming fresh from the owner's garden and skilfully prepared in front of you. The treatment rooms are cool and candlelit, with simple kanga-covered massage tables and sweet-smelling incense. There is a cold-water shower for post-scrub rinsing and a very chilled taarab music room for relaxing in before and afterwards.

Although not their raison d'être, Mrembo is also an impressively inclusive community project. The three local therapists have disabilities: two, Ali and Zubeiri, are deaf, and Asha is blind. Trained in therapeutic massage by professional therapists from African Touch (a Canadian-funded, community-based organisation in Kenya), they have benefited enormously in confidence and social standing from their practical education and employment. Each has an able-bodied assistant at Mrembo to ease understanding, though Ali will cheerfully encourage you to try a little Kiswahili sign language, using the alphabet poster for guidance.

For a lazy afternoon of complete beauty pampering or a simple massage or manicure while the sun's at its peak, Mrembo Traditional Spa is a great place to while away the time with a cup of refreshing ginger tea and friendly staff. It is a true oasis of calm in the centre of Stone Town, and an experience not to be hurried.

this spa charges around US$40–45 for massages & other treatments.

Nurture by Natasha [362 C6] Kenyatta Rd; m +255 714 888000; ⌚ 09.00–20.00 daily. This well-signposted owner-managed spa on the triangular junction with Shangani Rd offers a broad selection of treatments including massage, facials, pedicures & henna hand painting.

WHAT TO SEE AND DO

Spice tours and other excursions A spice tour has long been one of Zanzibar's most popular excursions into the interior of the island, giving visitors a chance to experience familiar flavours from the kitchen growing naturally. A typical tour lasts about 1½ hours and in addition to visiting a few spice plantations, tours will often include a walk around a cultivated rural homestead, as well as a visit to one of the island's ruins and a traditional Swahili lunch. The Princess Salme Tour operated by Zanzibar Different (page 360) is a particularly good example at around US$55 per person.

Other popular excursions from Stone Town include a boat trip to one or more of the nearby islands, a full-day trip snorkelling and sailing around Menai Bay, a visit to the dolphins at Kizimkazi, and a trip to Jozani Forest to see the endemic Kirk's red colobus. These trips can all be undertaken from anywhere on the island and organised through any of the tour operators (page 360).

Stone Town walking tour You can spend many idle hours getting lost in the fascinating labyrinth of narrow streets and alleys of Stone Town, and will almost inevitably hit most of the main landmarks within a couple of days of arriving. However, the following roughly circular walking tour through Stone Town will allow those with limited time to do their sightseeing in a reasonably organised manner (though they are still bound to get lost), and should help those with more time to orientate themselves before they head out to explore Stone Town without a map or guidebook in hand.

The obvious starting point for any exploration of Zanzibar Town is **Forodhani Gardens** [362 C2] (page 376), the open park between Mizingani Road and the main sea wall. Laid out in 1936 to mark the Silver Jubilee of Sultan Khalifa, the gardens are a popular eating and meeting point in the evening, and the staircase rising from the gardens to the arched bridge to the south offers a good view over the old town.

Three of the most significant buildings in Stone Town lie alongside each other overlooking the seafront behind the Forodhani Gardens. The **Palace Museum** [362 D1] (🕒 08.30–18.00 daily; admission US$3) is the most northerly of these, a large white building with castellated battlements dating from the late 1890s. The palace was the official residence of the Sultan of Zanzibar from 1911 until the 1964 revolution, after which it was renamed the People's Palace. For many years after this, it served as a government office and was closed to the public. Since 1994, however, it has housed an excellent museum, with a variety of displays relating to the early days of the sultanate, including a room devoted to artefacts belonging to Princess Salme. The graves of all the early sultans of Zanzibar are in the palace garden.

Next to the Palace Museum, the **House of Wonders** (**Beit al Ajaib**) [362 D2] (🕒 09.00–18.00 daily; admission US$5; closed for repairs in 2022) is a perfect rectangle, rising over several storeys, surrounded by tiers of impressive pillars and balconies and topped by a clocktower. It was built as a ceremonial palace in 1883, and was the first building on Zanzibar to have electric lights. Until recently it was the CCM party headquarters, but it is now home to the Museum of History and Culture, which houses about half of the eight planned permanent exhibitions (dedicated to the history of the Swahili Coast, and Zanzibar in particular). Sadly, it's crumbling more as the years go by: it suffered a partial balcony collapse in late 2012, a partial roof collapse in 2016, and more disastrous partial collapse that killed two people and injured several others on 25 December 2020. The building is likely to be closed for repairs for the foreseeable future, and some of its exhibits have been moved to the Zanzibar Museum of Art (page 377). If it is open during your stay in Stone Town, it is well worth a visit.

Moving along the road, and directly facing Forodhani Gardens, the **Old Fort** [362 C2] (🕒 07.00–19.00 daily; admission free, donations welcome) is probably the oldest extant building in Stone Town, built by Omani Arabs between 1698 and 1701 over the site of a Portuguese church constructed a century before that, remnants of which can still be seen in the inner wall. A large, squarish, brown building with castellated battlements, the fort ceased to serve any meaningful military role in the 19th century, since when it has served variously as prison, railway depot and women's

FORODHANI GARDENS

The Forodhani Gardens [362 C2] (Jamituri Gardens on some maps) are between the Arab Fort and the sea, overlooked by the House of Wonders. They were first laid out in 1936 to commemorate the Silver Jubilee of Sultan Khalifa (who ruled 1911–60), and were called Jubilee Gardens until the 1964 revolution. In the centre stands a podium where the band of the sultan's army used to play for the public. Nearer the sea is a white concrete arabesque arch, built in 1956 for the visit of Princess Margaret (sister of Queen Elizabeth II of the United Kingdom), but never officially used as the princess arrived at the dhow harbour instead. She did visit the gardens, however, and planted a large tree, which can still be seen today.

Forodhani has long been a popular place for local people and visitors in the evenings, lured by the waterfront gathering of stalls serving drinks and hot snacks. Years of excessive overuse and poor maintenance took its toll, though, and for several years 'gardens' was a euphemism for an unattractive, parched wasteland.

Wonderfully, things have changed. On 17 January 2008, the Aga Khan Trust for Culture, with approval from the Zanzibar government, finally began a major rehabilitation of the gardens. They had been in discussion about the project with the government since 2002 when the organisation first proposed comprehensive seafront rehabilitation. The aims of the project were to improve the infrastructure and to restore and preserve the civic components of the gardens, none of which had happened in the past as a result of overuse, disrepair and limited private refurbishment.

The project was completed in 2010, and the changes are plain to see. Everyone agrees that the new Forodhani Gardens are a vast improvement, with the practical introduction of wheelie bins, lighting and waste collections, a new sea wall of salvaged stone, an organised food court for the evening stall holders, three inviting cafés (page 367), a bandstand, a dhow-shaped adventure playground and tropical planting amid manicured lawns. We, like the Aga Khan, hope that this project will prove a catalyst for urban upgrading and economic opportunity, as well as aesthetically improving the remaining waterfront area.

tennis club. The interior of the fort is open to visitors, who can climb to the top of the battlements and enter some of the towers. There is a restaurant serving cold drinks (🕘 08.00–20.00 daily).

Heading southwest from the fort, under an arched bridge, the fork to your right is **Shangani Road**, the site of notable important buildings. Just before following this fork, to your left, the **Upimaji Building** was the home of the German merchant Heinrich Ruete (later the husband of Princess Salme) in the 1860s. To the left of the fork is a block of government offices which served as the **British Consulate** [362 B4] from 1841 until 1874, and next to that the **Tembo Hotel** [362 B3], a restored 19th-century building. As you follow Shangani Road around a curve, alongside the Park Hyatt Zanzibar, whose main building is part of the UNESCO-listed **Mambo Msiige building** [362 A4], you'll come out to a leafy green corner, **Kelele Square** [362 A4], where the Zanzibar Shipping Corporation Building, dating to around 1850, stands to your left and the Zanzibar Serena Hotel, formerly Extelcoms House, straight ahead.

Perhaps 100m past the Serena, to your left, you'll see the rear of **Tip House** [362 B5], a tall brown building that once served as the residence of Tippu Tip, the notorious 19th-century slave trader who helped explorers such as Livingstone and Stanley with supplies and route planning. The building is privately owned and is closed to visitors, but if you follow the alley around the rear of the house, you can see its huge carved front door from the street. Residents will sometimes show visitors around, although some 'guides' here are heroin addicts and visitors are advised to exercise caution. From here, wander up another 50m to the **Africa House Hotel** [362 C6], which served as the English Club from 1888 onwards. Neighbouring 6°South (page 367) is a good place to punctuate your walk with a cold drink or bite to eat.

From here, a small alley leads to **Kenyatta Road**, an important thoroughfare dotted with hotels, shops and restaurants, as well as a number of old buildings with traditional Zanzibari doors. Turn left and walk a short way downhill to the junction with Gizenga Street to visit the **Freddie Mercury Museum** [362 B3] (**m** +255 777 153232; **w** freddiemercurymuseum.com; 🕘 10.00–18.00 daily; entrance US$10/6 adult/child), whose namesake, the lead singer and frontman of Queen, was born in Zanzibar Town in 1946. Curated by the prominent Zanzibari photographer and hotelier Javed Jafferji and fellow Queen fan Andrea Boero, the museum is split into two main parts. The first and most interesting is a series of black-and-white photographs and other displays that relate to Zanzibar in the early 20th century, the Bulsara family and the ancient Zoroastrian religion to which they subscribed, and Farrokh's childhood on Zanzibar and education at a private school in Panchgani, India, which is where he started to call himself Freddie and played in his first band, the Hectics. The second part of the museum mainly comprises Queen-related memorabilia, none of which adds much in the way of Zanzibari context.

Follow **Kenyatta Road** southeast for about 300m, passing the somewhat unkempt **People's Gardens** [363 F6], originally laid out under Sultan Barghash for the use of his harem, until you reach the **Zanzibar Milestone** [363 F7]. This octagonal marble pillar shows the distance from Zanzibar Town to various settlements on the island and further afield.

Cross the gardens in front of the milestone to the distinctive **Zanzibar Museum of Art** [363 G7] (🕘 09.00–18.00 daily; admission US$2.50). Also known as the Peace Memorial Museum, this impressive edifice, with its distinctive dome, arabesque windows and whitewashed walls, looks like a mosque or basilica. For years 'museum' was something of a misnomer; however, with the closure and planned restoration of the House of Wonders (page 375), many exhibits have been moved here. The Zanzibari door at the back of the building is reputedly the oldest in existence.

From the museum, follow Creek Road northwards for about 400m, and to your left you'll easily pick out the imposing **Anglican Cathedral** [363 G3] (🕘 daily; admission US$5 inc guide & access to Slave Trade Exhibit), built by the Universities' Mission in Central Africa (UMCA) over the former slave market between 1873 and 1880. Tradition has it that the altar stands on the site of the market's whipping block, and the cellar of the nearby **St Monica's Hostel** [363 G5] (closed for renovation in 2023) is said to be the remains of a pit where slaves were kept before being sold. Sultan Barghash, who closed the slave market, is reputed to have asked Bishop Steere, leader of the mission, not to build the cathedral tower higher than the House of Wonders. When the bishop agreed, the sultan presented the cathedral with its clock. The foundation of the UMCA was inspired by Livingstone: a window is dedicated to his memory, and the church's crucifix is made from wood from the tree under which his heart was buried in present-day Zambia. Several other missionaries are remembered on plaques around the cathedral wall, as are sailors killed fighting the slave trade and servicemen who died in action in East Africa during World War I. Also at the hostel, the newly opened **East African Slave Trade Exhibit** [363 G3] lays out the full economic and social history of East African slavery from its origins to the post-slavery Empire years. It's a truly engrossing, if often appalling, exhibition.

A short distance further along Creek Road lies the **covered market** [363 G2], built at around the turn of the 20th century, and worth a visit even if you don't want to buy anything. It's a vibrant place where you can buy anything from fish and bread to sewing machines and secondhand car spares. Once you've taken a look around the market, follow Creek Road back southwards for 100m or so, passing the cathedral, then turn into the first wide road to your right. This is New Mkunazini Road, and if you follow it until its end, then turn right into Kajificheni Street and right again into Hamamni Street, you'll come out at the **Hamamni Baths** [363 E3] (🕘 09.00–17.30 daily; admission US$1.50), one of the most elaborate Persian baths on Zanzibar, built for Sultan Barghash; the caretaker will show you around for a small fee.

Barely 200m from the baths, on Cathedral Street, **St Joseph's Catholic Cathedral** [362 C4] is notable for its prominent twin spires, and was built between 1896 and 1898 by French missionaries and local converts. There are now few Catholics on Zanzibar, and the cathedral is infrequently used, but visitors are welcome when the doors are open. The best way to get here from the baths is to retrace your steps along Kajificheni Street, then turn right into the first alley (which boasts several good examples of traditional Zanzibari carved doors) until you reach an open area where several roads and alleys meet – Cathedral Street among them. If you're in this area, or indeed if you fancy some serious pampering, consider making an appointment at the nearby Mrembo Traditional Spa (page 374).

From the cathedral, continue northwards along Cathedral Street for perhaps 50m, then turn right into Gizenga Street, a good place to check out the curios at any of numerous small shops. If you follow Gizenga Street until you see the Old Fort to your left, you can conclude your walk by wandering back out to Forodhani Gardens. Alternatively, if you want to keep going, turn right opposite the fort into Hurumzi Street and, after continuing straight for about 300m, you'll come to the open square close to the Zanzibar Coffee House (a good place to take a break for a tasty snack and a drink; page 365). A left turn as you enter this square takes you past the **Aga Khan Mosque** [363 G2] and on to Jamatini Road, which after about 200m will bring you out at the seafront opposite the **Big Tree** [369 A5]. Known locally as Mtini, this well-known landmark was planted in 1911 by Sultan Khalifa and now provides shade for traditional dhow builders.

On Mizingani Road, just south of the Big Tree, the **Old Customs House** [369 A6], a large, relatively plain building dating to the late 19th century, is where Sultan Hamoud was proclaimed sultan in 1896.

From the open area next to the Big Tree, a left turn along Mizingani Road will take you back to the Old Fort, passing the above-mentioned buildings. Turn right into Mizingani Road, however, and after about 100m you'll pass the **Old Dispensary** [369 B5] (🕘 09.00–18.00 daily; admission free), an ornate three-storey building built in the 1890s. Restored to its former glory by the Aga Khan, the dispensary now also contains a small exhibition hall of old monochrome photographs of Stone Town, though it was closed for maintenance in 2022.

If the above directions seem too complicated, or you want further insight into the historical buildings of Stone Town, most tour operators can arrange a guided city tour for around US$15–20, but for something really special contact Anjam

Hassan at Zanzibar Different for his utterly infectious enthusiasm and knowledge of this city, its culture and people (page 360).

AROUND ZANZIBAR TOWN

Along the coast north of Zanzibar Town, stretching over a distance of about 5km, are several palaces dating from the 19th century. Built for the various sultans who ruled Zanzibar during this period, it was commonplace for these wealthy families to retreat from the heat, smell and disease of the city in the hotter months to less populated corners. Some of the palaces and homes are in good condition and worth a visit; others will appeal only to keen fans of historical ruins and those with exceptionally good imaginations.

Most people visit this area as a day trip from Zanzibar Town, but it is perfectly possible to base yourself in the small town of Bububu, which served as the terminus of a light (36-inch gauge) railway used to connect the north coast to the Old Fort in the early 1900s. The springs just outside the town supply most of Zanzibar Town's fresh water, and the name 'Bububu' presumably derives from the bubbling sound that they make. Of interest in town is a small, centuries-old mosque about 200m from the main crossroads, along the road back towards Zanzibar Town.

Between Zanzibar Town and Bububu lie the ruined palaces of Maruhubi and Mtoni, and Bububu is also the closest substantial settlement to the Persian baths at Kidichi and Kizimbani.

GETTING THERE AND AWAY Although some of the places mentioned below might be included in your spice tour, it is easy to visit most of them independently, using a combination of dalla dalla 502 or 534 (with frequent services to Bububu from the bus station on Creek Road) and your legs. Another possibility is to hire a car, scooter or bicycle from one of the tour operators (page 360).

WHERE TO STAY AND EAT *Map, page 380*

Fumba Beach Lodge m +255 778 919525; w fumbabeachlodge.com. Fumba was created in line with contemporary safari camps & the result is a fabulously original place, with clean lines & bold colour. The 26 beach-chic rooms & suites are understated & spacious with lovely vistas. A large infinity pool lies next to the lounge & open-sided restaurant, while an African spa & onsite dive centre keep guests entertained. The full-day picnic sailing trip around Menai Bay's islands makes for one of Zanzibar's most beautiful & indulgent outings. HB/FB. **$$$$$$**

Mangrove Lodge m +255 623 557426; w mangrovelodge.com. This peaceful, leafy & relaxed seaside retreat is located on a pretty slice of mangrove beach overlooked by a large freeform swimming pool. The Zanzibari–Italian owners have taken admirable measures to reduce the environmental impact of the lodge: no energy-devouring AC, cooking over fire, locally sourced construction materials, furnishings by local tailors. Sandy pathways through tropical gardens & lawns link the 10 pretty thatched bungalows, each with either a dbl or a sgl bed & a kitchenette. It's peaceful here – butterflies flutter around the orchard gardens, the restaurant looks over fishing boats bobbing on the bay, & sunbathers can choose between 2 secluded beaches. *From US$72 dbl. B&B.* **$$**

WHAT TO SEE AND DO

Mtoni Palace (m +255 782 500011; f) The ruins of Mtoni Palace lie a short distance north of Maruhubi, and can be reached along the beach. The oldest palace on Zanzibar, Mtoni was built for Sultan Said in the 1840s. A book written by his daughter Salme describes the palace in the 1850s. At one end of the house was a large bathhouse, at the other the quarters where Said lived with his principal wife.

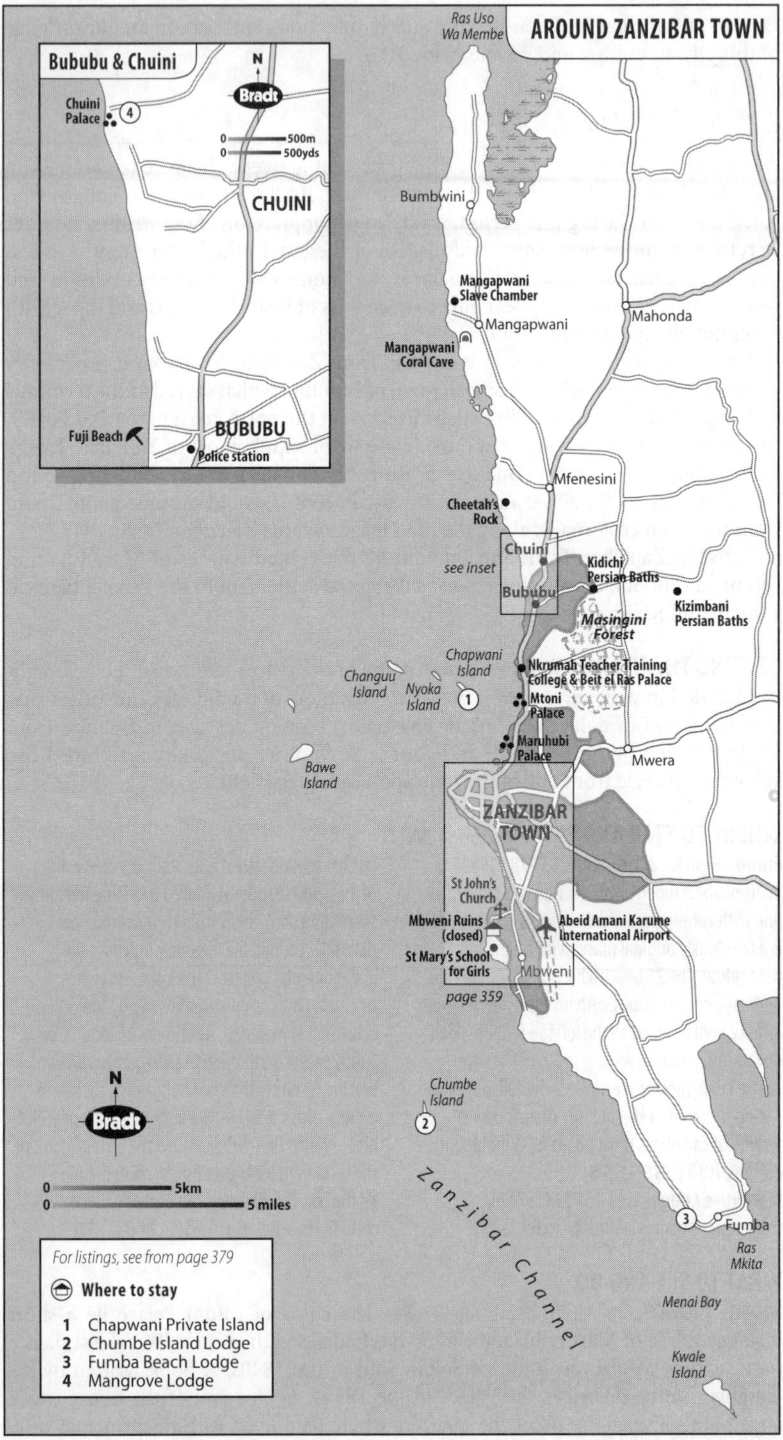

AROUND ZANZIBAR TOWN

Bububu & Chuini

Chuini Palace
4
0 500m
0 500yds
CHUINI
BUBUBU
Fuji Beach
Police station

Ras Uso Wa Membe
Bumbwini
Mangapwani Slave Chamber
Mangapwani
Mangapwani Coral Cave
Mahonda
Mfenesini
Cheetah's Rock
Chuini
see inset
Bububu
Kidichi Persian Baths
Kizimbani Persian Baths
Masingini Forest
Chapwani Island
Changuu Island
Nyoka Island
1
Nkrumah Teacher Training College & Beit el Ras Palace
Mtoni Palace
Maruhubi Palace
Mwera
Bawe Island
ZANZIBAR TOWN
St John's Church
Mbweni Ruins (closed)
St Mary's School for Girls
Abeid Amani Karume International Airport
Mbweni
page 359
Chumbe Island
2
Zanzibar Channel
3
Fumba
Ras Mkita
Menai Bay
Kwale Island

0 5km
0 5 miles

For listings, see from page 379

Where to stay

1 Chapwani Private Island
2 Chumbe Island Lodge
3 Fumba Beach Lodge
4 Mangrove Lodge

THE PRINCESS SALME TOUR

(w zanzibardifferent.com; bookings at least 1 day in advance) In 2008, the dedicated team at Mtoni Palace Conservation Project initiated a lovely tour combining a number of historical palaces and traditional ceremonies, as well as an informative spice tour and delicious Swahili lunch.

Escorted by a guide from the conservation project, small groups (up to 6) are taken around the evocative ruins of Mtoni Palace, Princess Salme's birthplace, in a colourful, thatched cart pulled by a donkey. They're then taken to Bububu for a traditional coffee ceremony with tasty local treats (kashata (peanut brittle) and candy-like halua). After a short walk, perhaps into the grounds of Salme's cousin's home, the group visits the lush Kidichi plantation area. Here, there's a guided tour of a spice farm before the farmer and his wife serve a deliciously fresh, homemade meal. Expect pilau rice, coconut curry, fish masala, roasted meats, stewed beans, kachumbari salad (East African coleslaw), an array of tropical fruits and spiced tea.

Heading back down the hillside after lunch in a private dalla dalla, there are great views towards the Indian Ocean and Stone Town before the vehicle arrives at the Kidichi Persian Baths (see below).

The tour leaves Stone Town at 08.30, returning at 14.00 and costs US$120 for one person, US$70 per person for two to three people, or US$50 per person for four to six people, including all entrance fees and lunch. It's an original and varied way to see these sites and enjoy traditional Zanzibari cuisine, and part of the charge is donated to the valuable work of the Mtoni Palace Conservation Project.

Gazelles and peacocks wandered around the large courtyard until Mtoni was abandoned around 1885. Now, only the main walls, roof and bathhouses remain, but members of the resident Mtoni Palace Conservation Project are working hard to restore significant sections and offer interesting guided tours. The palace was used as a warehouse in World War I, with evidence of this alteration still visible.

Kidichi and Kizimbani Persian Baths The Kidichi baths were built in 1850 for Sultan Said's wife, Binte Irich Mirza, the granddaughter of the Shah of Persia, and were decorated with Persian-style stucco. You can enter the bathhouse and see the bathing pool and toilets, but there is mould growing on much of the stucco. The baths lie about 3km east of Bububu; from the main crossroads follow the road heading inland (ie: turn right coming from Zanzibar Town) and you'll see the baths to your right after a walk of around 30 minutes. The Kizimbani baths are less attractive and less accessible on foot, lying a further 3km or so inland. The surrounding Kizimbani clove plantation, which is visited by many spice tours, was founded in the early 19th century by Saleh bin Haramil, the Arab trader who imported the first cloves to Zanzibar.

Mangapwani Slave Chamber Near the village of Mangapwani, some 10km north of Bububu, are a large natural cavern and a manmade slave chamber. This square cell cut into the coral was apparently built to hold slaves by one Muhammad bin Nassor Al-Alwi, an important slave trader. Boats from the mainland would unload their human cargo on the nearby beach, and the slaves would be kept here before being taken to Zanzibar Town for resale, or to plantations on the island. It is thought that some time after 1873, when slavery was officially abolished, the cave was used as a place to hide slaves, as an illicit trade continued for many years.

Menai Bay excursions The Menai Bay Conservation Area, to the south of Zanzibar Town, has a number of picturesque, uninhabited islands and sandbanks to explore, as well as some fascinating marine life. It's well worth taking a full-day excursion, either through Fumba Beach Lodge (page 379) if you're a guest, or with one of the two operators running trips: **Safari Blue** (w safariblue.net) or **Eco+Culture** (page 407). Take towels and waterproof shoes for wading out to the boat across coral rock.

ISLANDS CLOSE TO ZANZIBAR TOWN

Several small islands lie between 2km and 6km offshore of Zanzibar, many of them within view of Zanzibar Town and easily visited from there as a day trip. Boat transport to Chumbe arranged with an independent guide will cost around US$20, but you will pay more to go on an organised tour (see page 360 for tour operators). To cut the individual cost, it is worth getting a group together. Despite their individual attractions, these islands are quiet yet close to main shipping routes, so are not ideal overnight stays for those in search of either total isolation or entertainment and nightlife. Note that crossing to or from Zanzibar Town in an unlit boat at night is extremely dangerous.

CHUMBE ISLAND The coral island of Chumbe, along with several surrounding reefs, is gazetted as a nature reserve under the title of Chumbe Island Coral Park (CHICOP). The area is in near-pristine condition because it served as a military base for many years and visitors were not permitted. Snorkelling here is as good as anywhere around Zanzibar, with more than 350 reef fishes recorded, as well as dolphins and turtles. A walking trail circumnavigates the island, passing rock pools haunted by starfish, and beaches marched upon by legions of hermit crabs. Look out, too, for the giant coconut crab, an endangered nocturnal creature that weighs up to 4kg. Some 60 species of bird have been recorded on the island, including breeding pairs of the rare roseate tern, and the localised Ader's duiker, hunted out in the 1950s, has been reintroduced. Of historical interest are an ancient Swahili mosque and a British lighthouse built in 1904.

Visitors are encouraged to spend at least one night on Chumbe, and two or three would be perfect. Boat transfers are included in the overnight room rate and leave from the Mbweni Ruins a few kilometres south of Stone Town. Day trips are offered but only when the lodge isn't full, which means they can be booked no more two days in advance. The cost for a day trip is US$90 per person including transfers, lunch and a guided snorkelling excursion with equipment provided.

Where to stay and eat *Map, page 380*

✷ **Chumbe Island Lodge** m +255 777 413232; w chumbeisland.com; ⌚ mid-Jun–end Mar. Part of the Chumbe Island Coral Park (CHICOP), this superb, trail-blazing lodge is an example of truly eco-friendly accommodation. Bungalows are simple, clean, ingeniously designed & genuinely ecologically sensitive. The central area is a huge, star-shaped makuti structure – perfect for catching the sea breeze in the heat of the day. Fresh meals & drinks are served on the terrace (on the sounding of a gong), & there's a lovely upper deck of hammocks & chairs. Activities are all escorted & focus on learning about the surrounding environment & ecology, & include snorkelling (scuba diving is prohibited) on the nearby reefs, forest walks along the nature trail, & walks across the inter-tidal zone, with its plethora of rock pools. **$$$$$$**

CHANGUU (PRISON) ISLAND Lying in the Zanzibar Channel, 6km northwest of Zanzibar Town, Changuu is a coral-rag islet, also known as Prison Island and at one time Kibandiko Island. It was originally owned by a wealthy Arab, who used it as a detention centre for disobedient slaves. A prison was built there in 1893, but never used; today it houses a café, library and boutique. The island is home to several giant tortoises, gifted from the Seychelles in the 18th century, though numbers remain severely threatened. An entrance fee of US$5 per person must be paid in hard currency. The island has a small beach and there's reasonable snorkelling on the nearby reef. Daily tours to see the historical ruins and tortoises are organised by many of Stone Town's operators (page 360), invariably making the 20-minute crossing by dhow under sail. For a cheaper option, a local boat will take four people to the island for around US$30. There is a 27-room resort here too, **Changuu Private Island Paradise** (w hotelsandlodges-tanzania.com), but it is closed at the time of writing and unlikely to open in the foreseeable future.

CHAPWANI (GRAVE) ISLAND This long, narrow and very pretty island has been the site of a Christian cemetery since 1879. Most of the graves belong to British sailors who were killed tackling Arab slave ships, while others date from World War I, when the British ship *Pegasus* was sunk in Zanzibar harbour. The island also has a small swimming beach – good at low and high tide – and faces Snake Island, where thousands of egrets roost overnight. The indigenous forest supports about 100 Ader's duiker, large numbers of fruit bats and various coastal scrub birds. The giant coconut crab is often seen along the shore.

Between mid-June and mid-April, visitors can stay in one of the 11 semi-detached bungalows at **Chapwani Private Island** [map, page 380] (m +255 777 433102; w chapwani-resort-zanzibar-hotel.com; **$$$$$**). There's a nice pool tucked among the trees or, for a more natural dip, a tidal outlet in a coral crevasse on the northeast of the island makes a pleasant place to swim at high tide, and a good place to explore the starfish and barnacle-clad rock pools otherwise.

BAWE ISLAND About 6km due west of Zanzibar Town, Bawe has broad sandy beaches and a densely vegetated centre. In 1879, it was given to the Eastern Telegraph Company by Sultan Barghash to be used as the operations station for the underwater telegraphic cable linking Cape Town with Zanzibar, the Seychelles and Aden in Yemen. A second line was run from Bawe Island to the External Telecommunications building in the Shangani area of Zanzibar Town. The old 'Extelcoms' building has now been converted into the Serena Hotel, but the original phone line is largely redundant.

Lovely as the beach may be, it is firmly on the busy shipping route to Zanzibar Town and isn't visited as frequently as Changuu. In theory, it's possible to combine trips here with the tortoise excursions or simply arrange an out-and-back voyage with a boat captain in Zanzibar Town, though access prices do tend to be higher than those to Changuu. The 15-room **Bawe Tropical Island** (w hotelsandlodges-tanzania.com) is closed at the time of writing and unlikely to open in the foreseeable future.

NORTHERN ZANZIBAR

Ageing hippies, cool dudes, gap-year students and bright young things escaping European city jobs are all drawn to the white sand, stage-set palm trees, turquoise sea and sparkling sunshine of northern Zanzibar. Burgeoning guesthouses and vast resort complexes; beachfront activity overload and vibrant nightlife; an ever-expanding community and immense pressure on natural resources: these are the things that now characterise northern Zanzibar above its pleasant, white-sand beaches, warm sea, nautical heritage and good diving opportunities. Less than 2 hours' drive from Stone Town on the fast tar road past increasingly rural villages, this area mixes backpacker budget tourism with an increasing number of large, luxurious resorts. Focused around Nungwi village on the northernmost tip, and spreading near-continuously along the golden sands of Kendwa, on the northwest coast, this bustling centre appears to offer every component of the perfect holiday: a wide range of accommodation, watersports galore, fresh seafood washed down with daily cocktails, and a lovely ocean vista.

Once-small backpackers' bolt-holes have grown from a handful of rooms to resort hotels, mid-range places have added literally dozens of rooms to their original quota, whilst large-scale luxury or all-inclusive resorts now sit cheek-by-jowl on vast tracts of land around the north coast. Quite literally every beachfront plot from Ras Nungwi to Kendwa now has some tourist accommodation, either operational or under construction, and that has come at an aesthetic, social and environmental cost, but to the holidaymakers who flock here, it's a vibrant ocean spot.

GETTING THERE AND AWAY Nungwi lies about 60km north of Zanzibar Town, from where it can be reached by bus, tourist minibus or hired vehicle. The main road goes via Mtoni, Mahonda, Kinyasini and Kivunge, but the equidistant and more scenic route directly north of Mahonda to Mkokotoni, once the preserve of 4x4s only, is now wonderfully accessible on the new tar road. Either way, the drive takes around 90 minutes in a private vehicle, or in shared tourist minibuses, which stop in the centre of the action, beside Amaan Bungalows. Practically all hotels in Nungwi can arrange a transfer from Zanzibar Town or the airport (expect to pay around US$35–50 per car) or from anywhere else on the island.

Dalla dallas (no 116) leave Zanzibar Town for Nungwi every 30 minutes or so between 05.30 and 21.00. Alternatively, between 07.00 and 18.00 there are half-hourly public buses (route 14). Both depart from in and around Darajani terminal on Creek Road, and you should allow at least 2 hours for the drive. On arrival in Nungwi, the main stop is at the conspicuous traffic circle next to Nungwi Mosque and a Gapco filling station. Here a conglomeration of signs advertise accommodation and activities; with Stone Town to your back, head left for the main beach on the west coast and right for the east coast hotels. On foot, most properties are 10–15 minutes' walk from here.

 **WHERE TO STAY** The number of hotels and guesthouses in this area has grown tremendously in recent years, with the busiest beach to the southwest of the peninsula. While there's no shortage of accommodation – new or old – finding something that is both good quality and good value is more of a challenge. Listed below are a handful of our favourites.

Nungwi

Luxury

Essque Zalu Zanzibar [385 E1] **m** +255 778 683960; **w** essquehotels.com. One of northern Zanzibar's premier resort options, Essque Zalu is centred on an imposing makuti construction that's visible from quite a distance. The 40 spacious suites & 9 vast 4-bedroom villas are furnished beautifully with contemporary African fabrics, art & wallpaper. The focal point of the lush landscaped gardens is a huge saltwater pool, complete with whirlpool, water jets & multi-coloured lighting. There are 2 restaurants: the deli-style Market Kitchen & more upmarket à la carte Middle Eastern restaurant & shisha lounge at the end of The Jetty, which offers the ultimate sea

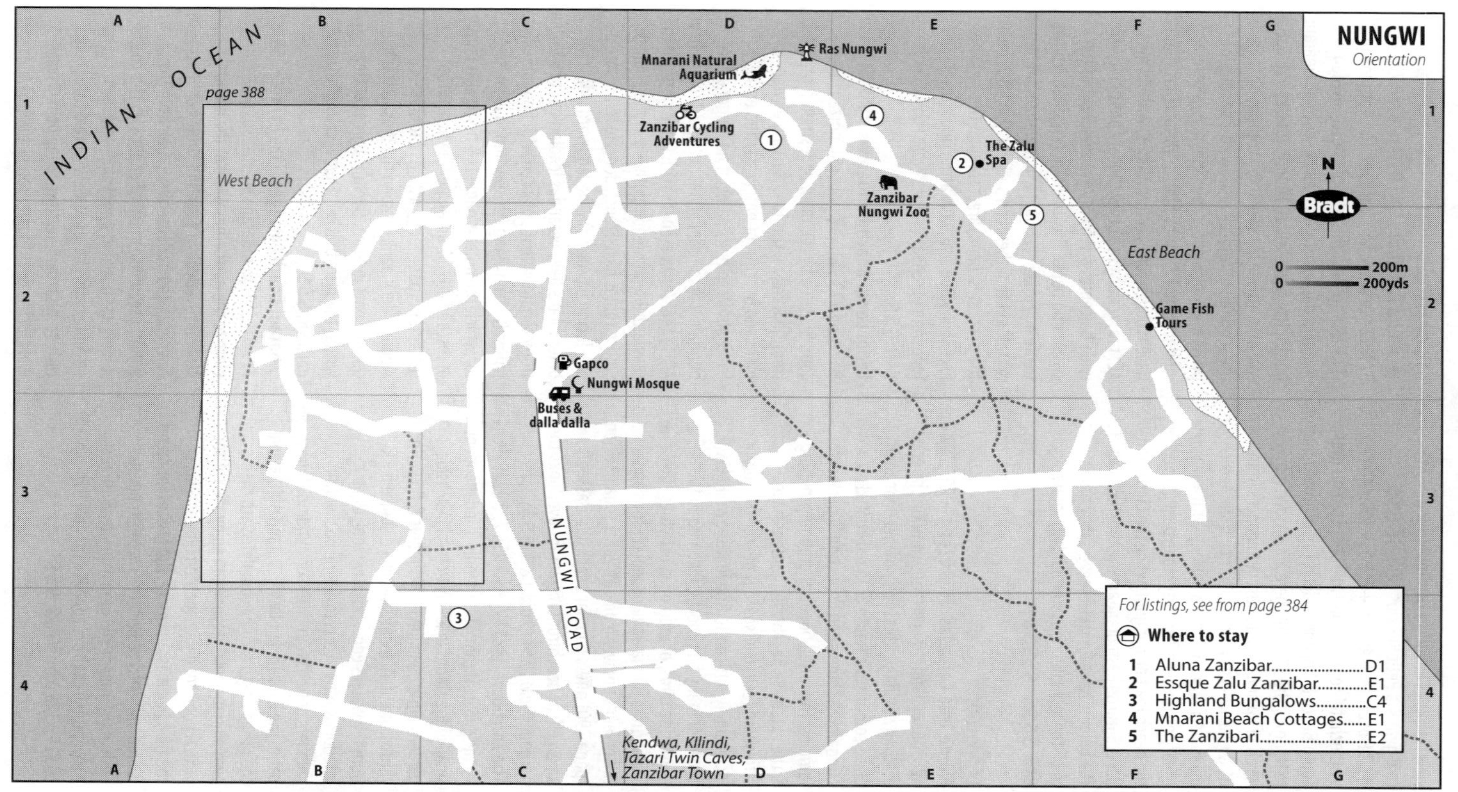

NUNGWI
Orientation
N
Bradt
0 200m
0 200yds
For listings, see from page 384
Where to stay
1 Aluna Zanzibar.........D1
2 Essque Zalu Zanzibar.........E1
3 Highland Bungalows.........C4
4 Mnarani Beach Cottages.........E1
5 The Zanzibari.........E2
INDIAN OCEAN
page 388
West Beach
East Beach
Game Fish Tours
The Zalu Spa
Zanzibar Nungwi Zoo
Ras Nungwi
Mnarani Natural Aquarium
Zanzibar Cycling Adventures
Gapco
Nungwi Mosque
Buses & dalla dalla
NUNGWI ROAD
Kendwa, Kilindi, Tazari Twin Caves, Zanzibar Town
A
B
C
D
E
F
G
1
2
3
4

view. Facilities include a pampering spa, super-cool gym & a Petit VIP kids' club. **$$$$$**

✷ **Z Hotel** [388 A5] m +255 699 109090; w thezhotel.com; ⌚ Jun–mid-Apr. Lording over South Beach & bringing a degree of city-boy bling to Nungwi, the 39 rooms here are divided into 6 levels of luxury, but all boast indulgences from AC & plasma TVs to Inaya toiletries & stocked minibars. Every room has a balcony with a sea view of varying degrees. The busy stone pool above the beach is a fine hangout, while the Cinnamon Bar & Saruche Restaurant are evening hotspots. The biggest issue for style-seekers may prove to be the less salubrious surrounding sprawl. *B&B*. **$$$$–$$$$$**

Upmarket

Flame Tree Cottages [388 C2] m + 255 752 526366; w flametreecottages.com. On the edge of Nungwi village, this lovely owner-managed place comprises a house & 15 red-roofed bungalows. some interconnecting & perfect for families. The raised pool is thoroughly inviting & the extensive beachfront gardens have a refreshing feeling of space & peace – something increasingly difficult to find in Nungwi. Relax in one of many hammocks, listening to the twittering birds, or indulge in activities such as a lemongrass oil massage or snorkel trips aboard the owner's dhow. An on-site Zanzi Yoga pavilion (page 390) offers popular beachside classes & an excellent beachfront restaurant overlooks the harbour. *From US$140 dbl. B&B*. **$$$**

The Zanzibari [385 E2] m +255 772 222919; w thezanzibari.com. This friendly & independent small lodge stands in lovely tropical beachside gardens amid bougainvillea climbers & flowering shrubs. Standard rooms are set a distance back from the water's edge, but have cool, clean interiors & offer access to a large pool with loungers dotted around the surrounding stone patio. The 2 luxury family villas stand right above the raised beach & come complete with their own plunge pool. Everyone can enjoy the clifftop jacuzzi pools for dhow-spotting dips or relax in the thatched massage room. The restaurant menu is predominantly seasonal & Swahili in flavour, with many ingredients grown on site, & there's a mezzanine chill-out zone & a friendly bar. *US$155/175 sgl/dbl B&B*. **$$$**

Moderate

✷ **Aluna Zanzibar** [385 D1] m +255 773 079125; w alunazanzibar.com. The epitome of stylish simplicity, this friendly Dutch-owned & -managed lodge stands a block south of Mnarani lighthouse & aquarium. Though it lacks a direct sea view, the lushly vegetated compound feels like a genuine tropical oasis, with 2 swimming pools & a cool outdoor spa. Split across several whitewashed 2-storey blocks, 18 spacious rooms have wooden floors & furnishings, walk-in nets, AC, fan, terracotta pots with leafy pot plants, & wide balconies & terraces overlooking 1 of the swimming pools. The excellent restaurant comes to life on Friday evenings when management & staff get together for a sociable fish BBQ. For the best rates, book direct through the website. Excellent value & already attracting a loyal following of repeat visitors. *From US$125 dbl B&B*. **$$$**

Langi Langi Beach Bungalows [388 A4] m +255 773 911000; w langilangizanzibar.com. Bisected by the main pedestrian footpath through Nungwi, this long-serving owner-managed beachfront hotel is staffed entirely by locals. Despite its name, it no longer offers bungalow accommodation, but all 32 rooms have AC, fans & Zanzibari beds with fitted nets. On the seaward side of the footpath is a 3-storey block whose rooms have French doors leading onto a sea-facing balcony. On the landward side, the older rooms have verandas leading out to a lovely tropical garden that's planted with bougainvillea, palms & ylang ylang (the perfumed Asian tree for which the hotel is named) & home to a family of rescued dik-dik antelope. The beachfront restaurant (page 389), with its cantilevered wooden deck, ranks among the most attractive dining spots in town. Overall, a great option within the price bracket. *From US$100/120 sgl/dbl B&B*. **$$$**

Mnarani Beach Cottages [385 E1] m +255 777 415551; w mnarani-beach-cottages.com. Close to the northernmost tip of the island, Mnarani overlooks a beautiful stretch of beach, & is separated by dense vegetation from the lighthouse; unlike most other plots on this coast, it feels less boxed in by development. Some of its en-suite rooms have sea views; others are set in lush, tropical gardens close to the pool. Kayaks, windsurfers & surfboards can be hired, & the lagoon in front of the hotel is a great place for kitesurfing. The bar has a cool, relaxed vibe, & the staff are some of the friendliest on the north coast. *From US$100 dbl B&B.* **$$–$$$$**

Budget

✷ **Casa Umoja** [388 B3] m +255 777 487570; w casaumoja.info. Set a short distance back from the busy waterfront this is a thoroughly laidback place with gentle Zanzibari–German owners & a lovely tropical garden shaded by tall palms & casuarinas. Rooms & bungalows are clean & spacious with simple furnishings, swept concrete floors, fans & a small veranda. There is a nice raised terrace, with plenty of spots under the trees to chill – swinging chairs, dbl hammocks & a baraza around the firepit for social evenings. *US$50/80 sgl/dbl. B&B.* **$$**

Highland Bungalows [385 C4] (10 rooms) m +255 757 619761; w highlandzanzibar.co.tz. Set behind a clearly marked white wall about 800m from the beach, this tranquil & leafy lodge is owned & managed by an agreeable German-Tanzanian couple. The circular makuti area, with its upstairs Sky Lounge, houses an inexpensive bar & restaurant. A separate gated area contains the rooms, which form a quadrangle around a freeform infinity pool set in a rustic grass garden with neat flowerbeds & shady pomegranate, sweet almond & flame trees. The bright & airy tiled rooms are simply furnished but have AC, fitted nets, small bathrooms & a private terrace. Attractive & well-priced lodge but some distance from the beach. *From US$53/63 sgl/dbl. B&B.* **$$**

Makofi Guesthouse [388 B6] (17 rooms & 2 dorms) m +255 777 484165; w makofiguesthouse.com. This top-notch backpackers stands in a shady sandy courtyard about 100m inland of the southern end of West Beach. The grounds are dotted with tables converted from old dhows & covered in colourful local fabrics. Dbl rooms are simply but brightly decorated & come with fan but no AC; most use a shared bathroom but some are en suite. There's also an 8-bed mixed dorm, a 4-bed female-only dorm, a lively bar, a well-priced restaurant & super-friendly staff, & management has also arranged a 10% discount with various service providers, restaurants & bars in Nungwi. *US$20pp dorm bed; from US$50 dbl.* **$–$$**

Kendwa *Map, page 391*

Exclusive

✷ **Kilindi** w elewanacollection.com. Exclusive, stylish & upmarket without being pretentious, Kilindi has a unique design reminiscent of a Greek Orthodox church. Accommodation is in white 2-tier domed pavilions that are accessed through heavy wooden Zanzibari doors & spread out across 20ha of dense, indigenous shrubbery overlooking a sweep of beach. With a personal butler to bring you whatever you may desire, including your meals, you may never wish to leave your pavilion. However, if you can be tempted away, there's an attractive, colonial chic restaurant & bar, a bijou spa & gorgeous infinity pool. One of Zanzibar's top spots! **$$$$$$**

Moderate

Kendwa Rocks m +255 774 415475; w kendwarocks.com. The 1st property to open on this stretch of beach, Kendwa Rocks had expanded to 65 rooms by the time it celebrated its 25th birthday in 2020. These range from semi-detached Coconut Bungalows, spread out in a semi-circle on a lovely stretch of seaside sand, to a 19-bed basic mixed dorm popular with groups of off-duty volunteers. The Mermaid Bar is the epitome of beachside drinking dens: a hip DJ messes on decks in the corner, smiling staff stand behind a well-stocked bar festooned with lists of cocktails, while sun-kissed travellers recline, chat & drink. On Sat nights (22.30 onwards) & at Full Moon the bar hosts live music & a huge beach party: a messy affair that's often still in full swing at sunrise. Revellers come from all over the island to experience the cocktails, bonfires, dance beats & acrobatic shows here. *B&B.* **$$$–$$$$$**

✷ **Natural Kendwa Villa** m +255 772 326460; w naturalkendwavilla.com. Some of the loveliest accommodation in Kendwa can now be found tucked behind the seafront resorts at this original, contemporary & charming hotel. The amiable Italian owner has put his heart & considerable experience into the gorgeous rooms, which are simple in style, elaborate in detail & blissfully spacious. The manicured tropical gardens slope around a lovely free-form pool & jacuzzi that make for a thoroughly enjoyable alternative to the busy beach. Dining is in the adjoining restaurant, which is a highlight in itself, & guests enjoy free day passes to beachfront Kendwa Rocks. *B&B.* **$$$$**

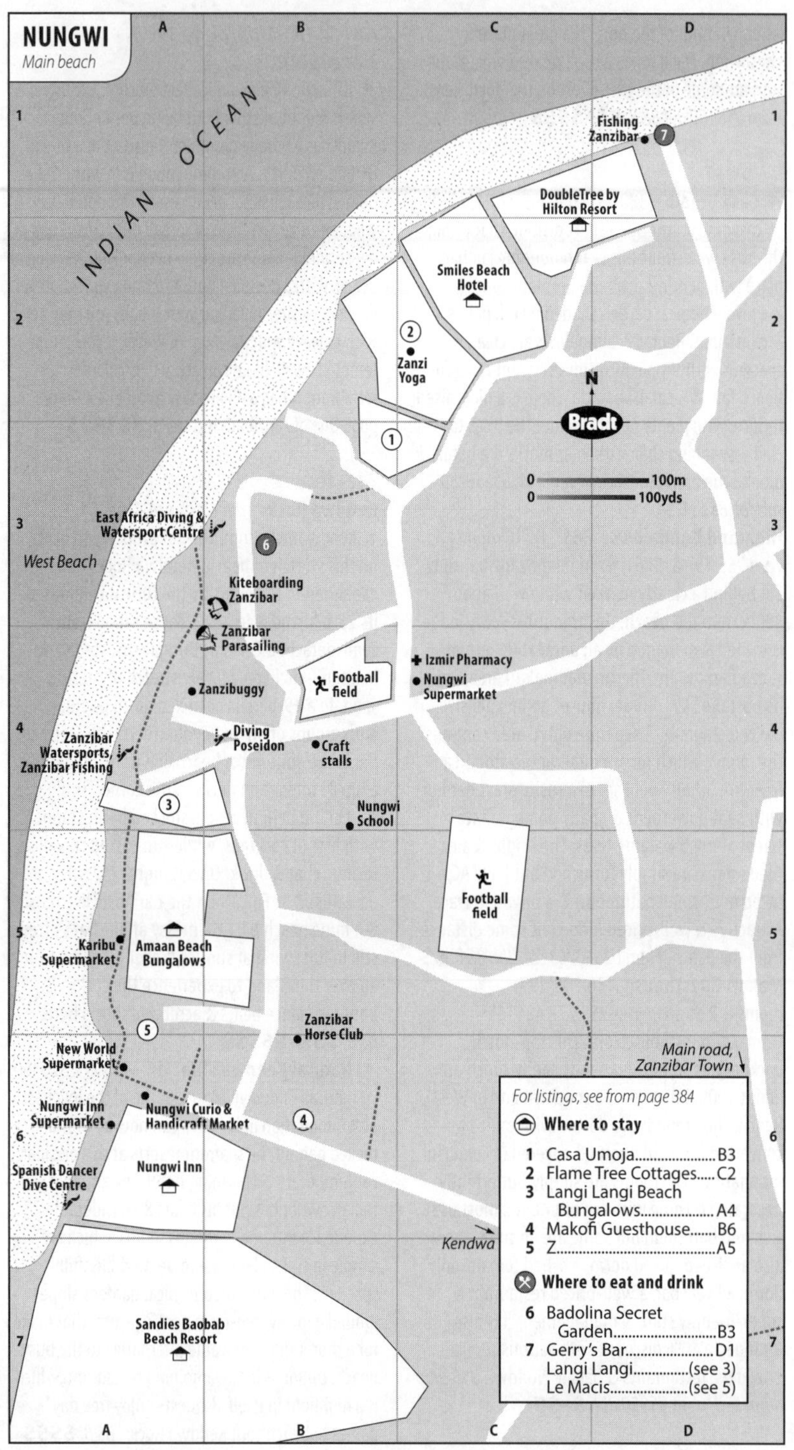

NUNGWI
Main beach
INDIAN OCEAN
West Beach
Fishing Zanzibar
DoubleTree by Hilton Resort
Smiles Beach Hotel
Zanzi Yoga
East Africa Diving & Watersport Centre
Kiteboarding Zanzibar
Zanzibar Parasailing
Football field
Izmir Pharmacy
Nungwi Supermarket
Zanzibuggy
Diving Poseidon
Craft stalls
Zanzibar Watersports, Zanzibar Fishing
Nungwi School
Football field
Karibu Supermarket
Amaan Beach Bungalows
Zanzibar Horse Club
New World Supermarket
Nungwi Inn Supermarket
Nungwi Curio & Handicraft Market
Spanish Dancer Dive Centre
Nungwi Inn
Kendwa
Sandies Baobab Beach Resort
Main road, Zanzibar Town
0 100m
0 100yds
Bradt
N
For listings, see from page 384
Where to stay
1 Casa Umoja....B3
2 Flame Tree Cottages....C2
3 Langi Langi Beach Bungalows....A4
4 Makofi Guesthouse....B6
5 Z....A5
Where to eat and drink
6 Badolina Secret Garden....B3
7 Gerry's Bar....D1
Langi Langi....(see 3)
Le Macis....(see 5)

Budget

✱ **SunSeaBar Hotel** m + 255 774 338066. Punningly woeful name notwithstanding, this sparkling white new beachfront block easily ranks as one of the best budget options in northern Zanzibar. It has a perfect location & offers comfortable accommodation in adequately sized & clinically clean rooms with AC & fridge. Most rooms have a sea view. There is no restaurant but plenty of others can be found within a 500m radius. *From US$70 dbl. B&B.* **$$**

WHERE TO EAT AND DRINK Nearly all the hotels and guesthouses in Nungwi and Kendwa have attached restaurants, many of which are open to guests and non-guests alike. Others are standalone places that tend to close and spring up again as if with the tide. A few stand out as worth investigating in their own right, as listed below, but do ask around for the current culinary hotspots.

Nungwi

✱ **Badolina Secret Garden** [388 B3] w badolinazanzibar.com; 🕘 11.00–23.00 daily. Opened in 2018 & already entrenched as one of Nungwi's most popular restaurants, Badolina offers a small but cosmopolitan menu of salads, Asian noodles & North African dishes such as hummus & shaksuka. Vegetarians are well catered for & it also serves great smoothies, juices, coffee & desserts. The attractive Zanzibar-meets-Mediterranean décor is offset by atmospheric contemporary music. $$

Gerry's Bar [388 D1] m + 255 777 430 006; w gerrysbar.com; 🕘 11.00–midnight daily. Situated at the north end of West Beach, this popular Nungwi sundowner & evening hangout has an open-sided makuti-shaded bar & live music area. Eat & drink inside or out, under shaggy palm umbrellas with the sand between your toes. Gerry's is a casual haunt, offering simple, well-cooked food, from rock lobster to chicken schnitzel & salads, an array of chilled beers & cocktails, & friendly staff. It hosts regular DJ sets, live-music shows & open-mic nights. Check the website for upcoming events. $$

Langi Langi Restaurant [388 A4] m +255 773 911000; w langilangizanzibar.com; 🕘 07.00–22.00 daily. Attached to Langi Langi Bungalows, this relaxed Swahili restaurant serves pizza, pasta, seafood grills & curries, while the brave can sample the Zanzibar Chili PiliPili menu – 'have fun in the sun don't get burn' warning included! The large cantilevered deck, complete with welcome sea breeze & rolling waves below, is very popular, so it's worth booking to guarantee a seafront table for dinner. Alternatively, dine inside amid the monochrome photos of Stone Town & antique objets d'art. $$

✱ **Le Macis** [388 A5] m +255 767 981861; w restaurantlemacis.business.site; 🕘 11.30–15.30 Mon–Sat & 18.30–21.30 daily. Nungwi's top standalone restaurant, set in a lovely green tropical garden, boasts an imaginative Afro-European fusion menu that uses locally sourced ingredients & reflects the nationality of its French owner & chef. Strong on seafood, it also has a good selection of pasta dishes, while dedicated carnivores can choose between the likes of beef bourguignon, grilled pork ribs & roast goat leg. It also serves excellent coffee & a tempting selection of desserts & cocktails. The only negative is the non-seafront location. $$–$$$

Kendwa *Map, page 391*

Fisherman Local Restaurant m +255 777 483977/871130; 🕘 07.00–22.00 daily. Every bit as unpretentious as its name indicates, this simple open-sided makuti roof structure on the main road through the village is kept cool by a bank of ceiling fans. Fresh seafood is the speciality, & it's usually very good, but it spreads its wings with a varied selection of stir-fries, curries, Swahili stews & the inevitable pasta & pizza. No alcohol served but you can bring your own. $–$$

✱ **The Lebanese Cuisine** m +255 688 031844; 🕘 07.00–22.00 daily. An unexpected & well-priced gem for those seeking culinary variety, this brightly decorated Middle Eastern restaurant specialises in Lebanese dishes such as hummus, falafel, shwarmas, tawook chicken & so on, supplemented by more typical seafood & other grills. Contrary to expectations, not only does it serve alcohol, but the walls are plastered with mischievous posters advocating its use. The coffee is great too. $–$$

HEALTH AND BEAUTY Temporary henna tattoos seem to be de rigueur in Nungwi, painted on to your skin by friendly local ladies as you lie under their makeshift palm shades on the beach. Be warned, however; the henna can badly mark bed linen, and hotel owners will charge for stains. It is also important to avoid black henna (pico): it is a synthetic dye and often results in bad allergic reactions, sometimes delayed by a few weeks, which requires medical treatment. For all-out African beach chic, hair-braiding services are also available, along with basic beach massages. Most of the more upmarket hotels around Nungwi have formal spas, with the following being outstanding:

The Zalu Spa [385 E1] m +255 778 683960; w essquehotels.com/wellness. Within the Essque Zalu Hotel (page 384), this small spa pavilion fans out into sweet-smelling treatment rooms, a Vichy shower room, a sauna/steam & gym area. Using Healing Earth products that blend the organic oils of indigenous African plants, the small team of therapists offer a range of beauty treatments, massages, body polishes & finishing touches from waxing to manicures. There are loungers amid the encircling gardens for pleasant pre- & post-treatment chilling, though the space is limited & it's not a place for all-day relaxing. *Facials US$120/90mins; body treatments US$80–280/60mins–3½hrs; manicures US$55/hr.*

Zanzi Yoga [388 C2] m +255 620 636935; w yogazanzibar.com. Founded in 2009, Yoga Zanzibar offers yoga classes & longer retreats. Based at Flame Tree Cottages (page 386), individual yoga tuition & longer retreats are available year-round by a registered teacher. Relaxation, pranayama (breathing techniques), sun salutations, asanas (postures) & reiki available.

SHOPPING

Nungwi There are several small shops in Nungwi village, where you'll find an array of cheap souvenirs, including carvings, paintings and jewellery, as well as essential items. Head inland across the football pitch behind Cholo's, and you'll find a small parade of shops including the long-standing Nungwi Supermarket [388 C4], a veritable Aladdin's den of imported luxuries from toothpaste and toiletries to chocolate and Pringles. Right next door, Izmir Pharmacy is the best stocked outlet of its type in Nungwi and it keeps long hours (⌚ 08.00–21.00 daily). Several craft stalls line the south side of this football field.

If you just need to grab a few essentials and don't want to stray too far from sunbathing, there are a couple of places on the south end of West Beach. Nungwi Inn Supermarket [388 A6], next to its namesake hotel, is very well laid out, clearly priced and stocks a good selection of snacks, drinks, toiletries and beach requisites such as sunscreen. The nearby New World Supermarket [388 A6] sells a similar range of goods, as well as a selection of beers and wines, but it is not nearly as nicely laid out.

For artwork and souvenirs, the fairly contained Nungwi Curio & Handicraft Market [388 A6] has steadily grown on the alley running perpendicular to West Beach between the Z and Nungwi Inn hotels. Known locally as the Maasai Market, on account of the majority of the traders' tribal background, you'll find some entertainingly named shacks and the organised approach to displaying the carvings and beadwork is to be commended.

Kendwa With the increase in accommodation and visitors, Kendwa now has a few small, local-style 'mini-markets', the pick being the unimaginatively named but well stocked Kendwa Mini-Market opposite the entrance to Gold Beach House. For wine, spirits, beer and other beverages, a couple of small but well-stocked bottle stores stand close to the entrance to Kendwa Rocks. For curios, there's an ever-

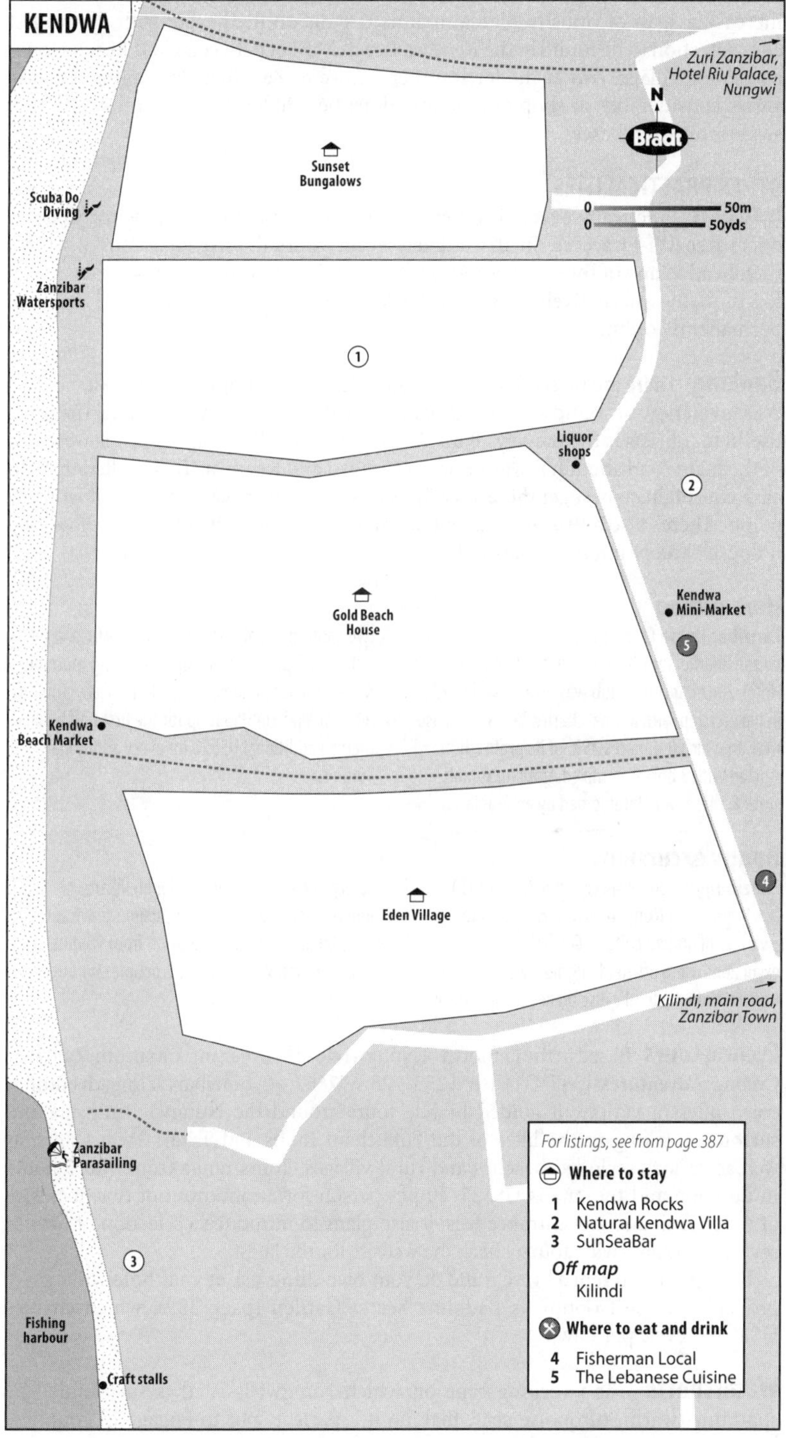
KENDWA
Zuri Zanzibar, Hotel Riu Palace, Nungwi
N
Bradt
0 50m
0 50yds
Sunset Bungalows
Scuba Do Diving
Zanzibar Watersports
1
Liquor shops
2
Gold Beach House
Kendwa Mini-Market
5
Kendwa Beach Market
Eden Village
4
Kilindi, main road, Zanzibar Town
Zanzibar Parasailing
3
Fishing harbour
Craft stalls
For listings, see from page 387
Where to stay
1 Kendwa Rocks
2 Natural Kendwa Villa
3 SunSeaBar
Off map
Kilindi
Where to eat and drink
4 Fisherman Local
5 The Lebanese Cuisine

increasing span of (mostly Maasai-manned) stalls on the beach, with the biggest concentration to be found at the Kendwa Beach Market between Gold Beach House and Eden Village, and at the far south end close to Zanzibar Parasailing. Quality varies considerably so shop around and don't be blinded by the sun into making second-rate purchases.

OTHER PRACTICALITIES

Internet Practically every accommodation option listed for Nungwi or Kendwa offers free Wi-Fi access. In the unlikely event yours doesn't, or it isn't working, then head to any of the smarter restaurants, order something to drink, and you can log in there. Alternatively, buy a local SIM card and a data bundle, and you'll be permanently online.

Banking There are no banks or bureaux de change in Nungwi or Kendwa, but two ATMs can now be found alongside the main road running between them. The more useful to tourists is the Barclays Bank ATM at the UP filling station on the west side of the main road about halfway between Nungwi and Kendwa. This is filled up with cash overnight so best get there as early as possible to be reasonably sure it won't be empty. There's also a PBZ ATM about 500m further south but at the time of writing it doesn't accept international cards.

Horseriding

Zanzibar Horse Club [388 B6] w zanzibarhorseclub.com. Situated behind the Z Hotel, Zanzibar Horse Club was established in 2019 in partnership with animal charity Zaaso (w zaaso.net), to which it donates 25% of its profits. It started with 3 horses of mixed Arabian/Somali stock & these were later joined by an Arabian & two spotted Appaloosas from South Africa. It offers a choice of guided excursions, including morning & evening beach rides, village tours, & swimming rides, at a rate of US$30pp for the first half hour, then an additional US$20 for every additional 30mins.

Buggy excursions

Zanzibuggy [388 A4] m +255 777 114030; f. Situated on Nungi Beach, this place offers a variety of guided cultural & adventure excursions using off-road buggies with automatic transmission, hydraulic disc brakes on all wheels, safety-certified roll cage & double A-arm independent suspension. Excursions leave at 09.00 & 14.00 daily, range in duration from 90mins to 3hrs, & cost US$80–120 for 2 people sharing.

Cycling tours Based in the far north of Nungwi close to Mnarani Aquarium, **Zanzibar Cycling Adventures** [385 D1] (m +255 778 677662; w zanzibarcyclingadventures.com) offers a variety of guided bicycle tours around the Nungwi Peninsula and surrounds, taking in the likes of the Fukuchani Ruins and Tazari Twin Caves, as well as various secluded beaches and rural villages. Tours range from 3 to 5 hours in duration and the rate is US$25–40 per person for a minimum of two, inclusive of water, fruit and any entrance fees. It also plans to introduce a selection of five- to seven-day island-wide tours; check the website for the latest.

If you prefer to rent a bicycle and do your own thing, ask at your hotel; otherwise probably the best option is Badolina Secret Garden (page 389), which charges US$5 per cycle per day.

Watersports The sweeping cape on which Nungwi is sited is surrounded by sparkling, warm, turquoise seas, making it a perfect spot to engage in countless water activities. Prices are all very similar; quality is highly variable. Listen to your instinct and other travellers' advice carefully when deciding who is currently offering the best trip.

Snorkelling and diving There are several competent dive operations on this stretch of coast, as listed below, and you can check what they offer and rates on their website. Divers are advised to talk seriously to the individual operators about safety, experience and ethos before signing up for courses or sub-aqua excursions. Knowledgeable, reliable operations include:

East Africa Diving & Watersport Centre [388 A3] m +255 777 416425; w diving-zanzibar.com. The oldest dive centre on the north coast, this excellent & highly efficient PADI 5* Gold Palm Resort has a beachfront office in Nungwi & bases within Essque Zalu & Z Hotel.

Scuba Do Diving [map, page 391] m +255 777 417157; e do-scuba@scuba-do-zanzibar.com; w scuba-do-zanzibar.com. For many years Kendwa's only dive operation, this highly professional & well-equipped beachfront dive centre is also involved in extensive community work.

Spanish Dancer Dive Centre [388 A6] m +255 777 417717; w divinginzanzibar.com. Based in an open rondavel on South Beach, Spanish Dancer is PADI 5* accredited & teaches in German, French, Spanish, English & Swahili.

Zanzibar Watersports [388 A4] m +255 773 165862; w zanzibarwatersports.com. With PADI 5* Gold Palm Instructor Development Centre status, Zanzibar Watersports has a beachfront base at Nungwi, as well as in Kendwa Rocks. Kayaks, wakeboarding equipment & sunset dhow cruises are also available.

Fishing Nungwi's proximity to some of Africa's best deep-sea fishing grounds – Leven Bank and the deep Pemba Channel – provides serious anglers some outstanding fishing opportunities. In addition to the weather-beaten local dhows that plough the coastal waters here, the following operators currently offer game fishing in fully equipped, custom-built boats. Check their websites for full information and the latest rates.

Fishing Zanzibar [388 D1] w fishingzanzibar.com. Established in 2005 & operated by Gerry Hallam (of Gerry's Bar), Fishing Zanzibar has 5 sport-fishing boats based in Nungwi, as well as a 50ft sailing yacht & 56ft Fountaine Pajot. Night fishing for broadbills is an option, as are live-aboard trips.

Game Fish Tours m +255 772 074766; w gamefishlodgezanzibar.wordpress.com. Firmly focused on the serious game-fishing market, this South African operation has 2 boats & runs half-day, night fishing & 2-day Pemba tours for reef & bottom fishing.

Zanzibar Fishing [388 A4] m +255 773 235030; w zanzibarfishing.com. Founded in 1998, this division of Zanzibar Watersports (see above) is extremely well kitted out for both professional fishermen & have-a-go holidaymakers.

Kiteboarding In recent years, kiteboarding has grown in popularity and Nungwi is no exception. Steady winds (approximately 15–20 knots) for most of the year, level beaches, warm clear water and protected, shallow lagoons make it a great place for both beginners and more experienced kiters. Check centres are certified by the International Kiteboarding Organization (IKO) if you are interested in quality assurance and training courses.

Kiteboarding Zanzibar [388 B3] w kiteboardingzanzibar.com. This IKO-certified operation uses up-to-date Cabrinha, NPX & Dakine equipment, with qualified, experienced staff on hand for safety & lessons.

Motorised watersports Nungwi now has several companies offering increasingly thrilling, motorised watersports. From stunt wakeboarding to sedate parasailing, and jet-ski safaris to fast-paced banana boats, the coastal waters are significantly busier and the range of activities vastly increased. Please consider carefully your own skill level, safety and the environmental impact of using powerful motorised machines like jet skis.

Zanzibar Parasailing [388 B3] w zanzibarparasailing.com. This well-established company is based in Kendwa but also operates out of a second office in Nungwi. It uses specially adapted boats, harnessing participants to a parasail & then winching them into the air from a platform at the rear of the accelerating boat. It's unquestionably thrilling & offers spectacular island panoramas. Solo or tandem 'flights' are possible, as is an optional dip in the sea on your descent. The flight itself is 10mins long, though several people may be on your boat, resulting in a trip lasting up to an hour. Wakeboarding & knee-boarding are also on offer. *Parasailing US$90/130 solo/tandem; wakeboarding & kneeboarding US$40–200 depending on duration.*

Zanzibar Watersports [388 A4] See page 393 for full details. Escorted jet-ski safaris (75mins) head from the Paradise Beach base in Nungwi to Tumbatu, where riders can have a quick swim before pushing on to Kendwa and back around the coast to the watersports centre. Drivers must be over 16 & no experience is necessary; passengers can be as young as 8. 2011 Yamaha 110 HP 4-Stroke jet-skis can also be hired for individual use. Parasailing, kite-surfing & waterskiing can also been arranged. *Jet-ski safari US$180/200 1/2 riders/bike; jet-ski rental US$50/15mins.*

WHAT TO SEE AND DO Most visitors come to this area to relax on the beach, swim in the sea and perhaps party at night. For local attractions, the small turtle sanctuary and terrific local coral reefs are still a draw. If you want a more cultural experience, head down the coast to the 16th-century Swahili ruins at Fukuchani and Mvuleni, the bustling, ramshackle market at Mkokotoni, or venture across the water to Tumbatu Island. Note that the lighthouse at Ras Nungwi is still in operation and, although it is not open to visitors anyway, no photography is allowed.

Mnarani Natural Aquarium [385 D1] m +255 773 719815; w mnaraniaquarium.org; ⌚ 09.00–18.00 daily; entrance US$10. Hawksbill turtles have traditionally been hunted around Zanzibar for their attractive shells, and green turtles for their meat. In 1993, with encouragement and assistance from various conservation bodies and some dedicated marine biologists, the local community opened the Mnarani Natural Aquarium, which is now the focal point of the Mnarani Marine Turtle Conservation Project.

In the shadow of the lighthouse (Mnarani meaning 'place of the lighthouse' in Swahili), at the northernmost tip of Zanzibar Island, the aquarium was created around a large, natural, tidal pool in the coral rock behind the beach. Originally set up to rehabilitate and study turtles that had been caught in fishing nets, the aquarium project expanded to ensure that local baby turtles were also protected.

Turtles used to nest frequently on Nungwi Beach, though sadly, in some part due to hotel lighting and visitor volume, this is now a rare occurrence. If a nest is found, village volunteers now mark and monitor new nests, while local fishermen rescuing turtles caught in their nets receive a small fee. The resulting hatchlings are carried to small plastic basins and small concrete tanks at the aquarium where they remain for ten months. By this time, they have grown to 25cm and their chances of survival at sea are dramatically increased. All bar one of these turtles are then released into the sea, along with the largest turtle from the aquarium pool. The one remaining baby turtle is then added to the pool, ensuring a static population of 17 turtles.

Currently, this equates to four hawksbills (Swahili: *ng'amba*), identified by the jagged edge on their shell, sharper beak and sardine diet, and 13 seaweed-loving green turtles (Swahili: *kasakasa*). The aquarium manager keeps a logbook detailing all eggs, hatchlings and releases.

In spite of the aquarium being little more than a glorified rock pool, it's fascinating to see the turtles at close quarters. Further, the money raised secures the project's future, and goes towards local community schemes – in a bid to demonstrate the tangible value of turtle conservation to the local population. With luck, this will lessen the trade in souvenir shell products and ensure the species' survival.

On a practical note, when timing your visit, the water is clearest about 2 hours before high tide (Swahili: *maji kujaa*).

Zanzibar Nungwi Zoo [385 E1] (m +255 774 899972; w zanzibarkilosasconservation.com; ⏲ 09.00–18.00 daily; entrance US$10) Registered as a conservation project with the Tanzanian government, this small zoo stands in a patch of natural vegetation roughly opposite Essque Zalu. Though its conservation credentials are difficult to confirm, it claims that all animals there were orphaned or otherwise rescued, and on our last visit, nobody present was able to address the issue of reintroduction into the wild. Either way, it offers the opportunity to get up close and personal with a variety of wildlife indigenous to Zanzibar, including blue and vervet monkey, bushbaby, dik-dik, rock python, flap-necked chameleon, leopard tortoise and Nile crocodile, and the inmates appear to be well cared for and in good condition.

Dhow-building and harbour activity Nungwi is the centre of Zanzibar's traditional dhow-building industry, where generations of skilled craftsmen have worked on the beach outside the village, turning planks of wood into strong ocean-going vessels, using only the simplest of tools. It is a fascinating place to see dhows in various stages of construction, but do show respect for the builders, who are generally indifferent towards visitors, and keep out of the way.

Fishing continues to employ many local men, who set out to sea in the late afternoon, returning at around 06.00 the following morning, taking their catch to the beach fish market. The spectacle is worth the early start, but if you don't make it, there's a smaller rerun at around 15.00 each day.

Cultural village tour (US$15pp) The base for the Nungwi Cultural Village Tours [385 D1] is adjacent to Mnarani Aquarium and run by the same volunteers. From the clearly marked bungalow, the 2-hour walks take in the aquarium, fish market (best visited early morning when the day's catches are landed), mosques, dhow-builders, basket-weavers and even touch on the uses of surrounding medicinal trees. A pleasant, guided trip, it offers visitors a different view of the community here, and gives photographers a great opportunity to capture the dhow-builders (always ask permission first). The money generated from these tours goes back into the community and is donated to a range of beneficiaries, from the kindergarten to the dhow-builders.

Tazari Twin Caves [385 C4] (m +255 777 261320/459102, w tazaricaves.blogspot.com; ⏲ 09.00–17.00; US$10pp inc guide) Rediscovered in 2013 by a local villager called Waziri, who was out looking for housebuilding material, the twin caves at Tazari have a long history of occupation, housing as they do several ceramic remains dating to the 11th or 12th century. More recently, it is thought that the caves served as a hiding place for captives held by Omani slave traders in the 19th century.

The first cave is 105m long and you can walk upright all the way through it before arriving at an opening where the roof has collapsed. It is noticeably the cooler of the two caves, perhaps because it is shallower or better ventilated, and is notable for its green coppery rocks, beautiful glittering crystalline outcrops, and a host of impressive stalactites, stalagmites and other drip formations, the most striking of which are likened by locals to a toothy shark and a giant snail. It is also home to plenty of bats and the pottery relicts discovered there are kept in situ.

The second, warmer, cave is similar in length but goes deeper underground, and requires some crouching to explore to the end, after which you need to return back to the same entrance. A pot has been placed near the entrance to collect the drinkable water that drips from its roof. Several striking formations can be found within this cave, variously resembling an elephant, an octopus and a jellyfish.

To get to Tazari Caves, head south from Nungwi along the main road towards Zanzibar Town for about 5km, then take the clearly signposted turn-off to the east and follow it for 400m to the guide office. For those without private transport, you could catch any southbound dalla dalla from Nungwi as far as the junction, then walk the last few hundred metres, or else take a piki-piki or taxi from Nungwi, rent a bicycle, or join a half-day tour with Zanzibar Cycling Adventures. The caves are relatively steep and slippery underfoot so wear solid walking shoes rather than flip-flops. Guided tours take about 45 minutes. Guides are very friendly and informative and will provide a torch, but it is worth bringing your own if you have one.

Attached to the caves is a 'chameleon centre' which keeps about 20 chameleons (all the same species) in a few cages, ostensibly to help educate locals that these beguiling lizards are neither dangerous nor magical. Sceptics could be forgiven for assuming the more pertinent motivation for the zoo is the opportunity to charge visitors an additional US$5 to see and touch its inmates.

THE EAST COAST

The east coast of Zanzibar is where you will find the idyllic tropical beaches of which you've dreamed: clean white sand lined with palms and lapped by the warm blue waters of the Indian Ocean. Some travellers come here for a couple of days just to relax after seeing the sights of Zanzibar Town, and end up staying for a couple of weeks. Visitors on tighter time restrictions always wish they could stay for longer.

The east coast is divided in to two discrete stretches by Chwaka Bay, which lies at the same latitude as Zanzibar Town on the west coast. Traditionally, the most popular stretch of coast is to the south of this bay, between Bwejuu and Makunduchi, but recent years have seen an increasing number of developments further north, between Matemwe and Chwaka. Most hotels have restaurants, and you can usually buy fish and vegetables in the villages, but supplies are limited. If you are self-catering, stock up in Zanzibar Town.

GETTING THERE AND AWAY The east coast can be easily reached by bus or dalla dalla from Zanzibar Town. North of Chwaka Bay, bus 6 goes to Chwaka (some continue to Uroa and Pongwe), 13 goes to Uroa (via Chwaka), 15 goes to Kiwengwa and 16 to Matemwe. South of the bay, bus 9 goes to Paje (sometimes continuing to Bwejuu or Jambiani) and 10 to Makunduchi. Chwaka Bay can sometimes be crossed by boat between Chwaka and Michamvi, with the help of local octopus fishermen. Most travellers prefer to use private transport to the east coast: several tour companies and some independent guides arrange minibuses (US$5–8pp each way). Unless you specify where you want to stay, minibus drivers are likely to take you to a hotel that gives them commission.

NORTHEASTERN ZANZIBAR Stretching from Nungwi on the northernmost tip of the island to the mangrove swamps of Chwaka Bay, the sand beaches of the northeastern coastline are breathtaking in length and beauty. Less than 1km offshore, waves break along the fringe reef that runs the length of the island, and the warm, turquoise waters of the Indian Ocean attract divers, swimmers and fishermen. Bordering the sand, an almost unbroken strip of picturesque coconut palms provides shade for traditional fishing villages and sunbathing honeymooners, and completes many people's vision of paradise.

The beaches along Zanzibar's east coast slope very little. Consequently, when the tide is out, the water retreats a long way, making swimming from the beach difficult. It does, however, allow for fascinating exploration along the top of the exposed reef. For diving in the area, One Ocean (w zanzibaroneocean.com) has offices in Kiwengwa and Matemwe, as well as at a number of hotels.

If you are staying in this part of Zanzibar, a worthwhile goal for a terrestrial day trip is the Kiwengwa Caves, which lie 3km inland of Kiwengwa within the 31km² Kiwengwa-Pongwe Forest Reserve. There are two near-contiguous caverns at the site. The longer cave is walkable for about 200m and it contains some truly impressive stalactites, stalagmites and other dripstone formations, along with an intimidating number of bats. The shorter cave is most notable for a beautiful skylight-like sinkhole 100m from the entrance and some interesting root systems that hang from the ceiling. Guided tours cost US$3 per person and leave from a manned visitors centre 800m south of a well-signposted junction on the main surfaced road running inland from Kiwengwa.

Where to stay and eat *Map, page 398*

The roughly 40km of coastline north of Chwaka Bay is lined with numerous lovely beaches and punctuated by a number of small traditional fishing villages, the most important of which – running from north to south – are Matemwe, Pwani Mchangani, Kiwengwa, Uroa and Chwaka. Hotels along this stretch of coast mostly fall into the mid-range to upmarket bracket, though good budget accommodation is available at Kiwengwa.

Exclusive

✱ **Matemwe Lodge** w asiliaafrica.com; ⌚ Jun–Mar. Smart yet informal, this quiet lodge comprises 14 stylish & well-equipped thatched cottages are perched on the edge of a low coral cliff with a superb view across to Mnemba Island. Lush tropical gardens lead to the swimming pools, dining area & sandy beach. Activities include snorkelling & sailing in dhows, fishing, diving, & escorted reef walks. The lodge supports the local community through the provision of fresh water, a primary school, 2 deep-sea dhows for fishing, & teaching English. Neighbouring **Matemwe Retreat** (**$$$$$$$**) offers 4 exclusive villas under the same management. **$$$$$$$**

✱ **Tulia Zanzibar** m +255 773 409377; w tuliazanzibar.com; ⌚ closed May. Set behind imposing timber gates in Pongwe, this beautiful resort is an oasis of calm, beauty & luxury modern design. It boasts beautiful indigenous botanical gardens, stylish sgl-storey suites with classic interiors blending European elegance with natural materials, & a poolside restaurant that serves some of Zanzibar's finest food. Aside from sophisticated chilling, guests (big & small) can giggle their way down the curvy water slide. One of the island's smartest & more sophisticated boutique hotels, with the benefit of a quiet seafront (if not beach) location & top-notch staff. **$$$$$$$**

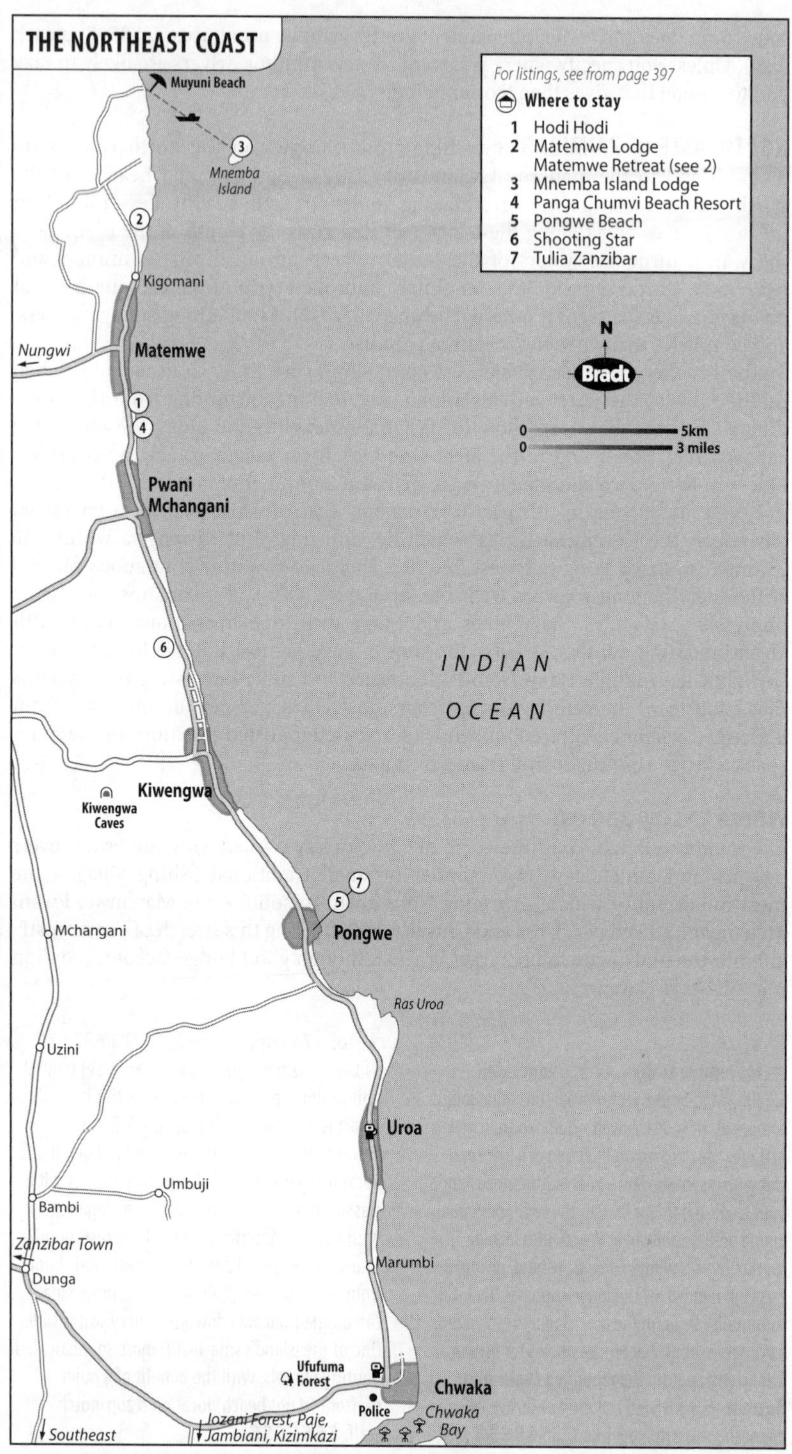
THE NORTHEAST COAST
For listings, see from page 397
Where to stay
1 Hodi Hodi
2 Matemwe Lodge
Matemwe Retreat (see 2)
3 Mnemba Island Lodge
4 Panga Chumvi Beach Resort
5 Pongwe Beach
6 Shooting Star
7 Tulia Zanzibar
Muyuni Beach
Mnemba Island
Kigomani
Nungwi
Matemwe
N
Bradt
0 5km
0 3 miles
Pwani Mchangani
INDIAN OCEAN
Kiwengwa
Kiwengwa Caves
Mchangani
Pongwe
Ras Uroa
Uzini
Uroa
Umbuji
Bambi
Zanzibar Town
Dunga
Marumbi
Ufufuma Forest
Chwaka
Police
Chwaka Bay
Southeast
Jozani Forest, Paje, Jambiani, Kizimkazi

Upmarket

✱ **Hodi Hodi** m +255 779 412603; w hodihodizanzibar.com. Set in the small village of Kilimajuu 2km south of Matemwe, this small, smart & welcoming lodge distils owner Julia Bishop's love of Africa, the sea & the environment into a gem of crafted beach-chic. It is all very low key, just as a homely beach retreat should be. On a tiny, picture-postcard little plot of coconut palms & ocean views, it consists of 3 houses: Poa, Toto & Dua, each with lovely open rooms & neat terraces overlooking the small garden & little oval pool. An honesty bar, daily cocktail hour & seasonal menu all make this a great spot for a quiet, chilled-out stay. *B&B*. **$$$$**

✱ **Pongwe Beach Hotel** m +255 773 169096; w pongwe.com; ⌚ closed May. This simple but well-managed & good-value 22-room lodge has a lovely beachfront location under a shady oasis of coconut palms within its own quiet cove. Some of the airy, whitewashed bungalows have garden views while others face out to sea. There's a lovely infinity pool, plenty of inviting hammocks & loungers, a small library, a kite for seaside entertainment, free kayak usage, an intimate tiered baraza lounge, tasty set-menu dinners & an array of other individual & group beach games. **$$$$**

✱ **SeVi Boutique Hotel** m +255 777 753220; w sevihotelzanzibar.com. Standing at the south end of a lovely curved beach, this terrific lodge lies on a pleasantly large & strikingly landscaped plot in Matemwe. The 14 bungalows are identical bar their view, with well-designed interiors & a veranda, shaded by banana trees & palms. The beachfront public areas are the real draw though: a bar/restaurant cantilevered over the beach, 3 inviting pools & the Tulia Spa in the centre of the gardens. *B&B*. **$$$$**

Shooting Star m +255 777 414166; w shootingstarlodge.com. Above Kiwengwa Beach, about 8km south of Matemwe, this is a social place whose 17 garden rooms, sea-view cottages & suites all feature Zanzibari beds & colourful Tingatinga pictures. An infinity pool & sundeck afford views over the ocean, reef & beach below. Dining is split across 3 shady areas, offering simple & filling meals, but it's the lively bar & relaxed lounge area that are the true heart of Shooting Star – & especially the lobster beach BBQ (extra US$45pp). Diving, snorkelling & fishing trips can be organised. **$$$$**

Zoi Boutique Hotel m +255 774 388662; w zoihotelzanzibar.com; ⌚ Jun–Apr. Formerly the Sunshine Hotel, Zoi occupies a relatively small plot on a sweeping curve of white sand in Matemwe. The immaculate gardens of raked stones & tropical trees, stylish architectural touches & calm efficiency lend this place a cool intimacy & prevent it from feeling claustrophobic. Light rooms are set in 2-storey chalets, some with private plunge pools & beach bandas. On the beachfront, the 2-tier restaurant & lounge overlooks a small, sailcloth-shaded infinity pool. The lively buzz will appeal to sociable young couples & urban escapists. **$$$$**

Moderate

* **Jafferji Beach Retreat** m +255 774 078441/2; w jafferjibeachretreat.com. Situated on Kigomani Beach north of Matemwe, this sister property to Stone Town's Jafferji House was converted from 2 beachfront family villas. Behind the modern beachfront facade, spacious & imaginatively decorated rooms evoke Zanzibar of old, with splashes of colour supplied by bright African fabrics. All rooms come with AC, fan, coffee station & flatscreen TV, & most also have a shared or private terrace with a full-on sea view. There's a large beachfront swimming pool, an excellent open-sided restaurant, & plenty of activities, including diving & snorkelling. Classy, laidback & superb value. *From US$120/149 sgl/dbl B&B*. **$$$**

Panga Chumvi Beach Resort m +255 777 344092; w pangachumvi.com. This locally owned 15-room place just south of Matemwe offers genuine eco-friendly accommodation just a stone's throw from a quiet stretch of beach. It has a varied selection of rooms & has a tranquil atmosphere. An on-site restaurant, complete with pizza oven, offers the usual Swahili fare. Community support is strong, with the owners heavily involved in Matemwe life & some interesting projects. Equally impressive is their real commitment to environmental awareness – an aspiration that many others on the island should embrace. *From US$70/90 sgl/dbl B&B*. **$$–$$$**

Budget

✱ **Lucrezia's Garden** m +255 622 159299; f. Owned & managed by a friendly hands-on Romanian-Tanzanian family that collectively speaks English, Spanish & Italian, this refreshingly non-institutional property in central Pwani

Mchangani comprises a 6-room 2-storey block overlooking a small swimming pool in a developing garden less than 500m from the beach. Spacious & well lit, the pastel-shaded rooms all come with AC, fan, modern bathroom & private terrace. Home-cooked Italian, Swahili and seafood meals can be prepared, or you can nip around the corner to the Waikiki Restaurant. Excellent value. *From US$50/55 sgl/dbl.* **$$**

✷ **Waikiki Resort** (16 rooms, 8 more under construction) m +255 777 877329; w waikikiafrica.com. This small Italian-English owner-managed resort in Pwani Mchangani provides budget travellers with a fun & offbeat option on a stretch of coast where upmarket all-inclusive resorts prevail. Life here focuses on the buzzing central restaurant, which is the most popular place for a bite in Pwani Mchangani. A variety of affordable makuti-roof bungalows, all with AC, fan, net & balcony, are dotted around the lushly vegetated beachfront property. On Fri it hosts a popular beach party & is perhaps best avoided by those seeking a quiet night. *From US$80 dbl. B&B.* **$$**

Mnemba Island The tiny island of Mnemba, officially titled Mnemba Island Marine Conservation Area (MIMCA), lies some 2.5km off the northeastern coast of Zanzibar, and forms part of the much larger submerged Mnemba Atoll. It is now privately leased by &Beyond and has become one of Africa's ultimate beach retreats. It cannot be visited without a reservation.

The island itself boasts wide beaches of white coral sand, fine and cool underfoot, backed by patches of tangled coastal bush and a small forest of casuarina trees. The small reefs immediately offshore offer a great introduction to the fishes of the reef for snorkellers, while diving excursions further afield allow you to explore the 40m-deep coral cliffs, a good place to see larger fish including the whale shark, the world's largest fish. The bird checklist for the island, though short, includes several unusual waders and other marine birds.

Getting there and away Overnight guests at Mnemba Island Lodge are chauffeur-driven from the airport or Stone Town to Muyuni Beach, north of Matemwe, from where it's a 15–20-minute ski-boat ride to the island.

Diving and snorkelling excursions to the reefs off Mnemba can be arranged through any dive school listed for Nungwi, Kendwa, Matemwe and elsewhere in northern Zanzibar (page 393). Many people also visit as a day outing from Stone Town; any tour operator or hotel there can put you in touch with a reputable operation.

Where to stay and eat

✷ **Mnemba Island Lodge** [map, page 398] andbeyond.com; ⌚ Jun–Mar. The crème de la crème of &Beyond's impressive portfolio, Mnemba Island Lodge is the height of rustic exclusivity. Overlooking the beach from the forest's edge, the 12 secluded, split-level bandas are constructed entirely of local timber & hand-woven palm fronds. Large, airy & open-plan, each has a huge bed & solid wooden furniture, softened with natural-coloured fabrics. The cuisine is excellent, with plenty of fresh seafood, fruit & vegetables, though guests may choose what, when & where to eat. A number of superb dive sites are within 15mins of the lodge. Up to 2 dives a day are included for qualified PADI divers, though courses are charged extra. There's also snorkelling, dbl kayaks, windsurfing, power-kiting, sailing, & fly or deep-sea fishing. Hot stone, aromatherapy, deep-tissue massage & reiki are all available too. Mnemba is unquestionably expensive, but its flexibility & service levels are second to none, & its idyllic location & proximity to outstanding marine experiences are very hard to match. **$$$$$$$**

JOZANI-CHWAKA BAY NATIONAL PARK (⌚ 07.30–17.00 daily; admission US$12 for a short guided walk or US$50 for a half-day hike) Zanzibar's only national park,

Jozani-Chwaka Bay protects a variety of wooded habitats, the most important of which are the largest surviving stand of the mature indigenous forest that once naturally covered much of the island, and the extensive mangroves that line the southern end of Chwaka Bay. The park extends for more than 100km² across the narrow low-lying isthmus that links the island's northwestern and southeastern components. The water table is very high and the area is prone to flooding in the rainy season, giving rise to this unique 'swamp-forest' environment. The large moisture-loving trees, the stands of palm and fern, and the humid air give the forest a cool, 'tropical' feel.

Jozani's main attraction is Kirk's red colobus, a beautiful and cryptically coloured monkey with an outrageous pale tufted crown. Unique to Zanzibar, Kirk's red colobus was reduced to a population of around 1,500 individuals in the mid 1990s, but recent researchers estimate between 1,600 and 3,000 individuals remain, whilst the IUCN (International Union for Conservation of Nature) classified it as endangered.

The forest used to be the main haunt of the Zanzibar leopard, an endemic subspecies long thought to be extinct until nocturnal footage was captured on a camera trap in June 2018. It is also home to Ader's duiker, a small antelope that may effectively now be a Zanzibar endemic, as it is probably extinct and certainly very rare in Kenya's Sokoke Forest, the only other place where it has ever been recorded. Several other mammal species live in Jozani, and the forest is one of the best birding sites on the island, hosting a good range of coastal forest birds, including an endemic race of the lovely Fischer's turaco.

When to visit Keen naturalists who want to watch wildlife undisturbed, or those who just like a bit of peace and quiet, should try to visit the reserve as soon as possible after it opens at 07.30 or in the early afternoon, as most tour groups from Stone Town come at about 09.00–10.00 on their way to the coast, or 15.00–16.00 on their way back. Wildlife tends to be rather subdued in the midday heat, so early morning is also the best time for spotting birds and watching monkey behaviour.

Getting there and away The entrance to the national park is clearly signposted on the main road between Zanzibar Town and the southern part of the east coast, north of the village of Pete. You can visit at most times of the year, but in the rainy season the water table rises considerably and the forest paths can be under more than 1m of water. The entrance fee includes the services of a mandatory guide and the mangrove boardwalk.

Many **tour companies** include Jozani on their east-coast tours or dolphin tours, but you can easily get here by frequent **public bus** (routes 9 or 10), **dalla dalla** (nos 309, 310, 324 or 326), hired **bike** or **car**. This road is well used by tourist minibuses and other traffic throughout the day, so after your visit to the forest you could flag something down and continue to the coast or return to Zanzibar Town.

Where to eat and drink *Map, page 404*

Although no overnight accommodation is available close to Jozani, there is now a very tempting restaurant for those who want to stop for lunch.

Jozani Maridadi Restaurant m +255 773 950022; e jozanimaridadi@outlook.com; ⌚ 10.00–16.00 daily. Set in lush green gardens about 1km southwest of the park reception, this attractive restaurant incorporates an open-sided makuti-roofed main building, a well-maintained swimming pool (usage of which is free to diners), a spa, & a rather bizarre domed building that was originally destined to be a jacuzzi. It offers the choice of a hand-eaten Swahili buffet (US$22pp) or a reasonably varied selection of seafood & other mains. $$$

What to see and do There are two guided nature trails, both of which must be explored in the company of an official guide in order to protect the monkeys from irresponsible tourists. Both trails start at the main reception, where you are unlikely to have to walk far to see both Kirk's red colobus and Sykes' monkey. Normally these animals are shy, and will leap through the trees as soon as they hear people approaching, but several troops that live around the reception are habituated to humans and can be watched at close quarters. This is ideal animal viewing – the monkeys are aware of your presence but not disturbed. They are not tame, and don't come close, but just get on with their usual feeding, playing, grooming or resting. As the colobus monkeys look so cute, some visitors have been tempted to try to stroke them or give sweets to them. This is very bad for the monkeys, but can be bad for tourists too – several people have been given a nasty nip or scratch (page 88). Look, but don't touch.

The more popular and cheaper short trail (US$12pp) takes up to 90 minutes to follow at a leisurely pace. It runs south from the reception for about 1.5km to a long thin mangrove-lined creek that extends inland from the island's south coast. Here, a fascinating mangrove boardwalk has been constructed, one of the few of its type in East Africa, so you can easily and harmlessly go deep into the mangrove to experience this unique ecosystem and look out for localised wildlife such as mudskippers (amphibious fish often seen on the mudflats) and the stunning aquamarine-coloured mangrove kingfisher (*Halcyon senegaloides*). This is also a community project, and revenue from visitors coming to the boardwalk helps fund local development projects.

The longer trail (US$50pp) runs north from the park reception to the Wangwani Wetlands, a 7km hike in either direction that usually takes around 5 hours in total. It is particularly recommended to serious birders and butterfly enthusiasts, or to anybody who wants to hike through the heart of the forest.

Zanzibar Butterfly Centre (ZBC; f ZanzibarButterflyCentre; ⏲ 09.00–17.00 daily; admission US$6) The Zanzibar Butterfly Centre aims to show visitors the forest's fluttering friends close up, as well as generating an income for local villagers and preserving the forest. Twenty-six local farmers have been taught to identify butterfly species, gently capture female butterflies, net small areas for breeding, harvest eggs, plant appropriate caterpillar fodder, and ultimately collect the resulting pupae for breeding the next generation. The pupae are then sold on to overseas zoos and live exhibits, or displayed for visitors to this centre in the large, netted tropical garden. Here, 200–300 colourful butterflies can be seen in the enclosure, making for a fascinating diversion and one of Africa's largest butterfly exhibits. There are good guides and clear informative signs to explain the project and butterfly lifecycle, and experienced photographers can get some wonderful shots. The income generated from visitors to ZBC is channelled back into further funding local conservation and poverty-alleviation projects, while the message is made clear to the communities that protecting the natural habitat of these insects provides much-needed income. The centre is a fun, worthwhile, 30-minute stop, and its location, just outside Jozani Forest, makes it a convenient addition to a forest trip.

SOUTHEASTERN ZANZIBAR Home to several of Zanzibar's most popular and developed beaches, the far southeast is linked to the main body of the island by the low-lying and relatively narrow forested isthmus protected within Jozani-Chwaka Bay National Park. Running from the north-pointing finger of the Michamvi Peninsula to the southern coastal curve bookended by Makunduchi and Kizimkazi, it offers, in many ways, a continuation of the powder-white sandy beaches and traditional fishing villages found from Matemwe to Chwaka Bay.

Coming from Zanzibar Town along the main road through Jozani Forest, the first coastal settlement you'll hit is **Paje**, a small fishing village situated at a junction, from where minor roads run north and south along the coast. The most important settlement north of Paje and south of Chwaka Bay is **Bwejuu**, a fishing village whose livelihood is linked to the gathering and production of seaweed. Several resorts catering to all budgets lie within a few kilometres' radius of Bwejuu. South of Paje, **Jambiani** is a substantial village that runs for several kilometres along the beach, while the more southerly town of **Makunduchi** lacks any real tourist development.

The **Michamvi Peninsula**, which demarcates Chwaka Bay, is very similar to the northeast of the island, with the same stunning powder-white beaches, barrier reef, palm trees and a significant tidal change.

Where to stay

Exclusive

Anna of Zanzibar (5 villas) **m** +255 773 999387; **w** annaofzanzibar.com. Staying at this small lodge in Dongwe feels like being welcomed into a friend's home. The 5 cosy but spacious villas are full of charm & fitted with minibars & a safe; for proximity to the sea, book villa 4 or 5. The villas surround the pool, which sits behind a lovely section of powdery sand, where dinners are served in suitable weather. On occasion, tasty 3-course meals are also eaten at the formal table in the dining room. The lounge is a popular place to kick back; there's a large satellite TV & DVD collection, plus a good range of novels & a pair of massage treatment rooms. **$$$$$$**

The Palms **m** +255 720 538148; **w** palms-zanzibar.com. Situated in Dongwe, The Palms is small & stylish, with a colonial feel, attracting affluent honeymooners lured by image & intimacy. In the colonnaded Plantation House, housing a bar/lounge, dining room & mezzanine library, antique furniture rests on highly polished floors, while old-fashioned fans spin in the high makuti thatch. In the 7 villas, huge rooms are classically elegant but with all mod-cons & a private outdoor plunge pool. They share a small swimming pool & each has a private banda overlooking the beach. Most activities take place at Breezes, which is right next door & under the same management. Min age 16. *AI*. **$$$$$$$**

Upmarket

✷ **Breezes Beach Club & Spa** **m** +255 720 538148; **w** breezes-zanzibar.com. A perennial favourite with honeymooners & families, Breezes is a large, efficient, family-run beach resort in Dongwe. Comfortable rooms are set in whitewashed villas with all the amenities of a good hotel. Facilities include a large swimming pool & a great stretch of sandy beach, plus plenty of watersports, including the independently owned Rising Sun Dive Centre (**w** risingsun-zanzibar.com). For landlubbers, there's a modern spa, yoga studio, fitness centre & tennis court. Several restaurants & bars complete the package, including a carved beach hut for dining *à deux* (but note that dinner at the smaller restaurants is not included in HB rates). Beach weddings, which must be arranged in advance, are increasingly popular here. *HB*. **$$$$**

✷ **Dhow Inn** **m** +255 777 525828; **w** dhowinn.com. In Paje, Dhow Inn's motto 'come as a guest, leave as family' rings true. 44 lovely, modern rooms are built in 2 neighbouring circles & 1 quadrangle, each of which encloses a whitewashed courtyard & swimming pool. Interiors are contemporary & thoughtfully finished, albeit set back from the water's edge. The atmospheric bar, Swahili charcoal grill & formal restaurant are all popular. Bike rental, beach volleyball, kitesurfing & massage treatments all available. *B&B/HB*. **$$$$**

Moderate

✷ **Bellevue Bungalows** [map, page 404] (13 rooms) **m** +255 718 384150; **e** bellevuezanzibar@gmail.com; **w** bellevuezanzibar.com. Perched on a coral rise north of Bwejuu, this consistently brilliant &

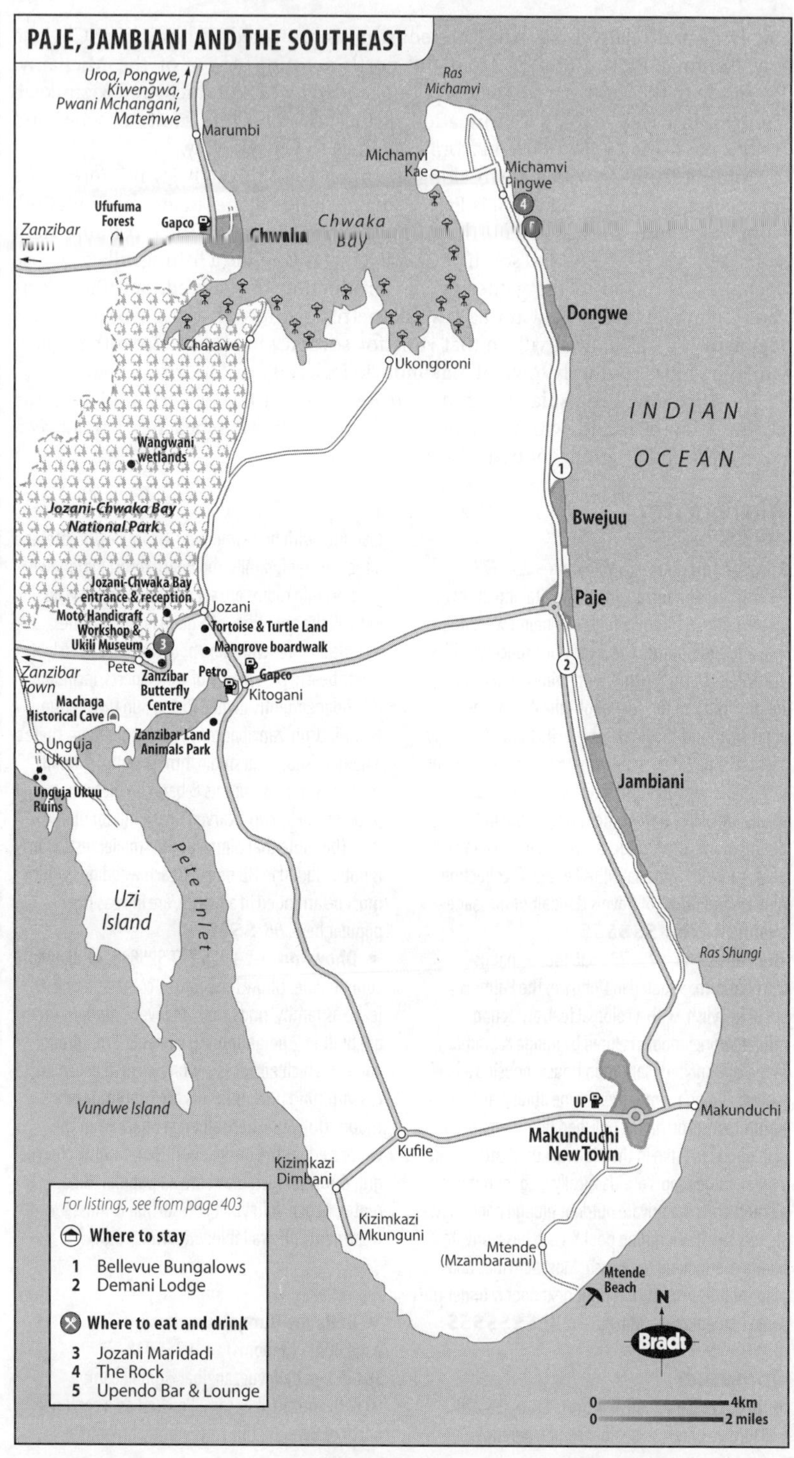
PAJE, JAMBIANI AND THE SOUTHEAST
Uroa, Pongwe, Kiwengwa, Pwani Mchangani, Matemwe
Marumbi
Ras Michamvi
Michamvi Kae
Michamvi Pingwe
Ufufuma Forest
Gapco
Zanzibar Town
Chwaka
Chwaka Bay
Dongwe
Charawe
Ukongoroni
INDIAN OCEAN
Wangwani wetlands
Jozani-Chwaka Bay National Park
Bwejuu
Jozani-Chwaka Bay entrance & reception
Paje
Jozani
Moto Handicraft Workshop & Ukili Museum
Tortoise & Turtle Land
Mangrove boardwalk
Pete
Zanzibar Town
Zanzibar Butterfly Centre
Petro
Gapco
Kitogani
Machaga Historical Cave
Zanzibar Land Animals Park
Unguja Ukuu
Unguja Ukuu Ruins
Jambiani
Pete Inlet
Uzi Island
Ras Shungi
Vundwe Island
UP
Makunduchi
Makunduchi New Town
Kufile
Kizimkazi Dimbani
Kizimkazi Mkunguni
Mtende (Mzambarauni)
Mtende Beach
For listings, see from page 403
Where to stay
1 Bellevue Bungalows
2 Demani Lodge
Where to eat and drink
3 Jozani Maridadi
4 The Rock
5 Upendo Bar & Lounge
N
Bradt
0 4km
0 2 miles

thoroughly relaxed Dutch-owned & -managed lodge is one of the best budget deals on the island. There are lush terraced gardens, the restaurant serves fresh healthy food, there's a super swimming pool, the rooms are filled with vibrant colour & it's only 50m from the beach. *US$80 standard dbl B&B.* **$$**

Blue Oyster Hotel (18 rooms) m +255 783 045796; w zanzibar.de. Set in lovely beachfront gardens in Jambiani, Blue Oyster remains one of the friendliest & best-value hotels in its range. Ground-floor rooms enclose a palm courtyard while others are in balconied 2-storey buildings. The wonderfully breezy 1st-floor restaurant, with a wide veranda overlooking the sea, offers a good selection of snacks, salads, pizzas & seafood & other grills. In front of the hotel a raised stretch of sand is perfect for sunbathing or a coconut-oil massage. *US$75–150 dbl, B&B.* **$$$**

Casa Beach Hotel m +255 773 696310; w casa-delmar-zanzibar.com; ⌚ Jun–Mar. Recently reopened following extensive renovations, the former Casa del Mar in Jambiani is run with impressive enthusiasm, skill & environmental awareness. Rooms are in thatched 2-storey houses, made almost entirely of organic material. The majority of the staff are Jambiani residents, & the school & clinic receive regular support. These credentials aside, the accommodation & friendly vibe are good reasons to stay, too. En-suite rooms are either 1- or 2-storey, both with balconies & the latter with a galleried bedroom high in the thatch, & a lounge (or children's room). Food is served in the shady restaurant, there's a new pool, & the lodge has its own boat for snorkelling trips *US$160/185 sgl/dbl B&B.* **$$$**

✷ **Driftwood Beach Lodge** m +255 774 236455; w driftwoodbeachlodge.com. Occupying a prime beachfront site in the heart of Jambiani, this intimate low-rise lodge has 8 recently renovated standard rooms, some with AC & others with ceiling fan only, as well as 2 newer bungalows with fan only. All are simply but brightly decorated with makuti roofs, local paintings, wooden bed, fitted net, modern bathroom & private terrace. A lovely infinity pool practically opens out onto the beach, while the open-sided restaurant/bar has a sociable atmosphere & serves a cosmopolitan menu of tasty seafood, curries, Chinese-French fusion dishes & Swahili cuisine. An unpretentious, well-priced gem. *From US$82/130 sgl/dbl B&B.* **$$$**

✷ **Mahali Zanzibar** m +255 778 382915; w mahalizanzibar.com. A Swahili name meaning 'The Spot', Mahali has lived up to its name by becoming one of Paje's most stylish & consistently popular places to stay since it was opened by its welcoming Dutch owner-managers in 2017. The 24 rooms are in 2-storey blocks that overlook a large beachfront swimming pool but are angled so that all have a partial sea view from the balcony. Smart but unfussy, the large & neat rooms all come with king-size 4-poster bed & fitted net, AC, fan, fridge, kettle & modern en-suite bathroom. The attached beach café is a gem but there are plenty of other restaurants within 5mins' walking distance. *From US$120 dbl B&B.* **$$$**

✷ **Villa Bahati Zanzibar** m +255 748 235949; w bahati-zanzibar.info. Owned & managed by an Austrian IYC-certified yoga instructor, this homely beachfront villa in Jambiani comprises a pair of 2-storey whitewashed coral rag Swahili-style buildings with makuti roofs & plentiful arches. Cool, spacious rooms are decorated in traditional Swahili style with antique Zanzibari beds, fitted nets, colourful local paintings on the walls, fan & AC, & large stylish bathrooms fitted with terrazzo stone or Moroccan-style concrete. B/fasts are taken on a wide terrace that overlooks a swimming pool & leafy tropical garden running down to the beach. It runs 10-day yoga & mindfulness courses in Feb & Oct/Nov. An on-site spa offers massages using locally made seaweed products. *From US$90 dbl B&B.* **$$–$$$**

Budget

Demani Lodge [map, page 404] m +255 778 889298; e demanilodge.com. Situated on the road between Paje & Jambiani, delightful Demani is a top choice for anyone on a tight budget who still wants a decent standard. Chill-out music, good vibes & interesting character added to a great recent renovation make it hard to beat for value. The 20 rooms stand in friendly circles around well-screened grounds & there's also the island's most immaculate dorm. A swimming pool, rainbow hammocks, a fire pit & a terrific all-you-can-eat Swahili night (Thu) make the 10min walk to the beach acceptable. One of the island's best budget deals. *From US$32/52 sgl/dbl, US$20 dorm bed B&B.* **$–$$**

BEACHED SEAWEED

From December to mid-February, some of the beaches on the east coast have large patches of brown seaweed washed ashore by the wind. This can be quite a shock if you expect pristine, picture-postcard tropical beach conditions. The seaweed normally stays on the beaches until the start of the rainy season, when it is carried back out to sea. After March, and up until November, the beaches are mostly clear.

✷ **New Teddy's on the Beach** (8 rooms & 2 dorms) m +255 773 096306; e info@teddys-place.com; w teddys-place.com. Formerly the Jambiani Beach Hotel but taken over by now new hands-on German owner-managers, New Teddy's is the busiest backpacker hangout in Jambiani, if not anywhere in the southeast. The renovated en suite rooms all have net, fan, local paintings on the wall & private balcony. The makuti-roofed dorms both have 12 bunk beds, fan, nets & private lockers. Situated right on the beach, the large palm-shaded gardens include a sociable beach bar serving cocktails & mocktails, a large swimming pool, a well-priced restaurant, & a handicraft shop. A standout option for sociable backpackers. *US$26pp dorm bed, US$70 dbl.* **$$**

Where to eat and drink

✷ **Bahari Pizza** m +255 624 940614; f BahariPizzaRestaurant. One of Jambiani's most popular & lively restaurants, Italian-owned Bahari is a fabulous makuti construction with a relaxed vibe, a great seafront location & an extensive menu dominated by excellent pizzas (more than 50 varieties straight from a wood-fired oven) & so-so seafood. Booking is advisable on Fri night, when a local band cranks out a mix of contemporary & traditional Tanzanian music. **$$**

✷ **Mr Kahawa** m +255 785 355105; w mrkahawa.com/restaurant; ⌚ 08.00–21.30 daily. Dutch-run Mr Kahawa (meaning Mr Coffee) is a stylish beachfront café that serves the best coffee on the east coast, plus delicious homemade baguettes, salads, cakes & smoothies. It occasionally hosts live music & a fair-trade craft & souvenir market. **$$**

The Rock Restaurant [map, page 404] m +255 776 591360; w therockrestaurantzanzibar.com; ⌚ 4 seatings daily, at noon, 14.00, 16.00 & 18.00. Perched on an undercut coral-rock outcrop marooned offshore of Michamvi Peninsula, The Rock has probably the most remarkable location of any Zanzibar restaurant. Accessed by wandering across the sand at low tide, or by boat or breaststroke at high tide, the local team in this dilapidated building serve up a simple 'catch of the day' & seafood pasta dishes. The views are terrific, the staff friendly & the experience unique. Call in advance or book online, especially if you're coming a distance. **$$$**

✷ **Upendo Bar & Lounge** m +255 777 770667; w upendozanzibar.com; ⌚ 10.00 until last customer leaves daily. On a gorgeous sweep of beach, this is the perfect place to while away an afternoon, where gentle bar staff mix tantalising cocktails & exotic mocktails. London lounge music is piped into the shady, cushion-covered beach barazas, & tasty treats are cooked to order. Sun brunches are an island institution, but it's worth a trip any time. Understated beach chic: a perfect place to just lose time. **$$$**

What to see and do

Watersports As with most of coastal Zanzibar, the main focus of the tourist agenda is swimming and sunbathing. Diving and snorkelling can be arranged anywhere along the southeast coast, while the main local of kitesurfing is Paje. The following operators are recommended.

Buccaneer Diving m +255 777 853403; w buccaneerdiving.com. This efficient 5* PADI dive school in Paje has a purpose-built classroom, a swimming pool for coursework & a resident team of experienced expat instructors & dive masters, who between them speak 4 languages.

Kite Centre Zanzibar m +255 777 846083; w kitecentrezanzibar.com; ⏱ mid-Dec–mid-Mar & mid-Jun–mid-Oct. Under the same Dutch management as the adjacent Mr Kahawa, this IKO-accredited activity outfit was one of original kiting operations on the island & it continues to offer high-quality, branded kit, lessons & courses with experienced instructors & a thoroughly exhilarating seaside diversion.

The Loop Watersports Centre m +255 773 696310; w theloopzanzibar.com. Run by a vastly experienced Italian sailor, this smart new watersports centre in Jambiani offers sailing excursions, kayaking, catamaran rental & quad bike trips.

Cycling Based in Paje's craft market, **Paje Bike Tours & Rental** (m +255 779 424173; w pajebiketours.weebly.com) rents out bicycles for US$10/49 per day/week and also offers a range of six reasonably priced guided 2–5-hour cycling tours to the likes of Jozani Forest, Kuza Cave and various snorkelling sites for US$20–45 per person (minimum group size two), depending on the duration. Check the website for full details.

Kuza Cave The coral rock that underlays southeast Zanzibar is riddled with limestone caverns carved by the sea or underground rivers around 250,000 years ago. The most accessible of these is Kuza Cave (m +255 777 672652; w kuzacave.com; ⏱ 08.00–18.00 daily; entrance & guided tour US$10), which lies inland of Jambiani and is well developed for tourism. Short guided tours are included in the entrance fee and include a detailed explanation of the caves geology and long history of human habitation, as well as an opportunity to swim in the beautiful and staggeringly clear freshwater pool at its base. In addition, a small café serves simple and inexpensive Swahili meals and cooking sessions, and a traditional drum and dance session is held there at 19.30 on Tuesdays. Kuza Cave lies just 600m west of the main surfaced road through Jambiani, and the turn-off is clearly signposted about 4.5km south of Paje Roundabout.

ECO+CULTURE JAMBIANI CULTURAL TOURS

Probably the island's best insight into genuine rural life, the Eco+Culture village tours are guided by Jambiani resident Ramadhan Issa (m +255 777 843021/665444; e rama20issa@gmail.com). Meet in the small, signposted hut in the centre of Jambiani (opposite the school), or be collected on foot from your hotel for these well-run, enlightening community-focused walks. A percentage of your fee goes directly towards community-development initiatives, a direct result of the organisation's original NGO status.

Depending on your enthusiasm and heat tolerance, tours last anything from a few hours to the best part of a day and take in many aspects of everyday life. Spend time helping the women make coconut paste, reciting the alphabet in unison at the efficient kindergarten and meeting the *mganga* (traditional healer). Kassim's presence, reputation within the community and ability to translate allow for genuine interaction with the Jambiani residents and a thoroughly engaging time.

Do be aware that of late there are a few villagers operating inferior copycat walks. It is well worth taking the time to seek out Ramadhan Issa or the Eco+Culture office, not only for his knowledge and friendliness, but also to be sure that your money is directed back into vital village projects.

KIZIMKAZI The small town of Kizimkazi lies on the southwestern end of the island, and is best known to tourists as the place to see humpback and bottlenose dolphins, both of which are resident in the area.

Getting there and away

Most tourists visit Kizimkazi on an **organised day tour** out of Zanzibar Town, which costs US$25–100 per person, depending on group size, season and trip quality, including transport to/from Kizimkazi, the boat, all snorkelling gear and lunch. Alternatively, the town can be reached independently in a **hired car**, or with **dalla dalla** 326 from Zanzibar Town.

Where to stay and eat

Karamba m +255 773 166406; w karambazanzibar.com. This attractive clifftop lodge is one of this coast's most appealing. Rooms have individual interiors, are decorated in nautical blues & whites, & boast outdoor baths or open-air showers hewn into coral rock. There are also 4 new duplex bungalows for up to 6 people & a honeymoon villa for rustic luxury. All rooms enjoy a sea view from the veranda though the harbour vista from the cushioned lounge/restaurant is arguably the finest of them all, with cocktails overlooking the sunset dhow activity making for a quintessentially Zanzibari experience. A Tanga-stone swimming pool, yoga, reiki & Ayurvedic therapies are also available. *B&B.* **$$$$**

✷ **Mama Root** (6 rooms) m+255 621 871002; w mamaroot.com. The most central option in Kizimkazi Mkunguni, this delightfully quirky Polish-Zanzibari-owned & -managed budget lodge comprises a converted 1990s villa overlooking the dhow harbour. Imaginatively & individually decorated, the rooms all have treated concrete floors painted with bananas & palm fronds, king-size or queen-size bed with fitted net & AC but no fan. African-style seafood meals are eaten communally, but they will gladly cater to vegetarian & vegan diets, ideally with some notice. This is a super-friendly & refreshingly unconventional set-up that will hold great appeal to sociable travellers, vegetarians & anybody seeking to connect with the local community or get in touch with their inner hippy. *US$60-70 dbl. B&B.* **$$**

✷ **The Residence by Cenizaro** 024 555 5000; w cenizaro.com. Set on a delightfully calm stretch of powdery beach 3km north of Kizimkazi, The Residence comprises 66 plush villas, each with its own large private terrace & generously sized swimming pool. They are divided into 6 categories, with varying views, sizes & number of bedrooms, but all are extremely well appointed with satellite TV, minibar, safe, bathrobes, slippers…the list goes on. Each guest is provided with a bicycle to explore the complex, but you can also give reception a call for a lift in a golf buggy. The main complex is spread over a number of buildings, including 2 superb restaurants, as well as a swimming pool with glass sides & the first hotel spa on Zanzibar to offer ohashiatsu, an energy-based massage therapy. There is good birding in the grounds, which extend across 32ha & retain plenty of indigenous vegetation, as well as troops of Kirk's red colobus & Sykes' monkeys. *HB/AI.* **$$$$$$$**

Sarabi Zanzibar m +255 776 863961; w sarabizanzibar.com. Situated 100m south of Kizimkazi Mkunguni dhow harbour, Sarabi (literally 'Mirage') opened in 2019 under the same dynamic Dutch management as Paje's Mahali Zanzibar. The 21 rooms & luxury suites are cheerful & tastefully decorated with terracotta tile floor, queen-size Zanzibari bed, fitted net, wooden furniture, AC & private terrace. The suites also have a sitting room, sea view & private plunge pool. Amenities include a private beach with parasols, an attractive swimming pool area & a good restaurant serving seafood, curries & Swahili cuisine. Overall, a very convenient, well-run, reasonably priced & attractive small resort. *From US$90 dbl B&B.* **$$–$$$**

What to see and do

Dolphin watching The best time of year to see the dolphins is between October and February. From June to September, the southerly winds can make the seas rough, while during the rainy season (March to May), conditions in the boat can be unpleasant. However, out at sea you're likely to get wet anyway. You should also protect yourself against the sun. Sightings used to be almost guaranteed, but it's not unusual now for groups to return without having seen a single dolphin. Sadly, as the disturbances from too many boats and people increasingly outweigh the benefits of food and shelter, this trend is likely to continue, with fewer and fewer dolphins appearing in Kizimkazi's waters.

Never encourage your pilot to chase the dolphins or try to approach them too closely yourself. With up to 100 people visiting Kizimkazi daily in the high season, there is genuine cause to fear that tourism may be detrimental to the animals. If you do get close enough and you want to try your luck swimming with the dolphins, slip (rather than dive) into the water next to the boat, and try to excite their interest by diving frequently and holding your arms along your body to imitate their streamlined shape.

Kizimkazi Mosque Hidden behind its new plain walls and protective corrugated-iron roof, the mosque at Kizimkazi Dimbani is believed to be the oldest Islamic building on the East African coast. The floriate Kufic inscription to the left of the mihrab (the interior niche indicating the direction of Mecca) dates the original mosque construction to AD1107 and identifies it as the work of Persian settlers. The silver pillars on either side of the niche are decorated with pounded mullet shells from the island of Mafia, and the two decorative clocks, which show Swahili time (6 hours' difference from European time), were presented by local dignitaries. However, though the fine-quality coral detailing and columns date from this time, most of the building actually dates from an 18th-century reconstruction. The more recent additions of electrical sockets and flex have not been installed with a comparable degree of style or decoration.

Outside the mosque are some old tombs, a few decorated with pillars and one covered by a small makuti roof. The pieces of cloth tied to the edge of the tomb are prayer flags. The raised aqueduct that carried water from the well to the basin where hands and feet were washed is no longer used: running water is piped straight into a more recently built ablution area at the back of the mosque.

Archaeological evidence suggests that when the mosque was built, Kizimkazi was a large walled city. Tradition holds that it was founded and ruled by King Kizi, and that the architect of the mosque itself was called Kazi.

Today, very little of the old city remains, but non-Muslims, both men and women, are welcome to visit the mosque and its surrounding tombs. It's normally locked, and you'll probably have to find the caretaker with the key (he lives nearby, but is usually under the trees near the beach a few hundred metres further down the road). Show respect by removing your shoes and covering bare arms and legs, if they aren't already. On leaving you'll be shown the collection box for donations.

PEMBA ISLAND

Lying to the northeast of the larger island of Zanzibar and directly east of the mainland port of Tanga, Pemba is visited by few travellers. While tourist facilities on Zanzibar have mushroomed in recent years, Pemba has changed little over the last decade, making it a particularly attractive destination for those seeking to 'get away from it all'.

Pemba has a more undulating landscape than Zanzibar, and is more densely vegetated with both natural forest and plantation. The main agricultural product is cloves, which Pemba produces in far greater abundance than Zanzibar, with the attendant heady aroma permeating much of the island.

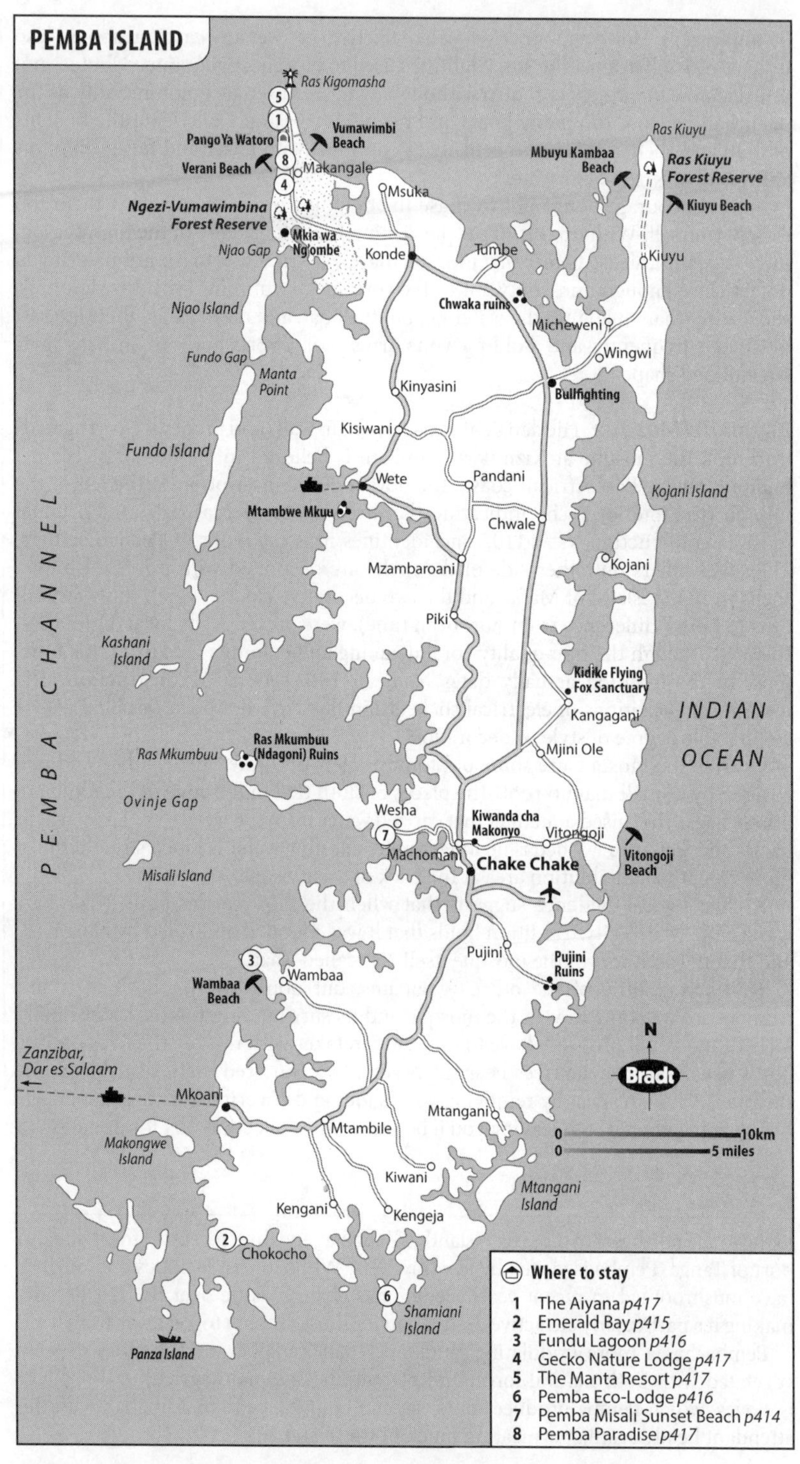
PEMBA ISLAND
Ras Kigomasha
Pango Ya Watoro
Vumawimbi Beach
Verani Beach
Makangale
Ngezi-Vumawimbina Forest Reserve
Mkia wa Ng'ombe
Njao Gap
Msuka
Konde
Tumbe
Ras Kiuyu
Mbuyu Kambaa Beach
Ras Kiuyu Forest Reserve
Kiuyu Beach
Kiuyu
Chwaka ruins
Micheweni
Njao Island
Wingwi
Fundo Gap
Manta Point
Bullfighting
Kinyasini
Kisiwani
Fundo Island
Wete
Pandani
Mtambwe Mkuu
Kojani Island
Chwale
Kojani
Mzambaroani
Piki
PEMBA CHANNEL
Kashani Island
Kidike Flying Fox Sanctuary
Kangagani
INDIAN OCEAN
Ras Mkumbuu
Ras Mkumbuu (Ndagoni) Ruins
Mjini Ole
Ovinje Gap
Wesha
Kiwanda cha Makonyo
Vitongoji
Machomani
Chake Chake
Vitongoji Beach
Misali Island
Pujini
Pujini Ruins
Wambaa
Wambaa Beach
N
Bradt
Zanzibar, Dar es Salaam
Mkoani
Mtangani
Mtambile
0 10km
0 5 miles
Makongwe Island
Kiwani
Mtangani Island
Kengani
Kengeja
Chokocho
Shamiani Island
Panza Island
Where to stay
1 The Aiyana p417
2 Emerald Bay p415
3 Fundu Lagoon p416
4 Gecko Nature Lodge p417
5 The Manta Resort p417
6 Pemba Eco-Lodge p416
7 Pemba Misali Sunset Beach p414
8 Pemba Paradise p417

There is nothing on Pemba to compare with Zanzibar's Stone Town, but it does boast a number of attractive beaches, as well as some absorbing ruins dating to the Shirazi era. During holidays, traditional bullfights are sometimes held, presumably introduced during the years of Portuguese occupation. The island is also a centre for traditional medicine and witchcraft, and it is said that people seeking cures for spiritual or physical afflictions come from as far away as Uganda and the Congo to see Pemba's doctors.

Accommodation is limited to just a handful of lodges, hotels and guesthouses. Most are geared to the diver in search of the island's renowned underwater attractions, including some exciting drift dives and the possibility of seeing some of the larger pelagics.

The island's largest town is Chake Chake. To the north lies the port of Wete, while to the southwest is the port of Mkoani, used by most passenger ferries. There are banks and post offices in Chake Chake, Wete and Mkoani, but none has ATMs, so taking cash is advisable. The main hospital is in Chake Chake, where there is also a ZTC office.

GETTING THERE AND AWAY

By air

Domestic services Daily services run between Dar es Salaam and Pemba, although all flights go via Zanzibar, and some may involve a change of plane. The duration of the flight is just over an hour. The modern terminal, located 7km southeast of Chake Chake, has few facilities – just a small shop selling drinks and snacks and a couple of toilets. Auric Air (w auricair.com), Coastal Aviation (w coastal.co.tz) and ZanAir (w zanair.com) all operate scheduled flights to Pemba from Dar es Salaam and/or Zanzibar and/or Tanga, with Coastal Aviation being particularly useful when it comes to connections to the Serengeti, Nyerere and other mainland safari destinations. Check the individual carrier's websites for up-to-date schedules.

Private plane charter If you can get a group together and charter a whole plane, it can sometimes be cheaper per person than buying a ticket on a regular flight. From mainland Tanzania and Kenya, travel agents in Dar, Nairobi or Mombasa will be able to help you – they will probably phone the airport or one of the local charter companies to see if anything is going your way. To book scheduled or charter flights to the mainland from Pemba, contact any of the airlines listed on page 356, or phone the airport control tower (☎ 024 245 2238) and enquire yourself. This is a fairly standard procedure – the charter companies often tell the tower if they're looking for passengers to fill spare seats.

For planes from Zanzibar Island, contact one of the local air-charter companies in Zanzibar Town. In high season there are flights at least every other day, so it's worth contacting the companies direct, or getting a travel agency to do it for you, to see if there's anything going (for contact details, see page 428).

By sea

The main ferry port on Pemba is at Mkoani in the south.

Azam Marine & Coastal Fast Ferries ☎ 022 212 3324; w azammarine.com. The best of the commercial passenger boats to Pemba from Zanzibar. It's a 4-times-weekly service, taking around 3hrs in either direction. It leaves Zanzibar for Mkoani at 07.30 on Wed, Thu, Sat & Sun, & Mkoani for Zanzibar at 07.30 on Thu, Fri & Sun, & at 09.00 on Tue. The fare is US$35/45 economy/1st class one-way). There is no direct service from Dar, but it is possible to leave form Dar at 18.00 the previous evening & travel via Zanzibar to Pemba, although this is a lengthy trip. There is also a weekly service between Pemba & Tanga, leaving Pemba at 14.30 on Sun & Tanga at 23.00 on Mon.

MV *Mapinduzi II* m +255 777 438739; w shipco.go.tz. Zanzibar Shipping Corporation (ZSC), the state-owned line, runs the new MV *Mapinduzi II* ('Revolution'). This Korean-built, cargo-passenger ship is generally used by local people because it is cheap (Mon & Fri; US$25/35 economy/1st class one-way), but some travellers on a tight budget also travel this way. Although this service is slow, the cabins are quite airy & comfortable. Under maintenance at the time of writing, it leaves Zanzibar for Mkoani on Mon & Fri at 07.30 & travels in the opposite direction at the same time on Tue & Sat.

Zan Fast Ferries w zanzibarfastferries.com. This new operator is the only one that runs between Zanzibar and Wete harbour, a 7hr trip. It departs from Zanzibar at 10.00 on Sun & 07.30 on Thu, & does the return trip from Wete at 07.30 on Mon & Fri.

GETTING AROUND Pemba's road system was given a boost in 2005 with the completion of the tarred road across the island from Mkoani to Konde, paid for by the World Bank. North of Konde, and elsewhere, however, most of the roads are pretty poor, with access to some of the outlying villages requiring **4x4** vehicles, particularly in the rainy season. A network of inexpensive **dalla dallas** connects most main points of interest on Pemba, starting up at 06.00 (or 04.00 during Ramadan), with the regularity of the service depending on the popularity of the route; one of the most frequent is the No 606, with several buses each day. Services to and from Mkoani are tied in closely with ship arrivals. Fares on the longer routes, such as Chake Chake to Mkoani, are around US$1 one-way, with shorter trips about half that. The most useful routes are listed below (though note that dalla dallas will stop to collect or drop off passengers at any point along their route).

601	Wete to Konde
602	Chake Chake to Konde
603	Chake Chake to Mkoani
606	Chake Chake to Wete
305	Chake Chake to Wesha (Chake's port)
316	Chake Chake to Vitongoji (5km east of Chake Chake)
319	Chake Chake to Pujini
330	Chake Chake to Wambaa
10	Wete to Wingwi/Micheweni

Other **buses** connect Chake Chake and, to a lesser extent, Wete, with outlying villages; for details, check with the station manager at the bus depot in each town.

Most **tour companies** on the island can arrange car hire with a driver at around US$60 per day. Recommended drivers include Zahran Yahya (m +255 776 171208; e zaharayahya1985@gmail.com), Mohammed Amir (m +255 777 430816), Said Mohammed (m +255 777 430201) and Suleiman Seif (m +255 777 431793). It is rare for tourists to hire cars in Pemba, and not the easiest thing to organise.

It's normally possible to arrange **bicycle hire** through your hotel reception for around US$10 per day, and **motorbike hire** for around US$22 per day.

CHAKE CHAKE This is the largest town on Pemba, and several centuries old, but it has never achieved a degree of importance comparable to Zanzibar Town. The busy market area and old port are pleasant to walk around, and seem very relaxed and untouristy after Zanzibar, but sightseeing is pretty much limited to the remains of an Omani fort near the modern hospital, part of which is now a good little museum.

Travel and tour operators The tourist who arrives in Chake Chake in the hope of organising something on the fly could well be disappointed, since the town is less geared to visitors than in the past. The best bets are:

Azam Marine w azammarine.com. Next to the market, this is the main agent for ferries to Zanzibar (page 356).

Coastal Travels m +255 777 418343; ⌚ 07.30–17.00. This helpful bureau is set up to handle bookings of Coastal Aviation flights between Pemba & Zanzibar, Tanga & Dar.

Msewe Travel ☎ 024 245 2774; e mseweto urs@gmail.com; f MseweTravelLtd. Managed by the very friendly & enthusiastic Kassim, Msewe is down a tiny side street just across the road from the Chake Hotel. The office provides lots of information on excursions, flights, ferries, diving, bullfighting & transfers. Other offices in Arusha & at Pemba Airport.

Where to stay *Map, page 413, unless otherwise stated*

There are a few central options, of which the Chake Hotel is easily your best bet. Sadly, one by one, the small collection of clean and basic guesthouses just north of town have closed down. Alternatively, there is the superior out-of-town Pemba Misali Sunset Beach Hotel.

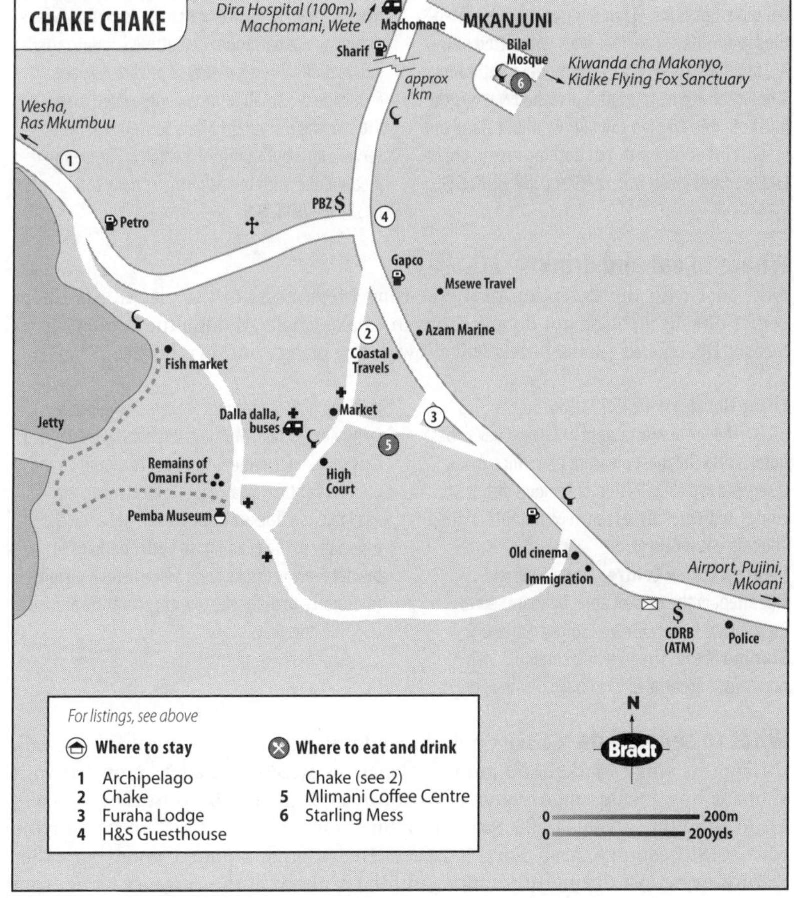

Archipelago Hotel m +255 654 473772/778 373737; e baraka@zanlink.com. Formerly the Hifadhi Hotel but now under the same competent ownership as Zanzibar Town's Archipelago Restaurant & Stone Town Café, this pale blue-&-white building with banks of mirrored windows has the look of a hospital or government department. The 13 rooms have Zanzibari beds with fitted nets, as well as AC, TV & decent bathrooms. It is also the only place in town with a swimming pool, which is set in small green gardens. A good restaurant is attached. Rather charmless, but well run. *US$50/85 sgl/dbl. B&B.* **$$**

✷ **Chake Hotel** m +255 777 766766; e chakehotel@outlook.com. Far & away the nicest & best-value option in Chake Chake, this couldn't-be-more-central new 8-room hotel has been converted from the old Barclays Bank building. Spacious, clean & agreeably decorated tiled rooms have Zanzibar beds with fitted net, AC, fan, flatscreen cable TV & modern bathroom. A good terrace restaurant is attached & it has the most reliable Wi-Fi in town. It wouldn't stand out in most other contexts, but nothing else in Chake Chake comes close. *US$52/60 sgl/dbl. B&B.* **$$**

Furaha Lodge (8 rooms) m +255 777 420822. This simple hotel has adequate rooms with bathroom & ceiling fan. No Wi-Fi. *US$26 dbl. B&B.* **$**

H&S Guesthouse (6 rooms) m +255 777 451266. Formerly Hotel Le Tavern & still known by that name locally, this very basic place stands on the main street above a small row of shops alongside the town's only traffic light. Run-down en-suite rooms have twin or dbl beds with nets, fans & dodgy plumbing. No Wi-Fi. *US$30 dbl or twin. B&B.* **$**

Pemba Misali Sunset Beach [map, page 410] (20 villas) m +255 776 531214; w oceangrouphotel.com. North of Chake Chake, near the village of Wesha, Pemba Misali Sunset Beach's row of pea-green villas occupies a pretty waterfront spot, with sea views for all, albeit mangrove not powder-sand beaches. All rooms have wooden king-size or twin beds, nets, AC, fans, a shiny white bathroom & shuttered, handcrafted louvre doors. There's plenty of privacy & space, & outside is a small terrace. Cantilevered over the sea, the restaurant offers sunset views while serving up a buffet mix of Swahili & European meals along with the fisherman's daily catch. *US$80 dbl B&B.* **$$**

Where to eat and drink *Map, page 413*

Note that with the exception of the Starling Mess, none of the places listed here serves or sells alcohol, nor do any shops in Chake Chake, though the Pemba Misali Sunset Beach and Chake hotels will allow you to bring your own bottle.

Chake Hotel m +255 777 766766; ⌚ 07.30–21.00. The terrace restaurant at Chake Chake's best hotel is also the most pleasant place for a meal. It serves a typical selection of seafood dishes & curries, with friendly & relatively prompt service. The coffee is excellent. $

Mlimani Coffee Centre Down a narrow side street in the market area, Milmani serves inexpensive freshly brewed spiced coffees. $

Starling Mess Situated in Mkanjuni 2.5km northeast of central Chake Chake, Pemba's only drinking hole stands in a garden-like military camp next to Bilal Mosque. 2 separate open-sided bars serve beer, wine & spirits to consume on the premises or take away. Simple local meals are available too. The atmosphere can get a rowdy, especially in the evening, so better perhaps to buy take-away drinks & eat elsewhere. A pikipiki (motorbike taxi) for the town centre costs around US$1.50 one-way.

What to see and do Chake Chake has a dusty charm that is revealed by a walk through its small market and around its narrow streets and alleys crowded with shops selling a wide range of goods. Worth a visit is the **Pemba Museum** (⌚ 09.00–16.30 Mon–Fri, 09.00–16.00 Sat–Sun; admission US$3). Located in part of the town's 18th-century Arab Fort, it retains the original wooden door, but other features were lost during restoration, and the cannons at the entrance came from

Wete. Clearly laid-out exhibits cover every aspect of Pemba's history, economy and culture and of particular interest is the display on the ruins of Pemba, and the room on the island's maritime history and boatbuilding. Also, several rooms are set out to represent the interior of a Swahili house, while related displays focus on individual aspects of Swahili culture, from initiation and burial rituals to the use of herbal plants and traditional musical instruments. Visitors are accompanied around the exhibitions by a guide.

Excursions

Kiwanda cha Makonyo (☎ 024 245 2221; **w** zstcznz.org; admission US$5) Meaning 'Industry for Clove-buds' Kiwanda cha Makonyo is a state-run distillery where essential oils are extracted from cloves and other plants. Guided tours run you through the production process, and the resultant oils and associated organic products are sold on site. A pikipiki should cost around US$2 one-way, or you could take dalla dalla no 316.

Kidike Flying Fox Sanctuary (**m** +255 777 472941/429280; ⏲ 09.00–18.00 daily; admission US$5/1 adult/child) Just 7km north of Chake Chake is Kidike, home to more than half of Pemba's flying foxes. At the reserve, a local guide will show you the pathways through the forest to see the 4,000 flying foxes that roost in the treetops, feeding and, of course, flying overhead with their distinctive silhouette. Several tour operators run trips here, and individual drivers charge around US$25 from Chake Chake, including entrance. Alternatively, you can take a dalla dalla from Chake Chake, then walk the 45 minutes or so along the 3.5km track to the reserve.

Ras Mkumbuu Ruins About 14km west of Chake Chake, these well-preserved ruins lie at the tip of a long peninsula. Thought to have been one of the largest towns on the coast during the 11th century, Ras Mkumbuu may also have been the site of the earlier port of Qanbalu. Today, the remains of a mosque are visible, albeit overgrown, along with several pillar tombs.

The most enjoyable way to reach Ras Mkumbuu is by boat, perhaps combined with a visit to Misali Island. While there is a road from Chake Chake, the final 5km is negotiable only on foot or by bike.

Pujini Ruins This site is about 10km southeast of Chake Chake. You can walk there and back in a day, but it is easier to travel by hired bike or car. The ruins are the remains of a 13th-century Swahili town, known locally as Mkame Ndume ('milker of men'), after a despotic king who forced the inhabitants to carry large stones for the town walls while shuffling on their buttocks. The overgrown remains of the walls and ditches can be seen, as can a walkway which joined the town to the shore, some wide stairways that presumably allowed access to the defensive ramparts, and the site of the town's well.

MKOANI AND THE SOUTH The smallest of the three main towns on Pemba, Mkoani is the main arrival point for boat services from Zanzibar and Dar es Salaam.

Where to stay and eat *Map, page 410*

Emerald Bay (7 rooms) **m** +255 789 759698; **w** emeraldbay.co.tz. Through forested hills southwest of the main tar road, Chokocho is a remote valley village, beside a natural harbour, and the stepping-off point for Emerald Bay: a friendly, low-key resort. The 3-storey central area, complete with its castellated roof terrace, is traditionally built with white Omani arches & red concrete floors, with spacious, dbl-storey makuti-roof rooms either side. Inside, they are plainly decorated; outside each has a small veranda. There is a new mosaic swimming pool, along with a few simple makuti umbrellas & coir loungers. Sea swimming is not possible directly in front of the hotel, which is predominantly mangrove, but complimentary trips are offered daily to nearby picture-perfect sandbanks. Meals receive regular praise, & the terrace dining area offers lovely bay views. This is a quiet, remote spot & not a place for jam-packed days of activities or long beach walks. *FB rates inc 1 free excursion daily*. **$$$$**

✷ **Fundu Lagoon** (18 rooms); m +27 (0)87 0735184; w fundulagoon.com; ⌚ mid-Jun–mid-Apr. In the south of the island, this upmarket & romantic hideaway is accessed by boat from Mkoani, & is extremely popular with honeymooners. En-suite tented rooms, with verandas overlooking the sea, nestle among the trees. Meals, predominantly seafood, are served in the restaurant or at the end of the jetty, with regular BBQ & Swahili nights. Snorkelling, kayaking & fishing are on offer, & there's a fully equipped dive centre; less strenuous are sunset dhow cruises, boat trips to Misali Island, & village excursions. There's also a treatment room, & a games room with satellite TV. *FB*. **$$$$$$$**

Pemba Eco-Lodge m +255 777 415551; w pembalodge.com; ⌚ May–Mar. With an emphasis on the 'eco', this is the vision of enthusiastic Pemban Nassor Ali. The 4 dbl & 1 family timber-frame bungalows are constructed from natural materials, featuring solar-powered lighting & composting toilets, but also a building design that harnesses the breeze from the Pemba Channel. Access to the lodge is an adventure by traditional (though motorised) boat through the beautiful mangroves, dinner is 'catch of the day' cooked over a gas flame, & there's an honesty bar. Come for ecological sensibility & peace on a deserted beach, not luxury. *HB*. **$$$**

NGEZI PENINSULA Jutting out from the northwestern corner of Pemba, the Ngezi Peninsula hosts the island's main cluster of beach resorts. On the eastern side of the peninsula, the beautiful Vumawimbi Beach comprises miles of dazzling white sand flanked by the pristine forest of the Ngezi-Vumawimbina Forest Reserve. The west coast is flanked by the long expanse of Verani Beach with, at its northern end, a place called Pango Ya Watoro ('the cave of the fugitives') and offers great snorkelling and diving opportunities.

Getting there and away Makangale, the largest village on the Ngezi Peninsula, lies about 55km north of Chake Chake via Chwale and Konde. The first 45km of road, as far as Konde, is surfaced and in decent condition. After that it is unsurfaced and in poor condition, finally passing through Ngezi-Vumawimbina Forest Reserve for 4km before emerging at Makangale. Most of the accommodation options on the peninsula lie between 2km and 5km past Makangale on a labyrinth of rough sandy roads that are somewhat erratically signposted.

Regular dalla dallas run from Chake Chake to Konde and some continue to Makangale via the reception to Ngezi-Vumawimbina Forest Reserve. It also easy enough to pick up a pikipiki (motorbike taxi) in Konde or (more cheaply) Makangale to take you to your lodge; it shouldn't cost more than around US$5 per person.

Alternatively, and especially if you want to go on to one of the beaches, you could try to hire a car (with or without driver) in Chake Chake, for which you can expect to pay US$50–70 for the day. Self-drivers should get through in any car in most conditions, but the road is pretty sandy so a 4x4 is preferable, especially after rain, and you may need to stop to ask directions once past Makangale.

All the lodges on the peninsula can arrange transfers with trusted local drivers; expect to pay around US$40–45 per person.

Where to stay and eat *Map, page 410*

All the lodges on the Ngezi Peninsula lie along its west coast facing towards the distant Tanzanian mainland.

Exclusive

The Aiyana m+255 672 644118; w theaiyana.com. This lovely lodge stands in lush gardens on a picture-perfect crescent at the north of the island. The 30 luxury thatched villas all boast a gorgeous view across the powder sand to the turquoise ocean waters, with private outdoor space & stylish, contemporary interiors to match. The surrounding courtyards & gardens are filled with palms, tinkling fountains, bougainvillea-covered pergolas & fragrant frangipani & lily beds; the seafront is idyllic. So given the setting & views, simply chilling comes highly recommended here. For the more active, diving & snorkelling are good, the usual range of island excursions are on offer, & there's a beautiful spa. Meals are served either in the colonnade restaurant or around the resort & beach, with a variety of cuisine on offer. **$$$$$$**

✷ **The Manta Resort** m +255 776 141429; w themantaresort.com; ⌚ Jun–Apr. Boasting a truly stunning location on Pango Ya Watoro Beach, this exclusive all-inclusive Swedish-Zimbabwean family-run resort caters to divers & landlubbers alike. There are 6 seafront villas built on stilts affording a panoramic view across the Pemba Channel, plus garden rooms, some family-friendly, some basic. A central area serves as dining room, bar, lounge & lobby, with a big terrace looking out to sea & steps leading down to a powder-sand beach, with a 2-tiered beach bar: beware sea urchins. There is a spa, pool & a PADI dive centre, plus floating in the Indian Ocean in front of the hotel, a timber cube, boasting a dbl room 3m below the surface of the sea! Guests benefit from a location that offers a wide range of birdlife & some interesting walks to the lighthouse, Vumawimbi Beach & Ngezi Forest (5km). **$$$$$$**

Moderate

Gecko Nature Lodge m +255 773 176737; w swahiligecko.com. Located about 2km west of Makangale, this unpretentious lodge stands above a sand-&-rock beach that offers decent swimming at high tide. Cool & spacious bungalows contain a dbl bed raised up on a plinth, colourful bedding & nets, & en-suite solar-heated shower. The lodge is home to Swahili Divers, a PADI 5* Resort run by a passionate & exceptionally experienced & knowledgeable team of divers (see below). Snorkellers, sunbathers & cruisers are more than welcome to hop on board, too. Birdwatching tours to see Pemba's 4 endemic species can be arranged, & are free for guests who pre-book as birders, but forest fees are extra (page 419). Kayaking, fishing, yoga, paddleboarding, local hikes & trips to Ngezi-Vumawimbina Forest are also on offer. Aside from making sure everyone has a good time, the lodge is trying hard to maintain a low carbon footprint & to work with the local community. From backpackers to chilled families & hardcore divers, this is a super spot for a low-key beach break. *From US$60/70 sgl/dbl, US$20pp dorm B&B*. **$–$$**

Pemba Paradise m +255 777 800773; w pembaparadise.com. Set on the west coast of the peninsula between Gecko Nature Lodge & The Aiyana, Pemba Paradise, which opened in 2017, is a welcome addition to the island's mid-range offerings. The 21 clean & simply furnished rooms & suites all have a veranda, & suites also boast sea views & daybeds, which can be used to accommodate children. Amenities include a large swimming pool, diving with the Manta Resort (see left) or Swahili Divers (see below) & island-wide excursions. *From US$70 dbl. B&B*. **$$**

What to see and do The main activities on the Ngezi Peninsula are the usual seaside pastimes of sunbathing and swimming.

Snorkelling and diving The protected reef immediately in front of the Manta Resort (see above) offers superb snorkelling. Excursions can be arranged though two dive shops: Swahili Divers at Gecko Nature Lodge or 360 Dive at the Manta Resort. These dive shops also arrange diving excursions to a number of excellent sites along the 30km reef system running south from Ras Kigomasha (Pemba's northernmost headland) to the south of Fundo Island. The pick among these is arguably Manta Point, just off Fundo Gap, a great circular dive, affording regular ray sightings, as its name would suggest, although the number of mantas has significantly dwindled with overfishing. Other top sites are Swiss Reef (a fantastic 3km-long submarine topography of rolling reefs near Ras Kigomasha), Mandela Wall (a sheer vertical wall, up to 45m deep, that you can drift along for almost 4km) and The Aquarium (a shallow snorkel-friendly site, rich in reef fish and small pelagic fish, off the northern end of Njao Island.

Ras Kigomasha Lighthouse (Admission US$4) A rather futuristic 27m-high cast-iron construction built by the British in 1904 and renovated in 2002, Ras Kigomasha Lighthouse stands close to the most northerly tip of the Ngezi Peninsula (and of Pemba) about 1km north of the Manta Resort. It's possible to walk there along the beach from any of the resorts on the peninsula, but only at low tide, so do check carefully before setting out – though if you don't time it correctly, there is an alternative route back through the fields. Ask at the nearby lighthouse keeper's house for permission to climb the 95 narrow steps to the top, which offers some outstanding views out to sea and across the lush green landscape of northern Pemba. Humpback whales are often seen from the lighthouse from September through to November.

Coconut Crab Tours (Depart 19.00; US$15pp) Initiated by a research project developed by the University of Exeter in the UK and the University of California in the USA, these walking tours are designed to engage community support for the conservation of Pemba's last surviving population of the coconut crab *Birgus latro*, a massive nocturnal omnivore with pincers strong enough to break open a coconut. Five local guides are involved in the project and tours usually take 60–90 minutes, with virtually a 100% chance of spotting the crab. It can be arranged through any lodge on the peninsula, with one-third of the fee going to the guide and the remainder earmarked for community-development projects.

KWANINI MARINE CONSERVATION AREA

An affiliate of the Manta Resort (page 417), the Kwanini Foundation (w kwaninifoundation.org) was established in 2008 with the goal of conserving the spectacular coral reefs and biodiverse marine habitat off Pemba in collaboration with the local fishing communities on the Ngezi Peninsula. In 2013, with government permission and the cooperation of local communities, it established the Kwanini Marine Conservation Area as a no-fishing zone protecting a 1km stretch of reef offshore of the Manta Resort. The reserve has since seen a massive increase in fish numbers and diversity, helping the project gain further community support for the concept of setting aside designated no-fishing areas that serve as breeding grounds for future generations. The foundation also supports several community education and other projects using funds raised by the Manta Resort, which allocates US$30 of its per person room rate to the foundation, and levies a conservation fee to all guests who join the daily morning snorkelling trip there. Snorkelling trips to the conservation area are highly recommended: the diversity of the coral reefs and the fish that inhabit them is truly sensational, and you are also likely to see oddities such as the superbly camouflaged stonefish, the psychedelic devil firefish (whose spiked spines are highly venomous) and stingrays.

Ngezi-Vumawimbina Forest Reserve (m +255 777 324030/772 674844; ⌚ 07.30–15.30 daily; admission & guided tour US$10pp) Extending south from Vumawimbi Beach to the southern shore of the Ngezi Peninsula facing Njao Island, this 29km² forest reserve protects the largest surviving tract of the indigenous forest that covered much of Pemba into the 19th century, since when more than 95% of it has been cleared for cultivation. One of the highlights of Pemba, especially if you have an interest in wildlife, it is home to most of the non-marine mammals, birds and reptiles that occur on the island, and offers the opportunity to discover it as it once was.

The reserve covers just 29km² but the variety of soil types has resulted in a wide range of vegetation, with more than 350 plant species having been identified. This includes the endemic Pemba palm or mpapindi (*Dypsis pembana*), whose red seeds are attractive to birds. The forest is home to 30 mammal species, most notably the Pemba flying fox, Pemba vervet monkey and the nocturnal Zanzibar tree hyrax. The introduced Kirk's red colobus, a striking long-fringed monkey that occurs naturally only on Zanzibar, is sometimes seen by tourists. Ngezi Forest supports around 130 bird species, and it is the best place to see the endemic Pemba scops owl, Pemba green pigeon, Pemba sunbird and Pemba white-eye.

Getting there and away The reserve's reception is on the north side of the unsurfaced main road to the Ngezi Peninsula about 5km west of Konde. The road then passes through the forest for about 4km before emerging at the southern end of the village of Makangale. For self-drivers, it shouldn't take much more than an hour to get there from Chake Chake and might be up to 30 minutes from the various lodges on the peninsula. Using public transport, your best option coming from Chake Chake or Wete is to catch a dalla dalla to Konde, then, unless it continues to Makangale, to pick up a pikipiki (motorbike taxi) to the reception office. All the lodges on the peninsula can arrange day trips to the forest, and Gecko Nature Lodge specialises in birding excursions there.

Activities The most popular activity in the forest is a short nature trail that runs south from the main road opposite the reception office. The reserve also offers excellent birdwatching, though you need a good local guide to stand a serious chance of ticking off all the endemics.

Main nature trail Starting directly opposite the reception office, this 2km guided nature trail takes about 1 hour and can only be done with a guide from the office. It runs mainly through moist forest, but also passes large forest-fringed ponds, and the main emphasis is on trees and other plants, particularly those with traditional medicinal uses. The guides will also show you a small colony of Pemba flying foxes, which roost in the trees; butterflies are plentiful, but wildlife viewing is otherwise quite hit-and-miss. The odds of seeing any of the endemic birds on this walk are very small, but you may see the likes of malachite kingfisher, crowned hornbill, palm-nut vulture and Fischer's turaco, especially in the vicinity of the pools. The trail also passes through the so-called Joshi Ruins, which comprise the rusting remnants of the sawmill installed by their namesake in 1951 and abandoned in 1964. Wildlife tends to be most conspicuous in the early morning, but this is also when mosquitoes are most active.

Birdwatching For most visiting birders, the prime target in Ngezi-Vumawimbina is the four avian species endemic to Pemba and to a lesser extent the endemic subspecies. Of the four endemics, the most easily seen are the Pemba sunbird and Pemba white-eye, both of which are common enough in the reserve but more easily seen in hotel gardens and other wooded but non-forested habitats. The Manta Resort is particularly good for both species, as to a lesser extent is Gecko Nature Lodge, which is also a favourite haunt of the lovely African paradise flycatcher.

A good spot for general birding, the oddly named PC Pond (short for Promotion Centre and pronounced 'Pissy Pond') lies in the northern part of the park near central Makangale. The pond is as good a place as any to look for the endemic sunbird and white-eye, and it is worth scanning the canopy of the fringing forest for the endemic Pemba green pigeon and endemic subspecies of black-bellied starling, as well as crowned hornbill, Fischer's turaco, broad-billed roller and blue-cheeked bee-eater. Water-associated species likely to be seen include African fish eagle, palm-nut vulture, and African pygmy goose, little grebe, African moorhen and malachite kingfisher. To get to PC Pond, you need to drive north through Makangale for about 1km past the school, then turn right onto a well-signposted but otherwise inconspicuous track that leads to the shore after less than 1km.

More productive for birding than the trails through the forest interior is the 4km of road between the reserve reception and Makangale. This passes through some atmospheric primary forest but is wide enough to offer good views into the canopy, and taken slowly it should yield all the above-mentioned birds along with a range of other coastal forest species. This site offers your best chance of spotting the local subspecies of African goshawk, which is most likely to be flying fleetingly and directly across the road. It is also where local guides usually start looking for the Pemba scops owl, a russet nocturnal species best located by listening for its distinctive monosyllabic call at dusk, then playing back a recording to flush it out.

If you're serious about seeing all the endemics, you will need a local guide and should be prepared to dedicate a full day and evening to the excursion. You could make an arrangement with one of the guides at the reception, but they will ask around US$50 and you will need to provide your own transport to get to the best sites. A more straightforward option is to arrange a day tour with Gecko Nature Lodge/Swahili Divers, which charges US$35 per person (minimum two people) for a day tour inclusive of transport, an expert guide and an evening session to look for the owl.

16

Mafia Archipelago

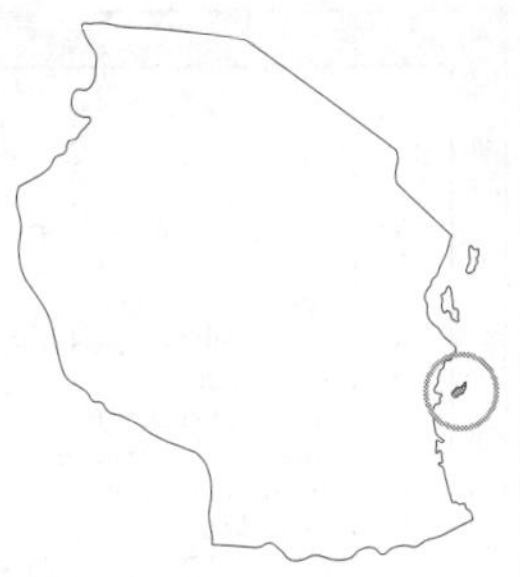

While Zanzibar is entrenched as probably the most popular ocean resort in East Africa, the small archipelago around Mafia Island, 160km to its south, remains virtually unknown. Yet a trickle of visitors over recent years, probably no more than a few thousand annually, have been unanimously singing the island's praises.

Mafia lacks an equivalent to Zanzibar's atmospheric Stone Town, so it cannot be recommended as an alternative destination for those whose primary interest is culture or history, However, its winning combination of small, high-quality lodges, some of the Indian Ocean's finest offshore diving and snorkelling, and a conspicuous absence of hassle and crime make it the ideal destination for those seeking an exclusive but low-key island retreat. Paradoxically, perhaps, Mafia also has considerable potential for budget travellers seeking a truly off-the-beaten-track and adventurous experience.

The Mafia Archipelago, which lies approximately 20km east of the Rufiji River Delta in central Tanzania, probably became isolated from the mainland some 20,000 years ago. The archipelago consists of about 15 sandstone and coral-rag islands and numerous smaller atolls and sandbars, none of which reaches an elevation above 80m, and all but two of which are little more than 1km^2 in extent. The central island, known today as Mafia, is by far the largest, approximately 50km long by 15km across. The second-largest island, Juani, now boasts an impressive turtle conservation project, whilst tiny Chole Island, sandwiched between these two larger islands, was the local centre of trade in the Omani era and is now home to an award-winning lodge.

The archipelago's population (46,850 in the 2012 census and probably more than 50,000 today) lives in rustic fishing communities and farming villages dotted all over the archipelago, although many of the islands are theoretically uninhabited. The largest town and port on Mafia Island is Kilindoni in the southeast, the site of the airstrip, and the main landing point for dhows from the mainland. A couple of hotels can be found along the beach from Kilindoni, as well as a few local guesthouses in the town itself, but the centre of upmarket tourist development is Chole Bay on the southeastern side of the island. Here a number of tourist lodges, ranging in standard, line the coast around Utende, roughly 10km from Kilindoni by road. Further accommodation options are found on Chole Island within the bay, and more recently on the private islands of Fangove and Thanda.

VEGETATION

Natural vegetation on Mafia ranges from tidal mangrove thickets (eight species of mangrove grow here), marshland, heath and scrubby coastal moorlands to palm-wooded grassland and lowland rainforest, although the evergreen forest was cleared for coconut plantations in the 1980s. Baobabs are prominent along with the

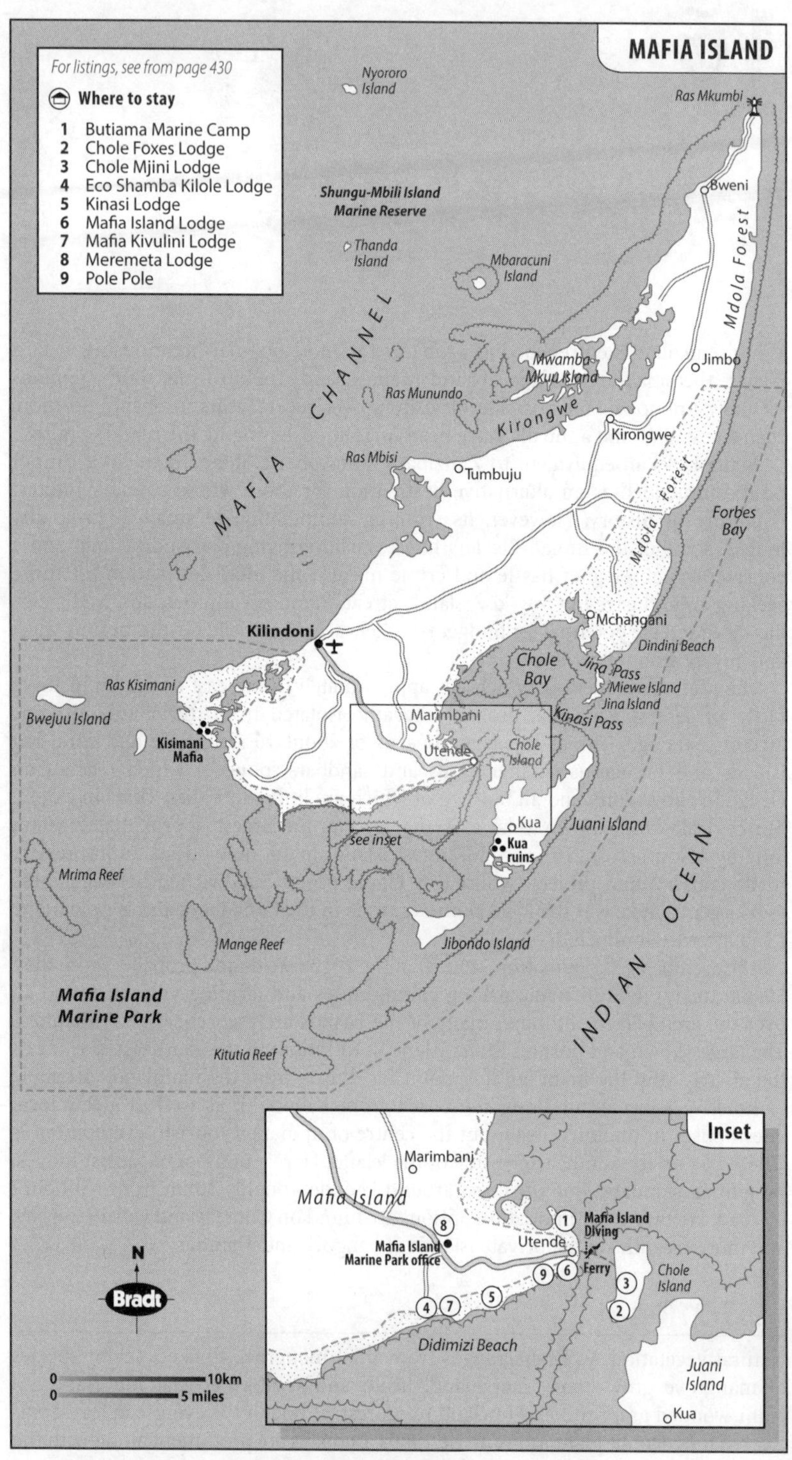
MAFIA ISLAND
For listings, see from page 430
Where to stay
1 Butiama Marine Camp
2 Chole Foxes Lodge
3 Chole Mjini Lodge
4 Eco Shamba Kilole Lodge
5 Kinasi Lodge
6 Mafia Island Lodge
7 Mafia Kivulini Lodge
8 Meremeta Lodge
9 Pole Pole
Nyororo Island
Ras Mkumbi
Bweni
Shungu-Mbili Island Marine Reserve
Thanda Island
Mbaracuni Island
Mdola Forest
MAFIA CHANNEL
Mwamba-Mkuu Island
Jimbo
Ras Mnundo
Kirongwe
Kirongwe
Ras Mbisi
Tumbuju
Mdola Forest
Forbes Bay
Mchangani
Kilindoni
Dindini Beach
Chole Bay
Jina Pass
Miewe Island
Jina Island
Ras Kisimani
Kinasi Pass
Bwejuu Island
Marimbani
Kisimani Mafia
Utende
Chole Island
Kua
Juani Island
see inset
Kua ruins
Mrima Reef
INDIAN OCEAN
Mange Reef
Jibondo Island
Mafia Island Marine Park
Kitutia Reef
Inset
Marimbani
Mafia Island
Mafia Island Diving
Utende
Mafia Island Marine Park office
Ferry
Chole Island
Didimizi Beach
Juani Island
Kua
N
Bradt
0 10km
0 5 miles

native *Albizia*. A patch of coastal high forest, the Chunguruma Forest towards Ras Mbisi, is a dense tree canopy interlaced with lianas and having an abundant floor covering of ferns.

WILDLIFE

MAMMALS A large, reed-lined lake in central Mafia, probably a relic lagoon dating from when the island was joined to the mainland, harbours about 20 hippos that were washed out to sea during flooding in the Rufiji River system. Unpopular with locals, they eat from the rice farms at night and can cause considerable damage, but are hard to see. Other island fauna includes a colony of Seychelles flying fox (*Pteropus seychellensis*), a species of giant fruit bat that also occurs on the Comoros and Seychelles but is found nowhere on mainland Africa. Bush pigs are found in Mdola Forest and Juani Island. The pigs eat the cassava from farms on Juani, so are a menace to farmers, who try to trap them where possible.

Mdola Forest stretches along the east coast of Mafia Island for about 30km, from Bweni to Chole Bay, and has a high level of diversity, as well as a number of endemic species, such as the blue duiker, a subspecies endemic to Pemba and Mafia. Other fauna includes at least one bushbaby species, the genet and the black-and-rufous elephant shrew. Monkeys (Sykes' and vervet) and squirrels were introduced for the pot by the Portuguese.

REPTILES AND INSECTS The leaf-litter toad has been recorded in Mdola Forest, and may be endemic to Mafia; the writhing gecko is found both in Mdola Forest and on the Tanzanian mainland. The monitor lizard is known locally as *kenge*. Butterflies (there are five endemics) are best seen in the wet season, particularly around Ras Mbizi and mangroves, which flower during the rains.

BIRDS More than 120 species of bird have been recorded on Mafia, including five different types of sunbird. The island is of particular interest for its concentrations of resident and migrant shorebirds, which have breeding grounds in northern Europe but come to Mafia from October to March for the nearby mangrove estuaries, where they feed on the mudflats. Waders include ringed plover, crab plover, grey plover, Mongolian plover, great sandplover, curlew, whimbrel and turnstone, and the island is also a nesting area for fish eagles and open-billed storks.

MARINE LIFE Of far greater ecological importance than Mafia's terrestrial habitats is the immensely rich marine environment, which provides some of the finest snorkelling and diving sites in the Indian Ocean. It may be surprising that the biodiversity of the Rufiji–Mafia complex has global significance, and of 21 sites in East Africa it has been described as having 'one of the world's most interesting and diverse ecosystems'. The coral-reef habitats around Mafia have a diversity of species rivalled only by rainforests, with at least 380 species of fish and 48 of coral. The beds of seagrass (12 species of which are found here, the only flowering plants to have colonised the sea) and the deep open waters support some of the planet's most endangered marine life.

Four species of turtle live in Mafia's waters, and two of these use Mafia as a nesting ground. The hawksbill (*Cretmochelys imbricata*) lays eggs between December and January; the green turtle (*Chelonia mydas*), between April and June. The East African coast is one of the last strongholds for the critically endangered dugong (*Dugong dugon*), and during the 1960s and 1970s these gentle sea cows

KITU KIBLU: RESPONSIBLE MARINE ENCOUNTERS

Kitu Kiblu ('a little blue thing') was established to offer responsible marine encounters with whale sharks for visitors and also to support the work of the Mafia Island Whale Shark Conservation Society (WHASCOS), which aims to raise awareness about whale sharks and their conservation. It is a highly principled organisation, with a clear understanding of how solid, long-term conservation must be approached. Staff work hard to demonstrate the whale sharks' worth to the authorities who are able to protect them and they believe fervently in the whale sharks' right to live free and undisturbed. They understand sharks' importance within the ecosystem, and support scientific research to better understand whale-shark behaviour and how to interact with them without harming or harassing them.

Half-day encounter trips offer visitors utterly incredible experiences with the whale sharks, and always in a safe and respectful way. On board traditional dhows, guests not only have the chance to spot and swim with these amazing animals, but also to be guided by knowledgeable people, able to translate the whale sharks' behaviour and explain their biology. Resident marine biologists involved in current research may also be on board, giving opportunities to gain real insight into these fish and the area's conservation projects. It is as eye opening as it is magical.

For budding marine conservationists, there is also a well-organised internship programme, offering hands-on experience of scientific research and working at sea. From spot pattern data collection and 3D photometry to rural development projects, up to eight interns at a time can join the team on two- to twelve-week placements from October to February, working and staying at the Kitu Kiblu Magemani beach camp. Interns even learn to sail and scuba dive while they are there.

If you are in Mafia during whale-shark season, you can book Kitu Kiblu trips directly (**m** +255 784 520799; **e** info@kitukiblu.com; **w** kitukiblu.co.tz) or through your tour operator, dive operator or hotel.

were regularly caught in the shark nets of Mafia's fishermen. Despite two separate sightings in 1999, there are fears that the dugong may now be extinct here.

The lowland coastal forest of the eastern seaboard has been 'recognised as a critical site for biodiversity', and the intertidal flats are important for octopus, while in the open sea marine mammals like the humpback whale give birth and nurse their young. Sadly the demand for shark-fin soup in the Far East is one contributor to diminished populations of shark along the coastline. The large pelagics such as marlin, billfish and tuna also inhabit the deeper sea.

Oceanographers often talk of the Rufiji River Delta–Mafia–Kilwa area being one extended ecosystem. It's particularly exciting that a coelacanth was caught here in 2003. Archaeologists have found fossils of this very rare, bony fish which dates back to the era of the dinosaurs, and today's specimens are almost identical.

From October to April, whale sharks (*Rhincodon typus*) are seen in the area. Peaceful creatures, sometimes in excess of 20m in length, they are the world's largest fish, and survive on a diet of plankton. Kitu Kiblu, in Kilindoni, is the headquarters of the Mafia Island Whale Shark Conservation Society and during the season offers regular dhow excursions for research scientists and guests to visit these gentle giants, which are spotted mainly on the western side of the island off the shore of Kilindoni.

There are a few other operators in recent years who have begun offering trips, most with reasonable responsibility; however, it is very important to familiarise yourself with the whale shark code of conduct (page 438) for your own safety and the animals' protection. It is our view that Kitu Kiblu (page 424) are still the gold standard for care, quality and responsibility when it comes to these magical marine encounters.

CLIMATE

The Mafia Archipelago experiences a tropical climate tempered by ocean breezes. Rainfall averaging 2,000mm a year occurs mainly between April and May, although November can also be wet. February and March are hot and humid, while a strong southerly wind, the *kusi*, blows during July. The best holiday period is from June until mid October, when the islands enjoy blue skies with temperatures kept pleasant by light coastal breezes. The water temperature varies from 24°C to 31°C while the air temperature rarely exceeds 33°C or drops below 20°C.

HISTORY

Little is known about the early history of the Mafia Archipelago, but presumably it has been settled for millennia, and it may well have participated in the ancient coastal trade with Arabia. The eminent archaeologist Neville Chittick regarded Mafia as a strong candidate for the 'low and wooded' island of Menouthesias, described in the 1st-century *Periplus of the Erythraean Sea* as being two days' sail or 300 *stadia* (roughly 50km) from the river port of Rhapta (which, according to this theory, was situated in the Rufiji Delta; and if recent discoveries prove positive, is actually off Ras Mbisi; page 346). Although the anonymous writer of the *Periplus* also mentions the sewn boats and hollowed-out tree canoes that are still used widely on Mafia today (as they are elsewhere on the coast), several other aspects of the description count against Mafia. Two days rather exaggerates the sailing distance from the island to the Rufiji Delta; furthermore, either the *Periplus* was mistaken in its assertion that there are 'no wild beasts except crocodiles' on Menouthesias, or the crocs have subsequently vanished and the island's few hippos are a later arrival.

The earliest known settlement on the archipelago, Kisimani Mafia, was situated at Ras Kisimani in the far southwest of the main island. Archaeological evidence suggests that this town, which covered about 1ha, was founded in the 11th century, possibly by a favoured son of the Sultan of Kilwa. Several coins minted at Kilwa have been unearthed at the site, as have coins from China, Mongolia, India and Arabia, all minted prior to 1340. A second important town, Kua, was probably founded in the 13th century, again as a dependency of Kilwa, and it must surely have usurped Kisimani as the islands' political and economic hub soon after that. In its prime, Kua was thought to have been the second-largest city along what is now the southern coast of Tanzania, boasting seven mosques as well as a double-storey palace and numerous stone homesteads spread over an area of more than 12ha.

Following the Portuguese occupation of the coast, Kua was chosen as the site of a Portuguese trade agency in 1515, when a fortified blockhouse was built at the town. The name Mafia (more accurately Morfiyeh) was well established by this time, and the islands are marked as such on the earliest Portuguese naval charts. Several explanations have been put forward for the origin of this name (page 427). Because the archipelago lies 20km offshore, Mafia attracted a large influx of refugees from the mainland during the cannibalistic Zimba raids that dealt the final deathblow to so many coastal settlements during the late 16th century.

Control of Mafia changed hands frequently in the 17th century as Portugal's fortunes declined. An Omani naval raid in 1670 effectively terminated the Portuguese presence on the Mafia islands, and by 1598 the entire East African coast north of modern-day Mozambique was under Omani control. Little is known about events on the islands over the next two centuries. In about 1829, however, the archipelago was attacked by the cannibalistic Sakalafa of Madagascar, who succeeded in wreaking havoc at Kua, one of the few coastal towns left untouched by their Zimba forebears 250 years earlier. Kisimani, though also attacked by the Malagasy, stumbled on into the 1870s, when a devastating cyclone dealt it a final death blow, while Kua was abandoned to go to ruin.

One reason why Kua was not resettled after 1820 is that a new seat of the Sultanate of Zanzibar had been founded on the north end of Chole Island barely ten years earlier. Known as Chole Mjini (Chole Town), this settlement was also attacked by the Sakalafa, but it was soon rebuilt to emerge as the most important town on the islands. Chole became the established home of a number of wealthy Omani traders and slave owners, while the main island of Mafia, known at the time as Chole Shamba (Chole Farm), was occupied by newly established coconut plantations and the slaves who worked on them. Although Chole was not as directly involved in the slave trade as Pangani, Bagamoyo or Kilwa Kivinje, it was an important stopover for slave ships heading between Kilwa and Zanzibar, and the ruined mansions that survive today indicate that it was a very wealthy settlement indeed.

Mafia was part of the Zanzibar Sultanate throughout the Omani era, and it should have remained a part of Zanzibar in the colonial era, according to a treaty that placed it under British protectorateship along with Zanzibar and Pemba islands. However, in the complex Anglo-German treaty of 1890, Mafia was ceded to Germany in exchange for a part of what is now Malawi, and it has been administered as part of mainland Tanzania ever since. In 1892, Germany sent a local administrator to Chole, who constructed the two-storey Customs House that can still be seen on the beach today.

In 1913, Germany relocated its administration from Chole to the deeper harbour at Kilindoni on the main island. Two years later, Mafia was the first part of German East Africa to be captured by British forces. The island was subsequently used as the base for a series of aerial assaults on the German cruiser *Königsberg* which, having evaded capture in the Rufiji Delta, was finally sunk on 11 August 1915. A six-cent German Tanganyika Territory stamp overprinted 'Mafia' by the British and listed at £9,000 in the Stanley Gibbons catalogue makes philatelists one of the few groups of people aware of the existence of the islands.

ECONOMY

Coconuts were the main source of income for the islands until the 1970s, when the price of coconut products dropped, and the fishing industry grew in importance, thanks in part to the efficient production of ice on the island. Cultivated since the 19th century, coconuts remain a secure income source and, although the trees are still climbed by hand, some 30 tonnes are exported to Dar daily in dhows from all over the islands. There are three main harvesting periods in the year – after the rains, in October/November and in February/March – after which the nuts leave in sacks for processing elsewhere. Coconut products have a number of local uses: leaves are used for roofing; coconut coir makes doormats and ropes; ribs are used to make fishing traps and brooms; and the wood can also be used to make furniture.

Other produce grown on Mafia is used for subsistence farming, particularly the primary crop, cassava. Rice, sweet potato, maize, pumpkin, okra, banana,

WHAT'S IN A NAME?

There are a number of suggestions for the source of the archipelago's name, but it isn't derived from the Sicilian crime syndicate. It may have origins in the Arabic word *morfiyeh* meaning 'group', describing the archipelago of Mafia, or be named after the Ma'afir, an Arab tribe from Merku (Mocha) in present-day Yemen. An unlikely suggestion is that the name derives from the Arabic *mafi* meaning 'waste' or 'rubbish', or perhaps from the Kiswahili *mahali pa afya* meaning 'a healthy place to live'. The authors would be grateful for any further suggestions!

pineapple, passion fruit, lime, mango, oranges and tomato are also seen growing on the islands, some of which are exported to Dar. Cashew nuts are either sold locally or exported. At subsistence level, raffia fibre, medicinal plants and game (monkey, bush pig and duiker) play a little role. Mangrove trees provide many raw materials: their wood is used for building poles, and boatbuilding and repair. Dead mangrove branches are used for firewood; leaves, bark and fruit are all used for medicines and colour dyes. **Firewood** is collected to burn coral rag for lime, and also for charcoal, which is sold to locals, hotels, and the market at Kilindoni, as well as exported. The charcoal industry is now a disturbingly big business. The attempt at a ban on charcoal production on Zanzibar sadly created an instant market for Mafia. Mafia's hardwoods are now being removed at an alarming rate to fuel the trade to the Gulf States and, more locally, Forodhani's night market in Stone Town. This deforestation comes with a raft of aesthetic and environmental impacts for the island, notably significant erosion along the formerly wooded valleys, which act as important water channels during the rains.

The **sea** is vital to the livelihood of many of Mafia's inhabitants. Seaweed farming exists on a small-scale basis on Jibondo, with some questioning the sensibilities of introducing vigorous species from the Philippines within the marine park. It is grown on lines attached to wooden stakes across the seabed of shallow lagoons, and is dried on palm leaves, before being exported for processing into food additives. Traditionally the intertidal area has been the women's domain, where they fish for shellfish at spring tide. In the 1990s, however, men began collecting octopus on the intertidal flats as well, as fish catches were declining yet prices increasing. Today, 60% of octopus is caught by men, through free-diving or harpoon-fishing at low tide in Jibondo reef's rocky crevasses. Sea cucumbers are harvested mainly off Kilindoni's sandy seabed for export to Zanzibar or Dar, then out to the Far East, although thanks to over fishing, this practice is happening less. Fish is also exported. Chole and Jibondo were well known for their boatbuilding in the past, but activity decreased somewhat as secondhand fibre-glass boats were brought in. This traditional skill is in decline, although you can still see people working in the shipyards. The majority of the work is now repairing smaller dhows rather than building large cargo-carrying boats. Put simply, the depletion of hardwood forest reserves has resulted in the cost of timber doubling every three years, so maintaining existing boats rather than building them anew is increasingly necessary.

RELIGION AND CULTURE

The majority of the islanders are Muslim, but there are also many Christians, and both religions are sometimes mixed with local beliefs which are older in origin.

While traditionally reserved, the islanders are tolerant of visitors provided they dress discreetly and behave in a manner in keeping with local customs. Mafia women wear the colourful patterned kanga of the Swahili coast, and on weekends and religious holidays men exchange Western dress for the long, white *kanzu*. Older folk who remember the British era can speak some English, as can staff working at the tourist lodges, but it can help to know a little Swahili when talking to other islanders.

Mafia is a conservative society, and the passing visitor is unlikely to be asked for handouts. Children who beg from tourists are quickly reprimanded by their elders. Please make sure that you, and your travelling companions, keep it this way.

GETTING THERE AND AWAY

BY AIR The most efficient way of getting to Mafia is on a scheduled light-aircraft flight from Dar es Salaam. The flight path to Mafia is within sight of the Rufiji River Delta, at $40km^2$ the largest delta in East Africa with the region's greatest concentration of mangroves. The views are impressive; the dhows look tiny as they go about their fishing unfeasibly far from shore. At the time of writing, and after much stalling, the new 1.9km runway is finally under construction in Kilindoni, so a bumpy arrival on Mafia's uneven gravel airstrip should soon be a thing of the past. The airport has a simple waiting room and visitors holding a hotel reservation will be met at the airport for their transfer. If you don't have a reservation, most of the lodges have representatives who speak English, and can radio the lodges to organise accommodation subject to availability.

In addition to using one of the airlines listed on page 356, you can also **charter planes** to Mafia from a range of companies in Dar es Salaam and Zanzibar, with the cost of a small aircraft from Coastal or Tropical coming in at around US$900. Note that an airport **departure tax** of US$15 per person is payable in cash on leaving Mafia, although most flights now include this in the ticket price.

Airlines

Coastal Aviation w coastal.co.tz. 2 daily flights from Dar (30mins; US$140 one-way) with connecting flights to Zanzibar, Pemba, Arusha & elsewhere. Also 1 daily flight from Songo Songo to Mafia (25mins; US$173 one-way).

Safari Airlink w flysal.com. 2 daily flights from Dar to Mafia via Zanzibar & other destinations along the coast, then on to the various national parks. Check website for schedule & prices.

BY BOAT The options for budget travellers who wish to visit Mafia are limited to boats that connect Kilindoni to the mainland. Many of these dhows are uncomfortable and crowded and the trip can take anything from 10 to 24 hours; the safety record is none too inspiring either. Equally, if it's too windy, none will sail. Nevertheless, if you do want to take a boat, make sure you check that they're properly licensed to carry passengers or vehicles, and at the very least have marine radios and life jackets on board.

For the incorrigible, it is worth checking tides at w tide-forecast.com/locations/Dar-Es-Salaam-Tanzania/tides/latest, as boats to Mafia have to arrive at high tide, and often leave on a high tide, too. In Kilindoni, a jetty has been in use for some time, despite being half-built. Should it ever be finished, it would mean that boats no longer have to restrict their arrival to high tide, which might lead to a more regular service.

The closest mainland port to Mafia is Kisiju, 30km from Dar, and 45km southeast of Mkuranga on the Kilwa road. From the Kariakoo bus depot in Dar, take a bus to

MAFIA ISLAND MARINE PARK

023 240 2526; w marineparks.go.tz

Over the past 2,000 years, turtle-shell, mangrove poles and seashells have been part of East Africa's trade to Arabia. By the 1960s, however, it had become clear that natural resources were not coping with human progress. In Tanzania, dried and salted fish, exported to the mainland, contributes more to the national protein consumption than meat and poultry combined. Dynamite fishing became very popular on Tanzania's coast, despite the destruction that it causes to fish populations and to coral. Small-mesh, beach-seine nets were catching all sizes of fish, again damaging populations. In some areas the only source of building materials has been coral, used as bricks and in the production of lime: this was the second-largest industry on Mafia at one time. Mangrove wood is very hard, insect-resistant and makes excellent building material, so vast areas were cleared to provide timber, fuelwood, farmland and salt pans for salt production.

In the 1970s, four islands were declared marine reserves to slow the damage, but in the absence of facilities to police the park, fishermen ignored the rules and continued as usual. By 1995, it was clear that conservation had become an urgent priority, so the following year a partnership of investors, communities and the government set up the Board of Trustees of Marine Parks and Reserves of Tanzania, and on 6 September 1996, an area of Mafia extending across 822km^2 was gazetted as Tanzania's first marine park, to protect the ecosystems as well as the future livelihood of coastal people. The park embraces most of the southern and eastern shore of Mafia, including Chole Bay and associated reefs, a number of isolated atolls to the south of the main island, and the reefs enclosing Juani, Jibondo and Bwejuu islands.

The marine park now owns seven boats and has one full-time park warden plus many rangers. The park authorities are aiming to co-operate and collaborate with local residents, using community-based projects to dispel conflict between groups. If the islands are to be protected, the success of the marine park is imperative. Mangroves trap river sediments that would be otherwise washed out to sea and, along with coral reefs, protect the shoreline from the erosion of rising sea levels. The natural forest shields the island's crops from storm damage from the ocean, and a healthy ecosystem helps in the recovery from natural disasters such as cyclones, hurricanes and floods. Significantly, wetlands have also been shown to provide clean water, perhaps the most significant issue in terms of sustainable development of the islands.

Kisiju and then a dhow to Mafia. Make sure you arrive in Kisiju before 14.30, when the last dhow usually leaves for Mafia. Another possibility from Dar es Salaam is via Kimbiji, easily reached by catching the motor ferry from the city centre to Kigomboni (boats leave every 10 minutes or so and take 5 minutes), then a dalla dalla direct to Kimbiji (about an hour). There are also dhows connecting Mafia to Kilwa Kivinje. Finally, a rather sporadic service runs from Niamisati in the Rufiji Delta once a day, leaving around midday and arriving in Kilindoni 6 hours later, before departing for the return journey at around 08.00. To reach Niamisati it's a 3–4-hour drive from Dar, or 2 hours' taxi ride from Mbalala. There is also a 04.00 departure from Kilindoni to Kisiju, though this is fundamentally a coconut-export vessel that happens to allow passengers on board.

GETTING AROUND

The island's infrastructure is generally basic. Hardly any villages are connected to mains water or electricity and there is only one tarred road from Kilindoni to Utende. Throughout the rest of the island the best you'll find is a bouncy sandy track. Vehicles are few, mainly Land Rover pick-ups and 4x4s belonging to the hotels and other organisations. Most local people use bicycles and motorbikes to get around, although the former are quite hard work on the sandy roads. **Bicycles** can be rented by arrangement with most lodges, whilst **motorbikes** are available for hire from Whale Shark Lodge.

A not very reliable **minibus** runs every 3 hours or so between Kilindoni and Utende charging less than US$1 one-way. It seats a minimum of 12 and has no fixed timetable – it departs when it's full. **Dalla dallas** shuttle between Kilindoni and Utende, picking people up along the way. They're not the most comfortable means of getting around, but are a good way of meeting local people and really getting to understand life on Mafia. Alternatively, a **motorbike taxi** can be picked up in Kilindoni – but safety should be seriously considered first. **Hitchhiking** is an accepted means of getting about, but it usually entails a long wait. Islanders also use *jahazis*, widely referred to in English as dhows, to commute between Kilindoni and outlying villages on Mafia, and for inter-island travel.

Free **maps** of Mafia can be obtained from the friendly Mafia Island Marine Park office, an obligatory stop to pay fees en route from the airport to all Utende lodges.

WHERE TO STAY AND EAT *Map, page 422, unless otherwise stated*

Mafia isn't really the place for easy backpacking, but budget travellers who do come here may stop in Kilindoni itself. Meanwhile, the majority of Mafia's tourists head straight through town and over to one of the more upmarket small lodges in Utende or on Chole Island. For **camping**, there is a fully kitted-out campsite at Big Blu in Utende (page 434) and, if you have your own tent, Meremeta (page 432) offers camping for US$10 per person including breakfast. It is possible that camping may also return at Whale Shark Lodge. Otherwise, check with the marine park authorities before camping independently, as it's not legal to camp in Tanzania unless you're in a specified area – don't take any chances.

KILINDONI *Map, page 435*

The guesthouses here are all pretty basic, with little to draw travellers to most of them. They are still generally better in value and appeal than their price-matched Zanzibari counterparts, but a far better bet is to head to the more upmarket Butiama Beach or the simple treehouses at Kitu Kiblu Magemani.

Upmarket

✷ Butiama Beach w butiamabeach.com. Bordering Mafia Island Marine Park only 10mins' walk south along the beach from Kilindoni, Butiama Beach is an immediately likeable lodge with sand pathways, well-tended lawns & lovely public areas. The 15 aquamarine bungalows are spacious, well-designed & comfortable, & tremendous care & creativity has gone into the colour-coordinated décor. The heart of the lodge is the circular seafront bar with its well-stocked bookshelf, snooker table & palm-shaded pool. Kayaks are available to explore the mangrove creeks, & a walk to the market or the morning fish auction offers a taste of village life. The beach here is better than many around Chole Bay, but snorkellers & divers must head to Chole Bay, a 20–30min drive, where Big Blu (page 434) is also owned by Butiama. **$$$$$**

Moderate

Butiama Bustani Hotel w butiamamafiaisland.com. Opened in 2015 under the name Kilindoni Magemani, this neat, efficient place has charming staff but lacks soul. The 10 rooms are in sgl-storey, red-roofed cottages at the back of a flat lawned area. Interiors are neat, cool & clean, with AC & satellite TV, locally made wooden furniture, fitted nets & marble bathrooms; outside, they have small terraces with neat flower beds. Recent additions include a raised swimming pool, an adjacent makuti-roof bar, & an à la carte restaurant catering to seafood lovers & vegetarians alike. There is no beach access & taxis will be necessary to get around. *From US$60/85 B&B*. **$$**

✱ **Kitu Kiblu** w kitukiblu.co.tz; ⌚ Jul–Mar. This is Chole Mjini for backpackers! Set on the forested slopes behind Kilindoni Beach, this delightful tented camp was built by the same husband-&-wife team as the ingenious treetop lodge of Chole Mjini (page 433). Each of the 5 stilted safari tents has a wraparound deck, a cool makuti-thatched roof & a spacious interior with a simple timber bed, electricity point & free-standing fan. Immaculate composting toilets & showers are in a shared ablution block. For socialising & chilling, there's a beachfront area & simple restaurant, an evening fire pit (ukuleles may even be on hand) & a stunning sand beach with a brilliant view of the dhows heading to the nearby harbour & sunsets on the watery horizon. Great value! *US$60/80 sgl/dbl B&B*. **$$$**

Budget

Ibizza Inn Ismalia St; m 0658 653160; w booking.com. The most comfortable & cleanest guesthouse in central Kilindoni, welcoming Ibizza Inn is a tangerine-coloured establishment set in well-tended gardens behind the main road. It has 12 bright, cheery & good-sized rooms with a wrought-iron bed, TV, large bathroom & optional AC. An outside restaurant serves Swahili meals, plays groovy African tunes & enjoys lovely views over the banana- & coconut-filled valley below. Used mainly by Dar professionals working at the hospital, it's well maintained, efficient & very good value. *US$30/35 sgl/dbl B&B*. **$**

UTENDE The number of accommodation options around Utende has increased in recent years, but thankfully remains at a low level and retains its escapist charm. There's a reasonable amount of choice, even for those on a tighter budget, although the more upmarket places remain the most popular.

Exclusive

Eco Shamba Kilole Lodge w ecoshambakilolelodge.com; ⌚ mid-Jun–mid-Apr. This quiet, peaceful & eco-friendly Italian-owned lodge comprises 6 individually themed chalets & suites, all thoughtfully decorated with ochre exteriors, traditional ceilings, reclaimed dhow furniture, fan, mosquito net & semi-open bathroom. A cosy 2-storey lounge is filled with wooden & coir-rope chairs, packed bookshelves & cats who steal the comfiest spots. Beach access is through a band of mangroves, baobabs & palms, but the main focus is diving. The lovely pool is used for novice/refresher dives, while the emerald lawns are perfect for candlelit Italian dinners or wine tastings. Substantial discounts offered for long stays. **$$$–$$$$**

Kinasi Lodge w kinasilodge.com; ⌚ Jun–end Mar. The lovely Indian Ocean hideaway stands in palm-shaded landscaped gardens above a lovely sandy beach. The 14 bungalows are individually decorated & named after a country or region with historical links to the Swahili Coast, but all boast Zanzibari queen-size beds enveloped in vast mosquito nets & stone verandas furnished with armchairs & hammocks. The multi-level, open-sided bar & lounge contains a top-notch reference library & comfortable couches, while the adjacent dining area stands alongside the swimming-pool & serves an eclectic fusion menu & themed dinners. There's a walk-in wine cellar & cocktail bar for pre-dinner drinks & canapés. A fully equipped watersports & PADI dive centre offers snorkelling trips, windsurfing, kayaking & game fishing. Other activities include dhow trips, village visits, mountain biking & 4x4 excursions. The Isis Spa has 3 treatment rooms, including the romantic Pharaoh bath. *FB*. **$$$$$**

✱ **Pole Pole** w polepole.com; ⌚ Jun–Mar. Combining elements of luxury with a rustic, unpretentious charm, this relaxed Italian-managed lodge (whose Swahili name translates as 'slowly,

slowly') stands in a garden of coconut palms & has a small beach with mangroves on either side. Connected by pathways of the softest sand, the 9 suites & bungalows are built almost entirely from organic materials & have private shaded verandas with relaxing Zanzibari daybeds, well-cushioned chairs & a sea view. Italian-influenced 4-course dinners are served in the airy restaurant; Swahili dinners are offered once a week or on request. Other amenities include a lovely sail-shaded swimming pool & masseuse service. A complimentary dhow trip, usually including some snorkelling & perhaps a BBQ picnic lunch, is normally offered every day & more remote diving, game fishing & island excursions are also offered. Ideal if you're looking for somewhere small, comfortable, chilled & fairly remote. **$$$$$$**

Upmarket

Mafia Island Lodge w mafialodge.com; 🕘 Jun–Apr. This large, functional government-built lodge stands on one of the island's few open palm-lined beaches, opposite the ruins of Chole Mjini. Now under experienced & welcoming Italian management, the lodge is architecturally uninspired but decent value & the 40 comfortable rooms have dark-wood furniture, built-in storage, terracotta tile floors & sea-facing French windows. Dives are arranged through the PADI-affiliated Mafia Island Diving (page 434), while the in-house Mafia Island Tours is the obvious choice for booking other excursions. **$$$$**

Moderate

Butiama Marine Camp w butiamamafiaisland.com. Under the same management as the neighbouring Big Blu Dive Centre, this budget camp offers accommodation in 5 palm-woven beach bungalows with mosquito nets & hot-water shower & 2 larger stone bungalows with AC. There's also a semi-circle of simple but well-kept twin tents, each with clean linen & 24hr electricity (plug point & light). Rooms are en suite but tents use a shared ablution block with clean showers & toilets. The chilled-out restaurant stands right on the beach & there's a lovely ocean-facing lounge area. Considerable discounts are available for room-&-dive combinations. *From US$30/50 sgl/dbl B&B*. **$–$$$**

Mafia Kivulini Lodge w mafiakivulinilodge.com. Opened in 2018, Kivulini means 'beneath the shade' in Swahili and it is an apt name for this small lodge set in a tranquil garden below 100-year-old mango & coconut palm trees. Simple but attractively decorated en-suite dbl & twin chalets have a makuti roof, Zanzibari bed with fitted nets, AC, fan & private balcony with comfortable seating. A restaurant serves curries, seafood & vegetarian dishes. Dives can be arranged through nearby Big Blu (page 434). It is not on the beach but free bicycles are available to ride there in 5mins. *From US$55 dbl B&B*. **$$**

Meremeta Lodge w meremetalodge.com. Boasting a conspicuous kerb-side location on the tar road just outside Utende, quirky Meremeta receives consistently favourable reviews for its friendly atmosphere & relaxed vibe. Rooms are a vision in pink, filled with carvings, ornaments & a fan, & have a private veranda. The open-sided, sand-floor dining room serves 2-course lunches & 3-course dinners & there's also a swimming pool. Active guests can rent quad bikes (US$75/hr) & motorbikes (US$50/hr) or use mountain bikes free of charge. It's not on the beach, but the charming & passionate owner will bend over backwards to ensure guests have the best possible stay. *US$50 dbl B&B*. **$$–$$$**

CHOLE ISLAND The two lodges on Chole are polar opposites: one an originally designed, ecologically friendly retreat; the other a bottom-of-the-scale backpacker hangout. Regardless of your accommodation choice, all visitors to the island must pay a US$10 per person village levy.

Chole Foxes Lodge w booking.com. Named after Chole's population of flying foxes, this small rustic lodge is owned & managed by a charming retired Tanzanian doctor & his wife. The neat bungalows have solar power, fans, wooden 4-poster beds, fitted nets & simple but clean bathrooms. A few coir-rope loungers are dotted about the garden, a seaside restaurant serves homemade seafood & other meals, & it can arrange tours on Mafia (tide dependent). *From US$23/42 sgl/dbl B&B*. **$$**

✷ **Chole Mjini Lodge** w cholemjini.com; ⌚ Jun–Mar. Interspersed with the baobab-studded 19th-century ruins at Chole Mjini, this fabulous lodge is emphatically not aimed for people seeking Sheraton-style luxury or a conventional beach retreat (there is no electricity & the waterfront is overgrown with mangroves), but taken on its own terms it ranks among the most original & aesthetically pleasing lodges on the East African coast. The 9 individually decorated bungalows, some set on stilted platforms & others alongside a large baobab, are made almost entirely of local organic materials & contain a large dbl bed, walk-in net, open wardrobe & dressing area & a padlocked wooden box for valuables. There is also a converted 6-berth, 40ft wooden dhow where guests can spend a night or 2 on the water or fly-camp on a secluded beach. There's no dive centre, swimming pool or sandy beach here, but scuba activities can easily be arranged & it usually offers a couple of complimentary organised walks, snorkel trips or sandbar excursions daily. **$$$$$$**

DIVING *with Jean de Villiers*

Many people visit Mafia purely for its diving, which is often considered the best anywhere in East Africa. It's easy to dive two sites outside the bay on a single outing; the trip out and back can also be great for fishing, sunbathing, sailing and dolphin spotting. The marine park off Chole Bay is home to 48 species of coral, including giant table corals, delicate sea fans, whip corals and huge stands of blue- and pink-tipped staghorn coral.

As well as the spectacular variety of reef fish there are turtles and large predatory fish such as grouper, Napoleon wrasse and barracuda. Stingray, manta rays (rare) and several species of shark are encountered in Kinasi Pass. November to January is best for the more common black-tip and white-tip reef sharks. The corals of Chole Bay, in the heart of the marine park, have recovered dramatically from damage caused by El Niño (of 1997–98) and the destructive fishing practices used before the establishment of the park, and the number of fish is now increasing again. The number of manta rays has sadly decreased significantly in recent years.

Almost all Mafia's best diving is in depths of less than 26m. Between June and September you can dive only within the lagoon-like Chole Bay, albeit in almost any weather. For the more challenging dives outside the bay, you have to wait until the calmer conditions from mid September to November. Outside the bay the average size of the fish is bigger, and you've a good chance of seeing a 2–3m grouper; these are friendly and let you come quite close. Inside the bay, visibility from June to September tends to be 10–15m, whereas from October to February it can be 25m, and high tide gives better visibility than low tide. Mafia is good for beginner divers, as it's very safe inside the bay. However, diving outside the bay on an outgoing tide can be extremely dangerous, with strong currents that can sweep you out to sea: if you miss your rendezvous with a boat, the next stop is Mogadishu. Make sure you check the tides before you set out.

When diving in the open ocean, divers are advised always to carry two means of signalling: one audible (a whistle or air horn) and one visible (an inflatable surface marker, a flare, strobe light or mirror). In addition, always wear a full wetsuit as protection against exposure, and drink water before commencing a dive. Don't take any risks or push the safety boundary while diving here; it's a long way to the nearest decompression chamber in Zanzibar. Note that you can't buy diving insurance in Tanzania – you must have this before you travel; it can be arranged online.

All of the lodges on Mafia offer diving excursions as well as full PADI courses, and those operators listed on page 434 offer specialist diving courses with every conceivable type of dive site – reefs and bommies, channels, walls, caves, drift, ocean and night dives. All these are accessible in a day, while diving safaris catering for 12 people can be arranged to destinations further afield such as Ras Mkumbi, Forbes Bay southeast of Mafia, and the spectacular reef complex around the Songo Songo Islands, which lie about 80km south of Mafia and about 50km north of Kilwa, and so require an overnight trip.

DIVE OPERATORS There are a number of dive operations in Mafia – all listed below – and details of the various courses and packages they offer, as well as rates, can be obtained from their websites. It's worth organising any specialist or 'learn to dive' courses in advance to guarantee space and talk through the options. The majority of operators are very good, and if you are planning on learning to dive on Mafia, it's well worth completing the e-learning scheme before you travel. It allows you to undertake the 'classroom' work online in advance, and so avoid spending your holiday reading up on the facts and physics! Do also remember to check if you need medical clearance to undertake any planned courses, so that this can be arranged in good time.

Big Blu Mafia Island Dive Centre w bigblumafia.com. Adjacent to Butiama Marine Camp, this dedicated dive centre on the fringe of Utende Beach is one of the island's largest scuba operations & offers a comprehensive selection of packages.

Blue World Diving w divingmafiaisland.com. Based at Kinasi Lodge (page 431), this small PADI 5*centre has professional staff & good equipment. Night diving is occasionally possible but requires a minimum of 4 divers, & other specialisms such as Medic First Aid can be arranged.

Mafia Island Diving w mafiadiving.com. Operating at the heart of Utende Beach since 2005, this long-standing dive shop offers high-quality snorkelling, diving & sailing experiences. From deep diver to underwater photography, night diver to peak performance buoyancy, or coral, sea turtle, seahorse or shark-awareness specialisms, there are knowledgeable, multi-lingual staff on hand to teach in & out of the water.

AROUND MAFIA ISLAND

Although Mafia is predominantly visited for its waters, many choose to explore the islands beyond the marine park. It's easiest to arrange this through one of the lodges. For a good English-speaking guide, ask for either Moussa from Big Blu or Halfani at Mafia Island Diving (see above), who was sponsored through school by Pole Pole, where he also once worked. Having extensively researched these islands, Halfani is now also a knowledgeable snorkel guide. To go it alone, you could either hire a bike or negotiate a price with the 4x4 drivers parked in Kilindoni to take you on an excursion.

KILINDONI All arrivals on Mafia pass through Kilindoni, the main town as well as the island's airport and sea port, but few visitors venture into Kilindoni for any length of time. New by East African standards, the town was established by the Germans in 1913 on discovering that Chole Island lacked a deep-water anchorage. While it has none of the Arab architecture of Stone Town on Zanzibar, its coral and lime-mortar shop-houses with quaint signs and rusting corrugated-iron roofs exude an ambience of old Indian Ocean days.

At first, Kilindoni appears to have all the accoutrements of a small town: a district hospital, school (complete with science laboratories), police station, bank, petrol station, post office, airport, mosque and churches. Then suddenly the sandy road opens into a square full of clothes for sale, music and activity, as well as a cluster of tuk-tuks awaiting business.

Peaceful rather than bustling, the **market** is the centre of local life. Tomatoes, chillies, potatoes, onions, limes, coconuts, dried prawns, bananas, cassava and whatever the trader can get his hands on are arranged in little piles. A large amount of food here is from Dar, grown elsewhere on the Tanzanian mainland. Spices are from Zanzibar, naturally, all wrapped up in little plastic packets. Baobab seeds for kids to chew are sold in piles and the fish stalls are pungently gathered together a little further off. Other stalls sell pottery, kangas and secondhand clothes, and if you're brave enough to buy a homemade snorkelling/diving mask, ingeniously made of pieces of metal stapled to thick black rubber, it'll set you back US$2.50. In stark contrast to the ramshackle surroundings, there are a few video rental stores and a surprising number of mobile phone shops, with some unexpectedly up-to-date models available; it seems everyone in town owns one, and Wi-Fi is generally available at even the local guesthouses.

A number of small **local shops** are of interest to the visitor, and most are found on the square or just off it down one of the five road branches. Here various stalls, shacks and shops sell a surprising variety of goods for such a small place. A couple of local tailors tout for business while a tiny shack sells various snacks and sundries. On the square itself the **KMB MIN mini-market** sells cold Cokes and Fantas for US$0.50, as well as items such as chocolate, toilet paper and toothpaste, although note that suncream is a rare commodity – the locals don't use it so it's next to impossible to find. If you're desperate, lighter-skinned lodge staff might be able to lend you some, but it's far better to come well prepared. The **Kisoma Store** sells basic stationery and offers internet access from four computers.

There are more stores on the road descending to the dhow landing, with the **Market General Supply Store** and the **Peace and Love** selling soft drinks. Off the main

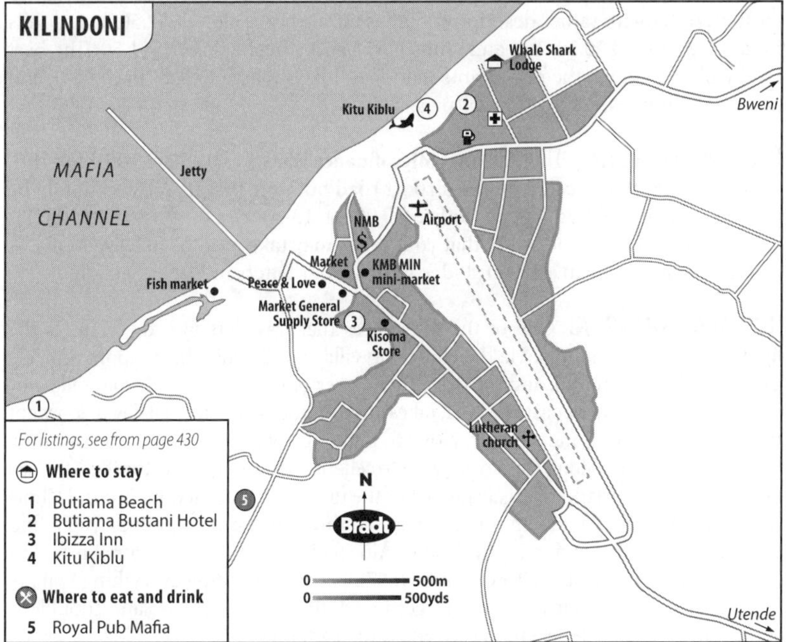

CATCH OF THE DAY – GET HANDS ON

If you decide to stay in Kilindoni, it's worth waking up early to experience the fishermen returning to shore with their overnight catch, and the ensuing spectacle of the fish auction and beachfront cooking. The dhows usually return around 06.30, hitting the beach just south of the jetty. Hauls of fish and octopus are brought ashore and sold in a noisy marketplace, before groups of local women set up all along the beach, laying out carpets of *dagaa*, a small pelagic fish, before scooping them into buckets by hand and cooking them in troughs of bubbling seawater over smoking logs on the sand. It's quite a remarkable scene, and you can always offer to help with the cooking. If you can stomach the gut-wrenching smell and handfuls of slimy fish, you will bring tremendous amusement to these hard-working local women and gain some insight into everyday island life. A great opportunity for some genuine community interaction.

square, Utende Road has a rather vulgar monument presented by the fish factory. On the left is a grey weather-beaten **mosque** and further along the Roman Catholic **church**, one of at least six churches.

The **landing** in Kilindoni usually has 15–20 jahazis moored on the beach. Whether unloading fish or mending their nets, the fishermen object strongly to being photographed, as do the people frying cassava chips and cooking octopus on small stoves under the trees.

Where to eat and drink A basic African establishment, the tiny **Royal Pub Mafia**, with a woven palm door, may be rather surprised by visitors, but sells local beers: Kilimanjaro, Tusker, Serengeti and Bin Bingwa for US$1, and Konyagi (a local firewater with rather descriptive flames on the bottle) for US$2.50. It also sells food: chips are US$0.50, egg and chips US$1 and a beef kebab US$1.50. The best food will be found at the restaurants in lodges, like Butiama Beach (page 430), and better guesthouses, such as Ibizza (page 431).

Other practicalities The **National Microfinance Bank** (⌚ 08.30–15.00 Mon–Fri, 08.30–12.30 Sat), is located on the airport road but note that its ATM can only be used by account holders. The **post office** (⌚ 08.00–13.00 & 14.00–16.30 Mon–Fri) is just past the bank, but be aware that your letter may take months to leave Mafia. A better option may be to ask your lodge to post your letters in Dar es Salaam.

NORTH OF KILINDONI One of the few places that travellers visit on Mafia is the lighthouse at Ras Mkumbi, via the charming village of Bweni. This is approximately 47km north of Kilindoni, and the drive there, over bouncy sand roads that follow or run parallel to the west coast of Mafia, takes about 2 hours direct, or all day if you want to include swimming and a picnic. Note, though, that while there are some stunning white-sand beaches along this coast, with excellent swimming opportunities, the sea on this side of the island is largely devoid of the underwater attractions around Chole Bay to the east. The excursion is best organised through one of the lodges; you'll find an English-speaking guide is invaluable. Alternatively, a full-day excursion to Ras Mkumbi with Mafia Island Tours costs US$75 per person. Bring everything you are likely to need from your hotel, not forgetting clothes to cover knees and shoulders, suncream and insect repellent in case you return after dark.

Driving across Mafia is a good way of seeing the island and finding out about everyday life. As you drive through the villages, you'll see crops of mangoes, pineapples, bananas, cassava and cashew nuts, as well as sweet potatoes, which grow after the rainy season. About 8km from Kilindoni is a picturesque swamp covered in mauve lotus. Small tilapia and catfish dart among the reeds. Further on, the old agricultural village of **Kirongwe**, with a tradition of making clay pots, counts a score of houses, a handful of shops and a market selling the usual dried octopus, bananas and coconuts. Beyond here the countryside is intensively cultivated with beans, pigeon pea and cassava, and – rather less attractive – numerous indications of slash-and-burn agriculture. Sykes' and vervet monkeys raiding the crops flee at the sound of any vehicle.

The north of Mafia is markedly different from the wetter southern part of the island, which is dominated by vast coconut plantations. After **Jimbo**, where you may see local blacksmiths working by the side of the road, the landscape suddenly becomes more undulating open grassland with outcrops of mia'a or palm, and baobabs similar to those on the mainland coastal plain. Birdlife is plentiful, with bee-eaters and lilac-breasted rollers flashing among the trees and large flocks of guineafowl scuttling off the road. While only about 30m above sea level, it is noticeably cooler here than on the coast.

Bweni village, built behind 2km of beach, has obvious potential for tourism development, with its traditional Swahili houses of coral and lime plaster dotted among slender coconut palms. You need to stop to collect the lighthouse key from a keeper in the village if you plan to visit, and will be soon surrounded by excited and curious children, delighted at the chance to shout '*Mzungu*!' at the unexpected visitor. Their behaviour is polite, however, and their fascination mixed with a fear of the unknown, although this is slowly changing. Bweni women are experts at weaving striped prayer mats from the palms on the plateau, and you only need to show interest for items to be shyly produced. The larger mats are 2.5m by 1.5m, and cost around US$4; smaller oval mats go for US$3.

The **lighthouse** at **Ras Mkumbi** is a 3km drive on a good stretch of road from Bweni. Built on coral rag on the northern tip of Mafia, it is worth climbing the 15m up to the top of the red-and-white structure for a spectacular view of the Mafia Channel lying between the archipelago and the mainland. The stretch of deep-blue water is reputed to offer some of the best big-game fishing in East Africa.

The grassy area in front of the lighthouse leads towards a rocky beach which offers half an hour or so of exploration at low tide. Black kites swoop low over the cliffs, while further out fishermen search for octopus in their race against the tide. It's possible to rent a bike from the village, or to go on a forest walk to see birds and monkeys. Snorkelling, fishing and diving trips can also be organised in this area.

KISIMANI MAFIA Kisimani (Kiswahili for 'the place of the well') lies on Ras Kisimani, at the south end of the island 30 minutes' drive from Kilindoni, or a 2-hour boat trip. The town was an important centre during the Shirazi domination of Kilwa between the 12th and 14th centuries (page 446). The hands of the sultan's chief mason were cut off after he built the palace, so that he could never repeat the task. The story goes on to claim that this was why a few months later Kisimani was inundated by the sea. There is little left of the submerged medieval settlement, but you can see the well for which it is named on the beach. Wandering about, you might find a few coins and pottery shards.

The shady coconut palms are a nice spot for a picnic, and there's a lovely beach with good birding and snorkelling, but bring everything you want to eat or drink.

WHALE-SHARK WATCHING: CODE OF CONDUCT

From October to March, Mafia's visitors are blessed with wonderful whale-shark watching opportunities. Visitors during this period are more than 90% likely to see these marvellous marine creatures and have the chance to swim with them – it is really magical. To minimise the disturbance to the whale sharks, ensure their time around Mafia continues well into the future, and to keep both whale sharks and watchers safe, relaxed and happy, it is imperative that both boat operators and swimmers adhere to strict guidelines when approaching, watching and interacting with these huge creatures. The negative effect of not doing so is significant. The whale sharks risk intense, unpleasant harassment, disrupted feeding and even being hit by speeding boats. The code of conduct aims to control and mitigate the impact of human presence and to ensure high-quality experiences.

Please take the time to read these guidelines, and choose carefully an operator who is familiar with, cares about and guarantees to abide by them. Insisting upon this will help to promote truly responsible whale-shark encounters.

GUIDELINES FOR BOATS

- All boats must observe a 50m 'Contact Zone' radius around whale sharks.
- Only one boat at a time may operate in the Contact Zone, and not for longer than 90 minutes, or closer than 10m.
- If a second boat arrives in the Contact Zone, it must stand at least 50m away. Any further boats must wait at least 100m away from the whale shark.
- Boat operators in the Contact Zone should approach from ahead of the shark's direction of travel when dropping swimmers into the water.
- The speed limit for boats in and near a Contact Zone is 2 knots and speeds greater than 5 knots are discouraged because of the high risk of collisions with whale sharks.

GUIDELINES FOR SWIMMERS

Swimmers in the Contact Zone **must not**:

- Exceed more than ten people in the water with one animal at any one time.
- Approach closer than 1.5m from the head or body and 3m from the tail fin.
- Attempt to touch or ride on the whale shark.
- Restrict the normal movement or behaviour of the whale shark.
- Use flash photography.
- Use any underwater motorised devices.

UTENDE The majority of Mafia's tourist lodges lie along the beach below this small village, at the end of the 15km road west from Kilindoni. Many of Utende's inhabitants are Makonde people from the mainland, who keep their fishing boats in Chole Bay. One or two shop houses sell strings of dried octopus and fish. Like everywhere else on Mafia, the village is quite safe to explore, being only 10 minutes' walk from any of the hotels. The beach in front of Utende (close to Mafia Island Lodge) is where local dhows leave for Chole Island.

Schools here are developing with aid from the lodges. A new primary school was built on the site of the old school, offering Standards 1–6, and nursery education for 31 pupils. Since 2000, this has been financed by Pole Pole who sponsor some of the pupils. The government was then helped to build another school building for seven to 14 year olds. Visitors are welcome to visit the projects of the non-profit community development organisation Karibuni Onlus, which aims to improve education and health care in Utende village and all over Mafia. They have sponsored students and contributed towards the building and upkeep of a school and a well in Utende, but they also provide volunteer doctors, distribute mosquito nets all over the island and are renovating a school in nearby Kiegeani. Mafia Island Tours (**w** mafiadiving.com) offers a trip to see the well and the school, plus learn about Karibuni Onlus's work for just US$5 per person, all of which goes directly to the organisation.

Utende also has a couple of small shops, and you'll notice a number of buildings made with cement blocks and corrugated iron. Although not picturesque, cement blocks are relatively cheap and an easy material for building, while corrugated-iron roofs last longer than a palm-leaf roof, which has to be replaced every three years or so.

For a fascinating insight into local life, visit the morning fish auction on the beach and see the night's catch sold and prepared. It is on a smaller scale to the fish preparation in Kilindoni (page 436), but still an eye-opening snapshot of Swahili island ways.

OTHER EXCURSIONS Most other villages on Mafia are inaccessible by road and, like the offshore islands, may be visited only by boat. Given advance warning, the lodges can usually arrange trips to visit them.

However, the most popular excursions are probably those to isolated sandbars. You'll sail to these from your lodge, and then the boat crew will set up some shade on the beach, and cook lunch over a barbecue. Meanwhile, you can relax, sunbathe, swim and snorkel with nothing around you except miles and miles of deep-blue ocean. Trips like these are included by some of the lodges, while others will charge you extra, depending on the destination (US$40–75 per person per trip is typical).

Away from the sandbars and the larger islands of Chole, Juani and Jibondo, a few smaller spots worth a mention include the following.

Mchangani This village is the end of an interesting excursion winding for nearly 3km up a creek on the north side of Chole Bay. Sykes' monkeys can be seen in the mangrove forests and fish eagles are commonly observed. The village lies on the east bank of the creek; it takes about an hour to reach by vehicle, or 90 minutes if you'd rather walk over sand and rock. Depart only on a high tide.

Dindini Beach Likewise accessible only at high tide, the beach faces the ocean from Mafia Island just north of Chole Bay, and from December to February can see big waves. Behind the beach is a large, sea-fed rock pool, which contains a variety of marine life. There are also low sand dunes and interesting vegetation on the coral rag.

Ras Mbisi Only 90 minutes by road from Kilindoni, Ras Mbisi has an ideal beach for picnics, swimming and snorkelling. Ras Mbisi Lodge, right on the beach, was razed to the ground by a devastating fire in 2016. Its resurrection is still very uncertain, but should accommodation spring up here, it's a great spot for beach escapists, and just after dawn the villagers put on a tremendous display of teamwork, hauling in their nets on the beach.

Mbaracuni Island Lying 12km northwest of Mafia, this island can be visited by arrangement. Uninhabited, quiet and said to be very beautiful, it is used by fishing dhows. This is a good place to see black kites and occasionally two or three fish eagles.

Miewe Another small, uninhabited island used by fishermen to clean and dry fish, Miewe can be visited for picnics, as can the sandbank of **Marimbani**. If you're interested in sailing a little further, and for a good chance of seeing dolphins, you can take a day excursion to the island of **Kitutia**. After a couple of hours under sail, you'll be rewarded by some stunning snorkelling on a reef which surrounds a pure-white sandbank. This is all covered by the sea at high tide, so the trip needs to be timed carefully.

ISLANDS AROUND MAFIA

CHOLE ISLAND Chole is the lush, tropical island lying to the west of the Kinasi Pass. With the adjacent islands of Juani and Jibondo, it forms a barrier between Mafia and the open ocean. The shallow reef in front is rich in soft corals, sea anemones and sponges, and, sloping to 15m, it is a good spot to practise drift diving. The bay itself is ideal for sailing, windsurfing and kite surfing. The town of Chole Mjini was the main urban centre on the archipelago for much of the 19th century, the home of wealthy merchants whose plantations lay on the main island of Mafia. Ruins dating from this era include a reasonably preserved **German Customs House** on the waterfront, and several more **ruined mansions** dating to the Omani era. A path behind the new market leading to the village brings you to a **prison**, whose broken cells are invaded by tangled tree roots. Farther along and also in ruins is a **Hindu temple**.

Hanging upside down in a nearby baobab is a colony of Seychelles flying foxes. Every evening these massive bats fly across Chole Bay to feed on the cashew nut and mango trees of Mafia, as well as marula fruit, figs and mangrove flowers. Like the Comoros bats they dip over the surface of the water – an action which scientists believe may be an attempt to rid themselves of parasites. A more enchanting local explanation claims 'they are washing before evening prayers'. Bats are nocturnal, so it's imperative for the continuation of the Chole colony that visitors allow them to sleep in the day, ensuring that neither they nor their guide throw stones at them, or shake their tree, just to wake them up and take photos of the bats in flight. Remember that it is a bat sanctuary.

Chole's human population was estimated at 5,000 during the early years of German rule, but today it is no more than 1,000. The islanders cultivate smallholdings of cassava, beans, mangoes, paw-paw, citrus (including very sweet oranges) and passion fruit. Encouraged by the lodges, these smallholdings have flourished and produce is now exported to Mafia, with the oranges also making their way to the mainland. Most of the menfolk fish, while many of the women are engaged in catching octopus beyond the mangroves at low tide. Winding past traditional houses, the path brings you to a beach where fishermen can be seen mending nets, or making sails and coconut-coir ropes. Chole was once a centre of boatbuilding, and boats are still repaired and occasionally built on the island. The boatyard is indicated on the circular walk available from Chole Mjini, about half an hour from the lodge.

The Norwegian Women's Front and Chole Mjini Lodge have been instrumental in much of Chole's development. They have funded the building of a hospital and a free clinic for the under fives, a kindergarten, a market and the Society for Women's Development (which runs savings and loan schemes). They have also helped to set up a school, so that children no longer have to walk across to Juani Island at low tide, and a learning centre to help educate adults.

For places to stay, see page 432. Note that Chole Mjini Lodge does not cater to passing custom or serve meals to non-residents.

Getting there and away The lodges at Utende (page 431) operate **boat trips** to Chole, or you can visit it independently from Mafia, or on a **'bat and village tour'** with Mafia Island Tours. A dhow dubbed the **'Chole taxi'** leaves the beach in front of Mafia Island Lodge every 30 minutes or so throughout the day – last sailing at 16.00 – a crossing of 10 to 15 minutes depending on the wind and tide, for a cost of US$0.60 one-way for visitors. It is also possible to charter a local boat across for a fee of about US$10.

On arrival you will need to hand over a village levy of US$10 per person – which goes straight to the village – payable at the Red Herring Café where the boat docks. You can also charge camera batteries here because there's no other electricity on the island. If you plan to stay more than a few hours on the island it is advisable to bring a picnic and refreshments from your hotel, and note that you'll have to wade a short distance from the boat. Make sure that you're wearing shoes, as there are stingrays in this area.

JUANI ISLAND The boat trip from Mafia to Juani, site of the ruined city of Kua, takes about 10 minutes longer than the one to Chole, but the island can be approached only at high tide. The landing, in a small bay sheltered by dense mangroves, is covered in thousands of opened oyster-shells, so remember to wear good shoes, as you'll have to wade to shore. Seafood is the staple diet on Juani, but, unlike Chole, Juani has no well water, and locals practise rain-dependent cultivation.

Beneath three big baobabs near the landing, your shoes crunch on the rocky paths of a buried civilisation. Bits of blue-and-white Shirazi pottery suggesting trade links with China are embedded in the dirt. In the past, people from the mainland came to Juani to bathe in a seawater cave reputed to have curative properties for rheumatism. It is a long, difficult walk across to the ocean side, where there are three protected turtle-nesting beaches (page 442). The Kua Channel slices a tiny chunk off Juani as it opens into Chole Bay. It makes a superb picnic excursion with birdwatching and swimming. A friendly grouper lives in one of the rock pools at the southern end.

The ruined city of **Kua** (page 443), spread across 6ha on the west coast of Juani, was the Shirazi capital of Mafia. It was one of the few East African ports to be continuously inhabited from medieval times into the early 19th century, when it was sacked by raiders from Madagascar. A trail hacked out of the undergrowth leads up to a large building shedding masonry: the former palace, still revered locally as a 'spirit place' where offerings such as bits of glass are left. The ruins here have been defeated by the powerful strangler figs that dominate a number of the walls, and the tomb of the sultan himself has been destroyed by a tree growing in its centre. The path passes other ruined edifices, including two 14th-century mosques and a series of tombs.

The buildings are made from coral rock and lime cement, which does not survive well in this sea air. Looking at cracks in the walls you wonder how long they will remain standing, with the occasional monkey as the only inhabitant. If you see the caretaker, he expects and deserves a small gratuity; ask him to show you the foundations of the house referred to in the box on page 443.

You depart on a beautiful sail home between the islands, watched by the scores of ibis on the mangroves. There is a guide and map of the ruins, as well as the report on its archaeology, in the library at Kinasi Lodge (page 431).

JIBONDO ISLAND Jibondo is a long, low-lying island another 20-minute sail from Juani. This traditional village community is rather different from the rest of Mafia, and the atmosphere is somehow more charged than in other villages. Coming ashore, a big **jahazi dhow** is one of the first things you see. Built 15 years ago, it has never been launched and is subsequently something of a museum piece, but the old men sitting under the quinine tree nearby have already learned its value to tourism, wanting to charge US$1 for a photo.

Behind the boat is a rather plain white **mosque**, built in 1979. Some of its furniture was taken from the queen's palace in the ruins at Kua, and it's worth wandering around the back to see the carved wooden door from Kua (by contrast, the window frames were made of wood from India). This is all set off by the pungent smell from the row of long-drop loos that literally drop into the sea. Jibondo does not have a fresh water supply, so the islanders depend on frequent deliveries from Mafia's main island.

Jibondo people are well known as shipbuilders and, as on Chole, use only traditional tools. Even the nails are handmade and the holes are plugged with local kapok and shark fat. Local women play a prominent role in trading as well as fishing. They also sail boats, which is unusual in African society, and are more affable and confident than women elsewhere. Jibondo people also collect and dry seaweed to export.

Another unusual aspect of Jibondo is that cultivation is carried out at one end of the island while the people live in an urban community at the other. The village,

TURTLE-HATCHING ECOTOURISM

Turtles have been nesting on Tanzanian beaches for millions of years, and thanks to a successful NGO called **Sea Sense** (m +255 783 965380; w seasense.org), visitors to Mafia can now witness this spine-tingling spectacle. Established in 2001, they work in partnership with the local community to promote the importance and protection of marine turtles and their habitats. Over the last 15 years, the initiative has been so successful that it has significantly increased the number and survival rate of turtle eggs, and in doing so, it has made sea-turtle ecotourism viable.

Managed by conservation officers and local 'Turtle Tour Guides', the ecotourism venture offers visitors a truly remarkable experience and also generates a sustainable source of revenue for the community. Aside from local staff employment and donations, the community also receives half of all ecotourism revenue to fund their own development projects, making them both aware and proud of the benefits that come from protecting their marine environment.

Between June and September, the baby turtles hatch in their hundreds on the eastern beaches of Juani Island and make their long sandy journey to the lapping waves of the Indian Ocean. It's a magical sight! Leaving by dhow from Utende, excited turtle enthusiasts arrive on Juani's western coast, before walking across the island's densely forested interior (45mins) and past the village, to reach the hatching beaches. Here, the Turtle Tour Guide will point out the subterranean nests, and thanks to impeccable monitoring, the near-exact time of hatching. Furiously flapping their fins, the tiny turtles appear through the parting grains of sand, allowing for close-up heart-melting viewing of their first steps into the sun. It's terribly exciting and very moving to watch them head down the beach and onwards with their life's journey, and well worth supporting if you're here.

You can book the Sea Sense turtle-hatching trip through any hotel or dive centre on Mafia (US$40 plus US$10 Sea Sense charity fee).

KUA'S REVENGE

The political relationship between Kisimani and Kua is unclear, but an intriguing if unverifable oral tradition recounted by T M Revington in an essay in *Tanganyika Notes & Records* suggests that it was not always amicable:

> The people of Ras Kisimani constructed a ship, and when it was finished and still on the stocks, they made a feast to which they invited the people of Kua. From amongst the guests they took by force several children, laid them on the sand, and launched the ship over their bodies. When the Kua people heard what had been done at Ras Kisimani, they were infuriated and thought out a scheme of revenge. Seven or eight years later, when they thought that the incident had been forgotten, an invitation was sent to the inhabitants of Ras Kisimani to attend a wedding at Kua. When the guests arrived in the evening they were ushered to a room that had been especially prepared beneath a house; the hosts one by one left their guests on the excuse of inquiring into the food, until only an old man remained to entertain them. This he did so well that the doors were bricked up without the guests perceiving it. The bodies are there to this day. So, too, is the sealed-off basement in which the bodies lie, according to the site's caretaker, who claims that it is situated below the ruins in front of his hut.

which consists of traditional Swahili-style houses with makuti roofs, is laid out in a grid pattern. As on Chole and Juani, there is no transport other than boats which shelter on the western side of the narrow neck of the island.

The island has one school, easily identified by the football field in front. If the tide is good for fishing, the children – encouraged by their parents – go straight out on the water, skipping lessons. In a year, only one child is likely to leave the island and go to secondary school on Mafia. There are, however, three *madrasas* on the island, where there is a strong Muslim faith. There are no other social services, and only a basic shop. On the other side of the island is **Flamingo Beach**, which makes an interesting 2-hour trek. The village trail and sailing dhow with Mafia Island Tours costs US$30.

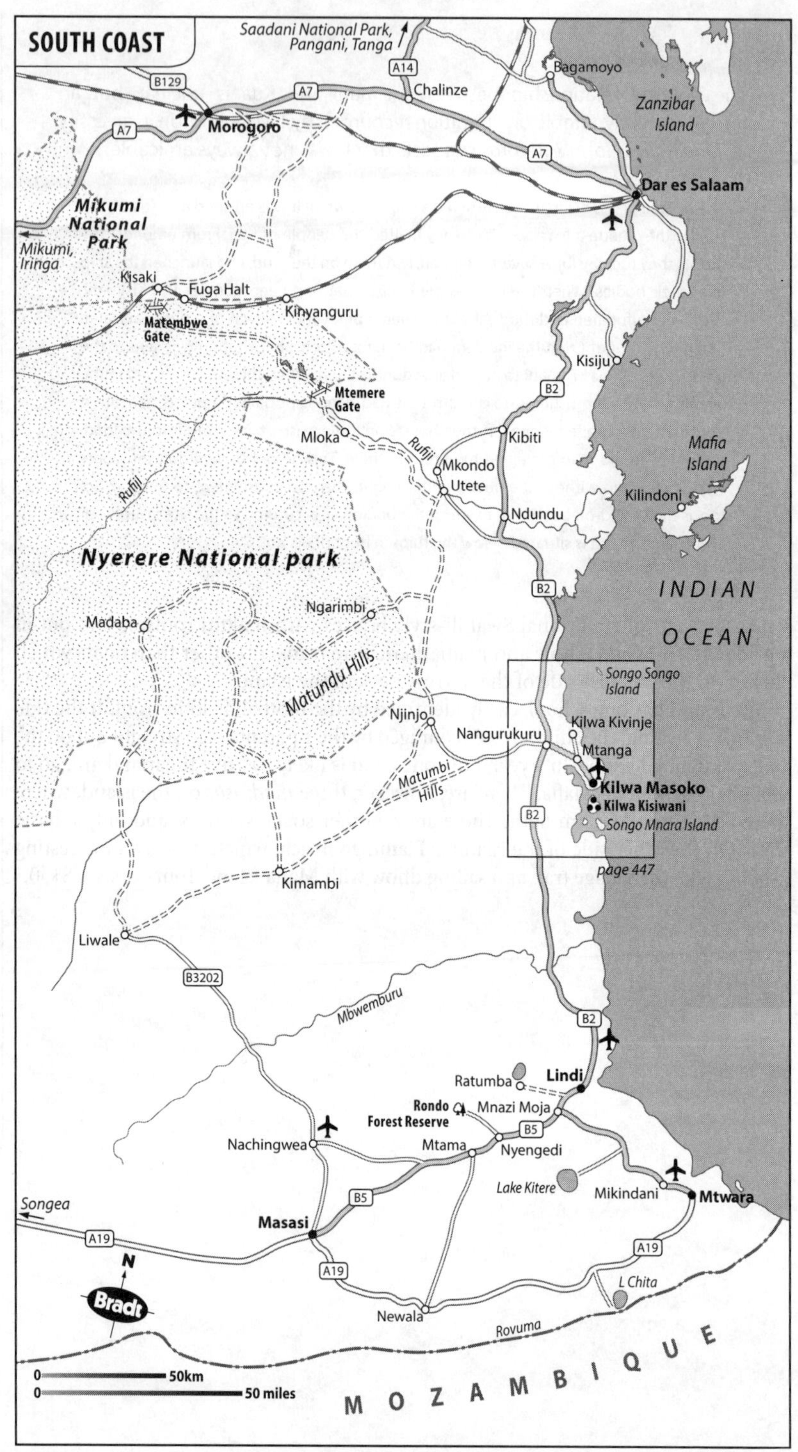

SOUTH COAST
Saadani National Park,
Pangani, Tanga
Bagamoyo
Chalinze
Zanzibar Island
Morogoro
Dar es Salaam
Mikumi National Park
Mikumi, Iringa
Kisaki
Fuga Halt
Kinyanguru
Matembwe Gate
Kisiju
Mtemere Gate
Mloka
Rufiji
Kibiti
Mkondo
Utete
Mafia Island
Kilindoni
Ndundu
Nyerere National park
INDIAN OCEAN
Madaba
Ngarimbi
Matundu Hills
Songo Songo Island
Njinjo
Nangurukuru
Kilwa Kivinje
Mtanga
Matumbi Hills
Kilwa Masoko
Kilwa Kisiwani
Songo Mnara Island
page 447
Kimambi
Liwale
Mbwemburu
Ratumba
Lindi
Rondo Forest Reserve
Mnazi Moja
Nachingwea
Mtama
Nyengedi
Lake Kitere
Mikindani
Mtwara
Songea
Masasi
L Chita
Newala
Rovuma
MOZAMBIQUE
N
Bradt
0 50km
0 50 miles

17

Kilwa and the South Coast

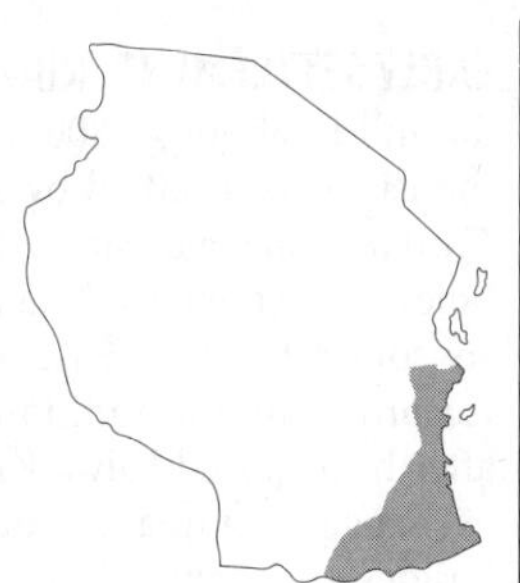

Situated 300km south of Dar es Salaam, the Indian Ocean island of Kilwa, separated from the mainland by a narrow palm-fringed channel, houses the ruins of the most architecturally ambitious and historically significant of the mercantile cities that lined the East African coast during the so-called Golden Age of Swahili. Inscribed as a UNESCO World Heritage Site in 1981 (together with the lesser ruins on Songo Mnara), this 20km^2 island once served as the apex of a cosmopolitan maritime trade that linked medieval Arabia, Asia and Europe to the gold mines of the African interior.

Somewhat confusingly, the name Kilwa – literally, 'Place of Fish' – today applies to three different settlements. Kilwa Kisiwani (Kilwa on the Island) is the name of the island-bound ruins and an adjacent fishing village that now supports a few hundred people. On the facing mainland, Kilwa Kivinje (Kilwa of the Casuarinas) is a slumbering 19th-century settlement steeped in history, while Kilwa Masoko (Kilwa of the Market), administrative capital of Kilwa District, is a relatively modern town that has served as the main regional hub of commerce and transport since the early 20th century.

For most visitors, Kilwa's main points of interest are its history and architecture. Kilwa Kisiwani and Kilwa Kivinje are possibly unique in that they collectively include well-preserved buildings that represent virtually every era of the past millennium of coastal history. But Kilwa is also a good place to immerse yourself in a traditional Swahili port-cum-fishing-village culture, and the surrounding coast is very attractive, with good angling and diving possibilities for those who can afford them.

HISTORY

Neglected by Tanzania's safari-based tourist industry and universally ignored in modern school curricula, Kilwa was, back in its medieval pomp, the most important settlement in subequatorial Africa. For more than 300 years, it was the commercial pivot of a gold-trading network that linked the interior of present-day Zimbabwe to Arabia, China and India. The most widely travelled man of the age, Ibn Battuta, ranked it as 'one of the most beautiful and well-constructed cities in the world'. And the city's finest buildings – the Great Mosque and the Sultan's Palace or Husuni Kubwa – formed the undisputed apex of Swahili architectural aspirations. Fortunately, while many details of Kilwa's past are open to conjecture, the combination of archaeological excavations, a few surviving contemporary descriptions and two known versions of the *Kilwa Chronicle* (written in 1520 under the supervision of the then-exiled sultan) means that the history of Kilwa is better understood than that of most medieval Swahili settlements.

EARLY SETTLEMENT Kilwa Kisiwani was occupied by the Shirazi precursors of the Swahili in about AD800, though little is known about this early period. In 1150, the island was settled by Ali bin Al-Hasan, whose father, according to the *Kilwa Chronicle*, had a dream in Shiraz in which 'he saw a rat with an iron snout gnawing holes in the town wall…a prophecy of the ruin of their country'. The father and his six sons set sail for East Africa, where they disembarked at seven different ports. According to this tradition, Ali was known locally as Nguo Myingi ('many clothes') after he acquired Kilwa Kisiwani from the 'infidel king' of the facing mainland in exchange for a quantity of cloth, 'some white, some black, and every other colour besides' sufficient to 'encircle the island'.

Tradition has it that Ali bin Al-Hasan ruled over Kilwa for 40 years, and his importance can be gauged by the fact that coins bearing his name – probably minted long after his death – have been found as far afield as Pemba and Mafia islands. The dynasty he founded endured for 150 years, and he is widely credited with establishing Kilwa as a significant trade centre, whose sphere of influence stretched at least as far as Mafia and quite possibly beyond it. The earliest surviving reference to Kilwa is in an Arabic document written in 1222, and while it is less than illuminating ('a town in the country of the Zanj'), it does confirm that Kilwa was by then a trade centre of significance.

Another Arabic document, written a few years later, goes further in describing Kilwa as the principal port between Mogadishu and Madagascar, confirming that the island port flourished under Ali bin Al-Hasan and his successors. Kilwa does, however, seem to have entered a period of political (though perhaps not economic) turmoil in the late 13th century, initiated by repeated conflicts with the indigenous Shanga Kingdom of the nearby island of Sanje ya Kati. According to the *Kilwa Chronicle*, the Sultan of Kilwa was during this period twice overthrown by the Shanga, who installed their leader in his place, though in both instances the upstart ruler was soon deposed by the islanders and a sultan of the Al-Hasan dynasty reinstalled. This instability in turn seems to have prompted a series of internal coups, culminating in 1300 with the ascent of Sultan Al-Hasan Mahdali, founder of the Mahdali dynasty.

THE GOLDEN AGE Al-Hasan Mahdali's was a short reign, as was that of his son and successor Sulaiman, who was killed by followers of the old sultan. Stability was finally restored during the reign of Sultan Al-Hasan bin Sulaiman (1310–32), a highly respected scholar who had studied in Aden and made the pilgrimage to Mecca, and it was maintained during that of his brother Daud bin Sulaiman (1332–56). These two brothers presided over what was almost certainly Kilwa's peak in international prominence and commercial prosperity. Al-Hasan is generally credited with the reconstruction of the Great Mosque and the domed extension to that building, and it was also he who built the splendid out-of-town palace now known as the Husuni Kubwa.

Kilwa at this time was the dominant town on the coast, with a population exceeding 10,000, the first coin mint in sub-Saharan Africa and an extensive well system which is still in use today. The Friday Mosque and Husuni Kubwa, the most impressive buildings on the island, if not the entire coast, date to this period. In addition to gold, Kilwa exported ivory and ebony, and imported such fineries as Eastern cloth and Chinese porcelain. The wealthy traders lived in houses of coral and some had small private mosques. Ordinary townsmen lived in mud-and-wattle huts. Even though some Arab traders settled on Kilwa, the vast majority of its occupants were local Swahili. The island was too small to be self-sufficient in

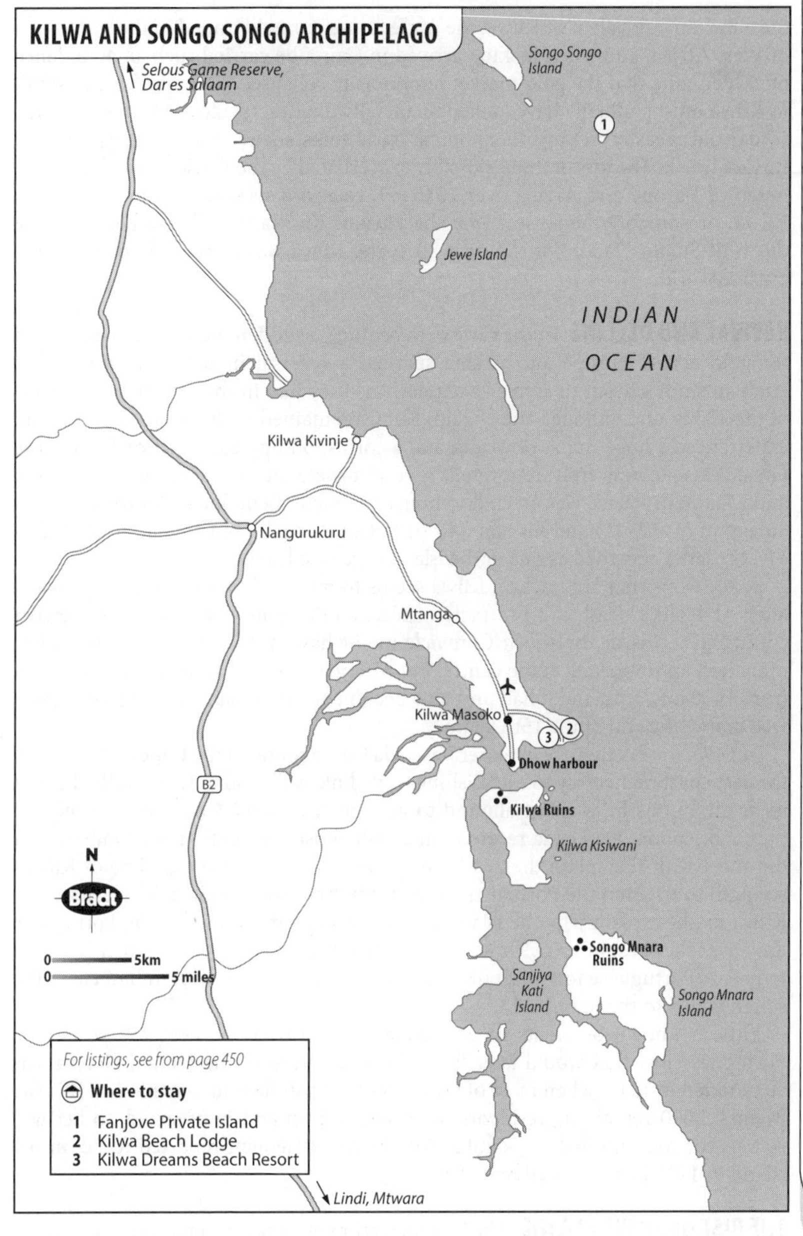

food, so had extensive agricultural interests on the mainland. The only surviving description of Kilwa in this era, penned by Ibn Battuta, the greatest globetrotter of his era, is reproduced on page 453.

Towards the end of Sultan Daud's rule, the maritime gold trade through Kilwa slowed almost to a standstill. The cause of this unexpected slump must have baffled the islanders, but almost certainly it was linked to the King of Timbuktu's trans-Saharan trek to the Mediterranean a few years earlier. Timbuktu, at this time, was the Sahelian equivalent of Kilwa, the trade funnel for gold mined in the rainforests of West Africa, and when its king arrived in Cairo, he carried such an abundance of golden gifts that the gold market temporarily collapsed. The long voyage south to Kilwa must suddenly have looked financially unattractive to Arabian merchants who could as easily pick up other popular trade items, such as ivory and tortoiseshell, further north. The loss of trade, possibly exacerbated by the Black Death that struck much of Europe and Arabia over 1346–49, caused a serious economic slump in Kilwa, presumably the reason why the Husuni Kubwa was abandoned after the death of Sultan Daud. For the next 50 years, Kilwa was almost forgotten by the outside world.

REVIVAL AND DECLINE In the early 15th century, a sudden increase in the demand for gold across Europe and Arabia sparked a reversal in Kilwa's fortunes. The Arabian ships started to arrive as regularly as they had in the commercial heyday of the 1330s, and although the Husuni Kubwa remained in disuse, the town centre experienced a huge influx of wealth and a corresponding construction boom. The Great Mosque was fully renovated, several ornate smaller mosques were built, and Makutani Palace was erected to house the incumbent Sultan Muhammad bin Sulaiman (1412–21) and his son and successor Al Malik bin Muhammad (1421–41), the latter regarded as one of the island's greatest leaders.

For reasons that are unclear, Kilwa seems to have slid backwards economically after Al Malik's death – a protracted succession dispute described in somewhat confusing terms in the *Kilwa Chronicle* might have been a factor in this. Kilwa remained an important trade centre, but Mombasa was steadily in the ascendant from 1450 onwards, and it had probably become the dominant coastal trade centre well before the end of the 15th century.

In 1498, the Portuguese explorer Vasco da Gama rounded the Cape and sailed up the east coast on his way to establishing trade links with India. He described Kilwa in detail, but as he was not allowed to go near the island, his report is probably pure fabrication. Da Gama received an equally hostile reception in Mombasa, but did meet with the sultan there, who may have exaggerated the decline of Kilwa's strength to frighten the Portuguese away from the coast. Da Gama's description of Kilwa might explain why the island was so heavily targeted when the Portuguese took over the coast in 1505. Three-quarters of Kilwa's residents were killed or forced to flee. A Portuguese fort was built, the gold trade moved to Mozambique and the sultan exiled to the mainland.

Little is known of events on and around Kilwa over the next 250 years. The Portuguese fort that would later form the foundation of the Omani Gereza was abandoned in 1512, when most of the garrison succumbed to malaria. In 1587, the island's 3,000 remaining residents were rounded up and imprisoned, to become rations for the cannibalistic Zimba. An Omani settlement reported to be on the island in 1712 had vanished by 1719.

THE RISE OF KILWA KIVINJE The first indication of Kilwa's re-emergence as a trade centre, and of the nature of its future trade, came in 1776 when the Sultan of Kilwa – presumably of Shirazi or indigenous descent – signed a contract to provide a French merchant from Mauritius with 1,000 slaves annually. That treaty fell through in 1784 when Kilwa was attacked by, and made subject to, the Sultan of Oman. The island was occupied by Omani agents, who left their mark in the form of the large fort (Gereza) on the waterfront, and minor restoration work to the Great Mosque and Makutani Palace.

In 1812, when HMS *Nisus* anchored off Kilwa, James Prior noted that the Gereza was still in use as the Omani governor's residence, but was unimpressed by the scattering of thatch huts that comprised the town, 'if town it should be called'. Within a few years, the Omani settlers evacuated the island to establish the mainland town of Kilwa Kivinje. Kilwa Kisiwani went into terminal decline thereafter – the last Sultan of Kilwa, interviewed by Lieutenant Christopher of the *Tigris* in 1846, was captured by the Sultan of Zanzibar and sent into exile before 1856.

Within years of its establishment, Kilwa Kivinje had become the centre of the southern slave trade. By the mid 19th century it was a very wealthy town, with up to 20,000 slaves passing through annually. Although the Sultan of Zanzibar outlawed the slave trade in 1873, it persisted out of Kilwa for longer than anywhere else, but had been stopped almost entirely by 1880. Many of Kilwa's slave traders established rubber plantations, and business continued to prosper. In 1886, Kilwa Kivinje became a German administrative centre, and it remained a town of regional importance during the first half of the 20th century. Since the end of World War II it has gradually been reduced to backwater status, with the more modern town of Kilwa Masoko serving as the regional headquarters.

KILWA AND GREAT ZIMBABWE

Kilwa's pre-eminence during the early 14th century is linked to broader patterns associated with the medieval gold trade out of Africa. The inland source of this gold was long shrouded in mystery, but we now know that the gold was mined in the southern interior, in the vicinity of Great Zimbabwe, the fabulous stone ruin for which the country Zimbabwe is named.

The mechanism of trade between Great Zimbabwe and the coast remains a matter of conjecture. It seems likely that the gold was carried on foot along the Zambezi Valley to the coastal port of Sofala (near modern-day Beira in Mozambique). It is assumed that, prior to the mid 13th century, local middlemen transported it northward along the coast from Sofala to Mogadishu (in present-day Somalia), which was then the most important trade centre on the Swahili coast – presumably reflecting the inability of contemporary Arab vessels to sail much further south within the annual monsoon cycle.

As the volume of coastal trade increased, however, improvements in Arab navigation and ship design allowed them to penetrate steadily further south. But Sofala would have been beyond their reach whatever they did, since the winds south of Kilwa are notoriously fickle. Nevertheless, it would have suited the merchants of Sofala to bring the centre of trade closer to home. And Kilwa would have been the ideal compromise: much closer to Sofala than Mogadishu or Mombasa, but still within reach of the Arab vessels. By the early 14th century, Sofala and Kilwa had assumed joint control of the gold trade, and it is often suggested that the Mahdali dynasty of Kilwa had its roots in Sofala.

That Kilwa and Great Zimbabwe were the most important subequatorial African cities of their age is beyond question. And clearly the prosperity of either city was dependent on that of the other. Yet the only surviving physical evidence of this link is a solitary Kilwa-minted coin that was unearthed at Great Zimbabwe a few decades back. Cultural and architectural parallels between the two cities are non-existent – indeed, no evidence exists to suggest that the coastal traders ever visited, or indeed knew of, Great Zimbabwe.

KILWA MASOKO

The most useful base in Kilwa District, this friendly, modern town boasts a good selection of budget and mid-range accommodation options, though it's of less inherent interest than its more antiquated namesakes. The nominal town centre, a small grid of dirt roads emanating from a central market, lies about 1km inland of the harbour, to which it is connected by a tar road. The town's smarter lodges lie a few hundred metres east of the main tar road along the attractively sandy baobab-lined Jimbizi Beach.

GETTING THERE AND AWAY

By air There are no longer any scheduled flights to Kilwa Airport, which lies 500m from the centre of Kilwa Masoko, but charters from Songo Songo, Dar es Salaam, Mafia Island or Nyerere National Park can be arranged through any domestic airline including Coastal Aviation (**m** +255 699 999999; **w** coastal.co.tz).

By road Kilwa Masoko lies about 320km south of Dar es Salaam, a drive that should take around 6 hours in a private vehicle. The road is fully surfaced but you need to branch left at the small junction town of Nangurukuru, from where it is about 10km to Kilwa Kivinje and 20km to Kilwa Masoko. Half-a-dozen **buses** leave Dar es Salaam for Kilwa daily (US$6.50; 6hrs), starting at the Mbagala ya Rangi terminus. Most reliable is the Mashallah Bus (**m** +255 688 067706), whose relatively comfortable buses leave Dar es Salaam at 06.30, 11.30, 13.00 and 15.00. With early-morning buses, book your ticket a day in advance and arrange to be collected by a taxi on the morning of departure.

WHERE TO STAY

Out of town *Map, page 447*

Exclusive

Fanjove Private Island **w** ed.co.tz. This low-impact solar-powered lodge stands on a small private island 5km southeast of Songo Songo Island (from which it is reached by dhow) & 40km north of Kilwa Masoko. The 6 2-storey A-frame bandas have wooden floors, makuti roofs, simple but stylish furnishing, bathroom open to the sky & a balcony facing the sandy palm-lined beach. Marine birds are plentiful & the island is home to the coconut crab, the world's largest terrestrial crustacean. **$$$$$$**

Moderate

Kilwa Beach Lodge ⊕ -8.89969, 39.51846; **m** +255 745 236372; **w** kilwa.co.tz. Situated on Pwani Beach 4km north of Kilwa Masoko, this owner-managed seafront lodge has an idyllic location on a former coconut palm plantation. The 6 whitewashed beach bands were constructed using local expertise & recycled or organic materials, & there is also a very pleasant campsite with a common ablution block. A relaxed seaside restaurant serves fresh seafood & caters to vegetarians. *From US$61/80 sgl/dbl B&B; camping US$10pp.* **$–$$**

Kilwa Dreams Beach Resort ⊕ -8.89804, 39.51806; **m** + 255 784 585330; **w** kilwadreams.com. Also on Pwani Beach, this small owner-managed lodge comprises a row of 7 airy blue cottages literally 10m from the sea. There's a good seafood restaurant with DSTV, & a very peaceful isolated atmosphere. It offers fishing trips & arranges safaris to Nyerere National Park. *US$90 dbl B&B.* **$$**

In town *Map, page 451*

Moderate

Kilwa Pakaya Hotel **m** +255 714 586405; **w** kilwapakayahotel.co.tz. The smartest lodge on Jimbizi Beach comprises a 2-storey accommodation block, a superb open-air seafood restaurant & a white sandy beach lined with makuti-shaded deckchairs. The 20 rooms come with AC, fan, coffee-/tea-making facilities & modern décor complemented by ethnic artwork on the walls. Upper-floor rooms have the better sea view. *US$95/115 sgl/dbl B&B, but check the website for special offers.* **$$$**

Kimbilio Lodge **w** ed.co.tz. This small beach resort stands in well-maintained gardens running down to a beachfront restaurant & wooden deck. The 6 cool & comfortable makuti-roofed huts

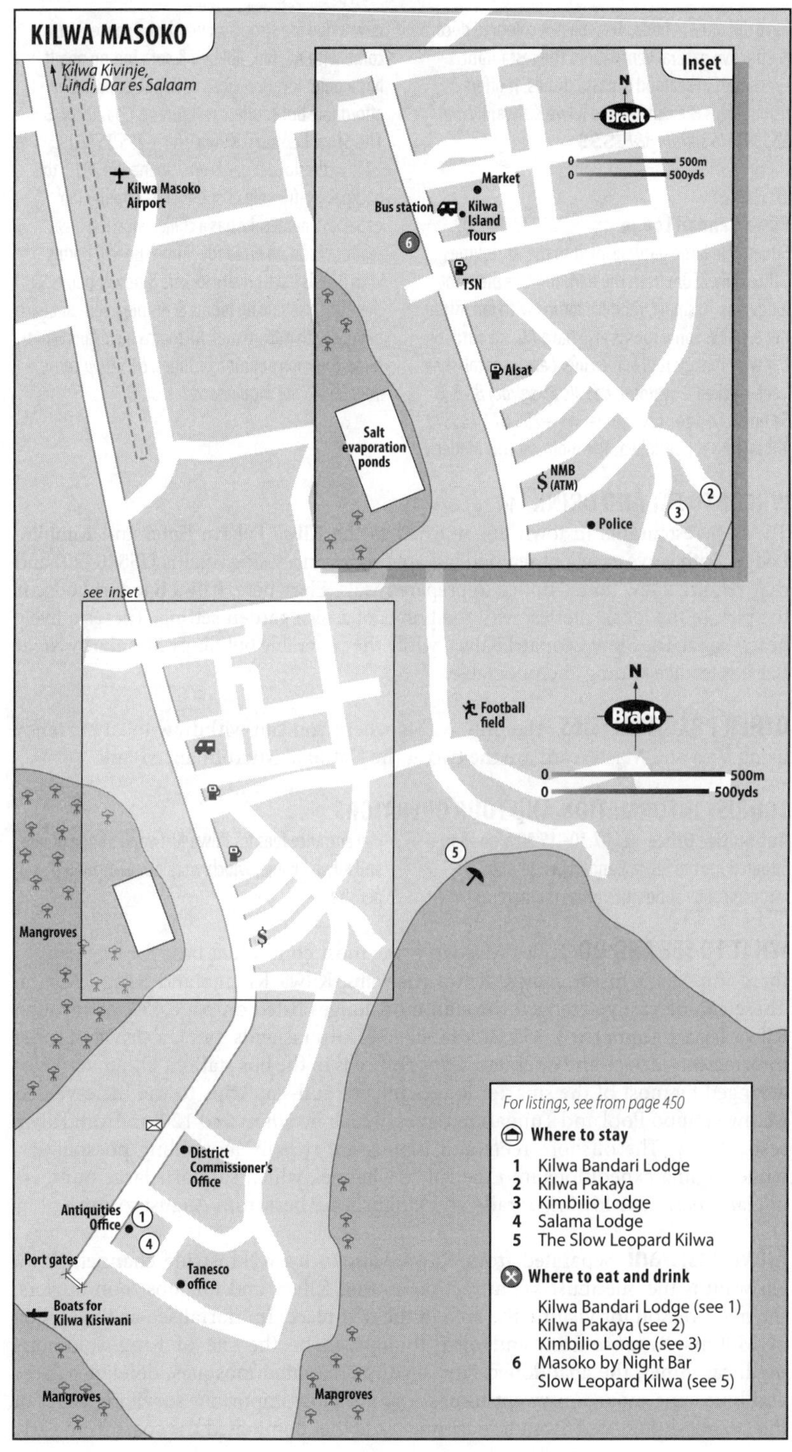
KILWA MASOKO
Kilwa Kivinje, Lindi, Dar es Salaam
Kilwa Masoko Airport
Inset
Market
Bus station
Kilwa Island Tours
TSN
Alsat
Salt evaporation ponds
NMB (ATM)
Police
0 500m
0 500yds
see inset
Football field
Mangroves
District Commissioner's Office
Antiquities Office
Port gates
Tanesco office
Boats for Kilwa Kisiwani
Mangroves
Mangroves
For listings, see from page 450
Where to stay
1 Kilwa Bandari Lodge
2 Kilwa Pakaya
3 Kimbilio Lodge
4 Salama Lodge
5 The Slow Leopard Kilwa
Where to eat and drink
Kilwa Bandari Lodge (see 1)
Kilwa Pakaya (see 2)
Kimbilio Lodge (see 3)
6 Masoko by Night Bar
Slow Leopard Kilwa (see 5)

have dbl or twin beds, nets, pastel-coloured décor & effective natural ventilation. The restaurant specialises in seafood & pasta dishes. It offers fishing trips & excursions to Kilwa Kisiwani. *From US$80/115 sgl/dbl B&B.* **$$$**

Budget

Kilwa Bandari Lodge m +255 713 748309. Situated in large gardens next to the Antiquities Office only 250m from the harbour, this pleasant lodge has 10 smart, modern rooms with fan, fitted net & DSTV. Some rooms also have AC. An outdoor bar with makuti roof serves inexpensive local-style beef, chicken & seafood. *US$20/25 sgl/dbl B&B.* **$**

Salama Lodge (20 rooms) m +255 673 735372; f salama-lodge-kilwa. The rooms at this modern new lodge are strong on wardrobe space & also come with AC, fan, dbl bed & sofa but no net. It has a quiet location close to the beach & a clean & affordable but soulless restaurant. *US$20 dbl.* **$**

The Slow Leopard Kilwa m +255 757 029 244; w theslowleopard.com. Opened in 2019, this backpacker-friendly offshoot of its popular Dar es Salaam namesake has a chilled vibe & a great seafront location on sandy Jimbizi Beach. Dorms with 8 beds have private lockers & power points, & there are also private rooms & simple open-air beach bandas with makuti roof. All rooms have fans & nets, & use common ablution facilities. *US$20pp dorm; from US$45 dbl, inc dinner & b/fast.* **$**

WHERE TO EAT AND DRINK *Map, page 451*

The best restaurants in town are attached to the **Kilwa Pakaya Hotel** and **Kimbilio Lodge**. Both serve excellent seafood but are on the pricey side (mains US$10–20) and may require a few hours' notice to prepare meals. Elsewhere, **Kilwa Bandari Lodge** is the pick of the local eateries, with the bonus of a nice garden setting. There's a lively beach bar at The Slow Leopard Kilwa, while the venerable but dingy **Masoko by Night Bar** has terrace seating and pool table.

OTHER PRACTICALITIES The only ATMs where you can withdraw local currency using Visa and Mastercard are the two at the National Microfinance Bank.

TOURIST INFORMATION AND TOUR OPERATORS

Antiquities Office 07.30–15.30 Mon–Sat. Situated next to Kilwa Bandari Lodge, the inconspicuous antiquities office is where you must pay entrance fees for Kilwa Kisiwani, Songo Mnara and Kilwa Kivinje, which work out at around US$10 per site.

WHAT TO SEE AND DO Kilwa Masoko is the most convenient base for day trips to three important historic sites: Kilwa Kisiwani, Kilwa Kivinje and Songo Mnara. These can be easily arranged through most lodges listed on page 450, or through Kilwa Island Tours (m + 255 715 463029; f kilwa.islands.tour), a private tourist information service and operator, whose office is in the bus station. Other activities arranged by most of the smarter lodges include full-day trips to the little-visited Maliwe Hippo Pool and Tungande Caves, which lie 90km and 120km from Kilwa respectively. The offshore reefs and islands are rich in snorkelling possibilities, while angling expeditions into the Kilwa Channel, which supports large numbers of giant marlin, yellowfin, dorado and kingfish, are best from August to April.

Kilwa Kisiwani Separated from Kilwa Masoko by a 2km-wide channel, Kilwa Kisiwani is the one must-see attraction around Kilwa, and for most non-anglers, the main reason for visiting the area in the first place. Immortalised as the Quiloa of Milton's *Paradise Lost*, and once thought to be the site of King Solomon's mythical mines, the abandoned city – with its haunted mosques, derelict palaces and lonesome monsoon-swept tombs – is the most important surviving relict of the Islamic-influenced Swahili maritime trade that dominated the coast from early medieval times until the arrival of the Portuguese, who sacked the city in 1505, a defeat from which it never recovered, despite several later reoccupations.

Set aside a half day for the excursion from Kilwa Masoko. Most people arrange a tour with their lodge, but you could theoretically make your own way there using the dhows that serve erratically as public transport, charging around US$1 per person one-way. Be warned, however, that this option is complicated by the fact you are required to travel with a local guide, who may well have a vested interest in encouraging you to pay more for a private charter. Either way, the trip usually takes 15–30 minutes each way, though in becalmed conditions it's been known to take an hour. An entrance fee equivalent to US$10 must be paid in advance at the Antiquities Office next to the Kilwa Bandari Lodge.

Even before you set foot on the island, as you cross the channel your eyes will be drawn to the partially collapsed quadrangular building on the beach. This is called the **Gereza**, a Swahili word meaning 'prison', but derived from a Portuguese word meaning 'church'. In fact, the Gereza on Kilwa was neither of these things, but a fort built by Omani Arabs in about 1800. It has thick coral walls and an impressive arched door, and incorporates the walls of a smaller Portuguese fort built in 1505. It has undergone extensive restoration work funded by UNESCO.

Uphill from the Gereza, you pass through the small modern village before arriving in the **medieval city centre**. It is difficult to gain much of a feel for the layout of the original town, since many of the smaller stone buildings have vanished without trace, largely through the removal of rubble as building material. But the

KISIWANI IN 1331

The first detailed eyewitness account of Kilwa was written by Ibn Battuta, a young Arabian lawyer and inveterate globetrotter who is estimated to have covered something like 120,000km (more than Marco Polo) in his thirst for fresh sights. Ibn Battuta arrived in Kilwa in 1331, when the port was at its commercial peak, possibly at the invitation of Sultan Al-Hasan bin Sulaiman, with whom he might well have crossed paths in Mecca:

> We…set sail for Kilwa, the principal town on the coast, the greater part of whose inhabitants are Zanj of very black complexion. Kilwa is one of the most beautiful and well-constructed towns in the world. The whole of it is elegantly built. The roofs are built with mangrove poles. The people are engaged in a holy war, for their country lies beside that of Pagan Zanj. The chief qualities are devotion and piety…The sultan…[is nicknamed] Abu Al-Mawahib (Giver of Gifts)…He frequently makes raids into the Zanj country, attacks them, and carries off booty, of which he reserves a fifth, using it in the manner prescribed by the Koran…
>
> The sultan is very humble: he sits and eats with beggars, and venerates holy men and the descendants of the prophets…One Friday as he was coming away from prayer…a faqir from Yemen stopped him and said 'O Abu Al-Mawahib'. He replied: 'Here I am, O beggar! What do you want?' 'Give me the clothes you are wearing!' And [the sultan] said: 'Certainly you can have them.' 'At once?' [the beggar] asked. 'Yes, immediately!'
>
> When this virtuous and liberal sultan died…his brother Daud became ruler, and acted in the opposite manner. If a poor man came to him, he said: 'The giver of gifts is dead, and has nothing left to give.' Visitors stayed at his court a great number of months, and only then did he give them something, so much that eventually no-one came to visit him.

THE LAST DAYS OF KILWA KISIWANI

With grim irony, the most detailed eyewitness account of Kilwa in its prime is included in *The Sack of Kilwa and Mombasa*, penned by Francisco de Almeida after he led the Portuguese attack on the island in 1505, and is interspersed with comments relating to the sacking:

> In Kilwa there are many strong houses several storeys high. They are built of stone and mortar and plastered with various designs...As soon as the town had been taken...they went to the palace and there the cross was put down. Then everyone started to plunder the town of all its merchandise and provisions.
>
> The island and town have a population of 4,000 people. It is very fertile and produces maize...butter, honey and wax. On the trees hang beehives like jars of three almudes' capacity, each closed with woven palm leaves...There are many trees and palms on the mainland, some of them different to those of Portugal...There are sweet oranges, lemons, vegetables, small onions, and aromatic herbs. They are grown in gardens and watered with water from the wells.
>
> Here also grows betel that has leaves like ivy and is grown like peas with sticks at the root for support. Wealthy Arabs chew the leaf, together with specially prepared limes that look like an ointment. They keep the leaves as if they were to be put on wounds. These leaves make the mouth and teeth very red, but are said to be most refreshing.
>
> There are more black slaves than white moors here: they are engaged on farms growing maize and other things...The soil is red, the top layer being sandy; the grass is always green. There are many fat beasts, oxen, cows, sheep and goats and also plenty of fish; there are also whales which swim around the ships. There is no running drinking water on this island. Near the island there are other small inhabited islands. There are many boats as large as a caravel of 50 ton and other smaller ones...They sail from here to Sofala, 255 leagues away.
>
> People here sleep raised above the ground in hammocks made of palm leaves, in which only one person can lie. Flasks of very good perfume are exported from here and a large

most important structures – the mosques and palaces – have been left untouched, largely because they are still sanctified by locals.

The **Great Mosque**, which would have been the focal point of spiritual life in medieval Kilwa, is the largest coastal mosque of its period, with 30 bays covering

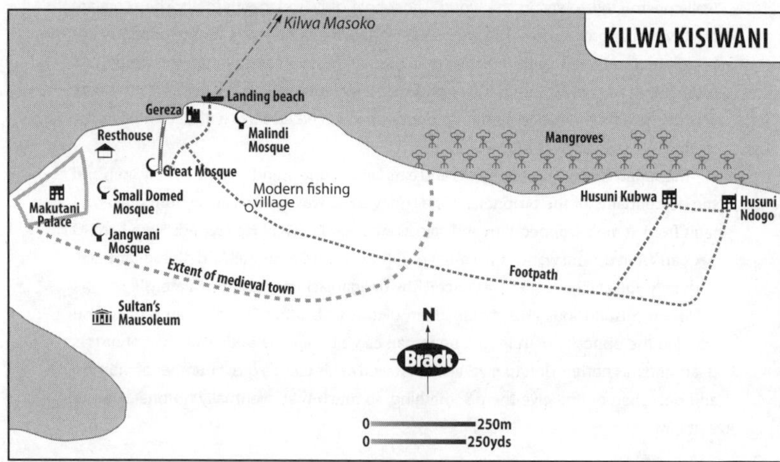

quantity of glass of all types and all kinds of cotton piece goods, incense, resin, gold, silver and pearls. The Grand Captain ordered the loot to be deposited under seal in a house. The fortress of Kilwa was built out of the best house there was. All the other houses were pulled down. It was fortified and guns were set in place.

Cotton is found in abundance. It is of good quality...The slaves wear a cotton cloth around the waist and down to the knees; the rest of the body is naked. The white Arabs and slave owners wear two pieces of cotton cloth, one around the waist down to the feet, and the other over the shoulders and reaching down to the first cloth. There are copper coins [but] no gold coin. The Grand Captain...saw 25 gazelle which had been let loose on the island...There are many vaulted mosques, one of which is like that of Cordova. All the upper-class Moors carry a rosary.

The contrast between the above and James Prior's 1812 description of the island during the brief Omani re occupation is striking:

The present town, if town it should be called, consists merely of a number of huts, scattered from the margin of the sea to a mile from its shore; the glittering white of only two stone houses enlivens and embellishes the cocoa-thatched metropolic...Quiloa seems to offer only ivory and tortoiseshell for commerce...The number of slaves formerly exported used to be many thousands, but at present the demand is confined to the Arabs, who do not take many. The articles principally in request here are arms, ammunition, dollars, tobacco, coarse cloths, and hardware. Refreshments...seem scarce, and the natives poor...The [Arab] people are generally good figures...they domineer over the Negro nations within their reach [and] sometimes make war to get more slaves, but more generally get them in traffic with people that come from a considerable distance in the interior. The common dress is a piece of cotton cloth wrapped around the middle, and extending to the knee, and another thrown loosely over the shoulders...They profess Muhammadism, but do not very strictly adhere to it.

about $100m^2$, and the best preserved and most aesthetically satisfying of all extant Shirazi buildings. The original mosque, erected c1050 under Ali bin Al-Hasan, was more modest in ambition than the present structure, and reputedly collapsed in the late 13th century. It was rebuilt in about 1320 under Sultan al-Hasan bin Sulaiman, who elaborated on the original design by adding an imposing wing of 16 domed ceiling cupolas supported by rows of tall arches – unquestionably the mosque's distinguishing architectural features. These ostentatious flourishes, intended to show off the contemporary wealth and sophistication of Kilwa, may also reflect architectural influences absorbed during the sultan's pilgrimage to Mecca as a teenager. It is to the immense credit of the masons involved that their handiwork remains in such fine shape over 700 years later.

Close to the Great Mosque, the so-called **Small Domed Mosque** dates to the 15th century and is also built over an older structure. This mosque has three bays, three aisles and seven ceiling domes, some still intact, but its fine decorations have been removed by modern visitors. Closer to the Gereza, the **Malindi Mosque** is a 15th-century construction associated with settlers from Malindi (Kenya), and was extensively renovated during the late-18th-century Omani occupation. **Jangwani Mosque**, a similar structure to the Small Domed Mosque, is now all but collapsed.

West of the mosques, the tall triangular **Makutani Palace** is still very well preserved. It was built and fortified in the 15th century after the Husuni Kubwa fell into disuse (page 446), and is enclosed by a low, crumbling 18th-century wall built by the Omani. A few hundred metres south of the Great Mosque, the **Sultan's Mausoleum** houses the tombs of many of Kilwa's most important sultans. All around town you'll see traces of the **ancient well system**, still used by the villagers today.

The eminent archaeologist Neville Chittick, who carried out excavations on Kilwa from 1958, regarded the **Husuni Kubwa**, perched on a low seafront cliff 1km east of the main ruins, as 'the only attempt to go beyond the merely practical and approach the grand'. Oddly, locals refer to the Husuni Kubwa as São Jago, reflecting a widespread local belief that it is of Portuguese origin (even the Department of Antiquities guides, who should know better, call it the Portuguese House). Persistent as this Portuguese association might be locally, it lacks historical foundation.

More likely the Husuni Kubwa was constructed by Al-Hasan bin Sulaiman as a palace and storehouse c1320 (almost two centuries before the Portuguese arrived) and was abandoned after two generations as it was too costly to maintain. In some aspects – its geometrical design, for instance – the clifftop palace is a typical Swahili building, but its scale and complexity are unprecedented, and it boasts many unique features. The building incorporates extensive domestic quarters, an audience court, several large ornamental balconies, a stairwell to the beach, and even a swimming pool. Few walls are still left standing after six centuries of disuse, but the ground plan is still clearly discernible.

Not far from the Husuni Kubwa, **Husuni Ndogo** superficially resembles a fort, but its purpose is a mystery. There is no comparable building elsewhere in East Africa, and it has variously and inconclusively been cited as a mosque, a storehouse, a minor residence and a fortified marketplace.

Kilwa Kivinje Less frequently visited than Kilwa Kisiwani, the rundown town of Kilwa Kivinje is no less absorbing in its own rather unfocused way. A living memorial to a more prosperous past, the broad impression is of a once-grand town returning to its fishing village roots – much of the main street consists of boarded-up shops, while mud huts are built on to the still-standing walls of old Omani dwellings and fortifications, many in good enough condition to allow you to imagine what they must have looked like 150 years ago.

The waterfront German Boma, the town's largest building, served as an administrative centre into the 1950s. A few years back, it looked to be just one powerful gust away from total collapse, but it is rumoured it may yet be converted to a lodge similar in style to its namesake in Mikindani. Between the Boma and a stone seawall, a cannon, presumably dating from World War I, stands on a common that comes complete with park benches. Behind the Boma a small monument commemorates two Germans who died in 1888. Nearby, the Mwembe Kinyonga

KILWA KIVINJE IN 1859

In February 1859, on their return trip from 'discovering' Lake Tanganyika, Burton and Speke diverted to Kilwa Kivinje to fulfil a promise made by Burton prior to starting the expedition. The town was, at the time, in the grip of a terrible cholera epidemic, and Burton wrote of how: 'corpses lay in the ravines and dead Negroes rested against the walls of the Customs House. The poorer victims were dragged by the leg along the sand to be thrown into the ebbing water of the bay; those better off were sewn up in matting. Limbs were scattered in all directions and heads lay like pebbles on the beach.' They did not stay in Kilwa Kivinje long.

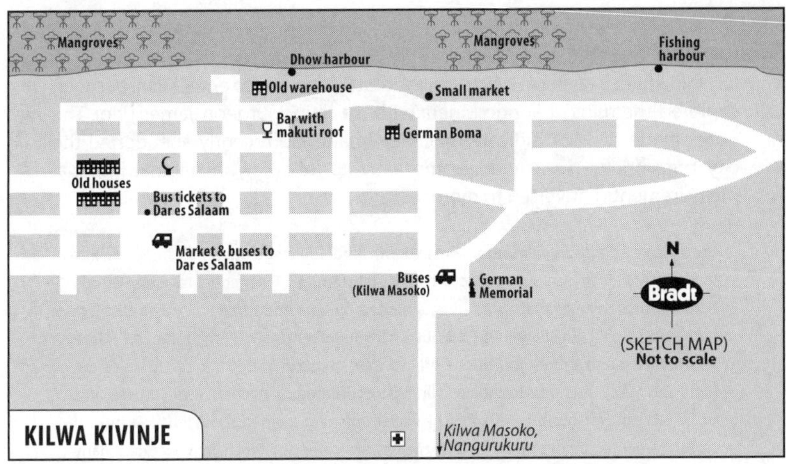

Memorial marks where the Germans executed by hanging several participants in the Maji-Maji Rebellion. Another relic of the German era is the covered central market. The roads radiating out from the market offer glimpses of Kilwa Kivinje in the 1940s and 1950s: double-storey buildings with ornate balconies, small homes with Zanzibari-style doors, and a few steel advertising boards that must date to the 1950s.

Historical interest aside, Kilwa Kivinje lies on an attractive beach surrounded by an extensive mangrove swamp, where odd little mud-skippers scuttle across the sand, and pairs of the beautiful mangrove kingfisher emit their high descending call from bare branches. It's also a very traditional Muslim town, marked by the characteristic Swahili reserve – though tourists remain a rare enough sight that you'll find no shortage of people wanting to practise their English on you. It's fascinating to watch the local fishermen at work along the beach to the south of the Boma, or youngsters preparing to smoke the day's catch in the back streets. Although Kilwa Island Tours run guided day tours to Kilwa Kivinje, it is easy enough to visit independently. Plenty of transport runs there and back from Kilwa Masoko, a 15–30-minute drive, depending on the number of stops. In theory, before visiting Kilwa Kivinje, you are required to pay an entrance fee equivalent to around US$9 at the Antiquities Office in Kilwa Masoko, but since it is a living working town, this rather unusual requirement is likely to be enforced only on a guided tour. Accommodation options in Kilwa Kivinje are uniformly dire, and eating-out options are limited to a couple of basic hotelis near the market.

Songo Mnara Island Set in the Songo Songo Archipelago, 10km south of Kilwa, Songo Mnara is the site of a second ruined town contemporaneous with medieval Kilwa. Little is known about the town's origin and history, but it was allegedly built by Ali Hussein, the founder of Kilwa, and the layout indicates that it was founded as a fortified outpost to defend the sea route into the harbour against naval attacks. Most constructions on Songo Mnara date from the 15th century or earlier, but – like Kilwa Kisiwani – the old town was occupied by Omani settlers in the late 18th century, and some renovation and new building occurred during this period.

The ruins on Songo Mnara lack the impact of those on Kilwa Kisiwani, but they have also suffered less damage through removal of building material, so they give a clearer idea of the layout of the ordinary houses and the town as a whole. The name Songo is ancient, but Mnara is a relatively modern appellation meaning 'tower', and

SONGO MNARA IN 1812

Captain Philip Beaver of HMS *Nisus*, the first British ship to enter Kilwa harbour, explored the ruins at Songo Mnara with the ship's surgeon James Prior. The notes made by Prior indicate that the Omani had recently abandoned the city they briefly reoccupied. Some extracts follow, with original imperial measurements converted to metric:

> We discovered a large well...about 6m in depth [and] hollowed out of calcareous rock... formerly enclosed by a wall, part of which is still standing. Further on, towards Pagoda Point, appeared several decayed huts, tenanted by bats and reptiles...The first object [after this] was a small cemetery, about 12m square, enclosed with stone and raised less than 1m above the ground; the graves were convexly raised...with stones at the head and feet...but no trace could we find of inscriptions...Attached [were] the remains of...a place of worship, above 7x4m. The walls remaining seemed about 5m high, built of stone, cemented by mortar formed by the bastard coral...in which were wedged many pieces of coconut shell, that seemed of no other use than of emblems...An arched door in front, and two in rear, formed the entrances, and a circular white stone raised above the ground may, perhaps, have received the inclined knee of many a humble supplicant for divine mercy...Two or three hundred metres from this spot lie the ruins of a stone building, larger than any at present possessed by the Quiloans, except the residence of the Sultan. Its apartments have been numerous...the walls are broad...and their height must have been considerable. Captain Beaver thought he could distinguish the remains of Saxon arches; but this resemblance is probably accidental.

refers to the tall but collapsed minaret of the main 15th-century mosque. A second large labyrinthine building with beautiful arched doors is generally referred to as the Sultan's Palace, but since the island had no sultan, it was probably the secondary residence of the Sultan of Kilwa.

A daily passenger boat connects Kilwa Masoko and Songo Mnara, weather permitting. You can also arrange private transport in a local fishing dhow, while the various lodges in Kilwa Masoko can arrange combined sightseeing and snorkelling day trips to the island, as can Kilwa Island Tours. For those with a serious interest in coastal archaeology, it would be possible, over the course of a day, to combine a visit to Songo Mnara with two other islands that contain substantial ruins. The first of these is the ruined town on **Sanje Mjoma**, which lies about 3km from Songo Mnara, and is noted for several large coral houses enclosed in courtyards with tall arched entrances. The second is **Sanje Ya Kati**, the capital of the Shanga people, a local tribe who resisted the rule of the Shirazi at Kilwa into the 13th century.

SOUTH OF KILWA

The 300km coastline that stretches south from Kilwa to the Rovuma River is seldom visited by tourists, with the exception of the occasional overlander or backpacker following the coastal route to Mozambique. It is nevertheless an area of some interest, with historic ports such as Lindi and Mikindani possessing a slightly time-warped atmosphere underscored by their crumbling German and Arab architecture, while the Mnazi Bay–Rovuma Estuary Marine Park close to the Mozambican border offers some fine snorkelling and diving.

LINDI The first urban centre you reach coming from Kilwa, Lindi is a compact and somewhat decrepit port that was founded in the 11th century, served as the capital of Southern Province prior to 1952 and remains the administrative hub of an eponymous region. Now home to around 80,000 people, it boasts a pretty location alongside the mouth of the Lukuledi Estuary, and is an important centre of coconut and cashew production, but otherwise has little to show for its long history. It's about 190km from Kilwa Masoko on a good surfaced road, and the drive usually takes around 3 hours, with several buses running along it daily, though most run directly from Dar es Salaam and stop to pick up and drop off passengers at the Nangurukuru junction for Kilwa.

Where to stay and eat

Malaika Hotel Market St; m +255 713 263335. This long-serving guesthouse is the pick of several basic cheap lodgings dotted around the town centre. It stands a couple of blocks west of the bus station & serves decent food. *US$10 dbl*. **$**

Sea View Beach Resort Waterfront Rd; f SeaViewBeachResortLindi; m +255 677 042 270. Lindi's top lodging, about 300m east of the bus station, boasts a great estuary view, an inviting swimming pool, a decent restaurant & spacious rooms with satellite TV, fridge, hot shower or tub & private balcony. *From US$48 dbl B&B*. **$**

MTWARA AND MIKINDANI The largest town on the south coast, supporting a population of 110,000 and connected to Dar es Salaam by regular buses and daily flights, Mtwara has a disjointed and unfocused layout that reflects an ambitious but unfulfilled development plan initiated by the colonial government after World War II. It is something of a travel dead-end, especially now the old coastal ferry crossing into Mozambique has largely been superseded by the new bridge across the Rovuma near Newala. Mtwara is a pleasant enough town without offering much in the way of sightseeing. However, the suburb of Shangani, a short walk north of the town centre, boasts a good swimming beach surrounded by coral flats dotted with rock pools.

Straddling the main road from Lindi 10km north of Mtwara, the closest thing to a tourist focus on the coast south of Kilwa is the small traditional port of Mikindani, with its sleepy old Swahili town of narrow alleys, balconied double-storey homesteads and carved Zanzibari doors. Named for the palms (*mikinda*) that flourish in the vicinity, the town peaked commercially in the late 19th century as an exporter of rubber and agricultural produce during the years that divided the abolition of the slave trade from German colonisation. Before that, in 1866, the explorer David Livingstone rested up in Mikindani for two weeks – citing it as 'the finest port on the coast' – before he embarked on his final, fatal expedition into the African interior.

Mikindani's best-known building, the German-built **Old Boma**, which dates to 1895, was restored to its former whitewashed pomp in 1998 by the non-profit organisation Trade Aid (w tradeaiduk.org) and now serves as a boutique hotel whose proceeds fund various local community projects. Below it, the so-called **Old Slave Market**, a restored German building that post-dates the slave trade by two decades, now houses a clutch of – very good – local craft shops and eateries. Opposite this, a **commemorative plaque** celebrating 'the reputed dwelling place of David Livingstone' is posted with some disingenuity on one of several two-storey balconied homesteads built by Arab or Indian merchants in the early 20th century. The ruined **German Customs House**, which stands on the waterfront next to the bus station, is of a similar vintage to the Old Boma, while the nearby **Aga Khan Building**, built in the mid 19th century by a wealthy Arab trader, is distinguished by its unusual staircase.

CROSSING INTO MOZAMBIQUE

Opened in 2010, the Unity Bridge, which crosses the Rovuma River between the Tanzanian town of Newala and its Mozambican counterpart Mueda, has rendered all but obsolete the established coastal cross-border route between Mtwara and Pemba (using a decidedly iffy ferry) for self-drivers.

To get to Newala coming from Kilwa, take a right fork at Mingoyo, 22km south of Lindi, then proceed inland along the 120km surfaced road to Masasi, from where a 75km dirt road leads towards Newala. There is also a rougher 140km dirt road running directly from Mtwara to Newala. With its bracing highland climate, Newala makes for a refreshing contrast to the sticky coast, and it is worth stopping at the Shimu ya Mungu Viewpoint, which looks over a vast escarpment down to the Rovuma Valley.

The road distance between Newala and Mueda is about 230km and the drive takes 5–6 hours, allowing for border formalities. The Tanzanian immigration shack lies 50km from Newala at the village of Masuguru, while the Mozambican immigration office is just after the bridge. You pass through some spectacular scenery as you descend into the Rovuma Valley then climb back on to the plateau on the Mozambican side. In Mueda, there are a few basic guesthouses offering en-suite rooms for less than US$10, the pick being Pensão Ntima.

There is still no public transport between Mueda and Newala, so backpackers must cross using the old coastal route and ferry from Mtwara to Palma. It is easy to get to the ferry from Mtwara, stopping first at the border post at Singa. Once formalities are complete, you can expect a bit of a feeding frenzy among the motorboat pilots and money-changers! If you have leftover Tanzanian money, this is your last chance to get rid of it. The passenger launch across the river takes 20 minutes and costs US$1 per person. The 40km from the Namoto border post to Palma takes 2 hours on public transport along a road as bad as the surrounding scenery is beautiful.

Be aware that Mozambique's northerly Cabo Delgado Province has been rendered unstable in recent years by a militant Islamist group which has launched violent attacks on several coastal towns and villages. You are therefore strongly advised to check the current situation before crossing into there from Tanzania.

Where to stay and eat

✱ The Old Boma m +255 784 360110; w mikindani.com. This imposing & lovingly restored 19th-century German administrative building is the most distinguished landmark in Mikindani & our favourite hotel anywhere on the south coast. Decorated in traditional Swahili style, the 9 airy rooms all have net, fan & hot bath, while the wooded grounds contain a swimming pool & excellent restaurant. *From US$65/105 sgl/dbl B&B.* **$$$**

✱ Ten Degrees South m +255 766 059380; w tendegreessouth.com. Another exceptional & popular tourist base in Mikindani, this budget-oriented lodge stands in a restored 1920s Swahili homestead & has a great garden restaurant. It offers diving & snorkelling expeditions outside Mikindani Bay & in Mnazi Bay–Rovuma Estuary Marine Park. The latter is possibly the best diving site in East Africa. *US$20/30 sgl/dbl, en suites US$60/70 sgl/dbl.* **$–$$**

Tiffany Diamond Hotel Makonde Rd, Mtwara; m +255 712 104141; w tiffanydiamondhotels.com. The smartest place in central Mtwara is this well-run but rather impersonal 3-star business hotel. The 44 rooms all have AC & sat TV. There is also a swimming pool & more-than-adequate restaurant. *From US$45/70 sgl/dbl B&B.* **$$**

18

Nyerere National Park

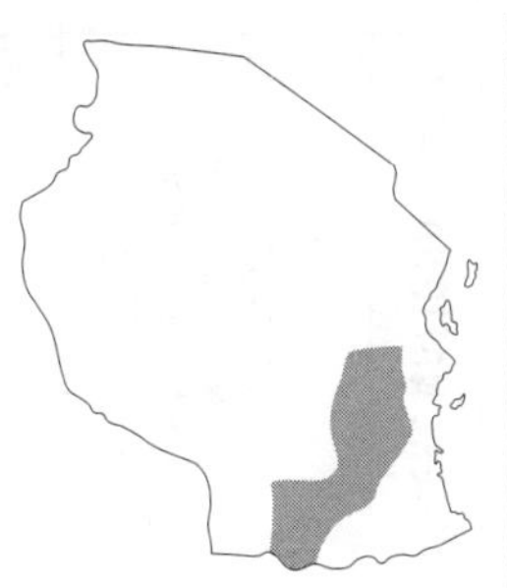

The largest national park anywhere in Africa, 30,893km² Nyerere (m +255 762 012700; e nyerere.tourism@tanzaniaparks.go.tz) is twice the size of the Serengeti National Park and slightly larger than Belgium or Lesotho. It was gazetted as a national park in 2019, prior to which it formed the northern half of what was then the world's largest game reserve, the 54,600km² Selous. The park forms the core of Africa's largest remaining tract of untrammelled bush, the 155,000km² Greater Selous–Niassa ecosystem, which also incorporates Mikumi and Udzungwa Mountains national parks, Kilombero Game Controlled Area, and Mozambique's 23,400km² Niassa Game Reserve. Bisected by the life-sustaining Rufiji River, this vast area of dry woodland supports what are probably the world's largest surviving populations of buffalo, hippo and lion (estimated at around 150,000, 40,000 and 4,000 respectively), and it is also the most important global stronghold for the endangered African wild dog. As recently as 2010, the Greater Selous was home to around 70,000 elephants, some 10% of the continental total, but the population has since declined significantly (see *Nyerere's Endangered Large Mammals*, page 466).

Nyerere's immense area is something of a red herring in touristic terms. True, this vast national park does attract a fraction of the tourist arrivals associated with the northern safari circuit. And accommodation is indeed limited to a dozen or so low-key camps that espouse an eco-friendly philosophy and thatch-and-canvas aesthetic, and whose combined bed capacity amounts to a few hundred clients. Yet a quick glance at a map will reveal that these tourist facilities are all compressed within a relatively small tourist circuit to the north of the Rufiji, a reserve-within-a-reserve that accounts for a tiny fraction of the park's total area. Furthermore, Nyerere's main tourist circuit is subject to ever-increasing numbers of day visitors, some staying from camps situated outside Mtemere Gate, others on a fly-in day safari from Zanzibar. As a result, the 'multiple vehicles looking for the same lion pride' phenomenon is more commonplace in Nyerere than some would have you believe, especially in the area closest to Mtemere Gate and Airstrip, and in the mid morning (usually from around 09.00) when the fly-in safaris arrive.

For all that, the public part of Nyerere is wonderfully atmospheric, a dense tract of miombo wilderness dominated by the compelling presence of the wide palm-lined Rufiji River and an associated labyrinth of interconnected lakes and channels. Arriving by light aircraft, as most visitors do, you'll sweep exhilaratingly above green-fringed channels teeming with hippos and waterfowl, swampy islets grazed by immense herds of elephant and giraffe, and exposed sandbanks full of drinking antelope and sleeping crocodiles. And once there, the opportunity to go on guided bush walks, take boat trips on the Rufiji or fly-camp around the lakes makes for a more thrilling and integrated bush experience than the repetitive regime of two daily game drives typical of other Tanzanian national parks. Be warned, however,

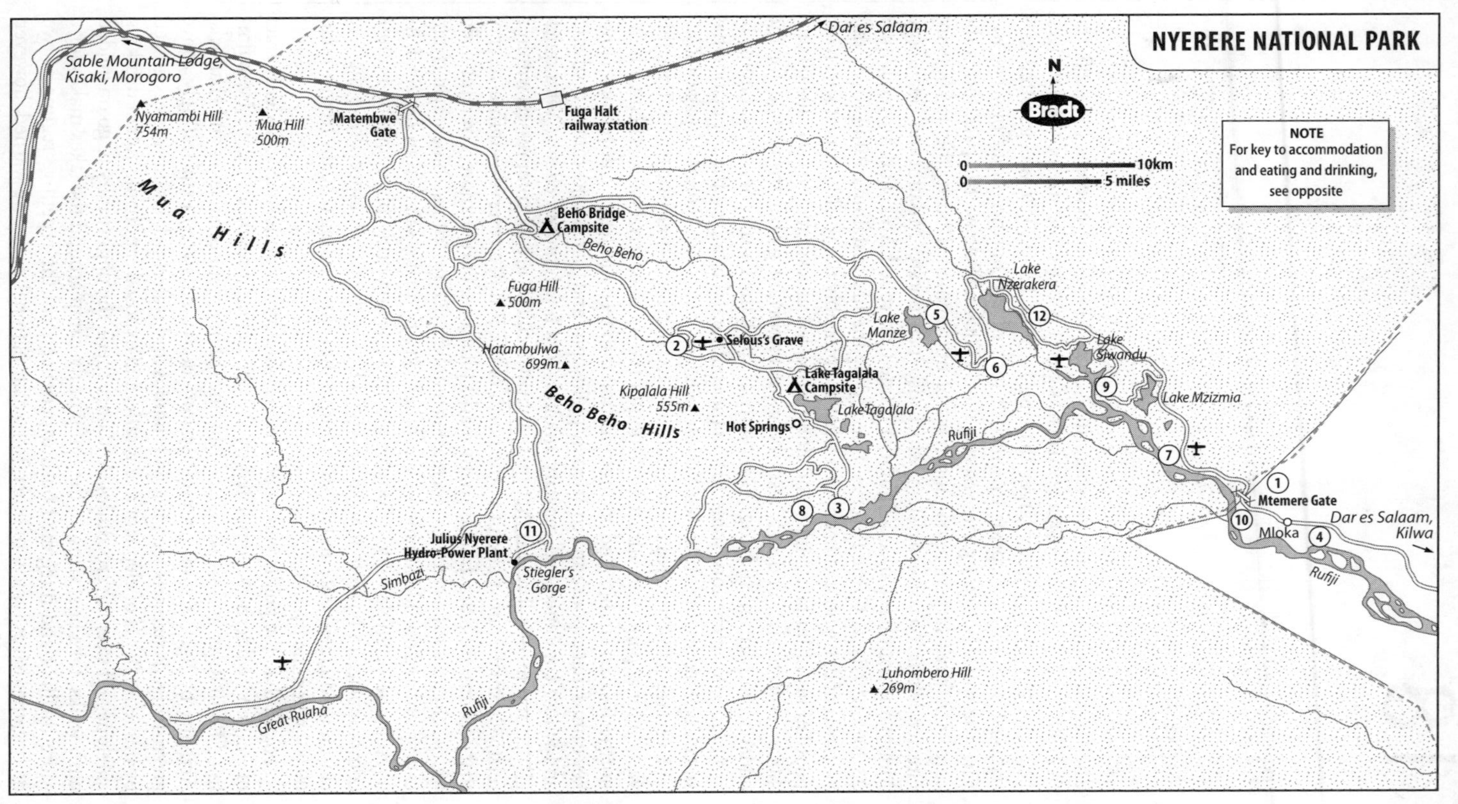
NYERERE NATIONAL PARK
NOTE
For key to accommodation and eating and drinking, see opposite
N
Bradt
0
10km
0
5 miles
Dar es Salaam
Sable Mountain Lodge, Kisaki, Morogoro
Nyamambi Hill 754m
Mua Hill 500m
Matembwe Gate
Fuga Halt railway station
Mua Hills
Beho Bridge Campsite
Beho Beho
Fuga Hill 500m
Selous's Grave
Hatambulwa 699m
Kipalala Hill 555m
Beho Beho Hills
Lake Tagalala Campsite
Lake Tagalala
Hot Springs
Lake Manze
Lake Nzerakera
Lake Siwandu
Lake Mzizmia
Rufiji
Mtemere Gate
Mloka
Dar es Salaam, Kilwa
Julius Nyerere Hydro-Power Plant
Stiegler's Gorge
Simbazi
Great Ruaha
Luhombero Hill 269m

that Nyerere's wilderness character, and the exposed nature of its rustic camps and lodges, means it is probably better suited to experienced safari-goers than to nervous neophytes.

ENTRANCE FEES

The park entrance fee is US$70 per person per day (dropping to US$60 from 15 March to 15 May) plus 18% VAT. For overnight visitors, a concession or camping fee is also levied: US$60 per person per night for a lodge, special camp or permanent camp in peak season (July to September), dropping to US$50 from October to June) or US$30 per person for a public campsite. Activities other than daytime game drives, for instance boat trips, night drives and guided walks also attract specific fees, ranging from US$20 to US$50 per person per activity. These fees will be included in the cost of most fly-in safaris. If you are paying yourself at the gate, you will need a valid Visa or Mastercard, as cash is no longer accepted.

WHEN TO VISIT

Nyerere is a highly seasonal game-viewing destination, and it tends to be hotter than other reserves in Tanzania due to its low altitude (much of the reserve lies below 100m above sea level). The optimum time to visit is the core dry season of June to September, when wildlife is prolific and temperatures are relatively tolerable. Game viewing is just as good over October and early November, but this the so-called 'suicide season' prior to the alleviating start of the rains, and the heat can be genuinely oppressive (especially as few camps have air conditioning, and some even lack fans). October is also when seasonal pockets of tsetse flies are most likely to lurk in the miombo woodland (though they are very seldom present in more open country or along the river itself). Game viewing tends to be less reliable during the early part of the rainy season, which runs from mid-November to February, but the scenery is lovely and green, and the birdlife is at its finest. Roads tend to become impassable and most camps close over part or all of April and May.

HISTORY

In 1859, Burton and Speke passed through what would later become the Selous Game Reserve (now Nyerere National Park), noting that the area lacked for any significant human settlements. This uninhabited state is partly explained by a profusion of tsetse flies (which carry livestock diseases) and the limited amount of permanent water south of the Rufiji River. Another factor, doubtless, would have been regular slave raids associated with the Arab trading post of Kisaki, today an overgrown village set on the northern boundary of the game reserve, but in the 19th century the junction of two main caravan routes into the interior. In 1905, the region was further depopulated when the German

NYERERE NATIONAL PARK

For listings, see from page 468

Where to stay and eat

1 Africa Safari Selous
2 Beho Beho
3 Kiba Point
4 Kumbu Kumbu Selous Riverside Camp
5 Lake Manze Camp
6 Roho ya Selous
7 Rufiji River Camp
8 Sand Rivers
9 Selous Impala Camp
10 Selous River Camp
11 Serena Mivumo River Lodge
12 Siwandu Camp

Off map

Sable Mountain Lodge

colonial authorities undertook a brutal series of raids in retaliation for the Maji Maji uprising. The section of the present-day Nyerere National Park lying to the north of the Rufiji River was gazetted in the same year, as a gift from Kaiser Wilhelm to his wife, earning it the local nickname Shamba la Bibi (The Woman's Field).

Selous (pronounced 'Seloo') was named in honour of Frederick Courteney Selous, who left England for Africa in 1871 as an athletic 18-year-old – his school pals called him The Mighty Nimrod – and spent the next four decades acquiring a reputation as perhaps the most accomplished hunter of his age. Selous served as Great White Hunter to the likes of Theodore Roosevelt, and was renowned as a writer of rollicking African hunting yarns, notably *A Hunter's Wanderings in Africa.* A staunch patriot, Selous was right-hand man to Cecil John Rhodes's campaign to annex present-day Zimbabwe to the British Empire, though he also achieved brief notoriety in 1899 for speaking out against England's war on the Boer Republics of South Africa.

In 1914, when war broke out between Britain and Germany, Selous was more than 60 years old, yet he unhesitatingly volunteered and was made Captain of the 25th Royal Fusiliers, winning a DSO in 1916. With his intimate knowledge of the bush, Selous was the automatic choice to head up the chase after the ragtag German guerrilla army that Colonel Von Lettow led through southern Tanzania for longer than a year, consistently evading or defeating the British troops. On New Year's Day 1917, the opposing troops converged on each other close to the banks of the Beho Beho River, and Selous was shot dead by a sniper. The most famous casualty of East Africa's so-called 'Battle of the Bundu', Selous was held in such universal esteem that Colonel Von Lettow, upon hearing of his death, described the old hunter as having been 'well known among the Germans, on account of his charming manner and exciting stories'.

Less than two years later, P H Lamb trekked to the site of the simple wooden cross that marked the spot where the sexagenarian Selous had fallen and was buried. 'It is', Lamb reported, 'a wild inhospitable district, the haunt of a great variety of big game, including elephants, giraffes and rhinos. Not more than four miles away is a warm salt spring running down into a salt lake, where hippos, wild ducks, egrets and numerous other wild fowls abound. But despite these alleviations it can hardly be called a fascinating part of the world, and the object of most people who have seen it will be to avoid it carefully in the future.'

While the opening sentences of Lamb's report could have been written yesterday, hindsight does lend a certain irony to his final prediction. Five years after Selous's death, the plains of the Shamba la Bibi were greatly extended by the British colonists to incorporate a number of existing game reserves south of the river, and the reserve was named in honour of the hero buried within it. In the 1940s, the colonial government moved the remaining tribes out of the area to combat a sleeping sickness epidemic, leading the reserve to be further extended to a remarkable 54,600km². Selous Game Reserve was inscribed as a UNESCO World Heritage Site in 1982, and far from being carefully avoided, the site of Selous's Grave lies within 15km of two of Tanzania's most exclusive safari lodges!

In November 2019, the Tanzania government split the Selous into two parts. The slightly larger northern section was gazetted as a new 30,893km² national park, and named in honour of President Julius Nyerere, the iconic founding father of independent Tanzania, while the south remained a game reserve to be used mainly for legal trophy hunting. Sceptics claim that the creation of what is now Africa's largest national park was partially designed to deflect criticism of the near-simultaneous commencement of the construction of the Julius Nyerere

Hydro-Electric Power Plant on the Rufiji as it flows through Stiegler's Gorge west of the main tourist circuit. The 130m high, 700m wide Stiegler's Dam will support a hydro-electric plant with a generating capacity of 235MW. The government of Tanzania defends the project on the basis that affordable electricity is vital to economic growth, but it has drawn widespread criticism from conservationists, on the basis that it will submerge and deforest 1,350 km² of pristine bush in the heart of the park and might also have a negative effect on the seasonal flow of Tanzania's largest and wildest river. Audrey Azoulay, Director General of UNESCO, has expressed concern that the dam 'is likely to have a devastating and irreversible impact on Selous's unique ecosystem', which might in turn lead to Selous losing its status as a World Heritage Site. Either way, the hydro-electric plant, originally scheduled for completion in June 2022, is almost certain to start operating during the lifespan of this edition.

GETTING THERE AND AWAY

PACKAGE SAFARIS Most safari companies in Tanzania (especially those based in Dar es Salaam) offer fly-in and drive-down packages of anything from two to seven nights in duration, sometimes combined with Ruaha National Park. All-inclusive rates for budget safaris based outside Mtemere Gate start at around US$250 per person per day, but safaris based at camps inside the park are far pricier.

BY AIR Coastal Aviation, Safari AirLink and Zan Air all operate daily scheduled flights connecting Nyerere to Dar es Salaam, Zanzibar and Ruaha. Before the park was created, most of the camps had their own airstrips, but now there are just two possibilities: Mtemere Airstrip, at the gate of the same name, is preferred by camps east of Selous's Grave, while Beho Beho Airstrip is used by more westerly camps.

BY ROAD There are a few possible routes, all ideally undertaken in a 4x4. The best choice will depend firstly on whether you are staying in one of the eastern or western camps, and secondly on whether you are coming directly from Dar es Salaam, or from Kilwa, or from elsewhere on the southern safari circuit, for instance from Ruaha, Mikumi or Udzungwa Mountains national parks.

To/from Dar es Salaam via Kibiti Coming directly from Dar es Salaam to any camp east of Selous's Grave, you'll use the 245km road to Mtemere Gate via Kibiti and Mloka, which takes up to 6 hours.

To/from Kilwa The most reliable option coming from Kilwa Masoko is a 255km route that entails following the Dar es Salaam road north for 160km to Ikwiriri, then turning left on to the unsurfaced road to Mtemere Gate

To/from the west The most reliable route coming from the west is the unsurfaced but reasonably maintained 140km Matombo road which connects Morogoro to Matembwe Gate via Kisaki. This route is suitable for linking up with the other southern reserves, or for direct visits from Dar es Salaam to camps west of Selous's Grave. Look out for some interesting roadside quartzite formations about 50–60km south out of Morogoro, just after the small town of Makuyuni, and for the forest-fringed Ruvu River (plenty of monkeys) between Mgazi and Kisaki. Coming from Ruaha, Mikumi or Udzungwa, there used to be a more direct route through the

NYERERE'S ENDANGERED LARGE MAMMALS

The second-most endangered of Africa's large carnivores, after the very localised Ethiopian wolf, is almost certainly the **African wild dog**, and the Selous's importance as a sanctuary for this fascinating pack animal is difficult to overstate. Recent surveys indicate that every part of Nyerere falls within the home range of at least one pack of wild dogs. The reserve's total population, estimated at more than 1,000–1,300 adults, is twice that of any other African country, let alone any individual game reserve, and represents around 20% of the global free-ranging population. Quite why Nyerere has been unaffected by the precipitous decline in wild dog populations elsewhere in Africa is an open question. Perhaps it is because the surrounding area is so thinly inhabited, minimising the wild dog's exposure to canid-borne disease and vengeful stock farmers. Perhaps, as suggested by biologists Scott and Nancy Creel, who spent the best part of a decade studying several packs of wild dogs in Nyerere, it is because its wild dogs face less competition from other large predators than they do in many other reserves. Quite possibly, it is simply a matter of good luck. Whatever the reason, Nyerere is probably the best place in Africa to see free-ranging wild dogs, with at least two packs living to the north of the Rufiji River. Wild dogs are highly mobile and wide-ranging creatures, but it's unusual for more than a few days to pass without one or another pack showing up somewhere around the lakes of the tourist circuit, and once sighted the pack is normally easy to locate until it moves off again. The best time to see wild dogs is thus the denning season, which usually runs from June to August.

Less glamorously, the Greater Selous–Niassa ecosystem is of particular significance to two antelope species classified as Low Risk Conservation Dependent by the IUCN. The 8,000 **sable antelope** that migrate through the area constitute by far the largest wild population anywhere in Africa. In 1998, DNA testing placed the sable of Greater Selous in the race *Hippotragus niger roosevelti*, formerly thought to be endangered, since the only confirmed population was a herd of 120 protected within Kenya's Shimba Hills National Reserve. The estimated 50,000 **puku antelope** resident within the greater ecosystem represent about 75% of the global population of this localised wetland species. Although a small proportion of the puku's range lies within the western boundaries of Nyerere National Park, the bulk is accorded a far lower level of protection within the adjacent Kilombero Game Controlled Area (page 487). Neither of these antelope is seen with any frequency in the main tourist circuit.

In common with several other East African conservation areas, the Greater Selous suffered greatly from commercial ivory poaching during the 1980s, its vulnerability exacerbated by its proximity to the then war-torn Mozambique. In 1976, the area's **elephant** population stood at around 110,000, which was probably an artificial high, arguably related to the fact that the protected area formed a relatively safe refuge for herds that might formerly have ranged more widely. The 1981 census indicated a relatively small numerical drop, possibly seasonal, to 100,000, but the next ten years saw elephants being poached at an alarming rate of roughly 20 per day, with the estimated population dropping to 55,000 in 1986 and 25,000 in 1989.

In 1988, fearing that elephants might be eliminated entirely from the then-Selous Game Reserve, the Tanzanian government launched the Selous

Conservation Programme with support from several international conservation agencies such as the Frankfurt Zoological Society, the African Wildlife Foundation and the World Wide Fund for Nature. This programme aimed to involve bordering communities in conservation activities, as well as raising funds for better policing of the reserve. Aided by the controversial CITES ban on ivory in the early 1990s, poaching was brought under control. By the year 2000, the population of the greater ecosystem was estimated at 70,000, probably about 80% of which was focused on Selous Game Reserve, and despite a post-millennial increase in poaching activity, it is thought that numbers held steady until 2010. Since then, however, a renewed outbreak of commercial poaching has resulted in the death of almost 80% of the ecosystem's elephants, reducing the population to around 13,000 in 2013, at which point some conservationists predicted they will be hunted out entirely by 2022. Fortunately, improved anti-poaching measures set in place in 2015 reversed the trend, and the elephant population now stands at around 16,000. Despite this, any regular visitor to Selous over recent decades will be conscious of a tangible decline in the frequency of elephant sightings.

In 1980, Selous's estimated herd of 3,000 **black rhinoceros** was the largest in any one East African conservation area. Until the mid 2010s, these creatures, classed as Critically Endangered, were still seen occasionally in the vicinity of Sand River Camp (which established the Selous Rhino Trust in 1995 to help fund an anti-poaching unit to monitor and protect the few rhinos that survived north of the Rufiji). However, a recent statement, released by the Department of Natural Resources and Tourism in March 2022, following a few reported sightings of a solitary female, affirms that rhinos are no longer present in Nyerere National Park.

Prior to the creation of Nyerere National Park, a significant factor in stemming poaching was the utilisation of almost 90% of Selous Game Reserve for low-volume trophy hunting. Whatever one might feel about the sort of individual who is prepared to pay vast sums of money to blow the brains out of a lion or elephant or kudu in the prime of its life, these hunting concessions – which still exist in the part of the reserve outside the national park – have several clear benefits in conservation terms. First, the lessors have a strong interest in driving poachers off their concessions, and thus play an important role in policing remote parts of the reserve. Second, the revenue derived from the hunting concessions and their patrons – far larger than the sums raised by less pugnacious forms of tourism – form an important source of funding for anti-poaching patrols and reserve management.

Setting aside ethical issues, the low-volume hunting does have several negative effects. The large tuskers that once characterised the region have been conspicuously absent since the 1990s, and although commercial poaching of the 1980s is primarily to blame for this, trophy hunting – which targets the most physically impressive specimens of most species – has not helped. It is also noticeable how skittish much of Nyerere's wildlife is – proof, say those who subscribe to the Nyerere myth machine, that the animals here are 'wilder' than in other reserves. A more plausible explanation, given that Nyerere is not *that* lightly trafficked, is that many of its animals regularly visit areas that lie outside the national park and are used for legal hunting.

southern part of Mikumi National Park, but this never carried much traffic and it has now fallen into disuse and cannot be recommended.

BY BUS No public transport runs into Nyerere (unless you count the stretch of the Tazara Railway that skirts it), and the only viable bus route there is from Dar es Salaam to Mloka, the village that lies about 6km by road outside the Mtemere Gate. There's only one bus daily, and this leaves Dar es Salaam from Majaribio Roundabout on Mahunda Street at around 07.00. The trip takes up to 7 hours and tickets cost around US$4. Selous River Camp will meet the bus by prior arrangement, and can arrange game drives and boat trips into the reserve from their camp outside Mtemere Gate. In Mloka village, there are also a few very basic and inexpensive local guesthouses aimed mainly at safari drivers.

WHERE TO STAY AND EAT

Map, page 462

Around a dozen small permanent camps and lodges are dotted in Nyerere National Park. The main cluster is centred on the eastern lakes circuit, which offers the most reliable game viewing in the reserve but is also the busiest area in terms of vehicle traffic. A trio of relatively isolated camps and lodges to the west of the lakes combine a more exclusive setting with more erratic game viewings. Further east, outside Mtemere Gate, is a string of riverside lodges and camps catering to more budget-conscious travellers. Most lodges also offer overnight fly-camping excursions, which entail sleeping beneath a glorified mosquito net on the shore of a lake teeming with hippos and crocs, and should be arranged in advance. Most accommodation within the reserve closes at the start of the rains (late March or early April), when internal roads tend to become impassable, and reopens in June.

EASTERN LAKES CIRCUIT Other considerations aside, the most rewarding camps in terms of pure game viewing tend to be those situated in the lake-studded east. Lakes Manze, Siwandu and Nzerakera support the park's densest wildlife populations, and are particularly good for lions and wild dogs. Roho ya Selous, Siwandu Camp and Lake Manze Camp lie in the heart of this prime game-viewing territory, as does the more ephemeral Maji Moto Camp, but the area is also easily accessed from Rufiji River and Impala camps. All the camps in this area offer boat trips on the Rufiji and/or one of the lakes, all of which are teeming with hippos, crocs and other wildlife.

Exclusive

✷ **Roho ya Selous** ⊕ -7.67493, 38.10190; **m** +255 736 500515; **w** asiliaafrica.com. Opened in 2017, Roho ya Selous (literally 'Heart of Selous') occupies a small promontory on the west side of Lake Nzerakera, just to the north of the inland delta formed by the Rufiji River, at the heart of the best game-viewing circuit in Selous/Nyerere. Nestled between tall riverine trees & widely spaced for privacy, the 8 spacious standing tents have a canvas roof, rustic stone floor, bamboo walls, & screened open side with a private bush view. Tastefully decorated in contemporary safari style, the tents also include a near-silent, low-power breeze cooling system & standing fans as well. The kidney-shaped swimming pool & restaurant offer views over a stretch of water that is alive with birds & attracts wildlife such as elephants, hippo & greater kudu. **$$$$$$$**

Selous Impala Camp ⊕ -7.71126, 38.16175; **m** +255 717 189167; **w** selousimpala.net. This unpretentious but attractive camp boasts a magnificent location overlooking a wooded channel alongside the Rufiji. The 6 stilted tents are furnished in a bright, warm style & come with fan, hot shower & private balcony. The expansive thatched lounge, communal deck & swimming pool look out over a stretch of the Rufiji regularly visited by elephants & other wildlife. **$$$$$$$**

Siwandu Camp ⊕ -7.67050, 38.12074; **m** +255 22 212 8485; **w** selous.com. This plush camp on Lake Nzerakera is divided into 2 separate camps: 1 containing 7 tents & the other 6, both with their own dining areas & good-sized swimming pools. Both provide accommodation in spacious stilted en-suite tents, which are set far apart from one another & have fans, open-air showers & private decks. The common lounge & dining area is a fabulous stilted treehouse lit by dozens of gas lamps at night. Game drives, boat trips, guided walks & fly-camping are all offered. A pontoon boat (larger than the usual Selous camp vessels) allows for relaxing lake trips with sundowners or meals. Overall it's a high-quality, professional operation that offers great guiding & pays attention to detail. **$$$$$$$**

Upmarket

✷ Lake Manze Camp ⊕ -7.66597, 38.06150; **w** ed.co.tz. This rustic & sensibly priced camp has a genuine wilderness feel & stunning location on the palm-fringed shores of Lake Manze. It also boasts perhaps the best game-viewing location of any camp in the park, especially when it comes to lion, elephant & wild dog. The 12 spacious & simply furnished standing tents, set on a wooden deck with a stone balcony, come with solar-powered hot shower & fan. The thatched lounge has a library & views to the hippo- & croc-infested lake. **$$$$$$**

Rufiji River Camp ⊕ -7.74500, 38.19410; **m** +255 754 237422; **w** rufijirivercamp.com. One of Nyerere's oldest lodges, the ever-popular & reasonably priced Rufiji River Camp stands in a lush stretch of woodland overlooking a magnificent stretch of the Rufiji River less than 2km from Mtemere Gate. The camp and river are alive with monkeys, hippos, crocs & waterbirds, & regularly visited by elephants. The 14 classic & suite tents are shaded by a thatch roof & set on a wide wooden platform with a balcony offering superb river views. Suites have private plunge pools. The wood-&-thatch dbl-storey restaurant/bar has plentiful seating & a swimming pool. Guides here are generally very experienced & many formerly worked as game scouts. **$$$$$$**

Moderate

Selous Maji Moto Camp Mobile; **m** +255 786 019965; **w** authentictanzaniasafaris.com. A welcome throwback to the old-school safari, this mobile camp is set up by request (min 2 nights) at a variable location on the banks of 1 of the 5 lakes, which means that elephant, hippo & other wildlife pass through on a regular basis. The focus is on game drives, but guided walks & river trips are offered, & since it is reserved for private parties of up to 8 people, individual guests can decide their day-to-day schedule in conjunction with an experienced guide. The emphasis is on providing guests with a down-to-earth & immersive bush experience, so while tents are comfortable enough, they come with narrow twin camp beds, bucket shower & portable loo, & are not suited to those seeking a high level of comfort. **$$$$$$**

WEST OF THE LAKES Scattered around the vast tract of northern Nyerere to the west of the main lakes circuit, the camps listed below generally offer decent wildlife viewing, as well as boat trips, in areas that attract refreshingly little tourist traffic. Most offer full-day game drives to the lakes circuit.

Exclusive

Beho Beho n -7.67373, 37.92059; **w** behobeho.com. This top-notch lodge comprises a main camp with 9 large stone cottages & the private Bailey's Banda, a 2-bedroom villa with its own swimming pool. All units are open fronted with king-size Zanzibari 4-poster bed, walk-in netting, stylish *Out of Africa* furnishings & indoor & outdoor shower. The dining area & swimming pool offer a fabulous view over the plains & the camp blends harmoniously into its setting on the footslopes of the westerly Beho Beho Hills. Although it is set away from the river, a permanent pool supports hippos & attracts other passing wildlife. Game walks are offered & it's the only place to run boat trips on bird-rich & croc-infested Lake Tagalala. Excellent game viewing can be had between the camp & Lake Manze, a relatively remote location where other tourist vehicles are scarce. The quality & enthusiasm of the guiding team deliver a consistently rewarding & well-informed bush experience. $$$$$$$

✷ **Sand Rivers** n -7.77907, 38.00880; **m** +255 787 595908; **w** nomad-tanzania.com. Set above a wide, sandy bend in the Rufiji River, this spectacular camp has a wonderfully isolated feel in an area infrequently visited by other vehicles. The 8 open-fronted stone-&-thatch suites are airy, elegantly decorated in African style, & come with king-size bed, walk-in netting & private balcony overlooking the river. Walking safaris, river trips & boat excursions are offered & guiding standards are exceptionally high. Game viewing is also excellent from camp, with hippo & crocodile resident in the river below, waterbuck & elephant making regular appearances, & plentiful birdlife. The stylish curved swimming pool stands under a large baobab tree. Meals are very good & eaten communally or separately as you prefer. About 1km downstream, Kiba Point, a separate camp of 4 units (each with private plunge pool), caters to private parties. $$$$$$$

Upmarket

Serena Mivumo River Lodge ⊕ -7.80931, 37.90027; **m** +255 786 999060; **w** serenahotels.com. Situated on the Rufiji at the eastern entrance to Stiegler's Gorge, 5km downstream of the new Julius Nyerere Hydro-Electric Power Plant, Mivumo has an unbeatable location in terms of scenery & the 12 modern suites are perhaps the most comfortable on offer in Nyerere, with wooden floor, leather furnishings, king-size bed, large bathroom with indoor tub & outdoor shower, as well as AC, which might offend the purists, but can feel very welcome in this muggy climate. There is also a large deck with a spectacular infinity swimming pool looking over the river. The one big drawback is that the surrounding miombo woodland supports low game densities & plenty of tsetse flies, which makes for unrewarding game drives unless you opt for the long full-day excursion to the lakes. $$$$$$

Moderate

Sable Mountain Lodge ⊕ -7.51631, 37.67627; **m** +255 713 323318; **w** tentwithaview.com. Set in a range of small hills 1km outside the western park boundary near Matembwe Gate, this lodge has 4 cottages, 5 tented bandas, a private villa & a separate rooftop suite, all with hot shower, toilet & 24hr electricity. A treehouse offering a grandstand view over a waterhole regularly visited by buffalo & elephant now includes a suite for overnight stays. The surrounding woodland is very thick, & guided walks offer the opportunity to see forest-associated species such as blue monkey, Angola colobus & the amazing checkered elephant shrew, as well as a host of forest birds including the exquisite Livingstone's turaco, a variety of hornbills & the vociferous forest weaver. Between Dec & May, sable antelopes move into the area. Game drives concentrate on the plains north of the lakes, which can be worthwhile seasonally, with very few other vehicles around. $$$$$

OUTSIDE MTEMERE GATE A more easterly string of riverside camps set outside Mtemere Gate offers useful access to the lakes' game-viewing circuit, and while these camps are less convenient than their counterparts, they also tend to be a lot cheaper. There are around a dozen camps outside the gate in total, but most are semi-functional and/or poorly tended. The three listed below stand out as the nicest, least ephemeral and best-run options in this area.

Moderate

Kumbu Kumbu Selous Riverside Camp ⊕ -7.84272, 38.38671; **m** +255 786 940848; **w** kumbukumbuselous.co.tz. Set on the lushly wooded south bank of the Rufiji 5km east of the reserve boundary as the crow flies, this well-managed camp is the smartest option outside Mtemere Gate. A large thatched dining & bar area leads to a small swimming pool overlooking the river, while accommodation is in large stilted tented units with king-size beds, walk-in nets, bright furniture, 24hr electricity & private balcony with river view. Some rooms also have a private plunge pool. Good value. $$$$

Budget & camping

Africa Safari Selous **m** +255 789 467 746; **w** africa-safari.com. Practically bordering

Mtemere Gate, this popular & well-run camp lacks for river frontage but has a genuine bush location overlooking a newly created waterhole designed to attract elephant & other wildlife. The spacious & attractively rustic bandas & smarter bungalows all have fitted nets, fan, organic décor & hot showers. The grounds are studded with baobabs & include a swimming pool, curio shop & attractive thatched dining area & bar. There is also a campsite. *From US$148/240 sgl/dbl FB.* **$$$**

✷ **Selous River Camp** ⊕ -7.76088, 38.22816; **m** +255 784 237525; **w** selousrivercamp.com. This relatively affordable camp has an idyllic riverside location outside Mtemere Gate & offers the choice of simple standing tents using common showers or en-suite mud huts. Travelers coming from Dar es Salaam by bus can be met at Mloka by prior arrangement. Amenities include a small swimming pool. Guided walks, boat trips & game drives into the park can be included in game activity packages of 2–5 nights' duration; see the website for full details. *From US$120/180 sgl/dbl FB.* **$$$$**

WHAT TO SEE AND DO

GAME DRIVES The main focal point of game drives for visitors staying at the camps to the east of Selous's Grave is a network of rough roads offering access to a series of five lakes fed by the Rufiji. This circuit to the north of the Rufiji is reliably rewarding, especially towards the end of the dry season, with the area around lakes Manze and Siwandu typically hosting the highest concentrations of wildlife. Among the most frequently seen ungulates are impala, common waterbuck, white-bearded wildebeest, buffalo and common zebra, but bushbuck, eland and greater kudu are also present, though often quite skittish. Giraffe are also numerous, most usually seen drinking at the lakes in the late afternoon – in such concentrations that the area is sometimes referred to as Giraffic Park. Oddly, though, giraffe are entirely absent from the part of Nyerere south of the Rufiji, which also forms a natural barrier between the ranges of the distinctive white-bearded and Niassa races of wildebeest.

The most conspicuous large carnivore in Nyerere is the lion, typically darker in coloration than elsewhere in Tanzania, and with a scragglier mane. At least two different pridal territories converge on each of the main lakes, and the lions are seldom seen too far from the water. This is partly because the lions of Nyerere tend to rely on an unusual opportunistic diurnal hunting strategy, resting up in the shade to wait for whatever ungulate happens to venture within pouncing distance on its way to drink. As a result, Nyerere probably offers a better chance of seeing a lion kill than almost any reserve in Africa.

Also very common is the spotted hyena, though the population here appears to be scruffier in appearance, and altogether shier, than its counterparts on the northern safari circuit. The endangered African wild dog is sporadically common: packs often cover large distances before settling in one area for a few days, so the typical pattern is a few days without any sightings then a few days when they are seen daily. Other large predators are seldom seen. Leopards, though probably quite common, tend to be very elusive and skittish. So far as we can ascertain, the cheetah has not been recorded in this part of the reserve since the 1980s, most likely as a result of competition with the dense lion population.

A good focal point for game drives out of more westerly camps such as Beho Beho and Sand Rivers is Lake Tagalala. Home to high densities of hippo and croc, this shallow lake is also the main dry-season source of drinking water in the area, so you will often see various antelope drinking at the shore. The birdlife here can be astounding. Conspicuous species include pink-backed and great white pelican, yellow-billed and open-billed stork, and a variety of lapwings, waders, ibises, egrets and herons.

BOAT EXCURSIONS Not to be missed, boat trips along the Rufiji River and/or lakes are an absolute highlight of any visit, particularly in the afternoon, when they usually culminate with a brilliant red sun setting behind the tall borassus palms and baobabs that line the wide sandy watercourse. Gulp-inducing dentist's-eye views of Nyerere's trademark gigantic crocs are pretty much guaranteed from a boat, as are close-up encounters with conferences of grunting, harrumphing hippos – and you'd be unlucky not to be entertained by herds of elephant, buffalo or giraffe shuffling down to drink.

A memorable aspect of the boat trips is the profuse **birdlife**. Characteristic waterbirds along this stretch of the Rufiji include yellow-billed stork, white-crowned and spur-winged plovers, various small waders, pied and malachite kingfishers, and African skimmer. Pairs of fish eagle and palm-nut vulture perch high on the borassus palms, seasonal breeding colonies of carmine and white-fronted bee-eater swirl around the mud cliffs that hem in some stretches of the river, and pairs of trumpeter hornbill and purple-crested turaco flap between the riparian trees. Worth looking out for among a catalogue of egrets and herons is the Malagasy squacco heron, a regular winter visitor, while the elusive Pel's fishing owl often emerges at dusk to hawk above the water.

If you are staying outside Mtemere Gate, be aware that most places run their boat trips on the stretch of river to the east of the reserve boundary in order to save on entrance and activity fees. As a result, wildlife viewing is less productive, with the likelihood of encountering the likes of elephant and giraffe diminishing to almost nothing a couple of kilometres outside the park, while hippos and crocodile are likely to be vastly outnumbered by cattle and their human herders. Birdlife remains prolific as you head further east, but far less so than it is within the reserve boundaries.

GAME WALKS AND FLY-CAMPING Walking within Nyerere is permitted in the company of an armed ranger, and all the camps offer this activity to their clients. It is a thrilling way to experience the African bush, but not for the faint of heart, as there is a real likelihood of encountering elephant or buffalo – even lion – on foot. Less dramatically, guided walks also offer a good opportunity to enjoy the reserve's wealth of woodland birds, as well as smaller stuff such as flowers and invertebrates.

Mikumi and Udzungwa Mountains National Parks

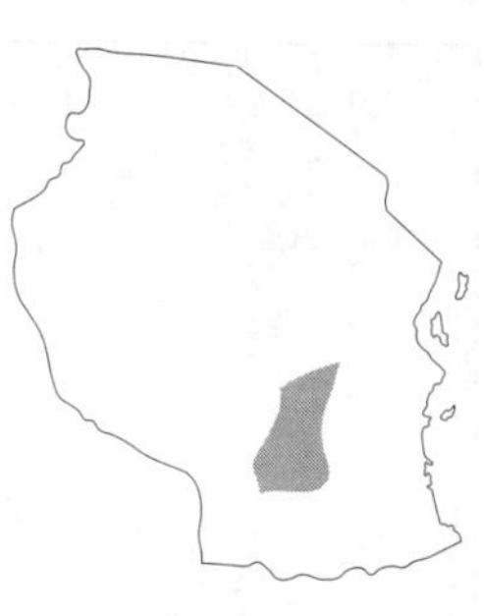

Some 320km southwest of Dar es Salaam, a pair of ecologically contrasting but equally underrated national parks flank the Tanzam Highway (the main road running towards the Zambian border). The closer of these national parks to Dar es Salaam is Mikumi, which protects a tract of classic African savannah and provides sanctuary for large herds of associated wildlife, notably buffalo, elephant and lion. Not far south of this, the hiker-friendly Udzungwa Mountains National Park protects the steep forested slope of a vast Eastern Arc mountain range that harbours a wealth of primates, birds and other species endemic to Tanzania. The only significant point of natural interest between Dar es Salaam and Mikumi is the Uluguru Massif, which rises to 2,638m above the substantial town of Morogoro and is of some ornithological significance as the sole preserve of two striking bird species found nowhere else in the world.

MOROGORO

This orderly town almost 200km inland of Dar es Salaam stands at the junction of the main road southwest to Mikumi and northwest to Dodoma. Set at an elevation of 500m at the base of the Uluguru Mountains, it is a fast-growing town, with an estimated population of 350,000 and a bustling fruit and vegetable market supplying fresh produce to Dar es Salaam. Architectural landmarks include the central **German-era railway station** [474 F1] and **Old German Boma** 1km along Boma Road [474 C4], but Morogoro is of interest mainly as the best base for exploring the little-visited Uluguru Mountains, the closest of the Eastern Arc ranges to Dar es Salaam, or a staging post en route to Mikumi or Ruaha national parks.

GETTING THERE AND AWAY The surfaced road from Dar es Salaam is in good condition and can usually be covered in around 4 hours, depending on traffic in the city suburbs. Buses leave hourly, cost around US$5 and terminate at Msamvu Station, 2km out of town on the Old Dar es Salaam Road. There are several operators of which JMC Express (**m** +255 754 354976; **w** jmc.co.tz), which continues to Dodoma, is the pick. A taxi from Msamvu Station to the town centre shouldn't cost more than US$2.

WHERE TO STAY AND EAT

Arc Hotel [474 G1] Old Dar es Salaam Rd; **m** +255 769 600240; **w** archotel-tz.com. Set 4km out of town, this popular Danish-run hotel has 28 comfortable en-suite rooms with DSTV & AC, & a

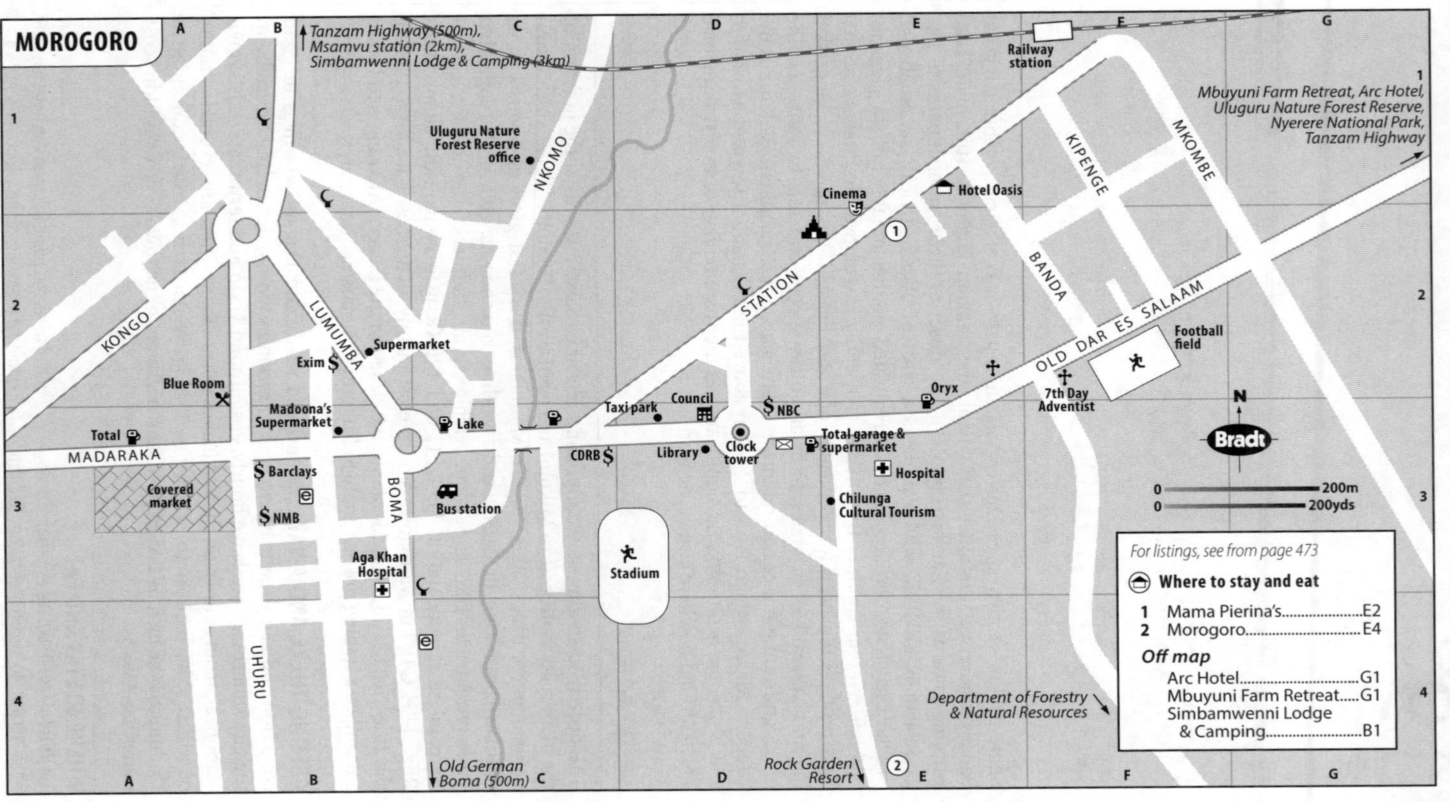

MOROGORO
Tanzam Highway (500m), Msamvu station (2km), Simbamwenni Lodge & Camping (3km)
Railway station
Mbuyuni Farm Retreat, Arc Hotel, Uluguru Nature Forest Reserve, Nyerere National Park, Tanzam Highway
Uluguru Nature Forest Reserve office
NKOMO
KIPENGE
MKOMBE
Cinema
Hotel Oasis
STATION
BANDA
OLD DAR ES SALAAM
Football field
KONGO
LUMUMBA
Supermarket
Exim
Blue Room
Madoona's Supermarket
Lake
Taxi park
Council
NBC
Oryx
7th Day Adventist
Total
MADARAKA
CDRB
Library
Clock tower
Total garage & supermarket
Hospital
Barclays
Covered market
NMB
BOMA
Bus station
Chilunga Cultural Tourism
Stadium
Aga Khan Hospital
UHURU
Department of Forestry & Natural Resources
Old German Boma (500m)
Rock Garden Resort
200m
200yds
Bradt
N
For listings, see from page 473
Where to stay and eat
1 Mama Pierina's.....E2
2 Morogoro.....E4
Off map
Arc Hotel.....G1
Mbuyuni Farm Retreat.....G1
Simbamwenni Lodge & Camping.....B1

restaurant serving Indian & other international cuisine. *US$50/65 sgl/dbl B&B.* **$$**

Mama Pierina's [474 E2] Station Rd; **m** +255 786 786913; **e** dshatzis@hotmail.com. This characterful central stalwart, owned by the same Greek family since the 1960s, but regularly renovated & upgraded, is a popular & friendly budget option. Behind the rooms there's a well-priced open-sided restaurant with a lovely view of the Uluguru. *US$14/20 dbl with fan/AC B&B.* **$**

Mbuyuni Farm Retreat [474 G1] ⊕ -6.74638, 37.75873; **m** +255 786 957587; **w** kimango.com. Situated 1.5km north of the main Dar es Salaam road 10km out of Morogoro, this lovely riverside retreat is on a German-owned organic farm specialising in herbal teas & spices. Accommodation is in 3 bungalows that each sleep 4 people & have a kitchen & wide balcony. More than 230 bird species have been recorded & it's a good self-drive base for exploring Uluguru. **$$$$**

Morogoro Hotel [474 E4] Rwegasore Rd; **m** +255 747 181817; **e** info@morogorohotel.com; **w** morogorohotel.com. This long-serving countrified hotel stands in green grounds adjoining a golf course about 1km southeast of the town centre in the shadow of the Uluguru. The 69 rooms & suites are clustered in domed chalets & have AC, fridge & sat TV. *From US$45/55 sgl/dbl B&B.* **$**

Simbamwenni Lodge & Camping [474 B1] (10 rooms) **m** +255 753 884496; **w** simbamwenni.com. Set in 2.5ha of tropical bird-filled gardens along the Ngerengere River 3km northwest of central Morogoro, this lovely owner-managed retreat offers accommodation in 10 chalets & furnished standing tents. You can also pitch your own tent. Management can arrange birding & walking trips into the Uluguru. *US$100 dbl chalet, US$40 dbl standing tent, US$10pp camping.* **$–$$**

WHAT TO SEE AND DO

Uluguru Nature Forest Reserve (☎ 023 293 4274; **w** nature-reserves.go.tz; entrance fee US$10) Immediately east of Morogoro, the Uluguru comprises two connected ranges that form part of the Eastern Arc formation and serve as the main water catchment for Dar es Salaam. North Uluguru, the dramatic backdrop to Morogoro, reaches an elevation of 2,150m, while the more remote South Uluguru rises to 2,638m. The massif's lower slopes are densely cultivated by the Luguru people for which it is named, but the forested upper slopes are protected within the 240km^2 Uluguru Nature Forest Reserve, which was amalgamated from three formerly disjointed forest reserves across the two ranges in 2007.

As with other Eastern Arc forests, Uluguru protects a wealth of endemics, including 135 plant species and ten reptile and amphibian species. Two endemic bird species are unique to Uluguru, the beautifully marked but elusive Uluguru bush-shrike and pretty nectar-eating Loveridge's sunbird, while other avian highlights include Mrs Moreau's warbler, Fulleborn's black boubou and Livingstone's turaco. A scenic highlight is the Hululu Waterfall, which tumbles into a natural swimming pool. A good network of hiking trails has now been developed, ranging from 1 to 8 hours in duration, and specialised ornithological guides are available.

For those with private transport, the main entrance to Uluguru Nature Forest Reserve lies about 8km from Morogoro and is clearly signposted as you approach the town from Dar es Salaam. However, you need to stop in Morogoro to sort out fees, guides and permits at the reserve office [474 C1] (Nkomo Rd).

Alternatively, a variety of tours into Uluguru are offered by community-based **Chilunga Cultural Tourism** [474 E3] (Rwegasore St; **m** +255 754 477582; **w** chilunga.or.tz), which stands opposite the main gate to Morogoro hospital. These range from a 2-hour round trip to Kigurunyembe ('Keep on Walking' in the Luguru language), where a forested stream harbours a variety of birds and monkeys, to an 8-hour trail running from Morogoro to Tegetero Mission through a part of the forest reserve where you might see the endemic Uluguru bush-shrike,

ROAD KILLS

The Tanzam Highway, the main trunk road through southern Tanzania, passes through Mikumi National Park for 50km, creating an unusual hazard for the local wildlife. Road kills have accounted for a significant number of animal fatalities ever since the park's inception, but the problem was exacerbated in the 1990s following massive improvements to the road surface, as well as the steady increase in heavy traffic as Tanzania emerged from the economic trough of the 1980s. Between 1992 and 1997, more than 450 large mammal road kills were reported from Mikumi. The most affected species were civet (110), impala (85), hare (50), buffalo (42), black-backed jackal (32) and baboon (23) – but speeding trucks also accounted for a leopard and ten lions, and somewhat incredibly contrived to kill seven elephants. In order to slow down the trucks and stem the carnage, the 50km stretch of public road running through Mikumi has subsequently been studded with speed bumps (sleeping policemen). As you drive through the park, you'll see prominent roadside signposts itemising species-by-species fines for colliding with various animals (elephants and giraffes attract a hefty US$15,000, while baboons are at the bottom of the pecking order, below civets, dik-diks and warthogs, at US$110). Despite this, as recently as 2016, the chief park warden of Mikumi reported that an average of 237 animals were killed annually by traffic.

Loveridge's sunbird and African violet. Another option is the full-day round-trip ascent of North Uluguru's 2,150m Lupanga Peak.

If you want to explore Uluguru independently, detailed data can be found at **w** easternarc.or.tz/mountain-blocks/uluguru/index.html.

MIKUMI NATIONAL PARK

The 3,230km² Mikumi National Park (**m** +255 767 536135; **e** mikumi@tanzaniaparks.go.tz) protects a combination of flat open grassland and wooded hills flanked by the Uluguru Mountains to the north and the Udzungwa to the south. It was gazetted in 1964, following the construction of the Tanzam Highway between Morogoro and Iringa, which opened up the formerly remote area to poachers. In 1975, the park was extended to share its southern boundary with Nyerere National Park, which means that Mikumi is now officially an extension of Nyerere, and quite a bit of wildlife migrates between the two.

Bisected by the Tanzam Highway as it runs southwest from Dar es Salaam, Mikumi is arguably the most accessible of all Tanzania's major safari destinations. Despite this, it has never featured prominently on tourist itineraries, possibly because the presence of a major trunk route, within earshot of most of the camps, is rather demystifying. Nevertheless, Mikumi is emphatically worth a night or two on any road safari through southern Tanzania, especially towards the end of the dry season, when wildlife concentrations compare favourably with Nyerere or Ruaha. It also makes for a relatively affordable one- or two-night safari destination out of Dar es Salaam, though it is best avoided over long weekends, when hordes of city dwellers flock down to the park to demonstrate their insensitivity to wildlife. At other times, once you're away from the main road, tourist traffic is actually very low by comparison with anywhere in northern Tanzania or even the main road loop through Nyerere.

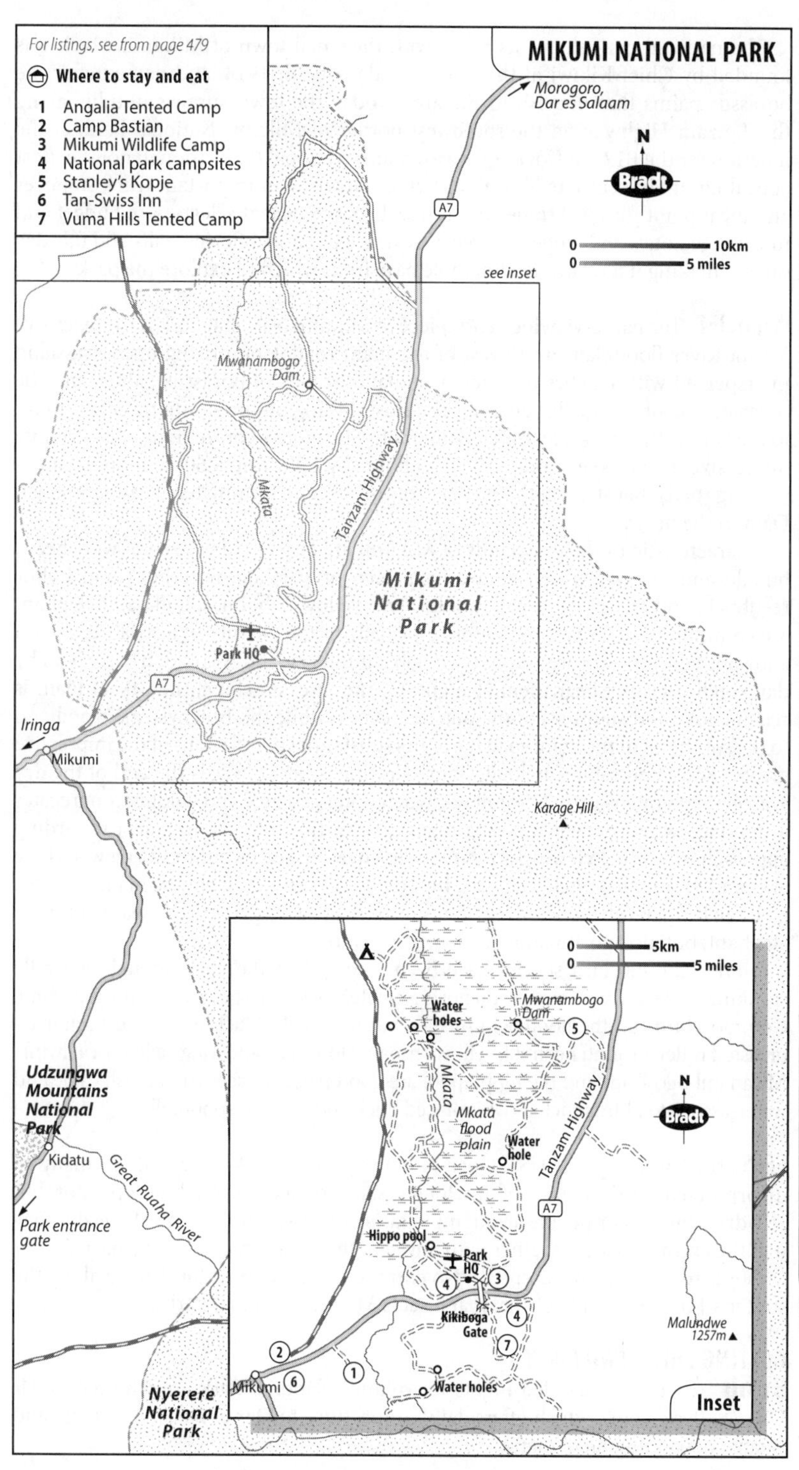
MIKUMI NATIONAL PARK
For listings, see from page 479
Where to stay and eat
1 Angalia Tented Camp
2 Camp Bastian
3 Mikumi Wildlife Camp
4 National park campsites
5 Stanley's Kopje
6 Tan-Swiss Inn
7 Vuma Hills Tented Camp
Morogoro, Dar es Salaam
N
Bradt
A7
0 10km
0 5 miles
see inset
Mwanambogo Dam
Mkata
Tanzam Highway
Mikumi National Park
Park HQ
A7
Iringa
Mikumi
Karage Hill
Udzungwa Mountains National Park
Kidatu
Great Ruaha River
Park entrance gate
Nyerere National Park
0 5km
0 5 miles
Water holes
Mwanambogo Dam
Mkata
Mkata flood plain
Water hole
Tanzam Highway
A7
Hippo pool
Park HQ
Kikiboga Gate
Malundwe 1257m
Water holes
Mikumi
Inset

The national park shares its name with the small town of Mikumi, which was founded by Chief Kikiwi of the Wavindunda tribe in 1914, and named after the borassus palms that flourish in the area. Today the town sprawls untidily along the Tanzam Highway on the southwest border of Mikumi National Park, at the junction for the B127 to Udzungwa Mountains National Park. Though not the most appealing urban centre in Tanzania, Mikumi town is an important truck stopover and focal point for local trade, and it now boasts a decent selection of budget and mid-range hotels and lodges, as well as several operators offering half- and full-day safaris, making it a relatively affordable base from which to explore the park.

WILDLIFE The game-viewing centrepiece of Mikumi National Park is the extensive Mkata River floodplain northwest of the main road. Comprising open grassland interspersed with patches of acacia woodland, stands of borassus palms, and the occasional baobab, the floodplain is the closest thing on the southern safari circuit to the Serengeti, and while the game might not be quite so prodigious, it is certainly impressive. It can be explored over 5–6 hours by following a 60km loop of game-viewing roads that starts at the main entrance gate and terminates at Mwanambogo Dam in the north.

Characteristic of the grasslands of Mikumi are large herds of zebra, wildebeest, buffalo and impala, as well as smaller parties of warthog, waterbuck and Bohor reedbuck, and troops of vervet monkey and yellow baboon. Giraffe and elephant are common on the main road loop, especially in the vicinity of acacia trees. Lion and spotted hyena are around in reasonable numbers, and if you don't see them by day you'll certainly hear them at night. Of the rarer antelope, the Mkata Plain is reliable for good sightings of the outsized eland, while the Brachystegia woodland to the southeast of the main road harbours substantial populations of the impressive greater kudu and sable antelope. Game viewing is best towards the end of the dry season (September–early November), when water is scarce and wildlife congregates around a few permanent watering holes. At this time of year, the most rewarding approach to wildlife viewing is often not to cover distances but to sit at a waterhole and wait to see what pitches up. The hippo pool 15 minutes from the main entrance gate can be incredibly rewarding in this respect, attracting a steady stream of thirsty elephant, buffalo and antelope to its muddy shores.

More than 400 bird species have been recorded in the park, though generally speaking the less-visited woodland hosts a greater variety of species than the grassland. Common birds on the floodplain include bateleur eagle, black-bellied bustard, lilac-breasted roller, ground hornbill, yellow-throated longclaw and long-tailed fiscal, while Mwanambogo Dam and the hippo pool are good places to see African fish eagle and water-associated birds such as white-faced duck and African spoonbill.

FEES The entrance fee is US$30 per 24 hours plus 18% VAT. Fees will normally be incorporated into the price of any longer safari booked through an operator, but self-drive visitors or people arranging safaris out of Mikumi town will need to pay it at the entrance gate (together with any camping and vehicle fees) using a Visa or Mastercard (cash is not accepted). No entrance fee is charged for driving along the stretch of the Tanzam Highway that bisects Mikumi National Park.

GETTING THERE AND AWAY

By air The only scheduled flights to Mikumi National Park are with **Safari Air Link** (w flysal.com), which offers daily connections to Dar es Salaam, Nyerere and Ruaha, depending on demand.

By road Road safaris to Mikumi usually run from Dar es Salaam, a 300km drive that should take around 6 hours in a private vehicle. The main Kikiboga Entrance Gate, on the Tanzam Highway about 15km northeast of Mikumi town, is always accessible, even in an ordinary saloon car, but a 4x4 may be required inside the park. Between November and April, the black cotton soil of the Mkata floodplain often becomes waterlogged, placing the main game-viewing circuit out of bounds, so check road conditions in advance. Traditionally, Mikumi is often combined with a road safari to Nyerere and/or Ruaha, and it makes for an ideal stopover driving between the two parks.

By public transport Bisected by the Tanzam Highway and serviced by the small town after which it is named, Mikumi is the only Tanzanian reserve to offer the combination of large numbers of plains animals and easy access from a reasonably substantial urban centre on a major thoroughfare. Mikumi town is readily accessible on public transport – any bus or dalla dalla heading between Dar es Salaam and Iringa or Mbeya can drop you there – but while you are likely to see a fair amount of wildlife from the main road, this isn't quite the same as spending time in the park itself. Fortunately, Mikumi is now serviced by several local operators offering guided safaris in open vehicles, including the reputable Tan-Swiss Inn and Camp Bastian. Going rates are around US$200/250 per group (up to six) for a half/full day, inclusive of driver/guide, fuel and vehicle entrance fees, but exclusive of the entrance fee of US$30 per person.

WHERE TO STAY AND EAT *Map, page 477*

A trio of well-run lodges and camps set within the reserve boundaries all feel like very good value by comparison with their counterparts in the more popular Ruaha and Nyerere. Several cheaper options are now available in Mikumi town and in the buffer area separating it from the national park.

Inside the park

Mikumi Wildlife Camp ⊕ -7.34488, 37.13603; **m** +255 778 919525; **w** mikumiwildlife.com. This underrated & reasonably priced lodge lies 1km from the Tanzam Hwy inside Kikiboga Entrance Gate, which is also the start of the park's best game-viewing circuit. The 9 large stone cottages overlook a pair of waterholes that attract a steady stream of zebras, giraffes & elephants, the occasional passing lion or hyena & a resident flock of habituated marabou storks. Elephants are also rather partial to sipping the water in the small swimming pool! The proximity to the main road means that the rumble of passing trucks vies with the nocturnal howling of the hyenas. **$$$$**

National park bandas **w** tanzaniaparks.go.tz. Situated inside the park only 3km from Kikiboga Entrance Gate, this complex of comfortable cottages is a great base from which to explore Mikumi on a budget. *US$50/75 sgl/dbl B&B.* **$$**

National park campsites **w** tanzaniaparks.go.tz. There are 3 campsites near the main gate, with ablution blocks & firewood but no water. *Standard campsites US$30pp, special campsites within the park US$50pp.* **$$–$$$**

✱ **Stanley's Kopje** ⊕ -7.16943, 37.19929; **m** +255 754 237422; **w** stanleyskopje.com; ⊕ closed Mar–May. Situated on a small rocky hill (kopje), this archetypal bush lodge is the only one in Mikumi to lie far enough from the Tanzam Highway that the tranquillity of the bush isn't interrupted by the occasional rumble of passing trucks. The thatched restaurant/bar & swimming pool are perched on a small hill offering superb views in all directions, while the 12 spacious tents are raised on wooden platforms around the hill's base. There's plenty of wildlife around as it lies in the middle of the excellent Mkata Plains road circuit. Day trips to Udzungwa Mountains National Park are arranged by request. **$$$$$–$$$$$$**

Vuma Hills Tented Camp ⊕ -7.38788, 37.14802; **m** +255 754 237422; **w** vumahills.com; ⊕ closed Mar–May . Under the same management as Stanley's Kopje, this 16-tent camp, set among the thick Brachystegia woodland of the Vuma Hills southeast of the Tanzam Highway, is a popular long-weekend retreat from Dar es Salaam. The classic safari tents are perched on stilted wooden platforms & offer a fabulous view over the wooded plains. Meals are prepared with fresh produce sourced from the nearby highlands & there is a small swimming pool. Vuma Hills is probably the most atmospheric & aesthetically pleasing lodge in Mikumi, with traffic from the main road only faintly audible, but there isn't a great deal of game around camp or in the nearby vicinity. **$$$$$–$$$$$$**

Outside the park

Angalia Tented Camp ⊕ -7.39024, 37.02148; **w** angaliatentedcamp.com. Set on a tract of woodland about 1km south of the main road & a similar distance west of the national park boundary, this old-fashioned safari camp has a real bush feel, with plenty of wildlife noises at night. It comprises 5 well-spaced-out stilted bungalows & a simple but appealing stone-&-thatch dining area & bar. It arranges game drives into Mikumi & day visits to Udzungwa. Good value. **$$$$**

Mikumi town

Camp Bastian **m** + 255 718 244507; **w** campbastian.com. This pleasant suburban camp stands in large fenced grounds about 300m north of the main road, more or less opposite Tan-Swiss. Small but neat stone bungalows have mat ceilings, red polished floors, hot showers, standing fans & private balconies. There are also 3-bedroom family units & a campsite. It offers good-value half-/full-day 4x4 game drives into Mikumi. *From US$55/75 sgl/dbl B&B. Camping US$10pp B&B.* **$$–$$$**

Tan-Swiss Inn **m** +255 755 191827; **w** tan-swiss.com. This bright & well-priced lodge stands in well-tended grounds on the Dar es Salaam side of Mikumi town. The 20 spacious tiled dbl rooms with AC, fan, net & DSTV are great value. There's a swimming pool & an excellent restaurant with outdoor or indoor seating. Half-/full-day 4x4 game drives into the park are offered by the on-site Samkalina Tours & Safaris. *From US$60/70 sgl/dbl B&B, camping US$8pp.* **$$**

UDZUNGWA MOUNTAINS NATIONAL PARK

The 1,990km² Udzungwa Mountains National Park (☎023 2934316; **e** udzungwa@tanzaniaparks.go.tz) was gazetted in 1992 to protect the northeastern portion of the eponymous mountain range, which is the largest component in the Eastern Arc formation. In common with the other Eastern Arc mountains (page 473), it consists of ancient crystalline bedrock that was pushed above the surrounding plains by upward faulting at least 100 million years ago. It has a wide elevation variation, rising from 250m to the 2,576m Luhombero Peak, and although some 75% of the indigenous cover has been lost to human encroachment over the past two millennia, the 2,000km² of surviving forest, protected within the national park and a number of smaller forest reserves, is the most substantial of any Eastern Arc range. It is also the most biodiverse forest habitat in Tanzania, supporting a rare wealth of endemic species, many of which are comparatively recently discoveries.

Despite its ecological significance, Udzungwa is a rather esoteric destination, suited more to keen walkers, primate enthusiasts and birdwatchers than to conventional safari-goers. Although the entrance gate is accessible by road, the steep eastern slopes and forest interiors protected within the park are accessible on foot only, using a network of well-maintained guided day trails. That said, the park makes for a straightforward addition to any southern safari itinerary taking in Mikumi, offering the opportunity to break with the standard regime of twice-daily game drives and stretch your legs a bit.

FLORA AND FAUNA Udzungwa is unique within East Africa in that it boasts an unbroken cover of closed-canopy forest spanning the full transition from lowland forest communities at 250m above sea level, through to montane forest communities at above 2,000m. The eastern escarpment of the Udzungwa supports submontane rainforest with a canopy reaching to 50m tall in some areas. Central and southern parts of the plateau consist of rolling hilly country covered in grassland, miombo woodland and scattered patches of Afromontane forest. Elevation decreases gradually to the west where there is arid woodland, and semi-desert conditions in the rain shadow of the mountains. This variety of habitats makes Udzungwa a strong contender for the accolade of Tanzania's most important terrestrial biodiversity hotspot, with more than 25% of the plant species recorded in the mountains being endemic.

The level of faunal endemism is the highest of any East African range. Several species of reptile, amphibian and invertebrate are unique to the Udzungwa, many of them first described in the last 30 years (page 484). The most celebrated of these forest residents are the five endemic primate species, namely Udzungwa red colobus, Sanje mangabey, kipunji monkey, Matunda dwarf galago and mountain dwarf galago. What is most remarkable about the first three of these endemics is their geographical isolation from other closely allied species. The mangabeys are otherwise restricted to the Congolese and Guinean rainforests, thousands of kilometres to the west, the one exception being a localised species endemic to forests along Kenya's Tana River. Likewise, the red colobus group is primarily West African in distribution, though they range through the Lake Tanganyika region, and endemic species do occur on Zanzibar Island and the Tana River. And the kipunji is a recently discovered species so unusual it is placed in its own monospecific genus (page 488). Of the five, only Udzungwa red colobus – common around the entrance gate and in the grounds of Udzungwa Forest Camp – is readily seen by casual visitors.

Numerous other large mammals are present in the mountains. Common primates include Angola colobus, yellow baboon, blue monkey and vervet monkey. The most readily seen antelope are bushbuck and the diminutive red duiker and blue duiker, but the higher slopes probably harbour the largest single population of Abbott's duiker, an endangered Tanzania endemic. The oddball chequered elephant shrew is the most striking of the smaller forest mammals, but a wide range of small predators include Lowe's servaline genet, which was first described in 1932 based on a single pelt and wasn't recorded again until one was captured during a live trapping survey in 2000. In addition, a number of typical savannah and woodland species are resident in the higher plateaux or pass through the park on a regular basis, including lion, elephant, leopard, buffalo and sable antelope.

The Udzungwa Mountains are particularly alluring to birdwatchers, with more than 400 species recorded, including at least 25 of the 32 species unique to the Tanzania–Malawi Endemic Bird Area. Species that generate a high degree of interest among visiting birdwatchers are the Nduk eagle-owl, dappled mountain robin, spot-throat, Swynnerton's robin, white-chested alethe, white-winged apalis, Chapin's apalis, banded green sunbird, Usambara weaver and Kipengere seedeater. Three bird species, the Iringa akalat, rufous-winged sunbird and Udzungwa forest partridge, are often cited as endemic to the Udzungwa Mountains. (In fact, the akalat has been recorded in a handful of other forests, while a similar partridge discovered in the remote Rubeho Mountains in 2003 was originally assumed to be a geographically isolated race but is now considered most likely to be specifically distinct.) It should be noted that several of the more interesting birds of Udzungwa are more or less absent from the eastern footslopes protected within the national park. For this reason, dedicated birdwatchers are advised to skip the national park

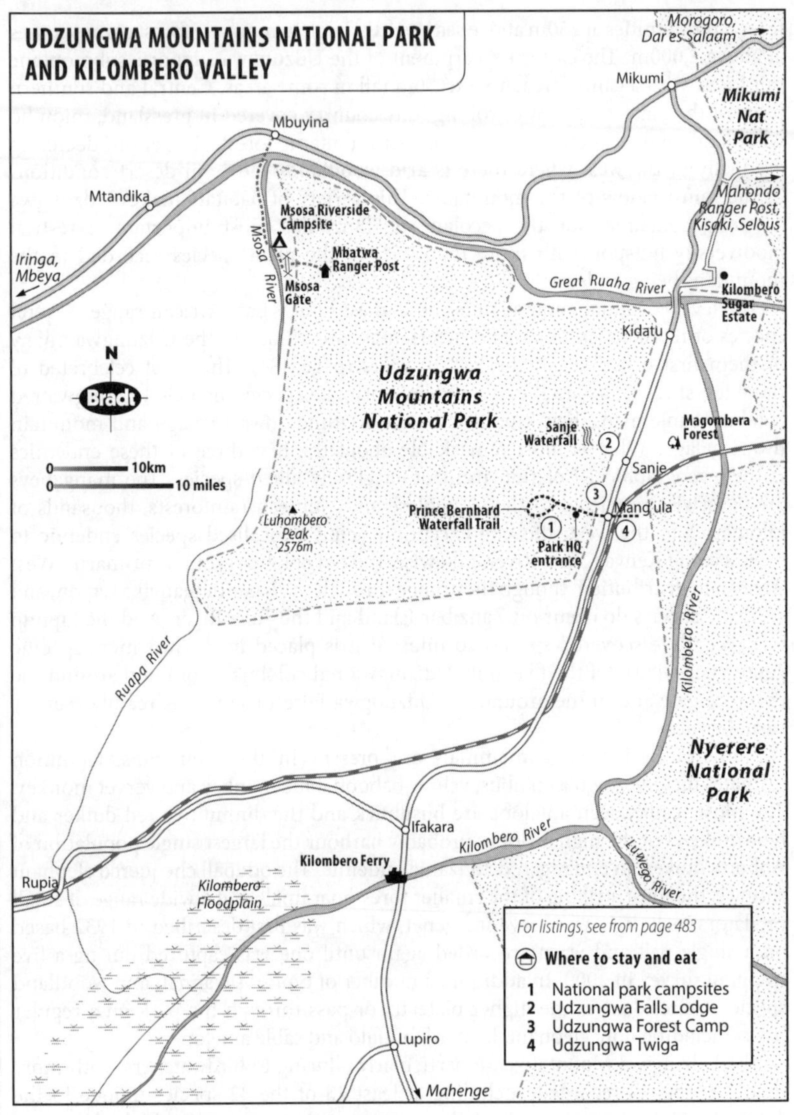

in favour of the forest reserves on the western side of the mountains for a realistic chance of seeing the Udzungwa specials; see page 475 for details.

FEES AND FURTHER INFORMATION The entrance fee of US$30 plus 18% VAT must be paid at the main park entrance. It is forbidden to walk without a guide, so you will also need to pay a guide fee of US$20 plus VAT per hike per party. For longer hikes, you need to be accompanied by an armed ranger, which costs another US$20 plus VAT per party. The office can also arrange porters, who will carry up to 20kg apiece at a charge of around US$10 per porter depending on which trail you are hiking. All fees must be paid by Visa or Mastercard; cash is not accepted, irrespective of the currency.

GETTING THERE AND AWAY

By air Auric Air (w auricair.com) operates a daily flight between Dar es Salaam and Iringa that stops by prior arrangement at Illovo Airstrip on the Kilombero Sugar Estate about 20km from the park entrance.

By road Coming from the direction of Dar es Salaam, or anywhere else along the Tanzam Highway, you need to turn south on to the B127 to Ifakara at the junction town of Mikumi. The main entrance gate lies about 55km along this road at the village of Mang'ula, on the west side of the road opposite the Twiga Hotel. The B127 is surfaced as far as Kidatu, 37km south of Mikumi, but the stretch after this is unsurfaced and can be very rough. Even so, the drive from Mikumi shouldn't take much more than an hour (so it's easy to visit Udzungwa as a day trip from Mikumi National Park, or vice versa). For details of the back route between Kidatu and Nyerere National Park via the southern sector of Mikumi National Park, see page 465.

As many as a dozen buses run between Mikumi and Ifakara daily, all passing the park entrance gate at Mang'ula. Many of these buses come from (or continue to) Morogoro or Dar es Salaam, but if you don't use a direct bus from one of these towns, the best place to pick up Ifakara-bound transport is at the junction in Mikumi town. The 2-hour trip costs around US$3.

WHERE TO STAY AND EAT *Map, page 482*

National park campsites w tanzaniaparks.go.tz. A series of campsites has been cut into the forest along the stream immediately uphill of the park headquarters at Mang'ula. They are very attractive, but given the greater affordability & better facilities at the private camps listed here, they are unlikely to attract any but the most dedicated or extravagant of campers. *US$30pp.* **$$**

Udzungwa Falls Lodge ⊕ -7.73952, 36.92562; m + 255 789 638583; w udzungwafallslodge.com. Situated on the park boundary about 10km south of Kidatu & a similar distance north of Mang'ula, this smart lodge lies in densely forested gardens alive with bird & insect song. The rambling grounds include a 3km walking trail from where red colobus & mangabey are seen with some frequency, & the large freeform swimming pool is shaded by leafy boughs. Accommodation is in 10 ivy-clad circular stone 2-storey buildings that each contain 4 rooms, all with AC, fan, fitted nets, DSTV, fridge, tea-/coffee-making facilities & private balconies with views into the canopy (best from the upper floor). The décor is a bit old-fashioned & it lacks the bush feel of Udzungwa Forest Camp, but it will appeal more to those who prefer proper hotel rooms. *US$140/240 sgl/dbl HB.* **$$$$**

✷ **Udzungwa Forest Camp** ⊕ -7.83461, 36.88984; m + 255 758 844228; w udzungwaforestcamp.com. Also known as Hondo Hondo after the 3 species of noisy hornbill that proliferate in the area, this superb tented camp stands in large gardens bordering the national park on the outskirts of Mang'ula. There is the choice of comfortable standing tents with open-roof bathrooms or more basic thatched huts using a common ablution block. Camping is also permitted. The camp is a haven for wildlife lovers: several primate species including the endemic Udzungwa red colobus are semi-resident, forest birds are prolific, & elephants & leopards occasionally pass through by night. The management is an excellent source of advice about Udzungwa hikes (detailed maps & route descriptions are available at reception). Other activities include dugout canoe trips on the Kilombero River, day safaris to Mikumi National Park, guided hikes in Magombera Forest & self-guided cycling excursions. *US$80/96 sgl/dbl B&B (hut); US$206/276 sgl/dbl (tent); US$10pp camping.* **$$–$$$$**

Udzungwa Twiga Hotel ⊕ -7.84853, 36.88929; m +255 787 280250; w tanzaniaparks.go.tz. Situated in large & well-wooded gardens practically opposite the park entrance gate in Mang'ula, this long-serving hotel is now under national park management & looks all the better for it. The 13 rooms come with AC, fan, net, DSTV & en-suite hot shower. A decent & inexpensive restaurant/bar has indoor & garden seating. *US$50pp B&B plus 18% VAT; payment by Visa or Mastercard only.* **$$$**

SECRETS OF THE FOREST

Until the 1980s, the Udzungwa Mountains and environs were poorly known to scientists, certainly by comparison with the more accessible Usambara or Uluguru ranges. The main reason for this is that early biological exploration in the Udzungwa concentrated on more developed and easily accessible parts of the central and southern plateau. Forests visited were mostly secondary with widespread Afromontane species. Only in more recent times have researchers visited the primary forests along the eastern escarpment, resulting in a flurry of new discoveries.

The endemic **rufous-winged sunbird** (*Cinnyris rufipennis*), for instance, was first described in 1984, while the **Udzungwa forest partridge** (*Xenoperdix udzungwensis*) was discovered in 1991. The story behind the discovery of the partridge is that two Danish biologists working in the mountains noticed an unusual pair of feet swimming in a chicken stew that had been prepared for them by a local cook. The next day, a local guide snared them another 'wild chicken', and it turned out to be an unknown fowl more closely related to the forest partridges of Asia than to any African bird. Since then a second population of the partridge, now regarded to be a discrete species, has been discovered in the Rubeho Mountains 150km to the north. Placed in their own genus, these two Eastern Arc forest partridges are relicts of an otherwise extinct lineage that dates back more than 15 million years, when the forests of East Africa and Asia were linked via the Middle Eastern coast.

The endemic **Sanje mangabey** (*Cercocebus sanjei*) was unknown to Western science in 1979, and the circumstance of its discovery by the ecologists Katherine Homewood and Alan Rodgers illustrates just how little attention the area had previously received from biologists. Homewood, studying the red colobus at Sanje Waterfall while suffering from a fever, heard a distinctly mangabey-like whooping call. At first she thought she was hallucinating with fever or that Rodgers was somewhere nearby playing a recording of a mangabey call as a joke. But Homewood's guide Langson recognised the call as that of a monkey, known locally as *n'golaga*, and different from a baboon or red colobus. The next day, Langson led the researchers to a troop of monkeys sitting high in the canopy, and their suspicion was confirmed: these were definitely a type of mangabey, furthermore one significantly different in appearance from the closest population, which lives about 1,000km further north on Kenya's Tana River. Langson, incredulous that this large monkey, with its loud and distinctive call, could have been overlooked by other *wazungu*, casually mentioned that an orphaned *n'golaga* was resident in Sanje village on the main Ifakara–Mikumi road. The excited researchers rushed to

WHAT TO SEE AND DO

Hikes Several walking trails have been cut through the forested eastern slopes, most of them leaving from the main entrance gate at Mang'ula. The more popular trails are described below:

Prince Bernhard Waterfall Trail (2km; 45–60mins) Named after the late Prince Consort of the Netherlands who attended the park's official opening in 1992, this short flat trail leads to a small but pretty waterfall no more than 1km from the entrance gate. Taken slowly, the trail can be remarkably rewarding. Blue monkey and the endemic Udzungwa red colobus (actually grey and white the village, and there they were able to photograph the tame young mangabey, which clearly belonged to an undescribed race or species. Twenty years after it was discovered, the Sanje mangabey had the dubious distinction of being the solitary East African species included on a list of the World's 25 Most Endangered Primates compiled by the IUCN Primate Specialist Group. In 2006, it was joined on that list by the kipunji monkey, a newly discovered species endemic to southern Udzungwa and Mount Rungwe (page 488).

While the endemic birds and mammals tend to receive the greatest attention, the abrupt recent decline in the population of an amphibian endemic to the Udzungwa illustrates how precarious the situation of a range-restricted species can be. One of seven species in a genus of toads endemic to Tanzania, the yellow-streaked **Kihansi spray toad** (*Nectophrynoides asperginis*) is so tiny that an adult can fit on a human fingernail, and unusual among amphibians in that it does not lay eggs, but rather gives birth to a brood of live miniatures. When it was first described in 1996, the Kihansi spray toad was thought to number around 17,000 in the wild, despite having the smallest range of any known vertebrate species, a mere 20,000m^2 of ferny terrain sustained by the spray from a single waterfall on the Kihansi River. Since its discovery, the toad population has plummeted, partly due to the diversion of most of the gorge's water to feed a government hydro-electric dam that generates a third of the nation's electricity supply, then in 2005 as a result if an outbreak of amphibian disease called chytrid fungus. In 2009, the IUCM listed Kihansi spray toad as Extinct in the Wild, and this is still its official status today. However, a captive breeding programme maintained at a few zoos in the USA has led to the reintroduction of large numbers of toad into Kihansi Gorge since 2012; according to some sources the wild population now stands at more than 5,000 individuals.

The list of Udzungwa endemics grows with practically every passing year, a prominent fairly recent discovery being the **Matunda dwarf galago** (*Galagoides udzungwensis*) in 1996. Furthermore, three endemic species of bird have been discovered in the Kilombero Valley immediately southwest of Udzungwa, and it has been noted that several Eastern Arc specials likely to occur within the Udzungwa Mountains National Park have yet to be actually recorded there. In more recent times, scientists were excited by the discovery of the world's largest species of elephant shrew, the **grey-faced sengi** (*Rhynchocyon udzungwensis*), which was first photographed in 2005 and described in 2008. One can only guess at how many birds and other creatures endemic to the Udzungwa still await scientific discovery.

with a bright orange fringe) are common in the area and likely to be seen. Look out, too, for the shy red duiker, which often emerges on to the trail in the early morning and towards dusk, and for the bizarre checkered elephant shrew with its tan-striped flanks and habit of crashing noisily through the litter. Birding is erratic and can be quite frustrating, but you can be reasonably sure of seeing the outsized trumpeter and crowned hornbill, the lovely green-headed oriole (listen for its repetitive four-note song in the canopy) and the brightly coloured forest weaver, whose gentle fluting call is all around. If you sit quietly at the waterfall in the early morning or evening, you might see monkeys come to drink at the pool below it.

Sanje Waterfall Trail (7km; 3–4hrs) This is the most popular day hike, a round trip of at least 4 hours' duration leading to the Sanje Waterfall – in fact a series of falls that plunge more than 100m down over three separate stages, with a pool at the base where swimming is permitted. This trail offers excellent forest birding, and you can be practically sure of seeing the Udzungwa red colobus as well as black-and-white colobus. The Sanje mangabey was first heard by researchers in

BIRDING IN THE WESTERN UDZUNGWA

David Moyer

A reasonable assumption made by many birders visiting Tanzania is that the place to seek out the Udzungwa Mountains' endemics and near-endemics is in the national park, but this is not the case. Although birding in the eastern forests of the national park is very rewarding, and key species such as rufous-winged sunbird and Swynnerton's robin might be seen above Sanje Waterfall, the most alluring endemic – the Udzungwa forest partridge – has yet to be recorded in this area. The best chance for seeing that species, and other specialities, is in fact in the forests on Luhombero Mountain (the tallest point in the national park) and on Ndundulu Ridge and Nyumbanitu Mountain in the adjacent West Kilombero Forest Reserve, all of which lie in the western part of the range and are not realistically approached from Mang'ula. The best time to go looking for forest birds is from September to early December.

The gateway to the western forests is Udekwa, which lies 3 hours from Iringa by road. Before visiting, a permit must be obtained from the Catchment Forestry Office in Iringa, though you might also be able to do this at the village government office in Udekwa. To get to Udekwa, follow the Tanzam Highway out of Iringa towards Mikumi for 45km to Ilula, and ask there for the turn-off to the east.

On reaching Udekwa, report to the village government office near the primary school. After introductions are complete and fees or permits presented, ask the village chairman or secretary to assist with the selection of porters. (Never select porters on your own – if anything goes wrong, you are less likely to receive help from the village government!) Make an agreement with the porters to meet you at Chui Campsite (7km into the forest reserve at the end of the motorable track) very early the next morning and start the expedition from there.

From Udekwa or Chui, you can go to one of two campsites. The more accessible is in Luala Valley, a grassy glade in the forest on the Ndundulu Ridge at an elevation of 1,900m, meaning it can be very cold at night, especially from June to August. Take good raingear as it can be wet at any time. Luala is a 5–6-hour walk from Chui Campsite, and can be very steep and tiring in places. After about 1½ hours, you enter the forest and head up the ridge along a path that offers good birding. From Luala, the forest trails to the northeast towards Luhombero Mountain are a good place to find Udzungwa forest partridge and rufous-winged sunbird.

Alternatively, you can go to Mufu Camp, where the partridge was originally discovered. This is about a 6-hour walk from Chui, also quite steep. It is situated right in the middle of the forest and dappled mountain robin, Iringa akalat, Swynnerton's robin and Nduk eagle owl (as well as Udzungwa forest partridge) may be seen around the camp.

the vicinity of the waterfall, but it is not normally resident in the area, and is unlikely to be seen by casual visitors. The area around the waterfall is legendarily rich in butterflies, including several endemic taxa, with activity typically peaking from mid morning to mid afternoon. Visitors with a vehicle have the option of using a shorter trail by driving back along the Mikumi road towards the Sanje ranger post, which lies a few hundred metres below the base of the waterfall.

Hidden Valleys Trail (14km; 6–8hrs) This quite demanding trail follows a big loop around the large peak rising behind the park entrance gate. It starts at Campsite Three, just after the turning for the park headquarters, and arrives back on the trail from Njokamoni Waterfall, leading into Udzungwa Forest Camp. It's a long steep walk that climbs to above 1,000m, so you should plan to leave early. It is necessary to take a ranger on this hike, as well as a guide, as there are large mammals deep in the forest. Once you've climbed the sometimes steep trail to the ridge, you walk through a series of grassy valleys often frequented by elephants.

Mwanihana Trail (38km; 3 days) The longest existing hike leads to Mwanihana Peak, which is the second-highest point in the range at 2,150m, and it entails two nights' camping on the mountain. This is the only trail that exposes visitors to the closed-canopy montane forest and grassland habitats of the range's higher slopes. As such, it provides the best chance within the national park of encountering the rare Abbott's duiker and larger mammals such as buffalo and elephant, as well as some of the more interesting birds. Prospective hikers will need to have their own camping gear, and to carry all the food they will need. An armed ranger is mandatory, owing to the presence of potentially dangerous animals, and a porter is recommended if you want to make the most of the hike.

Other activities

Mangabey tracking The most reliable way to see these shy terrestrial monkeys – which tend to avoid forest margins where they face competition for food with baboons – is to join the researchers who spend their days studying a habituated troop resident in the forest uphill from the park headquarters. No additional fee is charged for this, but it is best organised a day ahead, and cannot be done on Sundays, which is the researchers' day off. Morning is the best time to look for the mangabeys, and you should expect a walk of up to 2 hours to locate them, depending on how close they are to the road.

Magombera Forest Set on a sugar estate about 30 minutes' drive from Mang'ula, this isolated patch of lowland forest, roughly 20km^2 in extent and bounded by the Tazara Railway to the north and Nyerere National Park to the east, is likely to be set aside as a formal forest reserve during the lifespan of this edition. For wildlife enthusiasts, it makes for an alluring alternative to the popular national park, boasting the densest known population of Udzungwa red colobus alongside the more widespread Angola colobus and blue monkey. It is also a good place to look for forest, forest-fringe and marsh-associated birds, including Peter's twinspot, broad-billed roller, marsh tchagra and Pel's fishing owl. An endemic chameleon and tree frog have also been recorded. Guided visits cost US$20 per person and must be arranged through Udzungwa Forest Camp (page 483).

Kilombero Valley Flanked by the Udzungwa Mountains to the northwest, this untrammelled 4,000km^2 floodplain follows the course of the Kilombero River

KIPUNJI!

While interviewing Nyakyusa subsistence hunters in early 2003, biologists Tim Davenport and Noah Mpunga of the Southern Highlands Conservation Programme were first alerted to the possibility that an unusual monkey might inhabit the forests of Mount Rungwe, a 2,960m dormant volcano set in the southern highlands close to the border with Malawi. Initially, the researchers assumed that this creature, known locally as *kipunji* (see page 38 for a photo), was a form of blue monkey, or one of the many spirit animals integral to Nyakyusa culture.

The combination of steep terrain, thick undergrowth and the animal's shy nature meant that several months passed before the biologists obtained a clear sighting of a kipunji. But when they did, in the Livingstone Forest (now part of Kitulo National Park) in December 2003, it confirmed their growing suspicion that this elusive canopy-dweller, with its unique 'whoop-gobble' alarm call, was a previously undescribed monkey species – the first to be discovered in Africa in more than two decades.

Also known as the highland mangabey, the kipunji is almost exclusively arboreal and it boasts an unusually shaggy coat, presumably an adaptation to the chilly nocturnal temperatures that characterise the upper slopes of Rungwe and Kitulo. Almost 1m long, it is grey-brown in colour, with a long crest standing erect on its head, elongated cheek whiskers and an off-white belly and tail. It lives in medium-sized troops that forage in the safety of the canopy (up to 50m high), and is thus most likely to be located by its distinctive call.

Given that Tanzania is among the most biologically well known of African countries, it is remarkable that this distinctive large mammal managed to elude scientists into the 21st century. But more bizarre still is that having remained invisible for so long, the same monkey was effectively discovered twice by

(and various tributaries) before its confluence with the Great Ruaha. Set aside as a relatively lowly Game Controlled Area, it is East Africa's largest low-altitude wetland, a significance acknowledged when it was accepted as Tanzania's second Ramsar site in 2011. Much of the wetland is seasonal, but there are also extensive permanent swamps at Kibasira and in the far southwest on the Kihansi River.

A western extension of the Greater Selous–Niassa ecosystem, the valley forms an important dry-season feeding ground for up to 5,000 elephant, while large numbers of hippo, crocodile and buffalo are resident alongside an estimated 50,000 puku, representing about 70% of the global population of this kob-like antelope. The valley also made ornithological headlines in 1986 with the discovery of the previously undescribed Kilombero weaver (now illustrated in all recent East African field guides), and it is also home to bird species in the genus *Cisticola* that still await formal designation. It also supports an impressive checklist of unusual water-associated birds, notably shoebill, African skimmer, Madagascar squacco heron, Pel's fishing owl, half-collared kingfisher and coppery-tailed coucal. Udzungwa Forest Camp (page 483) arranges dugout canoe excursions on the river and it can also put together overnight excursions to the colonial-era Itete Catholic Mission. Longer excursions into the Kilombero Valley can be arranged through the affiliated **Wild Things Safaris** (w wildthingsafaris.com).

independent research teams working at sites more than 350km apart. In May 2004, before Davenport had announced his discovery, Caroline Ehardt and Trevor Jones identified what appeared to be an undescribed mangabey in the remote Ndundulu Forest Reserve in the Udzungwa Mountains. And as chance would have it, one of the first confidants to whom Ehardt divulged her exciting secret – over a sociable beer in a Dar es Salaam bar – was none other than a rather astounded Davenport. Having recovered from the mutual shock of their joint discovery, the two teams subsequently prepared a joint paper describing the new species for the May 2005 edition of *Science* magazine.

Subsequent genetic tests have determined that the kipunji is more closely related to baboons than the superficially similar mangabeys, and it has been assigned to a new genus *Rungwecebus*, the first to be discovered in Africa since 1923. Although it is conceivable that further populations await discovery, its known range is restricted to three sites – the semi-contiguous Rungwe and Livingstone forests as well as the isolated Ndundulu Forest bordering Udzungwa Mountains National Park – with a total extent of less than 75km². In 2006 and 2008, the kipunji earned the dubious distinction of being listed among The World's 25 Most Endangered Primates; it has since been removed from this list, not because numbers have increased but rather as a result of more endangered taxa having been identified. It is assessed as Critically Endangered on the IUCN Red List, with a total population estimated at 1,100 individuals, and it remains vulnerable to subsistence hunting, illegal logging and other unmanaged resource extraction. Fortunately, since the kipunji was discovered, much of its small range has been incorporated into Kitulo National Park, and there is also a possibility that Udzungwa Mountains National Park will be increased in extent to include Ndundulu.

20

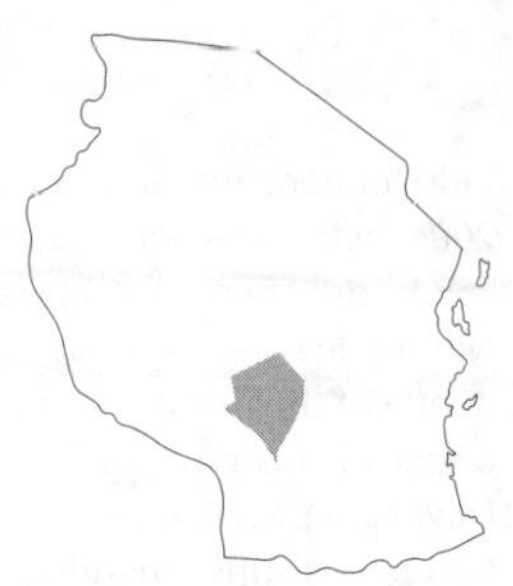

Ruaha National Park and Iringa

Neither as popular as Serengeti/Ngorongoro, nor as widely publicised as Nyerere, Ruaha National Park is nevertheless one of East Africa's finest safari destinations. Set in the vast semi-arid central interior, its eastern boundary formed by the Great Ruaha River, this vast park is often – and justifiably – cited by the cognoscenti as Tanzania's best-kept game-viewing secret (an accolade for which the only other real contender is Katavi National Park). Indeed, the sheer volume and variety of wildlife on show in Ruaha can be truly spectacular, particularly towards the end of the dry season, when elephants seem to lurk around every corner. Meanwhile the park's rugged slopes, studded with mighty baobab trees, underscore a compelling wilderness character that seems increasingly savoury in this day of package safaris and hundred-room game lodges. Although many people fly to Ruaha, the gateway town by road is Iringa, which lies on the Tanzam Highway 500km southwest of Dar es Salaam and 110km east of the national park entrance gate.

IRINGA

Perched at 1,500m on a steep escarpment rising immediately north of the Tanzam Highway, Iringa is an important regional administrative centre, with an estimated population of 175,000 supplemented by a substantial contingent of foreign volunteers and NGO workers. The compact town centre, which overlooks the Ruaha Valley, is studded with old German and Asian buildings, and the old market is an excellent place to buy the rugs and baskets for which the region is famed. It is the principal town of the Hehe people, who provided the most sustained resistance to German colonisation of any tribe in the Tanzanian interior (page 494) and its name is a corruption of the Hehe word *lilinga*, a reference to the large fort built by Chief Mkwawa at Kalenga southwest of the modern town. Iringa is of interest to tourists mainly as the springboard for road safaris into Ruaha National Park, but other places of interest include the central Boma Museum and the out-of-town Isimila Stone Age Site and Mkwawa Museum.

GETTING THERE AND AWAY

By air **Auric Air** (w auricair.com) offers daily flights between Dar es Salaam, Ruaha National Park and Iringa, optionally stopping off at Kilombero Airstrip (for Udzungwa Mountains National Park). Tickets cost US$160.

By road Iringa lies 2km from the Tanzam Highway along a steep ascent road that branches west at Ipogoro junction 500km southwest of Dar es Salaam and 390km northeast of Mbeya. Allow up to 9 hours to drive directly from Dar es Salaam, 4 hours from Mikumi, and 6 hours from Mbeya.

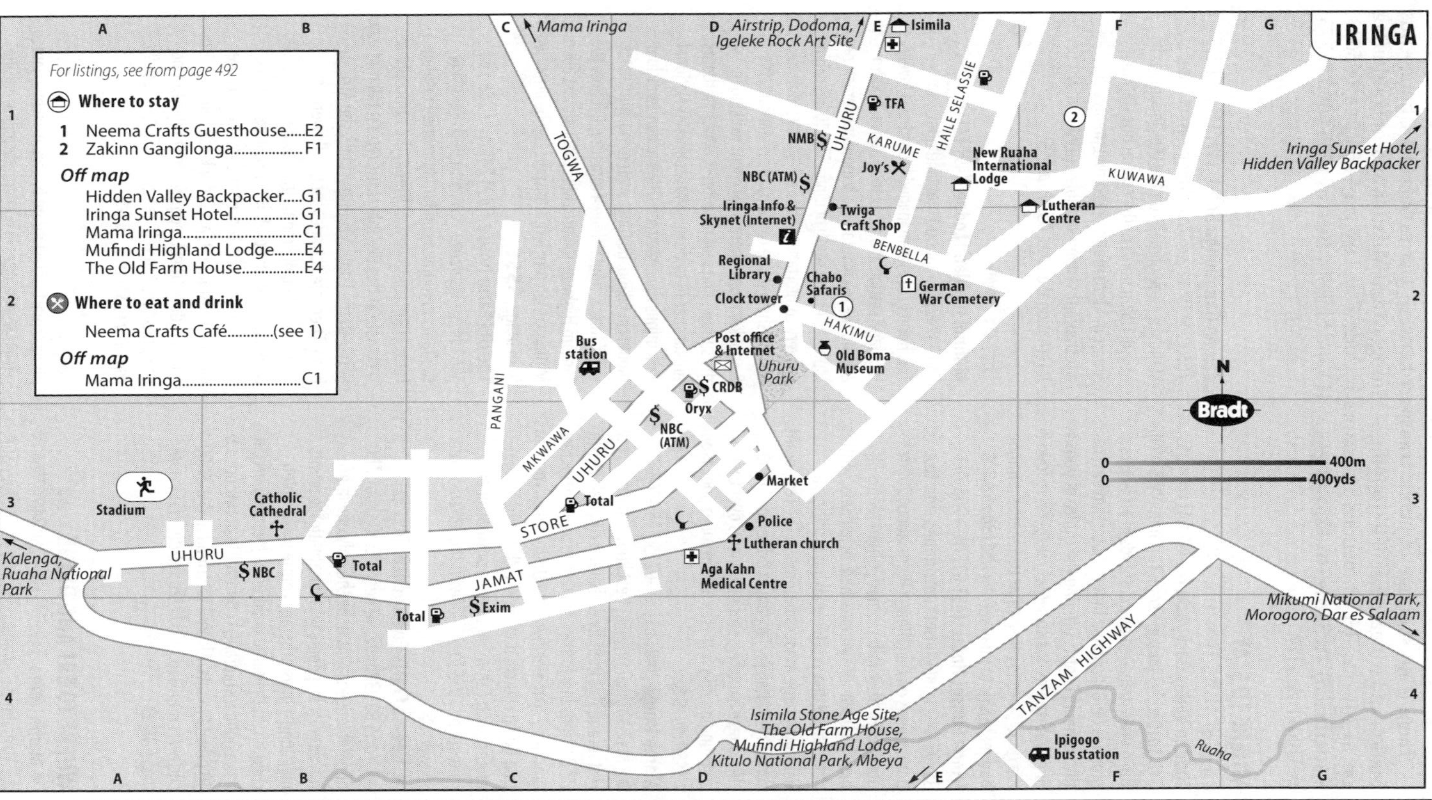
IRINGA
For listings, see from page 492
Where to stay
1 Neema Crafts Guesthouse.....E2
2 Zakinn Gangilonga..................F1
Off map
Hidden Valley Backpacker.....G1
Iringa Sunset Hotel.................G1
Mama Iringa..............................C1
Mufindi Highland Lodge........E4
The Old Farm House................E4
Where to eat and drink
Neema Crafts Café............(see 1)
Off map
Mama Iringa..............................C1
Mama Iringa
Airstrip, Dodoma, Igeleke Rock Art Site
Isimila
TFA
HAILE SELASSIE
UHURU
KARUME
NMB
NBC (ATM)
Joy's
New Ruaha International Lodge
KUWAWA
Lutheran Centre
Iringa Sunset Hotel, Hidden Valley Backpacker
Iringa Info & Skynet (Internet)
Twiga Craft Shop
BENBELLA
Regional Library
Chabo Safaris
German War Cemetery
Clock tower
HAKIMU
Post office & Internet
Uhuru Park
Old Boma Museum
TOGWA
Bus station
CRDB
Oryx
NBC (ATM)
PANGANI
MKWAWA
Market
Total
Police
Lutheran church
STORE
Stadium
Catholic Cathedral
UHURU
NBC
Total
JAMAT
Exim
Total
Aga Kahn Medical Centre
Kalenga, Ruaha National Park
400m
400yds
Mikumi National Park, Morogoro, Dar es Salaam
TANZAM HIGHWAY
Isimila Stone Age Site, The Old Farm House, Mufindi Highland Lodge, Kitulo National Park, Mbeya
Ipigogo bus station
Ruaha

There is no shortage of **public transport** between Dar es Salaam's Ubungo Bus Station and Iringa, most of it stopping at Morogoro and Mikumi, and/or continuing on to Mbeya. Recommended operators include Dar Lux (m +255 744 666643; f darluxco), Al Saedy (m +255 713 013541) and Shabiby Bus (m +255 654 777773; w shabiby.co.tz).

WHERE TO STAY

In & around town

Hidden Valley Backpacker [491 G1] m +255 748 101080; w booking.com. This homely & well-run owner-managed hostel stands in attractive grounds on Gangilonga Ridge about 1km east of the Lutheran Centre. Offering the choice of dorms or private rooms, it also serves inexpensive food & is a good place to meet other travellers & arrange budget safaris to Ruaha. *From US$13pp B&B.* **$**

Iringa Sunset Hotel [491 G1] m +255 743 359971; w iringasunset.com. Iringa's smartest hotel stands on Gangilonga Ridge about 200m north of Hidden Valley. Smart, bright rooms all have a queen- or king-size bed, fitted nets, writing desk, sat TV, tea-/coffee-making facilities, a balcony & large modern bathroom. The restaurant serves good Italian, Tanzanian & Indian cuisine, the terrace bar offers stunning views over the surrounding hills & there's a swimming pool. *From US$80 dbl.* **$$**

Mama Iringa [491 C1] m +255 746 476650; f MamaIringaTanzania. Best known for its restaurant, this friendly & characterful Italian-run B&B stands in a former convent in large attractive grounds 2.5km northwest of Uhuru Rd en route to Don Bosco church. It offers the choice of budget rooms using common showers or smarter en-suite rooms. *US$10/25 dbl with shared/en-suite showers.* **$**

✷ **Neema Crafts Guesthouse** [491 E2] m +255 683 380492; w neemacrafts.com. This popular lodge claims to be the only one in Africa run entirely by people with disabilities & profits help fund a physiotherapy centre for disabled children. In the same building as Neema Crafts, it has a good restaurant, comfortable dormitories & 10 private rooms. Alcohol is forbidden & a 22.00 curfew is imposed. *US$11/20 sgl/dbl, US$8 dorm bed, B&B.* **$**

Zakinn Gangilonga Hotel [491 F1] m +255 763 454525; w zaki.co.tz. This pleasant hotel stands in large gardens on the Old Dodoma Rd about 1.5km north of the central bus station. Smart modern rooms are complemented by a restaurant serving sensibly priced local & international dishes. *US$45 dbl.* **$**

Out of town

Mufindi Highland Lodge [491 E4] m +255 754 237422; w mufindihighlandlodge.com. This homely owner-managed lodge has a lovely highland setting at an elevation above 2,000m among the tea plantations & montane forests of Mufindi, 130km south of Iringa. The 10 log cabins are very comfortable, while a 2-storey stone-&-wood fishing lodge contains the restaurant, bar & snooker room. There is excellent walking in the surrounding montane forest, which harbours similar species to Udzungwa Mountains National Park minus the endemics. Other activities include mountain biking, boating, swimming, horseback excursions & trout fishing. From Iringa, follow the Tanzam Highway towards Mbeya for almost 80km to Mafinga, then turn left. Transport can be arranged from Iringa. **$$$$**

The Old Farm House [491 E4] m +255 754 306144; w kisolanza.com. Situated alongside the Tanzam Highway on family-owned Kisolanza Farm 60km southwest of Iringa, the atmosphere & climate at this likeable rustic retreat fall midway between the English countryside & the African bush. There are cottages set in a flowering private garden, dbl rooms in a stable bunkhouse, & separate campsites, both with hot showers, for private campers & overland trucks. Facilities include a restaurant, a bar & a kiosk selling fresh farm produce (meat, eggs & vegetables but no dairy products) to self-caterers. *US$45–120 dbl, camping US$8pp.* **$–$$$**

WHERE TO EAT AND DRINK

✷ **Mama Iringa** [491 C1] m +250 746 476650; f MamaIringaTanzania; ⌚ noon–21.30 Tue–Sun. Iringa's smartest restaurant has an attractive garden setting & specialises in homemade Italian cuisine, ranging from the predictable pizzas & pasta dishes to the more unusual likes of lasagne, gnocchi, ravioli & grills. *Mains are in the US$5–8 range.* $

Neema Crafts Café [491 E2] m +255 683 380492; w neemacrafts.com; ⌚ 07.00–19.00 Mon–Sat. Attached to the eponymous craft shop, this chilled 1st-floor café is a favourite with aid workers & expatriates thanks to its extensive & inexpensive menu of sandwiches, paninis & light meals. Beverages include fresh ground coffee & delicious smoothies & juices but no alcohol. Staffed by deaf people from the workshop, they've created an ingenious ordering system whereby you write down what you'd like & then turn on a flashing light to let them know. $

TOUR OPERATORS

Chabo Safaris [491 D2] m +255 754 893717; w chaboafricasafari.com. A good contact for budget safaris to Ruaha, Chabo has its own cheap guesthouse in Tungamalenga, the closest village to the national park accessible on public transport. It can arrange a full-day safari out of Iringa or Tungamalenga, as well as transfers between the two.

Kamweme Heritage Tours m + 255 659 740849; w kamwenetoursiringa.blogspot.com. This small operator offers 2–3hr walking tours of Iringa town, incorporating visits to the market & several historic buildings, for US$15pp. It can also arrange cooking classes, village visits & day excursions to archaeological sites such as Isimila & Igeleke.

Kusini Safaris w kusini-safaris.com. Run by Iringa-based wildlife photographer & safari guide Paul Tickner, this small operator specialises in tailor-made photographic safaris to Ruaha. Paul will guide safaris personally by request.

WHAT TO SEE AND DO

Old Boma Museum [491 E2] (w fahariyetu.net; ⌚ 09.30–18.00 daily; entrance US$5/3 foreign adults/children) This museum is set in the old German Boma, a Swahili-influenced stone-and-brick-faced building that was constructed c1900, and used as the regional administrative headquarters from the end of World War I until 2014, when it was restored to its original design as part of the Fahari Yetu Project under the University of Iringa. Various displays in the museum detail the prehistory of the area, local Hehe cultural practices, and the history of Iringa from the late 19th-century reign of King Mkwawa to the modern era.

Neema Crafts Workshop [491 E2] (w neemacrafts.com) This admirable vocational workshop for deaf and disabled youngsters produces a variety of handmade paper products (from material as varied as pineapple leaves and elephant dung), as well as Maasai-influenced beadwork, patchwork quilts and rugs for sale to visitors. Free guided tours are available, after which you can pop upstairs for a coffee at the attached café (see above).

Igeleke Rock Art Site [491 E1] (⊕ -7.72528, 35.71448; m +255 766 662777; ⌚ 07.30–18.00 daily; entrance US$3) Although less well known and extensive than the rock art of Kondoa, the paintings on the Igeleke Shelter, a prominent rock outcrop on the northwest outskirts of Iringa, are similar in style and vintage, with the oldest figures thought to be around 3,000 years old. At least 30 well-preserved red-ochre figures of humans are depicted, along with wildlife such as giraffe and elephants, and various red, black and white geometric figures. The site lies about 500m west of the main road to Dodoma, 6km north of the town centre, close to Igeleke Primary School. Guides are available at the site (around US$3 per party) or you can arrange a guided tour through Neema Crafts, Kamweme Heritage Tours or the Old Boma Museum. The site also offers fabulous views towards the Dodoma escarpment.

Isimila Stone Age Site [491 E4] (🕘 09.00–16.00 daily; entrance US$10) South of Iringa off the Tanzam Highway, Isimila (or Isimilia) is a seasonal watercourse that has yielded one of the world's richest assemblages of Stone Age tools. The significance of the site was first recognised in 1951 by a local schoolboy who collected two

CHIEF MKWAWA AND UHEHE

The area around Iringa is known as Uhehe: homeland of the Hehe, the dominant regional military force during the late 19th century (the name Hehe derives from the warriors' feared *hee-hee* battle cry) and the most successful in initially resisting German colonisation. The Hehe Empire took shape c1850 under Chief Munyigumba, who asserted control over about 100 ntemi chieftaincies to forge a centralised polity ruled from Lungemba, 10–15km south of modern-day Iringa. The formation of Uhehe coincided with a trend towards centralisation in the Tanzanian interior, a phenomenon attributed to the threat posed by militant Ngoni warriors coming from the south, and the economic opportunities created by coastal slave caravans.

In 1879, Munyigumba died (the tree under which he was reputedly buried can still be seen at Lungemba), prompting a violent secession dispute. Tradition has it that Munyigumba had appointed his younger brother Muhalwike as his successor, or failing that had asked that the empire be divided between his two eldest sons. Instead, his son-in-law Mwamubambe seized the throne by force, and had Muhalwike and one of the chosen royal sons killed. The other son, only 21 years old at the time, was forced into exile. But Mwamubambe lacked popular support, and the Hehe elders conspired with the exiled heir to overthrow him. Mwamubambe and 1,000 of his warriors were killed in battle at a place now known as Lundamatwe – 'where skulls are heaped'.

Munyigumba's only surviving heir was appointed Chief of the Hehe, and he took on (or subsequently acquired) the throne name Mkwawa, a diminutive form of Mukwavinyika – 'conqueror of lands'. Mkwawa established a capital at Kalenga, 15km west of present-day Iringa, and embarked on a series of military campaigns to expand his empire into other territories traversed by the coastal trade caravans. Mkwawa demanded substantial levies from the passing slavers, and he also sold them any enemies captured in battle by the Hehe. By the mid 1880s, the military prowess of the Hehe and tactical skills of Mkwawa were legendary among follower and foe alike.

In 1888, as Mkwawa continued to expand his territory ever coastward, Germany secured its first permanent foothold on the East African mainland at Bagamoyo. Initially, the Germans were preoccupied with asserting their legitimacy at the coast. By 1891, however, Germany had not only quelled a series of coastal rebellions, but it had also gained nominal custody over the interior of modern-day Tanzania by treaty with Britain. In response to these ominous developments, Mkwawa mobilised his army, announcing that Uhehe would remain an independent state irrespective of the lines drawn on maps in Europe. Germany, meanwhile, recognised that Mkwawa, more even than Chief Mirambo of Nyamwezi, was likely to prove the most formidable obstacle to realising its nominal rule over the interior.

In July 1891, the German Commissioner Emil von Zelewski led a formidably armed expedition of 13 German officers and 570 African troops and porters into Uhehe, razing several villages on the way, then shooting dead the trio of envoys rucksacks full of stone implements, amongst them a 40cm-long axe weighing 4kg. Formal excavations by American universities took place over 1957–58 and 1969–70.

The watercourse at Isimila has yielded its wealth of ancient tools because it cuts through a series of sediment layers deposited on the bed of a shallow lake that

sent by Mkwawa to open negotiations. Mkwawa interpreted this as an open declaration of war, and – quietly keeping tabs on the German progress – he set a trap for the invaders at a rocky gorge on the Little Ruaha River near Lugalo, 15km east of Iringa. On 17 August, as Zelewski and his troops set up camp, some 3,000 Hehe warriors armed with spears and a few guns surged across the shallow river, closing in on the German troops to enforce hand-to-hand combat. Within 15 minutes, Zelewski and all but three of the German officers, and 140 of the Africans under his command, lay dead. Mkwawa boosted his armoury by making off with hundreds of rifles and many rounds of ammunition. A monument to Zelewski and the other slain officers still stands at Lugalo today.

Following this victory, Mkwawa fortified Kalenga, raising a 4m-high stone enclosure around the royal village, and surrounding that with a deep trench. He also tormented the Germans by launching surprise attacks on their positions, on one occasion wiping out an entire garrison at Kondoa. The Germans lusted for revenge but bided their time, gradually isolating Uhehe by forging alliances with neighbouring chiefs unsympathetic to Mkwawa. On 28 October 1894, the Germans set a row of cannons high on a hill above Kalenga, and bombarded the fortified capital for two days, before descending to the fort to pit their bayonets against the Hehe spears in hand-to-hand combat. The Germans easily took possession of the fort, then destroyed the ammunition store and confiscated the chief's stockpiles of ivory and guns.

Mkwawa proved to be more elusive. Having fled Kalenga when defeat became inevitable, he spent the next four years roaming through Uhehe, inflicting occasional guerrilla attacks on German garrisons. His success in evading the Germans can be attributed to the loyalty of his subjects, who refused to give away his position. No German knew what Mkwawa looked like, and even when the German Governor offered a reward of 5,000 rupees for Mkwawa's head, it was to no avail. The chief's luck eventually ran out on 19 June 1898, while encamped at Mlambalasi, 50km west of Iringa. A German garrison surrounded the camp, and Mkwawa, facing certain defeat, shot himself rather than being taken captive.

The German sergeant who arrived at the fatal scene cut off Mkwawa's head and took it to Iringa. Mkwawa's decapitated corpse was buried at Mlambalasi, but his skull was taken to the Bremen Anthropological Museum in Germany. There it would remain until 1954, when – 56 years to the day after Mkwawa's death – Sir Edward Twining handed it over to Mkwawa's grandson, Chief Adam Sapi Mkwawa. The skull was displayed unceremoniously at the Mkwawa Museum in Kalenga until 1998, the centenary of Mkwawa's death, when it was finally interred alongside the chief's body at Mlambalasi. A memorial to Mkwawa, still widely revered in Tanzania for his resistance to colonisation, was unveiled at the same time – it can be reached along an 11km road signposted to the right 40km out of Iringa en route to Ruaha National Park.

For further information, check out the website **w** mkwawa.com, which describes several sites associated with Chief Mkwawa.

flourished for a few thousand years before drying out 60,000 years ago. The tools mostly date from when the lakeshore was inhabited by Stone Age hunter-gatherers, and though they aren't the oldest unearthed in East Africa – similar implements of half a million years old are known from Oldupai Gorge and other sites – they do form an unusually varied and numerous showcase of late Acheulean workmanship. The site museum houses a selection of these tools, including several pear-shaped hand-axes, as well as picks, cleavers, hammers and cutting stones.

The site has also thrown up the fossilised bones of several large mammals, giving a good impression of what the area's large fauna must have looked like at the time. These include several extinct pig species, including a giant variety far larger than any that survives today, one extinct antelope, and a giraffe-like ungulate with large antlers and a relatively short neck. The fossilised bones and teeth of the extinct *Hippopotamus gorgops* – another extinct species with telescoped projecting eyes – are protected in a shelter on site. Ten minutes' walk from the Stone Age site, a scenic gully studded with 10m-high sandstone pillars carved by the extinct river looks like the set of a Lilliputian cowboy movie.

Isimila lies about 2km from the Tanzam Highway, along a clearly signposted turn-off about 20km southwest of Iringa. If you don't have private transport, you could hire a taxi from Iringa (expect to pay US$20–30 for the round trip), or ask any southbound bus to stop at the junction, from where it's a 20-minute walk to the archaeological site. Drinks are available, and an informative booklet written by Neville Chittick in 1972 is often on sale.

Kalenga This small village on the banks of the Ruaha was the site of Mkwawa's fortified capital before it was destroyed by German cannon fire in 1894. A small site **museum** (🕘 09.00–16.00 daily; entrance US$10) in the village houses several of Mkwawa's personal effects, including some of his clubs, spears and guns. Outside the museum stand the tombs of Mkwawa's son and grandson, Chief Sapi Mkwawa and Adam Sapi Mkwawa, the latter famous in his own right as the first Speaker of Parliament in independent Tanzania. About 500m from the museum is the tomb of the German Commander Erich Maas, who died in the Battle of Kalenga.

The museum caretaker will happily take you around the village, which seems pretty unremarkable to the untrained eye, but is in fact dotted with relics of Mkwawa's capital: the remains of fortified walls, the mound used by the chief to address his people, and the foundations of his home. The caretaker will also point out the ridge from where the Germans unleashed the barrage of cannon fire that destroyed the capital. This hill has since become known as Tosamaganga (throwing stones), and is now the site of a quaint 1930s Italian mission.

Pick-up trucks to Tosamaganga and Kalenga leave Iringa every hour or so. They wait for passengers at the end of the surfaced road 200m past Samora Stadium. At Kalenga you will be dropped off next to the market, from where it is a 5-minute meander through the village to the museum. Keep asking for directions. If your Swahili is limited, asking for Mkwawa will get you further than asking for a museum.

Kitulo National Park Gazetted in 2005, this rather obscure 413km^2 national park is the first such entity in tropical Africa to be created primarily for its floristic significance. It protects the Kitulo Plateau, the country's largest and most important montane grassland habitat, perched above 2,600m between the Kipengere Range and the Poroto and Livingstone mountains, and incorporating two of the highest peaks in the Southern Highlands: the 2,961m Mount Mtorwi and the 2,929m Chaluhangi Dome. Known locally as 'Bustani ya Mungu' (God's

Garden) and elsewhere as the 'Serengeti of Flowers', the plateau hosts one of the world's great floral spectacles between November and April. This is when its 350 documented species of vascular plant come into bloom, among them 45 types of terrestrial orchid, the yellow-and-orange red-hot poker (*Kniphofia kirkii*) and various aloes, proteas, geraniums, giant lobelias, lilies and aster daisies. More than 30 species are Tanzanian endemics, and at least three are endemic to the plateau itself. Listed as an Important Bird Area, the plateau is also home to breeding colonies of blue swallow and Denham's bustard, as well as mountain marsh widow, Njombe cisticola and Kipengere seedeater. The national park also incorporates the expansive Livingstone Forest, a mosaic of bamboo thicket and Afromontane forest that is one of the few strongholds of the kipunji monkey (an Endangered southern Tanzanian endemic discovered in 2003; page 488) and also harbours the very localised Abbott's duiker and Rungwe dwarf galago.

Coming from the north, two roads connect the Tanzam Highway to Matamba, which is the gateway village to Kitulo and site of the national park head office (⊕ -8.98652, 33.93565; m +255 767 536130; e kitulonp@tanzaniaparks.go.tz). The better of these is a gently ascending 30km road that runs from the village of Mfumbi about 250km southwest of Iringa and 80km east of Mbeya. The more spectacular but slower (and after rain, more dangerous) alternative, running south from the Tanzam Highway at Chimala about 10km further west, is a road called 'Hamsini na Saba' ('57') in reference to the number of hairpin bends along its length.

The park entrance fee is US$30 per person plus VAT, and guides can be arranged for US$20. From Matamba, it's a 1-hour drive or 3-hour walk (no public transport) to the edge of the plateau. There are a few inexpensive guesthouses with en-suite rooms in Matamba, among them **Mtanganyika Lodge** (US$13 dbl; **$**), **Super Eden Guesthouse** (m +255 763 654441; US$8 dbl; **$**) and **JM Ngogo Resort** (m +255 757 303540; **$**). The only option within the park is wild camping, which costs US$30 per person. Organised trips and guided hikes can be arranged through Kitulo Cultural Tourism Enterprise (m +255 757 741195; f kituloculturaltourism), a well-organised community project based in Matamba.

RUAHA NATIONAL PARK

Ruaha (m +255 754 144400; e ruaha@tanzaniaparks.go.tz) is one of East Africa's most biodiverse and rewarding safari destinations. Tanzania's second-largest national park, it protects a wild 20,220km^2 tract of wooded rocky slopes, open plains and seasonal wetlands that drain into the Great Ruaha River. Home to large numbers of elephant, Ruaha is also generally very reliable for lion sightings, and it's also a good place to look for leopard, cheetah and African wild dog. Other attractions include an unusually varied selection of ungulates and some excellent birdwatching. Above all, perhaps, Ruaha possesses a wild and untrammelled feel that has made it the favourite of many regular East African safari-goers. This wilderness feel is reflected in Ruaha's accommodation, which comprises no more than a dozen small and exclusive camps, scattered far more widely than their counterparts in Nyerere.

Ruaha's remote location – more than 600km from Dar es Salaam, including a rough and dusty 110km drive west from Iringa – means that the overwhelming majority of visitors fly in to one of these camps, which generally offer all-inclusive upmarket packages incorporating expertly guided game drives and in some cases guided walks. But Ruaha is also becoming a popular target for more budget-conscious travellers thanks to a proliferation of small lodges that lie between the

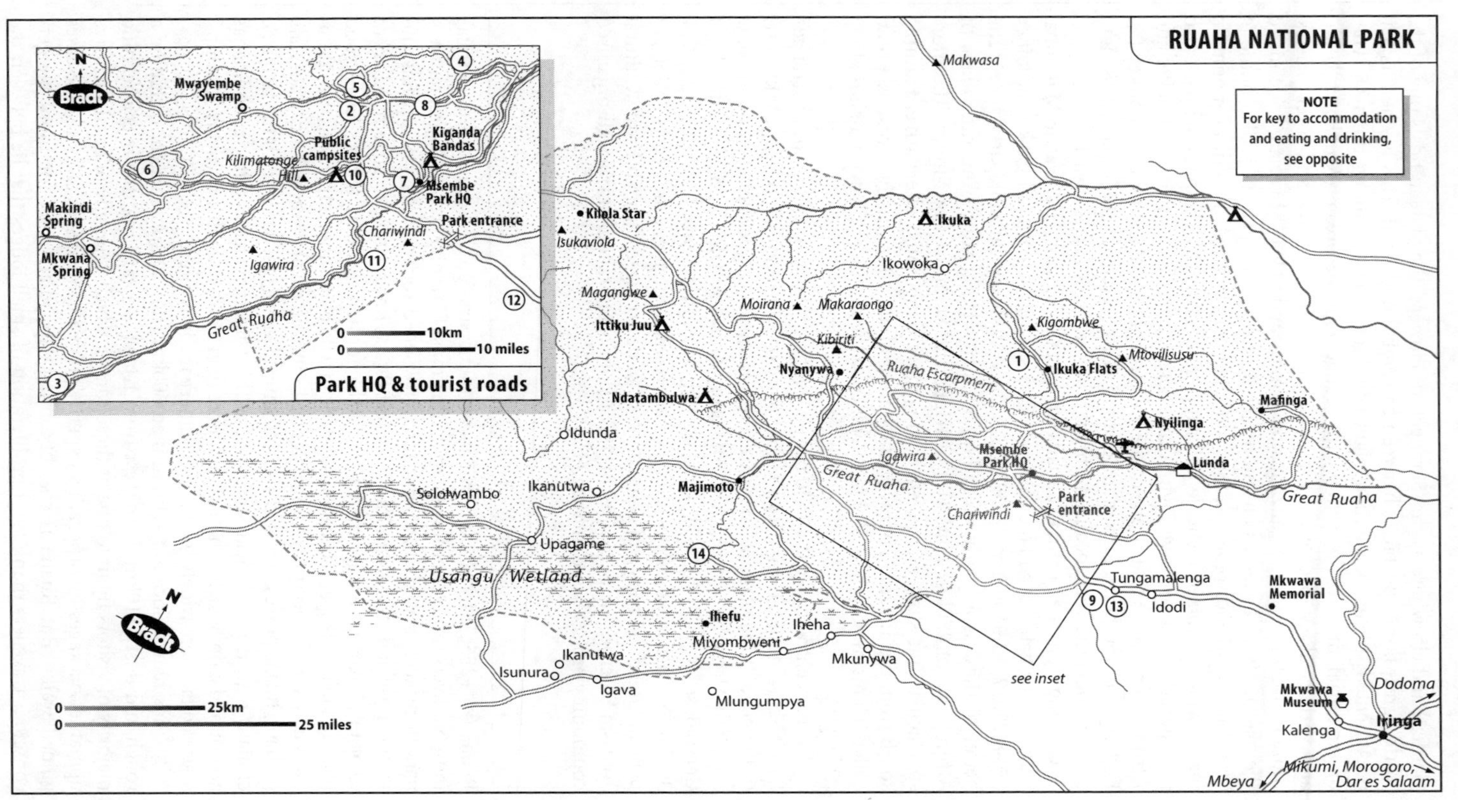

RUAHA NATIONAL PARK
NOTE
For key to accommodation and eating and drinking, see opposite
Makwasa
Kilola Star
Isukaviola
Ikuka
Ikowoka
Magangwe
Moirana
Makaraongo
Kigombwe
Ittiku Juu
Kibiriti
Mtovilisusu
Nyanywa
Ruaha Escarpment
Ikuka Flats
Mafinga
Ndatambulwa
Nyilinga
Idunda
Igawira
Msembe Park HQ
Lunda
Great Ruaha
Solotwambo
Ikanutwa
Majimoto
Chariwindi
Park entrance
Great Ruaha
Upagame
Tungamalenga
Usangu Wetland
Idodi
Mkwawa Memorial
Ihefu
Iheha
Miyombweni
Mkunywa
Ikanutwa
Isunura
Igava
Mlungumpya
see inset
Mkwawa Museum
Dodoma
Kalenga
Iringa
Mbeya
Mikumi, Morogoro, Dar es Salaam
N
Bradt
0 25km
0 25 miles
Park HQ & tourist roads
Mwayembe Swamp
Public campsites
Kiganda Bandas
Kilimatonge Hill
Msembe Park HQ
Makindi Spring
Mkwana Spring
Park entrance
Chariwindi
Igawira
Great Ruaha
0 10km
0 10 miles

main entrance gate and Tungamalenga 18km to its east and offer day safaris into the park. Ruaha is best visited between July and November, when animals concentrate around the river. Internal roads may be impassable towards the end of the rainy season (March to May).

RUAHA NATIONAL PARK

For listings, see from page 502

Where to stay

1 Ikuka Safari Camp
Jabali Private House (see 2)
2 Jabali Ridge
3 Jongomero Camp
4 Kigelia Ruaha
5 Kwihala
6 Mdonya Old River Camp
7 Msembe Camp
8 Mwagusi Safari Camp
9 Ruaha Hilltop Lodge
10 Ruaha Kilimatonge Camp
11 Ruaha River Lodge
12 Tandala Safari Camp
13 Tungamalenga Camp
14 Usangu Expedition Camp

HISTORY Little is known about Ruaha prior to the colonial era. While the area was certainly visited by tribes such as the Hehe of Iringa and Gogo of Dodoma, it seems likely that the combination of tsetse flies and a semi-arid climate precluded much in the way of permanent settlement. In 1910, the German colonial administration included the area in the Saba River Game Reserve, and it later formed the southeastern part of the Rungwa Game Reserve, as gazetted by Britain in 1946. The modern park was created in 1964, three years after independence from Britain, and it was vastly expanded in 2008 following the addition of a 9,500km^2 tract of bush and seasonal wetland including the Usangu Floodplain (a vast seasonal wetland that flows into the Great Ruaha). As a result, Ruaha now extends over 20,220km^2, making it one of the continent's largest national parks. No less significantly, Ruaha forms the core of an unfenced 50,000km^2 network of contiguous protected areas that functions as a more or less self-contained ecosystem.

GEOGRAPHY AND VEGETATION With an altitudinal range of 750–1,868m, Ruaha is nowhere near as hot or humid as Nyerere, though daytime temperatures of 40°C are regularly recorded over October and November before the rains break, and tsetse flies can be a cause for aggravation, particularly in the vicinity of Jongomero and Mdonya Old River camps. Rainfall is highly seasonal, with almost all the annual average of 500mm falling between late November and early May, and the remainder of the year being very dry. The best game viewing is from May to November, but the bush is greener and prettier from January to June, and birding peaks during the European winter months of December to April.

The vegetation of Ruaha is transitional to southern miombo and eastern savannah biomes, for which reason the number of plant species identified is almost twice as many as Nyerere. A wide variety of habitats is represented, including swamp, grassland and acacia woodland, though the dominant vegetation type is miombo or Brachystegia woodland. Several areas support an impressive number of large baobab trees, creating a setting strongly reminiscent of the northern circuit's Tarangire National Park. The Great Ruaha and tributary watercourses such as the Mwagusi are lined with patches of riparian woodland, supporting a variety of Ficus trees (a favourite with birds when fruiting), as well as the oddball sausage tree (named for its long narrow pods) and groves of the striking mlala palm.

WILDLIFE Ruaha's floral diversity is mirrored by the variety of wildlife likely to be seen over the course of a few days. The most common ungulates are impala, common waterbuck, bushbuck, buffalo, zebra and giraffe, all of which might be encountered several times on any given game drive. The park lies at the most southerly extent of the range of several East African ungulate species, including

THE GREAT RUAHA RIVER

Ruaha is named after the Great Ruaha River, a 475km-long tributary of the Rufiji that flows along the national park's southeast boundary for 160km and serves as an important wildlife magnet in the dry season. The name Ruaha is a corruption of *luhava*, which simply means 'river'; its local Hehe name is actually Lyambangori. It has a catchment area of 83,970km^2 and is fed by several wide seasonal tributaries – notably the Mwagusi, Mdonya and Jongomero rivers – that flow through the heart of Ruaha National Park. The Great Ruaha itself was perennial until the early 1990s, since when it has regularly ceased flowing in the dry season as a result of rice farming, a pair of hydro-electric dams, and various other disruptions upstream of where it reaches the park boundary. And while elephants are capable of digging into the sandy riverbeds of the Great Ruaha and its tributaries for drinking water, the prospect of it drying up regularly is a potential ecological disaster for most other wildlife resident in the national park. It also has ramifications further afield: the Rufiji, Tanzania's largest waterway, is formed by the confluence of the Great Ruaha and Kilombero in the west of Nyerere National Park. Fortunately, the Usangu Wetland, the main headwater for the Great Ruaha, was incorporated into the national park in 2008, which will hopefully allow the government to place more stringent regulations on the usage and flow of water close to its source.

lesser kudu and Grant's gazelle. Yet it also harbours a number of antelope that are rare or absent in northern Tanzania, most visibly the splendid greater kudu – including some of the most handsomely horned males you'll come across anywhere in Africa – but also the more elusive roan and sable antelope.

The Greater Ruaha ecosystem supports a massive elephant population, despite the outbreak of commercial poaching that reduced numbers from around 70,000 in 1970 to 7,000 in 1990. The elephant population had recovered to around 32,000 in 2009, when a fresh outbreak of poaching reduced it to 15,000 in 2015. Elephant poaching is now under control, numbers are gradually recovering and sightings are as good as certain, especially in the late dry season, when 100-strong herds can be seen along the stretch of river between Ruaha River Camp and the Mwagusi confluence. The most impressive pair of tusks weighed in the 20th century (combined weight 201kg) adorned an individual shot in Ruaha in the 1970s, but the poaching of the recent past means you're unlikely to see anything comparable these days. As recently as the late 1990s, Ruaha's elephants tended to be quite jumpy, and vehicles were frequently warned off by loud trumpeting. This no longer seems to be the case, presumably due to an increased tourist presence and a decrease in poaching in areas frequented by tourists.

Ruaha is an excellent park for big cats. Lions are numerous, with as many as 20 prides resident in the main developed part of the park, and prides tend to be unusually large, often containing more than 15 adults and sub-adults. Indeed, it is unusual to go a day in Ruaha without seeing lions, which are very habituated to vehicles. The park also boasts a justified reputation for good leopard sightings, particularly in the vicinity of Kilimatonge Hill, and they seem to be less skittish than in many game reserves. Cheetah are most often encountered on the open Lundu Plains to the northeast of the Mwagusi River, an area known locally as the Little Serengeti.

Ruaha is an important stronghold for African wild dogs, though exact numbers are unknown, and sightings are not as common as they used to be, probably due to competition with lions. Nevertheless, several packs are semi-resident, though their wide ranges mean that movements are difficult to predict. Visitors who particularly want to see wild dogs should try to visit in June or July, when they are normally denning, and are more easy to locate than at other times of year. Black-backed jackal and spotted hyena are both very common and easily seen, and the rarer striped hyena, though seldom observed, is found here at the southern limit of its range. The bat-eared fox is also quite common and often seen denning towards the end of the dry season (October and November).

BIRDLIFE Ruaha offers some excellent birding, with an impressive total of 574 species recorded, a figure that seems likely to increase with further study of the recently appended Usangu Wetlands. As with mammals, an interesting mix of southern and northern species is present. Of particular note are substantial and visible populations of black-collared lovebird and ashy starling, Tanzanian endemics associated with the Maasai Steppe found here at the southern extreme of their distribution. By contrast, this is perhaps the only savannah reserve in East Africa where the crested barbet – a colourful yellow-and-black bird whose loud sustained trilling is a characteristic sound of the southern African bush – replaces the red-and-yellow barbet. Two other noteworthy species, both recently described based on observations within the national park, are the Ruaha red-billed hornbill, a locally abundant Tanzania endemic, and the Ruaha chat, a variant of Arnot's chat associated with western Tanzania and eastern Rwanda. Raptors are well represented, with bateleur and fish eagle probably the most visible large birds of prey. The watercourses support a good range of aquatic birds.

FEES AND FURTHER INFORMATION The entrance fee is US$30 per person per 24 hours plus 18% VAT. Overnight visitors staying at a private lodge or camp must also pay a concession fee of US$30. These fees are normally incorporated into the price of any safari booked through an operator, but self-drive visitors will need to pay by Visa or Mastercard (cash is not accepted).

Two excellent books are usually sold at the entrance gate: Sue Stolberger's *Ruaha National Park: An Intimate View* (Jacana, 2012) is an exemplary field guide to the park's plants and smaller wildlife, while Robert Glen's thorough 106-page *Annotated Checklist of the Birds of Ruaha National Park* (self-published, 2011) is a must for birders. Useful online resources include w ruahanationalpark.weebly.com and w theruahanotes.com.

GETTING THERE AND AWAY

By air The most straightforward way to reach Ruaha is by air. **Coastal Aviation** (w coastal.co.tz) flies daily from Dar es Salaam and Nyerere National Park, while **Safari Air Link** (w flysal.com) runs a daily shared charter from Dar es Salaam to Ruaha via Mikumi and Nyerere in the high season, and also flies twice weekly to Katavi and Mahale national parks. Fly-in packages, often combined with a visit to Nyerere can be arranged directly through the lodges listed on page 502, or through any other safari operator, and a minimum stay of three nights is recommended.

By road The park entrance gate lies 110km west of Iringa along a fair dirt road that takes about 2 hours to cover and usually requires a 4x4. The road passes through Kalenga, former capital of Chief Mkwawa, after about 15km, and another 25km further along it passes the signposted side road north to Mlambalasi, site of the Mkwawa Memorial erected in 1998. Another 20km or so closer to Ruaha, the road branches into two forks, which converge shortly before the entrance gate. There is no substantial difference between the two options in terms of distance or quality, but you need the left fork if you intend to stay at accommodation around Tungamalenga road.

No public transport runs into the national park, but it is possible to bus as far as Tungamalenga, 27km east of the entrance gate. The bus leaves Iringa's central bus station at 13.00 and passes through Tungamalenga at 18.00, then comes past again on the return trip at around 05.00 the next morning, arriving back in Iringa at 10.00 or so. Both the lodges in Tungamalenga can arrange full-day safaris into the park for around US$200–250, inclusive of 4x4 with seating for up to six passengers, driver/guide, fuel, vehicle entrance fees, but exclusive of the personal entrance fee of US$30 plus VAT. Ruaha Hilltop Lodge, about 5km closer to the park, can provide a free transfer from Tungamalenga by arrangement and also arranges day safaris at a similar price. Alternatively, you can hire a 4x4 directly from Iringa, through Chabo Safaris, but this is a far costlier option than bussing.

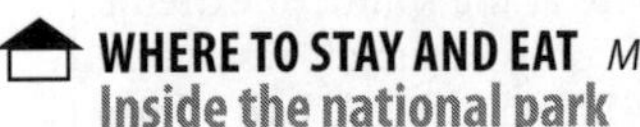

WHERE TO STAY AND EAT *Map, page 498*

Inside the national park

Exclusive

✷ **Ikuka Safari Camp** ⊕ -7.54204, 34.880203; m +255 763 598027; w ikukasafaricamp.com. Set on a tall ridge offering views to the Mwagusi River 5km to the south, this spectacular camp is owned & managed by a family with years of experience in the safari industry. The 6 open-fronted, canvas-sided, thatch-roofed suites each have king-size bed, a large modern bathroom, a brightly coloured sitting area & a stilted wooden balcony positioned to catch the welcome breeze & to make the most of the wonderful view. Architecture throughout is organic & stylish, while the extensive use of local white quartzite rocks gives it an individualistic feel. There's a swimming pool & excellent food, which is normally eaten communally, though individual parties can eat alone if preferred. **$$$$$$$**

Jabali Private House ⊕ -7.61566, 34.83989; m +255 736 500515; w asiliaafrica.com. Situated close & similar in feel to Jabali Ridge, this luxurious 3-bedroom house is aimed at private groups & family parties of up to 6 people. **$$$$$$$**

✷ **Jabali Ridge** ⊕ -7.61500, 34.83901; m +255 736 500515; w asiliaafrica.com. One of the most sumptuous & architecturally innovative lodges anywhere in Tanzania, Jabali Ridge is built into an outcrop of majestic granite boulders that offer expansive views over a wild baobab- & palm-studded landscape to the Mwagusi River. Connected by a network of stilted walkways, the 8 striking & luxurious bandas are spaced out between the boulders & have louvered floor-to-ceiling shutters that can be closed during the evenings or opened completely during the day. Each banda has a private veranda with a soft seating area shaded by a chunky wooden fringe canopy. The minimalist beach-house-meets-bush décor uses earthy colours throughout, & the heavy wooden-framed king-size beds are enclosed by mosquito nets. Amenities include an infinity pool & spa. The food is absolutely superb. It stands in a game-rich part of Ruaha & walking safaris, game drives & night drives are all on offer. **$$$$$$$**

Jongomero Camp ⊕ -7.90560, 34.5690; w selous.com; ⌚ closed Apr–May. Among the most overtly luxurious camps in Ruaha, Jongomero comprises 8 spacious standing tents, all with private balconies, & a welcome swimming pool. The camp is carved into dense woodland fringing the seasonal Jongomero River 2km upstream of its confluence with the Ruaha, where a semi-permanent pool hosts a resident pod of around 50 hippos. Jongomero's isolated location 60km southwest of the main entrance gate means that there's so little tourist traffic it functions much as a private game reserve, but it takes a little more effort to see wildlife than in other areas of the park. Birdlife within camp can be excellent, with Livingstone's turaco topping the gaudiness stakes, while the localised swift-like Böhm's spinetail is distinguished by its distinctive bat-like fluttering. **$$$$$$$**

Kichaka Expeditions Mobile; m +255 766 956627; w kichakaexpeditions.com. Based in the remote northeast of Ruaha some 4hrs from the nearest airstrip, this small operator runs 3 different 3-tent mobile camps, each of which is usually booked exclusively for 1 group of up to 6 people, ensuring a very intimate experience. The focus is on guided walks & game drives in a corner of the park where you're unlikely to see other tourists. Camps move periodically, depending on which areas the owner-managers decide to explore next. **$$$$$$–$$$$$$$**

Kigelia Ruaha ⊕ -7.55891, 34.95846; **m** +255 787 595908; **w** nomad-tanzania.com. Named after the sausage trees (*Kigelia africana*) that line the seasonal Ifuguru River on whose bank it stands, this rustic yet elegant camp offers accommodation in 6 secluded standing tents with king-size beds, hot outdoor showers & private balconies. The open-sided lounge is filled with solid wooden furniture, made from reclaimed dhow wood, & tasty 3-course meals are served outside, weather permitting. It has a prime location for game drives, offering good access both to the road circuit around the confluence of the Mwagusi/Ruaha rivers & to the 'Little Serengeti Plain' to its north. **$$$$$$$**

Kwihala ⊕ -7.59103, 34.83695; **m** +255 736 500515; **w** asiliaafrica.com; ⌚ Jun–Dec. This classic low-footprint safari camp comprises 6 spacious standing tents strung along the lushly forested banks of the seasonal Mwagusi River. It combines the down-to-earth, pack-up-and-go feel of a mobile camp with the tasteful décor, comfortable amenities, attentive service & excellent food characteristic of all Asilia's properties. It is well placed for game drives along the Mwagusi River. **$$$$$$$**

✷ **Mwagusi Safari Camp** ⊕ -7.60676, 34.92767; **m** +44 (0) 7525 170940; **w** mwagusicamp.com. Situated on the forested north bank of the seasonal Mwagusi River, this alluring & long-serving family-run camp combines a thrilling bush atmosphere with top-notch service – most memorably, starlit communal dinners around a campfire in the riverbed. The 10 walk-in tents are each enclosed in a wood, thatch & reed shelter and strung along a stretch of riverbank that offers excellent inhouse game-viewing, with elephant & greater kudu regularly putting in an appearance & plenty of birds hopping around the trees. It also has possibly the best location of any Ruaha lodge when it comes to game drives, with leopards regularly being sighted in the area & several lion prides resident. For early risers, the free early-morning bird walk around the camp is a lovely way to start the day. **$$$$$$$**

Usangu Expedition Camp ⊕ -8.225936, 34.453539; **m** +255 736 500515; **w** asiliaafrica.com; ⌚ Jun–Nov. Opened in 2022, this is the only camp in the Usangu Wetland, a vast & largely unexplored seasonal floodplain about 50km (2hrs' drive) southwest of Jongomero Airstrip. Set in a patch of miombo woodland on the edge of the floodplain, the 4 tents are relatively basic by Asilia standards, but still come with solar power, hot shower, flush toilet & nets, while meals are cooked on an open fire & enjoyed under the stars, weather permitting. In addition to game drives & walking safaris, you can explore the waterways by boat or head out into the field with researchers from the affiliated Douglas Bell Eco Research Station. The emphasis here is very much on a holistic bush experience rather than ticking off the Big Five, but all the wildlife found in other parts of Ruaha is present & birding is outstanding. **$$$$$$$**

Upmarket

Mdonya Old River Camp ⊕ -7.68576, 34.65139; **w** ed.co.tz. This determinedly rustic camp lies on the wooded banks of the 'old' Mdonya River, which has not flowed in earnest since the river changed course a couple of decades ago. Comfortable standing tents have king-size beds, private balconies & solar-heated water, while the culinary emphasis is on tasty home-style cooking, usually eaten communally beneath the stars. The riverbed is an important wildlife passage & plenty of animals come past daily, most abundantly elephant, impala, warthog & giraffe, but also the occasional nocturnal visitor such as lion, honey badger, genet & bushpig. Birding is superb, with the likes of purple-crested turaco, bearded woodpecker, crested barbet, black-necked weaver, orange-breasted bush-shrike & green-winged pytilia among the colourful & conspicuous residents. **$$$$$$**

Ruaha Kilimatonge Camp ⊕ -7.66804, 34.87892; **m** +255 786 019965; **w** authentictanzaniasafaris.com. This private mobile camp is set up by request for a minimum of 2 nights at a superb location on the bank of the seasonal Mdonya River as it flows past Kilimatonge

Hill, a massive granite dome that towers overhead. It lies in superb big cat country, with lions often passing within a few metres of the tents at night & a near guarantee of leopard sightings on the surrounding rocks. Reserved for private parties of up to 8, it is emphatically aimed at those seeking an intimate in-your-face bush experience as opposed to stylish safari chic. Tents are simple & contain 2 narrow camp beds, bucket shower & portable loo. **$$$$$–$$$$$$**

Ruaha River Lodge ⊕ -7.76567, 34.87057; **w** tanzaniasafaris.info. Ruaha's oldest & largest lodge boasts a magnificent hillside setting above a set of rapids on the Great Ruaha River 15km from the entrance gate. Owned & managed by the same family since it opened in the 1980s, it still remains well run, good value & perfectly located for game drives. The 24 spacious & breezy stone cottages all have walk-in nets, a comfortable sitting area, hot shower & balcony with river view. There are 2 dining & bar areas, 1 situated alongside the river, the other on a hill overlooking it. Elephants pass through all the time, & you'll also see hyraxes scuttling on the rocks, hippos yawning in the river & other wildlife coming down to drink. **$$$$$$**

Budget & camping

Msembe Camp ⊕ -7.68382, 34.93546; **m** +255 754 144400; **e** ruaha@tanzaniaparks.go.tz. Situated at the park HQ, close to the Great Ruaha in an area of extensive open plains teeming with game, this offers the choice of older prefabricated dbl & family bandas that get seriously hot during the middle of the day, & more modern & comfortable new bandas. Bedding, firewood & water are provided, & drinks & simple meals can be bought at the nearby staff canteen, but all other food must be brought with you. Payment must be made with Visa or Mastercard; cash is not accepted. *Old banda US$30pp, new banda US$50pp, camping US$30pp.* **$$**

Outside the national park

The camps listed here lie alongside the Iringa road between the main national park entrance & the village of Tungamalenga 18km to the east. They are all a lot cheaper than their counterparts within Ruaha, & arrange day safaris into the park.

Moderate

Tandala Safari Camp ⊕ -7.76935, 35.00553; **m** + 255 755 680220; **w** tandalacamp.com. Situated 6km outside the entrance gate along the Tungamalenga road, this attractive bush camp overlooks a seasonal river in a private conservancy buffering the national park, & makes for a good compromise between the costlier accommodation within the park & more basic options further east. The comfortable en-suite tents stand on stilted wooden bases, while facilities include an attractive makuti restaurant & bar area alongside a small swimming pool. The greater kudu for which the camp is named is quite common in the surrounding woodland, while a waterhole attracts a steady stream of wildlife in the dry season, including elephant on most days. Because it lies outside the national park, activities such as night drives, guided game walks & fly-camping are offered on the property. Game drives into the park are offered as an extra. **$$$$$**

Budget

Ruaha Hilltop Lodge ⊕ -7.82820, 35.06501; **m** + 255 784 726709; **w** ruahahilltoplodge.com. Situated on a steep hillside 16km from the park entrance gate & 2km from Tungamalenga, this well-organised lodge is comfortably the pick of a few budget options in the vicinity. Small but clean thatched bandas come with fitted nets, bright ethnic fabrics, hot shower, solar power & private balcony. There's a stunning view from the restaurant/bar area, & the management can arrange transfers from Iringa, free transfers from Tungamalenga to coincide with the bus, game drives into the park & guided walks into the surrounding hills. Good value. *US$95pp FB.* **$$$**

Tungamalenga Camp ⊕ -7.835126, 35.09461 **m** +255 745 679158; **e** tungacamp@gmail.com. This well-run camp & curio shop is situated on the southwest edge of Tungamalenga village about 18km from the park entrance gate. Neither the setting nor the small en-suite bandas, each with 2 beds & netting, compare with the far nicer Ruaha Hilltop Lodge, but it is considerably cheaper. Camping, with access to clean ablutions & a self-catering area, is permitted. There is a good restaurant & it can organise game drives into the park. *US$65pp FB, camping US$10pp.* **$$$**

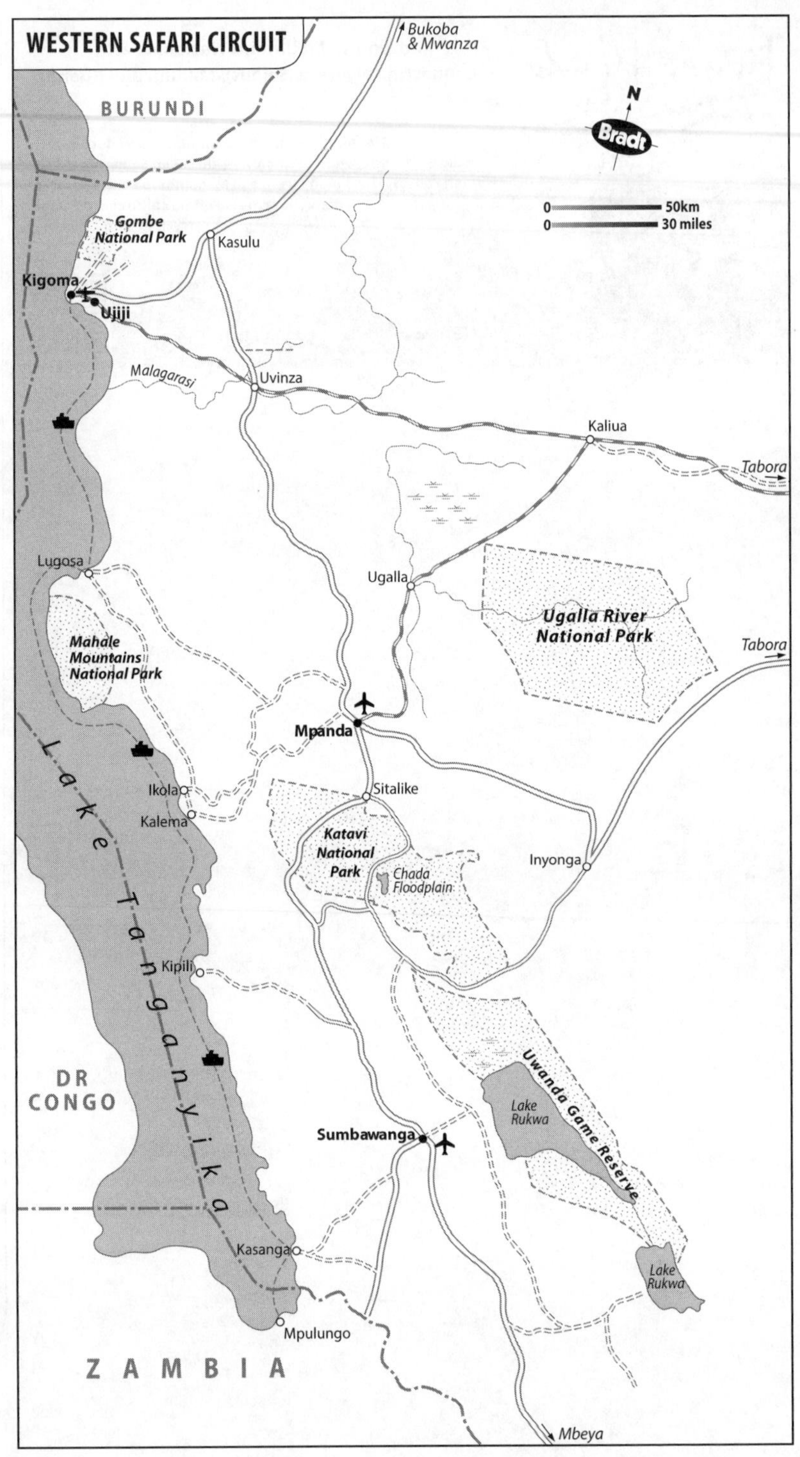

WESTERN SAFARI CIRCUIT
Bukoba & Mwanza
BURUNDI
N
Bradt
0 50km
0 30 miles
Gombe National Park
Kasulu
Kigoma
Ujiji
Malagarasi
Uvinza
Kaliua
Tabora
Lugosa
Ugalla
Ugalla River National Park
Mahale Mountains National Park
Tabora
Mpanda
Lake Tanganyika
Ikola
Kalema
Sitalike
Katavi National Park
Chada Floodplain
Inyonga
Kipili
Uwanda Game Reserve
DR CONGO
Lake Rukwa
Sumbawanga
Kasanga
Lake Rukwa
Mpulungo
ZAMBIA
Mbeya

21

The Western Safari Circuit

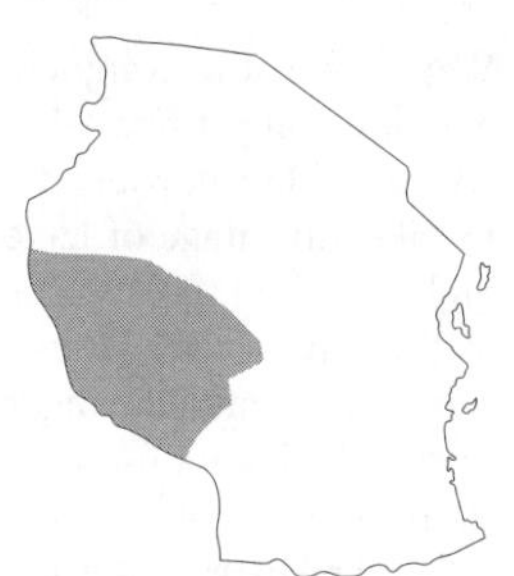

Tanzania's remote and little-visited wild west is dominated by serpentine Lake Tanganyika, which follows the contours of the Albertine Rift Valley for 675km and attains a depth of up to 1,435m, making it the longest and second-deepest freshwater body anywhere in the world. Bisected by the Congolese border, Lake Tanganyika is a very beautiful apparition, hemmed in on either side by a tall and verdant escarpment, and with crystal-clear water that lends credence to its reputation for being the world's least polluted lake. The lake is at least 3 million years old, stands at an elevation of 730m, and is fed by more than 50 rivers and streams, but its sole outlet is the Lukuga River, which flows out only in years of exceptional rainfall. Its isolation from similar habitats explains its exceptional biodiversity, which includes more than 500 fish species (page 510). Economically, the most important of these is the *dagaa*, a tiny plankton-eater that lives in large shoals and is sun-dried on the lakeshore for sale throughout western Tanzania. Indeed, a characteristic sight along any inhabited part of the Lake Tanganyika shore is the nocturnal spectacle of hundreds of small fishing boats lit by small lamps and bobbing in the waves like a low-lying swarm of fireflies.

Western Tanzania's main tourist attraction is a trio of excellent national parks that offer a very different experience from the better-known likes of the Serengeti and Selous. Fringing the eastern shore of Lake Tanganyika are Mahale Mountains and Gombe national parks, both of which support chimpanzee communities that were first habituated to human visitors by researchers in the 1960s, and now rank among the most approachable wild populations anywhere in Africa. Some distance east of the lake, Katavi National Park is a more conventional game-viewing destination, protecting a range of plains animals similar to more accessible southern reserves such as Ruaha and Nyerere, but visited by far fewer tourists. Of these parks, Katavi and Mahale function mainly as world-class upmarket fly-in destinations, and are otherwise quite difficult to access. By contrast, Gombe – best known as the former stomping ground of the iconic Jane Goodall – is very accessible on public transport from the nearby port of Kigoma, and thus well suited to independent travellers wanting to track chimps on a tighter budget.

KIGOMA

The largest port on the east shore of Lake Tanganyika, with a population estimated at 230,000, Kigoma sprawls attractively across hilly, green slopes rising from Kigoma Bay, a deep natural harbour hemmed in by the Bangwe Peninsula. The town was established by the German colonials, who favoured it over the nearby Arab slave-trading centre of Ujiji as a regional administration centre, and its ascendancy was sealed in February 1914, months before the outbreak of World

War I, with the completion of the railway line from the coast. Kigoma today is an easy-going town with a cinematic African port ambience and unexpectedly cosmopolitan flavour, thanks to the cross-border businessmen who gather there to take advantage of Lake Tanganyika's status as an international free-trade zone. Sightseeing in the town centre is pretty much restricted to the German-era railway station and Kaiser House (the two are reputedly linked by a subterranean escape tunnel excavated during World War I), but popular day outings include the historic port of Ujiji and, for swimming, Jakobsen Beach. In a 1943 *Tanganyika Notes and Records* article about the distribution of chimpanzees in Tanzania, Captain Grant, a former District Officer, recalled that 'it was a rare but occasional sight to see a family party on the lakeshore inside Kigoma Bay opposite the township'. You'd have to imbibe some seriously heavy stuff to be treated to such an apparition today, but Kigoma does remain the best springboard for chimp tracking in Gombe National Park and a potential starting point for independent visits to Mahale Mountains National Park.

GETTING THERE AND AWAY

By air **Precision Air** (w precisionairtz.com), **Air Tanzania** (w airtanzania.co.tz) and **Auric Air** (w auricair.com) all fly to Kigoma from Mwanza, Tabora and/or Dar es Salaam. The airport is located about 5km southeast of the town centre, and taxis are available.

By rail Kigoma is the inland terminus of the central railway, which connects it to Dar es Salaam via Tabora and Dodoma twice weekly, an inexpensive and often fascinating but rather ponderous 36-plus-hour journey across 1,200km of the thinly inhabited African interior. The schedule is posted at w trc.co.tz/pages/long-distance-train and bookings can be made at w booking.trc.co.tz/?lang=en.

By boat The Marine Services Company Limited (w mscl.co.tz) operates a weekly passenger service linking Kigoma to most other Tanzanian ports on Lake Tanganyika (but it no longer runs to Bujumbura in Burundi or Mpulungu in Zambia). The venerable MV *Liemba* (page 513), which usually covers this route, had been withdrawn for repairs in 2022, but it will hopefully resume operations during the lifespan of this edition. In addition, 'lake-taxis' (essentially the aquatic equivalent of dalla dallas) connect Kigoma to Gombe National Park (page 519).

By road Kigoma is a long way from most other major urban hubs by road (for instance, around 1,500km from Dar e Salaam, 1,200km from Arusha or 1,000km from Dodoma) and so almost all visitors arrive and leave by air, rail or water. However, the roads there are now in good shape, and daily buses take about 10 hours to cover the 650km to/from Tabora, which has bus links on to Arusha, Dodoma and Dar es Salaam.

WHERE TO STAY *Map, page 509*

Moderate

Kigoma Hilltop Hotel m +255 692 632659; w kigomahilltop.com. Perched on a cliff overlooking Kigoma Bay 2km south of the town centre, this quality hotel has a large swimming pool, watersports equipment, fishing, snorkelling & private beach. The 30 comfortable chalets have AC & DSTV & the Sangara Restaurant serves tasty Indian & Western dishes. No alcohol is sold or permitted in public spaces, but it can be consumed in the rooms. *From US$101/153 sgl/dbl B&B.* **$$$**

Lake Tanganyika Hotel m +255 713 293490; w laketanganyikahotel.com. The former Railway

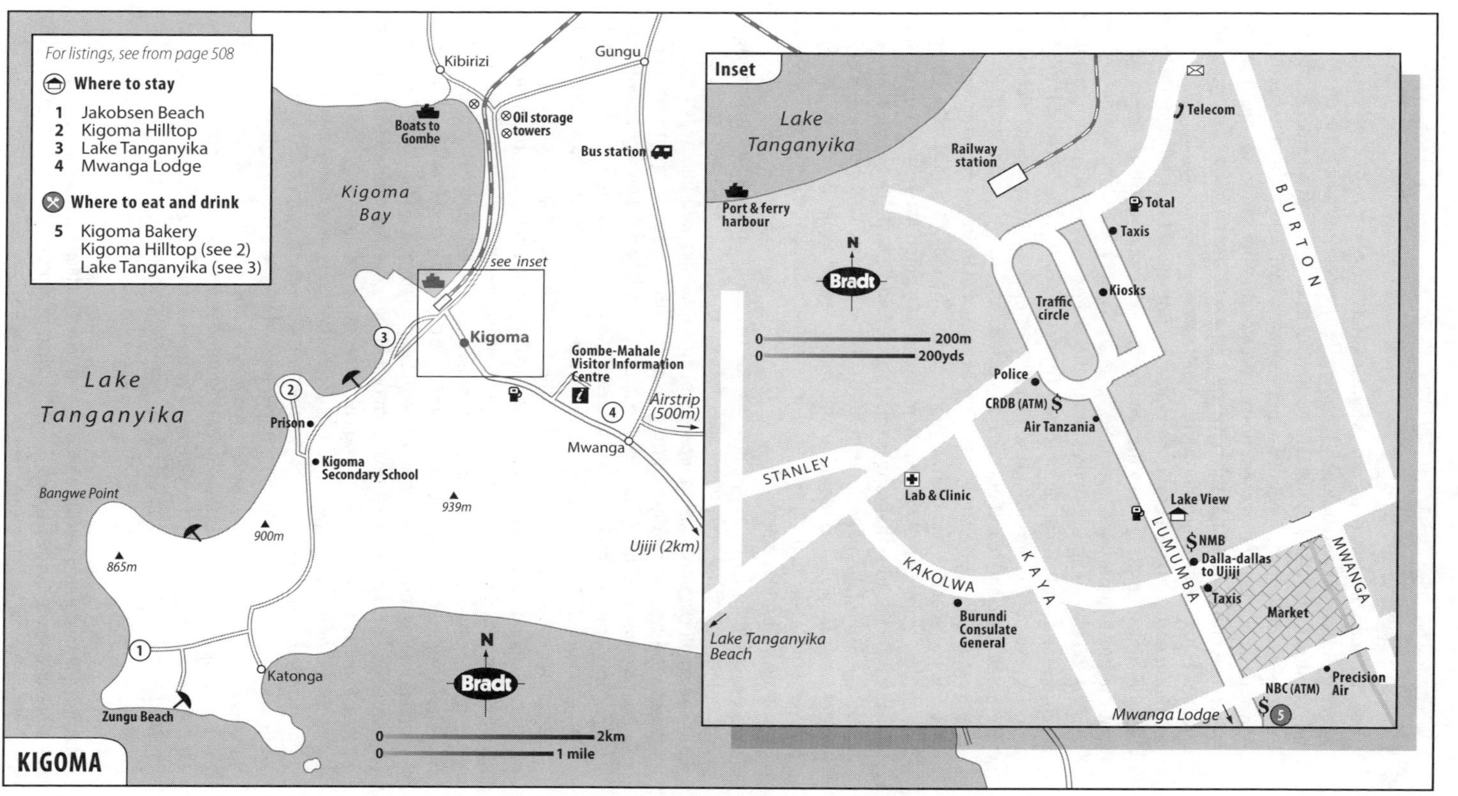
KIGOMA
For listings, see from page 508
Where to stay
1 Jakobsen Beach
2 Kigoma Hilltop
3 Lake Tanganyika
4 Mwanga Lodge
Where to eat and drink
5 Kigoma Bakery
Kigoma Hilltop (see 2)
Lake Tanganyika (see 3)
Kibirizi
Gungu
Boats to Gombe
Oil storage towers
Bus station
Kigoma Bay
see inset
Kigoma
Lake Tanganyika
Prison
Kigoma Secondary School
Gombe-Mahale Visitor Information Centre
Airstrip (500m)
Mwanga
Ujiji (2km)
Bangwe Point
939m
900m
865m
Katonga
Zungu Beach
N
Bradt
0 2km
0 1 mile
Inset
Lake Tanganyika
Railway station
Port & ferry harbour
Telecom
Total
Taxis
Kiosks
Traffic circle
BURTON
0 200m
0 200yds
Police
CRDB (ATM)
Air Tanzania
STANLEY
Lab & Clinic
Lake View
LUMUMBA
NMB
Dalla-dallas to Ujiji
Taxis
Market
MWANGA
KAKOLWA
KAYA
Burundi Consulate General
Lake Tanganyika Beach
Precision Air
NBC (ATM)
Mwanga Lodge
5

CICHLIDS OF THE GREAT LAKES

The staggering diversity of Tanzania's terrestrial fauna is old news, but few people are aware that Tanzania also probably harbours the greatest freshwater fish diversity of any country in the world. Significant portions of all of Africa's three great freshwater bodies – lakes Victoria, Tanganyika and Nyasa–Malawi – lie within the borders of Tanzania, and each one of them hosts a greater number of fish species than any other lake in the world bar the other two. Which of the three lakes supports the greatest fish diversity is an open question, since new species are regularly discovered and large parts of the lakes remain practically unexplored by ichthyologists. Lake Victoria almost certainly takes the wooden spoon, because it is relatively young, but the most conservative estimates for lakes Nyasa–Malawi and Tanganyika are around 500 species apiece – a greater number of freshwater species than are found in Europe and North America combined. The actual tally may well be closer to 1,000 species in each lake, of which more than 90% are endemic to that particular lake.

All well and good to trot out the boring statistics, but the greater significance of the great lakes' fish diversity is that it is the product of the most dramatic incidence of explosive speciation known to evolutionists. The majority of these fish species are cichlids – pronounced 'sicklids' – members of a perch-like family of freshwater fishes called cichlidae that ranges through the Middle East, Madagascar, Asia and South and Central America. It is in Africa's three largest lakes, however, that this widespread family has undergone an unprecedented explosion of evolutionarily recent speciation that has resulted in it constituting an estimated 5% of the world's vertebrate species!

The cichlids of Africa's great lakes are generally divided into a few major groupings, often referred to by scientists by their local Malawian names, such as the small plankton-eating *utaka*, the large, pike-like and generally predatory *ncheni*, the bottom-feeding *chisawasawa*, and the algae-eating *mbuna*. People who have travelled in any part of Africa close to a lake will almost certainly have dined on one or other of the *tilapia* (or closely related *oreochromis*) cichlids, large ncheni that make excellent eating and are known in Malawi as *chambo*. To aquarium keepers, snorkellers and scuba divers, however, the most noteworthy African cichlids are the *mbuna*, a spectacularly colourful group of small fish of which some 300 species are known from Lake Nyasa–Malawi alone.

The mbuna of Lake Nyasa–Malawi first attracted scientific interest in the 1950s, when they formed the subject of Dr Geoffrey Fryer's classic study of adaptive radiation. This term is used to describe the explosion of a single stock species into a variety of closely related forms, each of which evolves specialised modifications that allow it to exploit an ecological niche quite different from that exploited by the common ancestral stock. This phenomenon is most likely to occur when an adaptable species colonises an environment where several food sources are going unused, for instance on a newly formed volcanic island or lake. The most celebrated incidence of adaptive radiation – the one that led Charles Darwin to propose the theory of evolution through natural selection – occurred on the Galápagos Islands, where a variety of finch species evolved from one common seed-eating ancestor to fill several very different ecological niches.

Hotel doesn't quite match up to the Hilltop in terms of upkeep & service, but the lakeshore setting only a short walk from the town centre is perfect. Comfortable rooms have AC, DSTV & private balconies with lake views. *From US$70/85 sgl/dbl.* **$$**

The explosive speciation that has occurred among Africa's cichlids is like Darwin's finches amplified a hundredfold. The 500 or more cichlid species present in each of Lake Tanganyika and Lake Nyasa–Malawi are evolved from a handful of river cichlids that entered the lakes when they formed about 2 million to 3 million years ago. More remarkable still is that the 200 or so cichlids in Lake Victoria – many of which are now extinct or heading that way – have all evolved from a few common ancestors over the 10,000–15,000 years since the lake last dried up. In all three lakes, specialised cichlid species have evolved to exploit practically every conceivable food source: algae, plankton, insects, fish, molluscs and other fishes. Somewhat macabrely, the so-called kiss-of-death cichlids feed by sucking eggs and hatchlings from the mouths of mouth-brooding cichlids! No less striking is the diverse array in size, coloration and mating behaviour displayed across different species. In addition to being a case study in adaptive radiation, the cichlids of the great lakes are routinely cited as a classic example of parallel evolution – in other words, many similar adaptations appear to have occurred independently in all three lakes.

Not only have cichlids undergone several independent radial explosions in all three of Africa's great lakes, but the same thing has also happened in microcosm in many smaller lakes throughout the continent. Uganda's Lake Nabugabo, for instance, harbours five endemic cichlid species, all of which must have evolved since the lake was separated from Lake Victoria by a sandbar less than 4,000 years ago.

Why cichlids and not any of several other fish families is a question that is likely to keep ichthyologists occupied for decades to come. One factor is that cichlids are exceptionally quick to mature, and are thus characterised by a very rapid turnover of generations. They also appear to have an unusually genetically malleable anatomy, with skull, body, tooth and gut structures readily modifying over a relatively small number of generations. Their capacity to colonise new freshwater habitats is boosted by a degree of parental care rare in other fish – the mouth-brooders, which include all but one of the cichlid species of Lake Nyasa–Malawi, hold their eggs and fry in their mouth until they are large enough to fend for themselves. Most fascinating, bearing in mind that the separation of breeding populations lies at the core of speciation, there is mounting evidence to suggest that cichlids have a unique capacity to erect non-physical barriers between emergent species – possibly linked to a correlation between colour morphs and food preferences in diverging populations.

Tanzania's lake cichlids are never likely to rival the country's terrestrial wildlife as a tourist attraction. All the same, it is mildly astonishing that, at the time of writing, virtually no snorkelling or diving facilities exist for tourists visiting the Tanzanian shores of any of the three great lakes. Lake Tanganyika, in particular, already lies at the core of a nascent tourist circuit incorporating the game-rich plains of Katavi National Park and chimp tracking in the lakeshore forests of Gombe and Mahale Mountains. What more logical extension is there to this circuit than snorkelling and diving excursions – already offered by lodges on the small Zambian stretch of lake frontage – in a lake that has justifiably been described as a 'unique evolutionary showcase'?

Budget & camping

✷ **Jakobsen Beach** m +255 789 231215; w kigomabeach.com. Set on an attractive swimming beach signposted off the Katonga road 3km past the Kigoma Hilltop Hotel, this low-key Norwegian-owned resort stands in large grounds inhabited by zebras, otters, vervet monkeys & a profusion of birds. There are 4-bedroom & 2-bedroom houses, 2 beach cottages, 3 furnished standing tents & a campsite. No food is available but facilities include a BBQ area, self-catering kitchen & a shop stocking various dry goods. It has kayaks, snorkelling gear & mountain bikes for hire, & can arrange transport to Gombe. *Rooms & tents US$22pp, camping US$8pp with your own tent or US$12pp in theirs.* **$$**

Mwanga Lodge m +255 712 961921. About the best of several cheapies strung along Lumumba Rd as it climbs southeast from the railway station towards Ujiji, this simple guesthouse has clean rooms with nets. *US$5/6 dbl with common/en-suite showers.* **$**

WHERE TO EAT AND DRINK *Map, page 509*

The restaurants at the **Kigoma Hilltop** and **Lake Tanganyika** hotels can both be recommended for Western and Indian meals, though the former doesn't serve alcohol.

If you're stocking up on food before heading to Gombe or Mahale Mountains, the central **market** and the shops immediately around it are very well stocked with fresh fruit and vegetables and imported tinned and other packaged goods. The **Kigoma Bakery** bakes fresh bread every morning.

OTHER PRACTICALITIES

Foreign exchange The NBC and CRDB banks both have ATMs that accept foreign cards. There is no private bureau de change.

Swimming Local people swim with apparent impunity at the sandy beach bar next to the prison, but that doesn't necessarily mean it is free of bilharzia. The best bathing spot is Jakobsen Beach, provided you don't mind paying the daily entrance fee equivalent to US$2.50 per person. The swimming pool at the Kigoma Hilltop Hotel is open to non-residents for a small fee.

Tourist information Independent travellers heading to Gombe or Mahale should check in with the helpful Gombe–Mahale Visitor Information Centre (m +255 785 291416) for the latest lowdown on public transport and fees.

AROUND KIGOMA

Ujiji This sprawling lakeshore port is where the immortal enquiry 'Doctor Livingstone, I presume?' was made by Stanley on 10 November 1871 (page 514). Ujiji's historical significance does, however, extend beyond the utterance of one Victorian banality. For centuries, it was the main port from which the salt mined at nearby Uvinza was transported across the lake to the present-day eastern Congo. In about 1800, Ujiji was settled by Arab traders from the coast, and began its rise to prominence as the lakeshore terminal of the most important ivory and slave caravan route to Bagamoyo, eventually to be governed by an agent of the Sultan of Zanzibar. Ujiji is also where, in 1858, the exhausted Burton and Speke – the former with an ulcerated jaw and practically paralysed below the waist, the latter partially blind and driven close to dementia by an insect that had burrowed into his ear canal – arrived on the shore of the 'Sea of Ujiji'.

For all its historical associations, Ujiji is something of a backwater, and although it displays some Swahili influences one wouldn't normally associate with this part of the country, anybody who expects to find a thriving market town will be disappointed. But if you have come as far as Kigoma, it is difficult to resist making the short trip to the **monument**, set under a shady mango tree, whose brass plaque reads 'Under the mango tree which then stood here Stanley met Livingstone 10th

THE MV *LIEMBA*

This 800-ton steamer, reputedly the world's oldest operating passenger ship, was out of service in 2022 but should hopefully be running again by the time you read this. Originally called the *Graf van Goetzen*, it was railed in pieces from Dar es Salaam to Kigoma shortly before World War I. It was assembled at Kigoma, then embarked on an aborted maiden voyage to Kasanga carrying 700 soldiers, after which the Germans sank it in the Malagarasi River mouth rather than letting it fall into enemy hands. In 1927, Britain and Belgium undertook the costly task of rescuing the *Graf van Goetzen* from its watery grave, and renamed it *Liemba* (according to Livingstone, the local name for Lake Tanganyika).

Since the late 1920s, the *Liemba* has steamed up and down the lake almost continually. The oft-repeated story that it interrupted its schedule to feature in the film *The African Queen* is a complete myth (the film was shot on Lake Albert in Uganda), but the *Liemba* was used by the United Nations High Commission for Refugees (UNHCR) to transport more than 75,000 Congolese refugees back to their homeland following the overthrow of the dictator Mobutu Sese Seko in May 1997, and was used in 2015 to ferry refugees fleeing Burundi.

Prior to being docked for repairs, the *Liemba* undertook a round trip between Kigoma and Mpulungu (Zambia) every two weeks, stopping at several small ports on the lakeshore south of Kigoma. It departed from Kigoma at 16.00 on alternate Wednesdays, to arrive in Mpulungu at around midday Friday, then to turn back at around 16.00 Friday and arrive in Kigoma late on Sunday afternoon. When it will resume operation, and whether it will stick to the same schedule, is uncertain. Assuming it does, fares are inexpensive and it is worth paying the small extra for first-class (clean, comfortable and lockable two-berth cabins) or if that is full, second class (scruffier but adequate lockable four-bed cabins). Third class is deck only, which is fine for shorter hops, but risky for luggage on overnight trips. A restaurant/bar serves inexpensive meals, as well as cold beers, sodas and imported wines and spirits.

The most significant port to travellers is Lugosa, the closest disembarkation point to Mahale Mountains National Park. There is nowhere to dock here, or at most other villages, so the ferry is greeted by a floating market selling dried fish and other foodstuffs, while passengers are ferried to and from the shore on rickety fishing boats. Viewed from the upper decks this is a richly comic sight. If you are disembarking, however, it is a rather nightmarish experience, the hold seething with passengers climbing over each other, the ticket officer frantically trying to identify and extract fares from the newcomers, and small boats at the exit gate ramming each other trying to get the best position.

November 1871'. A smaller monument dedicated to Burton and Speke stands alongside it. The adjacent **Dr Livingstone Memorial Museum** (🕘 09.00–16.00 daily; entrance US$10) consists of several large and virtually empty rooms, one of which contains a few ineptly executed and comically captioned paintings of the great explorer, as well as life-size papier-mâché statues of Stanley and Livingstone doffing their caps in greeting.

UJIJI, 10 NOVEMBER 1871

In March 1866, Dr David Livingstone, the most famous and arguably the greatest explorer of his – or perhaps any – era, set off from the coastal port of Mikindani with the aim of resolving the whereabouts of the source of the Nile. Almost nothing concrete was heard of Livingstone over the next few years, and rumours of his death vied with equally difficult-to-substantiate rumours of his imminent return to the coast. So it was that in 1869, the American journalist Henry Morton Stanley, then on assignment in Spain, received a telegram from his editor at the *New York Herald* bearing a simple command that would take him two wearisome years to fulfil: Find Livingstone! The rest, as they say, is history.

In his autobiography, published in 1909, Stanley recalled the momentous day:

> We slept at a chief's village in Ukaranga, with only one more march of six hours, it was said, intervening between us and the Arab settlement of Ujiji, in which native rumour located an old, grey-bearded, white man, who had but newly arrived from a distant western country. It was now 235 days since I had left the Indian Ocean and 50 days since I had departed from [Tabora]... At cockcrow...we strengthened ourselves with a substantial meal, and, as the sun rose in the east, we turned our backs to it, and the caravan was soon in full swing on the march... About eight o'clock we were climbing the side of a steep and wooded hill, and [from] the very crest...I saw, as in a painted picture, a vast lake in the distance below, with its face luminous as a mirror, set in a frame of dimly blue mountains... For hours I strode nervously on...brushing past the bush on the hill-slopes and crests, flinging gay remarks to the wondering villagers who looked on...in mute surprise, until near noon, when, having crossed the last valley and climbed up to the summit of the last hill: Lo! Lake Tanganyika was distant from us but half a mile...
>
> Hard by the lake shore, embowered in palms, on this hot noon, the village of Ujiji broods drowsily. No living thing can be seen moving to break the still aspect of the outer lines of the town and its deep shades... I rested awhile, breathless from my exertions; and, as the stragglers were many, I halted to reunite and reform for an imposing entry. Meantime, my people improved their personal appearance; they clothed themselves in clean dresses, and snowy cloths were folded round their heads. When the laggards had all been gathered, the guns were loaded to rouse up the sleeping town. It is an immemorial custom, for a caravan creeps not up into a friendly town like a thief. Our braves knew the custom well; they therefore volleyed and thundered their salutes as they went marching down the hill slowly, and with much self-contained dignity. Presently, there is a tumultuous stir visible on the outer edge of the town. Groups of men in white dresses, with arms in their hands, burst from the shades, and seem to hesitate a moment, as if in doubt; they then come rushing up to meet us, pursued by hundreds of people, who shout joyfully, while yet afar, their noisy welcomes.
>
> The foremost...cried out: 'why, we took you for Mirambo and his bandits, when we heard the booming of the guns. It is an age since a caravan has come to Ujiji. Which way

A good surfaced road covers the 6km between Ujiji and Kigoma. A regular dalla dalla service runs back and forth between the two ports, leaving Kigoma from next to the market every 5 minutes or so. The signposted junction for the monument lies on the outskirts of central Ujiji – the conductor will drop you off there if you ask for 'Livingstone'. From here, it's a 5-minute walk along a straight road, and you'll quite likely be accompanied by a few vociferous children re-enacting Stanley's 19th-century description of arriving in Ujiji to a mob that 'bawled a jangling chorus of "Jambo"'!

did you come? Ah! You have got a white man with you! Is this his caravan?' Being told it was a white man's caravan by the guides in front, the boisterous multitude pressed up to me, greeted me with salaams, and bowed their salutes. Hundreds of them jostled and trod upon one another's heels…when a tall black man, in long white shirt, burst impulsively through the crowd on my right, and bending low, said 'Good morning, sir,' in clear, intelligent English.

'Hello!' I said. 'Who in the mischief are you?'

'I am Susi, sir, the servant of Dr. Livingstone.'

'What! Is Dr. Livingstone here in this town?'

'Yes, sir.'

'But, are you sure; sure that it is Dr. Livingstone?'

'Why, I leave him just now, sir.'

'Well, now that we have met, one of you had better run ahead, and tell the Doctor of my coming.'

The same idea striking Susi's mind, he undertook in his impulsive manner to inform the Doctor, and I saw him racing headlong, with his white dress streaming behind him like a wind-whipped pennant. The column continued on its way, beset on either flank by a vehemently enthusiastic and noisily rejoicing mob, which bawled a jangling chorus of 'Jambo' to every mother's son of us, and maintained an inharmonious orchestral music of drums and horns. I was indebted for this loud ovation to the cheerful relief the people felt that we were not Mirambo's bandits, and to their joy at the happy rupture of the long silence that had perforce existed between the two trading colonies of [Tabora] and Ujiji.

After a few minutes we came to a halt. The guides in the van had reached the marketplace, which was the central point of interest. For there the great Arabs, chiefs and respectabilities of Ujiji had gathered in a group to await events; thither also they had brought with them the venerable European traveller who was at that time resting among them. The caravan pressed up to them, divided itself into two lines on either side of the road, and, as it did so, disclosed to me the prominent figure of an elderly white man clad in a red flannel blouse, grey trousers, and a blue cloth, gold-banded cap.

Up to this moment my mind had verged upon non-belief in his existence, and now a nagging doubt intruded itself into my mind that this white man could not be the object of my quest, or if he were, he would somehow contrive to disappear before my eyes … 'It may not be Livingstone after all,' doubt suggested. If this is he, what shall I say to him? My imagination had not taken this question into consideration before. All around me was the immense crowd, hushed and expectant, and wondering how the scene would develop itself.

Under all these circumstances I could do no more than exercise some restraint and reserve, so I walked up to him, and, doffing my helmet, bowed and said in an inquiring tone:

'Dr. Livingstone, I presume?'

Smiling cordially, he lifted his cap, and answered briefly: 'Yes.'

GOMBE NATIONAL PARK

Gazetted as Gombe Stream Game Reserve in 1943 and upgraded to its current status in 1965, Gombe National Park (**m** +255 689 062303; **e** chimps@tanzaniaparks.go.tz) is best known for the ground-breaking chimpanzee research project initiated there in the 1960s by Jane Goodall. Yet, surprisingly, Gombe remains a rather remote and low-key national park, one whose popularity has diminished

CHIMPANZEES

Almost certainly, you'll hear them before you see them: from somewhere deep in the forest, an excited hooting, just one voice at first, then several, rising in volume and tempo and pitch to a frenzied unified crescendo, before stopping abruptly or fading away. Jane Goodall named it the 'pant-hoot' call, a kind of bonding ritual that allows any chimpanzees within earshot of one another to identify exactly who is around through each individual's unique vocal stylisation. To the human listener, this eruptive crescendo is one of the most spine-chilling and exciting sounds of the rainforest, and an almost certain indicator that visual contact with humankind's closest genetic relative is imminent.

It is perhaps our close evolutionary kinship with chimpanzees that makes these sociable black-coated apes so enduringly fascinating. Humans, chimpanzees and bonobos (pygmy chimpanzees) share about 95% of their genetic code, and are all more closely related to each other than to any other living creatures. Superficial differences notwithstanding, the similarities between humans and chimps are consistently striking, not only in the skeletal structure and skull, but also in the nervous system, the immune system and in many behavioural aspects – bonobos, for instance, are the only other mammals to copulate in the missionary position.

Chimpanzees don't live in troops, but extended communities of up to 100 individuals, which typically roam the forest in small socially mobile subgroups comprising a few close family members. Male chimps seldom leave the community into which they were born, but females usually migrate into a neighbouring community after reaching adolescence. A high-ranking male will occasionally attempt to monopolise a female in oestrus, but non-hierarchical promiscuity is more normal. A young female might mate with any male that takes her fancy, but older females tend to form close bonds with a few specific males, sometimes allowing themselves to be monopolised by a favoured suitor for a period, but never pairing off exclusively in the long term.

Male chimp society is strongly hierarchical. Every community has an alpha male (though alpha coalitions between a dominant and a submissive sibling also have been recorded), and most other adult males have a clear place in the pecking order. The role of the alpha male, not fully understood, is evidently quite benevolent – chairman of the board rather than crusty tyrant. This is probably influenced by his relatively limited reproductive advantages over potential rivals, most of whom he will have known for his entire life. Other males in the community are generally supportive rather than competitive towards the alpha male, except when a rival consciously contests the alpha position, which certainly isn't an everyday occurrence. In Mahale's Mimikere Community, for instance, an alpha male called Ntologi held that status almost continually from 1979 until his death in 1995.

Prior to the 1960s, chimps were assumed to be strict vegetarians. This notion was rocked when Jane Goodall witnessed a group of chimps hunting down a red colobus monkey, something now known to be common behaviour, particularly during the dry season when other food sources are depleted. Over subsequent years, an average of 20 kills has been recorded in Gombe annually, with red colobus being the prey on more than half of these occasions, though young bushbuck, young bushpig and even infant chimps have also been victimised and eaten. In the dry season, visitors are quite likely to see an attempted hunt, but a successful kill is less commonplace. The normal modus operandi is for four or five adult chimps to encircle a colobus troop, then for another chimp to act as a decoy, sowing deliberate confusion in the hope that it will drive the monkeys into the trap, or cause a mother to drop her baby.

Chimp communities are essentially stable and peaceful entities, but intensive inter-community warfare has been observed at both Mahale and Gombe. In Mahale, one of the two communities habituated by researchers in 1967 had exterminated the other by 1982. A similar thing happened in Gombe, where the Kasekela Community split into two discrete communities that coexisted peacefully for some years. In 1974, however, Goodall discovered that the Kasekela males were methodically persecuting their former allies, isolating them one by one, and tearing into them until they were dead or terminally wounded. By 1977, the splinter community had vanished entirely.

Fatal attacks within a community are more unusual, but they have been known to occur from time to time. The brutal assassination of the Mimikere Community's alpha male Pimu is a recent case in point. Researchers regarded Pimu to be an unpopular leader, since he displayed unusually high levels of aggression to other males, and frequently made violent sexual advances to females. Pimu's unpopularity was confirmed in October 2011, four years after he achieved alpha status, when a group of high-ranking males, including his predecessor Alofu and eventual successor Primus, set upon him, kicking, biting and beating him with logs, then left him to die.

Chimpanzees are essentially inhabitants of the west and central African rainforests, and the Tanzanian population of perhaps 2,000 individuals represents less than 1% of the continental total. Somewhat paradoxically, however, much of what is known about wild chimpanzee society and behaviour stems from the ongoing research projects that were initiated in Gombe and Mahale Mountain national parks back in the 1960s. One of the most interesting patterns to emerge from the parallel research projects on these two populations is a number of social and behavioural differences that can only be described as cultural.

A striking difference between the two populations is their food preferences. Of the plants that occur in both national parks, as many as 40% that are used as a food source by one community are left untouched by the other. In Gombe, for instance, you'll often see chimps in the vicinity of oil palms, whose nut is treated as something of a delicacy. Exactly the same palms are found at Mahale, but the chimps were not recorded eating from them until as recently as 2010. Likewise, the 'termite-fishing' behaviour first recorded by Jane Goodall at Gombe in the 1960s has a parallel in Mahale, where the chimps are often seen 'fishing' for carpenter ants in the trees. But the Mahale chimps have never been recorded fishing for termites, while the Gombe chimps are not known to fish for carpenter ants.

At Mahale, you're bound to come across chimps grooming each other with one hand while holding each other's other hand above their heads – once again, behaviour that has never been noted at Gombe. More than any structural similarity, more even than any single quirk of chimpanzee behaviour, such striking cultural differences – the influence of nurture over nature if you like – bring home our close genetic kinship with chimpanzees.

in recent decades thanks to a decline in backpacker traffic precipitated to some extent by the introduction of chimp tracking in several sites in Uganda. Despite this, it remains a thoroughly worthwhile destination. True, the more southerly Mahale Mountains National Park is much larger, and correspondingly wilder in atmosphere, but Gombe is the more accessible goal for independent travellers. Furthermore, Mahale Mountains aside, it is difficult to think of anywhere else in Africa that offers an in-your-face encounter with wild chimpanzees as regularly as Gombe – one of the most extraordinary and memorable wildlife experiences our planet has to offer!

FEES The entrance fee of US$100 per 24 hours plus VAT is applicable only to time spent in the forest, not to time spent in the rest camp. To independent travellers, for whom a two-night stay is enforced by the lake-taxi schedules, this means that you need only pay entrance fees for those days when you track chimps. In addition to the entrance fee, you need to pay US$20/25 per person per 4-hour/full-day guided walk. All fees must be paid by Visa or Mastercard – cash is not accepted.

FLORA AND FAUNA Gombe extends over 52km² of hilly terrain climbing from the lakeshore, at an elevation of 773m, to above 1,500m at the top of the rift escarpment. At no point measuring more than 3.5km from east to west, the narrow national park is bisected by 13 streams that carve steep valleys into the rift escarpment before flowing into the lake. This rugged topography is covered not in the rainforest one might expect of a reserve whose best-known inhabitants are chimpanzees, but rather in thick Brachystegia woodland that gives way to narrow belts of lush riparian forest along the river courses.

Gombe is most widely associated with a renowned chimpanzee research project that was initiated by Jane Goodall in 1960 and now ranks as the world's longest-running study of an individual wild animal population. Goodall was originally sponsored by Louis Leakey, an anthropologist and palaeontologist who believed his protégé's lack of scientific training would allow her to observe chimpanzee behaviour without preconceptions. After initial difficulties trying to locate her subjects, Goodall overcame the chimps' shyness through the combination of a banana-feeding machine and sheer persistence. Since the late 1960s Goodall's work has achieved both popular and scientific recognition. Her painstaking studies of individual chimps and the day-to-day social behaviour of troops have been supplemented by a series of observations confronting conventional scientific wisdom. Observations that initially caused controversy – tool-making, inter-troop warfare and even cannibalism – have since been widely accepted. Much of Goodall's work is described in her books *In the Shadow of Man* and *Through a Window*, which are highly recommended to interested readers (page 545). Fifi, a three-year-old when Goodall first arrived at Gombe in 1960, was regularly seen by tourists until shortly before her death in 2004.

Although chimpanzees hog the limelight, Gombe harbours a surprisingly varied fauna for a park of its small size. Fascinating in their own right are the beachcomber olive baboons that hang out in front of the rest camp. These have been the subject of ongoing research since 1967,

A NOTE ON CHIMPANZEES

Chimpanzees are susceptible to many of the same diseases as people, so if you are unwell, do not visit the park – even a common cold has the potential to kill a chimpanzee, which may not share your immunity!

and – like their larger and more celebrated cousins – they are apparently oblivious to the presence of humans, without showing any of the aggression one normally associates with baboons that forage close to habitations. Other primates include vervet, blue, red-tailed and Uganda red colobus monkey, the last frequently seen while searching for chimps.

Most of the other mammals found here are secretive or nocturnal, and are seldom seen by visitors. The only part of the park where you may walk unguided is along the lakeshore and in the immediate vicinity of the rest camp, which is a good place to seek out some of the 287 bird species recorded in the park. Of particular note are the palm-nut vultures and African fish eagles that perch on palms and other trees along the lakeshore, and the gem-like Peters's twinspot, a normally elusive forest bird that is tame and easily spotted within the rest camp. Other striking birds that might be seen at Gombe include blue-breasted kingfisher, Schalow's turaco, Ross's turaco, Luhder's bush-shrike and mountain wagtail.

GETTING THERE AND AWAY The southern boundary of Gombe National Park lies 16km north of Kigoma, and the Kasekela Research Station and Rest Camp is situated on the lakeshore about 8km further north (access to which is by boat only). It is one of the few national parks in East Africa that is easily accessed on public transport and can only be explored on foot, making it an excellent goal for independent travellers.

Organised tours and private charters The main operator is Mbali Mbali, which manages the only lodge in Gombe (see below), and can put together a variety of all-inclusive package excursions for one to twelve people using their own motorboat to do the 25-minute transfer. Transfers can also be arranged through the park visitor centre in Kigoma; these cost US$300 return for up to eight passengers.

Independent visits The cheapest way to get to Kasekela is with one of the inexpensive lake-taxis that run between Kibirizi Beach, 3km north of Kigoma, and Mwamgongo village on the park's northern boundary. These lake-taxis stop by request at all lakeshore settlements on the way, Kasekela Rest Camp included. At least two boats ply the route daily, generally leaving from Kibirizi between 13.00 and 14.00 and taking up to 4 hours to get to Kasekela. On the return trip, the lake-taxis generally pass Kasekela between 07.00 and 08.00 and arrive at Kibirizi 2–3 hours later. The uncovered lake-taxis can become uncomfortably hot in the sun, so bring a hat, sunscreen and drinking water.

WHERE TO STAY AND EAT

Kasekela Rest Camp m +255 785 291416; w tanzaniaparks.go.tz. This lakeshore camp has a few simple twin bandas with nets & screened porch but no fan. Camping is permitted, too, but since it is more expensive, there's no advantage unless the bandas are full (unlikely, but safest to check in advance at the park office in Kigoma). You can bring food with you (there are limited self-catering facilities) or eat at the canteen for around US$10–15. A staff shop sells biscuits & a few other basic foodstuffs, & visitors are welcome to visit the staff bar, which is stocked with beer & sodas. The baboons are likely to attack anybody who carries food outdoors, or to knock down any tent with fresh fruit or vegetables inside. *Rooms US$20pp, camping US$30pp.* **$**

Mbali Mbali Gombe Lodge m +255 692 700600; w mbalimbali.com; ⌚ closed Mar–Apr. Formerly called Gombe Forest Lodge, this luxury tented camp fringes Mitumba Beach at the northern end of the park. The 7 tents stand on raised wooden platforms spaced out along the lakeshore. **$$$$$$**

WHAT TO SEE AND DO In addition to organised chimp tracking, guided night walks are offered at US$20 per person, and it is permitted to explore the forest-lined beach immediately around camp without a guide.

Chimpanzee tracking The park's population of roughly 100 chimpanzees is divided across three communities. The habituated Kasekela Community studied by Jane Goodall is the largest, comprising about 45 individuals, and its territory lies in the central part of the park, around the Kasekela research centre, rest camp and river. To see the chimpanzees, however, you will need to go on a guided walk from the research centre, which costs US$20 per party and may or may not involve some fairly strenuous walking on steep slopes. During the dry season, when the chimps tend to forage on the lower slopes of the escarpment, it often takes less than an hour to locate a group. In the wet season, when the chimps forage higher and walking conditions are tougher, it could take 3 or 4 hours. Either way, the best time to track chimps is shortly after sunrise, because the guides normally know where they nested the previous night, and are thus likely to find them quite easily.

MAHALE MOUNTAINS NATIONAL PARK

Scenically reminiscent of Gombe but on a far grander scale, the 1,613km² Mahale Mountains (e sokwe@tanzaniaparks.go.tz) is quite simply one of the most beautiful national parks anywhere in Africa, and it also ranks as arguably the top chimpanzee-tracking destination anywhere on the continent. Some 30 times larger than Gombe, the park occupies a mountainous knuckle that juts into Lake Tanganyika some 150km south of Kigoma. It is dominated topographically by the Mahale Range, a stretch of the Rift Valley Escarpment that rises sharply from the lakeshore to the 2,462m Nkungwe Peak, and six other peaks that exceed 2,000m in elevation. Even without the forested peaks, the crystal-clear waters and deserted sandy beaches that characterise this part of Lake Tanganyika would be thoroughly alluring, but as it is, the setting is scenically reminiscent of a volcanic island beach resort somewhere deep in the Indian Ocean – with the added bonus that these forests are inhabited by a rich variety of birds and primates, including an estimated 900 chimpanzees divided across 13 communities. This includes the habituated Mimikere community, which currently numbers 75 individuals.

HISTORY Gazetted as a national park in 1985, Mahale Mountains was one of the last parts of East Africa to be explored by outsiders. The British naval officer Verney Lovett Cameron passed below the mountains in 1873 on his way to becoming the first European to cross equatorial Africa from the Indian to the Atlantic coastline, and gave brief mention to them in *Across Africa*, the book he published in 1877. Aside from sporadic visits to the lower slopes by the White Fathers based at Kalema between 1911 and 1916, however, the area was ignored until 1935, when Dollman exhibited a chimpanzee skull found at Mahale to the Linnaean Society of London. No European is known to have ascended the highest peak in the range before 1940, and it was only in 1958 that a team of Oxford scientists started serious scientific exploration of the area.

In 1961, Mahale was one of several areas visited by a team of Japanese primatologists, led by the University of Kyoto's Toshisada Nishida, who were looking for a suitable site to study chimpanzees. The expedition agreed that Mahale was the most promising site, and in 1965 a permanent research centre was established at Kasoge, about 1km inland of the lakeshore, close to the present-day

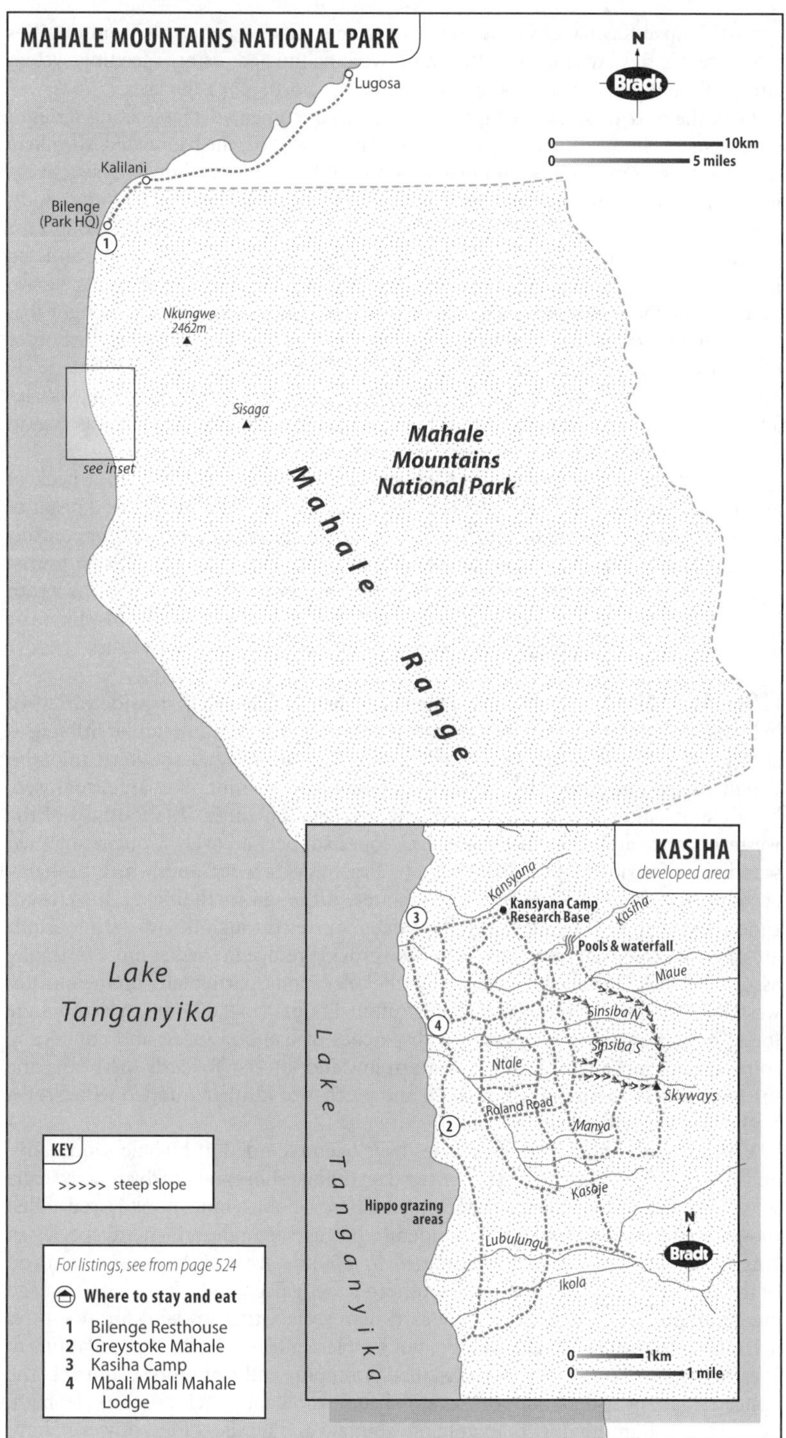
MAHALE MOUNTAINS NATIONAL PARK
N
Bradt
0 10km
0 5 miles
Lugosa
Kalilani
Bilenge
(Park HQ)
1
Nkungwe
2462m
Sisaga
see inset
Mahale
Mountains
National Park
Mahale
Range
Lake
Tanganyika
KEY
>>>>> steep slope
For listings, see from page 524
Where to stay and eat
1 Bilenge Resthouse
2 Greystoke Mahale
3 Kasiha Camp
4 Mbali Mbali Mahale Lodge
KASIHA
developed area
Kansyana
Kansyana Camp
Research Base
Kasiha
Pools & waterfall
Maue
Sinsiba N
Sinsiba S
Ntale
Skyways
Roland Road
Manya
Kasoje
Hippo grazing
areas
Lubulungu
Ikola
Lake Tanganyika
0 1km
0 1 mile

tourist camp at Kasiha. Over the course of the next five years, the two communities whose territories lay closest to the camp were habituated, using a feeding system similar to that pioneered by Jane Goodall further north along the lake.

Over the next 15 years, the Japanese scientists documented a fascinating series of developments in the local chimpanzee population. In 1967, the habituated Mimikere and Kajabala communities comprised about 100 and 27 individuals respectively, with territories that bordered each other. During the early years of the study, however, the smaller community gradually shrank in number, partially through the migration of females to the neighbouring territory, partially because of a protracted inter-community war that resulted in several fatalities, including the killing of two successive alpha males in the Kajabala Community. In retrospect, it is thought that the catalyst for this feud was the placement of a banana feeding station on the border of the two communities' territories, which led to frequent hostile encounters. By 1982, no adult males were left in the Kajabala Community, and the surviving females and youngsters were integrated into the Mimikere Community, which was free to occupy its former rival's territory.

In the years that followed, the Mimikere community declined from a peak of around 120 individuals in the 1970s to fewer than 50 in 2006, mainly as a result of infectious diseases spread by tourists. This led to the introduction of stricter controls (for instance, the use of face masks and the imposition of a 1-hour limit on tourist visits), since when the community has increased to around 75 individuals. The Kyoto University project at Mahale Mountains continues to this day, with the Mimikere or 'M' Community being the main subject of study, as well as of tourist visits.

FLORA AND FAUNA The elevation range of Mahale is reflected in its wide variety of habitats, with a floral composition that reflects a unique combination of influences associated with the eastern savannah, western rainforest and southern miombo woodland biomes. Altogether, some 15 different plant communities are recognised, but in simplistic terms there are four main vegetation zones. The foothills of the western slopes and most of the eastern slopes support a cover of open-canopied woodland of various types, dominated by Brachystegia woodland, which probably accounts for about 60–70% of the park's area. Although small in area, the closed-canopy riparian woodlands that follow watercourses through the western foothills are of great ecological significance, as they provide refuge to species more normally associated with rainforest habitats. At higher elevations, particularly on the moister western slopes, which receive an average annual rainfall of 2,000mm, Afromontane forest predominates, interspersed with patches of bamboo forest and containing some species more typical of the western lowland forests. Towards the peaks, the forest gives way to montane grassland and patches of heather studded with Protea bushes and other flowering plants.

Chimps aside, eight primate species have been recorded in Mahale Mountains, and at least five are likely to be encountered on the lakeshore and nearby Brachystegia woodland. These are yellow baboon, Uganda red colobus, blue monkey, red-tailed monkey and vervet monkey. An endemic but as yet undescribed subspecies of Angola colobus is more or less confined to a 50km^2 tract of Afromontane forest of the higher slopes. The doctrinal southern lesser galago and silver greater galago are common but more likely to be heard than seen. Other lowland forest species are similar to those found at Gombe, but supplemented by isolated populations of West African species such as brush-tailed porcupine and giant forest squirrel. The eastern slopes of Mahale support savannah and woodland species such as elephant, lion, African hunting dog, roan antelope, buffalo and giraffe. Lions, however, have killed several chimps in the forest, and African hunting dogs were once recorded on the beach! Warthogs used to be quite common in the vicinity of the lakeshore camps, but they been hunted out in recent years. By contrast, the nocturnal bushpig is often heard rooting noisily around the camps at night, and its dung is seen regularly on forest walks.

Almost 400 bird species have been recorded in Mahale. Among the more colourful and interesting ones likely to be seen close to the tourist lodges are crowned eagle, scaly francolin, crested guinea-fowl, Ross's turaco, giant kingfisher, blue-cheeked bee-eater, trumpeter hornbill, crested malimbe and Vieillot's black weaver. The Afromontane forest of Mahale is the only place in Tanzania where the rare bamboo warbler and Stuhlmann's starling have been recorded. It is also home to the Kungwe apalis, a localised Albertine Rift Endemic, as well as endemic subspecies of Bocage's akalat, yellow-throated woodland warbler and yellow-bellied wattle-eye.

FEES AND FURTHER INFORMATION The entrance fee is US$80 plus VAT per 24 hours. Chimp tracking is included in this fee, though an additional guide fee of US$20 per party plus VAT is levied for all forest walks. If you are staying at one of the private camps, fees will be dealt with through your operator. If you arrive independently, all fees must be paid by Visa or Mastercard – cash is not accepted.

Mahale National Park is also the subject of a beautiful coffee-table book entitled *Mahale: A Photographic Encounter with Chimpanzees*, by Angelika Hofer, Michael Huffman and Gunter Ziesler (Sterling Publishing, 2000) – it is out of print but cheap secondhand copies are still available at online booksellers such as Amazon. For an accessible academic behavioural overview of the habituated chimp community at Mahale, a recommended read is *Chimpanzees of the Lakeshore* (Cambridge University Press, 2012) by Toshisada Nishida, who founded the chimp research project here in the 1960s and remained involved in it until his death in 2011.

GETTING THERE AND AWAY Mahale is a more popular goal for organised fly-in tours than Gombe, but it is lot more difficult to reach on public transport.

Organised tours Fly-in safaris are best arranged through one of the two lakeshore camps (see page 519 for contacts). Nomad, which manages Greystoke Mahale, currently runs a twice-weekly scheduled flight connecting Mahale to Katavi and Arusha (with the option of being picked up at most airstrips in the Serengeti or Tarangire national parks, or anywhere else in between). This runs every Monday and Thursday in both directions, giving the option of a three-, four- or seven-night stay. Mbali Mbali, which manages Kungwe Beach Lodge, can also arrange a wide variety of fly-in packages, as well as motorboat transfers from Kigoma.

Independent visits Self-driving to Mahale Mountains, or reaching it on public transport, is an adventurous but doable option, especially in the dry season. Four local landmarks are of significance in the trip. Two are villages outside the park boundaries: Lugosa, which lies 15km north of the park, and Kalilani, the site of the airstrip, almost immediately outside the northern boundary. Within the park, the park headquarters at Bilenge, 1km south of Kalilani, is where all park fees must be paid. Kasiha Camp, 10km further south, is the usual starting point for chimp tracking and other forest walks.

For self-drivers, a rough 220km road now runs south from Kigoma to Bilenge via Lugosa and Kalilani. The drive entails an inexpensive and straightforward ferry crossing at Ilagala. Depending on when it was last graded, the road can usually be covered in about 4 hours in the dry season, but the last 20m past Lugosa may be impassable after heavy rain, in which case you would need to negotiate a boat transfer to Bilenge with a local fisherman (expect to pay US$20 per party).

Using public transport, at least one dalla dalla travels daily between Kigoma and Lugosa. It might sometimes continue to Kalilani, or even Bilenge, if you are prepared to pay a bit extra. Failing that, you shouldn't have a problem arranging a boda-boda (motorbike taxi) or boat to the park headquarters. Another option is a local lake-taxi service that runs between Ujiji and Kalilani daily, but be warned that this is crowded, unsafe, uncovered, and can take more than 24 hours to cover the distance.

More appealing, if and when it resumes operation, is to use MV *Liemba* (page 513) to travel between Kigoma and Lugosa. Coming as a round-trip from Kigoma, it is scheduled to depart on its southern leg at 16.00 on every alternate Wednesday, and it generally arrives at Lugosa between midnight and 02.00 on Thursdays. For the return trip, it passes Lugosa at any time between 21.00 on Saturday and 06.00 on Sunday, arriving in Kigoma about 10–12 hours later. Once at Lugosa, you can arrange a boda-boda or boat transfer to Bilenge, or walk the flat 15km footpath that more or less follows the lakeshore between them.

WHERE TO STAY AND EAT *Map, page 521*

Exclusive

✷ **Greystoke Mahale** m +255 787 595908; w nomad-tanzania.com; closed Apr–May. Set on a sandy private beach 3km south of Kasiha tourist camp, this wonderful Tarzan-goes-upmarket camp combines a high level of comfort with an organic feel. The stylish 2-storey dining & reception area is a wood, thatch & canvas construction with a good library of reference books. Accommodation is in 6 open-fronted 2-storey wood-&-makuti cottages with king-size bed, a large dressing area, a private veranda running out to the beach, & an en-suite hot shower connected to the main room by a wooden walkway. The setting is spectacular, with the jungle & mountains behind you & the beach in front, & the food, service & guiding are up to Nomad's usual impeccable standards. Chimp tracking is the main activity, usually undertaken in the morning straight after an early b/fast. In the afternoon, you can take a guided forest walk, swim in the lake, snorkel among the adjoining rocks, or hop aboard a dhow to visit the centre of the lake or check out a nearby river inlet inhabited by hippos. **$$$$$$$**

Upmarket

Mbali Mbali Mahale Lodge m +255 692 700600; w mbalimbali.com; closed Mar–15 May. Formerly Kungwe Beach Lodge, this pleasant tented camp stands on a secluded sandy beach near the Sisimba River mouth about halfway between Greystoke & Kasiha. The 10 standing tents each have a large dbl bed & en-suite flush toilet & shower, while the dining & lounge area consists of a large raised wooden construction on the beach. **$$$$$$$**

Budget

Bilenge Resthouse m +255 734 916752; e mahale.tourism@tanzaniaparks.go.tz. Primarily aimed at visiting park officials but also open to tourists, this 6-room resthouse has a pretty, isolated location above the lakeshore 300m from the main headquarters buildings. Drinks are available at the staff bar & basic local meals can easily be arranged with the staff at the headquarters. Note that, although all park fees must be paid at Bilenge, all chimp-tracking excursions leave from Kasiha, for the simple reason that it lies within the territory of the habituated chimp communities. *US$40pp.* **$$$**

Kasiha Camp m +255 734 916752; e mahale.tourism@tanzaniaparks.go.tz. Also the main departure point for chimp tracking, Kasiha Camp lies in a glade of mango trees about 100m inland of the lakeshore. The 10 twin bandas all have netting; some are en suite while others use common showers. There is no electricity or running water, but kerosene lamps & bucket showers are available, or you can swim in the lake. No food is available, so you'll need to bring everything with you, whether you want to self-cater or arrange a local cook. Beers & other drinks can be bought at the park headquarters, which you will need to visit in order to pay park fees before coming to the rest camp. Camping is not permitted. *US$40pp.* **$$**

WHAT TO SEE AND DO A variety of forest walks are offered, not only chimp tracking but also more general hikes in search of monkeys and birds. A popular short hike leads up the escarpment to a pretty waterfall on one of the several streams that babble down towards the lake shore. More ambitiously, you can climb from the lakeshore camps to the 2,462m peak of Nkungwe, but it's a long and tiring day out, involving an altitudinal ascent of around 1,700m. A guide fee of US$20/25 per person is charged for 4-hour/full-day walks. Some of the camps also offer boat trips and snorkelling in the lake. The beaches are idyllic for swimming, despite the occasional presence of crocodiles, and it is rather awe-inspiring to look up at the mountains and recognise that you are paddling roughly midway in elevation between the highest peak on the escarpment and the deepest point on the floor of the world's second-deepest lake!

Chimpanzee tracking Mahale's main attraction is undoubtedly tracking through the territory occupied by the Mimikere chimpanzee community, which was first habituated more than 50 years ago and now comprises around 75 individuals, almost all of whom have been accustomed to visits by rangers, researchers and/or tourists since the day they were born (the exception being female migrants from other communities). The habituated chimps here are incredibly relaxed around people, so much so that they often brush past human visitors on the forest trail, flagrantly ignoring the 10m rule imposed by the park authorities for their own safety. That said, the habituated community at Mahale occupies a far larger territory

CHIMPANZEE TRACKING CODE OF CONDUCT

Chimps are susceptible and lack immunity to many diseases carried by humans. In order to prevent potentially fatal infections, the park authorities have introduced a stringent code of conduct at Mahale and Gombe. The most important rules are as follows:

- No person under the age of 12 is permitted to track chimps.
- If you have any cold-like symptoms or viral infections, you may not track chimps.
- A surgical mask is issued to all trackers at the start of the walk. Use this to cover your nose and mouth whenever you are close to chimpanzees.
- Try to maintain a distance of at least 10m from chimps, moving back when they approach you (as they often do).
- Do not eat, drink, urinate or defecate within 250m of chimpanzees; if you are caught short ask your guide to dig a deep hole at a suitable site.
- Do not leave personal belongings on the ground as chimps are curious animals and your belongings can transmit disease.
- Do not litter.
- No more than six visitors (plus one guide) are permitted close to the chimps at any one time.
- Maximum viewing time is 1 hour. If the chimps are moving and viewing is interrupted, the stopwatch is paused until they have been relocated, but tracking is not permitted for longer than 3 hours after the initial sighting.

than the chimps at Gombe, which means that locating them can entail quite a long walk, especially when they are on the upper slopes. As a rule, the odds of finding the chimps easily improves towards the end of the dry season, from July to October, when they tend to stick to the lower slopes of the mountain, and are seldom more than a 60-minute walk from the tourist lodgings on the lakeshore. During the rainy season of November to April the forest trails are tougher underfoot, and the chimps are often more difficult to locate, so a flying visit might well result in disappointment. But at any time of year, you'd be extremely unfortunate to spend three or four nights in the park and not encounter any chimps at all. A US$20 per-party guide fee is charged for tracking chimpanzees in Mahale.

KATAVI NATIONAL PARK

In the 1980s, when Tanzania's elephant- and rhino-poaching crisis peaked, Nicholas Gordon, author of *Ivory Knights,* described Katavi National Park as 'isolated and unloved, and in need of support'. Since then, its stock has risen considerably. In 1998, the original 2,250km^2 set aside by President Nyerere was extended southeast to cover 4,471km^2, making it significantly larger than the established Mikumi and Tarangire national parks. Meanwhile, the solitary concrete bunker that once served as its only tourist accommodation has been supplemented by a trio of top-notch tented camps catering to the top-end fly-in market. Even so, Katavi retains a truly remote wilderness character, and while tourist numbers have increased gradually over recent years, it is one of the few safari destinations where you're likely to see more lions that you are other people. Indeed, if any national park deserves the well-worn accolade of 'Africa's best-kept game-viewing secret', it is surely Katavi, with its plentiful lions and elephants, large herds of buffalo, and what is possibly the continent's densest concentrations of hippos. In short, the perfect goal for anybody seeking a true bush experience!

FLORA AND FAUNA Katavi lies within the Rukwa Rift, an easterly extension of the Albertine Rift that culminates in the extensive Lake Rukwa Basin. Covered in dense Brachystegia woodland, the park is bisected by the seasonal Ikuu, Katuma and Kapapa rivers, which converge to become the Kavu, a major effluent of Lake Rukwa. Flanked by open floodplains, the rivers also run through a trio of larger shallow depressions whose fine alluvial dust and yellowing grass are transformed into vast wetlands at the height of the rainy season. These are Lake Katavi (on the Katuma River 2km west of the B8 between Mpanda and Sumbawanga), Katasunga Floodplain (to the west of the alternative main road via Ikuu Bridge and Usevia) and Lake Chada (at the confluence of the Katuma and Kapapa 3km east of the Ikuu–Usevia road). The name Katavi, incidentally, is said locally to derive from Katabi, a deified traditional healer who lived close to the eponymous lake.

Wildlife viewing is best during the late dry season, when the rivers are reduced to sluggish muddy streams, in parts little more than a metre wide, that form the only source of fresh water for miles in any direction. Lions are abundant, with several different prides' territories converging on each of the so-called lakes. Spotted hyenas are regularly sighted in the early morning, while leopards are common but elusive in the fringing woodland. At least three African wild dog packs currently roam the park, but sightings are erratic except when they are denning at a known location.

Around 2,500–4,000 elephants have a range centred on Katavi, and sightings are common. A notable feature of the park is its thousand-strong buffalo herds – at least three or four such herds roam along the river and associated floodplains. Other ungulates often seen on the floodplains are zebra, giraffe, hartebeest, topi, impala, Bohor reedbuck and Defassa waterbuck. The woodland is less rewarding for game, at least in terms of volume, but it is where you are most likely to encounter eland, sable and roan antelope, which are drawn to the open grassland only at the very end of the dry season.

Most remarkable of all, perhaps, are the spectacular numbers of hippo that converge on any stretch of the river sufficiently deep to wallow in during the dry season. There are several pools where hundreds of hippo can reliably be seen, flopped all over each other like seals at a breeding colony. These huddled concentrations consist of several different pods that wouldn't associate during the rains, when they are able to disperse more widely into the seasonal marshes and lakes. As a result, there is fierce territorial competition between rival males. Bloody fights are an everyday occurrence, with dominance over any given hippo pool often passing from one bull to another several times in the course of a season, and the rejected behemoths being forced to spend their days foraging on the plains alongside the buffalo and zebra. We've not encountered anything like this anywhere else in Africa – the hippo density per kilometre of riverfront must be comparable to that of the Rufiji River or the Victoria Nile, except that instead of occupying a wide, deep river the hippos are squeezed into a shallow, muddy stream!

And if the rivers dry up altogether, as they do most years in September or October, the few thousand hippos associated with them all relocate to a series of muddy pools fed by natural groundwater springs below Ikuu ranger post. Here, you might see more than 500 individuals in one muddy wallow, lying cheek to cheek not only with each other, but also with impressively proportioned adult crocodiles, a foe they would normally avoid. Another great spot for wildlife watching in dry conditions is Massawe Hippo Pool, which lies 500m east of the main road 5km south of Ikuu Bridge, and often attracts large numbers of thirsty elephants and other wildlife from mid-morning into the afternoon.

The rivers also harbour large concentrations of water-associated birds such as yellow-billed, open-billed and saddle-billed stork, pink-backed pelican, African spoonbill, giant kingfisher, and numerous herons, egrets and lapwings. Particularly notable is the flocks of hundreds of black-capped night heron that roost along the Ikuu River immediately west of Ikuu Bridge. Raptors are well represented, with fish eagle, bateleur and white-backed vulture prominent. The acacia grove around Katavi Tented Camp is a particularly rewarding spot for woodland birds such as little bee-eater, Tanzania red-billed hornbill, lilac-breasted roller, orange-breasted bush-shrike, black cuckoo-shrike, African golden oriole, African paradise flycatcher and crested barbet. A characteristic sound of the floodplain is the gurgling chuckle of yellow-throated sandgrouse, which flock along the river to drink about 2 hours after sunrise and shortly before sunset.

WHEN TO VISIT Katavi is a classic dry-season reserve. During the rainy season, the inundated black cotton soil renders the seasonal tracks more or less impassable, wildlife viewing is erratic as the animals disperse far and wide, and the sweltering heat, combined with hordes of mosquitoes and other insects, can be highly uncomfortable. During the late dry season, by contrast, the three main floodplains attract copious concentrations of wildlife, with numbers usually peaking between August and early November.

FEES The entrance fee is US$30 plus VAT per 24 hours. If you arrive independently, all fees must be paid by Visa or Mastercard – cash is not accepted. The only place

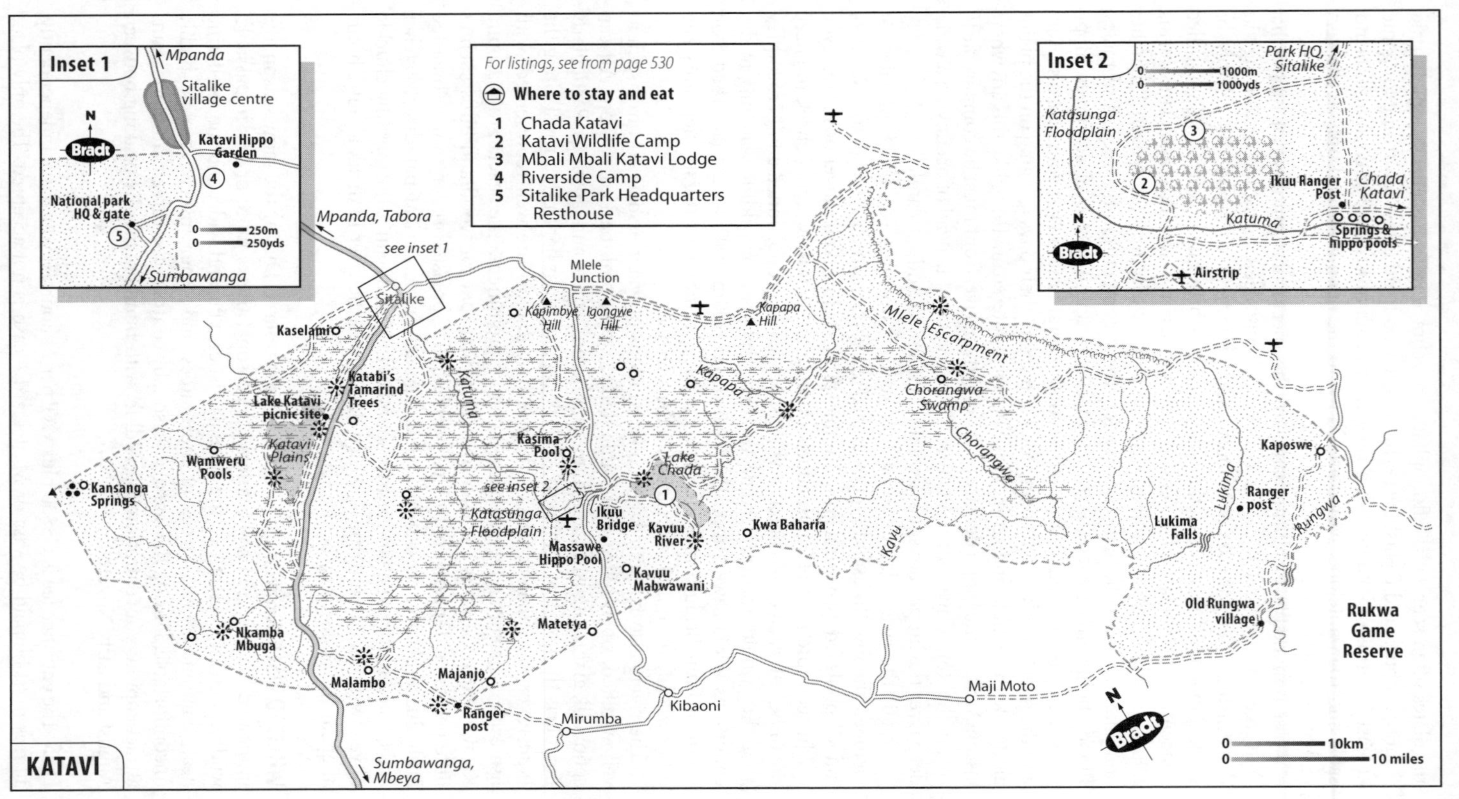
KATAVI
Inset 1
Mpanda
Sitalike village centre
Katavi Hippo Garden
National park HQ & gate
Sumbawanga
0 250m
0 250yds
For listings, see from page 530
Where to stay and eat
1 Chada Katavi
2 Katavi Wildlife Camp
3 Mbali Mbali Katavi Lodge
4 Riverside Camp
5 Sitalike Park Headquarters Resthouse
Inset 2
0 1000m
0 1000yds
Park HQ, Sitalike
Katasunga Floodplain
Ikuu Ranger Post
Chada Katavi
Katuma
Springs & hippo pools
Airstrip
Mpanda, Tabora
see inset 1
Sitalike
Mlele Junction
Kapimbye Hill
Igongwe Hill
Kapapa Hill
Mlele Escarpment
Kaselami
Katuma
Kapapa
Katabi's Tamarind Trees
Lake Katavi picnic site
Katavi Plains
Chorangwa Swamp
Chorangwa
Kasima Pool
Wamweru Pools
Lake Chada
Kansanga Springs
see inset 2
Katasunga Floodplain
Ikuu Bridge
Kavuu River
Kwa Baharia
Kavu
Massawe Hippo Pool
Kavuu Mabwawani
Kaposwe
Lukima
Ranger post
Rungwa
Lukima Falls
Old Rungwa village
Rukwa Game Reserve
Nkamba Mbuga
Matetya
Malambo
Majanjo
Ranger post
Mirumba
Kibaoni
Maji Moto
Sumbawanga, Mbeya
0 10km
0 10 miles

where this payment can be made is the park headquarters (m +255 767 536128; e katavi@tanzaniaparks.go.tz) on the outskirts of Sitalike. No entrance fee is charged for using the two public roads connecting Sitalike to Sumbawanga or Mlele junction to Usevia. It is, however, illegal to deviate from these two main roads without having paid park fees, so anybody driving up from Sumbawanga must go to Sitalike before they undertake any game drives.

WARNINGS Katavi is notorious for its voracious tsetse flies, which can be a real nuisance, though fortunately they are commonest in thickets and woodland and rather less numerous on the floodplains that comprise the main game-viewing circuits. Self-drive visitors should also be aware that internal roads are mostly in poor condition, and signposts are non-existent, which – given that the game tends to be concentrated in a few specific areas – makes it well worth hiring a guide from the park headquarters. Take local advice before exploring the park beyond the main roads during the rainy season (November to March).

GETTING THERE AND AWAY Although most visitors to Katavi fly there, it can also be visited from Mpanda, a smallish but fast-growing town that lies 35km north of the Sitalike park headquarters. Mpanda is quite remote (1,180km from Dar es Salaam, 1,000km from Arusha and 750km from Dodoma) but it is now connected to all these towns by decent surfaced roads. There are also now a few scheduled Air Tanzania (w airtanzania.co.tz) flights from Dar es Salaam to Mpanda, and an inexpensive thrice-weekly rail service runs there from Tabora, at the junction of the main lines from Dar es Salaam to Kigoma (Lake Tanganyika) and Mwana (Lake Victoria). If you need to overnight in Mpanda itself, the pick of an indifferent bunch is Mpanda Lodge (Kigoma Rd; m +255 764 907001) but a more attractive base for a budget safari is Riverside Camp in Sitalike (page 530).

By air Most people fly to Katavi. **Safari Airlink** (w flysal.com) flies from Ruaha to Katavi and Mahale then back every Monday and Thursday, continuing to Dar es Salaam the same day, and also connecting to Nyerere and Dar es Salaam on the day before or after. On the same days, Nomad Safaris (which operates Chada Camp in Katavi and Greystoke Camp in Mahale) runs a flexible scheduled air service connecting both parks to Arusha via any specified airstrip in the Serengeti, Tarangire or elsewhere in between.

By road The main entrance gate and park headquarters are situated at the northern extreme of the park 1km south of the village of Sitalike, 35km south of Mpanda and 200km north of Sumbawanga. The main road between these towns is now surfaced for most if its length and well-maintained, so the drive from Mpanda to Sitalike can be done in 30–45 minutes, while the drive from Sumbawanga takes about 3 hours. Make sure you carry enough fuel, since there is nowhere to fill up between Mpanda and Sumbawanga. Using public transport, a few buses and dalla dallas run from Mpanda to Sitalike daily, taking about an hour in either direction. From Sitalike you can walk to the park headquarters in about 15 minutes, crossing a river with a resident hippo pod.

For people driving themselves, the excellent game-viewing circuit around the Chada and Katasunga floodplains is most easily reached by following the public road that branches east at Sitalike for 20km to Mlele Junction, then heads south towards the small town of Usevia outside the southern boundary of the park. Initially, this road isn't very promising, passing through dense Brachystegia woodland that is sparsely populated with game. That changes 25km south of Mlele Junction, when you reach Ikuu Bridge. You should see plenty of hippos, crocodiles and waterbirds at Ikuu Bridge, and tracks run either side, east towards the Chada Floodplain and west towards Ikuu Ranger Post and the Katasunga Floodplain.

WHERE TO STAY AND EAT *Map, page 528*

Exclusive

Chada Katavi ⊕ -6.93584, 31.25005; **m** +255 787 595908; **w** nomad-tanzania.com; ⊕ closed 16 Nov–31 May. This superb old-style tented camp sprawls in a glade of tall acacia trees overlooking the Chada Floodplain. The 6 tents are set on wooden platforms & come with king-size bed, bucket shower & eco-toilet. There is also a well-stocked library & shady dining area. The feel is pure untrammelled Africa – no concrete or stone structures, no neat footpaths, no lawns, no fences, just a few tents in a patch of pristine woodland regularly traversed by elephant, lion & other large mammals. It is precisely this air of uncluttered rusticity that lends Chada its exclusivity & the wilderness atmosphere takes on a heightened immediacy at night, when it's not unusual to hear several prides of lion & numerous hyenas calling simultaneously, while elephants crash through the surrounding bush. Not for the faint of heart, perhaps, but in its own understated way arguably the most exciting camp in Tanzania. The guiding & food are to the usually high standard associated with Nomad. **$$$$$$$**

Upmarket

Katavi Wildlife Camp ⊕ -6.89710, 31.16207; ☎ (UK) +44 (0)1452 862288; **w** tanzaniasafaris.info; ⊕ closed Mar–May. Overlooking Katasunga floodplain close to Ikuu Ranger Post, this rustic tented camp comprises 9 standing tents set on stilted wooden platforms below a makuti roof. All units have 2 ¾ or 1 queen-size bed, large en-suite bathroom, & wide balconies with chairs & hammock overlooking the floodplain, so you're afforded exceptional game viewing right from your tent. There are also 2 family units, each comprising 2 en-suite tents & shared plunge pool. **$$$$$$**

Mbali Mbali Katavi Lodge ⊕ -6.88729, 31.17143; **m** +255 692 700600; **w** mbalimbali.com; ⊕ closed Mar–May. This attractive camp has a striking communal area with a swimming pool on the raised wooden deck, & a great location for wildlife watching from camp. The spacious en-suite standing tents are set on raised wooden decks & have a makuti roof shaded by palms & tall riparian forest, & come with generator electricity, king-size bed, deck with seats & swing chair, & uncluttered contemporary furnishings. *US$680/1,010 FB sgl/dbl inc activities & soft drinks Jun–Oct, low-season discounts.* **$$$$$$**

Budget & camping

National park campsites Self-sufficient travellers with private transport may camp at a number of places in the park, including sites overlooking the Chada & Katavi floodplains. Campsites are basic, with firewood but no drinking water. *US$30pp, plus park entrance fees & VAT.* **$$**

Riverside Camp ⊕ -6.62941, 31.144797; **m** +255 767 754740; **w** riversidecampkatavi.weebly.com. Owned by the bush-savvy son of a former park warden, this well-organised & friendly camp in Sitalike has a pleasant location alongside the Katuma River bordering (but outside) the national park. There are adequate en-suite rooms, camping facilities & a restaurant. It can also arrange a 4x4 for game drives at US$200 for up to 6 people, including driver, fuel & vehicle entrance fees, but not individual entrance fees. *US$15pp room, US$5pp camping.* **$**

Sitalike Park Headquarters Resthouse ⊕ -6.63227, 31.13897; **w** tanzaniaparks.go.tz. Situated at the park headquarters 1km south of Sitalike, this well-equipped resthouse is aimed primarily at visiting Tanapa officials but also open to tourists. Basic meals are available & there's a staff bar. *US$30pp plus 18% VAT.* **$$**

Appendix 1

LANGUAGE

SWAHILI Swahili, the official language of Tanzania, is a Bantu language that developed on the East African coast about 1,000 years ago and has since adopted several words from Arabic, Portuguese, Indian, German and English. It spread into the Tanzanian interior along with the 19th-century slave caravans and is now the lingua franca in Tanzania and Kenya, and is also spoken in parts of Uganda, Malawi, Rwanda, Burundi, Congo, Zambia and Mozambique.

In Dar es Salaam, Zanzibar, Arusha, Moshi and the northern game reserves, you can get by with English well enough. If you travel in other parts of the country, you will need to understand some Swahili. And even if you are sticking to tourist areas, it is polite and can be useful to know a bit of Swahili.

There are numerous Swahili–English dictionaries on the market, as well as phrasebooks and grammar books, and most can be ordered from online sellers such as Amazon. For anybody serious about learning Swahili, Joan Russell's long-standing but recently upgraded *Teach Yourself Swahili* (TY Complete Courses, 2010) is the best choice, and the book comes with two invaluable CDs, though it is quite pricey at around US$40. A useful dictionary for travellers is Nicholas Awde's *Swahili-English/English-Swahili Practical Dictionary* (Hippocrene Books, 2000), which costs around US$30.

For short-stay visitors, all these books have practical limitations. Wading through a phrasebook to find the expression you want can take ages, while trying to piece together a sentence from a dictionary is virtually impossible. In addition, most books available are in Kenyan Swahili, which often differs greatly from the purer version spoken in Tanzania.

The following introduction is not a substitute for a dictionary or phrasebook. It is not so much an introduction to Swahili as an introduction to communicating with Swahili-speakers. Before researching this guide, my East African travels had mainly been in Kenya, Uganda and parts of Tanzania where English is relatively widely spoken. We learnt the hard way how little English is spoken in most of Tanzania. I hope this section will help anyone in a similar position to get around a great deal more easily than we did at first.

Pronunciation

Vowel sounds are pronounced as follows:

a	like the a in *father*
e	like the e in *wet*
i	like the ee in *free*, but less drawn out
o	somewhere between the o in *no* and the word *awe*
u	similar to the oo in *food*

The double vowel in words like *choo* or *saa* is pronounced like the single vowel, but drawn out for longer. Consonants are in general pronounced as they are in English. *L* and *r* are often interchangeable, so that *Kalema* is just as often spelt or pronounced *Karema*. The same is true of *b* and *v*.

You will be better understood if you speak slowly and thus avoid the common English-speaking habit of clipping vowel sounds – listen to how Swahili-speakers pronounce their vowels. In most Swahili words there is a slight emphasis on the second-last syllable.

Basic grammar Swahili is a simple language in so far as most words are built from a root word using prefixes. To go into all of the prefixes here would probably confuse people new to Swahili – and it would certainly stretch my knowledge of the language. They are covered in depth in most Swahili grammar books and dictionaries. The following are some of the most important:

Pronouns

ni	me	*wa*	they
u	you	*a*	he or she
tu	us		

Tenses		***Tenses (negative)***	
na	present	*si*	present
ta	future	*sita*	future
li	past	*siku*	past
ku	infinitive	*haku*	negative, infinitive

From a root word such as *taka* (want) you might build the following phrases:

Unataka soda	You want a soda
Tutataka soda	We will want a soda
Alitaka soda	He/she wanted a soda

In practice, *ni* and *tu* are often dropped from simple statements. It would be more normal to say *nataka soda* than *ninataka soda.*

In many situations there is no interrogative mode in Swahili; the difference between a question and a statement lies in the intonation.

Greetings There are several common greetings in Swahili. Although allowances are made for tourists, it is rude to start talking to someone without first using one or another formal greeting. The first greeting you will hear is *Jambo*. This is reserved for tourists, and a perfectly adequate greeting, but it is never used between Tanzanians (the more correct *Hujambo*, to which the reply is *Sijambo*, is used in some areas).

The most widely used greeting is *Habari?*, which more or less means *What news?* The normal reply is *Nzuri* (good). *Habari* is rarely used by Tanzanians on its own; you might well be asked *Habari ya safari?*, *Habari yako?* or *Habari gani?* (very loosely, *How is your journey?*, *How are you?* and *How are things?* respectively). *Nzuri* is the polite reply to any such request.

A more fashionable greeting among younger people is *Mambo*, especially on the coast and in large towns. Few tourists recognise this greeting; reply *Safi* or *Poa* and you've made a friend.

In Tanzanian society it is polite to greet elders with the expression *Shikamu*. To the best of my knowledge this means *I hold your feet*. In many parts of rural Tanzania, children will greet you in this way, often with their heads bowed and so quietly it sounds like *Sh…oo*. Don't misinterpret this by European standards (or other parts of Africa where *Mzungu give me shilling* is the phrase most likely to be offered up by children); most Tanzanian children are far too polite to swear at you. The polite answer is *Marahaba* (I'm delighted).

Another word often used in greeting is *Salama*, which means peace. When you enter a shop or hotel reception, you will often be greeted by a friendly *Karibu*, which means *Welcome*. *Asante sana* (thank you very much) seems an appropriate response.

If you want to enter someone's house, shout *Hodi!* It basically means *Can I come in?* but would be used in the same situation as *Anyone home?* would in English. The normal response will be *Karibu* or *Hodi*.

It is respectful to address an old man as *Mzee*. *Bwana*, which means *Mister*, might be used as a polite form of address to a male who is equal or senior to you in age or rank, but who is not a *Mzee*. Older women can be addressed as *Mama*.

The following phrases will come in handy for small talk:

Where have you just come from?	*(U)natoka wapi?*
I have come from Moshi	*(Ni)natoka Moshi*
Where are you going?	*(U)nakwenda wapi?*
We are going to Arusha	*(Tu)nakwenda Arusha*
What is your name?	*Jina lako nani?*
My name is Philip	*Jina langu ni Philip*
Do you speak English?	*Unasema KiEngereze?*
I speak a little Swahili	*Ninasema KiSwahili kidigo*
Sleep peacefully	*Lala salama*
Bye for now	*Kwaheri sasa*
Have a safe journey	*Safari njema*
Come again (welcome again)	*Karibu tena*
I don't understand	*Sielewi*
Say that again	*Sema tena*

Numbers

1	*moja*	30	*thelathini*
2	*mbili*	40	*arobaini*
3	*tatu*	50	*hamsini*
4	*nne*	60	*sitini*
5	*tano*	70	*sabini*
6	*sita*	80	*themanini*
7	*saba*	90	*tisini*
8	*nane*	100	*mia (moja)*
9	*tisa*	150	*mia moja na hamsini*
10	*kumi*	155	*mia moja hamsini na tano*
11	*kumi na moja*	200	*mia mbili*
20	*ishirini*	1,000	*elfu (moja)* or *mia kumi*

Swahili time Many travellers to Tanzania fail to come to grips with Swahili time. It is essential to be aware of it, especially if you are catching buses in remote areas. The Swahili clock starts at the equivalent of 06.00, so that *saa moja asubuhi* (hour one in the morning) is 07.00, *saa mbili jioni* (hour two in the evening) is 20.00, etc. To ask the time in Swahili, say *Saa ngapi?*

Always check whether times are standard or Swahili. If you are told a bus leaves at nine, ask whether the person means *saa tatu* or (Swahili) *saa tisa* (standard). Some English-speakers will convert to standard time, others won't. This does not apply so much where people are used to tourists, but it's advisable to get in the habit of checking.

Day-to-day queries The following covers such activities as shopping, finding a room, etc. It's worth remembering that most Swahili words for modern objects, or things for which there would not have been a pre-colonial word, are often similar to the English. Examples are *resiti* (receipt), *gari* (car), *polisi* (police), *posta* (post office) and – my favourite – *stesheni masta* (station master). In desperation, it's always worth trying the English word with an *ee* sound on the end.

Shopping The normal way of asking for something is *Ipo?* or *Zipo?*, which roughly means *Is there?*, so if you want a cold drink you would ask *Soda baridi zipo?* The response will normally be *Ipo* or *Kuna* (there is) or *Hamna* or *Hakuna* (there isn't). Once you've established the shop has what you want, you might say *Nataka koka mbili* (I want two Cokes). To check the price, ask *Shillingi ngape?* It may be simpler to ask for a brand name: Omo (washing powder) or Blue Band (margarine), for instance.

Accommodation The Swahili for guesthouse is *nyumba ya wageni*. In my experience *gesti* works as well, if not better. If you are looking for something a bit more upmarket, bear in mind *hoteli* means restaurant. We found self-contained (*self-contendi*) to be a good keyword in communicating this need. To find out whether there is a vacant room, ask *Nafasi zipo?*

Getting around The following expressions are useful for getting around:

Where is there a guesthouse?	*Ipo wapi gesti?*
Is there a bus to Moshi?	*Ipo basi kwenda Moshi?*
When does the bus depart?	*Basi itaondoka saa ngapi?*
When will the vehicle arrive?	*Gari litafika saa ngapi?*
How far is it?	*Bale gani?*
I want to pay now	*Ninataka kulipa sasa*

Foodstuffs

avocado	*parachichi*
bananas	*ndizi*
bananas (cooked)	*matoke/batoke*
beef	*(mnyama ya) ngombe*
bread (loaf)	*mkate*
bread (slice)	*tosti*
coconuts	*nazi*
coffee	*kahawa*
chicken	*kuku*
egg(s)	*(ma)yai*
fish	*samaki*
food	*chakula*
fruit(s)	*(ma)tunda*
goat	*(mnyama ya) mbuzi*
maize porridge (thin, eaten at breakfast)	*uji*
maize porridge (thick, eaten as staple with relish)	*ugali*
mango(es)	*(ma)embe*
meat	*mnyama*
milk	*maziwa*
onions	*vitungu*
orange(s)	*(ma)chungwa*
pawpaw	*papai*
pineapple	*nanasi*
potatoes	*viazi*
rice	*pilau*
rice (cooked plain)	*wali*
rice (uncooked)	*mchele*
salt	*chumvi*
sauce	*mchuzi/supu*
sugar	*sukari*

tea (black/milky)	*chai* (*ya rangi/maziwa*)
vegetable	*mboga*
water	*maji*

Days of the week

Monday	*Jumatatu*
Tuesday	*Jumanne*
Wednesday	*Jumatano*
Thursday	*Alhamisi*
Friday	*Ijumaa*
Saturday	*Jumamosi*
Sunday	*Jumapili*

Useful words and phrases

afternoon	*alasiri*
again	*tena*
and	*na*
ask (I am asking for…)	*omba* (*ninaomba…*)
big	*kubwa*
boat	*meli*
brother	*kaka*
bus	*basi*
car (or any vehicle)	*gari*
child (children)	*mtoto* (*watoto*)
cold	*baridi*
come here	*njoo*
European(s)	*mzungu* (*wazungu*)
evening	*jioni*
excuse me	*samahani*
far away	*mbale kubwa*
father	*baba*
friend	*rafiki*
good (very good)	*mzuri* (*mzuri sana*)
goodbye	*kwaheri*
here	*hapa*
hot	*moto*
later	*bado*
like (I would like…)	*penda* (*ninapenda...*)
many	*sana*
me	*mimi*
money	*pesa/shillingi*
more	*ingine/tena*
morning	*asubuhi*
mother	*mama*
nearby	*karibu/mbale kidogo*
night	*usiku*
no	*hapana*
no problem	*hakuna matata*
now	*sasa*
OK or fine	*sawa*
only	*tu*
passenger	*abiria*
pay	*kulipa*
person (people)	*mtu* (*watu*)
please	*tafadhali*
road/street	*barabara/mtaa*
shop	*duka*
sister	*dada*
sleep	*kulala*
slowly	*polepole*
small	*kidogo*
soon	*bado kidogo*
sorry	*pole*
station	*stesheni*
stop	*simama*
straight or direct	*moja kwa moja*
thank you (very much)	*asante* (*sana*)
there is	*iko/kuna*
there is not	*hamna/hakuna*
thief (thieves)	*mwizi* (*wawizi*)
time	*saa*
today	*leo*
toilet	*choo*
tomorrow	*kesho*
want (I want...)	*taka* (*ninataka...*)
where	(*iko*) *wapi*
yes	*ndiyo*
yesterday	*jana*
you	*wewe*

Useful conjunctions include *ya* (of) and *kwa* (to or by). Many expressions are created using these; for instance *stesheni ya basi* is a bus station and *barabara kwa Mbale* is the road to Mbale.

Health

flu	*mafua*	recover	*pona*
fever	*homa*	treatment	*tiba*
malaria	*malaria*	cure	*ponyesha*
cough	*kikohozi*	injection	*sindano*
vomit	*kutapika*	bone	*mfupa*
swollen	*uvimbe*	death	*mauti*
injure	*jeraha*	to examine	*vipimo*
weak	*dhaifu*	to fall down	*kuanguka*
pain	*maumizu*	to bleed	*kutokwa na damu*

MAA *Emma Thomson*

Maa is the language of the Maasai. It does not exist in written form, so the spellings below are approximate.

Greetings

Father/elderly man, I greet you	*Papa…supai*
Warrior/middle-aged man, I greet you	*Apaayia…supai*
Young woman, I greet you	*Siangiki…supai*
Boy, I greet you	*Ero…supai*
Girl, I greet you	*Nairo…supai*
Mother/middle-aged woman, I greet you	*Yeyio…takwenya*
Grandmother/elder woman, I greet you	*Koko…takwenya*
How are you?	*Koree indae?*
Are you fine/healthy?	*Kira sedan/kira biot?*
My name is…	*Aji…*
What is your name?	*Kekijaa enkarna?*
I come from…	*Aingwaa…*
Where do you come from?	*Kaingwaa?*
Goodbye	*Serae*

Numbers

1	*nabo*	13	*tomon ok ooni*
2	*are*	14	*tomon o ongwan*
3	*ooni*	15	*tomon o imiet*
4	*ongwan*	16	*tomon o ille*
5	*imiet*	17	*tomon o opishana*
6	*ille*	18	*tomon o isiet*
7	*naapishana*	19	*tomon o odo*
8	*isiet*	20	*tikitam*
9	*naudo*	100	*iip nabo*
10	*tomon*	1,000	*enchata nabo*
11	*tomon o obo*	2,000	*inkeek are*
12	*tomon o are*	3,000	*inkeek ooni*

Shopping

How much does it cost?	*Empesai aja?*
I want/need it	*Ayieu*
I don't want/need it today	*Mayieu taata*
I will buy this one	*Ainyang ena*
I will buy these	*Ainyang kuna*

I won't buy anything today	*Mainyang onyo taata*
I haven't got any money	*Maata empesai*

Useful words and phrases

Thank you	*Ashe*
Thank you very much	*Ashe naleng*
Take it (used when giving a gift)	*Ngo*
I receive it (used when accepting a gift)	*Au*
Leave me/it alone (to children)	*Tapala*
Go outside (to children)	*Shomo boo*
May I take a picture?	*Aosh empicha?*
Yes	*Ee*
OK	*Ayia*
No, I don't want you to	*A-a, mayieu*
Stop it	*Tapala*
Expression of sympathy (like '*pole*' in Swahili)	*Kwa adei*

AFRICAN ENGLISH Although many Tanzanians speak a little English, not all speak it fluently. Africans who speak English tend to structure their sentences in a similar way to how they would in their own language: they speak English with Bantu grammar.

For a traveller, knowing how to communicate in African English is as important as speaking a bit of Swahili, if not more so. It is noticeable that travellers who speak English as a second language often communicate with Africans more easily than first-language English-speakers.

The following ground rules should prove useful when you speak English to Africans:

- *Unasema KiEngereze?* (Do you speak English?). This small but important question may seem obvious. It isn't.
- Greet in Swahili then ask in English. It is advisable to go through the Swahili greetings (even *Jambo* will do) before you plough ahead and ask a question. Firstly, it is rude to do otherwise; secondly, most Westerners feel uncomfortable asking a stranger a straight question. If you have already greeted the person, you'll feel less need to preface a question with phrases like 'I'm terribly sorry' and 'Would you mind telling me' which will confuse someone who speaks limited English.
- Speak slowly and clearly. There is no need, as some travellers do, to speak as if you are talking to a three-year-old; just speak naturally.
- Phrase questions simply and with Swahili inflections. 'This bus goes to Dodoma?' is better than 'Could you tell me whether this bus is going to Dodoma?'; 'You have a room?' is better than 'Is there a vacant room?' If you are not understood, don't keep repeating the same question; find a different way of phrasing it.
- Listen to how people talk to you, and not only for their inflections. Some English words are in wide use, others are not. For instance, lodging is more likely to be understood than accommodation.
- Make sure the person you are talking to understands you. Try to avoid asking questions that can be answered with a yes or no. People may well agree with you simply to be polite.
- Keep calm. No-one is at their best when they arrive at a crowded bus station after an all-day bus ride; it is easy to be short-tempered when someone cannot understand you. Be patient and polite; it's you who doesn't speak the language.

Appendix 2

GLOSSARY

Acacia woodland	type of woodland dominated by thorny, thin-leafed trees of the genus *Acacia*
AICC	Arusha International Conference Centre
banda	a hut, often used to refer to hutted accommodation at hotels and lodges
boda-boda	motorcycle taxi
boma	traditional enclosure or homestead; administration building of the colonial era
Brachystegia woodland	type of woodland dominated by broad-leaved trees of the genus *Brachystegia*
bui-bui	black cloth worn veil-like by women, mainly in Islamic parts of the coast
bwana	mister (polite term of address to an adult man)
Chama Cha Mapinduzi	ruling party of Tanzania since independence (CCM)
cichlid	family of colourful fish found in the Rift Valley lakes
closed canopy forest	true forest in which the trees have an interlocking canopy
dalla dalla	light vehicle, especially minibus, serving as public transport
dhow	traditional wooden seafaring vessel
duka	kiosk
endemic	unique to a specific country or biome
exotic	not indigenous; for instance plantation trees such as pines and eucalyptus
fly-camping	temporary private camp set up remotely from a permanent lodge
forex bureau	bureau de change
guesthouse	cheap local hotel
hoteli	local restaurant
indigenous	naturally occurring
kanga	colourful printed cloth worn by most Tanzanian women
KIA	Kilimanjaro International Airport
kitenge (pl *vitenge*)	similar to *kanga*
koppie (or *kopje*)	Afrikaans word used to refer to a small hill such as those on the Serengeti
mandazi	deep-fried doughball, essentially the local variant on a doughnut
mishkaki	meat (usually beef) kebab
mzungu (pl *wazungu*)	white person
NCA	Ngorongoro Conservation Area

ngoma	Swahili dance
Omani era	period when the coast was ruled by the Sultan of Oman, especially 19th century
savannah	grassland studded with trees
self-contained room	room with en-suite shower and toilet
Shirazi era	medieval period during which settlers from Shiraz (Iran) dominated coastal trade
taarab	Swahili music and dance form associated particularly with Zanzibar
Tanapa	Tanzania National Parks
ugali	stodgy porridge-like staple made with ground maize meal
woodland	area of trees lacking a closed canopy

Appendix 3

ENDEMIC AND NEAR-ENDEMIC BIRDS OF TANZANIA

ENDEMICS Full list of confirmed and probable species confined to Tanzania:

Grey-breasted spurfowl (*Pternistis rufopictus*) Serengeti and vicinity; common in scattered woodlands around Seronera.

Udzungwa forest partridge (*Xenoperdix udzungwensis*) Discovered 1991 in Udzungwa. Estimated population 3,500–4,000.

Rubeho forest partridge (*Xenoperdix obscuratus*) Discovered in Rubeho Highlands 2003, described as a new species 2005. Population may be <1,000.

Pemba green pigeon (*Treron pembaensis*) Confined to Pemba Island, greyer underneath than the mainland equivalent, but unmistakable in its limited range.

Fischer's lovebird (*Agapornis fischeri*) Feral population exists in Kenya, but naturally endemic to Serengeti and vicinity, where common.

Yellow-collared lovebird (*Agapornis personatus*) Feral population exists in Kenya. Common in Tarangire and semi-arid parts of central Tanzania.

Tanzanian red-billed hornbill (*Tockus ruahae*) Recently described, range centred on Ruaha National Park, where common.

Pemba scops-owl (*Otus pembaensis*) Very rare. Confined to Pemba Island.

Nduk eagle-owl (*Bubo vosseleri*) Eastern Arc forests including Usambara, Uluguru and possibly Udzungwa. Now often lumped with Fraser's eagle-owl.

Usambara nightjar (*Caprimulgus guttifer*) Recent debatable split from mountain nightjar. Usambara Mountains and possibly other Eastern Arc ranges.

Beesley's lark (*Chersomanes beesleyi*) Recent split from the spike-heeled lark. Population <1,000 in short grasslands west of Kilimanjaro.

Uluguru mountain greenbul (*Arizelocichla neumanni*) Recent split from mountain greenbul. Uluguru forests.

Yellow-throated mountain greenbul (*Arizelocichla chlorigula*) Recent split from mountain greenbul. Forests of Udzungwa, Ukaguru and Nguru.

Montane tiny greenbul (*Phyllastrephus albigula*) Split from tiny greenbul in 2009. Usambara and Nguru.

Usambara thrush (*Turdus roehli*) Recent split from olive thrush. Usambara and Pare forests.

Usambara akalat (*Sheppardia montana*) Forests of western Usambara.

Iringa akalat (*Sheppardia lowei*) Udzungwa and other Eastern Arc ranges.

Rubeho akalat (*Sheppardia aurantiithorax*) Discovered in Rubeho Mountains in 1989.

Ruaha chat (*Myrmecocichla collaris*) Proposed new species. Present Ruaha and Katavi.

Winifred's warbler (*Bathmocercus winifredae*) Also known as Mrs Moreau's warbler. Udzungwa, Rubeho, Uluguru and some other Eastern Arc ranges.

Usambara hyliota (*Hyliota usambara*) Recent split from southern hyliota, endemic to the East Usambara.

Kilombero cisticola (*Cisticola* sp) Recently discovered and undescribed. Kilombero Valley.
White-tailed cisticola (*Cisticola* sp) Recently discovered and undescribed. Kilombero Valley.
Reichenow's batis (*Batis reichenowi*) Eastern Arc forest canopies.
Banded green sunbird (*Anthreptes rubritorques*) Udzungwa, Nguru, Uluguru and Usambara.
Rufous-winged sunbird (*Cinnyris rufipennis*) Discovered in 1981. Udzungwa Mountains.
Rubeho double-collared sunbird (*Cinnyris* sp) Recently discovered in Rubeho Mountains.
Moreau's sunbird (*Cinnyris moreaui*) East Usambara, Udzungwa and other Eastern Arc ranges.
Loveridge's sunbird (*Cinnyris loveridgei*) Uluguru Mountains.
Usambara double-collared sunbird (*Cinnyris usambaricus*) Usambara and Pare mountains.
Pemba sunbird (*Cinnyris pembae*) Confined to Pemba Island.
Pemba white-eye (*Zosterops vaughani*) Confined to Pemba Island.
Tanzania broad-ringed white-eye (*Zosterops eurycricotus*) Split from montane white-eye in 2017; forest on Kilimanjaro, Meru and three other massifs in northeast Tanzania.
South Pare white-eye (*Zosterops winifredae*) Controversial split from mountain white-eye. South Pare Mountains.
Uhehe fiscal (*Lanius marwitzi*) Confined to highlands around Iringa.
Uluguru bush-shrike (*Malaconotus alius*) Rare. Forest canopies in Uluguru.
Ashy starling (*Lamprotornis unicolor*) Central plains. Common in Tarangire and Ruaha.
Rufous-tailed weaver (*Histurgops ruficauda*) Serengeti, Ngorongoro and Tarangire national parks.
Kilombero weaver (*Ploceus burnieri*) Recently described. Kilombero Valley.
Usambara weaver (*Ploceus nicolli*) West Usambara, Uluguru and Udzungwa mountains.
Kipengere seedeater (*Serinus melanochrous*) Southern highlands.

NEAR ENDEMICS Several species have a range confined to Tanzania and one neighbouring country:

Fischer's turaco (*Tauraco fischeri*) Coastal Tanzania and Kenya.
Sokoke scops-owl (*Otus ireneae*) Eastern Usambara and one locale in Kenya.
Red-faced barbet (*Lybius rubrifacies*) Kagera region, nudging into Uganda and possibly Rwanda.
Friedmann's lark (*Mirafra pulpa*) Grassland at base of Kilimanjaro, Tanzania and Kenya.
Athi short-toed lark (*Calandrella athensis*) Grassland in Tanzanian–Kenyan border between Rift Valley and Lake Victoria.
Sokoke pipit (*Anthus sokokensis*) Coastal forest; Kenya and northern Tanzania.
Red-throated tit (*Parus fringillinus*) Serengeti–Mara ecosystem.
Dappled mountain robin (*Modulatrix orostruthus*) Udzungwa, East Usambara and one locale in Mozambique.
Spot-throat (*Modulatrix stictigula*) Eastern Arc, nudging into Malawi.
Stripe-faced greenbul (*Arizelocichla milanjensis*) Eastern Arc, nudging into Kenya.
Sharpe's akalat (*Sheppardia sharpei*) Eastern Arc, nudging into Malawi.
Swynnerton's robin (*Swynnertonia swynnertoni*) Montane forests of Eastern Arc, Mozambique and Zimbabwe.
Schalow's wheatear (*Oenanthe schalowi*) Rocky grassland, southern Kenya and northern Tanzania.
Tanzanian illadopsis (*Illadopsis distans*) Recent split from pale-breasted illadopsis; forest interiors in Kenya and Tanzania.
Long-billed forest warbler (*Artisornis moreaui*) Also known as Mrs Moreau's tailorbird. Eastern Usambara and one locale in Mozambique.
Black-lored cisticola (*Cisticola nigriloris*) Southern highlands, extending into Malawi.

Kungwe apalis (*Apalis argentea*) Albertine Rift endemic; isolated population in Mahale Mountains.

Karamoja apalis (*Apalis karamojae*) Serengeti Plains and northeast Uganda.

Long-billed forest warbler (*Artisornis moreaui*) Also known as Moreau's tailorbird. Eastern Usambara and one locale in Mozambique.

Red-capped forest warbler (*Artisornis metopias*) Also known as African tailorbird; Eastern Arc through to north Mozambique.

Fulleborne's black boubou (*Laniarius fuelleborni*) Eastern Tanzania, nudging into Malawi.

Grey-crested helmet-shrike (*Prionops poliolophus*) Serengeti–Mara ecosystem, into Kenya.

Hildebrandt's starling (*Lamprotornis hildebrandti*) South Kenya and north Tanzania.

Abbott's starling (*Pholia femoralis*) Pare Mountains, other forested locales in Kenya.

Kenrick's starling (*Poeoptera kenricki*) Montane forests in Tanzania and Kenya.

Amani sunbird (*Hedydipna pallidigaster*) Coastal forests, Tanzania and Kenya.

Taveta weaver (*Ploceus castaneiceps*) North Tanzania and south Kenya.

Tanzania masked weaver (*Ploceus reichardi*) Swamps in Tanzanian–Zambian border region.

Montane marsh widowbird (*Euplectes psammocromius*) Southern highlands, extending into Malawi.

Appendix 4

FURTHER INFORMATION

BOOKS

History and biography A limited number of single-volume histories covering Tanzania are in print, but many are rather dated and textbook-like in tone. Useful starting points include Kimambo, Maddox and Nyanto's *A New History of Tanzania* (Mkuki Na Nyota Publishers, 2017) and Robert Maxon's very readable and recently revised *East Africa: An Introductory History* (West Virginia University Press, 3rd edition, 2009). Also highly recommended is Richard Hall's *Empires of the Monsoon: A History of the Indian Ocean and its Invaders* (HarperCollins, 1996), a highly focused and reasonably concise book that conveys a strong historical perspective thanks to the author's storytelling touch and his largely successful attempt to place the last 1,000 years of East and southern African history in an international framework. A more concise and modern book covering similar ground is Charles Cornelius's *History of the East African Coast* (CreateSpace, 2015). Considerably more bulky, and working an even broader canvas, John Reader's *Africa: A Biography of the Continent* (Penguin, 1998) has met with universal praise as perhaps the most readable and accurate attempt yet to capture the sweep of African history for the general reader.

Several books document specific periods and/or regions in African history. Good coverage of the coastal Swahili, who facilitated the medieval trade between the gold fields of Zimbabwe and the Arab world, is provided in J de Vere Allen's *Swahili Origins* (James Currey, 1992). Among the better popular works on the early era of European exploration are Hibbert's *Africa Explored: Europeans in the Dark Continent* (Penguin, 1982) and two excellent biographies by Tim Jeal: *Livingstone* (Yale University Press, revised and expanded edition, 2013) and *Stanley: The Impossible Life of Africa's Greatest Explorer* (Faber & Faber, 2007), the latter voted *Sunday Times* 'Biography of the Year' in 2007. Alastair Hazel's informative *The Last Slave Market* (Constable, 2011) describes the East African slave trade and efforts to close Zanzibar's slave market from the viewpoint of Dr John Kirk, who was then the British consul to Zanzibar. For an erudite, compelling and panoramic account of the decade that turned Africa on its head, Thomas Pakenham's gripping 600-page tome *The Scramble for Africa* (Abacus, 1992) was aptly described by one reviewer as '*Heart of Darkness* with the lights switched on'.

Field guides and natural history

General *East African Wildlife* by Philip Briggs and Ariadne Van Zandbergen (Bradt, 2nd edition, 2015) is a handy and lavishly illustrated one-stop handbook to the fauna of East Africa, with detailed sections on the region's main habitats, varied mammals, birds, reptiles and insects. It's the ideal companion for first-time visitors whose interest in wildlife extends beyond the Big Five but who don't want to carry a library of reference books.

Mammals The pick of the field guides, especially if your interest extends to bats and other small mammals, is Jonathan Kingdon's *Field Guide to African Mammals* (Bloomsbury, 2nd edition, 2018), which also contains a goldmine of information about the evolutionary relationships of modern species. Its more compact counterpart is the same author's *Kingdon Pocket Guide to African Mammals* (Bloomsbury, 2020). Chris and Tilde Stuart's *Field Guide to the Larger Mammals of Africa* (Struik Publishers, 2006) is well suited to space-conscious travellers who are serious about putting a name to all the large mammals they see.

Not a field guide in the conventional sense so much as a guide to mammalian behaviour, Richard Estes's superb *The Safari Companion* (Chelsea Green, 1999) is well organised and informative but rather bulky for casual safari-goers.

Birds Zimmerman, Turner, Pearson, Willet and Pratt's *Birds of Kenya and Northern Tanzania* (Christopher Helm, 3rd edition, 2005) is a contender for the best single-volume field guide available to any African country or region. I would recommend it to any serious birder sticking to northern Tanzania, since it provides complete coverage for the northern safari circuit, the Usambara and Pare mountains and Pemba Island, and although it stops short of Dar es Salaam and Zanzibar, this wouldn't be a major limitation. Unfortunately, the gaps in its coverage would limit its usefulness south of Dar es Salaam or in the Lake Victoria and Lake Tanganyika region.

For any birding itinerary extending to parts of Tanzania west of the Serengeti or south of the Usambara, the best option is the *Field Guide to the Birds of East Africa* by Stevenson and Fanshawe (Helm, 2nd edition, 2020), which provides comprehensive coverage of the whole of Tanzania, as well as Kenya, Rwanda and Burundi, and contains very accurate plates, good distribution maps and adequately detailed text descriptions.

Another quality field guide that provides full coverage of East Africa is *Birds of Africa: South of the Sahara* by Ian Sinclair and Peter Ryan (Struik Publishers, 2nd edition, 2010), which describes and illustrates the 2,100-plus species recorded in the region. Should you already own it, or be planning more extensive travels in Africa, then this guide will more than suffice for Tanzania. But if your African travels will be restricted to East Africa, you are probably better off buying a more focused field guide.

Other field guides The past few years have seen the publication of a spate of high-quality field guides to other more specialised aspects of East Africa's fauna and flora. Among the more interesting of these titles are Najma Dharani's *Field Guide to Common Trees and Shrubs of East Africa* (Struik, 3rd revised edition, 2019) and a simply magnificent *Field Guide to East African Reptiles* by Stephen Spawls, Kim Howell, Harlad Hinkel and Michele Menegon (Bloomsbury, 2022). Drewes, Spawls and Howell's *Pocket Guide to the Reptiles and Amphibians of East Africa* (Bloomsbury, 2006) is also highly worthwhile.

National parks An excellent introductory handbook to all Tanzania's national parks and other major conservation areas is Olli Marttila's misleadingly named *The Great Savanna* (Auris Publishers, 2011). This includes a very useful overview of conservation in Tanzania, and detailed (20–30-page) descriptions of each park and reserve, including lesser-known ones such as Rubondo Island, Mkomazi and Amani. There is also a useful pocket field guide to mammals and select birds at the back.

In the early 1990s, Jeanette Hanby and David Bygott wrote a series of excellent booklets covering Serengeti National Park, Tarangire National Park and Lake Manyara National Park. These were published by Tanapa and can still be bought for US$5–10 from street vendors and bookshops in Arusha, and possibly at some safari lodges. The same authors have written an equally informative and widely available self-published booklet covering the Ngorongoro Conservation Area.

Those with an interest in ape behaviour would do well to read Jane Goodall's books about chimpanzee behaviour, *In the Shadow of Man* (Collins, 1971) and *Through a Window* (Weidenfield & Nicolson, 1990), based on her acclaimed research in Tanzania's Gombe National Park. A more visually attractive alternative is the coffee-table book *Mahale: A Photographic Encounter with Chimpanzees* by Angelika Hofer, Michael Huffman and Gunter Ziesler (Sterling Publishing, 2000).

Coffee-table books The best book of this sort to cover Tanzania as a whole is Paul Joynson-Hicks's *Tanzania: Portrait of a Nation* (Quiller Press, 2001), which contains some great down-to-earth cultural photography and lively anecdotal captions. It is stronger on cultural, landmark and scenic photography than on wildlife photography, for which M Iwago's superb *Serengeti* (Thames and Hudson, 1987) has few peers, although Reinhard Kunkel's stunning *Ngorongoro* (Welcome Enterprises, 2006) is certainly one, while Boyd Norton's more recent *Serengeti: The Eternal Beginning* (Fulcrim, 2011) is also very handsome and has better text. For more wide-ranging pictorial coverage of Africa, look no further than the comprehensive *Africa: Continent of Contrasts*, with text by Philip Briggs and photography by Martin Harvey and Ariadne Van Zandbergen (Struik Publishers, 2005).

Health Self-prescribing has its hazards so if you are going anywhere very remote consider taking a health book. For adults, Jane Wilson-Howarth's excellent *The Essential Guide to Travel Health* (Cadogan, 2009) is out of print, but the same author has a new and similar book *Staying Healthy When You Travel: Avoiding Bugs, Bites, Bellyaches and More* scheduled for publication by Companion House in late 2023. If travelling with the family look at *Your Child Abroad: A Travel Health Guide* by Jane Wilson-Howarth and Matthew Ellis (Bradt, 2nd edition, 2014).

Fiction Surprisingly few novels have been written by Tanzanians or about Tanzania. An excellent novel set in World War I Tanzania is William Boyd's *An Ice-Cream War*, while the same author's *Brazzaville Beach*, though not overtly set in Tanzania, devotes attention to aspects of chimpanzee behaviour first noted in Gombe.

A Tanzanian of Asian extraction now living in Canada, M G Vassanji is the author of at least one novel set in Tanzania and the Kenyan border area, the prize-winning *Book of Secrets* (Macmillan, 1994). This is an atmospheric tale, with much interesting period detail, revolving around a diary written by a British administrator in pre-war Kenya and discovered in a flat in Dar es Salaam in the 1980s. Vassanji is also the author of *Uhuru Street*, a collection of short stories set in Dar es Salaam. The most prominent Tanzanian-born novelist is Abdulrazak Gurnah, a Zanzibari now living in the UK whose books are mostly set in East Africa. His best-known novels are *The Last Gift* (Bloomsbury, 2012), *Desertion* (Bloomsbury, 2005) and *Paradise* (Bloomsbury, 1994), which was shortlisted for the Booker and the Whitbread Prize.

MAPS A number of maps covering East Africa are available. The best is the Austrian-published Freytag-Berndt 1:2,000,000 map. By far the most accurate and up-to-date dedicated map of Tanzania is the 1:400,000 *Tanzania Travel Map* published by Harms Verlag (**w** harms-ic-verlag.de). Electronic maps can be downloaded from **w** tracks4africa.co.za on to some GPS receivers and smartphones.

A series of excellent maps by Giovanni Tombazzi covers most of the northern reserves, as well as Kilimanjaro, Mount Meru and Zanzibar. Colourful, lively and accurate, these maps are widely available throughout northern Tanzania, and are probably the most

TANZANIAN MUSIC

From traditional percussion and chants to Congolese-style guitar pop and a home-grown style of contemporary hip hop called bongo flava, Tanzania has a rich and varied musical culture, and – unlike a few years back – it is increasingly well represented on CD and streaming services. The following short list includes some of the most interesting material on offer:

Bi Kidude: Zanzibar (Retroafric, 2007) The first solo recordings by the gravel-voiced Queen of Taarab, a centurion who first performed in the 1920s and was an active member of the Zanzibari music scene until she passed away in 2013.

Lady Jaydee: Ya 5 – The Best of Lady Jaydee (Machozi, 2012) The cream of the four studio CDs recorded by this very popular and multiple award-winning artist, one of the few to have given international exposure to bongo flava.

Mohamed Ilyas: Taarab (Chitu-Taku, 2009) A soulful modern taarab recording by one of Zanzibar's most legendary singers backed by a 16-piece orchestra.

Siti Binti Saad: The Legendary Mumbai Recordings (Retrotan, 2021) Born on Zanzibar in 1880, the celebrated 'mother of taarab' Siti Binti Saad recorded more than 100 (mostly long lost) 78rpm sides prior to her death in 1950. This welcome release – the first dedicated to her pioneering music in the modern era – collects 16 tracks she recorded for the Gramophone Company in Mumbai in 1929 and 1930.

Siti Muharam: Siti of Unguja (On the Corner, 2020) Showcasing the voice of the great-granddaughter and musical heir of Siti Binti Saad, this award-winning album presents a decidedly modern take on taarab, blending traditional Zanzibari sounds with electronica and eclectic Middle Eastern influences.

user-friendly maps I've seen in East Africa. Each map shows details of the appropriate conservation area in both the dry and wet seasons, and is liberally dotted with illustrations of common trees and other points of interest. Giovanni has also produced a map covering the whole northern safari circuit, useful to those who don't want to splash out on the entire series of more detailed maps. Also recommended are the new Harms Verlag maps to Ngorongoro Conservation Area, Lake Manyara National Park and Zanzibar Island.

WEBSITES The following offer information on Tanzania and Zanzibar:

w **dailynews.co.tz** Current news.
w **thecitizen.co.tz** Current news.
w **ntz.info** Wide-ranging archive of material about northern Tanzania.
w **tanzaniatourism.com** Tourist board website.
w **tanzaniaparks.com** Current information and entrance fees for all the country's national parks.

Various Artists: Bongo Flava – Swahili Rap from Tanzania (*Out Here, 2006*) A rare international release featuring 70 minutes of modern Swahili hip-hop by 14 artists, mostly recorded in Dar Es Salaam.

Various Artists: Rough Guide to the Music of Tanzania (Rough Guides, 2009) Traditional music, 80s guitar pop and bongo flava all get an airing on this genre-spanning and highly recommended introduction to Tanzania's musical heritage.

Various Artists: Taarab 3 – Music of Zanzibar (Globestyle, 1989) Excellent and well-annotated introduction to Zanzibar's distinctive taarab music, mostly played by small bands and recorded in the 1980s, also featuring one of the best recordings by the legendary Bi Kidude.

Various Artists: Tanzania Instruments (SWP, 2009) A fascinating countrywide tour of traditional instrumentals performances – ranging from Lake Victoria to Zanzibar – recorded by the legendary Hugh Tracey in 1950.

Various Artists: Tanzania Vocals (SWP, 2009) Another culture-hopping rerelease of material recorded by Hugh Tracey in 1950, this *a capella* selection includes atmospheric Maasai chants and a 600-strong mixed-sex Chagga choir recorded on the footslopes of Kilimanjaro.

Various Artists: Zanzibara Vol. 3 – The 1960s Sound of Tanzania (Buda, 2007) Highlife-influenced and infectiously poppy guitar-driven *muziki wa dansi* (dance music) recorded by the likes of the Jamhuri Jazz Band and Atomic Jazz Band in the late 1960s and early 1970s.

Vijana Jazz Band: The Koka Koka Sex Battalion (Sterns Africa, 2011) Showcasing one of the most exciting and popular purveyors of East African rumba-style *muziki wa dansi*, this includes a great selection of toe-tappers recorded in the 1970s and 1980s.

COVID-19

Please note that some of the research for this guide was carried out during the Covid-19 pandemic. Because of the impact of the crisis on tourism, some businesses or services listed in the text may no longer operate. We will post any information we have about these on **w** bradtguides.com/updates. And we'd of course be grateful for any updates you can send us during your own travels, which we will add to that page for the benefit of future travellers.

Ninth edition published May 2023
First published 1993
Bradt Guides Ltd
31a High Street, Chesham, Buckinghamshire, HP5 1BW, England
www.bradtguides.com
Print edition published in the USA by The Globe Pequot Press Inc,
PO Box 480, Guilford, Connecticut 06437-0480

Project Manager: Susannah Lord
Cover research: Pepi Bluck, Perfect Picture

ISBN: 9781784777142

British Library Cataloguing in Publication Data
A catalogue record for this book is available from the British Library

Photographs All photographs in guidebook and on covers by Ariadne Van Zandbergen (www.africaimagelibrary), unless otherwise stated.
Front cover Male lion (*Panthero leo*), Serengeti National Park
Back cover African elephant (*Loxodonta africana africana*), Tarangire National Park; plains zebra (*Equus quagga*), Serengeti National Park; on safari in Arusha National Park
Title page, clockwise from left Leopard (*Panthera pardus*) drinking, Loliondo Reserve, Serengeti National Park; topi (*Damaliscus lunatus*) in Serengeti National Park; white-fronted bee-eater (*Merops bullockoides*) colony nesting in the bank of the Rufiji River, Nyerere National Park

Maps David McCutcheon FBCart.S; colour map relief base by Nick Rowland FRGS

Typeset by Ian Spick, Bradt Guides
Production managed by Jellyfish Print Solutions; printed in India
Digital conversion by www.dataworks.co.in

Acknowledgements

PHILIP BRIGGS

This would be a poor guidebook indeed were it not for the industry support and hospitality that has made it possible for me to explore Tanzania so thoroughly during the course of researching various editions of this book over the past 30 years. To the many safari companies and airlines that have helped ferry me around Tanzania over the years, to the myriad lodges, hotels and camps that have accommodated me, to William Mwakilema, Beatrice Kessy and Pascal Shelutete of Tanzania National Parks, to Peter Makutiani and Chris Timbuka of the NCAA, and to Franklin Alexander at Ministry of Natural Resources and Tourism, I would like to express my utmost gratitude.

I am also indebted to my wife, travel companion and photographic collaborator Ariadne Van Zandbergen; to my co-author Chris McIntyre, his wife Susan McIntyre and the staff of Expert Africa; to my parents Roger and Kay Briggs for shuttling us to and from O R Tambo Airport so many times I've lost count; and to the many Bradt staffers past and present who have laboured hard on all nine editions of this book to date.

CHRIS MCINTYRE

Primarily my thanks go to Philip Briggs, my co-author, for kindly allowing me to have a modest input into what was his creation and has always been his book. Then to numerous people in Tanzania, mostly on the islands, who I know will forgive me for only crediting them properly in the Zanzibar book.

In the UK, thanks especially to James Denny, Lyndsey Marris, and Richard Trillo. All are African experts in their own right; all work closely with me at Expert Africa; and all got involved with extensive research trips – contributing significantly to various sections of this text. Finally, my love and thanks to my wife, Susie, who undertook the lioness's share of our hard work, on the islands and back in the UK, as she pulled together a detailed and comprehensive update to our Zanzibar book, which forms the basis of the Zanzibar section in this guide.

Index

Page numbers in **bold** indicate main entries; those in *italics* indicate maps

INDEX OF ADVERTISERS

THE BRADT STORY

In the beginning

It all began in 1974 on an Amazon river barge. During an 18-month trip through South America, two adventurous young backpackers – Hilary Bradt and her then husband, George – decided to write about the hiking trails they had discovered through the Andes. *Backpacking Along Ancient Ways in Peru and Bolivia* included the very first descriptions of the Inca Trail. It was the start of a colourful journey to becoming one of the best-loved travel publishers in the world; you can read the full story on our website (bradtguides.com/ourstory).

Getting there first

Hilary quickly gained a reputation for being a true travel pioneer, and in the 1980s she started to focus on guides to places overlooked by other publishers. The Bradt Guides list became a roll call of guidebook 'firsts'. We published the first guide to Madagascar, followed by Mauritius, Czechoslovakia and Vietnam. The 1990s saw the beginning of our extensive coverage of Africa: Tanzania, Uganda, South Africa, and Eritrea. Later, post-conflict guides became a feature: Rwanda, Mozambique, Angola, and Sierra Leone, as well as the first standalone guides to the Baltic States following the fall of the Iron Curtain, and the first post-war guides to Bosnia, Kosovo and Albania.

Comprehensive – and with a conscience

Today, we are the world's largest independently owned travel publisher, with more than 200 titles. However, our ethos remains unchanged. Hilary is still keenly involved, and **we still get there first**: two-thirds of Bradt guides have no direct competition.

But we don't just get there first. Our guides are also known for being **more comprehensive** than any other series. We avoid templates and tick-lists. Each guide is a one-of-a-kind expression of an expert author's interests, knowledge and enthusiasm for telling it how it really is.

And a commitment to wildlife, conservation and respect for local communities has always been at the heart of our books. Bradt Guides was **championing sustainable travel** before any other guidebook publisher. We even have a series dedicated to Slow Travel in the UK, award-winning books that explore the country with a passion and depth you'll find nowhere else.

Thank you!

We can only do what we do because of the support of readers like you – people who value less-obvious experiences, less-visited places and a more thoughtful approach to travel. Those who, like us, take travel seriously.